D1784882

# Roof Construction Manual

## Pitched Roofs

Eberhard Schunck
Hans Jochen Oster
Rainer Barthel
Kurt Kiessl

BIRKHÄUSER – PUBLISHERS FOR ARCHITECTURE
BASEL · BOSTON · BERLIN

EDITION DETAIL
MUNICH

The original German edition of this book was conceived and developed by **DETAIL**, Review of Architecture in association with Clay Roof Tile Study Group, Bundesverband der Deutscher Ziegel-industrie e.V.

Authors:

Eberhard Schunck, Prof. Dipl.-Ing., architect
Chair of Building, Munich Technical University

Hans Jochen Oster, Dipl.-Ing., architect

Rainer Barthel, Prof. Dr.-Ing.
Chair of Structural Engineering, Munich Technical University

Kurt Kiessl, Prof. Dr.-Ing.
Professor of Building Climate, Faculty of Architecture,
Bauhaus University, Weimar

Assistants:
Eva Bodemer, with
Alexander Blank, Christian Brinkmeier, Ralf Elias, Oliver Grassmann, Christian Kovac, Robert Pawlowski, Frank Ressel, Christian Salz
Loadbearing structure: Herbert Markert

Editorial services:
Heide Wessely
Editorial assistants: Claudia Fuchs, Heike Werner
Drawings: Nicola Kollmann
CAD assistants: Markus Betz, Peter Lingenfelser, Isabel Mayer, Emese Köszegi, Elisabeth Krammer, Axel Müller-Engelhardt, Andrea Saiko, Linda Werner

Assistants on previous editions:
Marc Gerhard, Albrecht Hanser, Hansjörg Kehnel, Harald Konsek, Swenja Nölting, Uli Rüb, Martin Schibel, Hubert Schmickler, Peter Schmidt, Matthias Stumpfl, Hubert Vollmer, Bettina Vismann, Markus Wacker, Thomas Ziegler



Printed on acid-free paper produced from chlorine-free pulp. TCF ∞

ISBN 3-7643-6986-8

Layout and production: Peter Gensmantel, Cornelia Kohn, Andrea Linke, Roswitha Siegler

Printed in Germany

Translators (German/English):
parts 1 – 3: Gerd Söffker, Philip Thrift, Hannover
part 4: Ingrid Taylor, Munich

A CIP catalogue record for this book is available from the Library of Congress, Washington, D.C., USA

Bibliographic information published by Die Deutsche Bibliothek
Die Deutsche Bibliothek lists this publication in the Deutsche Nationalbibliografie; detailed bibliographic data is available on the internet at http://dnb.ddb.de.



This book is also available in a German language edition (ISBN 3-7643-6896-9).

Specialist advisers:

| | |
|---|---|
| Thatch | Norbert Hofmann, Berend Meyer |
| Wooden shakes/ shingles | Gerhard Beyer, Bettina Horsch, Andreas Rapp, Eckart Schwab, Ludwig Weiss |
| Natural and fibre-cement slates | Heinrich Baum, Georg Guntermann, Ewald A. Hoppen, Karin Kirchner, Gaston Lemmé, Ulrich Lutter, Frank Rummel, Wolfgang Schinkel, Wolfgang Wagner, Franz Wierschem |
| Asphalt shingles | Heinz Blass, Ernst P. Giercke, Brigitte Liess |
| Clay roof tiles | Leonhard Froschauer, Klaus Göbel, Heinz Zanger, Paul Zielinski |
| Concrete roof tiles | Heinrich Baum, Horst Pavel |
| Glass | Georg Babioch, Edmund Hahn, Heinz Krewinkel |
| Corrugated bitumen sheeting | Ulrich Franke |
| Fibre-cement corrugated sheeting | Gaston Lemmé, Bernhard Rohde |
| Metal profiled sheeting | Kunibert Breuer, Hubert Wittur |
| Sheet metal roof coverings | Friedolin Behning, Kunibert Breuer, Gert Bröhl, Stephan Christensen, Rainer Schulze-Rettmer, Hermann Wenzel, Friedhelm Wiesel, Hans-Peter Wilbert |
| Green roofs | Roland Appl, Gerd Harzmann |
| Membranes | Carsten Moritz |
| Secondary water-proofing/covering layer | Gaston Lemmé, Hans Peter Raidt |
| Drainage | Friedolin Behning |

# Contents

**Part 1 · Pitched roofs – past and present**

Eberhard Schunck



**Part 2 · Fundamentals**

Loadbearing structure

Rainer Barthel



Building science

Kurt Kiessl

Design

Eberhard Schunck and Hans Jochen Oster



Layers and materials



**Part 3 · Construction details**

Eberhard Schunck and Hans Jochen Oster



**Part 4 · Built examples in detail**

Eberhard Schunck and Hans Jochen Oster



**Appendix**

# Preface

The first *Roof Construction Manual* goes back to the beginnings of a successful series of building handbooks, which in the meantime comprises seven volumes. Although the completely new edition of 1991 had twice been updated and augmented, new legislation, directives, standards and technical guidelines plus new construction methods have made this comprehensive revision necessary. All the existing chapters were brought up to date and some were totally recast. Even the introductory chapter demonstrates the topicality of the subject – with reference to the current situation in the building industry. The chapter covering the loadbearing structure is also new. It now includes the actions on the roof and the transfer of loads from the roof covering to the loadbearing structure, and besides the most significant traditional roof frameworks also looks at long-span roofs.

The building science chapter now outlines not only the indispensable scientific principles but, for the first time, the methods of calculation based on the new energy economy legislation, with all the references that legislation contains.

All the roof covering materials from the former manual reappear in this book. These constitute an important resource within the range of traditional roof coverings and represent the current state of these materials.

However, new types of roofing materials are also dealt with; for instance, membranes get their own chapter for the first time. This is the first publication we know of that illustrates the construction principles in this form.

And the chapter on energy gains is new – for this subject plays an increasing role for the pitched roof.

Within the realms of production and erection we show the current status of prefabrication and offer suggestions for employing prefab solutions to achieve economic pitched roofs. Furthermore, the principles for designing a modular roof are explained, coupled with ideas on how to proceed in the development of modular systems.

Refurbishment is a task that will gain more importance in the building industry in the future. This topic was therefore included, taking into account various cases of damage and corresponding refurbishment options.

The examples at the back of the book include many contemporary buildings that reflect the state of roof technology and the aesthetic spectrum of today's architecture. However, a number of classic examples are also shown, together with details that have been published only rarely and then mostly incomplete. For the first time, a glossary of the more common specialist terms complements the index.

The idea behind the *Roof Construction Manual* is not merely to present ready-made construction formulae but rather to set out the principles for the construction and design of the roof as a climatic envelope. These include:

- basic knowledge about the loadbearing structure and its interaction with the roof covering,
- knowledge of the scientific principles affecting the building in conjunction with the new editions of DIN standards and statutory instruments,
- information about the construction principles of pitched roofs in terms of the problem of ventilated and non-ventilated forms of construction,
- a deeper understanding of the roof covering materials and the jointing options,
- an overview of the options for gaining energy and their integration within the pitched roof,
- an understanding of the special problem of moisture and how to overcome this with the help of current findings,
- an awareness of the flow mechanisms acting on the roof and the consequences for the airtightness and its design,
- knowledge of insulating materials together with their physical properties and how they should be used,
- and finally, an impression of the materials, types and design of drainage systems.

In order to illustrate these principles, construction drawings show simple applications. These are supplemented by appropriate actual examples.

The publisher and authors hope that the knowledge assembled in this book will serve to extend the understanding of the construction and the design skills required for the complex tasks of roof construction.

The publisher and authors

# Part 1 Pitched roofs – past and present

**A status report**

The origins of the pitched roof stretch back to the beginnings of human civilisation. Its advantages are undisputed. It is an ideal upper enclosure to the building envelope. Its inclined surfaces discharge precipitation quickly and reliably. The small-format structure is very easy to maintain and the elements of the roof covering are mostly very durable.

Only briefly was the superiority of the pitched roof called into question as the flat roof enjoyed a major boost with the development of modern architecture in the 1970s and threatened to overtake the pitched roof in terms of popularity. Today, the pitched roof has regained first place. A large majority in our society these days regards the pitched roof as the very embodiment of the roof per se, meeting society's expectations in terms of appearance.

In the first part of this book we shall attempt to instil an understanding of the forms and methods by presenting a historical review of roofing technology.

First, we look back to the 19th century, when industrialisation revolutionised all areas of production. We shall examine the question of to what extent building technology at that time had reached the level of development of other areas of production, and whether it benefited from other disciplines even then. After that we investigate the motives that determined the development of technology and building technology. Later, we trace further progress throughout the 20th century up to the present day. We establish the basis for our modern-day construction methods by considering the individual materials, particularly with respect to the two most important aspects that dominate today's society: economy and ecology. Finally, the use and form of the roof are explained in order to set out the boundaries and our options for action.

# Roofing materials and techniques in the 19th century

## Changes to the building industry in the 19th century

Starting in the mid-18th century, fundamental changes took place – first in England then also in France and Germany – that strongly influenced each other. Populations increased at an ever faster rate, industrial production was stepped up and the mechanisation of production systems expanded.
The increasing population density in the towns and cities presented new challenges for the building industry in terms of multistorey construction, transportation and infrastructure. The new production plants demanded quickly erected buildings to cover large open spaces, and early single-storey sheds were modelled on churches. The liberal theories of Adam Smith in England and the first social welfare policies in France brought about an increase in wages. Thus, in order to avoid a rise in the cost of production, the building industry, too, turned to mechanisation.

### The evolution of building science

The constant expansion of mechanisation and the associated population density had an influence primarily on the use, and hence the design, of buildings. The wide range of stylistic elements to solve construction problems with standard architecture took on a subsidiary role. Thus, the engineering dimension became separated from the artistic, often purely decorative dimension. Engineers, freed from the burden of artistic design, could now devote themselves to technical problems and the demands of industry. They were well equipped to do so because the intensive scientific investigations, in progress since the middle of the 18th century were now, at the beginning of the 19th century, beginning to bear fruit.
In 1823 Claude-Louis-Marie-Henri Navier, the father of structural engineering, summed up the knowledge of his age in a comprehensive work. The development of projective geometry by Gaspard Monge enabled the complex systems of three-dimensional objects to be analysed. The increasing importance of the science of building manifested itself in the founding of the “Ecole des Ponts et des Chaussées” in the year 1747. For the first time, building technology was taught in its own school. After the Ecole Polytechnique was

1.1 Foundry building, Sayner Works, Bendorf, 1828-30, Carl Ludwig Althans

established in 1794–95 in Paris, technical universities followed in Prague (1803), Vienna (1815) and Karlsruhe (1825).
The divergence of engineers and artist-architects began very early in France and reinforced the position of the engineer. As Anatole de Baudot said in 1889: "The influence of the architect has been diminishing for a long time, and the engineer, the modern person *par excellence*, is beginning to replace him. If the engineer were to replace the architect completely, the latter could without doubt disappear without his art being extinguished altogether."[1]

## Iron, glass, concrete – the new building materials

Innovations in society, industry and science gave iron, glass and concrete, which hitherto had only been used as secondary materials, a new importance.

### Iron

Iron had long been used in the building industry. However, it was not until the 19th century that production methods that enabled iron to be employed on a larger scale were devised. Since Henry Cort had lowered the carbon content using the puddling method (1784) and produced usable wrought iron, and Henry Bessemer had replaced manual methods of introducing air by mechanical ones (1855), forgeable iron ("ingot steel") had become inexpensive and available in large quantities. Iron was first used in England for bridge-building (Coalbrookdale, 1771–79) and later also in buildings. The possibilities were quickly recognised in France, too, (corn market, Paris, 1809–11) and Germany (east choir of Mainz Cathedral, 1827).

### Glass

Developments in the production of glass, which took place in the latter half of the 18th century, had, by the beginning of the 19th century, already led to the manufacture of panes of glass measuring 2.5 x 1.7 m. During the first 30 or so years of the 19th century the production of glass became so cheap that it could be used in great quantities for windows and roofs.

### Concrete

Concrete had been known as a building material for more than 2000 years. However, only after 1824 could it be used irrespective of the place from which the pozzolana was obtained – thanks to the production of "artificial cement" by the Englishmen John Smeaton, James Parker and Joseph Aspdin. The most important invention, in which Joseph Monier (1867), Edmund Coignet (1861), Josef Luis Lambot (1855) and Thaddeus Hyatt (1877) played a part, was, however, to make this material, hitherto only suitable for components in compression, suitable for components in tension, too, through its combination with iron reinforcement.

## Developments in roofing techniques and roofing materials

While the methods of roof covering had not changed significantly for hundreds, indeed thousands of years, the Industrial Revolution initiated a series of momentous changes.

### Natural stone

Roofs had been covered with cleaved stone material by the Romans, but was not rediscovered until the 11th century in France. While granite, gneiss, limestone and sandstone were only of local significance, clay slate was used in many parts of Europe (Germany, England, France, Austria, Hungary). The spread of this type of roof covering, likewise clay roof tiles, was attributable to the ban on combustible materials – reed, straw, wood – for roof coverings. This ban had been in place since the devastating fires of the Middle Ages, but it was not until the establishment of building authorities in the 19th century that this ban could be properly enforced. Ingenious methods were developed in England, France and Germany to improve the old methods of laying slates. This form of roof covering became particularly popular along the major waterways leading from the slate quarries.
The introduction of the steam engine at first simplified the mining of slate underground. Later, the labour-intensive splitting and dressing of the slate on site was also carried out by machine. The decisive change came in 1844 with the introduction of standard size slates. The slates could now be manufactured using a template in workshops protected from the weather at the various quarries and mines. The interchangeability this brought about, the good supplies and the extensive network of roads and the new railways led to a real "slate boom" starting in the 1870s, which only ended with the outbreak of the First World War.

### Clay roof tiles

Roof coverings of fired clay tiles had been around for 4000 years and by the start of the 19th century had undergone the greatest development. Owing to their clearly defined production stages (preparation, shaping, firing), they were predestined for the changeover to industrial production.

Circular kilns
With the increase in industrialisation, the demand for combustible material for use as fuel became a problem in all areas of production. Throughout Europe, the new steel furnaces, lime and cement kilns, and the growing use of steam engines, called for enormous quantities of wood and led to ecological problems. Although the traditional materials wood and peat had been supplemented or replaced by coal, shortages and the rising cost of fuel also played a major role in the production of roof tiles. Processes had to be found that consumed less combustible material. After many trials Hoffmann and Licht succeeded in 1858 in inventing the circular kiln, which, through multiple

1.2

usage, enabled the energy requirement to be reduced by two-thirds compared to the conventional charcoal kilns. Just how important and revolutionary this invention was for the roof tile industry is demonstrated by the fact that 10 years after the first kiln was built, some 640 circular kilns were in operation worldwide.

Clay roof tile machines
The industrialisation of roof tile production had been investigated continuously since the beginning of the 19th century. The first stage in its development was marked by the invention of the roof tile machine by Carl Schlickeysen in Berlin in 1854. These machines were called extruders after the characteristic die. They united the preparation of the clay, shaping and cutting in one machine. The development of the dry press represented further progress. This created better conditions for the firing process and enabled more accurate products to be produced. Finally, the increasingly refined shapes of the interlocking clay tiles could only be produced in moulding presses. With his invention of the turret press in 1881, Wilhelm Ludowici from Jockgrim near Karlsruhe managed to combine the operating speed of the extruder with the refinements of the moulding press. This development paved the way for an inexpensive roof covering material.

Forms
The shapes of the clay roof tiles themselves also underwent further development. Initially, using an extruder meant tiles could only be shaped about their longitudinal axis; this gave rise to the extruded clay roof tile.
Shallower roof pitches and the desire to incorporate additional sealing functions within the overlap led to evermore specialised forms; clay roof tiles shaped in this way were called interlocking clay tiles. The first experiments with these forms were carried out in 1847 by the Gilardoni brothers based in the Alsace region. Wilhelm Ludowici, named many times as the inventor of the interlocking clay tile, did not patent his double Roman clay tile until 1881. This type, with small modifications, is still produced today. Ludowici also developed and manufactured numerous special forms and built the first completely ceramic roof.

**Cement**
Even before the industrial production of "artificial cement" in Germany, Adolph Kroher, based in Staudach in Bavaria, produced his Staudacher roof tiles in 1844. He used his own cement made from fired mineral deposits from the region around Staudach and the sharp sand from the flood plains of the Tyrol. He used this rapid-setting "natural" cement to manufacture two forms: one that he called the "slate-type" diamond form and an "ogee form", which today we would call a pantile.
These tiles exhibited remarkable properties. Their low water absorption and the associated frost resistance rendered shallow pitches possible. The tiles were very rigid and, above all, cheap. The inventor's remark regarding their deceptive resemblance to natural slate illustrates the laborious evolutionary path that building materials often have to travel before their own material characteristics are acknowledged by society.
Following initial production on hand-moulding tables, Peter Jörgensen from Haseldorf in Schleswig-Holstein took out various patents for presses and apparatus in 1882; these permitted more rational production. He and Hartwig Hüser from Bonn-Oberkassel experimented with various formats and forms. In this way Jörgensen produced a trapezoidal roof sheet before 1882, with a double rebate on all sides and hence with a high resistance to rain penetration. Following official awards at exhibitions in Vienna (1873) and Nuremberg (1882), the new material became particularly popular for roof coverings, especially after industrial production meant that it was available in great quantities. By 1899 there were already nine manufacturers of "cement sheets" in Germany, offering a wide range of different forms.

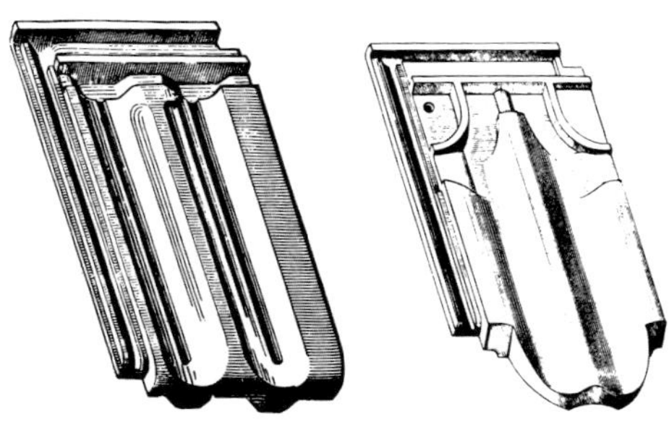

1.3

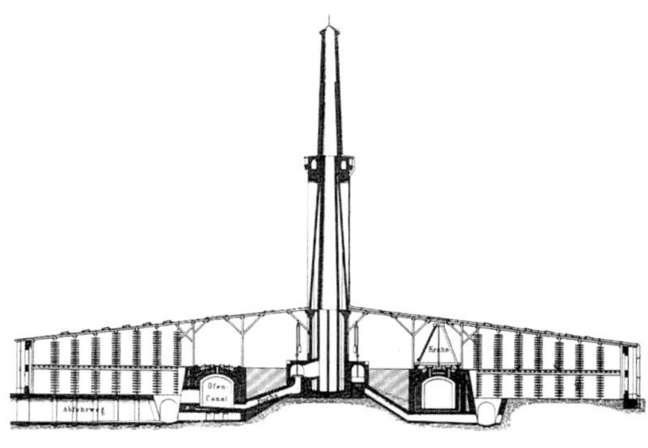

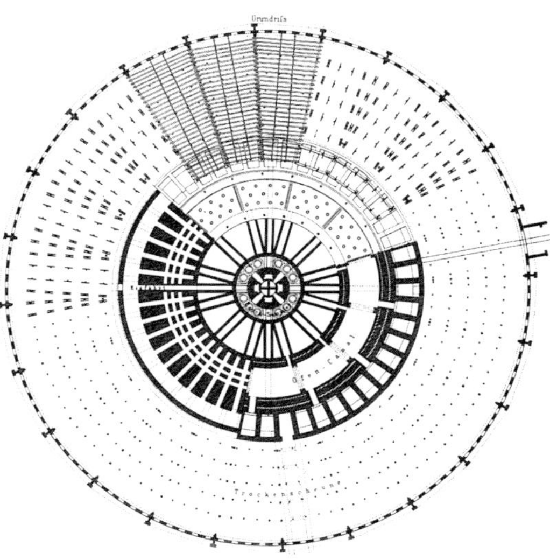

1.4

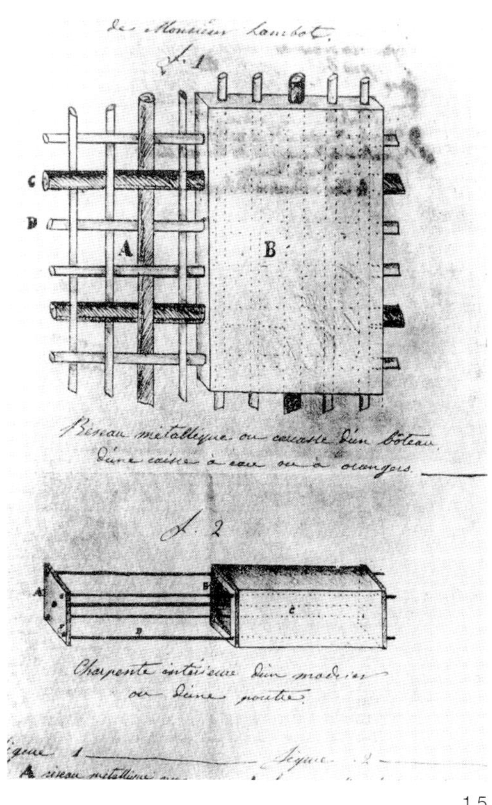

1.5

1.2 The production of cast glass using the method devised by L. de Nehou, taken from the encyclopaedia by D. Diderot and J.B. D'Alembert (1773)
1.3 Double Roman clay tile and overlapping clay tile by Wilhelm Ludowici, 1881 and 1882
1.4 The circular kiln invented by Hoffmann and Licht, 1858, saved two-thirds of the fuel consumed previously.
1.5 Extract from patent application for production of reinforced concrete by J. Louis Lambot, 1885 – 12 years before the Monier patent

[1] Taken from a speech by Anatole de Baudot on French architecture past and present, Paris, 1889. Anatole de Baudot was a pupil of Henri Labrouste and Viollet-le-Duc. He built the first church with a reinforced concrete frame – St Jean de Montmartre in Paris.

**Asbestos, asbestos cement**

The fibrous, highly durable mineral called asbestos by the Greeks had been used as a thread for spinning and weaving even in early civilisations.

In seven years of trials Ludwig Hatschek from Austria succeeded in combining this material economically with cement, and applied for a patent in 1900. His small-format roof sheets were inexpensive and highly resistant to heat, cold, moisture and fire.

Good bending strength combined with low weight enabled profiled sheets to be manufactured in large formats, producing simple and economical roof structures.

These properties, as well as its excellent durability led to a rapid expansion in the use of this material for roofing, both as flat shingles and profiled (corrugated) sheets.

**Metals**

Metals such as bronze, copper and lead were used for roof coverings in ancient times. In the 19th century metal roof coverings became much more widespread.

Sheet metals

The decisive step in the manufacture of large, thin metal sheets was the introduction of the rolling process; this continuous process replaced the expensive and complicated casting of individual pieces. After the rolling of lead began in England around 1670, this method was applied to copper at the start of the 18th century, to zinc in 1805 and to iron in 1818. The use of sheet iron as a roofing material first became realistic after the introduction of galvanising on a larger scale. Until then, repainting every three or four years was too costly and the risk of corrosion too great. Stanislaus Sorel introduced economic hot-dip galvanising in England in 1836 and in the same year took his invention to France. From then on, inexpensive galvanised sheet iron gradually replaced the zinc sheets that had been gladly used up until that time to finish off the shallow roof pitches of diverse structures. The city centres of Innsbruck, Passau and Salzburg owe their roofscapes to these 19th-century innovations. Zinc, copper and lead were also favoured when the search for a characteristic expressive form or the desire for greater mouldability required this. By the end of the 19th century, aluminium, which had only recently become available, was also used as a roofing material. Its first major application was in 1897 for the cupola of the San Gioacchino Church in Rome. While the production of the material had largely been

1.6

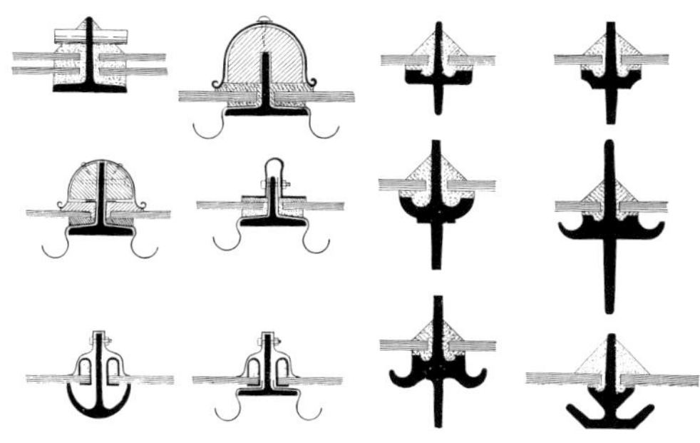

1.7

1.8

1.9

industrialised, laying techniques, based on welted and soldered joints, were restricted to manual methods.

Roofing sheets
Sheet iron's good mouldability often led to expensive roof coverings like slate being initiated by the less expensive iron. The most effective and simplest use of sheet iron was to give it a corrugated form. This invention, too, came from England, and was introduced into Germany in 1851.
This shaping – ideally suited to this material – was advantageous for good water run-off, for jointing high longitudinal laps and for tightly sealed transverse laps. The good load-carrying capacity, good dimensional stability and low weight led to the spread of corrugated iron right around the globe.

1.6 The centre of Salzburg has many shallow-pitched roofs finished with sheet metal.
1.7 A selection of glazing bars used on glass roofs in the 19th century, from: Obderbecke
1.8 Palm House, Kew Gardens, London, 1844–48, Richard Turner and Decimus Burton
1.9 One of the first aluminium roof coverings: San Gioacchino church, Rome, 1897

[2] The gardener John Claudius Loudon developed the first "prefabricated greenhouses", contracted the manufacture of these to the W. & D. Bailey company and sold them with the help of the prototype built at his house in Bayswater, London. One of the most elegant of these was built in Langport, Somerset, in 1817. In: John Hix, The Glass House, London, 1981, p. 19.
[3] A. Obderbecke, Der Dachdecker und der Bauklempner, Leipzig, 1901
[4] Adolf Loos, Trotzdem, reprint, Vienna, 1982, p. 200

**Glass**
The use of glass as a roofing material saw England demonstrate her leading role again. Between the years 1816 and 1829 glass production in England rose from 1000 to 6000 tonnes. The method commonly used, initially only for palm houses and the like, of clamping the panes of glass onto the loadbearing iron glazing bars had been established in the 1820s.[2] However, this system was soon extended to other types of building in which lightweight, well-lit and long-span constructions were desirable. In 1829 Charles Percier and Pierre François Fontaine provided a glass roof for the Galerie d'Orleans in Paris.
The Crystal Palace, designed by Joseph Paxton for the Great Exhibition of 1851 in London, brought together all the relevant experiences into one consummate system. It constituted both the archetype of the industrially produced building and the prototype for innumerable glass-covered single-storey sheds throughout Europe.
By the end of the century there existed a well-developed, highly diverse technology that stretched from simple wooden glazing bars to highly elaborate, metal ones with channels for draining condensation.
Putty and felt were used to seal the joints, and the flat or curved panes were held in place with spring-like clamping bars in the most diverse forms.

**Asphalt, tar, bitumen**
The sealing materials asphalt and pitch – known in ancient Babylon – were rediscovered in the 19th century and employed for both shipbuilding and buildings. The specialist publications from around the turn of the 20th century claim that tar-saturated felts had been used in Sweden and Finland as early as 1800.[3] This knowledge was first disseminated in Germany in 1826 by Wilhelm August Lampadius, the inventor of coal gasification. The oldest roofs with tar-saturated felt – on the Baltic Sea coast – have been around since 1830; in 1860 there were already 28 factories in Germany producing tar-saturated felts.
The wood-cement roofs of the Silesian master cooper Samuel Häusler dating from 1839, and described euphorically by Adolf Loos as the most ingenious invention "for thousands of years", consisted of several layers of packing paper glued together on site with expensive pitch and tar and subsequently covered with sand and gravel.[4] The paper served as "reinforcement" in the tar-paper layer. It was soon replaced by bituminous felt. The patents for this came from America in 1896, where large quantities of bitumen occurred as a by-product of the petroleum distillation industry.
This form of roof covering permitted very shallow roof pitches and used easily produced joints, which meant that operatives with only minimal training could also build them. Low weight and affordable price promoted its expansion. In the end, the tar and bitumen roofing felts created the conditions for the introduction of flat roofs, which very quickly became indispensable for modern architecture.

## New criteria

Looking back at the 19th century we can see that all the principal inventions appeared in two relatively short bursts: between 1825 and 1860, and between 1880 and 1900. Taking a somewhat global view, we can say that our present pitched roof technology is essentially based on these inventions and has only advanced in terms of the automation of the production processes. The origins and motives for these innovations can be summed up as follows:

1.10

**Roof technology as a "by-product" of technical development**

To a great extent, the development of roof technology was governed by developments in industry as a whole. Only in the realms of roof tiles, asbestos cement and roofing felt were most new solutions worked out specifically for the building, or rather the roofing, industry. In metal roofing, glass and cement the roofing industry benefited quite clearly from technical progress in metallurgy, the glass industry and the invention of "artificial cement". However, innovations in other fields were also recognised rapidly and incorporated into roofing.

**Human resources**

The value of manual labour became increasingly significant. Shorter working hours were called for – and introduced – in England and later also in Germany. For the first time there were efforts to save not only material but also labour costs.

**Problems with quantities**

Shorter production times were also desirable in order to deal with the enormous volume of building materials required to cope with the rapid growth of industry and the huge increase in the urban population.

**The construction period**

We can assume that developers were always impatient and equated the construction period with a financial expense. However, in the boom building years of the 1870s onwards the time-span from turning the first sod to occupying the building rose to become a quality in itself. Benjamin Franklin's saying "Remember that time is money" from his "Advice to a Young Tradesman, written anno 1749" became a driving force.[5]

1.11

1.10 The Crystal Palace, London, 1851, Joseph Paxton, shown here in a contemporary coloured drawing
1.11 Worker with pick and shovel, etching, from Tom F. Peters loco citato

[5] Tom F. Peters, Time is Money: Die Entwicklung des modernen Bauwesens, Stuttgart, 1981

# Further developments in the 20th century

## Changes in the 20th century

The 20th century brought magnificent and enormous progress in science. The discovery of quantum mechanics has revolutionised thinking in science and questioned the principle of causality. Chemistry and biochemistry have given mankind almost creator-like tools with which to work. Microelectronics is on the way to completely redesigning our everyday and working lives, also substituting our memories, regulative intervention and foresight. And the question of how the search for the fundamentals of life can be continued in the light of ethical frontiers is being asked far more often than ever since the arrival of nuclear energy. The prerequisites for human labour have changed fundamentally. Increasing awareness of health issues and standards of living have brought about an overall reduction in working hours, making workers a precious resource. Progress in the field of mechanisation has made most everyday commodities affordable for a large majority of our society. The introduction of microelectronics in the control of manufacturing processes has speeded up production while maintaining the same level of quality. The global relationships between ecology and economy were first revealed when the Club of Rome published its work in 1972. This initiated a discussion about the sensible application of energy in the industrialised world, which led to a rethink by responsible planners.

Improving communications technology and the means of communication available to us have brought production and trade between regions and nations closer together. The resulting globalisation is leading to change in the organisation of resources and the manufacture of goods of all kinds.

### Economy

Many people in the industrialised world today enjoy a standard of living that in the past was reserved for the privileged few. Crucial for this was the establishment of competition as a central (market) principle of our society. In this way, economic relationships have a direct influence on the appearance of our towns and cities, and hence also on our roofscapes.

**Economy – architecture**

Economic ups and downs have a more direct effect on construction than on other sectors of industry in our Western society. For example, more efficient use of building land in New York and Chicago led to the birth of the skyscraper. Conversely, periods of economic hardship have led to more rational and more economic methods of construction, and hence often also to the loss of many traditional skills. In terms of roof construction this initially affected the use of natural materials, whose extraction, transport or maintenance was too expensive. Countless thatched, wooden shingle and stone slab roofs disappeared from our roofscapes.

However, such changes are often countered by efforts to preserve old methods and prevent the destruction of exemplary structures. The understandable desire of people to preserve a familiar appearance often entails a balancing act for the designer. Forms originally resulting from the type of construction become ornaments – the "scars" of outdated production techniques.[6] This also applies when natural materials characterised by manual work, e.g. slate or reed, are imitated by forms stemming from large-scale production.

**The cost factors of the building material**

After satisfying constructional requirements and taking into account durability, the price will continue to be crucial in the choice of building material. But environmental stipulations and the taxes accompanying these mean that "ecological" factors such as primary energy requirement, emissions during production and further environmental effects are increasingly playing a role in calculating the price. Where short-term cost efficiency is not the top priority, environmental compatibility already frequently determines the choice of building material. Within the life cycle of a structure, capital outlay, fitting out, maintenance and disposal costs must be added together.

1.12

1.12 Strand of DNA with its typical double-helix structure, from: Faszination der Technik, Augsburg, 1996

[6] Theodor W. Adorno, Ohne Leitbild, Parva Aesthetica, Frankfurt, 1967, p. 107

**Material costs**
Extraction of raw materials, production, transport and storage costs together make up the material cost. The abundance of deposits, cost or rationalisation (e.g. mining of German slate) and possibly land rehabilitation measures play a role in the extraction of the raw material. The cost of production depends on the forming processes required to turn it into a building material, and on the method of production selected. Extensive automation is just as likely as energy-saving measures and forms that reduce the consumption of the raw material. Further developments in the preparation and forming of building components could change the textures and colours of our roofs, while automation processes are important for the continuance of types and methods of roofing, and hence for the desired diversity. Energy and transport policies will play a bigger role in the proportion of freight costs in future.

Erection
The time taken for erection is, in the long term, undoubtedly an important factor in the cost of a roof. Unlike with the extraction of raw materials and manufacturing, mechanisation and automation quickly come up against construction-related limits. The size of a roofing unit has a considerable influence; there is an almost linear relationship between this and erection time. As in other branches of industry there is a tendency in the building industry to transfer production to protected, enclosed plants, and restrict the work on site to the assembly of prefabricated components. The primary advantages are: greater reliability in the construction sequence, more efficient rationalisation options, better-quality products, better working conditions, and independence from the vagaries of the weather. To be able to compete on price, integrated components that combine several functions must undergo further development. The larger the prefabricated component, the more care can be taken in forming connections and joints. The number of layers and hence the sequence of successive operations also needs to be looked at in detail. In the meantime, therefore, the tendency has been to erect simpler roof structures with fewer but more efficient layers, which has seen a corresponding reduction in the cost of erection.

The roof in service / lifetime
Computers and the pressure of economic framework conditions for the active management of property in the corporate sense ("facility management") has changed the former simple approach to building maintenance. High labour costs for care, maintenance and repairs plus rising energy costs for air-conditioning are hence becoming important criteria for buildings and thus roof design. Both the durability of the materials used and the ease of repairing the construction are vital for keeping maintenance costs low. In this sense, all overlapping elements and sheet-type coverings offer the best conditions for replacing any number of damaged parts.
Even just a short time ago, the decision to build a low-energy building meant almost inevitably minimising the windows, that source of "energy leaks". The demands of users for daylighting, information and communication with the outside world have meanwhile led to the development of high-quality forms of glazing. The extra costs, measured in relation to usage and the overall cost of the structure, fluctuate within justifiable limits.
Even in the age of disposable products, buildings are among the long-term investments.

Financial institutions continue to provide mortgages with repayment periods of up to 50 years for land and property. They have faith in these objects because they reach a corresponding age. As the roof represents a primary guarantor for the life span of a building, the highly stressed parts must be made from particularly durable materials. The roofing materials available today are essentially resistant to the effects of the weather; however, they often do not equal the service life of the complete building. It is therefore advisable to increase the resistance of these materials. In the case of metals, high-quality alloys may be the answer,

1.13

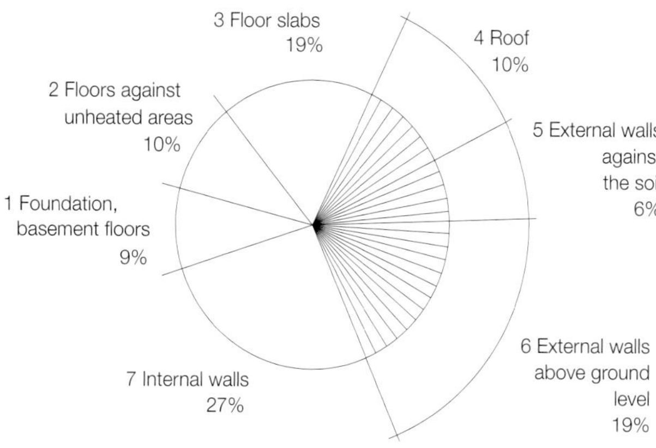


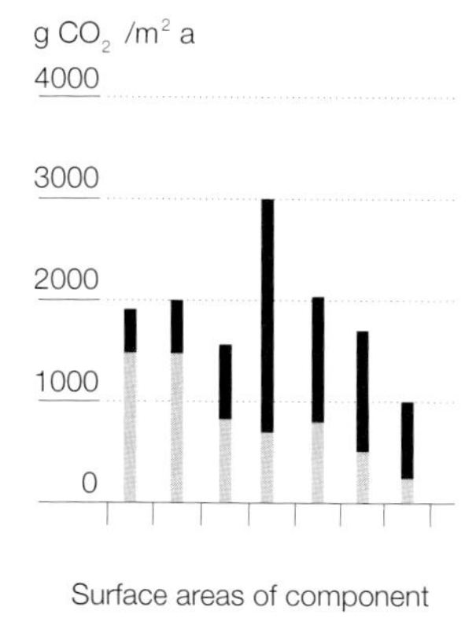


1.14

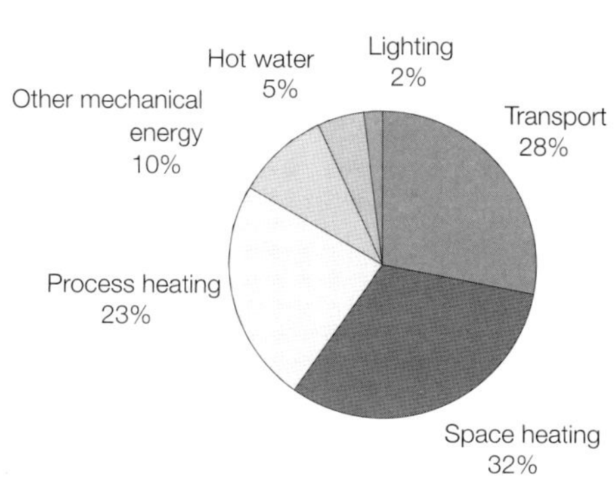


1.15

or coatings of more resistant metals or plastic. The firing process alone makes ceramic materials resistant. Improvements in the form of glazes or water- and dirt-repellent surfaces ("lotus effect") are possible. Concrete and fibre-cement – not vulnerable to frost and heat and thus ideal as building materials – are given coatings to make them sufficiently resistant to moisture and immissions.
Turning to natural stone, the high resistance of slate makes it highly recommendable. However, the cost of extraction and preparation make it unsuitable for widespread use.

Deconstruction, disposal
The debate about health risks (e.g. from the former all-round building material asbestos, from chemical timber preservatives, or the fibres of insulating materials) and the growing awareness of environmental concerns have led to the expected costs of demolition and disposal also being taken into the calculation. Crucial criteria here are: the reusability of whole components, the recyclability of the materials employed (metals), or their easy disposal (mass components). From this point of view, demountable constructions are desirable.

1.13 Vrin in Grisons: Old, natural roofing materials have been replaced by cheaper alternatives due to economic constraints.
1.14 The two diagrams show the optimisation potential with respect to the greenhouse effect for a typical residential building. The potential is particularly great for the external walls and the roof construction, which together constitute about 35% of the entire surface area of a building. From: Klaus Daniels loco citato
1.15 Space heating as a proportion of the total energy consumption in Germany. From: Stephan Oberländer, Judith Huber, Gerhard Müller loco citato

[7] Ernst Ulrich von Weizsäcker, Amory B. Lovins, L. Hunter Lovins, Faktor Vier. Doppelter Wohlstand – halbierter Naturverbrauch, Munich, 1995
[8] Dennis Meadows, The Limits to Growth, A Report for the Club of Rome's Project on the Predicament of Mankind, Stuttgart, 1972

**Economy – ecology**
The constantly growing world population, increasing prosperity and the associated consumer behaviour, also in numerous newly industrialised countries, and the lack of incentives to handle finite natural resources carefully transform measurable growth from a source of prosperity into a risk for our civilisation.[7] Evolution in the natural world, so research teaches us, is dominated by the fundamental principle of minimum input for optimum output. However, the fixation on economic "competition" has been revealed as a dangerous one-sided interpretation of this "economic" principle. In the long term, only the careful handling of raw materials can guarantee the survival of humankind. Ecology must be integrated into our system via the economy factor. Whether we are in the position to include the social and ecological "price" of our material prosperity will become a survival issue for our civilisation. People's increasing awareness of environmental themes and the growing political pressure have had the effect of advancing ecology and sustainability to become important economic factors. In view of the quantities of materials and energy used in the construction industry, it is essential to place ecological demands on building.

## Ecology

### Ecology as a new ethic

The work of the Club of Rome marked a turning point in the assessment of environmental problems.[8] This was accelerated by the oil crisis of 1974, which made it clear that energy reserves were not infinite, even for wealthy Europe. Even though the effects did not lead to any noticeable catastrophes, it was obvious that the growing environmental pollution represented a hitherto unknown threat to mankind. The increasing carbon dioxide content of the air, the plight of the forests suffering from the effects of acid rain, pollution of the oceans and the growing hole in the ozone layer, the risks of accidents and the unsolved disposal problems of the nuclear power industry, and further aspects with an impact on the environment are topics for public discussion. The social awareness of this has also come about due to a changed view of our planet as "Spaceship Earth" (Buckminster Fuller). Finally, a new ethic and hence changes in the political landscape of Germany have evolved through ecological issues.

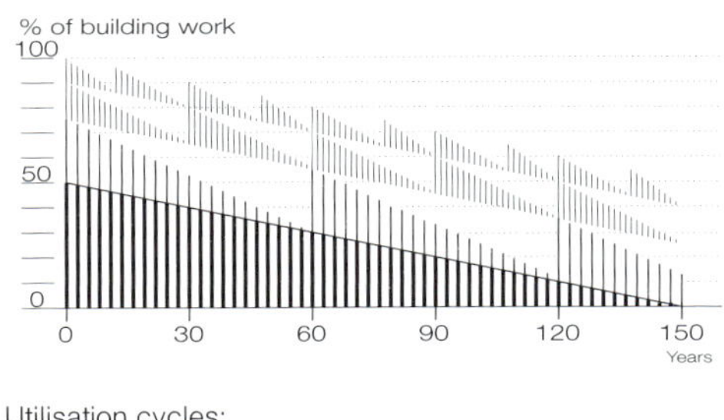


Utilisation cycles:
IIII Services
IIII Facade
IIII Fitting-out
IIII Structure
1.16

1.16 In non-monolithic constructions the weakest member (frequently the joint) makes periodic renewal necessary. Besides ecological problems, this gives rise to material costs that make the building, viewed over its entire service life, more expensive.
A method of construction designed to rationalise operations is hence better – also economically – only in the short term. From: Klaus Daniels loco citato

1.17 Holiday retreat in Dyngby, Denmark, 2001, Claus Hermansen

1.18 Expo Dome, Pavilion of the USA at the 1967 World Exposition in Montreal, Buckminster Fuller

9 Stephan Oberländer, Judith Huber, Gerhard Müller, Das Niedrigenergiehaus – ein Handbuch mit Planungsregeln zum Passivhaus, Stuttgart, 1997

10 SIA Documentation D 0123 Hochbaukonstruktion nach ökologischen Gesichtspunkten, SIA, Zurich, 1995

11 Klaus Daniels, Low-Tech, Light-Tech, High-Tech, Basel/Boston/Berlin, 1998, p. 182

12 Frederic Vester, Neuland des Denkens. Vom technologischen zum kybernetischen Zeitalter, Munich, 1985

13 Klaus Daniels loco citato

**Climate**

The third United Nations Climate Conference took place in Kyoto in 1997. In the Kyoto Protocol, for the first time, an attempt was made to agree on a timetable for limiting the emissions of greenhouse gases into the Earth's atmosphere on a global scale. This can be achieved in the first instance by energy economy measures which limit emissions causing the greenhouse effect, cut costs and save resources. At a national level in Germany, new energy economy legislation has now replaced the former Thermal Insulation Act. The goal is to minimise the total energy consumption of a building with all its consequences for the environment and the climate: operating a building still accounts for 50% of total energy consumption.[9]
Climate protection requires, however, not only the "green" production of energy and its thrifty use in a building, but also a critical evaluation of the building materials. In this context the emissions of pollutants from the materials used in the building during all phases of its life cycle must be assessed; in other words, construction, use and disposal. These days building materials are therefore evaluated according to their influence on the greenhouse effect ($CO_2$), acidification ($SO_2$) and their proportion of "grey" energy (primary energy content), as is applied in Switzerland's building materials catalogue SIA D 0123.[10] According to Klaus Daniels the optimisation potential for reducing the greenhouse effect is greater for the roof than for all other parts of the building.[11] Every structure signifies a loss of area for vegetation and hence a change in the microclimate. This fact spawns the question of whether the roof surface can play an active part in improving the external microclimate. One possibility is to plant vegetation on the roof surface; this improves the local environment and also increases the thermal mass of the building.
The simplest way of providing planting on the roof is to build a lattice using lathing or scaffolds. Planting on a layer of soil prevented from slipping calls for a special type of construction. However, this method has a long tradition in Scandinavia and in the northern regions of America.

**Energy**

In Germany energy imported from abroad is still unrivalled in terms of price. However, it is only a question of time before alternative forms of energy become profitable. The roof can make an active contribution here. As the upper termination to the building, the roof is particularly suitable for exploiting solar and wind energy due to its exposed position, even though the natural conditions in our latitudes are not always perfect.
The artistic treatment of the technical components necessary for exploiting these energy sources and their integration into the roof in a uniform architectural language will be an important task. It seems obvious to seek this uniformity in the choice of materials – materials related to those of the structure and the roof covering.
The one-sided fixation on competition to regulate the market currently leads to economies being made at the expense of resources. Ecological decisions are still regarded as unprofitable. Only moral values and legislative support provide openings for promoting alternative energy sources. Furthermore, we have a responsibility to take into account energy consumption and environmental impact due to the production and disposal of the building materials chosen.

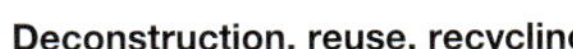

**Deconstruction, reuse, recycling**

One of the eight fundamental rules of biocybernetics as formulated by Frederic Vester in his main work *Neuland des Denkens* ("New Frontiers of Thinking") is the principle of recycling.[12] This term, which expresses the law of the material life cycle, is also extremely important for building. The biggest role for the recycling of buildings here is that it should be possible to detach building materials from an overall construction without releasing hazardous substances. The make-up of a structure should therefore be conceived in such a way that this non-hazardous demolition, and hence the separation of the individual layers, is possible. Only then can a building material be reused. The criteria for the recycling of the materials to be considered during design are: material homogeneity, the separability of different materials, the use of just a few materials, the identification

1.17

of materials and the technical conditions for sensible demolition. These criteria are specified in the Swiss catalogue mentioned above. The scarcity of materials after the Second World War forced builders to reuse building materials to a great extent. They applied two principles:

First, small components were detached from larger constructions for use in a suitable way. Among these were tiles and bricks. It would be worth investigating the relationship between this constraint on materials and the resulting architectural language.
The second recycling method applied was the somewhat more involved crushing and reforming. These days we would call it "downcycling". As in ancient Rome, tiles and building rubble were used in opus caementitium; for example, new bricks were formed from crushed brick, which even as facing masonry evolved its own character.
In principle, these two methods are still valid today.
A roof covering of overlapping elements creates good conditions for reusability. However, the erection of these small elements is expensive. But buildings built from just a few, simple materials have a longer life expectancy. Calculated properly, it can be worthwhile to invest in higher labour costs instead of ever more ingenious materials. For example, roofing systems incorporating energy system components are often unsuitable for easy transformation owing to the diverse materials they contain. Harmonising the demands of energy systems with those of recycling and economic construction are challenges we must face.

#### Flexibility, change

If a system is to remain viable, it must be able to adapt in order to respond to the changing requirements of the outside world.
This adaptability cannot be solved by design alone. This was shown in the 1970s by the demands for maximum multifunctionality. The multifunctional buildings erected at great expense were not optimised for any usage. The adaptability of buildings, which in our fast-moving times is an indispensable requirement, must be possible through conversion or deconstruction. In addition, materials in composite components have different service lives, and the weakest link (frequently the joint) leads to periodic renewal becoming necessary. A method of building aimed solely at rationalising working operations is hence only economical in the short term.[13]
The pitched roof with its multi-layer construction, its replaceable and easily separated components, is well suited to changes. Demolition required by new environmental situations can be carried out essentially non-destructively.
A design employing panels, sheets and tiles is such a successful method for guaranteeing adaptability that it could be transferred to other aspects of building.

### The science of building in the 20th century

At the start of the 20th century structural analysis was based on the elastic theory. The engineer had collections of "ready-made" formulae and tables for the design of repetitious, statically indeterminate structures. The complicated relationships between several dynamic variables were handled using alignment charts and nomograms. Graphical structural engineering was highly popular owing to its intelligibility and ease of use. At the same time the properties of the materials, in particular reinforced concrete, were the subject of intensive research, and the associated theories were unified, improved and recast. It was in 1901 that Emil Mörsch laid the foundation for modern reinforced concrete design. Robert Maillart investigated the theory of flat slabs. Walter Bauersfeld, Franz Dischinger and Ulrich Finsterwalder formulated the membrane theory and adapted it to the needs of reinforced concrete.
Eugène Freyssinet introduced serviceable prestressed concrete to the building fraternity in 1928. Its development was continued by, above all, Finsterwalder, Dischinger and Fritz Leonhardt. During the 1930s Friedrich Bleich was the main driving force behind the development of limit state design. This was based on plastic theory, the advantages of which lay in the realistic modelling of the loadbearing mechanism.
In the field of materials technology, cast steel was rediscovered and applications for cables developed further. The use of concrete was enriched through the introduction of fibre-reinforced, lightweight, high-strength and self-compacting concretes. Plastics have meanwhile become an indispensable part of modern building technology. In recent years in particular, more attention has been devoted to composite building materials to achieve optimum use of their individual properties or to improve their overall behaviour.
The computer conceived by Konrad Zuse in 1941 began to displace graphical methods of structural analysis in the early 1960s. This enabled some long-established numerical methods of computation to be solved. Thanks to finite element methods (FEM), mainly the work of Argyris, Kelsey, Turner and Clough, the problem of multiple static indeterminacy in the design of structures was conquered. Thus there began a rapid and, even now, accelerative development whose fruits are available to architects and engineers in the form of CAD (computer aided design), CAM (computer aided manufacturing), databases, Internet, FEM, structural optimisation programs and other electronic aids.

### The building industry and new building materials

#### Industrialisation and production

Industrialisation has benefited in all branches from advances in science and technology. It has made the commodities of our civilisation affordable and available in great quantities. While automation seems to replace human labour in some sectors, industrialisation in the building industry progresses only very slowly, and sometimes even regresses. For instance, precast reinforced concrete components, in particular for the construction of universities in the 1970s, had advanced such that a noticeable potential for savings in production and sales could be expected. The large quantities necessary for profitable production were, how-

1.18

1.19

1.20

ever, never achieved owing to the multitude of competing suppliers. In the wake of the oil crisis, a flagging building industry and the use of over-conservative methods of construction led to such a slump in demand for these products that they are no longer part of the industrial building portfolio. The same thing happened to building systems, which in the early 1970s were a common sight on the European building market, primarily for schools.
For the most part, the great advances in metallurgy had an effect on the highly stressed components in mechanical engineering and the aerospace industry. The construction industry acquired high-strength steel and stainless steel. One interesting invention was Cor-Ten steel, which prevented further corrosion due to the rapid formation of a protective oxidation layer. Unfortunately, however, complete drying after exposure to the weather – an essential prerequisite for this self-protection – was often not guaranteed.
Glass technology delivered the greatest advance in building. Methods of production enabled a better quality at lower prices and the diversity of products provides for many new applications today.
Research into concrete resulted in new chemical additives providing better quality, which led to additional functions such as waterproofing. The development of self-compacting and high-strength concrete meant that this traditionally conservative mass material could be counted among the group of "high-tech" building materials.
Plastics offer a wide range of products whose development and production started in the 1920s. A building industry without plastics is these days inconceivable and they fulfil important insulation, sealing and covering tasks in the modern roof.

## Forms of roofing and materials

### Overlapping elements

The oldest method of covering a roof – with small-format overlapping elements – still has many advantages. Its adaptability to suit different shapes and slopes, ease of repair, the allowance for movement, and above all the texture of animated roof surfaces, outweigh the cost of manufacture and laying. Better preparation of the materials and improved methods of production have adapted the quality of this form of roofing to the technical requirements of our age.

1.19 Thatched roof of reed in Denmark
1.20 Roof covering of wooden shingles
1.21 Granite slabs on the roof of a sheep stall in Vals, Grisons
1.22 Flat clay tiles, cotton mill in Campione

Thatch
Reed and straw are primarily used when called for by landscaping and conservation requirements. As marshy areas have disappeared from the German landscape, there is less and less reed available, which is why it must be imported these days. Straw, on the other hand, is available in sufficient quantities. Energy economy requirements are met by these materials, but their high cost, maintenance and fire risk force them into the niche market of historical roof coverings.

Wooden shingles
At the start of the 1970s the number of shingle roofs was steadily diminishing. However, in the course of the general renaissance of wood as a building material during that decade, wooden shingles were rediscovered as a roofing material. One of the reasons for this was because the imported western red cedar and eastern white cedar exhibit good weathering resistance.
Although wood is a renewable resource, it is not always ecologically friendly. Many of the types of wood used today come from ecologically sensitive forests and the trip across the Atlantic requires high energy consumption. Great quantities of energy are also consumed in production and erection, and in protecting the wood against fire, pests and mould. The availability of resin-rich larch wood and the development of ecologically justifiable preservatives for indigenous timber will determine the spread of wooden shingles in Germany in the future.

Natural stone
The triumph of the flat roof, dwindling resources and irrational methods of production brought about the almost complete demise of the slate industry in the mid-1970s. Since then, new sources of this material in Spain and other countries have been brought on line and production further rationalised. This fact, coupled with the general popularity of pitched roofs and the requirements of historic building conservation, has led to a renaissance of the slate roof. Ingenious roofing techniques, which were already used by the Romans for their buildings along the Rhine and reached their climax in the buildings of the Baroque, give this durable material with its low primary energy requirement good chances despite the time-consuming erection necessary in our aggressive economic climate.

1.21

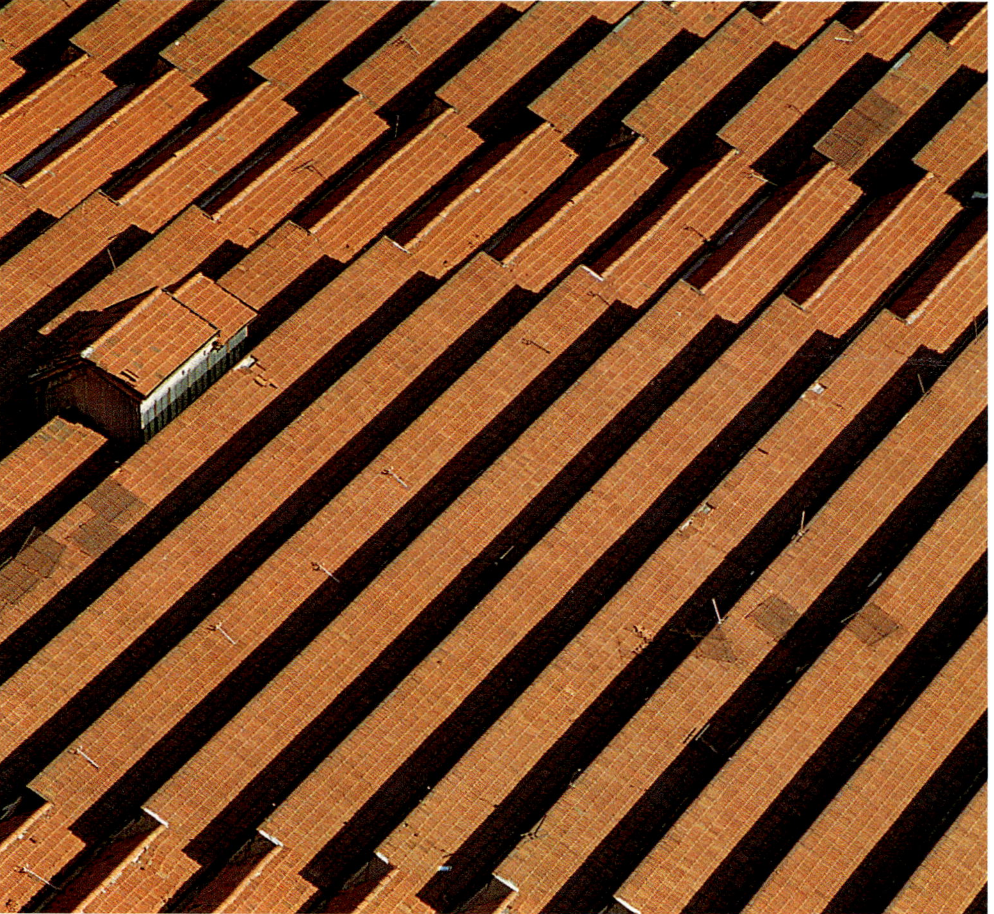

1.22

1.23

1.24

1.25

Clay tiles
Improvements have been seen in all areas of roof tile production. Both the extraction of the raw materials and their preparation have been mechanised and automated. Tunnel kilns started replacing circular kilns around 1950 and enabled the continuous but, above all, precisely controlled firing process necessary for industrial production. The manufacturing process was fully mechanised and controlled mainly automatically. In this way, this traditional type of roof covering was able to become economically efficient.
The form of the tiles became increasingly refined so that today there is a large selection available. The limits are determined by the tolerances of the material and the firing process. In Germany the quantities of raw materials required can be covered by indigenous deposits and the primary energy requirement, which is constantly being reduced, lies in the middle for roof covering materials. These durable tiles (lasting 80–100 years) can be reused after crushing. In many respects this is a "green" building material.
Although laying tiles is labour intensive and so cannot be counted among the cheaper alternatives, tiles will continue to play a significant role in the long term.

Concrete
The production of concrete roof tiles was largely a manual operation long into the 20th century. In 1925 roof tile machines were exported from Denmark to England, where in 1936 some 203 million roof tiles were sold by one company alone. The most notable phase in the development of these tiles was brought about by the demand for inexpensive roofing materials in the post-war years. Today, automation is on a par with that of clay tile production. Almost unlimited cement and sand resources are available in Germany and can be extracted without causing problems (through reactivation of the mines).
Environmental pollution caused by cement production can be prevented these days by suitable measures. The primary energy requirement for concrete roof tiles is in fact lower than that for clay products. Disposal in landfill sites presents no problems and concrete roof tiles removed from buildings are taken back by manufacturers for reuse. Forms and production techniques are equal to those of clay tiles. In fact, precision is even better than with clay tiles. Prejudice against concrete as a building material has mainly come about through the many badly planned large structures. Concrete roof tiles present no health risks and are a sensible alternative to clay roof coverings.

Fibre-cement
The fibre-cement available these days contains no asbestos. The production of asbestos cement products has increased steadily since the introduction of asbestos as a building material. Since 1982 the inhalable asbestos fibres once used have been replaced by Dolanit and Kuralon (synthetic fibres based on polyacryl nitrite and polyvinyl alcohol). These non-disruptable fibres are much (1300 times) thicker than asbestos fibres and hence cannot be inhaled. They are combined with cellulose process fibres.
The test results for the new material reveal values just as good as the old material in terms of mechanical and chemical behaviour. Many products have been in use since 1982. This durable and easily worked material is therefore still available for unrestricted use in the future.

Bitumen
Although originally developed for large areas, rolls of bitumen roofing felt have led to the development of small-format, flat overlapping elements. These shingles with their special surface finishes are more suitable for shallow roof pitches than their natural stone counterparts. They are easy to cut and fit, lightweight and inexpensive. A simple but ingenious laying technique makes them ideal for do-it-yourself builders.

**Sheet metals**
Since the introduction of the industrial rolling process for sheet metal, this has been used for many shallow roof pitches with critical sealing demands. Another advantage is that metal is non-combustible. Although production has been automated and rationalised, which means that better and more consistent material quality can now be guaranteed, the methods of laying sheet metal have hardly changed since 1900. Just as in the past, joints are made manually by folding and soldering, although folding machines now ease the work on site.

Lead
Were it not for the more frequent use of this material in other countries, the low number of complete lead roofs in Germany would make mention of this material unnecessary. Further, its good mouldability makes it adaptable and it is very popular for transitions. Low reserves, high transport costs, high primary energy requirement and, above all, the health risks associated with lead mean that its use must be limited to unavoidable situations. Otherwise it should be replaced by other materials.

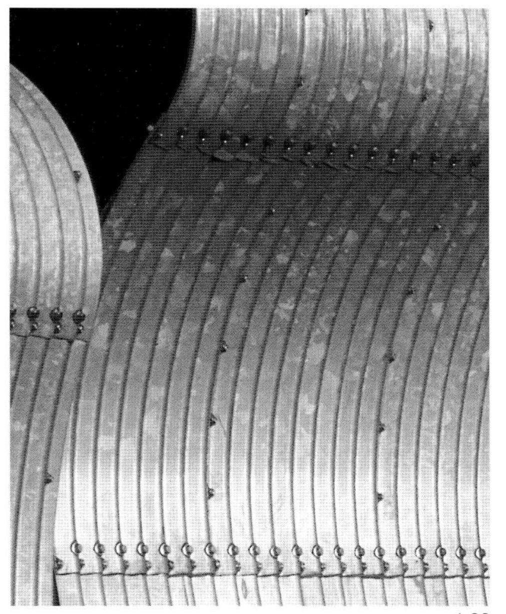

1.26

Copper
After aluminium, copper has the next highest primary energy consumption. Resources are limited, and 99% lie outside Germany. These disadvantages are balanced by the high recovery rate and the long life span (exceeding 100 years). Fears that acid rain could convey dangerous quantities of copper from the roof into the soil and groundwater have been disproved by extensive calculations carried out by Otto Franqué.[14]

Steel
Steel scores relatively well on the ecological scale thanks to the deposits of iron ore available and the good reuse quotas for scrap iron. The risk of corrosion has been minimised by improvements in galvanising (Sendzimir process). This process permits an even coating of zinc, the thickness of which can be controlled, that still adheres after shaping the steel. Owing to abrasion and aggressive atmospheres, however, the life expectancy of a galvanised sheet steel roof is nowhere near as high as that of the other metals used for roof coverings. Sheet steel in the form of coils and plates should therefore be given an additional weatherproof coating or laminated with plastic film. The further development of these methods will show just how much sheet steel we can expect to see in roofing in the future.

Zinc
The single fundamental new development in metal alloys in the 20th century took place in the 1960s and involved zinc to which copper and titanium were added to produce titanium-zinc. Its high primary energy requirement is unfortunately not offset by any satisfactory recycling (downcycling).[15] Resources in Germany have been exhausted and transport from Australia and North America involves great amounts of energy. However, this new material is predicted to last 80–100 years thanks to its corrosion resistance and low degradation rate. This justifies its frequent use. Zinc does not present any health risks; abraded zinc that manages to enter the soil does not reach a value that could be considered harmful. It is one of the non-hazardous heavy metals because it does not accumulate in the body but is excreted.[16]

Aluminium
Owing to its low weight, good workability and resistance to corrosion, this material is frequently used for roofs as well. As with the other sheet metals, laying techniques have remained conventional. But poor in ecological terms is Germany's dependence on imports from overseas and the high energy requirement during production, which puts aluminium at the top of the primary energy requirement table for metal

1.27

1.23 Lead sheet in Greenwich
1.24 Fibre-cement sheeting in Denmark
1.25 Concrete tiles on a building in Laibach by Jože Plečnik
1.26 Sheet metal panels: bicycle shed in Sakai-cho, Japan, 1999, Shuhei Endo
1.27 Sheet metal panels, chrome steel: Liner Museum, Appenzell, 1996–98, Gigon & Guyer

[14] Dr Otto Franqué, Wechselwirkungen zwischen Kupfer und Umgebung, in: Baumetall, issue 2/86, Berlin
[15] Tobias Waltjen et al., Ökologischer Bauteilkatalog: Bewertete gängige Konstruktionen, Vienna, 1999
[16] Wend Burggraef, Die Eigenschaften von Zink unter besondere Berücksichtigung des Umweltschutzes, study of available literature

roof coverings – three times higher for this obliging and durable material than, for example, steel. The service life of 50+ years (the oldest application still in use today was built in 1897) cannot completely outweigh this disadvantage. In order to justify the use of aluminium, almost 100% recycling is desirable. That could be achieved with an intensive environmental policy and corresponding education. Acid rain may liberate ions from aluminium, which then enter the soil. However, 8% of the Earth's crust consists of aluminium compounds so that a minimal addition of aluminium from human sources can hardly cause any problems. High concentrations may, however, damage very fine plant roots.

**Sheets**
The term "sheet" covers all roofing elements that are clearly much larger than overlapping elements (e.g. clay/concrete roof tiles, slates); these are, as it were, the "big brothers" of the overlapping elements. New building materials and production techniques have made possible larger formats than those of natural products. Their big advantage over overlapping elements is fewer loadbearing components; these lightweight sheets can themselves carry more and so purlins can be spaced further apart and the loadbearing structure reduced accordingly. In addition, less labour is needed for larger units. These advantages can be best exploited in simple roof structures. Sheets are therefore usually employed for straightforward applications. They are also less expensive for multi-layer constructions. Their low cost of erection makes sheets particularly suitable for industrial prefabrication.

Metals
It had already been realised in the 19th century that shaping sheet metal produced improvements in stability. The corrugated sheet iron invented during this period has not lost any of its advantages today. It can only be compared with those few apparently simple ideas with a rich harvest of positive consequences – like the shaping of roof tiles. The sine-wave form was joined in the 1950s by the trapezoidal form from the USA; additional profiling resulted in even better load-carrying ability but, above all, these sheets had a better bearing on the roof structure. Steel trapezoidal sheets are produced with various finishes and coatings to protect against corrosion. Preservation of this protective layer is a prerequisite for their durability. Various coatings are available, for aluminium sheets as well, governed basically by aesthetic aspects.

Fibre-cement
Developments in corrugated fibre-cement sheets can be attributed to results in metal forming. Compared to inexpensive corrugated sheet iron they have the advantage of a life span of 50–70 years. As moss and lichen grow well on fibre-cement sheets, this building material is often considered on a par with natural products.

Bitumen
Corrugated bitumen sheets have been produced since 1950. They have the same advantages as corrugated sheet iron. They are multilayer (laminated), easily worked and inexpensive sheets.

Glass
The boom years of glass-roofed buildings and passages came to an end at the close of the 19th century. Glass roofs degenerated to roofs with glass rooflights. Only in horticultural buildings did glass roofs continue to prevail. However, architects like Bruno Taut and Peter Behrens carried this fascination for transparent roofs into the 20th century so that glass as a roofing material for buildings other than greenhouses never quite died out. But it was not until the late 1950s that developments in glass roofs were given a new momentum. Contemporary

1.28

architecture would be inconceivable without the pane of glass as a roofing material. Of all the roof covering materials, glass has undergone the greatest development in terms of production, size, quality and, primarily, the diversity of products available. There is not enough space here to discuss the individual steps that begin with the Fourcault glass drawing process in 1905 and end with the float glass process common today. All materials for glass production in Germany are essentially obtained from domestic deposits. The primary energy requirement for standard flat glass is indeed relatively high but much less than that for metals. Recycling used glass is becoming increasingly important.

The greenhouse effect that retains long-wave heat radiation within a glazed room is an important starting point for gaining energy from solar radiation. The various techniques range from reflective coatings for thermal insulation in summer and winter to gas-filled or low-gas cavities between the panes of double glazing. Intermediate layers in panes of laminated glass can reflect or admit light and energy, according to frequency. However, these layers can also be temperature- or voltage-controlled in order to regulate the transmittance of energy. Finally, photovoltaic elements are readily integrated into laminated glass panels.

Glazing without putty – called patent glazing – is based on the laying techniques of the 19th century. Since the 1970s it has become more diverse and more reliable so that combining various types of glass and coatings allows well-coordinated overall designs to be constructed.

As a rotproof, durable building material with which the human dream of sheltered "living as if in the open air" becomes true, glass still has a great potential for development.

1.29

1.30

1.28 Sheet metal: Wallraf-Richartz Museum and Ludwig Museum, Cologne, 1980–86, Busmann + Haberer

1.29 Glass: Maximilian Museum, Augsburg, 2000, Augsburg Building Authority, structural engineers: Ludwig + Weiler

1.30 Glass: extension to the Louvre, Paris, 1988–93, I.M. Pei & Partners, structural engineer: Peter Rice Although the inverted pyramid in the Louvre Carrousel does not serve as a roof, it illustrates the great progress made in modern glass design.

Plastics

Today, we understand plastics – for building or other purposes – to be materials made from macromolecular organic compounds produced from animal or vegetable products (in the form of oil, gas or coal) that exhibit a plastic status in certain phases of their processing. Following the first fully synthetic plastics made from phenolic resins (Bakelite), polyacryl and polystyrene appeared after the First World War. These were joined by polyvinyl chloride and polyvinyl acetate in 1930, and during the first half of the 1940s the range of products multiplied to the many types we know today. Glass-fibre reinforced sheets on a polyester basis (GRP) appeared on the market in 1950. Today, there are plastic sheets of polyvinyl chloride (PVC), polymethyl methacrylate (PMMA, plexiglass) and polycarbonate (PC). The shaping of these materials to improve their stability when used as sheets has been drawn from the repertoire of metal-forming techniques. They are available in sine-wave or trapezoidal profiles and as flat sheets with strengthened edges or ribbed surfaces. They can also be employed as transparent or translucent roof coverings.

As the raw materials are primarily obtained from crude oil and natural gas, Germany and many other countries are highly dependent on imports. In addition, the extraction of oil, its transport and processing raises ecological and health issues. When we consider the loss of calorific value, the primary energy requirement is higher than that of most metals. Recycling is currently only possible with a high energy input (pyrolysis) and is associated with a loss in quality (melting down). Biological decomposition is limited and extremely slow, which is why plastics pollute the environment. Risks stemming from the constituent substances have not yet fully been researched. It is believed that vinyl chloride is carcinogenic. Likewise, softeners such as PCB, solvents (benzene, glycols) and fillers may be health risks. In a fire, chlorine gas (from PVC) and cyanate compounds (from polyurethane) are released. These dangers would seem to suggest restricting the use of plastics to areas in which they cannot be replaced or long-term usage is guaranteed. The machining of various plastics, their effects, their recycling and disposal must be weighed against the advantages in each individual situation.[17]

**Flexible sheeting**

Roofing felts

A dynamic development has taken place in the realm of roofing felts since the dawn of the 20th century. The obliging "roofing felt", which was so easy to work with, enjoyed high growth rates, initially on pitched roofs and then on the flat variety. After the Second World War bitumen was used exclusively until the arrival of the first synthetic roofing felt in the mid to late 1950s. Today, bitumen roofing felts without protective layers are only used on pitched roofs for buildings of secondary importance.

Grass-covered roofs

Bitumen roofing felts are regaining importance as a run-off layer for grass-covered pitched roofs. As the basic product for these felts is essentially obtained from crude residual asphalt, a waste product of crude oil distillation, its availability depends on the quantity of oil processed – or consumed. This also applies to synthetic roofing felts. The primary energy requirement, measured in terms of the weight per m$^2$ necessary, is negligible. The ecological benefits of such a roof are very high. Internally, there is the thermal mass and cooling effect in summer, and externally, the effect on the microclimate. In a pitched roof, the risk of root penetration by the plants suitable for such applications is extremely low, provided care is taken during construction and the pitch is sufficient.

We can expect the increasing significance of "green" issues to lead to more planted roofs in the future although these are at the moment considerably more expensive and more complicated than conventional types of roofing.

**Membranes**

The evolution of membranes began with the appearance of synthetic roofing felts in the mid-1950s. Membranes can be used for independent loadbearing, i.e. membrane, structures.

1.31 Grass-covered roof: library, Delft, 1993–98, Mecanoo
1.32 Millennium Dome, London, 2000, Richard Rogers Partnership
1.33 Schlumberger Development Centre, Cambridge, 1985–88, Michael Hopkins & Partners

[17] Burkhart Schulze Darup, Bauökologie, Wiesbaden/Berlin, 1996

1.31

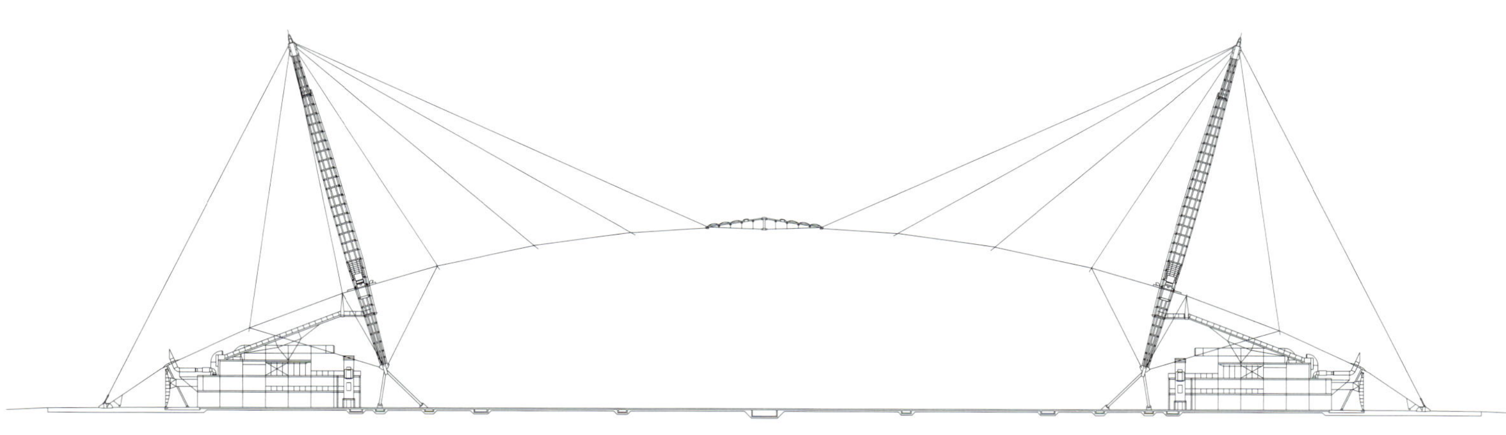

1.32

Owing to their low self-weight, membrane structures allow the design of highly efficient roofs, which in multi-shell and multi-layer designs can also serve as a proper building envelope. Isotropic and anisotropic sheet materials are used for their production. Isotropic materials have the same physical properties in all directions. They essentially consist of fluoropolymer films, of which the ethylene-tetrafluoroethylene (ETFE) variety is most common. ETFE has a high tension and tearing resistance, and is also resistant to weathering and ageing. Permanent structures achieve service lives of at least 25 years. The material – up to 95% translucent – can be printed to achieve various lighting effects. Anisotropic materials are textiles made from natural, synthetic and chemical fibres. A great choice of PVC, PTFE and silicone coatings enable a whole range of requirements to be met.
When it comes to recycling, the same applies as for plastics. Composite textiles are difficult to separate into their constituent components, which means that disposal in a landfill site or incineration are the only options. However, its high calorific value makes PVC-coated polyester popular with the operators of waste incineration plants.
Until recently, membranes were considered an exotic roofing material. Their highly efficient load-carrying abilities and their adaptability to suit various functions has seen their popularity grow in recent years. The further development of membranes will affect many areas of building in the near future.

Summary and outlook

The rising cost of human labour has led to mechanisation and automation in the realm of roof coverings, too. The material quality of synthetic products has been improved and refined. Shaping and jointing has become better and more reliable, meaning that there is now a wealth of roofing materials and forms available. On the other hand, methods of laying these roofing materials have changed only marginally. This means that the small-format variety demands a large manual input during erection. Trials to reduce this workload have been repeatedly carried out; trials that involve dividing up the roof into larger elements that can be prefabricated off the building site.
A broad spectrum of prefabrication methods are on offer today. These range from pure loadbearing structures to which roof covering layers have to be added, to complete elements merely waiting to be joined together on site. The pitched roof will in future gain importance as a source of energy. Modular constructions in which large-format elements are allocated different tasks could represent one way forward for the future.

1.33

# Use and form

### Use and the form of the roof

There have always been roof forms geared to a particular usage. For example, deep buildings were stepped back in order to illuminate the interior, as was the case with religious buildings with a basilica-type cross-section. In industrial buildings the complexity of the production processes, their interaction and mutual dependence increasingly called for flat, "isotropic" buildings. It was obvious that such buildings should be finished off with a flat roof. However, the easier planning of the layout that resulted from these flat roofs led to a weakening of the relationship between plan layout and roof form. So it is not trite to point out today that the special needs of the use of a building can determine the character of a structure. The fact that this is also expressed in the roof form and that the use of a building can thus be directly expressed by the roof form has become forgotten in the age of the flat roof.

### Using the roof space

The roof space has always been used. In earlier civilisations in which buildings were little more than a roof, no distinction was made between roof space and living quarters. Later, as these were separated for reasons of heating, the latter was generally used for storage. However, open roof spaces also existed for architectural reasons, as the early Christian and Romanesque churches demonstrate. Today, the roof space is put to many uses.

#### Simple uses without special demands on the interior climate

This includes the storage of goods for which temperature fluctuations are unimportant. The roof space can be hot or cold, dirty, or affected by driving snow. This traditional usage does not introduce any new problems and so is not discussed further here.

#### Uses involving an exposed structure

Wide-span structures often reach a structural depth equal to the useful height below. If the loadbearing structure is integrated into the space, the effective height of the space extends as far as the underside of the roof covering. In such interiors designing the structure becomes an important task because it is an

1.34

1.34 Sogn Benedetg chapel, Sumvitg, Grisons, 1985–88, Peter Zumthor
1.35 Centennial Hall, Bochum, 1902, H. Schumacher

[18] Institute for Climate, Environment and Energy, Wuppertal, quoted in: Volker Wöhrl, Der überforderte Alleskönner, Süddeutsche Zeitung, No. 86/2002, Munich

architectural element defining the space. We must give credit to the 19th century for rediscovering and recording the beauty of single-storey shed structures. They are usually found in unheated, semi-open spaces, e.g. railway stations, market halls, factories or large exhibition buildings. One characteristic of this type of building was that the lighting was integrated into the overall architecture by means of large expanses of glazing. This tradition is continued by many architects – with outstanding results.

**Living in the roof space**

The value of building land in densely populated regions and large cities led to the practical climate buffer of the open roof space being turned into living quarters during the 19th and 20th centuries. Mansard roofs began to appear in the urban landscape. This characteristic roof with its cranked shape was named after François Mansart. It has two advantages: the usable floor area of the roof space approaches that of the storeys below, and the number of storeys and the eaves height can remain within building authority stipulations. However, this roof form existed even before Mansart gave it his name. Such living quarters without an overlying buffer zone were subject to extreme temperature fluctuations, and thus reserved for servants and the poor. Looked at purely from this historical perspective, it is therefore astonishing to find that living under the roof has remained a favourite, indeed is even growing in popularity.

Building land has become a valuable commodity. In light of the fact that in Germany alone 120 ha of land are lost to man-made constructions every day, with far-reaching ecological consequences, building land must be utilised as efficiently as possible.[18] So the task is to provide an interior climate for the living quarters under the roof that meets modern standards.

Two reasons for living in the topmost storey are to escape from the noise and exhaust fumes of the streets below and to benefit from better lighting conditions. A lift spares us the long climb up the stairs. The hierarchy of storeys in the urban apartment block has been reversed. Sloping external walls are regarded as cheerful and cosy. Is this a combination of a longing for the simple life and an atavistic search for security?

1.35

Nevertheless, the problems of living under the roof should not be underestimated. Multi-skin constructions providing thermal insulation and moisture control make the roof a technically complicated "inclined outside wall". Openings to admit light and air, indispensable for healthy living conditions, do not always contribute to improving the aesthetics of the roof surface. As a rule, the inappropriately large dormer or roof windows disrupt the roof structure and are sources of problems.

Proper storey or roof storey?
Basically, the question is whether it would not be better to add another full storey in order to use the building land to the full. The cost is usually lower than that of a fully fitted-out roof space, when the available floor space is calculated according to the DIN standard. Is it really just a cunning exploitation of the legal elbow room that leads to an apartment under the roof? The definitions and legislation that exist solely to clarify the number of storeys and the roof would seem to prove this point. But if an apartment under the roof is desired, the pitch of the roof should be as steep as possible. The roofing material thus lasts longer and the rest of the construction is less vulnerable to damage. A climatic buffer zone around and above the living quarters improves the internal climate. Where this is not possible, multi-layer constructions with adequate ventilation are the only answer.

## Using the roof surface

### Solar energy

In Central Europe solar radiation reaches annual values of approx. 1050 kWh/m². It would seem obvious to exploit this source of energy from the sun. In Germany three-quarters of all surfaces available for energy purposes are roof surfaces; of this figure about two-thirds are pitched roofs.[19] So from the annual figure of approx. 112 TWh of solar-generated electricity, or about 25% of Germany's annual electricity needs, around 67 TWh could be generated on pitched roof surfaces each year.
But the lack of adequate storage options means the anticyclical behaviour of solar radiation and energy consumption initially prevents satisfactory utilisation of the roof surface for energy production. Nevertheless, the potential for generating energy on the pitched roof is very significant in the light of dwindling resources. It is therefore important to continue developing the engineering and architectural aspects of solar energy systems for roofs.
The following two methods are available for exploiting solar energy:

Solar energy heating systems
This is the straightforward method of using solar energy. A fluid medium is heated by the energy absorbed from the radiation. This in turn heats up the actual water in the system. This type of solar energy system is also useful for backing up other heating systems.
Flat-plate collectors are available in various sizes and represent the simpler variation of the system. Vacuum collectors are technically more advanced and about twice as efficient. The vacuum tubes, any number of which can be coupled together, are about 2 m long. Both types of collector occupy only one part of the roof surface, so integration is often a problem.

Photovoltaic systems
These systems, in which light is converted directly into (d.c.) electricity, are currently burdened by the high production costs of the components and the overall setup; and technical developments are currently lagging behind expectations. The greatest development potential is expected to come from thin-film technologies, with the copper-indium-diselenite (CIS cells) variety (degree of efficiency of 10–15%) being promised the best chances. In 1999 the German government launched the "100 000 roofs photovoltaic programme" with electricity generated by solar energy being sold into the public grid. For the first time there was an incentive for widespread use and hence new momentum for further development. The size of the glass modules housing the cells varies depending on the number of cells. Once again, the problem of incorporating these systems into the roof surface has not yet been satisfactorily solved.

1.36

1.37

1.38

## Health

A prime goal of building is to create an internal climate for users that smooths out the seasonal and daily climatic fluctuations. The interior, in which we live and work for most of our lives, should provide optimum conditions for our well-being. Humidity of 40–50%, temperature of 18–23 °C and adequate daylight with a natural spectrum and radiation balance are desirable. This places quite a burden on the roof.

**Interior climate**

The unoccupied roof space used as a buffer is an important factor for a balanced climate in the rooms below. If this intermediate space is omitted, very high demands are placed on the roof construction to meet the standards of a proper storey. Multi-skin designs ensure that moisture problems do not arise and that the boundaries of the room are warm. In doing so, the mass of the materials used for floors and walls plays a major role owing to their thermal storage capacity. Once the problem of cooling has been overcome, heating the inside surface of the roof (wall-mounted heating) may contribute to increasing the comfort in the – in climatic terms – highly stressed roof.

1.36 Attic apartment, London, 1996, Brooks Stacey Randall
1.37 The effects of a badly designed, badly built and badly maintained attic apartment: Carl Spitzweg, Der arme Poet, 1893
1.38 Pictorial comment by Adolf Loos on the converted roof space. From: Adolf Loos, Trotzdem, reprint, Vienna, 1982
1.39 Federal Ministry for Economic Affairs, Berlin, 2001, Baumann & Schnittger. Solar panels can provide shade and improve the appearance of glass roofs.

[19] M. Kaltschmitt, Wind- und Solarstrom im Kraftwerksverbund, Heidelberg, 1995
[20] P. Krusche, D. Althaus, J. Gabriel, Ökologisches Bauen, Wiesbaden/Berlin, 1982
[21] Federal Office of the Environment, Umweltfreundliche Beschaffung (manual for taking environmental protection into account in public administration and procurement), Wiesbaden/Berlin, 1987
[22] Katalyse Umweltgruppe and Gruppe für ökologische Bau- und Umweltplanung, Das ökologische Heimwerkerbuch, Hamburg, 1985

**Materials**

Our well-being must be guaranteed by the materials used in the construction. Legislative measures have partly reduced the risks mentioned below.

Internal lining

The materials used for the internal lining may not contain any substances that are hazardous to health. Such substances may occur in chipboard (formaldehyde), timber preservatives (PCP) and the constituents of paints (aromatic and aliphatic solvents).

Loadbearing structure and insulation

The impregnated preservatives used in timber roofs may contain dangerous solvents (e.g. PCP). Thermal insulation made from rigid plastic foam sheets may contain toxic gases. Fibrous insulating materials made from mineral or glass fibres with and without surface finishes suffer from abrasion of microparticles, which can then lead to bronchial irritation.

Roof coverings

While the minimal radioactivity of clay materials can be ignored, metals raise questions of health risks. But if we ignore the energy requirement and emission of pollutants during production, with the exception of lead, the metals suitable for roof coverings – copper, zinc, steel, aluminium – can be regarded as safe for our health. They all occur in the human body and in healthy soils. Despite this, high individual concentrations can cause damage. The heavy metal lead should be replaced by other metals wherever possible.[20,21,22]

## Form

The roof is part of a complex system of relationships determined by the most diverse tasks and requirements. This affects the form of the roof.

The most important relationship is between the roof and the rest of the building envelope, which it protects. Together they form an indivisible unity: the structure. Like the structure, the roof is also determined by three equally important parameters: use, construction and form. However, it also interacts with the landscape and the built environment. After looking at use and construction separately, we shall investigate the conditions affecting the form and the interaction between roof form and environment.

### Roof forms – basic forms and their derivation

A word on the characteristics of roof forms

A long tradition of observation has produced a hierarchy among pitched roofs. The simplest form is the monopitch roof. This suffers from being primarily associated with ancillary buildings, a predicament that architects have desperately been trying to overcome since the beginning of the 20th century. The duopitch roof is regarded as somewhat more advanced because it embodies the reassuring symmetry of classical architectural forms. The hipped roof, demanding a certain distance on all sides, is regarded as the most genteel and most stately; it has been used in many miniature forms to imitate former mansion houses. Curved roof forms evolved for constructional reasons and were reserved for the domes of religious buildings. They assume a special position in classification of buildings. Although a curved surface only comes about as a result of the structurally pragmatic shell form, it attracts more attention than a roof of flat surfaces.

1.39

1.40

It is interesting to note that this age-old affinity between form and importance was first abandoned by the post-modernists, which highlights the re-evaluation aspects within this architectural movement.
Attempts by architects to create a fluid transition between outside wall and roof – a design approach simply borrowed from the aircraft or automotive industries – are illogical in the construction of buildings. Radiation and precipitation mean that the roof is subject to a much higher climatic load than the vertical wall it is supposed to protect. Using a wall material for the roof may be inadequate, and a high-quality roof covering for the outside wall too elaborate and expensive.

## The parts of the roof

The overall appearance of the roof is governed by the material, its texture, the material-related roof pitch and the arrangement of its constituent parts. Forming them to suit the material is inseparable from the overall form of the roof, and also influences its character. The various parts of the roof are shown in the illustration on the facing page.

**Constructional tasks**
The following notes are intended to show which constructional tasks each individual part of the roof – ridge, verge, eaves – has to fulfil. A more detailed treatment of this subject can be found in the chapter entitled "Construction details".

Edges
The edges are the ridge, the verge and the eaves. In the case of a gable roof, the ridge povides a waterproof junction between two adjoining roof surfaces. The construction of the ridge must permit small movements of the roof surfaces. In ventilated designs the ridge, as the highest point, is the ideal place to incorporate ventilation outlets. The ridge of a monopitch roof must also allow for some movement between roof surface and adjoining construction. An overhanging ridge to a monopitch roof protects the wall below. If a multi-skin construction is involved, its whole edge must be protected against the weather.
The verge must fulfil similar tasks to the ridge of a monopitch roof. It need not be ventilated but ventilation does no harm. The verge, too, must be able to move essentially independently of the outside wall below. Sensibly, it overhangs and thus provides protection for the wall underneath. Finally, the side of the roof construction must be clad (barge board), as with the ridge of a monopitch roof.
Functions similar to those of the monopitch roof ridge and verge have to be fulfilled by the eaves as well. As the bottom edge of the roof they must guarantee that precipitation can drain into a gutter or drain clear of the roof covering. Providing ventilation inlets for the roof construction is another important task for the eaves.

1.40 Due to their frequent use for religious buildings, curved roofs, above all domes, have taken on a special position in the system of values for roofs, as here in Siena, Italy.

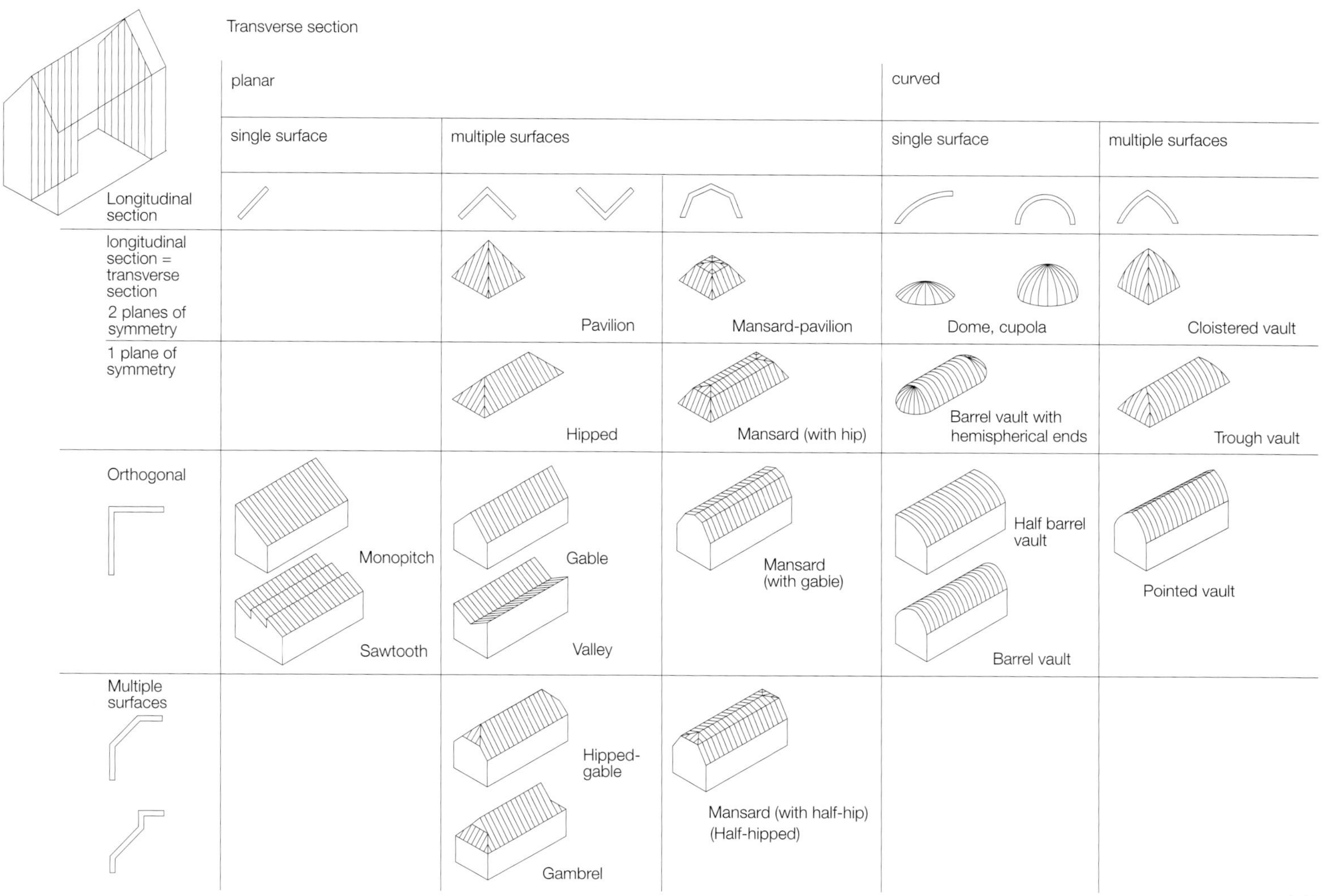

| Transverse section | planar | | | curved | |
|---|---|---|---|---|---|
| | single surface | multiple surfaces | | single surface | multiple surfaces |
| Longitudinal section | | | | | |
| longitudinal section = transverse section<br>2 planes of symmetry | | Pavilion | Mansard-pavilion | Dome, cupola | Cloistered vault |
| 1 plane of symmetry | | Hipped | Mansard (with hip) | Barrel vault with hemispherical ends | Trough vault |
| Orthogonal | Monopitch<br>Sawtooth | Gable<br>Valley | Mansard (with gable) | Half barrel vault<br>Barrel vault | Pointed vault |
| Multiple surfaces | | Hipped-gable<br>Gambrel | Mansard (with half-hip) (Half-hipped) | | |

1.41

1.41 Roof forms: basic forms and their derivation
1.42 Roof edge forms
1.43 Types of dormer window: a) eyebrow dormer, b) shed dormer, c) gablet, d) gable-end dormer

## Arrises

The arrises are the ridge of a gable roof, plus hips, valleys, troughs, cranks and steps.
The arrises of the roof surface must be able to accommodate the movements of the individual adjoining areas. The ridge, which in a gable roof can also be regarded as an edge, has already been described above.
It is harder to incorporate ventilation outlets in the hip – very similar to the ridge of a gable roof – if the entire ventilation is to be routed via the hip.
The valley, as a water collection and draining channel, raises problems of waterproofing. If ventilation around the valley is necessary, the depth of water required leads to additional constructional requirements. Continuous ventilation underneath must be solved together with the hip.
Cranks and steps link and demarcate different roof pitches or raise the upper roof surface with the same pitch. They are distinguished by their different constructional details. While the crank enables the roof surface to continue uninterrupted, allowing for a certain degree of movement, the step divides it into two parts. The careful design of a crank often leads to a step, above all when preformed parts are not available for the change of direction of various pitched surfaces. Provided adequate precautions are taken against water ponding, driving snow and driving rain, a step can also incorporate ventilation inlets.

## Openings

Openings in the roof surface are intended to admit light and air into the roof space – a requirement that contradicts the protective nature of the roof. Water run-off for rooflights in the plane of the roof surface is achieved by incorporating the rooflight scale-like in the roof covering material. Basically, the inclusion of openings restricts ventilation underneath the roof surface; ventilation above the opening is complicated and expensive.
Dormer windows have the advantage that they can be covered with the same roofing material as the rest of the roof surface. Ventilation problems are easier to solve with shed dormers than with rooflights in the plane of the roof. However, the height of a shed dormer is limited by the general pitch of the roof. Other types of dormer windows do not suffer from this dis-

| Surface | |
|---|---|
| Edges | ridge, verge, eaves |
| Arrises | ridge, ridge of gable roof, hip, valley, trough, crank, step |
| Penetrations<br>Openings | chimney etc., window, dormer window |
| Junctions | wall |

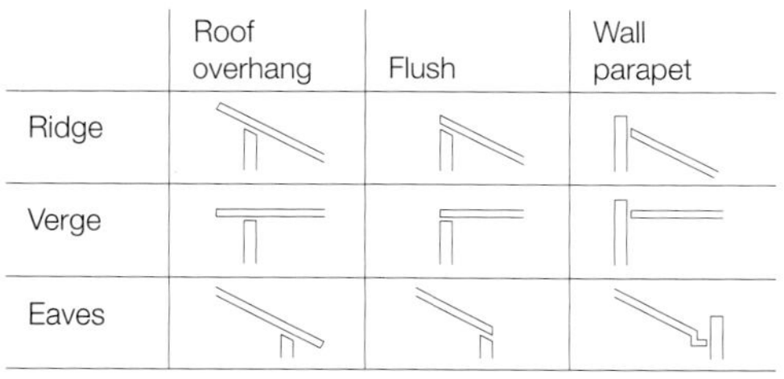

| | Roof overhang | Flush | Wall parapet |
|---|---|---|---|
| Ridge | | | |
| Verge | | | |
| Eaves | | | |

1.42

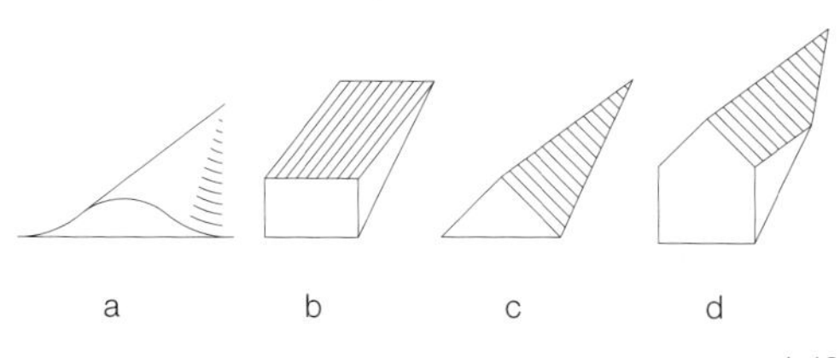


1.43

1.44

advantage but they involve a larger number of small hips, valleys, verges and eaves. Ventilation of these forms is therefore more complicated than with the shed dormer. The most logical solution for an opening – in terms of the roof covering – is the eyebrow dormer because it exhibits no sharp hips and valleys and can be covered together with the rest of the roof surface. However, its size is limited.

Penetrations and transitions
Roof penetrations present similar constructional tasks to openings in the plane of the roof. In the case of a wide penetration, the transition to the roof surface above is the most important one to solve. A narrow penetration makes use of a saddle, i.e. a saddle-shaped metal flashing connected flexibly to the rising component and the roof covering. Wide penetrations call for a drain channel, which must be deep enough to accommodate the expected quantities of water, and have a functioning overflow. Including ventilation for the underside of the roof at this point is extremely complicated.

**Design and form**
We shall take the three most important parts of the roof – ridge, verge, eaves – to illustrate the relationship between the design and the form of a roof.

Roof overhang
A roof overhang offers the best conditions for a long-lasting construction. The protective functions of the components below are guaranteed in ideal fashion. The independent movement of roof and building can be reliably incorporated, as well as ventilation.
It is interesting to note that this form was long neglected in the sequence of architectural fashions. We are now witnessing a comeback of this sensible method.

Flush arrangement
The desire to achieve compact and angular building envelopes is expressed in flush roof terminations. These forms contradict, in principle, the constructional tasks of these details. Box gutters at eaves and verge can help to prevent damage if properly planned and installed. Despite this, protection for the building, as provided by the roof, is not always achieved.

1.44 Grass-covered roof in Norway
1.45 Profiled tiles need flat surfaces
1.46 Small tiles are suitable for curved surfaces: valley in old German slating

External wall parapet
The need to allow both roof and building to move can be readily fulfilled when the external walls extend above the roof surface to form a parapet. Ventilation inlets and outlets are also incorporated relatively easily. If the architectural intention of such a parapet is also transferred to the eaves, this produces a gutter with many technical problems. It is advisable to allow the roof to overhang at the eaves.

## Roof form and use

#### Roof space and heated usable space

The roof with a cold and ventilated roof space is a common sight. We still appreciate the tranquil roof surface interrupted by just a few ventilation openings as a refreshing contrast to the "facade". The constructional and building science issues also favour the roof remaining a "roof". However, if it should assume the role of a heated usable room, we should ask ourselves whether its form and surface should not be treated completely differently, for aesthetic reasons. The "sloping external wall" has not yet been treated logically; for the constructional and use-related requirements must produce different results and not a conventional roof surface with multiple penetrations. Developments could move in the direction of a sloping facade, corresponding to the degree of utilisation. The result might well be a better affinity with the external wall below and not just a modified roof surface.

#### The roof as an energy provider

Using the roof to satisfy energy requirements leads to a completely different aesthetic when we use conventional roofing materials. Glass enclosures to collectors and photovoltaic panels are a striking contrast to tiles, corrugated sheets, sheet metals or roofing felt. Previous attempts by the industry to produce these elements to match the dimensions of the roof coverings have proved unsatisfactory due to the difference in appearance. Neither uniform panels nor uniform materials are available. It would seem prudent to choose a type of roofing that corresponds to the technical character of the energy-generating components, or to choose a roof form such that the energy systems occupy a clearly demarcated area, e.g. at a different level. But it would seem to be most sensible to seek a material harmony, and choose the single roofing form that accomplishes this – a roof covering of flat panes of glass. If as much energy as possible is to be generated by rooftop systems, the most logical solution is to cover the entire roof with energy components. Appropriate options are shown in the chapter "Energy production".
The logical development of roof-mounted energy systems will lead to a re-appraisal of the roof. Over time this will change our view of the roof.

#### Planting on the roof

Roofs covered with vegetation contribute to improving both the internal and external climate. Certain construction details are necessary at verge, eaves and ridge on this type of roof. In turn, these details lead to a certain roof form. However, the question arises as to which roof forms are suitable, in principle, for grassy and floral landscapes. Although small settlements in northern Europe provide examples of green roofs on apparently normal pitched roofs, the form issue must be carefully considered in our culture, our urban landscape.

#### Roof form and material

There is a close relationship between roof form and roof covering. This simple fact threatens to be relegated to the background: films, adhesives and sealing compounds are becoming universal remedies for experiments in form and arbitrary design. If any material can be used for virtually any form, we lose our feeling for the material itself and lose the skill to employ materials in a way that suits their character.

#### Materials and roof coverings

A roof covering of thatch is suitable for complicated transitions and penetrations only to a limited extent. Roofs of reed and straw therefore demand simple, steep forms with chimneys that penetrate the ridge and whose surfaces are, at best, interrupted only by eyebrow dormers. Even flat overlapping elements of wood, stone and synthetic materials call for steep pitches. These small-format building components make them suitable for covering valleys, gently curved surfaces and those made up of distinct areas. Infill sheets, as are necessary with pyramidal or conical roof forms, can only be built with flat overlapping elements; such roofs cannot be covered with profiled overlapping elements, especially the most highly developed interlocking roof tiles. Their transverse and longitudinal rebates require them to be assembled to form a homogeneous surface, which must be essentially flat. However, the rebates acting as rainwater channels permit a shallower pitch. For this reason, profiled overlapping elements should be used on geometrically simple, flat and – preferably – shallow pitches. When used with additional sealing strips, profiled sheets can be used on very shallow pitches. Their low weight and high loadbearing capacity recommends them for single-storey shed roofs with long spans.

1.45

1.46

Sheet metals are readily formed. Virtually any curved shape can be covered. This is proved by the many church cupolas and Baroque onion domes. Their welted joints lend a roof a certain texture. Good workability and ease of jointing has led to sheet metals being accepted as "right" on shallow or steep pitched roofs. Sheet metals are not tied to any particular pitch.

Roofing felts are extremely adaptable. They are easy to work with and connect to other parts of the building. The material itself can be used in a rich diversity of shapes. But the plain surface of this material usually restricts it to areas that are not generally visible, to buildings of lower importance, or to waterproof layers hidden below grass.

This list of the properties of roof covering materials shows that each material has a range of applications that are right for it. If this applicability is blurred and adulterated without good reason, a finely tuned technology plus an important traditional craft is put at risk. Our perception is fooled, our ability to differentiate between technical methods weakened, and our building tradition thereby endangered.

#### Roof pitch

The mutual dependence of material and roof form is most evident in the pitch. Materials suitable for shallow pitches can also be used on steeper ones, but – with the exception of sheet metal – the reverse is never true without elaborate framing. A steeper roof pitch basically means greater protection against damage and hence a longer service life. However, as the pitch increases, so does the surface area of the roof and hence the quantity of materials and cost for the roof structure and the roof covering. Consideration must therefore be given to just how steep the pitch should be to satisfy economic and artistic requirements. Careful thought is necessary here to free steep roofs from the overdone pointed gables of the Middle Ages.

1.47

1.47 The lack of understanding of the relationship between material, roof form and building was illustrated by Franz Hart in his especially durable bastard form of the "bungalow".
1.48 Roof and external wall form a unity: granite roof covering in Corippo, Ticino
1.49 In his "Winslow Residence" Frank Lloyd Wright separates the roof from the bulk of the building, River Forest, Illinois, USA, 1893–94
1.50 Homogeneous envelope of slate panels: private house in Sarzeau, France, 1999, Eric Gouesnard

### Roof form and building

Although roof and building should be designed as a whole, this unchallenged thesis in the history of building is, however, frequently abused. During periods in which transport difficulties limited the availability of building materials, the resources available in the neighbourhood determined the uniformity of a building. Climatic conditions and limited constructional options also led to features being shared by roof and external wall. Today, the variety of materials and enormous choice of constructional methods would seem to offer inexhaustible options. We therefore need to develop an awareness of the overall system so that the two primary components – roof and building – are compatible. In order to achieve this unity, design and construction of roof and building must be considered together. If an unmistakable duopitch roof is chosen, this calls for a geometrically simple plan shape. As illustrated, some types of roof covering lead to specific, rigidly defined surface forms, which reveals that the decision for a roof form begins with the material itself. The design process – plan layout – external wall – roof form – roofing material – must therefore be approached from both directions. There have doubtless been many examples in the past of clever architects who defied this rule. Nevertheless, it is part of our teaching tradition to preserve the relationship between material, building and roof. The outcome of the lack of appreciation of this tradition was first seen in the 20th century, as Franz Hart showed us so pointedly by way of the "bungalow" in the first edition of the *Roof Construction Manual*.

1.48

**Unity and separation**
They are two principal – and equal – options for the relationship between roof and building:

Unity
The unity of roof and building is achieved when just one material is chosen for the external walls and the roof. We see this unity in the case of stone, wood and clay bricks/tiles on many impressive examples of anonymous structures. Very soon after the invention of "artificial cement", monoliths were also built of concrete. Coated and uncoated metals now serve to shroud a building with a homogeneous envelope. However, it has been shown that the effects of sunlight, rain and snow cause different weathering effects on the roof compared to the vertical external walls.

Separation
As the constructional conditions for roof and building are not identical, the second approach is to separate the two parts: the roof structure provides a canopy over the bulk of the building. This reproduces the primary functions of the two components in obvious fashion. This approach has been with us since ancient times and still attracts outstanding architects. As a rule, lightweight roofing materials reproduce this conception better than the heavyweight variety. But even with a roof covering of overlapping elements, this separation is still achievable, as can be seen on Frank Lloyd Wright's "Winslow Residence".

Shaping, detail
As mentioned earlier, the appearance of a building and its roof is essentially governed by the form of the individual parts. This includes general details such as the roof overhang at eaves and verge, and fine details such as the profile of the edges. Connections to parts of the building and the design of three-dimensional corners are important here. But above all, this shaping calls for care and attention; the history of architecture has shown us that the presence or absence of such attention plays a very prominent role in the overall visual, and psychological effect of a structure.

1.49

## Roof form and environment

Not only should the roof and the building form a harmonious pair, the building must also fit in with its immediate natural and built environment.

**Roof form and the natural environment**
Subordination
The first shelters were more intrinsic to their environment when the natural materials used to build them were left untreated. The less these materials were worked, the more were roof and building a part of their surroundings. Today, as our natural environment is often disrupted by widespread development, it is one of the duties of our society to leave the rest as untouched as possible. So situations repeatedly occur in which a necessary building at an exposed location within the landscape has to be designed, so that its bulk, height and roof or wall materials are subordinate to the natural surroundings. The most important factors here are the bulk and height of the building. To achieve this subordination, natural roofing materials such as straw, reed, wood or stone are best used. An uninterrupted continuum can be accomplished with planting on the roofs, provided the external walls are kept low.

1.50

Integration
Integrating structures into their natural surroundings is another approach; for it is not always the prevailing desire to camouflage a building completely. We are accustomed to seeing this type of solution. For example, we would regard a textured, red clay tile roof as a desirable component of the landscape, provided its overall proportions are acceptable. In this respect, the ageing process of the roofing material plays an important role. The firing process brings about a variegated colouring in the untreated roof tiles. The ageing process gives uncoated concrete and fibre-cement products a rough surface in which the natural aggregates gain emphasis. Lichens or algae thrive here and so lend the whole a dynamic texture. Metals oxidise to form a patina. Glass can reflect its surroundings or, through its transparency, preserve them.

Contrast, prominence
However, it may also be desirable to declare our respect for the natural world by contrasting it with the products of human activities. This might be the case when a continuation of the surroundings using man-made means would lead to confusion and adulteration of the immediate environment. Materials that hardly alter are suitable for such applications. As a rule, these are coated materials. Their permanence, their almost absolute unnaturalness, disengages them from their surroundings and enables both to express their identity. Buildings that, owing to their use, occupy an exposed position in the landscape become points of orientation. Lighthouses, windmills and water towers once belonged to this class of structure; today it is chimneys, wind turbines and transmitter masts that occupy such positions. Society has always erected buildings that occupy a high priority in our system of values and have employed particular architectural means to highlight this. Numerous religious edifices prove that they were considered to be an intensification of nature. Their roofs made a valuable contribution to this notion.

**Roof form and the built environment**

A new quality appeared as soon as human beings ceased to build their shelters isolated in the natural environment, but instead congregated them in settlements. In addition to the effect of the individual building there was also its interaction with others to consider. As individual grasses make up a meadow, and individual trees a forest, individual buildings formed a settlement, and individual roofs a roofscape. Each single building had to create and underline this overriding quality. In doing so, the roof played an important role because of its dominant position in the overall appearance of a settlement. A few typical relationships are worth explaining.

Association and unity
In early times the availability of a material and the relevant techniques led to a settlement having a uniform appearance. As roofing materials and roof form are closely interrelated, a uniform roof covering material luckily reduced the number of forms possible. The common typology gave rise to homogeneity and power of expression, as can be seen in towns with many medieval buildings. Basically, all roof covering materials can create this unity: cities like Innsbruck and Salzburg are characterised by sheet metal, Bern and Nördlingen by clay tiles.

Variety and pluralism
Historical developments led to a very heterogeneous roofscape in many places. The diversity of materials and roof forms has various causes. Devastating fires in the Middle Ages put an end to many roofs of straw and reed, or wooden shingles, so these disappeared from the urban landscape.
Cheaper materials were often used in times of economic deprivation. Dwindling resources led to substitutes being introduced, and the cost of labour made some types of roofing too expensive. This resulted in a lively diversity, which in many places also created a chaotic picture, particularly where lack of thought, and the desire for short-term profits led to old types of roofing being replaced by new ones. Architects today have a whole range of materials and means of expression at their disposal. In legislative terms, the architectural language employed is essentially deregulated. When development plans limit the choice of materials and forms, this is seen as a constraint. However, both opportunities and risks are involved. The heterogeneous multiplicity of our structures can be regarded as a reflection of our society. Accordingly, it is wrong to channel our built environment – because of an indeterminate longing for harmony, as we suspect in the

1.51

1.51 Integrating the building into its natural surroundings: pavilion in Zeewolde, Netherlands, 2001, René van Zuuk
1.52 Structural shaping: Olympic Stadium, Munich, 1968–72, Behnisch + Partner

towns of the Middle Ages – into a form that does not correspond to our society. As we can only make judgements from appearances to which we have become accustomed, there is no absolute right or wrong for the appearance of our buildings. Perhaps we enjoy the homogeneous textures of uniform roofscapes precisely because we have such a variety at our disposal today.

Prominence
Buildings with a high value in our society are emphasised within the urban landscape and thus illustrate our system of values. While prominent buildings might appear excessively dominant in natural surroundings, they are an enrichment of the built environment; they form points of orientation for the local inhabitants. Sprawling urban landscapes without constructional highlights emphasise how important it is to have such points from which to gain our bearings. Roofs, too, reflect the social position of buildings. For example, important buildings are given domes whose materials can be seen from afar and accentuate the appearance of curved surfaces. One famous example is the glazed ceramic covering of to the shell roofs of the Sydney Opera House by Jørn Utzon (see p. 402).

**Semantic observations**
Treating the roof as the archetypal form of building is afflicted with a whole host of meanings. As the uppermost protective part of a building, as a part taken to be representative of the whole, it embodies the thoroughly important concept of "home" – something intrinsic to the development of our society.
Without claiming to be a methodical catalogue, the sources of this importance are examined here in order to place the technical tasks of a roof in relation to its semantic cargo.

Constructional shaping
The external form of the roof is based on understandable constructional principles. As with every tried-and-tested basic form, several tasks are combined to form one solution. For example, a steep pitch first and foremost results in a simple loadbearing structure. The inclined timbers of the duopitch roof are very easily stabilised and readily extended to any length. The steeper the pitch, the easier it is to accommodate horizontal forces and to use the roof space created. In addition, the sloping surface is ideal for draining rainwater.
The first roofing materials taken from nature had to be joined to form a weather-resistant surface. What could be more obvious than combining the components (pieces of bark, leaves and thatch) in such a way that the upper pieces were laid on top of the lower ones and thus covered the space below like scales? So basic forms were devised that differed from others using natural materials.
Forming these materials into roofing components was carried out in different ways depending on the cultural conditions. These conditions gave rise to manual skills that determined appearance through the construction and the surface. These skills were passed on as an important cultural asset and defined the roof in terms of construction, surface texture and colour. This experience finally became part of our phylogenetic recollection and hence also affects our individual experiences.

Significance
The roof, as the most important element of a building, becomes significant for the elementary functions of the entire building. It therefore penetrates deep into our language and gives rise to sayings like "under one roof", which sometimes no longer relates literally to the built structure.

Protection
The roof is inseparable from the concept of protection. Once we are beneath a roof, it protects us from the outside world. In the German language Heidegger cleverly points out the linguistic link between the verbs "to build", "to live" and "to be". He traces the Middle High German etymological roots of these verbs and arrives at words meaning "to be satisfied" and "protection against pursuit", finally ending on "free" and "freedom". He therefore shows us that building, leading to the house and the roof, forms a union with the existence of mankind.[23]

1.52

1.54

The most important human needs and the prerequisite for our individual existence are deeply embedded in the idea of a building, and above all with the pitched roof and its form.

### Demarcation – exaltation

The separation of a space from the outside world is a basic human need. This formation of a space is represented most impressively by the roof. Roofing over a place, separating it from the sky, gives it its own identity. The canopy, which originally had a protective function, protecting against sun or rain, is a word that embodies this meaning.[24] Such a demarcation represents a prominence or exaltation of that which is located beneath the roof. To have a fixed roof over our heads and demonstrate our social standing by owning our own house is one of the yearnings of mankind. People have built special roofs on buildings that appeared important to them and hence demonstrated their status. Such signal designs become embedded in our consciousness through long tradition, and in conjunction with power and honour give rise to their own definition of beauty.

### Function and importance

The form of the roof depended on constructional necessities. Its exposed position has made the roof a symbol for the most important functions of our homes. So the roof form is also associated with meanings that are deeply ingrained in our human existence. The pitched roof carries with it part of our cultural heritage and can no longer be detached from it. Today's architect, poring over his designs, has the task of employing such encumbered components without bias. We are living in an age in which crucial changes are necessary in our architectural activities. The roof cannot be left aside. Our designer must separate the roof from its mythical connotations and subject it fairly to the changes that the environment and society demand. Consistent handling of new tasks can lead to forms that steer us away from experiences linked with ideas of beauty. As a glance back at history shows, new appearances must justify their existence and first conquer the associated new definition of beauty through their recognition as a sociological necessity.

1.53

1.53 The roof as a crown: canopy in Göllersdorf, 1740–41, Lukas von Hildebrandt

1.54 Society has always emphasised buildings that it holds in special esteem: Blue Mosque in Istanbul

[23] Martin Heidegger in: Bauen Wohnen Denken, presentation at the Darmstadt Conference on 6 August 1951 in: Mensch und Raum, Bauwelt Fundamente 94, ed. Ulrich Conrads and Peter Neitzke, Braunschweig, 1991

[24] "Baldachin" is another word for canopy and is derived from Baldacco, an early Italian name for Baghdad. It has probably been so well preserved in the German language owing to the fact that it contains the word for roof – "Dach".

# Part 2 Fundamentals

#### Loadbearing structure

The roof is part of both the building envelope and the loadbearing structure. The mutual dependency of the roof covering and its supporting construction form the focal point of this chapter. The emphasis is not on structural analysis and design but on the conception of the construction and the way it works.
After introducing the actions, the various constructions and the way they carry the loads are dealt with in order to draw attention to the requirements of different roof coverings. As the roof can also be an important element for stabilising the entire building, principal options for bracing the building are discussed. A few examples of historical roof structures are described in addition to the traditional varieties. The section "Loadbearing structures for pitched roofs" offers a brief insight into the principal structural systems possible. A detailed treatment of this subject would exceed the scope of this book.
References to standards are confined to new editions, which follow the European concept of Eurocodes; some of these are only available in draft form at present. In detailed instances, German standards are referred to, as well as Swiss and Austrian codes.

#### Building science

In the light of the extensive specialist works of reference available covering thermal and sound insulation, moisture control and fire protection, it was the intention to confine the information in this book to matters affecting the roof. However, it became clear that this would not be possible without explaining the fundamentals of this science. Therefore, the most important basic concepts, with the terms in common use today, form the beginning of each section. Interesting phenomena and their practical significance for pitched roofs are then explained in context.
The revision of DIN 4108 to include new requirements and methods of analysis is reflected in the sections "Thermal performance" and "Climate-related moisture control".
Germany's new Energy Economy Act is looked at in somewhat more detail because of its topicality. This section presents reviews of the fields of application, requirements and methods of analysis as far as is feasible here. As this new statutory instrument attaches more importance to thermal performance in summer, airtightness and thermal bridges, these are treated in more deta l in the "Building science" chapter. Current developments and findings in moisture control are referred to in particular.

#### Materials for roof coverings

This chapter is a speciality of the *Roof Construction Manual*. We outline all the principles with which a designer can create proper constructions. Consequently, this chapter is both preparation for and supplementary to "Part 3 Construction Details". The information here has been updated in terms of both the technical regulations and standards and the availability of products and their properties. Furthermore, new sections such as "Membranes" and "Energy production" have been added. Finally, the ecological aspects of the materials have been investigated more closely and refurbishment options added.

#### Design

There has recently been heated debate about the question of "to ventilate or not to ventilate?" The constructiona aspect of this is discussed under the "Design principles" to supplement the building science chapter. The section entitled "Prefabrication" presents an overview of the products currently available on the market. The presentation of the principles necessary for the development of a modular roof goes one step further. A catalogue of the elements is intended to help the novice become acquainted with this subject.

# Loadbearing structure

**Rainer Barthel**

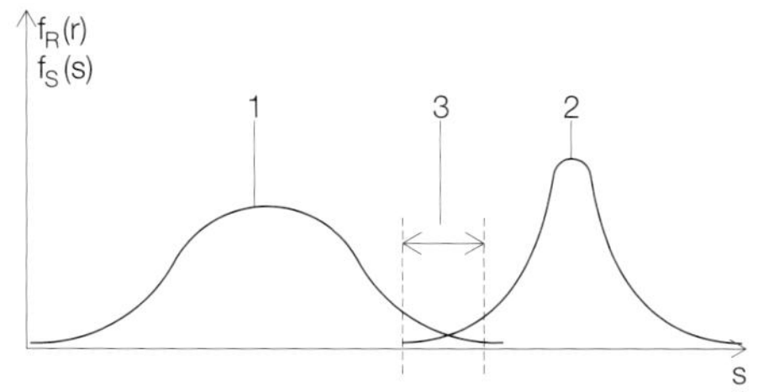


2.1.1.1 Schematic diagram of normal probability curves for actions $f_S(s)$ and resistance $f_R(r)$: 1 action, 2 resistance, 3 definition of safety factor v.

Roofs must be able to withstand a multitude of actions. The primary actions are:
- dead loads
- imposed loads
- wind, snow and ice loads
- temperature fluctuations
- actions during construction
- fire

## Actions

Like the overall structure, the roof must be designed and built in such a way that the potential actions to which it is subjected cause neither collapse nor unacceptable deformations during erection and use. The collapse of a building, or individual parts thereof, is prevented by providing adequate load-carrying capacity. Likewise, a building's serviceability in accordance with specified conditions (e.g. maximum permissible deformations) must be guaranteed in order to ensure that it can be used for its intended purpose.
The load-carrying capacity and serviceability must guarantee a suitably adequate durability over the entire intended period of use of the building. These fundamental requirements of a building cannot be guaranteed absolutely but only with a reasonable degree of reliability. In order to define a reasonable and adequate level of safety, a consistent safety concept is necessary. The safety concept on which European and most national standards are based employs a system of degrees of probability, to take into account the various statistical distributions of the respective variables and the scatter of the measured values (figure 2.1.1.1). This safety concept applies to both the loads/forces (actions) and the components subjected to those loads (resistances). The required level of safety is defined for each basic variable (actions, resistances, geometric properties) by way of partial safety factors.

"Characteristic values" are specified for the actions according to the probability of their occurrence. To do this, a basic breakdown according to chronological variability is first necessary:
- permanent actions, e.g. self-weight, fixed attachments (generally immovable),
- variable actions, e.g. imposed, wind and snow loads (generally movable),
- exceptional actions, e.g. fires, earthquakes.

The permanent actions exhibiting only a little scatter are generally taken into account by way of an average value. The time-dependent, variable actions are specified by characteristic values so that the probability of their not being exceeded within any one year is 98%. Taking an assumed service life of 50 years, this means that this value will, on average, be reached or exceeded once. So the characteristic values describe actions that can realistically occur during the lifetime of a structure. These values do not contain any factor of safety.
From this we can deduce that for a shorter service life, e.g. temporary structures, or during construction, the design wind and snow loads can be reduced.
In order to guarantee a certain level of safety, the characteristic values are multiplied by partial safety factors during analysis of the load-carrying capacity. For dead loads this is normally 1.35, for imposed, wind and snow loads 1.50.
The partial safety factor for dead loads used in the serviceability analysis is 1.00. The partial safety factors for variable loads are reduced by factors and "frequency values".
The simultaneous action of various loads (e.g. snow and wind) must be taken into account. As we assume that several loads do not act with their full characteristic values simultaneously, the standards provide rules for combining these loads and use lower "combination values".

The following standards deal with actions:
- Eurocode 1 part 1
- DIN 1055 parts 1–10
- DIN 1055 part 100
- SIA 160 (Switzerland)
- ÖNORM B 4001, B 4010 to 4014–1 (Austria)

Parts 1, 3, 4 and 5 of DIN 1055 were only available in draft form as this book went to press. The following explanations regarding dead, imposed, wind and snow loads reflect this status of the standards. Furthermore, there are rules for dealing with actions in the specifications covering particular types of construction.

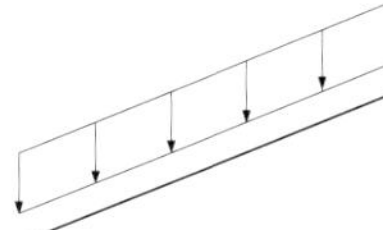

2.1.1.2 Uniformly distributed load acting vertically, loading related to roof surface, e.g. dead loads.

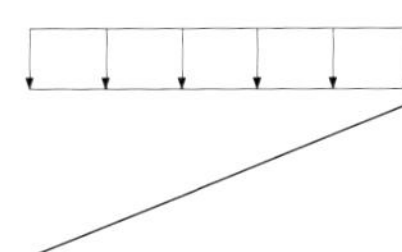

2.1.1.3 Uniformly distributed load acting vertically, loading related to projected plan area of roof surface, e.g. imposed loads, snow loads.

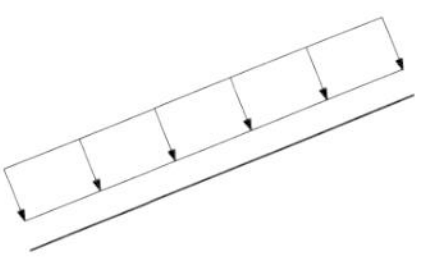

2.1.1.4 Load acting perpendicular to roof surface, loading related to roof surface, e.g. wind loads.

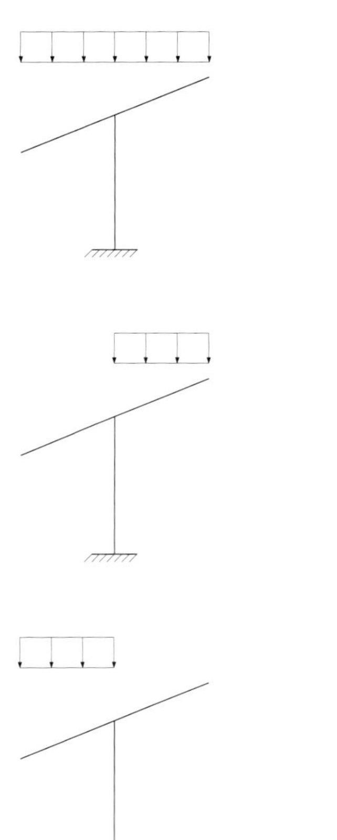

2.1.1.5 Worst-case application of imposed loads

**Dead loads**

Dead loads are permanent and immovable actions caused by the self-weight of loadbearing and non-loadbearing components, e.g. insulation, roof covering. They may be added together to form a common action. Table 2.1.1.7 gives characteristic values for the dead loads of building materials and roof coverings. These are average values.

It should be remembered that for accurate calculations and for components which, regarding their stability and serviceability requirements, are sensitive to deviations from these values, the values for types of roof covering exhibit a relatively wide scatter compared to other dead loads, and that the values specified here are average values. More accurate values for specific cases can be obtained from the test certificates of the products.

A partial safety factor of 0.90 is provided for analysing the safety against displacement, which is, for example, important for securing the roof structure and roof covering against wind suction. This safety factor takes into account the fact that the dead load has a beneficial effect in this case.

Dead loads of loose gravel and tipped materials on roofs must be regarded as variable actions. The loads from service installations should also be considered as movable actions when there is a probability of their being altered at some time in the future.

**Imposed loads**

Imposed loads are actions that may change with time and, generally, can change their position, e.g. persons, movable objects etc. The imposed loads acting on the roof should be assumed to act in their most unfavourable constellation with respect to the loadbearing system.

Pitched roofs are generally not subject to foot traffic, apart from normal maintenance measures and repairs. Nevertheless, a uniformly distributed imposed load should be allowed for on pitches below 40°. This is specified in table 2.1.1.6 and relates to the projected plan area of the roof surface. A figure of 0.75 kN/m² should be used for pitches below 20°, which may be more than the expected snow load, depending on the snow zone. But it is not necessary to add the imposed load to the snow load.

In addition, a local minimum load-carrying capacity must be guaranteed, especially if there is no adequate transverse distribution of the loads. A point load (from a person) of 1 kN at any position must be allowed for. This point load does not need to be added to the uniformly distributed imposed load. In the analysis it is considered to be distributed over a square measuring 50 x 50 mm.

This point load is relevant both for designing the roof covering itself, and for the sheathing, rafters, purlins and top chord of trusses that carry the roof covering directly. In the case of tiling battens, two point loads of 0.5 kN each should be considered to act at the outer quarter points of the span.

Lightweight glazing bars may be analysed using a point load of 0.5 kN at an unfavourable position when the roof is only accessible using crawling boards and ladders.

A uniformly distributed imposed load of 3 kN/m² should be assumed for walkways that form part of a prescribed escape route.

| Roof pitch | $q_k$ kN/m² | $Q_k$ kN |
|---|---|---|
| ≤ 20° | 0.75 | 1.0 |
| ≥ 40° | 0 | 1.0 |

$q_k$ = uniformly distributed load
$Q_k$ = point load

2.1.1.6 Characteristic values for imposed loads on roofs accessible only for standard maintenance purposes and repairs; intermediate values may be interpolated linearly [11]

A uniformly distributed imposed load of 4 kN/m² should be taken for rooftop terraces. The tipped soil on roof gardens and planted roofs is not included in the imposed load. It should be considered separately as a variable action, i.e. it must be applied so that it has the most unfavourable effect with respect to the loadbearing construction. This takes into account the fact that tipped soil could be rearranged at any time. On a pitched roof surface the resulting negative lift of the tipped material must be considered.

Roof spaces that, because of the dimensions of their cross-section, are only accessible to a limited degree should allow for an imposed load of 1 kN/m². Roof spaces here means attics and lofts with a clear headroom of max. 1.80 m below monopitch or duopitch roofs, unsuitable for use as living quarters.

| Metals | [kN/m³] |
|---|---|
| aluminium | 27 |
| lead | 114 |
| copper | 89 |
| brass | 85 |
| steel and welding steel | 78.5 |
| zinc | 72 |
| **Concrete** | |
| reinforced concrete (DIN 1045) | 25 |
| aerated concrete, gross density class 0.40–0.80 (DIN 4223) | 5.2–9.5 |
| lightweight concrete | 10.5–20.5 |
| **Stone** | |
| granite | 28 |
| slate | 28 |
| **Timber** | |
| softwood, general | 5 |
| glued laminated timber | 4–5 |
| chipboard | 5–7.5 |
| plywood | 4.5–8 |

Primary building materials according to draft of DIN 1055 part 1

| Clay and concrete tiles | | [kN/m²] |
|---|---|---|
| Concrete roof tiles with multiple tail ribs and upstand longitudinal rib | | |
| up to | 10 tiles/m² | 0.50 |
| more than | 10 tiles/m² | 0.55 |
| Concrete roof tiles with multiple tail ribs and upstand longitudinal rib | | |
| up to | 10 tiles/m² | 0.60 |
| more than | 10 tiles/m² | 0.65 |
| Clay bullnose tiles (to DIN EN 1304) [10], 155 x 375 mm and 180 x 380 mm, and concrete bullnose tiles | | |
| on slip-tiled roof (including shingles) (ancillary building) | | 0.60 |
| on double-skin and crown-tiled roof (including tiling battens) | | 0.75 |
| interlocking clay Reform tile, flat pan tiles (to DIN EN 1304) [10] | | 0.55 |
| Glass rooflight tile with type of roof covering as above | | |
| large-format pantiles, up to 10 tiles/m² [10] | | 0.50 |
| small-format clay bullnose tiles and special formats (church roofing tile, bullnose steeple tile, etc. to DIN EN 1304) [10, 29] | | 0.95 |
| flat pan tiles, pantiles (to DIN EN 1304) [10] | | 0.45 |
| flat pan tiles, pantiles laid in bituminous sheets over battens [10] | | 0.55 |
| Under-and-over tiles (with mortar) [10] | | 0.90 |
| Extruded interlocking clay tiles (to DIN EN 1304) [10] | | 0.60 |

| Sheet metal | | [kN/m²] |
|---|---|---|
| aluminium (0.7 mm thick, including 24 mm roof decking) [10] | | 0.25 |
| profiled aluminium sheeting, 80 mm deep, 0.8 mm thick, without roof decking [29] | | 0.04 |
| profiled aluminium sheeting, on battens [20] | | 0.08 |
| corrugated/trapezoidal profile and ribbed aluminium sheeting [10] | | 0.05 |
| double welt joints in titanium-zinc or copper, 0.7 mm thick, including sheathing and 24 mm roof decking [10] | | 0.35 |
| copper sheet with double welt joints [20] (copper 0.6 mm thick, including 22 mm roof decking) | | 0.30 |
| galvanised ribbed steel sheeting (to DIN 59231), | | |
| including battens [10] | | 0.15 |
| including sheathing and 24 mm roof decking [10] | | 0.30 |
| profiled steel sheeting (trapezoidal or ribbed profile) [10] | | |
| 26 mm deep: | nom. thickness 0.75 mm | 0.075 |
| 121 mm deep: | nom. thickness 1.50 mm | 0.24 |
| corrugated sheeting (galvanised steel, including fixings, to DIN 59231) [10] | | 0.25 |
| zinc with core roll joints, including 22 mm roof decking [10, 20] | | 0.30 |

| Slate | [kN/m²] |
|---|---|
| "old German" slating and standardised slating on 24 mm roof decking, including roofing paper underlay and decking [10] | |
| single lap | 0.50 |
| double lap | 0.60 |
| rectangular slating [10] on battens, | |
| including battens | 0.45 |
| on 22 mm roof decking, including sheathing and decking | 0.55 |

| Fibre-cement tiles and sheets | [kN/m²] |
|---|---|
| "German" bond on 24 mm roof decking, including sheathing and decking [10] | 0.40 |
| double-lap bond on battens, including battens [10] | 0.38 |
| horizontal bond on battens, including battens [10] | 0.25 |
| short corrugated sheets (housing sheets) [10] | 0.24 |
| corrugated sheets to DIN EN 494, according to Austrian standard B 3422, on battens [10, 20] | 0.20 |

| Other roof coverings | [kN/m²] |
|---|---|
| corrugated plastic sheets (profile to DIN EN 494), without purlins, including fixings, made from fibre-reinforced polyester resins (density 1400 kg/m³), | |
| sheet thickness 1 mm [10] | 0.03 |
| ditto, but with capping | 0.06 |
| corrugated plastic sheets on battens [20] | 0.20 |
| PVC-coated polyester textile, without supporting structure [10] | |
| type 1 (tearing strength 3.00 kN per 50 mm width) | 0.0075 |
| type 2 (tearing strength 4.70 kN per 50 mm width) | 0.0085 |
| type 3 (tearing strength 6.00 kN per 50 mm width) | 0.01 |
| Reed and straw, including battens [10] | 0.70 |
| shingles, including battens [10] | 0.25 |
| glazing, without glazing bars [10] | |
| patterned glass, single glazing | 0.27 |
| patterned glass, double glazing | 0.54 |

| Glazing, including frames | [kN/m²] |
|---|---|
| plain glass, 5 mm thick [29] | 0.25 |
| wired glass, toughened glass, 6 mm thick [29] | 0.35 |
| laminated safety glass, 8 mm thick [20] | 0.40 |
| surcharge for each extra 1 mm thickness of glass [20] | 0.03 |

| Sandwich panels | [kN/m²] |
|---|---|
| in steel, 70–140 mm (according to manufacturer's details) | 0.11–0.17 |
| in aluminium, 85–125 mm (according to manufacturer's details) | 0.07–0.09 |

| Bitumen and synthetic roofing felts | [kN/m²] |
|---|---|
| bitumen and polymer base roofing felt to DIN 52130 and 52132 [10] | 0.04 |
| bituminous and synthetic roofing felt, including bonding materials, per layer [20] | 0.05 |
| bitumen and polymer base built-up felt to DIN 52131 and 52133 [10] | 0.07 |
| bitumen roofing felt with metal foil inlay to DIN 18190 part 4 | 0.03 |
| non-woven glass-fibre bitumen roofing felt (DIN 52143) [10] | 0.03 |
| synthetic roofing felt [10, 29] | 0.02 |
| uncoated bituminous roofing felt (DIN 52129) and uncoated bitumen roofing felt (DIN 52126) [10, 29] | 0.02 |
| insulation (glass fibre or mineral wool) per 10 mm thickness [29] | 0.02 |
| rigid fibreboards [29] | 0.05 |
| timber roof decking, 24 mm [29] | 0.14 |

2.1.1.7 Dead loads of roof coverings
[10] Draft of DIN 1055 part 1
[20] Austrian standard B 4010
[29] Swiss standard SIA 160

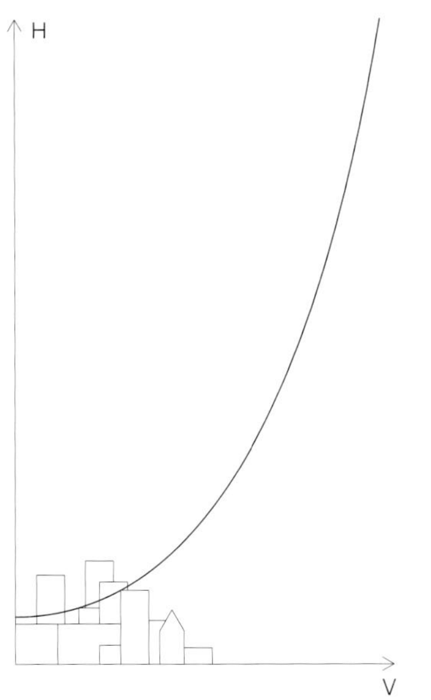


2.1.1.8 Wind profile – how wind speed changes with height above ground level [30]

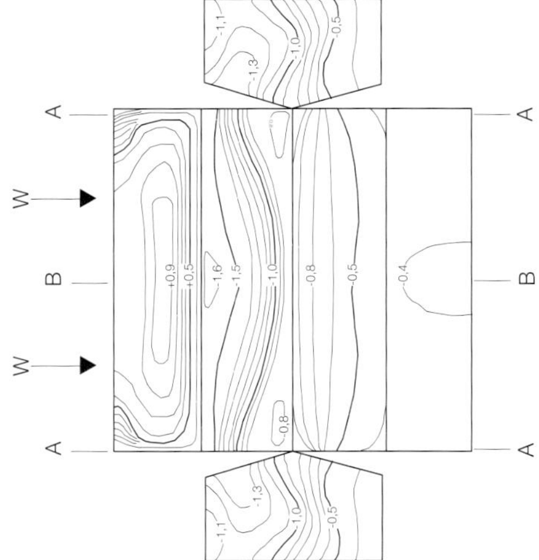


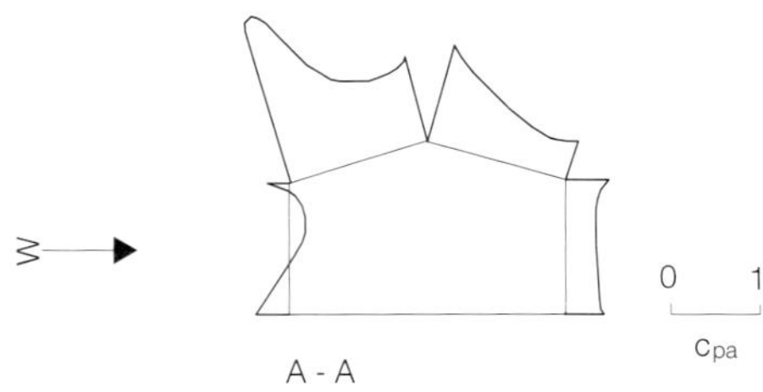


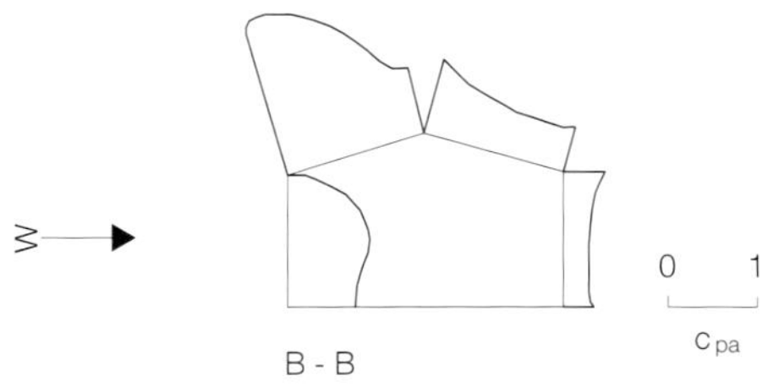


2.1.1.9 Pressure distribution on a building with a gable roof; roof pitch 15°, ratio of height to length to width = 0.5:2:1 [30]

**Wind loads**

The wind load depends on wind speed and direction, as well as the shape, dimensions, surface characteristics and permeability of the structure.

The wind load is made up of pressure, suction and friction effects. Pressure and suction act perpendicular to the surface of the building, and with partly open buildings and those with a permeable envelope there are also internal pressures to be taken into account. Frictional drag can be relevant on large structures with certain types of surfaces.

In the first place the wind load depends on the wind speed. The laws of physics allow us to assign a dynamic pressure to a certain wind speed.

| Scale | km/h | m/s | Description | General effects |
|---|---|---|---|---|
| 0 | 0–1 | 0–0.3 | calm | Smoke rises vertically |
| 1 | 1–5 | 0.3–1.5 | light air | Direction shown by smoke only, wind vanes not affected |
| 2 | 6–11 | 1.6–3.3 | light breeze | Breeze felt on face, leaves rustle, wind vanes move |
| 3 | 12–19 | 3.4–5.4 | gentle breeze | Leaves and small twigs in motion, light flags extended. |
| 4 | 20–28 | 5.5–7.9 | moderate breeze | Small branches move, dust and paper rise |
| 5 | 29–38 | 8.0–10.7 | fresh breeze | Small trees in leaf sway, crested wavelets on inland water |
| 6 | 39–49 | 10.8–13.8 | strong breeze | Large branches in motion, telegraph wires whistle |
| 7 | 50–61 | 13.9–17.1 | moderate gale | Whole trees in motion, walking inconvenient |
| 8 | 62–74 | 17.2–20.7 | fresh gale | Twigs break off, walking impeded |
| 9 | 75–88 | 20.8–24.4 | strong gale | Slight structural damage |
| 10 | 89–102 | 24.5–28.4 | whole gale | Trees uprooted, structural damage |
| 11 | 103–117 | 28.5–32.6 | storm | Widespread damage |
| 12 | >117 | >32.6 | hurricane | Very rare inland, very severe damage |

2.1.1.10 Beaufort scale for estimating wind speed [25]

$$q = \rho/2 \cdot v^2$$

q = dynamic pressure [N/m$^2$]
ρ = air density [kg/m$^3$], normally 1.25 kg/m$^3$
v = wind speed [m/s]

2.1.1.11 Relationship between dynamic pressure and wind speec

$$w = c \cdot q$$

w = wind pressure [N/m$^2$]
c = aerodynamic coefficient
q = dynamic pressure [N/m$^2$]

2.1.1.12 Relationship between dynamic pressure and wind speed on part of object

In order to determine the actual wind pressure on the surface of a building we need to consider the overall shape of the building and the way this disrupts the wind flow. This can usually only be carried out in wind tunnel tests in which the wind pressure is measured at the surface of a model. In relation to wind speed, the pressures measured can be used to determine aerodynamic pressure coefficients.

It is difficult to determine specific values for the wind load assumptions. Only at high altitudes can we assume the wind to exhibit a laminar flow. At ground level the flow is always turbulent due to the roughness of the ground, caused by topography, vegetation and man-made objects. Wind speed therefore fluctuates quite severely over time and depending on the exact location. The loads on a roof caused by wind are accordingly very complex and can be calculated only approximately. The aerodynamic pressure coefficients measured on an object in the wind tunnel also vary considerably across a surface, showing distinct differences at the edges of a roof and at projections (figure 2.1.1.9).

In the European standards the following method for determining wind loads on structures has become established: as in meteorology, a reference speed is defined. This is measured at a height of 10 m above ground with few interruptions. This is the average value over a period of 10 minutes with a probability of 0.02 against being exceeded within one year, i.e. the speed is exceeded – statistically – once every 50 years.

Very strong gusts dependent on local conditions are hardly considered in the average value because they reach their maximum speed for only a few seconds. Wind zone maps for rough characterisation of the wind climate have been drawn up using these measured and average wind speeds. Five zones are defined for Germany; the reference speed and dynamic pressure are specified for each zone. They apply to sites up to 800 m above sea level (figures 2.1.1.19 and 2.1.1.20).

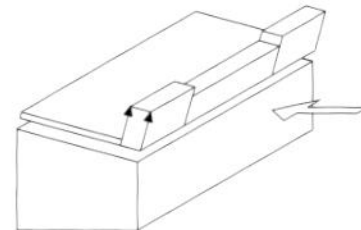

2.1.1.13 Monopitch roof, 15° pitch, distribution of suction loads

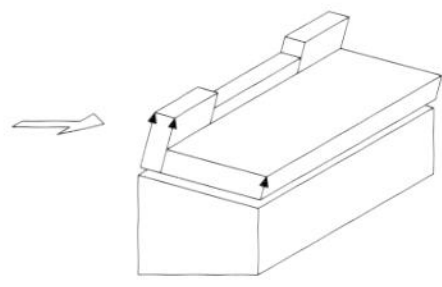

2.1.1.14 Monopitch roof, 15° pitch, distribution of suction loads

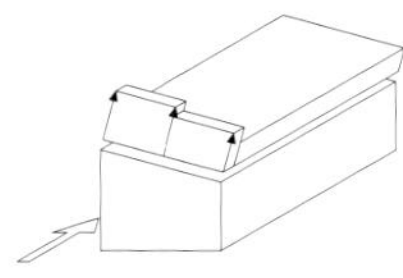

2.1.1.15 Monopitch roof, 15° pitch, distribution of suction loads

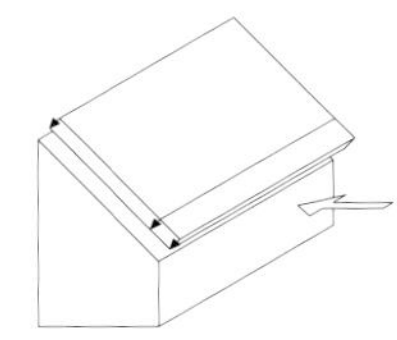

2.1.1.16 Monopitch roof, 45° pitch, distribution of pressure loads

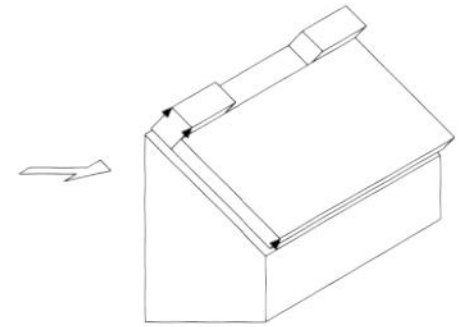

2.1.1.17 Monopitch roof, 45° pitch, distribution of suction loads

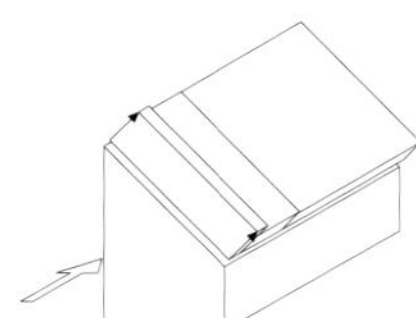

2.1.1.18 Monopitch roof, 45° pitch, distribution of suction loads

However, these reference speeds are not sufficient to determine a specific design wind load. The actual peak wind speeds during brief gusts must be considered. The peak speed used in the wind load assumptions is the highest wind speed averaged over a gust duration of 2–4 seconds. In addition to the wind zone, the immediate local surroundings and the height of the building influence this figure.

To take account of the local surroundings, four topography categories have been defined to describe the roughness of the ground:

- category 1: open sea and flat terrain without obstructions
- category 2: terrain with hedges, individual houses and trees
- category 3: suburbs, industrial areas and forests
- category 4: urban districts

However, as equilibrium profiles are only achieved over distances exceeding 50 km of homogeneous topography, category 2 can be generally applied for practical purposes in Germany. This is recommended in the standard. However, differentiation in individual cases is permitted.

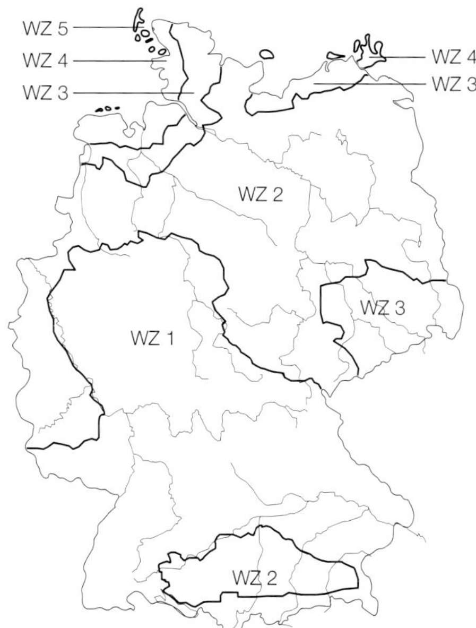


2.1.1.19 Wind zones map [12]

| Wind zone | $V_{ref}$ [m/s] | $q_{ref}$ [kN/m²] |
|---|---|---|
| 1 | 22.5 | 0.32 |
| 2 | 25.0 | 0.39 |
| 3 | 27.5 | 0.47 |
| 4 | 30.0 | 0.56 |
| 5 | 30.0 | 0.56 |

$V_{ref}$ = reference wind speed
$q_{ref}$ = associated dynamic pressure

2.1.1.20 Wind zones [12]

Equations are provided for taking height above ground level into account. They are based on the height above ground level and the reference dynamic pressure. For simplicity, on structures up to a height of 25 m the wind speed pressure may be assumed to act constantly up to certain levels.

| Wind zone | Dynamic pressure q [kN/m²] | | |
|---|---|---|---|
| | 0 m – 8 m | 8 m – 20 m | 20 m – 25 m |
| 1 | 0.55 | 0.70 | 0.80 |
| 2 | 0.65 | 0.85 | 1.00 |
| 3 | 0.80 | 1.05 | 1.20 |
| 4 | 0.95 | 1.25 | 1.45 |
| 5 | 1.25 | 1.50 | 1.70 |

2.1.1.21 Dynamic pressures for low-rise structures [12]

Generally, it should be assumed that the extreme wind speed can occur with the wind blowing in any direction. If reliable statistics are available, the relevance of direction may be taken into account. [12]
The aerodynamic coefficients $c_p$ are specified in the standard [12] for the orthogonal wind directions 0°, 90° and 180°. However, these represent the highest value occurring within a range of ±45° about the given orthogonal direction. This means, for example, that wind blowing onto a corner does not need to be investigated separately.
The coefficients are specified for

- flat roofs
- monopitch roofs
- gable and valley roofs
- hipped roofs

separately and related to individual areas of the roof surface. (Flat roofs are roofs with a pitch less than ±5°.)

As the coefficients $c_p$ are averaged over a certain area but the magnitude of the wind pressure fluctuates severely, the loaded area must be considered in each case when designing individual loadbearing members. The $c_p$ values are therefore specified separately for a loaded area of 10 m² and 1 m², the values for 1 m² naturally being much higher.

Space precludes us from reproducing the extensive tables of $c_p$-values – up to 0.8 for wind pressure and up to 2.8 for suction – here. The wind suction loads are larger than the wind pressure loads for all types of roof. The highest suction loads occur mainly in the region of the edge onto which the wind is blowing, and at the corners. The suction load case and the pressure load case must be analysed for shallow roof pitches.

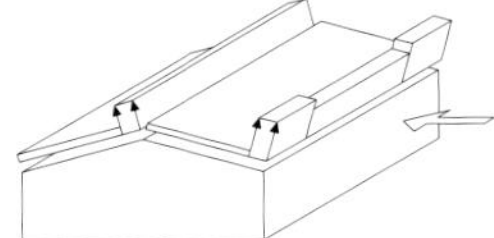

2.1.1.22 Gable roof, 15° pitch, distribution of suction loads

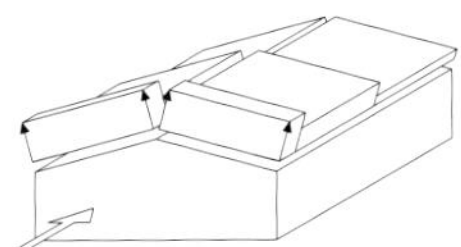

2.1.1.23 Gable roof, 15° pitch, distribution of suction loads

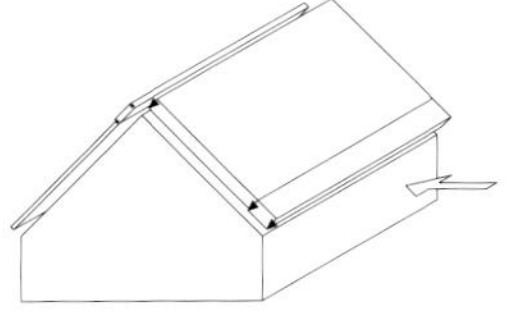

2.1.1.24 Gable roof, 45° pitch, distribution of pressure loads on windward side, suction loads on leeward side

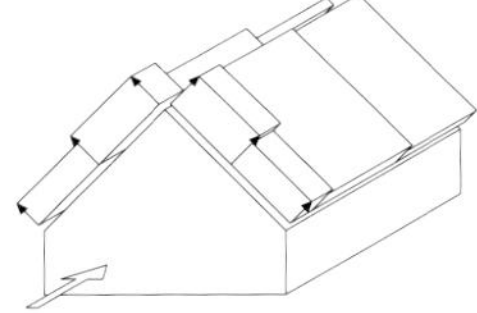

2.1.1.25 Gable roof, 45° pitch, distribution of suction loads

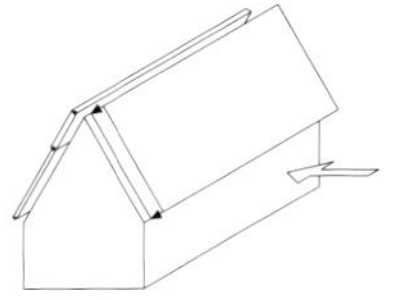

2.1.1.26 Gable roof, 60° pitch, distribution of pressure loads on windward side, suction loads on leeward side

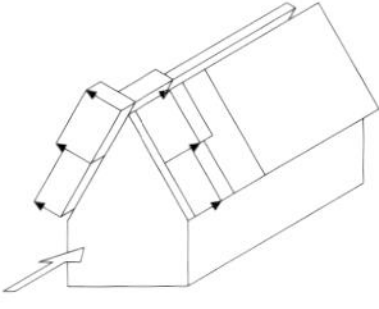

2.1.1.27 Gable roof, 60° pitch, distribution of suction loads

Wind load distributions are illustrated in general terms for a number of examples in figures 2.1.1.13 to 2.1.1.18 and 2.1.1.22 to 2.1.1.27. They are calculated for wind zone 2, a building height less than 8 m and with the $c_p$-values for a loaded area of 1 m². In the case of a monopitch roof with 15° pitch, the highest wind suction load occurs when the wind blows onto the taller long side (figure 2.1.1.14). In this example the suction load is 1.82 kN/m² at the corners, 1.30 kN/m² along the edges and 0.78 kN/m² over the surface.

The pressure/suction acting on the soffit of a roof overhang can be taken to be equal to the value acting on the adjoining wall surface; the pressure/suction on the top of the roof overhang is the same as on the adjacent roof surface. The wind pressure/suction should be increased by 10% when analysing the stability of the building envelope and its anchorage.

When analysing larger loadbearing members it should be remembered that the given wind pressures for the individual areas need not act simultaneously. They may indeed belong to different wind directions. The resulting influence on a variable under consideration may need to be investigated. This applies, in particular, to long-span frames and arches. One generally conservative estimate is to equate the beneficial load components to zero.

If necessary, internal pressure within the building may need to be considered in addition to the external pressure. The internal pressure depends on the size and position of openings in the building envelope; $c_p$-values for buildings with permeable and open external walls are specified. A wall with a proportion of openings between 1 and 30% (permanent or possibly open during a storm) is classed as permeable. All types of doors which, in connection with the use of the building, may be opened during a storm must be taken into account, but not windows. A wall with a proportion of openings exceeding 30% is classed as completely open. The pressure coefficients on the inner surfaces of buildings open at the sides are specified separately.

Special coefficients are given for free-standing canopies. The roof surfaces of such canopies are not divided into individual areas and the coefficients are not differentiated according to the loaded area of loadbearing components. However, when investigating the roof covering, an increased suction load should be assumed along a peripheral strip 1 m wide.

The wind load may be reduced for temporary structures and buildings under construction.

| Type of snow | Density (kN/m³) |
|---|---|
| newly fallen snow | 1.0 |
| snow that has been lying for a few hours or days | 2.0 |
| snow that has been lying for a few weeks or months | 2.5–3.5 |
| wet snow | 4.0 |

2.1.1.28 Average density of snow [8]

$$s = m_{\mu i}\, s_k$$

$m_{\mu i}$ = shape coefficient for snow load
$s_k$ = characteristic value of snow load on ground [kN/m²]

2.1.1.29 Relationship between snow load on roof and snow load on ground [13]

**Snow loads**

Snow loads are primarily dependent on the location of the structure, local climate, height above sea level and topography. They are also dependent on the shape of the building, surface roughness and the roof's thermal insulation characteristics. The wind may cause drifting and local accumulations of snow. Concentrated, high local loads can result from snow sliding down onto lower sections of a roof. The icing-up of drainage systems or rain that has fallen on snow can lead to extreme loads. The specific weight of snow is variable and generally increases over time.

A snow load on a roof is generally determined in two steps, as follows:
A basic snow load is defined. This is deduced from meteorological observations of the snow coverage or the water equivalent on the natural surface of the Earth. This snow load on the ground is primarily dependent on the geographical location of the site and its height above sea level.

The second step relates the loads to the roof by multiplying them with coefficients. In doing so, various influences are taken into account, e.g. shape and pitch of roof surface, accumulations of snow due to drifting or sliding.

This procedure forms the basis of the European standard. Accordingly, the new draft of DIN 1055 also includes the following method: Characteristic values for regional snow zones and height above sea level are defined for snow loads on the ground. Each snow zone is assigned an intensity Z. Using this value and the height above sea level, the characteristic snow load on the ground is determined with the help of mathematical equations or diagrams. In Germany the increase in snow load with height above sea level is roughly parabolic.

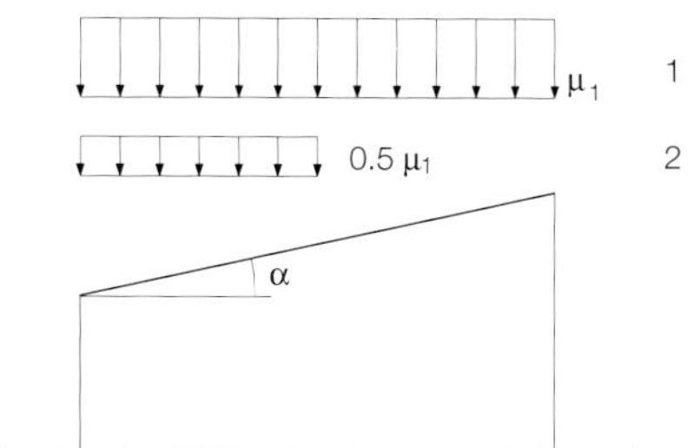


2.1.1.30 Snow load on monopitch roof: 1 full load, 2 half load applied as worst case [13]

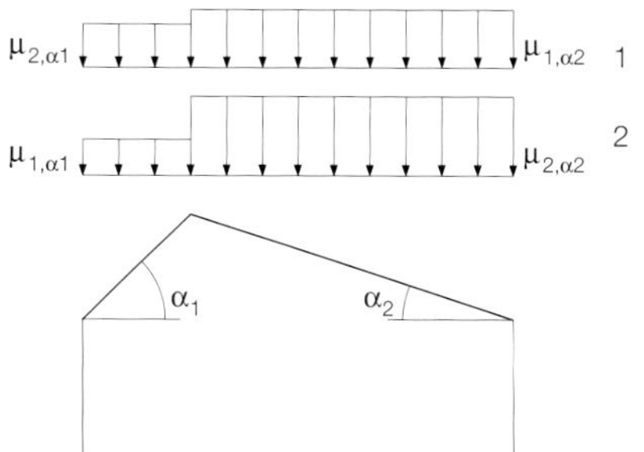


2.1.1.31 Snow load on gable roof taking drifting into account: 1 prevailing wind from the right, 2 prevailing wind from the left [13]

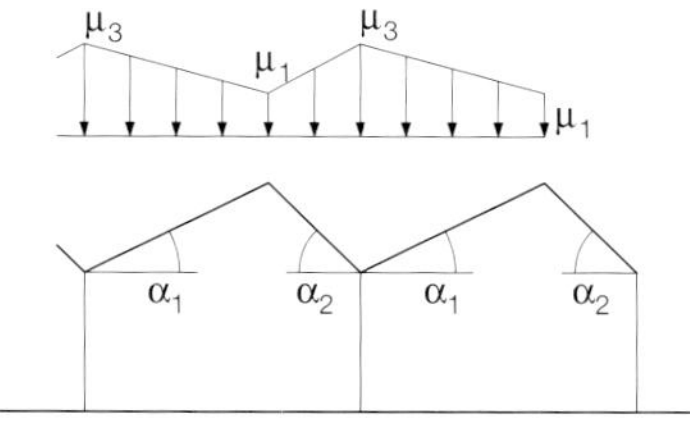


2.1.1.32 Snow load in roof valleys [13]

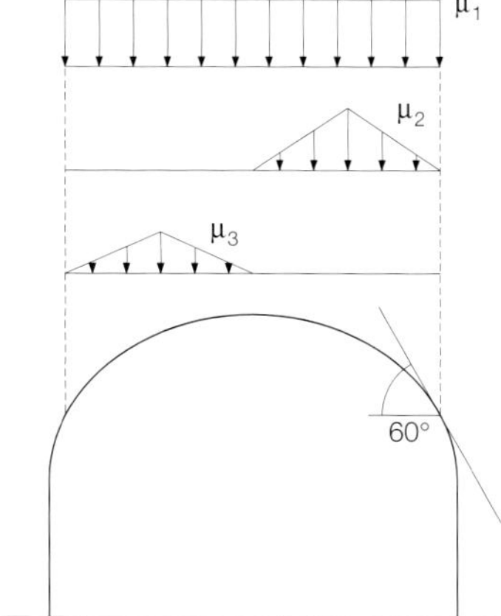


2.1.1.33 Snow load on barrel vault roof [13]

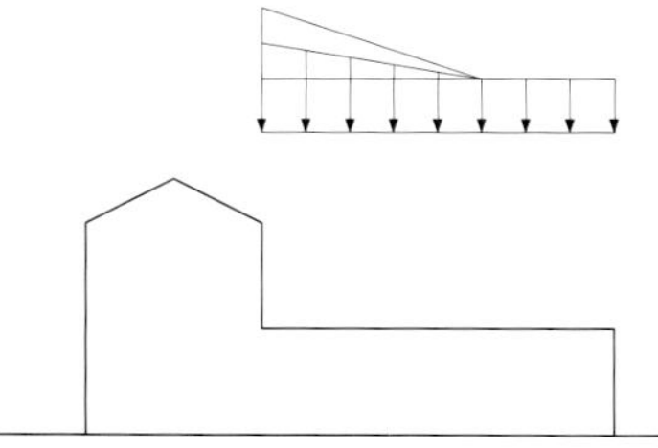

2.1.1.34 Snow load at abrupt change in height [13]

We distinguish between two regions in Germany when describing snow zones: the "central European region" and the "Alpine region". These regions are taken from the European snow load map. The snow zone map for the central European region is shown in figure 2.1.1.35. The non-shaded area in southern Germany belongs to the Alpine region and is shown on a separate map not given here.

The actual snow loads assumed for various roof forms according to the roof pitch are determined using the shape coefficients $\mu_1$ to $\mu_3$ (figure 2.1.1.37).

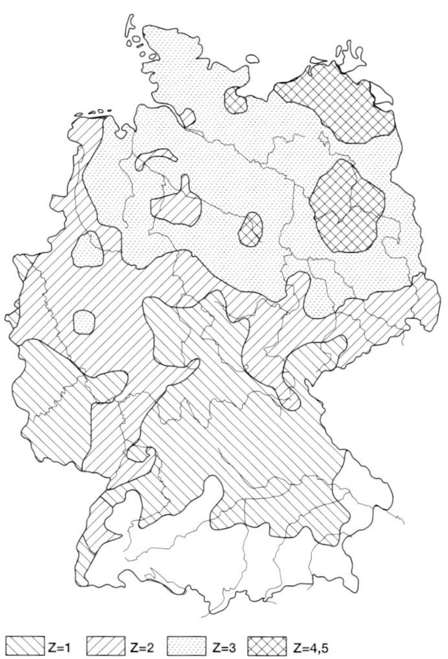


2.1.1.35 Central European region snow zones map [13]

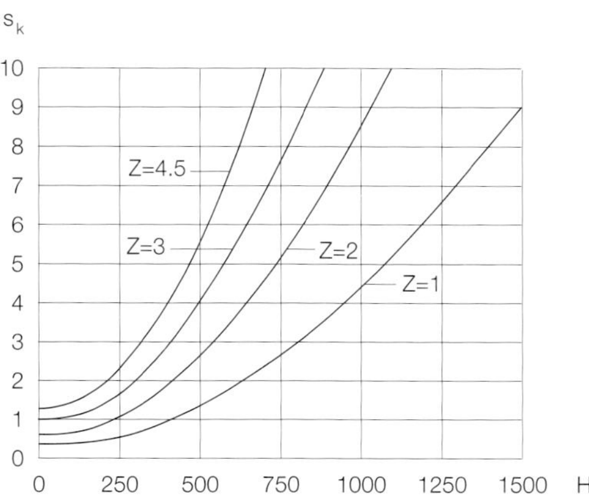


H = altitude of site above sea level
$s_k$ = snow load on ground

2.1.1.36 Snow load $s_k$ on ground in the central European region [13]

The shape coefficient $\mu_1$ is taken to be 0.8 for roof pitches less than 15°. The value is not equal to one because the snow load on roofs is generally less than that on the ground because of the drifting effect. The factor decreases for steeper pitches because snow tends to slide off the roof. On roofs with a pitch greater than 60° the snow slides off completely, provided obstructions (chimneys etc.) do not prevent it from doing so. The shape coefficient is then taken to be zero.

An additional shape coefficient $\mu_2$ takes account of drifts of snow on the lee side of the roof (figures 2.1.1.30 and 2.1.1.31).
A third shape coefficient μ3 is available for taking into account drifts of snow on sawtooth and similar roofs (figure 2.1.1.32).

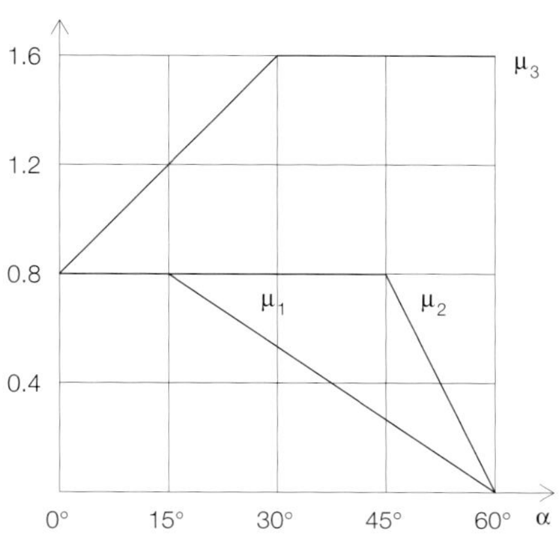


2.1.1.37 Shape coefficients for snow load in relation to roof pitch [13] for monopitch, gable and valley roofs

There are special values for snow loads on barrel vaults (figure 2.1.1.33). Advice is also given on snow loads resulting from snow sliding onto lower levels and drifting adjacent to walls and projections (figure 2.1.1.34).
Snow that overhangs at the eaves is a special case and must be allowed for by way of a line load along the eaves, as well as the load on snowguards and roof-mounted objects resulting from masses of snow at risk of sliding.

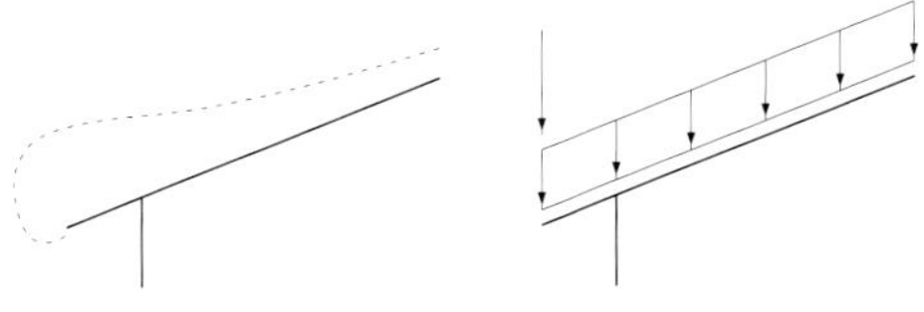

2.1.1.38 Taking account of an accumulation of snow at eaves [13]

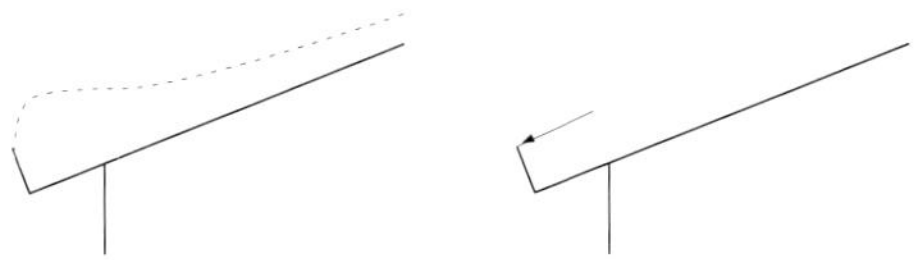

2.1.1.39 Taking account of an accumulation of snow behind snowguard [13]

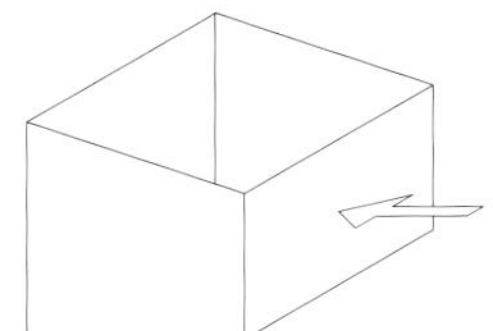

2.1.2.1 Four vertical plates (shear walls)

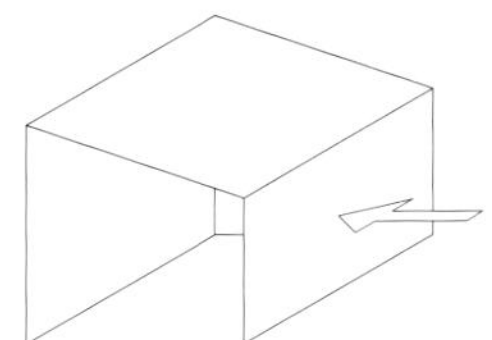

2.1.2.2 Three plates plus one roof plate

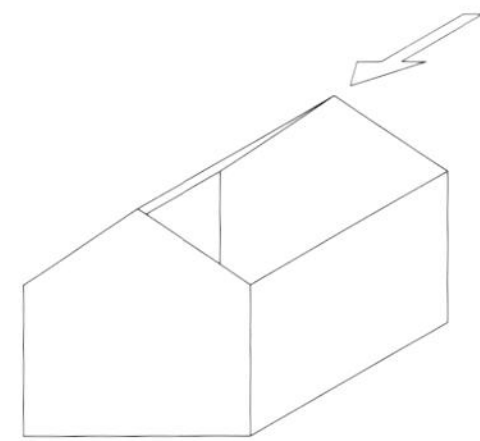

2.1.2.3 Gable roof, bracing to apex of gable

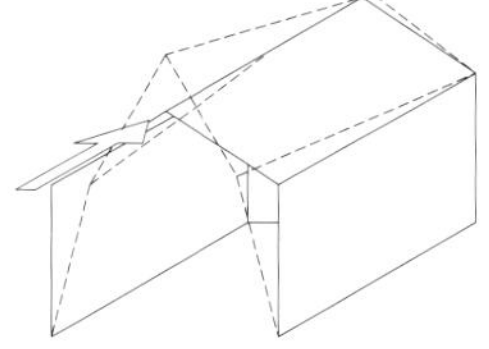

2.1.2.4 Gable roof, three plates plus roof plates

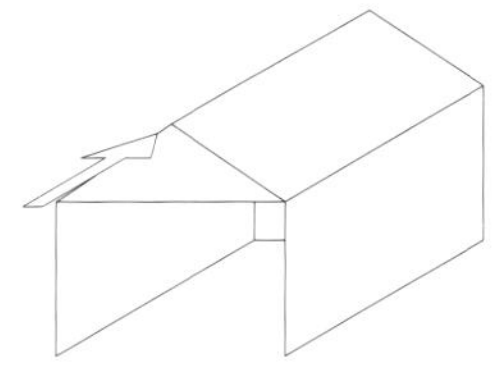

2.1.2.5 Gable roof, plate in gable

2.1.2.6 Barrel vault

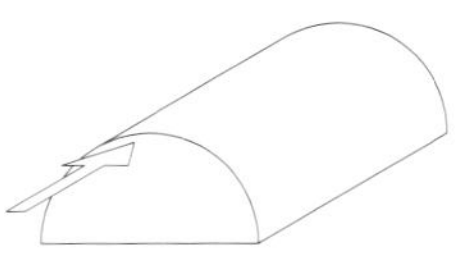

2.1.2.7 Barrel vault with end plates

## Bracing

#### The roof as part of the bracing system

The roof surface has a special significance in terms of providing the necessary bracing to the building. A considerable proportion of the overall bracing can be arranged within the roof surface. And both the roof structure itself and its individual components have to be braced.

The bracing should be planned at the draft design stage and treated as part of the design. If considered too late, bracing arrangements can influence a design considerably and seriously alter the intended architectural appearance of a building.

Generally, the bracing members of a building are those parts of the construction that must be provided in addition to the primary loadbearing structure to guarantee the stability and serviceability of the overall system and its members.

The loads acting on these constructions are the result of:

- external actions such as wind forces and seismic loads,
- forces due to out-of-plumb effects and imperfections, as well as forces for stabilising components at risk of buckling and overturning.

#### Plate effects

The mutual stability of plates in a three-dimensional arrangement is crucial. According to its definition, a plate can only carry loads in the plane of the plate; it cannot carry bending moments or loads acting perpendicular to the plate. In a structure these loads must be carried by other loadbearing members.

Four vertical, mutually supportive plates are each stabilised along their common edges. The four upper corners are fixed (figure 2.1.2.1).

Three vertical plates forming an open rectangle on plan require the addition of a roof plate to form an effective bracing system. As the plates can twist, the roof plate must prevent displacement at the open side. This applies to both flat and pitched roofs (figure 2.1.2.2).

In a building comprising four vertical, mutually supportive plates and a gable roof form, the tops of the gables must be supported horizontally. In order to restrain the ridge, at least one roof surface must be formed as a plate (figure 2.1.2.3).

A building that is open at the side and has three plates on plan and two plates forming a gable roof is unstable (figure 2.1.2.4). The two roof plates and the two side plates could twist. To prevent this, the gable at least requires a plate (figure 2.1.2.5).

We should mention the special case of a roof with surfaces at different pitches. Only a roof surface with the same pitch can act as a plate. No plate forces can be transferred across the change of pitch at the ridge/crank without vertical forces due to the change in direction ensuing – and these must be carried by the roof structure. The greater the pitch of the roof surfaces (i.e. the steeper the roof in the case of a gable roof), the larger these forces are due to the change in direction.

A barrel vault held along the bottom edges and subjected to a horizontal force in the longitudinal direction can also twist. It can be stabilised with end plates (figures 2.1.2.6 and 2.1.2.7).

#### Wind girders

Single-storey shed frameworks are used as an example in the following to illustrate a few of the bracing options. The wind girders shown can be replaced by plates if the dimensions and structural design permit.
Each axis of the building must be braced. In the transverse direction of a single-storey shed this can be achieved with columns restrained in the transverse direction (figure 2.1.2.8) or by means of frames (figure 2.1.2.9). In the longitudinal direction of the single-storey shed, wind girders in the facade provide the necessary bracing.

Wind forces acting on the gable facade can be transferred into the purlins of the roof structure by way of cladding posts. The purlins must in turn be connected to wind girders and thus also provide lateral restraint to the main beams. The wind girders act like horizontal trusses and transfer the forces to the side walls (figure 2.1.2.13). As with plates, wind girders also lead to negative lift at the ridge, which generates a load on the main beams (figure 2.1.2.14).

Instead of a wind girder in the plane of the roof consisting exclusively of X-bracing in tension, K-bracing may be used. But in this case all diagonals must be capable of accommodating compression forces as well (figure 2.1.2.9). The individual transverse axes of the single-storey shed can be held horizontally via a truss in the plane of the roof running the length of the building (figure 2.1.2.10).

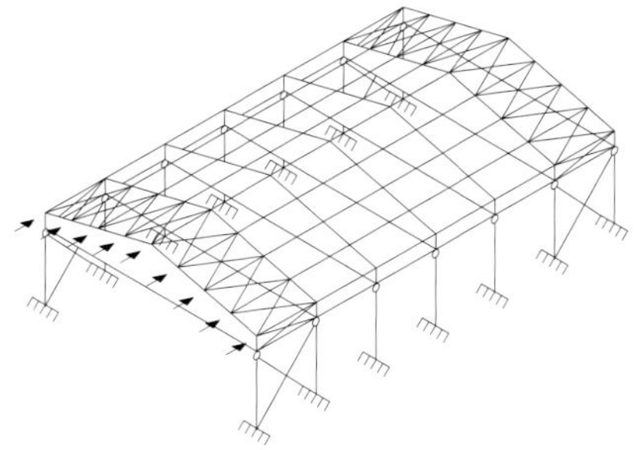
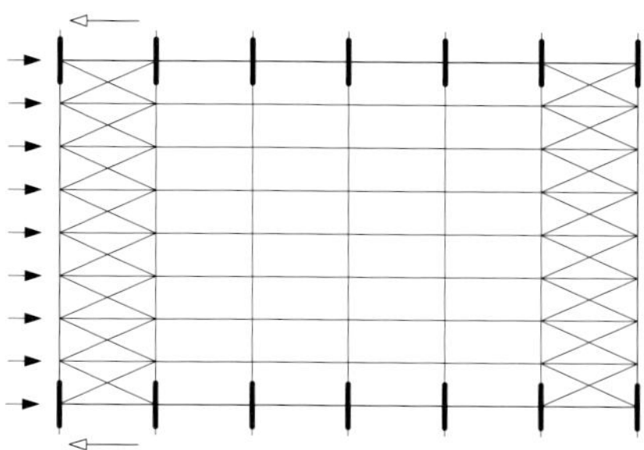

2.1.2.8 Fixed-based columns, wind girder to resist wind forces in the longitudinal direction

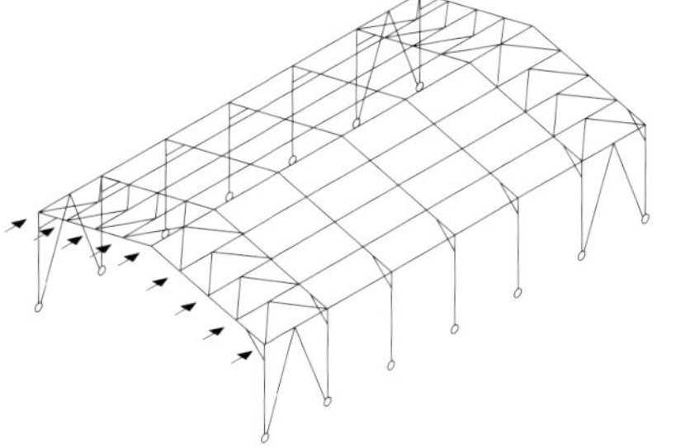
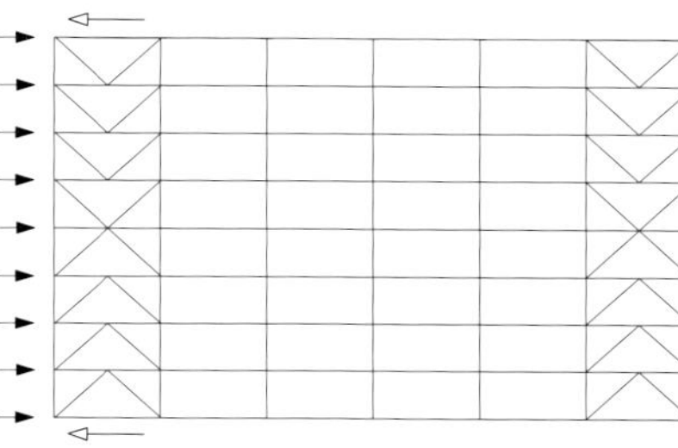

2.1.2.9 Frames in the transverse direction, K-bracing to resist wind forces in the longitudinal direction

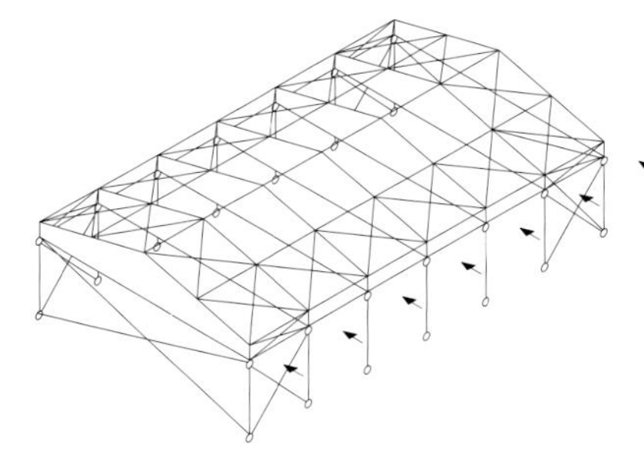
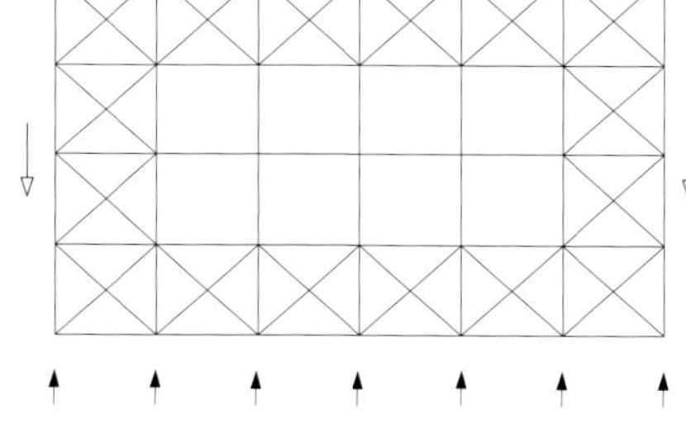

2.1.2.10 Wind girders in roof and gable wall to resist transverse wind forces

2.1.2.11 Bracing in the longitudinal direction

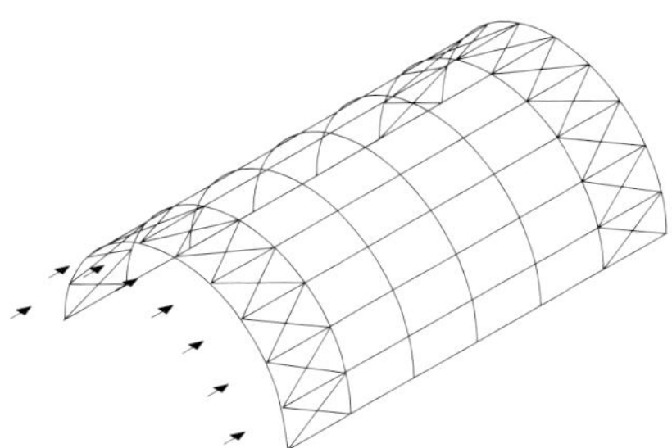
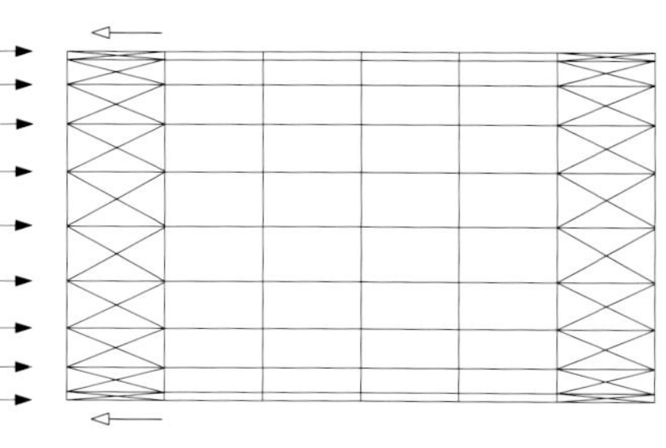
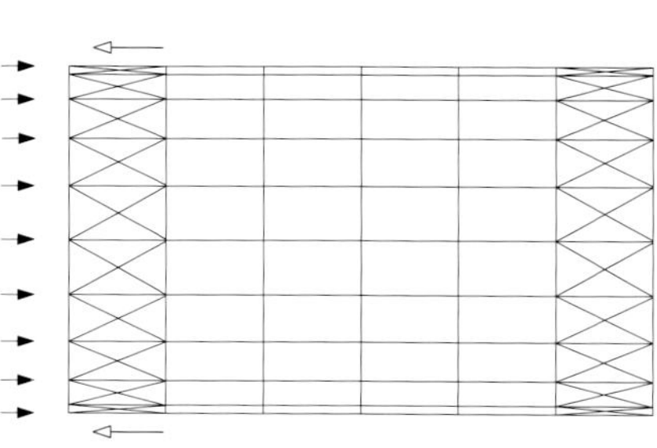

2.1.2.12 Arch construction, wind girders providing bracing in the longitudinal direction

The transverse horizontal forces acting on the single-storey shed are concentrated at the gable walls, from where they can be transferred to the foundations. Frames and fixed-base columns are not necessary. However, this bracing concept presumes a corresponding design freedom at the gable walls.

On steep roofs the negative lift due to wind girders can be considerable. Wind girders cantilevering towards the ridge are an advantageous alternative when the negative lift occurring here can be short-circuited at the eaves by a horizontal connection between the supports (figure 2.1.2.15).

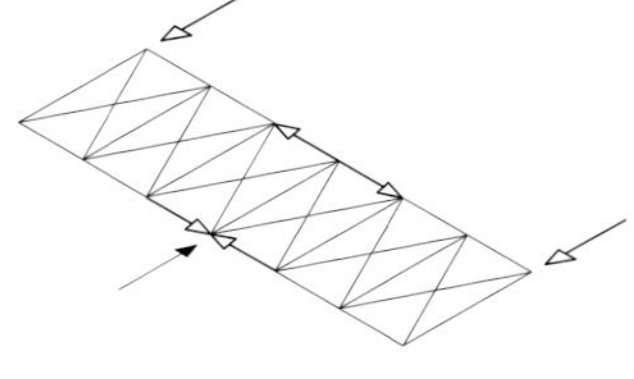

2.1.2.13 Horizontal wind girder

2.1.2.14 Wind girder in duopitch roof, with negative lift at ridge

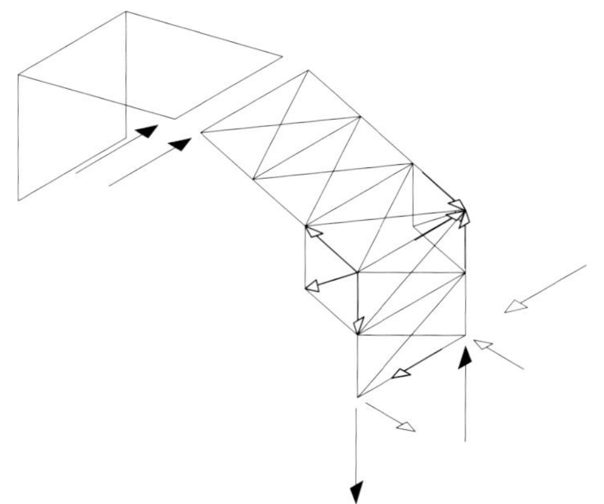

2.1.2.15 Cantilever wind girder, with negative lift at eaves

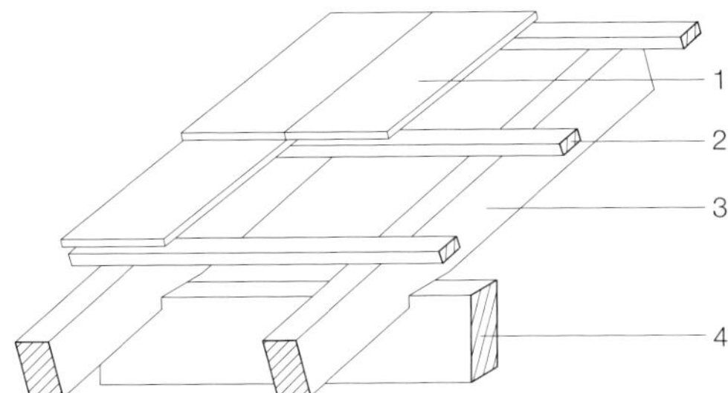


2.1.3.1 Roof covering over an open roof space: 1 Overlapping elements, 2 battens, 3 rafters, 4 purlin

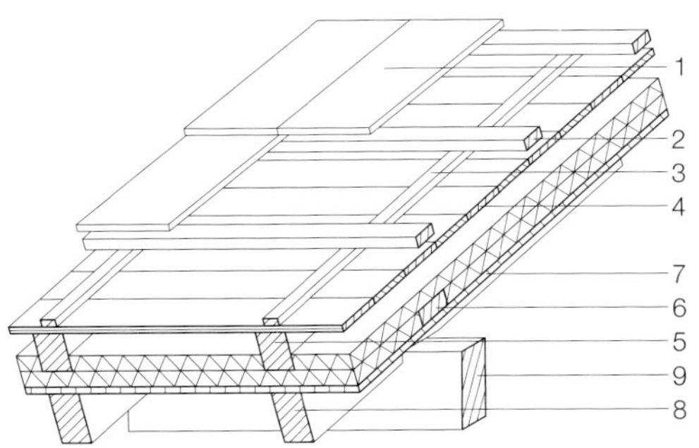


2.1.3.2 Overlapping elements over cold deck: 1 Overlapping elements, 2 battens, 3 counter battens, 4 roof decking, 5 spacer rafters, 6 spacer purlin, 7 roof decking, 8 rafters, 9 purlin

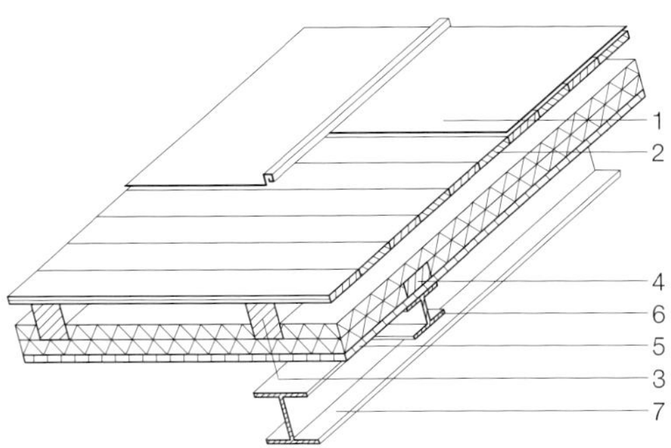


2.1.3.3 Sheet metal on roof decking (cold deck): 1 sheet metal, 2 sheathing, 3 spacer rafters, 4 purlin plate, 5 roof decking (timber derivative board), 6 purlin, 7 main beam

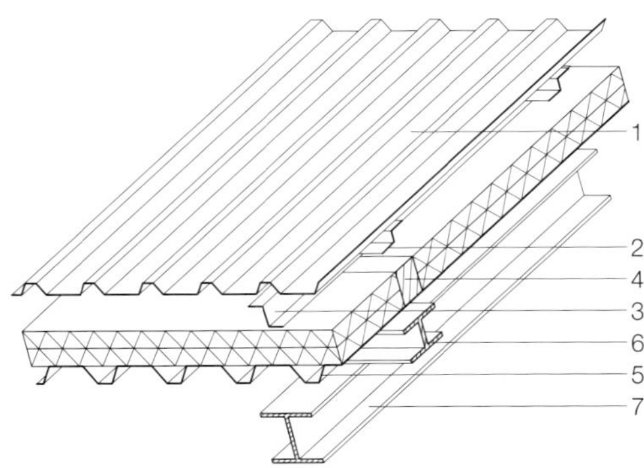


2.1.3.4 Metal sheeting to topside and underside of cold deck: 1 trapezoidal profile sheeting, 2 horizontal Z-section supporting sheeting, 3 Z-section spacer in direction of roof pitch, 4 timber spacer, 5 trapezoidal profile sheeting, 6 purlin, 7 main beam

## From roof covering to loadbearing structure

**Transferring the load from the roof covering to the primary loadbearing structure**

The way the loads are carried by the roof covering and transferred into the primary loadbearing structure is described below for eight typical roof systems. The examples chosen are described in detail in the chapter "Construction details". The loadbearing members are treated individually.

The roof may be made up of numerous different elements. The choice of elements and their arrangement is essentially governed by thermal, sound, moisture and fire aspects, but must also satisfy structural and aesthetic demands.

The loads acting on the surface of the roof must be transferred via the individual construction elements into the primary loadbearing structure and from there into the subsoil. We distinguish between loadbearing and non-loadbearing members. Loads uniformly distributed over an area are converted into linear or point loads. The direction of span can change from member to member; loads can be carried along one or two axes (figure 2.1.3.5).

The loads act perpendicular to the roof surface as a pressure or suction (wind forces) and as vertical forces (dead, snow, imposed loads). The forces acting vertically can be resolved into a component perpendicular to the roof surface and a component parallel to the roof surface (negative lift) (figure 2.1.3.6). Both components have to be transferred through the construction.

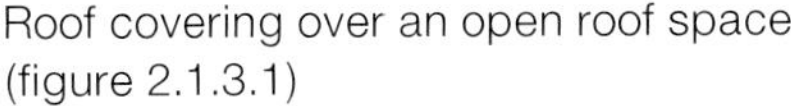

Roof covering over an open roof space (figure 2.1.3.1)

The individual overlapping elements carry the uniformly distributed loads and transfer them to the tiling battens as a linear load. The tiling battens span across several rafters and, in structural terms, act as a continuous beam. They are subject to uniformly distributed (linear) loads both perpendicular and parallel to the roof surface (bending about two axes). The tiling battens are carried on the rafters as point loads and the rafters in turn are carried by the purlins. Every member has a loadbearing function. The fixings must ensure that the negative lift is transferred from the point of action to the primary loadbearing structure.

Overlapping elements over cold deck (figure 2.1.3.2)

The individual overlapping elements carry the uniformly distributed loads and transfer them to the tiling battens as a linear load. The tiling battens transfer the loads via the counter battens and the roof decking to the "spacer" rafters. The counter battens and the roof decking are supported directly and continuously on the "spacer" rafters so that they cannot be considered as loadbearing. However, they have

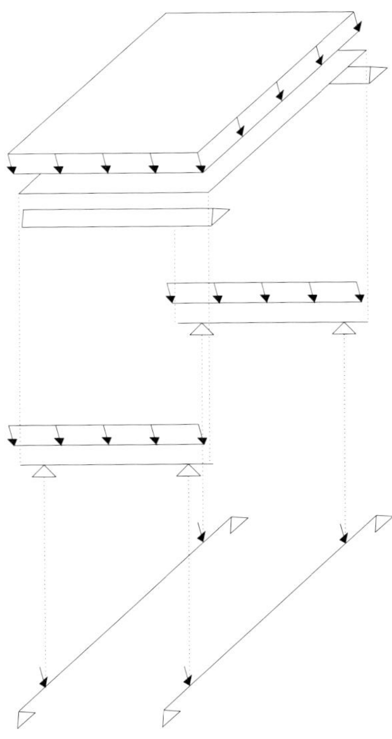

2.1.3.5 Uniformly distributed loads (per m$^2$, per m length), point loads

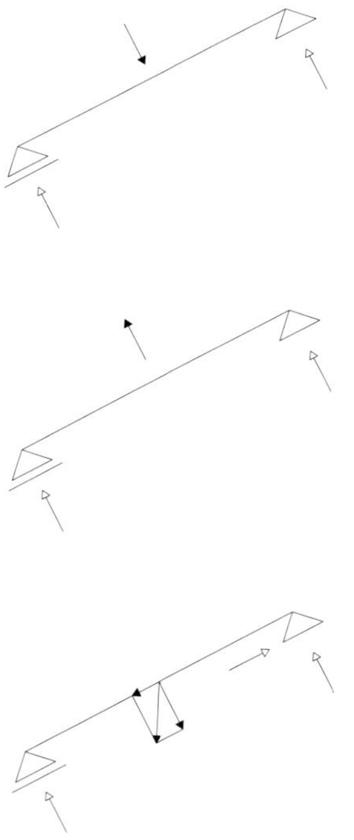

2.1.3.6 Loads acting on the surface of the roof

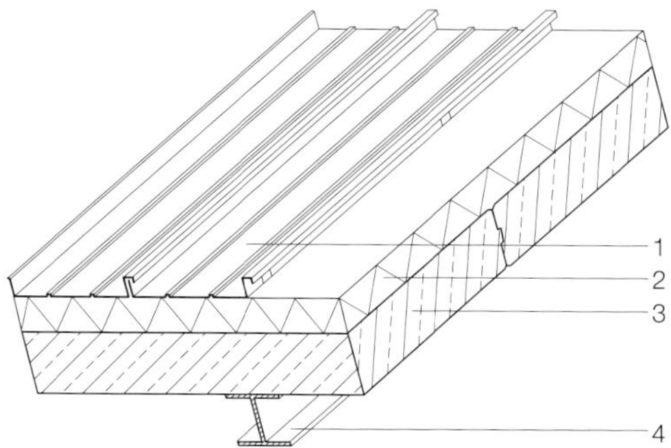


2.1.3.7 Ribbed metal sheeting on rigid thermal insulation and aerated concrete planks:
1 ribbed metal sheeting, 2 rigid thermal insulation, 3 aerated concrete planks with tongue and groove joints, 4 main beam

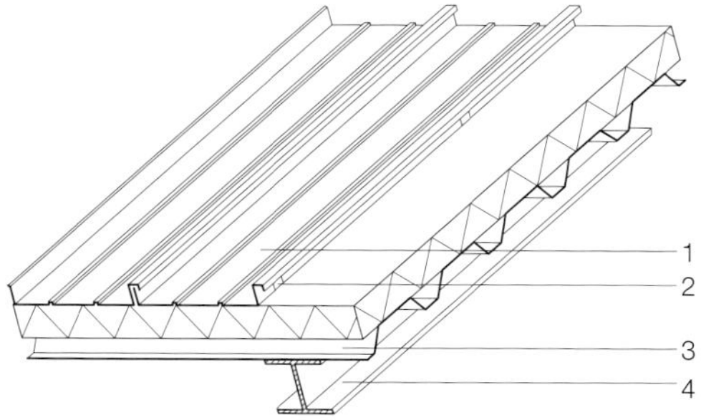


2.1.3.8 Ribbed metal sheeting on trapezoidal metal sheeting:
1 ribbed metal sheeting, 2 metal brackets passing through thermal insulation, 3 trapezoidal profile sheeting, 4 main beam

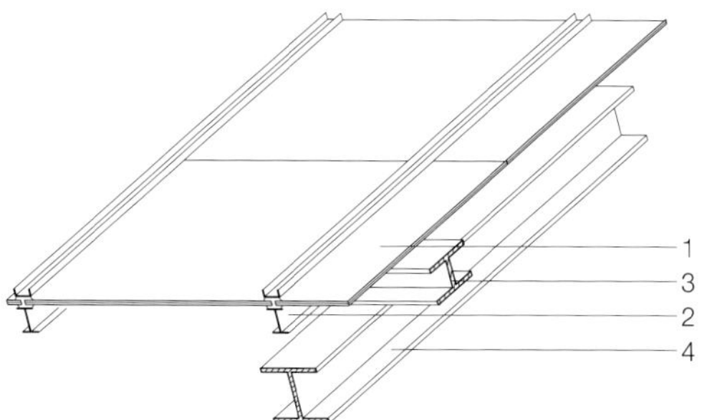


2.1.3.9 Double glazing on structural steelwork:
1 glass, 2 glazing bars, 3 purlin, 4 main beam

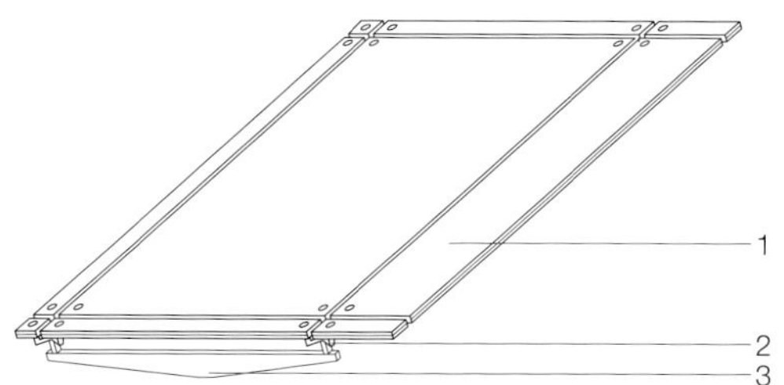


2.1.3.10 Discretely supported panes of glass on structural steelwork: 1 glass, 2 separate fixings, 3 steel bracket

to be joined together in such a way that the negative lift and uplift forces can be transferred. The "spacer" rafters are supported at close centres on the "spacer" purlins and must therefore span over this distance. The "spacer" purlins, which do not have to span any distance, transfer the load through the second (lower) layer of roof decking onto the loadbearing rafters. The upper and lower layers of roof decking are not classed as loadbearing in this case; they do not assist in carrying the external loads or the considerable dead loads, i.e. clay tiles.
The technical specification for loadbearing roof decking, as described below, does not apply in this case.

Sheet metal on roof decking (cold deck) (figure 2.1.3.3)
As the sheet metal is supported across its entire area, it is non-loadbearing. The roof decking is loadbearing in this case. It carries the external loads and spans as a continuous system between the "spacer" rafters. These are supported on the purlin plates, which are in turn carried continuously on the purlins. The "spacer" rafters are hence loadbearing members, which have to span between the purlins. The timber derivative boarding to the soffit is non-loadbearing.

Metal sheeting to topside and underside of cold deck (figure 2.1.3.4)
The roof covering of trapezoidal profile metal sheeting carries the external loads. It spans in the direction of the roof pitch and is carried on closely spaced horizontal cold-formed sections, which in turn are supported by similar sections spanning between timber spacers. These timber spacers distribute the loads onto the trapezoidal profile metal sheeting forming the soffit. This spans from purlin to purlin and is thus the loadbearing member.

Ribbed metal sheeting on rigid thermal insulation and aerated concrete planks (figure 2.1.3.7)
The ribbed metal sheeting is supported across its entire area by the rigid thermal insulation, which is also fully supported on the concrete planks. The metal sheeting must be anchored through the thermal insulation to resist wind suction and prevent slippage. The aerated concrete planks carry the loads and span between the main beams without requiring intermediate support in the form of purlins. The aerated concrete also contributes to thermal insulation.

Ribbed metal sheeting on trapezoidal metal sheeting (figure 2.1.3.8)
The ribbed metal sheeting is supported on the trapezoidal metal sheeting by means of metal brackets passing through the thermal insulation. The ribs ensure a load-carrying capacity in the direction of the fall. The ability to carry bending loads perpendicular to this direction is adequate for small spans; therefore, the thermal insulation does not need to carry any loads. All the loads are carried by the metal brackets. The trapezoidal metal sheeting forming the soffit spans between the main beams without the need for purlins or secondary beams.

Double glazing on structural steelwork (figure 2.1.3.9)
The panes of glass carry the uniformly distributed external loads and – spanning in one direction only – transfer these to the glazing bars. The glazing bars thus carry a uniformly distributed linear load and span between the purlins.

Discretely supported panes of glass on structural steelwork (figure 2.1.3.10)
Each pane of glass is held at its four corners. The panes of glass carry the uniformly distributed external loads and – now spanning in two directions – transfer these to the fixings at the corners. These fixings are attached to short cantilever brackets, which transfer the loads to the purlins.

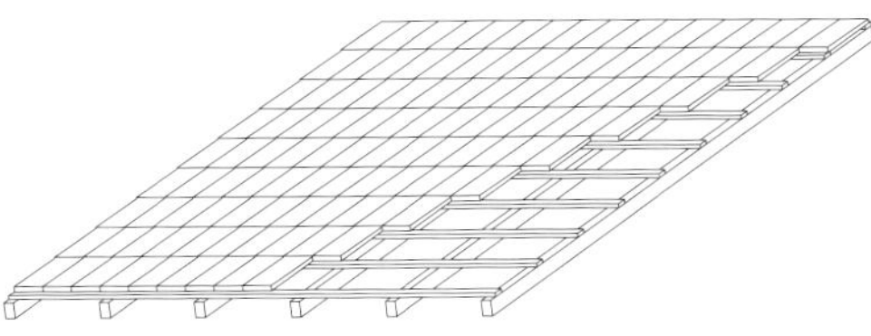

2.1.3.11 Overlapping elements on battens

**Overlapping elements on battens**

This type of roof covering uses clay or concrete roof tiles or small-format sheets. They are supported on horizontal tiling battens (figure 2.1.3.11).
The overlapping elements transfer uniformly distributed loads, self-weight, wind pressure and snow loads onto a linear support – the tiling batten. The negative lift caused by the loads acts parallel to the roof surface and is transferred to the battens by means of screws, nails or nibs on the underside of the overlapping elements.
The self-weight of the overlapping elements counteracts wind suction. Despite this, on parts of the roof subject to greater suction forces, especially along the edges and at the corners, it is often necessary to anchor the overlapping elements by means of nails, screws or tile clips (figure 2.1.3.12). The respective product information provides suitable guidance for calculating the fixings necessary in a particular case. [33] Irrespective of the fixings calculated, any type of small-format roofing unit (tiles etc.) must always be fixed along the edges (verge, ridge, hip etc.) and all such roof coverings must be fixed on roof pitches exceeding 65°.

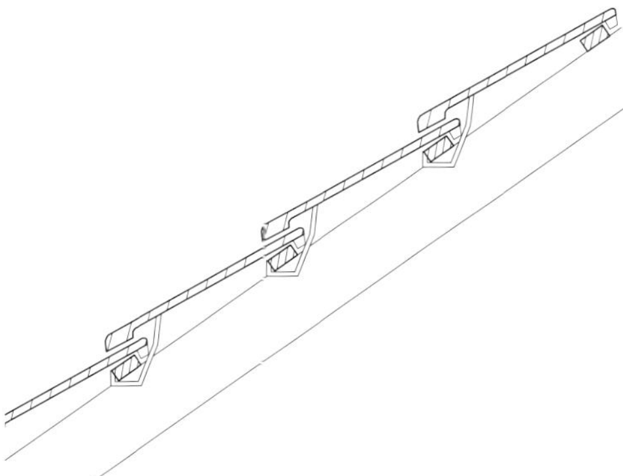

2.1.3.12 Tile clips to prevent uplift

The size of these tiles etc. determines the spacing of the tiling battens. Depending on the product, the spacing can vary from about 200 to 500 mm. The span of the battens is determined by the spacing of the rafters. This is usually between 700 and 1000 mm.

Tiling battens should be made from timber of grade 1 quality [7, 33], be at least 24 mm thick and have a cross-sectional area of at least 1100 mm². Larger cross-sections may be necessary depending on the choice of fixings or the required load-carrying capacity, or to limit deflection. A structural analysis is not required for tiling battens with sizes that have been proved in practice; this is 24 x 48 mm for rafters at 700 mm centres, 30 x 50 mm for 800 mm centres, and 40 x 60 mm for 1000 mm centres. A structural analysis should be carried out for other spans or cross-sections. This should allow for the finished roof covering with the corresponding loads and a repair load of two point loads of 0.5 kN each at the outer quarter points of the span.

Tiling battens are generally fixed to the rafters with a single nail. In the case of narrow rafters it may be advisable to mitre the ends of the battens.

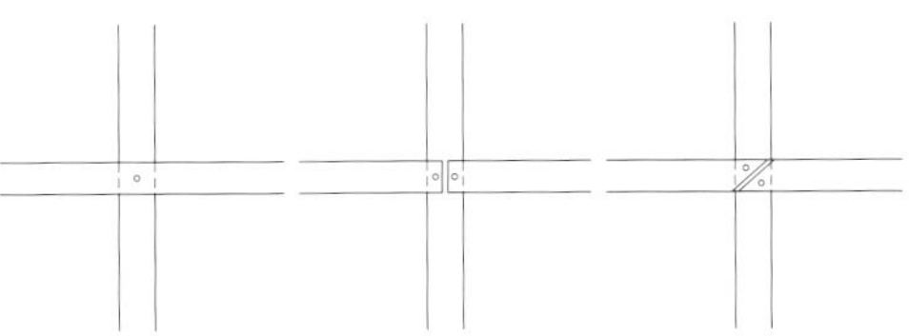

2.1.3.13 Batten-rafter fixing and butt joints between battens (over rafters)

Counter battens are positioned below the tiling battens in order to provide a ventilation cavity. The depth of the counter battens is primarily governed by the ventilation requirements. Their width depends on the fixings employed to attach the tiling battens and to attach the counter battens to the rafters or roof decking. These fixings must be able to transfer the entire negative lift acting on the roof covering to the supporting construction.

It is, in principle, possible to accommodate and transfer horizontal loads along the length of the battens. However, without an appropriate analysis, tiling battens may not be considered to provide lateral restraint to a top chord in compression. The sizes of tiling battens in general use can be considered to provide lateral restraint to rafters and the top chord of trusses at risk of buckling if (after [3]):

- the span of the roof does not exceed 15 m
- the spacing of the rafters or trusses does not exceed 1.25 m
- the rafter or truss top chord is at least 40 mm wide
- the depth of a rafter does not exceed four times its width

In addition, for transferring the load, care should be taken to ensure that the prescribed nail spacing is maintained, at the butt joints between battens as well. Special splice plates are required for narrow truss top chords.
The battens transfer the horizontal loads only along their length. Wind girders, diagonal bracing or roof plates are necessary to transfer the loads to fixed supports. The connection between the members must adequately transfer the forces involved.

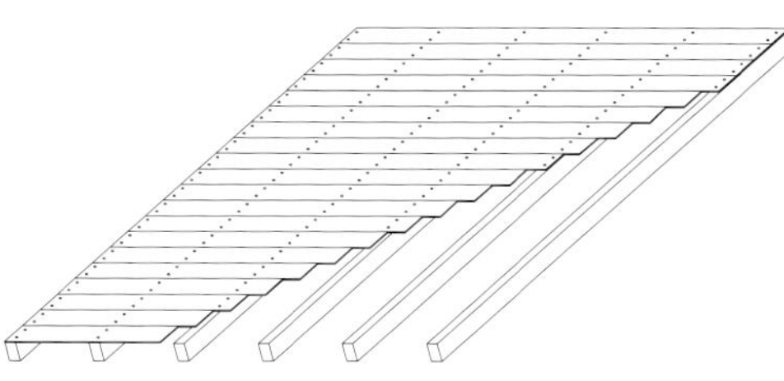

2.1.3.14 Roof decking made from timber boards or planks

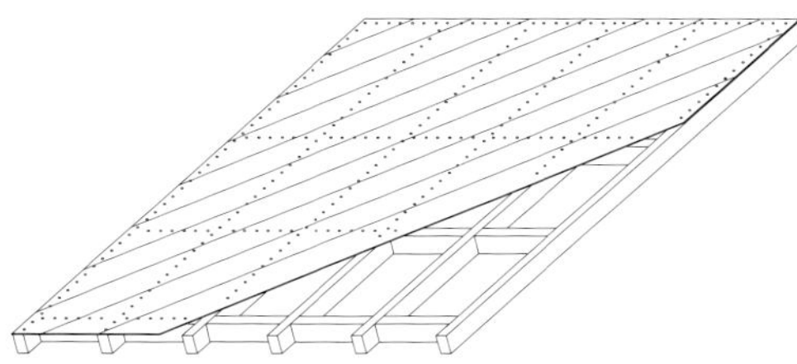

2.1.3.15 Roof decking made from timber planks attached diagonally to form a roof plate

### Timber roof decking

Timber roof decking is a loadbearing, plate-type component made of boards, planks or timber derivatives that carry the waterproofing, wind and snow loads. They are accessible only for maintenance and repair purposes.

The deflection of roof decking is generally limited to l/200 under total load and max. l/100 under self-weight and a point load of 1 kN (i.e. one person).

### Timber boards and planks

The usual spans for timber boards are 800 to approx. 1200 mm for lightweight roofs, and for timber planks, e.g. up to 60 mm thick, up to approx. 3000 mm. Boards must be at least 24 mm thick and have a cross-sectional area of at least 1400 mm² (width at least 60 mm), provided the fixings and the required load-carrying capacity do not call for a larger cross-section. [3]

In order to guarantee a certain distribution of any point loads, tongue-and-groove (or equivalent) joints are required between boards or planks. [3] An equivalent measure might be the provision of metal fastenings.
Boards and planks must be fixed at every support. Butt joints parallel to the supports may only be positioned over supporting components (rafter, purlin, beam).

It is possible for boards to carry horizontal loads in the longitudinal direction. Roof decking made from separate boards may be considered to provide lateral support to roof trusses if (after [3]):

- span of truss does not exceed 12.5 m
- spacing of trusses does not exceed 1.25 m
- truss chords are least 40 mm wide
- permanent load of truss is less than 50% of total load
- length of roof surface is greater than 80% of truss span but less than 25 m
- each board is at least 120 mm wide
- each board is fixed to every chord and at every butt joint with at least two nails
- butt joints between boards are offset by at least two times the truss spacing
- width of butt joint is max. 1 m

The boards transfer the stabilising loads in the horizontal direction only. In order to carry the loads to fixed supports, the boards must be connected to wind girders or roof plates.

A roof plate can only be formed with a single or double layer of diagonal boards. The boards should be fixed to both longitudinal and transverse supports (figure 2.1.3.15).

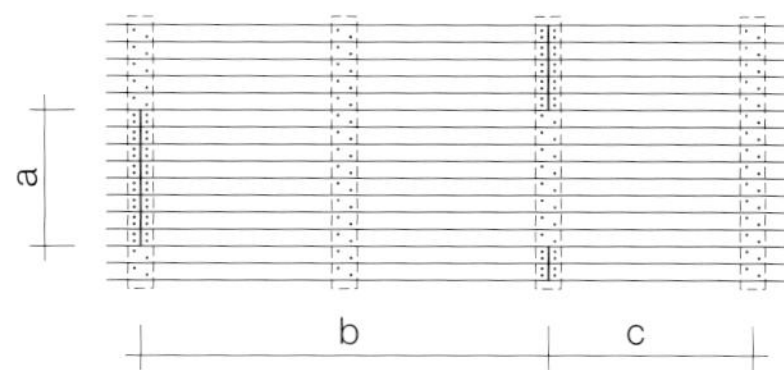


2.1.3.16 Roof decking of individual planks for providing lateral support to rafters and compression chords: a width of butt joint, b offset between butt joints (at least two bays), c spacing of rafters/trusses

### Boards of timber derivatives

The timber derivatives suitable for roof decking are:

- LVL (laminated veneer lumber) (e.g. Kerto)
- multi-ply solid timber boards
- building-grade plywood (min. 5 plies, min. 6 mm thick, for bracing purposes only min. 3 plies)
- OSB (oriented strand board) (min. 8 mm thick)
- synthetic resin-bound chipboard (min. 8 mm thick)
- cement-bound chipboard (min. 8 mm thick)
- wood-fibre boards (min. 6 mm thick)

Common spans for roof decking of timber derivatives – for lightweight roofs and provided a plate effect is not required – are:

- up to approx. 1.60 m for 27 mm thick LVL (e.g. Kerto Q), up to approx. 3.00 m for 57 mm thick
- up to approx. 0.80 m for 18 mm thick building-grade plywood, up to approx. 1.60 m for 30 mm thick
- up to approx. 0.80 m for 22 mm thick synthetic resin-bound chipboard, up to approx. 1.20 m for 36 mm thick

The boards should be laid in a regular pattern at right angles to the rafters or beams. They should be fixed at every support and be interconnected at every unsupported edge by tongue-and-groove or equivalent joints. Butt joints parallel to the supports may only be positioned over supporting components (rafter, purlin, beam) (figure 2.1.3.17).

Gaps should be left between the boards to allow for possible expansion. The width of these gaps should be 2 mm per board length for chipboard, and 1 mm per board length for building-grade plywood.

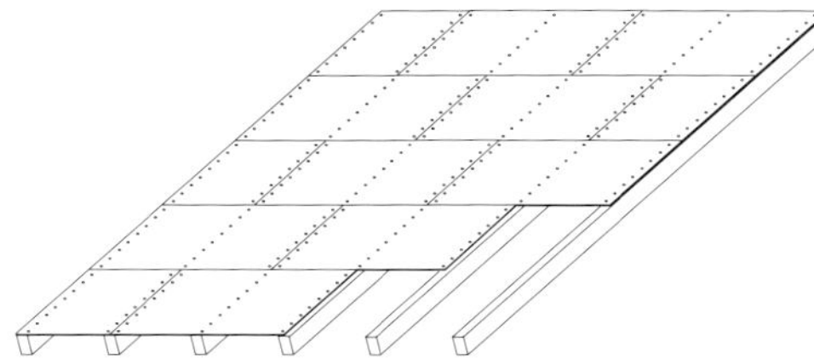

2.1.3.17 Roof decking made from timber derivative boards, offset arrangement perpendicular to rafters, without plate effect

Special care must be taken with roof decking to provide adequate anchorage against wind suction. The uplift forces must be transferable from the roof covering into the primary loadbearing structure by means of appropriate fixings. However, a structural analysis is not usually required for houses and structures with a similar form and construction, provided a number of conditions, as given in DIN 1055 part 4 [4], are fulfilled. For example, roof pitch, height of building and roof overhang must not exceed certain values, and the boards or sheets must be fastened with a minimum number of nails per square metre of roof surface.

**Roof decking as roof plate**

It would seem obvious to use a flat decking as a stiffening plate. External forces, e.g. wind on a gable wall, or bracing loads from the primary loadbearing structure, can be carried by a roof plate over a certain span. The supports to the plate can be bracing members in the facade or walls that can accommodate the support reactions and transfer these further. A plate effect is made possible by the interaction of the boards with their supporting construction (rafters, purlins, beams). The supporting construction is a connection transferring the forces between the boards. Shear forces are essentially transferred along the edges of the individual boards. The chords along the edges of the plate are subjected to tension and compression. Pin-type fastenings are generally used for the connections.

The deflection in the plane of the plate as a result of the plate loadbearing effect may not exceed l/1000. A lower limit applies for deflection as a result of simultaneous bending due to vertical loads than for roof decking without plate effect; in this case the deflection should not exceed l/400 under total load.

Timber derivative boards should be positioned offset and have shear-resistant connections along the four edges. If necessary, shear-resistant connections, possibly through timber splice plates, must be provided along the edges at right-angles to the supports. They can be nailed to the ribs/rafters at an angle. The boards should be nailed to the splice plate (figures 2.1.3.18 and 2.1.3.20).
A shear-resistant connection along the edges at right-angles to the ribs is not necessary for small horizontal loads and small dimensions, provided a series of conditions are complied with, as outlined in the draft of DIN 1052 [9] (figure 2.1.3.19).

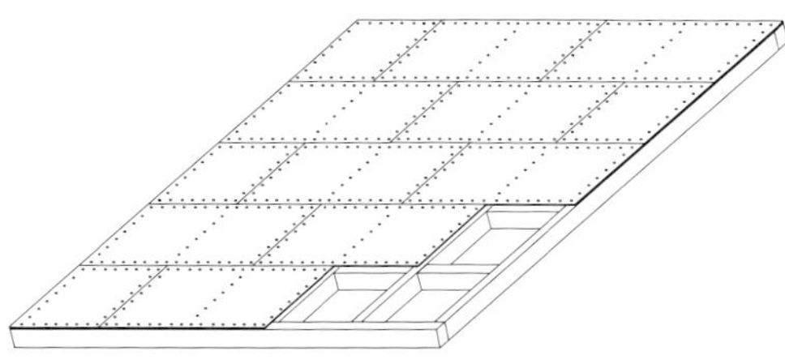

2.1.3.18 Stiffening plate made from timber derivative boards, with shear-resistant connections between boards and framing on all four edges

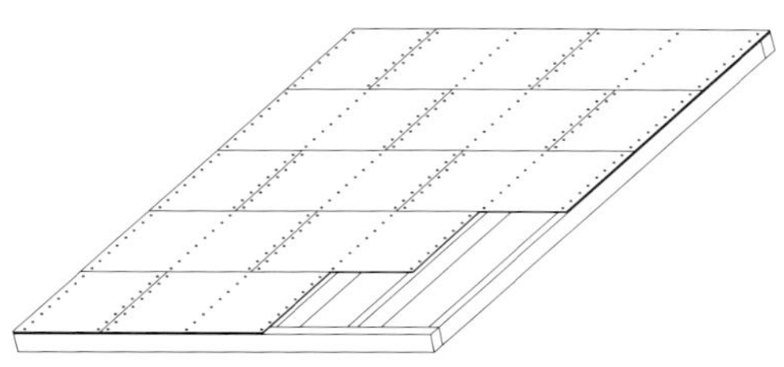

2.1.3.19 Stiffening plate made from timber derivative boards, for small dimensions and small loads, no shear-resistant connections between boards and framing on edges parallel to span

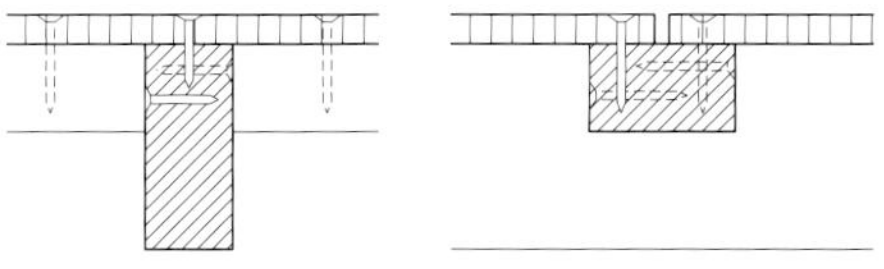

2.1.3.20 Timber splice plate for shear-resistant connection between timber derivative boards: side view, section [9]

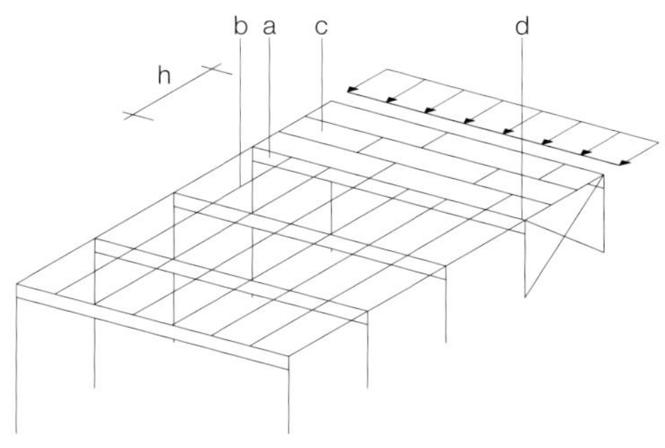


2.1.3.21 Roof plate of timber derivative boards for resisting wind forces: a main beam (chord), b rib (purlin, rafter), c board, d board support, h structural depth of plate

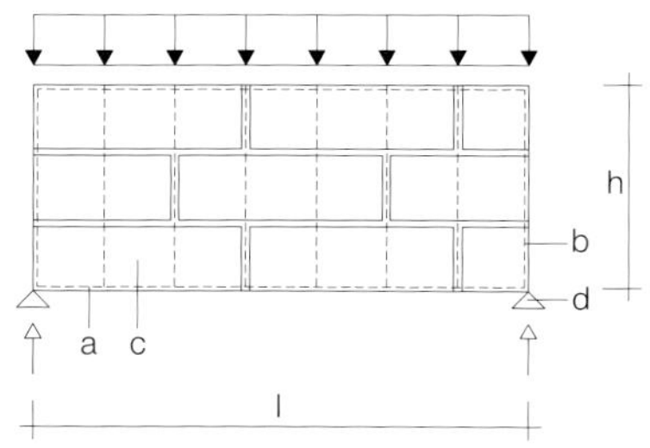


2.1.3.22 Roof plate with supported butt joints between boards in the direction of loading and unsupported butt joints parallel to the span: a main beam (chord), b rib (purlin, rafter), c board, d board support, h structural depth of plate, l span of plate

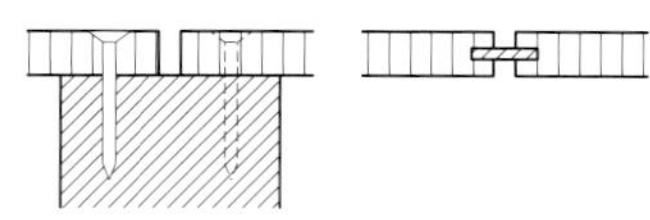

2.1.3.23 Butt joint over rib, unsupported butt joint [3]

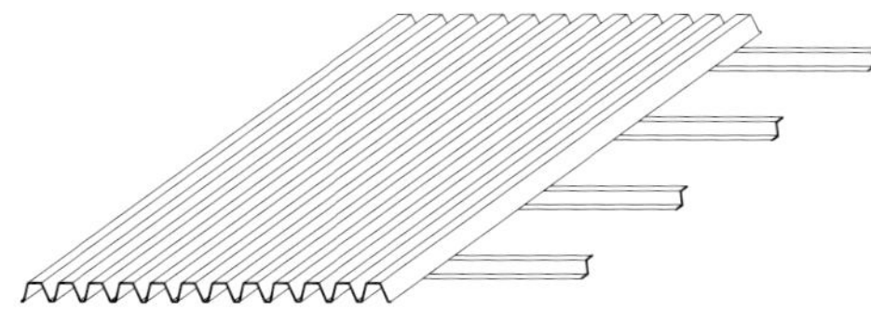

2.1.3.24 Roof covering of steel trapezoidal profile sheeting over short spans

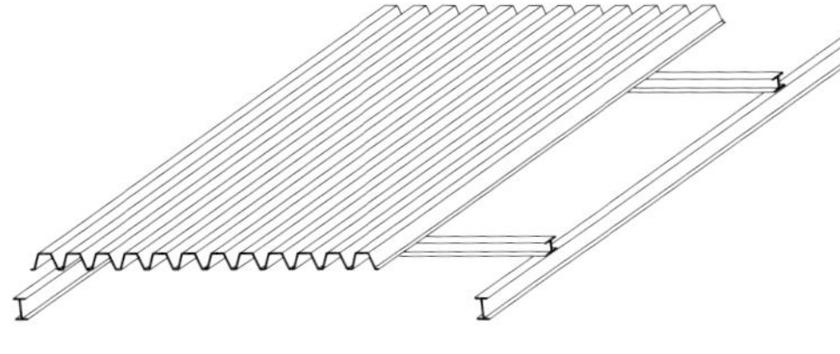

2.1.3.25 Roof covering of steel trapezoidal profile sheeting spanning between purlins

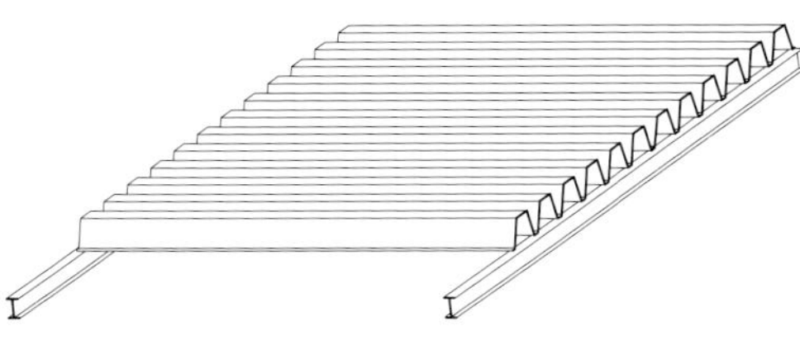

2.1.3.26 Deep steel trapezoidal profile sheeting spanning between main beams

**Trapezoidal profile sheeting**

Trapezoidal profile sheeting is cold-formed from flat metal sheets and exhibits parallel trapezium-shaped ribs. They may be of steel or aluminium; only steel trapezoidal profile sheeting is dealt with here. The specification and detailing of trapezoidal profile sheeting are covered in DIN 18807 part 1 [5] and part 9 [6]. They can only carry loads in the direction of the ribs, acting like beams in bending with top and bottom flanges and intermediate webs. The flanges and webs can be stiffened by further profiling. The bending capacity perpendicular to the ribs is very low.

The load-carrying capacity of steel trapezoidal profile sheeting depends primarily on the depth of the profile and the gauge of the metal. Depths are usually between 10 and 160 mm, but profiles up to 210 mm deep are available. The metal is between 0.75 and 2.00 mm thick. The sheets are available in widths of 600–1000 mm and lengths of up to 25 m; the standard length is 9 m. Load-carrying capacities and maximum spans are generally based on tests and can be found in the approval certificates; table 2.1.3.27 provides an overview. As their use as single-span sheets would be very uneconomic, the continuous effect over at least two bays should be exploited. Spans between 3 and 6 m are common for roofs but there is one profile available for spans of up to 10 m. It is possible to arrange smaller spans on purlins, or larger spans directly on roof trusses. The profiles can be butted together rigidly in the longitudinal direction. For roofs the deflection of steel trapezoidal profile sheeting subjected to a total vertical load is limited to [5]:

- l/150 when used as the waterproof roof covering
- l/150 when used as the lower loadbearing element in double-skin roofs
- l/300 when used as the loadbearing element below the waterproof roof covering (warm deck)

Special care is required with the fixings and the construction details at the supports because the force transfer with thin metal represents a potential source of damage. Minimum widths of supports are given in the approval certificates; min. 60–160 mm for intermediate supports of steel or timber, min. 40 mm for end supports, provided the trapezoidal profile sheeting is fixed directly after being laid. Otherwise, a minimum support width of 80 mm, for masonry at least 100 mm, must be ensured. Unsupported longitudinal edges of trapezoidal profile sheets must be stiffened by specially shaped sheet metal profiles. It is possible to form cantilevers in the direction of the ribs. At the unsupported end it should be ensured that a 1 kN point load is distributed over a width of at least 1 m. This transverse distribution can be achieved by, for example, sheet metal angles or timber planks, where each rib of the sheeting must have a tension-resistant fixing to the transverse spreader. [5]

Special fixings are available to suit the material thickness, e.g. self-tapping and self-drilling screws, machine screws, for fixing the sheeting to the supporting construction. Blind rivets and self-drilling screws are suitable for joining the sheets together and to other sheet metal items. The forces that can be carried and the necessary spacings are given in the corresponding approval certificates [15] (see also p. 186 and [24]).

A plate effect is not possible when the trapezoidal profile sheets are fastened only at the supports. However, longitudinal forces can be transferred in the direction of the ribs. Trapezoidal profile sheeting can therefore provide lateral restraint to beams and girders, provided that the sheeting can in turn transfer the longitudinal forces to a bracing member, e.g. a wind girder.

| Manufacturer's code | Profile designation: depth/rib spacing | Nominal thickness | Self-weight | Structural systems q=1.20 kN/m² | | |
|---|---|---|---|---|---|---|
| | | $t_n$ mm | g kN/m² | 1 span | 2 spans | 3 spans |
| IP | 35/207 | 0.75 | 0.073 | 0.88 | 1.10 | 1.10 |
| PP | | 0.88 | 0.085 | 1.36 | 1.70 | 1.70 |
| PS | | 1.00 | 0.097 | 1.78 | 2.22 | 2.22 |
| TBS | | 1.25 | 0.121 | 2.20 | 2.98 | 2.73 |
| UB | | | | | | |
| WU | | | | | | |
| PS | 48.5/250 | 0.75 | 0.075 | 1.77 | 2.21 | 2.21 |
| HSW | | 0.88 | 0.088 | 2.50 | 3.13 | 3.13 |
| WU | | 1.00 | 0.100 | 2.77 | 3.58 | 3.42 |
| TBS | | 1.25 | 0.125 | 2.99 | 4.01 | 3.69 |
| WU | 80/307 | 0.75 | 0.081 | 1.70 | 2.12 | 2.12 |
| | | 0.88 | 0.095 | 3.31 | 4.14 | 4.14 |
| | | 1.00 | 0.108 | 3.56 | 4.77 | 4.40 |
| | | 1.25 | 0.136 | 3.85 | 5.17 | 4.76 |
| HSW | 101/275 | 0.75 | 0.091 | 4.14 | 5.55 | 5.12 |
| | | 0.88 | 0.107 | 4.30 | 5.76 | 5.31 |
| | | 1.00 | 0.121 | 4.43 | 5.94 | 5.48 |
| | | 1.25 | 0.152 | 4.81 | 6.45 | 5.94 |
| FI | 106/250 | 0.75 | 0.100 | 4.35 | 5.84 | 5.38 |
| HSW | | 0.88 | 0.117 | 4.60 | 6.17 | 5.69 |
| | | 1.00 | 0.133 | 4.82 | 6.46 | 5.95 |
| | | 1.25 | 0.167 | 5.20 | 6.97 | 6.43 |
| UB | 111/275 | 0.75 | 0.090 | 4.23 | 5.67 | 5.25 |
| | | 0.88 | 0.106 | 4.39 | 5.89 | 5.46 |
| | | 1.00 | 0.121 | 4.54 | 6.08 | 5.63 |
| | | 1.25 | 0.151 | 4.87 | 6.53 | 6.05 |
| TBS | 126/326 | 0.75 | 0.092 | 4.66 | 5.31 | 5.79 |
| | | 0.88 | 0.108 | 4.93 | 6.70 | 6.14 |
| | | 1.00 | 0.123 | 5.16 | 7.00 | 6.41 |
| | | 1.25 | 0.153 | 5.57 | 7.56 | 6.93 |
| FI | 135/310 | 0.75 | 0.097 | 4.96 | 6.10 | 6.16 |
| HD | | 0.88 | 0.114 | 5.25 | 6.97 | 6.51 |
| WU | | 1.00 | 0.129 | 5.48 | 7.35 | 6.81 |
| UB | | 1.25 | 0.161 | 5.93 | 7.95 | 7.36 |
| HSW | 158/250 | 0.75 | 0.121 | 5.89 | 7.63 | 7.28 |
| PS | | 0.88 | 0.142 | 6.23 | 8.36 | 7.71 |
| UB | | 1.00 | 0.161 | 5.48 | 7.35 | 6.81 |
| | | 1.25 | 0.201 | 7.04 | 9.44 | 8.70 |
| UB | 165/250 | 0.75 | 0.120 | 6.00 | 7.60 | 7.45 |
| | | 0.88 | 0.141 | 6.33 | 8.40 | 7.86 |
| | | 1.00 | 0.160 | 6.61 | 9.00 | 8.21 |
| | | 1.25 | 0.200 | 7.20 | 9.75 | 8.90 |

2.1.3.27 Maximum spans for different types of steel trapezoidal profile sheeting for roofs [m] [27]

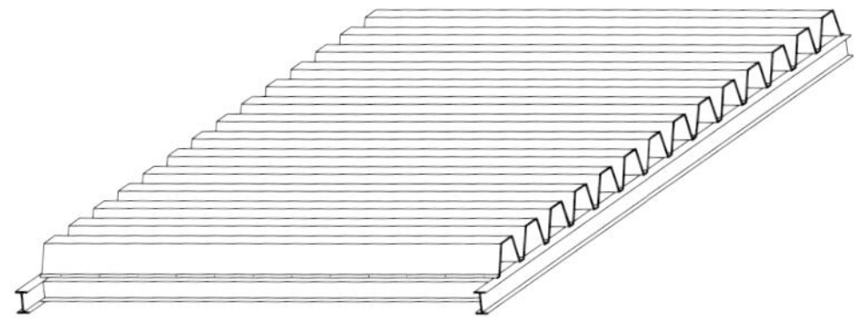

2.1.3.28 Roof plate made from steel trapezoidal profile sheeting fixed to longitudinal and transverse members

**Steel trapezoidal profile sheeting as roof plate**
Trapezoidal profile sheeting can act as a plate, e.g. as a substitute for wind girders. External loads, e.g. wind, and bracing loads can be carried over certain spans in addition to the vertical loads. However, shear diaphragms must be formed in order to do this. Shear diaphragms consist of trapezoidal profile sheets and peripheral edge supports. In this situation continuous shear-resistant connections are required between the trapezoidal profile sheets, and between the sheets and the four edge supports. The trapezoidal profile sheets prevent racking, i.e. distortion of the rectangular sheet into a parallelogram, where the edge supports are subjected to tension and compression.

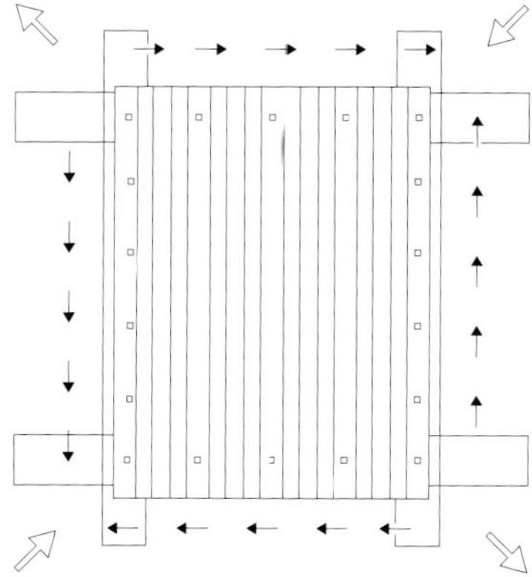

2.1.3.29 The shear diaphragm effect

Longitudinal edge supports that simultaneously act as, for example, purlins, may not have any pinned joints in the region of the shear diaphragms because that would be a discontinuity for the deformation of the trapezoidal profile sheeting.

The details regarding type and number of fixings as given in the individual approval certificates must be strictly adhered to. Temporary wind girders may be necessary during construction. Larger shear diaphragms can be subdivided into smaller rectangular bays by including secondary beams. These beams can either serve to transfer loads or assist the trapezoidal profile sheeting in carrying vertical loads.

The loads to be carried by the shear diaphragms are generally point loads, e.g. loads from cladding posts due to wind pressure or suction. A distinction should be made between forces to be transferred in the direction of the profiling or perpendicular to it. In the latter case, additional beams are necessary to transfer the forces evenly into the shear diaphragms. If the forces are to be transferred in the direction of the profiling, such beams are only required when the forces exceed a certain value dependent on the respective profile.

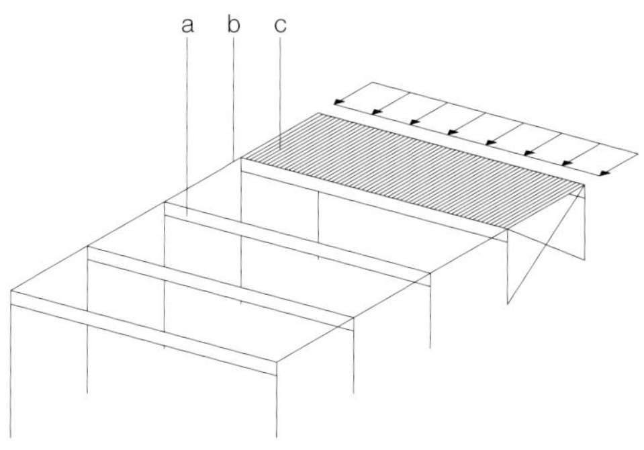


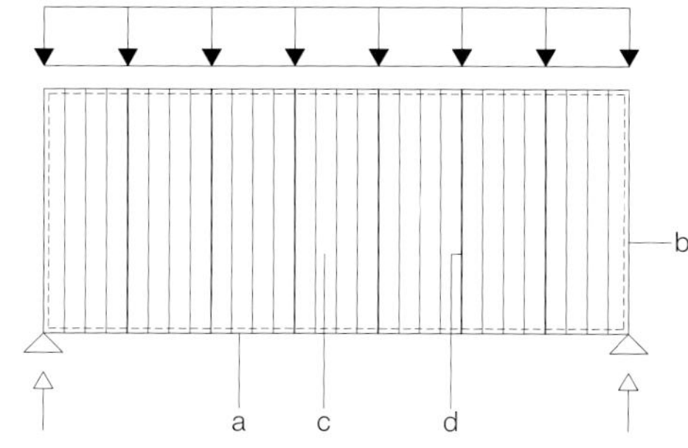


2.1.3.30 Roof plate made from steel trapezoidal profile sheeting, loaded in the direction of the ribs: a main beam, b edge beam, c trapezoidal profile sheeting, d longitudinal butt joints between sheets (unsupported)

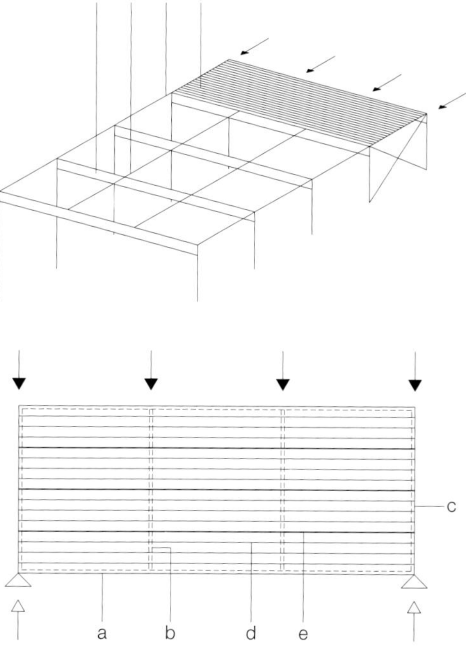


2.1.3.31 Shear diaphragm made from steel trapezoidal profile sheeting, loaded perpendicular to the ribs: a main beam, b secondary beam, c edge beam, d trapezoidal profile sheeting, e longitudinal butt joints between sheets

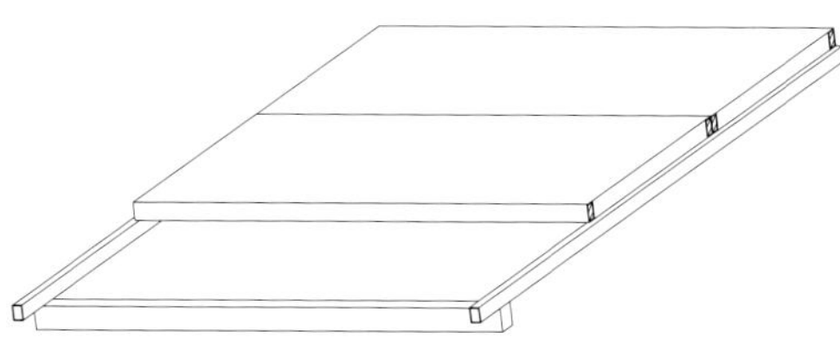
2.1.3.32 Timber panels

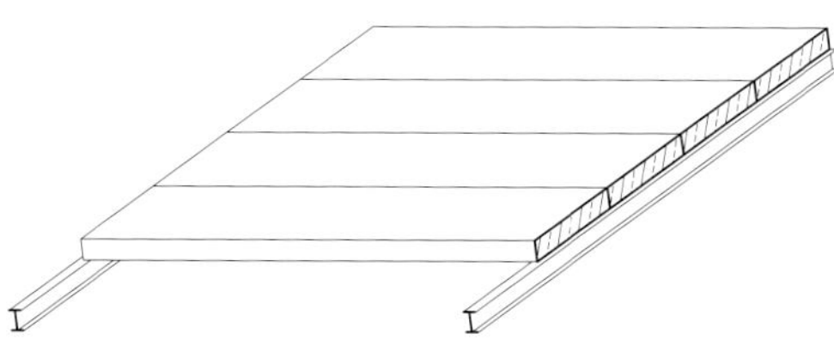
2.1.3.33 Reinforced aerated concrete planks

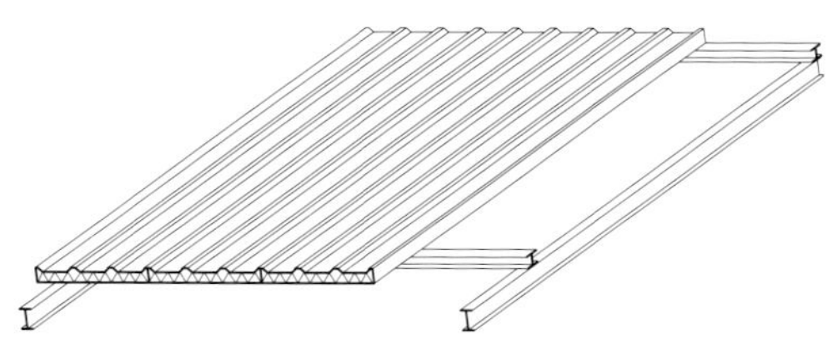
2.1.3.34 Sandwich panels

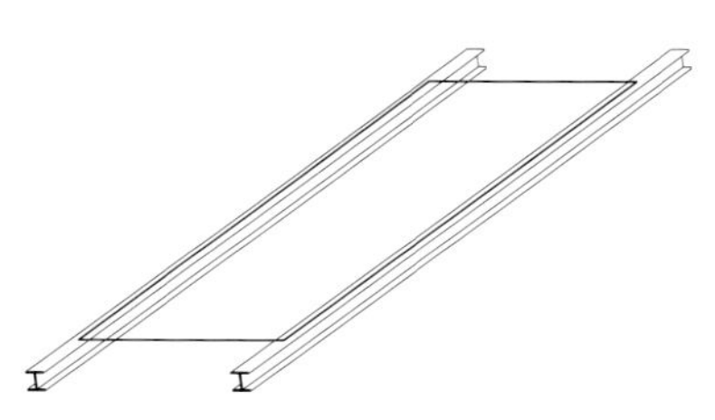
2.1.3.35 Glass supported along two edges

**Solid timber panels**
Panels of solid timber can consist of strips or planks placed on edge and glued or nailed together. They may also be made from plywood with three or five plies glued together. These panels can be laid parallel with or perpendicular to the eaves. Solid timber panels up to 200 mm thick can span distances of up to about 7 m. The customary spans of 3.5–4.5 m between purlins result in thicknesses of about 100–140 mm.

When glued, this type of roof can provide a plate effect. However, nailing does not generally provide the required stiffness.

Solid timber panels can be joined together at the ridge without the need for purlins so the loadbearing effect is comparable with that of a couple roof.

**Timber panels**
Timber panels consist of vertical ribs faced with planks on one or both sides. The ribs may be of sawn timber, laminated timber or timber derivatives. The facing can consist of diagonal planking or boards of timber derivatives. The ribs and facing are nailed or glued together continuously to produce a composite effect. These panels have ribs on all edges and may have intermediate ribs.
Timber panels usually span between 5 and 6 m, but with a suitable depth can span 10 m or more. Such panels can be combined to form roof plates (figure 2.1.3.32).

**Aerated concrete planks**
Roofing panels of reinforced aerated concrete are available in lengths up to 8 m and widths between 0.50 and 2.50 m. They are normally 200–240 mm thick. The customary spans are approx. 5.0 to 6.5 m. They can be laid parallel or perpendicular to the eaves (figure 2.1.3.33).

The individual planks should be joined together with mortar in both the transverse and longitudinal directions, and provided with reinforcement in the joints and concrete anchors. They are fixed to the supporting structure by metal retaining straps.

A plate effect can be achieved with suitable reinforcement to the planks and detailing of the joints. The span of the roof plate can be parallel or perpendicular to the planks. A reinforced concrete ring beam may be required.

**Sandwich panels**
Sandwich panels consist of an upper and lower facing of profiled steel or aluminium sheet and a core of rigid foam or mineral wool. The core is bonded to the facing to produce a loadbearing composite cross-section. A large number of different panels is available. Some are up to 24 m long, but the panel width is frequently 1 m; thicknesses lie between 40 and 140 mm. They can be used for short spans of, for example, 1.20 m, or as three-span panels with spans of up to approx. 6.00 m.

According to the profiling, the panels are laid in the direction of the roof pitch and span from purlin to purlin. They are fixed to the supporting construction by screw fasteners with appropriate sealing washers (figure 2.1.3.34).

**Glass**
Compared to other materials in the building industry, glass has a special significance. Although glass does possess elastic properties and is relatively strong, particularly in compression, it can fail without any apparent warning. Glass is brittle and lacks the ductility that characterises steel, for example. Local stress peaks that occur at scratches on the surface or at the supports cannot be eliminated through plastic behaviour of the material. If the strength is exceeded locally, the complete component fails. It must therefore always be assumed that a pane of glass could fail, and overhead glazing is required to exhibit a residual load-carrying capacity after it has failed.

Laminated safety glass is employed for overhead glazing. It consists of toughened or heat-treated glass and an intervening layer of plastic. This plastic film guarantees the residual load-carrying capacity after failure of the glass itself. Compared to toughened glass, heat-treated glass has the advantage that larger pieces are formed upon breakage, and so in conjunction with the film, heat-treated glass exhibits a higher residual load-carrying capacity and presents less danger from falling fragments of glass. Generally, therefore, laminated safety glass made from heat-treated glass is specified for overhead glazing. Safety rules for the use of panes of glass supported on linear, continuous supports (figure 2.1.3.35) can be found in [32]. Although they exhibit very good residual strength, panes of laminated safety and heat-treated glass supported on individual, discrete fixings are not yet covered by any standard. For an overview of forms of construction and the state of the art, the reader is referred to [28] and [2].

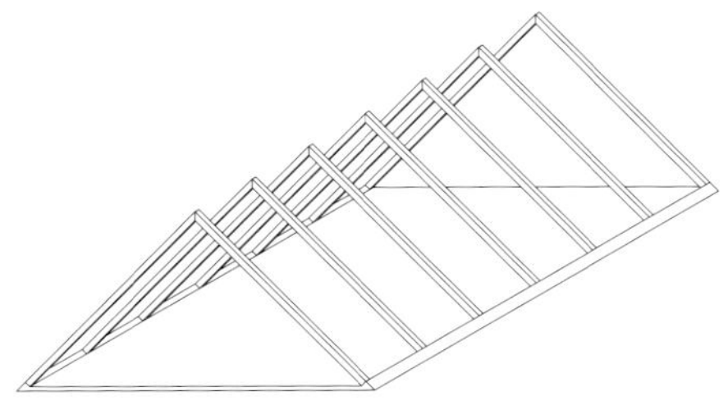

2.1.4.1 Close couple roof

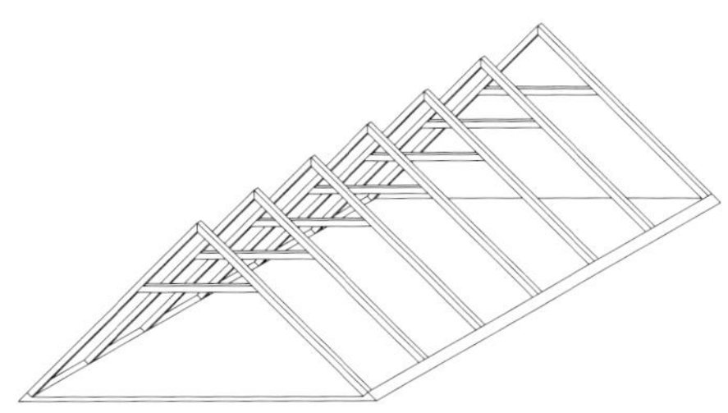

2.1.4.2 Collar roof

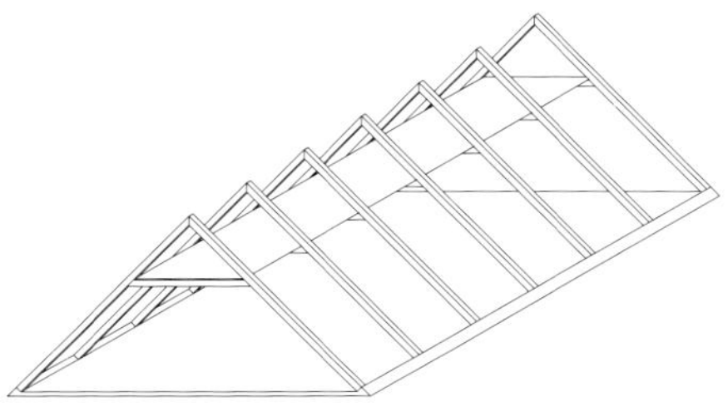

2.1.4.3 Stable collar roof with plate at collar level

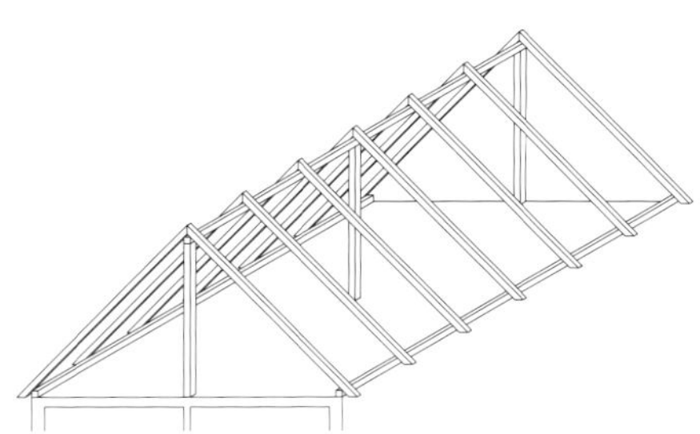

2.1.4.4 Purlin roof with ridge and eaves purlins

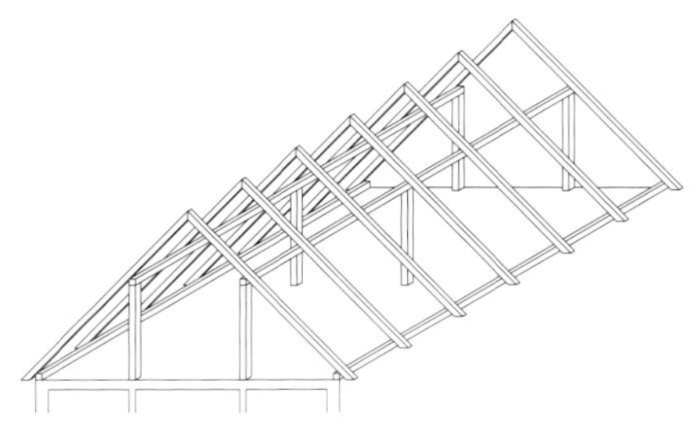

2.1.4.5 Purlin roof with intermediate purlin

## Timber pitched roofs

### Close couple and collar roofs

Close couple and collar roofs are common for pitched roofs with pitches of about 30–60°. The span of a traditionally built close couple roof is around 8 m, with a maximum of 10 m; the spacing of the rafters lies between 750 and 1000 mm.

Compared to the purlin roof, the advantage of the close couple or collar roof is the absence of posts in the roof space and the smaller quantity of timber required. The disadvantages are the work required at the rafter supports and restrictions on the position and size of openings and dormer windows. Intersections at roof level over L-shaped or non-rectangular plans are also problematic.

The close couple roof employs a pair of rafters, which give each other mutual support at the ridge, and a tie at the base to resist horizontal thrust. The rafters are subjected to tension and compression. The tie can be formed by a reinforced concrete slab or by ceiling joists. A minimum roof pitch is necessary because otherwise the compressive forces in the rafters would be too large (figure 2.1.4.1).

A collar roof is a close couple roof with an additional horizontal tie linking each pair of rafters. With a symmetrical loading, the collar tie acts as an additional horizontal intermediate support for the rafters. With an asymmetric load, e.g. wind, the collar tie can be displaced together with the rafters. This is an imperfect system. As the collar ties are in compression, lateral support in the horizontal direction, provided by longitudinal timbers (top beams), may be advisable. The collar ties can simultaneously act as ceiling joists in fully fitted out roof spaces (figure 2.1 4.2).

In the stable version of the collar roof, the plane of the collar tie is fixed horizontally by providing a horizontal wind girder or a horizontal plate connected to the gable walls or other bracing components. The rafters therefore have a horizontal support at the level of the collar tie even with asymmetric loads (figure 2.1.4.3).

The hinge forces at the ridge can be transferred via contact and splice plates or halving joints (figure 2.1.4.6).
The connection of the collar tie to the rafter should not weaken the rafter cross-section, because at this point the rafter is subjected to a support moment. Using a pair of members to form the collar tie is therefore a neat solution (figure 2.1.4.7).

The vertical and horizontal components must be resisted at the base of the rafter. This can be achieved by using a specially shaped reinforced concrete abutment (figure 2.1.4.8) or via a suitable connection with the ceiling joist suitable for transferring the forces.

The design of a roof overhang requires special detailing (figure 2.1.4.9). A dwarf wall of masonry is not possible because of the horizontal thrust it has to resist. A dwarf wall of limited height made from reinforced concrete is possible when the reinforcement is suitably designed and connected with the floor slab via a rigid corner detail.

### Purlin roof

In the purlin roof the rafters are supported on longitudinal members – the purlins. The rafters are considered to be single-span beams spanning between the ridge purlin or intermediate purlin and eaves purlin, or continuous beams spanning between ridge purlin, intermediate purlin and eaves purlin. The purlins are supported on walls or posts in the roof space. The rafters do not exert a horizontal thrust at the base as in a close couple roof, but are essentially subjected to bending. Vertical loads cause exclusively vertical support reactions.
A tie at the base is therefore unnecessary (figure 2.1.4.4).
Both monopitch and duopitch roofs can be built as purlin roofs. The purlin roof can also be built over more complicated plan layouts. The provision of several purlins makes large roof structures possible (figure 2.1.4.5).

Compared to the close couple roof, shallower roof pitches are possible, right down to the flat roof. The purlin roof can be regarded as a raised timber joist floor. But there is a limit to the steepness of such a roof: pitches exceeding 35° are complicated. As with the close couple roof, the rafter spacing is 750–1000 mm.

The rafters should be supported on the purlins in such a way that the loads can be transferred vertically into the purlin. This is achieved by cutting a notch (birdsmouth) in the rafter to produce a horizontal support face. This birdsmouth should be as small as possible to prevent the rafter cross-section from being excessively weakened. This is particularly important with continuous rafters, which are particularly highly stressed by the support moment at the intermediate purlin (figure 2.1.4.11). This usually results in an eccentric loading being placed on the purlin, which therefore must be prevented from twisting.

The rafter support at the base is best suited to transferring transverse horizontal forces from wind because it is closest to the floor or ceiling plate at this level. Every rafter should therefore be fixed in position horizontally and transverse to the roof. The eaves purlin must be anchored accordingly. The upper purlins can therefore

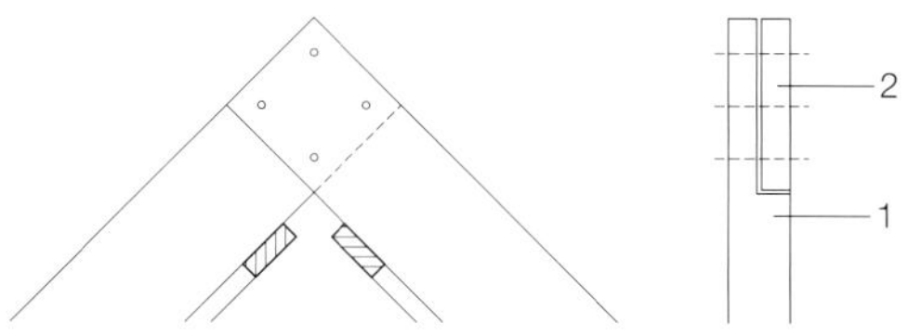


2.1.4.6 Ridge detail of close couple roof: 1 rafter, 2 halving joint

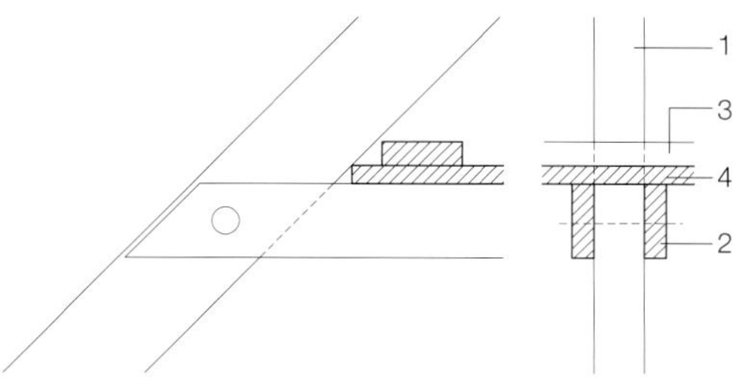


2.1.4.7 Rafter-collar connection, collar roof: 1 rafter, 2 collar (two pieces), 3 longitudinal member, 4 plate (stable collar roof)

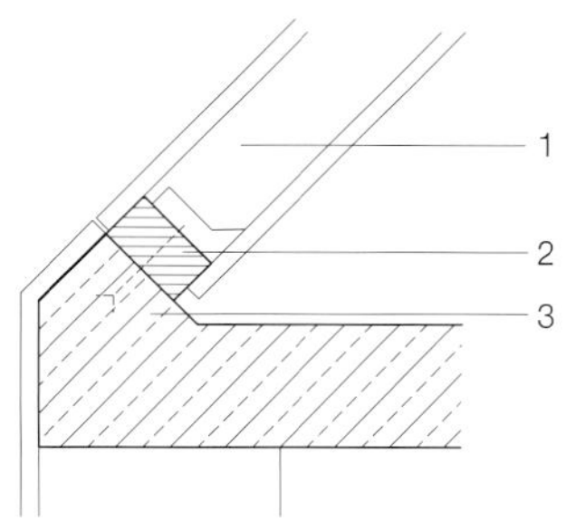


2.1.4.8 Detail at base of rafter, close couple roof: 1 rafter, 2 wall plate, 3 abutment

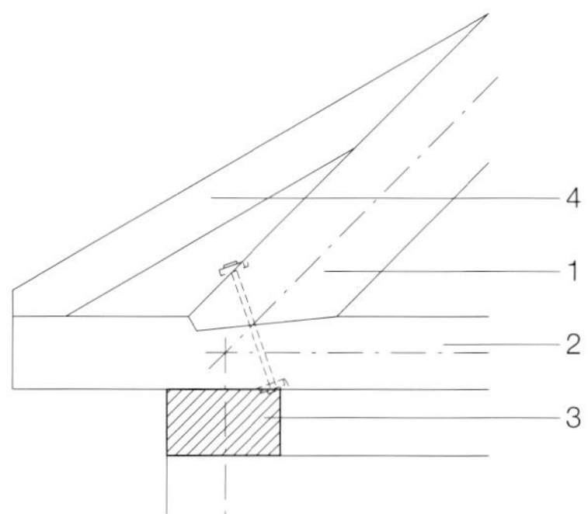


2.1.4.9 Detail at base of rafter, close couple roof: 1 rafter, 2 tie beam, 3 wall plate, 4 sprocket

be supported on pin-jointed posts as they are fixed in position horizontally by the rafters. Owing to the generally shallow roof pitch, the horizontal forces are considerably lower than those acting on close couple or collar roofs.

The rafters meeting at the ridge should be connected together even though the structural system of the purlin roof does not provide for any transfer of forces at the ridge. However, a connection is shown in order to secure the rafters against uplift forces due to wind suction at the ridge. Direct contact between the rafters should be avoided, for example, by means of splice plates and a few retaining nails, so that large compression forces cannot build up between the rafters (figure 2.1.4.10). Otherwise, our purlin roof could turn into a couple roof, which could lead to displacement and damage at the base of the rafter.

As with ceiling joists, openings can be created between the rafters of a purlin roof by using trimmers. Any rafters interrupted by the opening are replaced by trimming members. Roof overhangs are simply arranged by allowing the rafters or purlins to cantilever. Long overhangs require suitable details to prevent uplift (figure 2.1.4.12).

A propped purlin roof is characterised by the intermediate purlin acting as the immovable horizontal support for the rafters and thus resisting wind forces. This is achieved by providing suitable propping to the posts. The base of the rafter is only secured against wind suction and considered as not held in the horizontal direction in the structural analysis. This is advantageous for dwarf walls of timber or masonry, which cannot resist horizontal forces. However, the propped purlin roof is no longer very popular because it restricts the useful area within the roof space (figure 2.1.4.13).

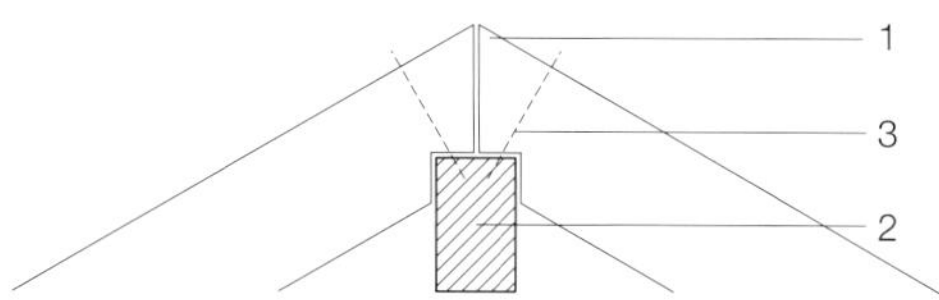


2.1.4.10 Ridge detail of purlin roof: 1 rafter, 2 ridge purlin, 3 nails

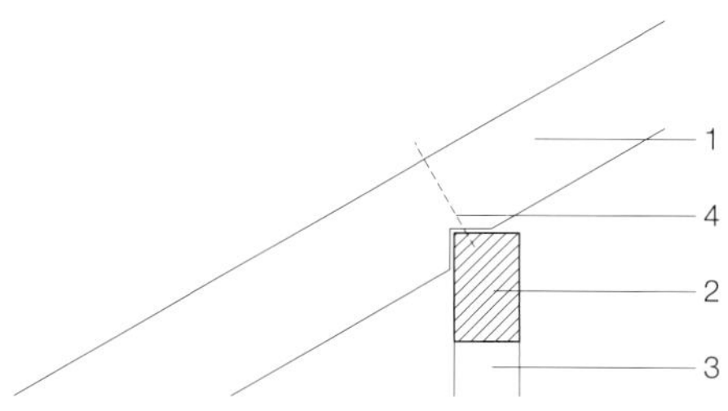


2.1.4.11 Detail at intermediate purlin, purlin roof: 1 rafter, 2 intermediate purlin, 3 post, 4 nail

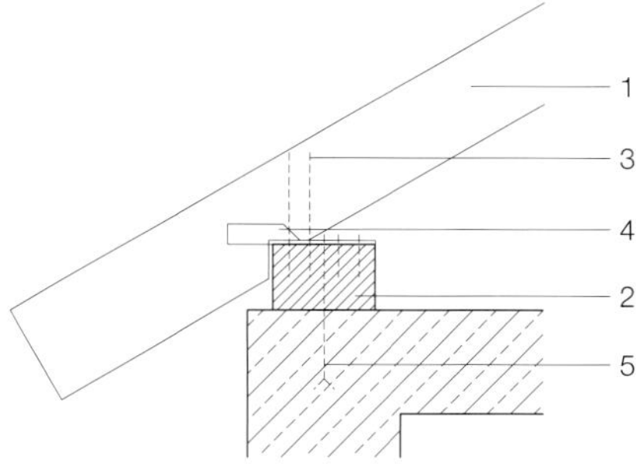


2.1.4.12 Detail at eaves purlin, purlin roof: 1 rafter, 2 eaves purlin, 3 nails, 4 rafter retaining strap, 5 anchor bolt

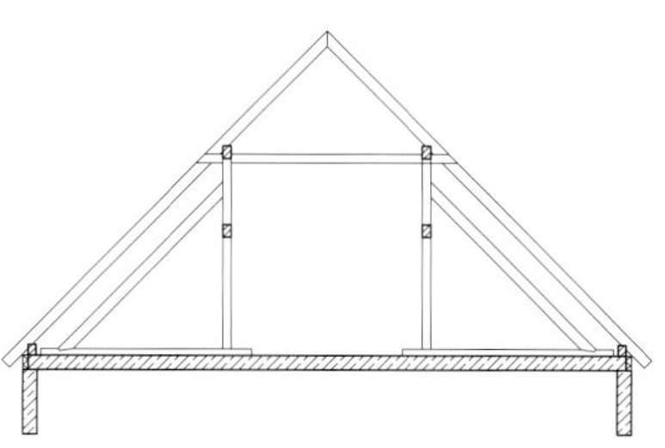

2.1.4.13 Propped purlin roof

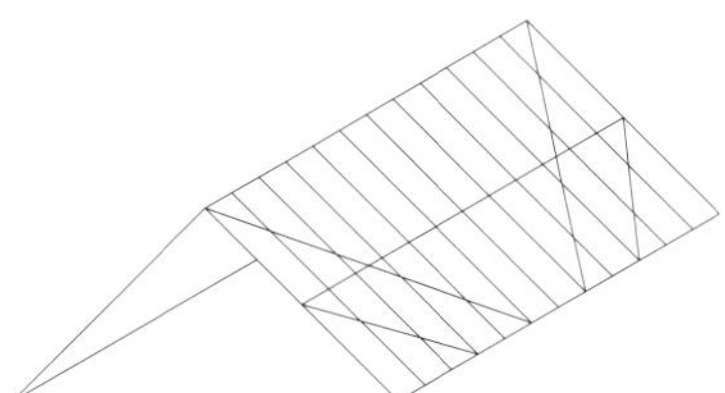

2.1.4.14 Timber diagonal braces beneath the rafters

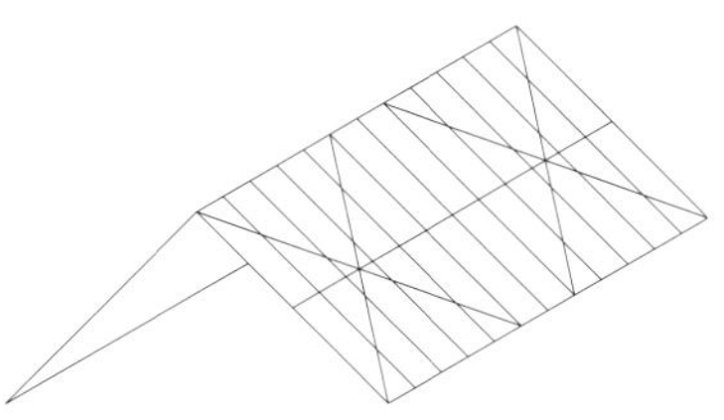

2.1.4.15 Steel diagonal braces over the rafters

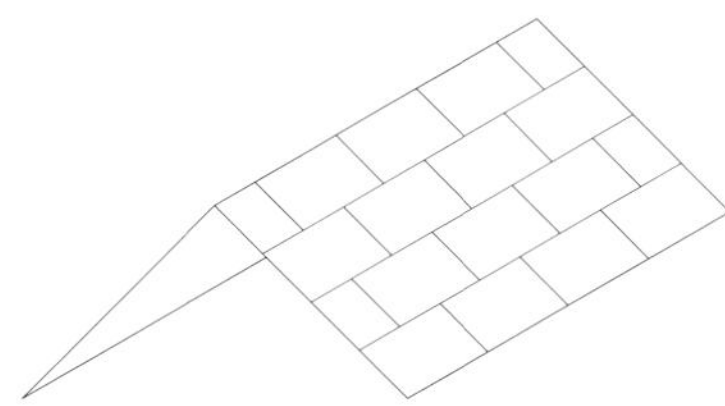

2.1.4.16 Roof plate made from timber derivative boards

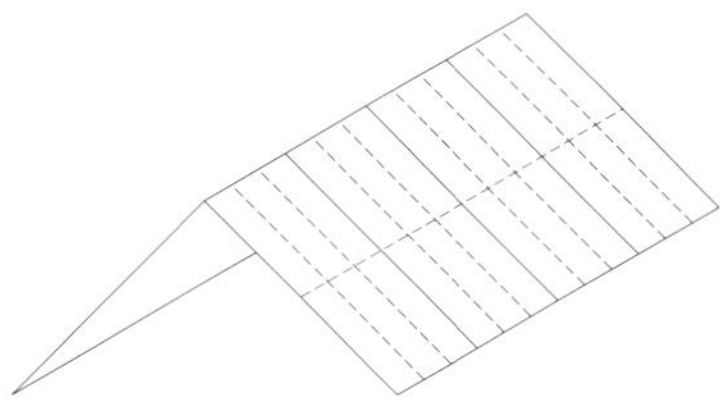

2.1.4.17 Roof plate made from timber panels

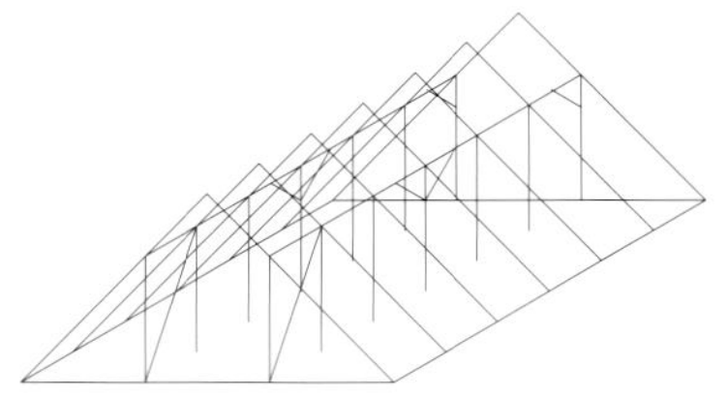

2.1.4.18 Purlin roof with kneebraces

**Bracing the timber pitched roof**

In the transverse direction the bracing to the close couple, collar and purlin roof is provided by the pairs of rafters themselves and the rafter fixings, and in the propped purlin roof by the propping arrangement. A plate at the level of the collar tie can provide additional stiffening for the collar roof.

In the longitudinal direction the roof structure must resist horizontal forces from wind acting on the gable walls. It must also resist forces to support the rafters against overturning and buckling, eccentricity and imperfections in the construction. Special bracing arrangements are necessary for this

Timber gable walls can be supported horizontally by tiling battens or roof decking when the force transfer is guaranteed by appropriate nailing. Masonry gable walls, too, must generally be supported horizontally by a suitably braced roof structure. In a purlin roof the horizontal forces from the gable wall can be resisted by the purlins. The connection between gable wall and purlin may, for example, be anchors fixed to a concrete capping beam along the top edge of the gable wall. Close couple and collar roofs require additional horizontal timbers along the ridge or edge members at the level of the collar tie connected to the gable wall.

The horizontal loads must be transferred by the tiling battens, roof decking or purlins into bracing constructions. These may be diagonal braces or roof plates.

Diagonal timber bracing can be designed to resist tension and compression. The disadvantage is that they usually have to be fixed beneath the rafters and are a nuisance when fitting out the roof space. They must be fixed to every rafter. At the bottom end the connection must ensure that the entire force is transferred to the loadbearing construction, which can be complicated (figure 2.1.4.14).

Diagonal steel bracing can only accommodate tension and must therefore always be provided in the form of X-bracing (figure 2.1.4.15). This, too, should be fixed to every rafter. The detail at the bottom end requires special attention. An uplift force, one force acting inwards and one parallel to the eaves must be transferred into the supporting construction. This task can be solved in a variety of ways. Figure 2.1.4.19 shows an anchorage that is usually adequate for the roof of a detached house. The diagonal brace is turned around the rafter to provide adequate length for a nailed fixing. The extra block on the eaves purlin prevents the rafter from overturning and resists the horizontal force in the direction of the eaves. The rafter-purlin anchor transfers the uplift force into the eaves purlin, which in turn is attached to the supporting construction anchor bolts.

Roof plates made from timber derivative boards or timber panels can accommodate and transfer horizontal forces in the longitudinal direction of the roof through the plate effect (figures 2.1.4.16 and 2.1.4.17). As the plate effect cannot be carried over the ridge, these act as cantilever plates. They cantilever from the bottom edge, which forms the support, in the direction of the ridge. Furthermore, it should be noted that timber derivative boards laid on the rafters in the longitudinal direction of the roof form butt joints parallel to the direction of the force. They should normally be supported to create a shear-resistant connection. To avoid this extra work, special measures must be taken and an appropriate analysis provided.

For purlin roofs there is a traditional way of transferring the horizontal forces in the longitudinal direction of the roof: by providing kneebraces between the purlins and their posts (figure 2.1.4.18).

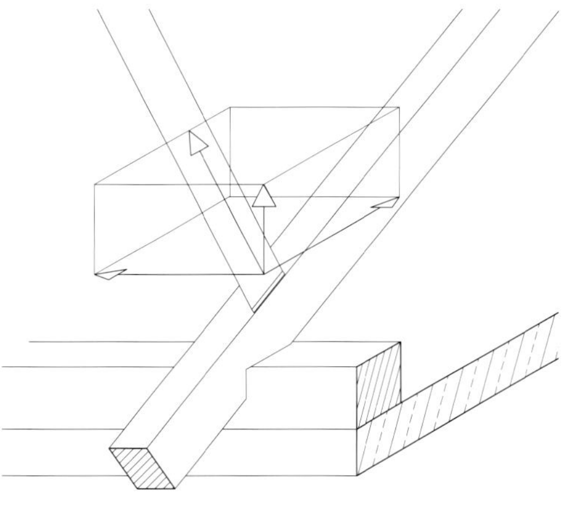

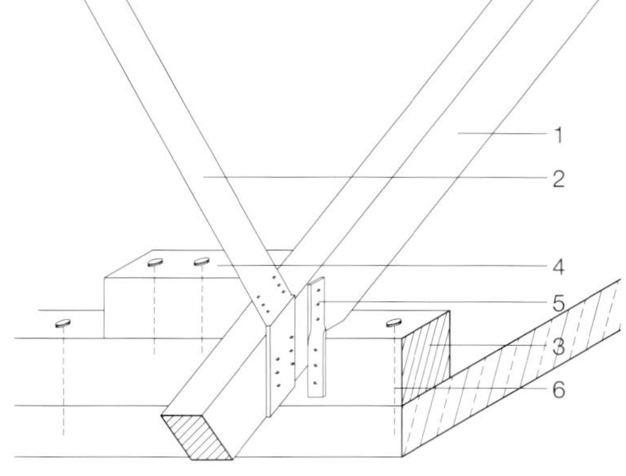


2.1.4.19 Diagonal brace connection: 1 rafter, 2 diagonal brace, 3 eaves purlin, 4 timber block, 5 rafter-purlin retaining strap, 6 anchor bolts

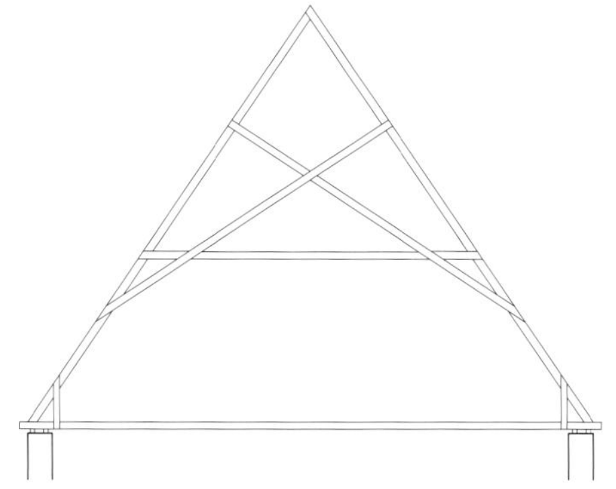

2.1.4.20 Collar roof with St Andrew's cross bracing plus struts (ashlars) at base

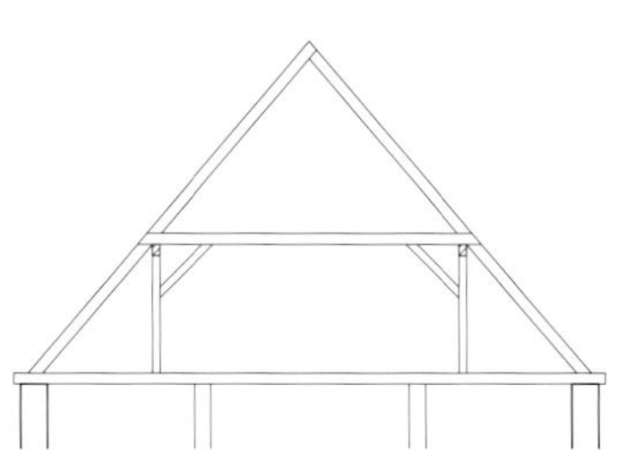

2.1.4.21 Collar roof with queen posts and kneebraces

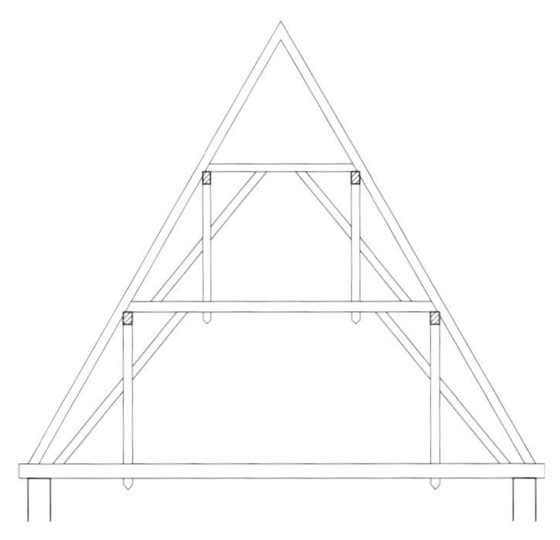

2.1.4.22 Collar roof with queen posts and vertical framing at two levels plus passing braces

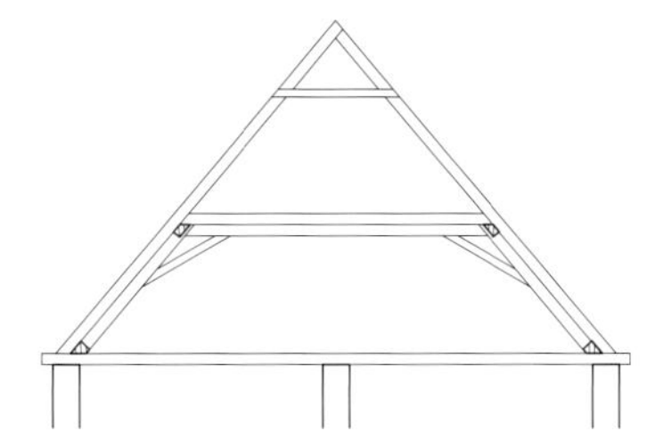

2.1.4.23 Collar roof with framing in plane of roof plus kneebraces

**Historical roof structures**

Historical roof structures are seldom pure purlin or couple roofs. Large roof structures are usually collar roofs supported and braced by various constructional measures.

Two rafters connected at the ridge with a halving joint and a tie beam to resist the horizontal forces is generally the basic form. Collars divide the roof space into storeys. Not every pair of rafters includes a collar. If vaulting extends into the roof space, collars are only possible on certain axes. The collars for the pairs of rafters in between then become short hammer beams, which are joined to the rafters via vertical posts or via trimmers to the continuous collars.

St Andrew's cross bracing was a popular way of stiffening large roof structures; these are joined to the rafters and one or more collars by way of halving joints (figure 2.1.4.20). Wide-span collars can be supported by posts and horizontal members (collar purlins) running the length of the roof. A single king post supports a collar in the middle, two queen posts support a collar near its connection with the rafters. This arrangement can be further braced by means of kneebraces or passing braces in both the transverse and longitudinal direction and arranged in several storeys (figures 2.1.4.21 and 2.1.4.22).

The framing in the plane of the roof transfers the loads via suitable struts directly into the external walls. This relieves the collars. Twin framing in the plane of the roof includes a straining beam directly beneath the collar that resists the horizontal compression (figures 2.1.4.23 to 2.1.4.26).

Vertical and inclined framing is usually positioned at every fourth or fifth pair of rafters. The collar purlin running the length of the roof supports the collars at the intermediate pairs of the rafters without framing. St Andrew's cross bracing between neighbouring frames brace the roof structure in the longitudinal direction. Hangers provide intermediate support for collars and ties with long spans. The tensile forces in the hangers are transferred into struts, which in turn are supported on an inclined or vertical frame (figures 2.1.4.24 to 2.1.4.27). It is possible to use several hangers in conjunction with trussed frames. The roof structure can be important for the stability of the entire building as the extra load of the roof structure contributes to the stability of the masonry. The trusses can help to resist horizontal forces from vaulting, provided friction between the timber and the apex of the masonry vaulting is permissible.

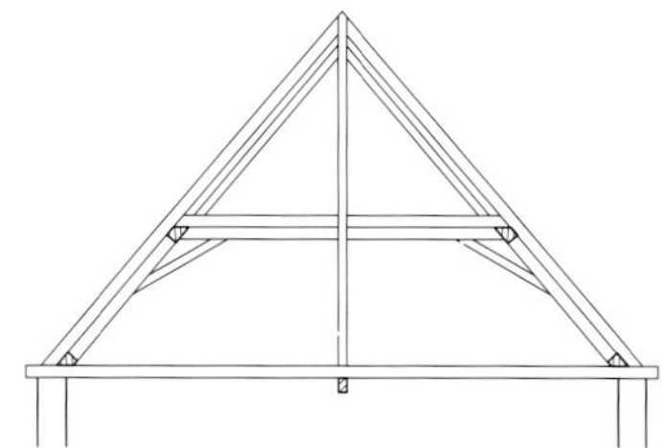

2.1.4.24 Collar roof with framing in plane of roof plus king post

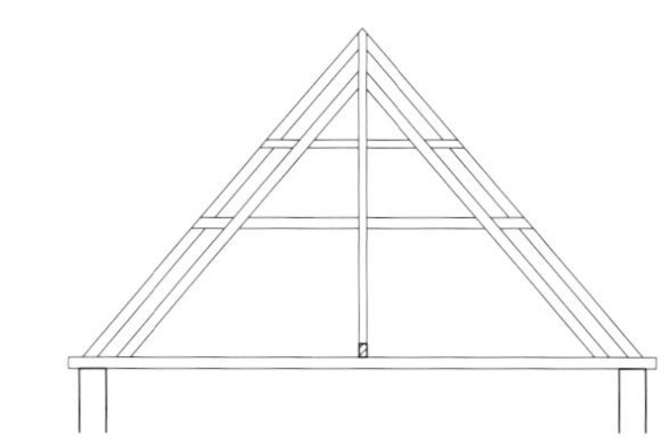

2.1.4.25 Collar roof with secondary spars parallel to rafters plus king post

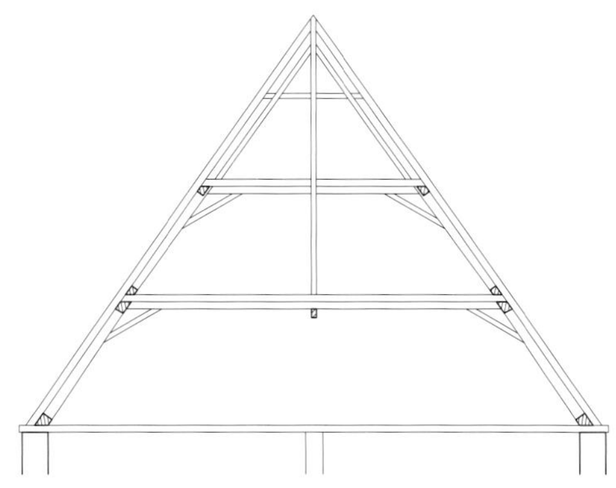

2.1.4.26 Three-storey collar roof with framing in plane of roof plus king post

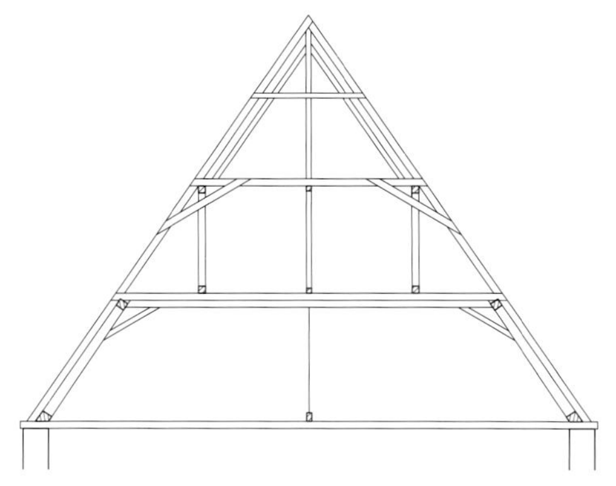

2.1.4.27 Three-storey collar roof with framing in plane of roof, queen posts and vertical framing plus king post

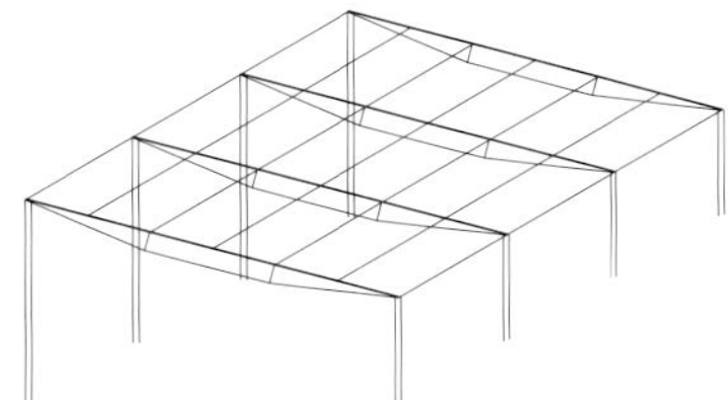

2.1.5.1 Addition of plane frames

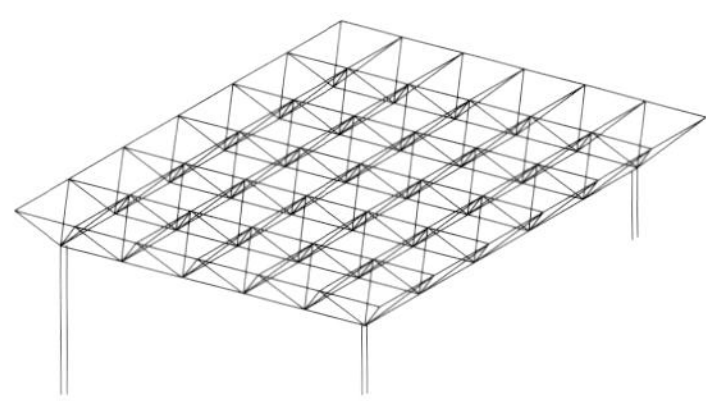

2.1.5.2 Space frame

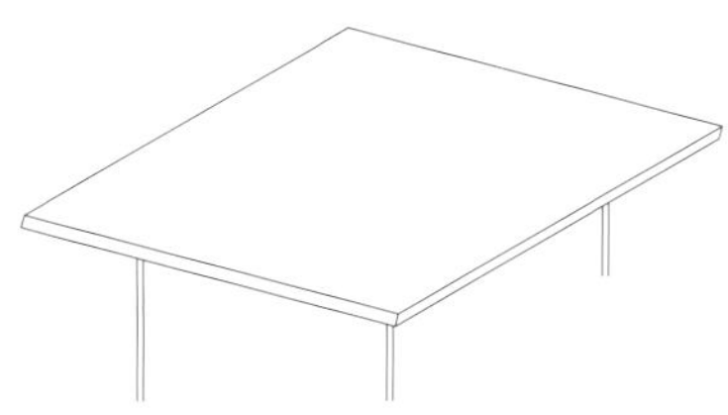

2.1.5.3 Flat stressed-skin structure

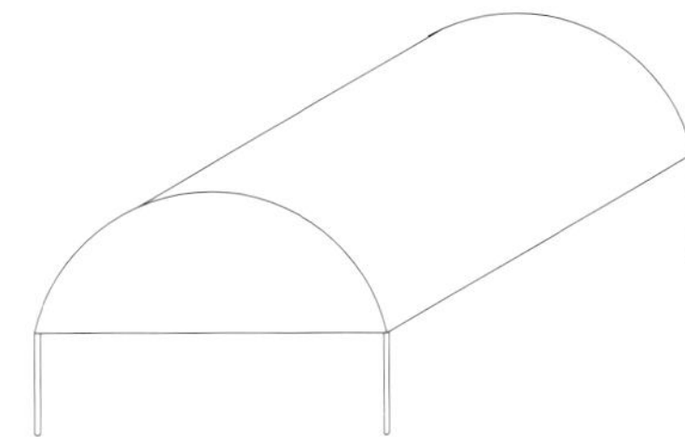

2.1.5.4 Stressed-skin structure in single curvature

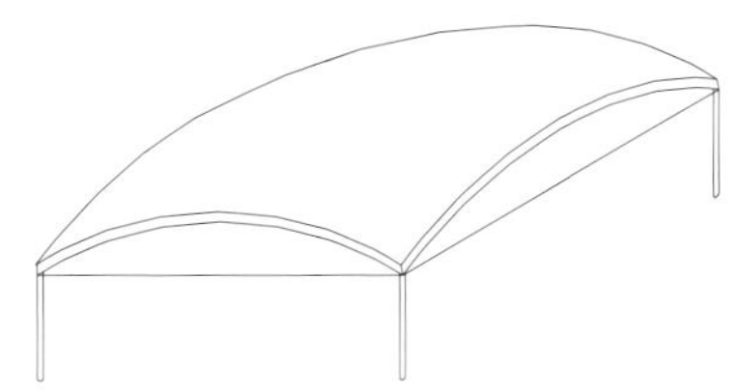

2.1.5.5 Stressed-skin structure in double curvature

## Loadbearing structures for pitched roofs

### Structural systems for pitched roofs

There is an infinite variety of loadbearing structures for pitched roofs. All structural systems that are suitable for flat roofs can, in principle, also be employed for pitched roofs. Added to this are all the loadbearing systems in which extra height over the span is either advantageous for the structural action or indeed characteristic of that system, e.g. a couple roof, or an arch or cable structure.

Uniformly distributed roof loads can be transferred to individual columns or walls over a certain span. This can be done in different ways. The principal systems can be divided into two- and three-dimensional frameworks, and flat, single- and double-curvature stressed skins.

Two-dimensional frames include beams in bending supported on columns, trusses, plane frames, systems with slung or arched framing. The construction, loading and load transfer takes place in one – normally vertical – plane. To carry uniformly distributed roof loads, two-dimensional frames are generally added together to form three-dimensional systems – primary structures and secondary structures perpendicular to them. Multiple layers with alternating directions of span are possible (e.g. purlins-rafters-battens). However, a roof covering, e.g. tiles, is necessary to carry the uniformly distributed load on the roof surface, which converts the uniformly distributed load into linear or point loads.

Space frames are three-dimensional structures. Loadbearing action in two directions is possible. An additive arrangement of independent structures is not required. A space frame can support the roof surface at numerous points. A suitable roof covering is required to carry the uniformly distributed load; this must be able to convert this distributed loading into point loads.

Stressed-skin structures such as slabs, membranes or shells can support the roof covering across their entire area, or even form the roof covering itself. Depending on their form, stressed-skin structures can themselves span over the building or be supported on a primary loadbearing structure. The loads acting on a flat stressed-skin structure are carried by way of bending in one or two axes, on a curved stressed-skin structure by way of vault or shell action.

Examples of feasible structural systems for flat or single- or double-curvature roof surfaces are discussed below.

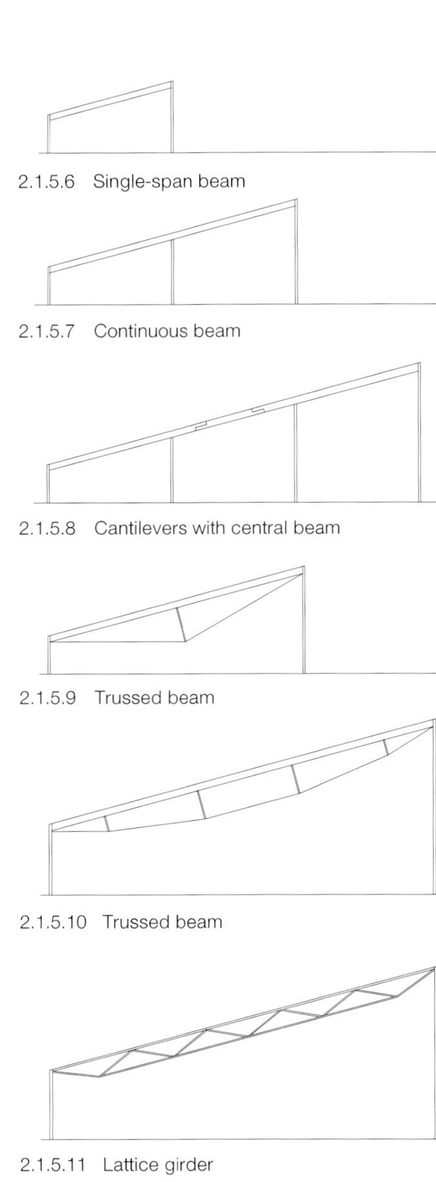

2.1.5.6 Single-span beam

2.1.5.7 Continuous beam

2.1.5.8 Cantilevers with central beam

2.1.5.9 Trussed beam

2.1.5.10 Trussed beam

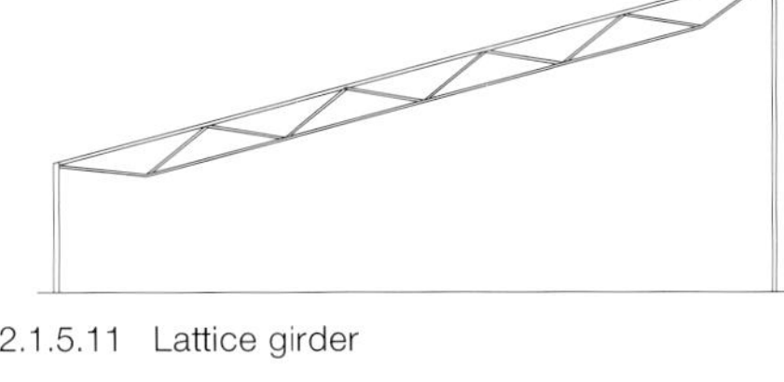

2.1.5.11 Lattice girder

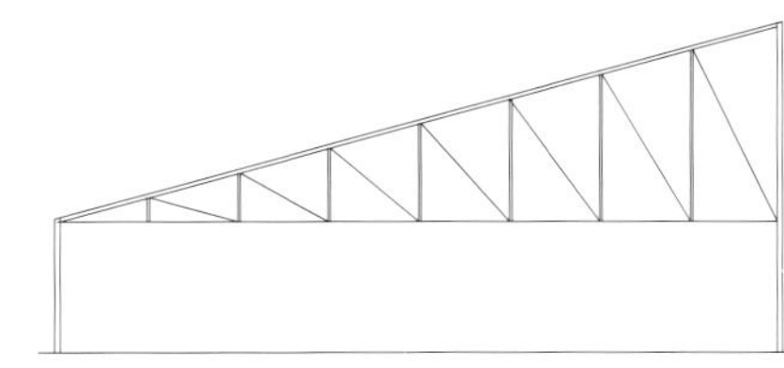

2.1.5.12 Lattice girder

2.1.5.13 Cranked beam

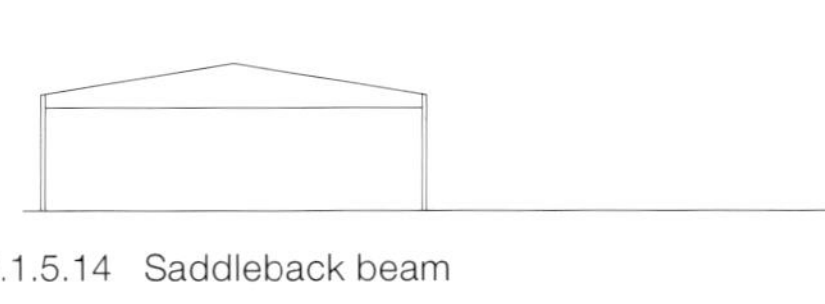

2.1.5.14 Saddleback beam

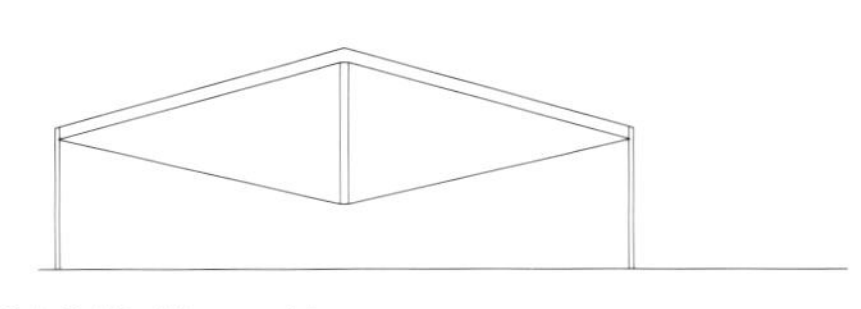

2.1.5.15 Trussed beams

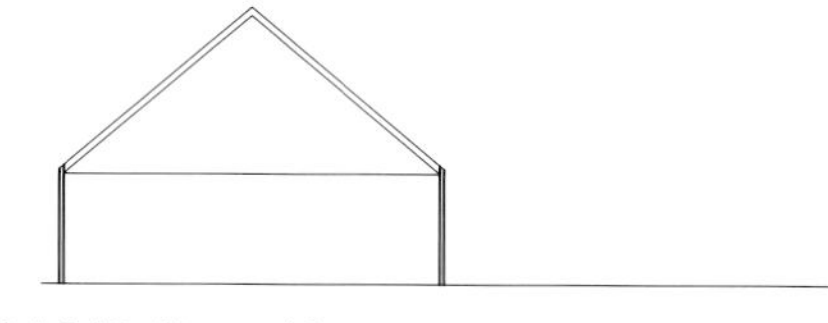
2.1.5.16 Trussed frame

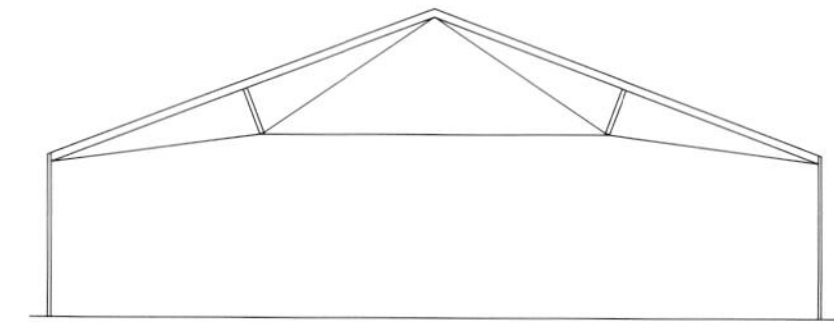
2.1.5.17 Polonceau truss

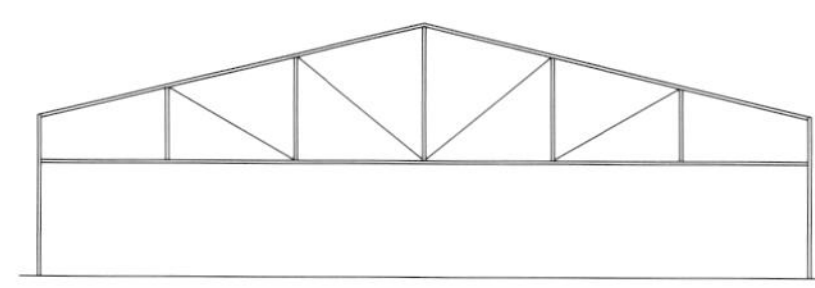
2.1.5.18 Lattice girder

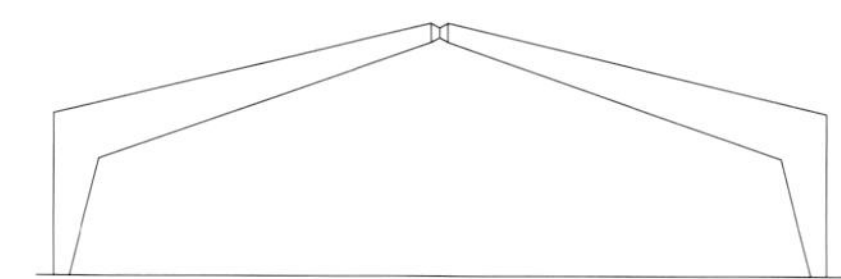
2.1.5.19 Frame

2.1.5.20 Frame with raking column arrangement

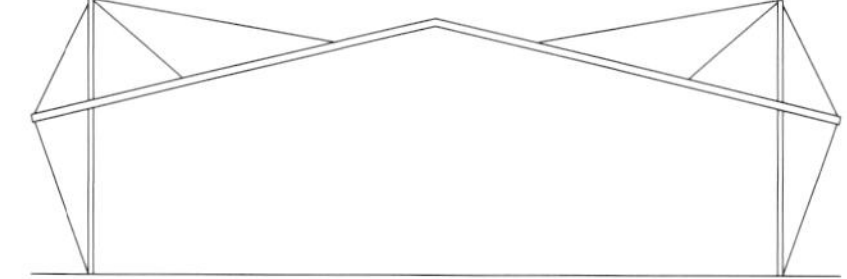
2.1.5.21 Guyed arrangement

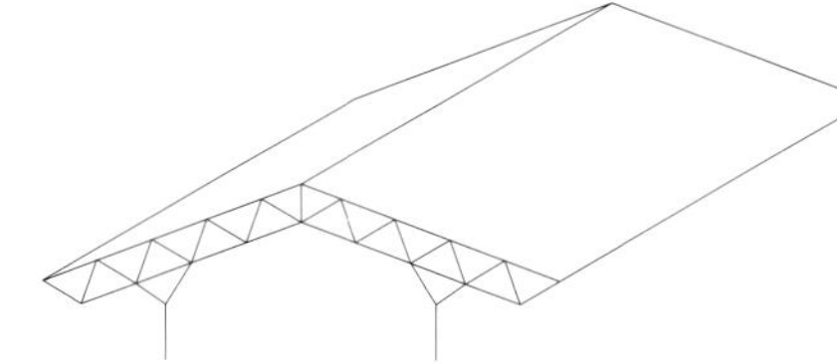
2.1.5.22 Space frame

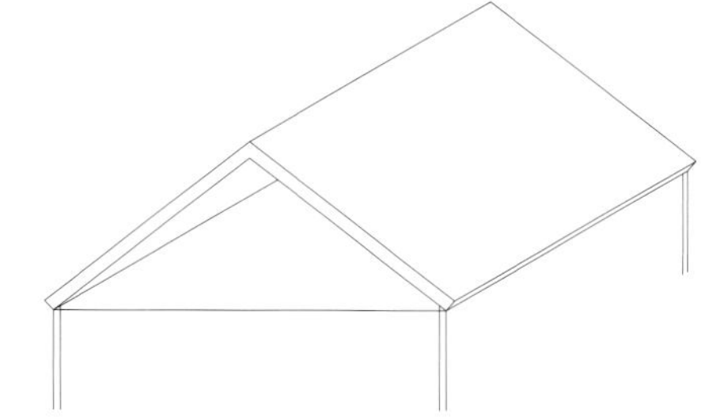
2.1.5.23 Folded plate structure

**Flat surfaces**

Beams with a constant cross-section arranged as single-span beams spanning from column to column, as continuous beams spanning over several columns, or as cantilevers with a central beam, are suitable for short spans. Their spacing is governed by the nature and size of the secondary beams. As the span lengthens, the weight of a solid beam increases disproportionately, making it advisable to differentiate the beam cross-section and resolve the bending stresses into tensile and compressive stresses.

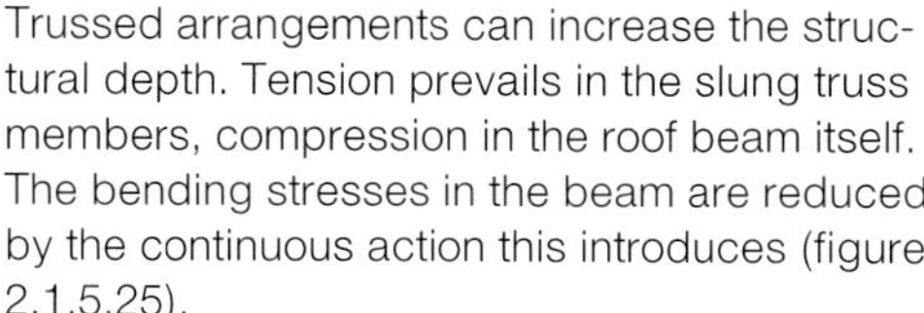

Trussed arrangements can increase the structural depth. Tension prevails in the slung truss members, compression in the roof beam itself. The bending stresses in the beam are reduced by the continuous action this introduces (figure 2.1.5.25).

A trussed frame is produced by two mutually supportive members with their bases held together by a tie. The traditional close couple roof consists of such trussed frames. The rafters are thereby subjected to compression and bending. Over longer spans the beams themselves can be trussed or constructed as girders. The Polonceau truss (figures 2.1.5.17 and 2.1.5.28) consists of two mutually supportive, trussed members with a tie that spans not from base to base but between the two trusses.

In trusses, bending is systematically resolved into tension and compression. Trusses comprise top and bottom chords, posts and diagonals. The arrangement determines which members are in tension and which in compression. Those in tension can be appropriately slender. Trusses may only be loaded at their nodes. Single-span and continuous systems are possible. Like a deep beam in bending, the top chord of a truss requires lateral restraint to prevent buckling or overturning. Secondary members and the formation of a roof plate can provide the necessary restraint. The most diverse roof forms can be realised with trusses (figure 2.1.5.26).

Frames comprise columns and beams. No additional bracing elements to accommodate horizontal forces are necessary in the plane of the frame. This makes frames especially suitable for single-storey sheds in which intervening columns are undesirable (figure 2.1.5.27). Furthermore, the use of a frame can reduce the structural depth of the beam because the columns resist part of the bending. Both vertical and horizontal reaction forces occur at the supports. Corresponding foundations or tension members between opposing supports are therefore essential.

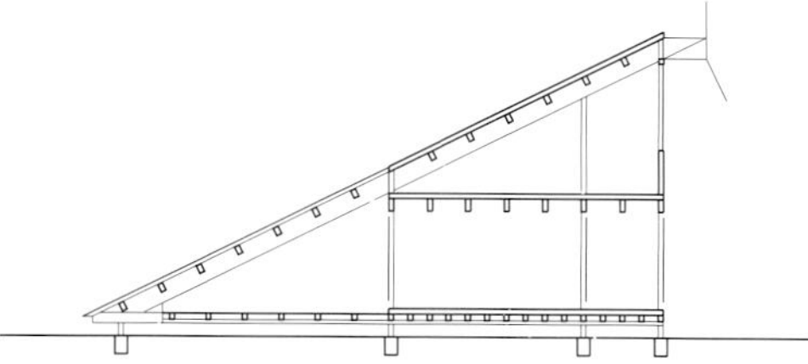
2.1.5.24 Private house in Regensburg, two-span timber beam

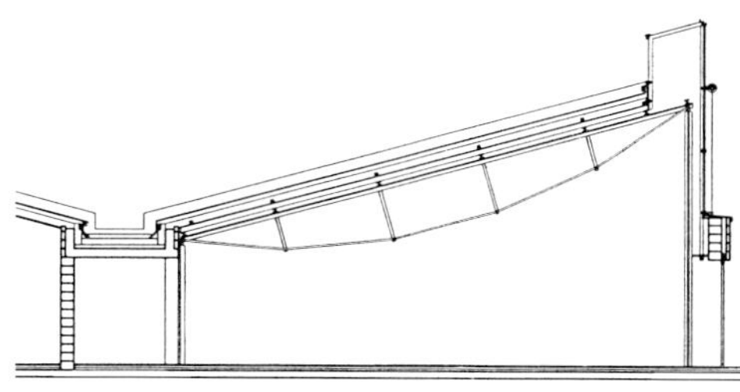
2.1.5.25 Church in Nuremberg-Langwasser, trussed timber beam

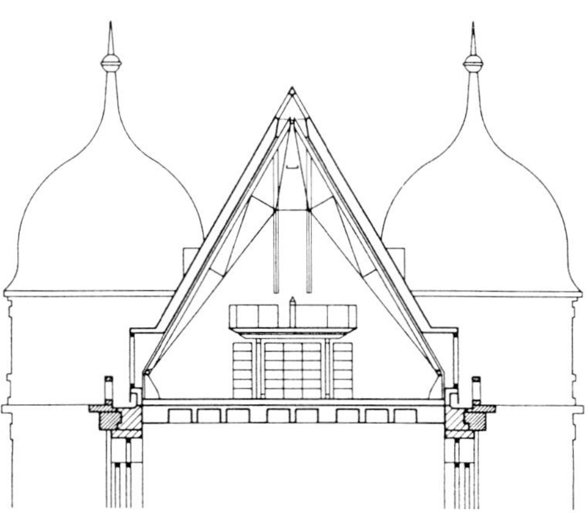
2.1.5.26 Gottesau Castle, Karlsruhe, new steel roof structure

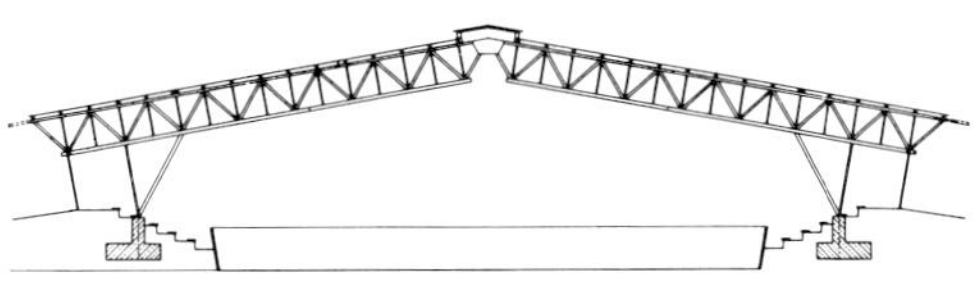
2.1.5.27 Riding arena in Riem, three-pin frame consisting of lattice girders and raking column arrangement

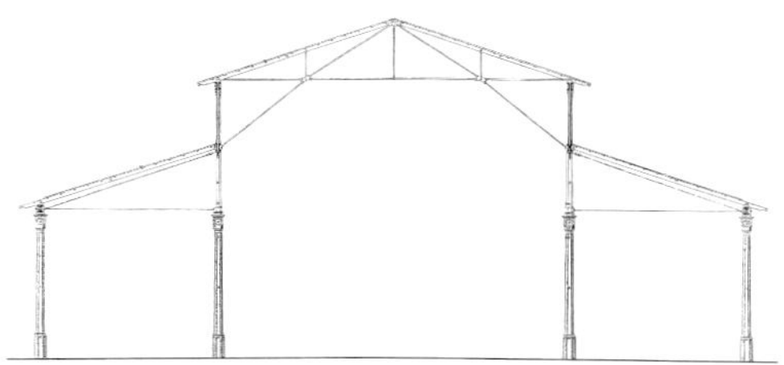
2.1.5.28 Schrannenhalle, Munich, Polonceau truss guyed back to create a frame action

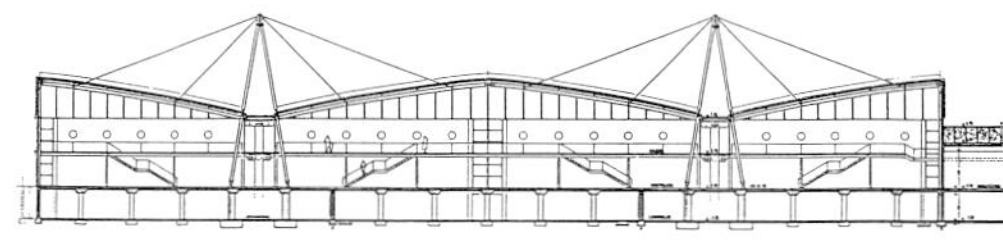

2.1.5.29 Aerospace wing of the German Museum in Munich

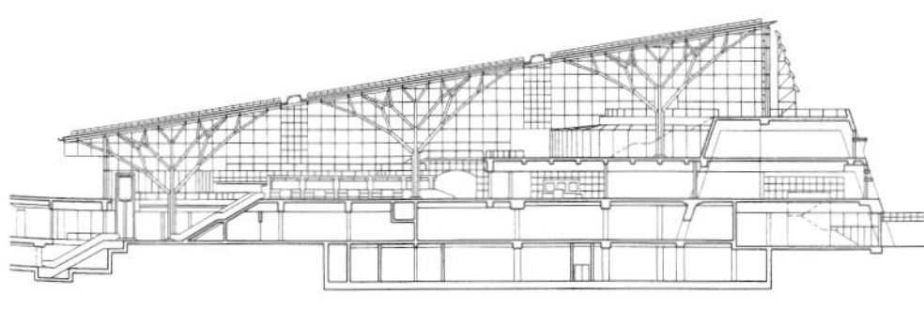

2.1.5.30 Terminal at Stuttgart airport, three-dimensional branching columns

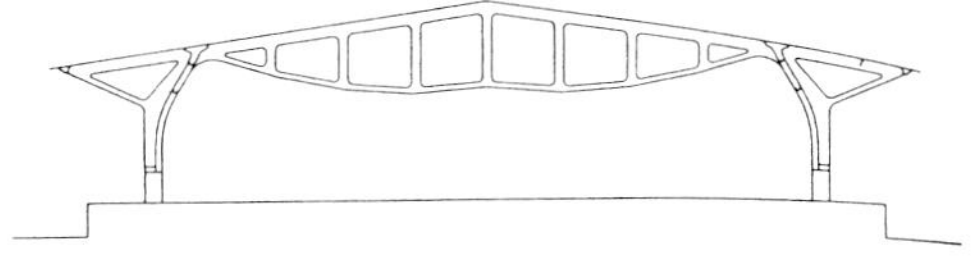

2.1.5.31 Chiasso warehouse, reinforced concrete roof on trussed beams

Frames can be formed from solid-web sections, trusses or systems with slung or arched framing.

Guyed arrangements from masts positioned at the sides or centrally permit lightweight and long-span structures. In structural terms, these correspond to slung framing (figure 2.1.5.29). Space frames can be used for a whole variety of roof forms. There are numerous ways of shaping space frames. Most space frames employ pin-jointed members subjected to tension or compression only. In contrast, three-dimensional branching systems employ rigid connections between the individual members. The structure must also possess a certain bending strength to resist asymmetric loads and provide stability against buckling.
Flat stressed-skin structures for flat surfaces are mainly the province of reinforced concrete slabs. These can be supported by downstand beams and carry bending moments in one or two directions. Flat slabs without downstand beams are conceivable for shallow pitches (figure 2.1.5.30).

**Roof surfaces in single curvature**
In the additive use of plane frames, i.e. with primary and secondary structural systems, it is sufficient to curve one element, e.g. the primary structural system, and place secondary beams on it (figure 2.1.5.32). Beams in bending can be curved so that cantilever, single-span, continuous and slung frame beams are feasible for curved roof surfaces. Girders can also be curved, even though curved chords in addition to tension or compression also undergo bending, which strictly speaking no longer corresponds to the definition of a girder (figure 2.1.5.33). An arch effect is then possible when rigid abutments and an adequate rise are available. The arch is then loaded mainly in compression. Particularly slender arch profiles are feasible when guys are used to stabilise the arch against buckling and asymmetric loads.

Tension structures can be built from cables or stiff components fabricated in a suitable form. Bracing against uneven loading can be provided by the bending strength of the tension member, by pretensioning with the help of cables or by a surcharge, as with the suspended roof (figure 2.1.5.34). The barrel vault or shell is a stressed-skin structure in single curvature. The barrel vault spans in the direction of the arch from support to support, while the shell spans in the longitudinal direction as well and creates a three-dimensional structural system.

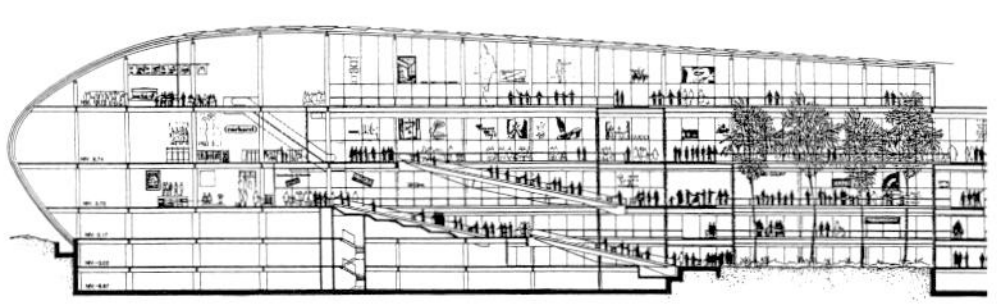

2.1.5.32 Supermarket, Bercy, curved beams in bending continuous over several columns

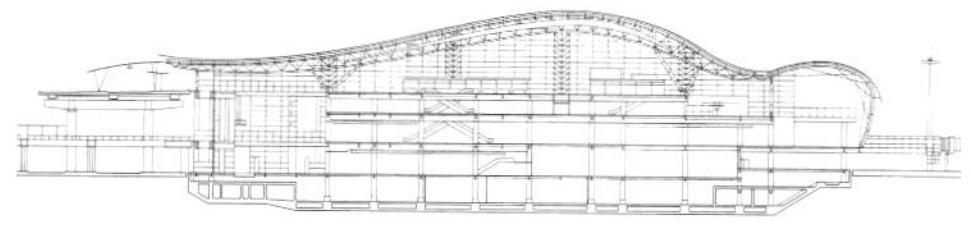

2.1.5.33 Terminal at Kansai airport, curved lattice girder

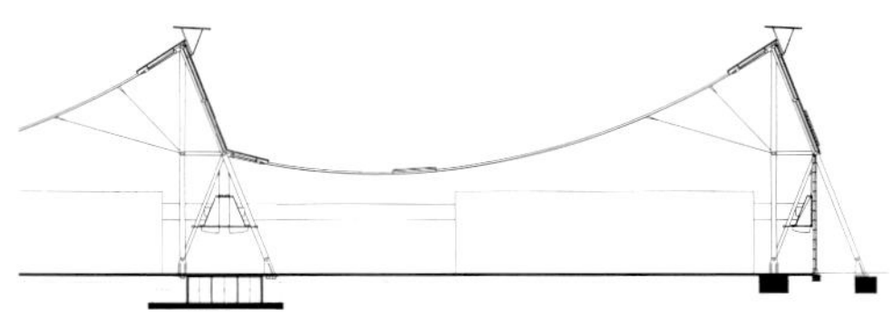

2.1.5.34 Exhibition hall No. 26, Hannover trade fair grounds, suspended roof

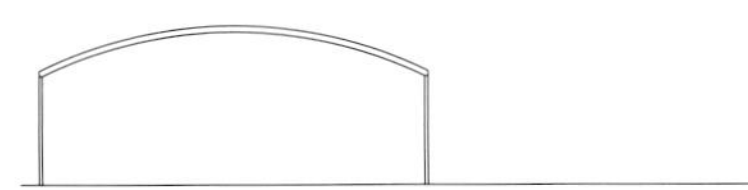

2.1.5.35 Curved single-span beam

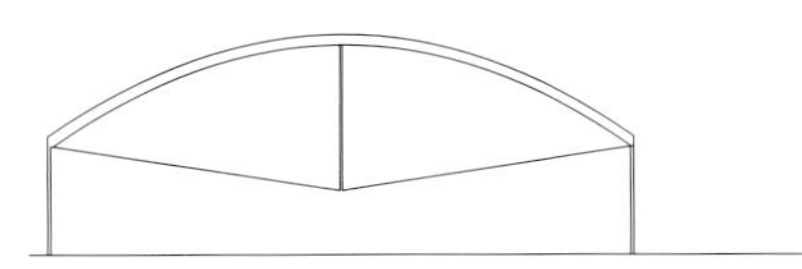

2.1.5.36 Trussed curved beam

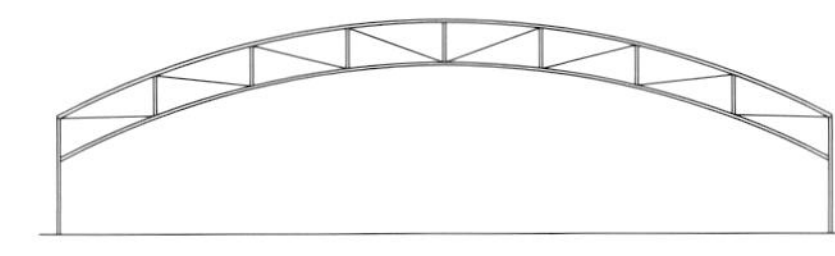

2.1.5.37 Curved lattice girder

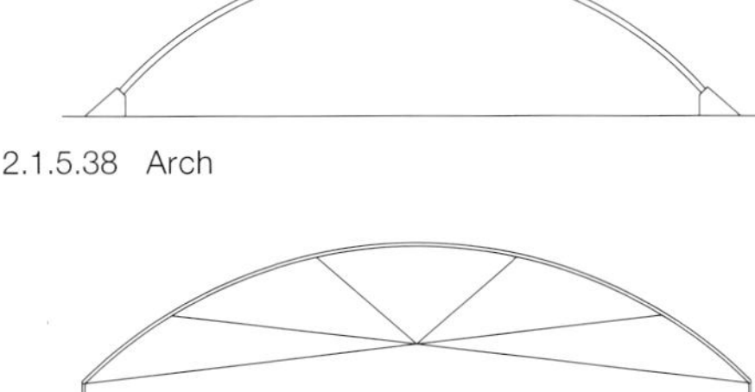

2.1.5.38 Arch

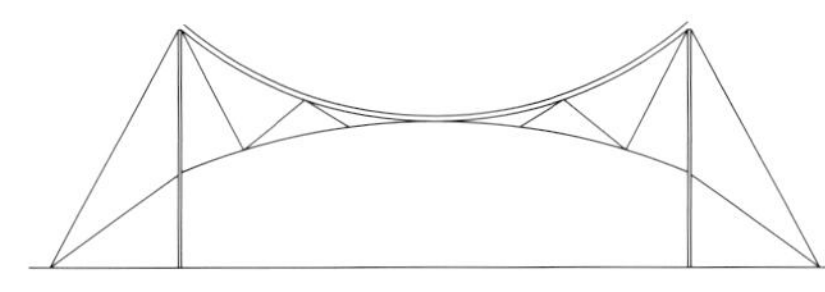

2.1.5.39 Guyed arch

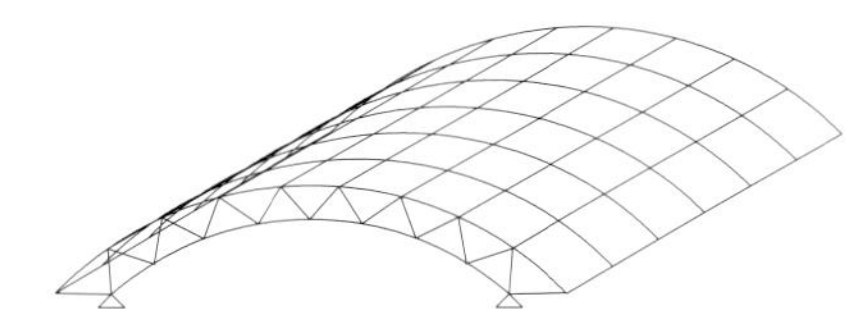

2.1.5.40 Prestressed cable structure

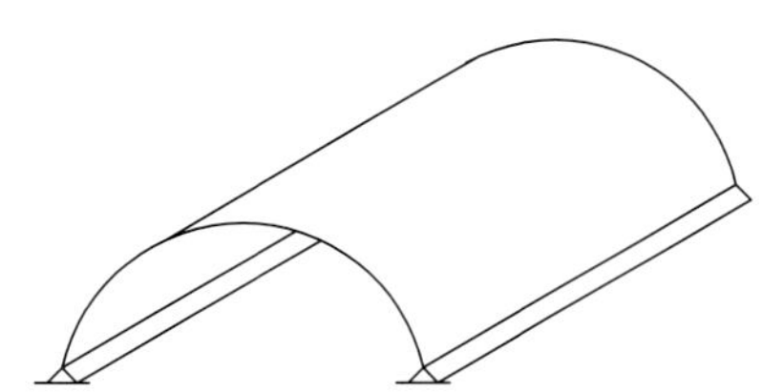

2.1.5.41 Curved space frame

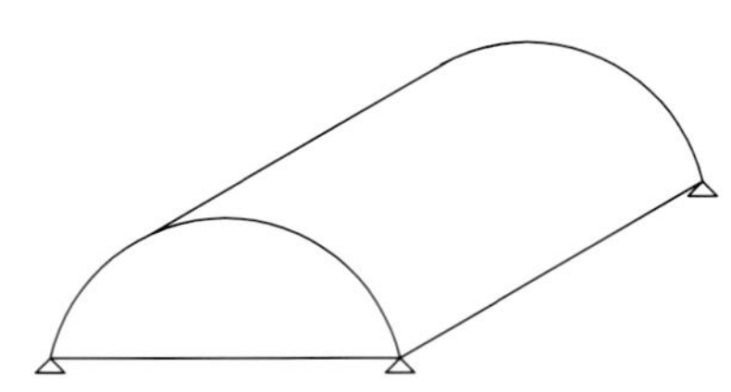

2.1.5.42 Barrel vault

2.1.5.43 Barrel shell

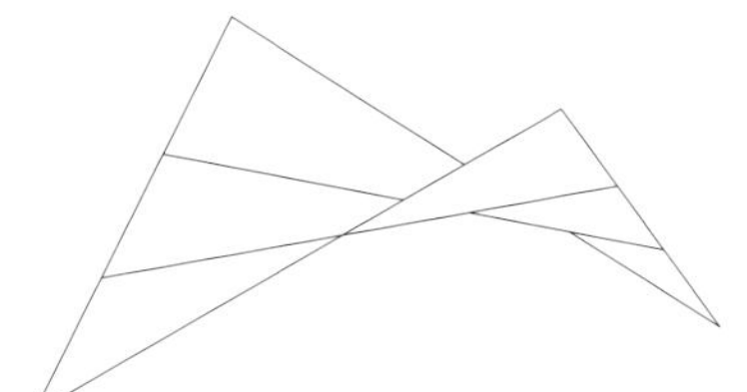

2.1.5.44 Hyperbolic paraboloid

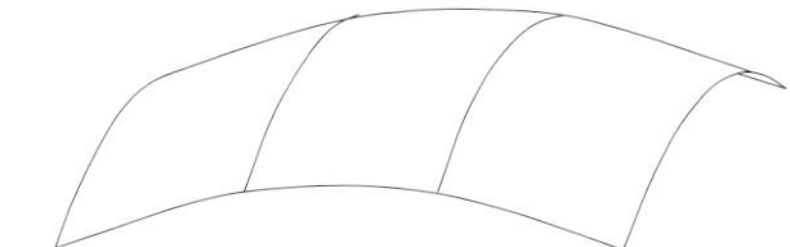

2.1.5.45 Ribbed shell

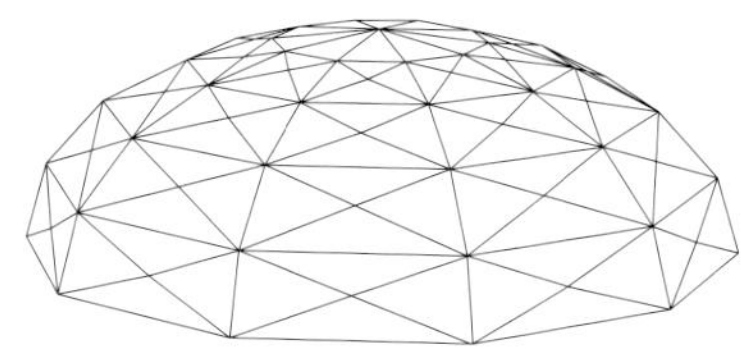

2.1.5.46 Ribbed dome

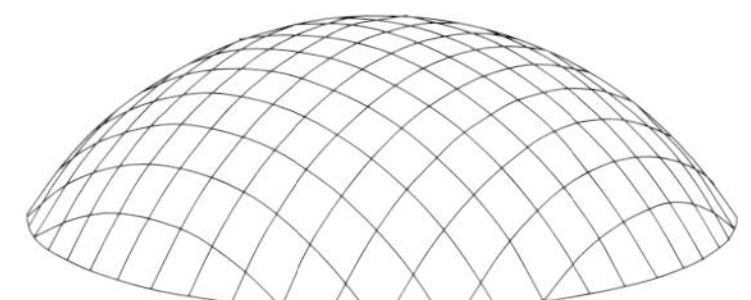

2.1.5.47 Lattice dome

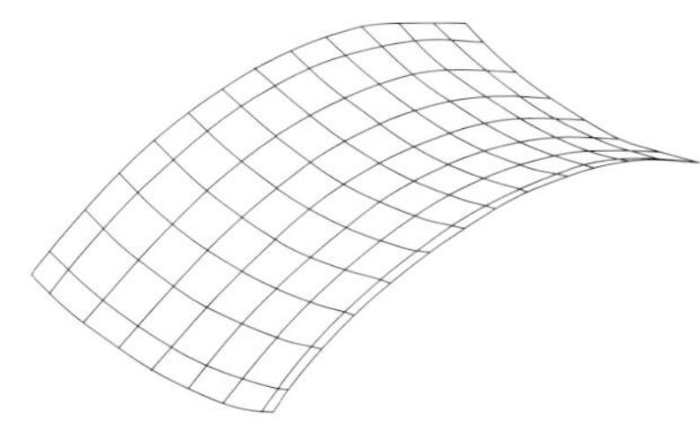

2.1.5.48 Cable lattice

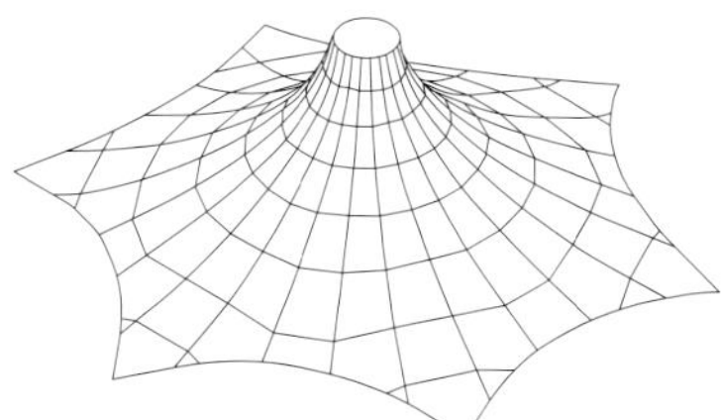

2.1.5.49 Tent

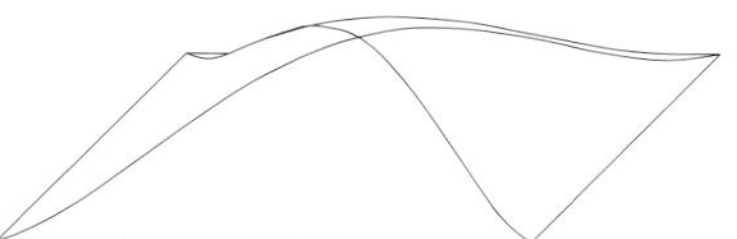

2.1.5.50 Air-supported membrane

**Roof surfaces in double curvature**

A surface in double curvature is an ideal form for lightweight stressed-skin structures, such as shells and membranes. The prerequisite is that the curvature is sufficient and that the edges and the supports can be suitably designed. Accordingly, we distinguish between two principal types of structure: those that gain their structural effect from the double curvature, e.g. a dome of meridian and circumferential ribs, a hyperbolic paraboloid shell of reinforced concrete, or a pretensioned cable network; and those that support a curved surface but where this is not an essential characteristic of their structural action, e.g. a structure comprising a number of curved beams in bending.

The hyperbolic paraboloid can be generated from straight elements as a translation surface. This property can be used to advantage, e.g. by using straight boards for the formwork of a reinforced concrete shell. However, the structural action of the shell takes place not along the straight lines but preferably in the direction of the curvature. Trapezoidal profile sheeting between two twisted edge members also produces a hyperbolic paraboloid surface due to the twisting of the ribs. The primary loadbearing effect here takes place along the straight ribs and is a bending action.

The prerequisite for shell action, apart from the curved form, is resistance to tension, compression and shear. It is possible to resolve a shell surface into a framework. Here it is essential to prevent angular rotation between the individual members (figure 2.1.5.51). This is possible by employing a triangular arrangement or X-bracing within the mesh.

Membranes and cable networks, which can accommodate tension but not compression, must be pretensioned in order to remain stable under different loads (figure 2.1.5.52).
Saddle roofs, i.e. with opposing curvatures, can be pretensioned mechanically. Pneumatically tensioned membranes are, for example, air-supported buildings. These are essentially surfaces curving in the same direction.

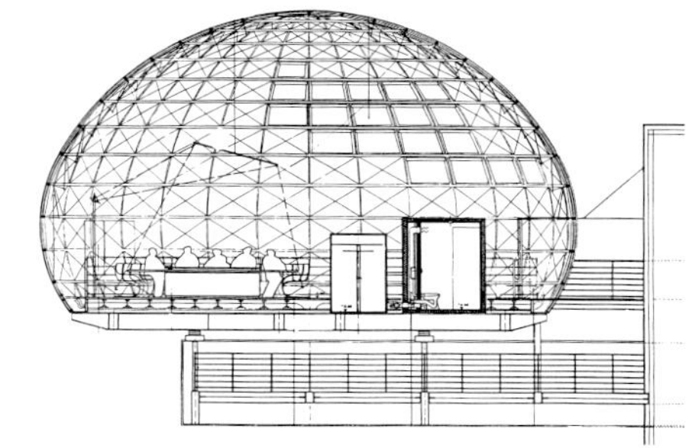

2.1.5.51 Conference hall, Lingotto, ribbed dome

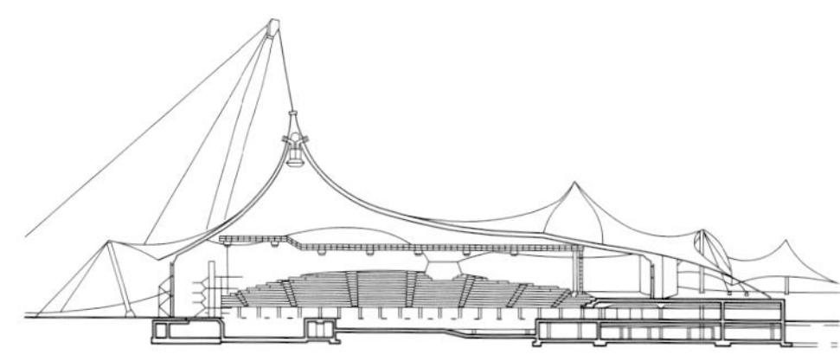

2.1.5.52 Olympic swimming pool, Munich, prestressed cable lattice

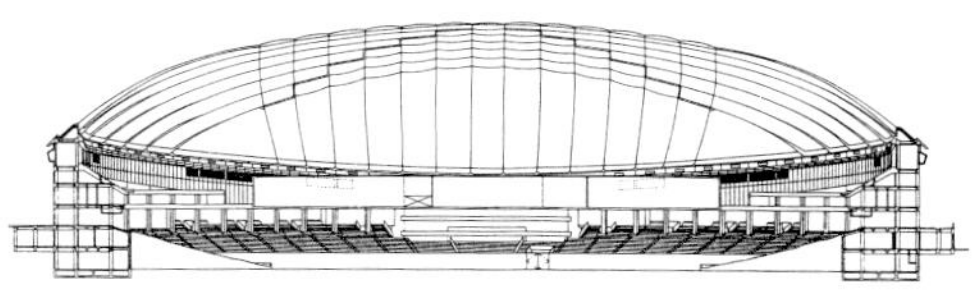

2.1.5.53 Tokyo Dome, air-supported membrane roof reinforced with cables

2.1.5.54 Exhibition hall, Camorino, reinforced concrete shell in double curvature

**References**


[01] Binding, Günther: Das Dachtragwerk; Munich: Deutscher Kunstverlag, 1991
[02] Bucak, Ömer: Glas im konstruktiven Ingenieurbau; in: Stahlbau Handbuch; Cologne: Stahlbau-Verlagsgesellschaft mbH, 1996
[03] DIN 1052 pt 1: Structural use of timber; design and construction; Apr 1988; Berlin: Beuth-Verlag, 1988
[04] DIN 1055: supplement to DIN 1055 pt 4, Mar 1969
[05] DIN 18807: Trapezoidal sheeting in building; pt 1: trapezoidal steel sheeting; General requirements and determination of loadbearing capacity by calculation; pt 3: trapezoidal steel sheeting; Structural analysis and design; Berlin: Beuth-Verlag
[06] DIN 18807: Trapezoidal sheeting in building; pt 9: Aluminium trapezoidal sheeting and their connections; application and construction; Berlin: Beuth-Verlag
[07] DIN 18334 (Dec 2000): Contract procedures for building works – Part C: General technical specifications for building works; Carpentry and timber construction works; Berlin: Beuth-Verlag, 2000
[08] Eurocode 1 – Basis of design and actions on structures – pt 2–3: Actions on structures; snow loads
[09] E DIN 1052 (May 2000, draft): Design of timber structures – General rules and rules for buildings; Berlin: Beuth-Verlag, 2000
[10] E DIN 1055-1 (Mar 2000, draft): Actions on structures; pt 1: Densities and weights of building materials, structural elements and stored materials; Berlin: Beuth-Verlag, 2000
[11] E DIN 1055-3 (Mar 2000, draft) Actions on structures; pt 3: self-weight and imposed load in building; Berlin: Beuth-Verlag, 2000
[12] E DIN 1055-4 (Mar 2001, draft): Actions on structures; pt 4: wind loads; Berlin: Beuth-Verlag, 2001
[13] E DIN 1055-5 (Apr 2001, draft): Actions on structures; pt 5: Snow loads and ice loads; Berlin: Beuth-Verlag, 2001
[14] Halász, Robert von; Scheer, Claus: Holzbau-Taschenbuch, vol. 1; Berlin: Ernst & Sohn, 1996
[15] IfBt: Deutsches Institut für Bautechnik, Berlin
[16] Informationsdienst Holz: Arbeitsgemeinschaft Holz e.V.; Düsseldorf
[17] Mehlhorn, Gerhard: Der Ingenieurbau; Berlin: Ernst & Sohn, 1996
[18] Natterer; Herzog; Volz: Holzbau Atlas Zwei; Munich: Institut für internationale Architektur-Dokumentation GmbH, 1996 & 1999
[19] ÖNORM (Austrian standard) B 4001: Design loads in building; general basic data for calculation in building construction; Vienna: Österreichisches Normungsinstitut, 1981
[20] ÖNORM B 4010: Design loads in building; dead loads of building materials and components; Vienna: Österreichisches Normungsinstitut, 1982
[21] ÖNORM B 4012: Design loads in building; variable actions; imposed loads; Vienna: Österreichisches Normungsinstitut, 1997
[22] ÖNORM B 4013: Design loads in building; snow and ice loads; Vienna: Österreichisches Normungsinstitut, 1983
[23] ÖNORM B 4014 pt 1: Design loads on structures; static wind loads (non-sway loads); Vienna: Österreichisches Normungsinstitut, 1993
[24] Petersen, Christian: Stahlbau; Vieweg-Verlag 1993, p. 765
[25] Rackwitz, Rüdiger: In: Der Ingenieurbau p. 185; Berlin: Ernst & Sohn, 1996
[26] Rybicki, Rudolf: Faustformeln und Faustwerte für Konstruktionen im Hochbau, Systeme – Dimensionen – Masse, pt 1 Geschoßbauten; Düsseldorf: Werner-Verlag, 1980
[27] Schneider, Klaus-Jürgen: Bautabellen für Architekten; Düsseldorf: Werner-Verlag, 2001
[28] Schulitz, Helmut; Sobek, Werner; Habermann, Karl: Steel Construction Manual; Munich: Institut für internationale Architektur-Dokumentation GmbH, 1999
[29] SIA (Swiss standard) 160: Actions on structures; Zürich: Schweizer Ingenieur- und Architekten-Verein, 1989
[30] Sockel, Helmut: Aerodynamik der Bauwerke; Braunschweig: Vieweg & Sohn, 1984
[31] Stahlbau Arbeitshilfen; Sandwichelemente; Bauen mit Stahl; Düsseldorf
[32] Technische Regeln für die Verwendung von linienförmig gelagerter Überkopfverglasung (DIBt Notes, June 1998)
[33] Zentralverband des Deutschen Dachdeckerhandwerks: Fachregeln für Dachdeckung mit Dachziegeln und Dachsteinen

# Building science

Kurt Kiessl

## Thermal performance

The thermal performance of the building envelope is the primary requirement for guaranteeing a comfortable and hygienic interior climate. The minimum requirements for thermal performance in winter also play a role in protecting the construction from climate-related moisture damage, as well as saving heating energy and thus improving economic efficiency. The minimum requirements for thermal performance in summer concern constructional measures for limiting the heating of the interior during the summer and hence for cutting the running costs of air-conditioning systems. Requirements for thermal insulation measures designed to save energy are a matter for public concern, and there is legislation to regulate energy-saving construction and protection of the climate. These requirements to limit the energy demands of and in buildings are embodied in Germany's new Energy Economy Act, which came into force on 1 February 2002; for the first time, the total energy requirement of a building in its construction and building services was considered.

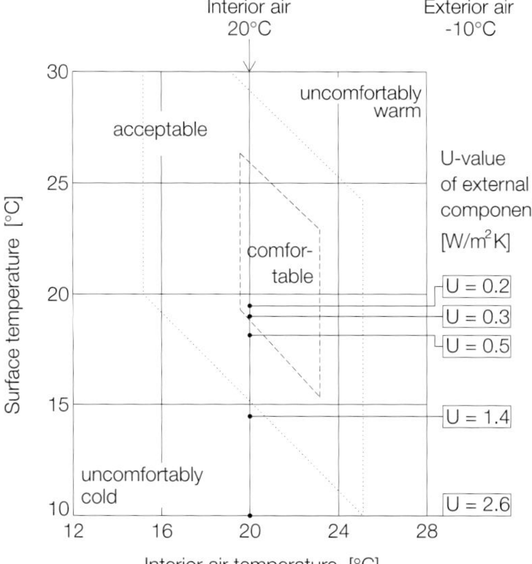


2.2.1.1 Thermal comfort depending on temperature of interior air and surfaces (based on [58]). Examples: surface temperatures for different U-values of external component and prescribed interior/exterior temperature difference.

One area that is relatively free of problems is thermal comfort because the important parameter affecting it is surface temperature (radiation exchange), which is directly influenced by the degree of thermal insulation.
This can be seen in figure 2.2.1.1, which gives a simplified example for an internal air temperature of 20°C and external air temperature of -10°C. In this case the pitched roof, with a thermal transmittance value of less than 0.2 W/m²K (the current standard), does not present any problems in terms of thermal comfort.

Hygiene aspects of thermal performance essentially concern the risk of reaching the critical surface moisture level (condensation, mould). Here again, a thermally insulated pitched roof does not lead to any problems. However, this presumes that thermal bridges have been avoided by constructional means at the critical points, penetrations and junctions.

#### Basic terminology (definitions, symbols, parameters)

The most important variables for thermal performance are given in table 2.2.1.2. Other physical parameters, symbols and units of measurement are specified in DIN EN ISO 7345. The reader is referred to, for example, [39, 55] for additional explanations of the physics involved in buildings.

Assumptions for thermal performance calculations
The boundary conditions for temperature are considered to remain constant over a sufficiently long period of time (average values), which means steady-state relationships with heat flows constant over time. This assumption is permissible when considering thermal and energy effects in terms of average values.

One-dimensional relationships for heat transmission through building components are still specified, which means assuming homogeneous, plane layers parallel to the surfaces and a constant heat flow always perpendicular to the plane of the component. Two- or three-dimensional heat transmission, as occurs, for example, at thermal bridges (corners, junctions, reveals etc.), cannot be taken into account by this approach. In these instances complex, multi-dimensional computational methods help to determine the corresponding deviations, which are then incorporated into the one-dimensional calculations using corrective factors.

| Symbol | Designation | Unit |
|---|---|---|
| A | Area | m² |
| F | Factor | – |
| $F_C$ | Reduction factor for sunshading | – |
| Q | Heat, heat energy | Ws or J |
| R | Total thermal resistance | m²K/W |
| $R_{se}$ | External surface resistance | m²K/W |
| $R_{si}$ | Internal surface resistance | m²K/W |
| $R_T$ | Thermal resistance | m²K/W |
| S | Solar gain index | – |
| U | Thermal transmittance | W/m²K |
| V | Volume | m³ |
| T | Thermodynamic temperature | K |
| a | Joint permeability coefficient | m³/ mhdaPa$^{2/3}$ |
| c | Specific heat | J/kgK |
| d | Thickness | m |
| $f_{Rsi}$ | Temperature factor for internal surface | – |
| g | Total energy transmittance of glazing | – |
| h | Surface conductance | W/m²K |
| q | Heat flow rate | W/m² |
| m | Mass | kg |
| n | Air change rate | 1/h |
| $n_{50}$ | Air change rate for 50 Pa pressure differential | 1/h |
| t | Time | s |
| ρ (Rho) | (Bulk/Gross) density | kg/m³ |
| θ (Theta) | Celsius temperature | °C |
| Φ (Phi) | Heat flow | W |
| λ (Lambda) | Thermal conductivity, design value for thermal conductivity | W/mK |
| Λ (Lambda) | Thermal conductivity coefficient | W/m²K |
| Ψ (Psi) | Linear thermal transmittance | W/mK |

2.2.1.2 Symbols and units for thermal performance parameters

#### Mechanisms of heat transmission

Practically all transmission mechanisms play a part in transporting the heat through a building component. These are briefly outlined below, together with the laws of physics that govern

| Material | ρ [kg/m³] | c [J/kgK] |
|---|---|---|
| Mineral materials | ~ 300–3000 | ~ 1000 |
| Rigid foams | 10–65 | ~ 1400 |
| Mineral wool | 10–200 | ~ 1000 |
| Air | ~ 1.25 | ~ 1000 |
| Timber | ~ 700 | ~ 1600 |
| Water | ~ 1000 | ~ 4200 |
| Glass | ~ 2500 | ~ 750 |
| Steel | ~ 7800 | ~ 450 |

2.2.1.3 Specific heat of materials

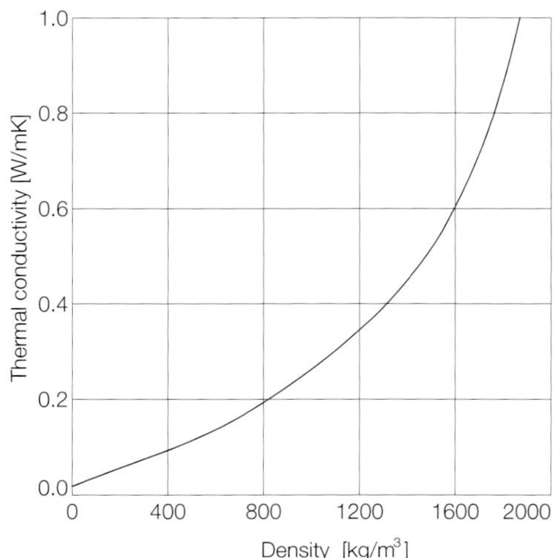


2.2.1.4 Thermal conductivity of building materials in relation to density (dry state, average values; Fraunhofer IBP, Holzkirchen)

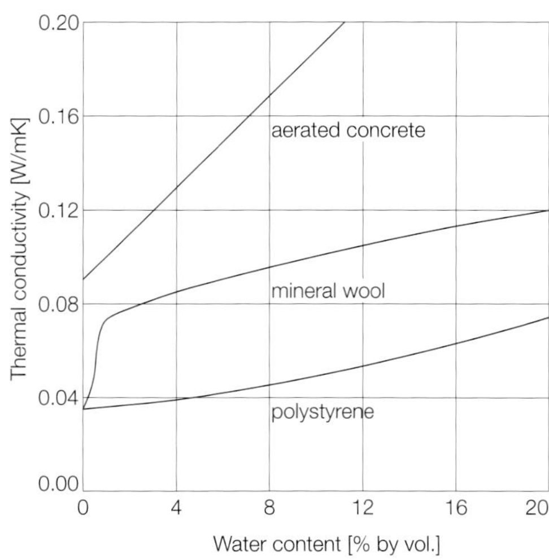


2.2.1.5 Influence of moisture on the thermal conductivity of building materials (hotplate method; FIW, Gräfelfing)

their behaviour. From this we can derive the definitions for the basic variables relevant to thermal performance.

Heat storage
The heat capacity of a material is important for heating or cooling processes, i.e. non-steady-state processes changing with time. The quantity of heat energy stored can be calculated from the following equation:

$$Q_{Sp} = m \cdot c \cdot \Delta\theta$$

Taking the gross or bulk density $\rho = m/V$ or $m = \rho V$, we get:

$$Q_{Sp} = V \cdot \rho \cdot c \cdot \Delta\theta$$

Table 2.2.1.3 gives examples of the specific heat capacity of various materials. Specific design values for c can be obtained from DIN EN 12524.

Heat conduction
Heat conduction takes place in solids, liquids and gases. The heat flow due to conduction can be calculated from the following equation:

$$\Phi_{cd} = A \cdot \lambda \cdot \frac{\Delta\theta}{d}$$

The critical material property is thermal conductivity λ. This essentially depends on the density and moisture content of the building material (see figures 2.2.1.4 and 2.2.1.5). Relating the heat flow to the surface area penetrated gives us the heat flow rate:

$$q_{cd} = \frac{\Phi_{cd}}{A} = \lambda \cdot \frac{\Delta\theta}{d} = \frac{\Delta\theta}{d/\lambda} = \frac{\Delta\theta}{R}$$

From this we can derive the definition of thermal resistance R of a material layer of thickness d:

$$R = \frac{d}{\lambda}$$

Practical figures for the thermal conductivity of common building materials are:

| | |
|---|---|
| metals | approx. 50–400 W/mK |
| concrete | 1.5–2.5 W/mK |
| masonry | 0.2–1.2 W/mK |
| timber | 0.13–0.20 W/mK |
| insulating materials | 0.02–0.10 W/mK |
| stationary air | approx. 0.025 W/mK |

Heat convection
Heat transmission by convection is linked to a flowing medium, e.g. air, water. We distinguish between
- free convection,

due to temperature and hence density differences, e.g. convection currents in enclosed, air-filled spaces (double glazing) where the boundary surfaces are subjected to different temperatures, and
- forced convection,

due to overall pressure differences, e.g. air flows through a building due to leaks and the pressure/suction effect of the wind flowing past the building.
The heat flow due to convection can be calculated as follows:

$$\Phi_{cv} = \rho \cdot c \cdot \dot{V}\, \Delta\theta$$

where
$\rho \cdot c$ = heat capacity [J/m³K] (for practical purposes we can take 0.34 Wh/m³K for air)
$\dot{V}$ = flow rate [m³/h]
$\Delta\theta$ = temperature change of medium [K]

The convection assumption is used, for example, to determine ventilation heat losses, where the rate of flow can be represented as the product of interior air volume and air change rate:

$$\dot{V} = V_R \cdot n$$

The temperature change here refers to the difference between heated interior air and cold exterior air. The air change rate n [h⁻¹] specifies how many times the interior air volume is replaced by external air every hour.

Radiation
Heat transmission through radiation requires a space (vacuum, gas) permeable to radiation and takes place in the form of electromagnetic waves. The characteristic variable is the wavelength λ, specified in µm or nm. A body radiates heat (energy) in relation to its temperature across a certain wavelength range (spectrum) – the higher its temperature, the shorter is the wavelength of the radiation emitted. The wavelength ranges of interest here are as follows:
Short wave:
UV (ultraviolet, $\lambda < 0.380$ µm)
VIS (visible light, $0.380 \le \lambda \le 0.780$ µm)
Long wave:
IR (infrared, heat radiation, $\lambda > 0.780$ µm)
Examples:
sun, $T \approx 6000$ K
wavelength spectrum approx.
$0.280 < \lambda < 2.5$ µm
radiator, $T \approx 330$ K
wavelength spectrum approx. $2.5 < \lambda < 50$ µm

- Radiation balance

When radiation, e.g. from the sun, strikes a surface of a building element, the total energy is divided into a component reflected from the surface, a component absorbed by the surface and, for transparent components (e.g. glass), a transmitted component according to the equation:

$\Phi_e = \Phi_e \cdot \rho_e + \Phi_e \cdot \alpha_e + \Phi_e \cdot \tau_e$ or
$\rho_e + \alpha_e + \tau_e = 1$

where
$\Phi_e$ = total radiation energy, e.g. sun [W]
$\rho_e$ = direct reflection index [-]
$\alpha_e$ = direct absorption index [-]
$\tau_e$ = direct transmission index [-]

These physical variables relevant to radiation depend on the wavelength and angle of incidence of the radiation. On glass, for instance, as the angle of incidence decreases, so $\alpha_e$ and $\tau_e$ tend towards zero and $\rho_e$ tends towards one. This is significant for the transmission of light or energy through glazing. These properties are determined for various wavelength ranges according to DIN EN 410.

- Short-wave radiation (sun)

The intensity of radiation across the solar spectrum incident on the surfaces of building elements is given by the following equation:

$I = \Phi_e/A$ [W/m²]

The absorption component contributes to heating up the element. A heat source ensues at the surface whose intensity is given by the equation:

$I_{abs} = I \cdot \alpha_e$

Typical values for the maximum solar radiation intensity are given in figure 2.2.1.6. Further details concerning local radiation intensities can be found in the preliminary edition of DIN 4108 part 6. The short-wave part of the spectrum $\alpha_e$ can be estimated essentially according to the colour of the surface (light colour = low $\alpha_e$, dark colour = high $\alpha_e$). When considering a component in energy terms in connection with absorption, these values are averaged for the effective range of the solar spectrum (300–2500 nm). Table 2.2.1.7 provides guidance on the figures to be expected.

- Long-wave radiation

The emission of long-wave radiation from surfaces subjected to low temperatures (heat radiated from surfaces of building components, radiators etc.) should be calculated according to the Stefan-Boltzmann law. It is proportional to the long-wave emission index e of the surface.
The emission index of a surface depends on the wavelength. The perceived colour of the surface is irrelevant here; in this wavelength range snow is practically "ideal black"! The e-values are measured for the relevant IR range and given as practical, average values.
Practical examples of e-values for surfaces:

| | |
|---|---|
| mineral building materials | ~ 0.9 |
| timber | ~ 0.9 |
| metal, polished | ~ 0.02–0.05 |
| metal, matt | ~ 0.4–0.8 |
| glass | ~ 0.3–0.9 |
| radiator enamel | ~ 0.93 |
| snow, ice | ~ 0.97 |

Long-wave radiation dominates for heat transmission through double or multiple glazing but is irrelevant for heat losses to the atmosphere from the surfaces of building components.

- Radiation exchange between roof and surroundings

The practically constant simultaneous radiation exchange processes – in different regions of the spectrum – for the external surfaces of roofs, with their thermal and moisture-related consequences, are important. We must distinguish between what happens during the day and what happens at night. During the day solar absorption takes place to a greater or lesser degree, according to the orientation of the surface, the intensity of incident solar radiation and the solar absorption index. The emission of long-wave radiation varies according to cloud cover and the emission index of the roof surface. Only by considering this overall balance (short and long wave) is it possible to derive the thermal status of the roof surface. This can lead, for example, to even light-coloured metal roof coverings (low $\alpha_e$ but also low e) being heated up quite noticeably at low solar absorption and low emission. At night, on the other hand, the emission of long-wave radiation alone can in some circumstances lead to a marked (over)cooling of the roof surface (3–5 K below external air temperature). With a relative humidity of 75% and air temperatures in the range 10–20°C this can lead to condensation forming when the roof has cooled to approx. 4 K below the air temperature, and with a relative humidity of 85% when the roof is just 2.5 K below the air temperature. The phenomenon of frost forming on roofs at night in early summer is not unknown. The significance of these effects – when the outside of the material is damp or wet – is seen in increased reverse diffusion during the day within the roof cross-section, with possible interstitial condensation, and possible condensation problems for the outer parts of the cross-section (tiles, battens, roofing felt, insulation) at night. To what extent this can lead to critical situations may need to be determined using more accurate moisture-thermal analyses or measurements, depending on climate, roof make-up and material properties.

**Heat transmission through components**

The heat transmission includes the heat transfer to the inner surface of the component, the heat flow through the component and the heat transfer between outer surface and surroundings. Figure 2.2.1.8 illustrates this path.

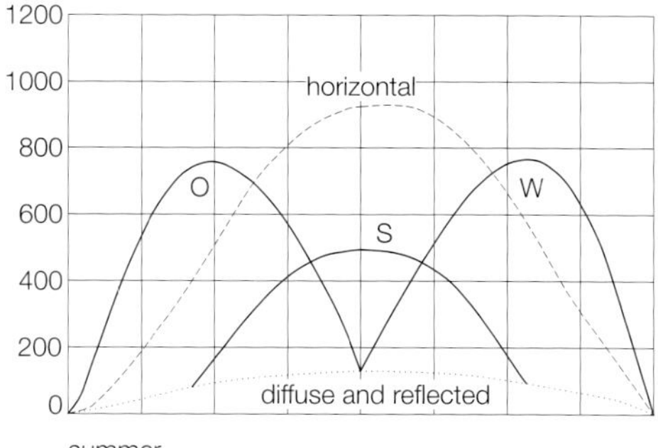


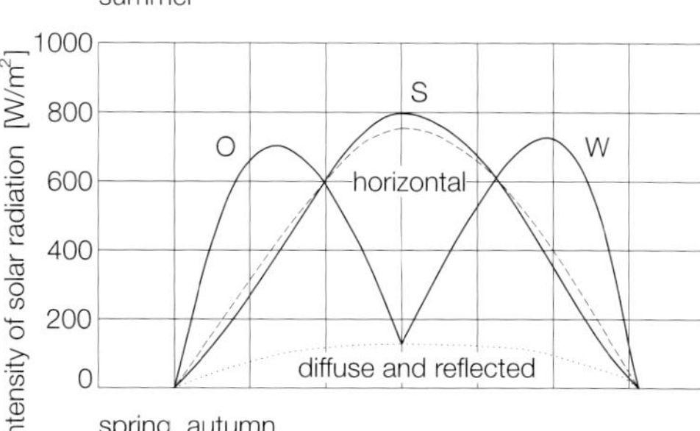


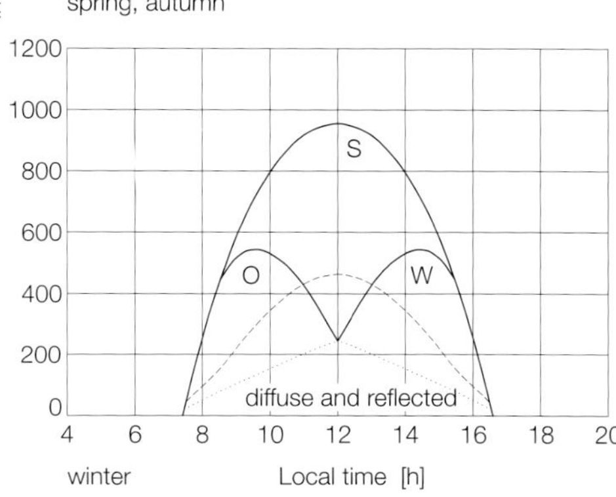


2.2.1.6 Daily profiles of direct and diffuse incident solar radiation intensity on component surfaces facing different directions during different seasons

| Surface | Radiation absorption index α |
|---|---|
| Wall surfaces: | |
| • light-coloured paint finish | 0.4 |
| • opaque paint finish | 0.6 |
| • dark-coloured paint finish | 0.8 |
| Engineering bricks | 0.8 |
| Light-coloured facing masonry | 0.6 |
| Roofs (property): | |
| • brick-red | 0.6 |
| • dark surface | 0.8 |
| • metal (polished) | 0.2 |
| • roofing felt (sanded finish) | 0.6 |

2.2.1.7 Typical values for the radiation absorption index of various surfaces within the solar spectrum relevant for energy analyses [11]

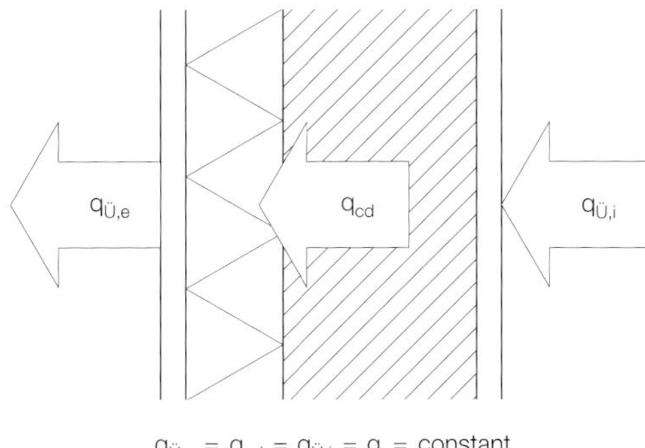


2.2.1.8 Heat flow rates for steady-state heat transmission through building component

Heat transfer (surfaces)
The convection and long-wave radiation components of the heat flow are assessed and, for a simplified analysis, added together to obtain the heat transfer. DIN EN ISO 6946 specifies approximate methods for determining the components due to convection and radiation.

This addition of the components gives the total heat flow rate for the heat transfer and provides the definitions for thermal transmittance and surface resistance:

$$q_{ü} = h \cdot \Delta\theta = \frac{\Delta\theta}{1/h} = \frac{\Delta\theta}{R_s}$$

The design values for surface resistance according to table 2.2.1.9 should be used for thermal performance analyses (see DIN 4108 part 2, DIN EN ISO 6946).

| | Direction of heat flow | | |
|---|---|---|---|
| | Upwards | Horizontal | Downwards |
| $R_{si}$ | 0.10 | 0.13 | 0.17 |
| $R_{se}$ | 0.04 | 0.04 | 0.04 |

2.2.1.9 Surface resistances [m²K/W]

Heat flow is defined as being horizontal with an angular tolerance of ±30°, so it also applies to components inclined at up to 60° to the horizontal.

Thermal transmittance (component)
The thermal transmittance concerns individual layers and components consisting of one or more layers, or parts of a component made from homogeneous layers, and describes the heat transmission between the two surfaces of the component or layer.

- Components with one or more homogeneous layers

Thermal resistance and thermal transmittance are given by the following equation:

$$q = \frac{\theta_1 - \theta_2}{d/\lambda} = \frac{\theta_1 - \theta_2}{R} = \Lambda \cdot (\theta_1 - \theta_2)$$

where

one layer: $R = d/\lambda$
more than one layer:
$R = R_1 + R_2 + \ldots = \Sigma_i R_i = \Sigma_i (d/\lambda)_i$

- Air layers

Heat transmission through layers of air is composed of the components for heat conduction, heat convection and long-wave radiation. In practical terms this results in a total thermal resistance. The layers of air within the cross-section of the component have to be considered – in terms of their thermal resistance – like homogeneous layers perpendicular to the heat flow, provided the following conditions are fulfilled:

a) thickness ≤ 300 mm, no exchange of air with interior
b) thickness < 1/10 of other dimensions of the surface
c) plane-parallel boundary surfaces with $\varepsilon \geq 0.8$

See DIN EN ISO 6946, appendix B, for other cases.

We must distinguish between three types of air layer, where the cross-section of an opening is specified per m length of component for vertical air layers and per m² of component area for horizontal air layers.

| Thickness of air layer [mm] | Direction of heat flow | | |
|---|---|---|---|
| | Upwards | Horizontal | Downwards |
| 0 | 0.00 | 0.00 | 0.00 |
| 5 | 0.11 | 0.11 | 0.11 |
| 7 | 0.13 | 0.13 | 0.13 |
| 10 | 0.15 | 0.15 | 0.15 |
| 15 | 0.16 | 0.17 | 0.17 |
| 25 | 0.16 | 0.18 | 0.19 |
| 50 | 0.16 | 0.18 | 0.21 |
| 100 | 0.16 | 0.18 | 0.22 |
| 300 | 0.16 | 0.18 | 0.23 |

Intermediate values may be obtained by linear interpolation.

2.2.1.10 Thermal resistances of stationary air layers [m²K/W]

1) Stationary air layers
Layers of air are considered to be stationary when the only openings to the exterior (if any) are those required for pressure compensation or for draining the opening, and do not result in any movement of the air within the layer, and the cross-section of any opening is ≤ 500 mm². The design values to be used for the thermal resistance of air layers $R_g$ according to DIN EN ISO 6946 are given in table 2.2.1.10 in relation to thickness and direction of heat flow.

"Horizontal" also includes heat flows ±30° to the horizontal here.

2) Poorly ventilated air layers
Layers of air with openings to the exterior with a cross-section of 500–1500 mm² are considered to be poorly ventilated. Take half the corresponding value given in table 2.2.1.10 as the design value to be used for the thermal resistance of such an air layer. If the thermal resistance of a component layer on the outside between air layer and exterior exceeds the value 0.15 m²K/W, the maximum value of 0.15 m²K/W should be used.

3) Well-ventilated air layers
Layers of air are considered to be well ventilated when there are openings to the exterior with a cross-section > 1500 mm². In this case the thermal resistances of the air layer and all other layers between layer of air and exterior can be ignored. Instead, an external surface resistance – between inner boundary surface of air layer and air flow within the layer – equal to the internal surface resistance of the same component (according to table 2.2.1.9) should be used.

Heat transmission parameters
The intervening total resistance governs the heat transmission through components, on the way from surrounding air 1 to surrounding air 2. Various methods of analysis to determine the transmission parameters to be considered in each case have been prescribed for realistic cross-sections, consisting either of homogeneous individual layers or of differently constructed adjacent sections.

- Components with one or more homogeneous layers

In the general case (multi-layer) a succession of resistances are activated as heat flows through the component (see figure 2.2.1.8). The total thermal resistance is the sum of the surface resistances and the thermal transmittance of the component (sum of layer resistances):

$$R_T = R_{si} + R_1 + R_2 + \ldots + R_{se} = R_{si} + R + R_{se}$$

This gives us the thermal transmittance as the parameter for the heat transmission through the component:

$$U = \frac{1}{R_T}$$

From this U-value we obtain the transmission heat loss through the component:

$$q_T = U \cdot (\theta_i - \theta_e)$$

- Components with one or more homogeneous and non-homogeneous layers

This concerns components with different sections or segments with various adjacent layers in the plane of the component. A typical case

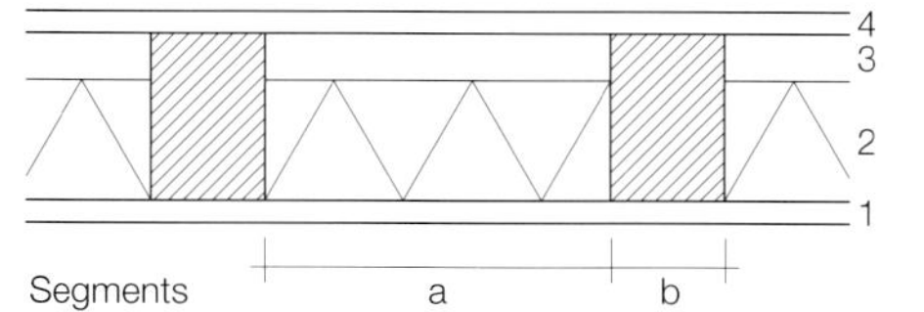


2.2.1.11 Non-homogenous component cross-section consisting of segments and layers. Area proportions of segments: e.g. $f_a = 0.80$, $f_b = 0.20$; $f_a + f_b + ... = 1$

of this is, for example, the close couple roof. An approximate method according to DIN EN ISO 6946 should be used for such cross-sections (see figure 2.2.1.11). Using this method an average thermal resistance for the complete non-homogeneous cross-section can be determined with reasonable accuracy. The method is only suitable for determining total transmission heat flows through the non-homogeneous section; temperature calculations for individual parts cannot be derived from the heat flow determined in this way.
A representative section of the non-homogeneous cross-section (e.g. rafters and space between) is broken down according to all element widths and layer thicknesses that occur. The area components $f_a$, $f_b$, $f_c$ ... on the section of component under consideration should be determined for all the sections a, b, c ... resulting from this breakdown. The resulting total number of layers (also sub-layers of a material) should be specified together with respective thickness and thermal conductivity. This breakdown into separate elements and the differentiated weighting of the heat flows in relation to area, always perpendicular to the plane of the component, produce a maximum and minimum value for the thermal resistance of the complete construction, which in reality lies in between. The final result is an arithmetic mean.

1) Maximum value $R'_T$
First, the thermal resistances $R_{Ta}$, $R_{Tb}$ etc. have to be calculated per section (homogeneous layers) according to the equation:

$$R_{Ta} = R_{si} + R_{a1} + R_{a2} + ... + R_{se}$$

From this we get the maximum value $R'_T$ as follows (corresponding to the area-related weighting of the flows per section):

$$R'_T = \left( \frac{f_a}{R_{Ta}} + \frac{f_b}{R_{Tb}} + ... \right)^{-1}$$

2) Minimum value $R''_T$
First, the thermal conductivity (inverse of resistance) has to be calculated per layer (uniform thickness over total width), weighted according to proportion of area. From these we determine fictitious resistances per total layer $R_1$, $R_2$ ... accordingly. The minimum value $R''_T$ is then calculated as follows:

$$R_1 = \left( \frac{f_a}{R_{a1}} + \frac{f_b}{R_{b1}} + ... \right)^{-1}$$

$$R''_T = R_{si} + R_1 + R_2 + ... + R_{se}$$

3) Parameters – average values and relative error
The arithmetic mean of the maximum and minimum values is taken as the average thermal resistance RT of the non-homogeneous component and forms the basis of further energy flow analyses:

$$R_T = (R'_T + R''_T)/2$$

We determine the thermal transmittance U for the non-homogeneous component from $R_T$:

$$U = \frac{1}{R_T}$$

The U-value here also governs the transmission heat losses through non-homogeneous components.

According to analyses of energy flows, an average thermal resistance for non-homogeneous cross-sections can be derived from the average thermal resistance as follows:

$$R_m = R_T - (R_{si} + R_{se})$$

A maximum relative error e [%] can be specified for estimating uncertainties:

$$e = \frac{(R'_T - R''_T)/2}{R_T} \cdot 100\%$$

**Thermal insulation**

The thermal insulation in the roof plays an especially important role in modern thermal performance concepts. A relatively high level of insulation, in relation to the component, can be installed here relatively easily. This can mean that, for example, better-than-average thermal insulation can be achieved in the roof at lower cost than in other parts of the building envelope; this could reduce the cost of other components so that, in the end, a more economic solution can be expected with the same standard of quality in terms of energy. The recommended level of thermal insulation in the roof according to the latest stipulations is < 0.25 W/m²K for new buildings, < 0.20 W/m²K for low-energy buildings and < 0.30 W/m²K for refurbishment work. This translates into a minimum insulation thickness of 160 mm for new buildings with a customary thermal conductivity of 0.04 W/mK, to well over 200 mm when striving to achieve enhanced standards (low-energy, passive-energy buildings, see also [63]).

| Application code | Permissible deviation of measured | |
|---|---|---|
| | average value from nom. thickness d | single value from average value |
| W | +5 mm or 6%[1) ]<br>−1 mm | ±5 mm |
| WL | +15 mm<br>−5% | ±10 mm |
| WD, WV | +5 mm<br>−1 mm | ±3 mm |

1) The larger figure governs

2.2.1.12 Application codes for fibre insulating materials with permissible thickness tolerances

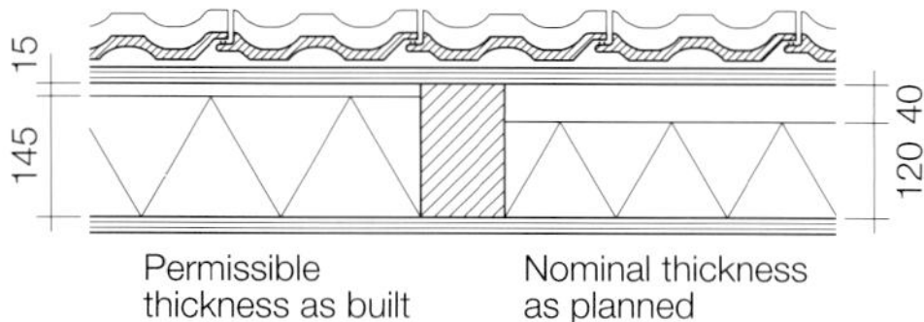


| | |
|---|---|
| Nominal thickness of insulating batts | 120 mm |
| Permissible deviation of average value | +15 mm |
| Permissible deviation of single value from average value | +10 mm |
| Permissible total thickness of insulating batts | 145 mm |

2.2.1.13 How the ventilation cross-section in a roof construction can be affected by the thickness of fibre insulating batts type WL, which are still within permissible thickness tolerances.

Thickness tolerances
The permissible deviation from the nominal thickness of a ready-made product is an important parameter, particularly for fibre insulating materials. Details can be found in the standards covering insulating material products (see, for example, [1]) and must be adhered to.
Permissible deviations in thickness can have fatal consequences for the function of a ventilated roof with a ventilation cross-section that is already at the minimum (see figures 2.2.1.12 and 2.2.1.13).

Loose insulating materials
Loose insulating materials in the form of flakes, fibres, granular organic or inorganic materials, waste or recycled products or renewable resources are suitable for filling cavities and thus upgrading the existing thermal insulation of a building. All these tipped or poured materials possess a low diffusion resistance. It should be noted that organic fibre materials have a relatively high sorption capacity and should not be exposed to high relative humidities for long periods. Although this impairs their thermal insulation effect to a lesser extent than one might expect, the increase in weight can lead to the fibres becoming compacted in vertical cavities and thus leaving parts of the cavity without insulation, which can produce considerable thermal bridge effects. Compacting the material during installation can counteract this effect. The fire behaviour of such materials should also be looked at carefully.

Organic fibre materials can achieve the minimum fire protection class required (B 2) by adding flame retardants (salts, borates). For further details of thermal insulating materials see the section "Thermal insulation" [1, 59].

**Thermal bridges**

Thermal bridges are localised points on building components at which the heat flow away from their inner surfaces is greater than adjacent areas and hence their temperature is lower. In principle, we can distinguish between material and geometric thermal bridges, but in practice various complex combinations of both occur.

A material thermal bridge, e.g. support/space, is caused by the different thermal conductivities of adjoining materials. Geometric thermal bridges, e.g. corner of external wall, are caused by a greater surface area around the heat loss (cold surface) than at the corresponding area of heat gain (warm surface), which on the whole creates a type of cooling surface effect. Two-dimensional heat flow/temperature fields, e.g. external wall corner over height of room, are designated linear thermal bridges. Point-like thermal bridges with three-dimensional fields occur, for example, at the corners of rooms or at pipe penetrations. They are a local effect and are usually ignored in energy flow analyses owing to their small proportion in terms of the surface area of the building envelope. In contrast, linear thermal bridges must be analysed under the new thermal performance requirements because their proportion of the area of the heat-exchanging envelope is no longer negligible; they add considerably to the total transmission heat losses of a building.

Thermal bridge analyses, thermal bridge catalogues

The effects of thermal bridges can now be determined theoretically using multi-dimensional numerical methods. Such analyses also form the basis for thermal bridge catalogues [41, 42, 43, 56]. The key variables in such calculations are the minimum interior surface temperature and the increased heat flow compared to the non-disrupted area. A temperature factor $f_{Rsi}$ (dimensionless surface temperature) is determined from this for the point of minimum surface temperature; this gives the surface temperature value for any temperature boundary conditions ($\theta_i$, $\theta_e$) under constant conditions:

$$f_{Rsi} = \frac{\theta_{si} - \theta_e}{\theta_i - \theta_e}$$

The increased heat loss compared to the non-disrupted area is taken into account by a length-related thermal transmittance coefficient $\Psi$ for linear thermal bridges thus:

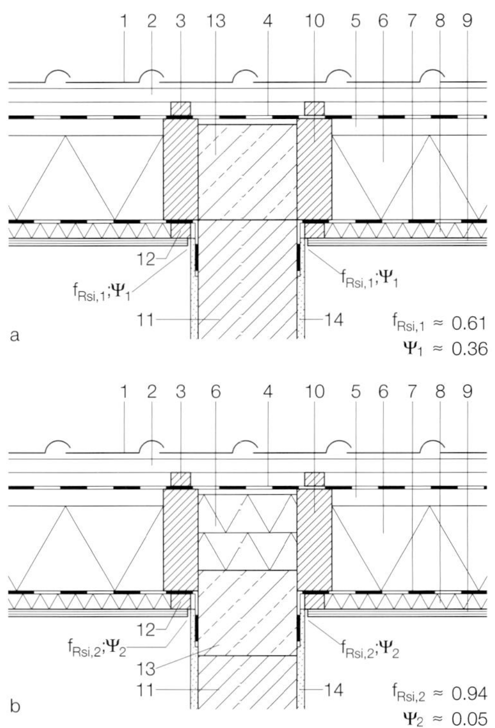


| No. | Material | ρ [kg/m³] | d [cm] | λ [W/(m K)] |
|---|---|---|---|---|
| 1 | Clay roof tiles | – | – | – |
| 2 | Tiling battens | – | – | – |
| 3 | Counter battens | – | – | – |
| 4 | Roofing felt | – | – | – |
| 5 | Ventilated air layer | – | 4 | – |
| 6 | Thermal insulation | – | 20 | 0.04 |
| 7 | Vapour barrier | – | – | – |
| 8 | Thermal insulation | – | 4 | 0.04 |
| 9 | Plasterboard | 1100 | 1.25 | 0.21 |
| 10 | Rafters (b = 80 mm) | 600 | 24 | 0.13 |
| 11 | Masonry | 1400 | 24 | 0.70 |
| 12 | Edge framing | 600 | 4 | 0.13 |
| 13 | Reinforced concrete | 2400 | 24 | 2.10 |
| 14 | Gypsum plaster | 1200 | 1.5 | 0.35 |

2.2.1.14 Thermal bridge effect in the region of an intersecting partition, with and without thermal insulation over top of masonry [63]

$$\Phi_{T,l} = (U \cdot A + \Psi \cdot l) \cdot (\theta_i - \theta_e)$$

and by a point-related thermal transmittance coefficient $\chi$ for point-like thermal bridges:

$$\Phi_{T,p} = (U \cdot A + \chi) \cdot (\theta_i - \theta_e)$$

The thermal transmittance coefficients $\Psi$ [W/mK] and $\chi$ [W/K] are also known as thermal bridge loss coefficients. Further detailed information on thermal bridge analyses can be found in DIN EN ISO 10211 parts 1 and 2. Figure 2.2.1.14 shows a practical example of the effect of a thermal bridge on a pitched roof. Here, a partition penetrates the underside of the roof construction; (a) shows a detail without and (b) with additional insulation over the top of the masonry. Taking $f_{Rsi}$ = 0.61 and assuming temperatures of $\theta_i$ = 20°C and $\theta_e$ = 0°C, without the additional insulation the surface temperature is approx. 12°C at the critical point. With an interior humidity of 50% this would lead to mould growth, which is unacceptable according to today's standards. And with $\Psi$ = 0.36 the additional thermal bridge losses, related to the roof, are correspondingly high. Thermal insulation on top of the masonry similar to that used in the roof cross-section overcomes these problems.

Typical solutions

The new thermal performance requirements take account of thermal bridge effects and measures to limit them. In order to avoid mould growth and higher transmission heat losses, suitable construction details for potential thermal bridges are given in DIN 4108 supplement 2. The application of the typical solutions given in that publication is, for example, a condition for the simplified analysis of residential buildings according to the Energy Economy Act.

**Airtightness**

The building envelope transmits heat and must therefore be sealed airtight around joints, junctions, penetrations, and likewise around composite or layered planar components, e.g. roofs. Air flows through components must be prevented. This is necessary to minimise uncontrolled ventilation heat losses and promotes an essentially definable guarantee for the minimum air change rate necessary for hygienic conditions. The importance of airtightness of the building envelope becomes clear when we realise that with modern levels of thermal insulation roughly half the heating energy is employed to cover ventilation losses. The airtightness of the building envelope achievable in practical terms should therefore be checked by measurements.

Measurements

The blower-door method (see DIN EN 13829) that should be used here determines the leakage flows present for a specified pressure difference of 50 Pa between the interior of the building and its surroundings.
The $n_{50}$-value (air change rate for $\Delta p$ = 50 pa) is determined. Conditions for energy analyses of airtightness and the operation of ventilation systems are derived from this variable (see, for example, DIN 4108 parts 6 and 7, Energy Economy Act).

Practical implementation

The best possible airtightness is achieved by minimising penetrations at the planning stage and through comprehensive specifications concerning workmanship. Careful workmanship and supervision are called for so that the inevitable problem areas are kept to an absolute minimum in practice. If necessary, service

| | Component | | Thermal resistance R m²K/W |
|---|---|---|---|
| 1 | External walls; walls to occupied rooms adjacent to roof spaces, drive-through passages, open corridors, garages, soil | | 1.2 |
| 2 | Walls between different premises; residential party walls | | 0.07 |
| 3 | Walls to staircases | to staircases with essentially lower interior temperatures (e.g. indirectly heated staircases); interior temperature $\theta_i \le 10$ °C, but staircases at least not affected by frost | 0.25 |
| 4 | | to staircases with interior temperatures $\theta_i > 10$ °C (e.g. in office buildings, business premises, teaching establishments, hotels, restaurants and residential buildings) | 0.07 |
| 5 | Floors separating apartments or working areas with different occupiers; floors below rooms between insulated pitched roof surfaces and dwarf walls of occupied roof spaces | generally | 0.35 |
| 6 | | in centrally heated office buildings | 0.17 |
| 7 | Floors to occupied rooms without basements below | directly adjacent to the soil for room depth ≤ 5 m | 0.90 |
| 8 | | over a non-ventilated cavity adjacent to the soil | |
| 9 | Floors below unused roof spaces; floors below crawl or even narrower spaces; floors below ventilated rooms between pitched roof surfaces and dwarf walls to occupied roof spaces, thermally insulated pitched roof surfaces | | |
| 10 | Floors over basements; floors adjacent to enclosed, unheated corridors or similar. | | |
| 11 11.1 | Floors (also roofs) separating occupied rooms from the outside air | downwards, adjacent to garages (also heated), drive-through passages (also with doors) and ventilated crawl spaces [1)] | 1.75 |
| 11.2 | | upwards, e.g. roofs to DIN 18530, roofs and floors below terraces; upside-down roofs<br><br>The U-value of an upside-down roof is to be-calculated according to DIN 4108 part 2 using corrective factors ΔU. | 1.2 |

1) Increased thermal resistance owing to cold floor.

2.2.1.15 Min. values for thermal resistance of components to DIN 4108 part 2 [7]

installation levels should be provided to avoid subsequent installations (e.g. power sockets) disturbing the airtightness layers. DIN 4108 part 7 contains comprehensive details for achieving an airtight building envelope. These typical details can be taken as a reference solution for airtight construction to satisfy thermal insulation and moisture control requirements. Examples related to pitched roofs can be found in the chapters "Construction details" and "Layers and materials".

**Requirements for thermal performance**

The thermal performance requirements, according to the current status of the statutory instruments, can be divided into winter and summer specifications, with minimum requirements plus energy-saving requirements to limit energy consumption. The figures for heated roof spaces and pitched roofs are summarised in table 2.2.1.15, updated to February 2002.

Thermal performance in winter

The purpose of quoting minimum requirements for thermal performance in winter (to DIN 4108 part 2) is to create the basis for hygienic living conditions, to protect against damaging moisture effects in building components and to provide minimum standards for saving energy.

Minimum requirements for non-transparent components

- Monolithic components, m' ≥ 100 kg/m²

As a distinguishing criterion, the mass per unit area m' is calculated from the total mass of the component related to its area. The current minimum requirements for the thermal resistance of such components is given in table 2.2.1.15. The stipulations of DIN EN ISO 6946 (see above) apply for calculating the thermal resistance, including air layers.

- Lightweight components, m' < 100 kg/m²

A minimum thermal resistance R = 1.75 m²K/W should be adhered to for lightweight external walls, ceilings below roof spaces not fitted out, and roofs. The enhanced requirement applies only to the infill sheets of frame structures; but in these cases the complete component must also comply with an average figure of R = 1.00 m²K/W.

- Buildings with low interior temperatures ($12°C \le q_i < 19°C$)

The requirements given in table 2.2.1.15 apply here as well, except components according to line 1. For these the minimum value should be R = 0.55 m²K/W.

Fundamental boundary conditions must be observed when determining thermal perfomance.

Minimum requirements for thermal bridges

- To avoid mould growth:

The requirements are deemed to have been satisfied for

a) corners of external components with the same construction when the components satisfy the requirements for minimum thermal insulation according to table 2.2.1.15,

b) thermal bridges constructed according to DIN 4108 supplement 2.

In all other cases it must be proved that the surface temperature or temperature factor $f_{Rsi} = (\theta_{si} - \theta_e)/(\theta_i - \theta_e)$ satisfies the condition

$$\theta_{si} \ge 12.6°C \text{ or } f_{Rsi} \ge 0.7$$

at the most unfavourable position.

Boundary conditions for analysis: see DIN 4108 part 2.

This means that a relative humidity $\phi_{si}$ = 80% is not exceeded at the most unfavourable point on the interior surface, which according to the current level of knowledge is assumed to be adequate to prevent mould growth (see also DIN EN ISO 13788).

Proving the absence of condensation on a surface is hence no longer a criterion. Small amounts of condensation are tolerated for short periods.

- To avoid increased transmission heat losses:

Owing to their limited size in comparison with the building envelope, three-dimensional thermal bridges can be ignored in this context. However, the increased transmission heat losses through a two-dimensional thermal bridge must be investigated for each component (method according to DIN EN ISO 10211 part 2, see above) or a global approach employed for the entire building (see preliminary edition of DIN 4108 part 6 or Energy Economy Act). Thermal bridge details to DIN 4108 supplement 2 are deemed to be adequately insulated. Components projecting into the surroundings, or walls with l > 0.5 W/mK that project into the non-insulated roof area, are not permitted.

Requirements for airtightness

For the reasons outlined above, requirements have been expressly formulated in DIN 4108 part 2 to deal with the problem of airtightness. These concern joint permeabilities derived from measurements for the joints between components and joint permeability coefficients for windows and external doors. Composite components or layers of components must be airtight, which has a direct significance for roof construction.

Thermal performance in summer

The earlier recommendations concerning thermal performance in summer have become requirements in the new DIN 4108 part 2 or rather the current draft thereof (DIN 4108-2/A1). The aim, within the scope of energy-saving efforts, is to exploit the constructional options to limit the build-up of heat in the interior during the summer and thus avoid, as far as possible, the use of energy for air-conditioning and cooling systems. It is assumed that if the new constructional requirements are adhered to, acceptable interior temperatures will be exceeded only rarely. This means that the primary influencing parameters per room, i.e.

- solar heat gains via the windows,
- mass of interior components,
- possible ventilation, in particular night-time ventilation,

need to be taken into account right from the planning stage. In addition, it should be noted that building components with dark colours and, in particular, windows on several facades have a negative effect.
Contrary to the considerations concerning window sizes with respect to thermal performance in summer, it should be noted that

- smaller windows reduce the desired level of daylight in the interior, and
- the desired passive solar gains in winter through generously sized south-facing windows can cause problems in the summer (sun-blinds).

The simplified method according to the draft of DIN 4108-2/A1, considered to be adequate in normal cases, e.g. residential buildings, includes a solar gain index (related to the glazing and the room), which may not exceed a maximum permissible value (depending on climate and constructional parameters).
Before performing the analysis a check should also be carried out to see whether an analysis is actually required. An analysis is not necessary when the values given in table 2.2.1.16 are not exceeded for window area proportions per elevation $f = A_W/A_{Facade}$ (also roof surfaces). Further, no analysis is required for detached and semidetached homes whose windows face east, south or west and have permanent external sun-blinds with a reduction factor $F_C \leq 0.3$ (e.g. roller/folding shutters). In all other cases proceed as follows:

| | Inclination of window to horizontal | Orientation of window and facade | Window area proportion [1] f % |
|---|---|---|---|
| 1 | 60–90° | south, east, west | 20 |
| 2 | | north-east, north north-west | 30 |
| 3 | 0–60° | all orientations | 15 |

[1] The area proportion f is the ratio of the window area (clear structural opening) to the area of the facade (overall dimensions) in the compass direction under consideration.

Note: The specified window area proportions are based on the climatic data of climate region B according to the preliminary edition of DIN 4108 part 6.

2.2.1.16 Permissible values of window area proportions below which an analysis of summer thermal performance is unnecessary [7]

Determining the solar gain index
The solar gain index S should be calculated for the room under investigation according to the draft of DIN 4108-2/A1 using the equation:

$$S = \frac{\Sigma (A_W \cdot g_{total})}{A_g}$$

where
$A_W$ = window area (clear structural opening)
$g_{total}$ = total energy transmittance of glazing including sun-blinds
$A_G$ = net plan floor area of room

The figures for all the windows in the room are added together. The simplified total energy transmittance $g_{total}$ is determined as follows:

$$g_{total} = g \cdot F_C$$

where
g = total energy transmittance of glazing
$F_C$ = reduction factor for permanent sun-blinds

Typical figures for the g-values of transparent components, which are normally intended for perpendicular incident radiation, can be found in DIN 4108 part 6; $F_C$-values for sun-blinds are given in DIN 4108 part 2. In the case of canopies, loggias and awnings it must be ensured, through appropriate shading, that no direct sunlight can strike the window.

Requirements
The calculated solar gain index S may not exceed a maximum value $S_{max}$

$$S \leq S_{max}$$

The maximum value is made up of a constant basic value and certain factors:

$$S_{max} = S_o + \Sigma\Delta S_x$$

where
$S_{max}$ = maximum permissible solar gain index
$S_o$ = basic value for building; $S_o = 0.12$
$\Delta S_x$ factors for climate region (A, B, C), type of construction, night-time ventilation (if applicable), sun-blind, inclination of window, north orientation.
The factors for the individual parameters for determining the permissible maximum solar gain index are specified according to a bonus system in the draft of DIN 4108-2/A1.
The assessment of summer thermal performance makes use of three climate regions according to table 2.2.1.17. The given room limit temperatures should be exceeded only marginally and reasonably (approx. 10%) when keeping to $S_{max}$. Maximum values for average monthly outside temperatures according to

| Summer climate region | Features of region | Max. interior temperature °C | Max. average monthly outside temp. θ [°C] |
|---|---|---|---|
| A | cool summers | 25 | $\theta \leq 16.5$ |
| B | moderate s. | 26 | $16.5 < \theta < 18$ |
| C | hot summers | 27 | $\theta \geq 18$ |

2.2.1.17 Summer climate regions with associated features [33]

DIN 4108 part 6, appendix A, should be used to determine the respective climate region for the building's location.

**Energy-saving thermal insulation – Energy Economy Act**

German legislation for energy-saving thermal insulation to the building envelope as formulated in the 1995 Thermal Insulation Act has now been incorporated into a building-related overall energy concept. Since February 2002 the Energy Economy Act (*Energieeinsparverordnung*, published in: Federal Gazette, part 1, No. 59, dated 21 Nov 2001, p. 3085), which is a combination of the Thermal Insulation and Heating Systems Acts, regulates the entire energy requirements of a building, covering thermal losses via the building envelope (thermal insulation requirements) and the operation of heating systems, hot water provision and, if applicable, mechanical ventilation systems (systems requirements).
The aim of the new Act – besides a further reduction in carbon dioxide emissions and the stimulation of increased use of renewable energy sources – is to cut the heating energy requirement by approx. 30% compared to the values achieved by the 1995 Act. There is sufficient flexibility for energy-saving measures to focus on either providing a high-level of thermal insulation or highly efficient HVAC systems. A minimum level of thermal insulation (roughly the same as the 1995 Act) must be maintained. The Energy Economy Act has therefore deliberately been turned into a planning instrument that calls for coordination between construction and services at an early stage of planning [40].

Parameters affecting the construction
The following parameters influence the heating energy requirement and are taken into account using corresponding variables:

- Building form (planning)

Compact forms with low A/V ratios have a positive effect on the energy consumption.

- Thermal insulation to building envelope

The U-values of all envelope components determine the total transmission heat loss – the better the thermal insulation of a component, the more significant the thermal bridge effect is.

- Air exchange between interior and exterior

Limited by extensive airtightness of building envelope and defined permeability of functional joints, e.g. openable windows.
Variables:
joint permeability coefficient a of windows and glazed doors (classification according to DIN EN 12207 part 1, depending on height of building);
air change rate n [$h^{-1}$];
The better the thermal insulation of the envelope component, the more significant is the proportion of ventilation heat losses.

- Heat capacity

Significant in the case of intermittent heating (e.g. night-time shutdown) and when using internal heat sources and solar energy gains.
Variable: effective heat capacity $C_{eff}$ (see DIN 4108 part 6 for calculation)

- Solar heat gains

Constructional (passive) use of solar irradiation to reduce the heating energy requirement.
Absorption on opaque components
Variable: solar absorption index $\alpha_s$ – effect not very significant (depends on colour);
Radiation transmission through glazing
Variable: total energy transmittance g – more marked effect

Parameters affecting HVAC systems
HVAC is the abbreviation for heating, (mechanical) ventilation and air conditioning, and in this context is also taken to include provision of hot water. The energy consumption of these systems is characterised by a series of losses incurred on the way from the heat producer (e.g. boiler) to the place where the useful heat is required (e.g. radiator). These losses have to be balanced against all the energy required to run the system (final energy requirement), including all ancillary energy needs (e.g. electricity for pumps). The energy required to extract the raw materials, convert them into an energy medium, and supply that medium up to the point where it is fed into the building (primary energy requirement) must also be taken into account.
The following variables are employed to define the total energy chain:

- (Operation-related) plant cost index e

This takes into account the plant's efficiency (losses, degrees of efficiency, ancillary energy needs) for each HVAC system.

- Primary energy evaluation factors $f_p$

These identify the primary energy value of different energy media; they are given in table 2.2.1.18, which is based on the preliminary edition of DIN 4701 part 10.

- (Primary energy-related) total plant cost index $e_p$

This takes into account all plant losses for HVAC systems, as well as the cost of supplying the primary energy (basically the product of e and $f_p$, determined according to the preliminary edition of DIN 4701 part 10).

Terminology

- Consumption

The amount of heat or energy actually consumed under real usage conditions.

- Requirement

Amount of heat or energy calculated theoretically for specified boundary conditions.

- Space heating requirement

Identifies the amount of heat to be supplied to a room or heated area of a building in order to maintain the interior temperature (from a balance of the losses/gains in the room).

- Heating energy requirement

Identifies the amount of energy to be supplied to the heating system to cover the space heating requirement and the losses of the heating system (included in the plant cost index).

- Final energy requirement

Identifies the amount of energy to be supplied to all the systems to cover the space heating energy requirement and the hot water energy requirement, including all plant losses and ancillary energy requirements (from the point where the energy medium is fed into the building).

- Primary energy requirement

Identifies the amount of energy required to cover the final energy requirement plus all further amounts of energy in upstream process chains for providing the energy medium (from extraction of raw materials to provision of energy medium at building).

Symbols, definitions of main variables
The most important symbols and definitions used in the Energy Economy Act are summarised in table 2.2.1.19. [40] This table is basically related to the simplified method (heating period audit method) for residential buildings as permitted by the Energy Economy Act.

| Energy medium | | $f_P$ |
|---|---|---|
| Fuel[1] | heating oil EL | 1.1 |
| | natural gas H | 1.1 |
| | LPG | 1.1 |
| | coal | 1.1 |
| | lignite | 1.2 |
| Local/district heat. from co-generation plant[2] | fossil fuel | 0.7 |
| | renewable fuel | 0 |
| Local/district heat. from heating plant | fossil fuel | 1.3 |
| | renewable fuel | 0.1 |
| Electricity[3] | mixed sources | 3.0 |

[1] Reference variable: lower calorific value (LCF) $H_u$
[2] Figures are typical for average local/district heating from co-generation)
[3] 2.0 when using thermal storage heaters

2.2.1.18 Primary energy evaluation factors

| Symbol | Unit | Designation | Notes |
|---|---|---|---|
| A | $m^2$ | Heat-transmitting enclosing surface area of building | external dimensions (building-system boundary) |
| $V_e$ | $m^3$ | Heated volume of building | governed by A |
| $A/V_e$ | $m^{-1}$ | Ratio, variable for building form | ref. variable for requirements |
| $A_N$ | $m^2$ | Usable floor space of building | ref. variable for requirements/ proof: $A_N = 0.32 \cdot V_e$ |
| V | $m^3$ | Heated (permissible) volume of air | $V = 0.76\ V_e$ (buildings up to 3 full storeys) $V = 0.80\ V_e$ (all other cases) |
| $Q'_p$ | kWh/m³a | Annual primary energy requirement (related to $V_e$) | for non-residential bldgs |
| $Q''_p$ | kWh/m²a | Annual primary energy requirement (related to $A_N$) | $Q''_p = (Q''_h + Q''_w) \cdot e_p$ (for res. bldgs) |
| $Q''_h$ | kWh/m²a | Anual energy requirement (related to usable floor space) | $Q''_h = Q_h/A_N$ |
| $Q''_W$ | kWh/m²) | Hot water heating requirement (related to usable floor space) | for residential bldgs: $Q''_W = 12.5$ kWh/m²a |
| $e_p$ | – | Total plant cost index | related to primary energy |
| $Q_h$ | kWh/a | Annual heating requirement | see prelim. ed. DIN 4108 pt 6 |
| $H_T$ | W/K | Specific transmission heat loss | $H_T = \Sigma (F_{x,i} \cdot U_i \cdot A_i) + \Delta U_{WB} \cdot A$ |
| $F_{x,i}$ | – | Temperature correction factor | per component |
| $\Delta U_{WB}$ | W/m²K | Thermal bridge allowance | related to total enclosing surface area |
| $H_V$ | W/K | Specific ventilation heat loss | $H_V = 0.34 \cdot n \cdot V$ |
| n | $h^{-1}$ | Air change rate with natural ventilation | $n = 0.7\ h^{-1}$ without proof $n = 0.6\ h^{-1}$ with proof of $n_{50} \leq 3\ h^{-1}$ |
| $H'_T$ | W/m²K | Specific, area-related transmission heat loss | related to heat-transmitting enclosing surface area |
| $Q_S$ | kWh/a | Solar heat gains | see prelim. ed. DIN 4108 pt 6 |
| $Q_i$ | kWh/a | Internal heat gains | see prelim. ed. DIN 4108 pt 6 |

2.2.1.19 Symbols and units for analyses required by the Energy Economy Act (simplified method)

| Application | Requirements/analyses/references | |
|---|---|---|
| 1. (New) building to be erected | | |
| 1.1 Generally in new buildings | Airtightness of building envelope<br>Guarantee of minimum air change rate | EnEV<br>DIN 4108 pt 7 |
| | Maintenance of minimum thermal performance | DIN 4108 pt 2 |
| | Minimisation of thermal bridge effects and consideration in transmission heat loss | EnEV<br>DIN 4108 pt 6<br>DIN 4108 supp. 2 |
| 1.2 Residential buildings with normal interior temperatures (≥ 19°C) | Usable area-related primary energy requirement | EnEV<br>DIN 4108 pt 6 |
| | Envelope area-related transmission heat loss | DIN 4108 pt 6 |
| | Summer thermal performance (if window area proportion > 30%) | DIN 4108 pt 2 |
| 1.3 Non-residential buildings with normal interior temperatures (≥ 19°C) | Volume-related primary energy requirement | EnEV<br>DIN 4108 pt 6 |
| | Envelope area-related transmission heat loss | DIN 4108 pt 6 |
| | Summer thermal performance (if window area proportion > 30%) | DIN 4108 pt 2 |
| 1.4 Buildings with low interior temperatures (> 12°C, < 19°C) | Envelope area-related transmission heat loss | EnEV<br>DIN 4108 pt 6 |
| 1.5 Buildings with heated volumes ≤ 100 m³ | Max. U-values of external components to table 2.2.1.22 | EnEV |
| 2. Existing buildings and plants | | |
| 2.1 Modifications to ext. components (at least 20% of component area) | Max. U-value of component (see table 2.2.1.22)<br>Alternative:<br>Requirements/Loss parameters for total building after modifications ≤ 1.4 x new building requirements | EnEV |
| 2.2 Extension of heated volume of building by at least 30 m³ | Requirements for extension as for new building | EnEV |
| 2.3 Retrofitting requirements | Replacement of old boiler<br>Insulation of hot water pipes and fittings<br>Insulation of floor over topmost storey | EnEV |
| 3. Heating and hot water systems | Please refer to EnEV for details of requirements regarding commissioning of heating boilers, distribution systems, hot water systems, control systems, insulation of pipes etc. | |

2.2.1.20 Applications and requirements/analyses according to the Energy Economy Act (EnEV), with cross-references

| $A/V_e$ ratio | Annual primary energy requirement $Q''_p$ [kWh/m²a] related to usable area of building | | $Q'_p$ [kWh/m³a] related to heated volume of building | Specific transmission heat loss $H_T'$ related to heat-transmitting enclosing surface area $H_T'$ [W/m²K] | |
|---|---|---|---|---|---|
| | Residential buildings except those in column 3 | Residential buildings with hot water provision mainly provided by electricity | other buildings | Non-residential buildings with a window area proportion ≤ 30% and residential buildings | Non-residential buildings with a window area proportion > 30% |
| 1 | 2 | 3 | 4 | 5 | 6 |
| ≤ 0.2 | $66.00 + 2600/(100 + A_N)$ | 88.00 | 14.72 | 1.05 | 1.55 |
| 0.3 | $73.53 + 2600/(100 + A_N)$ | 95.53 | 17.13 | 0.80 | 1.15 |
| 0.4 | $81.06 + 2600/(100 + A_N)$ | 103.06 | 19.54 | 0.68 | 0.95 |
| 0.5 | $88.58 + 2600/100 + A_N)$ | 110.58 | 21.95 | 0.60 | 0.83 |
| 0.6 | $96.11 + 2600/(100 + A_N)$ | 118.11 | 24.36 | 0.55 | 0.75 |
| 0.7 | $103.64 + 2600/(100 + A_N)$ | 125.64 | 26.77 | 0.51 | 0.69 |
| 0.8 | $111.17 + 2600/(100 + A_N)$ | 133.17 | 29.18 | 0.49 | 0.65 |
| 0.9 | $118.70 + 2600/100 + A_N)$ | 140.70 | 31.59 | 0.47 | 0.62 |
| 1 | $126.23 + 2600/(100 + A_N)$ | 148.23 | 34.00 | 0.45 | 0.59 |
| ≥ 1.05 | $130.00 + 2600/(100 + A_N)$ | 152.00 | 35.21 | 0.44 | 0.58 |

2.2.1.21 Requirements (max. values) according to the Energy Economy Act for the annual primary energy requirement and the specific transmission heat loss related to the $A/V_e$ ratio

Note: There are differences between the symbols used in the Energy Economy Act and the preliminary edition of DIN 4108 part 6, on which the Act is actually based. The usable floor area of the building defined in relation to the volume should not be confused with the floor space of living quarters either.

Applications, requirements
Table 2.2.1.20 shows the relationships between main requirements/analyses and applications according to the Energy Economy Act. Table 2.2.1.21 shows the maximum permissible values for annual primary energy requirement in relation to $A/V_e$ ratio and the specific transmission heat losses related to the heat-transmitting enclosing surface area according to the Energy Economy Act.
If modifications are carried out on external components around heated interiors which constitute ≥ 20% per surface area of the component, or for external walls and external windows (including rooflights) ≥ 20% per orientation of the component, the Energy Economy Act specifies certain maximum permissible U-values for the modified or replaced component. Modifications to pitched roof surfaces or affecting the heated roof space include:

- renewal of outer components (roof covering, cladding, roof decking),
- addition or renewal of inner lining,
- installation of thermal insulation,
- addition of thermal insulation or lining to walls around unheated roof spaces or to external gable walls,
- addition or renewal of roof lights,
- replacement of glazing.

In these cases the maximum U-values given in table 2.2.1.22 must be adhered to.

Analyses according to Energy Economy Act
Audit-type methods of calculation should be used to analyse the requirements. These are based on DIN EN 832 and, to meet national requirements (boundary conditions, simplifications), are implemented using the preliminary edition of DIN 4108 part 6 in Germany.
The latter standard specifies two methods for determining the annual space heating requirement: a detailed approach – the monthly audit method – with detailed analysis options, and a simplified approach – the period audit method (also known as the heating period audit method) – with global assumptions and omissions for certain applications. The variables required for plant should be determined according to the preliminary edition of DIN 4701 part 10. The annual primary energy requirement of a building $Q_p$ – the critical variable in the Energy Economy Act – is calculated from the annual space heating requirement $Q_h$, the annual hot water heating requirement $Q_W$ and the primary energy-related (total) plant cost index $e_p$ from the following equation:

| Component modified, replaced or installed for the first time | $U_{max}$ [W/m²K] normal interior temperature | low interior temperature |
|---|---|---|
| external wall | 0.35 or 0.45 | 0.75 |
| window in plane of roof surface | 1.7 | 2.8 |
| glazing | 1.5 | – |
| inclined roof surface*) | 0.30 | 0.40 |
| wall to unheated room | 0.40 or 0.50 | – |

*) The requirement is deemed to be satisfied for retrofitted insulation between the rafters when the maximum possible insulation thickness is installed (available space, justifiable cost).

2.2.1.22 Max. U-values for external components in the case of modifications to existing buildings according to the Energy Economy Act (components affecting the roof)

$$Q_p = (Q_h + Q_W) \cdot e_p$$

The inclusion of $Q_W$ is only relevant for residential buildings and a global figure is used. In certain circumstances the annual space heating requirement $Q_h$ required in his calculation can, alternatively, be calculated using one of the aforementioned methods, which are briefly explained below.

• Monthly audit method
The detailed monthly audit method according to the preliminary edition of DIN 4108 part 6 is basically regarded as a method of determining $Q_h$ for planned residential and non-residential buildings with normal interior temperatures. This method allows a number of influencing variables to be taken into account in detail, e.g. glass extensions, transparent thermal insulation, solar absorption, unheated periods, individual thermal bridge effects, heat storage effects, usability of heat gains, panel radiators, mechanical ventilation, etc. The basic audit equation is:

$$Q_h = Q_l - \eta \cdot Q_g$$

where
$\eta$ = degree of utilisation
l = losses
g = gains

• Evaluation of thermal bridges
Thermal bridge effects in buildings with normal and low interior temperatures are included in the specific transmission heat loss $H_T$ by way of a thermal bridge allowance as follows:

$$H_T = \sum_i (F_{x,i} \cdot U_i \cdot A_i) + \Delta U_{WB} \cdot A$$

The thermal bridge allowance $\Delta U_{WB}$ can be determined using one of three options:
a) as a global allowance for the entire surface area of the building envelope without analysing thermal bridge effects in detail,
$\Delta U_{WB} = 0.10$ W/m²K
b) as a reduced global allowance for the entire surface area of the building envelope when using the typical details given in DIN 4108 supplement 2,
$\Delta U_{WB} = 0.05$ W/m²K
c) through detailed individual analyses using $\Psi$-values.

This creates an incentive for high-quality detailing.

• Evaluation of airtightness
The airtightness of the building envelope manifests itself in the ventilation heat losses. However, besides the defined air permeabilities, e.g. at windows, uncontrollable infiltration air changes are impossible to exclude completely in practice. The specific ventilation heat losses are calculated according to the equation:

$$H_V = 0.34 \cdot n \cdot V$$

The Energy Economy Act specifies conditions for assuming a global air change rate, based on the requirements for airtightness introduced by the building authorities in DIN 4108 part 2 and its cross-references to DIN 4108 part 7. These are:
a) $n = 0.7\ h^{-1}$ for natural ventilation without measurements,
b) $n = 0.6\ h^{-1}$ for natural ventilation with measurements that prove the figure of $n_{50} \leq 3\ h^{-1}$ is complied with,
c) proof that the figure of $n_{50} \leq 1.5\ h^{-1}$ is complied with in every case of mechanical ventilation; the assumed air change rates in this case are determined by the plant in use. Here again, details and systems that take full account of energy requirements are rewarded.

• Period audit method (simplified method)
The simplified method may be used only for residential buildings with natural ventilation and a window area proportion ≤ 30%. The similar audit approach for determining $Q_p$ is carried out once for the heating period with some global assumptions and hence is valid as proof of the annual primary energy requirement. The hot water heating requirement $Q_W$ and the plant cost index $e_p$ should be calculated as shown above. Losses and gains are again balanced, but in a simplified form, to determine the annual space heating requirement $Q_h$.

The equation for specific transmission heat loss

$$H_T = \sum_i F_{x,i} \cdot U_i \cdot A_i + 0.05 \cdot A$$

uses a global thermal bridge allowance of 0.05 W/m²K for the entire area of the building envelope A. The thermal bridge details given in DIN 4108 supplement 2 must be employed. The specific ventilation heat loss, depending on the quality of airtightness, is calculated according to the following equation:

$$H_V = 0.34 \cdot n \cdot V$$

$$= 0.19 \cdot V_e \quad \text{(without measurements, } n = 0.7\ h^{-1}\text{)}$$
$$= 0.163 \cdot V_e \quad \text{(with measurements, } n = 0.6\ h^{-1}\text{)}$$

Here, the volume of air to be taken into account is assumed to be constant at $V = 0.8V_e$. Solar gains via the windows are taken into account with a global figure assuming constant solar irradiation per orientation over the entire heating period (see DIN 4108 part 6). A global figure is also used for internal gains: $Q_i = 22\ A_N$. For further details plus requirements to be met by HVAC systems, the reader should consult the Energy Economy Act in conjunction with the preliminary editions of DIN 4108 part 6 and 4701 part 10.

Energy requirement certificate
An energy requirement certificate should be drawn up to provide details of analyses and parameters and hence the quality of the building in terms of energy usage. The nature and content of this certificate are currently under discussion.

Workmanship
As will be shown later in more detail in the chapter "Design", thermal insulation to a pitched roof can be installed
- over the rafters,
- between the rafters, or
- beneath the rafters.

Combinations of these, e.g. for subsequent additional insulation, are also possible, provided they do not impair the functions of the existing roof layers. Furthermore, vapour barriers or wind breaks on the inside really must be installed without gaps, and the minimum cross-section of ventilation layers must be maintained.
The advantage of insulation above or beneath the rafters is that the minor thermal bridge effect of the rafter is practically eliminated. When retrofitting insulation below the rafters (without a vapour barrier on the inside), it should be ensured that – besides reducing the size of the roof space – if there is already a vapour barrier below the existing insulation between the rafters, the new thermal resistance of the internal insulation should not exceed approx. 20% of the total resistance. Otherwise, there is a risk of condensation or mould growth on the old vapour barrier.

## Climate-related moisture control

Climate-related moisture control includes scientifically based measures taken to help prevent critical moisture levels or moisture contents being reached within the cross-section of a building envelope component as a result of the natural climatic effects acting on both sides of the component. The critical climatic effects to which building envelope components are exposed are the humidity of the interior air on the inside and the natural humidity of the surrounding air plus rain on the outside. Equally important are the internal and external temperature gradients. Critical moisture levels are found when, for example,

- the relative humidity of the air adjacent a surface exceeds a certain limit,
- the dew point is reached and condensation water collects on or in non-sorptive materials within the component cross-section, or
- sorptive materials exhibit high moisture contents well above the equilibrium moisture content.

Such cases usually damage the materials or impair the insulating effect of thermal insulating materials. We know that proper moisture control is the prerequisite for good thermal performance. Climate-related moisture control also includes the phenomenon of capillarity during rainfall and the necessary subsequent release of moisture through evaporation. In the case of pitched roofs this concerns the water absorption of roof coverings, e.g. clay/concrete tiles, although other effects such as growth of algae or lichens, or the frost resistance of these materials are also involved here. The waterproofing of structures (components in contact with the soil, waterproof coverings to flat roofs/terraces etc.) is not considered to be part of climate-related moisture control. These aspects focus on permanent waterproofing in the direct presence of water. However, there are consequences here for climate-related moisture control in the case of sealed roof coverings, e.g. pitched sheet metal roofs.

**Basic terminology (definitions, symbols, parameters)**
A water molecule, with a diameter of ~ 0.28 nm, is relatively minute but possesses a high charge polarity (which causes the physical features of water). Moisture is water in its various aggregate and bonded conditions in a water-sorptive substance (e.g. air, building materials).
The most important variables, symbols and units of measurement are summarised in table 2.2.2.1; some of these have yet to be published in the latest standards. Please refer to DIN EN ISO 9346 for further definitions on the subject of mass transfer. Additional explanations of the scientific principles can be found in, for example, [39, 55].

**Moisture and moisture transport**
The complex processes involved in the transport of moisture through building components in practical situations and under natural conditions are due to the fact that moisture is transported in both vapour and liquid forms; the mechanisms are governed by different scientific laws and the building materials react differently, permitting either all phenomena simultaneously or preventing particular mechanisms. Simulation methods and practical computer programs, which are mentioned briefly at the end of this chapter, exist to deal with these processes realistically.
The fundamental moisture effects (in air and in solids) and the moisture transport assumptions employed in practice are summarised below for the simplified practical evaluation of moisture control issues.

Humidity of the air, dew point
- Partial pressure of water vapour

The atmosphere is a mixture of gases, one component of which is water vapour. Each component possesses its own partial pressure $p_i$, and the sum of all the partial pressures produces the total atmospheric pressure.
- Saturation water vapour pressure

At a certain temperature, water vapour is present in air in gaseous form only up to a certain maximum concentration. This temperature-dependent saturation state is characterised by the saturation water vapour pressure $p_{sat}$. The saturation pressure increases as the temperature rises. This dependence can be calculated using the following empirical formula given in DIN EN ISO 13788.

$$p_{sat} = 610.5 \cdot \exp[(A \cdot \theta)/(B + \theta)] \ [\text{Pa}]$$

when $\theta \geq 0°C$: $A = 17.26$, $B = 237.3$
when $\theta < 0°C$: $A = 21.87$, $B = 265.5$

The relationship is shown as a graph in figure 2.2.2.2 (see DIN EN ISO 13788 for tables).

| Symbol | Designation | Unit |
|---|---|---|
| D | Water vapour diffusion coefficient | m²/h |
| G | Water vapour diffusion flow | kg/h |
| $M_c$ | Quantity of condensation water per unit area (formerly: $m_{W,T}$) | kg/m² |
| $M_{ev}$ | Quantity of water evaporating per unit area (formerly: $m_{W,V}$) | kg/m² |
| W | Water vapour diffusion transmittance coefficient (formerly: Δ) | kg/m²hPa |
| $W_w$ | Water absorption coefficient (formerly: w) | kg/m²h^1/2 |
| Z | Water vapour diffusion resistance (formerly: 1/Δ) | m²hPa/kg |
| g | Water vapour diffusion flow rate (formerly: i) | kg/m²h |
| p | Partial pressure of water vapour | Pa |
| $p_{sat}$ | Saturation water vapour pressure | Pa |
| w | Mass of moisture content per unit volume | kg/m³ |
| u | Moisture content per unit mass (formerly: $u_m$) | kg/kg or % by weight |
| $s_d$ | Water vapour diffusion-equivalent air layer thickness | m |
| δ (Delta) | Water vapour permeability | kg/mhPa |
| μ (My) | Water vapour diffusion resistance factor | – |
| ν (Ny) | Humidity of air per unit volume | kg/m³ |
| ϕ (Phi) | Relative humidity of air (formerly: φ) | – or % rh |
| ψ (Psi) | Moisture content per unit volume (formerly: $u_v$) | m³/m³ or % by volume |

2.2.2.1 Symbols and units for moisture control parameters

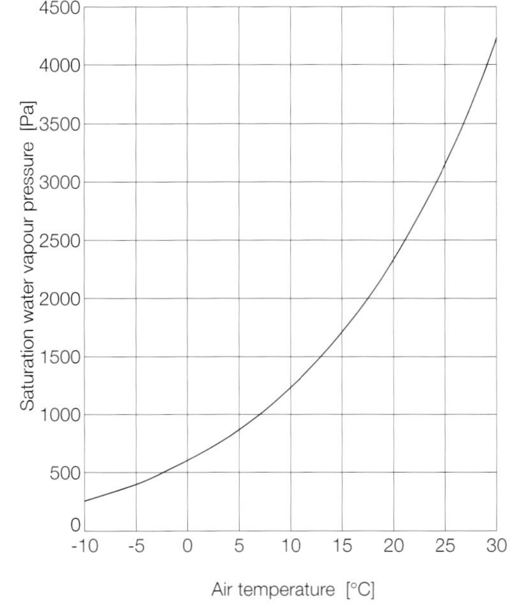


2.2.2.2 Saturation water vapour pressure in relation to air temperature

At higher temperatures $p_{sat}$ rises noticeably and at 100°C reaches the total atmospheric pressure. This is significant for moisture trapped below the waterproof layer of a roof, which in summer can heat up to 70-80°C (blisters), and for reverse diffusion inwards as the roof heats up in summer, making the integral moisture in roofing materials (e.g. timber decking, rafters) evaporate into the interior.

- Relative humidity of the air

The relative humidity is the ratio of the actual vapour pressure to the maximum possible saturation pressure at the current temperature:

$$\phi = \frac{p}{p_{sat}} [-] \quad \text{or} \quad \phi = \frac{p}{p_{sat}} \cdot 100\% \; [\% \text{ rh}]$$

The relative humidity is therefore itself dependent on temperature through $p_{sat}$ – for a constant actual vapour pressure – and increases as the temperature drops, or decreases as the temperature rises. This means that a higher relative humidity occurs only due to the lower temperature of, for example, a colder point on the inner surface of a component.

- Dew point temperature

The dew point temperature is the temperature at which the current vapour pressure becomes the saturation vapour pressure. It can be estimated from the saturation curve, calculated from the above equation or taken from DIN EN ISO 13788.

Moisture content, sorption

- Moisture storage

Water can be stored in building materials in different ways: by chemical reaction, by swelling or by sorption (physical accumulations on inner surfaces; reversible; adsorption, desorption). Sorption behaviour depends on the interaction between building material and water molecules, and on the pore structure. Accordingly, we can distinguish between hygroscopic substances (hydrophilic + fine pores + large inner surfaces; high sorption water content, e.g. timber, fine-pore mineral building materials) and non-hygroscopic substances (hydrophobic or hydrophilic with extremely small inner surfaces, coarse pores; very low sorption water content, e.g. clay tiles, most insulating materials).

- Sorption isotherms

As a characteristic function of the moisture storage capacity of a material, the sorption isotherms specify the equilibrium state between the ambient relative humidity and the concurrent water content of a material at a certain temperature (figure 2.2.2.3). Used as a surface finish, sorptive substances help to buffer moisture from severely fluctuating interior humidities, e.g. plaster, wood panelling. It is also important that the sorption moisture depends on the relative humidity of the air, and so wetting or drying processes, e.g. at the surface of a component, can only be triggered by temperature changes.

Water vapour diffusion

As a transport mechanism for the vapour phase, water vapour diffusion takes place as a result of vapour pressure differences. Figure 2.2.2.4 illustrates the principle of water vapour diffusion through building components or layers thereof.

The vapour pressures on both sides are determined by the respective relative humidity and saturation vapour pressure for the respective air temperature. We assume that the vapour pressure of the respective surrounding air also applies at the surface. Mass transfer effects can be ignored. The diffusion flow G or the diffusion flow rate g can be calculated from Fick's law of diffusion:

$$\frac{G}{A} = g = \delta \cdot \frac{\Delta p}{d}$$

From this we can derive the diffusion resistance $Z = d/\delta$ [$m^2$ h Pa/kg] and the diffusion coefficient $W = 1/Z$ [kg/$m^2$ h Pa]. The diffusion resistance index μ and the diffusion-equivalent air layer thickness $s_d$, derived from the above, are used for practical purposes.

- Water vapour diffusion resistance index (μ-value)

The μ-value of a material (see table 2.2.2.5) is defined as a ratio for simplicity. It specifies the diffusion resistance of a building material layer in relation to a layer of air of the same thickness and at the same temperature. With equal layer thicknesses this is equivalent to:

$$\mu = \frac{\delta_o}{\delta} \quad [-]$$

$\delta_o = 6.76 \times 10^{-7}$ kg/m h Pa for water vapour diffusion in air. The water vapour permeability δ of a material is determined by measurements according to DIN EN ISO 12572.

Therefore,
μ = 1 for air, and
μ > 1 for a building material.

- Water vapour diffusion-equivalent air layer thickness ($s_d$-value)

The $s_d$-value is a parameter used in practice for the diffusion resistance of a layer of a material and is defined by the μ-value and layer thickness d as:

$$s_d = \mu \cdot d \; [m]$$

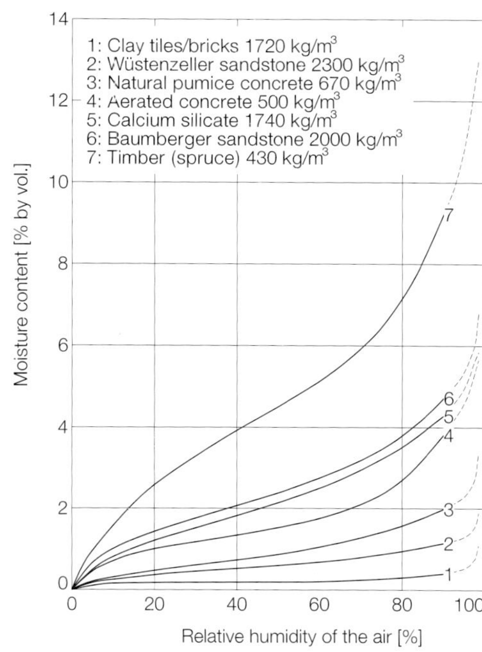


2.2.2.3 Sorption isotherms for various building materials (measurements by Fraunhofer IBP, Holzkirchen)

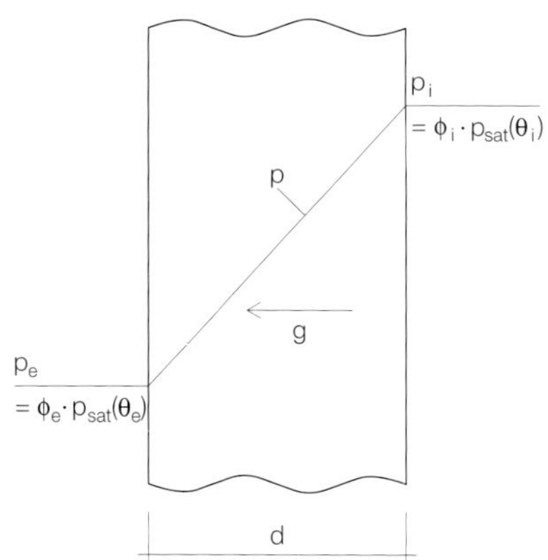


2.2.2.4 Schematic presentation of the steady-state water vapour diffusion through a building component as a result of partial vapour pressure differences between inside and outside

| Material | μ-value [–] |
|---|---|
| Plasters | 10 – 30 |
| Clay brickwork | 5 – 10 |
| Clay roof tiles | 40 |
| Concrete | 50 – 150 |
| Concrete roof tiles | 100 |
| Rigid expanded polystyrene foam | 20 – 100 |
| Mineral wool | 1 |
| Bitumen roofing felt | 2000 – 80 000 |
| Construction-grade timber | 50 – 200 |
| Chipboard | 50 |
| Plasterboard | 10 |

2.2.2.5 μ-values of materials

| Material | $s_d$-value [m] |
|---|---|
| Polyethylene film, 0.15 mm | 50 |
| Polyethylene film, 0.25 mm | 100 |
| Aluminium foil, 0.05 mm | 1500 |
| Gloss paint | 3 |

2.2.2.6 $s_d$-values of materials

| Material | w-value kg/m²h$^{0.5}$ |
|---|---|
| Clay bricks | 10–30 |
| Clay roof tiles | 2–3 |
| Clay roof tiles, siliconised | ~ 0.1 |
| Plasters | < 2 |
| Aerated concrete | 4–8 |
| Spruce, axial | ~ 0.5 |
| Spruce, radial | ~ 0.25 |
| Dispersion paint | 0.05–0.2 |

2.2.2.7 Approximate w-values of various building materials

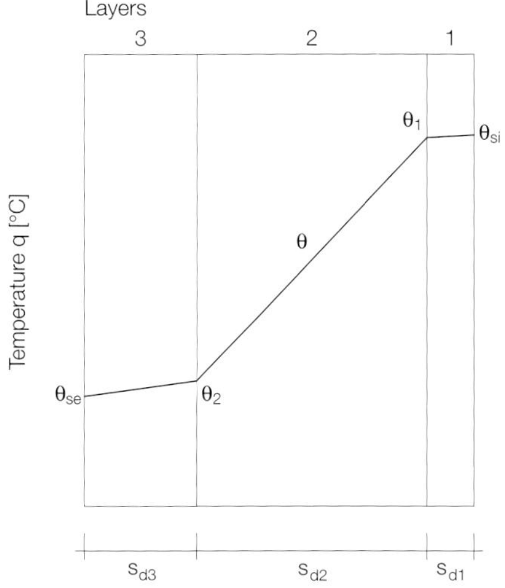


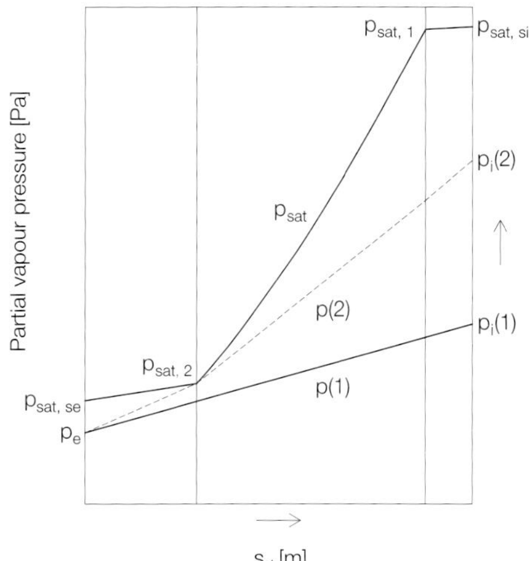


2.2.2.8 Steady-state temperature and vapour pressure distribution across a multi-layer component on an $s_d$ scale for determining condensation effects

In multi-layer arrangements the $s_d$-values of the individual layers are added together to produce a total resistance. Design values for μ are included in the preliminary edition of DIN 4108 part 4 and in DIN EN 12524. Such $s_d$-values are normally specified for building or ancillary materials which are either relatively thin and exhibit high μ-values (e.g. foils) or whose thickness cannot be classified (e.g. paints, impregnation substances) (see DIN EN 12524 for typical values).
In accordance with DIN 4108 part 3 the $s_d$-value is used to describe the openness to diffusion of layers of building components. Accordingly,
open to diffusion: $s_d \leq 0.5$ m
diffusion-retardant: $0.5 < s_d < 1500$ m
diffusion-resistant: $s_d \geq 1500$ m
See table 2.2.2.6 for examples of $s_d$-values.

Water vapour convection
This phenomenon is the transport of water vapour in the flow of moist air as a result of total pressure differences. The warmer and moister the air, the lower is its density and the easier it is for free convection currents to form with respect to colder and drier air. The forced convection of moist air in or through the building envelope components is triggered by the flow of air around the building, e.g. as a result of wind pressure/suction effects. These occur in ventilation layers designed for the purpose, which are connected to the outside air only and remove moisture from the component, or as a result of leaks at joints or a lack of airtightness in components due to poor workmanship, thus allowing air to flow between interior and exterior. The airtightness measures required to counter uncontrolled ventilation heat losses (see DIN 4108 part 7) thus gain considerable additional significance due to these moisture control aspects.
This applies in particular to efficiently thermally insulated pitched roofs, where moist, warm interior air should be prevented from penetrating – through leaks – into the roof construction. In comparison to diffusion, amounts of moisture larger by a factor of 100 or 1000 can be transported here. When this large quantity of moisture reaches the cold zones around the thermal insulation it condenses and inevitably leads to moisture-related damage over time. This problem can be eliminated by introducing airtightness measures, preferably on the inside, and ensuring these are properly carried out.

Capillarity
Contact between a material with active capillaries and liquid water results in capillary action sucking the water into the material. Almost all porous mineral building materials exhibit this capillarity, but even timber or timber derivatives can absorb water. Wettable substances with capillary-like pores can be made water-repellent by using hydrophobic surface treatments, e.g. impregnation, coatings, paints, which considerably reduces their wettability and hence their capillary suction capacity. Capillarity is determined for practical purposes according to the draft of DIN EN ISO 15148 and with the help of the water absorption coefficient w (in future: $W_w$) according to the empirical "root-t law":

$$m_w = w \cdot \sqrt{t}$$

where
$m_w$ = mass of water absorbed per surface area [kg/m²]
w = water absorption coefficient [kg/m²h$^{0.5}$]
t = absorption time [h]
See table 2.2.2.7 for examples of w-values.

For pitched roofs capillarity is in practice only important for roof coverings of clay/concrete tiles etc. exposed to rainfall or condensation. The w-value is used to help assess frost resistance or the growth of lichens and mosses where there is a clear connection. However, it should be noted that other material parameters such as microstructure strength, absorption and, above all, drying behaviour ($s_d$-value) are also important for such assessments. For example, with glazed clay roof tiles the engobe finish has little influence on the w-value, but drying behaviour is significantly influenced by higher $s_d$-values. Clay roof tiles can achieve good water-repellent properties, e.g. by using hydrophobic coatings ("siliconisation") (see investigations in [48]). But this does raise the question of how long this essentially positive effect lasts under intensive weathering conditions and, in particular, ultraviolet radiation.

**Condensation and evaporation within the component cross-section**

Condensation within the component
Condensation water can only collect within a building component in the case of water vapour diffusion under non-isothermic conditions, i.e. with a temperature drop over the cross-section and diffusion in the direction of the temperature drop. But this only happens when the vapour pressure on the warm side is higher than that on the cold side. Figure 2.2.2.8 illustrates the principle of condensation within a multi-layer building component; DIN 4103 part 3 contains more detailed information. Assuming a temperature distribution and associated $p_{sat}$-line over the cross-section on an $s_d$-scale, no condensation takes place as long as the straight p-distribution line does not touch the $p_{sat}$-line, e.g. for $p_i$ in case (1).
As $p_i$ rises, e.g. up to case (2), the p-distribution line touches the $p_{sat}$-line like a string under tension. This corresponds to the formation of a tangent to the saturation line drawn between $p_i$ and $p_e$. The vapour pressure p cannot be greater than the saturation vapour pressure at any point. There is a kink in the p distribution

line at the point where it touches the $p_{sat}$ line; this is where the condensation takes place. This graphic method for determining possible condensation in a multi-layer building component is also known as the "Glaser method" [38]; it forms the basis for assessing the condensation risk according to DIN 4108 part 3.
Calculating the quantity of condensation water: The quantity of condensation water $m_{W,T}$ (in future: $M_c$) per surface area at the point of the kink in the p distribution line over a period of time $t_T$ (condensation period) is calculated from the difference in the mass flows diffusing to and away from the point of contact. Equations for various cases are given in DIN 4108 part 3.

Evaporation of condensation water from the component cross-section
The second part of the "Glaser method" deals with whether the quantity of condensation at a particular point can be released to the surroundings on both sides within a certain time by diffusion under different temperature and humidity conditions. It is assumed here that a saturation vapour pressure, corresponding to the temperature (new temperature distribution) prevailing at this point, is present at the point of condensation. The condensation water diffuses away towards both surfaces.
Calculating the quantity of water evaporating: The potential quantity of water evaporating $m_{W,V}$ (in future: $M_{ev}$) per surface area from the condensation level over a period of time $t_V$ (evaporation period) is calculated from the sum of the mass flows with the same diffusion resistances $s_{di}$ and $s_{de}$ diffusing away towards the two surfaces, as for condensation, but taking into account the new boundary conditions. The equations are given in DIN 4108 part 3.

#### Moisture control layers

Moisture control layers in a pitched roof can be classified as follows in terms of climate-related moisture control (protection against rainwater/condensation water):

- Roof covering

Roof coverings consisting of overlapping elements (clay/concrete roof tiles, slates, etc.) must be rainproof. This rainproof quality is usually attained when the standard roof pitches as given in the guidelines of the roofing trade [64] are adhered to (depending on type, form, interlock, overlap). More severe conditions may make it necessary to introduce additional measures with respect to the underlying roofing felt, even the provision of a waterproof felt.

- Roofing felt, boarding, sarking

Thermally insulated pitched roofs are generally provided with a layer of roofing felt, boarding or sarking below the roof covering, which may also be dictated by any additional rainproofing measures required. Sheets of roofing felt may be bonded together or simply overlapped and nailed.
In addition to draining small amounts of rainwater that may penetrate the roof covering or condensation water that collects on the underside of the covering, the roofing felt, boarding, etc. also acts as a temporary roof covering during construction.

- Vapour barrier, windbreak

Diffusion-retardant layers on the inside are necessary with practically all thermally insulated roof constructions. The order of magnitude of the $s_d$-value depends on the type of roof covering (open/resistant to diffusion; ventilated/non-ventilated). Plastic sheeting (0.15 or 0.25 mm polyethylene, > 0.05 mm polypropylene, etc.), aluminium foil (> 0.05 mm) or special papers (impregnated, bituminised) are the most common materials for an internal vapour barrier attached to the underside of the thermal insulation (see preliminary edition of DIN 4108 part 4 or DIN EN 12524 for μ- and $s_d$-values).
Equally important are airtightness layers, as mentioned in connection with water vapour convection. These, too, should be positioned on the inside if possible. They are usually provided in the form of a layer combining diffusion-retardant and airtightness functions. Careful sealing to prevent leaks is important for both these functions (see DIN 4108 part 7). However, board materials (plasterboard, chipboard, etc.) are also considered to be airtight when butt and edge joints are properly and permanently sealed. For further details see the chapters "Design" and "Layers and materials".

- Innovative vapour barriers

In recent years interesting new developments have produced vapour barriers with enhanced functional properties: materials with active capillaries and materials with adaptive moisture properties. [51, 52, 61] These materials result in, above all, improved drying towards the inside in summer while maintaining an adequate diffusion-retardant effect in winter. This is important in situations with an increased level of inherent moisture still present in roof deckings or rafters, or small amounts of rainwater or condensation water when this water is transported inwards towards cooler roof zones by reverse diffusion under higher outside temperatures. If a vapour barrier has been provided on the inside, condensation water can collect here in summer, which can lead to drying problems in the case of, for example, diffusion-resistant roofing felts or roof deckings with internal vapour barriers.
The vapour barrier with active capillaries (also known as "Hygrodiode") is made from overlapping polyethylene sheets and a core of non-woven cloth with active capillaries, which is in contact with the surrounding air on both sides. In summer any condensation water collecting on the insulation side of the vapour barrier is absorbed by the non-woven cloth and transported by capillarity to the inner surface, from where it can evaporate into the room.
The vapour barrier with adaptive moisture properties, a polyamide film, is able to adjust its diffusion resistance depending on the surrounding relative humidity of the air through reversible changes to its polymer structure. As figure 2.2.2.9 shows, its $s_d$-value of about 4 m up to approx. 40% rh is relatively high.
As the relative humidity increases, so its $s_d$-value decreases to about 1/10 of this value at around 80% rh and continues to drop towards the dew point. These are the desirable properties of an internal vapour barrier for the winter (approx. 40% interior humidity, diffusion-retardant effect) and the summer (high relative humidity on the insulation side as a result of temporary reverse diffusion flows; the film "swells" and thus enables the drying process).

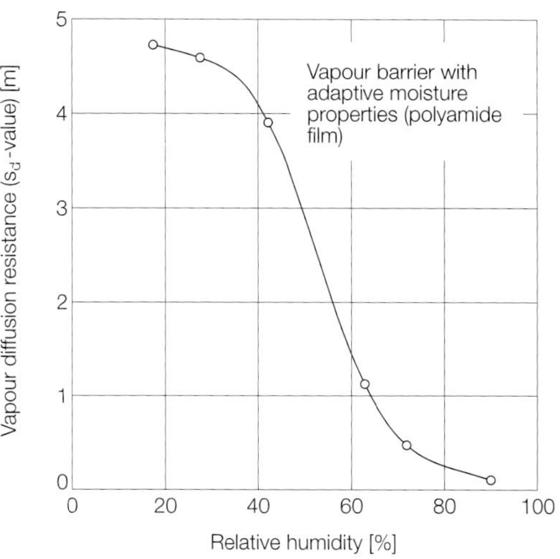


2.2.2.9 Variable $s_d$-value of vapour barrier with adaptive moisture properties in relation to the relative humidity of the air [52]

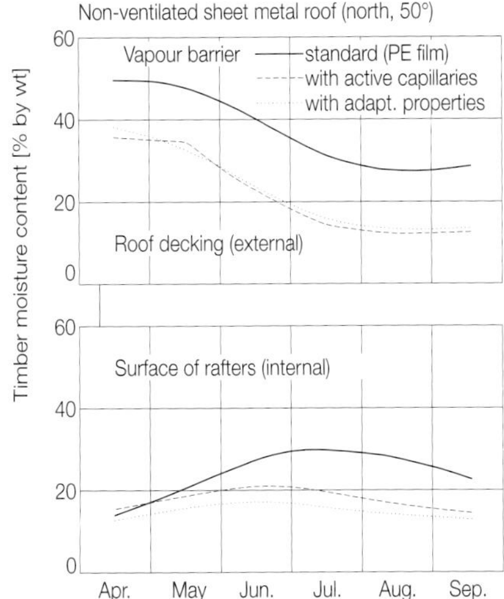


2.2.2.10 Measured moisture gradients for roof decking (external) and rafters (internal) on the north side of a 50° pitch, non-ventilated sheet metal roof with different internal vapour barriers [52]

The much higher drying potential of these two principles has been proved in field trials on a north-facing, non-ventilated sheet metal roof by means of the measured timber moisture gradient (roof decking, rafters) over a summer period. [52] Figure 2.2.2.10 shows the results of the measurements in comparison to the effect of a standard polyethylene film.

The vapour barrier with adaptive moisture properties is also used, for example, for refurbishing roofs from the outside; the continuous layer of film – between the rafters beneath the retrofitted insulation (i.e. on the inside) and around and over the rafters (i.e. on the outside) – does not present any moisture problems for the rafters owing to the special properties of the film. [44, 51, 52]

**Roof ventilation – openness to diffusion**

Roof ventilation is essentially provided for two reasons:

- To remove moisture penetrating into the roof construction from the outside or even from the inside, or moisture due to the construction (primary task).
- To dissipate part of the heat energy from the outer roof zones heated by solar radiation absorption during summer and thus help to prevent high temperatures in the roof covering, which also assists the summer thermal performance for the roof space (secondary task).

We distinguish between two types of roof construction according to the guidelines of the roofing trade [64] and moisture control aspects (DIN 4108 part 3):

- The ventilated roof with a ventilated layer of air directly above the thermal insulation
- The non-ventilated roof without a ventilated layer of air directly above the thermal insulation

The ventilated layer above the insulation is connected to the outside air via inlets and outlets at eaves and ridge. It could also be called a "lower ventilation level". A ventilated layer is usually included in conventional pitched roof constructions.

Irrespective of this, according to the type of roof covering we also distinguish between

- a ventilated roof covering using overlapping elements, e.g. clay/concrete roof tiles etc., on a linear supporting structure, e.g. battens and counter battens, beneath which air can flow in a defined cavity, and
- a non-ventilated roof covering using overlapping elements directly on a flat supporting structure, e.g. roof decking, where an exchange of air between the underside of the roofing elements and the surroundings takes place only via joints, gaps etc.

The ventilation layer directly beneath the roof covering is also connected to the outside air via inlets and outlets. It could also be called an "upper ventilation level". It is the conventional, tried-and-tested method of constructing roofs.

Flows in ventilation layers

In order to guarantee the intended function of the ventilation layer, it must be possible to set a flow of air in motion. This essentially depends on the resistance to the flow within this cavity. It is assumed that a planar cavity with flat sides requires a width of at least 20 mm for an effective flow of air (driven by wind pressure or convection currents) to take place under practical conditions. In normal building conditions the relevant flow resistance within the ventilation layer depends on a multitude of parameters. Liersch [54] and Pohl [57] have researched this complex topic in great detail.
It will always be the case that unevenness, projections, changes of cross-section, inlets/outlets, length of flow, slope of cavity, changes in direction, etc. lead to increased resistance to the flow of air and hence put effective ventilation at risk. The minimum figure of 20 mm quoted frequently for the cavity width is essentially correct in theory, but taking into account practical aspects of building it is recommended to increase this width significantly, depending on an estimate of the resistance to the flow. Particularly critical here with respect to ventilation above the insulation is when thicker layers of insulation are supplied even thicker but still within permissible dimensional tolerances, or when fibre insulating materials "expand" and thus "close off" a cavity of minimum width. In such cases the intended, necessary ventilation will be impaired. It may be necessary to provide spacers of some description.
Besides the construction itself (cross-section, roof pitch), the surrounding climate (wind profile, hours of sunshine) is also responsible for setting a flow of air in ventilation layers in motion. This leads to forced or free convection currents, but mostly a combination of both effects, resulting in flow velocities in ventilation layers of approx. 0.05–0.50 m/s being realised in pitched roofs in practice.

- Wind pressure

The wind flow around a building (see "Layers – Ventilation") is strongly influenced by the roof form. This leads to pressures on the windward side and suctions on the leeward side, and these are responsible for the infiltration air change of the building and forced flows within ventilation layers. It should be noted that the direction of flow within a ventilation cavity can change (eaves to ridge, ridge to eaves) with changing wind directions. The wind-induced average pressure differences are approx. 1–6 Pa, based on average wind speeds of 2–5 m/s. This leads to flow velocities of approx. 0.2–0.5 m/s in common ventilation layers.

- Convection currents

Thermal convection currents in ventilation layers occur only in pitched roofs. They are caused by temperature, i.e. pressure, differences between the air in the ventilation layer and the surrounding air. During periods with no wind movement (approx. 10% of the year) these convection currents are the sole means of "driving" the ventilation. An increase in the temperature of the air in either the upper or lower ventilation layer essentially depends on the solar radiation incident on the roof surface, and hence on its colour. In summer maximum surface temperatures for the roof covering may be:

| | |
|---|---|
| metal, matt finish | approx. 40°C |
| light colour, grey | approx. 50–60°C |
| brick-red | approx. 60–70°C |
| dark colour, brown | approx. 70–80°C |
| black, anthracite | approx. 80–85°C |

These temperatures occur only temporarily and underlying layers are not heated to the same extent. The steeper the roof, the lower the flow resistance in a ventilation layer, and the greater the temperature rise of the outside air, the more intensive are the convection currents in such ventilation layers. Average temperature rises in ventilation layers of customary pitched roofs of approx. 1–15 K lead to thermally induced flow velocities of approx. 0.05–0.30 m/s (measurements after [54]).

During periods without solar radiation (night), or on north-facing roofs or those permanently in the shade (which are generally cooler) it can happen that, for example, the direction of flow may reverse during radiation-induced night-time overcooling, i.e. the air flows from top to bottom and causes a suction effect at the ridge. With current standards of thermal insulation in the roof, this effect is augmented by the interruption of the heat flow outwards from the interior.

Ridge separation
Close couple and similar roofs normally have two ventilation layers. Ventilation inlets and outlets are provided at eaves and ridge for the desired dissipation of moisture via the respective through-flows. The ventilation layers of both roof surfaces converge at the ridge and are therefore linked in hydrodynamic terms (see figure 2.2.2.11).
If the roof surfaces are exposed to different climatic conditions, e.g. south- and north-facing, a higher wind pressure or intensive convection currents on the south side may cause warmer moisture-laden air to collect at the ridge outlet and be forced into the ventilation layers of the north side. Downward convection currents thus occur on this side, promoted by the cooler cross-section, particularly at night. This means there is a direct supply of moisture to both ventilation layers on the north side, with an associated increase in the sorption moisture of the cooler timber there (battens, roof decking, rafters) and possibly condensation. In winter especially, when snow and ice also hinder ventilation through the roof covering, this can lead to moisture accumulating in the timber, or frost or condensation forming in the upper and lower ventilation layers, even without overcooling at night. Measurements of the moisture content of rafters on the north and south sides of a pitched roof have confirmed this effect [48, 52] (see figure 2.2.2.12).
It is therefore recommended to separate – using, for example, a vertical baffle – the ventilation outlets at the ridge of a steep pitched roof where such climatic conditions could occur (see figure 2.2.2.11).

To ventilate or not to ventilate? The pros and cons

- Upper ventilation layer

As extensive investigations have revealed (summarised in [48]), it is not absolutely essential to include a ventilation layer below a roof covering with high air permeability (e.g. pantiles). It is essentially the temperature of the roof covering that governs how small amounts of rainwater or condensation water or the inherent moisture in the tiling battens dry out. However, when using less permeable overlapping elements (e.g. bullnose tiles) or when there are penetrations, dormer windows, Velux-type windows, where larger amounts of rainwater could penetrate because of acknowledged sealing problems, a roof design incorporating counter battens and ventilation is recommended. It is then easier for any incoming rainwater to drain away and the tiling battens are not subjected to a build-up of moisture. Even in areas less exposed to the sun, i.e. on the whole, cooler roof surfaces, where there is a higher risk of condensation during overcooling at night, a ventilated roof covering is preferable, for purely practical reasons. The faster removal of residual or sorption moisture from the outer layers (clay roof tiles, battens, maybe the roofing felt) has a positive effect, also in conjunction with reverse diffusion into the roof construction during the summer.

- Lower ventilation layer

The continuing debate surrounding the non-ventilated roof, which started in the early 1990s, has also led to the introduction of this type of roof, with its considerable practical advantages and proven beneficial moisture behaviour, as a standard type of construction. Provided both the outer skin (ventilated or air-permeable roof covering) and the roofing felt permit diffusion, omitting the ventilation layer between insulation and roofing felt brings clear advantages (see also [48, 49]):
a) The space between the rafters can be filled completely with insulation.
b) It avoids an increase in the sorption moisture of the timber (roof decking, rafters) and condensation collecting on the underside of the roofing felt, and dripping into the insulation as a result of the inflow of outside air and overcooling at night. The timber remains, on the whole, drier.
c) Roofing felt that allows diffusion and an internal vapour barrier with a relatively low $s_d$-value (approx. 2 m) favour the drying-out of moisture inherent to the construction, and possibly any moisture accumulating in winter, both inwards and outwards. Drying takes place more quickly.
d) Chemical timber preservatives can be avoided with an appropriate coordination of the $s_d$-values inside and outside.
e) The construction is simpler and hence cheaper because there is no need for special detailing at ventilation inlets and outlets, the problem of a possible separation at the ridge is easier to solve or is superfluous, and the relatively complicated details required to guarantee ventilation around dormer windows, Velux-type windows etc. are no longer necessary.

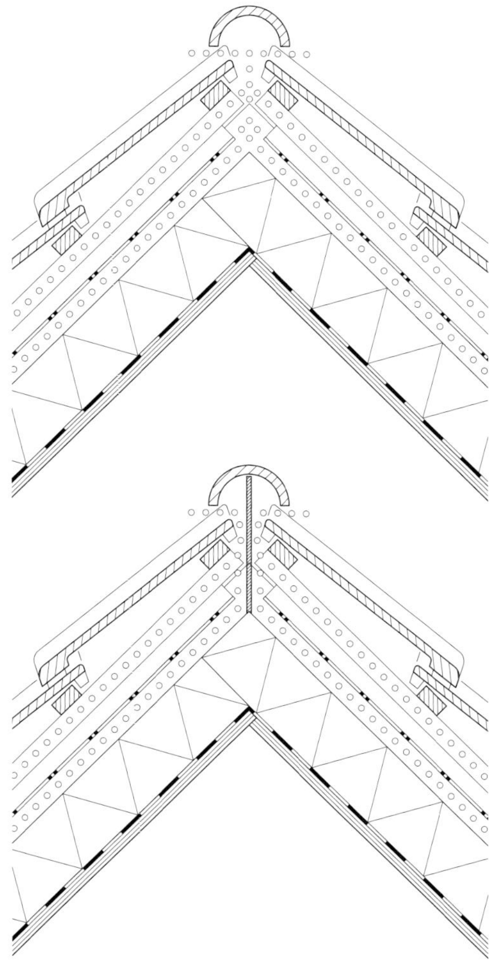

2.2.2.11 Roof construction with two ventilation levels, with and without separation at the ridge [48]

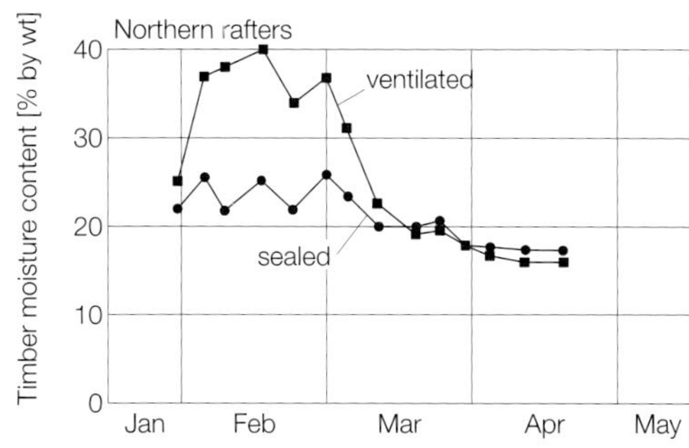


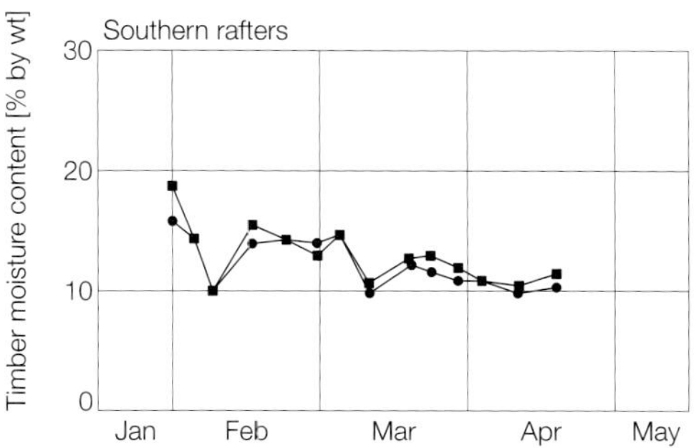


2.2.2.12 Measured rafter moisture content gradients on the north and south side of a "ventilated" roof and a "sealed" roof without ventilation layers [47, 48, 52]

However, it should be noted that such roofing felt allowing diffusion also promotes reverse diffusion from outside to inside during the summer. So in these roofs care should be taken to prevent high levels of sorption moisture in the region of the roof covering (roof covering materials, timber) or larger amounts of rainwater remaining below the roof covering for longer periods (ventilated roof covering, materials with low sorption or capillarity). Furthermore, it should be ensured that the $s_d$-value on the inside is not too high and so allows moisture to be released inwards (special vapour barrier materials can further accelerate the drying process).
Completely omitting an internal vapour barrier in roofing felts with extremely low $s_d$-values (approx. 0.02 m) is theoretically possible but should be studied very carefully. Such an extreme openness to diffusion can be impaired in the outward direction in winter through longer periods of icing, or through soiling of the roofing felt in badly polluted conditions.
According to DIN 4108 part 3 an internal vapour barrier with an $s_d$-value ≥ 100 m should be provided in non-ventilated roofs resistant to outward diffusion. Types of construction that require a high resistance to diffusion are generally problematic, especially with close couple or collar roofs, because reliable sealing of the vapour barrier is difficult in practice and vulnerable to mistakes, and because it is difficult for the moisture inherent in the construction or moisture penetrating into the roof through leaks to escape again by way of diffusion. Even though investigations [52] have revealed that adequate moisture can be released inwards where roof surfaces exposed to sunshine with an internal $s_d$-value reduced to about 2 m, or when a vapour barrier with adaptive moisture properties is provided, this type of construction should still be avoided if possible. In winter there is also the problem of "flanking diffusion", as shown in figure 2.2.2.13, e.g. via gable masonry or intersecting partitions with comparatively low μ-values. In this case diffusion flows penetrate into the roof construction and condensation takes place in the cold zone. This condensation cannot escape outwards via the ventilation, or inwards via the vapour barrier. Severe damage has already been reported in such cases. [60]
Conventional ventilation above the thermal insulation is, however, necessary when particular roof pitches, types of construction or climatic conditions call for waterproof and hence essentially diffusion-resistant roofing felts or sheet metal roofs. A ventilated pitched roof then requires an internal vapour barrier with an $s_d$-value of at least 2 m. All the topics already mentioned – flow, ventilation cross-section, inlet/outlet resistance, ridge separation, moisture ingress from the surrounding air and overcooling, construction complexities and space for thermal insulation not fully usable – are important for such roofs and must be taken into consideration. There is no problem of reverse diffusion from the roof covering inwards in this case. Nevertheless, the drying options inwards are important and should not be ruled out by high $s_d$-values.

#### Requirements for moisture control

The requirements for climate-related moisture control of external components are laid down in DIN 4108 parts 2 and 3. They involve avoiding critical surface moisture levels and limiting condensation within the component cross-section. It is presumed that the pitched roofs comply with requirements for minimum thermal performance and airtight construction.

Avoidance of critical surface moisture levels
The conditions for critical surface moisture levels are specified in conjunction with the minimum requirements for thermal performance around thermal bridges in DIN 4108 part 2. Unlike in the past, it is not the avoidance of surface condensation water that is important but rather – in line with the generally stricter minimum requirements for thermal performance – the avoidance of mould growth. To guarantee this at the most unfavourable point, the value of 80% rh taken these days for the critical surface moisture level at this point may not be exceeded.
The latest findings regarding the avoidance of mould growth on and in building components are taken from [62]. Besides the critical moisture level, these also take into account a substantial temperature influence and the effect of the underlying substrate. An assessment method specified in [62] will probably be included in measures to combat mould growth, which are currently being discussed by a standard drafting committee.

Limiting condensation within the component
The occurrence of condensation within the component cross-section (see above) may not damage or impair the function of building materials or thermal insulating materials. According to DIN 4108 part 3 condensation is considered harmless under the following conditions:

- There is no damage to the material (e.g. corrosion, mould).
- Condensation water collecting during a condensation period must be able to dry out again during a subsequent evaporation period.
- Maximum permissible condensation quantities for wall and roof constructions are
  1.0 kg/m²: generally
  0.5 kg/m²: when the material at the point of condensation (usually a boundary layer) does not exhibit capillarity (e.g. insulating materials).
- A condensation-related increase in the moisture content of 5% by wt for timber or 3% by wt for timber derivatives is not exceeded (exceptions: wood-wool and multi-ply lightweight building boards).

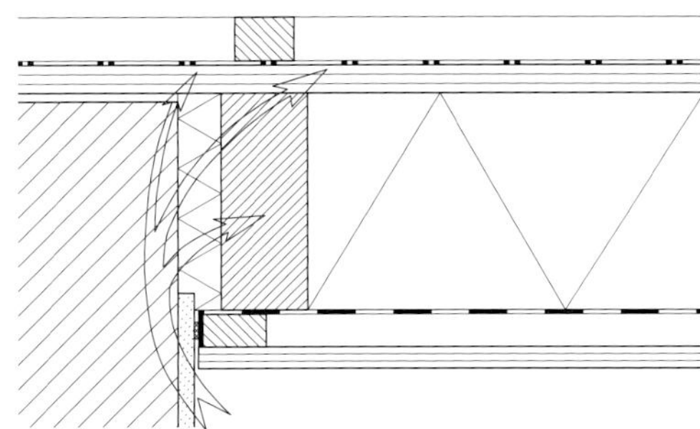
2.2.2.13 "Flanking diffusion" from a room into the roof construction via intersecting components [52, 60]

DIN 4108 part 3 specifies a method for analysing the condensation and evaporation quantities. This method is based on Glaser's graphic diffusion method [38] and is a true diffusion model for assessing condensation. It is based on experience and specifies a condensation period of 60 days and an evaporation period of 90 days, with respective temperature and humidity conditions (block climate boundary conditions for non-air-conditioned residential, office or similar premises; see the notes in DIN 4108 part 3 for other conditions). This method applies only to the assessment of construction for moisture control purposes; it is not suitable for evaluating other (real) drying, wetting or moisture transport processes (see next section for realistic moisture calculation).

The design values for thermal conductivity and the typical values for diffusion resistance index according to DIN 4108 part 4 should be used in this analysis. Where two μ-values are given (scatter), the more unfavourable value should be applied according to the position of the layer, i.e. when the layer is on the inside of a possible condensation level, use the lower μ-value; when on the outside, the higher μ-value. These values should, however, also be retained for determining the evaporation quantity. To ensure a factor of safety, $s_d$ = 0.1 m should be assumed in the calculation for external layers with very low $s_d$-values, i.e. $s_d$ < 0.1 m, determined according to DIN EN ISO 12572.

The present edition of DIN 4108 part 3 is currently undergoing revision in connection with the necessary inclusion of a new method of analysis taken from DIN EN ISO 13788, which provides for a monthly audit of the condensation and evaporation quantities ("Euro Glaser method"). A modified method for assessing diffusion with new boundary conditions and taking national requirements into account is therefore expected to appear in 2003.

Roof constructions permitted without analysis
Besides the condensation analysis method, DIN 4108 part 3 includes a catalogue of constructions that do not require analysis. These are types of construction in which there is no risk of condensation water or other moisture occurring when

- the requirements for minimum thermal performance to DIN 4108 part 2 are satisfied (avoidance of mould),
- the construction is airtight to DIN 4108 part 7 (avoidance of convection-related condensation), and
- certain constructional parameters are adhered to.

In practical terms, these stipulations are best followed during the planning phase. If compliance is not possible, an analysis must be carried out using the aforementioned method. A moisture control analysis is not necessary for pitched roofs when the requirements of table 2.2.2.15 are fulfilled.

| | Roof construction | Requirement | |
|---|---|---|---|
| A | non-ventilated | R below internal vapour barrier<br>$R_u \leq 0.2 \cdot R_{ges}$ (generally; space between rafters) | |
| | 1) with ventilated roof covering or with non-ventilated roof covering and additional ventilated air layer below roof covering<br>($s_{de} : s_{di}$ ratio) | $s_{de}$ [m][1)]<br>$\leq 0.1$<br>$\leq 0.3$ [2)]<br>$> 0.3$ | $s_{di}$ [m]<br>$\geq 1.0$<br>$\geq 2.0$<br>$\geq 6 \cdot s_{de}$ |
| | 2) with non-ventilated roof covering<br>($s_{di}$ below thermal insulation) | $s_{di} \geq 100$ m [3)] | |
| | 3) with sealing<br>• for layers of thermal insulation<br>• aerated concrete roof without vapour barrier and without additional insulation<br>• upside-down roof | <br>$s_{di} \geq 100$ m<br>(none)<br><br>(none) | |
| B | ventilated | | |
| | 1) roof pitch < 5°<br>($s_{di}$ below thermal insulation<br>$R_u$ below internal vapour barrier) | <br>$s_{di} \geq 100$ m<br>$R_u \leq 0.2 \cdot R_{ges}$ | |
| | 2) roof pitch ≥ 5°<br>• depth of ventilation layer above insulation<br>• $s_d$-value below ventilation layer<br>• ventilation cross-section at eaves or at eaves and termination of monopitch roof<br>• ventilation cross-section for duopitch roofs at ridge and hip[4)] | <br>≥ 2 cm<br>≥ 2 m<br>≥ 2‰ of associated roof area; at least 200 cm²/m<br>≥ 0.5‰ of associated roof area; at least 50 cm²/m | |

1) $s_{de}$ or $s_{di}$: sum of $s_d$-values above or below thermal insulation and as far as next ventilated air layer.
2) The use of chemical timber preservatives can be avoided in non-ventilated roofs with $s_{de} \leq 0.2$ m when the conditions of DIN 68800 part 2 are satisfied.
3) It is difficult, perhaps impossible, for moisture to diffuse out of a non-ventilated roof with $s_{de} \geq 2$ m.
4) Separation at the ridge is advisable for roof surfaces subjected to different climatic conditions; non-ventilated roofs are more advisable with valleys or dormer windows.

2.2.2.15 Summary of requirements for roofs so that a moisture control analysis is not necessary (after DIN 4108 part 3)

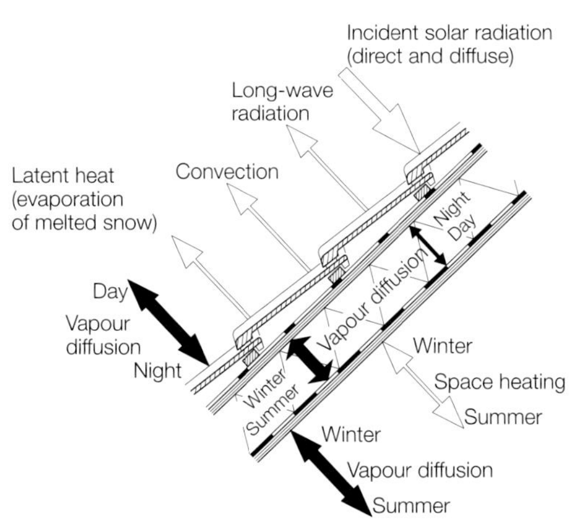


2.2.2.14 Hygrothermal processes in a pitched roof [52]

| Name of model | Authors | Dimension | Thermal conduction | Diffusion | Capillary conduction | Air flows | Moisture convection | Enthalpy transport |
|---|---|---|---|---|---|---|---|---|
| MATCH | Rode[1)] | 1 | + | + | + | + | + | + |
| WUFI-Pro 3.1 | Künzel, Schmidt, Holm[2)] | 1 | + | + | + | | | + |
| WUFI2d CFD | Künzel, Holm, Eitner[2)] | 2 | + | + | + | + | + | + |
| Delphin | Grunewald[3)] | 1 and 2 | + | + | + | + | + | |
| 1d-HAM | Hagentoft, Blomberg[4)] | 1 | + | + | | + | + | + |
| ConDry | Hedenblad, Arfvidsson[4)] | 1 | + | + | + | | | + |
| UMIDUS | Mendes, Ridley[5)] | 1 | + | + | + | | | + |

1) Tech. Univ. of Denmark; 2) Fraunhofer IBP; 3) TU Dresden; 4) Lund Univ.; 5) Prodeedings of Building Simulation, 99 Vol. 1, p. 277

2.2.2.16 List of computer programs for non-steady-state, realistic moisture calculations using complex models [53]

Realistic moisture calculation
Completely different, non-steady-state methods must be used for a realistic calculation of moisture transport processes in building components under natural climatic conditions. These take into account the sorption, diffusion and capillarity effects found in practice, possibly also moisture convection and the coupling with heat transfer. Special material property functions are necessary for such methods. They allow hourly climatic data to be used for more accurate analyses of building component moisture levels over the cross-section and over time, and even extrapolation to assess anticipated long-term behaviour. The principles behind such computational methods can be found in [45, 46, 50]. Figure 2.2.2.14 shows the complex conditions for moisture transport in a pitched roof. This also applies similarly to other building components, where sorption and capillarity effects are usually more severe (e.g. masonry). From this we can see that real processes cannot be assessed by way of simplified models, e.g. the standard diffusion method. A number of user-friendly computer programs are now available for non-steady-state, complex computational methods. These are listed in table 2.2.2.16 (see [53] for further information).

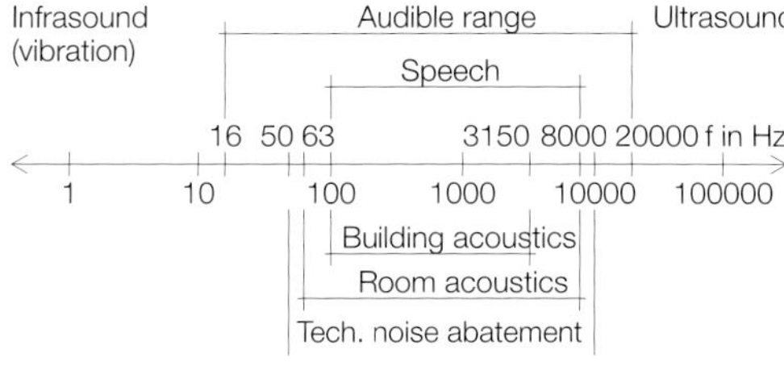


2.2.3.1 Acoustic frequency ranges [36]

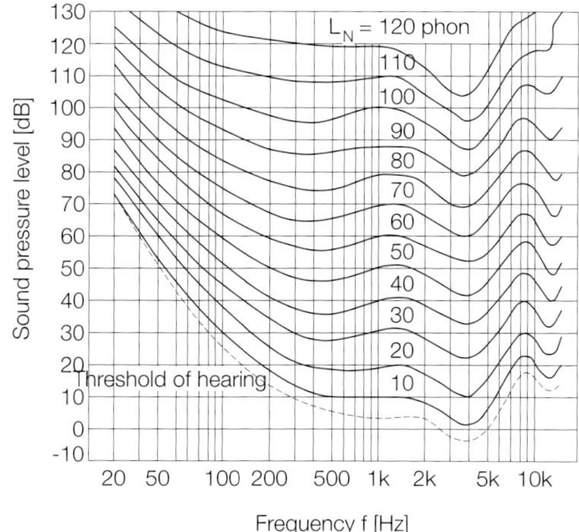


2.2.3.2 Lines of equal volume for sine-wave tones [36], e.g. 50 Hz/60 dB is perceived as 400 Hz/20 dB

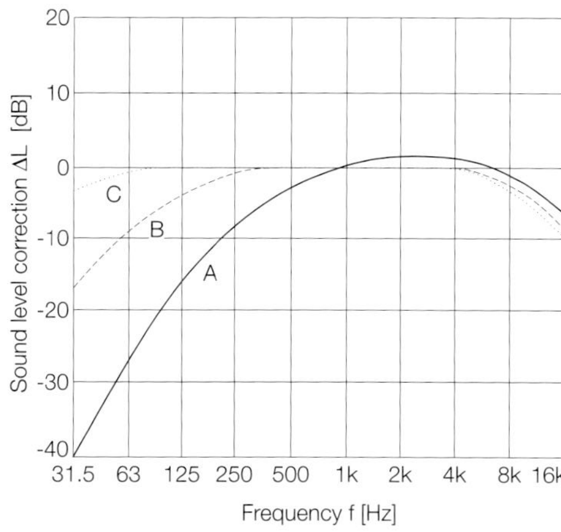


2.2.3.3 Frequency evaluation curves [36]

## Sound insulation

The task of sound insulation in building results from the need to design building components so that the effects of noise from other living quarters or working areas, from plant and from the external surroundings are no longer regarded as disturbing or annoying within the premises.
It is essential to include sound insulation measures right from the planning stage, for example, by designing the layout to limit noise from outside, grouping noisy and quiet zones, incorporating mass or acoustically effective layers in separating components, taking sound transmission via flanking components into account, avoiding joints and acoustic bridges, etc. Careful workmanship during construction is necessary because even minor inaccuracies, usually leading to acoustic bridges, can ruin the overall effect. Subsequent corrections or supplementary measures are usually complicated and hence expensive, or even impossible.
In terms of acoustics, the primary task of a pitched roof over occupied premises is to exclude external noise. Requirements are therefore placed on the external components. However, the roof should also be considered as a flanking component in the airborne sound insulation of party walls that separate adjacent premises beneath the same roof. The underside (inside) of the roof surface usually constitutes a large proportion of the total enclosing surface area of an occupied roof space, and can be usefully employed for acoustic purposes. This can have a beneficial effect on the acoustic quality of the room and the airborne sound insulation.

#### Basic terminology (definitions, symbols, parameters)

- Sound

The mechanical vibration of an elastic medium (e.g. air, water, building materials), especially in the frequency range audible to the human ear (from approx. 16 to 20 000 Hz); propagated in the form of sound waves characterised by frequency and wavelength; figure 2.2.3.1 shows the sound frequency bands of interest in buildings.

- Velocity of sound c [m/s]

The speed of propagation of the waves in an elastic medium; e.g. in air (dependent on temperature):
$c \sim 331 + 0.6\theta$ (with θ in °C for c in m/s);
in water approx. 1400 m/s, in concrete approx. 2900 m/s, in steel approx. 5100 m/s.

- Sound pressure p [Pa]

Alternating pressure of the vibrations, especially important in air, superimposed on the total atmospheric pressure; corresponds to the energy content of the sound wave.

- Sound intensity I [W/m²]

Sound energy per unit of time and surface area; proportional relationship: $I \sim p^2$

- Sound pressure level L [dB]

The practical, specified variable as a means of describing sound events in relation to the human ear; owing to the perception of sound pressures higher than $1 \times 10^6$ or sound intensities higher than $1 \times 10^{12}$, the sound pressure level – also known as the sound level for practical purposes – is defined as a logarithmic ratio in relation to the threshold value of the responsive hearing affected:

$$L = 10 \cdot \log(p/p_o)^2 = 20 \cdot \log(p/p_o)$$
$$= 10 \cdot \log(I/I_o) \text{ [dB]}$$

Threshold values:
$p_o = 20 \cdot 10^{-6}$ Pa or
$I_o = 1 \cdot 10^{-12}$ W/m²
Pain threshold: $p \sim 20$ Pa or $I \sim 1$ W/m²
The unit of measurement, the decibel (dB), has been defined for practical reasons and makes it easier to specify a finer gradation of levels based on the basic definition of level:
$L = \log (I/I_o) = 2 \cdot \log (p/p_o)$ [B = Bel]

- Volume level $L_N$ [phon]

Volume represents the subjective and frequency-related sound intensity as perceived by the human ear; curves of equal volume sensation are given in figure 2.2.3.2 in relation to sound pressure level and frequency; the volume level $L_N$ [in phon] is defined using the value of the sound pressure level at 1000 Hz; ranges of sensation for the human ear can be specified by means of the volume curves.
Sensation max.: at approx. 4000 Hz
high: approx. 400 to 6000 Hz
low: below approx. 200 Hz

- Evaluation of level

Consideration of the frequency-related perception of sound levels (auditory sensitivity) through frequency evaluation curves; they specify a sound level correction for a sound pressure level present in energy terms corresponding to the volume sensation (based on the physiological volume curves in figure 2.2.3.2); figure 2.2.3.3 illustrates the technical evaluation curves A, B and C for low, medium and high volumes – for practical purposes usually the A-weighted curve with level specified in dB(A); according to this a 100 Hz tone at 70 dB is perceived as a tone with 51 dB(A) (correction: -19 dB); practical examples of A-weighted noise levels are given in table 2.2.3.4.
For additional explanations relevant to building and room acoustics please refer to [36, 39, 55].

#### Sound transmission

Besides measures to influence sound directly at its source, sound insulation also involves reducing the transmission from the source to the listener by a required amount.

If source and listener are in the same room, sound attenuation measures are required (absorption, room acoustics). If source and listener are separated by a building component, that component must achieve an appropriate sound insulation effect (transmission, building acoustics). Figure 2.2.3.5 illustrates the difference: in sound attenuation only part of the incident sound intensity is reflected back into the room. The component absorbed by the surface (converted into heat = sound energy lost from the room) lowers the sound level in the room. In sound insulation it is the proportion of the incident sound intensity that penetrates the separating component and reaches the quiet room that interests us.

We distinguish between measures for airborne sound insulation or structure-borne sound insulation according to the nature of the acoustic excitation of the separating component – whether caused by airborne sound, e.g. through noise, or by structure-borne sound, e.g. impact sound or noise from services transmitted directly into the component.

**Sound attenuation**
Sound attenuation in a room is influenced by the acoustic absorption of the surfaces, and when people are assembled in a room also by the number of persons and possibly the type of seating. The degree of absorption in turn influences sound propagation or reverberation time in the room. The reverberation time represents a key parameter for assessing the comprehensibility of speech or enjoyment of music. In a simplified form it is related via Sabine's formula to the volume of the room and the equivalent sound absorption area as follows:

$$T = 0.163(V/A) \text{ [s]}$$

The sound absorption area in a room is given by the sum of the geometric area proportions multiplied by their respective absorption coefficient $\alpha_S$

$$A = A_1 \cdot \alpha_{S,1} + A_2 \cdot \alpha_{S,2} + \ldots \text{ [m}^2\text{]}$$

Optimum reverberation times, e.g. for a lecture theatre in a converted roof space, lie between 0.6 and 0.9 s for room volumes between 100 and 500 m³. The relatively large size of the underside (inside) of the roof surface can be usefully employed for improving room acoustics.

The reduction in level in the room to be attained through sound absorption measures is given by:

$$\Delta L = 10 \cdot \lg \frac{A_{after}}{A_{before}} \text{ [dB]}$$

Sound insulation
The sound insulation effect of a component separating noisy and quiet rooms is characterised by the measurable sound level difference $L_1 - L_2$ between the two rooms (figure 2.2.3.6). This allows the sound reduction index R to be defined as the characteristic value of the component's airborne sound insulation: the area of the separating component S and the absorption area $A_2$ for determining the sound reduction index of the component must be taken into account for the level measured in the quiet room $L_2$ as follows (correction):

$$R = L_1 - L_2 + 10 \cdot \log(S/A_2)$$

If the measurements are carried out in a laboratory under defined conditions without flanking transmissions, we obtain the theoretical sound reduction index R. When measurements are carried out on site with the usual flanking transmissions, we obtain the practical sound reduction index R'. There is a difference of about 2–3 dB between the two values:

$$R' \sim R - (2 \text{ to } 3) \text{ [dB]}$$

Airborne sound transmission paths
As shown schematically in figure 2.2.3.7, under practical conditions airborne sound is transmitted not only through the separating component itself with its constructional features, but also via the flanking components.
Starting with the airborne sound excitation in the noisy room, the paths shown are associated with different effects:

I: longitudinal flanking transmission
II: transmission via junction, integration, edge restraint (possibly joints)
III: direct airborne sound transmission
IV: acoustic bridges, e.g. through dynamically stiff connection between two leaves
V: leaks, joints with very high transmission component (sound insulation bridged)
VI: transmission via dynamically stiff coupled leaves at flanking segment
VII: transmission via dynamically stiff coupled single leaf plus longitudinal flanking transmission

In terms of the pitched roof acting as the separating element between a loud environment and an interior, we are primarily interested in the direct transmission paths III, IV and V. Flanking effects via rigid connections at the gable or party wall junction are possible, and connecting rafters in these areas should therefore be avoided. The roof construction itself may be involved as a flanking component in the transmission of sound to adjoining rooms. Appropriate precautions, e.g. the inclusion of mass, separation of components, attenuating connections, elastic seals (limited effect), can be taken for all transmission paths in order to achieve effective sound insulation.

| Level [dB(A)] | $I/I_0$ | Perception | Source of sound |
|---|---|---|---|
| 0 | 1 | threshold of hearing | |
| 10–20 | $10^1$–$10^2$ | not disturbing | leaves rustling |
| 30–50 | $10^3$–$10^5$ | | quiet music |
| 60–70 | $10^6$–$10^7$ | disturbing | loud conversation |
| 70–80 | $10^7$–$10^8$ | | road traffic |
| 90–100 | $10^9$–$10^{10}$ | damaging | heavy vehicles |
| 100–110 | $10^{10}$–$10^{11}$ | | loud machinery |
| 120–130 | $10^{12}$–$10^{13}$ | painful | propeller aircraft |
| 130–140 | $10^{13}$–$10^{14}$ | | jet fighter aircraft |

2.2.3.4 Examples of A-weighted sound levels of various sources

Sound attenuation (room acoustics, absorption)
Sound insulation (building acoustics, transmission)

2.2.3.5 Sketch of principle for distinguishing sound attenuation (room acoustics) and sound insulation (building acoustics)

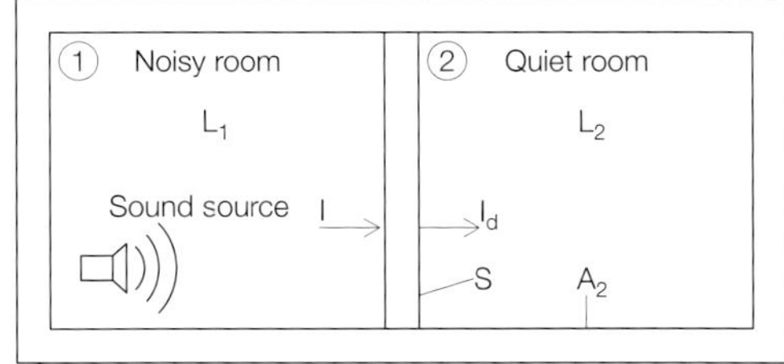


2.2.3.6 Schematic presentation of method for determining the sound reduction index of a partition

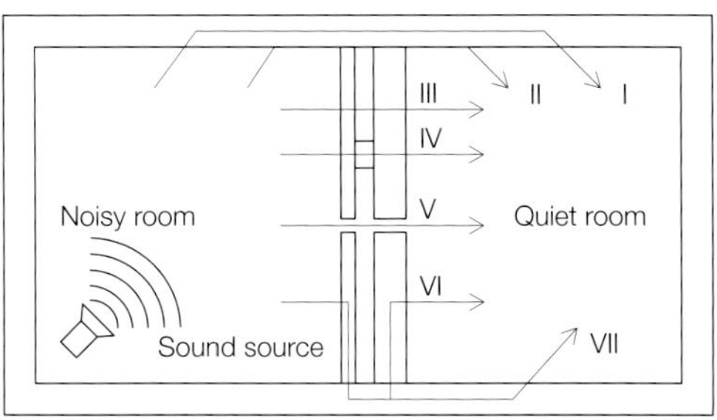


2.2.3.7 Paths for transmitting airborne sound between two rooms (Dept. of Building Science, Stuttgart University)

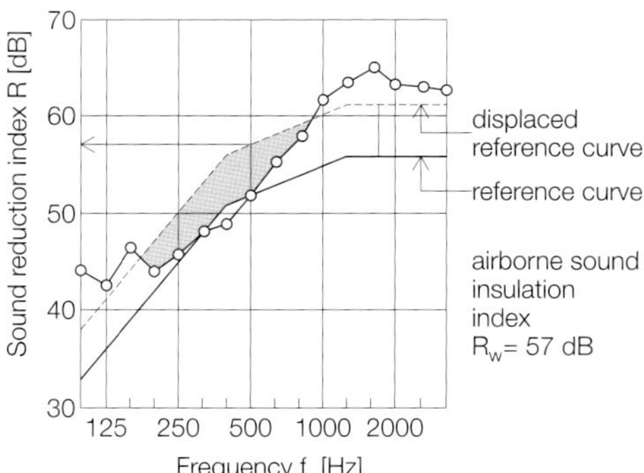


2.2.3.8 Schematic diagram of method for determining the airborne sound insulation index of a component [36]

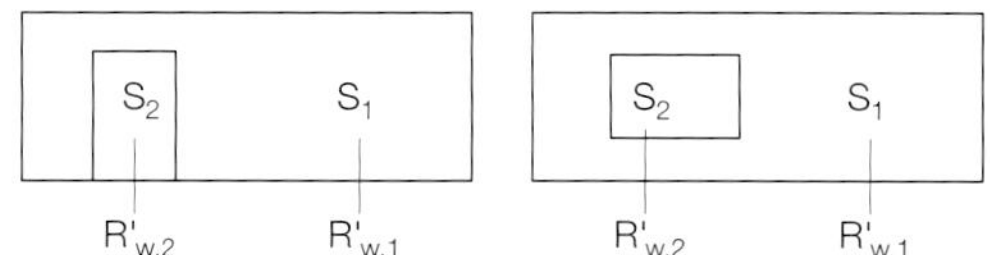


2.2.3.9 Examples of components comprising areas of different materials (door or window in a wall) [15]

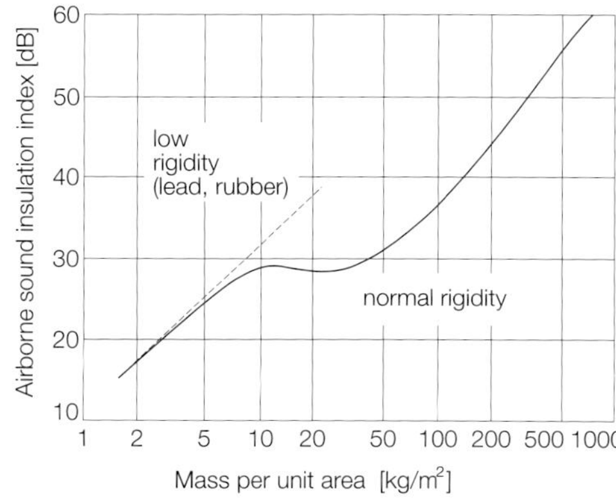


2.2.3.10 Airborne sound insulation index in relation to mass per unit area of non-rigid or rigid single-leaf components (slab-type components) [36]

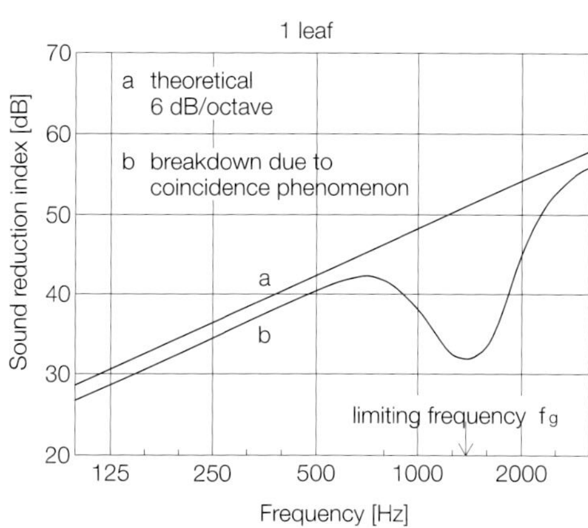


2.2.3.11 Schematic presentation of breakdown of sound reduction index of single-leaf components in the region of the limiting frequency [36]

**Airborne sound insulation**

The airborne sound insulation of building components attainable in practice should be assessed in terms of both our frequency-related perception of sound and the influence of building components and flanking components and their importance for sound transmission.

Airborne sound insulation index

These days we use the airborne sound insulation index $R_w$ to identify the airborne sound insulation of building components. This is a single figure based on practice according to DIN EN ISO 717 part 1. This involves a frequency-based evaluation of the individual values of the sound reduction index measured in 16 1/3-octave bands with the help of a prescribed frequency-related reference curve. This reference curve, as shown in figure 2.2.3.8 as measured for a typical component, is displaced up or down in 1 dB steps with respect to the measured curve so that the sum of all values below the curve (unfavourable measured values below the displaced reference curve; shaded area in figure) is as large as possible but does not exceed 32 dB in total. The value of the displaced reference curve at 500 Hz then represents the airborne sound insulation index. It is determined for laboratory ($R_w$) or typical building conditions ($R'_w$).

Resultant sound reduction index

The resultant sound reduction index $R'_{w,res}$ is calculated from the influences of the airborne sound insulation indexes of the individual elements and their individual areas $S_i$ for slab-type components made up of various elements, e.g. external wall and windows, roof surface and roof windows, internal wall and doors. The following equation is generally used:

$$R'_{w,res} = -10 \cdot \lg \left( \frac{1}{S_{tot}} \cdot \sum_{i=1}^{n} S_i \cdot 10^{-0.1 \cdot R'_{w,i}} \right)$$

The resultant sound reduction index for two elements of a building component, the most frequent case in practice (figure 2.2.3.9), can either be determined according to a diagram in DIN 4109 supplement 1 or by using the related surface proportions of the elements $f_i = S_i/S_{tot}$ as follows:

$$R'_{w,res} = -10 \cdot \lg \left(f_1 \cdot 10^{-0.1 \cdot R'_{w,1}} + f_2 \cdot 10^{-0.1 \cdot R'_{w,2}}\right)$$

If each element has a significantly different sound reduction index, the resultant is essentially governed by the smaller of the two individual values.

For a specified requirement for the whole component, e.g. total roof surface, and for a given sound reduction index for an element, e.g. roof window, the required sound reduction index for the remaining area, e.g. roof construction, can be calculated using the following equation:

$$R'_{w,2} = -10 \cdot \lg \left[ \frac{1}{S_2} \cdot \left(S_{tot} \cdot 10^{-0.1 \cdot erf\, R'_{w,res}} - S_1 \cdot 10^{-0.1 \cdot R_{w,1}}\right) \right]$$

Characteristic values for the sound insulation index of individual elements are used in the analysis according to DIN 4109 supplement 1. These already include the influence of common flanking transmissions where applicable.

Single-leaf components

The sound insulation of single-leaf components depends on their mass per unit area m² and on frequency. In acoustic terms, single-leaf also includes multi-layer components bonded together permanently across their entire surfaces to form one rigid layer. Theoretically, the following applies for the sound reduction index: a doubling of the mass per unit area or frequency (octave interval) is equal to a 6 dB increase in R; in practice it is usually only 4–5 dB. Figure 2.2.3.10 shows the relationship of the airborne sound insulation index to the mass per unit area. Note the influence of the component rigidity.

There is no increase in the airborne sound insulation index at the transition from non-rigid to rigid slab-type member, which is due to the coincidence phenomenon. This is seen in slab-type members with weights between approx. 10 and 50 kg/m² for the frequency range relevant in building work. In this range the sound insulation effect is reduced and hence offsets a mass-related increase in the sound reduction index.

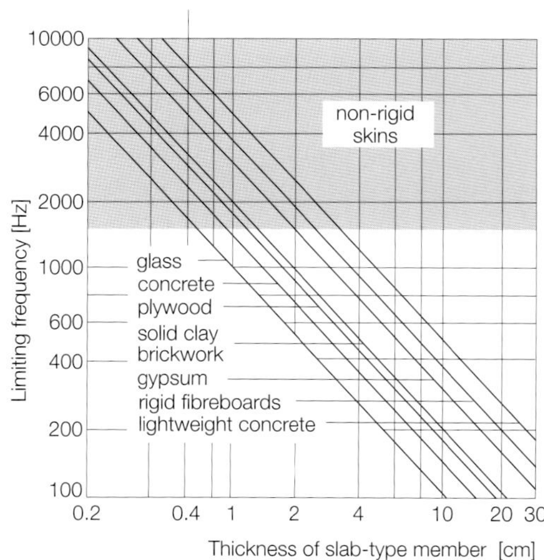


2.2.3.12 Limiting frequency of various materials in relation to the component thickness, with details of non-rigid segment [36]

Coincidence takes place when sound waves striking single-leaf plate- or slab-type members cause a projection of the sound wavelength equal to the wavelength of the member's natural oscillation. The lowest frequency at which this effect occurs is the limiting frequency $f_g$. The sound insulation effect breaks down in this frequency range. The limiting frequency of single-leaf components (slab-type members) can be determined by measurement or calculation. To satisfy the acoustic requirements of buildings, it should lie either below 100 Hz (rigid members) or above 2000 Hz (non-rigid members) (figures 2.2.3.11 and 2.2.3.12).

Double-leaf components
Double-leaf components can achieve a better sound reduction index with lighter construction and less overall thickness than equally heavy single-leaf components. The reason for this is the attenuating acoustic coupling of the two leaves. In practice, either the cavity is filled with a loose sound-insulating medium (usually fibre insulating materials – flow resistance critical) or the two leaves are fully bonded across their entire surface with a sound-attenuating material (usually soft foams – dynamic stiffness critical). However, the resulting mass/spring/mass dynamic system exhibits distinct resonance properties that lead to a noticeable breakdown in the sound insulation effect, especially in the region of the lowest natural frequency $f_R$. This frequency depends on the mass of the two leaves, the type of intermediate membrane and the spacing of the leaves. This can also be determined by measurement or by calculation, and for practical reasons it should lie below about 85 Hz. The effect that this resonance has on the sound reduction index can be seen in figures 2.2.3.13 and 2.2.3.14.
It is clear that a much higher sound reduction index can be attained above the natural frequency than in an equally heavy single-leaf component.

Flanking transmissions
The sound insulation of a partition is reduced by flanking transmissions, or even limited by enhanced sound insulation. A continuous pitched roof over terrace houses, for example, represents a flanking component for party walls between occupied rooms in adjacent properties in attic storeys and must comply with the sound insulation requirements of DIN 4109. For typical timber pitched roofs this is a lightweight flanking component with a total mass of approx. 100–130 kg/m². In order to minimise the (longitudinal) flanking transmissions through such components, non-rigid internal skins, airtight and sound-attenuated junctions with party walls, an acoustic break between continuous, sound-transmitting layers (outer skins, tiling battens), attenuating media in continuous cavities (fibre insulating materials) and similar measures will be needed. Such measures are feasible with a pitched roof and harmonise well with other criteria, e.g. thermal performance and moisture control.
Figure 2.2.3.15 illustrates a typical detail.

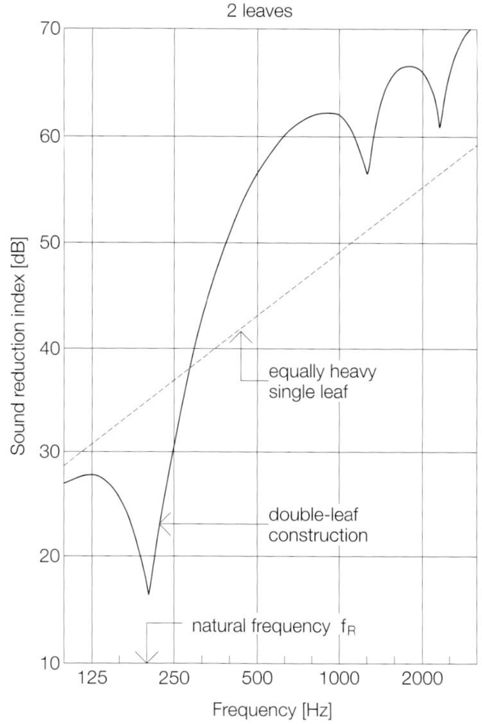


2.2.3.13 Schematic diagram of breakdown of sound reduction index of double-leaf components in the region of the natural frequency [36]

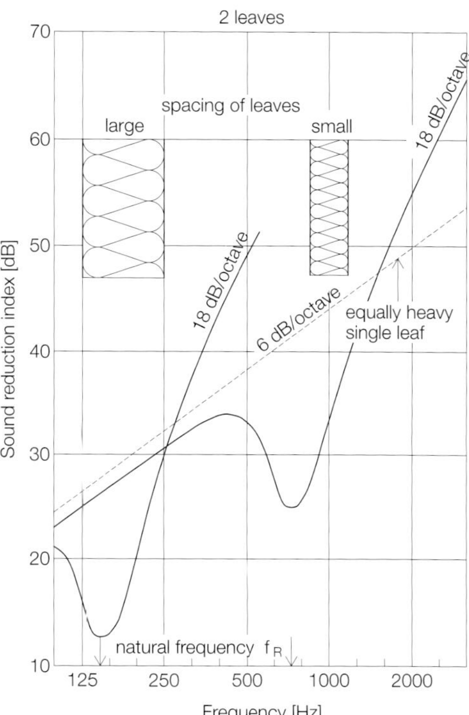


2.2.3.14 Schematic diagram of sound reduction index of double-leaf components with different spacing between leaves [36]

**Sound insulation for pitched roofs**
The purpose of sound insulation in a pitched roof forming part of the external envelope is to provide protection from external noise. Typical timber pitched roofs can usually be considered as approximating to lightweight double-leaf components, although the type of roof covering, additional outer skins if applicable and possible internal cladding do represent deviations from a simple double-leaf lightweight construction.

Requirements
The building authorities have introduced minimum requirements for the airborne sound insulation of external components according to DIN 4109 to protect against external noise, and these also apply to pitched roofs. DIN 4109 distinguishes between different types of external noise sources in order to determine the "relevant external noise level". These are: road, rail, water-borne and air traffic, and commercial and industrial plants. Seven noise level ranges with associated "relevant external noise levels" are specified for defining requirements (see table 2.2.3.16). For each noise level range there are resultant sound reduction index $R'_{w,res}$ requirements for the external component,

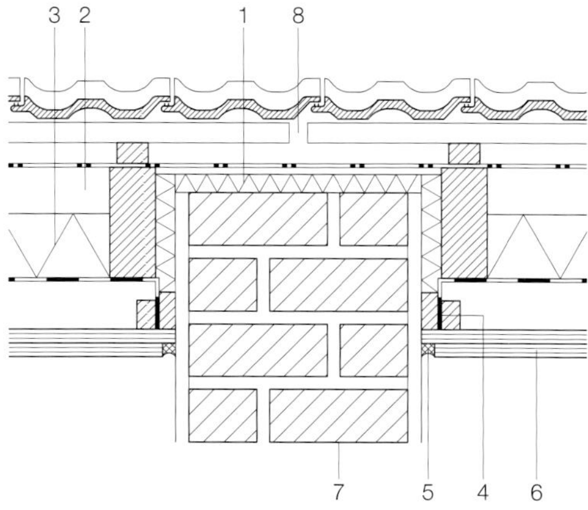


1 Mineral fibre batts on party wall and between party wall and rafters
2 Ventilation cavity
3 Layer of thermal insulation, mineral fibre batts, d = 80 mm, bulk density > 30 kg/m³
4 Sealed termination of airtight layer (polyethylene film, aluminium foil)
5 Permanently elastic jointing compound
6 Plasterboard, 2 x 12.5 mm
7 Party wall between residential premises
8 Gap between tiling battens

2.2.3.15 Junction with good acoustic properties between timber pitched roof and residential party wall

| Column | 1 | 2 | 3 | 4 | 5 |
|---|---|---|---|---|---|
| Line | Noise level | "Relevant external noise level" | Type of room | | |
| | | | Bedrooms in hospitals, clinics etc. | Occupied rooms in apartments, bedrooms in hotels etc., classrooms and similar | Offices[1] and similar |
| | | dB(A) | reqd $R'_{w,res}$ of external component [dB] | | |
| 1 | I | < 55 | 35 | 30 | – |
| 2 | II | 56–60 | 35 | 30 | 30 |
| 3 | III | 61–65 | 40 | 35 | 30 |
| 4 | IV | 66–70 | 45 | 40 | 35 |
| 5 | V | 71–75 | 50 | 45 | 40 |
| 6 | VI | 76–80 | [2] | 50 | 45 |
| 7 | VII | > 80 | [2] | [2] | 50 |

[1] No requirements are placed on the external components of rooms in which noise penetrating from outside contributes only marginally to the internal noise level owing to the activities performed in those rooms.
[2] The requirements in these situations should be specified according to local circumstances.

2.2.3.16 Requirements for airborne sound insulation of external components (after [14]), determination of required resultant sound reduction index

| Column/ Line | 1 | 2 | 3 | 4 | 5 | 6 | 7 | 8 | 9 | 10 |
|---|---|---|---|---|---|---|---|---|---|---|
| 1 | $S_{(W+F)}/S_G$ | 2.5 | 2.0 | 1.6 | 1.3 | 1.0 | 0.8 | 0.6 | 0.5 | 0.4 |
| 2 | Correction factor | +5 | +4 | +3 | +2 | +1 | 0 | −1 | −2 | −3 |

$S_{(W+F)}$: total area of external component of occupied room [m²]
$S_G$: plan area of occupied room [m²]

2.2.3.17 Correction factors for the required resultant sound reduction index given in table 2.2.3.16, according to room geometry (after [14])

including windows, which must be satisfied, depending on the use of the rooms. Corrective factors are employed to take account of the room geometry (see table 2.2.3.17).

Critical external noise levels for typical road traffic situations can be determined from the nomogram in figure 2.2.3.18, depending on the various traffic noise parameters. However, the noise level can also be determined by measurements (see DIN 4109, appendix B). Modified regulations must be observed in the case of aircraft noise (see Aircraft Noise Protection Act).

Analysis of requirements
Requirements for sound insulation can always be determined by measurement or calculation, or by using prescribed types of construction. This is regulated by DIN 4109 supplement 1 introduced by the building authorities. Reference examples are provided for timber pitched roofs which exhibit characteristic values of up to 45 dB for the airborne sound insulation index $R'_{w,R}$.
DIN 4109 supplement 2 or the draft of DIN 4109 part 10 include recommendations/suggestions for enhanced sound insulation measures which increase the $R'_{w,res}$ value of a roof by 5 dB compared to DIN 4109.

Basically, dense outer skins and heavier inner lining are required in order to ensure a sound reduction index of 50 dB or higher. The insulation thicknesses typical these days, often well in excess of 160 mm, also have an advantageous effect. Comparative measurements in [37] reveal that, for example, non-ventilated roofs with 160 mm thick insulation filling the space between the rafters achieve sound insulation figures in the region of 52 dB; by comparison, a ventilated construction with the same depth of rafter and insulation 60–120 mm thick reaches about 48–50 dB.

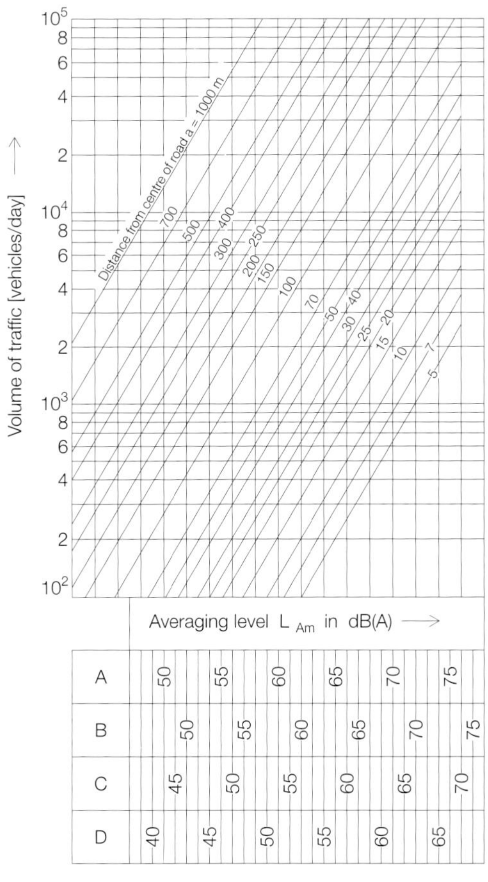


A Motorways and motorway feeder roads (HGV proportion: 25%)
B Trunk/main/secondary roads outside urban areas; roads on industrial estates (HGV proportion: 20%)
C Local/urban roads; main routes (2 to 6 lanes) (HGV proportion: 10%)
D Local/urban roads; in residential districts (HGV proportion: 5%)

The following surcharges may need to be added to the averaging levels:
+3 dB(A) if the point of reception of the sound is located on a road with uninterrupted development on both sides
+2 dB(A) if the road has a gradient exceeding 5%
+2 dB(A) if the point of reception of the sound is located less than 100 m from the next traffic light-controlled junction

2.2.3.18 Nomogram for determining the averaging level or the "relevant external noise level" for typical road traffic situations (after [14]).
Note: The free field propagation surcharge of 3 dB(A) has been taken into account here.

## Fire protection, corrosion protection

**Fire protection**

The aims of fire protection measures in buildings are:

- to protect persons (occupants, rescue services),
- to protect property (the assets of the occupier and third parties), and
- to protect premises (spread of fire to neighbouring premises)

in the event of a fire. Preventive structural measures essentially comprise the choice of building materials according to their behaviour in fire, the design of components to provide adequate fire resistance, and the division of the building into fire compartments in order to reduce the risk of the outbreak and spread of fire.

In Germany the building authority's stipulations regarding fire protection are laid down in the building code of each federal state. The requirements defined in those codes refer to the classification of the fire behaviour of building materials given in DIN 4102 part 1 and the fire resistance of components in DIN 4102 part 2. These define building material classes according to the combustibility of a material and hence the risk of outbreak of fire, and fire resistance classes based on the duration of fire resistance of components.

Building material classes
In principle we distinguish between incombustible (class A) and combustible (class B) materials, with each class subdivided further. Table 2.2.4.1 lists the classes together with their building authority designations. The allocation of a building material to a particular class can be proved by fire tests (e.g. furnace test to DIN 4102 part 1) or by assigning the material to a classified building materials group according to DIN 4102 part 4. The building codes do not permit the use of building materials of class B 3.

Fire resistance classes
The fire resistance class of a building component specifies the minimum length of time (in minutes) for which a component complies with certain criteria (e.g. loadbearing behaviour, heat transmission) in the standardised fire test to DIN 4102 part 2. The various fire resistance requirements of class F (for loadbearing or enclosing components, including roofs) are summarised in table 2.2.4.2. The allocation of a component to a certain fire resistance class can be proved by either fire tests to DIN 4102 part 2 or by constructing the component to meet the requirements of DIN 4102 part 4. The fire resistance class can be combined with a building materials class in order to achieve a differentiated designation or formulation of requirements for an individual case. Table 2.2.4.3 lists the allocation of requirements of the building code for a differentiated specification of fire resistance class F.

Flying sparks and radiant heat
Roofs and roof coverings must be able to withstand flying sparks and radiant heat from outside. This is achieved by the proper design of roof coverings with natural or man-made materials (slate, clay, concrete) or the use of at least 0.5 mm thick sheet metal on loadbearing construction, as well as by using intermediate layers of thermally insulating materials with two layers of bituminous roofing felt. Proof of resistance to flying sparks and radiant heat for other types of roofing must be confirmed by fire tests to DIN 4102 part 7.

**Corrosion protection**

Issues of corrosion protection primarily concern the metal elements used in roof construction. This essentially means sheet metal roof coverings, flashings etc. that are directly exposed to the atmosphere. Loadbearing elements of the construction, e.g. steel lattice beams or similar elements supporting heavy roof components, or lightweight steel constructions, can also come into contact with diffusion or ventilation flows with increased moisture levels and hence be subjected to an increased risk of corrosion. Besides chemical corrosion caused by the effects of moisture or aggressive moisture ("acid rain", air pollution), galvanic corrosion caused by contact between dissimilar metals is also important. Critical here are the positions in the electrochemical series of the two metals in contact.
Active measures to prevent corrosion consist of applying coverings, e.g. paints, dip/powder coatings, (hot-dip) galvanising, etc. compatible with the substrate. Regular inspection and maintenance of such measures is indispensable. The protective oxide coatings that form on some metals (e.g. sheet zinc, galvanised sheet steel) usually provide only limited protection.
Metals should be combined carefully in order to avoid galvanic corrosion. Table 2.2.4.4 shows suitable (+) and unsuitable (-) combinations of metals based on the guidelines of the plumbing trade. [65]

| Bldg. material cl. | Building authority designation |
|---|---|
| A | incombustible materials |
| A 1<br>A 2 | (pure organic)<br>(combustible constituents) |
| B | combustible materials |
| B 1<br>B 2<br>B 3 | not readily flammable materials<br>flammable materials<br>highly flammable materials |

2.2.4.1 Building material classes – classification according to behaviour in fire [2]

| Fire resistance class | Fire resistance in minutes | Designation |
|---|---|---|
| F 30 | ≥ 30 | fire-retardant |
| F 60 | ≥ 60 | |
| F 90 | ≥ 90 | fire-resistant |
| F 120 | ≥ 120 | highly fire-resistant |
| F 180 | ≥ 180 | |

2.2.4.2 Fire resistance class F – classification according to duration of fire resistance [3] with details of building code designations

| Description of requirements | Fire resistance class (satisfied by proof according to DIN 4102 pt 2 or 4) |
|---|---|
| fire-retardant | F 30–B, F 60–B |
| fire-retardant, with essential (loadbearing) parts made from incombustible materials | F 30–AB, F 60–AB |
| fire-retardant, all parts made from incombustible materials | F 30–A, F 60–A |
| fire-resistant | F 90–B |
| fire-resistant, with essential (loadbearing) parts made from incombustible materials | F 90–AB |
| fire-resistant, all parts made from incombustible materials | F 90–A |

2.2.4.3 Allocation of requirement designations and differentiated details for fire resistance class F

| | AL | Pb | Cu | Zn | SS | Steel |
|---|---|---|---|---|---|---|
| AL | + | + | – | + | + | + |
| Pb | + | + | + | + | + | + |
| Cu | – | + | + | – | + | – |
| Zn | + | + | – | + | + | + |
| stainless steel | + | + | + | + | + | + |
| steel | + | + | – | + | + | + |

2.2.4.4 Combinations of metals suitable (+) and unsuitable (-) in terms of galvanic corrosion

Corrosion of building materials, also called ageing or embrittlement, may occur in the synthetic materials used in roofs (roofing felt, boards, etc.). In these cases it can be the liberation of softeners or the effects of ultraviolet radiation that are significant. Corrosive effects stemming from synthetic materials can affect other materials and become significant in the event of fire. The release of caustic or toxic gases is not only a local health risk during a fire; they can also be disadvantageous when repairing the construction.
See the chapters on "Design" and "Layers and materials" for further details concerning the behaviour of metals and synthetic materials, and specific properties.

**References**


[01] Achtziger, J., and Zehendner, H.: Wärmedämmstoffe; in: Bauphysik Kalender 2001, Verlag Ernst & Sohn, Berlin 2001
[02] DIN 4102 pt 1: Fire behaviour of building materials and building components – Building materials; concepts, requirements and tests (May 1998)
[03] DIN 4102 pt 2: Fire behaviour of building materials and building components – Building components; definitions, requirements and tests (Sept 1977)
[04] DIN 4102 pt 4: Fire behaviour of building materials and building components – Synopsis and application of classified building materials, components and special components (Mar 1994)
[05] DIN 4102 pt 7: Fire behaviour of building materials and building components – Roofing; definitions, requirements and testing (Jul 1998)
[06] DIN 4108 supp. 2: Thermal insulation and energy economy in buildings – Thermal bridges – Examples for planning and performance (Aug 1998)
[07] DIN 4108 pt 2: Thermal protection and energy economy in buildings: minimum requirements for thermal insulation (Mar 2001)
[08] DIN 4108 pt 3: Thermal insulation and energy economy in buildings: protection against moisture subject to climate conditions; requirements and directions for design and construction (Jul 2001)
[09] DIN 4108 pt 3/corr. 1: Corrigenda to DIN 4108 pt 3 (Apr 2002)
[10] DIN V 4108 pt 4 (prelim.): Thermal insulation and energy economy in buildings: characteristic values relating to thermal insulation and protection against moisture (Feb 2002)
[11] DIN V 4108 pt 6 (prelim.): Thermal insulation and energy economy in buildings; calculation of annual energy use for building; amendment A1 (Nov 2000)
[12] DIN V 4108 pt 6 (prelim.)/A1: amendment A1 (Aug 2001)
[13] DIN 4108 pt 7: Thermal insulation and energy economy of buildings – Airtightness of building, requirements, recommendations and examples for planning and performance (Aug 2001)
[14] DIN 4109: Sound insulation in buildings; requirements and testing (Nov 1989)
[15] DIN 4109 supp. 1: Sound insulation in buildings; construction examples and calculation methods (Nov 1989)
[16] DIN 4109 supp. 2: Sound insulation in buildings; guidelines for planning and execution; proposals for increased sound insulation; recommendations for sound insulation in personal living and working areas (Nov 1989)
[17] DIN V 4701 pt 10 (prelim.): Energy efficiency of heating and ventilation systems in buildings – Heating, domestic hot water, ventilation (Feb 2001)
[18] DIN V 4701 pt 10 (prelim.) supp. 1: Energy efficiency of heating and ventilation systems in buildings – Diagrams and planning aids for selected systems with standard components (Feb 2002)
[19] DIN 68800-2: Protection of timber: preventive constructional measures in buildings (May 1996)
[20] DIN EN 410: Glass in building – Determination of luminous and solar characteristics of glazing (1998)
[21] DIN EN 832: Thermal performance of buildings – Calculation of energy use for heating; residential buildings (Dec 1998)
[22] DIN EN 12207 pt 1: Windows and doors – Air permeability – Classification (1999)
[23] DIN EN 12524: Building materials and products – hygrothermal properties – tabulated design values (Jul 2000)
[24] DIN EN 13829: Thermal performance of buildings – Determination of air permeability of buildings – Fan pressurization method (2000)
[25] DIN EN ISO 717 pt 1: Acoustics – Rating of sound insulation in buildings and of building elements – Airborne sound insulation (Jan 1997)
[26] DIN EN ISO 6946: Building components – Thermal resistance and thermal transmittance – Calculation method (Nov 1996)
[27] DIN EN ISO 7345: Thermal insulation – Physical quantities and definitions (1995)
[28] DIN EN ISO 9346: Thermal insulation – Mass transfer – Physical quantities and definitions (Aug 1996)
[29] DIN EN ISO 10211 pt 1: Thermal bridges in building construction – Heat flows and surface temperatures – General calculation methods (Nov 1995)
[30] DIN EN ISO 10211 pt 2: Thermal bridges in building construction – Calculation of heat flows and surface temperatures – Linear thermal bridges (Jun 2001)
[31] DIN EN ISO 12572: Building materials – determination of water vapour transmission properties (Sept 2001)
[32] DIN EN ISO 13788: Hygrothermal performance of building components and building elements – Internal surface temperature to avoid critical surface humidity and interstitial condensation – Calculation methods (Nov 2001)
[33] E DIN 4108 pt 2 (draft)/A1: Thermal protection and energy economy in buildings – minimum requirements for thermal insulation; amendment A1 (Feb 2002)
[34] E DIN 4109 pt 10 (draft): Sound insulation in buildings – Part 10: Proposals for improved sound insulation for housing (Jun 2000)
[35] E DIN EN ISO 15148 (draft): Building materials – determination of water absorption coefficient (Aug 1996)
[36] Fasold, W., and Veres, E.: Schallschutz und Raumakustik in der Praxis. Planungsbeispiele und konstruktive Lösungen; Verlag für Bauwesen, Berlin, 1998
[37] Fischer, H.-M., Koch, S., and Metzen, H.: Erhöhter Schallschutz im Steildach durch Sparrenvolldämmung; wksb 34 (1989), issue 27, p. 38
[38] Glaser, H.: Graphisches Verfahren zur Untersuchung von Diffusionsvorgängen. Kältetechnik 11 (1959), p. 345
[39] Gösele, Schüle, Künzel: Schall, Wärme, Feuchte; Bauverlag, Wiesbaden, 1997
[40] Hauser, G., and Maas, A.: Energieeinsparverordnung 2002 (EnEV). Verlag Bau + Technik, Düsseldorf, 2002
[41] Hauser, G., and Stiegel, H.: Wärmebrücken-Atlas für den Holzbau. Bauverlag, Wiesbaden, 1992
[42] Hauser, G., and Stiegel, H.: Wärmebrücken-Atlas für den Mauerwerksbau. 2nd ed., Bauverlag, Wiesbaden, 1993
[43] Hauser, G., Schulze, H., and Stiegel, H.: Anschlussdetails von Niedrigenergiehäusern. Wärmetechnische Optimierung – Standardlösungen; IRB-Verlag, Stuttgart, 1996
[44] Holm, A., and Künzel, H.M.: Feuchtetechnisches Verhalten von Holzsparren bei einer Dachsanierung von außen; IBP Note 27 (2002), No. 370
[45] Kießl, K.: Kapillarer und dampfförmiger Feuchtetransport in mehrschichtigen Bauteilen – Rechnerische Erfassung und bauphysikalische Anwendung; dissertation, Essen University, 1983
[46] Krus, M.: Feuchtetransport- und Speicherkoeffizienten poröser mineralischer Baustoffe – Theoretische Grundlagen und neue Messtechniken; dissertation, Stuttgart University, 1995
[47] Künzel, H., and Großkinsky, T.: Nicht belüftet, voll gedämmt: Die beste Lösung für das Steildach!; wksb 34 (1989), issue 27, pp. 1–7
[48] Künzel, H.: Dachdeckung und Dachbelüftung; IRB-Verlag, Stuttgart, 1996
[49] Künzel, H.: Steildächer. Die Normvorschriften sind überholt; Federal Building Gazette 46 (1997), issue 5, pp. 312–16
[50] Künzel, H.M.: Verfahren zur ein- und zweidimensionalen Berechnung des gekoppelten Wärme- und Feuchtetransports in Bauteilen mit einfachen Kennwerten; dissertation, Stuttgart University, 1994
[51] Künzel, H. M.: Feuchtesichere Altbausanierung mit neuartiger Dampfbremse; Federal Building Gazette 45 (1996), issue 10, pp. 798–801
[52] Künzel H. M., and Sedlbauer, K.: Steildächer – feuchte- und wärmetechnische Ausbildung; in: Bauphysik Kalender 2001; Verlag Ernst & Sohn, Berlin, 2001
[53] Künzel, H. M., Holm, A., and Sedlbauer, K.: Wärme- und Feuchteschutz; in: Beton Kalender 2002; Ernst & Sohn Verlag, Berlin, 2002
[54] Liersch, K.: Belüftete Dach- und Wandkonstruktionen, vol. 3; Dächer, Bauphysikalische Grundlagen; Bauverlag, Wiesbaden, 1986
[55] Lutz, P. et al.: Lehrbuch der Bauphysik; 4th ed., Teubner Verlag, Stuttgart, 1997
[56] Mainka, G.-W., and Paschen, H.: Wärmebrückenkatalog. Teubner Verlag, Stuttgart, 1986
[57] Pohl, W.-H.: Belüftete Dächer mit Metalldeckung. Feuchteschutz. Bauphysikalische Grundlagen, Fallstudien, Beispiele; pub.: RHEINZINK GmbH, Datteln, 1991
[58] Recknagel/Sprenger/Schramek: Taschenbuch für Heizung und Klimatechnik; 69th ed., Oldenbourg Verlag, Munich, 1999
[59] Reyer, E., Schild, K., and Völkner, S.: Kompendium der Dämmstoffe. 2nd ed., IRB-Verlag, Stuttgart, 2001
[60] Ruhe, C.: Nichtbelüftetes geneigtes Dach mit Sparrenvolldämmung. Wasserabtropfungen von der Decke im Sommer; Deutsches Architektenblatt 27 (1995), issue 8, pp. 1470–81
[61] Sagelsdorff, R., and Rode, C.: Eine wasserdurchlässige Dampfbremse als Hygrodiode. Schweizer Ingenieur und Architekt 1997, No. 36
[62] Sedlbauer, K.: Vorhersage von Schimmelpilzbildung auf und in Bauteilen; dissertation, Stuttgart University, 2001
[63] Werner, H., and Röder, J.: Konstruktion und Berechnung von Niedrigenergiehäusern; in: Bauphysik Kalender 2001; Verlag Ernst & Sohn, Berlin, 2001
[64] Zentralverband des Deutschen Dachdeckerhandwerks: Dachdeckerrichtlinien; Rudolf Müller Verlag, 2000
[65] Zentralverband Sanitär/Heizung/Klima: Richtlinien für die Ausführung von Metall-Dächern, Außenwandbekleidungen und Bauklempner-Arbeiten. St Augustin, 1994

# Design

Eberhard Schunck and Hans Jochen Oster

## Usage and requirements

The elementary function of a roof is to provide protection from precipitation in the form of rain, snow and ice. It must also be able to withstand the loads of wind and snow plus persons carrying out maintenance and repairs. Moisture control is also its task.
Use of the roof space for simple storage etc. calls for protection against driving snow and ingress of dirt, and a barrier against the wind. More demanding uses make it necessary to provide protection against extremes of heat and cold, and external noise. And if used as living quarters, additional problems of thermal performance and internal moisture must be taken into account. Finally, our current state of knowledge compels us to consider ecological issues and the use of the roof as a passive source of energy. So besides the climatic conditions, it is the use that primarily determines the choice of construction.

## Design principles

These days we have the technical means to respond to the manifold demands on the roof with a finely tuned series of different types of construction. The design principles consist of satisfying the various demands placed on the roof through the individual layers of the construction.

The current state of roof technology can be broken down into the following definitions:

- single-layer designs, where moisture and precipitation drains away on a covering layer,
- two-layer designs in which an additional, protective second layer – roofing felt or boarding – is introduced,
- three- or multi-layer designs in which the sealing layers and the insulating layer are separated by ventilation layers, and
- single-skin designs that integrate all the thermal, moisture-control and acoustic requirements into one element.

This approach – responding to different requirements with different layers – appears logical and sensible, but does entail a certain degree of extra work during erection. More layers means more junctions and connections are necessary, and hence, potentially, more chances of error. The single-skin principle would appear to overcome such problems.
Below, we first attempt to define the terms involved and then discuss the issue of ventilated or non-ventilated construction.

### Terms – definitions

Ventilated roof – ventilation layer above insulation
A ventilated roof according to the new edition of DIN 4108 part 3[1] is a roof with ventilated air layers positioned directly above the thermal insulation.

Non-ventilated roof – no ventilation layer above insulation
The new edition of DIN 4108 takes two sentences to describe this type of construction. The first tells us that there is no ventilated air layer positioned directly above the thermal insulation; however, the second says that a "non-ventilated roof" may nevertheless have other air layers!

Sheathing
This is laid on the roof before the uppermost layer of the roof covering and, together with this, forms a constructional unit.

Roofing felt, boarding, sarking
This is an autonomous "covering layer" or "waterproofing layer" that represents a rainproof roof even without the uppermost layer of the roof covering.

Covering and waterproofing
The new edition of DIN 4108 also makes a distinction between covering and waterproofing. A "roof covering" is a covering of overlapping elements, whereas "waterproofing" is the watertight bonding of sheets of material. In this context we can also make finer distinctions for sheathing, roofing felt, boarding and sarking, e.g. sheathing and watertight sheathing, sarking and watertight sarking.

### Ventilated – non-ventilated

Occupied roof spaces are described in the guidelines for the roofing trade as "ventilated designs", i.e. with a ventilated air layer directly above the insulation. However, since 1989 it has been observed that with roof surfaces subjected to different climatic conditions, moist, warm air can flow from the heated side facing the sun into the cooler part of the roof facing away from the sun and release moisture there (up to 100 g/m² in 24 h).[2] This effect is particularly noticeable when the layer above the air layer is unable to absorb much moisture (e.g. smooth roofing felt). This means that condensation cannot be absorbed and so saturates the layer of insulation below.

Ventilation layer above insulation
The tried-and-tested ventilated design has been assessed more critically since the above effect was first noticed. Nevertheless, this form of construction is still justifiable owing to the following undisputed advantages:

- Summer thermal performance can be improved by heated air masses escaping in the additional duct.
- The moisture accumulating is carried away irrespective of the cause – incoming rainwater, precipitation due to a temperature drop at the underside of the roof covering, moisture from the interior that has penetrated the vapour barrier and insulation.
- Ventilated designs help to compensate for errors and problems during construction, particularly when laying and joining the vapour barrier.
- Roof decking, which is frequently positioned above the air layer, improves the sound insulation.

However, positioning the ventilation layer above the insulation does have disadvantages:

- Greater heat loss via the air flow over an open-pore insulation, which also necessitates a thicker layer of insulation.
- When the insulation is placed between the rafters the dependence of the rafter depth on the sum of insulation thickness plus depth of air layer can lead to oversized rafters.

[1] DIN 4108 part 3, Jul 2001 ed.
[2] Künzel, H.; Großkinsky, T.: Nicht belüftet, voll gedämmt: Die beste Lösung für das Steildach, Wksb, issue 27, Ludwigshafen,1989

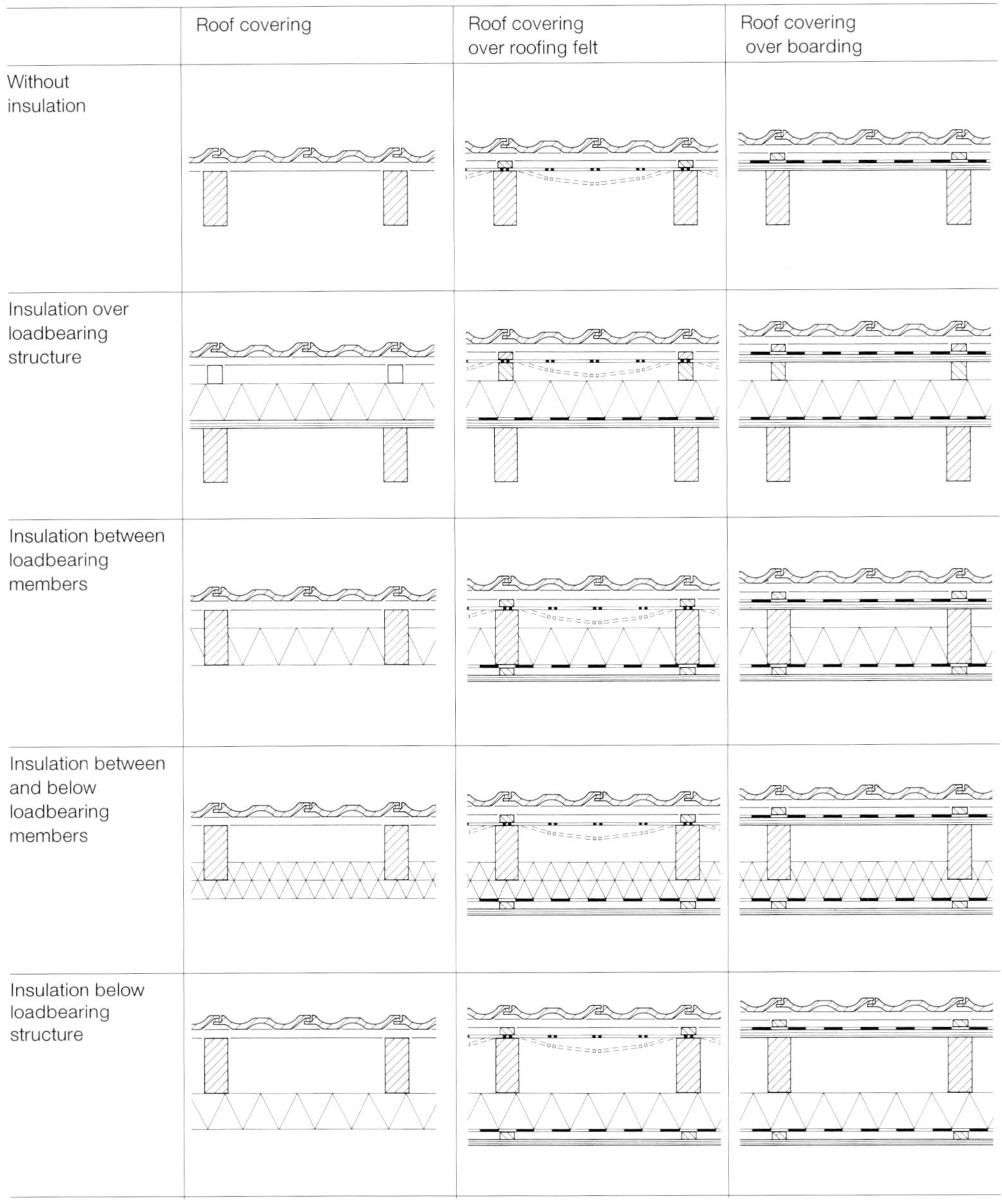


2.3.1 Ventilated design principles using the example of a roof covering of profiled overlapping elements

- The air cavity is regarded as being damp, which means that chemical timber preservatives are necessary.[3]
- A ventilated air layer above wide roof penetrations and in the region of hips and valleys is very complicated and expensive to build.
- The inlets and outlets required for ventilation call for extra work on site.

Figure 2.3.1 shows the main design principles of ventilated types of construction. The roof covering in the examples is profiled by overlapping elements laid by hand.

Without insulation
Designs without any thermal insulation are reserved for the simplest uses, such as open roof spaces and simple storage functions. Roofing felt or boarding can keep out wind, dirt and driving snow. Boarding is more useful than roofing felt as it also allows the standard pitch of the roof covering to be reduced slightly. In winter boarding is very useful if the roof covering itself cannot be laid immediately owing to poor weather conditions. In some climate zones the insulation value of a timber roof decking plus a layer of roofing felt is sufficient. Even simple sound insulation requirements can be fulfilled by this type of construction.

Insulation above loadbearing structure
This design principle has many advantages. The loadbearing structure remains exposed in the interior and is subjected to only minor moisture and temperature fluctuations. The thermal insulation is laid effectively without interruption over the rafters and the thickness can be determined completely independently of the loadbearing structure. Another advantage of this type of construction is that the vapour barrier can be installed in one plane and attached from above without interruption. The ventilation cavity is formed using counter battens or spacer rafters. However, as the thermal insulation is not normally rigid enough to secure the spacer rafters, purlins must be provided in the same plane as the insulation. These members interrupt the insulation and must therefore be made from a material of low thermal conductivity. This additional layer of purlins, normally of timber, requires a certain amount of work (and costs). This is the deepest type of construction.

Insulation between loadbearing members
The overall depth of the construction can be reduced but this type of roof can only function properly when the depth of the loadbearing structure clearly exceeds that required for the insulating and waterproofing layers. Otherwise adequate ventilation cannot be guaranteed. In principle, this type of construction is also suitable for refurbishment work. The disadvantages are that the layer of insulation is interrupted by the rafters and the vapour barrier must be carefully attached to the inside.

Insulation between and below loadbearing structure
This type of construction is required when the loadbearing structure is not deep enough and the overall depth of the construction has to be kept as slim as possible. Additional framing is required to fix the vapour barrier and inner lining. Here again, the vapour barrier must be carefully attached to the inside. This type of construction can also be used when fitting out the roof space at a later date.

[3] DIN 68800 Protection of timber; part 2: preventive constructional measures in buildings, May 1996 ed.; part 3: preventive chemical protection, Apr 1990 ed.

Insulation below loadbearing structure
If the structural depth available is insufficient, thermal insulation must be installed below the loadbearing structure. The cost and amount of work involved is roughly equal to the previous method. The thermal insulation must either be sufficiently rigid and suitable for attaching a vapour barrier and inner lining, or it must be interrupted by framing. The loss of interior space must be considered because the total construction is very deep.
The new requirements for the ventilation cross-section for ventilated roof designs without a theoretical analysis are included in the new edition of DIN 4108.[4] This also contains the requirement stipulating a maximum thermal resistance of 20% of the total construction for the layers below the diffusion-retardant layer (see "Ventilation").

No ventilation layer above insulation
The disadvantages of a ventilation layer above the insulation correspond to the advantages of no ventilation layer above the insulation:

- There is no air flow over the layer of insulation to cause additional heat loss.
- The total depth of the rafter can be used for insulation.
- As the insulation without an overlying ventilation layer is not subjected to moisture ingress from the outside, chemical timber preservatives can be avoided.
- Roof surfaces above wide roof penetrations and hip and valley areas can be built using the same construction principles as the rest of the roof.
- There is no need to include inlets and outlets.

However, an air layer must certainly be included below the roof covering. This serves to dissipate heat and drain incoming rainwater and condensation. It also helps to dry out saturated roofing components quickly. The water run-off layer above the insulation must be open to diffusion (max. $s_d \leq 0.2$ m) so that moisture present in the insulation can escape by diffusion. But non-ventilated layers of insulation also have disadvantages:

- The lack of an additional air duct above the layer of insulation downgrades the thermal performance in summer.
- Roof decking is not normally provided and so sound insulation is reduced.
- The film over the insulation that acts as a moisture barrier (with the necessary low $s_d$-value to allow drying by diffusion) may gradually become soiled over time and thus more resistant to diffusion. Layers of condensation and ice also increase the resistance to diffusion. Once the vapour barrier below the insulation is defective or damaged, the insulation can become saturated (a well-known problem) and the whole construction may even fail.
- Finally, the non-ventilated layer of insulation has to rely on a functioning vapour barrier with an $s_d$-value $\geq 100$ m. This means that all joints and connections to other components must be produced without any leaks. On a site-built pitched roof with insulation between the rafters this is only possible with the utmost care.

Non-ventilated, insulated roof designs generally have the following cross-sections:

Site-built roof with insulation between loadbearing members

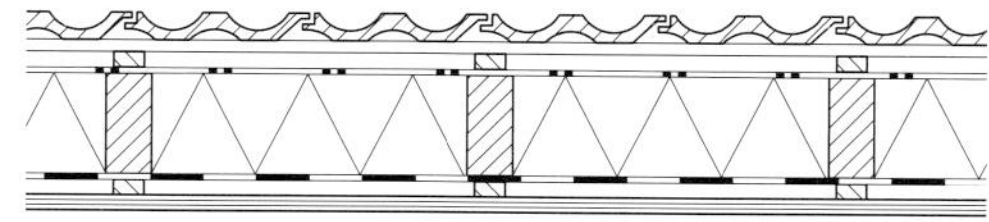

2.3.2 Non-ventilated design principle using the example of manual layering with insulation between the loadbearing members

The manual layering and building of a roof without a ventilation layer above the insulation and insulation between the rafters embodies all the aforementioned risks and disadvantages. Work is carried out on the underside of the pitched roof, overhead on a sloping surface – conditions that readily invite poor workmanship. In addition, the sealed junctions with other components are very often carried out by workers unfamiliar with the materials and techniques involved. The new edition of DIN 4108 therefore calls for defined ratios for the $s_d$-values of the layers above and below the thermal insulation. In certain types of construction (roof decking not ventilated and watertight roof covering) the standard prescribes an $s_d$-value $\geq 100$ m. To prevent the loss of the insulating effect in the event of insulation becoming saturated, it is recommended to use a special insulating material. Ventilation below the roof covering and the openness to diffusion of the layer above the insulation are indispensable constituents of this design. The new edition of DIN 4108 also contains the requirement stipulating a maximum thermal resistance of 20% of the total construction for the layers below the diffusion-retardant layer (see also the section "Ventilation").

[4] DIN 4108 part 3: 2001-07

Site-built roof with insulation over loadbearing members

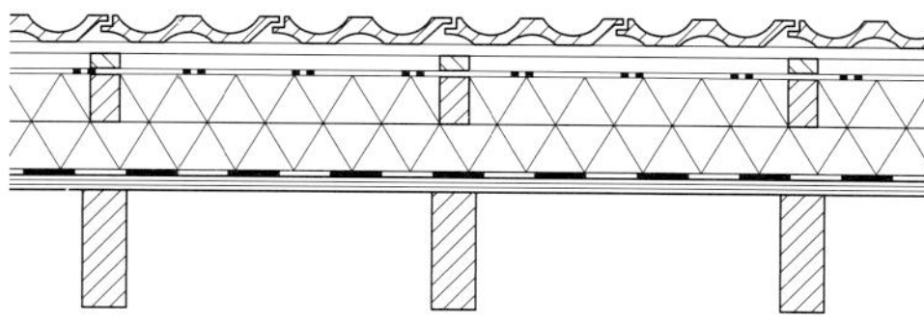

2.3.3 Non-ventilated design principle using the example of manual layering with insulation over the loadbearing structure

The problems outlined above would seem to favour of a type of construction in which the layer of insulation is positioned over the loadbearing structure.
This design enables optimum laying of the vapour barrier and hence reduces the risks of mistakes during construction. It also retains the advantages of the ventilation layer above the insulation as described earlier. But, as shown, the battens for the roof covering still have to be fixed and the overall depth of the construction is quite significant, although this is only occasionally a problem.

Factory jointing
As mentioned earlier, a non-ventilated design places very high demands on building components and their joints, and such demands are very difficult to satisfy with manual labour on site. Furthermore, the new Energy Economy Act contains more stringent requirements concerning thermal insulation and airtightness. Complex components and subassemblies are therefore increasingly available, thus reducing the manual input to simple assembly on site.

2.3.4 Non-ventilated design principle using the example of patent glazing

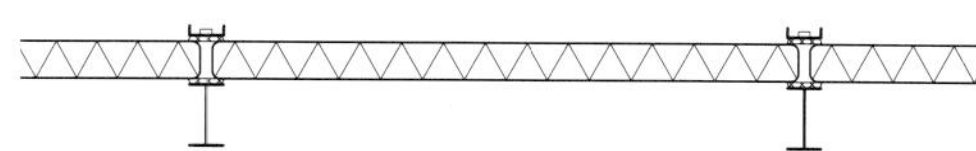

2.3.5 Non-ventilated design principle using the example of a panel clamped in place similar to patent glazing

The origins of industrial jointing can be found in the patent glazing designs (i.e. without putty) of the 19th century. In the construction of facades, industrial production and jointing started to make headway at the start of the 20th century. Since then a growing number of multifunctional components have been developed that are also suitable for use on pitched roofs. Today, transparent and opaque components with sealed joints are readily available.

The layers of these multi-layered constructions of glass and other materials are determined by their functions. They are dimensionally accurate in all directions, have geometrically specified joints and are characterised by simple, single-skin assembly on site.

Summer thermal performance must be taken into account using additional measures for both opaque and transparent units. For this reason, and owing to their industrial character, factory-jointed roofing elements have, up to now, mainly been used in less demanding industrial buildings and single-storey sheds. Progress in glass technology will, however, solve the sunshading problems. These roofs, which can contribute to active and passive energy gains, also have a role to play in housebuilding.

**Summary**

The new edition of DIN 4108 acknowledges roofs with no ventilation layer above the insulation as acceptable, modern designs. This means that we can use the aforementioned criteria to decide which type of construction – ventilated or non-ventilated – to choose for any particular situation.

With a ventilation layer above the insulation, the prime objective of the design is the proper functioning of the ventilation ducts. In other words, the ventilation ducts must be sufficiently large. In order to avoid moisture transport between roof surfaces exposed to different climatic conditions, the ventilation ducts must be separated at the ridge. To absorb any incoming moisture temporarily, the roofing felt or the supporting construction for the boarding should be made from an absorbent material.

With no ventilation layer above the insulation, the proper functioning of the vapour barrier is crucial. The utmost care is therefore necessary to ensure that the vapour barrier is laid without any gaps and sealed tightly against other components.

Irrespective of this, deciding to lay the insulation above the loadbearing structure always reduces the risks.

## Prefabrication

**Prefabricated elements for the pitched roof**

For centuries the pitched roof has been that part of the building with the greatest proportion of prefabrication and hence the smallest proportion of on-site assembly. Neither the roof structure nor the roof covering components are processed on site any more – they are simply assembled. The pitched roof is therefore predestined for further developments in the field of prefabrication.

In our age of computer-assisted design and electronically controlled production it is no surprise to discover that an impressive range of prefabricated elements is available for pitched roofs.

According to a survey carried out in 2000, there are about 70 manufacturers in Germany producing prefabricated roofing elements.[5] Useful information on 40 products from this wide range was scrutinised in more detail. However, here we are only interested in products for the building envelope or those products that combine building envelope and loadbearing functions; purely structural elements do not fall within the scope of the *Roof Construction Manual*. The products listed in table 2.3.6 can be divided into elements with the essentially manual connection of loadbearing parts to infill parts, hybrid constructions of loadbearing parts and flat layers, and generally industrially jointed, primarily flat elements. This survey reflects the situation in the autumn of 2000 and does not claim to be exhaustive.

Manual connection of loadbearing to infill parts

The following elements generally use linear supporting components with flat elements consisting of slab-type components, insulation and vapour barrier, combined in one unit. We shall consider them here in terms of their loadbearing parts.

Timber

Timber is used as the structural material for more than 50% of manually jointed constructions. The timber loadbearing members are connected to timber derivative boards or partial or full roof decking above or below the insulation. As a rule, the members can span from ridge to eaves. Such elements long have been produced by the woodworking industry. This means that tried-and-tested standard details are available for butt joints, ridge, eaves and verge. The arrangement of layers can be adapted to suit individual requirements. Only the roof covering has to be added on site to complete the roof construction.
Some of products use T-sections of glue laminated or solid timber for the structural members. Waffle or sandwich panels, with facings of timber derivative boards and a core of thermal insulation, are laid between these timber sections. The underside of the elements can generally remain exposed. The roof covering, together with any supporting members, is laid in the traditional way.

One manufacturer uses timber sections fixed to 50 mm thick concrete panels via an elastic shear-resistant connection. After the joints have been filled, the concrete surfaces are ready for painting. The roof covering and its supporting members are all that is required to complete the roof on site.

Metal

The tradition of fixing glass without putty has led to many forms of patent glazing. In these systems panes of glass or opaque panels are clamped tightly onto metal sections to hold them in place. The opaque panels are sandwich elements with metal facings or metal waffle units. No further components are required to finish the roof in these cases.

Hybrid construction

The second group of combined elements is the group of composite units. One manufacturer combines steel lattice beams with a concrete panel. The transverse joints are filled and the whole is thus ready for painting. To complete the roof all that is needed is the roof covering and its supporting members.
Another variation of composite construction uses V-shaped sheet steel beams between plywood at the top, and fibre-cement sheets at the bottom. Perforated sheet metal with good acoustic properties forms the inner lining. These very lightweight elements require no further work because their top surface is finished with synthetic roofing felt, which is overlapped and bonded during erection.

Industrial jointing of flat elements

Some of the elements shown here originate from other areas of the building envelope, but some were specially developed for pitched roofs. The current state of development enables us to distinguish between the following groups:

Sandwich element with timber facing

All-purpose panel with polyurethane insulation and without an additional vapour barrier, for spans up to 4 m.

Sandwich element and waffle panel with metal facing

These elements were introduced into the building sector over 30 years ago and have a layer of insulation made from polyurethane and mineral fibres. They can be used on spans of up to 4.5 m and are characterised by well-developed jointing techniques. After erection they provide all the functions necessary for a pitched roof without further additions.

Spans of up to 12 m are possible using a special version with loadbearing steel C-sections. These elements form a unit together with the C-sections. A roof covering of profiled metal sheets is required to complete the roof construction. The perforated soffit has good acoustic properties and remains exposed.

[5] Ressel, Frank: Vorfertigung am geneigten Dach – eine Marktanalyse; unpublished diploma thesis, Dept. of Construction, Munich Technical University, Prof. Eberhard Schunck, Oct 2000

| Type of loadbearing structure / Material of loadbearing structure | | Materials | Roof surface | No. of manufacturers | Max. span [m] | Typical lengths [m] | Typical widths [m] |
|---|---|---|---|---|---|---|---|
| | | Timber / Metal | | | | | |
| Manual jointing | Solid timber | 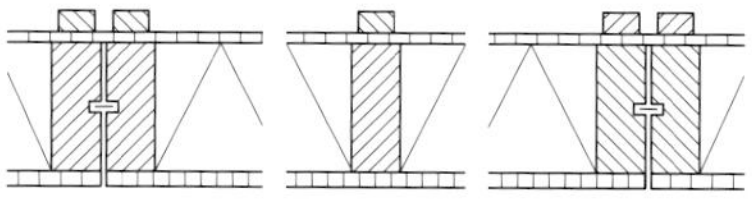 | Timber derivative boards, timber roof decking | 7 | 7.5 | 12 | 1.20 to 3.00 |
| | Solid timber | 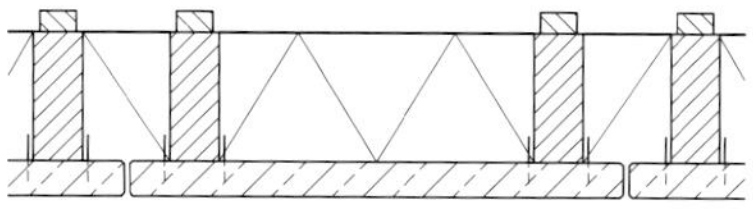 | Concrete | 1 | 5 | 9.25 | 1.04 to 2.25 |
| | Solid timber | 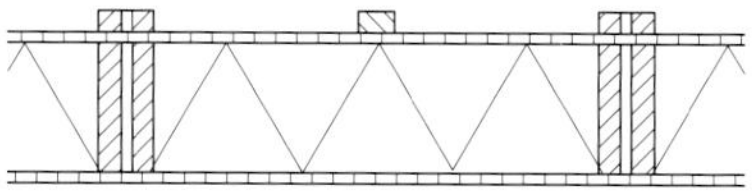 | Composite panel of timber derivative boards and expanded polystyrene core | 2 | 5 | 3.60 to 8.00 | approx. 1.00 |
| | I-section timber beam | 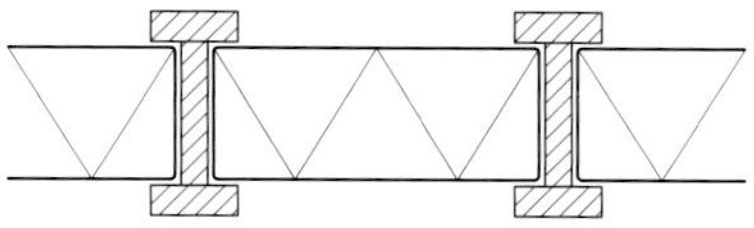 | Insulating panels of plastic foam or timber fibres | 5 | 5 | 2.50 to 10.00 | 1.00 to 1.25 |
| | Metal box section | 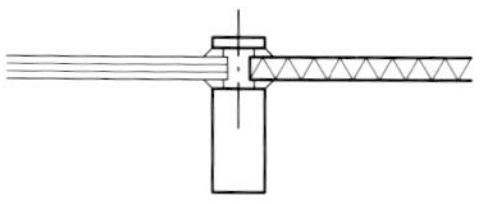 | Glass, sandwich panels of metal/expanded polystyrene | 3 | depends on support. constr. | 2.00 (Glass) 7.00 (opaque) | 0.875 (Glass) 1.00 (opaque) |
| | | Hybrid construction | | | | | |
| Hybrid construction | Metal lattice beam | 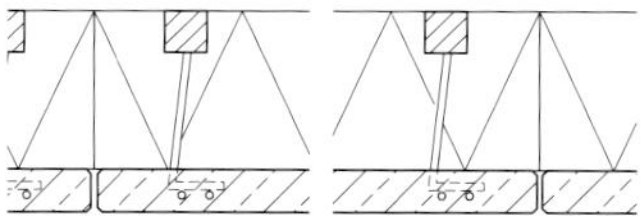 | Concrete | 1 | 7 | 16 | 3 |
| | Composite beam of sheet steel and timber | 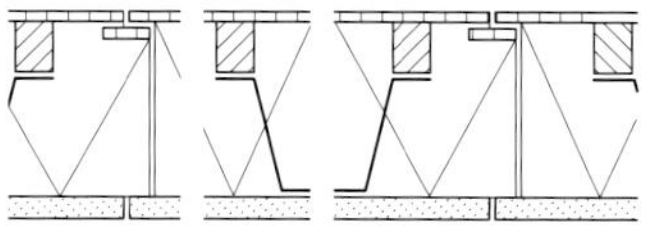 | Timber derivative and fibre-cement boards | 1 | 18 | 18 | 2.4 |
| | | Timber / Metal / Plastic | | | | | |
| Industrial jointing | Composite panel of timber derivative board and plastic foam | 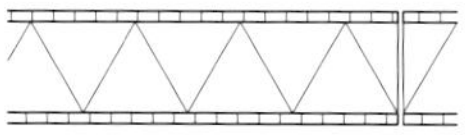 | Composite panel of timber derivative boards and plastic foam | 3 | 4 | 10 | 1.25 |
| | Composite panel of profiled sheet metal and plastic foam | 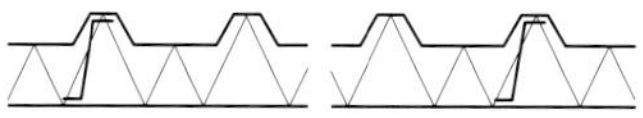 | Composite panel of profiled sheet metal and plastic foam | 5 | 4.5 | 24 | 0.90 to 1.20 |
| | Metal profiles | 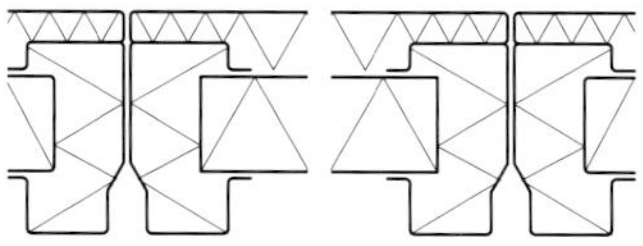 | Metal profiles filled with insulation | 1 | 12 | 32 | 2.4 |
| | Metal profiles | 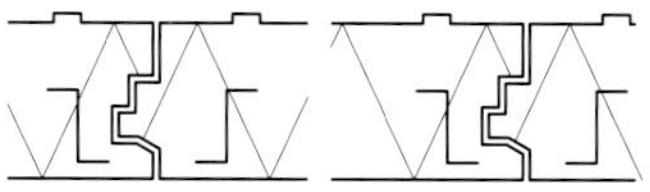 | Expanded polystyrene foam | 1 | 3 | 14 | 0.51 |
| | Translucent plastic (polycarbonate/PVC) | 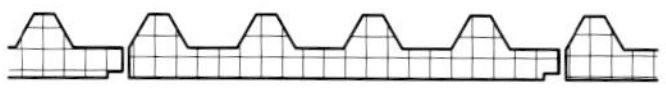 | Translucent plastic (polycarbonate/PVC) | 1 | 2.5 | 11.00 to 25.00 | 0.20 to 0.60 |

2.3.6 Prefabricated roofing elements; type of jointing

Plastic element with profiled steel reinforcement
This element, taken from a housebuilding system, is made from expanded polystyrene. It is very lightweight, has good thermal insulation properties (U = 0.22 W/m²K) and is suitable for spans up to 3 m. However, these are combustible elements of building materials class B 1 (not readily flammable).

Translucent plastic element
This element is an alternative to heavy glass and can be supplied in lengths up to 25 m. But again, these are combustible elements of building material class B 1 (not readily flammable).

**Summary**
The amazingly diverse range of prefabricated elements available has grown out of the long tradition of prefabrication for pitched roofs. That is why there are so many timber elements. Such elements contribute to simplifying erection and shortening the construction period. However, there are already some factory-made products made to a high technical standard that foreshadow the imminent dawn of the modular roof.

## The modular roof

**Prefabrication – modular roof**
It is only a small step from prefabrication to the modular roof. The advantages of modular construction become apparent when we look at this subject in more detail:

Quality of workmanship
In the light of the production figures, modular components combined into a system require careful development. They are therefore highly developed technical components and thus less vulnerable to problems.

Flexibility – interchangeability
Modular designs enable the replacement of individual elements for reasons of damage, change of function or improvement.

Construction time
The standardised production of modular systems means they can be delivered on time and erected quickly.

Costs
Assuming a sufficiently large production output, modular systems exhibit all the features of industrial production with its associated cost-reduction factors.

Production conditions
Modular systems are manufactured in production plants protected from the vagaries of the weather and thus ensure good working conditions.

| Loading kN/m² | dead load | 0.45 |
|---|---|---|
| | wind load | 0.56 to 2.56 |
| | snow load | 0.90 |
| | imposed load | 1.0 |
| Weather protection | rainproof | |
| Airtightness | class | 3 to DIN 12207 pt 1, vol.-related air permeability $n_{50} < 3\ h^{-1}$ |
| Thermal performance | alternative: Thermal Insulation Act | 0.22 W/m²K |
| Fire protection | building code | F30 |
| Sound insulation | DIN 4109 | 40 to 50 dB (stipulation) |

2.3.7 Requirements for roof elements (h < 20 m, snow load zone III, < 300 m above sea level, roof pitch < 45°)

Nevertheless, no modular roofing systems are yet available in Europe. Two of the reasons for this are outlined below:

Buildings as unique artistic objects
Buildings are still regarded as individual creations matching the respective urban needs. This understandable view is obviously held by many to preclude the completion of individual solutions with a ready-made roofing system. A change in our way of thinking, as has already happened with many other industrial products, has yet to take place here.

Initial risks
Modular roofing systems require more detailing than conventional solutions, especially when their parts are interchangeable. This makes them more complex and more costly than conventional roof designs. And while the output remains low, the lower costs associated with high numbers are not achieved. This entails risks for any company embarking on the development of a modular roof.

**Basis for design**
In the following we shall attempt to establish the basis for design for developing a modular roof. As the main application at present is the conversion of roof spaces into living quarters, our analysis will reflect the use of monopitch and duopitch roofs for accommodation purposes. This analysis is largely based on a study carried out at Munich Technical University.[6]

Elements of the modular roof – "product range"

Standard element
The modular roof, and hence the standard element, must comply with the normal demands placed on any roof. We shall consider a typical example (h < 20 m, snow load zone III, < 300 m above sea level, roof pitch < 45°):
• Adapter element
This element is a different size from the standard element and enables a modular roof system to be adapted to fit any size of roof or building.

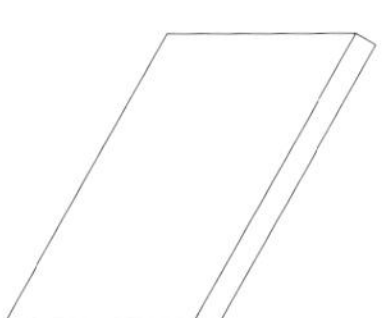

2.3.8 Standard element

• Edge element
The edges of the roof at ridge, eaves and verge need special treatment, which is carried out as a variation on the standard element.

Functional element
A modular system must include the following functional elements to guarantee the most important functions of a pitched roof:

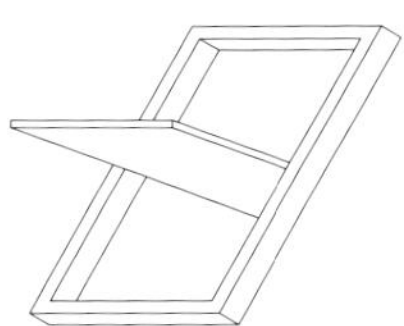

2.3.9 Window/gress element

• Window/egress element
This element must be transparent and openable in order to admit light and air, as well as provide access to the roof surface for maintenance purposes or as a means of escape.

[6] Elias, Ralf: Das Modulare Dach; unpublished diploma thesis, Dept. of Construction, Munich Technical University, Prof. Eberhard Schunck, Aug 2001

• Penetration element

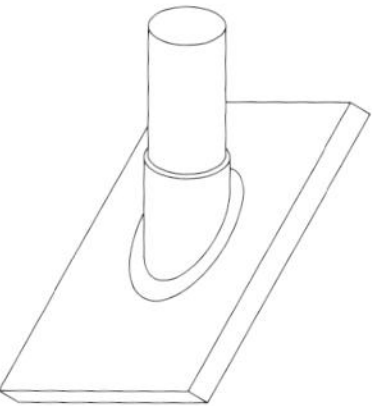

2.3.10 Penetration element

For flues, aerials, ventilation openings and services of all kinds to pass through.

• Energy element

In order to use the roof for solar energy purposes, our product range should include elements for the two most important solar energy components:

• collector panels
• photovoltaic panels

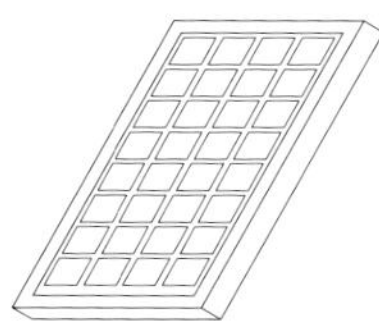

2.3.11 Energy element

**Position of primary loadbearing structure**

The primary loadbearing structure, which this analysis will not consider in detail, can be made from timber or steel. The following arrangements are conceivable:

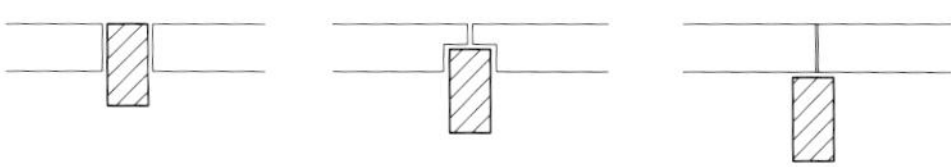

2.3.12 Position of primary loadbearing structure: between, intruding into and below elements

Positioning the primary loadbearing structure below the elements is preferred because this separates them from the structure and enables them to be readily replaced/exchanged. Cantilevering the elements beyond the walls of the building is also easiest when the primary loadbearing structure is positioned underneath.

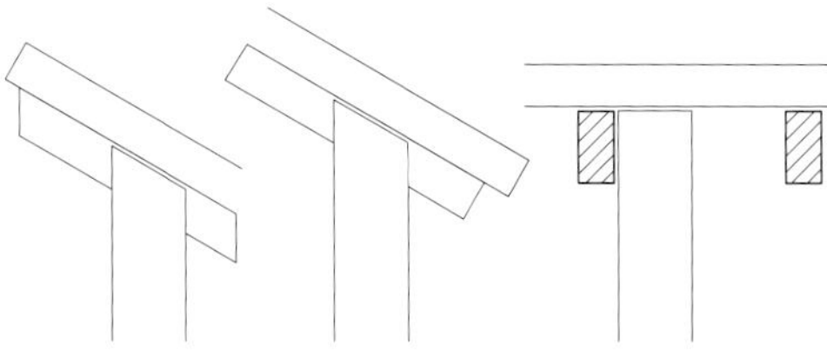

2.3.13 Roof overhang at ridge, eaves and verge

[7] Lewicki, Bohdan; Hochbauten aus großformatigen Fertigteilen, Warsaw, Arkady, 1966

Modular grid – dimensions

The search for the factors influencing the modular grid must take into account the conditions of the inclined surface because different pitches give rise to different plan dimensions in the plane of the roof. At best, the width of the element could be based on a plan dimension. So the standard dimensions result from the aforementioned functional elements. It is advisable to begin with the element that has fewest constraints.

Erection

If we assume erection without using cranes or other lifting equipment, it should be possible for two persons to transport and install each element. Assuming 30 kg per person[7], an element should not weigh more than 60 kg. And assuming a weight of approx. 45 kg/m², each element can cover approx. 1.33 m².

Window/egress element

The window element places the greatest demands on the dimensions because it is determined by the sight-lines of both seated and standing occupants.

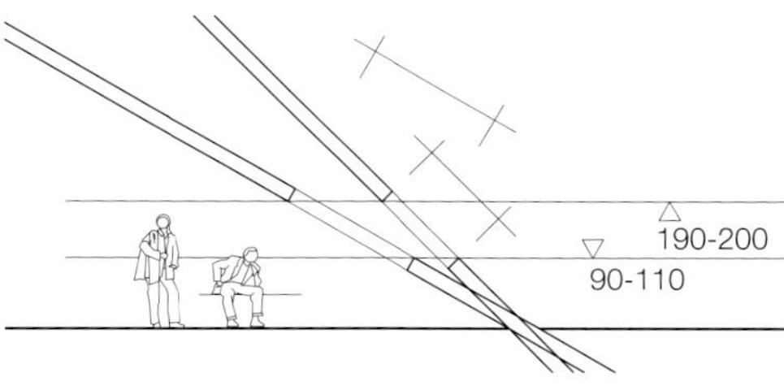


2.3.14 Position and size of window element for seated and standing occupants

If we assume a spandrel height of 900–1100 mm for the lower sight-line of a seated person, the window opening, depending on pitch, must be 1600–2200 mm long to guarantee an upper sight-line of 1900–2000 mm above the floor. The width of the window is based on the width of the human body, so that occupants can see through it comfortably; an average dimension of 700 mm can be assumed here. To this we have to add the width of the frame and the edges of the element, which results in an element width of 900 mm. The operation of a window that opens overhead places limits on the system, which means that the windows currently available are 1400 mm long. Taking into account the frame and edge of the element, we arrive at an element length of 1600 mm. Egress requires an opening measuring only 800 x 990 mm.

Penetration element

Steel flues with an outer diameter of 360 mm cover most requirements in housebuilding. Taking into account the clearance for fire protection purposes and the edge of the element, this results in a width of 760 mm and, with a 50° pitch, a length of 1310 mm.

Energy element

There are no minimum dimensions for energy elements. The photovoltaic panel element can be sized to fit 100 mm solar cells. A collector panel element could be designed to supply the water requirements of one person, i.e. 1–1.5 m².

Summary of conditions for element dimensions

If we take the optimum width of a window element and the optimum weight of an element for erection purposes, we get a length of 1400 mm, which does not coincide with the desirable sight-lines. But if we take the desirable window element length, we arrive at an element weight of 65 kg, which is just about tolerable. Alternatively, we could reduce the element width to 850 mm. Accordingly, we can assume an element to measure 1600 mm long and 850–950 mm wide.

Element construction

The make-up of the element is based on the principles described at the start of the next chapter. With an integrated, non-ventilated construction, the layers and their functions and materials are as given in table 2.3.16. Layers to provide protection from the sun can be added above the roof covering according to use. The thickness of an element is 120–180 mm, depending on the insulation chosen.

Joints between elements

In principle, both overlapping and sealed joints are conceivable. In order to achieve both, two sealing levels must be introduced. The upper one provides weather protection, the lower one protection from airborne and diffusion moisture.

| | Width (cm) | Length (cm) | Additional conditions |
|---|---|---|---|
| Erection | | | ≥ 60 kg, ~1.33 m² |
| Window element | ≤ 90 | ≥ 160 – 220 | |
| Egress element | ≤ 80 | ≥ 60 | |
| Penetration element | ≤ 75 | ≥ 131 | |
| Solar collector panel element | | | 1 to 1.5 m² |

2.3.15 Summary of conditions for element dimensions

| Layer | Function | Material |
|---|---|---|
| covering layer | overlapping or sealing<br>F30 | aluminium<br>titanium-zinc<br>plastic film<br>coatings<br>glass |
| upper supporting layer | span divided into 900 mm bays<br>sealed design – airtight<br>F30<br>contribution to sound insulation | profiled steel<br>profiled aluminium<br>profiled titanium-zinc<br>timber derivatives<br>glass |
| insulating layer | U-value < 0.22 ($W/m^2K$)<br>F30<br>sound insulation | fibre insulating materials<br>plastic foam<br>air layer |
| spacer loadbearing layer | in conjunction with supporting layers<br>spans up to 900 mm<br>thermal break<br>F30 | sheet steel sections<br>timber, timber derivatives |
| lower supporting layer | span divided into 900 mm bays<br>airtight, diffusion-resistant<br>F30<br>contribution to sound insulation | profiled sheet steel<br>timber derivatives<br>plasterboard<br>glass |

2.3.16 Element make-up

At the joints each element must fulfil all the standard requirements plus those concerning the fixing of the elements to the supporting construction.

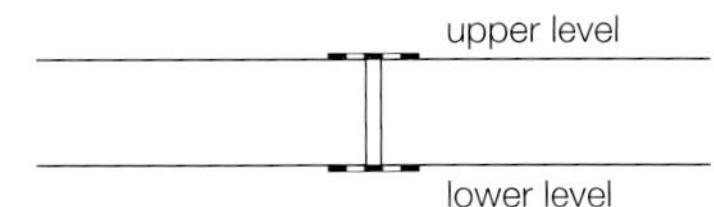


2.3.17 Longitudinal joint between elements

Overlapping joint
This type of element has a wedge shape. To guarantee interchangeability, the length of the overlap must be kept very small. As incoming rainwater can penetrate into an overlapping joint, the joint should be ventilated. It is advantageous to incorporate a channel into the joint for draining incoming rainwater.

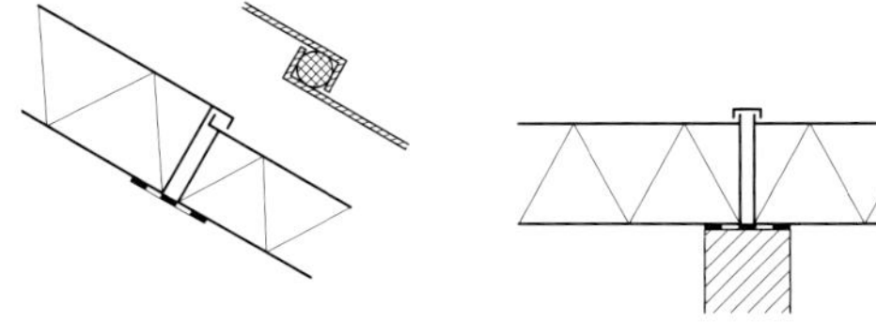

2.3.18 Overlapping joints, transverse and longitudinal

The lower sealing level is best guaranteed by a contact seal under constant pressure.

Sealing joint
It is more reliable to design the upper sealing level to be airtight as well. A contact seal, effective in both the longitudinal and transverse directions, is suitable for this. This calls

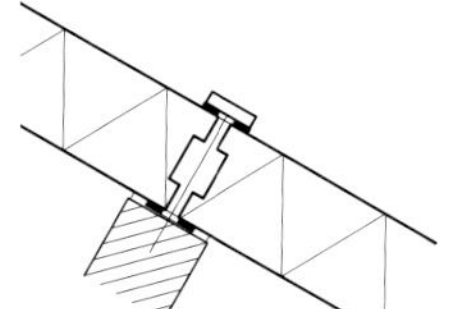

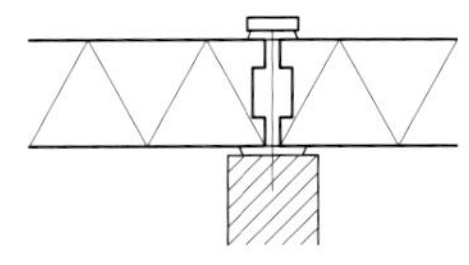

2.3.19 Sealing joints, transverse and longitudinal

for a primary loadbearing structure with purlin-type structural members in the transverse direction in the plane of the primary loadbearing direction as well. It is advisable here to drain any incoming rainwater that may have penetrated to the outside via a labyrinth-type sealing strip. It is not possible, or necessary, to ventilate the joint. This version corresponds to the latest thinking in facade and roof design. It is more reliable and guarantees simpler interchangeability.

**The elements**

The following illustrations provide a non-specific overview of the basic elements of a modular roof.

Standard element

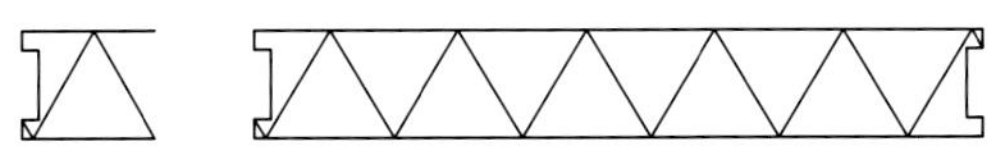

2.3.20 Standard element

Window/egress element
Figure 2.3.21 shows a window system with flush glazing as supplied by Lacker GmbH.[8]

2.3.21 Window/egress element

Penetration element
The size and shape of the penetration ellipse depends on the diameter of the pipe penetrating the roof, and the pitch of the roof. A collar with a Z-shaped folded sheet metal capping is required for the upper sealing level, and an annular flange, collar and vapour-proof film for the lower level.

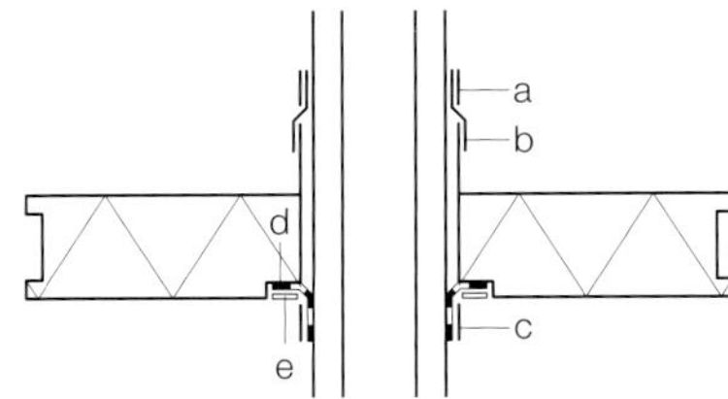


2.3.22 Penetration element: a collar, b Z-shaped capping, c collar, d film, e annular flange

Energy elements

Collector panel element

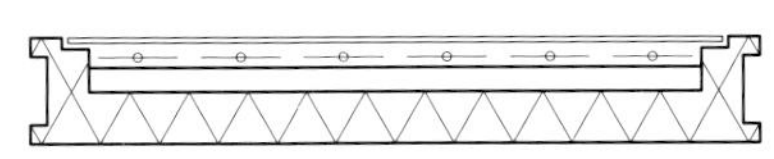

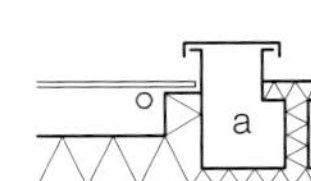


2.3.23 Solar collector panel element
a pipe duct

Figure 2.3.23 shows a collector panel as supplied by Solar-Energie-Technik GmbH.[9] To achieve the same element thickness as the standard element, a higher thermal insulation group has been chosen. The interior of the collector is partly ventilated. The elements are connected with pipes laid on site in the pipe ducts provided in each element. The bleed valve, accessible from outside, is also located here.

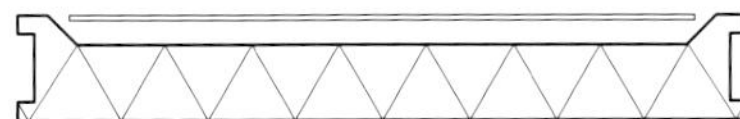

2.3.24 Photovoltaic panel element

Photovoltaic panel element
As the underside of the panel must be ventilated, to dissipate heat, the insulation must be thinner here but with a higher insulation value. The cables are laid in the joints between modules.

**Summary**
This appraisal of the most important aspects and conditions affecting the modular roof is intended to show that the work required for its development is not excessive and the technology does not stray beyond the bounds of techniques that are customary and proven in modern construction. The development work and its benefits lie primarily in the interchangeable nature of the parts. In principle, the pitched roof is an ideal starting point for modular fabrication in building.

[8] Lacker GmbH, Waldachtal
[9] Solar-Energie-Technik GmbH, Altlussheim

# Layers and materials

Eberhard Schunck and Hans Jochen Oster

A roof consists of various layers, each of which fulfills one of the tasks of the complete construction. We distinguish between the following individual layers:

| Main function | Secondary function |
|---|---|
| • Waterproofing/covering layer 1 | |
| checking rainwater | checking driving rain |
| draining rainwater | |
| carrying snow load | checking driving snow |
| carrying maintenance load | |
| blocking radiation | blocking out light |
| checking water-borne/ airborne particles | absorbing radiation and converting into energy |
| sound insulation | |
| fire protection | |
| • Loadbearing layer 1 (battens, roof decking) | |
| securing/supporting roof covering | |
| distribution of maintenance load | |
| distribution of snow load | bracing the structure |
| • Air layer 1 (ventilation below roof covering) | |
| heat dissipation | |
| removal of water vapour | |
| evaporation of condensation | |
| evaporation of residual water | |
| • Waterproofing/covering layer 2 (boards, roof. felt) | |
| draining incoming rainwater | draining rainwater during construction |
| draining condensation | |
| checking water-borne/ airborne particles | |
| checking driving snow | sound insulation |
| checking driving rain | |
| • Loadbearing layer 2 (roof decking) | distribution of imposed and snow loads during construction |
| sound insulation | |
| securing/supporting waterproofing and covering layer 2 | bracing the structure |
| • Air layer 2 (ventilation above insulation) | |
| evaporation of water vapour | |
| heat dissipation | |
| removal of residual gases | |
| • Insulating layer | |
| thermal insulation | |
| absorbing sound | |
| • Vapour control layer | |
| checking water vapour | |
| wind barrier | |
| dust barrier | |
| sound insulation | |
| • Inner lining | |
| boundary of interior | bracing the structure |
| sound insulation | |
| air barrier | |
| fire protection | |

The loadbearing layers were dealt with in an earlier chapter. The inner lining forms the transition between roof construction and interior; as it is primarily determined by appearance criteria, it will not be covered here. This chapter looks at the other layers in terms of their arrangement and importance for the construction.

## Covering and sealing

The uppermost layer of the roof construction must protect the building from precipitation of all kinds. There are basically two ways of doing so: either the water is drained away from the building via the quickest route, or it is intercepted before being drained away from a suitable point.

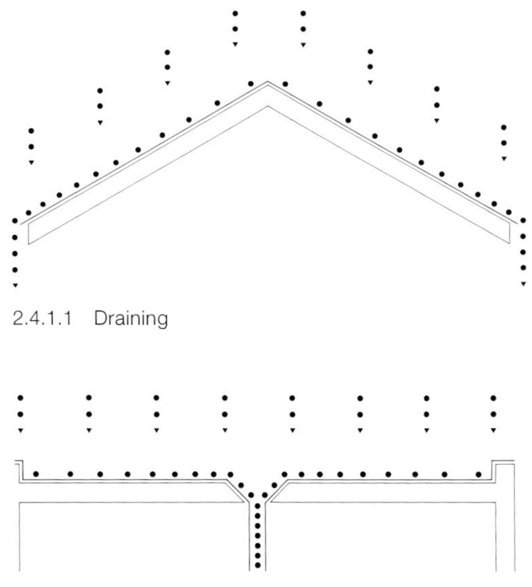

2.4.1.1 Draining

2.4.1.2 Checking

The first of these principles is the fundamental one behind the pitched roof, the second is the principle of the flat roof. There are various ways of achieving drainage.

## Overlapping joints

The materials available for roof coverings are available only in certain, limited sizes. The skill in covering a roof therefore lies in forming and arranging the individual pieces such that their joints also comply with the drainage principle.

Although a pitched roof must be rainproof, it does not need to be waterproof.

### Overlapping flat components

In the oldest of all methods, non-profiled parts are laid overlapping and offset in such way that all precipitation passing through the upper longitudinal joints drains down the roof, and from inside to outside. All flat overlapping elements, e.g. wooden shingles, slates, bullnose tiles, function in this way, and so do the multitude of overlaps between the pieces of straw or reed of a thatched roof. The disadvantage of this method is that the flat elements need to be overlapped more than once and require a relatively steep pitch.

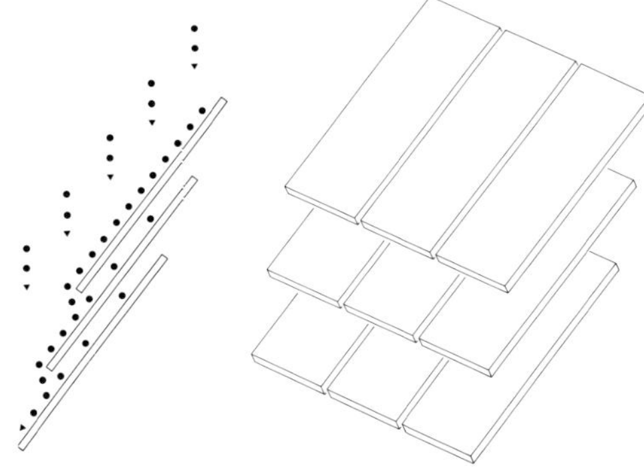

2.4.1.3 The principle of overlapping flat elements

### Overlapping profiled components

To overcome these disadvantages, even very early peoples started to shape their overlapping roofing elements so that the edges along the longitudinal joints were turned up and covered with another, separate component. Over the course of time this shaping became more and more specialised, leading to the types of overlapping elements we have today. The transverse joints were also included in this shaping process.

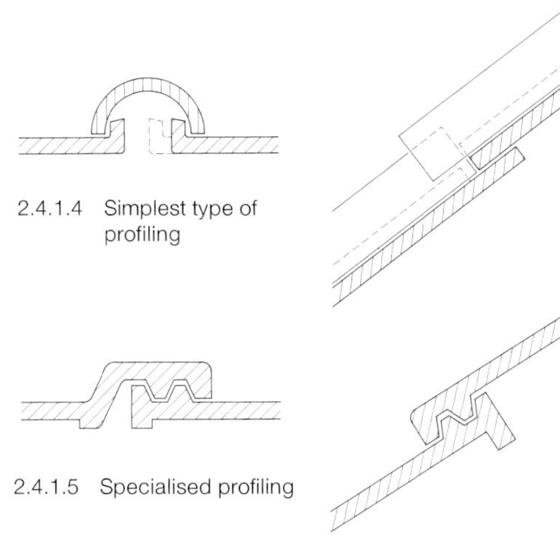

2.4.1.4 Simplest type of profiling

2.4.1.5 Specialised profiling

**Welting**

Sheet metals also use a protruding longitudinal joint and a shaped, overlapping transverse joint. However, welting seals the joint tighter and therefore enables shallower pitches to be used. The welted transverse joint is laid flat so that precipitation can drain across it.

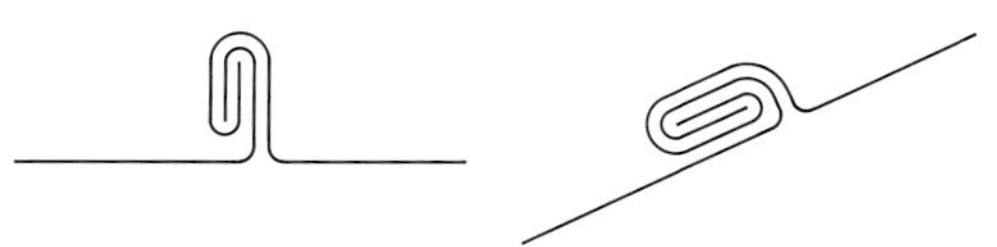

2.4.1.6 Welted longitudinal and transverse joints

## Sealed joints

**Clamping and clipping**

In the first roof coverings of this type flat panes of glass were clamped on to loadbearing glazing bars. Strips of tar-saturated felt were used to provide an almost watertight connection. Since the advent of resilient sealing strips made of synthetic materials, this clamping system has been used for flat panels of various materials (in addition to glass), and has become a standard roofing technique.

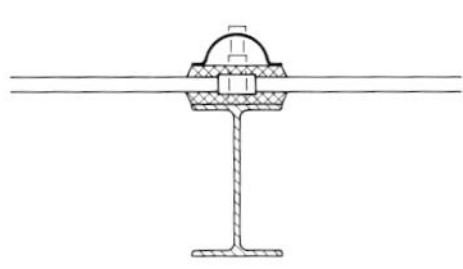

2.4.1.7 Panes of glass clamped to a glazing bar

**Soldering and brazing**

Joints in metal roof coverings can be made watertight through metallurgical reactions that allow the two pieces of metal to be fused. However, as large pieces of metal can experience thermal expansion problems, this method is suitable only for very small pieces.

2.4.1.8 Soldered or brazed connection

**Bonding and welding**

Bitumen and synthetic roofing felts are secured using bonding compounds and solvents, or by using a blow torch or hot air to melt the coating and thus join the layers of felt together. These joins are absolutely watertight, so these systems are also suitable for very shallow pitches according to the material used. The material itself can accommodate small movements.
This completes our brief look at the main roofing techniques available today. The choice of roofing material determines the appropriate method of jointing.

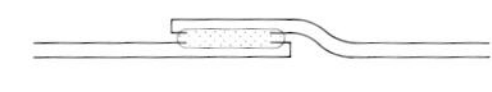

2.4.1.9 Bonded connection

## Forms of roof covering and materials

In this edition of the *Roof Construction Manual* roof coverings are classified according to their form rather than their material. The benefit of this is that the methods of jointing a particular form, which are used for various materials, need only be considered once. This becomes especially apparent when – as we might expect – the diversity of materials continues to increase as alternatives are added. This classification is retained throughout all parts of the book to make cross-references easier. The chart on p. 107 provides an overview of the most important forms of roof covering and materials together with their relationships. They are dealt with in detail in the following sections.

**Roof coverings · forms and materials**

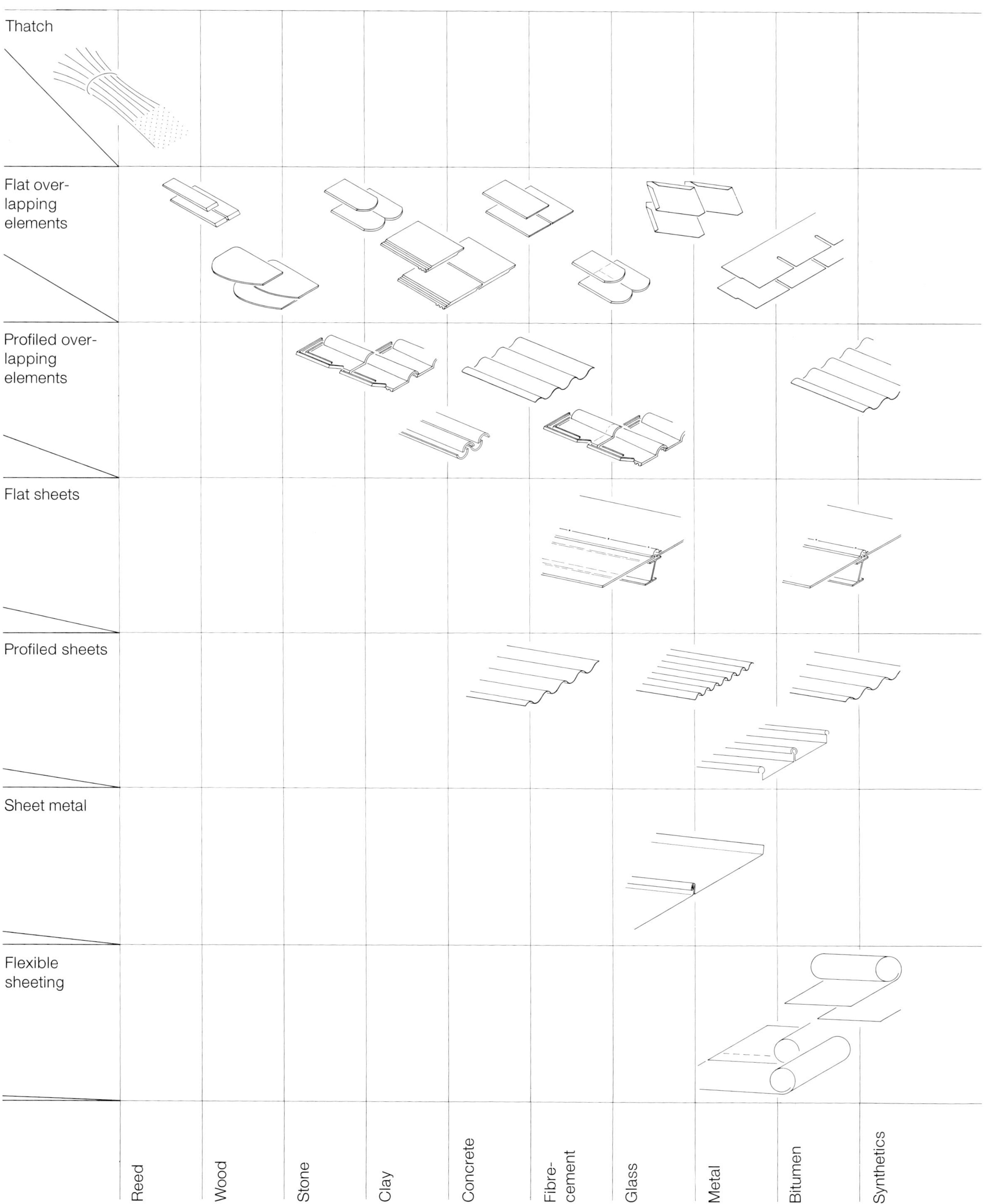

## Thatch
Materials, components, laying

### Materials
Sources, manufacture, properties

#### Sources
Reed grows throughout Central Europe on shallow banks alongside still or gently flowing water.
In Germany, the Netherlands, Denmark and Poland the type of reed used is an indigenous variety but is nevertheless usually imported (e.g. from the Balkan states). It grows to a height of 1.25–4 m and reaches a thickness of about 30 mm.
Bulrushes measure 2–4 m long and 2–3 cm thick.
Straw is a by-product of threshing cereals. Reed, bulrushes, or straw from rye and wheat can be prepared for use as roof coverings. The ridge is finished with reed, straw, turf or heather.

#### Manufacture
Reed is harvested during the cold months of the year (beginning of October to mid-March). [10] It is cut with a sickle, scythe or mower. The cut reeds are laid flat on the banks for a short time to dry naturally. When dry they are cleaned and combed with a special rake so that the long, dried leaves and broken reeds are removed. The cleaned reeds are then tied together about 20 cm from their bottom end to form bundles. These are then stored in the open air either standing upright or stacked lying down until needed.

#### Properties
Colour
Depending on the type of reed, the colour varies from sand to ochre, and turns grey within 1–2 years.

Form
Reeds should be up to 2 m long, thin (3–9 mm dia.) and straight, without damage, not stripped, healthy and mature. They should also be free from leaves and other plants. Reeds up to 3 m long can be used for an undercoat layer (see "Laying"). A proper thatched roof cannot be built with extra-long reeds alone. Rye straw must be as long as possible, fully grown, straight and clean. The straw should be threshed with a flail, but not flattened, and worked with the empty ears. Machine-threshed straw is not suitable for a thatched roof. Wheat straw is equally durable (quality as for rye straw), but is popular as a nest for mice!

Durability
Reed and straw are natural building materials vulnerable to various pests. These cannot be excluded permanently and so maintenance of the roof is important (see "Maintenance and repair").

| Pests | Damage | Remedy |
|---|---|---|
| Martens | damage to eaves | chasing away |
| Birds, primarily house sparrow | damage to ridge | chasing away |
| Insects, cockroaches | damage to thatch | powdered boric acid |
| Ants | nests | fresh insect powder, aniline oil solution, carbon tetrachloride |
| Bugs, beetles | nests | carbolic, cresol, hydrogen cyanide gas (gassing must always carried out by a pest controller) |
| Mosses | roots damage thatch | clean because otherwise humus collects for other plants and insects |

2.4.2.1 Pests and means of combating them

Physical behaviour
Thatched roofs of reed and straw "breathe" and filter the air, are open to diffusion and store the moisture. These roof coverings have thermal insulation properties; however, this may not be included in the analysis of thermal performance.

Behaviour in fire
Thatched roofs of reed and straw belong to building materials class B 3 (highly flammable materials) and are regarded as "soft roof coverings". Buildings with thatched roofs may not be positioned within 15 m of buildings with a "hard roof covering", or within 25 m of buildings with a "soft roof covering", and at least 5 m from outbuildings without their own fireplace or heating appliance. However, there are regional variations on these rules. [09]

### Components
Dimensions, edge components

#### Dimensions
The smallest unit in German thatching is the "Bund" (bundle – also known as a thrave, boulting, yealm, nitch), with a circumference of 45–85 cm, diameter of 14–17 cm and cross-sectional area of 160–580 mm² (measured 30–40 cm from root end).
Multiples of this are:
- "Draaf", "Stieg" (= 20 "Bund")
- "Schock" (= 60 "Bund")
- "Fimm" (= 100 "Bund")

| | Circumference [cm] | Diameter [cm] | Cross-sectional area [cm²] |
|---|---|---|---|
| Standard bundle | ~ 50 | 16 | 200 |
| Thick bundle | ~ 84–86 | 27 | 580 |
| Reeds imported from Hungary | ~ 60 | 19 | 288 |

2.4.2.2 Reed bundle dimensions

#### Edge components
Heather and turf can also be used to complete the ridge. Turf also serves as a flashing around a chimney, and overlapping boards can be used around chimneys or smoke-holes.

### Laying
Conditions for laying, fixing, additional measures, details, supporting construction, material requirements, maintenance and repair

#### Conditions for laying
The roof pitch should be ≥ 45°; ≥ 50° is better because at this pitch the wind cannot get under the thatch, but tends to compress it.
At these pitches the roof is secure against driving rain and snow. Rain penetrates the thatch up to 5 cm under normal conditions, and up to 10 cm in a storm. During a blizzard the thatch is absolutely secure against incoming snow (≥ 50°).

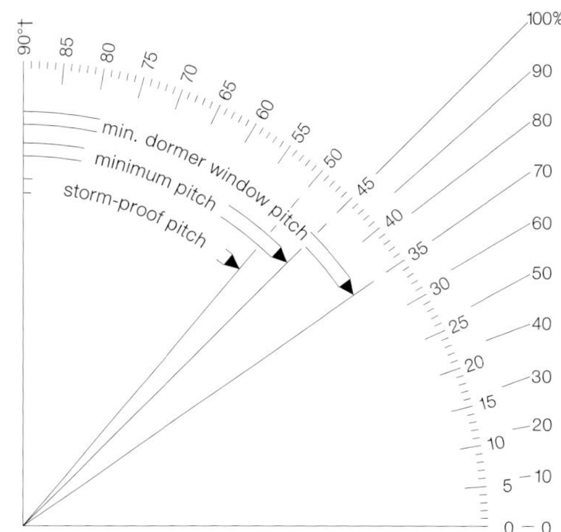


2.4.2.3 Standard roof pitches

A covering of reeds is 30–35 cm thick, a straw covering 25–30 cm. This tapers evenly from bottom (35 and 30 cm respectively) to top (30 and 25 cm respectively). [12]
A thin layer (2–3 cm) of reed or straw (undercoat) is spread over the battens. This is then covered layer by layer starting at the eaves and working towards the ridge, working in courses (horizontal) and lanes (vertical). The thatch is laid in the direction of the fall (except at hips, valleys and verges, see "Details") with the cut ends facing towards the eaves.
Valleys and hips may not intersect.
A ventilation space ≥ 6 cm must be kept open below the roof covering and battens.
Further ventilation openings are unnecessary because the thatch itself is adequately permeable to the air. [12]

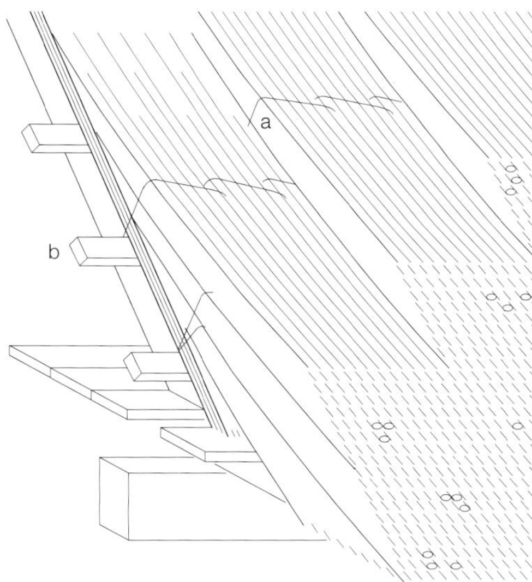

2.4.2.4 Stitched thatch: a stitch, b batten

**Fixing**

Stitching
The bundles are held progressively at intervals of 15–20 cm with wire tied around the battens. The wire extends roughly halfway into the covering layer. Each bundle is stitched in the middle of its length, with the bundle being pulled down firmly on to the batten. No wires should be visible on the surface of the roof. The pitch below the stitching must be ≥ 35°. [12]
The thatcher (outside) and an assistant (inside) push a wooden or metal thatching needle back and forth through the thatch and around the battens. Stitched thatch is becoming increasingly rare.

Fixing materials
The wire is at least 1.0–1.5 mm dia.; it is made from stainless steel (≥ 1.0 mm), plastic-covered steel (≥ 1.4 mm) or copper (≥ 1.5 mm). [12]

Binding
The bundles are held in place by sways tied to the battens every 15–20 cm with separate loops of wire. The roof covering is nicely compressed in this method because the sway can be tightened down against the thatch by twisting the ends of the wire with a pair of pliers. Only incombustible materials should be used for fixing. This method of laying can be carried out by one person. Using curved thatching needles is less strenuous than stitching with a straight needle.
As the spaces between the rafters sometimes need to be kept clear when converting a roof space for use as living quarters, these roofs can be re-thatched from outside without difficulties.

Fixing materials
The sways are made from "thumb-thick" hazel or willow sticks, or softwood battens (15 x 40 mm). Alternatively, rods (≥ 4.5 mm dia.) of galvanised steel or copper may be used, but they are at risk of being struck by lightning. The sways are held in place by 1.0–2.0 mm dia. wire made from stainless steel (≥ 1.0 mm), galvanised steel (≥ 1.4 mm) or plastic-covered steel (≥ 2.0 mm). [12]
Tarred twine (5 mm dia.) can be used instead of wire on very steep roofs. This subsequently contracts and creates a tight connection.

Fixing with brotches
The bundles are held in place by sways, which are fixed by individual willow brotches to a min. 10 cm thick undercoat, which in turn is stitched to the battens. Strength is achieved by the spreading action of the brotches. This type of fixing is still common in England and Ireland. [01, 02]

Fixing materials
Sways (see above) plus halved and twisted willow brotches, 1–1.5 mm thick and 50–60 mm long.

**Additional measures**
Additional measures should be taken in the case of enhanced requirements for securing the thatch. For example:
- with very large roofs
- with pitches shallower than recommended
- with an increased wind load

These additional measures could be:
- a steeper roof pitch
- a thicker covering
- boarding under the thatch

**Details**
Ridge, hip, eaves, valley, verge, chimney, dormer window

Angelner (Angeliter) ridge
(stitched thatch)
Two stitched ridge layers on both sides form the basis for this type of ridge. The upright ends of these layers coincide above the ridge. Each layer is double-stitched to the battens, with the stitches no farther part than 6–8 cm. To create the ridge filling, lower-quality thatch material and the trimmings from elsewhere on the roof are packed beneath the topmost course. The top two courses below the ridge consist of shorter bundles cut to a length of 90–130 cm.
In order to achieve a softer transition and higher strength at the ridge, short, thin bundles are used for this layer, with the thin ends fixed downwards on to the topmost courses. The ridge is then tapped down to the right height with the legget and gently rounded off on both sides. The bottom ends of the ridge layer are cut off to suit (see "Construction details – Thatch"). Necessary preparatory work includes covering the ends of the reeds at the smokehole, framing the chimney, and covering and trimming the topmost courses.

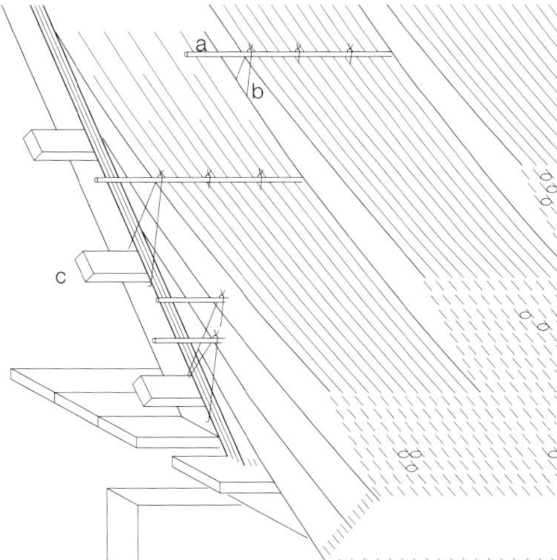

2.4.2.5 Tied thatch: a sway, b tying wire, c batten

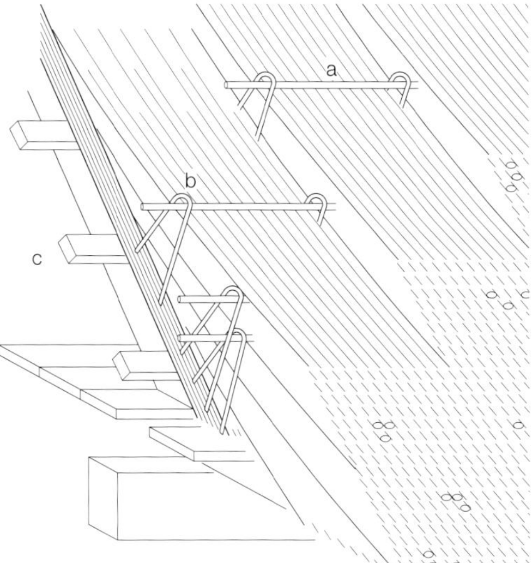

2.4.2.6 Fixing with brotches: a sway, b brotch, c batten

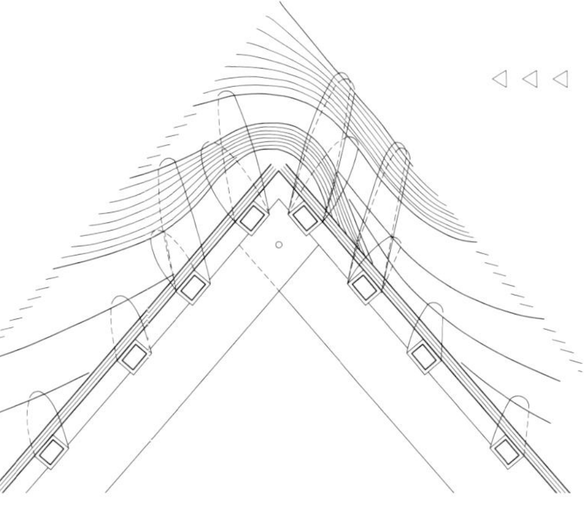
2.4.2.7 Mecklenburger ridge [08]: ◁◁◁ prevailing wind direction

Mecklenburger ridge
(stitched thatch)
Shorter topmost courses are not necessary with this type of ridge. The reeds of the two top courses are not cut short but instead curved over the ridge battens onto the other side and tucked below the topmost course there. A ridge layer is then stitched to these last two layers on the side facing away from the prevailing wind; the bundles projecting above the ridge are likewise bent over onto the other side. Finally, on the prevailing wind side a ridge layer with the cut ends upwards is double-stitched to each of the two final battens. The ends of the bundles are dressed upwards into shape and the bottom ends cut off to suit. This avoids a joint susceptible to rainwater penetration at the ridge.

Heather ridge
(tied thatch)
The top two courses on both sides are bent over the ridge battens. Their thin ends taper off on the opposite side and are firmly stitched to give the ridge a rainproof covering. To protect the ridge, a layer of heather – still moist – 90 cm wide is laid on the ridge such that it is 10–15 cm thick at the lower end and 25 cm over the ridge. Finally, oak cross-timbers each weighing 10–12 kg are placed on the ridge at a spacing of 30 cm. As the heather gradually sags, it is necessary to replenish the ridge every 2–5 years.

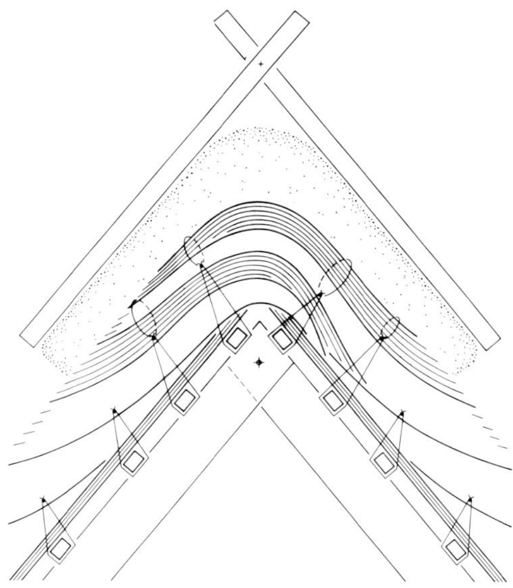

2.4.2.8 Heather ridge with cross-timbers

Heather ridge
(pegged)
The heather is fixed to the roof covering with about 100 timber pegs per metre of heather ridge. Each ridge capping requires about 100 additional timber pegs. The timber pegs are pointed, 1.5–2 cm thick and 30–60 cm long. Willow brotches (1 cm thick, 160 pcs/m) are sometimes used instead of timber pegs.

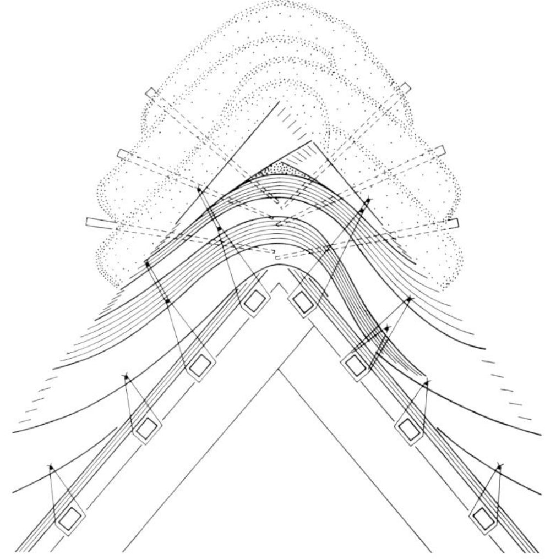

2.4.2.9 Heather ridge fixed with brotches

Hip
Hips are rounded off. The bundles point in the direction of the hip rafter. Additional (doubled) fixings are necessary here to withstand storm conditions. The bundles gradually return to the normal laying direction as we move away from the hip. Hipped roofs are secure in storms.

Eaves
The eaves are designed to have a horizontal overhang of 15–25 cm. The eaves are formed in two layers using the longest bundles available (preferably 150–200 cm). Laying commences at the hip or verge, with the first bundles being laid at an angle (see "Hip" and "Verge"). In order to introduce a certain tension into the entire roof covering, the lower eaves layer must be turned upwards by providing a tilting board or similar means to raise the level about 5–6 mm above the battens.
The upper eaves layer is attached overhanging by about 10 cm, likewise fixed turned up and finally dressed into shape with the legget (see "Construction details – Thatch").

Valley
Valleys must be 1.5 times the thickness of the rest of the roof and rounded off.
Raising the valley by nailing on additional, transverse battens, 20 cm long (top) increasing to 25 cm (bottom), is recommended. [12] It is advantageous to cover the bindings or stitches in the valley with bitumen roofing felt R 500. [11] This roofing felt inlay should be of such a size that the individual layers of thatch overlap ≥ 8 cm.

Verge
The cut ends of the roof covering form an overhang of 15–25 cm at each gable. The individual bundles are laid here at an angle (turned outwards at ≥ 30°). They gradually return to the normal laying direction again as we move away from the gable. To prevent damage at the verge during a storm, the bundles here must be long and thin and be placed under tension. They are fixed twice to the battens and turned upwards against a bargeboard (see "Construction details – Thatch") or pressed against the gable wall. A soft transition to board or wall can be achieved with a triangular fillet (50 x 25 mm), which increases the height above the battens. The gable masonry is taken up to the underside of the roof covering with just a half-brick leaf (starting approx. 50 cm below the roof covering) to ensure adequate working space.

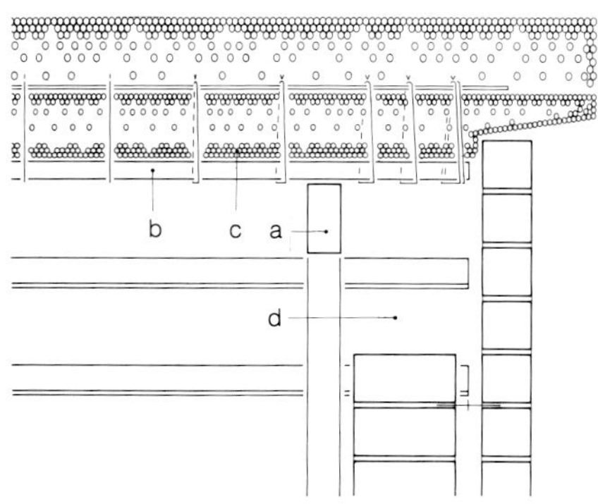


2.4.2.10 Verge without bargeboard: a rafter, b batten, c undercoat, d cavity providing space for tying

Chimney
The chimney passes through the ridge. Adding an extra half-brick leaf to the chimney stack above the roof level provides natural protection (approx. 30 cm above battens for reed, 25 cm for straw). The roof covering below the chimney consists of sheet metal, overlapping timber boards (fixed to hooks embedded in the masonry of the chimney) or heather. The last two courses of thatch are shortened, tucked under chimney stack and roof covering, and fixed with wire stitches every 6 cm (see "Construction details – Thatch").

Dormer window
The pitch of the roof to a dormer window should be at least 35°, preferably 45°. All junctions with dormer windows must be rounded off and packed out. The last course of thatch below the dormer window should be laid short and double-stitched with a visible stitch (see "Angelner ridge"). Overlapping boards can also be used at this position (see "Chimney"). The eaves detail for the dormer window should drain the rainwater onto the main roof surface well clear of the window.

**Supporting construction**

Battens

To produce tension in the bottommost course, either the supporting construction (tilting board, fascia board) should project 10–20 cm above the front edge of the rafters, or the bottommost batten should be at least twice as thick as the others. Similar details should be used at verges and at the eaves of a dormer window.

The spacing of the battens is normally 30–40 cm for reed, and 25–30 cm for straw. The top two battens should be spaced 25 cm apart, the bottom two 15–20 cm (measured from outside edge of fascia board or eaves batten). [12]

With a rafter spacing of about 100 cm and battens every 25–40 cm, battens measuring 40 x 60 mm are adequate; wider rafter spacings call for larger battens (50 x 60 mm or 50 x 70 mm). [12]

**Material requirements**

The quantity of reeds required per square metre of roof surface is calculated from the thickness of the covering (d) and the cross-sectional area (F) of a bundle as follows:

$d \cdot 100/F$ = No. of bundles

Some 10–12 bundles per square metre will be necessary, depending on their length and thickness. About 50 m of wire is required per square metre of roof surface to fix the thatch.

**Maintenance and repair**

Looked after carefully, a roof of reeds has a service life of 30–50 years – the steeper it is, the longer it lasts. A straw roof (or ridge) is not as durable.

So that the roof covering remains ventilated and does not rot, mosses and lichens must be removed (raked off) as necessary. Animal pests must be detected in good time and eradicated so that they do not damage the roof covering.

Any damage caused by storms or pests must be repaired without delay. This is carried out by stitching or tying loose layers from outside (or from inside if possible) and by filling the space left by bundles that have been driven inwards. A piece of wood is used to dress the new bundle to match the roof form.

To prevent the ingress of large amounts of condensation if ventilation is inadequate, use overlapping timber boards rather than large sheet metal flashings.

If thermal insulation is added at a later date, a clearance of ≥ 6 cm should be maintained between insulation and roof covering so that air can circulate freely. [12] If necessary, extra care must be taken with insulating materials that can swell up (swelling up to approx. 30%) (see "Building science, thermal performance"). Once the reed or straw has rotted away, or the roof covering has become so thin that the fixings can be seen and could therefore corrode, it is time to re-thatch the roof. Suitable material from the old covering can be reused. Components (e.g. dormer windows) that repeatedly suffer from rot should be roofed over with a steeper covering. Merely covering over a thin and damaged thatch with new layers of reed or straw is possible but is not recommended. During all subsequent work (renewal or recovering) it should be ensured that a clearance of ≥ 6 cm is maintained to other parts of the construction (e.g. boarding, thermal insulation). Thatched roofs are not accessible without using access equipment, e.g. S-hooks and poles. [12]

**References**


[01] Billett, M.: Thatching and Thatched Buildings; London: Hale, 1979

[02] Brown, R. J.: The English Country Cottage, 2nd ed.; London: Hale, 1988

[03] DIN 1055 pt 4: Design loads for buildings; imposed loads; wind loads on structures unsusceptible to vibration; Berlin: Beuth, 1986/1987

[04] DIN 1151: Drahtstifte rund; Berlin: Beuth, 1973 Superseded by: DIN EN 10230 pt 1: Steel wire nails; loose nails for general applications

[05] DIN 4102 pt 7: Fire behaviour of building materials and building components; roofing ñ definitions, requirements and testing; Berlin: Beuth, 1998

[06] DIN 18338: Contract procedures for building works – Part C: General technical specifications for building works; roof covering and roof sealing works; Berlin: Beuth, 2000

[07] DIN 68800: Protection of timber; pt 2: Preventive constructional measures in buildings; Berlin: Beuth, 1996; pt 3: Preventive chemical protection; Berlin: Beuth, 1990; pt 4: Measures for the eradication of fungi and insects; Berlin: Beuth, 1992

[08] Grützmacher, B.: Reet- und Strohdächer; Munich: Callwey, 1981

[09] Federal State Building Code of Schleswig-Holstein (section 40), 1975

[10] Nature Conservation Act of 18 March 1936

[11] Schattke, W.: Das Reetdach; Schleswig: Schleswiger Druck- und Verlagshaus, 1981

[12] Zentralverband des Deutschen Dachdeckerhandwerks; Fachverband Dach-, Wand- und Abdichtungstechnik e.V.: Regeln für Dachdeckungen mit Reet und Stroh; Cologne: R. Müller, 1988


## Wooden shakes and shingles

Materials, components, laying

### Materials

Species of wood, manufacture, properties

**Species of wood**

Narrow-ringed timber of the best quality is used for covering roofs. Typical, local species of wood are employed according to availability.

| | Argentina | Chile | Baltic states | UK | France | Canada | Central Europe | Eastern Europe | Scandinavia | South-east Europe | USA |
|---|---|---|---|---|---|---|---|---|---|---|---|
| Alerce[1)]<br>*Fitzroya cupressoides* | • | • | | | | | | | | | |
| Douglas fir<br>*Pseudotsuga menziesii* | | | | | | | • | | | | |
| Oak<br>*Quercus robur/petraea* | | | • | | • | | • | | • | • | • |
| Aspen<br>*Populus tremula* | | | • | | | | | • | | | |
| Spruce<br>*Picea abies* | | | • | | • | | • | • | • | • | |
| Sweet chestnut<br>*Castanea sativa* | | | | | • | | | | | | |
| Scots pine<br>*Pinus sylvestris* | | | | | | | • | • | • | | |
| Maritime pine<br>*Pinus pinaster* | | | | | • | | | | | | |
| Larch<br>*Larix decidua* | | | • | | • | • | • | | • | • | |
| Robinia<br>*Robinia pseudoacacia* | | | | | • | | | | | • | |
| Fir<br>*Abies alba* | | | | | | | • | | | | |
| Yellow cedar<br>*Chamaecyparis nootkatensis* | | | | • | | • | | | | | • |
| Western red cedar<br>*Thuja plicata* | | | | • | | • | | | | | • |
| Incense cedar<br>*Calocedrus decurrens* | | | | | | | | | | | • |
| White cedar<br>*Thuja occidentalis* | | | | • | | • | | | | | • |
| Southern cypress<br>*Taxodium distichum* | • | | | | | | | | | | • |

1) Alerce may no longer be imported under the treaty on protection of species.

2.4.3.1 Species of wood used for shakes and shingles, countries of origin [02, 04, 07, 22, 23, 27, 28, 32, 35]

**Manufacture**

Shakes or shingles are produced from one section of trunk that has previously been cut to the length of the shakes or shingles and divided into four or more bolts.

- Shakes are split by hand from the bolt using a mallet and froe. They have torn, sealed surfaces following the grain of the wood. The surface roughness varies with species of wood and quality of timber. Major unevenness is subsequently dressed with a drawknife, cutting the fibres of the wood to a greater or lesser extent. Shakes are manufactured from specially selected, straight-growing trees with a type of wood that is easily split.

- Shingles are sawn from the bolt. They have flat, smooth surfaces and all the fibres are most definitely cut. Only especially weather-resistant species of wood are suitable for being made into shingles. Sawing allows the use of species of wood that cannot be or are difficult to split.

The shakes or shingles are primarily produced by rift cutting (annual rings vertical to inclined), but also by radial cutting (vertical annual rings) of large-diameter trunks.

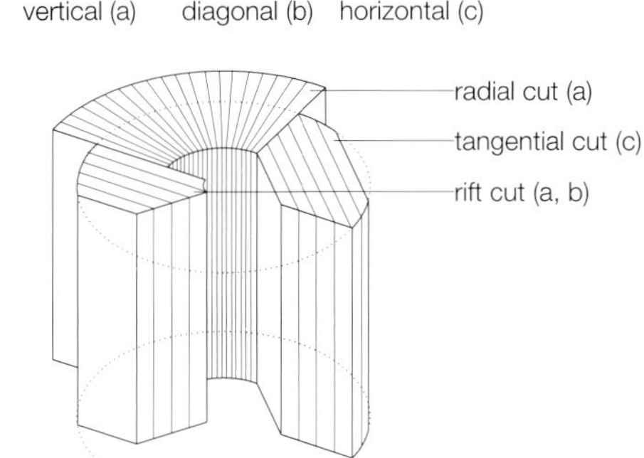


2.4.3.2 Alignment of annual growth rings

| | Radial/rift cut, annual rings vertical to diagonal | | | Tangential cut, annual rings horizontal | | |
|---|---|---|---|---|---|---|
| | split | sawn | grade[1)] | split | sawn | grade[1)] |
| Oak | • | • | 1 | | | |
| Spruce | • | | 1 | | | |
| Larch | • | • | 1 | • | | 1 |
| Fir | • | | 1 | | | |
| Yellow cedar | • | • | 1 | | • | 2 |
| Western red cedar | • | • | 1 | | • | 2 |

[1)] The grades agreed as usable in Germany may be classified differently in other countries.

2.4.3.3 Type of processing; classification [17, 36, 37]

Only shakes or shingles of grade 1 quality may be used for roof coverings, except in ancillary buildings.
Shakes or shingles of grade 2 quality may be used for wall cladding. [17]

| | Annual rings | Wood | Knots, imperfections |
|---|---|---|---|
| Grade 1 | vertical only | heartwood only | |
| Grade 2 | also curl, veins | also sapwood | in upper third |
| Grade 3 | curl, veins | sapwood | also in lower third |

2.4.3.4 Grades; classification

Split and sawn shakes and shingles

| | Oak | Spruce Fir | Scots pine | Larch | Yellow cedar | Western red cedar |
|---|---|---|---|---|---|---|
| Inclination of annual rings | vertical to inclined<br>90–30° inclination to width of shake or shingle | | | | | |
| Deviation of grain | up to 50 mm deviation from a line parallel to the side a distance of 300 mm from butt end of shake or shingle<br>grain runs primarily parallel to the side | | | | | |
| Right angle at butt end | deviation of up to 8% of width | | | | | |
| Colour | colour differences related to the natural properties of the wood | | | | | |
| Resin pockets | not continuous through wood | | | | | |
| Insect attack | not permitted | | | | | |
| Tolerances | length: +25/-6 mm; -6% for ≤ 10% of quantity supplied<br>width: ±5% of nominal dimension for shakes or shingles of equal width | | | | | |
| Parallelism | deviation ≦ 3% of length for 3% of quantity supplied | | | | | |
| Width of shake or shingle when nailed | normal width, 80 mm and over<br>20% of quantity supplied may be ≥ 75 mm wide<br>10% of quantity supplied may be ≥ 60 mm wide | | | | | |

2.4.3.5 Grading features [17]

Sawn shingles

| | Oak | Spruce Fir | Scots pine | Larch | Yellow cedar | Western red cedar |
|---|---|---|---|---|---|---|
| Fissures | provided the serviceability is not impaired | | | | | |
| Sapwood | not permitted | | | | | |
| Knots | not perm. | in upper third only if they are solid | | | not permitted | |

Split shakes and shingles

| | Oak | Spruce Fir | Scots pine | Larch | Yellow cedar | Western red cedar |
|---|---|---|---|---|---|---|
| Fissures | not permitted | | | | | |
| Sapwood | not permitted | | | | to a limited extent | |
| Knots | only in upper third | solid up to ≤ 20 mm dia. | | | not permitted on the front | |
| Deformation | deviation up to ≤ 4% of total of length + width | | | | | |

2.4.3.6 Grading features to DIN 68119; requirements for roofing shakes and shingles of grade 1 [17]

## Shaping

Shakes and shingles for roofing are usually given a tapered shape to allow air to circulate between their surfaces.

- Tapered shakes can be formed in one operation by turning the bolt through 180° after every splitting action. This produces shakes of unequal thickness with very rough surfaces that only rarely interlock with each other. Skill and care are therefore required when laying these shakes.
  Parallel shakes can be given a tapered shape in a second operation using a draw-knife.
  Parallel, double-thickness split shakes or sawn shingles can also be divided in two diagonally with a saw in a second operation. In both cases it is preferable to expose the split side to the weather. The surfaces here are less rough (split) or smooth (sawn).
- Parallel shakes are manufactured in one operation. These split shakes should be made exclusively from weather-resistant species of wood. The use of parallel-sawn shingles is not recommended.
- A 45° chamfer at the butt (i.e. bottom, thick) end is helpful. It limits later deposits and hence the growth of lichens and mosses on the roof.

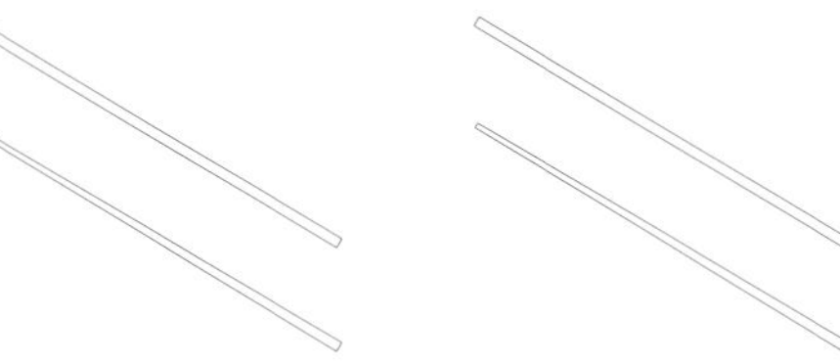

2.4.3.7 Section through shake or shingle; tapered and parallel; with chamfered butt end

**Properties**

Colour

Initially, shakes and shingles possess their natural wood colouring, but then turn grey due to the effects of the weather (particularly ultra-violet radiation) within about six months to about four years. Depending on the nature and severity of the weather, a light- to dark-grey patina develops on the surface.
Lime and cement mortars, metals and airborne pollutants can cause other discoloration.

Biological properties

Wood is an organic building material with hygroscopic properties. Wooden shakes and shingles absorb water during damp or wet weather, which makes them expand on the moist side and curve across the grain. In dry weather they release moisture, contract on the dry side and curve in the opposite direction. They therefore automatically create a clearance between each other and thus an air space to aid drying out.
Shakes and shingles with vertical annual rings move only moderately in their width and tend to curve and split less.
If wooden shakes and shingles are tightly packed on top of each other, they remain damp for longer, and when the moisture content remains above 20% for longer periods this creates an ideal breeding ground for insects and fungi.

| | Sapwood | Heartwood | Heartwood exposed to light | Annual rings |
|---|---|---|---|---|
| Alerce | white | light red-brown to red-brown | darkening to dark red-brown to red-violet | distinct, late wood clearly dark red-brown |
| Douglas fir | yellowish white to reddish white | yellowish brown to reddish yellow | darkening to reddish brown to dark red-brown | very clearly drawn, late wood clearly red-brown |
| Oak | yellowish white to grey-white | light brown to yellowish brown | darkening to dark yellow-brown to dark brown | more or less distinct, late wood dark brown |
| Aspen | sapwood and heartwood identical, grey-white to beige-white | | | less distinct |
| Spruce | sapwood and heartwood identical, yellowish white to reddish white | | darkening to yellowish brown | very clearly drawn, late wood clearly dark red-brown |
| Chestnut | grey-white | yellowish brown to dark brown | darkening | distinct |
| Scots pine | yellowish white to reddish white | reddish yellow | darkening to reddish brown | very clearly drawn, late wood clearly red-brown |
| Maritime pine | almost white | reddish yellow | darkening to reddish brown to red-brown | very clearly drawn, late wood clearly red-brown |
| Larch | yellowish white to reddish yellow | reddish beige to reddish brown | darkening to red-brown to dark red-brown | very clearly drawn, late wood clearly red-brown |
| Robinia | yellowish white to greenish yellow | yellowish green to greenish brown and light brown | darkening to gold-brown to chocolate brown | more or less distinct, late wood medium brown |
| Fir | sapwood and heart-wood identical, yellowish white to reddish white, grey shimmer | | | clearly drawn, late wood clearly red-beige |
| Yellow cedar | yellowish white | light yellow | darkening to pale brown to grey-brown | less distinct |
| Western red cedar | white | light red-brown to red-brown | little darkening | distinct, late wood dark red-brown |
| Incense cedar | white | reddish brown to chocolate brown | little darkening | less distinct |
| White cedar | white | yellowish brown | darkening | |
| Southern cypress | white | reddish yellow to red-brown/chocolate brown | | very clearly drawn |

2.4.3.8 Colours of sapwood and heartwood in as-supplied condition and after exposure to light [02, 03, 07, 22, 25, 30, 32, 35]

The sapwood of all species of timber has a low resistance and is therefore unsuitable for shakes or shingles. The sapwood of spruce and, in particular, pine is susceptible to blue stain fungus (discoloration).
Weather-resistant species of wood possess constituents (resins, acids) in the heartwood that help to combat insect attack and fungal growth; they do not normally require additional protection. Particularly weather-resistant species of wood are chestnut, oak, larch, robinia, yellow cedar and western red cedar. Constituents of various types of wood affect their compatibility with metals, as shown in table 2.4.3.9.

Timber preservatives

A three-layer covering (at least four layers in valleys), good ventilation behind the covering and the use of tapered shakes or shingles with a butt end chamfer are a good specification for protecting the wood. Space below the roof covering to allow air to circulate (counter battens) must be provided to ensure quick drying of the shakes or shingles. As shakes have rough, non-interlocking surfaces, good intermediate ventilation is ensured.
Preventive chemical timber preservatives are necessary in the case of a shallow roof pitch (< 18°), unfavourable climatic conditions or locations (shaded position, high relative humidity, inadequate air circulation, nearby trees, foliage, dust), pollutants and less weather-resistant species of wood. Chemical timber preservative should be applied according to DIN 68800 part 3.
Only pressure-impregnation with low-leaching salt solutions is advisable for larger roof areas.
Oil-based glazes and opaque paint finishes are possible, at best, on small ornamental roofs. The surface protection should not reduce the vapour-permeability of the wood, otherwise it will flake off in blisters.
Synthetic (polymer) roofing felts may not be used with impregnated wood containing oil.

| | Al | Cu | Pb | Steel stain. | Steel galv. | Steel paint. | Zn |
|---|---|---|---|---|---|---|---|
| Alerce | d | d | s | s | u | d | u |
| Douglas fir | | | | s | u | | |
| Oak | d | d | d | s | u | d | u |
| Aspen | | | | s | | | |
| Spruce | s | s | s | s | d | d | s |
| Chestnut | | | | s | u | d | u |
| Scots pine | s | s | s | s | d | d | s |
| Maritime pine | s | s | s | s | d | d | s |
| Larch | s | d | s | s | u | d | d |
| Robinia | | | | s | | | |
| Fir | s | s | s | s | d | d | s |
| Yellow cedar | s/d | d/u | s/d | s | u | d | u |
| Western red cedar | s/d | d/u | s/d | s | u | d | u |
| Incense cedar | | | | s | | | |
| White cedar | s/d | d/u | d/u | s | u | d | u |
| Southern cypress | | | | s | | | |

2.4.3.9 Materials for junctions and terminations [38]: s suitable, d discoloration/corrosion possible, u unsuitable without protection but with a suitable protective finish these materials can be combined for an unlimited period.

| Preservative | Applications | Protection |
|---|---|---|
| Containing oil but no solvent | | |
| Boiled linseed oil | Iv St | incomplete; re-treat every 2–5 years |
| Beeswax | Iv St | |
| Pigmented vegetable oils combined w. wax | P St | |
| Containing oil and solvent (PCP-free to DIN 68800) | | |
| w/o binding agent, sometimes dyed | P Iv W St | re-treat every 5–10 years |
| W. binding agent, unpigmented | P Iv W St | |
| Pigmented | P Iv W St | |
| Containing salt but no solvent | | |
| via a dip primer method with undercoat of blue stain primer via a non-pressure method with impregnating salts | | |
| CF salts | P Iv W | for low/moderate leaching |
| CFB salts | P Iv W St | |
| CK salts | P Iv W E | for high leaching |
| CKB salts | P Iv W St E | |
| CKF salts | P Iv W St E | |
| via pressure-impregnation | | |
| CFA salts*) | P Iv W | for moderate/high leaching, very effective, pollutant |
| CKA salts*) | P Iv W E | for high leaching, very effective, pollutant |

2.4.3.10 Timber preservatives [20, 29]: A arsenic, B boron, C chromium, F fluorine, K copper compounds; *) not permitted in Germany; P effective against fungi; Iv effective preventive treatment against insects; W suitable for wood exposed to the weather but not in permanent contact with water; E suitable for wood exposed to extreme conditions and in permanent contact with water; St suitable for painting, spraying and immersing in stationary plants.

| Species of wood | Density (air-dried) [g/cm³] | Bending strength [N/mm²] | Hardness (Janka scale) [N/mm²] | Shrinkage [%] per 1% moisture content change (5–20% range) | | Thermal conductivity (air-dried) [W/mK] | Resistance of unprotected heartwood against fungi in unfavourable conditions glong period with moisture content of timber > 20%) | Weather-resistant [1] | Mod. weather-resistant [2] | Not weather-resistant [3] | Impregnability of heartwood | Warping behaviour (stability) | pH value of heartwood | Notes |
|---|---|---|---|---|---|---|---|---|---|---|---|---|---|---|
| | $\rho$ | $\sigma_\perp$ | $HJ_\perp$ | radial | tangential | $\lambda_\perp$ | | | | | | | | |
| Alerce (softwood) | 0.33<br>0.44<br>0.54 | 60<br>61<br>88 | ~25 | 0.10<br>to<br>0.14 | 0.20<br>to<br>0.22 | 0.13<br>to<br>0.20 | ≥ 15 to 25 years, durable | • | | | moderate | very good | ~3.3 | Heartwood tree, v. narrow sapwood (< 2 cm), fine-consistent, no resin ducts; heartwood: constituents corrode metals (iron), discoloration; resistant to insect attack; readily worked, v. easily split; impregnable |
| Douglas fir (softwood) | 0.35<br>0.51<br>0.77 | 68<br>80<br>99 | 20<br>to<br>30 | ~0.15 | ~0.27 | 0.11<br>to<br>0.12 | ≥ 15 years, mod. durable | • | • | | very difficult | good | 3.3<br>to<br>4.2 | Heartwood tree, narrow/wide sapwood (3–6 cm), must be supplied w/o sapwood, narrow growth rings preferred; knotty, resin ducts/pockets; heartwood: 6–10% tanning agent corrodes metals (iron), discoloration (blue-grey); mod. acid/alkali resistance; mod. resistance to insect attack; elastic, readily worked, easily split, difficult to nail (w. wide growth rings); impregnable |
| Oak (hardwood) | 0.43<br>0.69<br>0.96 | 74<br>95<br>117 | 41<br>to<br>65 | 0.15<br>to<br>0.22 | 0.28<br>to<br>0.35 | 0.11<br>to<br>0.20 | ≥ 20 years, durable | • | • | | very difficult | good | ~3.9 | Heartwood tree, narrow sapwood (2–5 cm), must be supplied w/o sapwood, fine cracks; heartwood: 3–13% tanning agent corrodes metals (iron), discoloration (blue-grey to black); sensitive to alkalis; mod. termite resistance; elastic; limited workability (w. high proportion of late wood), easily split; impregnable |
| Aspen (hardwood) | 0.40<br>0.49<br>0.60 | 52<br>to<br>76 | ~29 | ~0.12 | ~0.25 | 0.15<br>to<br>0.19 | not durable | | | • | moderate<br>to<br>difficult | good | ~5.8 | Sapwood tree (heartwood formation delayed), very fine cracks; does not splinter; limited workability (needs sharp tools), cut faces felt-like, splittable; impregnable |
| Spruce (softwood) | 0.33<br>0.47<br>0.68 | 49<br>68<br>136 | 16<br>to<br>18 | 0.10<br>to<br>0.19 | 0.24<br>to<br>0.36 | 0.09<br>to<br>0.14 | ≥ 10 years, less durable | | • | • | difficult<br>to<br>very difficult | good | 4.0<br>to<br>5.3 | Ripewood tree (light heartwood), narrow growth rings preferred; knotty, many resin ducts/pockets; heartwood: constituents hardly corrode metals (iron), discoloration (pale grey); mod. acid/alkali resistance; vulnerable to insect attack; readily worked, easily split; impregnable |
| Chestnut (hardwood) | 0.54<br>0.62<br>0.68 | 63<br>77<br>91 | ~31 | ~0.14 | 0.21<br>to<br>0.26 | | ≥ 15 to 25 years, durable | • | | | very difficult | good | ~2.8 | Heartwood tree, narrow sapwood (2–5 cm), must be supplied w/o sapwood, fine cracks; heartwood: 7–16% tanning agent corrodes metals (iron), discoloration (blue-grey to black); mod. termite resistance; elastic; readily worked, splittable; impregnable |
| Scots pine (softwood) | 0.33<br>0.52<br>0.89 | 41<br>80<br>205 | ~25 | 0.15<br>to<br>0.19 | 0.25<br>to<br>0.36 | 0.12<br>to<br>0.14 | ≥ 10 to 15 years, less durable to mod. durable | | • | • | difficult<br>to<br>very difficult | good | 4.3<br>to<br>5.1 | Heartwood tree, narrow sapwood (2–10 cm), must be supplied w/o sapwood, narrow growth rings preferred; knotty, many resin ducts/pockets; heartwood: constituents hardly corrode metals (iron), discoloration (pale grey); mod. acid resistance; mod. resistance to insect attack; tough, readily worked, splittable; limited impregnability (w. high resin content) |
| Maritime pine (softwood) | 0.43<br>0.53<br>0.79 | 47<br>84<br>127 | | ~0.15 | ~0.30 | | less durable to mod. durable | | • | | very difficult | good | ~5.0 | Heartwood tree, wide sapwood, must be supplied w/o sapwood; knotty, many large resin ducts, resin pockets; heartwood: constituents barely corrode metals (iron), discoloration (pale grey); limited impregnability (w. high resin content) |
| Larch (softwood) | 0.44<br>0.59<br>0.85 | 64<br>93<br>132 | 35<br>to<br>37 | 0.14<br>to<br>0.18 | 0.28<br>to<br>0.36 | 0.12<br>to<br>0.13 | ≥ 15 years less durable to mod. durable | • | • | | very difficult | moderate<br>to<br>good | ~4.2 | Heartwood tree, narrow sapwood (1–3 cm), must be supplied w/o sapwood, narrow growth rings preferred; resin ducts; heartwood: constituents have low tendency to corrode metals (iron), discoloration (blue-grey); mod. acid/alkali resistance; elastic, tough; readily worked, easily split; limited impregnability (w. high resin content) |
| Robinia (hardwood) | 0.54<br>0.77<br>0.95 | 103<br>130<br>169 | ~77 | 0.17<br>to<br>0.24 | 0.32<br>to<br>0.38 | | ≥ 25 years, durable to very durable | • | | | very difficult | moderate | 4.1<br>to<br>5.3 | Heartwood tree, v. narrow sapwood (1–2 cm), fine cracks; heartwood: ≤ 26% tanning agent corrodes metals, discoloration (blue-grey); termite-resistant; v. elastic, v. tough; moderately workable, difficult to split & nail |
| Fir (softwood) | 0.35<br>0.45<br>0.75 | 47<br>68<br>118 | 18<br>to<br>29 | 0.10<br>to<br>0.16 | 0.28<br>to<br>0.35 | 0.09<br>to<br>0.14 | ≥ 10 years, less durable | | • | | moderate<br>to<br>difficult | good | 4.4<br>to<br>6.1 | Ripewood tree (light heartwood), narrow growth rings preferred; knotty, no resin ducts; heartwood: vulnerable to insect attack; mod. acid/alkali resistance; readily worked, easily split; impregnable |
| Yellow cedar (softwood) | 0.43<br>bis<br>0.55 | ~81 | | 0.04<br>to<br>0.09 | 0.06<br>to<br>0.20 | 0.10 | ≥ 20 years, mod. durable to durable | • | | | difficult<br>to<br>very difficult | good<br>to<br>very<br>good | | Heartwood tree, narrow sapwood (1–3 cm), must be supplied w/o sapwood; no resin ducts; heartwood: constituents corrode metals (iron, copper), discoloration probable, acid-resistant; not readily flammable; readily worked, difficult to split; impregnable |
| Western red cedar (softwood) | 0.33<br>0.37<br>0.46 | 48<br>54<br>55 | 15<br>to<br>20 | 0.07<br>to<br>0.10 | 0.20<br>to<br>0.24 | 0.09<br>to<br>0.10 | ≥ 20 years, mod. durable to durable | • | • | | difficult<br>to<br>very difficult | very<br>good | 2.5<br>to<br>3.5 | Heartwood tree, narrow sapwood (2–5 cm), must be supplied w/o sapwood; no resin ducts; heartwood: constituents corrode metals (iron, copper), discoloration (grey to blue-black); sensitive to alkalis; resistant to insect attack; readily worked, easily split; impregnable |
| Incense cedar (softwood) | 0.30<br>0.36<br>0.40 | ~56 | | | | | durable to very durable | • | | | | very<br>good | | Heartwood tree, wide sapwood (< 10 cm), must be supplied w/o sapwood; no resin ducts; heartwood: constituents corrode metals (acidic), discoloration probable; brittle, readily worked, v. easily split |
| White cedar (softwood) | 0.30<br>bis<br>0.45 | ~43 | ~14 | ~0.09 | ~0.18 | ~0.09 | ≥ 20 years, durable | | • | | moderate | good | ~3.5 | Heartwood tree, narrow sapwood, must be supplied w/o sapwood; knotty, no resin ducts; heartwood: constituents corrode metals (iron, copper), discoloration probable; readily worked, easily split |
| Southern cypress (softwood) | 0.27<br>0.50<br>0.65 | ~73 | ~23 | ~0.12 | ~0.21 | | mod. durable*) durable to very durable**) | • | | | moderate | good | <5.3 | Heartwood tree, narrow sapwood, no resin ducts; heartwood: constituents termite-resistant; moderately workable |

2.4.3.11 Characteristic values for timber [01, 02, 03, 06, 22, 23, 24, 25, 27, 30, 31, 32, 33, 34, 35, 38]; *) felled young, **) felled old; as roof shakes/shingles:
[1] also durable for decades without protection, [2] also durable for many years without protection, [3] chemical timber preservative necessary

Physical properties
According to DIN 1055 the weight per unit area for all types of wooden shakes and shingles is 2.5 kN/m² (see "Loadbearing structure"). Some species of wood are difficult to split. Furthermore, the elasticity and hardness of a few species of wood, e.g. robinia, makes nailing the shakes or shingles difficult; they may need to be predrilled. The rough split surfaces of shakes mean that the surfaces do not mate exactly. As the fibres at the surface are essentially undamaged, they absorb less moisture; and they dry out quicker owing to the better air circulation in between.
Shingles are easier to lay, fit together more snugly and therefore provide better protection from dust, driving snow and driving rain.
But their damaged surface fibres absorb more moisture and release it again more slowly owing to their tighter fit. Shakes are more durable than shingles.

Behaviour in fire
According to DIN 4102 part 7 the use of western red cedar shingles of grade 1 quality in a three-layer roof covering is classed as a "hard roof covering" (adequate resistance to sparks and radiant heat). The roof coverings of shingles made from Canadian yellow cedar and larch are also classed as "hard roof coverings" when they also have a butt end chamfer and are laid with a consistently ($\Delta_b$ = 2%) small joint width (1 to 5 mm, corresponding to their moisture content).
All other types of shake and shingle roof coverings are classed as "soft roof coverings".

## Components
Nailed shakes/shingles, loose-laid shakes/shingles

**Nailed shakes/shingles**
Nailed shakes/shingles are tapered or parallel in section. They are produced in lengths of 120–800 mm, preferably 300–600 mm. Depending on the source, width can vary from 60 to 350 mm. They should be divided when wider than 160 mm (European timber species) or 250 mm (overseas species). The nailed shakes/shingles preferred for roof coverings are ≥ 8 mm thick at the butt end.

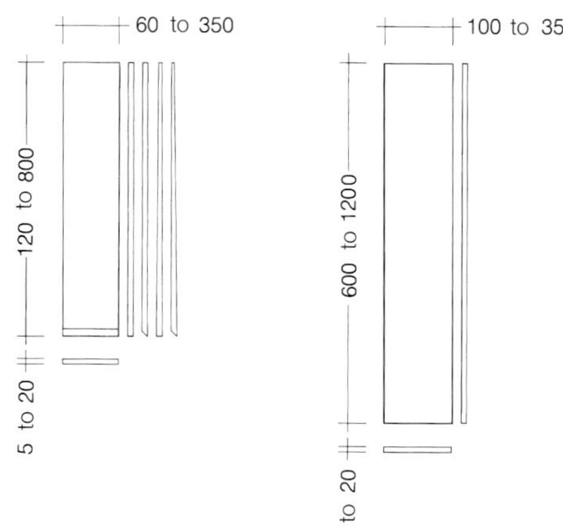

2.4.3.12 Nailed shakes/shingles: forms and dimensions (left); Loose-laid shakes/shingles: form and dimensions [38] (right)

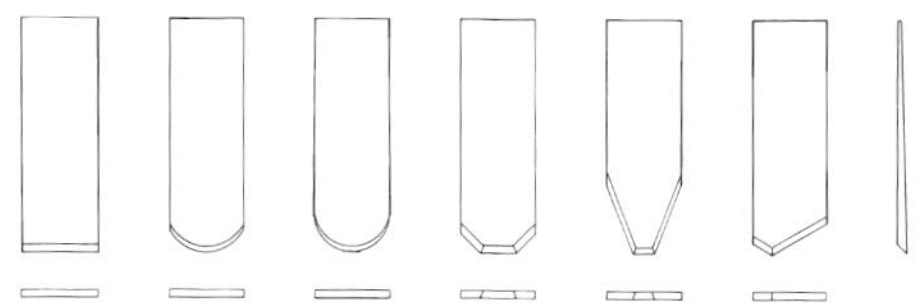
2.4.3.13 Ornamental shakes and shingles; forms [38]

Ornamental shakes or shingles
These are small, thin nailed shakes/shingles with specially shaped butt ends or special surface textures.

**Loose-laid shakes/shingles**
Loose-laid shakes/shingles are of equal thickness. They are produced mainly in lengths of 600–900 mm and widths of 70–300 mm. The thickness is ≤ 15 mm.

| Length | Width | Thickness | Parallel | Tapered |
|---|---|---|---|---|
| 120 to 300 | 60 to 150 | 5 to 10 | | • |
| ~ 400 | 70 to 350 | 8 to 10 | | • |
| ~ 450 | 70 to 350 | 8 to 12 | • | • |
| ~ 600 to 800 | 70 to 350 | 8 to 20 | • | • |
| 600 to 1200 | 100 to 350 | 15 to 20 | • | |

2.43.14 Dimensions of nailed shakes/shingles and loose-laid shakes/shingles [mm]

## Laying
Conditions for laying, fixing, additional measures, details, supporting construction, material requirements, maintenance and repair

**Conditions for laying**
Roof pitch
- Nailed shakes/shingles are laid in a three-layer bond, in four or five layers in valleys. The three-layer arrangement enables the roof surface to be better ventilated than with four or five layers, meaning that it can dry out quicker. As a rule, the length of shake or shingle does not vary across a roof surface. The use of longer shakes or shingles is advantageous on shallower roof pitches (< 30°). On roof pitches < 22° wooden shakes or shingles stay saturated for longer. The minimum pitch (22°) should always be maintained when using sprockets because most of the water accumulates at the eaves and this is also where snow lies longer.
- Loose-laid shakes/shingles are laid in a bond of at least three layers on a pitch of 17–22°. A steeper pitch is not possible because otherwise the stone weights roll off.

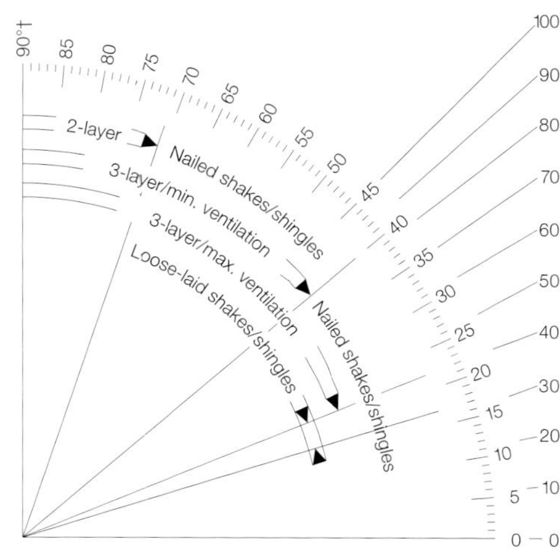

2.4.3.15 Standard roof pitches in relation to roof covering and ventilation [37, 38]

End overlap
The end overlap depends on the length of shake or shingle used and the pitch of the roof to be covered. The permissible minimum end overlap (between first and third layers) – or gauge – must be adhered to.
The side overlap for all loose-laid or nailed shakes/shingles must be ≥ 30 mm, and ≥ 20 mm between the first and third layers in the case of a three-layer bond.

| Length of shake/shingle | minimum overlap | | Gauge | |
|---|---|---|---|---|
| [mm] | 3-layer 22–90° [mm] | 2-layer 71–90° [mm] | 3-layer 22–90° [mm] | 2-layer 71–90° [mm] |
| 120 | 15 | 20 | 35 | 50 |
| 150 | 15 | 20 | 45 | 65 |
| 200 | 20 | 20 | 60 | 90 |
| 250 | 25 | 20 | 75 | 115 |
| 300 | 30 | 30 | 90 | 140 |
| 400 | 30 | 40 | 125 | 180 |
| 450 | 30 | 40 | 140 | 200 |
| 600 | 35 | 40 | 180 | 280 |
| 700 | 40 | 40 | 220 | 330 |
| 800 | 50 | 50 | 250 | 375 |

2.4.3.16 End overlap and gauge [38]; dimensions

Joints
With the exception of green (freshly cut) shakes or shingles and those still moist from pressure-impregnation, all shakes and shingles must be laid on the roof with

movement joints (1–5 mm) (see table 2.4.3.11 for swelling and contraction dimensions).

**Fixing**

Nailed shakes/shingles 60 mm wide are fixed with a single nail, all others with two nails. The use of shakes and shingles with a width > 160 mm (European timber species) or > 250 mm (overseas species) is not recommended. The edge distance of the nail must be 15–50 mm, and the next layer of shakes or shingles must overlap the nail by 30–40 mm. Visible nailing should be avoided. The nails are driven home flush but without damaging the fibres of the wood. Nails driven in too deeply lead to loosening or splitting of the shake or shingle due to the swelling and contraction movements. Only driving tools with a depth stop are permissible. Fixings should penetrate not more than 20 mm into the supporting construction. In contrast to the rules of the roofing trade, experts are in favour of fixing nailed shakes/shingles in the drier, upper part (at approx. 2/3 the length). This avoids multiple nailing and results in lower stresses and a lower risk of splitting. [05]
Loose-laid shakes/shingles are not fixed but held in place by a vertical load. A pole is laid diagonally across the courses every 4–6 courses. The pole is in turn weighted down with flat stones and fixed at the verge.

Fixing materials

The nails used have a flat head and a rough, twisted or grooved shaft, and are made from galvanised, preferably stainless, steel to DIN 17440 (only stainless steel nails are permissible with cedar shakes or shingles). Stainless steel staples (e.g. material No. 1.430 to DIN 17440) with a minimum diameter of 1.5 mm and a width of 10–12 mm are also suitable.

**Additional measures**

Additional measures are necessary when the reliability of the roof covering needs to be enhanced:

- on large roofs (long rafters)
- for roof coverings below the recommended roof pitch
- when several roof surfaces and valleys intersect at one point along the eaves
- with higher wind pressures
- with a high snow load
- with a build-up of melt waters

Additional measures could be:

- a steeper roof pitch
- a larger ventilation cross-section below the roof covering
- the use of shakes to improve surface ventilation and absorb less moisture
- the use of tapered shakes or shingles to improve the intermediate ventilation
- the use of longer shakes or shingles to reduce the number of joints
- the use of a more resistant species of wood
- pressure-impregnation with low-leaching salts
- boarding below the shakes or shingles
- roofing felt below the shakes or shingles

**Details**

Ridge, hip, eaves, valley, verge, junction with wall, chimney, dormer window

Ridge

The ridge capping is usually a three-layer overlapping arrangement. However, non-tapered shakes can also be laid in three layers in an alternating bond. The ridge capping should begin at the end facing away from the prevailing wind. According to ventilation requirements and wind situation, ventilation openings can be positioned on the leeward side at the ridge. The ventilation openings (at least the thickness of the counter battens) should include protective mesh screens. A strip of lead, copper or zinc can be laid below the horizontal ridge capping of alternating shakes or shingles. This exudes oxides and prevents the growth of mosses and algae. The species of wood used must be compatible with the metal (see table 2.4.3.9).

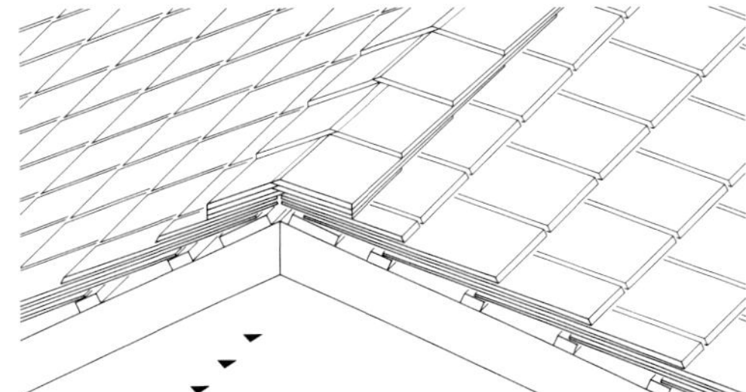

2.4.3.17 Ridge: alternating overlapping shakes or shingles; ▽ prevailing wind direction

Hip capping

This is preferred for roof pitches < 30°. The shakes or shingles projecting beyond the hip are cut off along the line of the hip and afterwards covered with three layers of shingles or shakes with alternating overlaps. This detail is also suitable for hips between roof surfaces at different pitches.

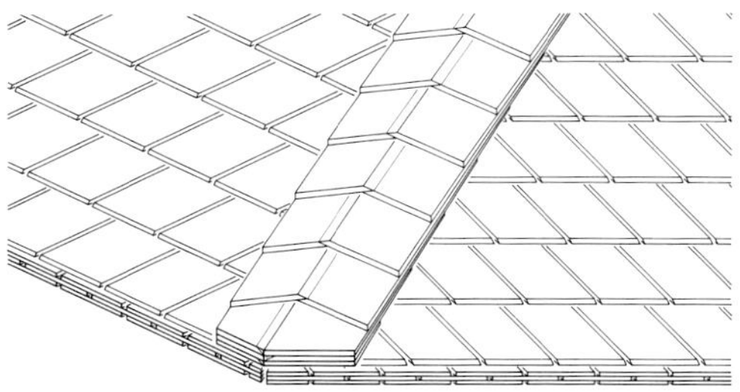

2.4.3.18 Hip capping: alternating overlapping shakes or shingles

Mitred hip

The roof covering starts at the hip and proceeds towards the body of the roof. The extent of the hip course is determined by chalk lines spanned to the left and right of the hip. The shakes or shingles on the hip are cut at an angle. Both these and the first shakes or shingles of each pair of rafters always have the same shape and can be manufactured using one template. When using uncut shakes or shingles (less waste and less work), the width of the hip course depends on the roof pitch and spacing of the battens.

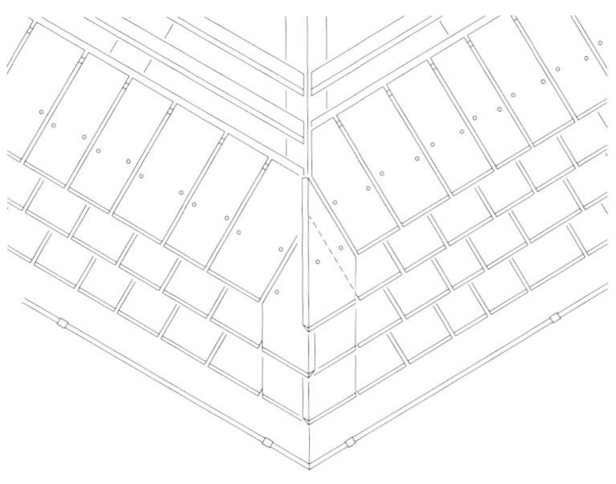

2.4.3.19 Mitred hip

Fanned hip

The sides of the shakes or shingles are bevelled and cut to suit the courses. This type of hip detail is only possible when the pitches of the adjoining roof surfaces are identical. Longer shakes or shingles are necessary for roof pitches < 30°, or additional measures must be taken. Rounded fanned hips are also feasible.

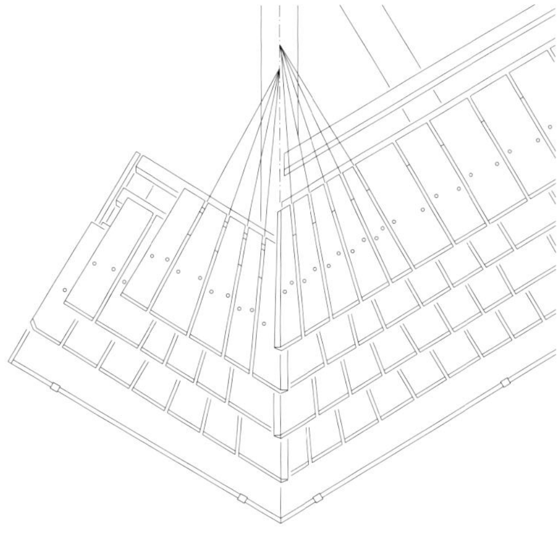

2.4.3.20 Fanned hip

Eaves

Without an eaves flashing the minimum overhang of the covering course must be 50–90 mm. With an eaves flashing the covering course must overhang at least 10–20 mm. The width of the eaves flashing that extends beneath the shakes or shingles depends on the roof pitch: 15 cm for > 30°, 20 cm for ≤ 30°.

The arrangement of the eaves course that leads to the smallest amount of water between the layers of shakes or shingles at the eaves is preferable.

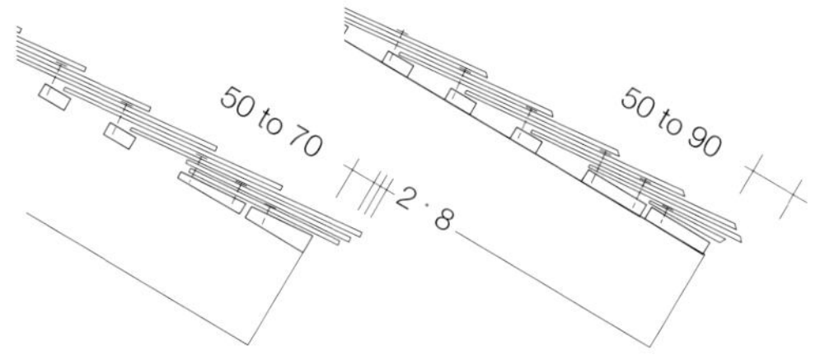


2.4.3.21 Eaves details [38]

Valley

Valleys of shakes or shingles without a metal underlay are only permissible with a valley rafter pitch ≥ 26° and at least four layers of shakes or shingles in the valley. The provision of a valley board underneath depends on the angle of the valley. The width of the valley board increases from 120 mm for a shallow pitch to 160 mm for a steep pitch; the thickness is 30 mm. Triangular fillets are positioned on both sides in order to create a smooth transition.

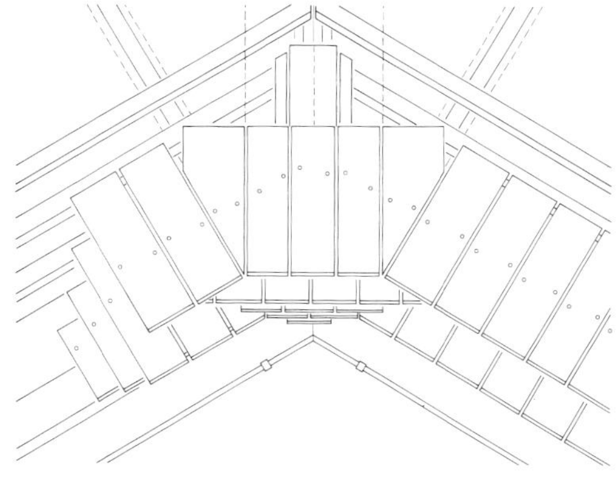

2.4.3.22 Semi-swept valley: covering and underlying layers

In the case of semi-swept valleys there are additional layers below the covering layers.

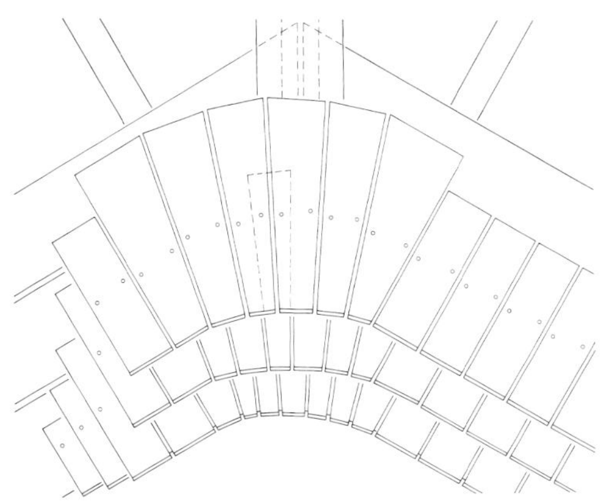

2.4.3.23 Swept valley with longer shakes or shingles in the valley

For swept valleys longer valley shakes or shingles are cut at an angle to suit.
Sheet metal valleys are necessary for valley rafter pitches ≤ 25° and can be provided in a channel form or flat on the valley board and bituminous felt with a sanded finish. The valley should be wide enough to clean (≥ 20 cm, able to carry maintenance load).
The flat sheet metal valley has a leg length of 250–300 mm with an upstanding seam ≥ 20 mm. So that the upstanding seam is not squashed at the edge, there should be a batten along the seam. The shakes or shingles must overlap the edge of the sheet metal by 100–120 mm along the sides.

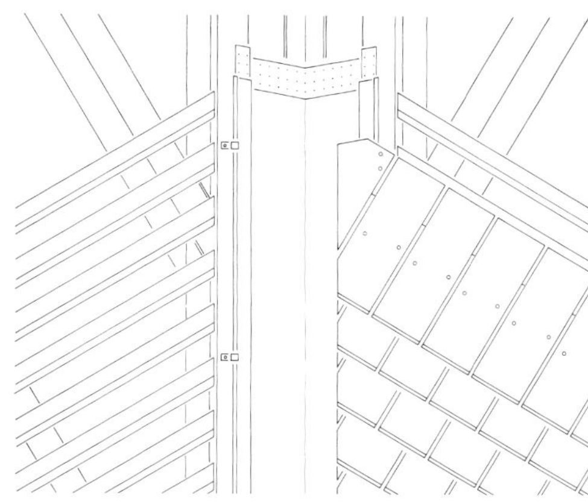

2.4.3.24 Open sheet metal valley

A channel-form sheet metal valley should be cut to a width ≥ 666 mm. The shakes or shingles must overhang the channel by 50–80 mm (see "Layers – Drainage").

Verge

Overhanging shakes or shingles must project beyond the wall construction by approx. 30 mm. To drain water away from the verge on to the roof surface, the butt end of the shakes or shingles can be cut at an angle on the verge side.

Junction with wall

The junction should be formed so that water running off the wall is drained away reliably. This is possible with a valley of shakes or shingles, but also with sheet metal soakers (most reliable sheet metal solution), a channel or a flashing. Sheet metal should be chosen in accordance with table 2.4.3.9.

Chimney

The flashings must be approx. 30 cm high, extend ≥ 20 cm below the shakes or shingles and have a saddle. The distance between shakes or shingles and chimney must be ≥ 10 cm so that the flashings can be cleaned easily.

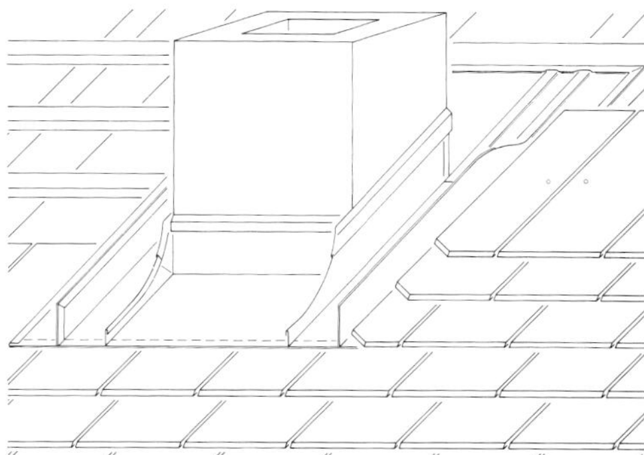

2.4.3.25 Flashings around chimney

Dormer window

Dormer windows should be built according to the recommendations for ridge, hip, valley, verge and wall junction details. Eyebrow dormers are the simplest and most reliable type because they produce the fewest problems. The ratio of height to width should not be less than 1:5 (see also "Construction details").

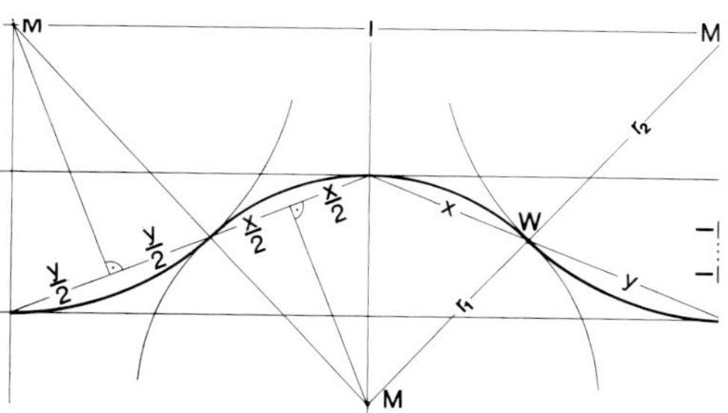


2.4.3.26 Eyebrow dormer window, construction of front curve; W chosen point of inflection

**Supporting construction**

Roofing felt, sarking

Roofing felt or sarking in the form of bitumen felt or plastic film is laid over an uninterrupted roof decking according to the requirements regarding the watertightness of the roof. The counter battens and battens necessary for a shake or shingle roof are then fixed to this film. Laying shakes or shingles directly on the roofing felt reduces their durability considerably because it precludes ventilation underneath. This means that higher moisture levels are maintained, which cause the wood to rot.

Battens

The counter battens determine the ventilation cross-section below the shakes or shingles. This must increase as the roof pitch decreases.

| Roof pitch | Shakes | Shingles |
|---|---|---|
| ≥ 40° | 24 mm | 30 mm |
| 26–39° | increase according to reduction in pitch | |
| ≤ 25° | 48 mm | 60 mm |

2.4.3.27 Counter batten thicknesses required; depth of ventilation layer [37, 38]

A minimum ventilation layer depth of 24 mm is required for a roof pitch ≥ 40° and should be doubled for roof pitches < 25°; intermediate values may be obtained by linear interpolation. The cross-section of the batten should be such that it does not whip. Battens are fixed to counter battens or rafters using nails to DIN 1151. Timber preservative for battens is to be applied in accordance with DIN 68800.

| Spacing of counter battens or rafters [mm] | ≤ 700 | ≤ 900 | ≤ 1000 |
|---|---|---|---|
| Battens (transverse or loadbearing battens) | 24x48 | 30x50 | 40x60 |
| Counter battens (longitudinal or for ventilation) | as required for ventilation | | |
| Battens laid directly on rafters | 30x50 | 40x60 | 40x60 |

2.4.3.28 Batten thicknesses required [mm] [38]

Roof decking
Structural roof deckings are best laid with gaps of 1–2 cm between the boards to improve air circulation. The thickness of the boards should be such that they do not whip. They should be fixed with at least two nails per board and rafter.

| Conventional decking thickness [mm] | | 18 | 19.5 | 22 | 24 | 28 | 30 |
|---|---|---|---|---|---|---|---|
| recomm. max. rafter spacing [mm] | tongue + groove rough boarding | 500 | 600 | 800 | 1000 | 1250 | 1500 |
| | narrow boards laid with gaps 120–160 mm | – | 500 | 600 | 700 | 800 | 1000 |
| | wide boards laid with gaps > 160 mm | – | 600 | 800 | 1000 | 1250 | 1500 |

2.4.3.29 Rafter spacing; thickness of roof decking [38]

**Material requirements**
The basic number of shakes or shingles is determined according to DIN 68119 part 1. In Germany the unit of measurement is the "Breitenmeter" (Bm):

"Breitenmeter" [m] = roof area [m$^2$]/gauge [m]

This represents the number of shakes or shingles with about 20% moisture content to be supplied for laying adjacent to each other; joints are not taken into account.
Include an allowance of about 5–10% of the quantity ordered for waste at hips, eaves, verges, dormer windows, etc.

**Maintenance and repair**
The service life of a shake or shingle roof depends on the roof pitch and the saturation of the wooden covering. A rule of thumb is that the pitch of the roof in degrees is roughly equal to the number of years the covering will last. The better the ventilation to the covering, the longer it will last. In order to keep the covering as dry as possible it should be maintained at regular intervals. Soiling, lichens, mosses and

| Length of shake or shingle[1] | 3-layer 22–90° pitch | | 2-layer[2] 71–90° pitch | |
|---|---|---|---|---|
| | Gauge | No. of shakes or shingles | Gauge | No. of shakes or shingles |
| [mm] | [mm] | [Bm/m$^2$] | [mm] | [Bm/m$^2$] |
| 120 | 35 | 28.57 | 50 | 20.00 |
| 150 | 45 | 22.22 | 65 | 15.38 |
| 200 | 60 | 16.67 | 90 | 11.11 |
| 250 | 75 | 13.33 | 115 | 8.70 |
| 300 | 90 | 11.11 | 140 | 7.14 |
| 400 | 125 | 8.00 | 180 | 5.56 |
| 450 | 140 | 7.14 | 200 | 5.00 |
| 600 | 180 | 5.56 | 280 | 3.57 |
| 700 | 220 | 4.55 | 330 | 3.03 |
| 800 | 250 | 4.00 | 375 | 2.67 |
| 900 | 280 | 3.60 | | |

[1] Gauges for intermediate lengths may be obtained by linear interpolation.
[2] 2-layer roof covering only used in exceptional cases.

2.4.3.30 Basic quantity of shakes or shingles required [38]

foliage should be removed as necessary because they retain rainwater and condensation and hence promote rotting and the growth of fungi. Cleaning can be carried out by sweeping with a stiff broom, washing with a high-pressure cleaner and/or spraying the roof surface with a 10% zinc/chlorine solution.
However, a properly built shake or shingle roof does not require special chemical timber preservative, either before or during its lifetime. Nailed shakes/shingles that are damaged or beginning to rot can be removed and replaced individually. This is easier when they are nailed near the top instead of being nailed according to the recommendations of the roofing trade because they are then not fixed through several layers of shakes or shingles. If the nailed shakes/shingles show signs of premature ageing, it is advisable to re-cover the entire roof with tapered shakes of a better timber quality and/or with a steeper pitch. Loose-laid shakes/shingles should be turned over and reversed every 5–10 years depending on species of wood and degree of exposure. When doing so, the shakes or shingles and the underlay should be thoroughly cleaned so that ventilation remains good. Crawling boards or similar means of access are required when maintaining or repairing such roofs.

**References**
[01] Alden, H. A.: Softwoods of North America, General Technical Report FPL-GTR-102; Madison: Forest Products Laboratory, 1997
[02] ARGE Holz e.V. and Verein Deutscher Holzeinfuhrhäuser e.V. (pub.): Informationsdienst Holz, Merkblattreihe Holzarten, 3rd ed.; Düsseldorf: ARGE Holz e.V., 1987
[03] Begemann, H. F.: Das große Lexikon der Nutzhölzer; Gernsbach: Dt. Betriebswirte-Verlag, 1981–94
[04] Bernard P. (ed.), team of authors: Encyclopédie des métiers: L´art dur couvreur (Bd. 3); Paris: Association ouvrière des Compagnons du Devoir, 1983
[05] Beyer, G.: Schindelleben verlängern, Tipps und Tricks für den richtigen Schindeleinbau; in: Holzkurier 1/98; Vienna: Österr. Agrarverlag, 1998
[06] Bosshard, H. H.: Holzkunde, vol. 1; Basel/Stuttgart: Birkhäuser, 1974
[07] Bramwell, M. (ed.), team of authors; The International Book of Wood; London: Mitchell Beazley, 1976
[08] Brennecke, W.; Folkerts, H.; Haferland, F.; Hart, F.: Dachatlas, Geneigte Dächer; Munich: Inst. f. intern. Architektur-Dokumentation, 1975–84
[09] Council of Forest Industries of British Columbia: Canadian Red Cedar Shingles and Shakes; Aachen, 1982
[10] Dietrichs, H.-H.: Fachkurs Holzkunde, chemical-technical data sheets; Leinfelden-E.: Konradin, 1988
[11] DIN 1055, Design loads for buildings, pt 1: Stored materials, building materials and structural members, dead load and angle of friction; Berlin: Beuth, 1978
[12] DIN 1151: Drahtstifte rd., Flachk.; Berlin: Beuth, 1973 Superseded by: DIN EN 10230 pt 1: Steel wire nails; loose nails for general applications
[13] DIN 4074 pt 1: Strength grading of coniferous wood; coniferous sawn timber; Berlin: Beuth, 1989
[14] DIN 4076: Terms and symbols in the field of wood; species of wood; Berlin: Beuth, 1985
[15] DIN 4102: Fire behaviour of building materials and building components; pt 7: Roofing; definitions, requirements and testing; Berlin: Beuth, 1987
[16] DIN 52181: Determination of growth properties of coniferous sawn timber; Berlin: Beuth, 1975
[17] DIN 68119: Wood shingles; Berlin: Beuth, 1996
[18] DIN 68364: Characteristic values for wood species; strength, elasticity, resistance; Berlin: Beuth, 2001
[19] DIN 68367: Determination of quality characteristics of sawn timber of broadleaved species; Berlin: Beuth, 1976
[20] DIN 68800: Protection of timber; pt 2: preventive constructional measures in buildings; Berlin: Beuth, 1996; pt 3: preventive chemical protection; Berlin: Beuth, 1996 & 1990
[21] DIN EN 350: Durability of wood and wood-based products – Natural durability of solid wood – Part 2: Guide to the natural durability and treatability of selected wood species of importance in Europe; Berlin: Beuth, 1994
[22] DRW-Verlag (pub.); team of authors: Holzlexikon; Leinfelden-E.: DRW Weinbrenner, 1988
[23] Frühwald, A., Schwab, E., Krause, H. A.: Eigenschaften einiger Plantagenhölzer aus Argentinien (Arbeitsbericht); Hamburg: Bundesforschungsanstalt für Holz- und Forstwirtschaft, 2000
[24] Giordano, G.: Technologica del Legno, vol. 3, pt 2; Torino: Unione Tipografico Editrice, 1988
[25] Grosser, D.: Fichte, Kiefer, Lärche, Esche, Kastanie, Douglasie; Düsseldorf: AG Holz e.V., 1984/85
[26] Güntzel, J. G.: Zurheide, E.: Holzschindeln; Freiburg: Ökobuchverlag, 1986
[27] Hall, M., Witte, J.: Maderas del Sul de Chile; Santiago de Chile: Deutscher Entwicklungsdienst, 1998
[28] Hoyet, J.-M. (ed.), team of authors: Guide Bardages Bois; Paris: Centre Technique du Bois et l´Ameublement et Editions Regirex; 1990
[29] Institut für Bautechnik: Holzschutzmittelverzeichnis; Berlin/Bielefeld/Munich: Erich Schmidt, 1999
[30] Langendorf, G., Schuster, E., Wagenführ, R.: Rohholz; Leipzig: VEB Fachbuchverlag, 1990
[31] Lohmann, U.: Holzhandbuch, 4th ed.; Leinfelden-Echterdingen: DRW, 1993
[32] Natterer, J.; Herzog T.; Volz, M.: Holzbauatlas Zwei, 2nd ed.; Munich: Inst. f. Intern. Architektur-Dokumentation, 1996 & 99
[33] Scholz, W.; Knoblauch, H. et al. (ed.): Baustoffkenntnis, 13th ed.; Düsseldorf: Werner; 1995
[34] Sell, J.: Eigenschaften und Kenngrößen von Holzarten; Zürich: Lignum, 1989
[35] Wagenführ, R.: Holzatlas, 5th ed.; Leipzig: Fachbuchverlag/Hanser, 2000
[36] Weiß, L.: Holzschindeln für Dach und Wand, Holzbau Technik, Jun–Sept 1986; Düsseldorf: Informationsdienst Holz, 1986
[37] Weiß, L.: Dach und Wand pt 1; unpubl. article, 1989
[38] Zentralverband des deutschen Dachdeckerhandwerks – Fachverband Dach-, Wand- und Abdichtungstechnik – e.V.: Regeln für Dachdeckungen mit Holzschindeln: Cologne: Rudolf Müller, 1986 & 1988

## Natural and fibre-cement slates

Materials, components, laying

## Natural slates

Raw materials, manufacture, properties

#### Raw materials

Slate originates from clayey sludge masses that were deposited on the seabed in the Devonian and Silurian periods some 450–350 million years ago. These masses were compressed at great depths. During the subsequent formation of mountain ranges, lateral pressures and corresponding moderate temperatures brought about realignment and a crystalline transformation in the rock.
Of the many different types of slate, clayey shale is the most suitable for use in building. Besides clay minerals (kaolinite, illite, montmorillonite) it also contains, above all, mica (muscovite, sericite), chlorite, quartz and feldspar. It possesses a fine-grained, extraordinarily close parallel microstructure of cross-linked layers of mica, which enable it to be easily split (riven) into thin sheets.

#### Manufacture

In Central Europe slate is obtained mostly from underground mines, below the weathering zone of 70 m, but in other countries also from open quarries.

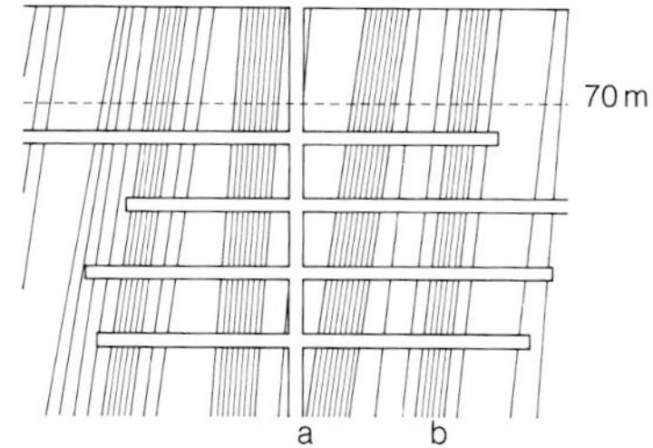


2.4.4.1 Schematic diagram of an underground slate mine; a slate pit, b slate strata [20]

Every deposit of slate has its own character, with different rock qualities occurring adjacent to each other even within a deposit.
Only 5–20% of the material extracted is actually used.
The slate is cut into large blocks at the mine or quarry and carefully separated from the wall by explosives or drilling. The blocks are split at the works into 5 mm (±1 mm) thick basic rectangular pieces. These are finished with a milling machine (works) or special hand tools (building site) to match a template or as required. The quality of the final product therefore depends both on the selection of slate for further processing and on the proper working of the material itself. Consequently, it is inadvisable to assess quality purely in terms of the source.

#### Properties

Colour

The colour of slate varies from one deposit to another, and therefore the slates used on a roof should all be supplied from the same source. German slate is blue-grey to black, but slate from other countries can be red, purple, light green or dark green. Care should be taken to ensure that the slates are of a consistent colour.

| Source | Colour after production | Colour after exposure to weather |
|---|---|---|
| B+F/Ardennes | green-grey, purple | no fading |
| BR/Gerais | black, grey-green, purple | little to no fading |
| | green | fades |
| CDN/Newfoundland | green-grey, purple | no fading |
| CDN/Quebec | dark grey to black | no fading |
| CZ/Bohemian-Moravian Highlands | blue-grey | no fading |
| D/Eifel/Moselle | blue-grey | no fading |
| D/Franconian Forest | blue-black blue-grey | no fading |
| D/Hunsrück | blue-grey | no fading |
| D/Sauerland | blue-grey | some fading |
| D/Thuringian Forest | dark blue to blue-black | no fading |
| E/La Coruna | blue-grey | no fading |
| E/Leon | dark blue-grey | no fading |
| E/Lugo | blue-black | |
| | dark blue-grey | no fading |
| | green | some total fading |
| E/Orense | dark blue-grey | no fading |
| E/Sistema Central | silver-grey, green-grey | no fading |
| F/Anjou | blue-grey | no fading |
| F/Bretagne | blue-grey | no fading |
| F/Pyrenees | | fades |
| UK/Cornwall | grey | fades |
| | blue-grey to green | some fading |
| UK/Wales | blue-grey to dark blue-grey | no fading |
| | violet-grey to blue-grey | no fading |
| | purple-grey to violet-grey | no fading |
| UK/Lake District | blue-green to green | no fading |
| UK/Scotland | blue-grey | gold-brown to light brown |
| Ireland | dark purple | |
| I/Liguria | blue-grey | severe fading |
| Norway | black-grey, green-grey | |
| | green | no fading |
| P/Porto | blue-grey | fades |
| USA/Vermont | dark grey with black stripes | partly grey-brown |
| | grey | grey-bronze |
| | grey to green-grey | grey-brown to grey-beige |
| | silver-grey to green-grey | no fading |
| | purple-grey with green-grey patches | no fading |
| | purple-grey to blue-grey | partly grey-beige |
| | blue-grey | |
| USA/Washington County | brick red | no fading |

2.4.4.2 Slate; colours [12, 18, manufacturers]

2.4.4.3 Slate extraction in Europe: ⚒ underground mines, + open quarries [21]

Chemical properties

Impurities in the stone and defects in the microstructure determine the chemical properties of natural slates.
Some impurities may react with carbonic acid ($H_2CO_3$) and sulphurous acid ($H_2SO_3$), which form when constituents of the air such as carbon dioxide ($CO_2$) and sulphur dioxide ($SO_2$) mix with water vapour ($H_2O$).
Damaging impurities are as follows:

- Calcite ($CaCO_3$) > 20% by wt is not permitted [27], and at > 5% an increase in the width of the gap is recommended in Germany and France. [12, 27] Limy (marly) slate is not suitable for use in industrial and marine atmospheres. [19] The 21-day acid vapour test (approx. 5% $H_2SO_3$ solution) is carried out to ascertain the resistance to acids. [08, 27]
- Oxidisable iron compounds lead to rusty efflorescence and cleaving of the mineral microstructure and (pyrite) to the leaching of compounds such as gypsum and alum [11]: pyrrhotine (FeS, pure: cream-brown; impure: dark grey or black), pyrite ($FeS_2$, light yellow), iron oxide (FeO, black), haematite ($Fe_2O_3$, red), goethite (FeOOH, ochre). [12, 15, 16] A visual inspection (colour/discoloration) serves to establish the presence of iron compounds, and the heating/odour test (pungent smell) the presence of sulphur compounds.
- Carbon (C) > 2% by wt [27], which promotes degradation by the weather. If this is washed out by the rain, the colour of the slate becomes lighter. Slate rich in carbon is soft.

The scratch test with a hard, pointed object is carried out to establish the presence of carbon. A dark scratch indicates carbon impurities, and a light scratch the lack of carbon. [11]

Coarse impurities of a wide range of minerals disrupt the microstructure. Their larger crystals, coarse particles or nodules reduce the density and cross-linking of the layers of mica, contributing to the loosening and thus the breakdown of the slate.

Mineral properties

Pure clayey shale is highly weather-resistant. The impurities in impure clayey shale promote the degradation by the weather but this damaging effect can be offset by the mineral microstructure. The quality of the slate therefore increases with the number and cross-linking of the layers of mica. The cohesion is determined by the density and cross-linking of these layers. As they increase, so does the probability that damaging constituents are enclosed effectively by mica. Adequate cross-linking is achieved with 40 or more layers/mm, complete cross-linking at 60–100 layers/mm.

| Long. bond / Transv. bond | Totally continuous | Partial continuity | Dis-continuous | Iso-lated |
|---|---|---|---|---|
| Highly developed bonding | | | | |
| Well developed bonding | | | | |
| Incomplete bonding | | | | |
| Totally separate | | | | |

2.4.4.4 Grades of clayey shale; abstract thin-section images [21]

In addition to assessing the slate according to its mineral composition, it is also helpful to assess it according to its cleavage plane microstructure. Only classes 1A, 2A, 1B and 2B are suitable for roofing (table 2.4.4.4a).

| Cleavage plane microstructure / Quality of stone | pure | im-pure | un-usable |
|---|---|---|---|
| Complete cross-linking | 1A | 2A | 3A |
| Good cross-linking | 1B | 2B | 3B |
| Incomplete cross-linking | 1C | 2C | 3C |

2.4.4.4a Classification of clayey shale [20]

Physical properties

Good quality slate should have a planar, consistent structure. It should be free from clefts (quartz), inclusions (ore, lime) and fissures. Visual inspection, feeling for spalling, bumps, depressions and cracks, plus a sound test (clear ring = dense, dry stone; dull thud = damp stone; clank = cracked stone) serve to assess the quality.

| | |
|---|---|
| Density (air-dried) | 2.7–2.89 $g/cm^3$ |
| Compressive strength | 140–250 $N/mm^2$ |
| Bending strength | > 40–87 $N/mm^2$ |
| Thermal conductivity | ~ 2 W/mK |
| Thermal expansion | ~ 0.005 mm/mK |
| Specific heat | ~0.8 J/gK |
| Temperature stability | ≥110°C |
| Behaviour in fire | building materials class A 1 incombustible, "hard roof covering" |
| Pore water content | 56% |
| Water absorption | 0.08–0.62% by wt |
| Swelling/shrinkage | 0.10–0.13 mm/m |
| Frost resistance<br>water ≤ 0.6% by wt<br>water > 0.6% by wt | <br>≥ 25 freeze-thaw cycles<br>≥ 100 freeze-thaw cycles |

2.4.4.5 Natural slates; characteristic values [17, 27, manufacturers]

Dimensional stability

The dimensions of natural slates produced in various fixed sizes using templates must lie within certain tolerances.

| | |
|---|---|
| Length/width deviation [mm] | ±5 |
| Deviation from right angle [%] | ±1 |

2.4.4.6 Geometric characteristic values; permissible dimensional tolerances for slates of the same size

## Fibre-cement slates

Raw materials, manufacture, properties

**Raw materials**

Fibre-cement is a composite material made from fibres and cement. Its constituents are (in terms of volume): 40% binder (Portland cement), 11% aggregates (ground limestone, ground fibre-cement), 2% reinforcing fibres (synthetic organic; polyvinyl alcohol, polyacrylonitrile), 5% process fibres (pulp), 12% water, 30% air (pores).

Asbestos fibres were originally used universally (asbestos-cement). However, since 1990 the production of building products in Germany has been completely converted to be free of asbestos fibres. Asbestos-cement is still produced in other European countries.

**Manufacture**

Forming

The raw materials are mixed together with an excess of lime-saturated water to produce a liquid sludge. This is picked up by cylindrical moulds through the blotting paper effect as a thin fabric (0.3–0.9 mm) and wound on format rollers to produce the final thickness. The coating of material produced in this way is vacuum-dewatered, cut open, trimmed to size and pressed (150 $N/mm^2$) to give the final slate thickness.

Colouring

Fibre-cement is naturally cement grey. Other colours can be obtained by spreading pigment during the manufacturing process (before winding up on the format rollers) onto the uppermost layer of the material. Fibre-cement can also be painted subsequently with suitable, conventional paints. Finished slates can also be given an open-pore acrylic coating.

**Properties**

Colour

The range of colours varies depending on the manufacturer. The durability of the colour also varies. However, only light-fast inorganic paints are used.

| Colour | RAL No. (approximate) |
|---|---|
| crystal white | 9001–9002 |
| light grey | 7035–7044 |
| dark grey | 7021–9011 |
| dark brown | 8002–8011 |
| brick red | 2001–8004 |
| classic red | 2001–2012 |
| dark green | 6011–6020 |
| blue-black | 5008 |
| graphite blue | 5007–5014 |
| pastel blue | 5024–6034 |

2.4.4.7 Fibre-cement slates; colour (RAL No. only approximate as the colours are not specified according to the RAL system) [09]

Fibre-cement slates can be supplied in special colours on request. The colours may change with atmospheric influences and environmental pollution.

Biological properties

Fibre-cement is resistant to fungi, bacteria (aerobic and anaerobic) and termites. Airborne deposits can form breeding grounds for algae and mosses, above all on non-coated slates.

Chemical properties

Brief exposure to damaging fluids and gases has no negative effects, provided the fibre-cement is cleaned immediately.

Crystals that destroy the microstructure of the material can form during the drying of certain salt solutions. Surface water on a fibre-cement roof, above all on non-coated slates, can give rise to reactions in the case of certain types of glass and aluminium.

It is not resistant to the long-term effects of:
- inorganic acids, e.g. $H_2CO_3$, $H_2SO_3$, HCl, nitric acid, phosphoric acid, acidic sulphate cooking liquors
- organic acids, oxalic acid, formic acid, lactic acid, acetic acid
- vegetable oils and fats
- solutions of magnesium salts, sulphates, ammonium salts, iron chloride
- warm distilled water
- hot condensation water
- aggressive water with pH < 6
- gases with a high concentration of Cl, $SO_2$, smoke (particularly in the condensation zone), $CO_2$, and other acid-forming gases
- $H_2S$ in combination with oxygen

It is resistant to the long-term effects of:
- alkaline solutions, aqueous chromate alkaline solutions, KCl, lime water, NaCl, saltpetre, soap, soda, tar, bitumen, liquid manure (provided the pH is not less than 6 and the sulphate content does not exceed 600 mg $SO_3$)
- oils, petroleum, petrol, benzole, toluene, xylene, coal-tar oil, neutral hydrocarbons (provided they are fat-free)
- dry gases (provided they cannot form acids with the water vapour in the material)
- $O_2$, $N_2$, $H_2$

Physical properties
The winding process aligns the fibres tangential to the cylindrical mould, i.e. in the longitudinal direction of the slates. These represent the tension reinforcement in the material, and in conjunction with the compressive strength of the cement they give rise to a product with a high bending strength. Fibre-cement is a high-quality concrete with corresponding material properties.

| | |
|---|---|
| Density, pressed<br>not pressed | 1.75 g/cm³<br>1.40 g/cm³ |
| Bending strength,<br>pressed ⊥/II<br>not pressed ⊥/II | <br>28.0 N/mm²/20.0 N/mm²<br>20.0 N/mm²/16.0 N/mm² |
| Permiss. bending strength | 6.0 N/mm² |
| Thermal conductivity | 0.58 W/mK |
| Thermal expansion | 0.010 mm/mK |
| Temperature stability | ~150°C |
| Behaviour in fire | building materials class A 2 incombustible "hard roof covering" [04] |
| Water absorption | ≤ 18% by wt |
| Swelling/shrinkage | 1.4 mm/m |
| Frost resistance | ≥ 50 freeze-thaw cycles ("frost-resistant" [06]) |

2.4.4.8 Fibre-cement; characteristic values [11, 17]

## Elements

General elements, edge elements

### Rectangular/square slates

#### General elements

The rectangular and square general elements are cut to various fixed sizes using templates. Natural slates are normally 4–6 mm thick with chamfered edges cut from below and are supplied without holes; fibre-cement slates are 4 mm thick with smooth, punched edges and are supplied with several holes.

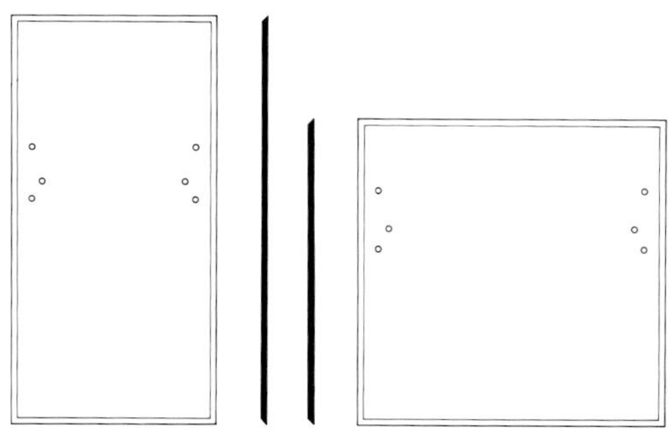

2.4.4.9 Rectangular and square slates; plans, sections and holes

| length x width [cm] | approx. weight per 1000 pieces [kg] natural slate | fibre-cement |
|---|---|---|
| 60 x 35 | 2890 | |
| 60 x 30 | 2410 | 1530 |
| 50 x 30 | 2070 | |
| 50 x 25 | 1720 | |
| 40 x 40 | 2265 | 1360 |
| 40 x 25 | 1380 | |
| 40 x 20 | 1100 | 680 |
| 35 x 35 | 1600 | |
| 35 x 25 | 1210 | |
| 35 x 20 | 970 | |
| 30 x 30 | 1205 | 770 |
| 30 x 20 | 750 | 510 |
| 30 x 15 | 620 | 380 |
| 27 x 18 | 600 | |
| 25 x 25 | 860 | |
| 25 x 20 | 600 | |
| 25 x 15 | 550 | |
| 22 x 15 | 480 | |

2.4.4.10 Rectangular and square slates, general elements; dimensions and weights [03, 09, 14, 24, 27]

#### Edge elements

The same rectangular/square elements are used at the ridge as for the surface of the roof; however, these are generally without holes. Special slates produced by working the rectangular/square slates with special hand tools on site are used at hip, eaves and verge. The slates required for valleys on slate roofs are produced from basic rectangular pieces (see table 2.4.4.21). The size of the basic pieces depends on the size of the slates required. Fibre-cement slates for valleys are produced in fixed sizes.

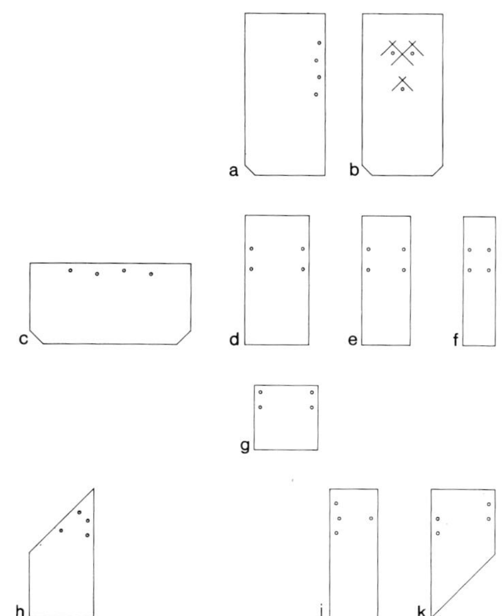


2.4.4.11 Rectangular and square slates, general and edge elements; selection [27]: a ridge slate, b key slate, c wide verge slate, d whole slate, e 3/4 slate, f 1/2 slate, g eaves slate, h hip slate, i valley slate, k valley slate

### Diagonal slates

#### General elements

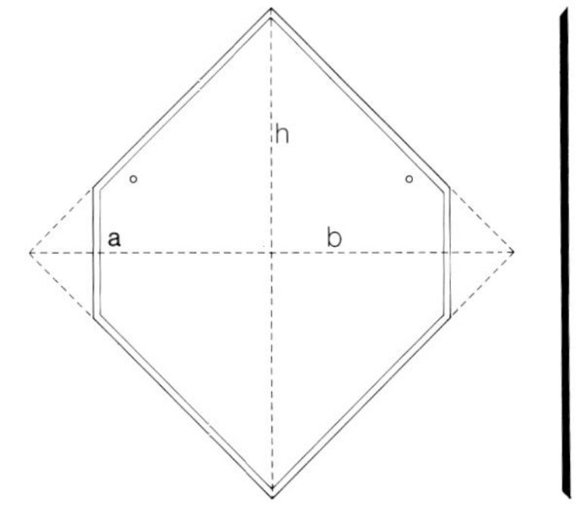


2.4.4.12 Diagonal slate; plan, sections and holes

The general elements with a diagonal shape are produced with templates in various diamond-like forms with fixed sizes. Their thickness and edges are as for rectangular/square elements. The different materials require different treatment at the tip (water drip): slate has an acute angle, fibre-cement a right angle (made from a square slate) or an obtuse angle. The splays are cut back further to suit the roof covering. Natural slates are supplied without holes, fibre-cement slates predrilled.

| length x width | splay | approx. weight per 1000 pieces [kg] | |
|---|---|---|---|
| h x b [cm] | a [cm] | natural slate | fibre-cement |
| 56.5 x 45.5 | 11.0 | | 1360 |
| 56.5 x 44.0 | 12.5 | | |
| 56.5 x 42.5 | 13.9 | | |
| 47.5 x 60.0 | 9.0 | | 1510 |
| 47.0 x 31.0 | 10.7 | 1400 | |
| 43.0 x 29.0 | 10.7 | 1100 | |
| 42.3 x 34.5 | 8.2 | | 770 |
| 42.5 x 33.0 | 9.6 | | |
| 42.5 x 31.5 | 11.0 | | |
| 42.5 x 30.0 | 12.5 | | |
| 38.0 x 25.0 | 10.7 | 900 | |
| 36.0 x 24.0 | 9.5 | 750 | |
| 33.0 x 21.0 | 7.3 | 650 | |
| 30.0 x 20.0 | 7.3 | 650 | |
| 29.0 x 19.0 | 7.3 | 450 | |
| 26.0 x 18.0 | 7.3 | 400 | |

2.4.4.13 Diagonal slates, general elements; dimensions and weights [03, 09, 14, 24, 27]

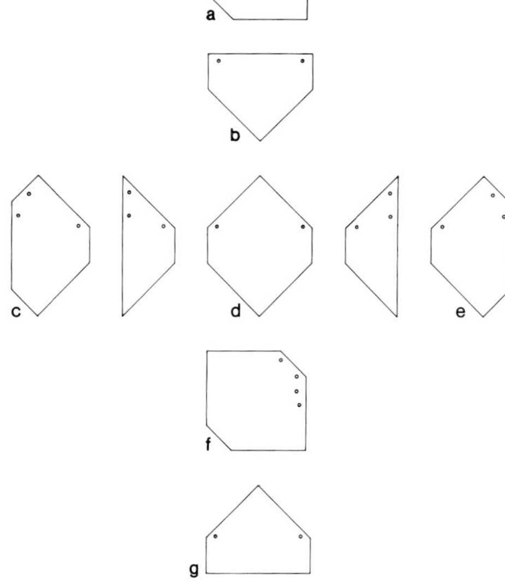


2.4.4.14 Diagonal slates, general and edge elements; selection [27]: a ridge slate, b top course slate, c verge slate, d standard slate, e verge slate, f eaves slate, g eaves slate

#### Edge elements

Special slates are used at ridge, hip, eaves and verge. They are produced on site from the standard diagonal slates using special hand tools. The slates required for valleys are made from basic pieces (see table 2.4.4.21).

## Curved slates

#### General elements

Various sizes of curved general elements, cut using templates, are available. Thickness as for rectangular/square elements. Natural slates are produced with chamfered edges, cut partly from below (back edge, tail, head), cut or sawn partly from above (front edge). Fibre-cement slates are supplied with smooth, punched edges. Both types are supplied with holes.

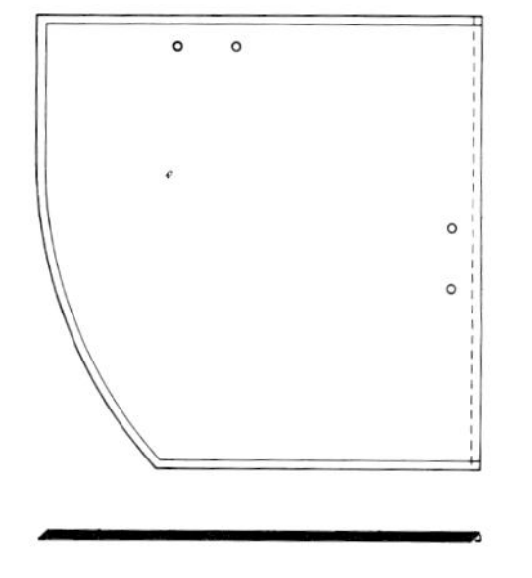

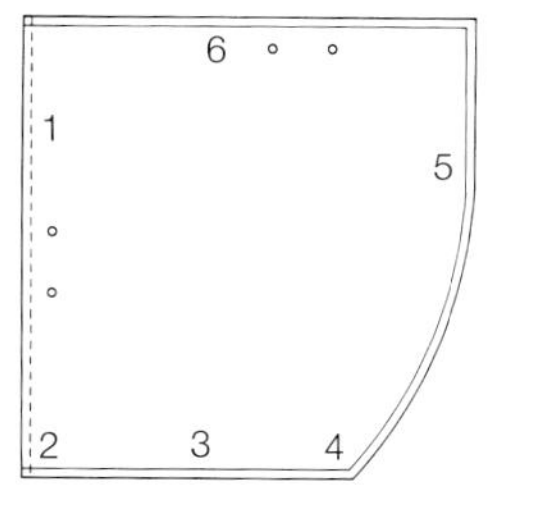


2.4.4.15 Curved slates, right and left; plans, sections and holes: 1 front edge, 2 toe, 3 tail, 4 heel, 5 back edge, 6 head

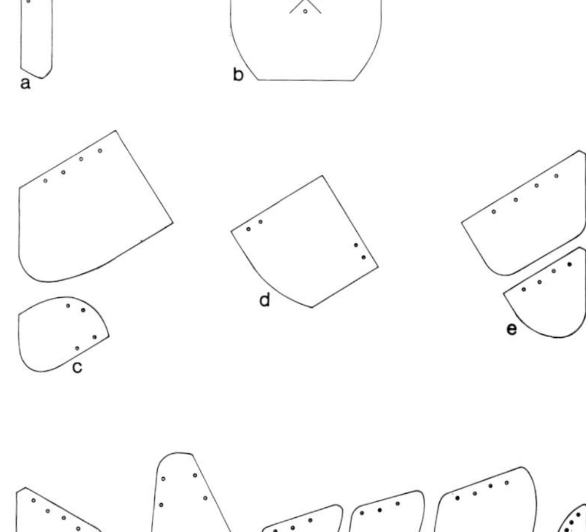


2.4.4.16 Curved slates, general and edge elements; selection [27]: a valley slate, b key slate, c verge starter slate, d standard slate, e verge end slate, f verge starter slate, g coursing slate, h short eaves slate, i standard eaves slate, k long eaves slate, l verge end slate

| length x width | approx. weight per 1000 pieces [kg] | |
|---|---|---|
| [cm] | natural slate | fibre-cement |
| 40.0 x 40.0 | | 1340 |
| 36.0 x 32.0 | | 955 |
| 30.0 x 30.0 | 1205 | 740 |
| 30.0 x 25.0 | | 615 |
| 25.0 x 25.0 | 860 | 510 |

2.4.4.17 Curved slates, general elements; dimensions and weights [03, 09, 14, 24, 27]

#### Edge elements

The same elements are used at the ridge as for the surface of the roof. Special slates produced by working basic pieces on site with special hand tools are used at hip, eaves and verge (see table 2.4.4.21). The slates required for valleys on natural slate roofs are produced from basic pieces (see table 2.4.4.21). Fibre-cement slates for valleys are produced in fixed sizes.

## Scalloped slates

#### General elements

The scalloped general elements of equal size are cut to various fixed sizes using templates, cut with a normal blow. The thickness and cross-section of slates are as for curved slates. They are supplied with at least three holes.

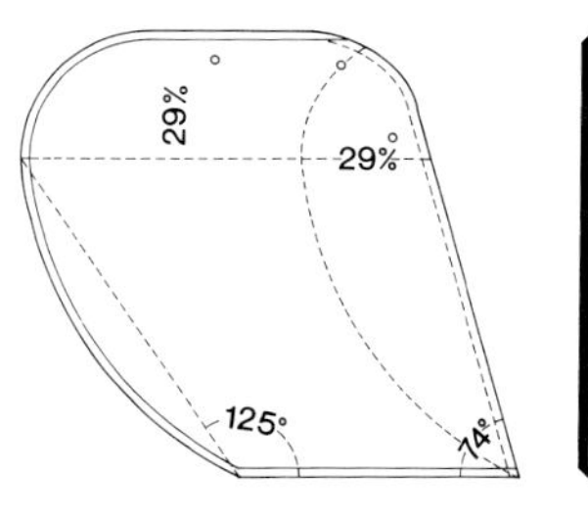


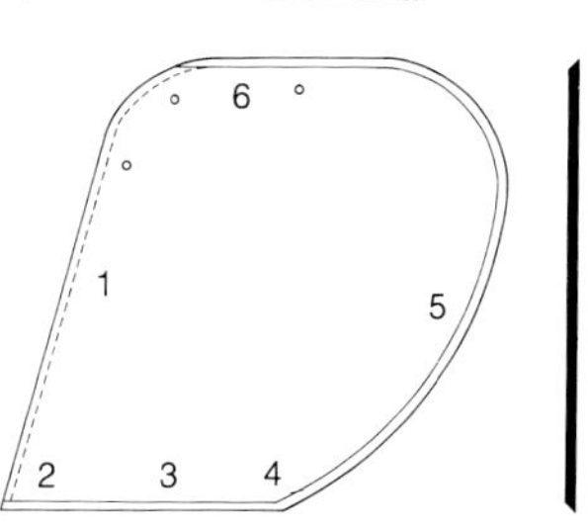


2.4.4.18 Scalloped slates (equal size), cut with normal blow, right and left; plans, sections and holes: 1 front edge, 2 toe, 3 tail, 4 heel, 5 back edge, 6 head

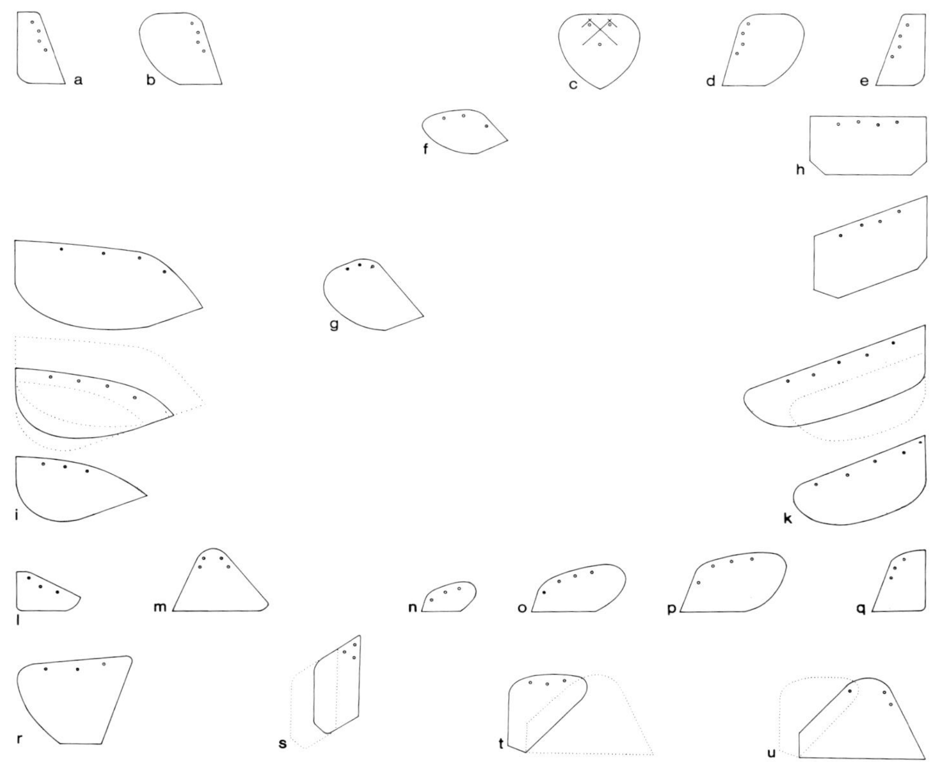


2.4.4.19 Scalloped slates (equal size), general and edge elements; selection [12]: a ridge starter slate, b ridge slate, c key slate, d ridge slate, e ridge starter slate, f special make-up slate, g standard slate, h wide verge slate, i verge starter slate, k verge end slate, l eaves end slate, m coursing slate, n short eaves slate, o standard eaves slate, p long eaves slate, q eaves starter slate, r draining slate, s valley slate, t valley transition slate, u channel slate

| length x width | approx. weight per 1000 pieces [kg] |
|---|---|
| [cm] | natural slate |
| 42.0 x 32.0 | 2000 |
| 40.0 x 32.0 | 1900 |
| 40.0 x 30.0 | 1750 |
| 38.0 x 30.0 | 1600 |
| 36.0 x 28.0 | 1400 |
| 34.0 x 28.0 | 1350 |
| 32.0 x 28.0 | 1250 |
| 32.0 x 25.0 | 1150 |
| 30.0 x 25.0 | 1050 |
| 28.0 x 23.0 | 900 |
| 26.0 x 21.0 | 690 |
| 24.0 x 21.0 | 640 |
| 24.0 x 19.0 | 590 |
| 22.0 x 21.0 | 530 |
| 22.0 x 17.0 | 460 |
| 20.0 x 15.0 | 360 |

2.4.4.20 Scalloped slates (equal size), general elements; dimensions and weights [03, 14, 27]

| length x width | approx. weight per 1000 pieces [kg] | |
|---|---|---|
| [cm] | natural slate | fibre-cement |
| 60.0 x 40.0 | 4030 | 2040 |
| 60.0 x 35.0 | 3530 | |
| 60.0 x 30.0 | 3030 | 1530 |
| 50.0 x 30.0 | 2520 | |
| 50.0 x 25.0 | 2100 | |
| 50.0 x 17.0 | 1170 | |
| 42.0 x 16.0 | 920 | |
| 42.0 x 14.0 | 820 | |
| 40.0 x 40.0 | 2250 | 1360 |
| 40.0 x 20.0 | 1100 | 680 |
| 40.0 x 14.0 | 770 | |
| 40.0 x 13.0 | | 440 |
| 37.0 x 15.0 | 760 | |
| 30.0 x 30.0 | | 770 |
| 30.0 x 20.0 | 750 | 510 |
| 30.0 x 15.0 | 620 | 380 |
| 30.0 x 14.0 | 590 | |

2.4.4.21 Edge elements (equal size), basic pieces (rectangular/square); dimensions and weights [03, 09, 14]

**Edge elements**

The same scalloped elements are used at the ridge as for the surface of the roof. Special slates produced by working basic pieces on site with special hand tools are used at hip, eaves and verge (see table 2.4.4.21). The slates required for valleys on natural slate roofs are produced from basic pieces (see table 2.4.4.21). Fibre-cement slates for valleys are produced in fixed sizes. The size of the basic pieces for scalloped edge elements of equal size depends on the size of the slates used on the roof surface.

## Scalloped slates of unequal size

**General elements**

The scalloped slates of unequal size cut with a normal blow are supplied graded according to slate length and width, those cut with a sharp blow according to slate length, in both cases without holes.

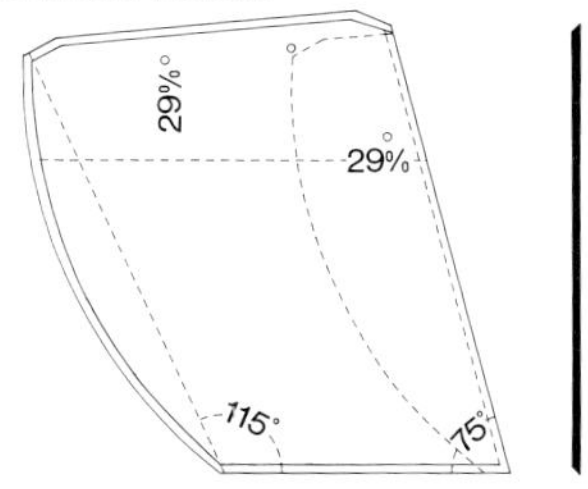


2.4.4.22 Scalloped slate (unequal size), cut with dull blow, right and left; plan, sections and holes [27]

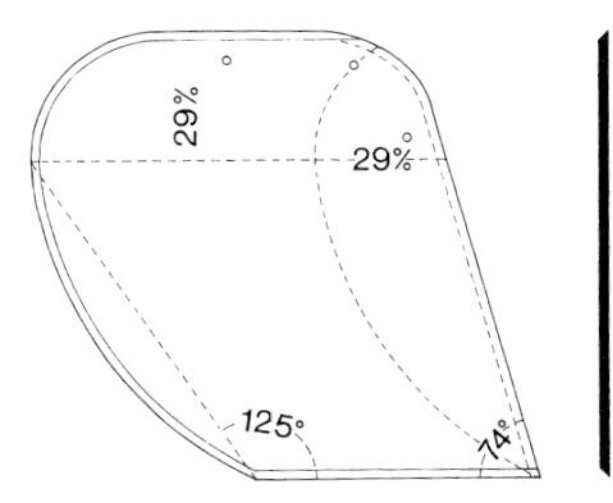


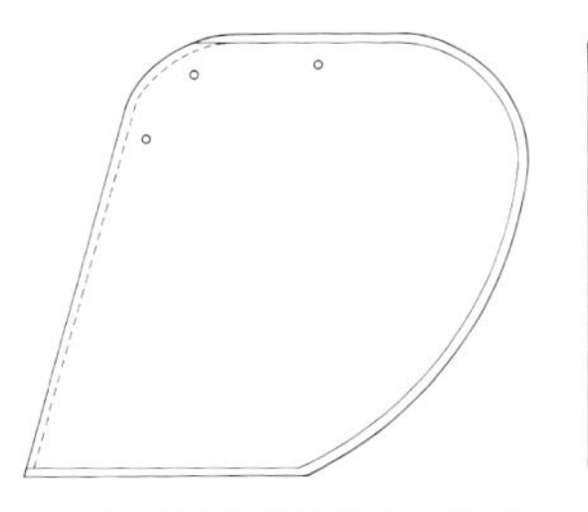

2.4.4.23 Scalloped slates (unequal size), cut with normal blow, right and left; plans, sections and holes; larger overlap (34%) with slate lengths < 150 mm [27]

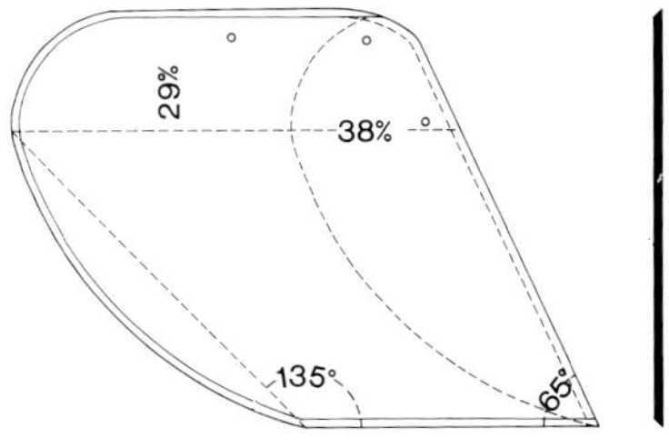


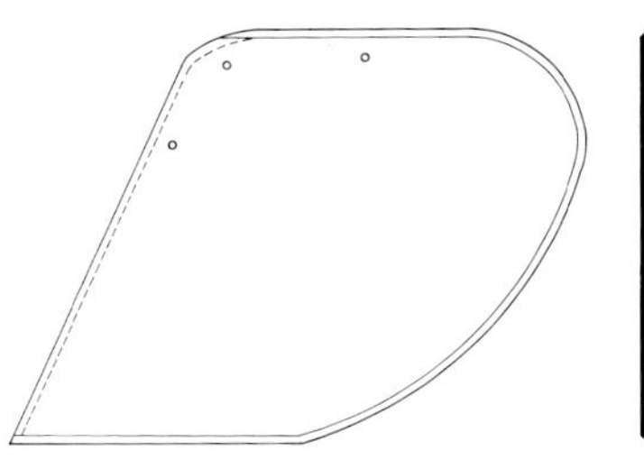

2.4.4.24 Scalloped slates (unequal size), cut with sharp blow, right and left; plans, sections and holes [27]

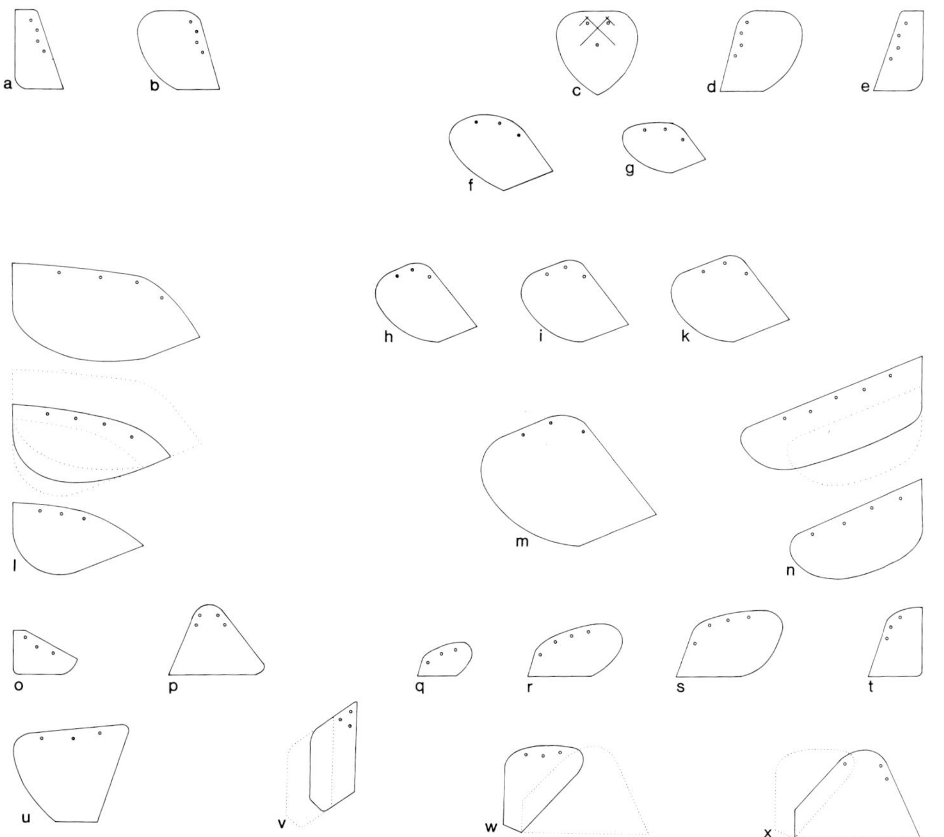


2.4.4.25 Scalloped slates (unequal size), general and edge elements; selection: a ridge starter slate, b ridge slate, c key slate, d ridge slate, e ridge starter slate, f 1/32 standard slate, g special make-up slate, h 1/8 standard slate, narrow, i 1/8 standard slate, normal, k 1/8 standard slate, wide, l verge starter slate, m 1/1 standard slate, n verge end slate, o eaves end slate, p coursing slate, q short eaves slate, r standard eaves slate, s long eaves slate, t eaves starter slate, u draining slate, v valley slate, w valley transition slate, x channel slate

These roof coverings are laid in a rainproof bond, sometimes horizontal on battens or roof decking, sometimes at a gradient on roof decking, at various standard roof pitches. The shallower the roof pitch and the greater the distance between ridge and eaves, the larger the slates should be. On curved roofs it can be advisable to vary the size of the roof slates in order to obtain a sealed roof covering.
Roof pitches shallower than recommended should not be used because they require waterproof roofing felt, sarking or boarding underneath. A roof pitch > 10° less than the minimum recommended pitch is not permitted, even with a waterproof layer underneath.

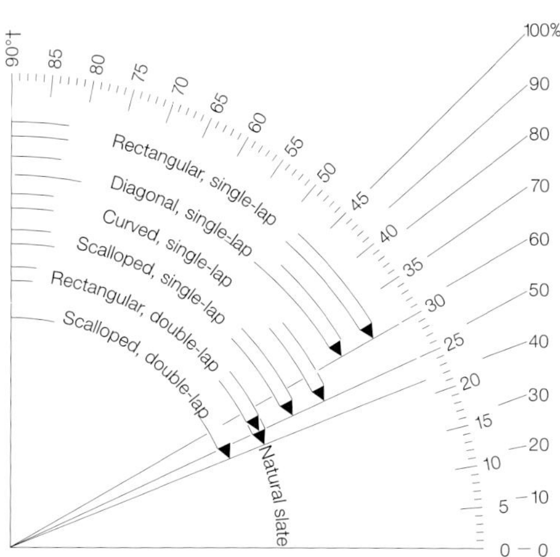


2.4.4.28 Standard proof pitches in relation to roof covering [24, 27]

| Slate type | length [cm] | width [cm] | approx. weight per vertical m | |
|---|---|---|---|---|
| | | | cut with normal blow | |
| | | | dressed | basic |
| 1/1 | 50–40 | 42–32 | 360 | 450 |
| 1/2 | 42–36 | 38–28 | 280 | 350 |
| 1/4 | 38–32 | 34–25 | 200 | 250 |
| 1/8 | 34–28 | 30–23 | 160 | 200 |
| 1/12 | 30–24 | 26–20 | 120 | 150 |
| 1/16 | 26–20 | 22–17 | 90 | 110 |
| 1/32 | 22–16 | 18–13 | 65 | 85 |
| 1/64 | 18–12 | 16–11 | 50 | 65 |

2.4.4.26 Scalloped slates (unequal size), cut with normal blow, general elements; dimensions and weights [03]

| Slate type | length [cm] | width [cm] | approx. weight per vertical m (basic) |
|---|---|---|---|
| Ola | 60–50 | 40–30 | 380 |
| OI | 50–40 | 30–27 | 240 |
| OII | 42–35 | 23–20 | 190 |
| OIII | 37–30 | 20–16 | 140 |
| OIV | 31–25 | 17–14 | 120 |
| KI | 55–45 | 17–12 | 145 |
| KII | 45–36 | 16–11 | 120 |
| KIII | 36–28 | 150–10 | 95 |
| KIV | 28–23 | 14–10 | 70 |

2.4.4.27 Scalloped slates (unequal size), basic pieces (rectangular); dimensions and weights [03]: O verge, K valley

#### Edge elements
The large slates required for the ridge are separated from the other slates before starting work. All the special pieces required for hip, eaves and verge can be produced by working the basic verge pieces on site with special hand tools (see table 2.4.4.27). The slates required for valleys are produced from basic pieces (see table 2.4.4.27).

### Laying
Conditions for laying, fixing, additional measures, supporting construction, maintenance and repair

#### Conditions for laying
A roof may be covered with rectangular, diagonal, curved, scalloped (single-lap/double-lap) or unequal scalloped (single-lap/double-lap) slates.

#### Fixing
All slates are fixed within the headlap or side lap. The fixing can be within the side lap below the headlap on roof surfaces exposed to severe wind conditions or those with a pitch > 70°.
The slates are normally nailed to timber battens or roof decking, while annular nails are used for roof deckings made from timber derivative boards (chipboard only V100G).
The holes must be cut from underneath when using forged slating nails or annular nails. They are drilled from above when using other types of fixing.
Clips or driven hooks can be (natural slate) or must be (fibre-cement) used with rectangular and diagonal slates (visible).

#### Fixing materials
The number of fixings and their materials for natural and fibre-cement slates are given in tables 2.4.4.29 and 2.4.4.30. Stainless steel must be used for the fixings on roof deckings made from timber derivative boards.

| General elements | Nails/annular n. | Hooks/clips |
|---|---|---|
| Rectangular slates | 2 and [2] or [1] | 1 (for 600 x 300 mm, 400 x 400 mm)[2] |
| Diagonal slates | 2 and [2] | 1[2] |
| Curved slates | 3[1] 2[1] and [2] | 1[2] (for 400 x 400 mm)[2] |
| Scalloped slates L ≥ 240 mm/ < 240 mm | 3/2[1] | |
| Edge elements | see "Details" | |

[1] natural slate, [2] fibre-cement

2.4.4.29 Fixings; minimum number [24, 27]

| Fixing | Natural slate | Fibre-cement |
|---|---|---|
| Nails/annular nails [1] | | |
| iron, 50 µm galvanised coating | | |
| punched | • | • |
| forged | • | |
| zinc, injection moulded | • | |
| stainless steel A2 [3] | • | • |
| copper | • | • |
| stainless steel screw A2 [1][3] | • | • |
| Hooks/clips [2] | | |
| stainless steel A2 [3] | | • |
| stainless steel A4 [4] | • | |
| copper | • | • |

[1] head dia. ≥ 10 mm, shaft ≥ 32 mm
[2] driving tip ≥ 32 mm
[3] material No. 1.4301
[4] material No. 1.4571

2.4.4.30 Fixings; materials [09, 24, 27]

**Additional measures**

Additional measures should be allowed for during planning and construction when enhanced requirements are placed on the reliability of the roof covering:

- with large roofs (long rafters)
- with roof pitches below the recommended pitch
- where the angle between roof surfaces is < 135°
- when several roof surfaces and valleys meet at one point along the eaves
- where higher wind pressures are expected
- where a high snowfall is expected
- where a build-up of melt water is expected

Additional measures could be:

- an increase in the roof pitch
- building up the battens or roof decking
- the use of larger slates
- natural slates cut with a sharp blow
- double-lap roof covering
- an underlay of rolled lead
- the provision of roofing felt, sarking or boarding below the roof covering

## Horizontal slating

Rectangular and diagonal slates

**Rectangular double-lap slating**

(see also "Laying")

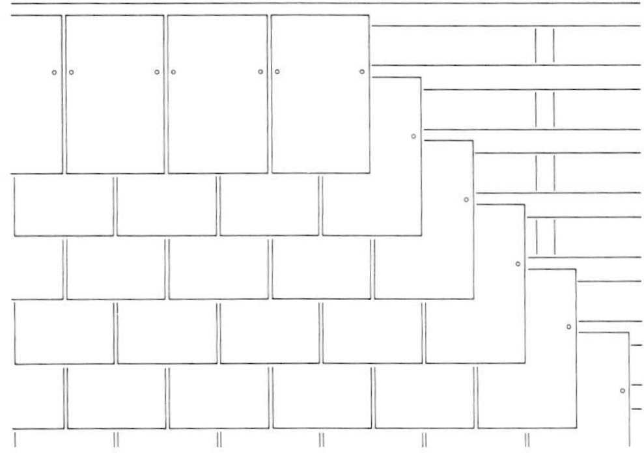

2.4.4.31 Rectangular double-lap slating

This type of slating, also known as English slating, makes use of rectangular or square slates. They form a regular pattern with a half-slate offset (joints between slates offset by half a slate width). They are laid in horizontal courses with a gap (3–6 mm) between adjacent slates and overlap by more than half the length of a slate, i.e. double-lap slating – the third course overlaps the first one according to table 2.4.4.32.

| Roof pitch [°] | Headlap [cm] | | | |
|---|---|---|---|---|
| | for slate size L x W [cm] | | | |
| | 60 x 35<br>60 x 30<br>50 x 30<br>50 x 25 | 40 x 40<br>40 x 25<br>40 x 20 | 35 x 35<br>35 x 25<br>35 x 20 | 30 x 30<br>30 x 20 |
| ≥ 22[1]<br>≥ 25[2] | 120 | 120[2] | – | – |
| ≥ 30 | 100 | 100 | – | 100[2] |
| ≥ 40 | 80 | 80 | 80[1] | 80[2] |
| ≥ 50 | 70[2] | 70[2] 60[1] | 60[1] | 60 |

[1] natural slate, [2] fibre-cement

2.4.4.32 Rectangular slating; minimum laps [09, 14, 24, 27]

The shallower the roof pitch and/or the longer the rafters, the larger the slate format and headlap are. This type of slating can be laid on battens or on roof decking with sheathing. [24, 27]

**Rectangular double-lap slating, details**

Ridge, hip, eaves, verge, valley, dormer window

Ridge, hip

At ridges and hips the courses on the side facing the prevailing wind must extend beyond those on the leeward side by ≥ 50 mm.
In exceptional cases the shallower roof surface at a hip can also project. A course with a capping of ridge units is laid at the ridge with a single (≥ 100 mm) or a double (natural slate ≥ 20 mm, fibre-cement ≥ 50 mm) side lap. Each slate should be fixed with at least four fixings offset within the side lap.
Driven hooks can also be used. End slates should be fixed with rustproof fixings (visible). The headlap of the ridge course over the top course on the roof surface must correspond to that of the courses on the roof surface. [24, 27]

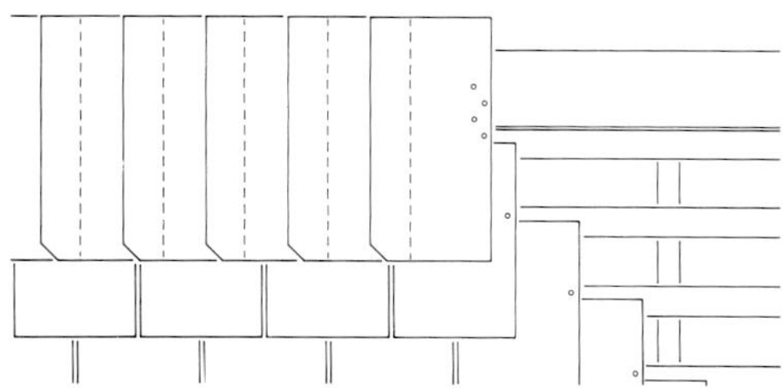

2.4.4.33 Rectangular double-lap slating; ridge capping

At roof pitches ≥ 45° the hip can be mitred but requires a single- or double-lap capping below this pitch. The headlap and side lap must match that of the slates on the surface of the roof. The side lap should not be less than a one-third offset (≥ 80 mm) for mitred, evenly laid cuttings. Hip cappings must overlap the slates on the surface of the roof ≥ 100 mm (fibre-cement).

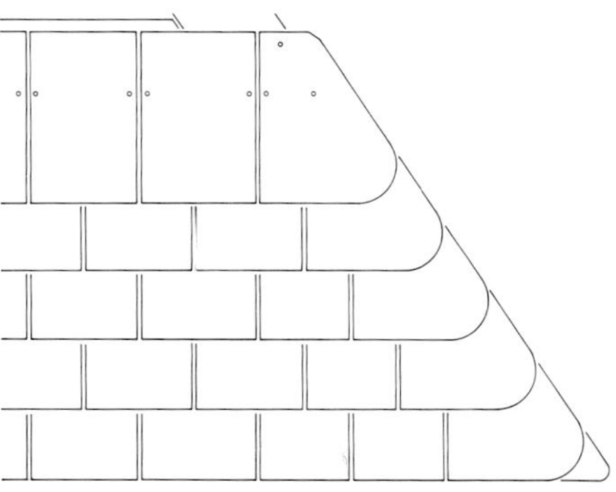

2.4.4.34 Rectangular double-lap slating; mitred hip

Each hip slate should have its upper outside corner splayed to help shed water and should be secured with at least three (mitred hip) or at least four (hip capping) fixings. Hip slates are also nailed in the case of a clipped/hooked roof covering. [24, 27]

Eaves

The undereaves course uses shorter slates, which are then fully covered by the eaves course (joints offset). They should be laid with an overhang of approx. 50 mm (on eaves flashing ≤ 50 mm) and secured with at least two fixings. The undereaves course should be packed up so that it has the same pitch as the roof courses. [24, 27]

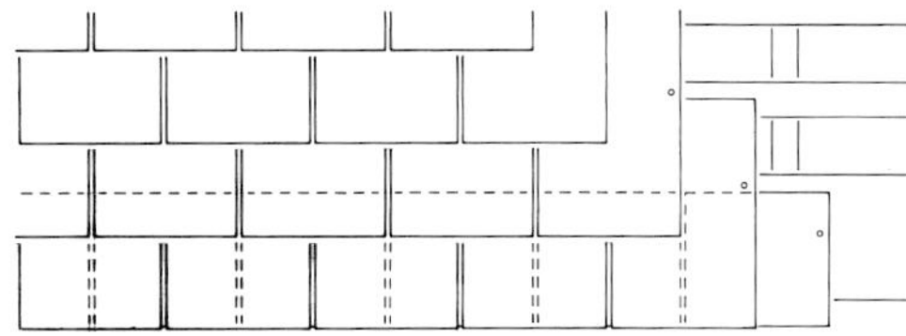

2.4.4.35 Rectangular double-lap slating; eaves

Verge
The roof courses continue up to the verge and the final slates overhang by approx. 50 mm. Side lap and headlap must be the same as for the surface of the roof. The lateral offset should not be less than one third (≥ 80 mm) for evenly laid cuttings.

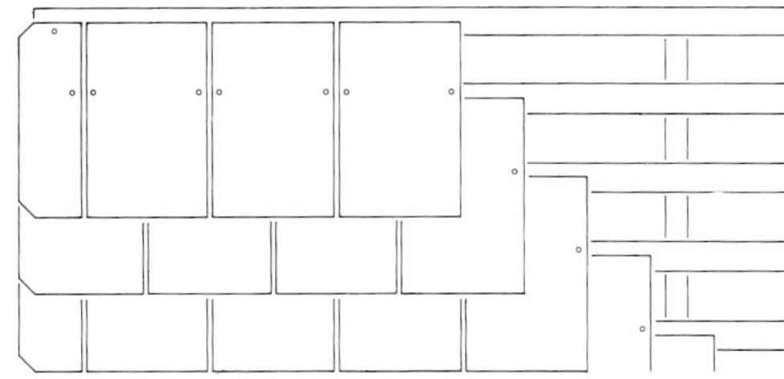

2.4.4.36 Rectangular double-lap slating; verge

The verge slates must be ≥ 12.5 cm (natural slate) or ≥ 15 cm (fibre-cement) wide and have corner splays and an edge profile (cut with a blow from above) that help shed water. They are to be secured with at least three fixings. Verge slates are also nailed in a clipped/hooked roof covering. [24, 27]

Valley
When the adjoining roof surfaces have the same pitch and are roughly the same size, the valley can be formed as a semi-swept or lined valley with ≥ 30° pitch (pitch of valley rafter). Both types of valley should be covered in triple-lap slating, where the fourth course overlaps the first by ≥ 10 mm. The valley slates should be laid with butt joints offset by half a slate. The slates should be 12–20 cm wide, cut from below or with sawn edges. Every valley slate is to be secured with at least two fixings. The upper termination of either type of valley is covered with a single-lap ridge course. [24, 27]

Semi-swept valley
This valley consists of upper and lower layers, with the upper courses bonded into the courses covering the surface of the roof and the lower courses fitted below the roof courses. The courses on the surface of the roof end at the valley with special slates made from basic pieces, cut off parallel with the line of the valley, at the upper layers in the valley. The side lap for evenly laid cuttings should not be less than a one-third offset of the upper slates.
The width of the valley is:
3 slates for a valley slate width of 12–15 cm
2 slates for a valley slate width of 15–20 cm

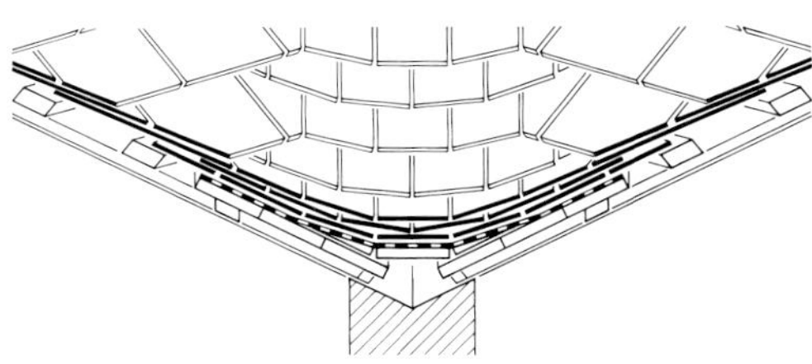

2.4.4.37 Rectangular double-lap slating; semi-swept valley

Lined valley
This valley consists of covering layers laid in an independent bond whose outer valley slates have a sharp-edged outside edge (cut with a blow from above) or a sawn edge. Apart from that, they must have an edge profile that helps to shed water.
The width of the valley is:
5 slates for a valley slate width of 12–15 cm
4 slates for a valley slate width of 15–20 cm

The courses on the roof surface continue up to the valley and must overlap the valley slates as follows:
≥ 10 cm for roof pitches ≥ 50°
≥ 12 cm for roof pitches ≥ 40°
Shallower valleys can be produced with metal soakers or a sheet metal underlay (see "Laying – Diagonal slating"). [24, 27]

Dormer window
An eyebrow dormer window can be covered with rectangular slates as a (re-entrant left-/right-hand) cheek valley. The ratio of the height to the width of the front of the window should not exceed 1:5. The angle of the apex of the dormer window relative to the main roof surface should be ≤ 12°; the pitch should not be less than 25° or the minimum recommended roof pitch. Gentle curvature at the apex and/or narrow slates are advantageous here.

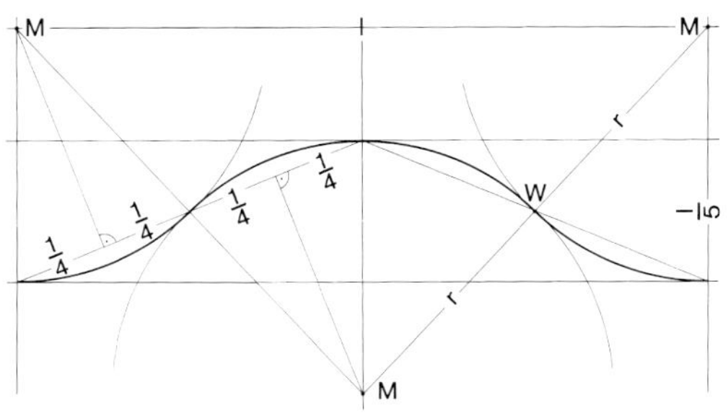


2.4.4.38 Eyebrow dormer window: construction of front curve; W chosen point of inflection [10]

If the courses on the roof surface above the dormer window have a bond with a half-slate offset, the height-to-width ratio of the front of the window should be 1:8.
Curved or rounded areas on a shed dormer window can also be covered as one surface using narrow rectangular slates. [27]

Roof penetrations
Built-in components such as step irons, walkway supports or snowguard fixings must be integrated into the roof covering in a rainproof manner and fixed firmly to the loadbearing structure. To prevent such items damaging the roof covering, they must be self-supporting (nails, screws) or attached to a sheet metal underlay that distributes the loads.

**Rectangular double-lap slating, material requirements**

$10\,000\,[(H - Ü)/2 \cdot B)] = x$ (pcs/m²)

where:
H = slate length
Ü = headlap + overlap between 1st and 3rd layers
B = slate width

**Diagonal slating**
(see also "Laying")

This type of slating uses diamond-shaped, sometimes square (fibre-cement), slates. They form a regular bond with a half-slate offset (joints between slates offset by half a slate width). They are laid with a single lap in horizontal courses with a gap (3–6 mm) between adjacent slates and with the tip overhanging ≥ 10 mm (fibre-cement ≤ 20 mm).

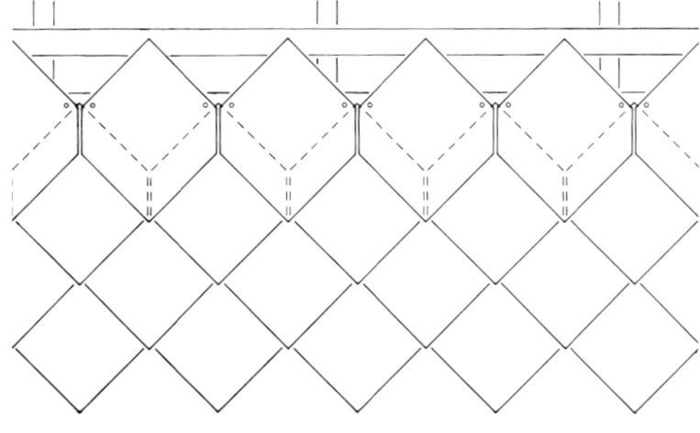

2.4.4.39 Diagonal slating

The minimum overlap (Ü) of the slates is given by the length of the splay (A) and the size of the overhanging tip (T) (see table 2.4.4.13) thus:

Ü = A + T

where
Ü = min. overlap, A = length of splay,
T = size of overhanging tip

| Roof pitch [°] | Headlap [cm] for slate size L x W [cm] | | | | | | |
|---|---|---|---|---|---|---|---|
| | 56.5 x 42.5<br>56.5 x 44.0<br>56.5 x 45.5 | 60.0 x 47.5 | 47.0 x 31.0<br>43.0 x 29.0<br>38.0 x 25.0 | 42.5 x 30.0<br>42.5 x 31.5<br>42.5 x 33.0<br>42.5 x 34.5 | 36.0 x 24.0 | 33.0 x 21.0 | 30.0 x 20.0<br>29.0 x 19.0<br>26.0 x 18.0 |
| ≥ 30 | 150 [2] | 130 [2] | 120 [1] | 140 [2] | | | |
| ≥ 35 | 140 [2] | 120 [2] | | 130 [2] | | | |
| ≥ 45 | 130 [2] | 110 [2] | | 120 [2] | 110 [1] | 90 [1] | |
| ≥ 55 | | | | 100 [2] | | | |
| ≥ 60 | | | | | | | 90 [1] |

[1] natural slate, [2] fibre-cement

2.4.4.40 Diagonal slating; roof pitches, suitable slate sizes [09, 14, 24, 27], minimum laps

Larger slate formats with longer splays and larger headlaps should be selected for shallower roof pitches.
Diagonal slating can be laid on battens or on roof decking with sheathing. [24, 27]

**Diagonal slating, details**

Ridge, hip, verge, valley

Ridge, hip

At ridges and hips the courses on the side facing the prevailing wind must project ≥ 50 mm beyond the courses on the leeward side.

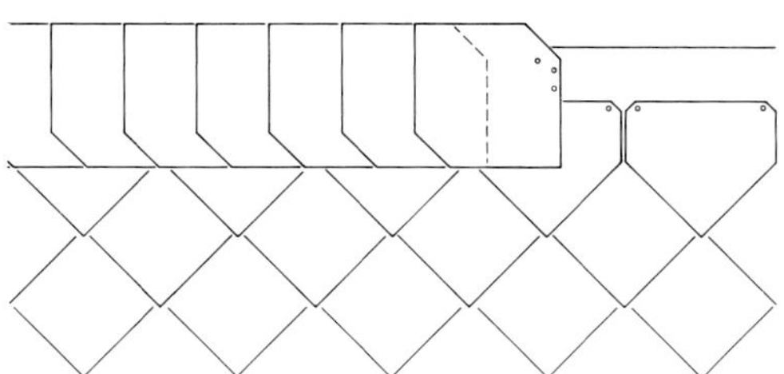

2.4.4.41 Ridge detail with diagonal slates

The ridge capping is formed with diagonal or rectangular ridge slates. Hips are formed with a capping. Overlaps and fixings as for rectangular slating.

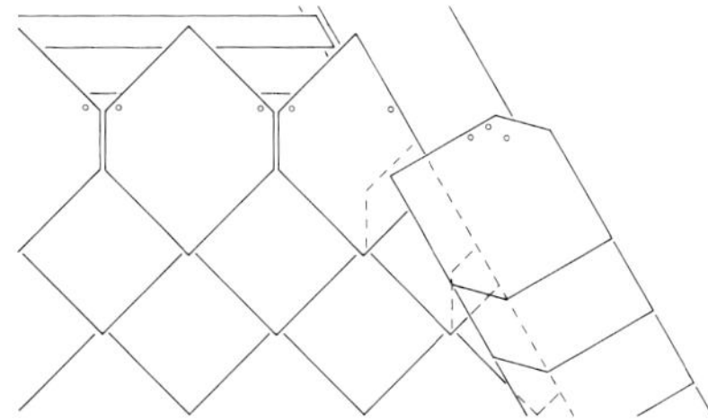

2.4.4.42 Hip capping with diagonal slates

Verge

An overhang of ≥ 50 mm should be maintained at the verge. Verges at right angles can be formed by simply allowing the courses to run up to the edge and then finishing off with half diagonal slates. However, verges at other angles must be capped with whole slates. The headlap between verge slates should be the same as that for slates on the surface of the roof. The side lap of a verge capping should overlap the roof surface ≥ 20 mm more than this headlap dimension.
The top and bottom outside corners of the slates are splayed to help shed water and for natural slate, in the overlapped area the edges are cut from above to help shed water. Verge slates should be secured with at least three fixings and also nailed in the case of clipped/hooked roof coverings.

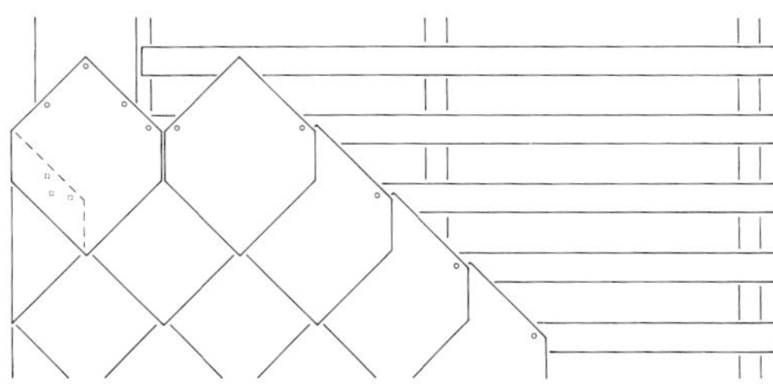

2.4.4.43 Diagonal slating; treatment at verge

Valley

Valleys with shorter or longer sheet metal linings are more suitable for shallower valley pitches than slate valleys. Please note the electrochemical series when specifying such a valley.

Closed valley with soakers

This valley consists of short metal soakers integrated into the roof covering. This type of valley is only permissible with equal roof pitches on both sides and when the slating on both roof surfaces meets at the line of the valley. With a valley rafter pitch ≥ 25° this type of valley is rainproof.
A piece of metal is laid below each course with a side lap of ≥ 150 mm. The headlap between the soakers must be one-third greater than that of the slates on the surface of the roof [24, 27] and is [26]:
≥ 140 mm for roof pitches ≥ 45°
≥ 160 mm for roof pitches < 45°
Each soaker should be fixed twice in the area of the headlap.
The slating on the roof surfaces can simply end at the soakers or can be cut from basic pieces parallel with the line of the valley. The side lap should not be less than a one-third offset (≥ 80 mm) for evenly laid cuttings. In every case 10–20 mm in the middle of the valley is to be kept clear for draining residual water.

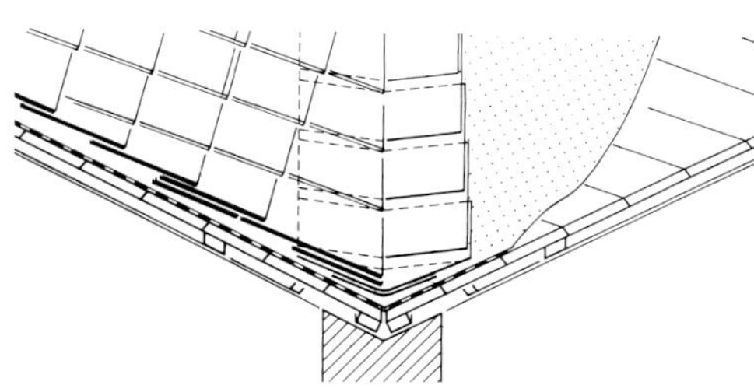

2.4.4.44 Diagonal slating; valley with soakers

Open valley with sheet metal

This type of valley consists of long pieces of sheet metal that can be laid rainproof at a valley pitch ≥ 15°. [26] The sheet metal lining is overlapped by the ends of the slating courses on the surface of the roof (making use of cuttings) as follows [27]:
≥ 120 mm for roof pitches < 50°
≥ 160 mm for roof pitches ≤ 50°
The shape and cutting of the sheet metal depends on the amount of water anticipated (see "Layers – Drainage"). The longitudinal sides of the sheet metal pieces are to be turned up ≥ 15 mm. It is recommended to provide a batten along these turned-up edges.
The sheet metal pieces in the valley must overlap each other by ≥ 120 mm or ≥ 150 mm (< 22°). [24, 26] They should be nailed within the headlap and clipped at the sides (at the turned-up edge).
The sheet metal valley must be 20 cm wide to permit access for cleaning. [24] It can be supported on battens at max. 16 cm centres or on roof decking.
Sheet metal valleys at shallower angles require special measures (channel, watertight). [26]

**Diagonal slating, material requirements**

$$10\,000/(C(L - A - Tü) \cdot B)/2) = x\ [pcs/m^2]$$

where:
L = diagonal length of slate
A = length of splay
Tü = tip overhang
B = width of slate

## Non-horizontal slating

Curved slates, scalloped slates of equal and unequal sizes

**Roof covering using curved or scalloped slates (German slating)**
(see also "Laying")

Slates with various ornamental shapes but equal sizes are used for German slating. The slates are laid in single- or (scalloped slates) double-lap in rising courses with the heel (water drip) overhanging and with the heels offset. This forms a regular bond.
The shallower the roof pitch, the steeper the gradient of the courses must be. Maximum and minimum gradients are specified for different roof pitches. At roof pitches > 70° the courses can also be laid without a gradient.

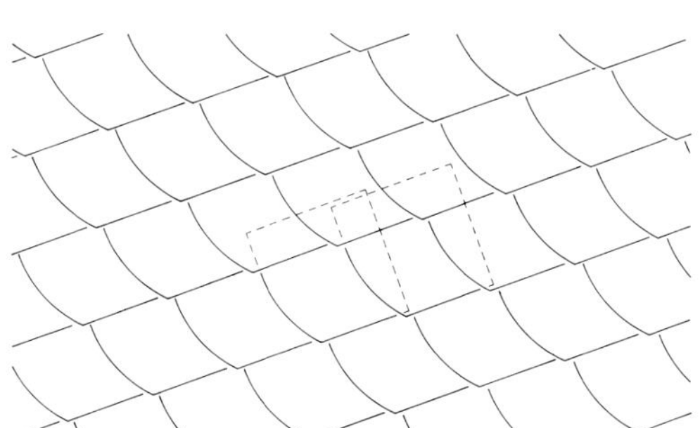

2.4.4.45 Slating with curved slates

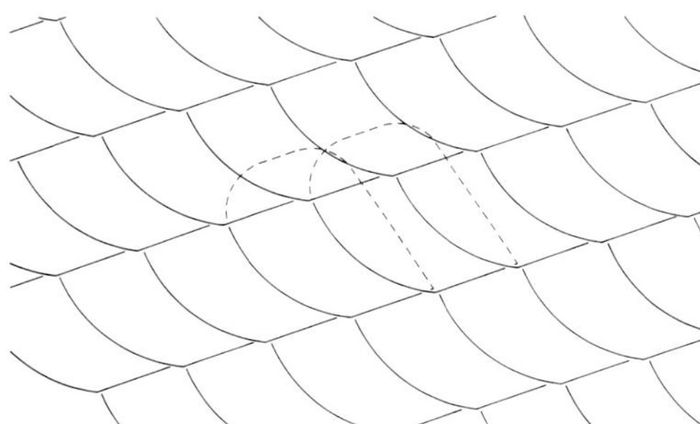

2.4.4.46 Single-lap slating with scalloped slates of equal size

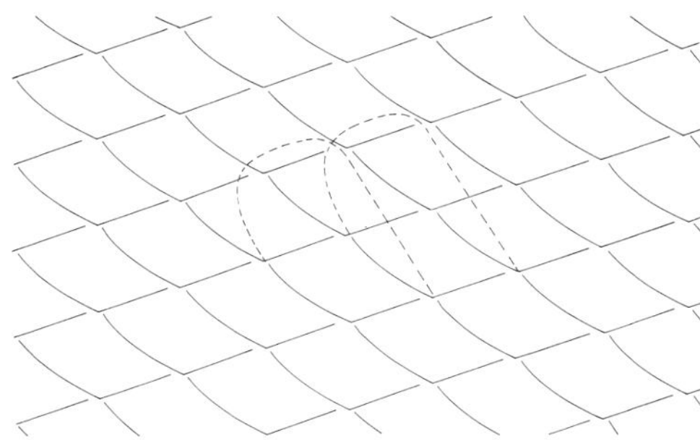

2.4.4.47 Double-lap slating with scalloped slates of equal size

The maximum course gradient for curved slates is 45° and for scalloped slates 37.5°, 37° and 32.5° for a dull, normal and sharp blow respectively.

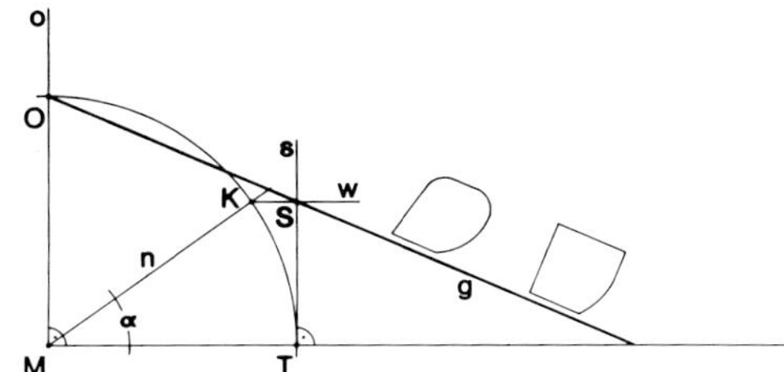


2.4.4.48 Calculating the minimum course gradient [03, 24, 27]: t line of eaves, o line of verge, K circle with any radius about M, n sloping line at chosen roof pitch, s perpendicular passing through T, w horizontal line passing through K, g course gradient line passing through O and S

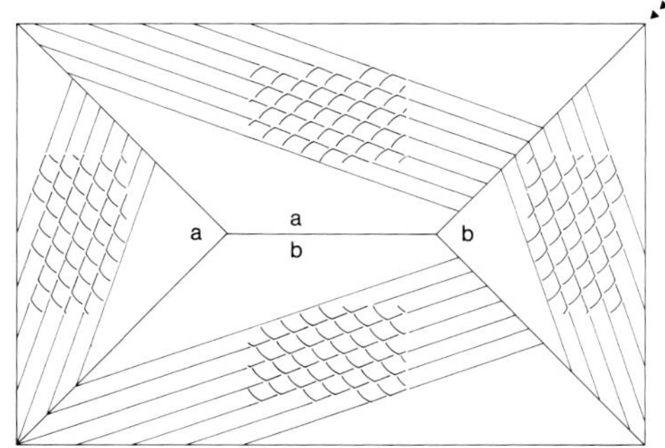


2.4.4.49 Slating directions in relation to prevailing wind direction: a left-hand slating, b right-hand slating; ▷ prevailing wind direction

There is left- and right-hand slating. The prevailing wind direction should be taken into account in order to achieve a rainproof roof covering; the gradient of the courses follows the direction of the wind. Table 2.4.4.50 gives the headlaps and side laps for curved slates, table 2.4.4.61 (normal blow) the values for scalloped slates.

| Roof pitch [°] | Headlap [cm] | | | | | |
|---|---|---|---|---|---|---|
| | for slate size L x W [cm] | | | | | |
| | 40 x 40 | | 30 x 30<br>30 x 25 | | 25 x 25 | |
| | H | S | H | S | H | S |
| ≥ 25 | 120[2] | 120[2] | 110 | 90 | – | – |
| ≥ 30 | 110[2] | 110[2] | 100 | 90 | 100[2] | 90[2] |
| ≥ 35 | 100[2] | 100[2] | 90 | 90 | 90[2] | 90[2] |
| ≥ 40 | – | – | 90[1] | 90[1] | 90[1] | 80[1] |
| ≥ 45 | 90[2] | 90[2] | 80 | 90 | 80[1][2] | 80[1]90[2] |
| ≥ 55 | 90[2] | 90[2] | 70 | 90 | 70[1][2] | 80[1]90[2] |

[1] natural slate, [2] fibre-cement

2.4.4.50 Curved slates; minimum laps [09, 14, 27]

Double-lap slating is only possible with large slates. In this case the slates of the third course overlap those of the first course by ≥ 20 mm.

The slates should be fixed within the headlap and side lap (curved slates, scalloped slates > 70°) or within the headlap (scalloped slates ≥ 70°).
Curved and scalloped slates are to be laid on a full roof decking with sheathing.

**Curved and scalloped slating, details**
Ridge, hip, eaves, verge, valley, dormer window

Ridge, hip
At ridges and hips the courses on the side facing the prevailing wind must project ≥ 50 mm beyond those on the leeward side. In exceptional cases the course on the shallower side of the roof can also project at the hip.
The ridge course is a capping laid in the same direction as the roof surface. This course consists of standard slates (curved slating) or ridge slates (scalloped slating) with a single side lap ≥ 100 mm and is secured in the area of the side lap with at least four fixings. Key slates should be nailed with rustproof fixings (visible).
The headlap of the ridge course over the course on the surface of the roof must be ≥ 100 mm or the same as the headlap between the slates on the surface of the roof.
The slating on the roof surface ends below the ridge course with specially cut slates. [24, 27]

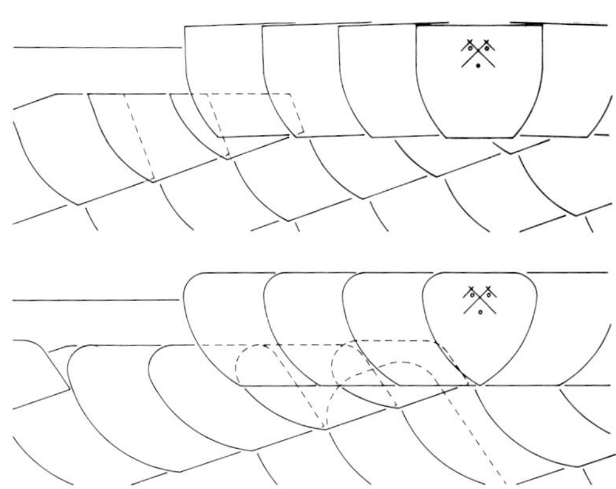

2.4.4.51 Slating with curved and scalloped slates; ridge capping

Hips are mitred and employ single laps. The roof covering here is laid as at the verge: the courses begin with two or three verge slates (parallel to the line of the hip with shaped back edges or vertical) and end with two verge slates (with the front edges aligned parallel to the other hip line), provided the maximum course gradient is not thereby exceeded. Furthermore, the hip must employ a capping whose slates match the chosen form of the slates on the roof surface and their outside corners must be splayed to help shed water.

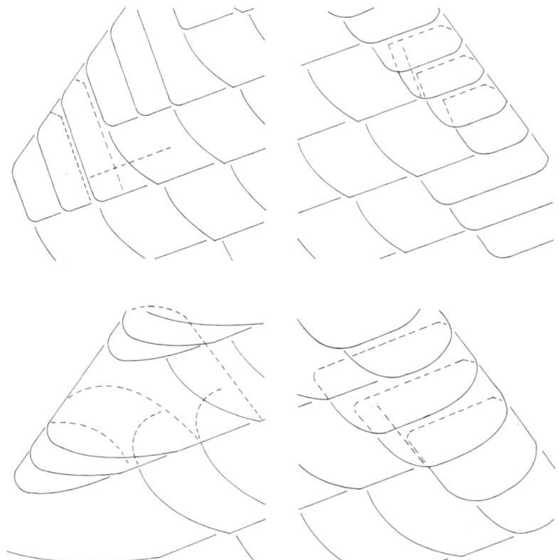

2.4.4.52 Slating with curved and scalloped slates; verge starter and verge end slates at a hip

The hip slates should be secured with at least 3 fixings (for fibre-cement at least 4). Verge end slates (fibre-cement) should also be secured with a clip.
The headlap between the hip slates must correspond to that used on the surface of the roof. The headlap of the hip course over the slates on the surface of the roof must be ≥ 100 mm (fibre-cement) or at least 20 mm greater (natural slates). [24, 27]

Eaves
The eaves makes use of eaves and standard slates or cut slates with an eaves course, all with single laps. The overhang of the roof covering is ≤ 50 mm at the eaves. Headlaps and side laps at the eaves must match those used on the surface of the roof. When using eaves and standard slates it is sensible to increase the side lap by using slates cut with a sharp blow and/or a larger heel offset. At the eaves course the side lap must be one-third larger (fibre-cement ≥ 120 mm) than that used on the surface of the roof. Eaves slates must be secured with at least 3 fixings. [24, 27]

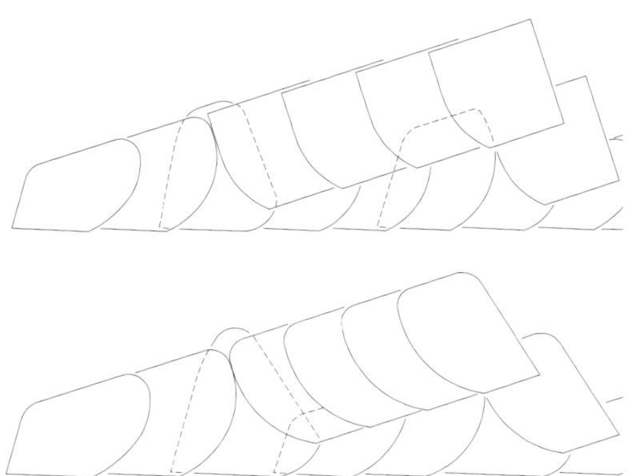

2.4.4.53 Slating with curved and scalloped slates; mitred eaves detail

Verge
The slating must overhang at the verge by approx. 50 mm. Verges are mitred with single laps. The start of the course is formed by two or three slates (undercloak, intermediate and starter slates for verges), and the end of the course consists of two slates (undercloak and verge end slates, or small and large verge end slates). These slates may be round, curved or straight as required. The outside corners of the slates are splayed to help shed water. Verge slates should be secured with at least 3 fixings (for fibre-cement at least 4). Headlaps and side laps must be at least equal to those used on the surface of the roof. [24, 27]

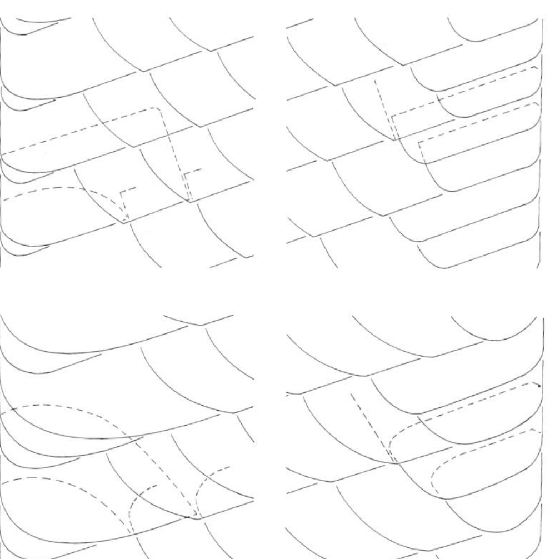

2.4.4.54 Slating with curved and scalloped slates; verge details at start and end of courses

There should not be a capping course at the verge because it is a risk in terms of rainproofing requirements.

Valley
The valley can be formed as a swept left- or right-hand valley when the roof pitches are not equal, as a swept heart valley when the roof pitches are equal, or as a lined heart valley when the pitch of the valley rafter is ≥ 30°.
The valley slates, ≥ 130 mm wide, are laid with single laps following the gradient of the courses. The back edges of the valley and valley transition slates should form a straight line.
It is preferable to use valley slates with a straight back edge and rounded or short splayed heel. The side lap of the valley and adjoining slates must be ≥ 65 mm or at least half the width of the valley slate. When using valley slates with a rounded back edge and long splayed heel, the side lap is increased by ≥ 10 mm. [27] The headlap of the valley course should be one-third greater than that used on the surface of the roof.

The topmost valley course is provided as a ridge course with single side laps; the valley slates below are cut to suit.
Eaves and top courses should be packed up to maintain the pitch of the slates on the surface of the roof. [24, 27]
In order to prevent the water from draining inwards, the front edges of the valley slates and the draining slates plus the back edges, i.e. sides, of the channel slate must have sharp edges (cut with a blow from above) or have sawn edges.

2.4.4.55 Edges of valley slates

Valley and adjoining slates should be secured with at least 3 fixings. Shallower valleys can be formed with sheet metal linings (see "Laying – Diagonal slating").

Swept left- and right-hand valleys
A swept left- or right-hand valley is chosen according to whether the roof surface to the left or the right exhibits a greater water run-off owing to its size or pitch and thus leads to a higher flow velocity.

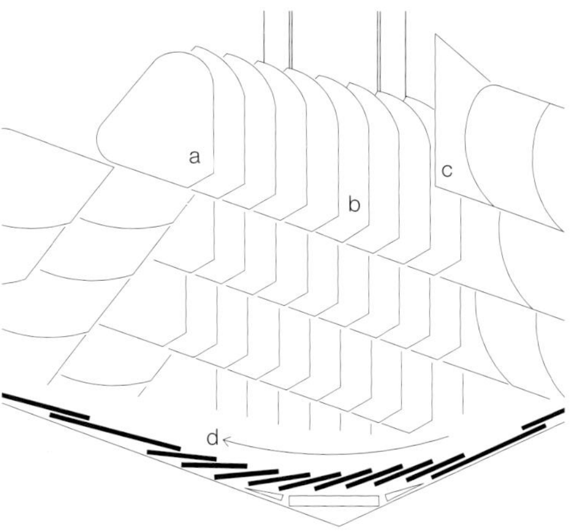


2.4.4.56 Slating with curved and scalloped slates; swept left-hand valley; plan and section: a valley transition slate, b valley slate with short splay, c channel slate, d direction of laying

The courses in the valley are laid in such a way that every valley course, starting from a roof surface course, is integrated into the courses of the adjoining roof surface. The valley courses should be rounded with channel and valley transition slates according to the direction of the slating on the neighbouring roof surfaces. Starting from the channel slate (from draining slate only for roof pitches ≥ 50°), the slating generally proceeds from the shallower/ smaller to the steeper/larger roof surface. The width of the valley must be equal to at least 7–9 valley slates.

Swept heart valley
When the roof pitch on both sides is the same and the roof surfaces are roughly identical in size, a swept heart valley can be used. Only valley slates with a straight back edge and rounded or short splay may be used here. Starting from the heart valley channel slate, positioned centrally about the line of the valley, at least 4 valley slates are laid left and right of this with the same course gradient on both sides. The valley courses are integrated as in left- and right-hand swept valleys. In the middle of the valley between the valley slates a narrow, 10–20 mm [10] water channel should be kept open on the heart valley channel slate. [27]

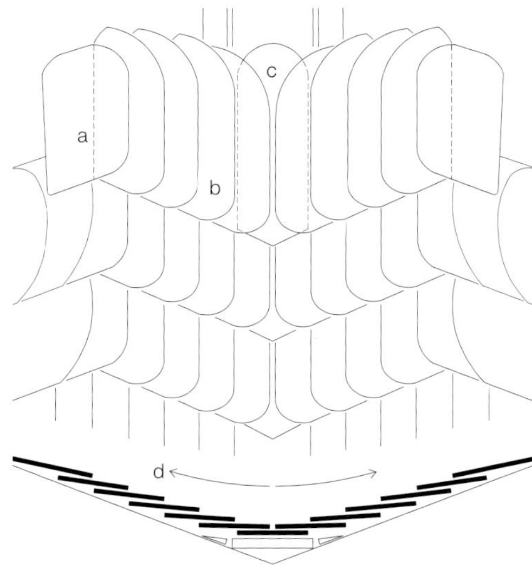


2.4.4.57 Slating with curved and scalloped slates; swept heart valley; plan and section: a valley transition slate, b valley slate with rounded corner, c heart valley channel slate, d direction of laying

Lined heart valley
When the roof pitches and roof areas on both sides are identical, we can also use a lined heart valley with its own coursing and gradient. The outside corners of the outer valley slates must be splayed to help shed water. The slates on the surface of the roof overlap the valley slates as follows [27]:
≥ 120 mm for roof pitches ≥ 40°
≥ 100 mm for roof pitches ≥ 50°
The whole length of the lined heart valley can be covered prior to the roof surfaces.

Dormer window
An eyebrow dormer window is covered as a cheek valley; ratio of curves and pitches as for rectangular double-lap slating. If covered as one surface with the main roof covering, the height-to-width ratio of the front of the window should be 1:8. ([27] and "Layers – Flat overlapping elements of clay and condrete")

**Curved and scalloped slating, material requirements**

22.7 to 34.6 pcs/m² depending on format and overlap.

**Slating with unequal scalloped slates (Old German slating)**
(see also "Laying")

On the roof surfaces the slating is laid with single or double laps and with a gradient (see "Laying – German slating"). We distinguish between single-lap slating cut with a dull, normal or sharp blow and double-lap slating cut with a normal blow, both on a complete roof decking with sheathing. Old German slating makes use of scalloped slates with different lengths and widths on one surface (random slating).

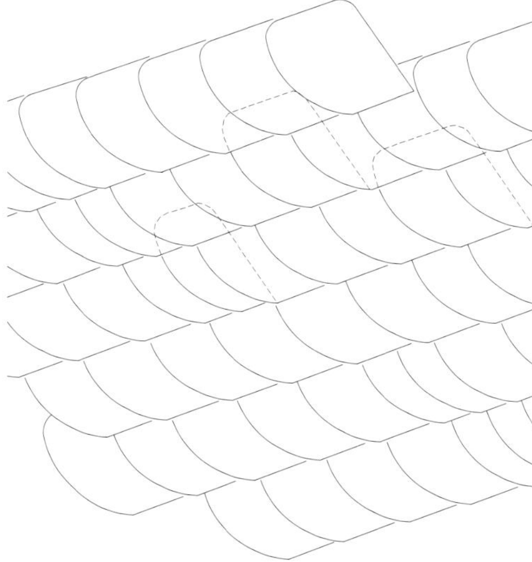

2.4.4.58 Single-lap slating with scalloped slates of unequal size

| Slate type | Length [cm] | Width [cm] | suitable for roof pitches [°] |
|---|---|---|---|
| 1/1 | 50–40 | 50–40 | ≥ 22–30 double-lap slating |
| 1/2 | 42–36 | 38–28 | ≥ 25–30 |
| 1/4 | 38–32 | 34–25 | ≥ 25–35 |
| 1/8 | 34–28 | 30–23 | ≥ 30–40 |
| 1/12 | 30–24 | 26–20 | ≥ 35–50 |
| 1/16 | 26–20 | 22–17 | ≥ 40–60 |
| 1/32 | 22–16 | 18–13 | ≥ 50 |
| 1/64 | 18–12 | 16–11 | ≥ 60 |

2.4.4.59 Scalloped slates; slate sizes and roof pitches [03, 14, 27]

Slating begins at the eaves with the largest slates. More and more smaller slates are used as we proceed towards the ridge (diminishing courses). The gauge of the courses must be finely graduated according to table 2.4.4.60. All courses should include both wide and narrow scalloped slates. In doing so, the visible difference in width must be ≥ 40 mm. It is permissible to lay two narrow slates on one wide slate or vice versa.

| Rafter length [m] | Difference in length [mm] | No. of types |
|---|---|---|
| ≤ 6 | ≥ 40 | 1 |
| ≤ 8 | ≥ 60 | 2 |
| > 8 | ≥ 80 | 2 to 3 |

2.4.4.60 Scalloped slates of unequal size; differences in length between slates at ridge and eaves

| Slate type | Length [cm] | Headlap (29%)*) / Side lap cut with normal/dull blow (29%)*) [mm] | Side lap cut with sharp blow (38%) [mm] |
|---|---|---|---|
| | 42 | 122 | 160 |
| | 41 | 119 | 156 |
| | 40 | 116 | 152 |
| 1/2 | 39 | 113 | 148 |
| | 38 | 110 | 144 |
| | 37 | 107 | 141 |
| | 36 | 104 | 137 |
| 1/4 | 35 | 101 | 133 |
| | 34 | 99 | 129 |
| | 33 | 96 | 125 |
| | 32 | 93 | 122 |
| 1/8 | 31 | 90 | 118 |
| | 30 | 87 | 114 |
| | 29 | 84 | 110 |
| | 28 | 81 | 106 |
| 1/12 | 27 | 78 | 103 |
| | 26 | 75 | 99 |
| | 25 | 73 | 95 |
| | 24 | 70 | 91 |
| 1/16 | 23 | 67 | 87 |
| | 22 | 64 | 84 |
| | 21 | 61 | 80 |
| | 20 | 58 | 76 |
| 1/32 | 19 | 55 | 72 |
| | 18 | 52 | 68 |
| | 17 | 50 | 65 |
| | 16 | 50 | 61 |
| 1/64 | 15 | 50 | 57 |
| | 14 | 50 | 53 |

*) Headlap is ≥ 120 mm for slate lengths > 42 cm

2.4.4.61 Scalloped slates; headlaps and side laps for single-lap slating [03, 27]

Laying the slates to overlap in the direction of the prevailing wind is recommended for Old German slating too; left- or right-hand slating ensues accordingly. Valleys are swept. Larger slates and/or slates cut with a sharp blow (owing to the slight increase in the side

lap) should be used according to the tables on shallower roof pitches or when enhanced requirements for the reliability of the roof covering apply. The minimum headlap and side lap depends on the size of the slate.
Double-lap slating is generally carried out with 1/1 to 1/12 slates on roof pitches of 22–30°. In double-lap slating the slates of the third course overlap those of the first course by ≥ 20 mm.

**Unequal scalloped slating, details**
The information given for scalloped slates of equal size (German slating) applies for the ridge, hip, eaves, verge, valley and dormer window details on roofs covered with unequal scalloped slates (Old German slating).

**Unequal scalloped slating, material requirements**

| | |
|---|---|
| Cut with normal blow: | ~ 32 kg dressed/m$^2$ |
| Cut with sharp blow: | ~ 36 kg dressed/m$^2$ |
| Double-lap slating: | ~ 45 kg dressed/m$^2$ |
| Verge slates: | ~ 10–12 kg basic/m, thereof 2 kg for undercloak and intermediate slates |
| Valley slates: | ~ 25–30 kg basic/m |
| Eaves slates: | ~ 4–7 kg basic/m |

**Supporting construction**
Sheathing
At least one layer of bitumen roofing felt (V13) with a sanded finish should be used as sheathing on top of the roof decking, laid lengthwise or crosswise on the roof decking with laps of ≥ 80 mm. Sheathing is also required at valleys. Both sheathing and boarding are also recommended as protection against dust, driving snow and driving rain (see "Layers – Secondary waterproofing/covering layer").

Battens
Battens should measure at least 24 x 48 mm when the roof covering is fixed to them with hooks. If the roof covering is nailed on, they should be 40 x 60 mm so that they do not whip during nailing. The spacing of counter battens (spacing of rafters) should not exceed 60 cm for natural slates or 80 cm for fibre-cement slates. Battens should be grade S10 to DIN 4074 part 1; one-third of each side of the batten should be free from wane. The size of the battens should be adjusted to suit greater loads or longer spans.

Roof decking
The roof decking must be complete, ≥ 24 mm thick and dry, and may not whip at any point. The boards should be ≥ 12 cm wide and fixed with two fixings. Boards ≥ 20 cm wide must be fixed with 3 fixings. The length of the nails must be equal to at least 2.5 times the thickness of the board. Timber must comply with grade S10 of DIN 4074 part 1.
The use of laminated veneer lumber (LVL) BFU 100G (DIN 68705 part 3) and glued laminated timber BSH 100G ≥ 22 mm thick is permissible in exceptional cases. These materials must be protected from the weather immediately (sheathing). The spacing of rafters should be ≥ 60 cm. A thicker roof decking should be chosen for greater loads or longer spans.
A continuous, wide board must be provided at the ridge. Below this, the roof decking should be closed off if necessary with narrow or tapered boards. The roof decking at a hip can run in the direction of the battens or parallel with the hip bay by bay. Intermediate counter batten pieces must be included (see "Layers – Ventilation") owing to the long spans of the battens and boards. Roof decking consisting of boards 16–18 cm wide and triangular fillets is required in valleys – at a lower level in lined valleys if possible – parallel to the line of the valley. [24, 25, 27] Nailable roofing panels (e.g. of aerated concrete) can also be used as an underlay for slating (min. 50 mm thick); care must be taken to choose the correct length of nail.

**Maintenance and repair**
A properly constructed slate roof covering should not cause trouble for many decades. However, natural slates with microstructure damage that was not detected during laying can fracture during the first 2–3 years due to the action of frost and heat.
In order to detect such material defects it is recommended to inspect a new roof after this period and to replace any damaged slates as necessary. Roofs with a shallow pitch or intersecting roof surfaces should therefore be inspected more often. Foliage, sludge and vegetable matter should be removed from valleys at regular intervals.
Replacement slates must have the correct format, thickness and colour.
Suitable fixings for repairs are hooks (tingles) made from copper or stainless steel (general elements) and copper wire bent to an S-shape (valley slates). Every replacement slate is held rigidly in place by notching its edge with the slater's hammer. Exposed nailing must be avoided at all costs.
Fixing slates with filler-type adhesives is not recommended. Such compounds hamper the drainage of water and therefore lead to damage.
The causes of more extensive damage may be the use of natural slates split too thin or a timber decking built in while it was still too moist, and which has subsequently twisted. In these cases the roof covering must be removed from the damaged area, partly or completely replaced and – after the roof decking has dried out – re-slated.

**References**


[01] Brennecke, W.; Folkerts, H.; Haferland, F.; Hart, F.: Dachatlas, Geneigte Dächer; Munich: Institut für Internationale Architektur-Dokumentation, 1980
[02] Braas Handbuch 94/96; ed. Braas Dachsysteme GmbH, Oberursel, 1993
[03] Deckungen mit Schiefer; ed. Rathscheck Schieferbergbau; Mayen, 1977
[04] DIN 4102: Fire behaviour of building materials and building components; pt 1: Building materials; concepts, requirements and tests; Berlin: Beuth-Verlag, 1981
[05] DIN 52103: Prüfung von Naturstein und Gesteinskörnungen; Bestimmung der Wasseraufnahme und Sättigungswert; Berlin: Beuth, 1988
Superseded by: DIN EN 13755 Natural stone test methods; determinaton of water absorption at atmospheric pressure
[06] DIN 52104: Frost-Tau-Wechsel-Versuch; Berlin: Beuth-Verlag, 1982
[07] DIN 52104 pt 1: Testing of natural stone; freeze-thaw cyclic test; methods A to Q; Berlin: Beuth, 1982.
Will be superseded by: DIN EN 12371: Natural stone test methods; determination of frost resistance
[08] DIN EN 12326: Slate and stone products for discontinuous roofing and cladding; pt 1: Product specifications; Berlin: Beuth, 2002; pt 2: Test methods; Berlin: Beuth, 1999
[09] Eternit (ed.): Planung und Anwendung, Dachplatten aus Faserzement; Berlin: Eternit AG, 2000
[10] Fingerhut, P.: Schieferdächer, 5th ed.; Cologne: Rudolf Müller, 2000
[11] Holzapfel, W.: Werkstoffkunde für Dach-, Wand- und Abdichtungstechnik, 10th ed.; Cologne: Rudolf Müller, 1999
[12] Hoppen, E. A.: Schiefer, natürlicher Baustoff für Kenner und Könner; Cologne: Rudolf Müller, 2000
[13] Jungblut, N.: Lehr- und Musterbuch über Schieferbedachungen, 3rd ed.; Mayen: Fachbücherverlag N. Jungblut, between 1925 & 1935
[14] Lutter, U.; Menn, M.: Das 1 x 1 der Schieferdeckungen; Bad Fredeburg: Arbeitsgemeinschaft Schiefer e.V., 2000
[15] Nickel, E.: Grundwissen in Mineralogie, pt 1–3, 2nd ed.; Thun: Ott, 1973 & 1975
[16] Römpp, H.: Chemie-Lexikon; Stuttgart/New York: Thieme, 1995
[17] Scholz, W.: Baustoffkenntnisse, 13th ed.; Düsseldorf: Werner Verlag, 1995
[18] Schwate, W.: Metamorphite, Naturstein Deutschland 2000; in: Stein 1/01; Munich Callwey, 2001
[19] Seuffert, O.: Geographical Institute of Darmstadt Polytechnic and Verein für Erdkunde zu Darmstadt e.V. (ed.): Geoökodynamik, vol. 12, issue 3; Darmstadt: Geoöko-Verlag, 1991
[20] Wagner, W.: Dachschiefer in der Lagerstätte; paper in Schriftenreihe des Schiefer-Fachverbandes, Deutschland e.V., 1992
[21] Wagner, W.: Die gesteinskundliche Analyse DIN 52201A. Transparenter Mineralbestand; paper, meeting of experts C.E.N./TC 128/SC8; in: Schriftenreihe des Schiefer-Fachverbandes, Deutschland e.V., 1994
[22] Wagner, W.: Kalk im Dachschiefer; in: DDH 7/88; Cologne: Rudolf Müller, 1988
[23] Wirschem, A.: Schiefer als Make-up; in: DDH 22/85; Cologne: Rudolf Müller, 1985
[24] Zentralverband des Deutschen Dachdeckerhandwerks, Fachverband Dach-, Wand- und Abdichtungstechnik e.V. (ed.): Regeln für Deckungen mit Faserzement, pt 1: Dachdeckungen mit Faserzement-Dachplatten; Cologne: Rudolf Müller, 1990
[25] Zentralverband des Deutschen Dachdeckerhandwerks, Fachverband Dach-, Wand- und Abdichtungstechnik e.V. (ed.): Hinweise, Holz und Holzwerkstoffe: Cologne: Rudolf Müller, 1997
[26] Zentralverband des Deutschen Dachdeckerhandwerks, Fachverband Dach-, Wand- und Abdichtungstechnik, e.V. (ed.): Fachregel für Metallarbeiten im Dachdeckerhandwerk; Cologne: Rudolf Müller, 1999
[27] Zentralverband des Deutschen Dachdeckerhandwerks, Fachverband Dach-, Wand- und Abdichtungstechnik e.V. (ed.): Fachregel für Dachdeckungen mit Schiefer; Cologne: Rudolf Müller, 1999

## Asphalt shingles

Materials, components, laying

### Materials

Raw materials, manufacture, properties

#### Raw materials, grades of bitumen

The raw material for bitumen is petroleum. The light distillates (petrol etc.), middle distillates (diesel and heating oil), heavy distillates (engine and lubricating oils) and finally bitumen are obtained in succession through evaporation and subsequent condensation (fractional distillation). The various grades of bitumen consist mainly of oily constituents, the "malthenes" and solid constituents distributed finely within them, the "asphaltenes". These are colloidal solutions in which the asphaltenes are present primarily as molecular agglomerations ("micelles"). [02, 05]
The following grades of bitumen are used for asphalt shingles:

Straight-run bitumen
The soft to medium-hard bitumen remaining upon distillation, preferably using a vacuum. [02]

Blown bitumen
Modified bitumen with a higher content of asphaltenes produced by blowing air into hot, fluid, soft, straight-run bitumen. The multitude of asphaltenes forms a cohesive framework ("gel" state) which considerably extends the irrange of plasticity. Blown bitumens exhibit a rubber-like elasticity with low plastic deformations. They soften at higher and become brittle at low temperatures. [04, 05]

Polymer-modified bitumen
A physical mixture or reaction product of straight-run bitumen (B 200, B 80) and polymers (12–30%). This gives rise to multi-phase materials whose behaviour and properties are essentially governed by their polymer content. They have a high extensibility and ageing resistance, and can also be adapted to meet special requirements (improved elastic properties, elastomers; extended plasticity range, plastomers; greater resistance to chemical attack). [02, 03]

Bitumen/Filler mixture
Bitumen containing fillers (fibrous, flaky, granular) such as rock flour (usually slate powder). The fillers improve weathering and impact resistance, reduce the tendency to flow and can lead to a certain extension of the range of plasticity. [02]

#### Manufacture

Asphalt shingles are produced from bitumen roofing felt. A base (inorganic: woven or non-woven glass-fibre fabric; organic: non-woven fabric of synthetic fibres; organic, not rotproof: felt base, mechanical pulp board) is dipped in straight-run bitumen and then coated on both sides with blown or polymer-modified bitumen. One side is then given a surface finish of mineral granules or chippings, or a metal foil facing. The shingles are punched out of this material. The base prevents the bitumen from flowing and tearing. The immersion process acts as an impregnation and forms the adhesive substrate for the covering layers of bitumen. Good adhesion of the surfacing is decisive for the service life of the layers of bitumen. This surface finish can be made from slate or basalt chippings, quartz sand or ceramic granulate. It must itself remain resistant to ultraviolet radiation and the effects of the weather for many years. It determines the appearance of the asphalt shingles and is available in various colours. Choosing light-coloured materials for the surfacing helps to reflect solar radiation and hence reduce the temperature within the layers of bitumen.

#### Properties

Physical properties
Bitumen and polymer-modified bitumen are thermoplastic materials; their hardness decreases as the temperature rises. As they heat up there is a constant transition from the solid to the liquid state.
Bitumen behaves elastically under the effects of low and short-term loading; longer-term loading results in plastic deformations. Elastic behaviour is also influenced by temperature; at low temperatures the elastic properties prevail, while with rising temperatures the plastic deformability increases. [02]

Behaviour in fire
The behaviour of asphalt shingles in fire must be tested and certified by an approved materials testing centre in accordance with DIN 4102. They are classed as a "hard roof covering", i.e. resistant to sparks and radiant heat.

Chemical properties
Bitumen is resistant to the effects of carbonic acid and other weak acids, inorganic alkaline solutions, salts and aggressive waters. It is not resistant to organic alkaline solutions and organic solvents (benzol, oil, benzene, carbon tetrachloride). Generally, the harder the bitumen, the greater its resistance to chemical

| Material | Origin | Colour |
|---|---|---|
| Slate chippings | Moselle Sauerland | blue |
| | Spain Ardennes | green |
| | Spain England | red |
| | Thuringian Forest | silver |
| Basalt chippings | | dark green dark grey black |
| Quartz sand | | white |
| Ceramic granulate | | various mineral paints |

2.4.5.1 Surface finishes, colours

| | | Straight-run bitumen | | | | | Blown bitumen | | | | | | Polymer-mod. bit. | |
|---|---|---|---|---|---|---|---|---|---|---|---|---|---|---|
| Applications | | B200 | B80 | B65 | B45 | B25 | 85/25 | 85/40 | 100/25 | 100/40 | 105/15 | 115/15 | SBS base | aPP base |
| Roofing felt and shingles | immersion compounds | • | • | • | | | | | | | | | | |
| | covering compounds | | | | | | • | • | • | • | | • | • | • |
| | adhesive compounds | | | | | • | • | • | • | • | • | • | | |
| Paints | emulsions | • | • | | • | • | | | | | | | | • |
| | paints, lacquers | | | | • | • | • | • | • | | | | • | • |
| Sealing materials | protective compounds, puttys | | | | • | • | • | • | • | • | | | | |
| | jointing compounds | • | • | • | • | • | • | • | • | • | • | • | | |
| Coverings | mastic asphalt | | | | • | • | | | | | | | • | |

2.4.5.2 Use of various grades of bitumen

| | Straight-run bitumen | | | | Blown bitumen | | | Polymer-mod. bitumen | |
|---|---|---|---|---|---|---|---|---|---|
| | B 200 | B 80 | B 65 | 85/25 | 85/40 | 100/25 | 100/40 | SBS base | aPP base |
| Penetration depth at 25°C [$10^{-1}$ mm] | 160 to 210 | 70 to 100 | 50 to 70 | 20 to 30 | 35 to 45 | 20 to 35 | 35 to 50 | 30 to 70 | 25 to 35 |
| Softening point (ring/ball) [°C] | 37 to 44 | 44 to 49 | 49 to 54 | 80 to 90 | 80 to 90 | 95 to 110 | 95 to 110 | 110 to 125 | ≥ 140 |
| Breaking point (Fraass) [°C] | ≤ –15 | ≤ –10 | ≤ –8 | ≤ –10 | ≤ –20 | ≤ –20 | ≤ –25 | ≤ –40 | –10 to –25 |
| Density at 25°C | 1.0 to 1.06 g/cm³ | | | | | | | | |
| Thermal conductivity | 0.16 W/mK | | | | | | | | |
| Water vapour diffusion resistance index | 100 000 | | | | | | | | |

2.4.5.3 Bitumen; physical properties [02]

attack. [02, 05] The application of heat causes the material to age due to the evaporation of lighter volatile constituents. The effect of heat and ultraviolet radiation also lead to reactions with atmospheric oxygen and hence to ageing phenomena due to the breakdown of molecular chains, thus causing the familiar hardening and embrittlement. Both processes take place very slowly and are confined to the surface for a long time.
The damage caused by oxygen also leads to the formation of water-soluble and degradation products with acidic reactions in water (ketonic acids). These cause corrosion of zinc, iron and other metals. PVC is not resistant to bitumen. [02] Bitumen can damage PVC roofing felts (see "Layers – Green roof").

| | Concen-tration [%] | Temperature up to about 30 °C | 65 °C |
|---|---|---|---|
| **Inorganic acids** | | | |
| nitric acid | > 10 | + | • |
| | < 10 | • | • |
| | 65 | – | – |
| hydrochloric acid | > 25 | + | • |
| | 36 | • | – |
| sulphuric acid | > 25 | + | • |
| | < 95 | – | – |
| fuming sulphuric acid (oleum) | | – | – |
| **Organic acids** | | | |
| formic acid | 40 | + | • |
| benzoic acid | | + | |
| butyric acid | | – | – |
| tannic acid | > 25 | + | |
| oleic acid | | – | – |
| phenols | | – | – |
| phthalic acid | | + | |
| tartaric acid | > 25 | + | |
| **Inorganic alkaline solutions** | | | |
| potassium hydroxide solution | | + | • |
| sodium hydroxide solution | | + | • |
| **Organic alkaline solutions** | | | |
| aniline | | – | – |
| pyridine and homologues | | – | – |
| triethanolamine | | + | |
| **Miscellaneous** | | | |
| waste water | | • | • |
| liquid manure | | + | |
| perhydrol | 30 | • | – |

+ resistant
• not resistant in every case – must be checked
– not resistant

2.4.5.4 Behaviour of bitumen exposed to the effects of chemicals [02]

Biological properties
Layers of bitumen can be penetrated by roots. Growths of algae (green algae, red algae) may occur in shady, permanently damp areas and lead to damage, e.g. cracking.

| Bitumen covering layer | Surface finish | Base [g/m²] | w x l [mm] | Thickness [mm] | Weight [kg/shingle] |
|---|---|---|---|---|---|
| polymer-modified bitumen | slate chippings | non-woven glass fibre/synthetic 140 | 1000 x 333 | 4.0 | 1.7 |
| polymer-modified bitumen | slate chippings ceramic granulate | non-woven glass fibre 135 | 1000 x 340 | 3.5 | 2.0 |
| blown bitumen 115/15 | basalt chippings ceramic granulate | non-woven glass fibre 125 | 1000 x 340 | 3.0 | 1.5 |
| blown bitumen 100/25 | ceramic granulate | non-woven glass fibre 105 | 1000 x 360 | 3.5 | 1.5 |
| blown bitumen | slate chippings ceramic granulate | non-woven glass fibre 130 | 1000 x 340 | 3.5 | 1.5 |
| blown bitumen 90/30 | slate chippings ceramic granulate | non-w. glass f. 50 lime-bitumen mortar non-w. glass fibre 80 | 500 x 300 | 6.0 | 1.5 |
| blown bitumen | ceramic granulate | mechanical pulp board | 1000 x 336 | 3.0 | 1.5 |
| blown bitumen | ceramic granulate | non-woven glass fibre 110 | 1000 x 336 | 3.0 | 1.7 |
| blown bitumen 115/15 | basalt chippings ceramic granulate | non-woven glass fibre 130 | 1000 x 340 | 3.0 | 1.6 |

2.4.5.6 Asphalt shingles; structure, forms, dimensions, weights

## Components

General components, edge components, grades, forms of supply

### General components

Asphalt shingles are rectangular in shape. They are preferably provided with two slits at the third points which divide the lower part of the shingle into several "tabs".
Strips, dots or patches of self-adhesive bitumen are applied to the top surface of the shingle. The underside of the shingle is covered with a separating layer (silicone strip, talcum powder) at the corresponding point to prevent shingles sticking together during storage.

The colour of the surface depends on the coating. It corresponds to the natural colours of the surface finish (sand, chippings) or is dyed to match these or to produce other colours (sand, chippings, ceramic granulate).

### Edge components

Edge components are not prefabricated but instead produced on site by cutting the standard shingles as required. All the necessary shingle types for covering ridge, eaves, hip, valley etc. can thus be produced.
To complement or replace continuous ridge ventilation, shingle roof vents can be incorporated. These are produced with a ventilation cross-section of 135 or 175 cm² (see "Layers – Ventilation").

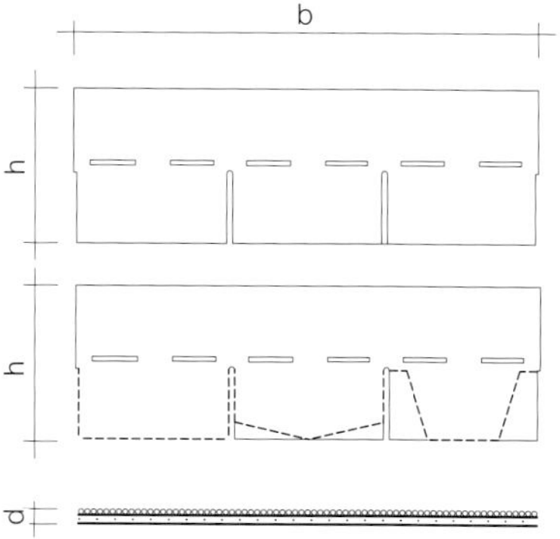


2.4.5.5 Asphalt shingle shapes; tab forms (rectangular, triangular, honeycomb); coating make-up (surface finish, bitumen covering, base immersed in bitumen, bitumen covering, separating layer) [06]

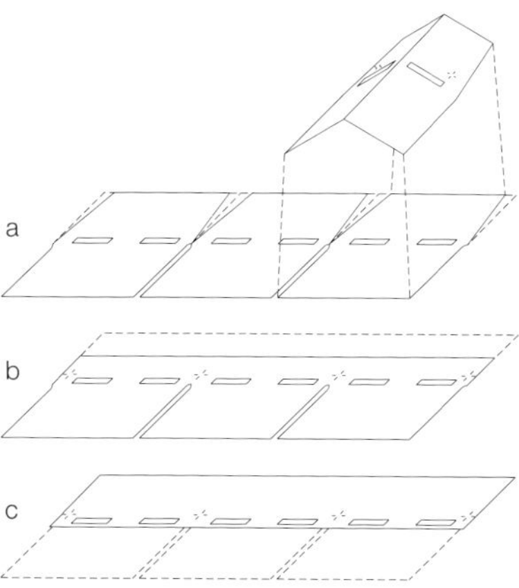


2.4.5.7 Cuttings: a ridge/hip/verge capping, b ridge course, c undereaves course

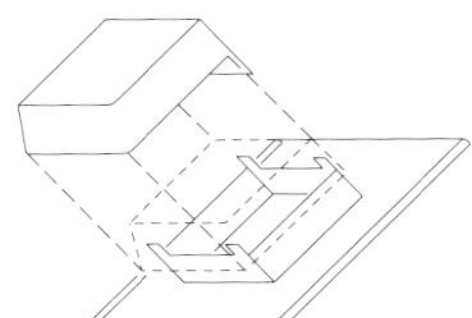

2.4.5.8 Individual vent

#### Grades

Asphalt shingles are divided into two classes. Class 1 complies with all climatic requirements in Europe, class 2 with only some of them.

| | | Grade 1 | Grade 2 |
|---|---|---|---|
| Base [g/m²] | average value | ≥ 110[1)] | ≥ 100[1)] |
| | single values | > 100[1)] | > 90[1)] |
| Bitumen covering [g/m²] | both sides | ≥ 1300 | |
| Adhesive area [%] | proportion of surface | | ≥ 15 |
| Blister formation [°C] | no blisters | ≤ 90 ± 2 | ≤ 80 ± 2 |
| Flow temperature [°C] | flow < 2 mm | ≤ 90 ± 2 | ≤ 80 ± 2 |
| Tensile strength [N] | longitudinal and transverse | ≥ 600[2)] | ≥ 400[2)] |

[1)] non-woven glass fibre, [2)] test strips 50 mm wide

2.4.5.9 Grades; requirements [03]

#### Forms of supply

Packet: The number of shingles in a packet varies from 15 to 30 according to their thickness. Pallet: 45–52 packets

### Laying

Conditions for laying, fixing, workability, auxiliary materials, additional measures, details, supporting construction, maintenance and repair

#### Conditions for laying

Asphalt shingles are laid in a double-lap horizontal bond with a half-tab offset. The third course must overlap the first and their slits must line up. The butt joints between bitumen shingles are 1–2 mm wide to accommodate temperature-related deformations. The properties of the material allow the shingles to adapt to any substrate. Minor curving of individual shingles and unevenness that can be seen on the top surface are not defects that impair the effectiveness of the roof covering. Horizontal and vertical chalk snap lines are necessary to ensure the even laying of the shingles.
An unobstructed ventilation depth of 60–100 mm (depending on pitch) below the shingles is recommended for dissipating solar heat gains (see "Building science – Thermal performance" and "Layers – Ventilation"). [06]

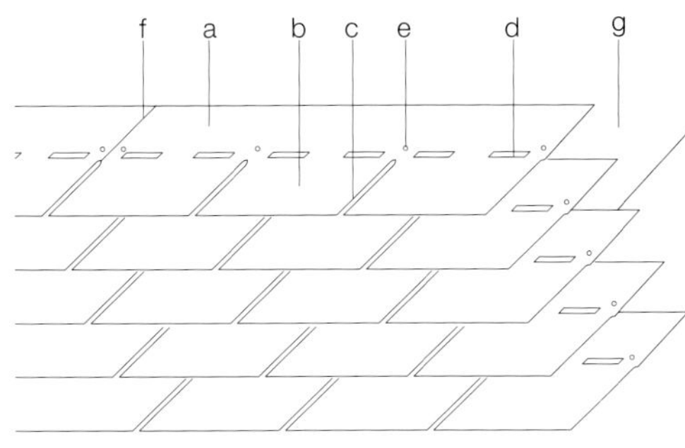


2.4.5.10 Roof covering: a shingle, b tab, c slit, d self-adhesive strip, e nailing point, f butt joint, g roofing felt [01]

Roof pitch
The standard roof pitch varies from 15° to 85° and depends on the length of the rafters.

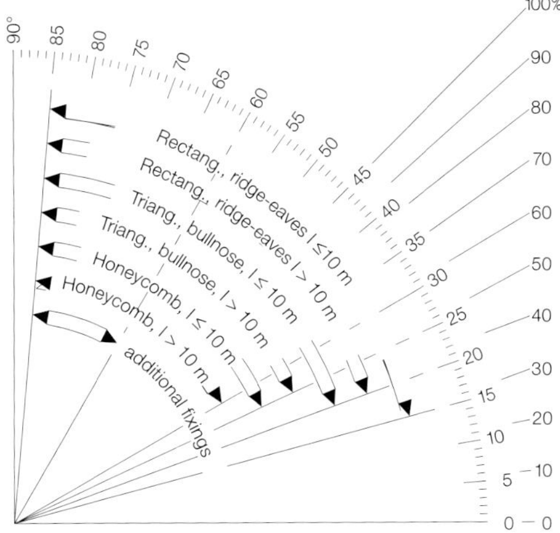


2.4.5.11 Standard roof pitches in relation to roof covering and distance between ridge and eaves

There is insufficient adhesion for laying on pitches > 85° because the weight of the shingle no longer presses down effectively on the adhesive. [01]

Laps
The headlap depends on the roof pitch. Shingles with sealing strips and large adhesive patches have a uniform lap of ≥ 45 mm. [06]

| Roof pitch [°] | min. lap ü [mm] [mm] |
|---|---|
| 15–24 | 100 |
| 25–34 | 80 |
| 35–44 | 60 |
| ≥ 45 | 50 |

2.4.5.12 Laps in relation to pitch [06]

Gauge, material requirements and the weight of the roof covering are all mutually dependent and can be calculated using the equations:

| Gauge [cm] | Material requirements [pcs/m²] | Weight of roof covering including fixings [N/m²] |
|---|---|---|
| $g = (h - ü)/2$ | $M = 1/(g \times w)$ | $D = G_s \times M$ |

w shingle width, D weight of roof covering, g gauge, $G_s$ weight of one shingle, h single length, M material requirements, ü lap

2.4.5.12 a Gauge, material requirements and weight of roof covering

#### Fixing

Rustproof clout nails to DIN 1160 are used to fix asphalt shingles to roof deckings of timber and timber derivatives. These nails have a large circular head with a diameter of ≥ 9 mm and must be at least 25 mm long, or at least 30 mm at multiple layers (ridge, hip etc.). The shaft of these stainless steel or copper nails must have a rough finish.

Fixings should be positioned above the adhesive patch where the headlaps vary, but within the large adhesive patches when the headlap is the same everywhere, thus securing the shingle underneath as well. Additional fixings in the upper corners of the shingles are necessary at roof pitches > 60°. [06] Special conical nails are used on lightweight concrete and pumice concrete planks. These must be hard enough to penetrate the compacted surface of the planks. Their pull-out strength must match that of nails in a timber loadbearing construction. [01, 06] The adhesive effect between individual courses takes place after a delay as it relies on the self-weight of the shingles and the self-adhesive strips, dots or patches being heated up by solar radiation. If the roof is covered at an unfavourable time of year (autumn), the adhesive effect is guaranteed by applying heat. [01, 06]

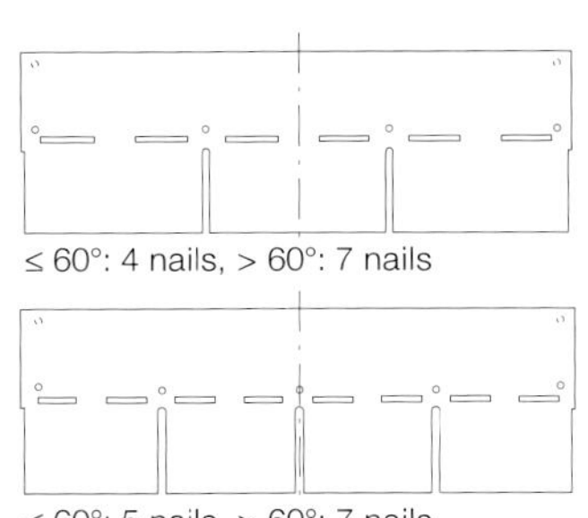


2.4.5.13 Fixing of shingles with several tabs; position of clout nails [01,06]

#### Workability

A knife or pair of scissors can be used to produce special pieces for ridge, hip, verge etc. Tools with a depth stop are allowed for nailing the shingles. A small blowlamp is sufficient to heat up the shingles in order to bend them or to guarantee adhesion between individual shingles when laying during cold weather; the self-adhesive patches and the underside of the overlying shingles are heated before being pressed together.

#### Auxiliary materials

The other materials required should be of the conventional quality or comply with the relevant standards [06]:

- aluminium sheet AlMn DIN EN 485
- lead sheet DIN 17640, DIN EN 12548

- copper sheet DIN 1787
- alloyed zinc sheet DIN EN 988
- stainless steel sheet DIN 17440, material No. 4571
- hot-dip galvanised steel sheet DIN EN ISO 1461
- bitumen roofing felt with inorganic base DIN 52143
- bitumen-based sealing and adhesive compounds
- bitumen primer
- synthetic coating

The following points should be taken into account when using metals:
- use only metals (Cu, V2A) that do not corrode when in contact with bitumen;
- coat with bituminous or synthetic paints up to ≥ 20 mm above the surface of the roof covering.

**Additional measures**

Additional measures should be allowed for during planning and construction when the reliability of the roof covering has to satisfy enhanced requirements:
- on large roofs (long rafters)
- for roof pitches below the recommended angles
- when several roof surfaces and valleys meet at one point along the eaves
- where increased wind pressures are expected
- where high snowfall or a build-up of melt water is expected

Additional measures include:
- a steeper roof pitch
- longer laps
- the inclusion of roofing felt, boarding or sarking underneath

**Details**

Ridge, hip, eaves, valley, verge, junction with wall, penetrations

Ridge

The shingles of the topmost course are cut off flush with the line of the ridge. To cover the ridge, cut 1/3 or 1/4 pieces from standard shingles. These are bent over the ridge so that they overlap the top courses on both sides equally.

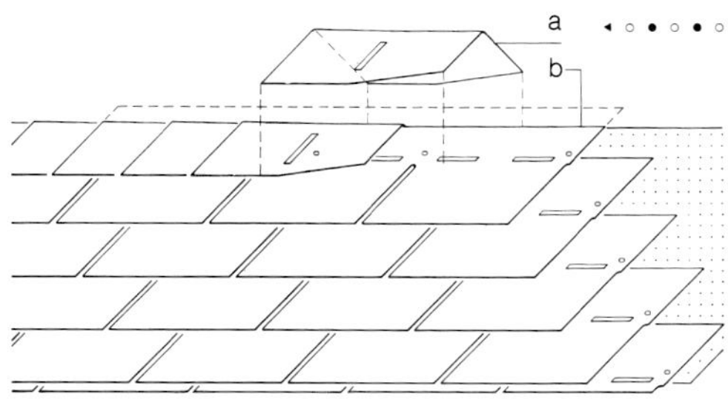


2.4.5.14 Ridge detail showing ridge course and ridge capping: a capping cut from shingle, b trimmed shingles; ◁ prevailing wind direction [01]

When laying in cold weather this ridge capping must be warmed first – carefully, to avoid causing cracks in the covering layer of bitumen. They are laid in the opposite direction from the prevailing wind and all nails are covered by the laps. In the longitudinal direction the third ridge piece overlaps the first by ≥ 10 mm. (For details of ridge ventilation see "Construction details – Asphalt shingles"). [01, 06]

Hip

The hip is covered in a similar fashion to the ridge. The courses on the surface of the roof are cut off parallel with the line of the hip and are covered by the hip capping.

Eaves

An eaves flashing is necessary. So that the first course has the same pitch as the rest of the roof surface, the edge of the eaves flashing can be raised by 10 mm by including a timber fillet or a feather-edge board.
The first course of asphalt shingles is cut off above the slits to form an undereaves course. The bottom edge of this course should be set back 10 mm from the edge of the eaves flashing. The next course of (full-size) shingles covers the undereaves course completely (bottom edges line up flush). The bottom edges of both courses thus stick together and provide mutual stiffening.
As a rule, the shingles are laid loose on the eaves flashing; they can be bonded at discrete points. Unprotected metal components, e.g. eaves flashing, gutter, require a coating to protect them from corrosion. [01, 06]

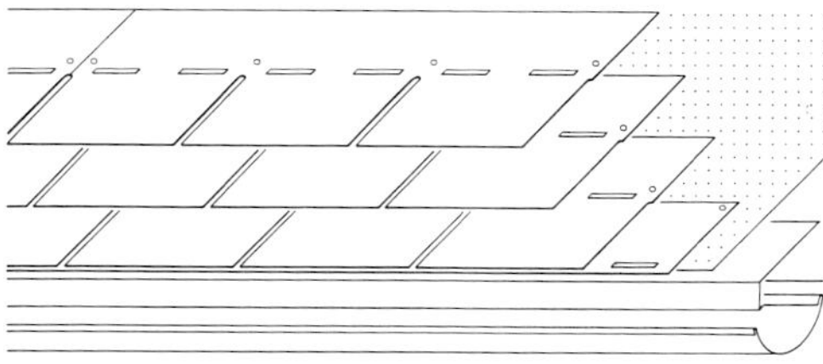

2.4.5.15 Eaves detail with undereaves course, eaves flashing and gutter [01]

Laced valley

The pitch of the valley should correspond to the recommended roof pitch, and depends on the length of the valley rafter.
Shingles laid alternately from different sides should include a valley board at pitches ≥ 25° to prevent the valley shingles tearing on the underside. They are cut off on both sides 300 mm from the line of the valley at the opposite chalk snap line. No nails should be positioned in the middle within a strip ≥ 300 mm wide. [06]

Semi-swept valley

To create a wide gutter, a valley can be formed with upper and lower layers (rectangular and bullnose shapes only) with a width equal to one or two tabs. The roof covering must employ a triple-lap bond (half-tab offset) on a valley board at the recommended roof pitch. The fourth course overlaps the first by ≥ 10 mm. Here again, no nails should be positioned in the middle of the valley. [06]

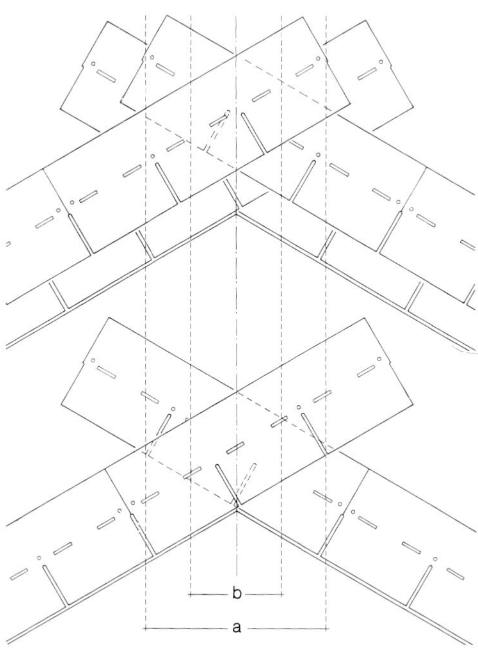


2.4.5.16 Laced valley; narrow valley gutter: a valley width, b no nails in this strip [01, 06]

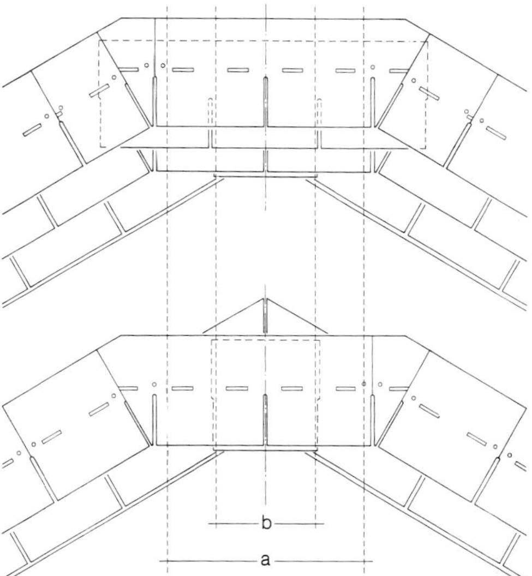


2.4.5.17 Semi-swept valley; valley gutter two tabs wide: a valley width, b no nails in this strip [01, 06]

Lined valley

The underlay below the valley gutter can be made from asphalt shingles, bitumen roofing felt or sheet metal protected against corrosion (See "Layers – Drainage"). The minimum valley pitch is ≥ 30°. The shingles on the surface of the roof must overlap the valley shingles by ≥ 120 mm and be cut off parallel with the line of the valley.

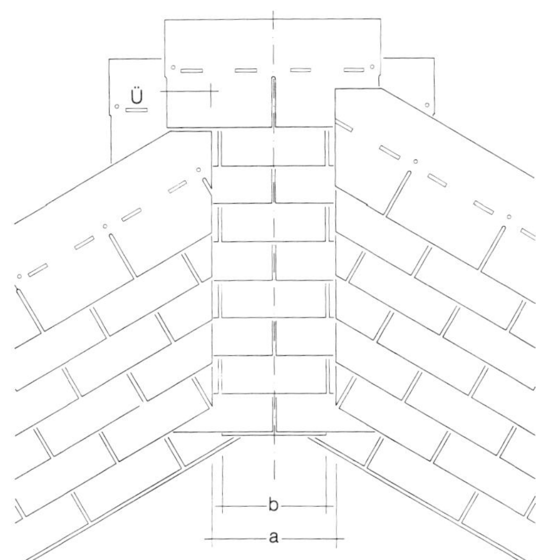


2.4.5.18 Lined valley: a valley width, b no nails in this strip, Ü = overlap [01, 06]

Shingle valleys (triple-lap) should be at least one tab wide. Sheet metal pieces should have turned-up edges on both sides. [01, 06]

Verge
A triangular fillet ≥ 30 mm high is usually fixed along the top edge of the gable. The sheathing and the courses of shingles are carried over this fillet and fixed with nails. A capping is laid over this, covering the fillet completely on the roof surface and with the vertical leg forming a drip at the top of the gable. Alternatively, a steeper triangular fillet can be used in conjunction with a sheet metal flashing. [06]

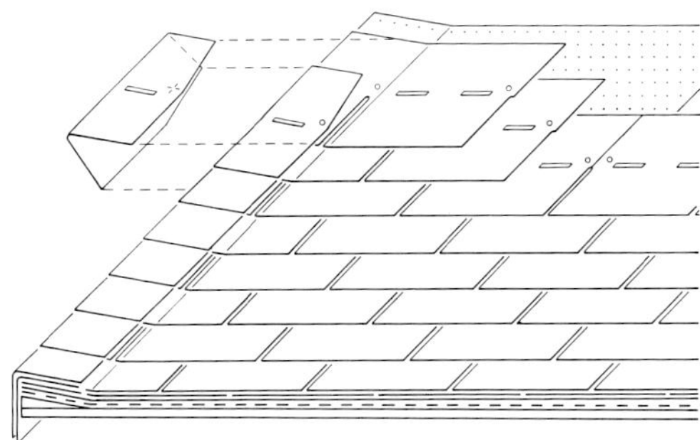

2.4.5.19 Verge detail with capping cut from shingles

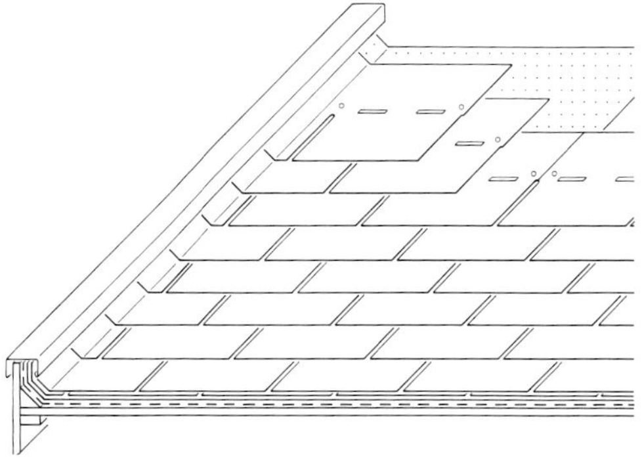

2.4.5.20 Verge detail with sheet metal flashing [01]

A verge capping is cut off at an angle. When laying during cold weather, the material must be must be warmed first – carefully, to avoid causing cracks in the covering layer of bitumen – before bending it into shape.
A verge detail employing a continuous sheet metal profile should include a turned-up edge. The courses of shingles are laid loose over this turned-up edge and overlap the sheet metal by ≥ 80 mm. The courses are not nailed or stuck down around the sheet metal profile. To prevent water being sucked below shingles laid flat, the top corner of each asphalt shingle is cut off at an angle. [01]

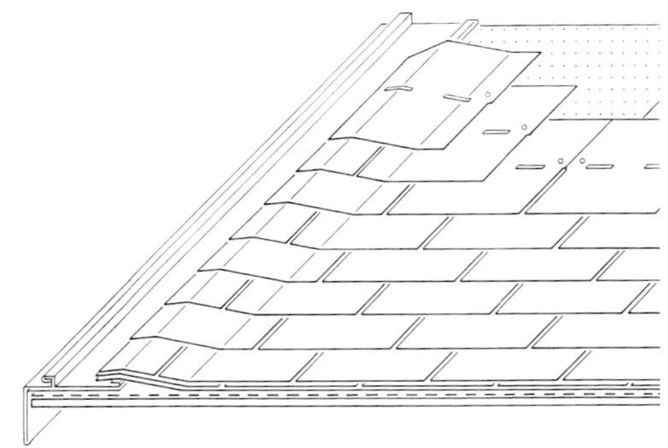

2.4.5.21 Verge detail with profiled sheet metal verge [01, 06]

Junction with wall
Such junctions can be realised with asphalt shingles or sheet metal flashings. When using shingles, a triangular fillet or feather-edge board must be included and the courses must be turned up the wall at least 80 mm (roof pitch ≥ 22°) to 100 mm (roof pitch < 22°). The junction must subsequently be protected by a capping strip or drip flashings let into a groove, fixed and sealed. [06]

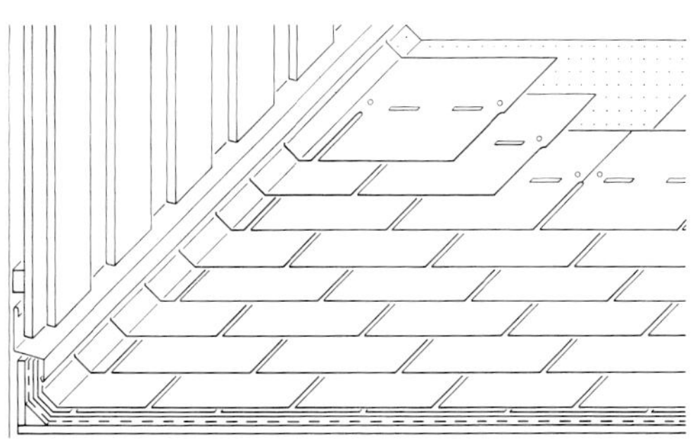

2.4.5.22 Wall junction detail with asphalt shingles turned up at wall

When using a sheet metal flashing, the horizontal leg should be ≥ 120 mm wide and include a turned-up edge. The adjacent shingle courses must overlap the metal ≥ 80 mm as at the verge. [01]

Metal soakers extend half a shingle tab below the roof covering and are the most reliable method of creating a junction with a wall. Junctions can also be formed with built-up felt roofing (cloth base).

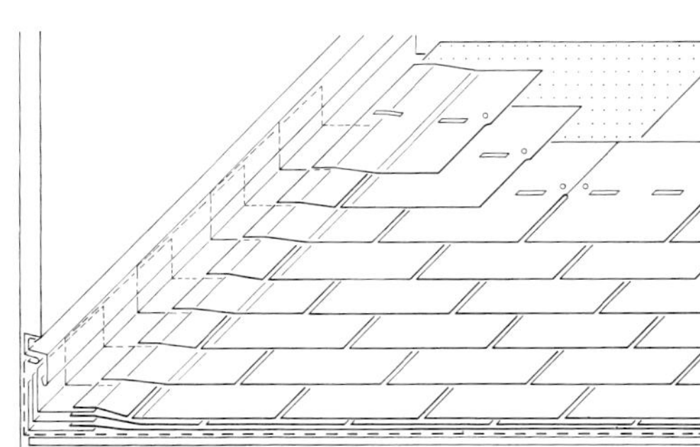

2.4.5.23 Wall junction detail with metal soakers

Penetrations
Penetrations are protected by a wide flange (≥ 120 mm) of metal (protected against corrosion) or another suitable material. The asphalt shingles overlap the flange by ≥ 80 mm and are not stuck down. The junction with the penetrating element (window, vent etc.) is carried out in a similar fashion to the junction with a wall. [01]
Mountings for lightning protection components, ladder fixings and snowguard supports are, if possible, incorporated during the laying of the roof covering. Lead sheet is laid underneath to distribute the load. [06]

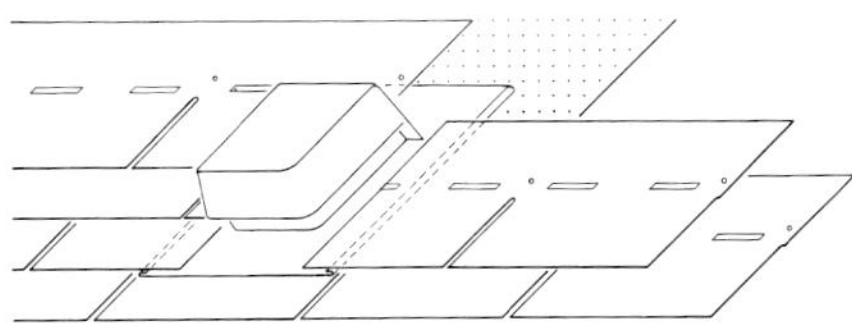

2.4.5.24 Roof penetration with sheet metal; individual vent

**Supporting construction**

Sheathing
One layer of bitumen roofing felt with an inorganic base is laid on the supporting construction before starting to lay the asphalt shingles. The rolls of material are laid parallel to the eaves. The overlap between rolls is ≥ 80 mm. They are fixed with clout nails (protected against corrosion) every 100 mm. [01, 06]
This sheathing remains fully effective for only a few years.

Roof decking
A flat, rigid supporting construction capable of accepting nails is required. Timber deckings of plain sawn boards must be at least 24 mm thick, tongue and groove boards at least 22 mm. The boards – dry, healthy and with no wane –

must be 80–160 mm wide and laid horizontally. Roof deckings made from timber derivatives must be 22 mm thick and should always be butt-jointed (offset) over the centre of the rafters. Timber roof deckings should be secured with 2 nails at right angles to DIN 18334, those made from timber derivatives with 6 nails/m² of roof surface.
Lightweight concrete planks must be laid flat. The joints between planks must be grouted flush with no sharp edges. [01, 06]

#### Maintenance and repair

The service life of an asphalt shingle roof covering may be 30 years or longer. The lighter the colour of the surface finish, the longer the shingles last.
So that the roof covering remains intact for this long period, it must be maintained at regular intervals. Carrying out work in good time prolongs the lifetime and protects the roof against serious damage during this period. [06]
Deposits, vegetable matter and foliage must be removed (brushed off) at regular intervals to prevent the formation of humus, the penetration of the shingles by roots and blocked gutters. Junctions and terminations require special attention. Metal components and flashings in contact with water, and thus at risk of corrosion, must be painted at regular intervals with a protective medium up to ≥ 20 mm above the surface of the roof. Asphalt shingles can be badly affected by the weather or suffer mechanical damage. Once they are cracked and worn they are no longer serviceable and must be replaced. It is advisable to replace the sheathing at the same time. An old roof can also serve as a substrate for a new covering of asphalt shingles. [06] However, this double roof covering is always recommended because it is not very even, and the thicker covering means that junctions and terminations can no longer be properly executed.

#### References

[01] ABC der Bitumen-Bahnen, Technische Regeln; ed. vdd Industrieverband Bitumen-Dach- und Dichtungsbahnen e.V.; Frankfurt/M.: vdd, 1991
[02] Braun, E.: Bitumen, Anwendungsbezogene Baustoffkunde: Cologne, R. Müller, 1987
[03] DIN EN 544: Bitumen shingles with mineral and/or synthetic reinforcement; Berlin: Beuth, 1998
[04] Rehm, G.; Werkstoffe im Bauwesen, vol. 1 & 2; manuscript; Stuttgart: Institute of Building Materials, 1984
[05] Scholz, W.; Knoblauch, H.; Ettel, W.-E.; Fleischmann, H. D.; Hiese, W.; Kutzner, J.; Kutzner, W.; ed. Hiese, W.: Baustoffkenntnis 13th ed.; Düsseldorf: Werner, 1995
[06] Zentralverband des Deutschen Dachdeckerhandwerks; Fachverband Dach-, Wand- und Abdichtungstechnik e. V.: Fachregel für Dachdeckungen mit Bitumenschindeln; Cologne, R. Müller, 2001

## Flat overlapping elements of clay and concrete

Materials, components, laying

### Clay

Raw materials, manufacture, properties

Raw materials
Clay roof tiles are formed from loam, clay or clayey materials and then fired. The clay is obtained from quarries with face shovels and other excavation plant. Deposits of pure clay are rare.The deposits usually contain quartz dust or quartz sand; in such cases we speak of loam. As a rule, clay roof tiles are made of loam with a clay content of 40–60%.

#### Manufacture

Preparation
As the natural deposits found do not always contain the right mixture of clay, the desired ratio has to be created subsequently. For instance, fat clays are made leaner by adding fine quartz sand or crushed fragments of clay roof tiles. Alternatively, fat clay can be added to sandy clay or heavy quartz constituents can be washed out in a centrifuge. Preparatory treatment breaks down the sedimentation structures of the loam or clay blocks. To do this, the coarse impurities are ground by heavy rollers in a pan mill, and the necessary additives such as lean/fat clay, fluidiser (lime) or substances to prevent efflorescence are fed into the clay mixer. Water is then added and over a period of 3–14 days (depending on type of clay and intended use) the mixture turns into a mouldable, homogeneous mass. The clay is ground down to the necessary grain size by the fine rollers of a pug mill.

Forming
Flat overlapping elements are usually produced by an extrusion process. The prepared raw material ready for forming is fed into a worm extruder with a die matching the required cross-section. Afterwards, the profiled ribbon of clay is cut to the required tile lengths. These are called wire-cut tiles, and both bullnose and interlocking tiles can be made by this extrusion process. [24]
Flat overlapping elements with an interlocking profile on all sides are produced in a press. These are called pressed tiles and include interlocking forms.
To give these tiles their shape, the extruder creates a flat ribbon of clay, which is then divided into "clots". These are fed to a turret press. A plunger forces the clots between the upper and lower dies, where they are pressed into the desired shape.

Colours

Natural colour
The natural colour of clay roof tiles is governed by the metal content of the raw material. Upon firing, iron hydroxides produce a deep red iron oxide. A higher manganese content gives rise to a dark brown colour. Light yellow clay roof tiles can be attributed to a low iron and high lime content. There are various ways of introducing other colours. [15]

Steam treatment
In this method clay roof tiles are produced by reducing the oxygen content in the iron oxide. After completion of finish firing, oil is introduced into the firing chamber, which removes the oxygen from the atmosphere through combustion. As the firing furnace is sealed to prevent the ingress of fresh air, the iron oxides in the clay are reduced to oxidulated iron. This results in a grey-blue colouring not unlike natural slate. Only clays rich in iron are suitable for steam treatment. [15]

Pigments
Owing to the elaborate and expensive technique involved, pigmented clay roof tiles are produced only very occasionally. Minerals that influence the colour after firing are added to the clay prior to its preparation. For instance, manganese compounds result in a dark brown colour. [15]

Engobe finish
This is the application – by immersion or spraying – of a matt, non-glaze-like coating prior to firing. Its purpose is to change the surface colour of the clay roof tile; however, the process has no influence on the quality of the tile. The engobe consists of a specially prepared clay slurry, to which appropriate minerals or metal oxides have been added to produce the desired colour. "Terra sigillata" – a glossy, open-pore, glaze-like coating – is also classed as an engobe. The material consists of readily melted clay that begins to sinter during firing and condenses to glass-like beads. However, as there is no final glass layer, this surface coating is not regarded as a glaze.

Glazing
Like the engobe, the glaze is applied to the moulded tile prior to firing. It consists of easily melted clay with a metal content, which may be coloured as required. This forms a glass-like, dense coating. The purpose of glazing is primarily aesthetic because it allows bright colours, black and white to be produced. Glazing achieves complete closure of the pores.

Firing process

The clay undergoes chemical changes during firing, resulting in final solidification. The sintering limit should not be reached for open-pore clay roof tiles. It is therefore necessary to heat the moulded tiles very slowly. In order to avoid steam blisters, they must be as dry as possible beforehand. They first pass through a drying chamber where the excess water is driven off at ≤ 120°C. The finish firing takes place at temperatures between 900°C and 1100°C (usually about 1050°C). Closed-pore clay roof tiles must be sintered and finish-fired at temperatures between 1200°C and 1300°C. After firing, the clay roof tiles must be cooled again just as carefully.

Correct coordination of these procedures is the prerequisite for an even colouring, the necessary elasticity and freedom from cracks, and the dimensional accuracy of the finished tiles. Duration of firing and firing temperature influence the hardness and weathering resistance of the tiles. The total firing process from heating to finish firing to cooling takes up to five days, depending on the quality of the clay and the properties of the moulded tiles. The tiles shrink by 8–10% for sandy clay, up to 12% for richer clays.

**Properties**

Colour

| Colour | Natural colour | Paler natural colour | Pigment | Engobe | Glaze |
|---|---|---|---|---|---|
| white | | | | | • |
| yellow | • | | | • | • |
| green | | | | • | • |
| blue | | | | • | • |
| red | • | | • | • | • |
| brown | • | | • | • | • |
| grey | | • | | • | • |
| black | | • | | • | • |

2.4.6.1 Colours

Chemical properties

Clay roof tiles are ceramic building materials and are wholly resistant to the effects of chemicals in the environment and to ultraviolet radiation. "Efflorescent salts, lime inclusions and other damaging substances should not be present in standard clay roof tiles in quantities that cause damage to such an extent that the clay roof tiles are made unsuitable for use as a rainproof roof covering. A small amount of segregation and chalking caused by salts is permissible." [10]

Quality control during production and monitoring by the manufacturer generally means that only good quality clay enters the production chain. In exceptional cases – with insufficient preparation – the clay may contain substances that influence its quality. These include calcium carbonate, quartz particles and organic materials, which have a bursting effect or cause hairline cracks, and efflorescent salts. These salts – all sulphur compounds – separate out under the effects of moisture and heat and migrate with the moisture to the surface, where they form a white coating. With large quantities of salt the clay roof tile is permanently damp and particles of clay can be spalled off by crystallisation. Barium carbonate can be added to counteract these effects; this binds the salts by forming insoluble barium sulphate. Another possibility is to siliconise the clay roof tiles. However, the silicon is washed out after a while and closes the pores until then.

As a rule, efflorescence on a roof is harmless and affects the appearance only temporarily. The standard permits a small amount of segregation.

Physical properties

Loadbearing capacity

Mechanical strength is tested by applying a point load.

| Roof tile type | Bullnose | Wire-cut interlocking clay<br>Pressed interlocking clay |
|---|---|---|
| Form | flat | flat exposed face |
| Loadbearing capacity [N] | ≥ 600 | ≥ 900 |

2.4.6.2 Loadbearing capacity, requirements [10]

Weight

The loading assumptions are specified in DIN 1055 part 1, section 7.11.1 (see Part 2 "Loadbearing structure").

Characteristic values

| | |
|---|---|
| Density | 1.6–2.0 [g/cm$^3$] |
| Bending strength | 8–30 [N/mm$^2$] |
| Tensile strength | 1–4 [N/mm$^2$] |

2.4.6.3 Characteristic values

Dimensional stability

Not only the protection from the weather depends on dimensional stability. This aspect also has an effect on laying the roof tiles and on their mechanical strength. Therefore, dimensions, twisting and warping must lie within the tolerances given in table 2.4.6.4. Checking dimensional stability relates to the deviation of two opposing clay tile corners from the plane of the tile.

| Roof tile type | Bullnose, wire-cut/pressed interlocking clay | |
|---|---|---|
| Form | flat, flat exposed face | |
| Length [mm] | ≤ 300 | >300 |
| Deviation from the flat [%] | ≤ 2.0 | ≤ 1.5 |
| Deviation from straightness [%] | ≤ 2.0 | ≤ 1.5 |
| Deviation in length/width [%] | +/- 2.0 | |

2.4.6.4 Geometric characteristic values; permissible tolerances [10]

Water permeability

Clay roof tiles must be permeable to water. Their natural porosity causes new clay roof tiles to absorb a relatively large amount of water; on average ≤ 0.5/≤ 0.8 cm$^3$/cm$^2$ per day may seep through. [10] After a while the pores become clogged with airborne dust and so the relative water permeability gradually decreases.

Frost resistance

Clay roof tiles must be resistant to frost. They should not suffer damage due to the effects of frost, i.e. surface crazing, spalling, bursting, fractures or slate-like cleavage. The tests to assess the frost resistance vary with the climatic zone [09, 10]:

- Test for the Benelux countries:
  ≥ 24 freeze-thaw cycles after vacuum impregnation with alternating frost exposure of the upper side, -15°C and -5°C/water-bath +15°C.
- Test for Austria, Switzerland, Czech Republic, Germany, Denmark, Iceland, Norway, Sweden and Finland:
  ≥ 150 freeze-thaw cycles after steeping with frost exposure of the upper side, -15°C, with sprinkling/water-bath +5°C to -10°C.
- Test for Spain, France, Greece, Italy and Portugal:
  ≥ 50 freeze-thaw cycles after vacuum impregnation with frost exposure on all sides, -15°C/water-bath +12°C.
- Test for United Kingdom and Ireland:
  ≥ 100 freeze-thaw cycles after steeping with frost exposure of the upper side, -15°C/warm air with sprinkling +3°C.

Behaviour in fire

Clay roof tiles are classed as an incombustible building material belonging to building materials class A 1.

## Concrete

Raw materials, manufacture, properties

#### Raw materials

The main constituents of concrete roof tiles are quartz sand (71%), Portland cement (18%) and water (7.5%). Added to this are rock flour made from limestone (3%), blastfurnace slag (hydraulic) and metal (mainly iron) oxides (0.5%) to provide colour. The upper limit of the grading curve for the sand is 4 mm.

#### Manufacture

Forming

The raw materials for the concrete are fed via an automatic metering plant into a mixer in accurate proportions by weight. After mixing, the fresh concrete is sent to the extrusion line. The concrete is placed on a profiled underlay and compacted under high pressure by the press-rollers. The compacted, profiled concrete leaves the extruder as a ribbon of material and is cut to length by pressure-controlled cutters. In the next operation the surfaces of the concrete roof tiles are refined. After this treatment the tiles spend 8–12 hours in hardening furnaces in which, at a defined temperature (50–60°C) and humidity, they reach their initial strength (60–70% of their final strength). The concrete roof tiles are then detached from the underlay and, following quality control measures, the surfaces are refined for a second time. Final hardening takes place during storage in the open air.

Coating

Concrete roof tiles are usually coated with an aqueous acrylate paint consisting of a polymer dispersion (~24%) on an acrylic-styrene basis, mineral flours and pigments (~17%) and water (~59%). This surface treatment is intended to protect the concrete against the effects of the weather, chemicals and mechanical damage. Crucial for the effectiveness of this surface protection is a low-porosity, compacted, close-grained substrate.

Colour

Theoretically, concrete roof tiles may be painted any colour. However, the range of colours is limited by the exclusive use of inorganic pigments. Only by using these can a light-fast colouring be achieved.
Concrete roof tiles are coloured by adding the pigments to the raw materials during mixing (homogeneous pigmentation). Colours such as black, brown, red and shades of these are possible using pure iron oxide pigments. Blue and green colours are achieved by using other inert metal oxides.
The slurries applied to the pigmented concrete roof tiles must have an even colouring. Here, an aqueous polymer dispersion serves as a binding agent for the pigments.

Concrete roof tiles are also produced with the natural colour of the concrete without any further colouring or surface treatment. Without this surface treatment, carbonation can lead to efflorescence on the surface of the tiles, although this is barely visible owing to the light grey colour of the concrete.

Surface finish

Apart from the roughness of the cement mortar, the surface of a flat concrete roof tile is smooth.

#### Properties

Chemical properties

Concrete can be attacked by chemicals through waters, soils and gases. These may have a solvent and/or expansive effect. Attack mainly takes place through diluted acids, which are formed in the air by gaseous pollutants. Examples of these pollutants are sulphur dioxide and nitrogen oxide, which dissolve in water to form sulphuric and nitric acid respectively ("acid rain"). The effect of solvent attack is confined to the surface and is negligible. But the expansive effect can burst the microstructure of the hydrated cement as a result of a severe increase in volume. Concrete technology measures to achieve adequate chemical resistance involve the choice of suitable materials, the production of dense concrete, and the very careful placing and curing of the concrete. [18]

Physical properties

Loadbearing capacity

Flat concrete roof tiles must reach the minimum loadbearing capacity given in table 2.4.6.5 at the latest 28 days after casting or upon leaving the precasting works.

| Type | without ribs | with ribs | |
|---|---|---|---|
| Form | flat | flat, flat exposed face | |
| Cover width [mm] | | ≤ 200 | |
| ≥ 300 | | | |
| Loadbearing capacity [N]*) | ≥ 550 | ≥ 800 | ≥ 1200 |

*) The loadbearing capacties for cover widths between 200 and 300 mm may be obtained by linear interpolation.

2.4.6.5 Loadbearing capacity, requirements [07]

Weight

The loading assumptions are specified in DIN 1055 part 1 (see Part 2 "Loadbearing structure").

Characteristic values

The manufacturers do not provide characteristic values for the materials.

Dimensional stability

Flat concrete roof tiles must be carefully stored for the whole of their long hardening time. Any deformations that occur may not exceed the values given in table 2.4.6.6.

| Roof tile type | without ribs | with ribs |
|---|---|---|
| Form | flat | |
| Deviation in cover width [mm] | +/-3 | +/-5 |
| Deviation in hanging length [mm] | +/-4 | |
| Deviation from a right-angle [mm] | +/-4 | |
| Deviation from the flat [mm, %]*) | ≤ 3, ≤ 1 | |

*) The higher figure governs.

2.4.6.6 Geometric characteristic values; permissible tolerances [07]

Water permeability, frost resistance

Well-compacted cement mortar or concrete has a low water permeability. The use of a low water/cement ratio (< 0.40) ensures that the hardened hydrated cement has few capillaries. Concrete roof tiles complying with the requirements of DIN EN 490 regarding loadbearing capacity (see tables 2.4.6.5 and 2.4.7.3) and water permeability (no dripping from the underside within 20 hours) are considered to be frost-resistant, provided these values are achieved after 25 freeze-thaw cycles. [08]

Behaviour in fire

Concrete roof tiles provide protection against sparks and radiant heat in accordance with DIN 4102. They are classed as an incombustible material belonging to building materials class A 1 to DIN 4102.

## Components

General elements, edge and special elements, form of supply

The components shown here are merely a selection from the complete range of clay and concrete roof tile products. Restricting the number of products is intended to assist clarity, as well as make the comparison and classification of the different forms easier.

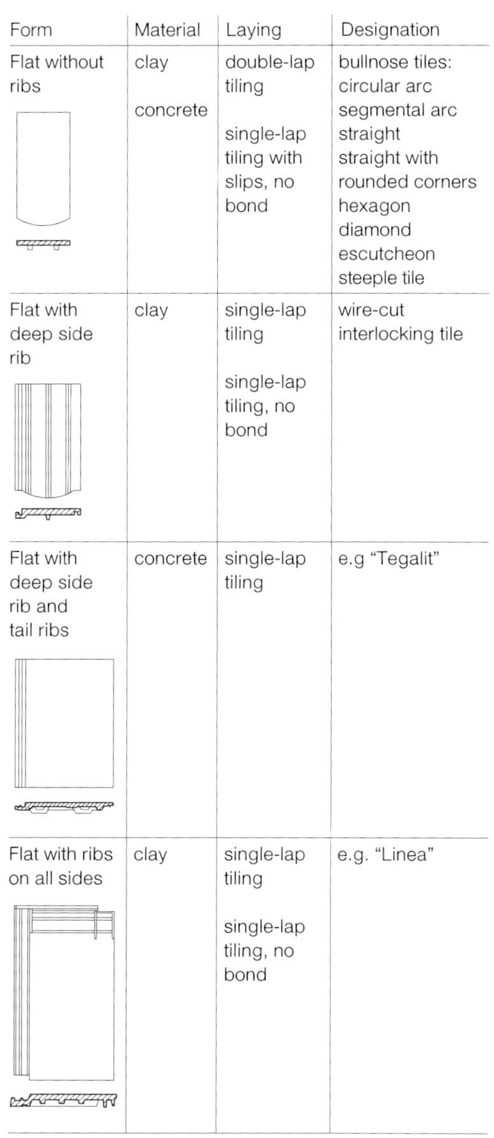

| Form | Material | Laying | Designation |
|---|---|---|---|
| Flat without ribs | clay<br>concrete | double-lap tiling<br>single-lap tiling with slips, no bond | bullnose tiles:<br>circular arc<br>segmental arc<br>straight<br>straight with rounded corners<br>hexagon<br>diamond<br>escutcheon<br>steeple tile |
| Flat with deep side rib | clay | single-lap tiling<br>single-lap tiling, no bond | wire-cut interlocking tile |
| Flat with deep side rib and tail ribs | concrete | single-lap tiling | e.g "Tegalit" |
| Flat with ribs on all sides | clay | single-lap tiling<br>single-lap tiling, no bond | e.g. "Linea" |

2.4.6.7 General elements

**General elements**

Flat overlapping elements without ribs (plain tiles) (see fig. 2.4.6.8)

- Bullnose tiles of concrete and clay

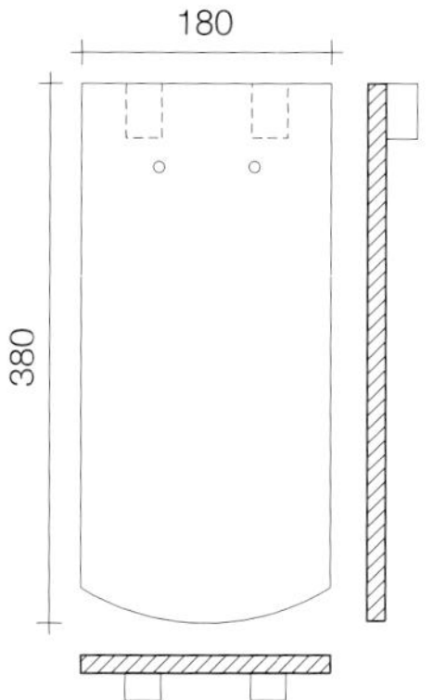


2.4.6.8 Bullnose tile; segmental arc [25]

Bullnose tiles consist of a plain element with one or two nibs. Near the head they normally have two holes for fixings.

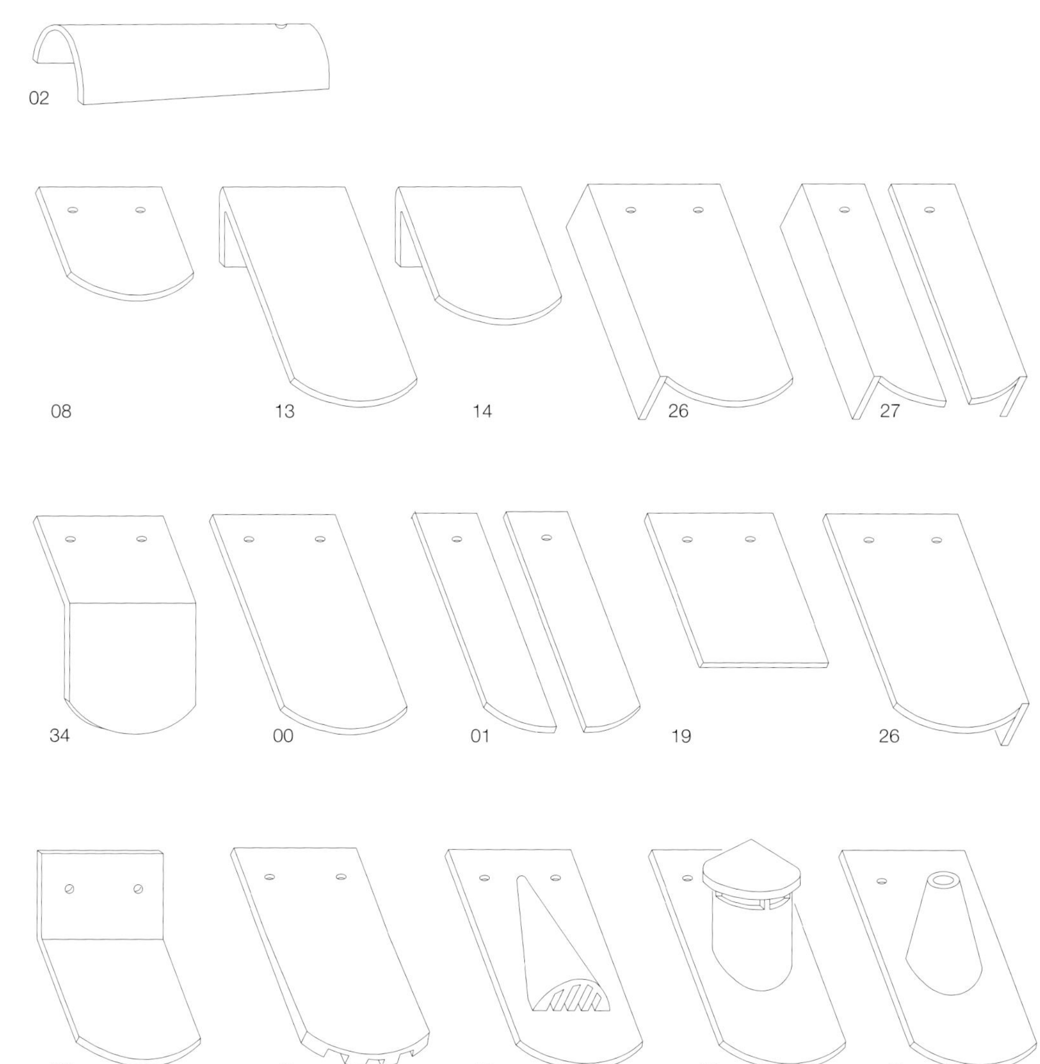


2.4.6.9 Bullnose tiles; general, edge and special elements; selection: 02 ridge or hip capping, 08 top course tile, 13 mono ridge tile, 14 mono ridge tile, 26 cloaked verge tile (left/right), 27 cloaked verge half tile (left/right), 00 standard bullnose tile, 01 bullnose half tile (left/right), 19 undereaves tile, 34 mansard tile, 38 angle tile, 42 ventilating tile, 44 tile with vapour vent, 45 tile with aerial mounting.
The numbers refer to table 2.4.6.16 and figure 2.4.6.18.

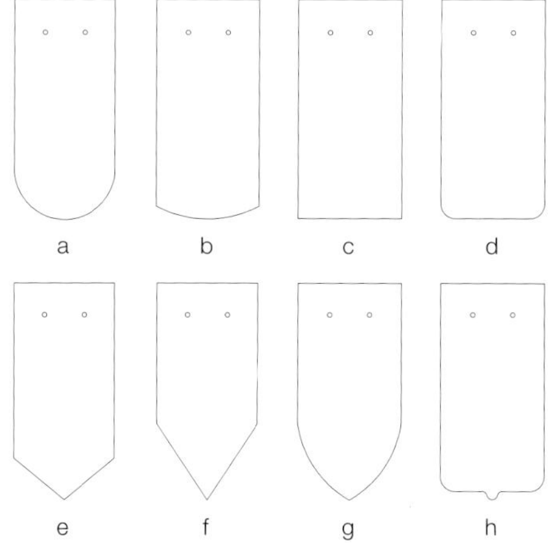


2.4.6.10 Bullnose tiles: a circular arc (with different dimensions to the steeple tile, b segmental arc, c straight, d straight with rounded corners, e hexagon, f diamond, g pointed arc, h escutcheon [25]

| | Concrete | Clay | | | | | | | |
|---|---|---|---|---|---|---|---|---|---|
| Forms | a | a | b | c | d | e | f | g | h |
| approx. weight [kg each] | 2.1 | 1.8 | 1.9 | 2.0 | 2.0 | 1.8 | 2.5 | 1.9 | 2.4 |
| Dimensions [mm] w x l x t | 168x420x14 | 160x380x5 | | | 180x380x5 | | | 140x280x5 | |
| approx.*) requirements [pcs/m²] | 35 | 40 | | | 35 | | | 68 | |
| Surface finish | smooth<br>red, brown speckled, slate grey on iron oxide basis | smooth, combed, brushed, grained<br>roughened<br>uncoated: natural red<br>coated: engobe colours<br>glaze colours | | | | | | | |

2.4.6.11 Bullnose tiles; characteristic values;
*) for double-lap or crown tiling

Flat overlapping elements with deep side ribs

- Wire-cut interlocking clay tile

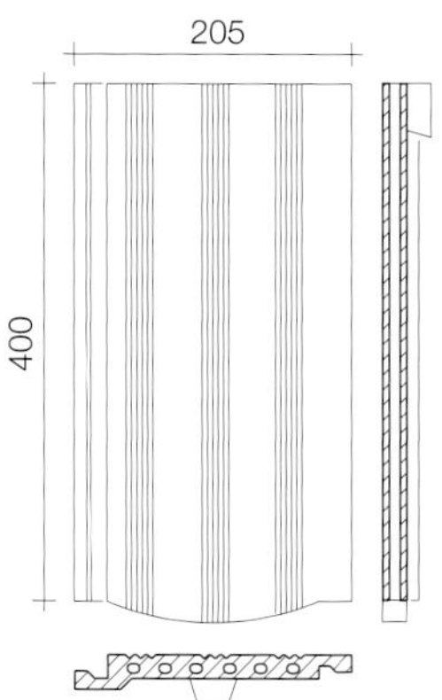


2.4.6.12 Wire-cut interlocking clay tile [25]

The wire-cut interlocking clay tile has a single, deep rib on both sides. When laid, this creates side joints – parallel to the grooves in the surface – facing upwards and open at the tail.

| approx. weight [kg each] | 2.5 | 3.0 |
|---|---|---|
| Dimensions w x l x t | 180 x 360 x 18 | 200 x 400 x 20 |
| approx. requirements [pcs/m²] | 20.5 | 16 |
| Surface finish | smooth/grooved; uncoated: engobe colours coated: engobe colours, glaze colours | |

2.4.6.13 Wire-cut interlocking clay tiles, characteristic values; w cover width, t thickness, l overall length

Flat overlapping elements with deep side ribs and tail ribs

- Flat concrete roof tile with deep side ribs

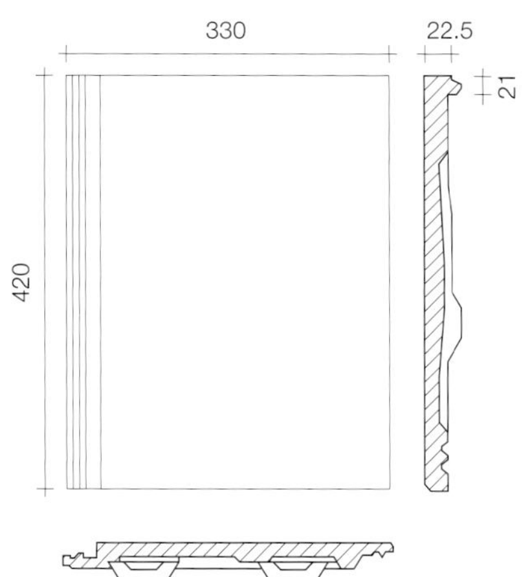


2.4.6.14 Flat concrete roof tile with deep side and tail ribs [03, 25]

Flat concrete roof tiles have deep twin ribs on each side and twin ribs at the tail. The ribs at the sides are visible from above as a joint in the roof covering and are open at the tail end.

Weight: approx. 5.3 kg each
Surface finish: smooth
dyed: red, dark brown, grey, dark grey, blue, dark blue
synthetic coating on acrylate basis
Requirements: approx. 10 pcs/m²

Flat overlapping elements with ribs on all sides

- Flat pressed interlocking clay tile.

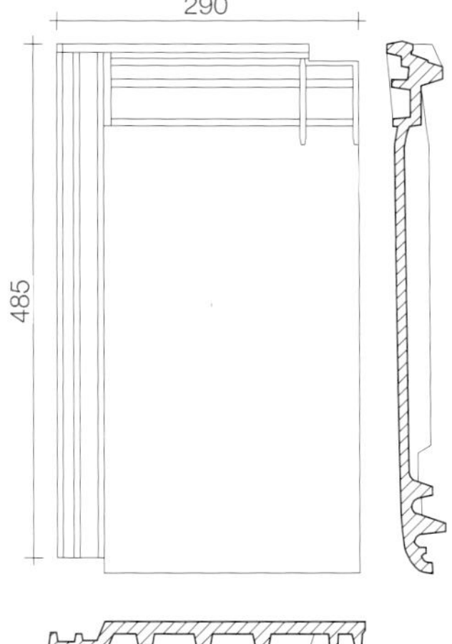


2.4.6.15 Flat clay roof tile with ribs on all sides

This flat pressed interlocking clay tile has twin ribs on all sides. These are deep on the two sides and are not covered. A rounded tail covers the end of the ribs.

Weight: approx. 4.0 kg each
Surface finish: smooth
uncoated: sinter red, sinter grey, sinter anthracite
Requirements: approx. 10.5 pcs/m²

**Edge and special elements**

According to the DIN standard the form of edge and special elements in clay and concrete is a matter for the manufacturers and is thus not standardised. These profiled parts must be designed so that, together with the standardised clay/concrete roof tiles, a proper roof covering can be achieved.

| | Clay | Concrete |
|---|---|---|
| 00 standard tile | • | • |
| 01 half tile | • | • |
| 02 ridge or hip capping / vent | • | • |
| 03 half ridge or hip capping | • | |
| 04 ridge or hip end tile, right-hand | • | • |
| 05 ridge end tile, left-hand | • | • |
| 06 ridge intersection | • | |
| 07 ridge/hip intersection tile | • | • |
| 08 top course tile | • | |
| 09 top course half tile | • | |
| 10 double roll verge/ridge intersection | • | |
| 11 ridge/verge cloaked intersection (left/right) | • | |
| 12 top course ventilating tile | • | • |
| 13 mono ridge tile | • | • |
| 14 mono ridge half tile | • | • |
| 15 double roll verge/mono ridge intersection | • | |
| 16 cloaked verge/mono ridge intersection | • | • |
| 17 top course tile | • | |
| 18 top course half tile | • | |
| 19 undereaves tile | • | • |
| 20 double roll verge/eaves intersection | • | |
| 21 cloaked verge/eaves intersection | • | |
| 22 cloaked verge/eaves intersection, half t. | • | • |
| 23 valley tile | • | |
| 24 double roll verge top course tile | • | • |
| 25 key top course tile | • | |
| 26 cloaked verge tile (left/right) | • | • |
| 27 cloaked verge tile (left/right) | • | • |
| 28 side abutment tile (left/right) | • | |
| 29 side abutment top course tile | • | |
| 30 wall abutment tile | • | |
| 31 wall abutment half tile | • | |
| 32 wall abutment double roll verge tile | • | |
| 33 cloaked verge/wall abutment intersection | • | |
| 34 mansard tile | • | • |
| 35 mansard half tile | • | • |
| 36 mansard double roll verge tile | • | |
| 37 mansard verge tile (left/right) | • | • |
| 38 angle tile | • | • |
| 39 angle half tile | • | |
| 40 angle double roll verge tile | • | |
| 41 cloaked angle verge tile (left/right) | • | • |
| 42 ventilating tile | • | • |
| 43 snowguard tile | • | • |
| 44 tile with vapour vent | • | • |
| 45 tile with aerial mounting | • | • |
| 46 rooflight tile | • | • |
| 47 step support tile | | • |
| 48 photovoltaic tile | • | • |

2.4.6.16 Edge and special elements; designations

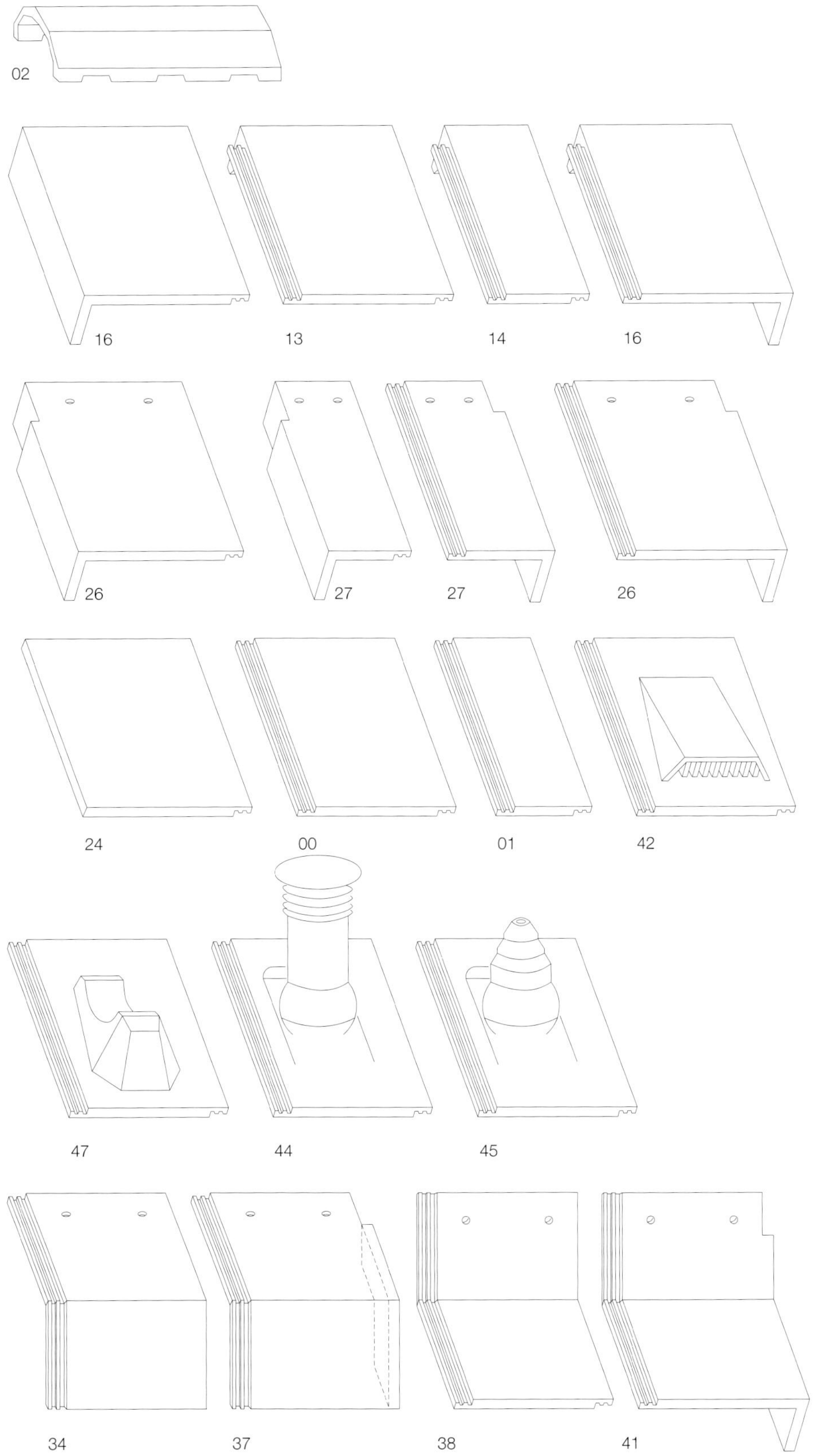

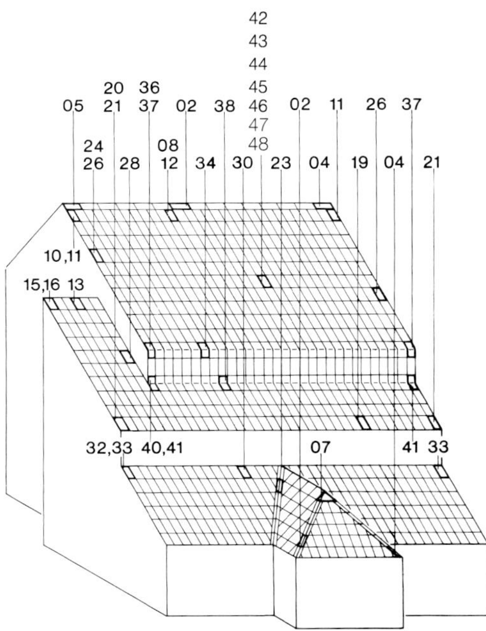


2.4.6.18 Clay and concrete roof tiles; edge and special elements

Not all the special tiles listed in table 2.4.6.16 and illustrated in 2.4.6.18 are available from every manufacturer. However, a number of manufacturers also produce ornamental tiles to match historical types. These ornamental tiles primarily involve ridge cappings and ridge finials.

#### Form of supply

As a rule, concrete and clay roof tiles are packaged in packets or stacked on pallets and delivered on goods vehicles equipped with a small loading/unloading crane.

### Laying

Conditions for laying, fixing, auxiliary materials, additional measures, details, supporting construction, maintenance and repair

#### Conditions for laying

The roofing trade guidelines and the details provided by the manufacturers should be followed when covering a pitched roof with clay or concrete roof tiles. If the recommendations are applied properly, such roofs are considered to be rainproof.

2.4.6.17 Flat concrete roof tiles; general, edge and special elements; selection: 02 ridge or hip capping, 16 cloaked verge/mono ridge intersection (left/right), 13 mono ridge, 14 mono ridge half tile, 26 cloaked verge tile (left/right), 27 cloaked verge half tile (left/right), 24 double roll verge tile (left/right), 00 standard tile, 01 half tile, 42 ventilating tile, 47 step support tile, 44 tile with vapour vent, 45 tile with aerial mounting, 34 mansard tile, 37 mansard verge tile (left/right), 38 angle tile, 41 cloaked angle verge tile (left/right).
The numbers refer to table 2.4.6.16 and figure 2.4.6.18.

Roof pitch
The recommended roof pitch is understood to be the minimum slope at which a roof covering has been proven rainproof under practical conditions without any additional measures. The recommended roof pitch should be increased by at least 5° for valleys. The recommended roof pitch should also be maintained at sprockets. Additional measures may be necessary under certain conditions.

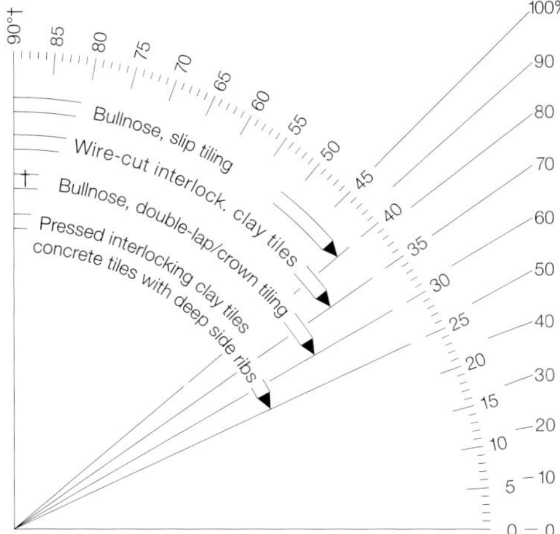


2.4.6.19 Recommended roof pitches in relation to roof covering [25]

Laps, clear spacing of battens
The headlap depends on the roof pitch and the form of the tiles. Tile length, headlap and clear spacing of battens are all interrelated. The clear spacing of the battens is the distance from the upper edge of a tiling batten to the next batten. The minimum headlap should not be reduced. The recommended headlaps are specified with the individual types of roof covering.
When not specified otherwise, the clear spacing of the battens for clay and concrete roof tiles, with and without interlocking ribs, is calculated as follows:

max. clear spacing of battens =
length of tile – min. headlap

The side lap of flat clay and concrete roof tiles with interlocking ribs is determined by the ribs. The headlap varies. Roof pitch and type of tile govern the minimum headlap.

**Roof covering of flat overlapping elements without ribs**
Bullnose tiles, types of tiling
- double-lap tiling
- crown tiling
- slip tiling

Double-lap and crown tiling can be carried out as follows:
- dry
- dry with internal bedding at transverse joints
- with mortar strip between bedding and covering layers,
- fully bedded in mortar, i.e. with mortar strip on bedding and covering layers
  This last method requires the approval of the tile manufacturer.

- Double-lap tiling

In double-lap tiling only one course of bullnose tiles is hung on each batten. The tiles are laid with a half-tile offset so that the pattern of joints is interrupted at every course. The covering layers overlap such that the third course just overlaps the first.

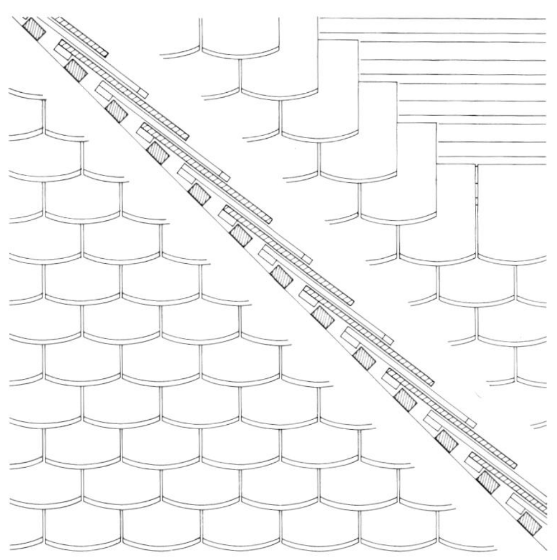

2.4.6.20 Double-lap tiling

The maximum clear spacing of the battens for double-lap tiling using bullnose tiles is as follows:

max. clear spacing of battens =
(length of bullnose tile – min. headlap)/2

| Roof pitch | headlap [mm] | |
|---|---|---|
| | clay | concrete |
| < 30° | 90 | 90 |
| | (additional measures are necessary) | |
| ≥ 30° ≤ 35° | 90 | 90 |
| > 35° ≤ 40° | 80 | 80 |
| > 40° ≤ 45° | 70 | 70 |
| > 45° ≤ 60° | 60 | 60 |
| > 60° | 50 | |

2.4.6.21 Minimum headlaps for double-lap tiling [25]

Eaves and ridge courses should be laid as for crown tiling unless special eaves and ridge tiles are being used.
Bullnose tiles are laid with a small gap (2–3 mm) between the sides of the tiles to accommodate settlement and movement of the roof structure.

- Crown tiling

In crown tiling two courses of bullnose tiles (bedding and covering layer) are hung on each batten. Again, the tiles are laid with a half-tile offset. Both layers together form one course and overlap the course below such that the pattern of joints of the covering layers forms a straight line from eaves to ridge.

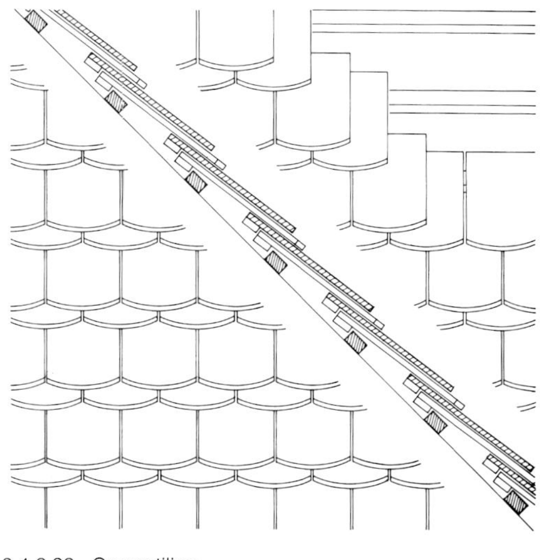

2.4.6.22 Crown tiling

The maximum clear spacing of the battens for crown tiling using bullnose tiles is as follows:

max. clear spacing of battens =
length of bullnose tile – min. headlap

| Roof pitch | headlap [mm] | |
|---|---|---|
| | clay | concrete |
| < 30° | 90 | 90 |
| 90 | (additional measures are necessary) | |
| ≥ 30° ≤ 35° | 90 | 90 |
| > 35° ≤ 40° | 80 | 80 |
| > 40° ≤ 45° | 70 | 70 |
| > 45° ≤ 60° | 60 | 60 |
| > 60° | 50 | |

2.4.6.23 Minimum headlaps for crown tiling [25]

• Slip tiling
This is a form of single-lap tiling, but without side laps. Eaves and ridge courses should be laid as for crown tiling. A slip ≥ 50 mm wide is laid beneath every side joint. The slips should not be visible from outside.

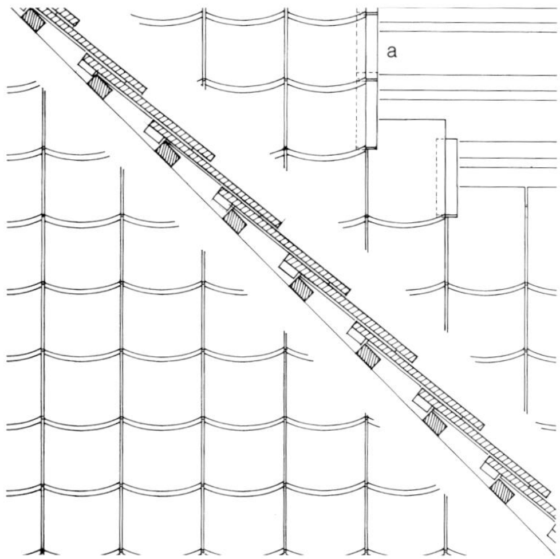


2.4.6.24 Slip tiling: a slip

The headlap and the rafter length determine the clear spacing of the battens for this type of tiling.

max. clear spacing of battens =
length of bullnose tile – min. headlap

| Roof pitch | Headlap [mm] | |
|---|---|---|
| | clay | concrete |
| < 40° | 170 | 170 |
| | (additional measures are necessary) | |
| ≥ 40° ≤ 45° | 160 | 160 |
| > 45° ≤ 50° | 150 | 150 |
| > 50° ≤ 55° | 140 | 140 |
| > 55° | 130 | 130 |

2.4.6.25 Minimum headlaps for slip tiling [25]

**Roof covering of flat overlapping elements with deep side ribs**
Wire-cut interlocking clay tiles

Wire-cut interlocking clay tiles can be laid with or without a half-tile offset. This tiling is carried out dry. The minimum headlap is 120 mm.

max. clear spacing of battens =
length of wire-cut interlocking clay tile – 120 mm

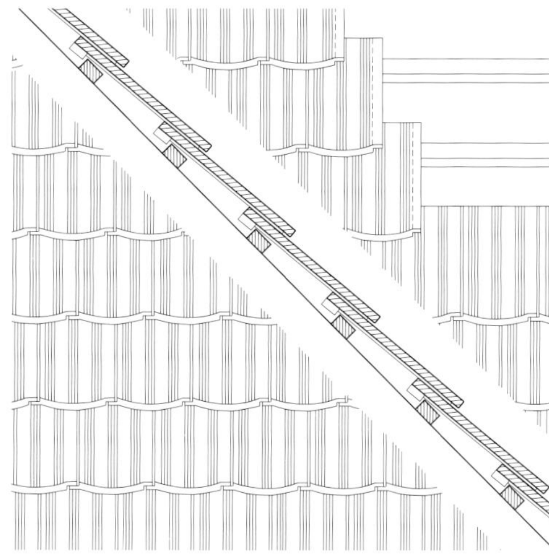

2.4.6.26 Roof covering of wire-cut interlocking clay tiles

**Roof covering of flat overlapping elements with side and tail ribs**
Concrete roof tiles

These concrete roof tiles are laid from right to left with a half-tile offset. The headlap varies. The cover widths of wire-cut interlocking clay tiles and concrete roof tiles with side ribs are determined in trials with 10 components (see “Profiled overlapping elements of clay and concrete – Laying”).

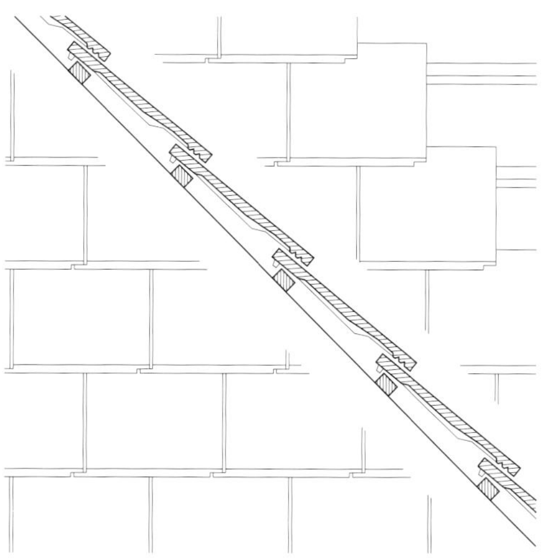

2.4.6.27 Roof covering of flat concrete tiles with deep side and tail ribs

| Roof pitch | Headlap [mm] |
|---|---|
| < 25° (additional measures are necessary) | 105 |
| ≥ 25° ≤ 35° | 95 |
| > 35° | 80 |

2.4.6.28 Minimum headlaps for concrete tiles with deep side and tail ribs [25]

**Roof covering of flat overlapping elements with ribs on all sides**
Pressed interlocking clay tiles

These tiles with ribs on all sides can be laid in a bond or with side joints aligned. Because they have deep side ribs, laying with a half-tile offset is recommended.

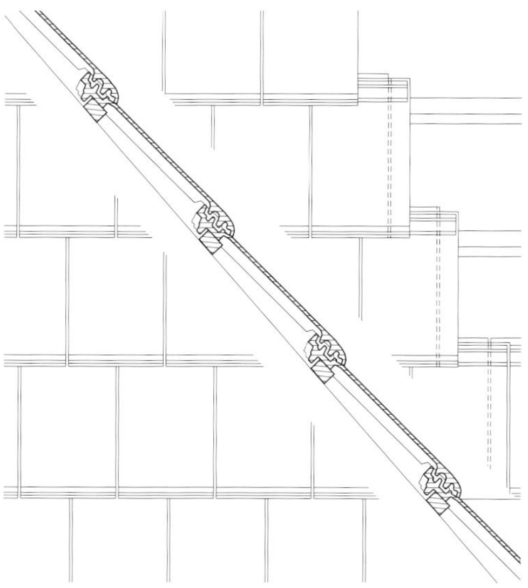

2.4.6.29 Roof covering of pressed interlocking clay tiles

The headlap and side lap are determined by the ribs. The cover length and cover width of pressed interlocking clay tiles are determined by trials in each case (see “Profiled overlapping elements of clay and concrete – Laying”).

**Fixing**
Generally, clay and concrete roof tiles are laid loose on the roof surface. However, if wind suction exceeds the self-weight of the covering layer, these tiles must be secured against uplift. Therefore, on steep roofs ≥ 65° all tiles must be fixed.
On less steep roofs, edges and corners – depending on roof form and roof pitch (see “Loadbearing structure – Wind loads”) – must be secured with a certain number of fixings.

$$n = (W - G)/BL$$

n number of fixings, W wind suction [kN/m$^2$], G self-weight [kN/m$^2$], BL design load (loading capacity) of fixing [kN/fixing] (BL ≥ 0.15 kN/fixing)

Such edges measure l/8 ≥ 1 m (l = shorter length of roof on plan) or ≤ 2 m (for l ≤ 30 m). Around penetrations (L ≥ 35 cm, W ≥ 50 cm) such as dormer windows and chimneys, an edge zone of l/2 ≥ 1 m ≤ 2 m (l = longer length of roof on plan) is recommended.
In these areas every third, better still every second or indeed every, roof tile in the covering layer should be fixed.

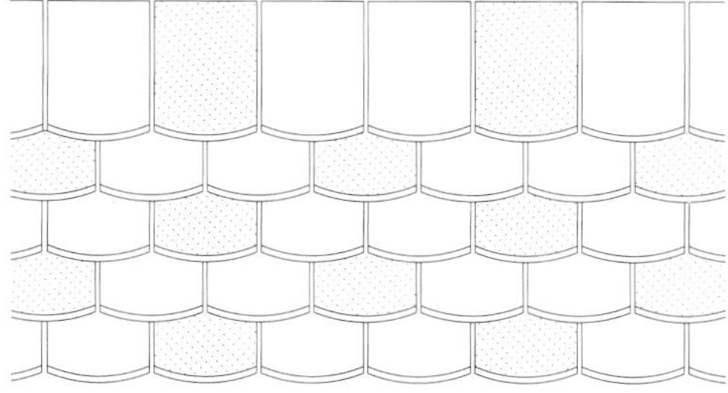

2.4.6.30 Fixings on the surface, at corners and edges

At the edges of the roof (ridge of monopitch or duopitch roof, hip, verge) all tiles should be fixed individually with a force of 0.6 kN/m.

Means of fixing
- Nails
- Annular nails
- Screws
- Clips

These must be at least protected against corrosion or – when exposed to the weather or in conjunction with bitumen sheets laid over the tiling battens – corrosion-resistant (steel with galvanising ≥ 50 μm, stainless steel)
- Binding wire

This must always be corrosion-resistant (copper, stainless steel).
- Mortar

(lime:cement:sand = 2:1:8)
This cannot be regarded as securing tiles against wind suction. [25]

**Auxiliary materials**
- Metals

Sheet aluminium, sheet copper, sheet zinc, milled laid and rustproofed iron in various thicknesses.
- Slips

Slips of wood, plastic or metal (length = tile length – 40 mm).
- Other materials

Bituminous felt, bituminous sheets laid over tiling battens, straw laid over tiling battens, glass wool, strips of glass fibre, felt and jute.

**Additional measures**
Additional measures should be allowed for during planning and construction when the reliability of the roof covering has to satisfy enhanced requirements:
- for roof pitches below the recommended roof pitch
- to meet the stipulations of the authorities
- in more severe climatic conditions (wind, driving snow, driving rain, humidity, solar radiation)
- for steep roof pitches
- for rooftop structures

Additional measures, depending on material and type of tiling, are:
- increasing the roof pitch
- providing mortar (≥ recommended roof pitch)
- bedding tiles in sheets laid over tiling battens (≥ recommended roof pitch)
- fixings
- roofing felt (≥ recommended roof pitch – 6°)
- boarding (≥ recommended roof pitch – 10°)
- waterproof roofing felt (< recommended roof pitch – 10°)
- thermal insulation systems that also fulfil the functions of boarding (see "Layers – Secondary waterproofing/covering layer")

**Details**
Ridge, hip, eaves, valley, verge, junction with wall, penetrations, dormer window, crank

Ridge
The ridge should be covered in the opposite direction to the prevailing wind. The ridge capping can be laid dry or bedded in mortar. In double-lap tiling the ridge course must be laid in such a way that no open side joints ensue. That can be achieved with a crown course or with a 3/4 bullnose tile as an additional covering layer.

Ridge capping laid dry
When laying the ridge capping dry, the tiling battens at the ridge must be attached a short distance back from the apex. On clay tile roofs the distance from the apex depends on roof pitch, batten thickness and type of tile. On roofs employing flat interlocking concrete tiles the topmost tiling battens on both sides are fixed about 40 mm back from the apex.
Prefabricated top course tiles should be hung on the battens at the ridge according to the roofing trade guidelines and the manufacturer's instructions and fixed in place. Bonnet ridge cappings in concrete or clay overlap each other at least 40 mm and are held in place with corrosion-resistant clips, nails or screws. Interlocking ridge tiles have a predetermined overlap.

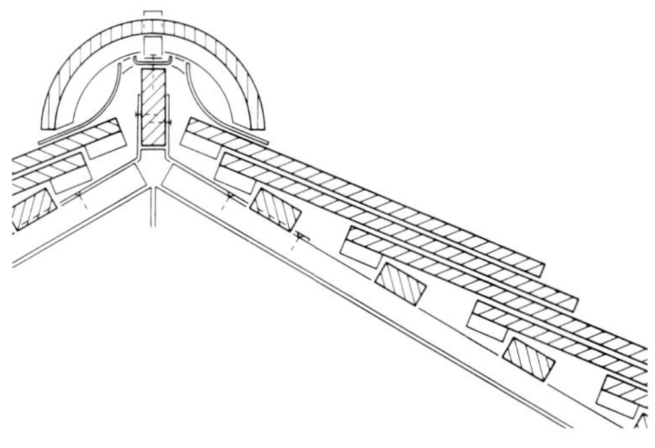

2.4.6.31 Clipped ridge; ridge capping with plastic ventilation element and adjacent crown tiling

Ridge capping bedded in mortar
The ridge tiles are mounted in such a way that the mortar recedes to leave the bottom outer edges of the clay or concrete ridge tile forming a drip edge. Bedding in a full bed of mortar is not permitted. A strip of mortar is also required on the narrow end of the bonnet ridge capping for bedding the next ridge tile.
Pigments may be added to the mortar.
Each end of the ridge is finished with an appropriate special end tile. These, too, may be sealed with mortar.
Ridge tiles laid in mortar should be additionally secured with at least one corrosion-resistant wire (≥ 0.5 mm) per ridge tile.

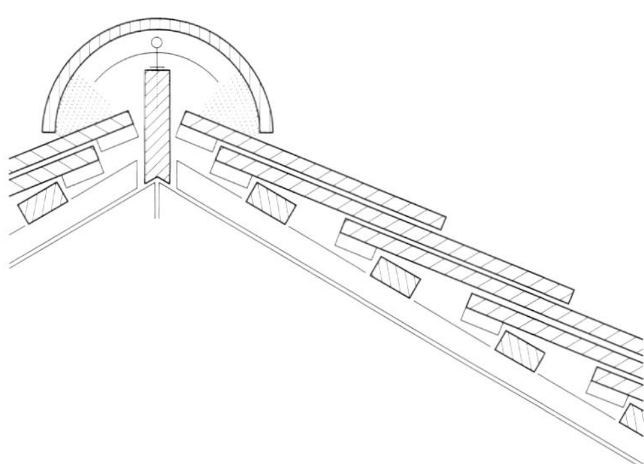

2.4.6.32 Ridge bedded in mortar; ridge capping with adjacent 3/4 bullnose tile; binding wire securing capping against uplift due to wind suction

Adequate vents at the ridge are necessary to complete the roof ventilation measures. Even excellent transverse ventilation cannot fully replace vents at the ridge. Ridge vent tiles can be substituted for standard ridge tiles along the whole length of the ridge (see "Layers – Ventilation").

Ridge to monopitch roof
This detail may use specially shaped clay or concrete tiles, folded sheet metal or a combination of both. These elements are available in various lengths.

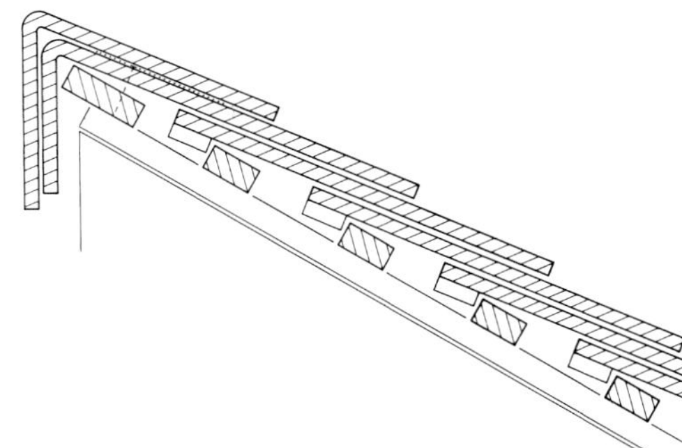

2.4.6.33 Ridge to monopitch roof, with nailed monopitch ridge bullnose tile and half-length monopitch ridge bullnose tile bedded in mortar

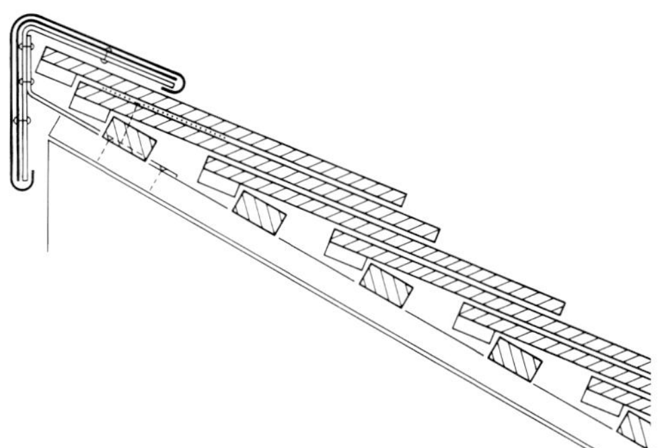

2.4.6.34 Ridge detail on monopitch roof; folded sheet metal

Elements for the ridge to a monopitch roof should be fixed to the construction below with screws, nails, clips or binding wire to prevent uplift. The special clay or concrete tiles supplied by various manufacturers are available with different vertical leg lengths. The ventilation is carried out either via a vent on the surface of the roof or – with an overhanging roof – via the soffit (see "Layers – Ventilation").

Hip

The clay or concrete roof tiles should be trimmed parallel to the hip such that there is only a narrow joint. Water must not be able to penetrate below the hip into the construction below. The trimmed clay or concrete roof tiles must be secured to prevent them sliding down the roof slope. The hip capping is laid dry, as at the ridge, or bedded in mortar. When bedding them in mortar, the hip tiles must be secured by rustproofed binding wire, nails, screws or clips attached to the battens on the hip. Otherwise, the hip capping bedded in mortar follows the same principles as for the ridge.

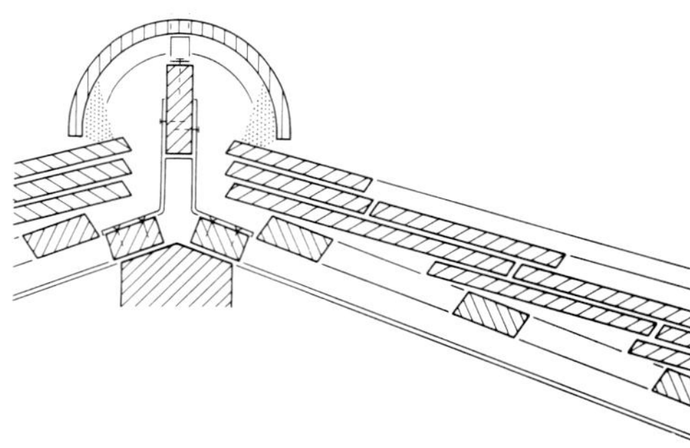

2.4.6.35 Clipped hip capping sealed with mortar

Eaves

The necessary ventilation openings should be allowed for when tiling the eaves. So that the eaves course has the same pitch as all subsequent courses, double battens, feather-edge boards or similar are required. The eaves course can be laid with or without projecting beyond the construction below. Bullnose tiles should be secured to prevent uplift.
The eaves course for double-lap tiling must be laid in such a way that there are no open side joints. This can be achieved with a crown course or with a 3/4 bullnose tile as an additional covering layer.

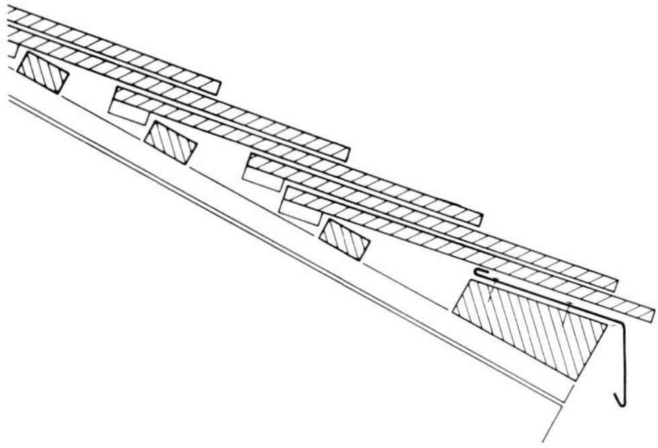

2.4.6.36 Eaves detail for crown tiling

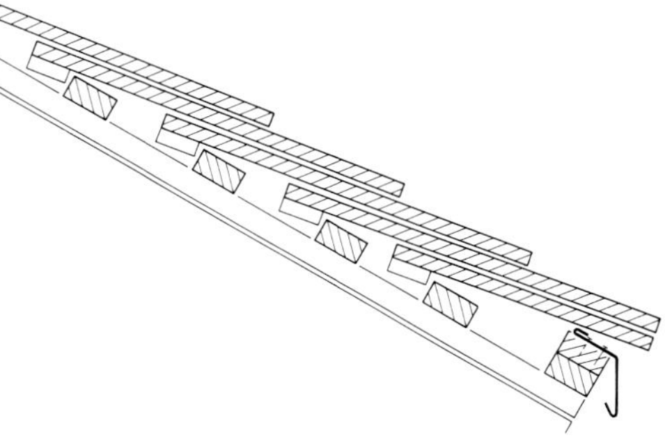

2.4.6.37 Eaves detail with 3/4 bullnose tile and under-eaves bullnose tile

Valley

Valleys for roof coverings of clay or concrete tiles are made of metal, PVC roofing felt, bullnose tiles or special valley elements. We distinguish between lined and semi-swept valleys. The valley pitch (pitch of valley rafter) may not be less than the recommended value.

Lined valley

In a lined valley the material in the gutter is not integrated into the roof covering on the roof surfaces. The roof covering overlaps the gutter by a prescribed amount.

• Sheet metal valley

The roof covering must overlap the metal gutter by at least 100 mm. Starting with the eaves course, the roof covering material is laid as close as possible to the gutter (accessibility) to match the form of the valley. The clay or concrete roof tiles projecting into the valley are cut off with a disc cutter, drilled, and screwed or nailed to the battens or tied with a corrosion-resistant wire. Depending on requirements, the sheet metal gutter can be provided as a flat sheet, as a sheet metal channel ($h \geq 20$ mm, $b \geq 80$ mm) – especially suitable for interlocking clay or concrete tiles with a low rafter pitch – or a deep sheet metal channel with one or two baffles (see "Layers – Drainage"). The pitch of the valley should not be less than 15° for a flat sheet gutter. [25, 26]

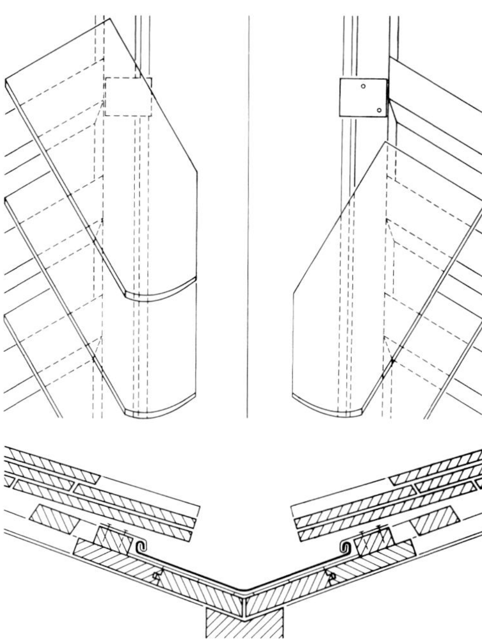

2.4.6.38 Lined valley with flat sheet metal valley

• Ribbed valley (see "Profiled overlapping elements of clay and concrete")

• Valley of bullnose tiles

Lined valleys with bullnose tiles are at least four tiles wide and always laid with a triple lap. The entire valley board should be covered with bitumen roofing felt with a coarsely sanded surface. To fix the gutter covering on steep roof pitches, thin battens can be nailed to the valley board. As valleys are always shallower than the adjoining roof surfaces, they also carry more water. The valley pitch of a lined valley with bullnose tiles must therefore be at least 30° [25] and the recommended roof pitch for bullnose clay or concrete tiling must be increased accordingly.

Semi-swept valley

In a semi-swept valley the courses on the roof surface are laid across the valley and match up with the courses on the other roof surfaces. Additional layers in the valley are integrated into these courses.

• Valley with metal soakers

Pieces of sheet metal are used for this type of valley. The clay or concrete tiles on the roof surface continue up to the middle of the valley, where they are cut to fit.

Every layer of tiles must have its own soaker underneath. The layers on both roof surfaces must therefore coincide. The soakers are integrated into the layers on the roof surfaces in such a way that they are not visible.

| Valley pitch | Headlap [mm] |
|---|---|
| ≤ 45° | 160 |
| > 45° | 140 |

2.4.6.39 Minimum headlaps for metal soakers [25, 26]

The layers on the roof surface must overlap the sides of the soakers by at least 200 mm. [25] This overlapping arrangement means that rainwater drains from soaker to soaker and, under normal conditions, no water can penetrate inwards. However, the pitch of the valley may not be less than 25°. [25]

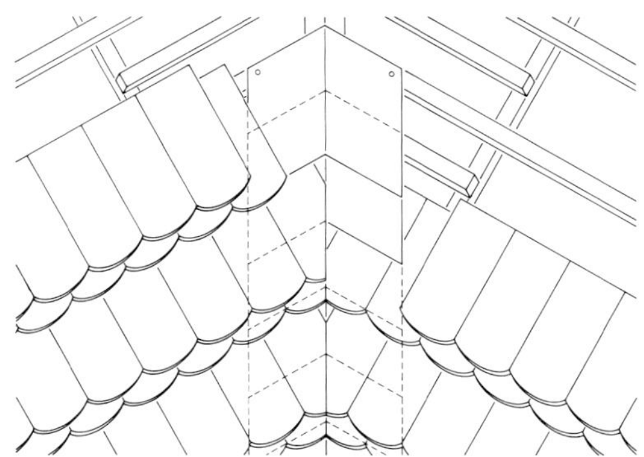

2.4.6.40 Mitred valley with metal soakers

• German semi-swept valley with bullnose tiles
Owing to the difference between pitch and length of roof surface and valley, the headlap must be such that the fourth tile overlaps the first by at least 10 mm. The outcome of this is that every course in the valley has to be divided into at least three layers, which makes it necessary to include an underlay. Valleys in double-lap and crown tiling are always laid with triple laps. The width of the valley should be no less than two whole tiles when the roof surfaces on both sides have the same pitch; otherwise, the width should be no less than one whole tile. As valleys carry a great deal of water, the pitch of a German semi-swept valley with bullnose tiles should not be less than 26°. There are other regional variations.

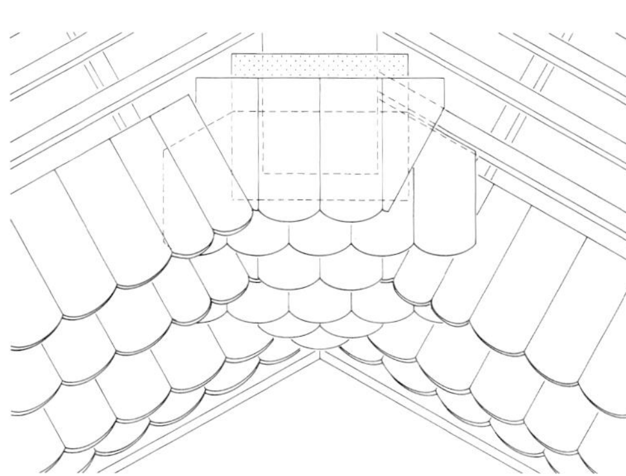

2.4.6.41 German semi-swept valley with bullnose tiles in double-lap tiling, width = 2 bullnose tiles

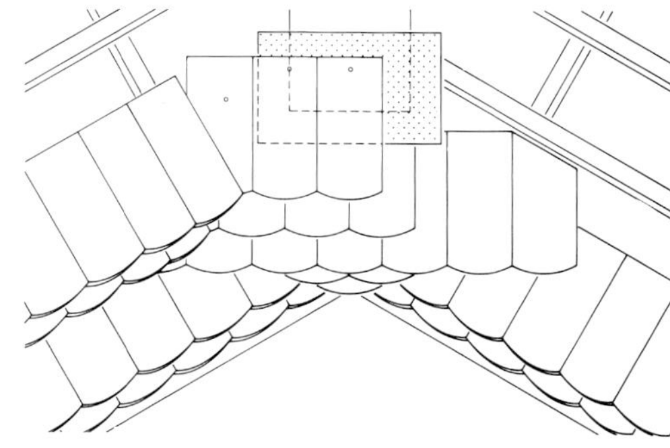

2.4.6.42 German semi-swept valley with bullnose tiles in crown tiling, width = 3 bullnose tiles

• Meschede valley
This type of swept valley makes use of special valley tiles to match the bullnose tiles on the roof surface and is only possible with double-lap tiling. Special valley tiles are available for valley pitches between 18° and 39°.

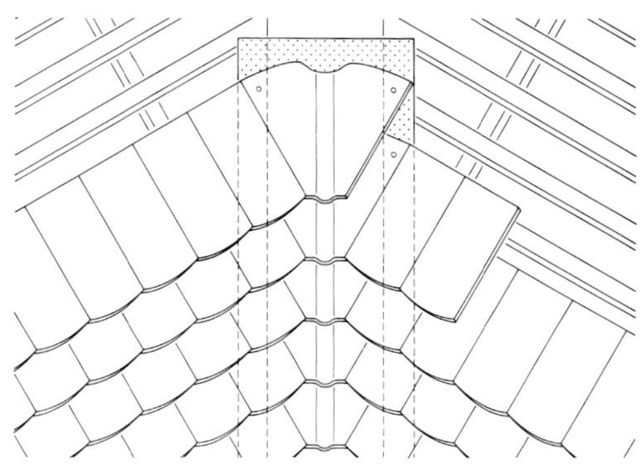

2.4.6.43 Meschede valley

• Swept valley
A swept valley is tiled with special tapering tiles. The valley board should first be covered with bitumen roofing felt. The minimum width of the valley is four tiles.
Double-lap tiling can only be used on a swept valley when the valley is short, e.g. between main roof and roof of gable- or hipped-end dormer. Otherwise, the swept valley is only possible with crown tiling at a pitch of at least 35°. [25]
Special valley tiles for the Meschede and swept valleys are no longer produced.

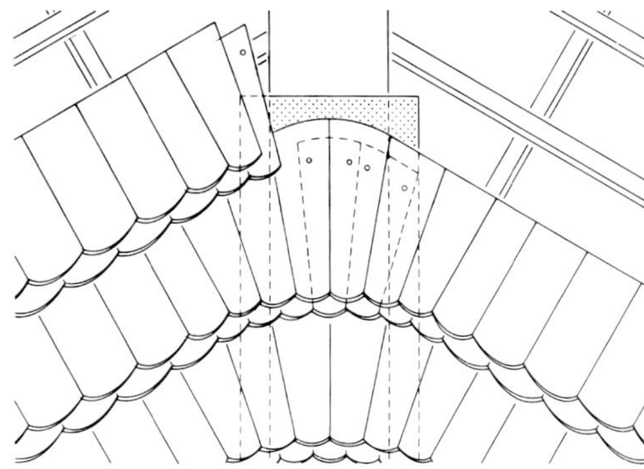

2.4.6.44 Swept valley

Verge
The detail at the verge can be realised in different ways:

- verge tile
- combination of general element and cloak
- sheet metal verge flashing
- verge gutter

All the verge elements – apart from the covering layer for crown tiling – must be fixed to the supporting construction. When laying verge tiles on masonry (verge without overhang), the distance between inside edge of verge tile and finished gable wall, or the outside edge of a timber frame, must be at least 10 mm. The tiling battens must be curtailed at least 20 mm short of any rendering. End tiles of concrete or

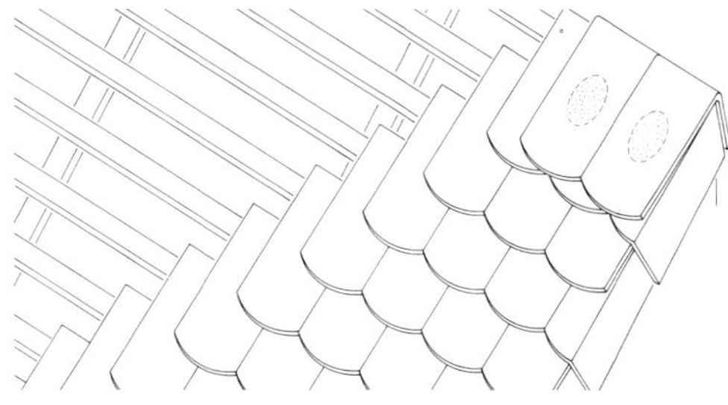

2.4.6.45 Verge without overhang, with special verge tiles

clay must project beyond the finished gable wall, or the outside edge of a timber frame, by at least 30 mm. The length of the building must be coordinated precisely with the overall width of the roof covering if there is no overhang at the verge. On the other hand, an overhang makes it easy to deal with any discrepancies.

Junction with wall
Water should never be drained towards the junction but rather away from it. As movements often take place at junctions (settlement, deflection etc.), the detail at this point must be able to accommodate these movements. The materials at the junction are often incorporated at an angle (folded sheet metal, tile fillets etc.) (see "Layers – Drainage").

Junction with wall at side
These junctions are realised with special tiles, metal soakers or metal flashings with a flat or channel gutter. Soakers must overlap at least one side joint in the roof covering (≥ 200 mm). In the case of a channel gutter, care should be taken to ensure that the tiles overlap by a sufficient amount.

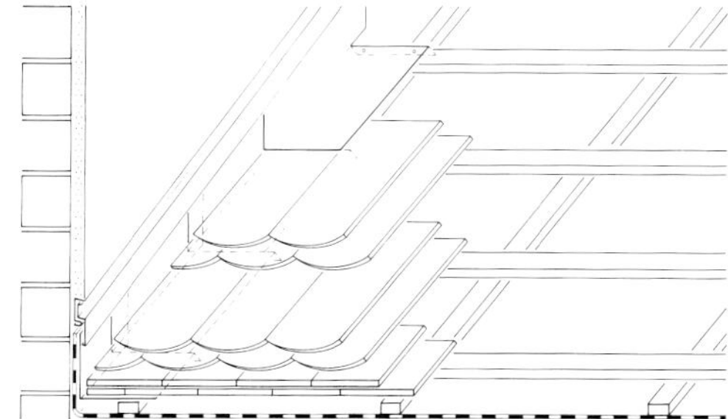

2.4.6.46 Junction with wall at side of roof slope, with metal soakers

Junction with wall at top of slope
Flashings should be turned up the wall for at least 100 mm above the level of the roof covering. They must overlap the clay or concrete roof tiles by an amount equal to the minimum headlap of the tiles on the roof surface. [24]

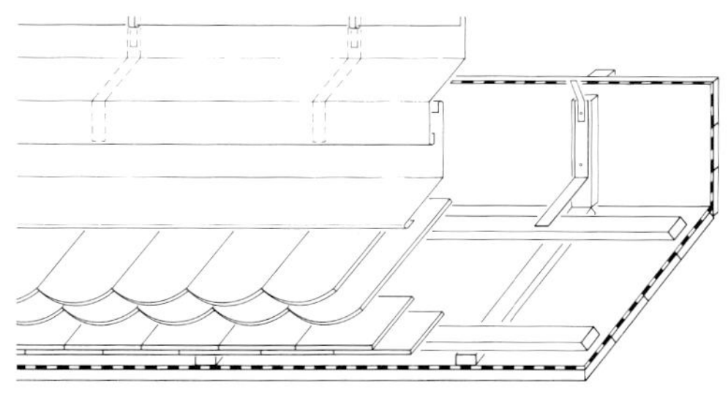

2.4.6.47 Junction with wall at top of roof slope

Junction with wall at base of slope
On a roof covering of overlapping elements a junction at the base of the slope is very much at risk because this is where waterproofing and ventilation are important. A back gutter should be formed and the gutter material turned up the adjacent wall at least 200 mm. There should be a clear space of at least 100 mm between the rising wall and the edge of the first course of tiles (see also "Construction details – Flat and profiled overlapping elements").

Penetrations
Snowguard supports, hooks for crawling boards, step irons etc. must be incorporated into the roof covering by means of a rainproof detail. They must be suitable for their intended purpose and be securely attached to the roof construction by screws, annular nails etc. Supports and hooks should not damage the roof covering when they are loaded. An underlay to distribute the load is recommended for snowguard supports, crawling boards and prefabricated special tiles. A lightning protection system should be planned before laying the roof covering so that lightning conductor mountings can be installed at the same time as the roof covering.

Roof windows and access openings
These should have a sufficiently wide frame to suit the type of roof covering. The minimum roof pitch specified by the manufacturer should be taken into account in the case of windows to living quarters. If the frame cannot cover the junction with the roof tiles, soakers must be used.

Dormer windows
The design and dimensions of rooftop structures should be coordinated with the roof covering. The roof surface should be divided horizontally and vertically in roofs with shed dormers, gable-end dormers etc. It should be remembered that the last row of tiles before the rooftop structure can be carried through. The vertical rows of tiles should be coordinated with the rooftop structures, taking into account the intended overhang at the verges so that the transition to the roof covering on the rooftop structure can be aligned with that on the main surface of the roof. The pitch of the roof to the rooftop structure should not be less than that recommended for the particular type of roof covering. The difference between the pitch of the apex of a shed dormer and the main rafters should be ≤ 12°.

The curves to the front face of an eyebrow dormer window should be calculated as follows:

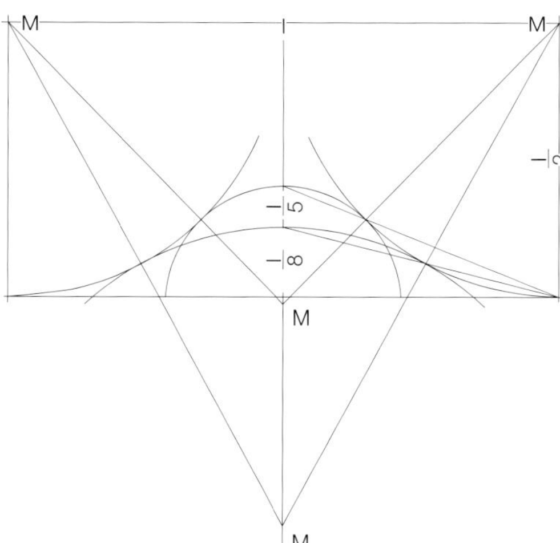


2.4.6.48 Eyebrow dormer window: construction of front curve

Either double-lap or crown tiling can be used on eyebrow dormers, and the ratio of the height to the width of the front face should not exceed 1:5 (see also "Construction details – Profiled clay and concrete tiles").

Crank
The transition from a steep to a shallow roof pitch (e.g. mansard roof) requires timber boards, special elements or sheet metal flashings. The clay or concrete roof tiles on the upper surface must project beyond the lower roof surface such that precipitation is drained onto it.
A transverse infill (e.g. mortar) may be necessary at the crank between the main roof surface and a shed dormer. The crank can be somewhat evened out with battens, boards, etc. If boarding is necessary with a shed dormer, it should be placed above the crank in the steeper roof surface.

**Supporting construction**
Battens
The cross-section of the loadbearing tiling battens should be chosen according to the spacing of the rafters and the weight of the clay or concrete roof tiles. It is not necessary to provide an analysis for the customary sizes.

| Rafter spacing [m] | | | |
|---|---|---|---|
| Bullnose tiles, double-lap tiling | ≤ 0.70 | ≤ 0.80 | ≤ 1.00 |
| Flat wire-cut interlocking clay tiles, other forms of tiling | | | |
| Flat concrete roof tiles | | ≤ 0.75 | ≤ 0.90 |
| Bullnose tiles, crown tiling | | ≤ 0.70 | ≤ 0.80 |
| Size of battens [mm] | 24x48 | 30x50 | 40x60 |

2.4.6.49 Batten sizes and rafter spacing in relation to roof covering [03, 25]

Tiling battens should have at least three sharp edges so that they are fixed with two edges on the rafters and the nibs on the tiles can hook over the upper edge of the batten, i.e. facing up the slope. If the fourth edge, i.e. the other upper edge facing down the slope, exhibits some wane, the quality of the battens is not impaired. This wane should not be wider than the smallest dimension of the batten. Battens with wane must be free of bark.

**Maintenance and repair**
Clay and concrete tiles, regardless of which type, need no regular maintenance. If installed correctly, they can last 50 years or more. However, it is recommended to inspect any roof of clay or concrete tiles at certain intervals because regular care prolongs the service life of the roof covering. The drying-out of the roof structure of a new building can cause movements, which may lead to damage to the roof covering (cracks in mortar strips and at the verge, damage to materials at ridges, hips, valleys and junctions). After a long period of use and the associated shocks and vibrations to which the roof is exposed, mortar strips in particular can suffer and must be renewed sooner or later.
Junctions may need to be inspected earlier, depending on their design and the materials used. Hip and ridge tiles must be made good

with mortar from time to time, depending on the weather conditions. If the mortar of a roof covering has become so brittle that it no longer functions as a binding agent between the roofing elements, the roof covering should be relaid and all worn parts replaced.
Torching the roof from outside can lead to rain penetration and thus to freezing (clay), and should therefore be avoided. No mortar should be visible from outside on any roof covering, except at ridges and hips. One exception is the mortar on a covering of bullnose tiles (side joint in double-lap and crown tiling). The mortar used here and for the internal strips should be based on white lime or hydraulic lime (no pure cement mortar).
If necessary, on roofs where the tiles are bedded in bitumen sheets laid over the tiling battens, the joints should be provided with mortar or an internal strip of mortar in order to maintain the flexibility and durability of these parts.
Flashings and safety installations (hooks, steps) should be checked for corrosion of the metal.
When converting a roof space at a later date, loadbearing components (rafters) should not be removed unnecessarily because the uneven deflection of the remaining rafters has a direct effect on the roof covering.
The new roof covering must be ventilated from below (counter battens ≥ 25 mm) and adequately fixed according to the guidelines of the roofing trade.
When converting the roof space, if airtightness of the internal vapour barrier and wind break are not anticipated, adequate ventilation above the thermal insulation should be ensured.
Direct contact between roof covering and thermal insulation must be avoided at all costs.
Subsequent coating of the roof covering, or covering layer, is not recommended. This changes the moisture relationships in the elements (clay tiles) so that their frost resistance can no longer be guaranteed.

**References**

[01] Arbeitsgemeinschaft Ziegeldach e.V. (pub.): Arbeitsblätter für Sanierung und Denkmalpflege, Ziegeldach; Bonn: Arb.-Gem. Ziegeldach, 1999
[02] Arbeitsgemeinschaft Ziegeldach e.V. (pub.): Deutsch-eingebundene Biberkehlen trocken gelegt; offprint from: DHH – Das Dachdecker-Handwerk pt 1 & 2; Bonn: Arb.-Gem. Ziegeldach, 1995 & 1999
[03] Braas Dachsysteme GmbH & Co. (pub.): Handbuch geneigte Dächer 1998/2000, 4th ed.; Oberursel: Braas, 1998
[04] Brennecke, W.; Folkerts, H.; Haferland, F.; Hart, F.: Dachatlas, geneigte Dächer; Munich: Institut für internationale Architektur-Dokumentation, 1980 & 1984
[05] Bundesverband der Deutschen Ziegelindustrie e.V. (pub.): Ziegel-Bauberatung, Ziegeldach; Bonn: Bundesverb. d. Dt. Ziegelindustrie, 1998
[06] DDH – Das Dachdecker-Handwerk, vol. 7: Dachziegel; Cologne: Rudolf Müller, 2000
[07] DIN EN 490: Concrete roofing tiles and fittings; product specifications; Berlin: Beuth-Verlag, 1994
[08] DIN EN 491: Concrete roofing tiles and fittings; test methods; Berlin: Beuth, 1994
[09] DIN EN 539: Clay roofing tiles for discontinuous laying – Determination of physical characteristics – Part 2: Tests for frost resistance; Berlin: Beuth, 1998
[10] DIN EN 1304: Clay roofing tiles for discontinuous laying – Product definitions and specifications; Berlin: Beuth, 1999
[11] DIN 1045: Structural use of concrete; design and construction; Berlin: Beuth, 1988
[12] DIN 4030: Assessment of water, soil and gases for their aggressiveness to concrete; Berlin: Beuth, 1991
[13] DIN 4226: Aggregates for concrete; Berlin: Beuth, 1983
[14] Hofmann, H. G.; Zipf, E.: Das Ziegeldach; Oestrich, 1966
[15] Holzapfel, W.: Werkstoffkunde für Dach-, Wand- und Abdichtungstechnik, 10th ed.; Cologne: Rudolf Müller, 1999
[16] Informationsdienst für neuzeitliches Bauen (pub.): d-extrakt-Arbeitsblatt 15, Planung und Konstruktion geneigter Dächer mit erhöhter Wärmedämmung; Bonn: Info-Dienst f. neuztl. Bauen, 1994
[17] Jungblut, H.: Die Biberschwanzziegel-Deckung (reprint); Mayen: 1938
[18] Krenkler, K.: Chemie des Bauwesens, vol. 1, Anorganische Chemie; Berlin: Springer-Verlag, 1980
[19] Leder, G.: Hochbaukonstruktionen, vol. III: Dachdeckungen; Berlin: Springer-Verlag, 1987
[20] Schmitt, H.: Hochbaukonstruktionen, 9th ed.; Braunschweig: Vieweg & Sohn Verlagsgesellschaft mbH, 1981
[21] Schneider, K. J. (ed.): Bautabellen, 6th ed.; Düsseldorf: Werner-Verlag, 1984
[22] Scholz, W.: Baustoffkenntnis, 13th ed.; Düsseldorf: Werner Verlag, 1995
[23] Sterly, H. J.: Kehlen im Ziegeldach, Unterkonstruktion – Berechnung – Ausführung; Cologne, Rudolf Müller 1984
[24] Zentralverband des Deutschen Dachdeckerhandwerks e.V. – Fachverband Dach-, Wand- und Abdichtungstechnik mit Hauptverband der Deutschen Bauindustrie e.V. – Bundesfachabteilung Bauwerksabdichtung (pub.): Fachregel für Dächer mit Abdichtungen – Flachdachrichtlinien; Cologne Rudolf Müller, 2001
[25] Zentralverband des Deutschen Dachdeckerhandwerks; (pub.) Fachverband Dach-, Wand- und Abdichtungstechnik: Regeln für die Deckung mit Dachziegeln und Dachsteinen; Cologne: Rudolf Müller Verlag, 1997
[26] Zentralverband des Deutschen Dachdeckerhandwerks, Fachverband Dach-, Wand- und Abdichtungstechnik e.V. (pub.): Fachregel für Metallarbeiten im Dachdecker-Handwerk; Cologne: Rudolf Müller, 1999

## Profiled overlapping elements of clay and concrete

Materials, components, laying

### Clay

Raw materials, manufacture, properties

#### Raw materials, manufacture

The raw materials and methods of manufacture for profiled clay roof tiles are the same as for flat clay tiles (see "Flat overlapping elements of clay and concrete"). However, the forming and therefore also the loadbearing capacity and the evenness values differ from those of flat clay tiles.

Forming
Profiled clay roof tiles are divided into pressed and wire-cut types according to the method of manufacture.
Of the profiled clay roof tiles, only the pantile is produced by means of extrusion. All the other profiled clay tiles with single and double ribs, plus over-tiles, under-tiles and flat pan tiles are produced by pressing. [13]

Physical properties

Loadbearing capacity
The requirements regarding loadbearing capacity are deemed to have been satisfied when the clay roof tiles do not fracture when subjected to a certain minimum load according to DIN EN 538.

| Type of clay roof tile | min. load [N] |
|---|---|
| under-and-over tiles | 1000 |
| all other types | 1200 |

2.4.7.1 Loadbearing capacity [05]

Evenness
The evenness values are different from those of flat clay roof tiles. Dimensions, twist and warping must lie within the ranges given in the table.

| Total length of clay roof tile | Evenness and straightness % |
|---|---|
| > 300 mm | ≤ 1.5 |
| ≤ 300 mm | ≤ 2.0 |
| Uniformity of transverse profiles of under-and-over tiles ≤ 1.5 mm | |
| Length and width dimensional tolerances for all forms (except under-and-over tiles) ≤ 2.0% | |

2.4.7.2 Geometrical properties [08]

Frost resistance
The minimum number of 150 freeze-thaw cycles corresponds to that for flat clay roof tiles.

## Concrete

Raw materials, manufacture, properties

**Raw materials, manufacture**

The raw materials, methods of manufacture and properties of profiled concrete roof tiles (except loadbearing capacity) are the same as for flat concrete tiles (see "Flat overlapping elements of clay and concrete").

Surface finish

Some types of tile are also provided with a granulated, rough surface, which is achieved by spreading a coloured (achieved by sintering) granulate over the tiles in a cement slurry. These concrete roof tiles are primarily used in regions with heavy snowfall because their rough surface lowers the risk of the snow sliding off the roof in large, dangerous avalanches. However, these tiles become soiled more quickly than those with a smooth surface.

Physical properties

Loadbearing capacity

Profiled concrete roof tiles must reach the minimum loadbearing capacity given in table 2.4.7.3 at the latest 28 days after casting or upon leaving the precasting works.

| | Loadbearing capacity[1] [kN] | |
|---|---|---|
| Cover width [mm][1] | > 20 mm[2] | ≤ 20 to ≥ 5 mm[2] |
| ≥ 300 | 2.00 | 1.40 |
| ≤ 200 | 1.40 | 1.00 |

[1] Loadbearing capacities for cover widths between 200 and 300 mm may be obtained by linear interpolation.
[2] Depth of profile

2.4.7.3 Loadbearing capacity [03]

Tolerances

| Direction | max. deviation [mm] |
|---|---|
| Hanging length or accuracy of right angles | +/- 4 |
| Flatness of cross-section | ≤ 3 |

2.4.7.4 Geometrical properties

## Components

General elements, edge and special elements

The components shown here are merely a selection of the complete range of clay and concrete roof tile products. Restricting the number of products is intended to assist clarity and make the comparison and classification of the different forms easier.

| Form | Material | Laying | Designation |
|---|---|---|---|
| Single trough without ribs <br>Over-/Under-tile | clay | in straight rows | under-and-over tiles<br>channel tiles |
| Single trough without ribs <br>Flat pan tile | clay | in straight rows | flat pan tile |
| Single trough without ribs<br>Pantile | clay | in straight rows | pantiles with<br>- short shoulder<br>- long shoulder |
| Single trough with raised side ribs plus tail ribs 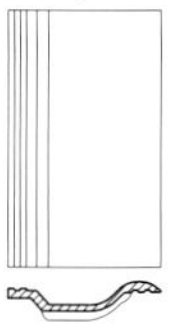<br>Interlocking tile* | concrete | in straight rows | Danube pantile |
| Profiled with ribs on all sides 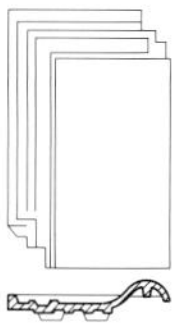<br>Interlocking tile* | clay | in straight rows | interlocking pantile<br>interlocking flat pan tile<br>flat pan w. flat roll<br>Reform tile<br>crown flat pan tile<br>Roman forms<br>combined under-and-over tiles<br>Karat tile |
| Double trough with raised side ribs plus tail ribs 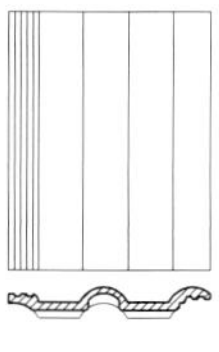<br>Double Roman tile | concrete | in straight rows | Frankfurter pantile<br>Heidelberger p.<br>Finkenberger p.<br>Ticino pantile<br>Taunus pantile<br>double pantile<br>Harzer pantile |
| Double trough with ribs on all sides 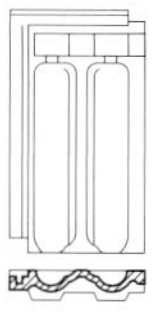<br>Double Roman tile | clay | in straight rows<br>in a bond | double Roman tile<br>tile with heart motif<br>profiled interlocking tile |

* no longer manufactured in Germany

2.4.7.5 General elements

**General elements**

Single-trough overlapping elements without ribs

- Under-and-over tiles

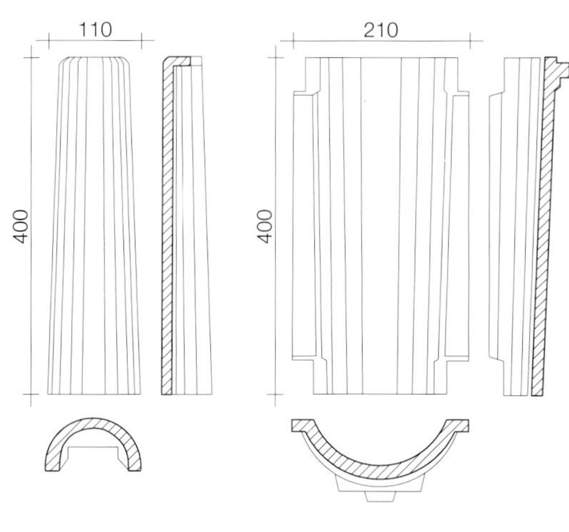


2.4.7.6 Clay over-tile (imbrex) [14]

2.4.7.7 Clay under-tile (tegula) [14]

The over-tile (imbrex) has a tapered profile with an open or closed head. The under-tile (tegula) has the same shape but is larger and open at head and tail.

| | |
|---|---|
| Weight: | over-tile: approx. 2.0 kg<br>under-tile: approx. 2.5 kg |
| Surface finish: | smooth<br>uncoated: natural red<br>coated: engobe colours<br>glaze colours |
| Requirements: | approx. 13 over-tiles/m$^2$<br>approx. 13 under-tiles/m$^2$ |

- Clay flat pan tile

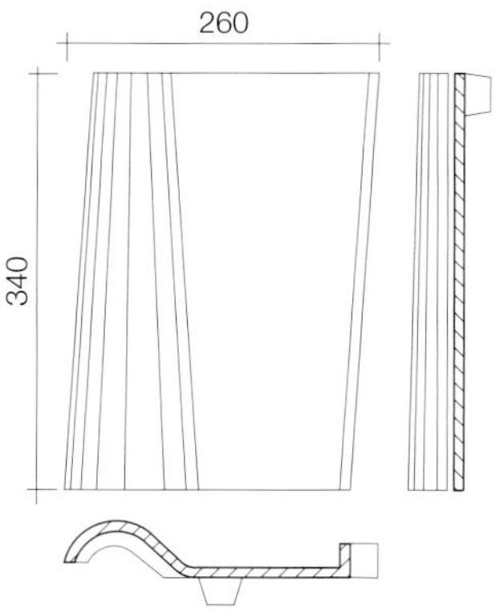


2.4.7.8 Clay flat pan tile [14]

This type of tile is flat with one side turned up about 15 mm, while the other side is in the form of a curved overlapping rim.

| | |
|---|---|
| Weight: | approx. 3.6 kg |
| Surface finish: | smooth<br>uncoated: natural red<br>coated: engobe colours<br>glaze colours |
| Requirements: | approx. 15 or 18 tiles/m$^2$ |

• Clay pantile

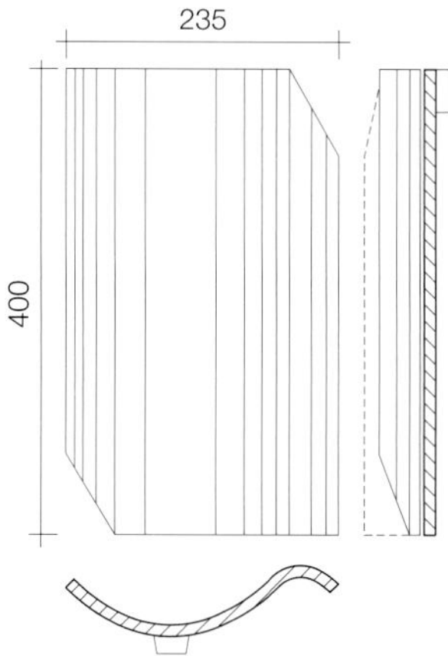


2.4.7.9 Clay pantile [14]

The pantile is in the shape of a wide trough with an overlapping rim on one side (S-shape). The right corner at the head and the left corner at the tail are both cut off at an angle to form either a short shoulder for tiling with overlapping shoulders or a long shoulder for tiling without overlapping shoulders. A single nib at the head is included for hanging the tile on the batten.

| | |
|---|---|
| Weight: | approx. 2.5 kg |
| Surface finish: | smooth<br>uncoated: natural red<br>coated: engobe colours<br>glaze colours |
| Requirements: | approx. 15 or 18 tiles/m² depending on type of tiling |

Single-trough overlapping elements with ribs on all sides

• Interlocking clay pantile

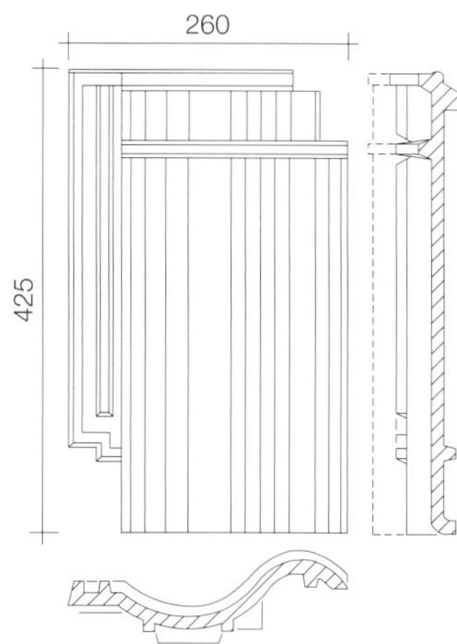


2.4.7.10 Interlocking clay pantile [5]

The interlocking pantile can have single or double ribs. The head can be provided with single, double or triple ribs. The headlap has a 30 mm range of adjustment.

| | |
|---|---|
| Weight: | approx. 3.0 kg |
| Surface finish: | uncoated: natural red<br>coated: engobe colours<br>glaze colours |
| Requirements: | approx. 15 tiles/m² |

• Clay Reform tile

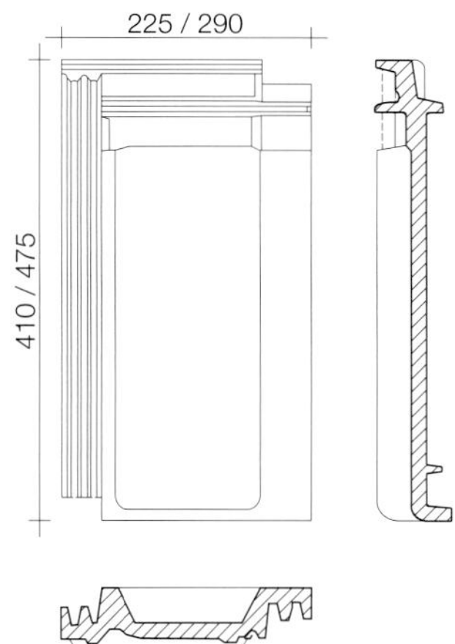


2.4.7.11 Clay Reform tile

The visible face of a single tile has the form of a flat trough with a flat overlapping rim. In use, the side ribs create a covered joint facing upwards.

| | |
|---|---|
| Weight: | approx. 3.0 kg |
| Surface finish: | uncoated: natural red<br>coated: engobe colours<br>glaze colours |
| Requirements: | approx. 11–15 tiles/m² |

• Interlocking clay flat pan tile

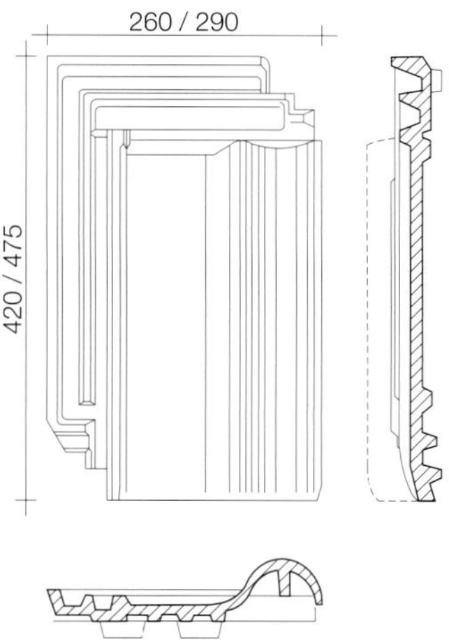


2.4.7.12 Interlocking clay flat pan tile

The interlocking clay flat pan tile is similar to the pantile. However, it has especially carefully formed ribs at the sides and at the head. The overlapping rim covering the side joint between individual tiles extends right down to the flat trough of the next tile. The self-cleaning effect of the side ribs is improved by channelling the water onto the trough below.

| | |
|---|---|
| Weight: | approx. 3.0 kg |
| Surface finish: | uncoated: natural red<br>coated: engobe colours<br>glaze colours |
| Requirements: | approx. 11–15 tiles/m² |

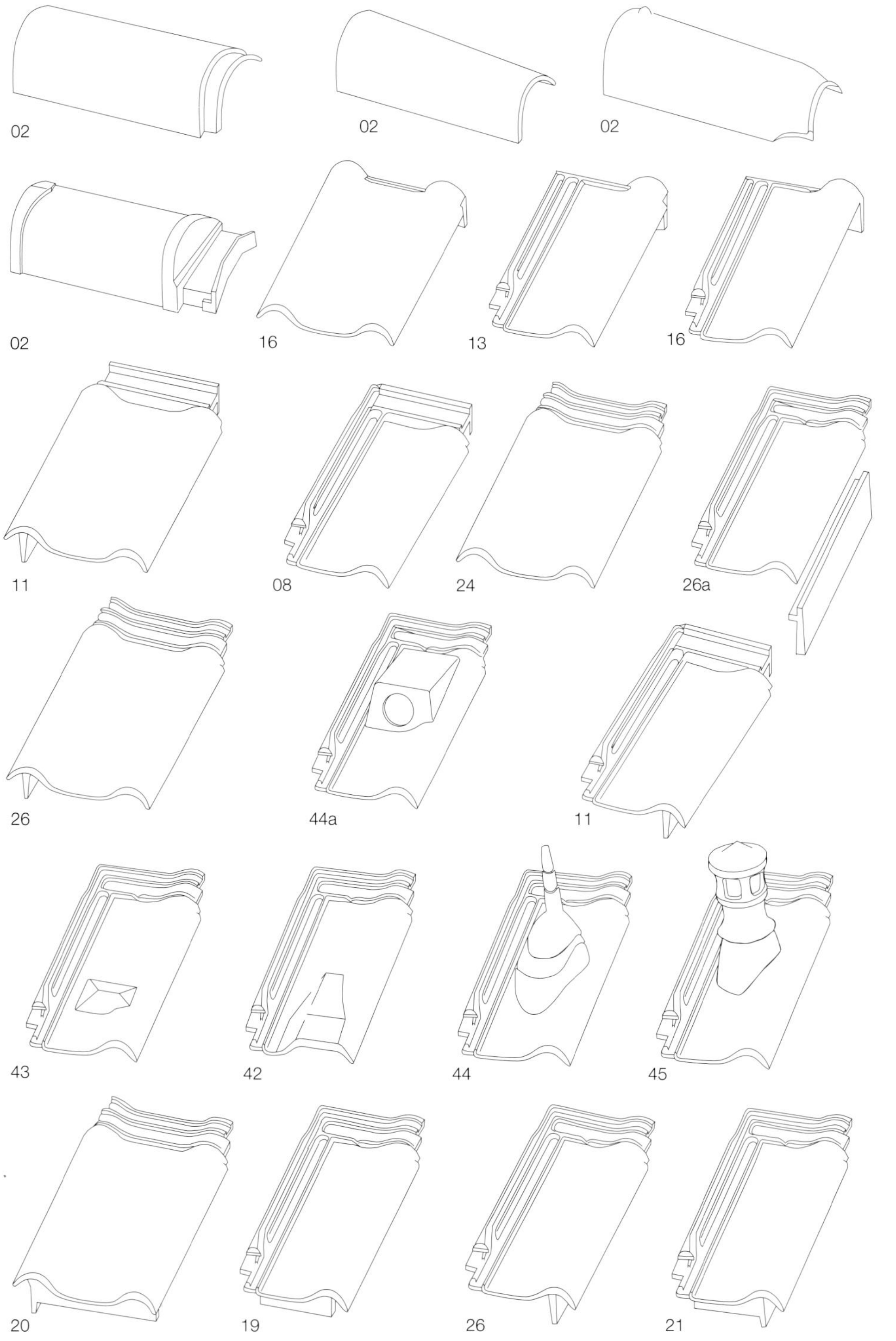

- Interlocking clay flat pan tile

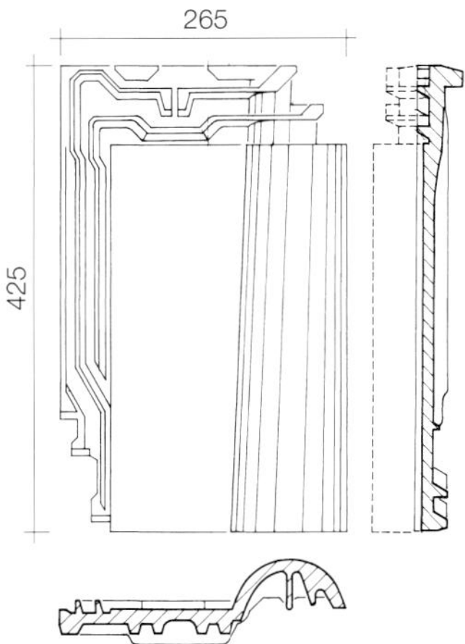


2.4.7.14 Interlocking clay flat pan tile [02]

Weight: approx. 3.0 kg
Surface finish: smooth
uncoated: natural red
coated: engobe colours
Requirements: approx. 15 tiles/m$^2$

- Interlocking clay flat pan tile, special form

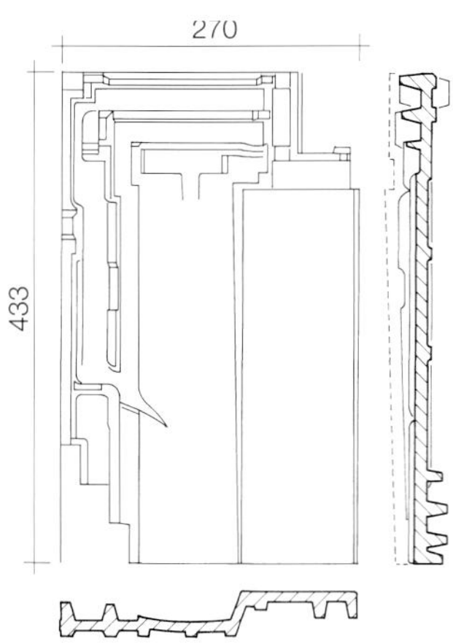


2.4.7.13 Interlocking clay flat pan tiles; edge and special elements, selection: 02 ridge/hip (ventilating) capping, 08 top course tile, 11 ridge/verge cloaked intersection (left/right), 13 mono ridge tile, 16 cloaked verge/mono ridge intersection, 20 double roll verge/eaves intersection, 21 cloaked verge/eaves intersection (left/right), 24 end tile (left/right), 26 cloaked verge tile (left/right), 26a verge tile with separate cloak (left/right), 42 ventilating tile, 43 snowguard tile, 44 tile with aerial mounting, 44a tile with opening for solar energy system, 45 tile with vapour vent.

The numbers refer to table 2.4.6.16 and figure 2.4.6.18.

Weight: approx. 3.5 kg
Surface finish: smooth
uncoated: natural red
coated: engobe colours
Requirements: approx. 15 tiles/m$^2$

• Clay tile with adjustable headlap

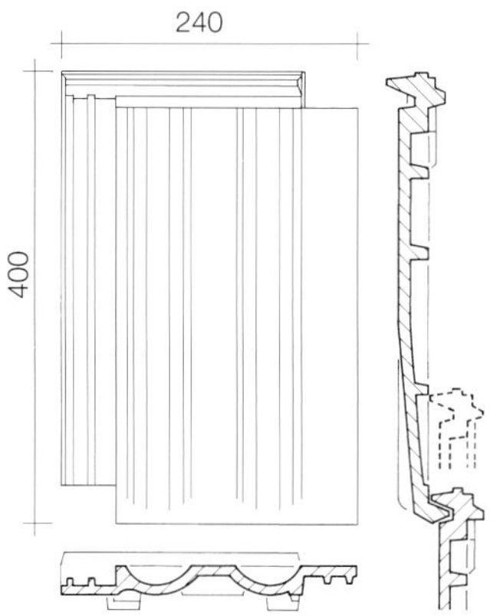


2.4.7.16 Clay tile with adjustable headlap

This type of tile has ribs on all sides. The design of the head and tail ribs allows the headlap to be adjusted. This avoids the need to reposition the tiling battens during re-roofing. The range of adjustment is at least 30 mm.

| | |
|---|---|
| Weight: | approx. 3.0 kg |
| Surface finish: | smooth<br>uncoated: natural red<br>coated: engobe colours<br>glaze colours |
| Requirements: | approx. 11–15 tiles/m² |

Double-trough overlapping elements with raised side ribs plus tail ribs

• Double Roman concrete tile

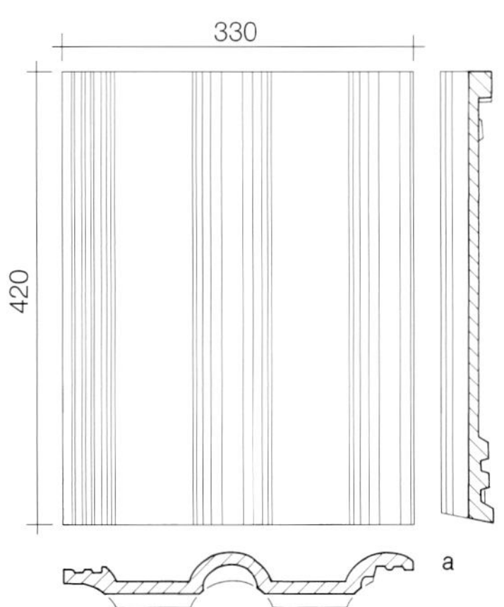


2.4.7.17 Double Roman concrete tile: a with symmetrical middle roll [01]

| | |
|---|---|
| Weight: | approx. 4.5 kg |
| Surface finish: | smooth or granulated<br>dyed: red, brown, grey, granite, blue, green, special colours |
| Requirements: | approx. 10 tiles/m² |

• Double Roman concrete tile

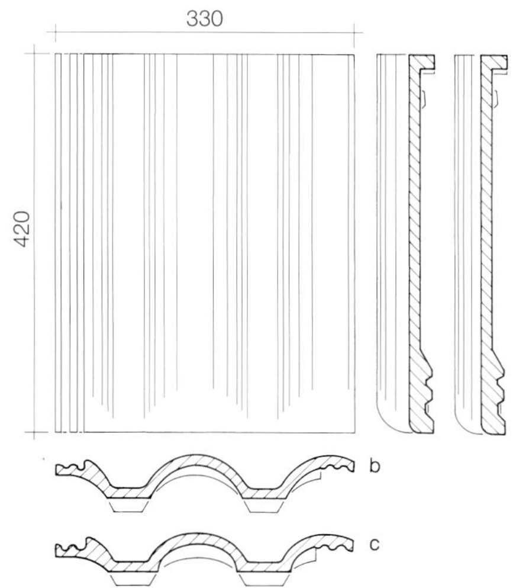


2.4.7.18 Double Roman concrete tile: b with higher middle roll, c with segmental middle roll [01]

| | |
|---|---|
| Weight: | approx. 4.5 kg |
| Surface finish: | smooth<br>dyed: red, brown, granite |
| Requirements: | approx. 10 tiles/m² |

• Double pantile

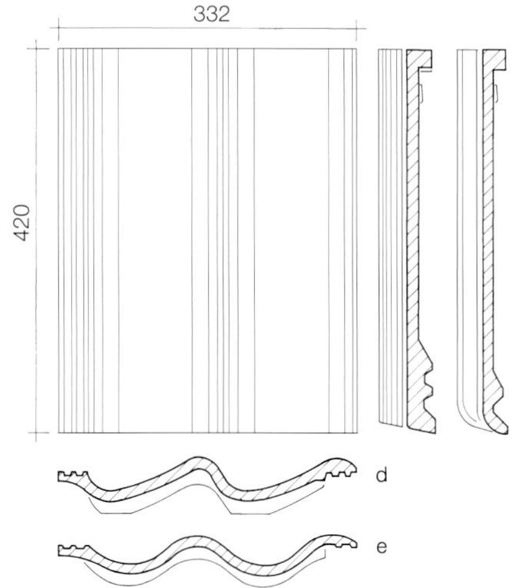


2.4.7.19 Double pantile: d with asymmetrical middle roll, e with symmetrical middle roll [01]

| | |
|---|---|
| Weight: | approx. 4.5 kg |
| Surface finish: | smooth<br>dyed: red, brown, granite, blue, green |
| Requirements: | approx. 10 tiles/m² |

Double-trough overlapping elements with ribs on all sides

• Clay French tile

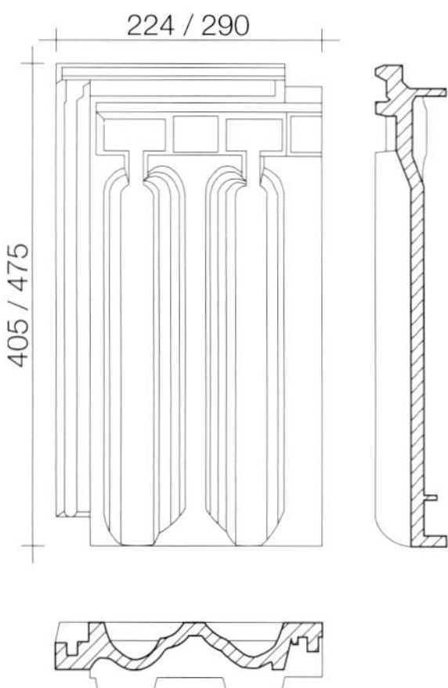


2.4.7.20 Clay French tile

| | |
|---|---|
| Weight: | approx. 3.0 kg |
| Surface finish: | smooth<br>uncoated: natural red<br>coated: engobe colours<br>glaze colours |
| Requirements: | approx. 10–15 tiles/m² |

These are pressed clay roof tiles with head and side ribs. They are produced with single or double ribs. The two troughs on the visible surface of the tile drain the precipitation reliably.

**Edge and special elements**

(see also “Flat overlapping elements of clay and concrete”)

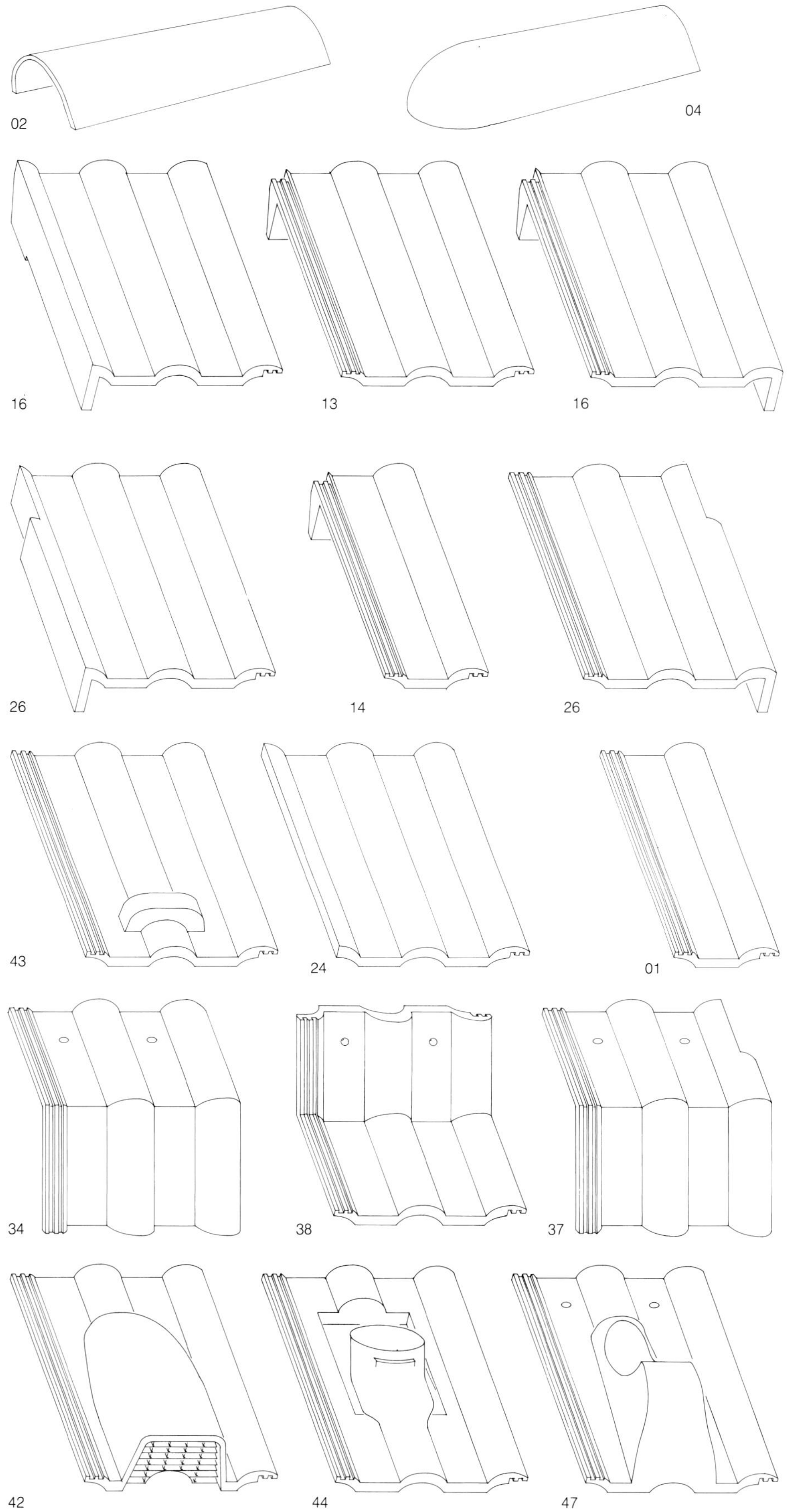

2.4.7.21 Concrete roof tiles; general, edge and special elements; selection: 02 ridge capping, 04 ridge or hip end tile, 16 cloaked verge/mono ridge intersection left/right, 13 mono ridge tile, 26 cloaked verge tile (left/right), 14 mono ridge half tile, 43 snowguard tile, 24 double roll verge tile, 01 half tile, 34 mansard tile, 38 angle tile, 37 mansard verge tile (right), 42 ventilating tile, 44 tile with vapour vent, 47 step support tile [01].
The numbers refer to table 2.4.6.16 and figure 2.4.6.18.

## Laying

Conditions for laying, fixing, additional measures, details, mainenance and repair

#### Conditions for laying

The same remarks apply here as for flat overlapping elements of clay and concrete.

### Roof pitch

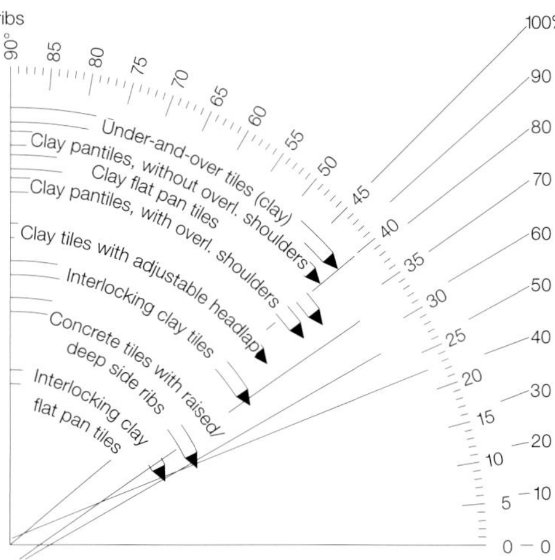


2.4.7.22 Recommended roof pitches in relation to roof covering

### Headlap

The headlap depends on the roof pitch and the form of the tiles. Tile length, headlap and clear spacing of battens are all interrelated. The clear spacing of the battens is the distance from the upper edge of a tiling batten to the next batten. The minimum headlap should not be reduced.
The side lap of profiled clay and concrete tiles with side ribs is predetermined by the ribs. The headlap can vary. Crucial for minimum headlap are roof pitch and type of component.

max. clear spacing of battens =
length of component – min. headlap

### Cover length

The headlaps and side laps of tiles with side, head and tail ribs are predetermined by the ribs. The average clear spacing of the battens, which corresponds to the cover length of these roof tiles, should be determined according to DIN 1304 using the tiles as supplied.
To determine the average clear spacing of the battens, two rows of 12 clay roof tiles each are laid on the ground with the heads touching the ground in such a way that the head ribs interlock (see figure 2.4.7.23). The dimensions between the nib of the first tile and the nib of the 11th tile when pulled apart and when pushed together are added together and then divided by 20. The result is the average clear spacing of the battens.

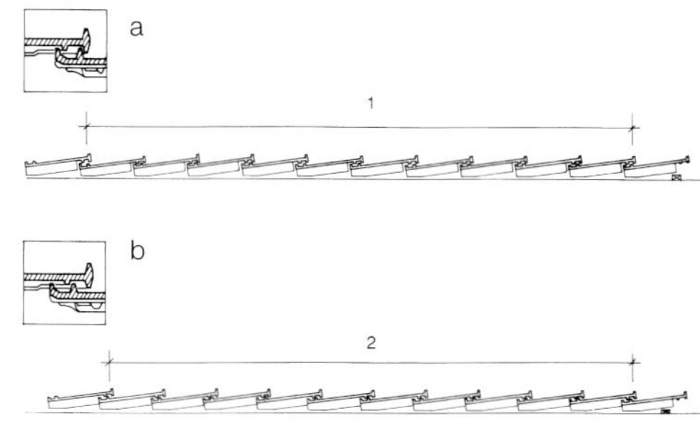


2.4.7.23 Calculating the average cover length, $L = (l_1 + l_2)/20$ (clear spacing of battens): a section through headlap of test tiles (pulled apart), b section through headlap of test tiles (pushed together)

This procedure is not necessary for concrete roof tiles. Here, the clear spacing of the battens is given by the length of the tile minus the headlap. The batten spacing at the ridge is a variable dimension; it depends on rafter pitch, batten thickness, the ridge tile and the tile of the top course.
The distance from the eaves also depends on the type of tile used and the detail at the eaves. The dimension is constant when using eaves tiles because the long tail rib closes off the roof construction at the eaves without any gaps. If standard roof tiles are used at the eaves, the batten spacing at the eaves may vary. [25]

Cover width
On hipped roofs without rooftop structures it is not usually necessary to divide up the roof surface in the transverse direction corresponding to the width of the clay or concrete tiles. All that is required is care when laying the tiles to avoid either pulling apart the side joints or pushing them together. Conversely, on gable roofs and hipped roofs with rooftop structures the roof surface must be divided up at ridge and eaves corresponding to the tiles used. The average cover width is determined as shown in figure 2.4.7.24.

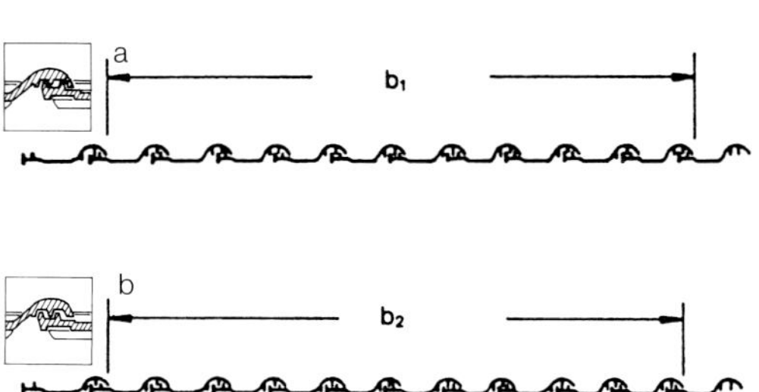


2.4.7.24 Calculating the average cover width, $B = (b_1 + b_2)/20$: a section through side lap of test tiles (pulled apart), b section through side lap of test tiles (pushed together)

**Roof coverings of single-trough profiled tiles**

Under-and-over tiles (clay)
The under-tile (tegula) should be hung on the batten in such a way that the over-tile (imbrex) can cover the ensuing space between two adjacent under-tiles. The under-tiles can be covered dry with an internal strip of mortar, clipped, or with a transverse strip of mortar. Laying the under-tiles in a full bed of mortar is not permitted.
The head of each over-tile is filled with mortar and each edge is "buttered" with mortar prior to placing it in position. Any openings visible from inside must be filled with mortar. The hollow spaces at the eaves must be closed off. Minimum headlap for under-and-over tiles is 80 mm.

max. clear spacing of battens = length of under-tile – min. headlap

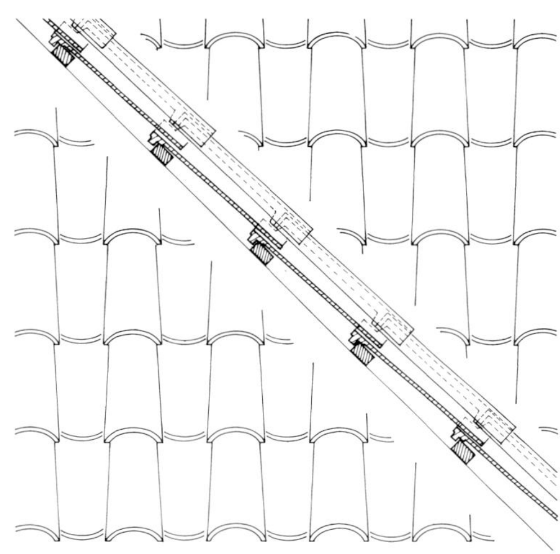

2.4.7.25 Tiling with clay under-and-over tiles

Clay flat pan tiles
These tiles are laid in straight vertical rows, i.e. without any offset between courses. The tiles are laid either dry with an internal strip of mortar, or with a transverse strip of mortar and side joints where an internal strip of mortar is not feasible. Minimum headlap for clay flat pan tiles is 80 mm.

max. clear spacing of battens = length of flat pan tile – min. headlap

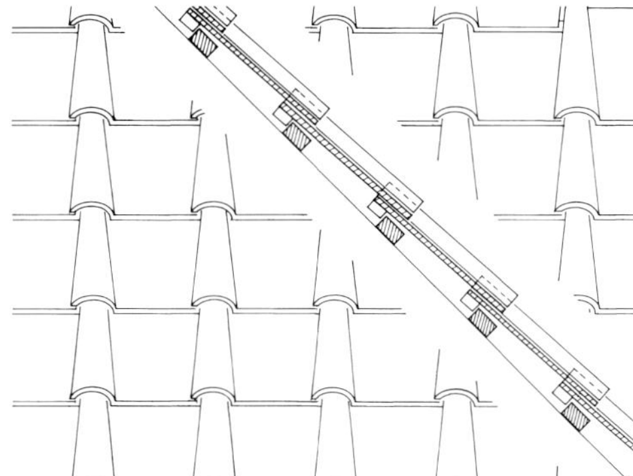

2.4.7.26 Tiling with clay flat pan tiles

Clay pantiles

These can be laid either with or without the shoulders overlapping. Both types of tiling can be carried out
- dry,
- dry, with tiles bedded in bitumen sheets laid over tiling battens,
- dry with internal strip of mortar (conservation work),
- dry on sheathing, or
- with transverse strips of mortar and side joints.

The side lap depends on the width and length of the overlapping rim and the type of tiling (with/without overlapping shoulders), although an adequate overlap must be maintained.

- Tiling with overlapping shoulders

This type of tiling employs clay pantiles with a short shoulder. Four layers of tiles overlap at the corners.

max. clear spacing of battens = length of pantile – min. headlap depending on roof pitch

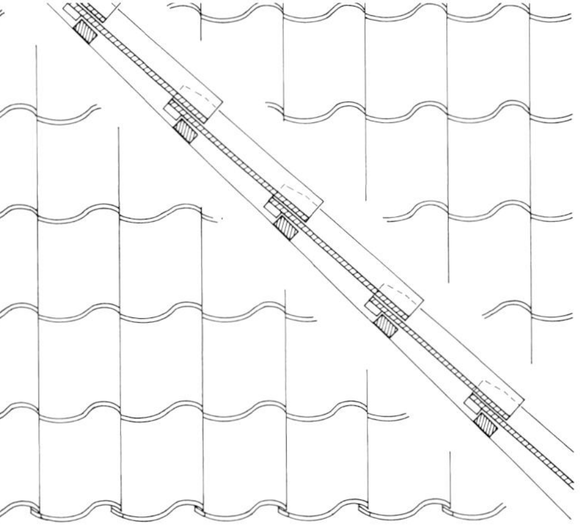

2.4.7.27 Clay pantiles; tiling with overlapping shoulders

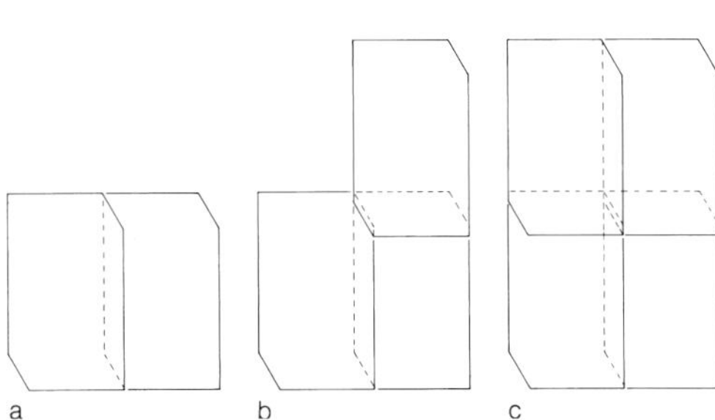


2.4.7.28 Four-tile corner (overlapping shoulders): a first operation, b second operation, c third operation

| Roof pitch | Headlap [mm] |
|---|---|
| 35° to 40° | 100 |
| > 40° to 45° | 90 |
| > 45° | 80 |

2.4.7.29 Minimum headlaps for clay pantiles with overlapping shoulders

• Tiling without overlapping shoulders
This employs clay pantiles with a long shoulder. Only three layers of tiles overlap at the corners.

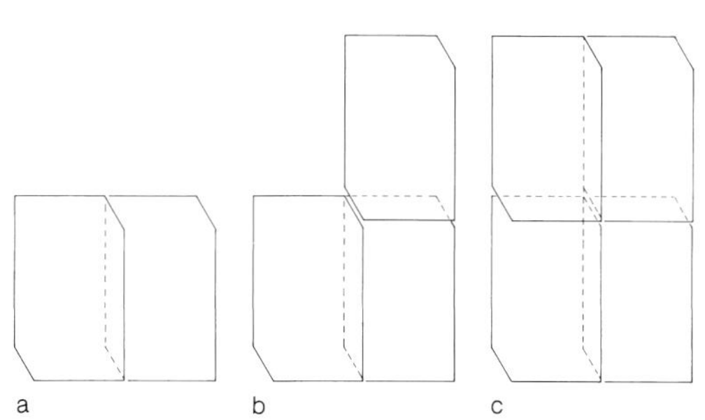


2.4.7.30 Four-tile corner (shoulders not overlapping): a first operation, b second operation, c third operation

The headlap is governed by the shoulder and is at least 70 mm. Roof pitches below 40° are not permitted.

max. clear spacing of battens = length of pantile – prescribed min. headlap

**Single-trough overlapping elements with raised side ribs plus tail ribs**

These concrete roof tiles are laid from right to left. The tiles are laid in straight vertical rows, i.e. with no offset between courses. The headlap varies. Minimum headlaps for concrete roof tiles with raised side ribs are as follows:

| Roof pitch | Headlap [mm] |
|---|---|
| < 22° (additional measures are necessary) | 100 |
| ≥ 22°<br>≤ 30° | 85 |
| > 30° | 75 |

2.4.7.31 Minimum headlaps for concrete roof tiles with raised side ribs

**Single-trough overlapping elements with ribs on all sides**

Covering a roof with these tiles can be carried out dry with or without an internal strip of mortar at the head joints. Ridge and eaves should be divided up according to the cover width calculated. The roof tiles are laid from right to left. With the exception of double Roman clay tiles, which can be laid in straight vertical rows or in a bond, all roof tiles with ribs on all sides are laid in straight vertical rows , i.e. without any offset between courses. The headlaps and side laps of these tiles are determined by their ribs.

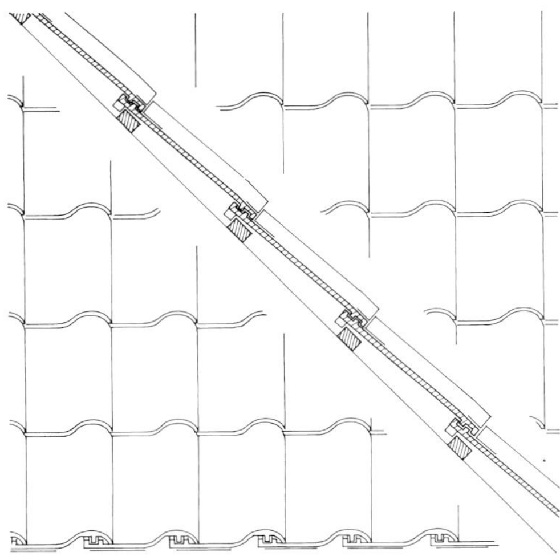

2.4.7.32 Tiling with interlocking clay tiles

**Double-trough overlapping elements with raised side ribs plus tail ribs**

These concrete roof tiles are laid from right to left. They are laid in straight vertical rows, i.e. with no offset between courses.

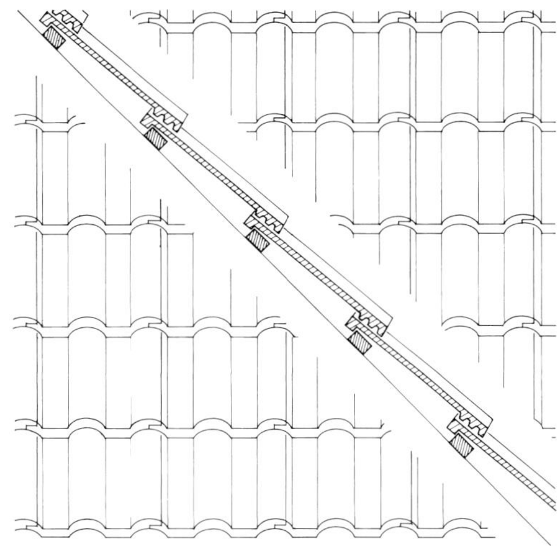

2.4.7.33 Tiling with double Roman concrete tiles

The headlap varies. Minimum headlaps for concrete roof tiles with raised side ribs are as follows:

| Roof pitch | Headlap [mm] |
|---|---|
| < 22° (additional measures are necessary) | 100 |
| ≥ 22°<br>≤ 30° | 85 |
| > 30° | 75 |

2.4.7.34 Minimum headlaps for double Roman concrete tiles

**Double-trough overlapping elements with ribs on all sides**

Covering a roof with these tiles is carried out dry. Ridge and eaves should be divided up according to the cover width (clay). The tiles are laid from right to left. The headlaps and side laps of these tiles are determined by the ribs.

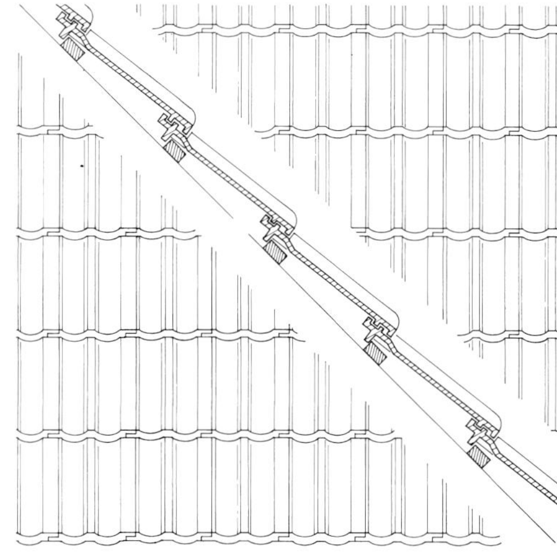

2.4.7.35 Tiling with double Roman clay tiles

Laying the tiles in a bond, i.e. with offset side joints, improves the rainwater run-off and the degree of rainproofing during storms, and is recommended for clay French tiles.

**Fixing**

(see "Flat overlapping elements of clay and concrete")
Calculations for the fixings are required for under-and-over tiling and any other types of roof covering that do not conform to the standard.

**Additional measures**

Apart from the additional measures listed under "Flat overlapping elements of clay and concrete", clay pantiles can also be bedded in special sheets laid over the tiling battens. These sheets, made from bitumen or synthetic material, must comply with the requirements of building materials class B 2 (flammable) to DIN 4102 part 1. They are laid in one operation together with the clay or concrete roof tiles. Care should be taken to ensure that the material of the sheets is compatible with any metal fixings or flashings being used. The sheets may not be used on roof pitches < 25°. Adequate ventilation underneath the roof covering is important when using these sheets on thermally insulated roofs. The sheets should be moulded to the shape of the tiling as they are laid. Regional customs or the requirements of building conservation may dictate the use of other materials, e.g. straw.

**Details**

Ridge, hip, eaves, valley, verge

Ridge

A roof covering of profiled tiles requires the topmost tiling battens on both sides to be positioned about 40 mm back from the apex. Apart from that, the detail at the ridge is the same as described under "Flat overlapping elements of clay and concrete". The ridge capping can be laid dry or in mortar.

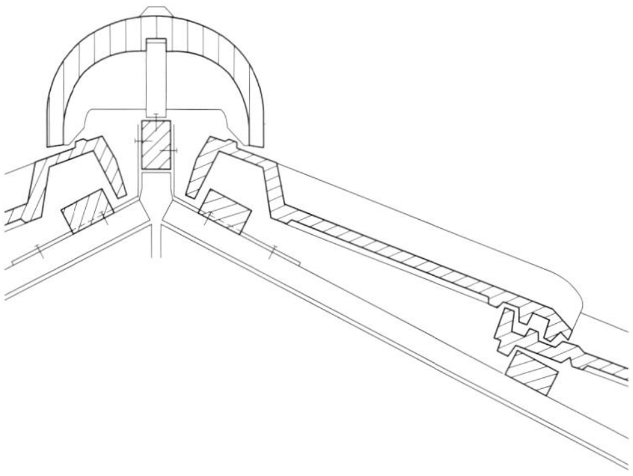

2.4.7.36 Clipped ridge capping with top course tiles

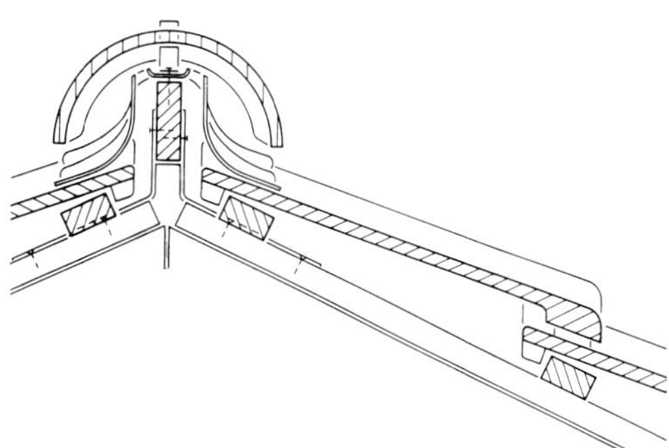

2.4.7.37 Clipped ridge capping with ventilating element

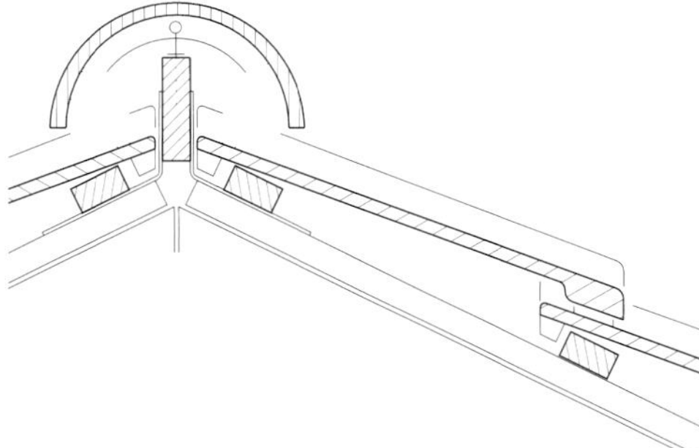

2.4.7.38 Ridge bedded in mortar; ridge capping secured against wind suction by means of binding wire (rare); analysis required for fixing

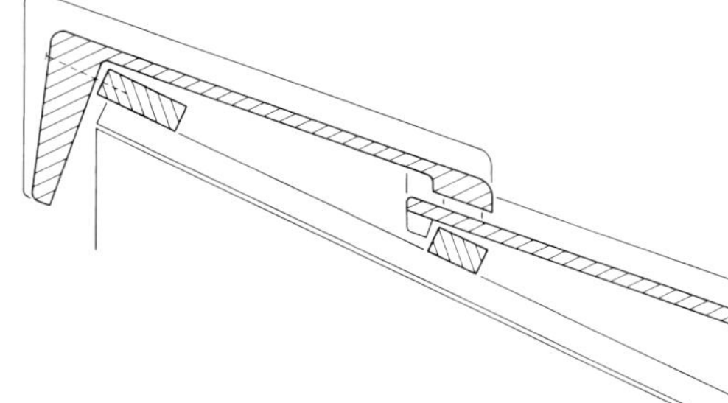

2.4.7.39 Ridge to monopitch roof, with screwed ridge tile

Hip

(see "Flat overlapping elements of clay and concrete")

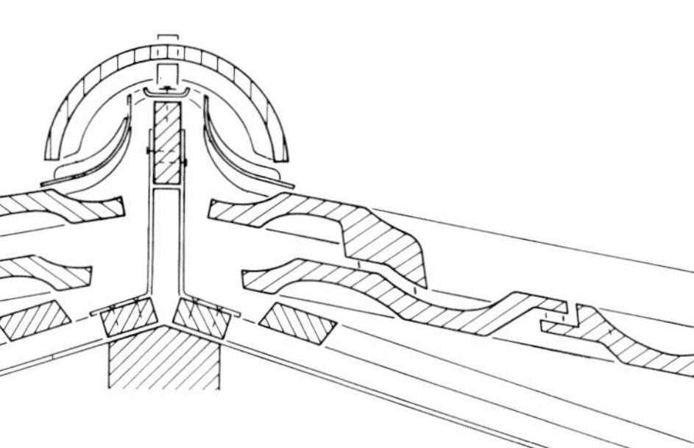

2.4.7.40 Clipped hip capping with ventilating element

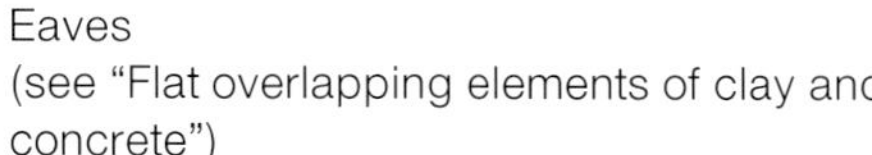

Eaves

(see "Flat overlapping elements of clay and concrete")

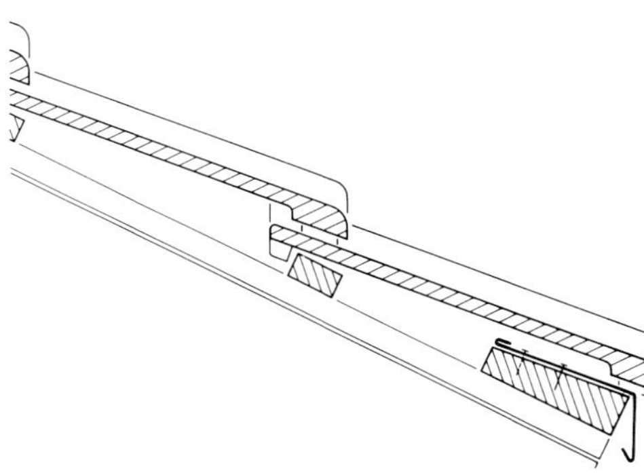

2.4.7.41 Eaves detail with eaves flashing and featheredge board

Valley

Only lined valleys are used with profiled roof tiles.

Lined valley

- Sheet metal valley (see "Drainage")

A sheet metal valley gutter should be provided with turned-up edges, except when using bullnose tiles (see "Flat overlapping elements of clay and concrete").

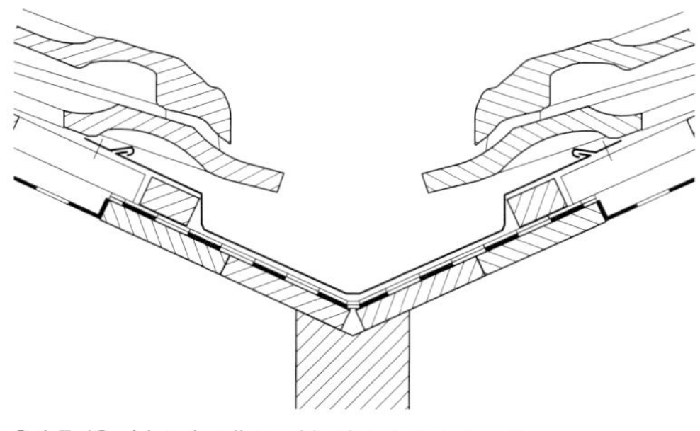

2.4.7.42 Lined valley with sheet metal gutter

- Ribbed valley

This is a prefabricated valley gutter made from coated aluminium. Strengthened middle and side ribs parallel to the line of the valley prevent water from being driven sideways beneath the roof covering, even with the wind blowing at an angle. The pieces of gutter material should have a headlap of 20 cm and the roof tiles should overlap the gutter by 8–10 cm.

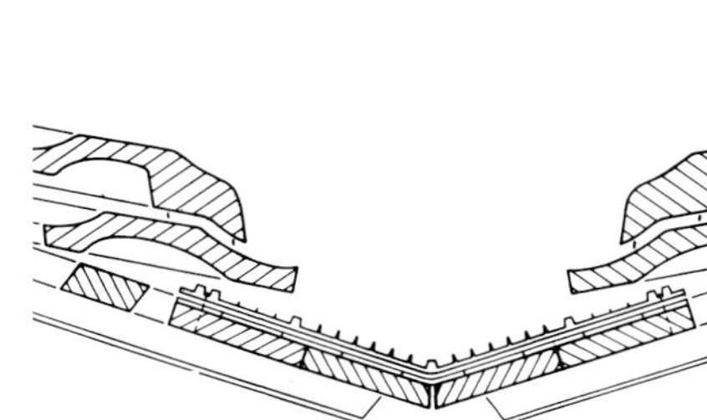

2.4.7.43 Lined valley with ribbed gutter

- Valley of special clay tiles

Here, the valley gutter is formed by special clay gutter tiles. These are available in forms and colours to match the tiles on the main surface of the roof.

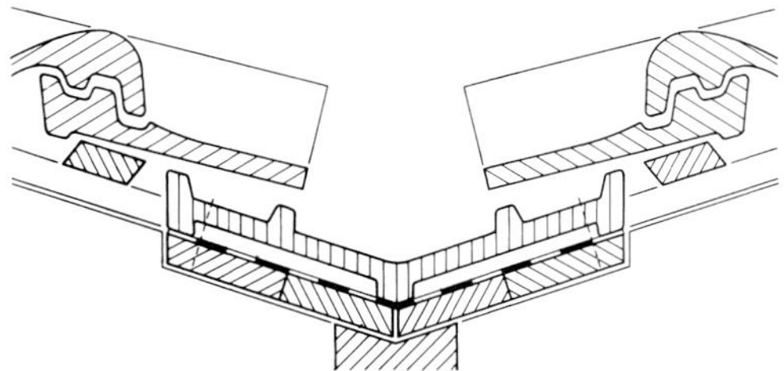

2.4.7.44 Lined valley with gutter of special clay tiles

- Triple pantile valley

The width of this valley gutter is equal to three pantiles. The middle – water channel – pantile is laid in the centre of the valley on a short piece of batten or – after removing the nib – bedded in strips of mortar transverse and at the sides. The pantile to the left is laid on the central pantile with a 4 cm side lap, and with 10 cm headlap. The pantile to the right is reversed and – after removing the nib – laid like the left-hand pantile so that it covers the edge of the central pantile and thus forms a watertight gutter. The tiles on the surface of the roof must overlap the gutterby ≥ 10 cm.

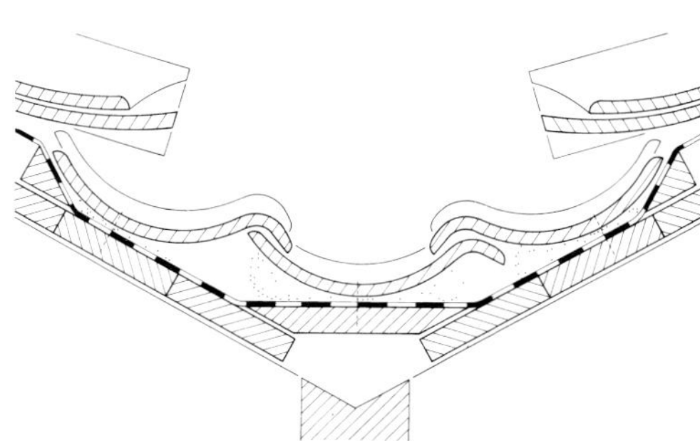

2.4.7.45 Triple-pantile valley gutter

Verge
(see "Flat overlapping elements of clay and concrete")

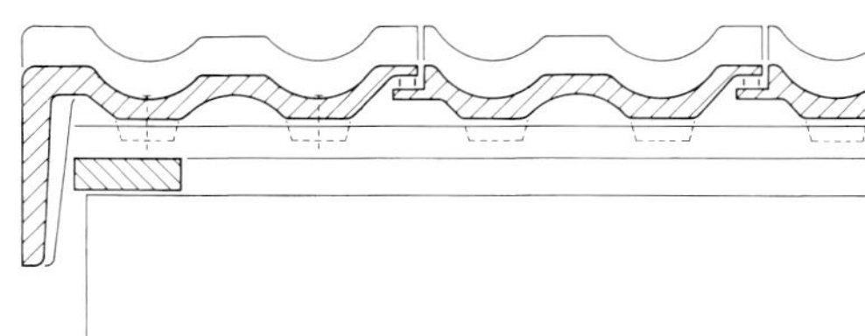

2.4.7.46 Verge detail with special cloaked verge tile

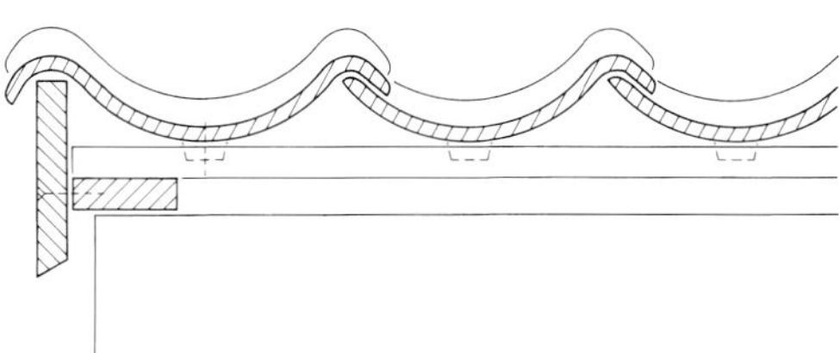

2.4.7.47 Verge detail with double-roll verge clay tile and profiled bargeboard

Dormer window
Dormers with flat roof surfaces, e.g. shed dormer, gable-end dormer, gablet, can be covered with any of the clay or concrete profiled overlapping elements provided the roof surfaces of the dormer can be matched to the size of the roof tiles. The recommended roof pitches apply as for the remainder of the roof surface.
Owing to their shape, only clay pantiles are suitable for covering eyebrow dormer windows. They are laid pushed together in the area of the main roof surface and pulled apart on the arch over the window.

For details of how to construct the curves of the front face, see "Flat overlapping elements of clay and concrete". However, for profiled elements the ratio of the height to the width of the front face should not exceed 1:8.

#### Maintenance and repair

For details of junctions with walls, roof penetrations, cranks, supporting construction and maintenance and repair, see "Flat overlapping elements of clay and concrete".

#### References

(see "Flat overlapping elements of clay and concrete")

## Glass roof coverings

Materials, components, laying

### Materials

Raw materials, manufacture, working the material, further treatment, coatings and surface treatment, properties

#### Raw materials

The glass used today as a building material is a soda-lime-silica glass. It is made from quartz sand, soda, limestone and dolomite, and is characterised by its good light transmittance and smooth, non-porous surface. Table 2.4.8.1 shows the composition of glass. Besides those listed here, small proportions of other materials are sometimes included to influence the properties and colour of the glass.

| Glass composition | | |
|---|---|---|
| silicon dioxide | ($SiO_2$) | 69% to 74% |
| calcium oxide | (CaO) | 5% to 12% |
| sodium oxide | ($Na_2O$) | 12% to 16% |
| magnesium oxide | (MgO) | 0% to 6% |
| aluminium oxide | ($Al_2O_3$) | 0% to 3% |

This composition is specified in EN 572 part 1 for the whole of Europe.

2.4.8.1 Glass composition specified for the whole of Europe [03]

| Chemical compound | Effect | Raw material |
|---|---|---|
| $SiO_2$<br>silicon dioxide | waterproofing<br>raises melting point<br>thermal fatigue stability<br>resistance to chemicals<br>resistance to UV radiation | quartz sand |
| $Al_2O_3$<br>aluminium oxide<br>$Fe_2O_3$<br>iron oxide | waterproofing<br>raises melting point<br>thermal fatigue stability<br>resistance to chemicals<br>resistance to mechanical damage | alumina |
| MgO<br>magnesium oxide | waterproofing | dolomite |
| CaO<br>calcium oxide | waterproofing | limestone, dolomite |
| BaO<br>Barium oxide | waterproofing | barytes |
| $Na_2O$<br>sodium oxide<br>$K_2O$<br>potassium oxide | solubility in water<br>lowers melting point<br>($Na_2O$ more than $K_2O$) | feldspar, potash, soda |

2.4.8.2 The effects of constituents and associated raw materials

#### Manufacture

The methods of production are similar for different types of glass. The main differences are in the forming of the glass. The raw materials are heated to such a high temperature that they reach a viscous state before being cooled down again.

The transparency of glass is the result of the inability of the melt to arrange its molecules in crystal lattices upon cooling. The structure is similar to that of a liquid; we speak of a "frozen melt" or a "supercooled liquid".

Production process

- Crushing the raw materials
- Mixing the components and adding scrap glass fragments (cullet)
- Melting down
- Refining to eliminate gaseous inclusions (seed, blibes)
- Forming
- Cooling

Forming

The types of glass are determined by the various methods of their production:

Sheet/plate glass

- Float glass

The melt is floated on the perfectly flat surface of a bath of molten tin and, after solidifying at the cooler end of the bath, is conveyed on rollers into the annealing lehr. This is now the most common method of production for transparent sheet or plate glass. Today, float glass is the most widely used type of glass and in most cases forms the basic product for all other types of glass.
Thicknesses available: 2–25 mm

- Drawn glass

A ribbon of glass is pulled upwards from the melting tank through slits, or simply from the surface, and cooled down either in a cooling shaft or a horizontal cooling duct. This method is only retained for producing very thin glass. The chemical and physical properties are the same as those for float glass.
Thicknesses available: 2–12 mm

- Cast or rolled glass

The glass melt is squeezed between a pair of rollers, or teemed directly on a stationary or moving table and subsequently rolled. The spacing of the rollers determines the thickness of the glass. Production takes place in cycles (now only for special types of glass) or continuously. The rollers can produce a texture or pattern on the surface. A spot-welded wire mesh can be laid in the liquid glass during the production process to create wired glass, with or without a pattern. The chemical and physical properties correspond to those of float glass; rolled glass is translucent, not transparent.
Thicknesses available: 3–10 mm

Profiled glass with or without wire inlay

This is a glass channel produced in a continuous casting and rolling method and bent into a U-shape during production. The glass itself is clear or coloured transparent soda-lime-silica glass.

Moulded or pressed glass

The melt is pressed into moulds and in the case of hollow items the two halves are fused together (e.g. glass blocks, glass roof tiles).

Borosilicate (heat-resisting) glass

This is produced like float or cast and rolled glass but contains, additionally, 7–15% boric oxide. Its composition gives it good thermal fatigue resistance and a high resistance to alkaline solutions and acids.
Thicknesses available: 3–15 mm

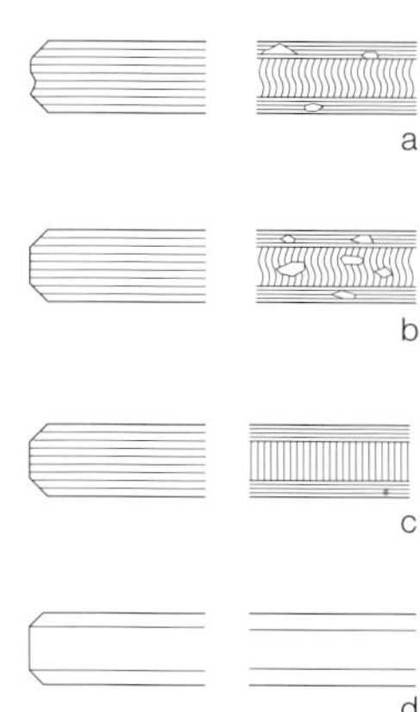


2.4.8.3 a arrissed edge, b edge ground to size, c ground edge, d polished edge [15]

**Working the material**

Edge working

The required size and shape of pane is obtained by snapping the glass along a scored line. The edges of panes built into frames are not normally given any special treatment.
The edges of toughened safety glass are arrissed, i.e. the sharp arrises are given a small chamfer to make them less dangerous but the edge remains otherwise rough.
A "ground-to-size edge" is where any high points on the edge projecting beyond a maximum dimension are ground off; blank spots remain.
A "ground edge" is ground completely smooth; no blank spots remain.
The edges of panes for use internally are polished for purely aesthetic reasons.
The visible edges of panes of wired glass with a non-stainless steel wire inlay should be coated with a clear lacquer to prevent the wires corroding where they have been cut through.
Panes of thermally toughened safety glass may not be worked (cut, drilled, ground) any further after being toughened. [04, 06]

Holes

Holes need to be drilled for discrete fixings and other reasons (see "Laying"). Minimum distances from corners and edges as specified by the manufacturer must be adhered to.

**Further treatment**

Toughening

- Thermally toughened safety glass

Finished panes are toughened by heating and quenching; this increases the tensile bending strength, impact resistance and thermal fatigue resistance. In contrast to non-toughened and heat-treated glass, which break into large, sharp fragments with a radial cracking pattern, thermally toughened safety glass breaks with a mesh-like pattern, resulting in small, blunt pieces (dice).

- Chemically toughened glass

The glass is immersed in a molten salt. The exchange of ions at the surface of the glass improves its resistance to mechanical and thermal strains, as with thermally toughened glass.

Bending, curving

- Bent glass

Flat panes are bent over a form while being heated. With a few exceptions (e.g. thick security glass), all types of glass and combinations thereof are suitable for this treatment. Bent glass can also be toughened by thermal or chemical means.

**Coatings and surface treatment**

Methods of production

One or more layers of inorganic substances (usually noble metals or metal oxides) are applied to the surface of the glass to improve properties of radiation and thermal performance. The coatings are applied either online, i.e. directly after the manufacture of the glass in the float plant, or offline in a later operation.

| | |
|---|---|
| Thermal performance | conductive metal coatings of:<br>gold, silver, copper, aluminium<br>low-emissivity coatings:<br>fluorine-doped tin oxide combined with silicon oxide<br>(at pos. 2 or 3 is better)<br>see figure 2.4.8.4 |
| Solar control | reflective, absorbent metal oxides of:<br>titanium, chromium, nickel, iron<br>enamel coatings made from ceramics<br>(at pos. 1, 2 or 3 combined with thermal insulation)<br>see figure 2.4.8.4 |

Anti-reflection coating
All glass-air interfaces are provided with coatings of different thickness and optical refractive index. This reduces the reflection to about 1% (e.g. shop windows).

Enamel coatings
Abrasion- and weather-resistant ceramic coatings applied to the finished pane of glass and fired (e.g. spandrel panels). [01, 10, 15]

Surface texture
One or both surfaces of a pane of rolled glass can be given a decorative finish using patterned rollers (more than 80 different types of glass are available, with and without wire inlay). The surface texture determines the translucency or transparency and the way in which the light is scattered or redirected. Float glass can be sandblasted, ground or etched with acid. This damage to the surface leads to an increased risk of soiling, lower strength and impaired transparency.

Positions of coatings

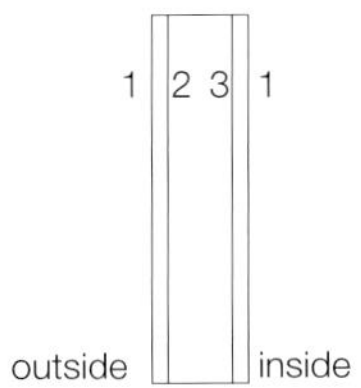


2.4.8.4 Position designations for coatings [15]

A coating can be applied to the inside, outside or cavity between the panes depending on type, structure or composition (follow the manufacturer's instructions). The coating is classified as follows according to its durability:
Class A:
The coating is applied to the glass surface facing outwards, which is directly exposed to the weather.
Class B:
The coating is applied to the glass surface not facing directly outwards and so is protected against direct exposure to weather. The coated glass can be used as single glazing.
Class C:
The coating is used only in the cavity between the panes in an insulating glass unit. The glass must be transported in special packaging and is prepared directly prior to the subsequent further processing.
Class D:
The coated glass is used only in the cavity between the panes and must be made up to form an insulating glass unit directly after production. It cannot be used as single glazing.
Class S:
The coated surface can be used both inside and outside and is suitable for special purposes (display windows, multiple glazing). [04, 15]

**Properties**
Colour

| Metal oxide | Colour |
|---|---|
| ferrous sulphide | brown, UV-absorbent |
| ferro | blue-green |
| ferric | brown, yellow |
| copper | blue, red |
| cobalt | blue, pink, green |
| manganese | violet (brown) |
| nickel | grey-brown, yellow, green |
| selenium | pale red |
| silver | citron yellow |
| gold | pink |
| uranium | lime green |
| chromium | green, yellow |
| silver halides | brown-grey, reversible colouring |

2.4.8.5 Metal ions for body-tinted glass

Normal clear glass can be given a colour by adding heavy-metal oxides to the melt (body-tinted glass), applying coatings of noble metals or metal oxides, or enamelling.

Physical properties

| | | |
|---|---|---|
| Density [g/cm³] | without wire inlay | 2.5 |
| | with wire inlay | 2.6 |
| Modulus of elasti. static, DIN 1249 [N/mm²] | not toughened | $7.3 \times 10^4$ |
| | toughened | $7.0 \times 10^4$ |
| Bending strength [N/mm²] of overhead glazing to DIBt | float glass | 12 |
| | toughened safety glass | 50 |
| | enamelled t. s. glass | 30 |
| | rolled and wired glass | 8 |
| | t. s. glass made from rolled glass | 37 |
| | laminated safety glass | 15 (25)[1] |
| Scratch hardness [Mohs] | | 5 to 6 |
| Softening temperature [°C] | | 520–550 |
| max. service temperature for thermally toughened glass [°C] | constant | 200 |
| | briefly | 300 |
| Thermal conductivity [W/mK] | | 0.8 |
| Coefficient of therm. expansion [mm/mK] | borosilicate glass | $3.1–6.0 \times 10^{-6}$ |
| | others | $9 \times 10^{-6}$ |
| Airborne sound insulation index [dB (A)] | glass thickness [mm] 3 to 19 | 22 to 38 |

[1] for lower pane

2.4.8.6 Characteristic values for glass [05, 07, 10, 16]

Chemical properties
Glass is highly resistant to chemicals, except hydrofluoric acid (HF) and concentrated alkaline solutions. Exposure to aqueous solutions, e.g. condensation in conjunction with industrial fumes, for a longer period can make, in particular, newly produced glass opaque. Such leaching can also be caused by the glass coming into contact with mineral plasters, fresh concrete or extremely alkaline cleaning agents. Glass is not sensitive to organic substances – apart from silicone, which tends to form bonds with the silicates in the surface of the glass. [10, 20]

Biological properties
UV-B radiation (short-wave ultraviolet radiation, 280–315 nm) is necessary for the formation of vitamin D and has a germicidal effect. Standard float glass is impermeable to UV-B radiation but types of glass with enhanced UV-B radiation permeability are available.

Environmental impact, recycling
The extraction of the raw materials from mines and quarries damages the landscape and the natural environment. Noise and dust are inevitable during the crushing of quartz sand, lime and dolomite.

Energy consumption
Complete production process for uncoated 4 mm float glass: 43.7 kWh/m²
Grey energy: 15.0 MJ/kg
Pollutants emitted during the complete production process for 4 mm float glass:
$CO_2$ 13.2 kg/m²
$SO_2$ 30 g/m²
$NO_x$ 94 g/m²
Emissions given off during the manufacture:
$SO_x$ 2.4 kg/t glass
$NO_x$ 1.4 kg/t glass

The energy consumption for coated glass is about 5% higher than that for uncoated glass. The grey energy value for insulating glass with argon gas in the cavity increases by only 0–1%.

Glass in use
Glass is not known to give off any pollutants once it has been installed in a building.

Recycling
Reuse takes place only to a limited extent because usually only production waste is recycled. Coloured and coated glass can only be intermixed to a certain degree or must be treated in some way.

Behaviour in landfill sites
Pigment residue and heavy metals are firmly embedded in the glass and are not liberated, or only after a very long time. [10]

Optical properties
The radiation relevant for buildings can be divided into three bands: ultraviolet radiation (~3%), wavelength 0–380 nm, visible light (~51%), wavelength 380–780 nm, and infrared

radiation (~46%), wavelength 780–2800 nm. Glass is impermeable to infrared radiation with a wavelength > 2800 nm. This gives rise to the greenhouse effect, i.e. objects heated up by short-wave radiation emit long-wave infrared radiation as a reaction to the increasing temperature. Most of this long-wave radiation is absorbed by the glass and some reflected back into the interior, thus heating it. [15]

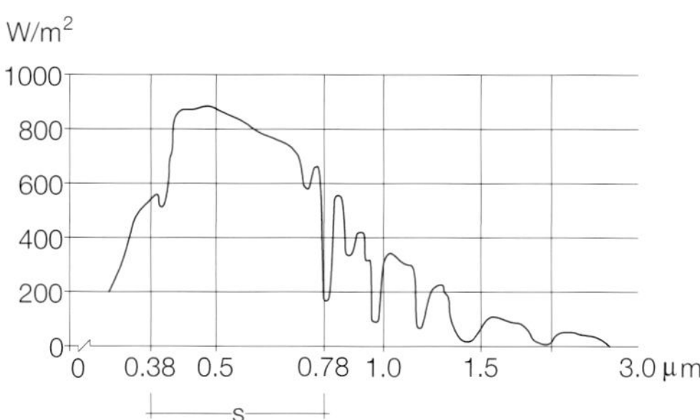


2.4.8.7 Solar spectrum at sea level; wavelength [nm], radiation intensity [W/m²], s = range of wavelengths visible to the human eye

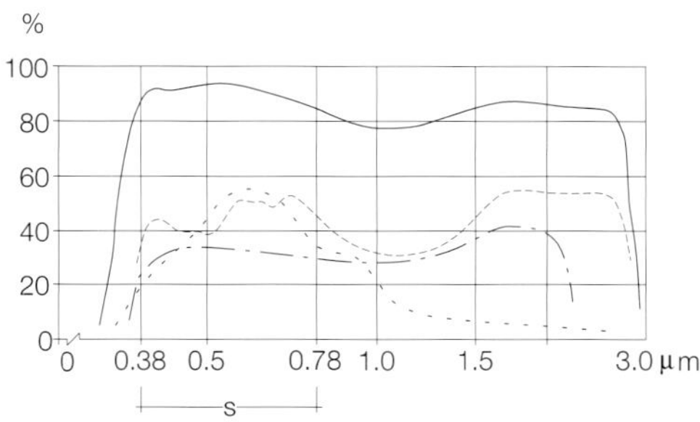


2.4.8.8 Transmission spectra of various solar-control glasses in comparison to clear float glass

The type and density of the glass, and its coating and colour determine the proportions and the spectral composition of the radiation passing through. The proportion of direct, straight, incident solar radiation that is lost through reflection depends on the angle of incidence. Reflection takes place at every glass-air interface (~4%). Minimum light transmittance values for various types of glass are specified in DIN 67507.

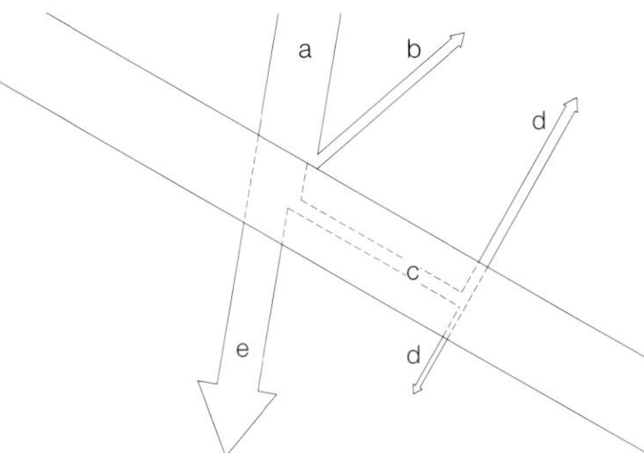


2.4.8.9 Radiation behaviour on glass: a incident radiation, b reflection, c absorption, d secondary dissipation, e transmission

Light transmittance
Typical values for non-tinted float glass are 85–90% for 4 mm glass and 69–81% for 19 mm glass.

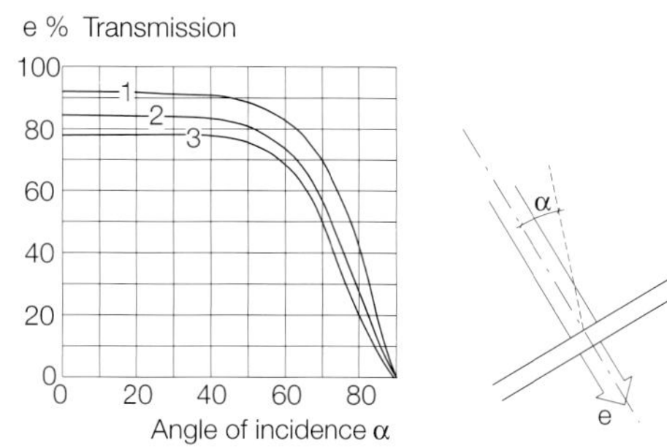


2.4.8.10 Light transmittance of clear glass in relation to angle of incidence [°] (measured from the perpendicular), transmittance [%]

## Components

**General elements**
The maximum dimensions given in the following tables are based on the technical possibilities of the manufacturers. The rule for overhead glazing is that panes of laminated safety glass made from float glass must be supported on all sides for spans ≥ 1.20 m. The pane aspect ratio may not exceed 3:1.

Single glazing
Protection against falling glass fragments, or a method of bonding the glass fragments together are required for glass roofs. Therefore, single glazing and the inner pane of double glazing units are made from laminated safety glass (in the future also heat-treated glass or a combination of both) or wired glass. However, the use of wired glass has not proved to be a good choice in recent years owing to corrosion and thermal problems. When using coloured rolled glass, the area of one pane should not exceed 1.5 m² and the pane aspect ratio should not exceed 1:2.2. [12, 17]

Laminated glass
This is a permanently bonded type of glass consisting of at least two panes plus a visco-plastic synthetic interlayer.
Laminated glass without safety properties
This can be used for sound insulation or for decorative purposes. The interlayer is made from a plastic film or casting resin.

Laminated safety glass
When broken the splinters and fragments of glass are held (bonded) together by the interlayer (usually PVB film, sometimes also casting resin). The fracture pattern is mesh-like, and the broken pane remains transparent.

Interlayer of polyvinyl butyral (PVB)
Normally, PVB film is used as the interlayer in laminated safety glass. It is particularly tear-resistant and can be employed in various thicknesses. The transparency we associate with glass can be very slightly impaired, depending on the thickness and number of films. By using various arrangements it is possible to create different types of security glazing resistant to vandals, intruders, bullets and explosives.

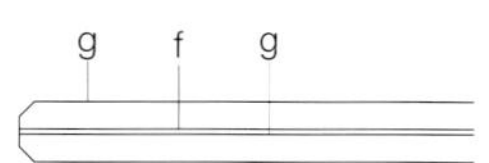


2.4.8.11 Laminated safety glass: g pane of glass, f PVB interlayer

Special interlayers
- Interlayer with heating wire (e.g. for thawing snowdrifts)
  The heat output is 1–30 kW/m²; toughened glass must be used for a heat output ≥ 5 kW/m²; max. size 2460 x 3750 mm.
- Interlayer with alarm wire
  An alarm is tripped when the pane is damaged and the wire broken.
- Interlayer of casting resin
  For use in acoustic-control glazing (see "Insulating glass – Sound insulation") or photovoltaic panels; can be completely/partly coloured with one or more pigments or films.
- Interlayer of water glass or gel containing water
  For use in fire-resistant glass (see "Insulating glass – Fire protection").
- Interlayer of polycarbonate
  For use in anti-intruder glazing.
- Coloured interlayers
  Coloured laminated (safety) glass is possible using coloured PVB film; the colours are not totally light-fast.
- Interlayer to block ultraviolet radiation (UV radiation permeability: 1%)
- Interlayer made from non-woven glass-fibre fabric or spun glass for light-scattering glazing.
- Interlayer of polyethylene film printed with holograms between two PVB films to redirect the daylight.
- Interlayers of electrolytes whose properties can be altered by applying an electric current (electrochromic); in this way a glazing unit can be alternately transparent and opaque.
- The use of thermotropic coatings (= combination of two synthetic materials) in laminated glass is currently undergoing development; at low temperatures these materials combine (= transparent) and at higher temperatures they separate and thus give the

glass a milky white appearance; the majority of the sunlight is then reflected. [10]

| Longest edge of pane [cm] | ≤ 8 mm thick | > 8 mm thick | with 1 single pane ≥ 10 mm thick |
|---|---|---|---|
| ≤ 100 | ± 10 | ± 15 | ± 25 |
| ≤ 150 | ± 15 | ± 20 | ± 30 |
| ≤ 200 | ± 15 | ± 20 | ± 35 |
| ≤ 250 | ± 25 | ± 30 | ± 40 |
| > 250 | ± 30 | ± 35 | ± 45 |

2.4.8.12 Laminated safety glass; permissible length and width tolerances [mm]

Insulating glass

Multi-pane insulating glass is a glazing unit produced from two or more panes of glass each separated by a sealed cavity framed by a hermetic edge seal that prevents the ingress of air, gas or moisture. The pressure in the cavity sealed against the external atmosphere depends on the altitude of the plant in which the glazing unit was manufactured. If insulating glass is transported to regions at a different altitude for use in buildings there, the pressure differential must be compensated for by means of an integral valve once a certain pressure differential has been exceeded. Gas-filled cavities are not possible in this case.
When used as a roof covering, the inner pane must be made from laminated safety or wired glass. Rolled glass can also be made into an insulating glass unit, normally with the patterned side facing outwards (to give a better edge seal).
Because there is such a multitude of types of patterned glass available, the possible combinations, dimensions and characteristic values can only be ascertained from the manufacturers.

Stepped insulating glass
Here, the upper pane of an insulating glass unit projects on one side. Stepped insulating glass can be used as an overlapping roof covering or – when laying stepped insulating glass with sealed joints – as a special eaves component. The projection should be at least 200 mm and the cantilevering pane should be made from toughened safety glass. Combinations with wired glass are also possible. [13, 15]
Max. size: 2000 x 3000 mm [13]

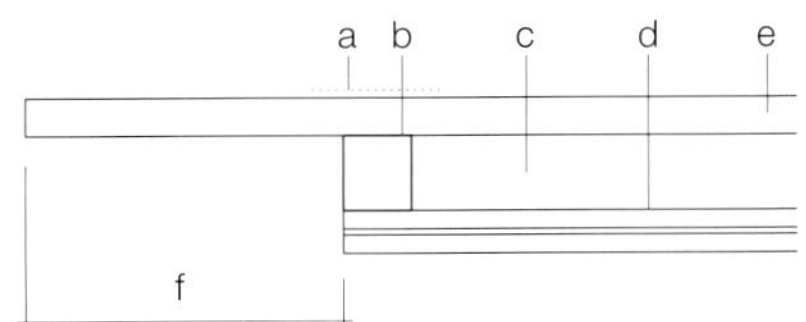


2.4.8.13 Stepped insulating glass; structure: a UV radiation protection, b hermetic edge seal, c cavity, d inner pane of laminated safety glass, e outer pane of toughened safety glass, f projection ≥ 200 mm

Hermetic edge seal
Today, the hermetic edge seal to the individual panes is almost exclusively produced by means of bonding. The spacer is usually made of aluminium, galvanised or stainless steel or plastic (polycarbonate with inlay of stainless steel foil as a diffusion barrier, or butyl). It is hollow, with perforations on the cavity side, and filled with a desiccant to soak up the residual moisture from air trapped during production. A double seal is common; this consists of a permanently elastic adhesive between spacer and pane and a 3–4 mm thick edge sealing over the spacer.
If the hermetic edge seal is exposed to incident solar radiation, silicone must be used for sealing (but without a gas filling because the rate of diffusion is markedly higher). [10, 13, 14, 15]

2.4.8.14 Hermetic edge seal on insulating glass: 1 outside, 2 inside, 3 metal spacer, 4 sealing level, 5 desiccant, 6 sealing level

**Insulating glass for special requirements**

Sound insulation
The following measures improve the sound reduction index of insulating glass:
- increasing the thickness of the panes
- reducing the stiffness of the panes (laminated glass with interlayer of casting resin)
- including an acoustic PVB film interlayer in laminated safety glass
- combining different thicknesses of individual panes (asymmetric double glazing, min. 30% difference in thickness)
- widening the cavity
- filling the cavity with a heavy gas (e.g. $SF_6$ argon, krypton or mixtures) [13, 14]

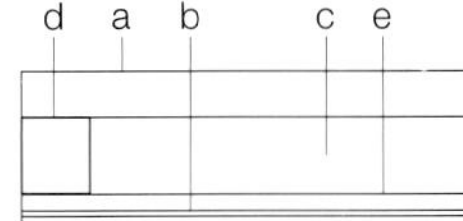


2.4.8.15 Structure of sound insulating glass: a glass pane, b casting resin interlayer, c filling of heavy gas, d hermetic edge seal, e pane of laminated safety glass

**Scattering and redirecting the light**

We distinguish between light-scattering and light-redirecting glass. These functions are achieved with stationary or tracking systems. Switchable glasses form a further group. These are divided into two main groups according to their method operation: tropic glasses (not coloured, purely a scattering function) and chromic glasses (coloured, with non-scattering functions). The weather-related variables temperature (thermo...) and radiation (photo...) or the user-related variables voltage application (electro...) and gas feed into the cavity (gaso...) act as the control signals. The glass then changes from the transparent to the opaque state. [15]

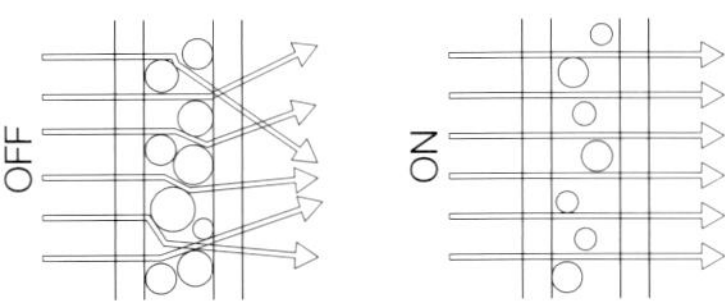


2.4.8.16 Micro-encapsulated liquid crystals without (left: opaque) and with (right: transparent) application of a voltage [14]

Properties of switchable glasses

| | g-value [%] | Light transmittance [%] | U-value of glazing system [W/m²K] | Appearance |
|---|---|---|---|---|
| Thermotropic heat-absorbing window | 0.18 to 0.55 | 0.21 to 0.73 | 1.28 | white to clear |
| Electrochromic window | 0.12 to 0.36 | 0.2 to 0.64 | 1.1 | blue to neutral |
| Gasochromic heat-absorbing window | 0.15 to 0.53 | 0.15 to 0.64 | 1.05 | blue to neutral |

Phototropic, electrotropic (electro-optical) and thermochromic glasses are still undergoing development and cannot be quantified at present. The values given here could change considerably over time as a result of further developments.

2.4.8.17 Overview of switchable glasses [15]

Scattering the light

Scattering the light allows us to achieve better illumination in the far corners of the interior and prevents glare due to direct sunlight. We distinguish between light-scattering glasses that can be processed to form all types of glass (thermal insulation, sound insulation, solar control) and those with a light-scattering filling in the cavity.

Transparent thermal insulation
Here, the cavity is filled with very fine plastic capillary or honeycomb structures, thin-walled narrow glass tubes, xerogels or aerogels. Any type of conventional sheet/plate glass can be used to enclose these materials.

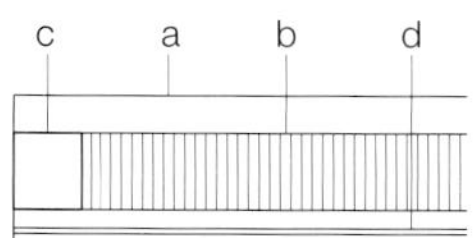


2.4.8.18 Light-scattering insulating glass: a pane of glass, b capillary infill, c hermetic edge seal, d pane of glass

| Type | Thickness [mm] | U-value [W/m²K] | g | $\tau_e$ | $\tau_v$ |
|---|---|---|---|---|---|
| G-HC-G | 50 | 1.01 | 0.78 | 0.71 | 0.80 |
| G-HC-G | 70 | 0.85 | 0.78 | 0.70 | 0.79 |
| G-A-G | 20 | 0.96 | 0.49 | 0.48 | 0.40 |
| G-G | – | 2.93 | 0.79 | 0.74 | 0.82 |

Physical characteristic values of transparent thermal insulation daylight elements (G = glass, HC = honeycomb structure, A = aerogel, g = total energy transmittance, τ = transmission, e = energy, v = visible)

2.4.8.19 Overview of various transparent thermal insulation elements [15]

Inlay of non-woven glass-fibre fabric
A light-scattering insulating glass with an air-filled cavity can be produced by using laminated glass with an interlayer of non-woven glass-fibre fabric.

Redirecting the light

We distinguish between diffuse redirection, selective shading with diffuse transmission, redirection of sunlight, and redirection systems not dependent on solar altitude angle. [17]

Diffuse redirection
Redirection of light from the north with holographic optical elements.

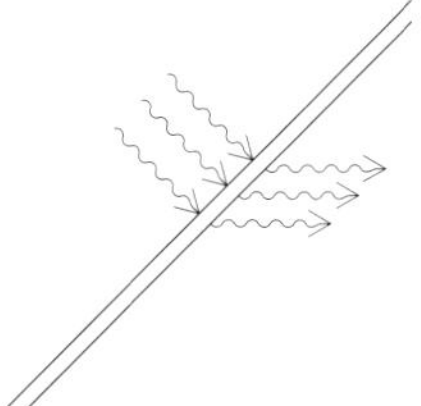

2.4.8.20 Diffuse redirection of the light

Selective shading with diffuse transmission
Prismatic plates, solar-control reflective grids, focusing by means of holographic optical elements and total reflection using holographic optical elements.

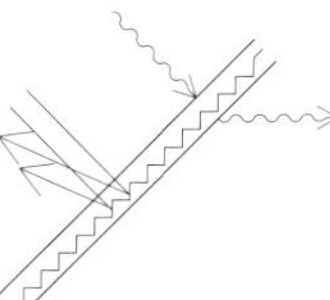

2.4.8.21 Transmission of diffuse light and selective reflection of direct sunlight

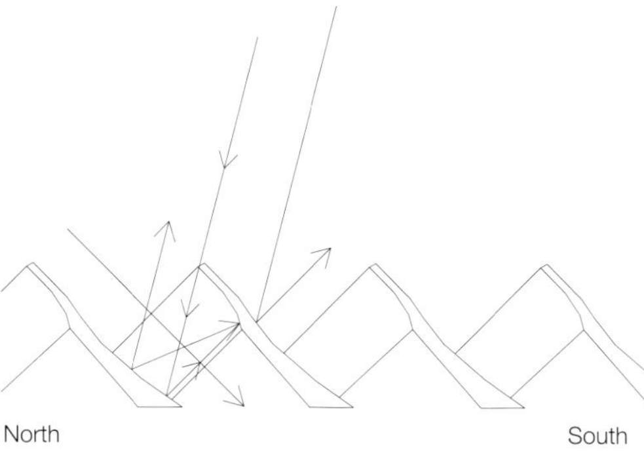


2.4.8.22 How a light grid works

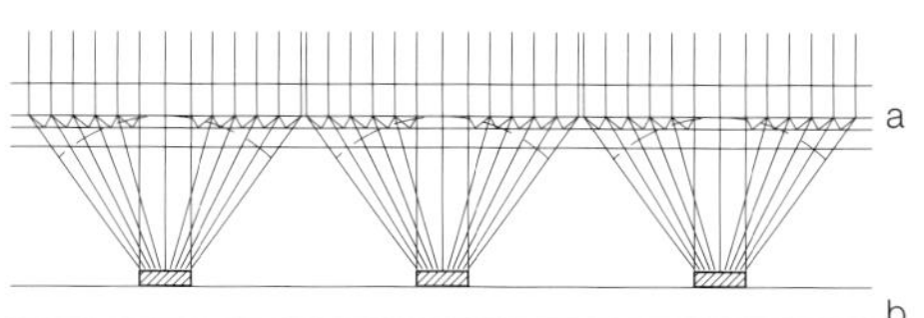


2.4.8.23 Laminated glass with a) focusing holograms, and b) pane of glass with solar cells

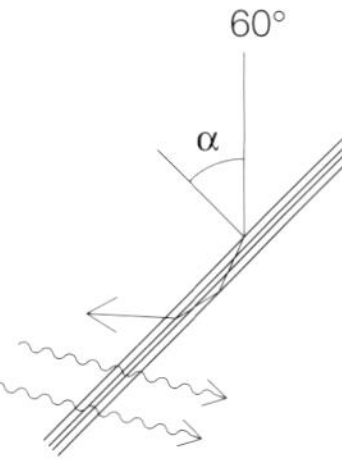


2.4.8.24 Direct incident light is refracted twice so that it is totally reflected; not effective for any other angle of incidence so transparent for diffuse light. [17]

Redirection of sunlight

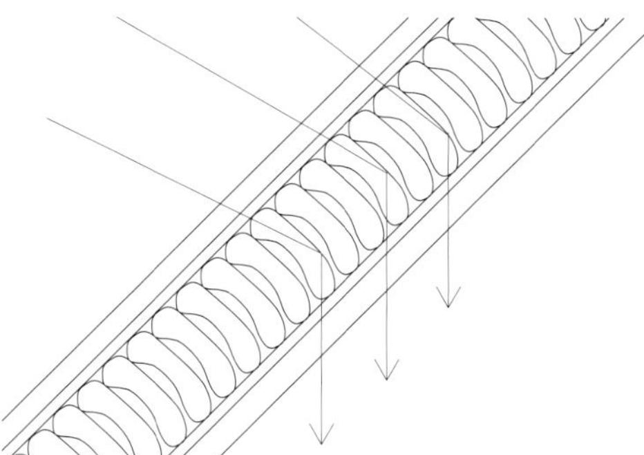

2.4.8.25 Direct incident light can be directed deep into the interior of the building by the acrylic glass louvres fitted in the cavity

Light redirection systems dependent on solar altitude angle

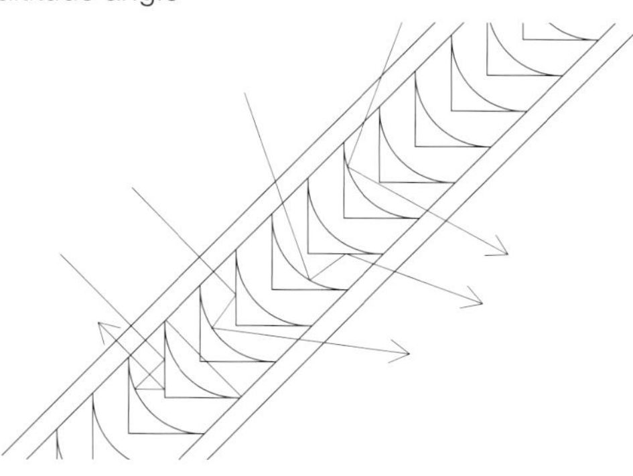

2.4.8.26 Glazing with reflective profiles

**Heat-absorbing glass**

A heat-absorbing glass is an insulating glass with at least one coated surface facing the cavity – which one is irrelevant for the thermal performance (U-value). The total energy transmittance can alter by about 5% according to the position of the coating, the colour, and the evenness of the colouring. For passive heat gains, a heat-absorbing glass should transmit as much solar energy as possible, i.e. have a high total energy transmittance (g) and a high light transmittance (t) in the visible range of the spectrum, and a low U-value.

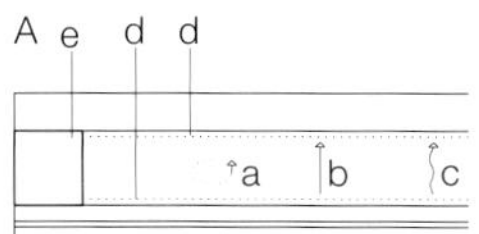


2.4.8.27 Insulating glass; heat losses: A outside, a convection, b conduction, c radiation, d coating, e hermetic edge seal (c = 67%, a + b + edge seal = 33%)

Enhanced thermal performance is achieved by using:

- triple glazing,
- a heat-reflecting coating,
- a gas-filled cavity – argon, krypton, xenon or mixtures ($SF_6$ is currently used but its main advantage is in improving the sound reduction index); xenon is now rarely used because the reserves of this gas are almost exhausted.

| Possible modified U-values according to Federal Gazette [W/m²K] | Cavity filling: Thickness of pane does not change U-value/Federal Gazette value; values in brackets apply to different coating | | | |
|---|---|---|---|---|
| | air | argon | krypton | argon/$SF_6$ |
| double glazing, | 1.8 | 1.5 | 1.1 | 1.5 |
| 12 mm cavity | (1.9) | (1.6) | (1.4) | (1.8) |
| double glazing, | 1.5 | 1.2 | 1.2 | 1.5 |
| 15/16 mm cavity | (1.6) | (1.4) | (1.4) | (1.9) |
| triple glazing, | no info | no info | 0.8 | no info |
| 2 x 8 mm cavity | | | (0.9) | |

2.4.8.28 Overview of various insulating glasses with gas filling [10]

## Solar-control measures

Lower total energy transmittance is achieved by using:

- mainly reflective and/or absorbent metal oxide coatings
- body-tinted, absorbent types of glass
- enamel or silk-screen printing
- film or foil in the cavity
- spun glass, non-woven glass-fibre fabric or capillary systems in the cavity
- sunshading (louvres etc.) in the cavity

(see "Scattering and redirecting the light")
Some solar-control coatings improve the U-value.

## Photovoltaic systems

Solar cells are integrated into the cavity of a laminated glass unit and convert the incident solar energy into an electric current. We distinguish between amorphous solar cells (degree of efficiency: 8%; appearance: translucent red/dark grey to opaque), monocrystalline solar cells (degree of efficiency: 16%; appearance: matt black/dark blue) and polycrystalline solar cells (degree of efficiency: 14%; appearance: light and dark blue). Casting resin is frequently used as the backing material. The size of these solar cells lies between 10 x 10 cm and 15 x 15 cm.
Another type is the thin-film solar cell (degree of efficiency: 6%; appearance: dark brown/black). The silicon is applied directly to the surface of the glass by vapour deposition. For details of cell sizes, please consult the manufacturers. The construction of a photovoltaic panel corresponds to that of an insulating glass element and can be integrated into the structure in a similar way. [14, 15]

| Characteristic values / Type of glass | Thickness of single pane [mm] | Cavity [mm] | Thickness of component [mm] | Light transmittance [%] | Total energy transmiss. [%] | Modified U-value [W/m²k] | approx. weight [kg/m²] | Airborne sound insulation index [dB] | max. dimensions [cm] |
|---|---|---|---|---|---|---|---|---|---|
| **Heat-absorbing glass** | | | | | | | | | |
| coated float glass (noble metal) | | | | | | | | | 321 x 600 |
| cavity: air | 4/4 | 12 | 20 | 76 | 57 | 1.7 | 20 | | |
| double | 8/8 | 15 | 31 | 74 | 59 | 1.4 | 40 | | |
| triple | 4/4/4 | 12/12 | 36 | 75 | 60 | 0.6 | 30 | | |
| coated float glass | | | | | | | | | 321 x 600 |
| (noble metal) | 4/4 | 12 | 20 | 77 | 58 | 1.4 | 20 | | |
| cavity: argon | 8/8 | 15 | 31 | 73 | 54 | 1.1 | 40 | | |
| double | 10/4 | 15 | 29 | 74 | 50 | 1.1 | 33 | | |
| triple | 4/4/4 | 15/15 | 42 | 66 | 45 | 0.6 | 30 | | |
| float glass cavity: krypton coated | | | | | | | | | 321 x 600 |
| (noble metal) | 4/4 | 12 | 20 | 77 | 58 | 1.0 | 20 | | |
| double | 8/8 | 15 | 31 | 73 | 54 | 1.0 | 40 | | |
| | 4/4/4 | 8/8 | 28 | 66 | 48 | 0.6 | 30 | | |
| triple | 4/4/4 | 12/12 | 36 | 66 | 45 | 0.5 | 30 | | |
| **Sound insulation glass** | | | | | | | | | |
| float glass | 8/4 | 12 | 24 | 75 | 59 | 1.6 | 30 | 37 | |
| cav.: argon, kryp- | 8/4 | 14 | 24 | 76 | 57 | 1.6 | 25 | 39 | |
| ton or mixture | 9.5/6 | 20 | 36 | 73 | 50 | 1.2 | 40 | 42 | |
| cast. res. interlayer | 20.5/9.5 | 20 | 50 | 67 | 44 | 1.7 | 75 | 56 | |
| lam. safety glass | 14/8 | 24 | 46 | 70 | 47 | 1.1 | | 51 | |
| **Solar-control glass** | | | | | | | | | |
| float glass cavity: argon metal oxide coating to inside of outer pane | | | | | | | | | 365 x 214 |
| silver | 6/4 | 15 | 25 | 7–28 | 8–25 | 1.3 | 25 | 35 | |
| blue | | | | 12–30 | 14–28 | | | | |
| grey | | | | 28 | 27 | | | | |
| body-tinted glass | | | | | | | | | no info |
| green | 6/4 | 15 | 25 | 60 | 40 | 1.3 | 25 | 35 | |
| grey | | | | 37 | 35 | | | | |
| bronze | | | | 44 | 38 | | | | |
| **Fire-resistant glass F 30** | | | | | | | | | |
| toughened safety g. cavity with alkali-silicate gel | 5/5/3/3 | 5/5/5 | 31 | 80 | | 4.9 | 63 | 42 | 124 x 200 |
| float glass cavity with alkali-silicate gel | 3/3/3/3 | 1.2/1.2/1.2 | 16 | 84 | | 4.9 | 40 | 41 | 190 x 310 |
| laminated safety glass | 3/3/3/3/4 | 1.5/1.5/1.5/28 | 28 | 71 | | up to 1.1 | 47 | 44 | 150 x 250 |

2.4.8.30 Characteristic values of insulating glass

| Direction | Inclination with respect to the horizontal | | | |
|---|---|---|---|---|
| | 0° | 30° | 60° | 90° |
| East | 93% | 90% | 78% | 55% |
| South-East | 93% | 96% | 88% | 66% |
| South | 93% | 100% | 91% | 68% |
| South-West | 93% | 96% | 88% | 66% |
| West | 93% | 90% | 78% | 55% |

2.4.8.29 Relative annual solar radiation intensity in relation to compass direction and inclination of solar panel [14]

## Fire-resistant glass

Fire-resistant glass has interlayers containing moisture that evaporates and thus consumes heat energy in the event of a fire; at the same time they become opaque and act as heat insulators. This means that the rise in temperature on the surface of the pane not directly exposed to the fire can be limited for a certain length of time and the transmission of smoke and radiant heat hindered. Laminated glass with alkali-silicate gel layers, normally consisting of four panes of glass (each 3 mm float glass) with a sealed frame (laminated aluminium strip), can be used as fire-resistant glazing (class F 30). In the event of a fire the first pane of float glass fractures, allowing the gel to foam up and form a protective shield. Testing and classification for fire-resistant classes F 30 to F 180 takes place in the built-in state according to DIN 4102 part 2. [10, 14]

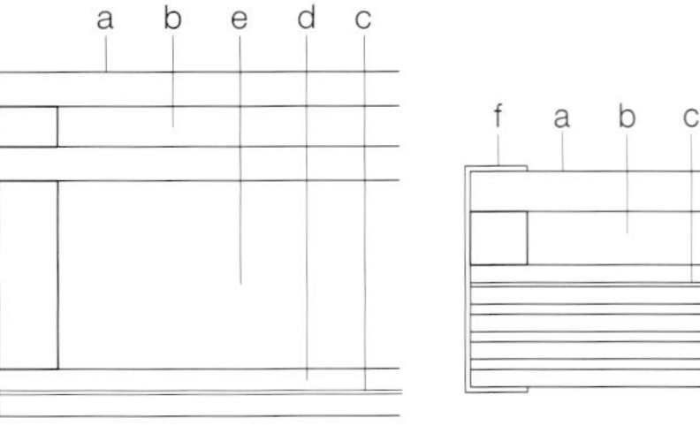


2.4.8.30 Fire-resistant glass
a float glass, b cavity, c PVB film (0.38 mm), d panes of 3 mm float glass, e layer of gel (≥ 28 mm/~1.5 mm), f enclosing frame (laminated aluminium strip)

**Edge elements**

Bent glass, special glass forms

Bent glass

In comparison with flat panes, bent glass has a lower optical quality and more generous dimensional tolerances. Higher costs (5–10 times higher) and longer delivery times can also be expected. Bent panes of glass are more rigid and can accommodate less deformation under loading.

The frame must allow for these tolerances due to the bending process.

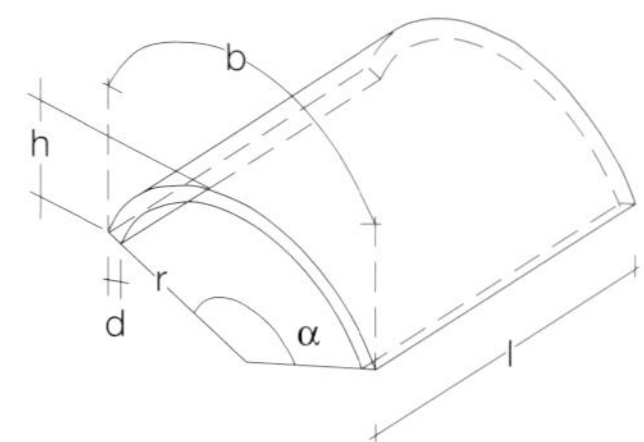


| Type of glass / Designation | Single glazing | Lam. safety glass | Tough. safety glass | Insulating glass |
|---|---|---|---|---|
| max. l x w [cm] | 250x400 | 250x400 | 213 x365 | 250 x400 |
| max. h [cm] | 80 | 80 | 40 | 80 |
| min. r [cm] | 5 | 8 | 20 | 12 |
| d [mm] | 5–19 | 5–19 | 5–19 | 5–19 |
| max α [°] | 120 | 120 | 120 | 120 |

2.4.8.31 Bent glass; dimensions: b development, h rise, l length, r radius

Insulating glass, special forms

Specially shaped panes with straight or curved edges can be cut from a rectangular piece of glass.

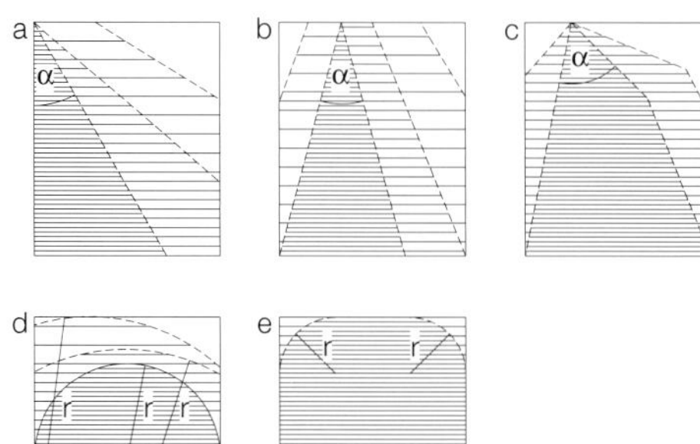


2.4.8.32 Insulating glass; special forms a to c = 1–3 straight cuts, d and e = curved cuts; a > 30°, r > 100 mm

Working

Components with cut-outs, holes and openings in the panes of glass are produced through scoring and snapping, drilling, and grinding. Sharp corners are not possible – rounded corners are essential.

Cut-outs or holes in insulating glass require toughened panes. [03, 21]

## Storage

Glass should only be stored upright in dry, ventilated conditions and covered with tarpaulins. Insulating glass should be protected from direct sunlight; otherwise there is a risk of heat cracking, particularly with coated, body-tinted, patterned, rolled or wired glass. The hermetic edge seal should also be protected from ultraviolet radiation to prevent premature ageing. [13]

## Laying

Building authority requirements, conditions for laying, covering, sealing, fixing, additional measures, details, sunshading, supporting construction, maintenance and repair

**Building authority requirements**

The German Building Technology Institute (DIBt) has drawn up "Technical rules for the use of overhead glazing on linear supports". Adhering to them means it is not necessary to obtain building authority approval in each individual case. These rules should be read in conjunction with the relevant federal state building code. They do not apply to bent glass. Generally, protection from falling fragments of glass, or a type of glass that bonds fragments together, is required on the inside of a glass roof covering. Single glazing and the inner pane of insulating glazing are therefore made from laminated safety glass or wired glass. However, owing to the risk of corrosion and thermal strains, the use of wired glass for overhead glazing is not recommended.

**Conditions for laying**

The unfavourable angle of incidence of the solar radiation means that a glass roof covering is subjected to higher temperatures. Additional thermal loads should therefore be avoided.

- Uniform ventilation of the inner and outer surfaces of the panes prevents a build-up of heat.
- The external wall at the eaves should be insulated to protect the overlying insulating glass from the ensuing heat radiation.
- The application of paint or adhesive coverings to panes of glass can lead to uneven heating.
- Any sunshading measures required should not be positioned too close to the glass (approx. 200 mm gap) in order to avoid a build-up of heat. Dark sunshading components emit long-wave radiation and heat the glass more than reflective, light-coloured components.
- Placing a thermal break between glazing bar and glazing wing/cap prevents a temperature gradient between edge and centre of pane. The edge cover should therefore be ≤ 20 mm, and there should be adequate ventilation to ensure that condensation in the base of the rebate is avoided or kept to a minimum and able to drain away.
- Extreme, heavy shadows lead to a temperature differential within the pane of glass.
- The cavity should not be wider than 15 mm (wired glass 10.5 mm), particularly with solar-control and heat-absorbing glass, because larger volumes of air in the cavity increase the pressure on the panes of glass.
- As glass and steel have different coefficients of thermal expansion, this aspect, together with increased heating of body-tinted or coated glass, can lead to the glass breaking. Solar-control glass/wired glass and wired glass/wired glass combinations should therefore not be used as insulating glass.
- If additional thermal loading cannot be avoided, the glass concerned should be toughened (not possible with wired glass).
- If the panes of glass are not identical (asymmetric double glazing), the thinner and less rigid pane is more likely to break because pressure differentials between cavity and external atmosphere cause it to deflect. The thinner pane should therefore be toughened for pane aspect ratios > 2:1. The inner pane may be max. 2 mm thinner than the outer pane when using solar-control and heat-absorbing glass. [13, 14, 16]

Roof pitch

The roof pitch for sealed transverse butt joints should be > 10° so that water drains away reliably from the panes and longitudinal butt joints. A build-up of water should be expected at transverse butt joints even at steeper roof pitches if the glazing wings/caps and, in certain circumstances, the preformed seals are not bevelled to suit the roof pitch.

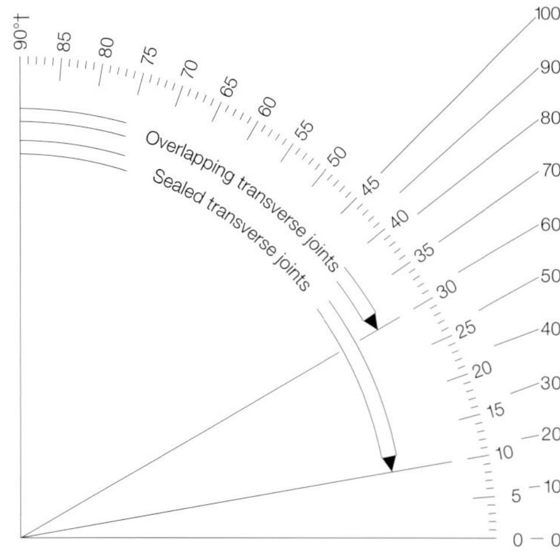


2.4.8.33 Roof pitch; recommendations of manufacturers and roofing trade

The roof pitch for overlapping transverse joints should be > 30° to prevent the ingress of moisture by capillary action or from a build-up of water.

Rebate
The dimensions for the rebate are specified in DIN 18544.
The edge cover g should be about 2/3 x h in the case of non-toughened glass, but not more than 20 mm.

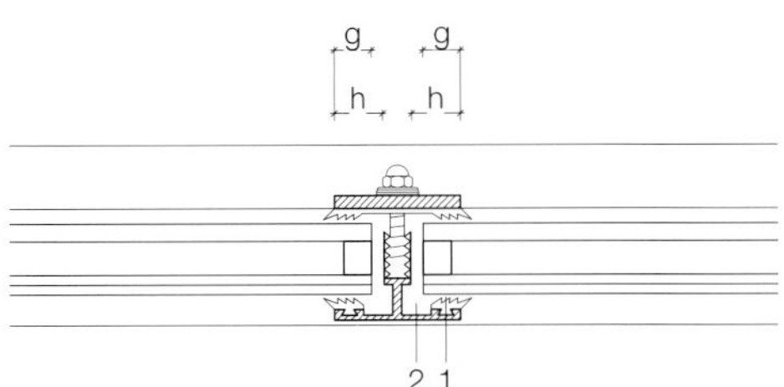


2.4.8.34 Rebate: h depth of rebate, g edge cover 2/3 x $h < 15$ mm for sloping glazing, 1 inner sealing level, 2 water run-off level in rebate

Draining and ventilating the rebate
Glazing systems with an open rebate, i.e. without seals/sealant, should be employed for glass roof coverings. Openings should be provided at the eaves for the ventilation and vapour pressure compensation of the rebate; and at the ridge for glazing over damp interiors. Any condensation or moisture from leaks must be intercepted and drained to the outside via the vapour pressure compensation openings. The water run-off level must lie below the inner sealing level.

| Longest side of glazing unit | Depth of rebate h [mm] for single glazing min. | multiple glazing min. |
|---|---|---|
| ≤ 1000 | 10 | 18 |
| 1000–3500 | 12 | 18 |
| > 3500 | 15 | 20 |

2.4.8.35 Depth of rebate: the depth of rebate may be reduced to 14 mm and the edge cover to 11 mm to allow for a narrow glazing bar with multiple glazing having an edge length of up to 500 mm; sloping glazing should generally have an edge cover $< 15$ mm. [13, 22]

**Covering**
Overlapping transverse joint

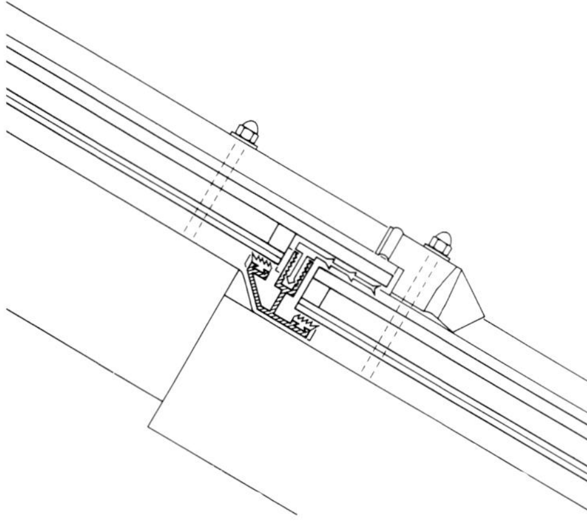

2.4.8.36 Overlapping transverse joint using stepped insulating glass [09]

Protection from the rain is ensured by the individual overlapping elements; an additional seal, chosen to suit roof pitch and overlap, protects against wind and a build-up of water. The overlap is formed by

- plane-parallel glazing units on a packed-up or stepped supporting construction.
- Stepped insulating glass can be laid on roof pitches ≥ 30°.

The minimum overlap is 100 mm. As the hermetic edge seal is not covered by fixing or sealing components at an overlapping transverse joint between insulating glass units, it must be made from a material resistant to ultraviolet radiation, or shielded against ultraviolet radiation by special measures:

- a metal coating of the overlying pane in this area
- a covering of sheet metal
- partial enamelling (outer pane of toughened safety glass)
- solar-control glass with a UV radiation transmittance $< 10\%$
- attaching a ventilated sheet metal shade
- applying a silicone coating

Tapered stepped insulating glass units can only be supplied to special order.
Seals and gaskets for use with an overlapping transverse joint seal it against wind, snow and a build-up of water caused by wind pressure, and prevent the upper pane of glass from lying directly on the lower one. The joint between seals at intersections must be carefully designed (mitred etc.). It is better to use special T-, L- and X-shaped pieces and move the joint away from this point. The best method is to employ prefabricated, vulcanised preformed gasket meshes.

**Sealing**
Sealed transverse and longitudinal joints

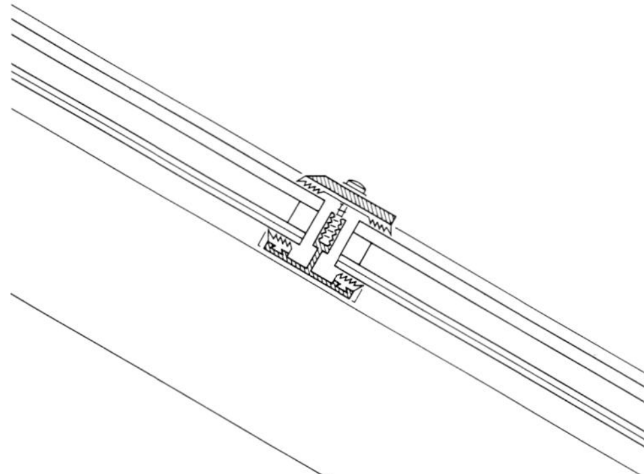

2.4.8.37 Transverse joint sealed with glazing cap

Protection from ingress of water is achieved solely through the seal. Sealing and support is accomplished with preformed seals or sealants and spacer tapes. These two options can be combined with respect to the seal on the side exposed to the weather and the interior.

Preformed seals may be self-clamping or held in place by glazing wings/caps. All the sealing materials used must be compatible with each other; the film used for the interlayer of laminated safety glass must also be taken into account. [22]

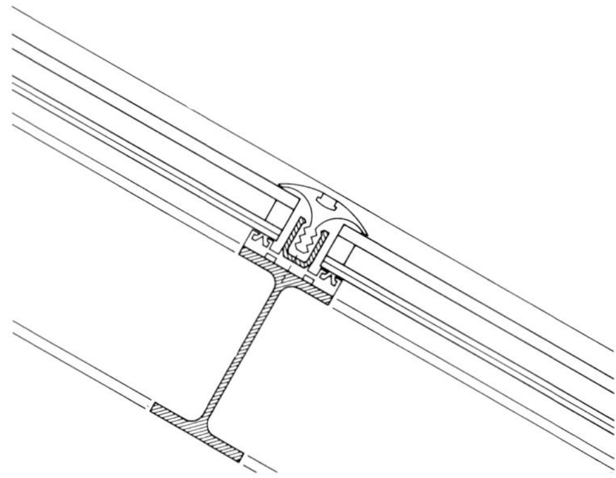

2.4.8.38 Transverse joint with self-clamping preformed seal

Sealing with preformed seals
Preformed seals provide a seal against water and air and guarantee elastic support for the glazing units.
Preformed seals must possess adequate deformability to compensate for their own tolerances, the permissible dimensional tolerances of the glazing units and glazing bars, and the permissible deflections. The hardness of the seal and its cross-section define the contact pressure necessary for a certain deformation and adequate sealing properties; a special pressure/compression diagram can be drawn up for every seal. The contact pressure should be limited to 5 N/mm edge of pane for insulating glass. If this pressure is generated by screws or other mechanical clamping elements, it must be applied in a controlled manner, e.g. using a torque wrench.

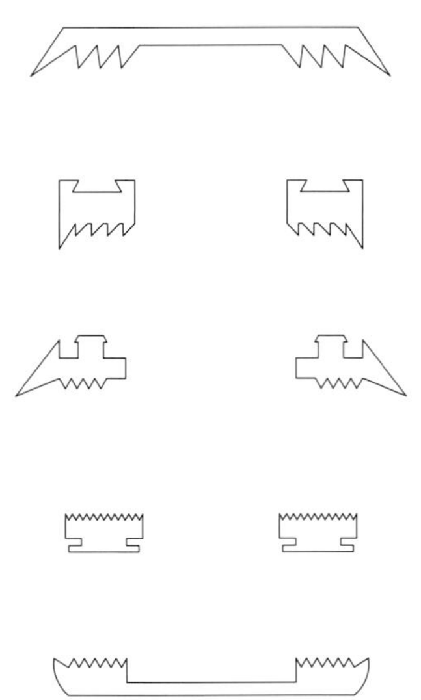

2.4.8.39 One- and two-piece preformed seals [09, 21]

The concentrated pressure of the screws must be transferred evenly to the preformed seal by a sufficiently stiff bar – according to material and cross-section. The spacing of the clamping elements should be < 25 cm. [12, 22]
Lipped preformed seals of silicone adhere better to glass than to EPDM profiles and permit subsequent sealing in problem areas. [13]
Preformed seals for sealing a butt joint can be made of one or two pieces. Two-piece profiles require a groove or tongue to prevent the seal slipping. One-piece profiles can be fixed by the penetrating clamping elements of the glazing wing/cap. The form and arrangement of the sealing lips varies. One-piece, internal profiles must be designed so that the level at which any condensation collects and drains lies below the inner sealing level. If fixings or clamping elements penetrate the seal, it should have a central bulb so that the penetration point lies above the water run-off layer.

The underside of the internal profile can be formed to match the cross-section of the glazing bar.

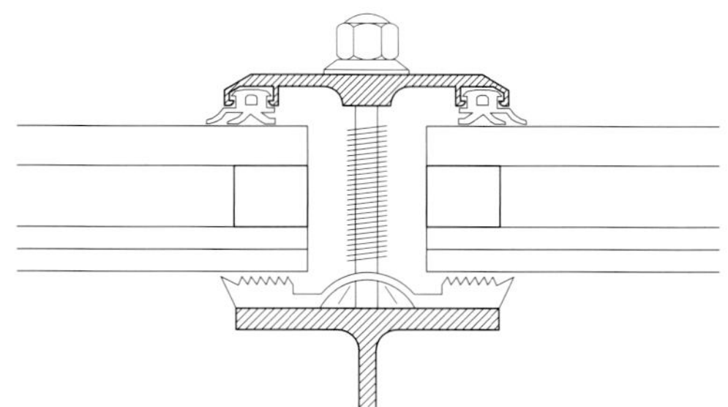

2.4.8.40 Sealed joint with preformed seals and glazing cap

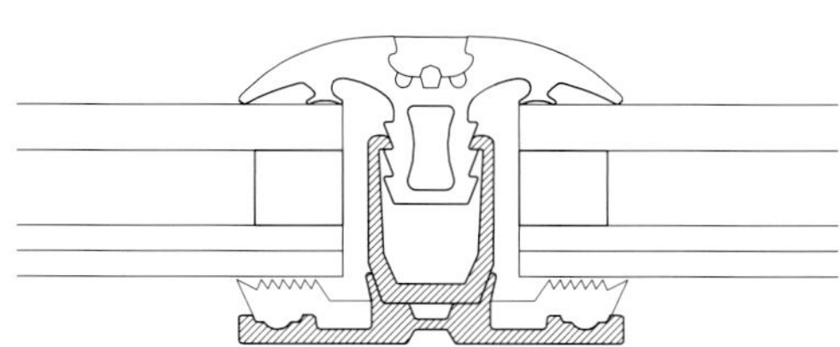

2.4.8.41 Self-clamping preformed seal [18]

Self-clamping preformed seals include a recess into which a filler strip – harder than the material of the seal – is pressed. This lends the sealing lips the necessary contact pressure, which, however, cannot be regulated or readjusted.

| Property | CR polychloroprene | EPDM ethylene-pro-pylenediene rubber | Silicon | PVC polyvinylchloride |
|---|---|---|---|---|
| Thermal behaviour | elastomeric | elastomeric | elastomeric | thermoplastic |
| Temperature range | –20°C to +70°C | –30°C to +90°C | –60°C to +180°C | –10°C to +40°C |
| Colours available | black | black | various | various |
| Corners | vulcanisation, bonding, injection moulding | vulcanisation, bonding, injection moulding | cold-cured with silicone adh. or injection moulding | |
| UV radiation resistance | good | good | good | limited |
| Permanent elasticity | high | high | high | high |
| Resilience | high | high | high | high |
| Ageing resistance | high | very good | extremely high | limited |
| Shore A hardness | 50 to 80° | 50 to 85° | 50 to 70° (for roof glazing) | |

2.4.8.42 Materials for preformed seals; properties and characteristic values [22, 23]

## Sealing with spacer tapes and sealants

### Spacer tapes

These guarantee elastic support to the pane of glass between glazing bar and glazing wing/cap, and the necessary joint width for the sealant.

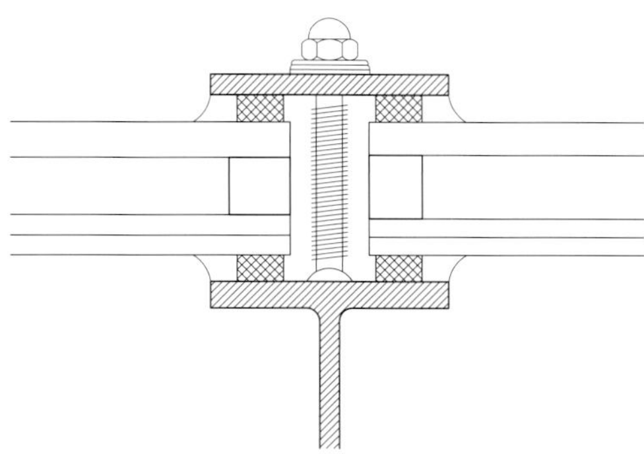

2.4.8.43 Sealed joint with spacer tapes and sealant

Spacer tapes are made from polyurethane, polyethylene or PVC foam, EPDM or polychloroprenes. In terms of compatibility with other materials, polyethylene foam is the best choice. If PVC, EPDM or polychloroprene are used, compatibility with the sealant must be tested beforehand. The Shore A hardness must be 60–70°. Mesh or fibre reinforcement prevents undesirable changes in length during installation.
The tapes must be sufficiently elastic to compensate for permissible dimensional tolerances and deflections. The width of the tape must be selected so that the width of the sealant adhering to the glass and the glazing wings/caps or glazing bars is at least 5 mm.
The greater the temperature fluctuations to which glazing bar or glazing wing/cap materials are subjected, the higher the shear strains on the sealant are owing to the differential thermal movement between panes and glazing bars or wings/caps. The thickness of the sealant appropriate to this load is ensured by the minimum thickness of the spacer tape. [22]

| Longest edge of glazing unit [cm] | Frame material | | |
|---|---|---|---|
| | wood | metal surface | |
| | | light | dark |
| l ≤ 150 | 3 | 3 | 3 |
| 150 < l ≤ 200 | 3 | 4 | 4 |
| 200 < l ≤ 250 | 4 | 4 | 5 |
| 250 < l ≤ 275 | 4 | 5 | 5 |
| 275 < l ≤ 300 | 4 | 5 | – |
| 300 < l ≤ 400 | 5 | – | – |

2.4.8.44 Minimum thickness [mm] of spacer tapes according to DIN 18545

### Sealants

These seal the glass against the ingress of air and water in an enclosing frame according to DIN 18361, and embed the glass so that expansion, contraction, shocks, vibrations, rattling, tension caused by temperature changes and mechanical influences can be compensated for or absorbed. DIN 18545 part 2 divides sealants into classes A to E according to their properties. These properties (plastic, elastic, hardening) are specified on the basis of the resilience (degree of re-formation after stretching or compressing). Distinctions are also made with respect to the number of components in the sealant, its curing behaviour, and basic raw materials groups. Sealants from the silicone and polysulphide basic raw materials groups are suitable for use with glass. Only sealants with a neutral behaviour with regard to the interlayer may be used with laminated safety glass in wooden or metal frames. [22]

**Fixing**

Setting blocks

Panes of glass are placed on setting blocks to ensure that they are supported and fixed without restraint. Loadbearing setting blocks transfer the self-weight component of the pane parallel to the slope to the supporting construction, and are subjected to heavier loads as the roof pitch increases. Spacer setting blocks hold the panes of glass in the correct position; they are made of a softer material than the loadbearing setting blocks.

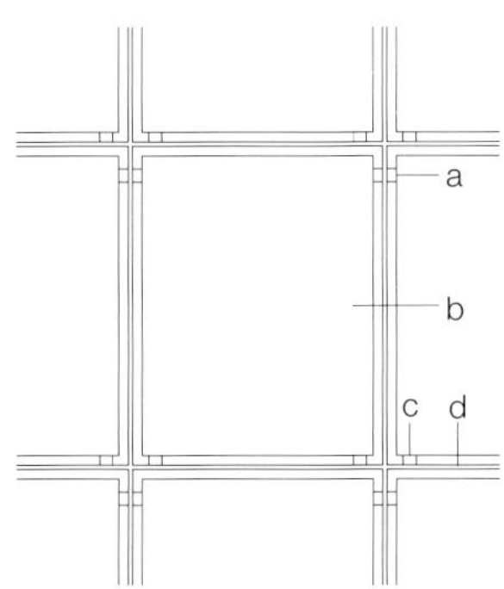


2.4.8.45 Setting blocks for fixed lights or sloping glazing: a spacer block, b pane of glass, c loadbearing block, d frame

Linear fixing

The panes of glass are held continuously along two, three or four sides.

- Fixing with glazing wings/caps

The panes of glass are held in place by steel or aluminium sections fixed to the glazing bars with screws. The spacing of the screws should be < 25 cm. The wings/caps must be removable to enable individual glazing units to be replaced. Deposits of dirt at fixings transverse to the roof pitch must be expected because the self-cleaning effect is hindered. Flat and bevelled sections improve the water run-off.

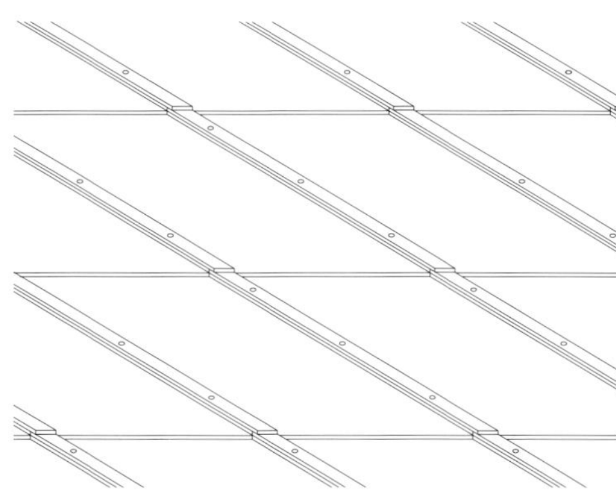

2.4.8.46 Glazing supported along two sides, with glazing wings/caps; overlapping transverse joints

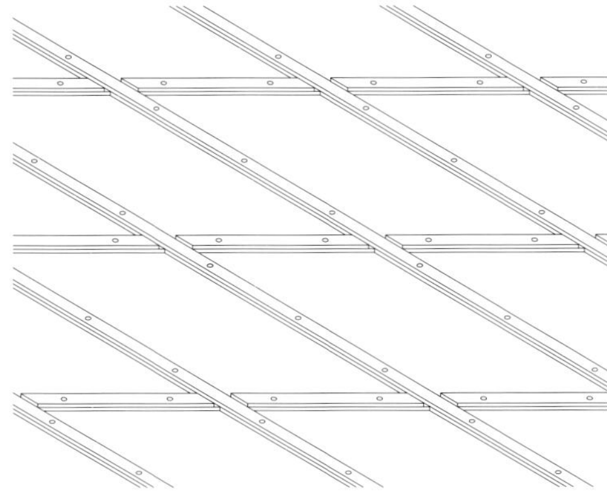

2.4.8.47 Glazing supported along four sides, with glazing wings/caps; sealed transverse joints

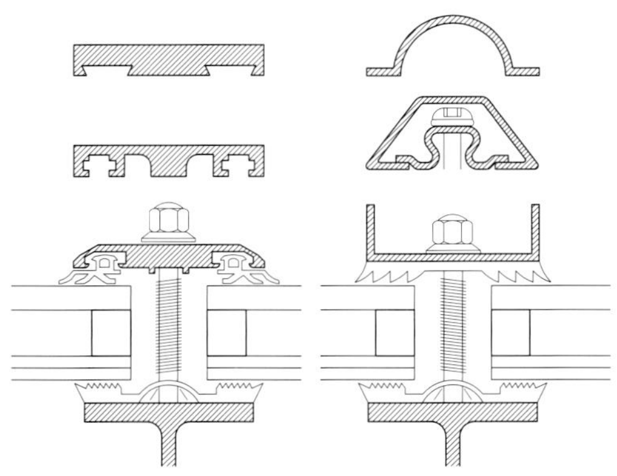

2.4.8.48 Fixing by means of glazing wings/caps [12, 21]

Preformed seals to DIN 7863 classes A to D are permissible for use with screwed glazing wings/caps. Wired glass is permissible only up to a span of 0.7 m in the main direction. The edge cover must be min. 15 mm. [02]

- Fixing with self-clamping preformed seals

The preformed seal is fixed by clipping it into serrations on a mating profile fixed to the glazing bar. The uplift due to wind suction must be resisted solely by the serrations.

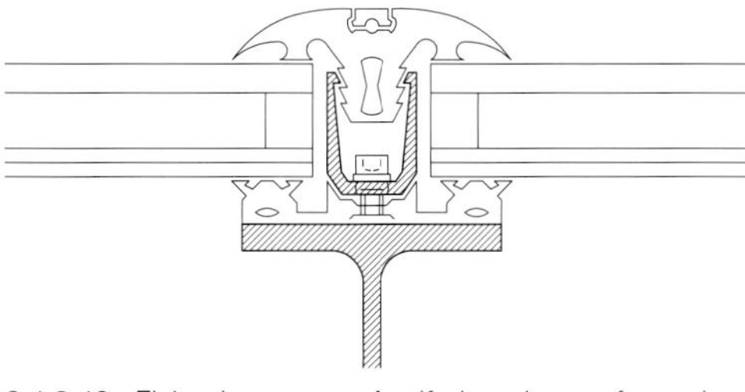

2.4.8.49 Fixing by means of self-clamping preformed seal [19]

- Fixing with silicone sealant

The panes of glass are bonded to the glazing bars with silicone. In Germany, to ensure resistance to wind suction when there are no additional mechanical fixings, this must be on two sides.

This means that the two other sides must be fixed with glazing wings/caps. Supporting glazing on two sides with sealants to DIN 18545 part 2 requires the use of class E sealants. When using coated glass, the coating may need to be removed around the sealant, or the sealant must be compatible with the coating. Industrial prefabrication can be carried out by providing an adapter frame at the works. The advantage of this over applying the sealant on site is that the work takes place under constant, controlled conditions.

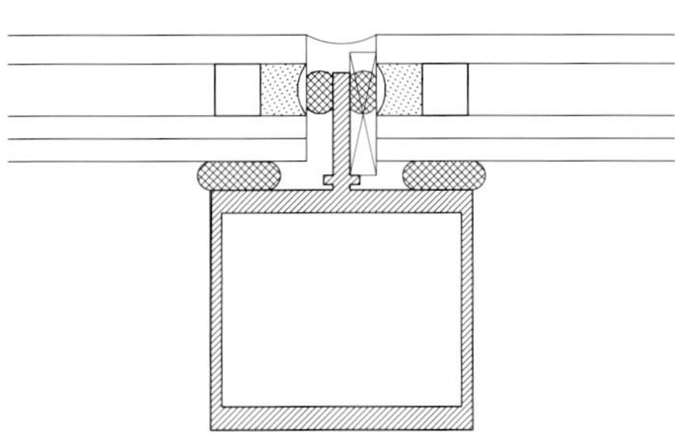

2.4.8.50 Fixing by means of silicone adhesive and adapter frame [21]

Discrete fixing

- Individual fixings in drilled holes

Fixings and sealing are kept separate in this approach.

Predrilled toughened glazing units are screwed to the supporting construction at the corners. As the bending and shear stresses in panes of glass held at discrete points are larger than those in panes of glass held along their edges, this requires thicker glass for the same dimensions.

In order to avoid additional stresses, articulated individual fixings are employed. A mounting with the hinge in the plane of the glass produces the lowest stresses in the glass.

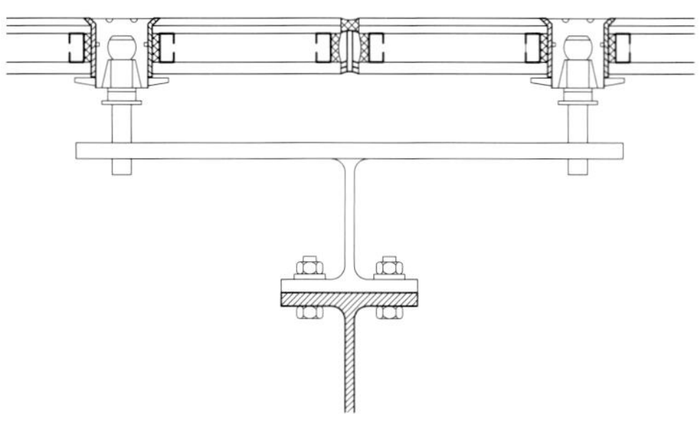

2.4.8.51 Individual fixings in drilled holes

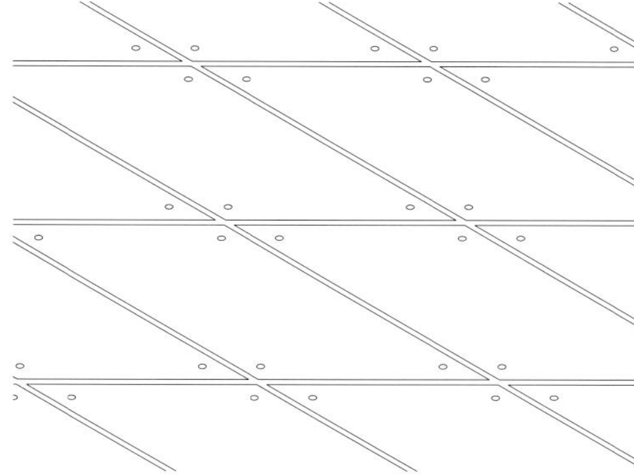

2.4.8.52 Individual fixings in drilled holes

- Individual fixings without drilled holes (clamp fittings)

The glazing units are held at the joints (or at corners or intersections). The load is transferred to the supporting construction via the setting blocks. As a rule, this is a cheaper alternative to drilling and screwing the glass because the drilling and associated hermetic edge seal around the hole for insulating glass is no longer necessary.

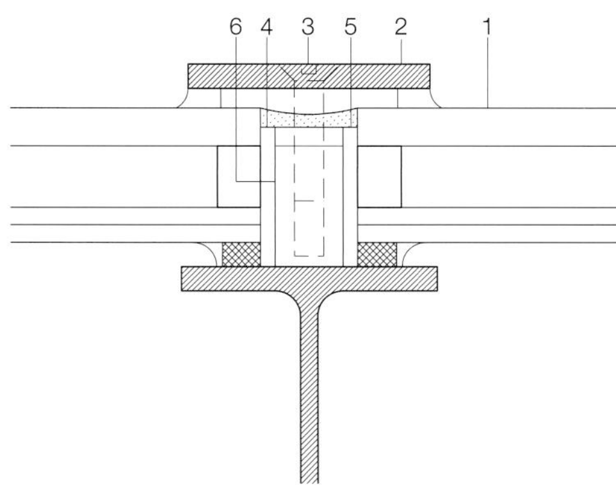


2.4.8.53 Individual fixings in the joint: 1 insulating glass, 2 clamping plate, 3 screw, 4 permanently elastic jointing material, 5 setting block, 6 mounting (welded on) with threaded socket

Thermal bridges

Thermal bridges between glazing wings/caps and glazing bars may lead to the formation of condensation. This depends on:

- the specific thermal conductivity of the material used for the connection; countermeasure: use screws with a low thermal conductivity – V2A and V4A steels are customary, mainly V4A for external applications; thermal break between glazing bars and glazing wings/caps created by the use of plastics with a low thermal conductivity (e.g. polyamide);
- the cross-sectional area conducting the heat; countermeasure: the heat transfer can be limited to isolated points by positioning the screws as far apart as possible, which calls for a correspondingly rigid glazing wing/cap;
- the ratio of the heat energy absorption on the inside to the heat energy dissipation on the outside; countermeasure: the larger the heat-absorbing surface internally and the smaller the heat-dissipating surface externally, the lower the tendency is for condensation to form.

**Additional measures**

Snow

In regions with a high snowfall it may be necessary to remove the snow from shallow pitched roofs and from areas such as troughs, shallow valleys etc.

- Removing the snow manually requires accessible non-glazed areas.
- The snow can be melted by laminated glass with electrical heating wires or glazing bars heated by hot water; however, this should be avoided for reasons of energy economy.

Watertightness

On shallow pitched roofs with overlapping glazing it may be necessary to seal the overlaps with a sealing material to prevent ingress of water blown back up the roof by the wind.

Condensation water

Water vapour condenses on the inner surface of a pane of glass depending on the humidity of the air, the internal and external temperatures and the U-value of the glazing. At a roof pitch of > 15° to 18° the condensation drains from the surface of the glass. At a roof pitch ≤ 15° condensation drips off the surface of the glass. Glazing with a higher U-value reduces the formation of condensation.

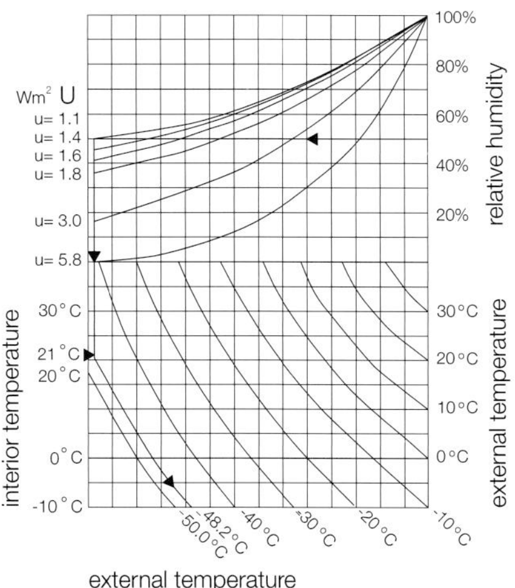


2.4.8.54 The external temperature at which condensation forms on the inside can be determined from the dew point diagram [13]

**Details**

Ridge to duopitch roof, ridge to monopitch roof, hip, eaves, valley, verge, junction with wall at side of slope, troughs, junction with wall at top of slope, internal/external angles, ventilation openings

The following descriptions and illustrations show the principles of these details. Details should be discussed with the manufacturers to establish whether the thickness of the thermal insulation shown is adequate.

Ridge to duopitch roof

The covering at the ridge may comprise an overlapping or sealed (with additional components) arrangement. Preformed sheet metal, glazing wings/caps and bent glass are particularly suitable for this detail.

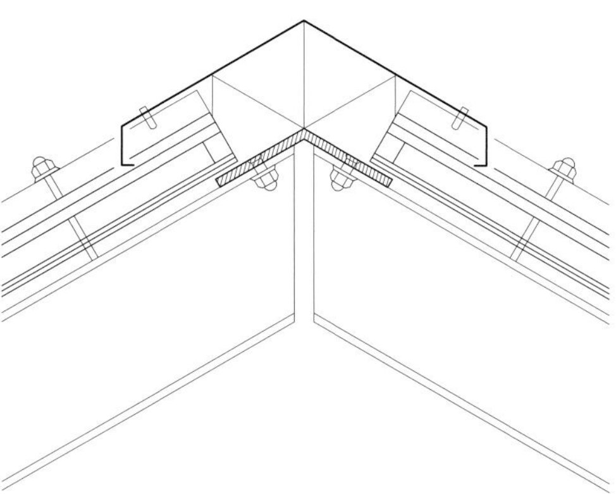

2.4.8.55 Overlapping transverse joints with sheet metal ridge; sketch of principle

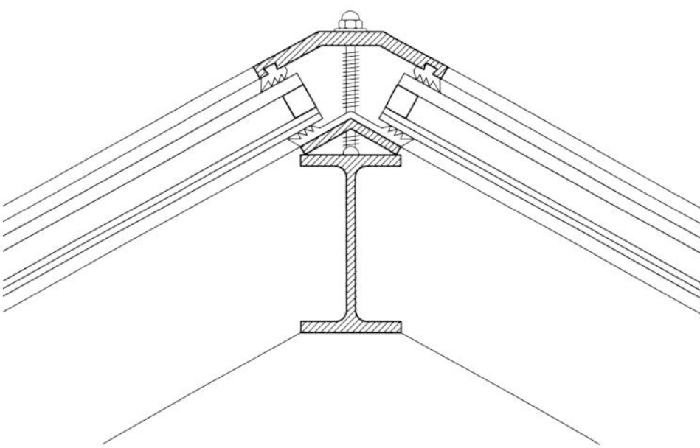

2.4.8.56 Sealed transverse joints with common glazing bar and specially formed glazing cap at ridge; sketch of principle

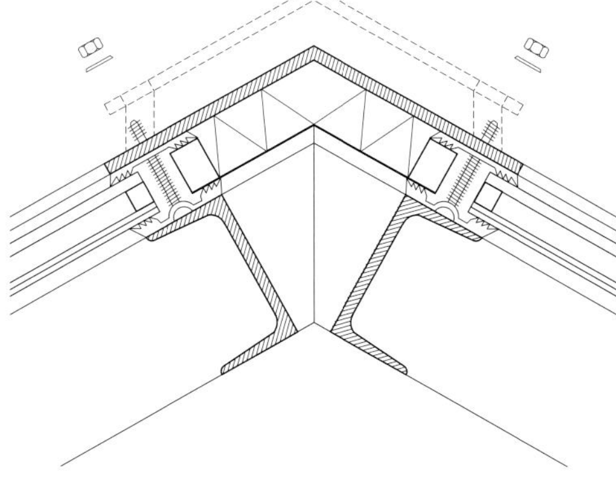

2.4.8.57 Sealed transverse joints with common glazing bar and specially formed glazing cap at ridge; sketch of principle

Movement during erection must be taken into account; elongated holes should be provided in the glazing wing/cap.

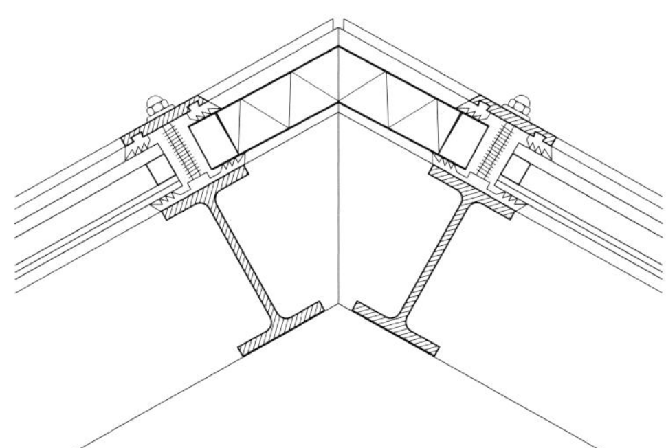

2.4.8.58 Sealed transverse joints with ridge made of multi-ply board; sketch of principle

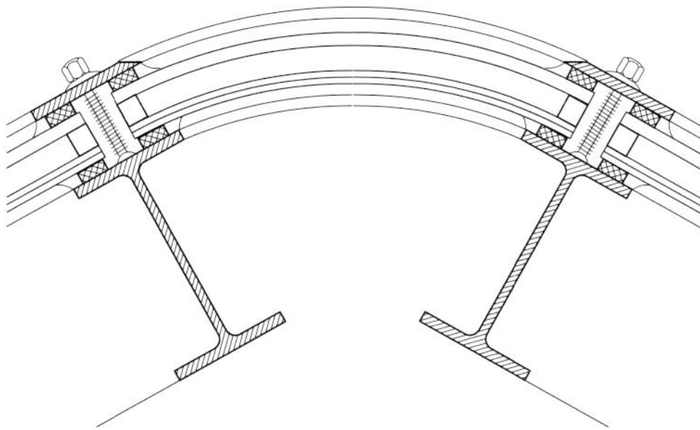

2.4.8.59 Sealed transverse joints with bent glass ridge; sketch of principle

As bent glass cannot accommodate any tensile or compressive stresses, it must be held in the rebate on all sides without restraint. There should be no voids between glass and rebate. Bent glazing bars and glazing beads are needed to support the glass in the direction of the longitudinal glazing bars. To guarantee the sealing effect, closely spaced fixings should be specified. Vapour pressure compensation openings for the rebates should be provided at the ridge when roofing over interiors with a higher humidity.

Ridge to monopitch roof
At the ridge of a monopitch roof the glazing bars can cantilever and create an overhang. Otherwise, the rules outlined for the ridge of a duopitch roof apply here as well.

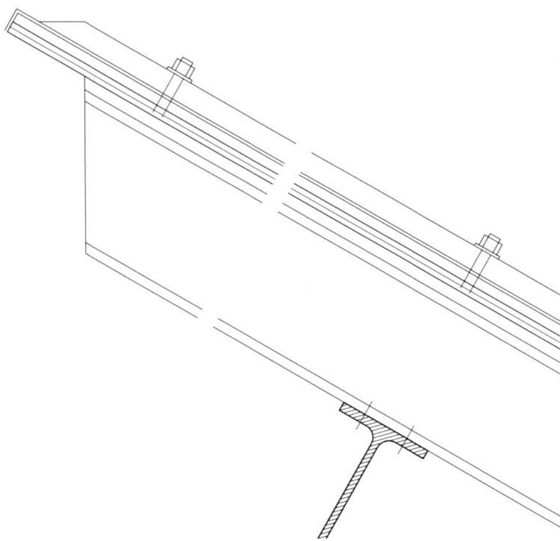

2.4.8.60 Ridge to monopitch roof, with projecting glazing bar; open, non-insulated construction

Hip
Trimmer glazing bars, preformed seals, glazing wings/caps and glazing units must all be cut at an angle to suit the detail at the hip glazing bar.

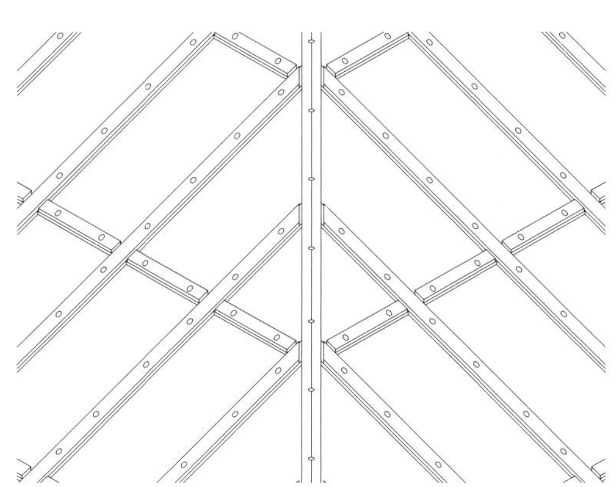

2.4.8.61 Hip detail

The ventilation to the underside of the glass – for glass supported only in the longitudinal direction too – is somewhat hampered by the resulting infill panels.

Eaves
Openings should be provided at the eaves for vapour pressure compensation and to drain condensation.

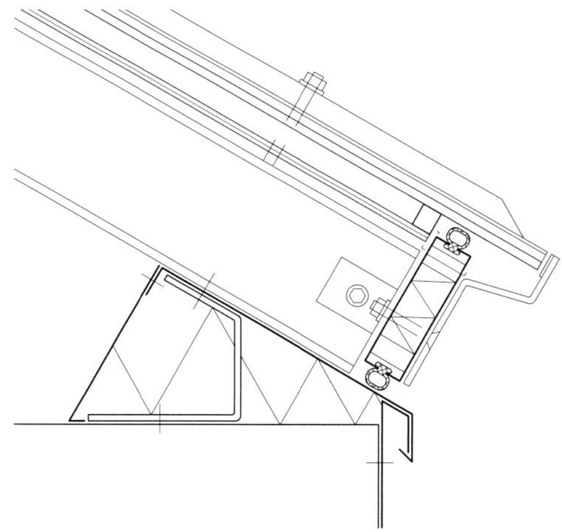

2.4.8.62 Eaves detail; overlapping transverse joints with stepped insulating glass [09]

Generally, the bottom edge of the projecting pane of glass in an overlapping arrangement must be held in position; the setting blocks to the inner pane may be sufficient when using stepped insulating glass on a shallow roof pitch, but the hermetic edge seal is subjected to higher stresses, which can lead to the service life of the insulating glass being reduced. Exposed glass edges must be ground to meet optical requirement or if there is a risk of injury. The projection of the upper pane can be ≥ 200 mm.

As wind suction peaks occur around the eaves, fixings may need to be provided at a closer spacing here. A drip flashing is sometimes advisable for a sealed arrangement.

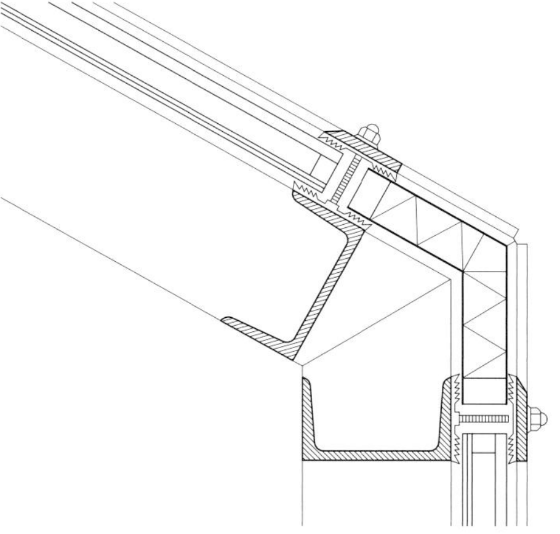

2.4.8.63 Sealed eaves detail; sketch of principle

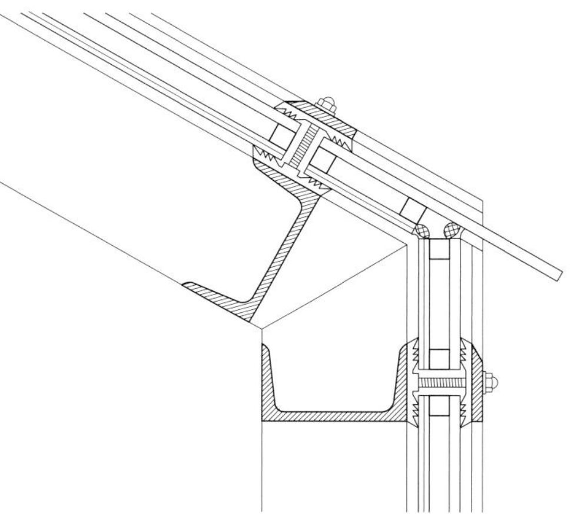

2.4.8.64 Overlapping transverse joints; glass eaves detail using stepped insulating glass

Valley
Vapour pressure compensation openings should be provided (also to drain condensation from the rebates). Glazing bars, preformed seals, glazing wings/caps and glazing units must all be cut at an angle to suit the detail at the valley glazing bar.
In overlapping arrangements an adequately sized channel can be provided to drain rainwater. If a sealed arrangement is being used, the additional sheet metal or specially shaped glazing wing/cap (see also "Movement during erection – Ridge") must be high enough or the sealing able to withstand the pressure of water collecting in the gutter.

The eaves-ridge ventilation at the valley may be slightly hindered on the inside of the panes by the resulting infill panels.

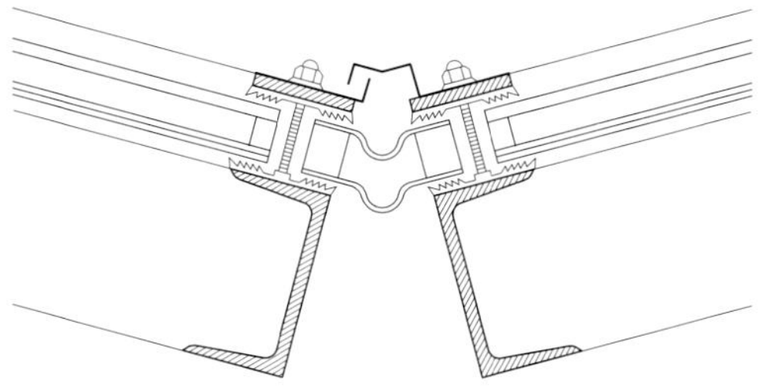

2.4.8.65 Sealed valley detail

Verge
Fixing and sealing can be carried out as for a standard longitudinal butt joint, although an insulated panel – corresponding to the glazing unit – may be used for the outside edge of the verge between internal and external preformed seal. If required, a special glazing wing/cap can prevent water draining onto the gable wall.

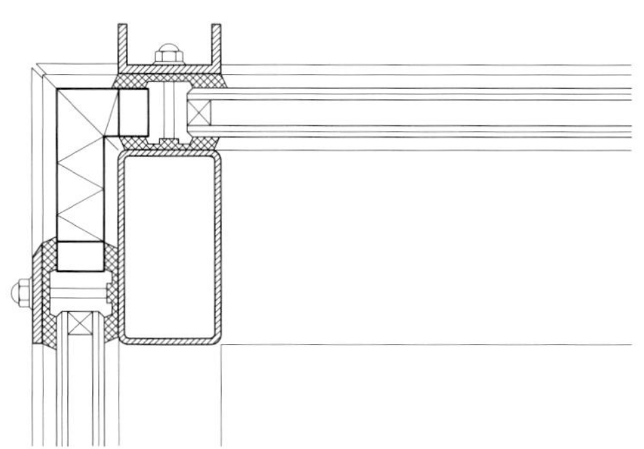

2.4.8.66 Sealed verge detail; sketch of principle

The junction with the gable wall can be realised as a sealed or overlapping arrangement. The size of overlap depends on the height of the building.

| Height of building (m) | < 8 | 8 to 20 | > 20 |
|---|---|---|---|
| Overhang (mm) | 50 | 80 | 110 |

2.4.8.67 Verge overhang in relation to height of building

Owing to the higher wind suction at the edge, fixings may need to be provided at a closer spacing here.

Junction with wall at side of slope
An angled junction must conform to the requirements of the standard and must be turned up the wall at least 10–15 cm above the water run-off layer. The detail must be able to compensate for movements of the structure, or the roof structure must be connected directly to the external wall. The junction must be permanently elastic, airtight and diffusion-resistant.

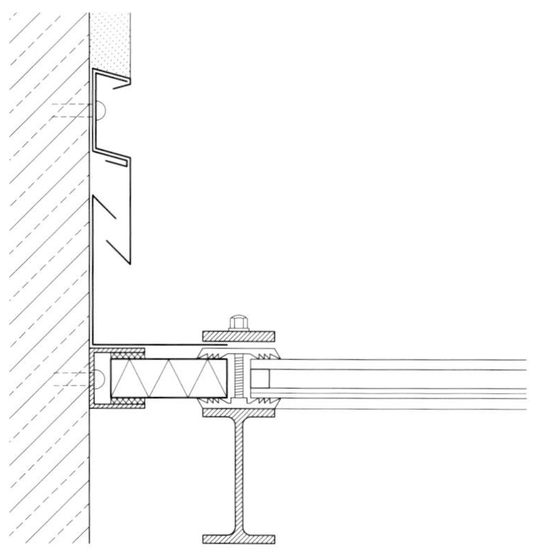

2.4.8.68 Junction with wall at side of slope; sketch of principle

Trough
Gutters here should have a longitudinal fall > 0.5%.
If the junction overlaps, the gutter must be of sufficient size. Openings should be provided for vapour pressure compensation, and for draining condensation from the rebates. In a sealed construction the gutter must also be large enough, unless the sealing can withstand the pressure of water collecting in the gutter. Snowdrifts can lead to excessive loads on the panes of glass and to a build-up of water. An accessible trough enables the snow to be removed manually.

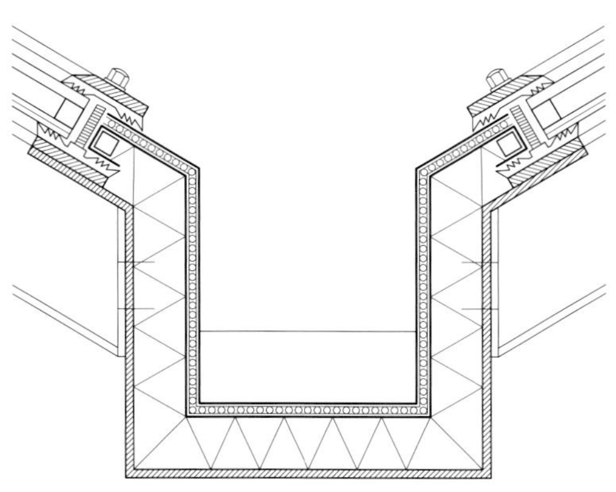

2.4.8.69 Trough detail; sketch of principle

Junction with wall at top of slope
Vapour pressure compensation openings for ventilating the rebates are necessary here on a roof over an interior with higher humidity. The detail must be able to compensate for movements of the structure, or the roof structure must be connected directly to the external wall.

An angled junction must be turned up the wall at least 10–15 cm above the water run-off layer.

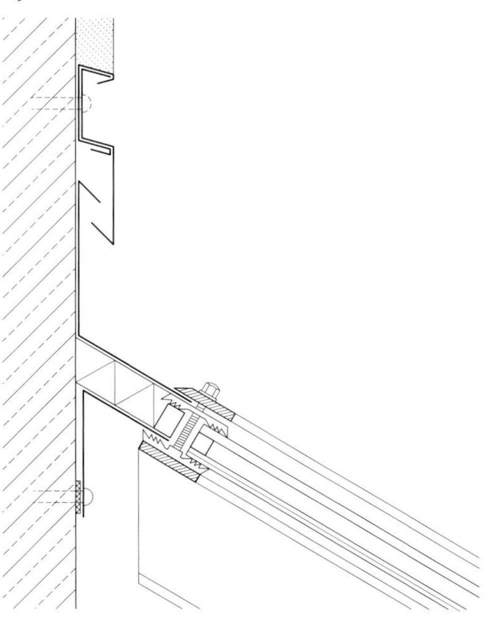

2.4.8.70 Junction with wall at top of slope; sketch of principle

Internal/external angles
These details can be achieved with suitably formed glazing bars and glazing wings/caps, or with separate standard sections.

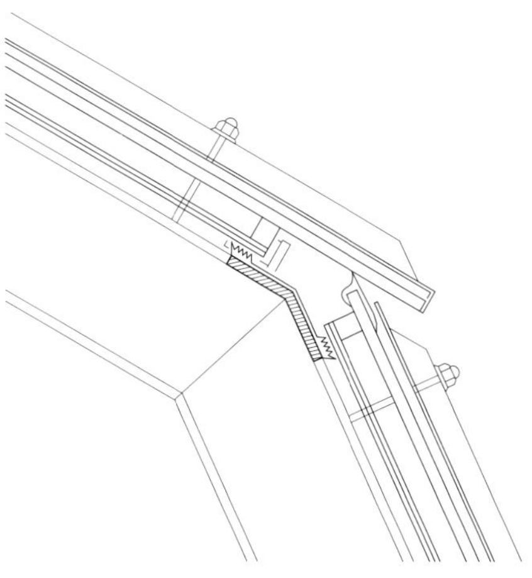

2.4.8.71 Mansard roof detail with overlapping transverse joints

Ventilation openings
These are in the form of sliding or hinged windows. The most effective type of ventilation is achieved by including means of ventilation at the highest point of the roof, with manual (pole etc.) or motorised (electric) opening/closing. The frame is pressed into place like a fixed light. There are opening mechanisms that react to smoke and closing mechanisms that react to wind and rain.

If an open window lies directly in front of a fixed light and the intermediate space cannot be adequately ventilated, solar-control or heat-absorbing glass cannot be used because it could heat up excessively. [18]

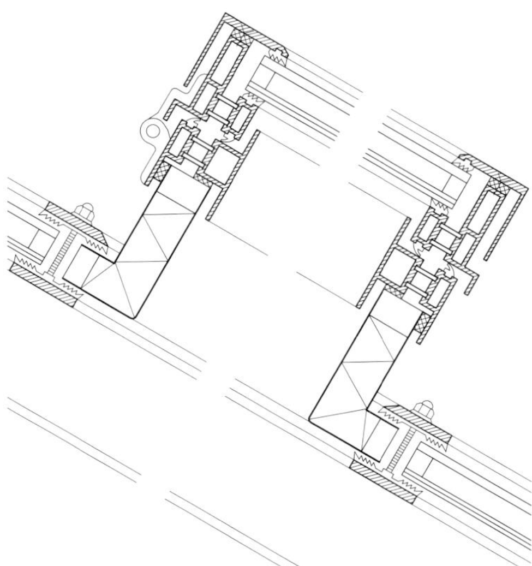

2.4.8.72 Opening light for ventilation

**Sunshading**

Temperatures of 65–70°C are reached in greenhouses without shading and ventilation, which can lead to the glass fracturing. Therefore, shading that functions even when the occupants are absent, and adequate ventilation, are essential.

Solar-control glass

Solar-control glass should have a total energy transmittance < 50% and a light transmittance L(tv) > 40%. As this cannot be adjusted, heat energy gains in winter are limited to the same extent and the level of daylighting is reduced throughout the year. Some types of glass alter the colours in the interior. Light-scattering or light-redirecting glass is a good way of preventing glare from direct sunlight.

Mechanical sunshades

The shading effect of rotating or sliding louvres can be adjusted to suit the level of sunlight. These louvres may be made of wood, metal, plastic or glass. As they have to be positioned outside to be fully effective, an elaborate design is required in order to withstand wind, rain and snow.

There should be sufficient clearance (10–20 cm) between shading and glazing to ensure good ventilation.

An adequate level of daylighting must remain. The colour of the incoming light should not be altered, certainly for some occupations. Shading from trees or climbing plants can augment or even replace mechanical sunshades.

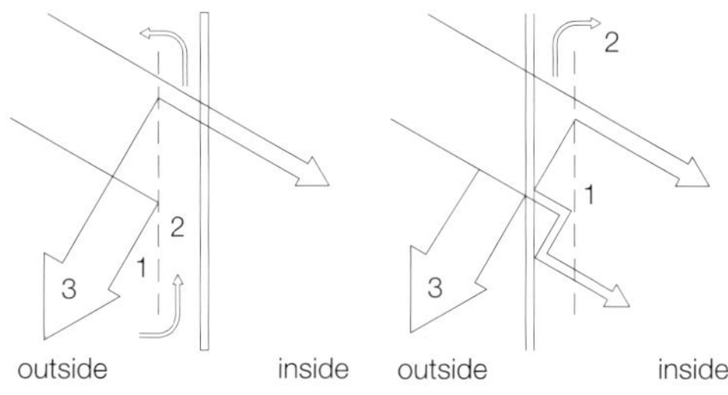


2.4.8.73 Comparison of external and internal sunshading: 1 sunshade, 2 convection, 3 reflection and absorption [15]

Orientation measures

In our latitudes there is a noticeable reduction in the level of incident radiation on north-facing roofs but only at a roof pitch ≥ 60°. Such roofs experience direct radiation only between April and August.

Ventilation

The ventilation should enable the air change rate up to 50/h to be regulated, which calls for openings in the roof surface amounting to 20–30%. Outlets should be positioned at the highest point of the space to be ventilated, inlets at the lowest point. An even distribution of the openings prevents thermal problems. If the outlets are larger than the inlets, this creates a negative pressure in the space, which in turn improves the ventilation. [21]

**Supporting construction**

The principles for establishing the thickness of the glass and its loadbearing supports are laid down in the DIBt's "Technical rules for the use of overhead glazing on linear supports".

The deflection of the supporting section may not exceed 1/200 – max. 15 mm – of the length of the pane to be supported. The requirements of the manufacturers apply for insulating glass: max. 1/300 of the span, but not more than 8 mm.

Suitable intermediate pads (e.g. rubber, plastic) must be provided between the glazing bars and the structure below to avoid galvanic corrosion. Panes of laminated safety glass with a span > 1.20 m must be supported on all sides; in this case the pane aspect ratio should be ≤ 3:1. When using laminated safety glass as single glazing or as the lower pane of insulating glass the total thickness of the PVB interlayer must be ≥ 0.78 mm. A thickness of 0.38 mm is permissible only with support on all sides, a pane aspect ratio ≤ 3:1 and a span in the main direction ≤ 0.8 m.

Glazing supported on two sides requires the use of sealants to DIN 18545 part 2 class E. Prefabricated preformed seals to DIN 7863 classes A to D are permissible with screwed glazing wings/caps.

Wired glass is permissible only up to a span of 0.7 m in the main direction. The edge cover must be ≥ 15 mm. The climate loading between cavity and surrounding air must be taken into consideration, as well as wind and snow loads, when using insulating glass. [02]

**Maintenance and repair**

Cleaning the glass surfaces regularly is recommended, especially in regions with a high level of airborne pollution.

If conventional methods of cleaning (water, sponge, leather cloth) prove inadequate, fine wire wool may be used. Splashes of mortar and sealant residue must be removed immediately.

The service life of glass is determined by the care with which it is installed and the maintenance of the seals. It should therefore be remembered that maintenance of the seal between glass and frame is almost more important than surface treatment of the sections. Glazing with putty and silicone seals must be maintained every five years. Preformed seals have a service life of about 20 years and must be replaced then, or earlier if damaged. Damaged or "fogged" insulating glass must be replaced because it is not possible to drain condensation that has entered the cavity of overhead glazing.

**References**


[01] Andrea Campagno: Intelligent Glass Facades; Basel 1999
[02] Deutsches Institut für Bautechnik: "Technische Regel für die Verwendung von linienförmig gelagerten Überkopfverglasungen"
[03] DIN EN 572 pt 1: Basic soda lime silicate glass products: Beuth-Verlag, 1994
[04] DIN EN 1096 pt 1: Glass in building – coated glass
[05] DIN EN 1863 pt 1: Glass in building – heat-strengthened soda lime silicate glass
[06] DIN prEN 12150 (prelim.): Glass in building – thermally toughened safety glass
[07] DIN 1249 pt 10: Chemical and physical properties
[08] DIN 1259: Terminology relating to glass products
[09] Eberspächer: product information
[10] ECOBIS 2000
[11] Fraunhofer Institute for Building Science
[12] Gartner: product information
[13] Gestalten mit Glas: pub. Interpane-Gruppe, 1997
[14] Glas am Bau: pub. Vegla 1999
[15] Glass Construction Manual
[16] Glashandbuch 2000; pub. Flachglas AG, 2000
[17] Institute for Lighting & Building Serivces, Cologne Polytechnic
[18] Mero: product information
[19] Okalux Kapillarglas GmbH: product information
[20] Scholz, W.: Baustoffkenntnis, 12th ed.; Düsseldorf: Werner-Verlag, 1991
[21] Schüco: product information
[22] Technische Richtlinien des Glaserhandwerks Nr. 1, Dichtstoffe für Verglasungen und Anschlussfugen
[23] Technische Richtlinien des Glaserhandwerks Nr. 13, Verglasen mit Dichtprofilen
[24] Technische Richtlinien des Glaserhandwerks Nr. 19, Linienförmig gelagerte Verglasungen

## Fibre-cement corrugated sheeting
Material, components, laying

### Material
Raw materials, manufacture, properties

#### Raw materials
The constituents of fibre-cement corrugated sheeting are essentially the same as those for fibre-cement slates (see "Flat overlapping elements – Fibre-cement slates"). The differences are in the forming and colouring of the elements.

#### Manufacture
Forming
(see "Flat overlapping elements – Fibre-cement slates")
In its unhardened state fibre-cement can be readily moulded into any shape. Each corrugated sheet is pressed into shape individually. For many details, specially formed pieces are produced on a large scale. However, one-off specials can also be manufactured to meet individual requirements. To do this, the mat of non-woven material is laid on an appropriate die. After a few hours the parts are sufficiently strong and can be removed from the mould. A 28-day period of natural curing follows, or the pieces can be autoclaved.

Colouring
(see "Flat overlapping elements – Fibre-cement slates")
To colour the surface of fibre-cement corrugated sheeting, the sheets are heated after about two weeks in the drying tunnel and coated with a synthetic resin dispersion (colourless or pigmented acrylate, open pores). Brown, red and grey are the standard colours available, but other colours can be supplied on request.

#### Properties
Chemical and physical properties
The chemical and physical properties correspond to those for fibre-cement slates.

Biological properties
In terms of resistance to environmental influences, fibre-cement corrugated sheeting is similar to fibre-cement slates. At present only production waste or sheeting damaged during transport is recycled.

Fire protection
Fibre-cement corrugated sheeting is classed as incombustible and, according to approval certificates, is in building materials class A 2 to DIN 4102 part 1.

Frost resistance
Fibre-cement corrugated sheeting must be frost-resistant, i.e. must withstand 100 freeze-thaw cycles and afterwards show no signs of spalling or cracking.

### Components
General elements, edge and special elements

A standard covering fibre-cement corrugated sheeting – DIN EN 494 – was introduced in 1995. However, in Germany every type of sheeting requires an approval certificate from the German Institute of Building Technology (DIBt).

#### General elements
We distinguish between "standard-pitch" and "narrow-pitch" fibre-cement corrugated sheets. The sheet designations describe the spacing of the crests of the corrugations and the depth of the sheet, as well as the number of corrugations per sheet.
The standard profiles available are profile 177/51 (5/6) and profile 130/30 (8). Profile 8 has a symmetrical cross-section, with both side edges pointing downwards, but one side edge of profile 5/6 points upwards (see also "Laying").
General elements are normally supplied with mitred corners (see "Laying"). Narrow-pitch corrugated sheets also have predrilled holes for fixings.
Prefabricated sheets are mainly produced for laying from right to left.

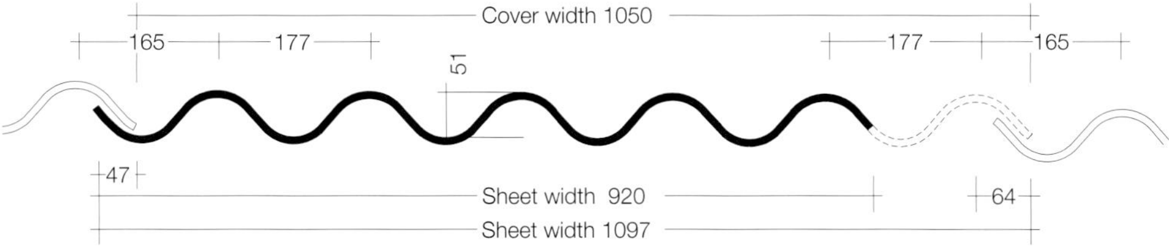


2.4.9.1 Profile 177/51; 5 or 6 crests for standard-pitch and narrow-pitch corrugated sheets [7]

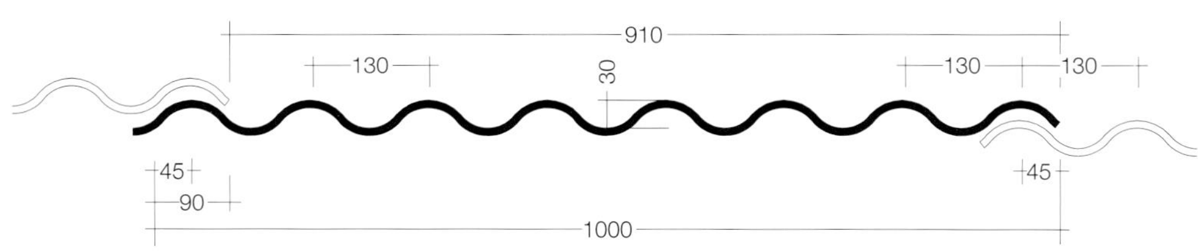


2.4.9.2 Profile 130/30; 8 crests [7]

| | Standard-pitch | | | | Narrow-pitch | | |
|---|---|---|---|---|---|---|---|
| Profile | 2500 | 2000 | 1600 | 1250 | 830 | 625 | Length [mm] |
| 5*) | 35.0 | 28.0 | 22.4 | 17.5 | 9.3 | 7.0 | Weight [kg] |
| 6 | | | | | 11.4 | 8.6 | |
| 8 | 32.6 | 26.1 | 20.9 | 16.3 | | | |

*) Refurbishment sheet 1650 mm

2.4.9.3 Common standard-pitch and narrow-pitch corrugated sheets; lengths, weights

| | d [mm] | w [mm] |
|---|---|---|
| Profile 177/51 (5) | 6.5 ± 0.5 | 920 ± 0.5 |
| Profile 130/30 (8) | 6.0 ± 0.5 | 1000 ± 0.5 |
| Narrow-pitch | 5.8 ± 0.5 | 1097 ± 0.5 |

2.4.9.4 Sheet thickness d [mm] and width w [mm] [7]

Corrugated sheets with planting
The uncoated sheet is given a retention mat of nylon (polyamide) at the works. On top of this is a 20 mm substrate layer suitable for extensive planting and landscaping. A strip around the periphery approx. 300 mm wide should be kept free from planting. Openings are cut through the retention mat at the fixings. Only stainless steel screws may be used for the fixings. Combinations with special elements are possible, depending on the manufacturer's recommendations. Once saturated with water, the self-weight of the sheets can reach 50 kg/m². They should be inspected once a year for undesirable vegetation with aggressive root systems, and to assess the nutrient content of the substrate.

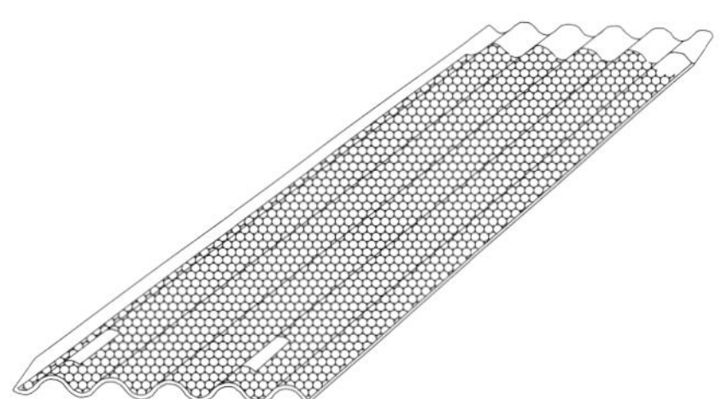

2.4.9.5 Corrugated sheet for planting, with open zones for fixings and laps

Cambered corrugated sheets
Profile 177/51 (5) can be supplied cambered with radii of 6–15 m. Standard shaped panels (see below) can be used for monopitch roof or wall junction details.

#### Edge and special elements
The range varies to a certain extent according to manufacturer. Edge elements are available for left and right, and upper and lower edges. Edge elements are also produced in other forms (e.g. with roll or as plain angle).

Components made of glass fibre-reinforced plastic for use as rooflights are available to match the respective standard profiles and standard lengths.

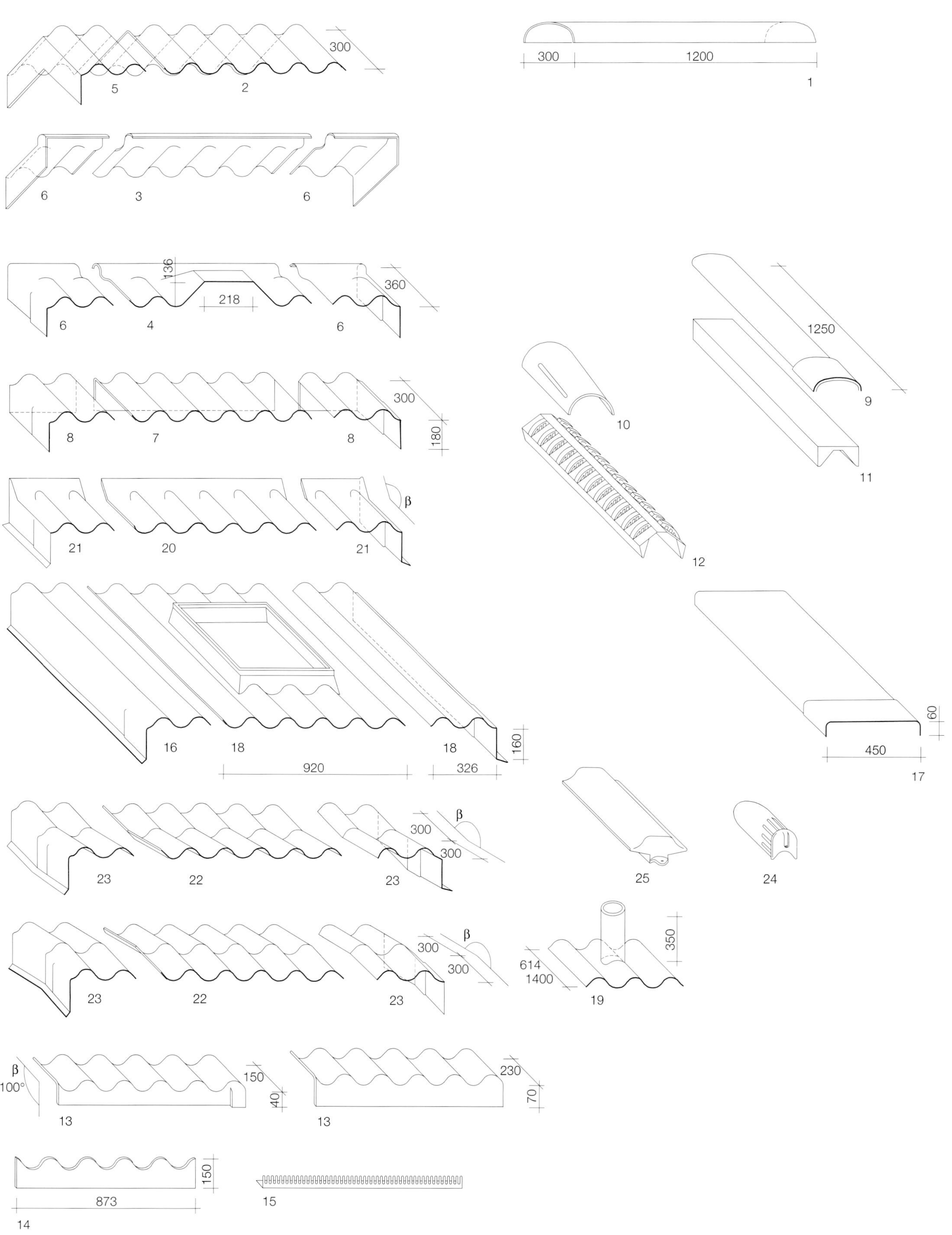


2.4.9.6 Standard-pitch and narrow-pitch corrugated sheets; edge and special elements (see table 2.4.9.7)

#### Edge and special elements

| | Key | Dim./Wt. | Std. pitch | | Narr.-pitch |
|---|---|---|---|---|---|
| Profile | | | 5 | 8 | 5 |
| 01 Ridge/hip capping | g | 17/m | • | • | • |
| 02 One-piece ridge capping | α<br>g | 10–15<br>8–12 | • | • | |
| 03 Two-piece ridge capping | α<br>g | 7–55<br>10.5 | • | • | • |
| 04 Two-piece ridge vent | lqSt<br>g | 2·162<br>11 | • | • | • |
| 05 One-piece gable/ ridge intersection | g | 4–5 | • | • | |
| 06 Two-piece gable/ ridge intersection | g | 6–8 | • | • | |
| 07 Mono ridge | ß<br>g | 75, 90<br>6.5 | • | • | • |
| 08 Mono gable/ridge intersection (left/right) | g | 6 | • | • | • |
| 09 Hip capping | g | 5 | • | • | • |
| 10 Hip capping | g | 5 | | | • |
| 11 Hip seal | g | 0.3 | • | • | • |
| 12 Ventilated hip seal (plastic) | lqm<br>g | 100<br>0.3 | | • | |
| 13 Eaves closure piece | g | 4 | • | • | • |
| 14 Profile closure | g | 1.4 | • | • | • |
| 15 Ventilating eaves profile filler (PUR) | lqm<br>g | 120, 200<br>0.1 | • | • | • |
| 16 Verge element (l/r) | g | 10–20 | • | • | |
| 17 Expansion joint hood | g | 19.5 | • | • | |
| 18 Roof penetration | g | 10 | • | • | • |
| 19 Pipe penetration (polyurethane) | ∅ R<br>α<br>g | 100–500<br>10–55<br>7–19 | • | • | • |
| 20 Apron flashing piece | g | 5 | • | • | • |
| 21 Apron flashing/ verge junction (l/r) | g | 4 | • | | • |
| 22 Mansard/angle element | g | 8 | • | | |
| 23 Verge element with mansard/angle (l/r) | g | 4–5 | • | | • |
| 24 Vent (polyurethane) | lqSt<br>g | 80<br>0.3 | • | • | • |
| 25 Vent (polyurethane) | lqSt<br>g | 180<br>5 | • | • | • |

2.4.9.7 Edge and special elements; dimensions, weights

g [kg] weight, α [°] roof pitch, β [°] angle, ∅ [mm] I.D. of pipe, lqSt [mm² each] ventilation cross-section per piece, lqm [mm²/m] ventilation cross-section per m

## Laying

Conditions for laying, fixing, additional measures, details, supporting construction, maintenance and repair

There are differences between laying standard-pitch corrugated sheets (l = 1.25–2.50 m) and narrow-pitch corrugated sheets (l = 0.625–0.830 m) with respect to prefabrication, roof pitch, laps, fixing and supporting construction.

#### Conditions for laying

As a rule, the sheets are laid in vertical rows from the eaves to the ridge. To protect the side laps from driving rain, it is advisable to cover the roof in the opposite direction from the prevailing wind. However, laying usually takes place from right to left.

Mitred corners
Without a mitred corner, four sheets would overlap at each corner.

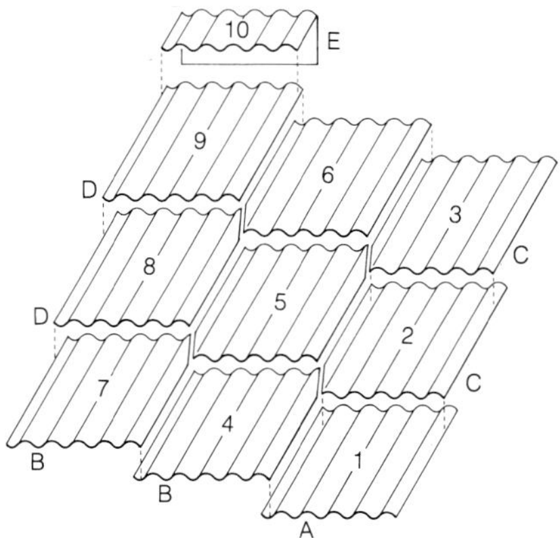


2.4.9.8 Standard-pitch or narrow-pitch corrugated sheets; laying sequence (1 to 9); sheet types (A, B, C, D, E)

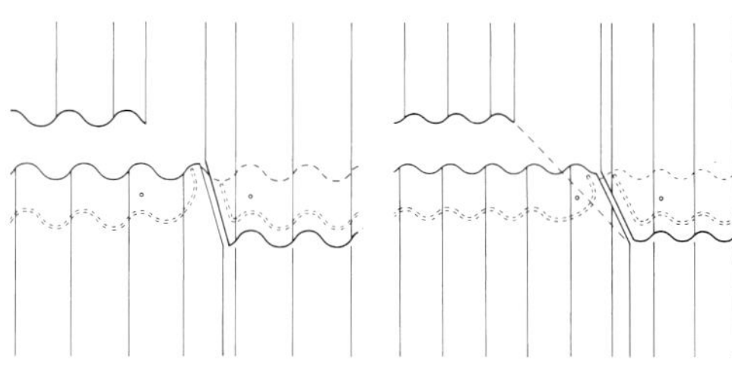

2.4.9.9 Fibre-cement corrugated sheets; mitred corners (with possible preformed seal inlay); left: profile 5/6; right: profile 8

In order to avoid restraint stresses, general elements are mitred (leaving a 5–10 mm gap) at two corners. Apart from the first and last sheets to be laid, all edge elements have just one mitred corner.
Corrugated sheets with or without precut mitred corners – in the case of narrow-pitch corrugated sheets mitred corners and drilled holes – are available for the main surface of the roof. Completely prefabricated corrugated sheets are mostly only available for laying from right to left. When laying is in the opposite direction, non-prefabricated sheets are used, and the mitred corners cut and holes drilled on site.
Non-prefabricated sheets or make-up sheets are used along the edges. Mitred corners and holes are provided here as required.

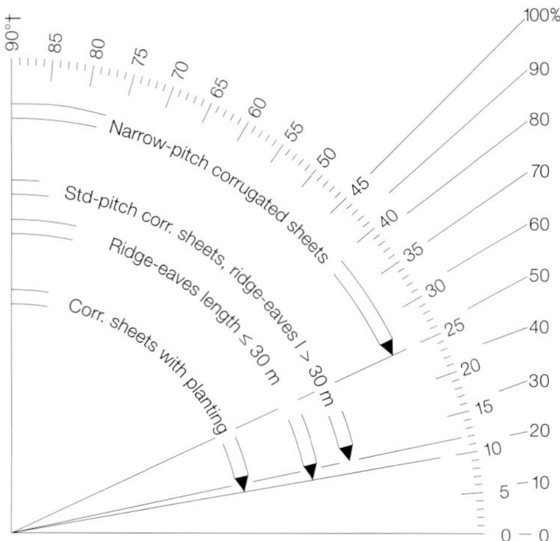


2.4.9.10 Recommended roof pitches [7]

Roof pitch
The recommended roof pitch for a roof covering of fibre-cement corrugated sheeting depends on the size of the roof. As the size increases, so does the load on the end laps at the eaves due to run-off water.
The recommended roof pitches are valid for rainproof roof coverings using standard-pitch and narrow-pitch corrugated sheeting without additional measures (see “Additional measures”).

Laps
The end lap depends on the roof pitch. This should be as uniform as possible over a roof surface.
Standard-pitch corrugated sheets with precut mitred corners are designed for a uniform end lap of 20 cm.

| Roof pitch | min. end lap | |
|---|---|---|
| | Standard-pitch | Narrow-pitch |
| ≤ 20° | 200 mm | |
| >20° ≤ 75° | 150 mm | |
| ≤ 25° | | 125 mm |
| >75° | 100 mm | |

2.4.9.11 Minimum end laps depending on roof pitch, without additional measures

cover length = length of sheet – end lap

The side lap of the sheets is 1/4 corrugation (47 mm) for profile 5 and 6, a complete corrugation (90 mm) for profile 8.

The cover widths for the different corrugated sheets are as follows: profile 5 873 mm, profile 6 1950 mm, profile 8 910 mm.

2.4.9.12 Side laps; ▶ prevailing wind direction; left: profile 5/6; right: profile 8

Overhang
The unsupported overhang (cantilever) of corrugated sheeting at eaves and ridge may not exceed 1/4 x max. permissible span. In the case of an overhang at the side, the last trough must be fully supported.

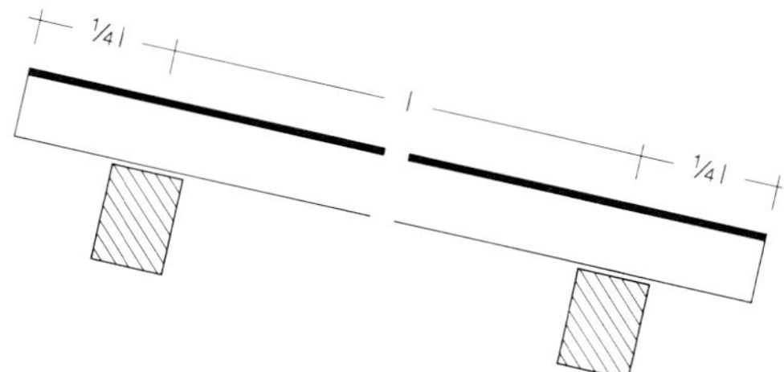


2.4.9.13 Ridge and eaves cantilevers

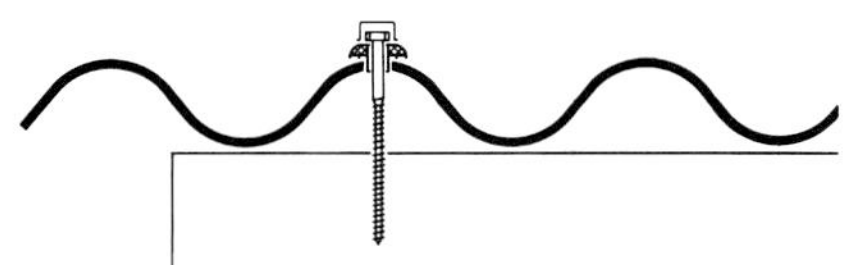

2.4.9.14 Overhang at side of sheet

Dimensional adjustment
Whole sheets are used wherever possible. If this is not feasible, the dimensions must be adjusted.
The individual adjustment in the longitudinal direction (eaves-ridge) can be achieved by using different standard lengths, longer overlaps (adapt mitred corners to suit), or by using make-up sheets. In the transverse direction (verge-verge) the dimensional adjustment can be achieved by employing make-up sheets, distributed over several courses if necessary.

**Fixing standard-pitch corrugated sheeting**
Every sheet must be fixed to the supports at four points at least. Additional fixings will be required on roofs with a pitch ≥ 35° and on buildings > 8 m tall, particularly at the edges (eaves and verge) to cope with wind suction peaks. The number of supports may need to be increased in certain circumstances.

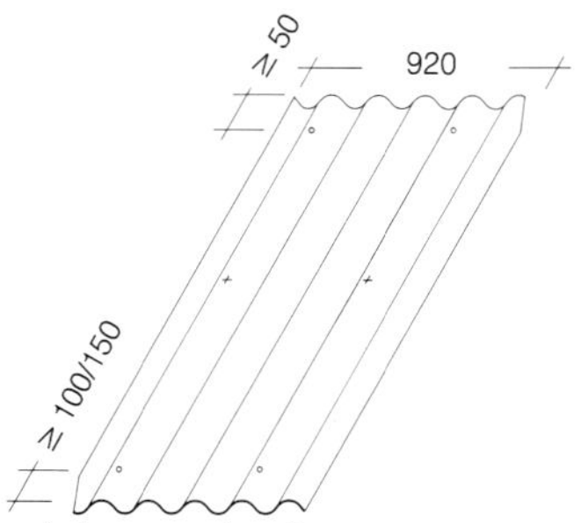


2.4.9.15 Profile 5; drilled holes for fixings at 2nd (3rd) or 5th crest

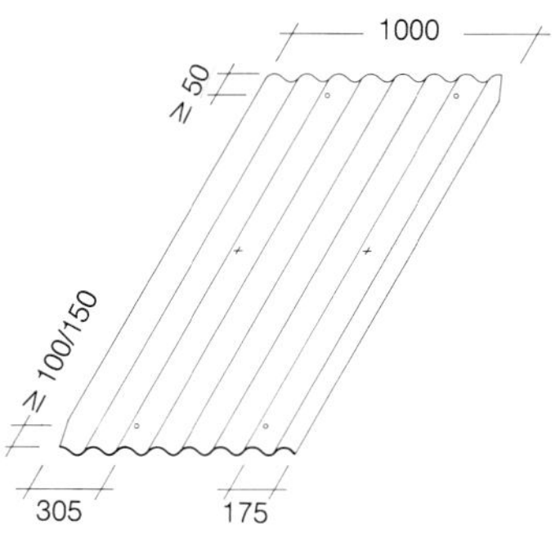


2.4.9.16 Profile 8; drilled holes for fixings at 2nd (4th), 6th or 7th crest

| Height of building [m] | Roof pitch [°] | No. of fixings profile 5 / profile 8 | | |
|---|---|---|---|---|
| | | normal | edge | corner |
| > 0 ≤ 8 | ≥ 7≤ 25 | 4 | 6 | 6/9 |
| | > 25 ≤ 35 | 4 | 6 | 6 |
| > 8 ≤ 20 | ≥ 7≤ 25 | 4 | 6/9 | 9/12 |
| | > 25 ≤ 35 | 4 | 6 | 6/9 |

2.4.9.17 Number of fixings in normal, edge and corner areas (for sheet length 2500 mm) [3]

The number of fixings will need to be recalculated for buildings > 20 high and in special cases with higher wind loads.
The spacing of the fixings from the upper or lower edge must be at least 50 mm. The sheets must therefore project beyond the support. Sheets are always fixed through the crest of a corrugation. Holes predrilled in the sheets are 11 mm diameter.

Fixing materials
Various screws and hooks are available to fix the sheeting to the supporting construction:

Timber purlins
- Hexagon-head wood screw, hot-dip galvanised (≥ 50 µm coating) to DIN 571/DIBt certificate

Penetration depth 36 mm with saddle-type sealing washer and small cap to protect from corrosion
7 x 60; edge and special elements
7 x 100; profile 8
7 x 120; profile 5
7 x 130, 7 x 150, 7 x 170; special details

Concrete structure
- Hexagon-head wood screw (see above) in plastic wall anchor

Steel purlins
- Steel hooks to DIN 17100, 6.25 mm dia., with M7 hexagon-head nut, hot-dip galvanised or stainless steel, shaped to suit purlin section (for I-sections and channel sections 80 ... 160 to DIN 1025/1026; hooks for IPB, IPBL and IPE sections to special order) or supplied straight for bending to suit on site, with saddle-type sealing washer and large cap to protect against corrosion
- Flange clamp fitting for I-sections and channel sections 80...160 to DIN 1025/1026, with hexagon-head nut, saddle-type sealing washer and large cap to protect against corrosion
- Self-tapping screws, hot-dip galvanised or stainless steel (with saddle-type sealing washer and small cap to protect against corrosion); 7.25 x 100 for profile 5, 7.25 x 80 for profile 8
- Self-drilling/tapping screws; no need to drill holes in sheet or steel section

All fixing materials must possess a pull-out or pull-over strength of min. 1.0 kN. For special elements the length of the fixing should be increased by 10 mm. Two-piece fixings are available for roof constructions subjected to severe vibrations (e.g. over crane bays).
All screws are positioned centrally on the purlin, all hooks on the ridge side of the purlin.
Saddle-type sealing washers made of plastic (UV-stabilised polyethylene) with a metal inlay are placed between head of fixing and corrugated sheet.

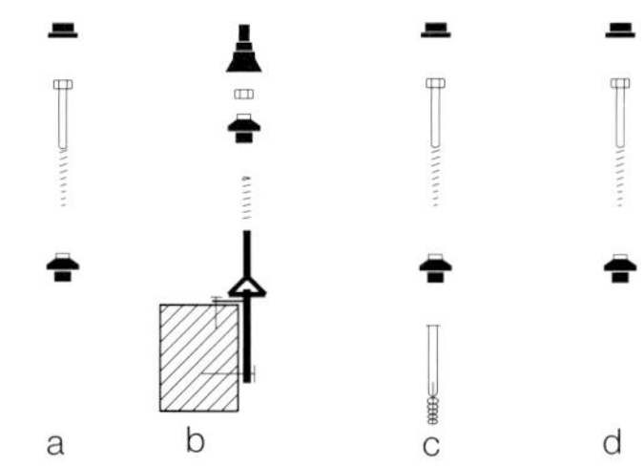


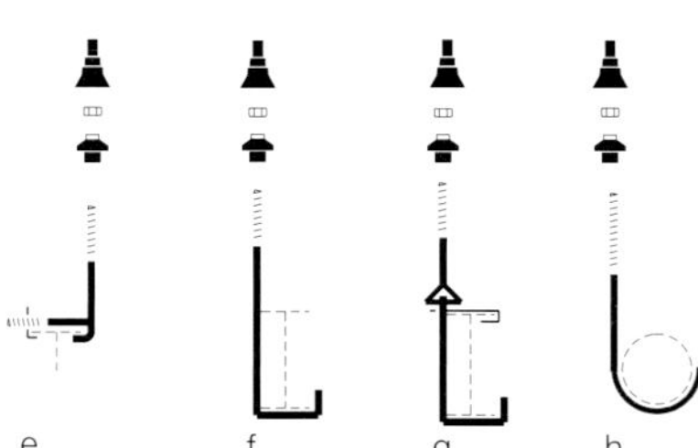


2.4.9.18 Fastenings: a wood screw, b two-piece fixing for timber, c wood screw with plastic wall anchor, d self-tapping screw, e flange (clamp) fixing, f and h hooks, g two-piece fixing for steel

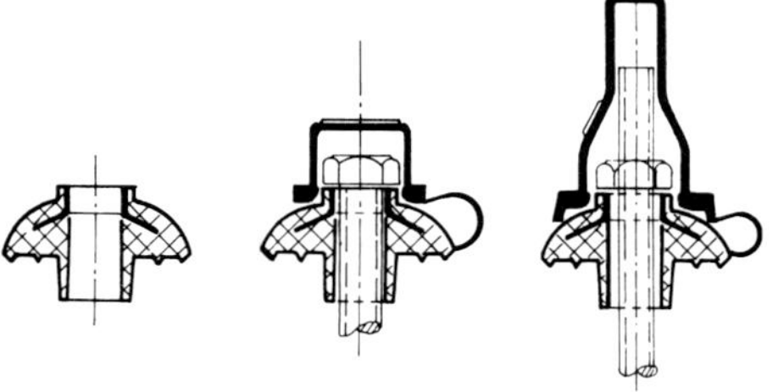

2.4.9.19 Sealing washers and protective caps for fastenings [03, 04]

**Fixing narrow-pitch corrugated sheeting**

Narrow-pitch corrugated sheets are fixed with roofing nails or screws at the second and fifth crest. General elements are predrilled, edge and special elements are drilled on site. The drilled holes must be suitable for the type of fixing chosen.

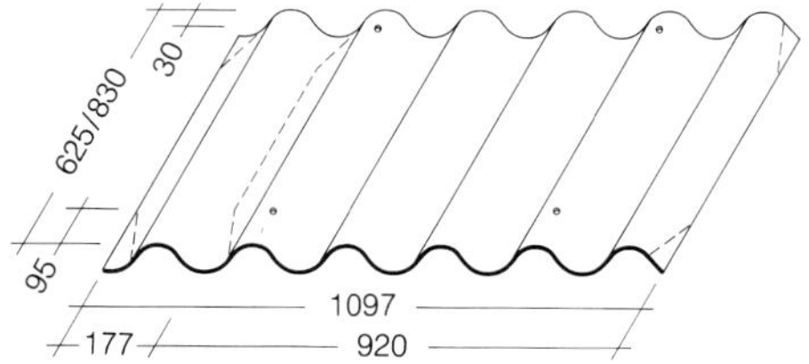


2.4.9.20 Drilled holes for fixings in profile 5/6; narrow-pitch corrugated sheets

| Height of building [m] | Roof pitch [°] | No. of fixings normal | edge | corner |
|---|---|---|---|---|
| > 0 ≤ 8 | ≤ 29 | 2N/S | 2N/S | 3N/S |
| | >29 | 2N/S | 2N/S | 2N/S |
| > 8 ≤ 20 | ≤ 30 | 2N/S | 2HS | 2HS |
| | >30 | 2N/S | 2N/S | 2N/S |
| > 20 ≤ 100 | ≤ 33 | 2N/S | 2HS | 2N/S |
| | >33 | 2N/S | 2N/S | 2N/S |

2.4.9.21 Number of fixings in normal, edge and corner areas to DIN 1055; N/S roofing nail or screw, HS hot-deep galvanised wood nail

Fixing materials

The standard fixings for narrow-pitch corrugated sheeting are roofing nails or screws or hot-dip galvanised wood screws with polychloroprene flat or saddle-type sealing washer; predrilled holes vary between manufacturers. More fixings may be required at the edges owing to the more severe wind suction loads. Edge elements (ridge capping etc.) are also each secured with two fixings.

Workability

Fibre-cement corrugated sheeting can be cut and drilled like wood with low-speed sawing and drilling equipment.
Drills: HSS or with tungsten carbide tip, jigsaws with interchangeable blades.
Depending on the quality of cut edge required, a line can be scored in the material and the material broken off with pincers.
Finer trimming work at cut-outs etc. can be carried out with a woodworking rasp. High-speed power tools must be fitted with dust extraction.

**Additional measures**

These are necessary when enhanced requirements regarding the reliability of the roof covering have to be met, e.g. if a roof pitch shallower than recommended is used, with complicated roof forms, higher wind pressures, heavy snowfall, a build-up of melt waters etc.

These include:

- a steeper roof pitch
- longer end laps
- longer sheets
- laying an 8 mm dia. preformed sealing strip in the end laps; on standard-pitch sheets 30 mm on the eaves side of the fixings (roof pitch ≥ 7°), on narrow-pitch sheets 50 mm below the ridge end of the sheet (roof pitch ≥ 10°)

| | Ridge-eaves length [m] | Roof pitch with sealed laps | without sealed laps |
|---|---|---|---|
| Standard-pitch corrugated sheet | ≤ 10 | ≥ 7° | ≥ 10° |
| | ≥ 10–20 | ≥ 8° | ≥ 10° |
| | ≥ 20–30<br>≥ 30 | ≥ 10°<br>≥ 12° | ≥ 12°<br>≥ 14° |
| Narrow-pitch corrugated sheet | ≤ 10 | ≥ 10° | ≥ 25° |
| | ≥ 10–20 | ≥ 12° | ≥ 25° |
| | ≥ 20–30 | ≥ 14° | ≥ 25° |
| | ≥ 30 | ≥ 15° | ≥ 25° |

2.4.9.22 Minimum roof pitches with additional measures [7]

- laying a 10 mm dia. preformed sealing strip in the end laps and sealing the side laps of profile 5 with a special preformed sealing strip (roof pitch 5–7°)

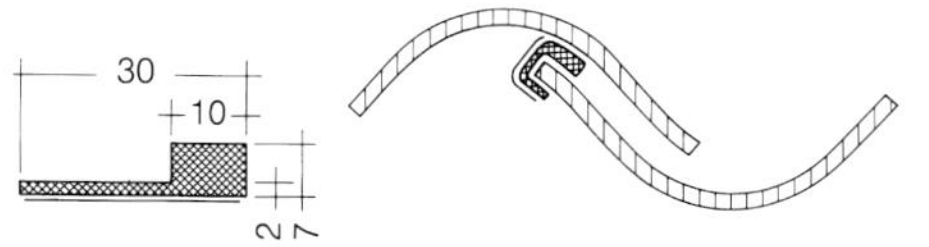


2.4.9.23 Standard-pitch corrugated sheet; profile 5; side lap with a special sealing strip [3]

- provision of boarding, sarking, roofing felt

**Details**

Ridge to duopitch roof, ridge to monopitch roof, hip, eaves, valley, verge, junctions with walls, penetrations, crank

Ridge to duopitch roof

When using a one-piece ridge capping, the corrugated sheeting must overlap in the same direction (opposite the prevailing wind). This means that on one side of the roof the sheets are laid from right to left, and on the other from left to right. Crests and troughs must line up exactly. It is important that the ridge capping fits snugly over the main roof sheets and no large gaps ensue. It is therefore recommended to select a ridge capping with a roof pitch 1–3° steeper than that of the general roof pitch.
In two-piece ridge capping it is not absolutely necessary for the profiles on either side of the ridge to line up exactly. A long cantilever will

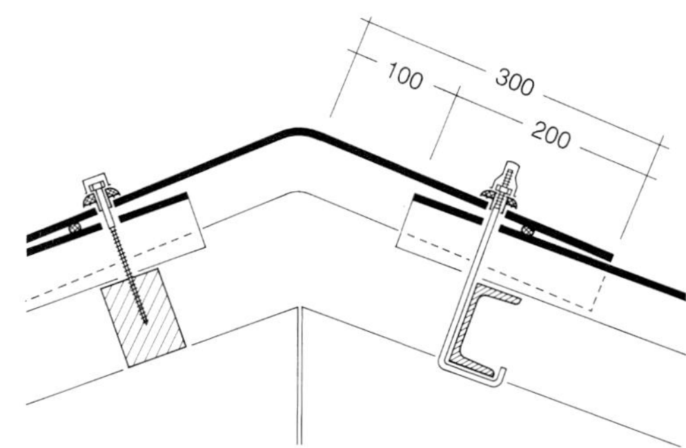


2.4.9.24 Ridge detail with one-piece ridge corrugated capping; fixings and sealing

need additional support or a ridge board. The two pieces of the ridge capping should be sealed along the length of the ridge with an 8 mm dia. preformed sealing strip in the overlap, as should the side laps in the transition (about 20 cm) between corrugation and capping of ridge element.

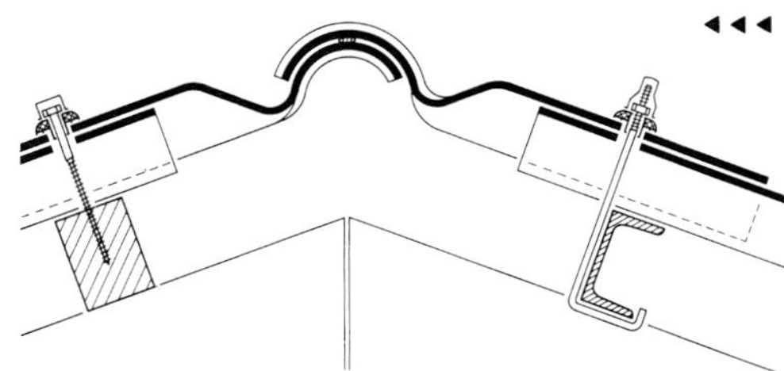

2.4.9.25 Ridge detail with two-piece ridge corrugated capping; supports and fixings; ◀ prevailing wind direction

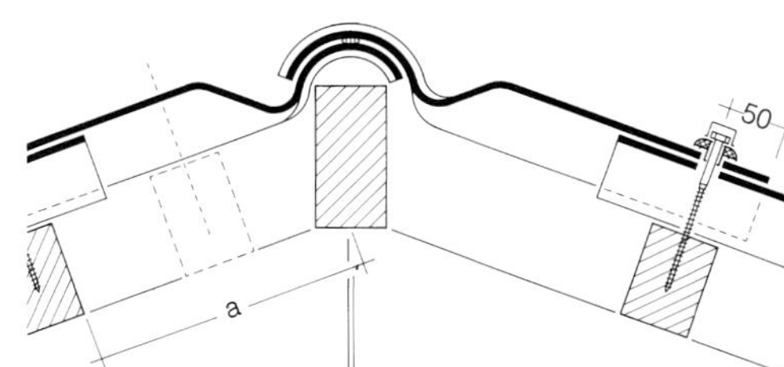


2.4.9.26 Ridge detail with two-piece corrugated ridge capping; support for longer cantilever

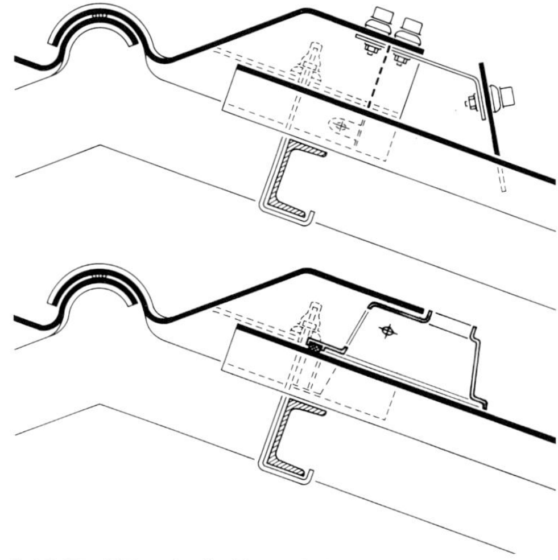

2.4.9.27 Ridge detail with ventilating capping (two-piece); top: screen; bottom: box; ventilation cross-section: screen 162 cm², box 122 cm²

The combination of two apron flashing pieces, two hood supports, two plastic guards (l = 1100 mm) and a hood piece (l = 1200 mm) creates a ventilated ridge detail with a ventilation cross-section of 250 cm²/m. However, this detail requires further treatment to make it secure against driving snow and driving rain (see "Construction details").

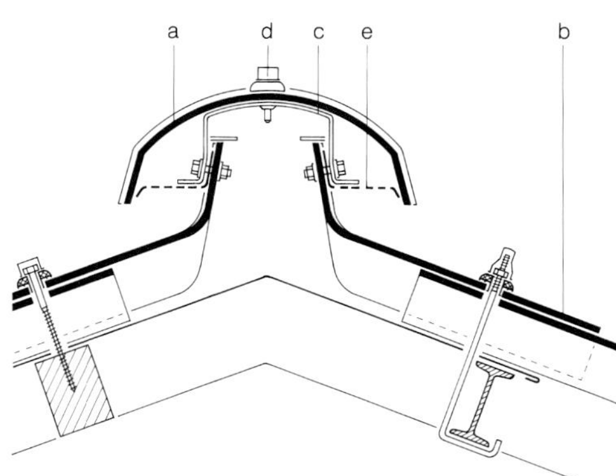


2.4.9.28 Ventilated ridge with hood: a hood, b apron flashing piece, c hood support, d fixing with saddle-type sealing washer and protective cap, e guard

Ridge to monopitch roof
An unsupported cantilever may project no more than 1/4 x max. permissible span beyond the last support. The openings between crests and support can be closed off with mesh, a profile closure or with mortar (reinforced if necessary). If special mono ridge elements are used, the length of the fixings must be increased by 10 mm.

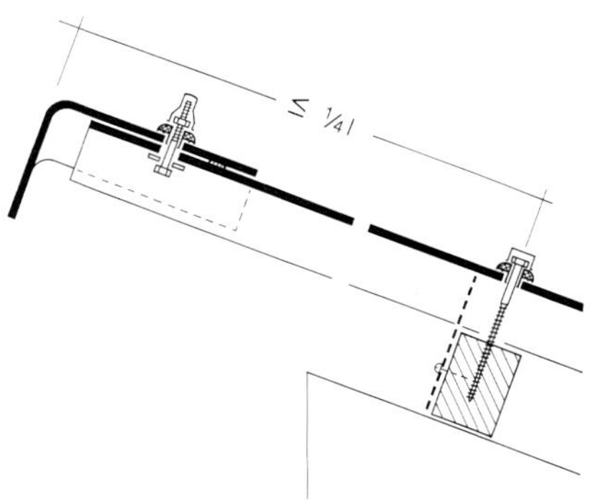


2.4.9.29 Eaves closure piece used at ridge of monopitch roof

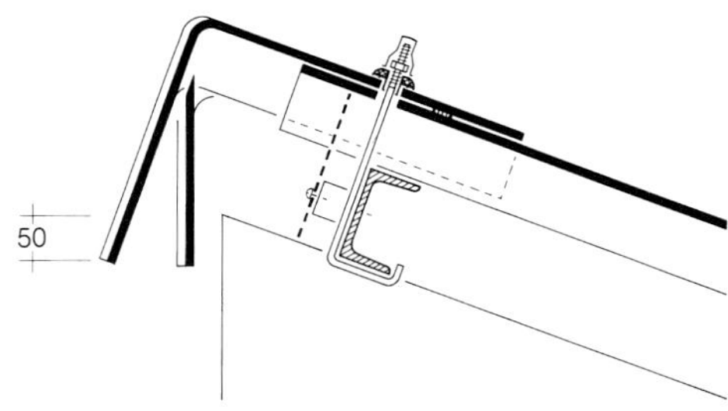


2.4.9.30 Mono ridge capping (75°/90°); fixing

Hip
The cut edges of the trimmed sheets must be placed together. A hip board or battens parallel to the line of the hip serve as a support. Hip cappings are fixed to a hip board with hexagon-head wood screws (with saddle-type sealing washer and protective cap). The depth of the hip rafter depends on the roof pitch. There are various options for sealing the hip:

- The void between corrugated sheeting and hip capping can be filled with mortar (reinforced if necessary) in chicken wire or wire hooks. The mortar should be pressed back behind the drip edge of the capping.

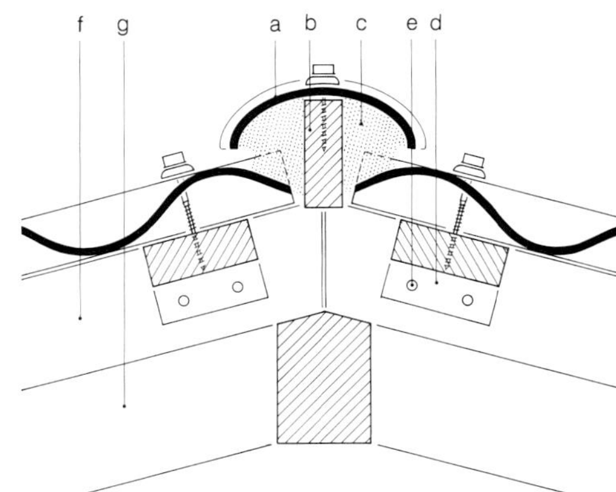


2.4.9.31 Hip bedded in mortar; support to hip capping and roof sheets; a hip capping, b hip board, c mortar, d cleat, e wood screw with sealing washer and cap to prevent corrosion, f trimming rafter, g purlin

- A strip of milled lead (w = 40 cm) can be laid between hip capping and hip board, pressed down over the cut ends of the corrugated sheets and fixed through them.

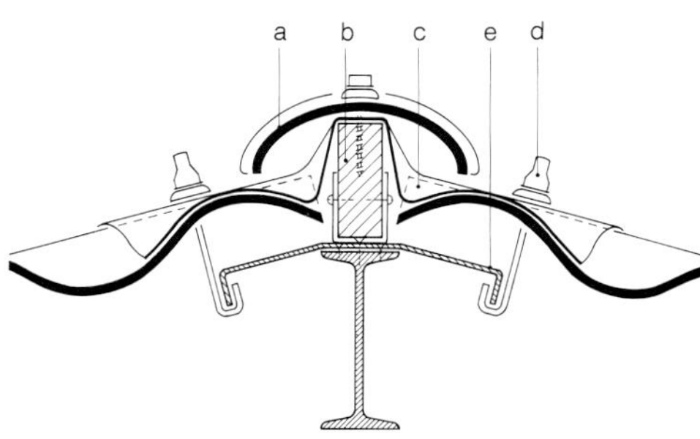


2.4.9.32 Hip with milled lead flashing: a hip capping, b hip board, c milled lead flashing, d hook fixing, e steel sheet with mountings

- Special plastic pieces (see "Edge and special elements") seal the joints between capping and corrugated sheets by way of flexible edge strips. Some versions (hip ventilating element) guarantee ventilation at the hip (see "Ventilation").

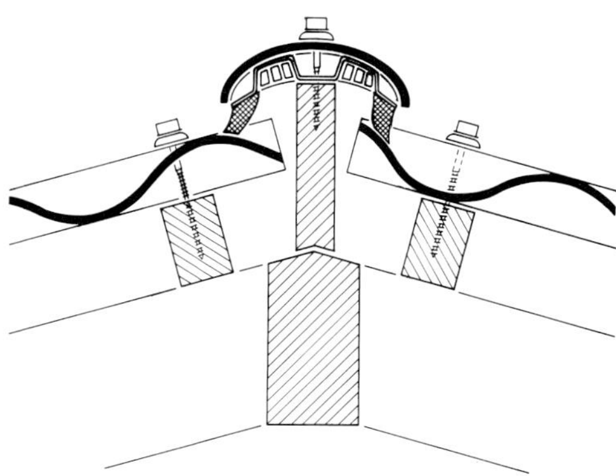

2.4.9.33 Hip with ventilating element and foam seal

Hip and ridge cappings must be cut to suit at the ridge-hip intersection. The sealing at this point is achieved with milled lead. This is cut and bent to suit on site, painted if necessary and fixed through the hip and ridge cappings.

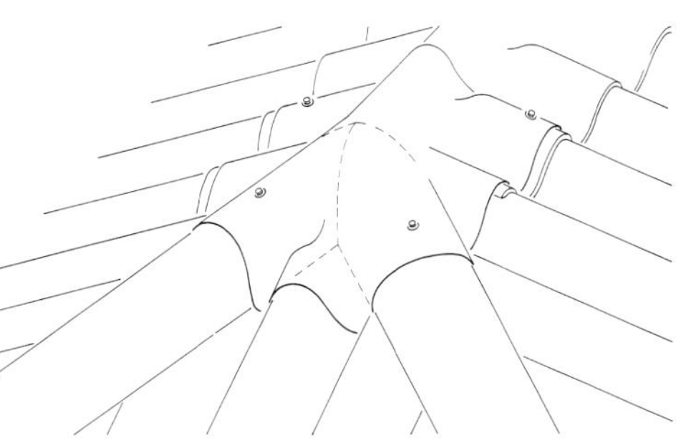

2.4.9.34 Hip-ridge intersection with milled lead flashing

Eaves
The sheets may cantilever no more than 1/4 of max. permissible span beyond the last support. The corrugated form of the sheets means that openings ensue between the supporting construction and the sheeting. Covered with wire mesh or similar to protect against birds, insects etc., these can serve as ventilation openings. However, they can be closed off as follows:

- Profile closure

This special element can be positioned tight up against the underside of the sheeting, or with a small gap. It is fixed with three screws (with plastic caps) to the sheeting, or the purlin.

- Eaves closure piece

This special element is drilled to suit on site and attached below the corrugated sheeting. A gap can be left between the vertical leg and the supporting construction for ventilation.

- Vented eaves closure piece
- Filling the gaps with mortar

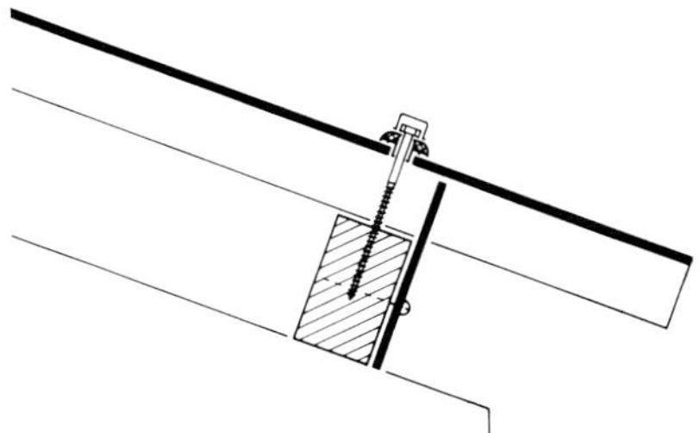

2.4.9.35 Eaves detail with profile closure; fixing

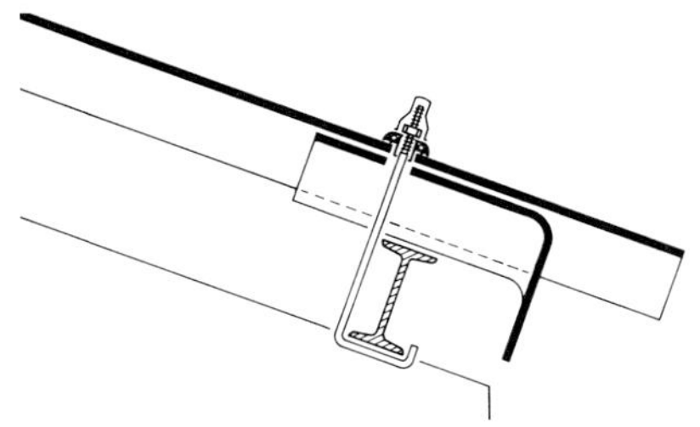

2.4.9.36 Eaves detail with corrugated eaves closure piece

Valley
The minimum pitch of the valley should be 17°. It is constructed as a lined valley with sheet metal or made watertight with synthetic or bitumen roofing felt extending ≥ 100 mm below the corrugated sheeting. To prevent the ingress of water, the valley should be positioned at a lower level (if necessary between two valley rafters). The voids between supporting construction and corrugations are sealed with mortar or special flexible hip sealing pieces (see figure 2.4.9.33) halved lengthwise. The top end of the valley is flashed with milled lead.

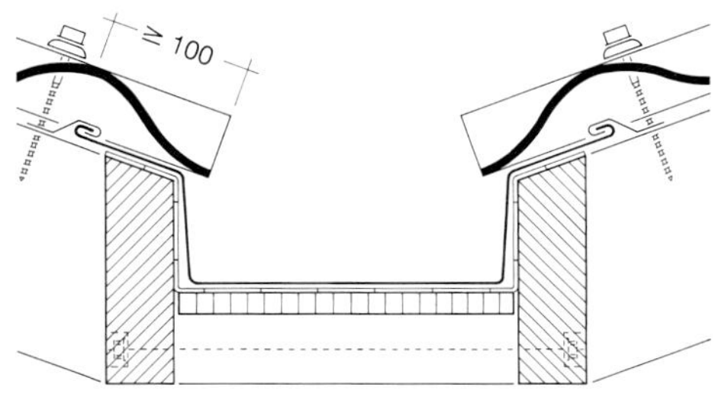


2.4.9.37 Lowered valley between two valley rafters

Verge
If the corrugated sheeting overhangs, the last trough should rest fully on the supporting construction. The sheeting must end with a downward corrugation. Whole sheets should always be used at the verge. The maximum overhang is 130 mm for profile 5, or 90 mm for profile 8. Special verge elements are drilled to suit on site and attached to the corrugated sheeting. Fixings at this point must be 10 mm longer than the standard fixings.

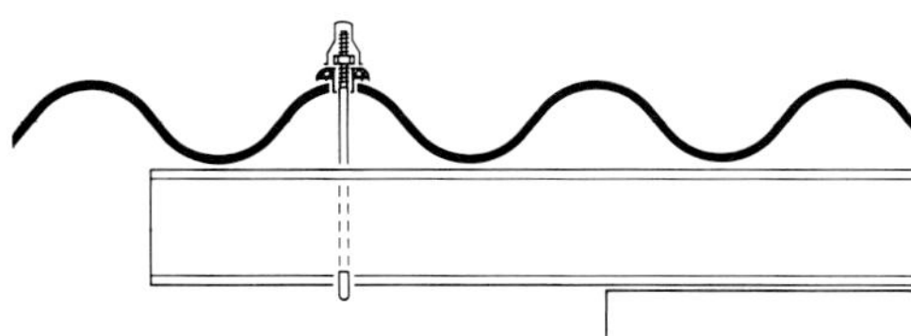

2.4.9.38 Verge detail showing side of sheet overhanging

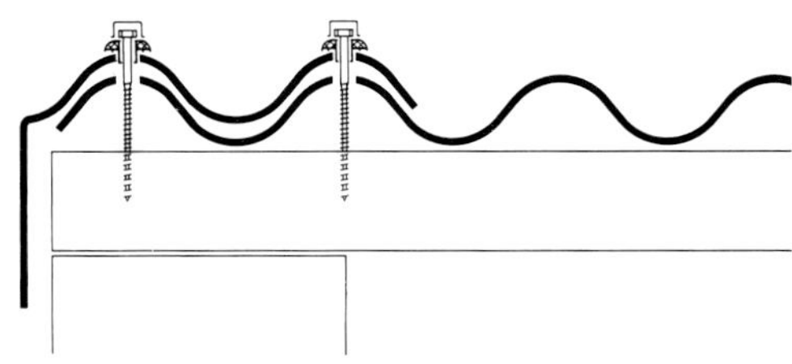

2.4.9.39 Verge detail with special verge element

Junctions with walls
A rigid connection between the corrugated sheeting and the wall must be avoided.

Junction with wall at side of slope

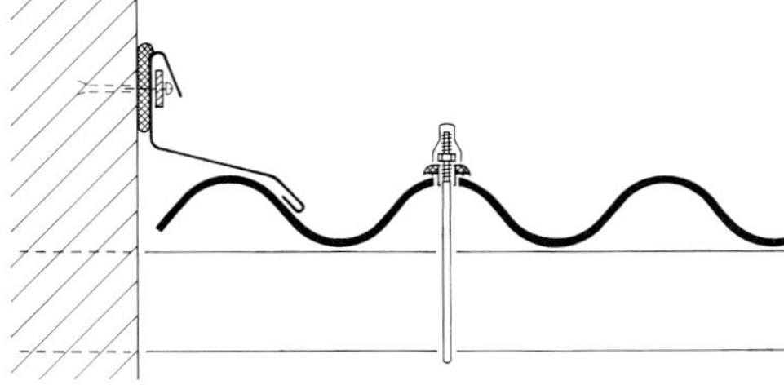

2.4.9.40 Junction with wall at side of slope, with metal flashing

The transition is created with a sloping piece of sheet metal. If the wall is not parallel with the line of the roof, the detail must be similar to that for a hip or valley.

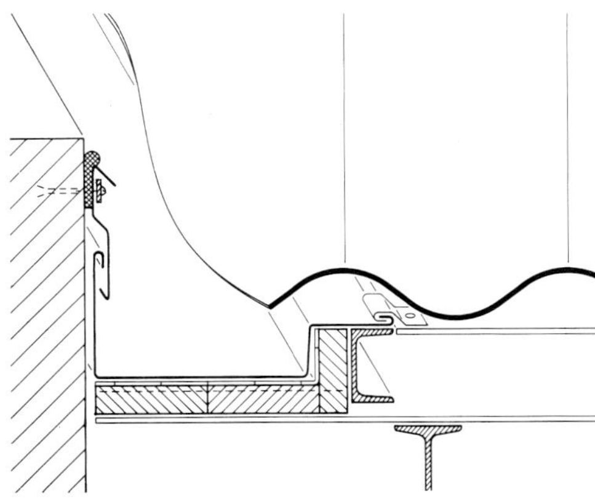

2.4.9.41 Junction with wall at side of slope (not parallel with corrugations), with gutter and sheet metal flashings

Junction with wall at bottom of slope
A back gutter at least 60 mm deep must be provided here (see also "Eaves" above). There is always a risk of a build-up of water in such a gutter, and so it should be kept short and have an adequate fall, outlet and overflow (see "Drainage").

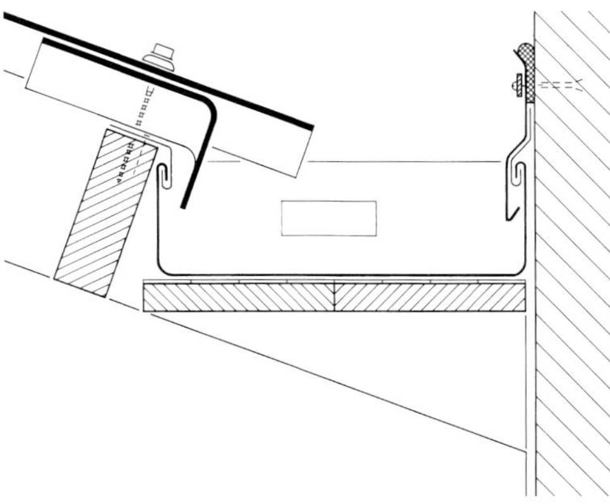

2.4.9.42 Junction with wall at bottom of slope, with corrugated eaves closure piece and back gutter

Junction with wall at top of slope
Special apron flashing pieces are normally used for this detail (see "Edge and special elements"). Their top edge is covered with a sheet metal flashing. If the wall is not straight or not exactly perpendicular to the line of the sheeting, it is possible to dress lead flashing over the corrugations and fix it through the sheeting.

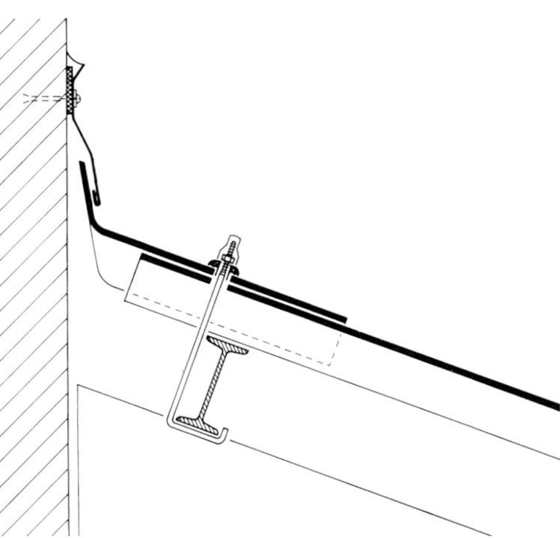

2.4.9.43 Junction with wall at top of slope, with apron flashing piece

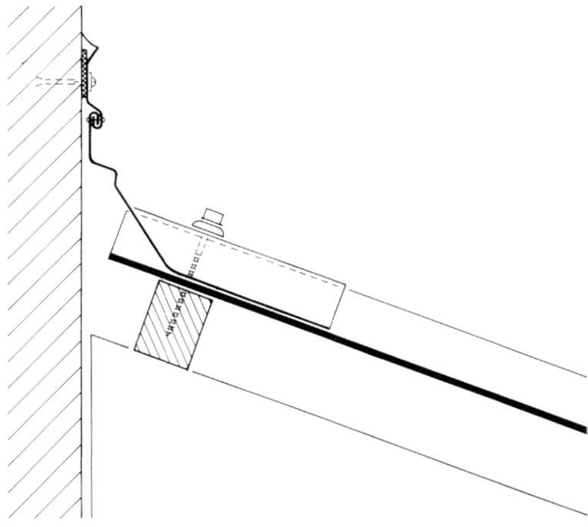

2.4.9.44 Junction with wall at top of slope, with milled lead flashing

Crank
If there is only a small difference in the two pitches (≤ 15°), it is sufficient to seal the sheets with putty or mortar. If the difference is > 15°, suitable cranked sheets must be employed.

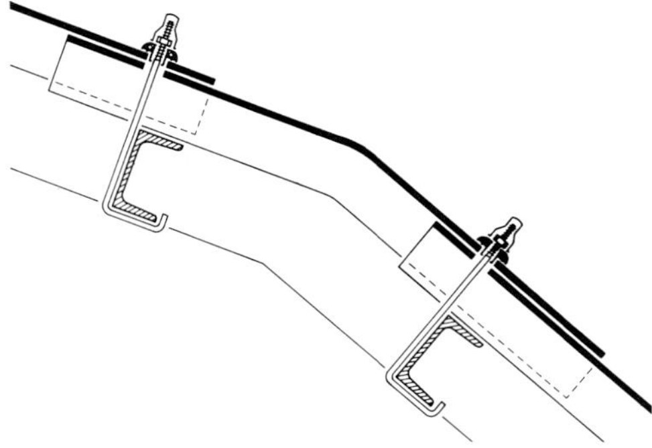

2.4.9.45 Crank > 15°, with special mansard roof element

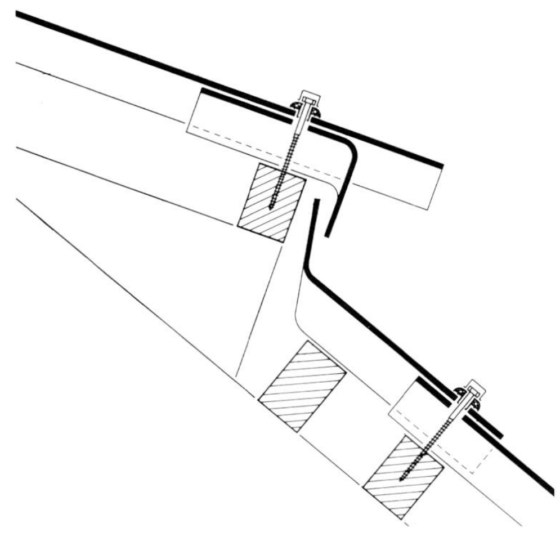

2.4.9.46 Crank > 15°, with corrugated eaves closure piece and apron flashing piece

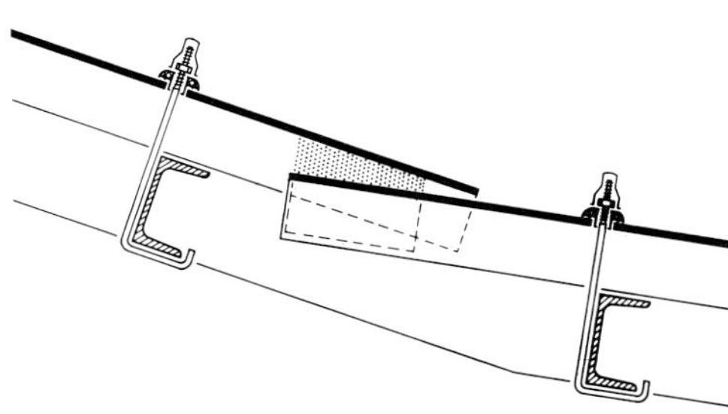

2.4.9.47 Crank ≤ 15°, with mortar or putty seal

Penetrations
A penetration may have a flexible (e.g. for chimneys) or rigid (e.g. for openings) arrangement. A flexible detail calls for the use of overlapping, sliding sheet metal aprons or milled lead. These are either integrated into the roof covering (sheet metal flashing) or firmly attached to the item penetrating the roof (milled lead). It should be ensured that the flashing at the rear is properly drained. Alternatively, a saddle flashing can be provided (see "Construction details"). Special cover frames made of fibre-cement or metal are available for windows.

Expansion joint
Special expansion joint hoods are used to cover expansion joints in the structure, where the supporting construction is also interrupted. They are fixed every 400 mm (staggered) with hexagon-head wood screws (see "Fixing materials").

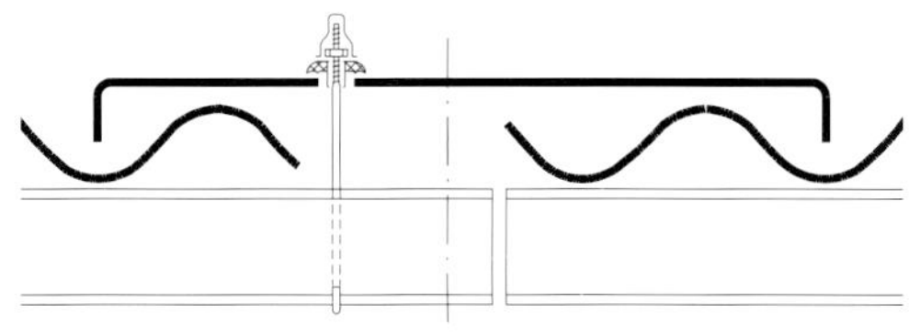

2.4.9.48 Fixing of expansion joint cover

**Supporting construction**

Boarding
When laying fibre-cement sheeting over interiors whose usage precludes any ingress of moisture (condensation, driven rain or snow etc.), boarding to act as a water run-off layer should be included (see "Layers – Secondary waterproofing/covering layer").

Supports for standard-pitch corrugated sheeting
Timber boards and purlins must be at least 60 mm wide, circular hollow steel sections at least 40 mm in diameter. Spacer strips (5 x 50 mm) must be provided at the fixings on a structural roof decking.

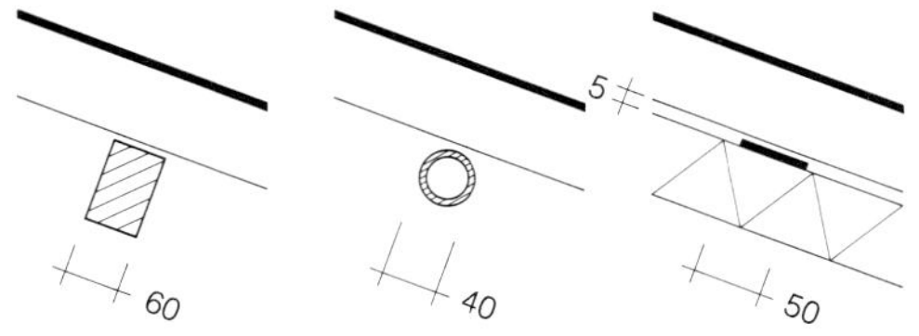


2.4.9.49 Supports for standard-pitch corrugated sheets

The spacing of the purlins depends on the length of sheet being used. The maximum permissible dimensions depend on the roof pitch or the magnitude of the loading.

| Roof pitch [°] | Permissible load [KN/m²] | Support spacing [mm] | Permissible load [KN/m²] | Support spacing [mm] |
|---|---|---|---|---|
| Profile | 5 (177x51) | | 8 (130x30) | |
| < 20 | 3.40 | ≤ 1150 | 1.70 | ≤ 1150 |
| ≥ 20 | 2.25 | ≤ 1450 | 1.70 | ≤ 1175 |

2.4.9.50 Permissible loads and spacing of supports [7]

Permissible loads are given in the DIBt approval certificate. If these are exceeded (e.g. in regions of heavy snowfall, sheets with planting), the purlin spacing must be recalculated.

Supports for narrow-pitch corrugated sheeting
Narrow-pitch corrugated sheets (rafter spacing ≤ 1.0 m) are generally laid on grade II timber battens, 40 x 60 mm; spacing of battens = 500 mm.

Prevention of falling through sheeting
Since 2002 fibre-cement corrugated sheeting has been supplied with reinforcing strips of plastic, which are integrated into every second corrugation and thus prevent accidents in which people fall through such roofs.

**Maintenance and repair**
Fibre-cement corrugated sheeting should be inspected from time to time for mechanical damage and excessive growth of moss. Any moss found should be removed and damaged sheets replaced. The low self-weight of corrugated sheets make them easy to replace. Crawling boards must be provided when working on fibre-cement corrugated sheeting. Unwanted vegetation must be removed annually from corrugated sheets with planting.

**References**

[1] Brennecke, W.; Folkerts, H.; Haferland, F.; Hart, F.: Dachatlas, Geneigte Dächer; Munich: Institut für Internationale Architektur-Dokumentation, 1975-84
[2] DIN EN 494: Fibre-cement profiled sheets and their fittings for roofing – Product specification and test methods
DIN 17100 Allgemeine Baustähle; Gütenorm
See also: DIN EN 10025, 10250 pt 1 and 2
[3] Eternit; product informationen, 2001
[4] Fulgurit; product informationen 2001
[5] Neufert, Ernst: Welleternit Handbuch; 10th ed.; Wiesbaden, Berlin: Bauverlag GmbH, 1974
[6] Scholz, W.: Baustoffkenntnis; 12th ed.; Düsseldorf: Werner-Verlag, 1991
[7] Zentralverband des deutschen Dachdeckerhandwerks: Regeln für Deckungen mit Faserzement, pt 3 (Wellplatten); Cologne: Rudolf Müller Verlag, 1993
[8] Zentralverband des deutschen Dachdeckerhandwerks/pub.: Dach-, Wand- und Abdichtungstechnik; Cologne: Rudolf Müller, 1987

## Corrugated bitumen sheeting
Material, components, laying

### Material
Raw materials, manufacture, properties

#### Raw materials
Corrugated bitumen sheets are made of straight-run bitumen (proportion 40–60%), primarily grade B 200, and cellulose fibres made from scrap paper (see "Flat overlapping elements – Asphalt shingles").

#### Manufacture
Corrugated bitumen sheets are manufactured from plain sheets made of cellulose fibres with a bitumen impregnation. The cellulose fibres are mixed with water to form a fibrous pulp. This is rolled flat, pressed into a corrugated shape and dried in a forming station.
In the one-layer process, the sheets are produced from a single homogenous layer, while in the multi-layer process several thin layers of cellulose fibres are bonded together.
The plain sheets are produced as a continuous band of material, which is then cut with a saw to the right format and impregnated with bitumen. The untreated sheets pass through a bath of bitumen and are completely impregnated by the bitumen.

Colour
The surface of the corrugated bitumen sheeting is treated to protect it from ultraviolet radiation and the effects of the weather, and to provide some colour. The normal method is to coat the surface or immerse the sheets in a dispersion paint on an acrylic resin basis. The standard colours are various shades of red, green, brown, black and anthracite. Special colours are also possible, depending on the manufacturer.
Granulate coatings are available in red, green, brown and blue.

#### Properties
Corrugated bitumen sheets are produced in two thicknesses:

| | |
|---|---|
| Type A | 3.0 mm |
| Type B | 2.4 mm |

Physical properties

| | |
|---|---|
| Weight | type A 2.6 kg/m² type B 2.2 kg/m² |
| Bending strength | 12.2 N/mm² |
| Coefficient of thermal expansion | ≤ 0.1% at δT = 50°C |
| UV radiation resistance | no change to surface |

2.4.10.1 Physical characteristic values [04]

Biological properties
Corrugated bitumen sheets exhibit only a limited resistance to fungi that attack wood, but are resistant to microorganisms. [07]

Chemical properties
Corrugated bitumen sheets are resistant to industrial atmospheres to DIN 50018 and to acids. They have only limited resistance to alkalis and ammonia. [06, 07]
Reactions with oxygen cause the formation of water-soluble degradation products, which can corrode zinc, iron and other metals (see "Flat overlapping elements – Asphalt shingles").

Moisture behaviour
Corrugated bitumen sheets have a low water absorption capacity and low water vapour permeability. The surface is frost-resistant.

Behaviour in fire
Corrugated bitumen sheets are classed as flammable (building materials class B 2) to DIN 4102 part 7. A coating of granulate (slate chippings) allows the material to be classed as a "hard roof covering", i.e. the roof is resistant to sparks and radiant heat.

### Components
General elements, edge elements, special elements, grades

#### General elements
Corrugated bitumen sheets are produced in various formats and profiles.
- Lightweight corrugated sheets are made of PVC or glass fibre-reinforced unsaturated polyester. They are available transparent or coloured.

Dimensions of profile

| Width w [mm] | Length l [mm] | Width $w_1$ [mm] | Depth h [mm] | No. of corrugations |
|---|---|---|---|---|
| 870 | 2000 | 62 | 28 | 14 |
| 930 | 2000 | 93 | 36 | 10 |
| 950 | 2000 | 95 | 31 | 10 |
| 950 | 2000 | 95 | 38 | 10 |
| 1060 | 2000 | 75 | 30 | 14 |

2.4.10.2 Standard formats for corrugated bitumen sheets [05]

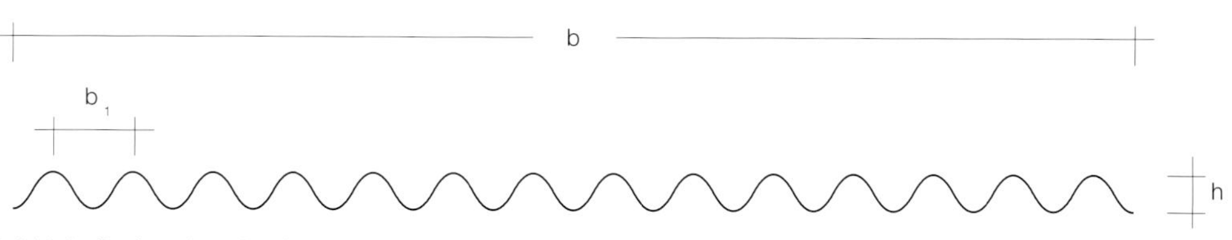


2.4.10.3 Designations for dimensions

#### Edge elements
Edge elements are also made of bitumen-coated fibres or plastic.
- The ventilating ridge capping is suitable for all roof pitches. It has a ventilation cross-section of 412 cm².
- Profile fillers made of plastic are required to close off the corrugations at ridge and eaves.
- The ridge capping made of bitumen-coated fibres can be bent to suit all roof pitches owing to the elasticity of the material. It is also used as a hip capping.
- The verge profile is also used for the ridge to a monopitch roof.
- Apron flashing pieces

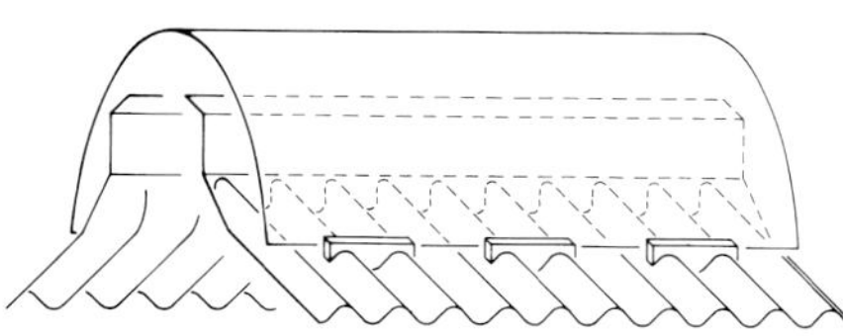

2.4.10.4 Ventilating ridge capping

2.4.10.5 Profile filler/closure

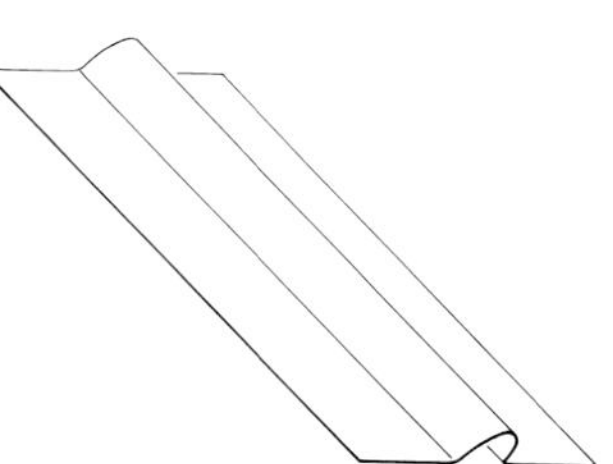

2.4.10.6 Ridge and hip capping

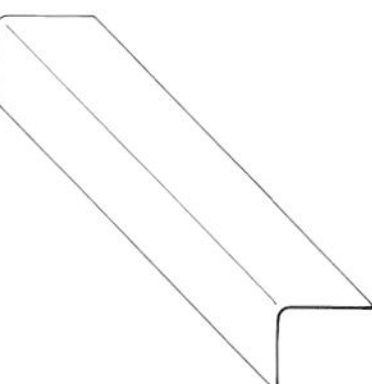

2.4.10.7 Verge profile

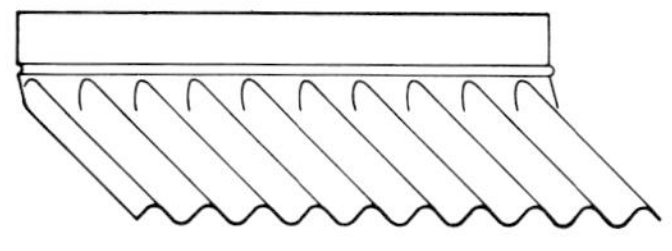

2.4.10.8 Apron flashing piece at top of slope

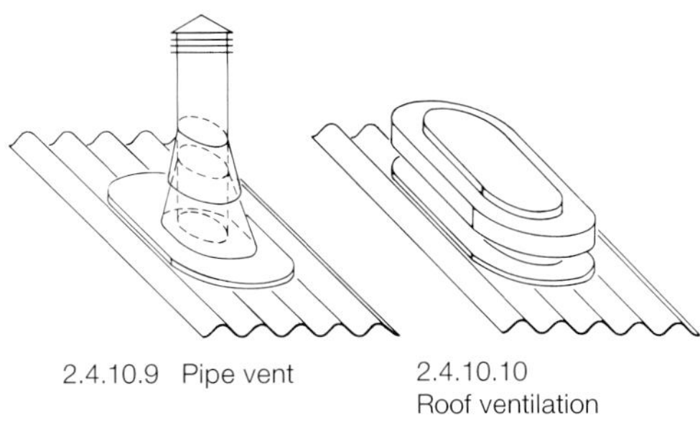
2.4.10.9 Pipe vent
2.4.10.10 Roof ventilation

**Special elements**

- Components with corrugated base plates made of plastic (hard PVC) for building into the roof are employed for penetrations (vents etc.).
- A pipe vent with adjustable pipe supports can be mounted vertically on any roof pitch.
- The roof vent has a ventilation cross-section of 175 cm².

**Grades**

Corrugated bitumen sheets must comply with DIN EN 534.

## Laying

Conditions for laying, fixing, additional measures, details, supporting construction, maintenance and repair

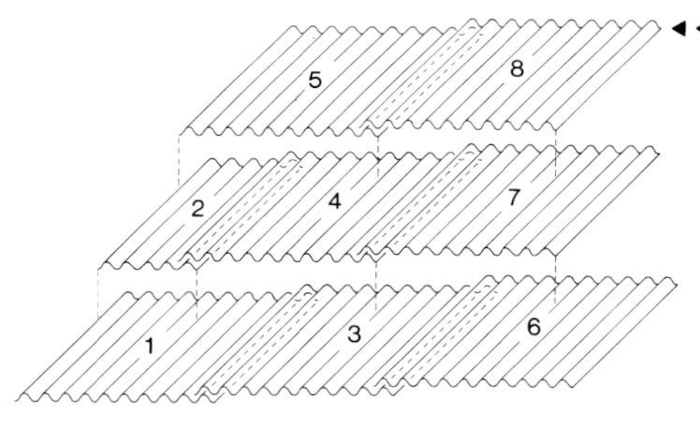

2.4.10.11 Laying the sheets offset in a bond; ◄ prevailing wind direction

**Conditions for laying**

Corrugated bitumen sheets are laid with the corrugations parallel to the slope of the roof. They are laid offset in a bond to avoid having to mitre the corners. The first sheet of every second course must be sawn in half. The sheets are laid in the opposite direction to the prevailing wind. The surface of the roof must be divided up straight and square. [05]

If precipitation drains from corrugated bitumen sheets onto metal items, the latter must be coated or painted to protect them from corrosion. [05]

Roof pitch

Corrugated bitumen sheets can be laid on roof surfaces with a pitch of ≥ 7°. The minimum roof pitch depends on the ridge-eaves length. [05]

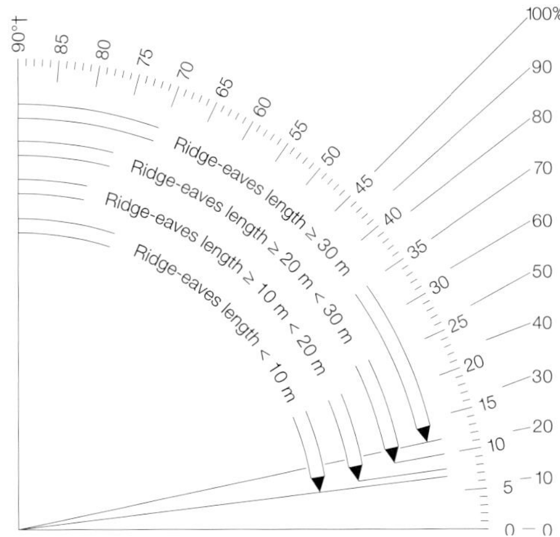

2.4.10.12 Minimum roof pitch

Laps

The side lap is equal to one corrugation. The end laps depend on the roof pitch. [05]

| Roof pitch [°] | head lap [mm] |
|---|---|
| ≥ 10 | ≥ 160 |
| ≥ 15 | ≥ 140 |

2.4.10.13 Head laps [04]

**Fixing**

Only approved rustproofed PVC-headed nails, countersunk nails with sealing washer or roofing nails with sealing washer may be used to fix corrugated bitumen sheets.
The sheets are fixed through the crests of the corrugations. There are no predrilled holes and all fixings are driven in perpendicular to the roof pitch to avoid deforming the sheets, and to ensure that the plastic sealing washers make proper contact with the material. Driving the nails in too far deforms the sheet. To prevent the sheets from moving apart, the second and the penultimate corrugations are secured first. Only after this are the intermediate fixings installed.
At the supports between the laps, every second crest is to be fixed, beginning with the first one. Every crest should be fixed at laps, eaves and ridges.

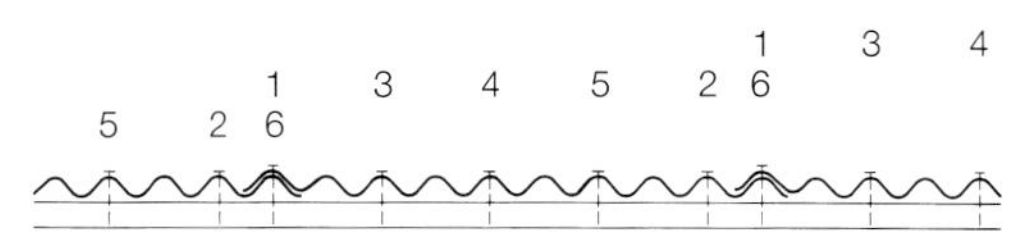

2.4.10.14 Fixings on the surface of the roof; sequence

The spacing of the fixings from the upper edge of the sheet should be ≥ 70 mm. At the edges every crest is fixed to every support over a width of 2 m. [05]

Workability

Corrugated bitumen sheets are very easy to work. Cutting across the corrugations is possible with a greased saw. In the longitudinal direction a special knife with a hooked blade can be used as well. [01, 02]

**Additional measures**

Additional measures should be taken when enhanced requirements are placed on the reliability of the roof covering. For example:

- with a high wind pressure
- with high snow loads
- with roof pitches ≤ 10°
- on large roofs
- when the roof space is in use

Additional measures include:

- increasing the minimum pitch by ≥ 3°
- increasing the side lap to two corrugations
- providing a minimum end lap of 200 mm
- providing sarking or roofing felt underneath
- providing watertight or rainproof boarding underneath

**Details**

Ridge, hip, eaves, valley, verge, junction with wall, penetrations

Owing to their similarities, details can be derived from those outlined for profiled metal and corrugated fibre-cement sheeting (see "Layers – Metal profiled sheeting and metal panels" and "Layers – Fibre-cement corrugated sheeting").

Ridge

At the ridge the corrugated bitumen sheets end about 50 mm below the apex. The ridge is constructed with a one-piece ridge capping that can be used for any standard roof pitch.

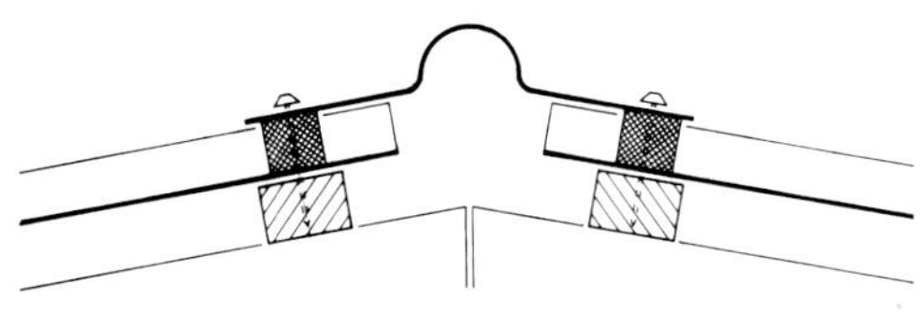
2.4.10.15 Ridge capping

These cappings are fixed through every crest on both sides of the ridge. The space between the straight edges of the ridge capping and the troughs of the corrugations must be closed off by inserting a profile filler. Adequate ventilation must then be ensured by other means. [05]

Hip
Ridge cappings are used on the hips as well. They are fixed through each crest of the adjoining sheets. Battens are laid along the hip to make sure that the sheets are firmly and continuously supported. [05]

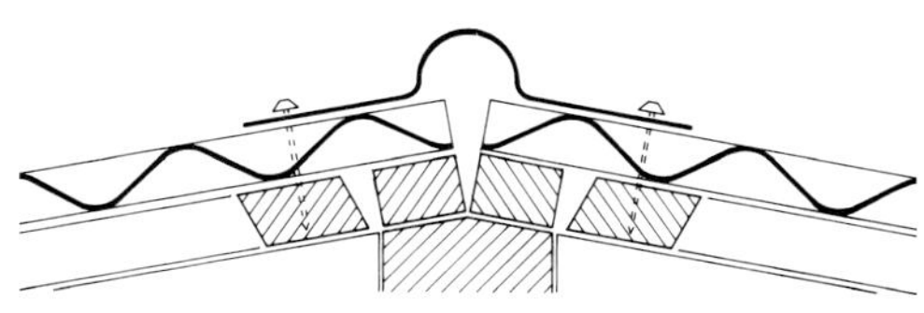

2.4.10.16 Hip detail with hip capping

Eaves
Sheets may project up to 50 mm beyond the edge of the last support. The crests of the corrugations must be closed off underneath with profile fillers, provided adequate ventilation is guaranteed by other means. [05]

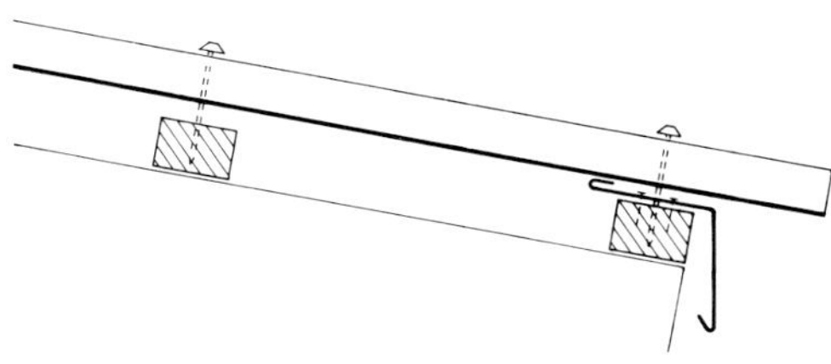

2.4.10.17 Eaves detail with overhang

Valley
Lined valleys are used with this type of roof covering. Their shape and the size of the overlap depend on the roof pitch. [05]

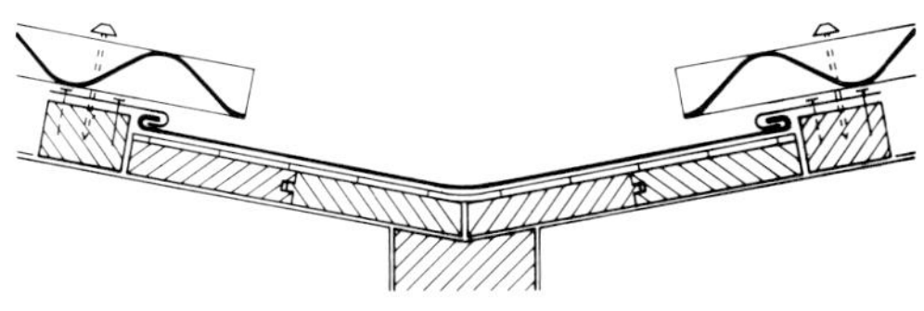

2.4.10.18 Lined sheet metal valley

Verge
A verge detail without a special verge profile requires the last corrugation to be fully supported. The projection should be no more than half a corrugation so that the last corrugation can still be fixed. Special verge pieces can be fitted on top, or underneath as a verge gutter. [05]

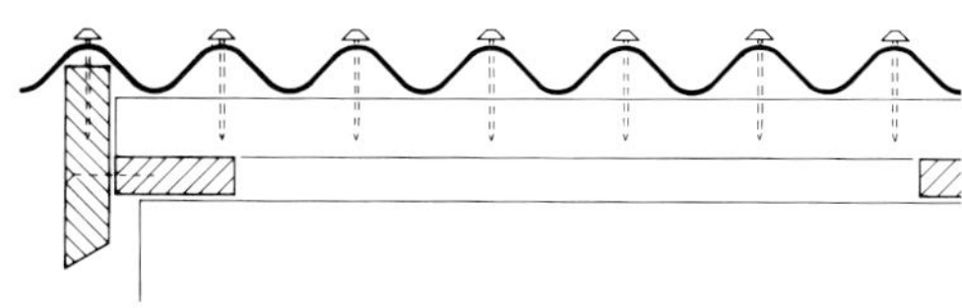

2.4.10.19 Verge detail with barge board

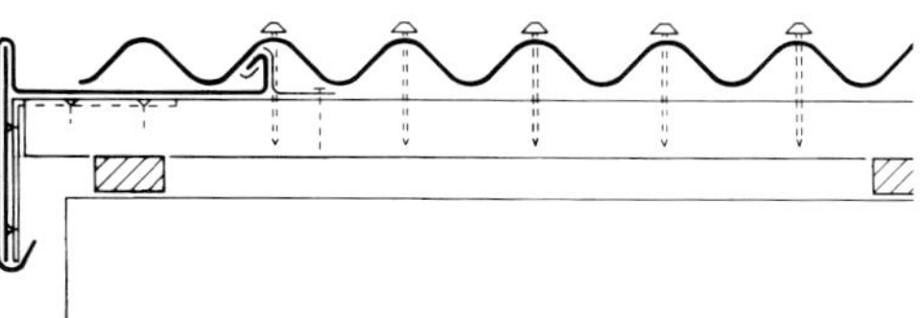

2.4.10.20 Verge detail with metal flashing

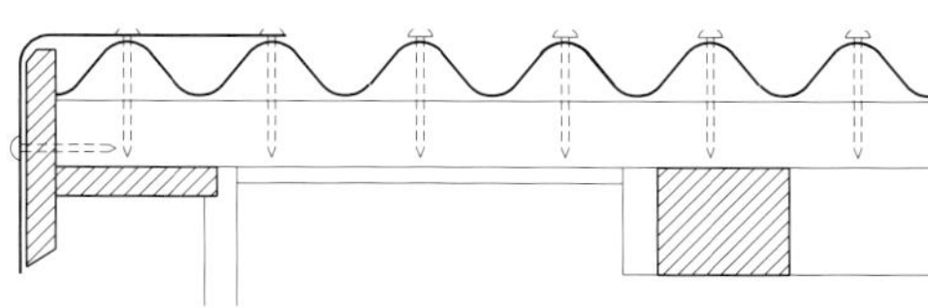

2.4.10.21 Verge detail with special verge profile

Junction with wall
The junction with a wall at the side of a slope is best carried out with sheet metal profiles, with a lap of one corrugation either above or below the sheeting. When exposed to the prevailing wind, this overlap should be increased to two corrugations. [05, 06]

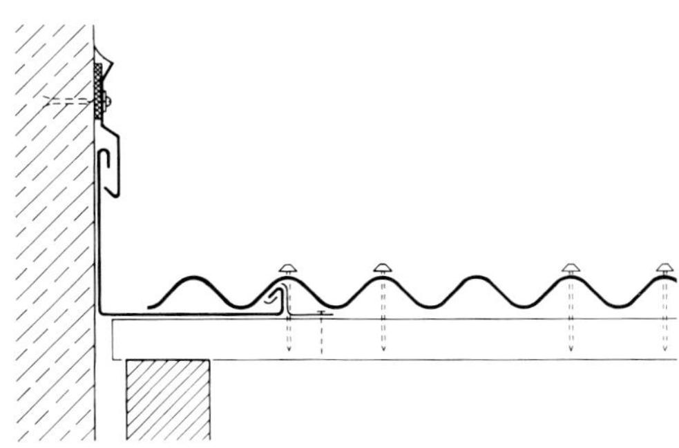

2.4.10.22 Junction with wall at side of slope, with metal flashing

Penetrations
It is best to use special pieces for roof vents and pipe vents. Their corrugated base plates are positioned on the roof surfaces with the standard end laps and side laps, and fixed at every crest. [05]
Junctions with chimneys are possible with the help of auxiliary materials arranged to suit on site.
Hooks for ladders and snowguard supports should be mounted around end laps. Packing up underneath is necessary to ensure the correct support for the corrugations.

**Supporting construction**
A roof covering of corrugated bitumen sheets is laid on battens or roof decking. Loadbearing timber battens should be ≥ 40 mm deep and ≥ 60 mm wide. Loadbearing battens or purlins must be installed at 90° to the corrugations and support the sheets over their full width. The spacing of battens is 30, 46 or 62 cm depending on the roof pitch, as well as on snow and wind loads. [05]
A roof decking below the sheeting is preferred on shallower roof pitches and/or with high snow loads. [07]
This should comprise boards 80–150 mm wide and 24 mm thick. As the nails have to be driven in to a depth of 40 mm, additional battens are necessary at fixings and supports. [05, 07]
All the falls of a roof surface must run parallel. Larger differences in the levels of the bearing faces of neighbouring supports should therefore be eliminated by packing up with timber, especially with loadbearing battens at spacings of 30 and 46 cm.
Corrugated bitumen sheets must always be laid directly on the supporting construction. Intermediate pads at the supports are not permitted.
A curved supporting construction must have a radius of 6 to 8 m. [02, 04]

Ventilation
Because water absorption capacity and water vapour permeability are low, adequate ventilation is not absolutely essential. At worst, corrugated bitumen sheets can suffer frost damage or deformations. The ventilation cross-section at the ridge should be approx. 20% greater than that at the eaves. [01, 02, 06]

**Maintenance and repair**
It is possible to repaint the sheets. Minor damage caused by hail etc. can be made good with bituminous cold adhesive or filler compounds made from butyl rubber. [06, 07]
Roof surfaces of corrugated bitumen sheets cannot be walked upon directly; access is only possible with crawling boards. Permanently installed means of access and crawling boards to DIN 274 part 2 should be provided for facilities requiring frequent maintenance (e.g. chimneys). Walkways should not introduce bending stresses into the corrugated bitumen sheets. [05] After a few years the surfaces can show signs of brittleness and fading, due to the effects of the weather; moss-like coatings can also appear. However, these do not impair the watertightness. [01, 02, 03]
Corrugated bitumen sheets are resistant to the weather, ultraviolet radiation and industrial atmospheres. Damage to individual sheets is easily remedied by replacing the sheets concerned. Their light weight and simple laying techniques make this possible without having to remove large areas of the roof covering. If the supporting construction is not damaged, the structural requirements permit and the existing roof covering is free from asbestos and other hazardous substances, new battens can be laid directly on an existing covering and the complete roof surface covered with new corrugated bitumen sheets. This enables refurbishment to be carried out over occupied premises regardless of the weather.

**References**
[01] Deutsche Landwirtschaftsgesellschaft e.V.; test report 3616
[02] Deutsche Landwirtschaftsgesellschaft e.V.; test report 3691
[03] Deutsche Landwirtschaftsgesellschaft e.V.; test report 3832
[04] DIN EN 534: Corrugated bitumen sheets
[05] Fachregeln des Dachdeckerhandwerks; ed. Zentralverband des Deutschen Dachdeckerhandwerks
[06] GUTTA-Werke product information
[07] Deutsche O.F.I.C. product information

## Metal profiled sheeting and metal panels

Materials, components, laying

## Materials

Raw materials, manufacture, properties

Profiled metal sheets are mainly produced from aluminium alloys, galvanised steel, or galvanised and coated steel. Profiled metal sheets of copper or stainless steel are much less common.

#### Raw materials

(see “Sheet metal roof coverings – Raw materials”)

#### Manufacture

Metal profiled sheeting is made from flat wide strips, the manufacture of which is outlined in the next chapter. The various surface finishes and coatings (bright-rolled, galvanised, galvanised and coated, colour-coated) serve both corrosion protection and aesthetic purposes. The coating is usually applied in a continuous process, and the flat metal sheets coated prior to profiling. Various synthetic materials are used for the coatings, usually in a liquid form, and less commonly as a rolled-on foil.
These coatings must be elastic and survive the profiling process without any cracking.
The profiled sheets are produced in a continuous production process through cold-forming on a train of precisely coordinated sets of profiled rollers. “Profiling produces the required profile in a series of graduated forming processes (a succession of pairs of rollers) from the flat wide strip to the finished profile. The depth and width of the profile to be produced determine the number of forming stations necessary. The deeper and wider a profile is, the more stations are required. The length of the sheets is essentially limited only by the type of transport.” [07, 14]

Manufacture of special elements
Special elements for ridge, eaves, verge, openings etc. are normally bent on bending presses, or, less often, rolled in cold-rolling plants. This restricts their length. [07]

#### Properties

(see “Sheet metal roof coverings – Properties”)

## Components

General elements, edge and special elements, product coding, forms of supply, storage

#### General elements

Profiled metal sheets are available in the standard sizes at all times. Special sizes within the maximum width are available on request.

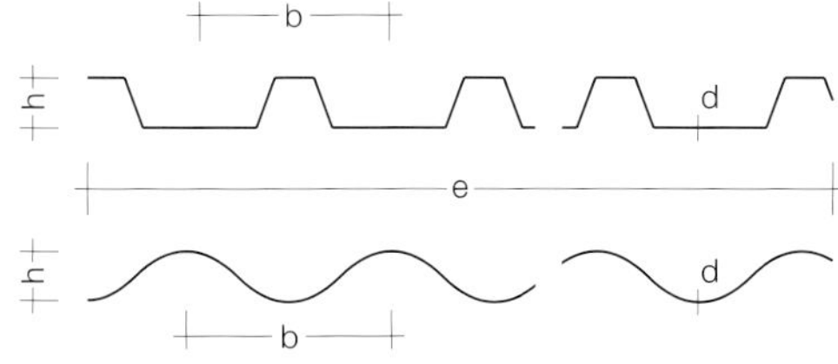


| | Trapezoidal/corrugated profiles | |
|---|---|---|
| | Aluminium [mm] | Galvanised steel [mm] |
| Trapezoidal profiles, hxb (selection) | 20x125<br>29x124<br>30x262<br>35x207<br>40x183<br>45x150<br>50x167<br>50x262<br>58x315<br>80x307<br>85x280<br>89x305 | 30x220<br>65x207<br>50x207<br>70x200<br>100x275<br>106x250<br>110x333<br>135x310<br>144x287<br>150x280<br>160x250<br>170x250<br>205x375 |
| Corrugated profiles hxb (selection) | 18x76<br>55x177 | 18x76 |
| Sheet thickness d | 0.5–1.5<br>typical 0.8 | 0.56–1.5<br>typical 0.75; 0.88 |
| Sheet width e | 600 to 1056 | |
| Length | 750–1600<br>(by road)<br>750–30 000<br>(by rail) | ≤ 20 000 |
| | special lengths on request | |
| Weight | 1.65–5.86 kg/m² | 7.5–16.7 kg/m² |

2.4.11.1 General elements; trapezoidal and corrugated profiles; forms and standard sizes [01, 02, 06, 07, 08, 09, 10]

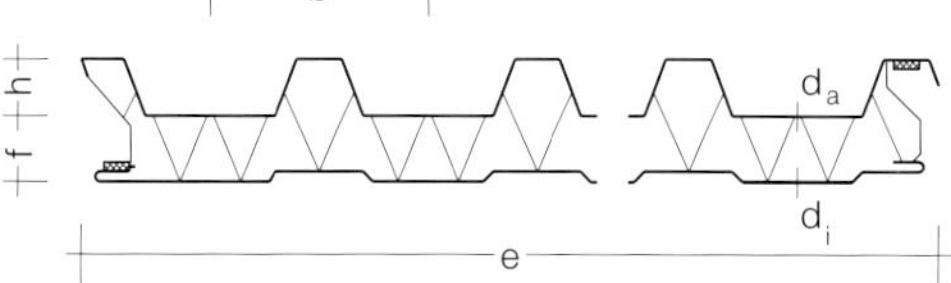


| | Composite panels of trapezoidal profiled sheeting and thermal insulation | |
|---|---|---|
| | Aluminium [mm] | Galvanised steel [mm] |
| Profile h/b (selection) | 30/333<br>35/333.3 | 30/333<br>35/333.3 |
| Sheet thickness<br>$d_i$ inside<br>$d_a$ outside | <br>0.40–0.55<br>0.50–0.70 | <br>0.40–0.55<br>0.50–0.70 |
| Insulation thickness f | 30–100 | 30–100 |
| Sheet width e | 1000 (1176) | 1000 (1176) |
| Weight [kg/m²] | 4.86–15.10 | 4.86–15.10 |
| Therm. transmittance U-value [W/(m²K)] | 0.23–0.71 | 0.23–0.71 |
| Thermal resistance 1/Λ [(m²K)/W] | 1.25–4.09 | 1.25–4.09 |

2.4.11.2 General elements; composite panels of trapezoidal profiled sheeting and thermal insulation; standard sizes [03]

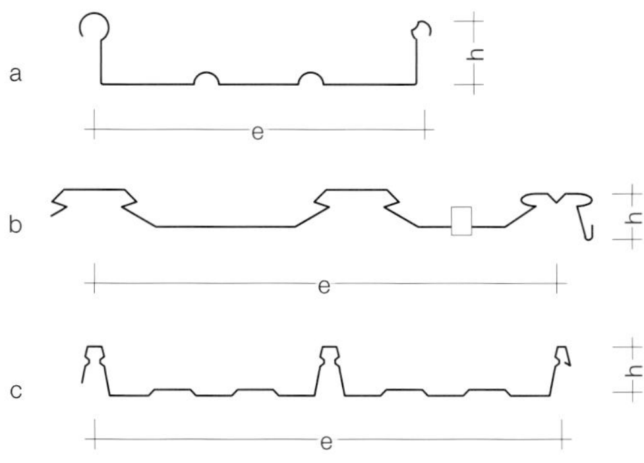


| | Ribbed profiles | | |
|---|---|---|---|
| | Aluminium [mm] | Copper (rare) [mm] | Galvanised steel [mm] |
| Depth h | 50, 65 | 47 | 35, 65 |
| Width e (No. of ribs) | 250 | 457 | 305 |
| | 305 | | 1000 |
| | 333 | | 250 |
| | 400 | | 333 |
| | 434 | | 400 |
| | 500 | | 500 |
| | 600 | | 600 |
| Thickness d | 0.7–1.2 typical 0.8 | 0.6 | 0.63–1.0 typical 0.75; 0.88 |
| Length | 1200–75 000 | ≤ 17 000 (by road) ≤ 30 000 (by rail) | ≤ 50 000 |
| Weight | 3.1–5.2 kg/m² | 7.9 kg/m² | 6.7 kg/m² |

2.4.11.3 General elements; ribbed profiles; forms and standard sizes, materials; a aluminium, galvanised steel, b galvanised steel, c copper [03, 06, 08, 09]

2.4.11.4 General elements; metal panels

Metal panels are supplied in a width (b) of 365 mm and standard lengths (l) of 2000 or 3000 mm. The thickness of the metal is 0.8 mm, the weight 7.89 kg/m².

**Edge and special elements**

Trapezoidal and corrugated sheeting can also be produced with a camber, i.e. concave in the longitudinal direction, and even in convex or conical-convex forms. They can be supplied in all standard sizes. Metal panels can also be laid on convex curving roof surfaces because joints, junctions and verge profiles can be supplied bent to suit.

Special elements are produced in all profiles for use at edges and junctions; they can also be made by hand to suit.

Profile fillers are required to close off the openings caused by the shape of the trapezoidal or corrugated sheeting. These are made from incombustible, heat-resistant plastic, are supplied on reels and are available in thicknesses of 30, 50 and 100 mm. Profile fillers are matched to the form of the respective metal profiled sheeting. If the openings are to be used for ventilation, soft vented fillers that follow the line of the profile can be installed.

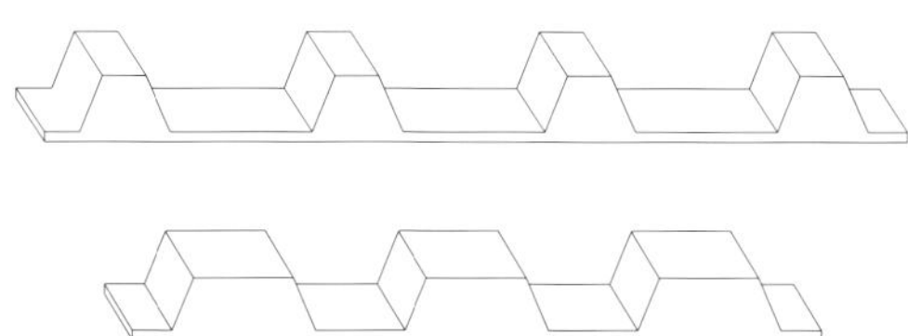

2.4.11.5 Edge and special elements; profile fillers

**Product coding**

In Germany metals and their alloys are designated by means of material numbers. These numbers provide precise information about group, grade, method of extraction and status of treatment. This is linked to an exact designation of the specific properties and the quality of every individual metal and metal alloy.

**Forms of supply**

Profiled metal sheets and metal panels are supplied stacked on pallets. Stacked coated components are protected by intermediate sheets of plastic film or oiled paper.

**Storage**

Profiled metal sheets should be stored under cover to protect them from soiling and the formation of condensation. Care should be taken not to exceed the permissible load on the roof construction when storing profiled metal sheeting temporarily on the roof.

## Laying

Conditions for laying, fixing, additional measures, details, supporting construction, maintenance and repair

**Conditions for laying**

Trapezoidal and corrugated sheets are laid in rows. Trapezoidal sheets should be laid so that the wider rib is always at the bottom. This means that the larger surface area is available for draining water reliably; the bearing surface of the sheets is then also larger.
To protect the side joints from moisture penetration, laying is carried out in the opposite direction from the prevailing wind. Ribbed sheets – with strengthening ribs on the face and turned-up edges – are fitted together and the edges welted. These side joints are therefore positioned above the water run-off layer. Any end (transverse) joints necessary lie below the water run-off layer; they are not watertight for a build-up of water below a certain roof pitch. Minimum roof pitches are therefore recommended for profiled and ribbed sheeting.

Panels are laid parallel to the eaves, from ridge to eaves or vice versa. Joint profiles, clipped to the battens or fixed directly to the timber roof decking, are laid at 90° to the eaves; the clips are hidden behind the roof covering, which lies on battens that match the profile chosen.

Roof pitch

The minimum roof pitch is essentially governed by depth of profile, length of sheeting (ridge-eaves length), the detail at the end joints, and the position and nature of penetrations.

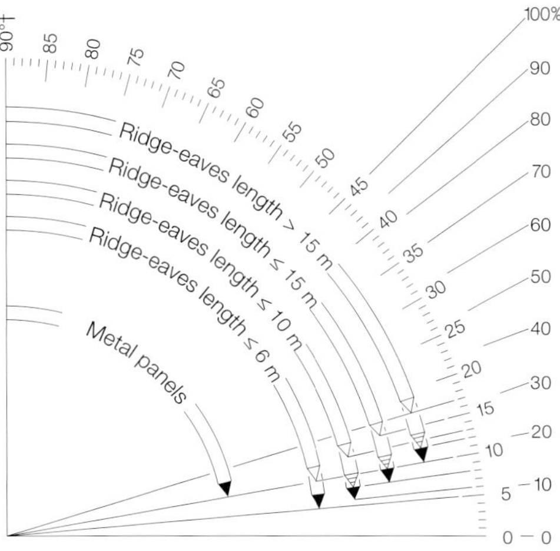


2.4.11.6 Minimum roof pitch in relation to ridge-eaves length and depth of profile h: ▽ h = 18–25 mm, ▽ h = 25–50 mm, ▼ h = > 50 mm [15]

A pitch < 5° should not be selected because airborne pollutants, dust and dirt can only be washed off with a certain velocity of run-off water.
If end joints are required and/or penetrations are located on the roof surface, the roof pitch should be increased.

Side joints

The edges of trapezoidal and corrugated sheets are overlapped and secured with screws, rivets or clips to guarantee a tight fit. The overlap is the width of one upper rib (corrugation).

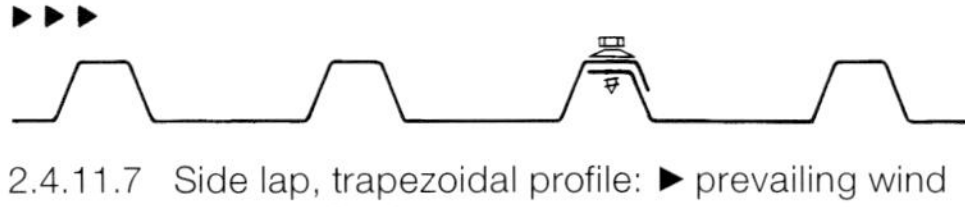

2.4.11.7 Side lap, trapezoidal profile: ▶ prevailing wind direction [07]

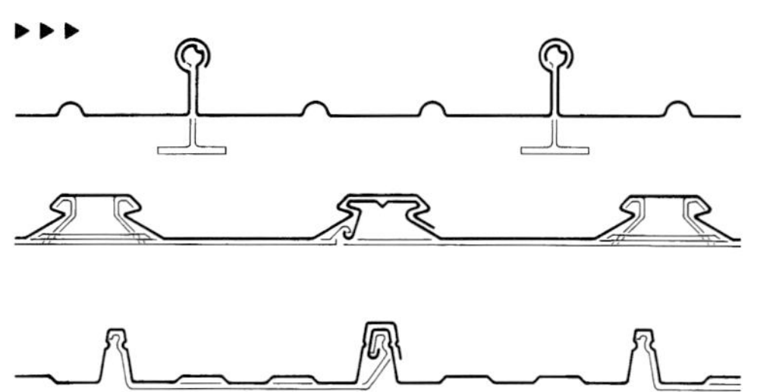

2.4.11.8 Side lap, ribbed profiles: ▶ prevailing wind direction [06, 08, 09]

A preformed strip seal should be laid in each side joint at a roof pitch ≤ 7° or in regions with high wind loads.

Ribbed sheets are fixed to retaining clips or strips. The overlap is equivalent to the roll width of one rib.

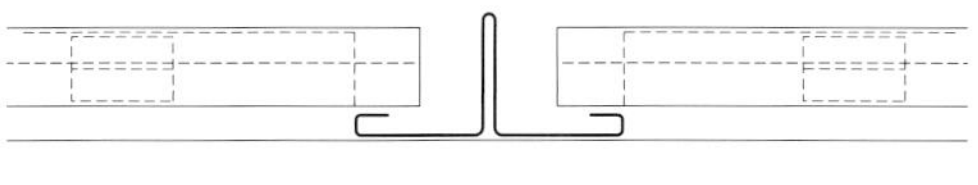

2.4.11.9 Side joint, metal panels [11]

Metal panels are laid with a head lap of 15 mm on joint profiles laid perpendicular to the eaves. They are fixed by simply hanging them on the matching battens.

End joints

If end joints in profiled sheeting are positioned in an area of run-off water, the minimum roof pitch should be increased. It is therefore advantageous to avoid end joints.

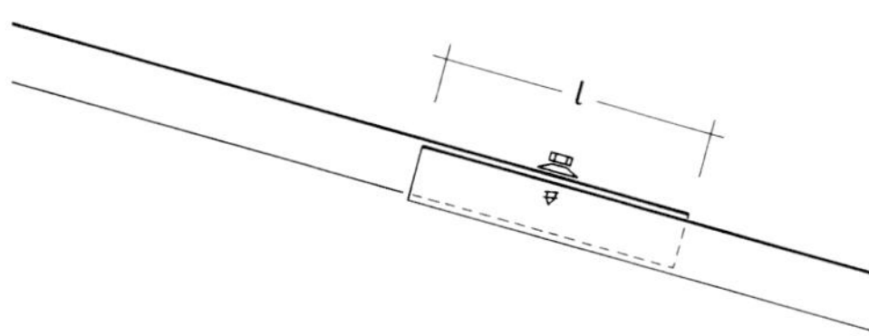


2.4.11.10 End lap, trapezoidal profile; lap length l, fixing [13]

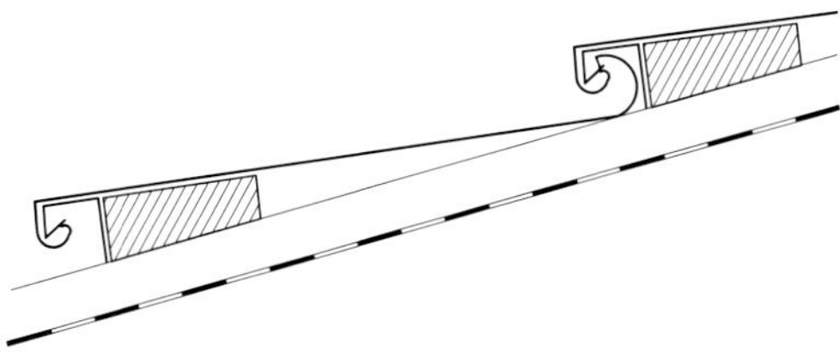

2.4.11.11 Headlap, metal panels [11]

The length of the end lap depends on the roof pitch and the wind loading.
Ribbed sheets should have a lap of 200 mm. The sheets are riveted, brazed/soldered or welded together. A preformed strip seal should be laid in each lap below a roof pitch of 7°.

**Fixing**

All fixings pass through the upper ribs of the profiled sheets (or crests of corrugated sheets) and into the supporting construction. Shaped pressure and capping pieces are installed between screw and profiled sheeting in order to achieve a good contact pressure.
A neoprene seal between pressure and capping pieces prevents the ingress of moisture.

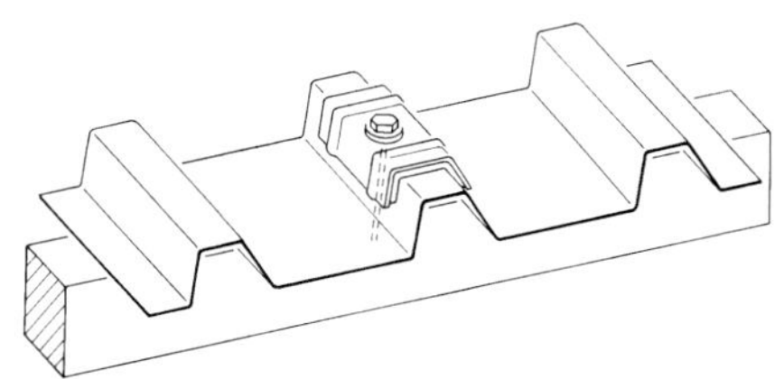

2.4.11.12 Fixing of trapezoidal profile; with screw, pressure and capping pieces [13]

To permit thermal expansion, elongated holes and sliding fixings are provided in addition to fixed points with sheet lengths > 5000 mm.

- Fixed points
  Fixed points secure the profiled metal sheets directly to the supporting construction and thus transfer the shear forces to the supporting construction.
- Fixing through elongated hole
  The larger holes to accommodate thermal expansion are covered by capping pieces shaped to match the respective profile.
- Sliding fixing
  The play in the fixing necessary to accommodate thermal expansion is already allowed for in the supporting construction. For example, a retaining rail can be screwed to the top flange of a Z-section.
  A sliding bracket can be clipped into this rail such that it can move freely within the profile.

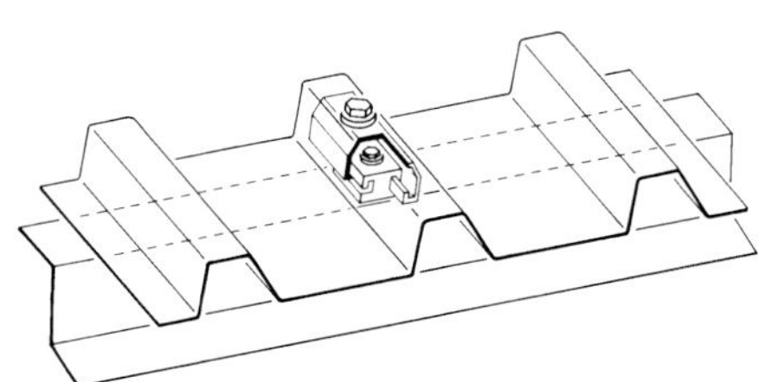

2.4.11.13 Fixing of trapezoidal profile; sliding fixing with sliding shoe on Z-section

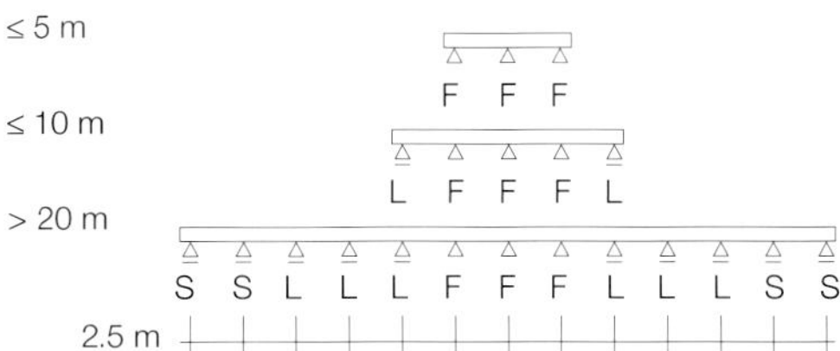


2.4.11.14 Arrangement of fixings for profiled sheeting in relation to sheet length: F = fixed point, L = elongated hole, S = sliding fixing

Ribbed sheets are connected to the supporting construction via hidden retaining clips or strips. They are fixed at the ridge or in the middle of the roof surface. At the ridge the sheets are riveted directly to the supporting construction. These rivets are covered by the ridge capping. However, the fixing in the middle of the roof surface is more common as it enables the ribbed sheets to expand both towards the ridge and towards the eaves. The smaller edge roll of the first ribbed sheet is riveted to the retaining clip and the rivet is hidden by the larger edge roll of the next sheet. In this case the ridge detail should take thermal expansion into account. A normal clip fixing can be regarded as allowing displacement.

Spacing of fixings

- For a purlin spacing ≤ 1500 mm, the profiled sheets should be fixed to every purlin in the longitudinal correction; with a purlin spacing > 1500 mm, the sheets should be connected together in addition with self-tapping screws, blind or compressible blind rivets at a spacing ≤ 500 mm.
- At least every second upper rib (crest of corrugation) should be fixed in the transverse direction, and every upper rib at laps and edges.
- Support at edges

Overhanging sides or outer, exposed profiled sheets should be additionally stiffened by a galvanised angle trimmer (≥ 0.7 mm thick). This is fixed every 333 mm (max.) with blind rivets or screws. Steel sections, steel, reinforced concrete or timber members are conceivable beneath every outer rib (corrugation). They are connected to the profiled sheets every 666 mm (max.) with powder-actuated fasteners or screws.

Fixing materials

Profiled sheets are fixed to the structure by means of a hammer-driven screws, annular nails, hook bolts, self-tapping screws, powder-actuated fasteners, screw fittings attached to powder-actuated fasteners, welding and clips. All fasteners must be made from corrosion-resistant, or at least corrosion-protected, materials and, in terms of the electrochemical series, correspond with the material of the profiled sheeting. Fasteners made from corrosion-protected materials that protrude above the roof surface should be protected with a cap of aluminium, stainless steel or weather-resistant plastic. [15]

2.4.11.15 Fixing for profiled sheets; pressure and capping pieces with neoprene seal [06]

Clips that match the profile of ribbed sheets are available to clip sheeting to matching retaining clips or strips. These are first fixed with stainless steel screws to the supporting construction.

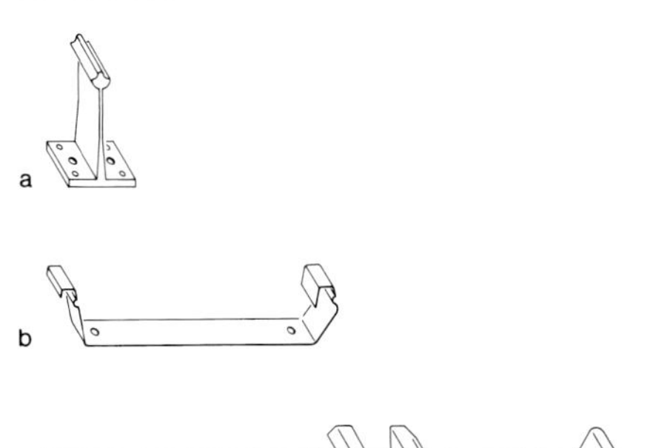


2.4.11.16 Fixings for ribbed sheets; fixing materials: a cut from extruded aluminium section, b and c made from folded sheet metal

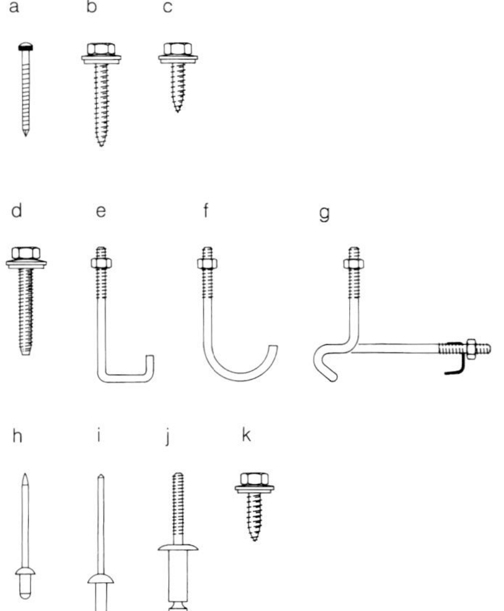


2.4.11.17 Fixings for profiled sheets; fasteners for timber structure: a aluminium or stainless steel annular nail with sealing washer, b and c aluminium or stainless steel screw grade 18/8 with washer and sealing washer; for steel or reinforced concrete structure: d self-tapping stainless steel screw grade 18/8 with washer and sealing washer, e L-bolt with nut, galvanised/stainless steel, M6...M10, f J-bolt with nut, galvanised/ stainless steel, M6...M10, g top flange clamp fitting with nuts, galvanised/stainless steel, M6...M10; for connecting profiled sheets together: h aluminium blind rivet with sealing washer, i aluminium blind rivet with enclosed mandrel and sealing washer, j compressible blind rivet with sealing washer, k aluminium or stainless steel screw grade 18/8 with washer and sealing washer [14]

Workability
Appropriate sheet metalworking tools and equipment can be used for working profiled metal sheeting and overlapping elements. Cutting on site should be kept to a minimum. Snips, nibblers, jig-saws and circular saws are suitable for cutting sheet metal. All swarf from cutting and drilling operations must be completely removed to prevent discoloration of the coating.

Disk cutters and other tools that create sparks and a great deal of heat should not be used as this can damage the coating.

**Additional measures**

Additional measures should be allowed for during planning and construction when the roof covering must satisfy enhanced requirements regarding its reliability. This is necessary when:

- roof pitch is below recommended minimum
- high winds, driving rain or driving snow are anticipated
- a build-up of rainwater is expected
- several roof surfaces and valleys intersect at one point along the eaves
- penetrations through the roof surface hinder the water run-off
- transverse joints cannot be avoided.

Additional measures include:

- a steeper roof pitch
- further sealing measures
- a longer end lap
- a wider side lap

**Details**

Ridge to duopitch roof, ridge to monopitch roof, hip, eaves, valley, verge, junctions with walls, trough, penetrations

Special details, e.g. ridge, hip, valley, verge etc. should be covered with special elements that are equivalent to the general roof covering in terms of rainproofing and other aspects. These special elements can often be obtained prefabricated. Otherwise they must be made by hand: they are usually restricted to plain sheets that are bent and cut to suit the profiled form of the main roof covering or metal panels.

Ridge to duopitch roof
The ridge capping is a piece of plain material cut and bent to match the profile exactly. A plastic profile filler is placed between this and the end of the sheeting at the ridge, the bottom of which is bent up ≥ 30 mm to protect against driving snow and rain. This ridge detail is not dependent on the type of profile chosen; the profiles on both sides of the roof do not have to line up either. If a profiled ridge capping is used, preformed strip seals (5 x 20 mm) must be laid in the lap between the profiled sheeting and the ridge capping. However, in this case the profiles on both sides of the roof do have to line up.

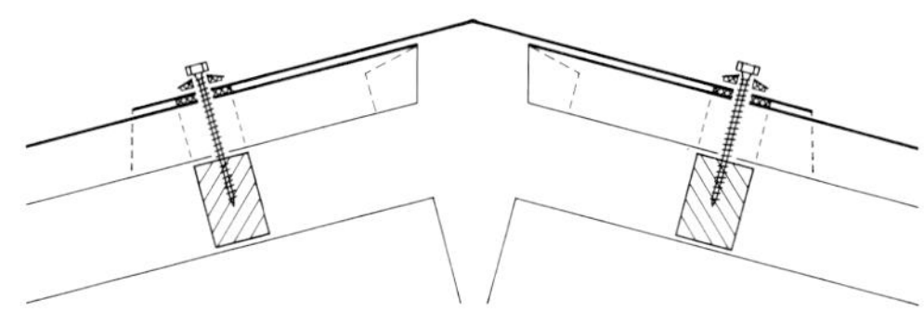

2.4.11.18 Ridge detail with plain sheet metal cut and bent down to close off troughs

The lap between ridge capping and sheeting is ≥ 200 mm in both cases. The longitudinal laps of the ridge capping should be offset from the laps of the general roofing sheets by at least one rib (corrugation).

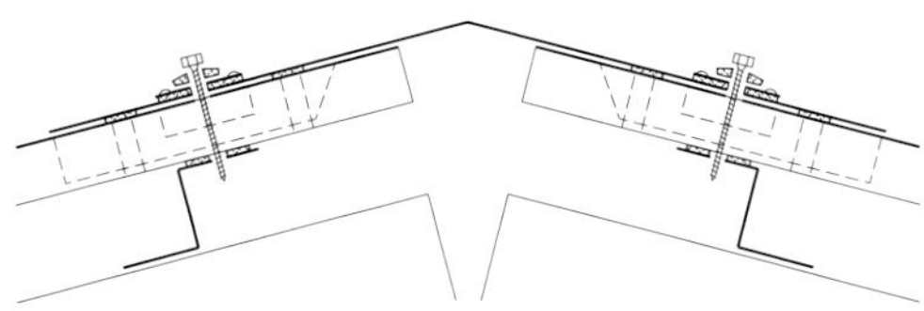

2.4.11.19 Ridge detail with profiled form to match roofing sheets

Neither of the above ridge details permits any ventilation. This is sufficient for small roofs but it is better to include a continuous vent at the ridge.

Ventilating ridge
First, bent plain material that matches the profile exactly is bent up at the ridge (h = 100-150 mm) to form an apron flashing.

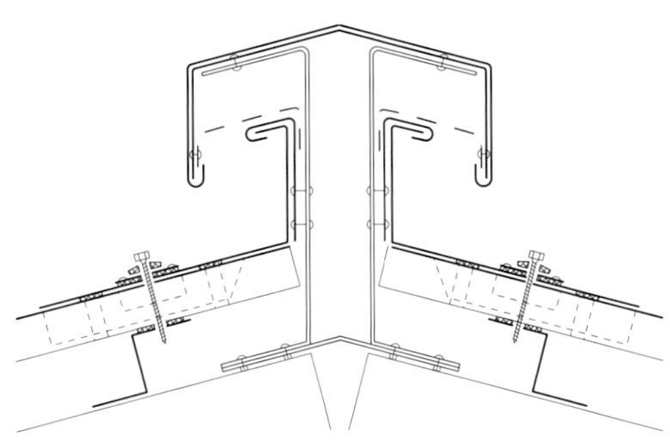

2.4.11.20 Ventilated ridge detail [05]

The continuous gap along the ridge (≥ 80 mm) is covered with a sheet metal hood. This is fixed either via spacers to the bent plain material or via special mountings to the top purlin. The bent plain material follows the profile of the sheeting. A preformed strip steel is placed in the lap between plain material and roof sheeting. If the bent plain material does not follow the profile of the sheeting, the troughs must be closed off with profile fillers; in addition, the bottom of the profiled sheeting must be bent up ≥ 30 mm at the ridge. Mesh screens or perforated sheet metal prevent birds and small animals entering the open ventilation cross-section.

Additional bending of the ridge hood and the apron flashing can increase the circulation of the air. Protection against driving rain and snow is thus also improved (see "Construction details – Metal profiled sheeting").

Ridge to monopitch roof
The termination at the ridge of a monopitch roof requires a special element that follows the profile of the roof sheeting. If bent plain material is used, it must be cut and bent to fit the profiling on the roof surface.

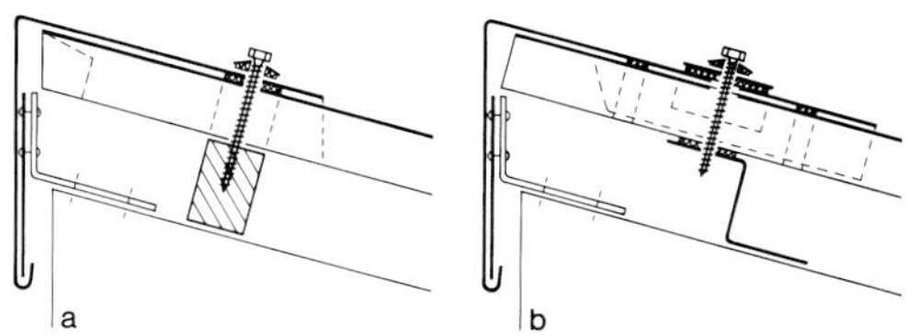


2.4.11.21 Detail at ridge of mono pitch roof: a with plain sheet metal cut and bent down to close off troughs, b with profiled form to match roofing sheets [14]

A profile filler is placed between sheeting and bent material to close off the openings; the bottom of the roof sheeting is also bent up ≥ 30 mm. The special elements or bent material at the ridge are screwed through the roof sheeting, and on the gable held with special fixings or a continuous clip.

Hip
The hip capping has to be made by hand to suit each individual situation. The sheets to close off the ribs (corrugations) and the profile fillers should be marked out and cut to suit on site. To limit the ingress of moisture, the bottom of the sheeting is bent up ≥ 30 mm adjacent to the hip. Preformed elements that follow the line of the profile are not produced.

Ventilating hip
(see "Ventilating ridge" above)
The hip capping need not be placed at an angle.

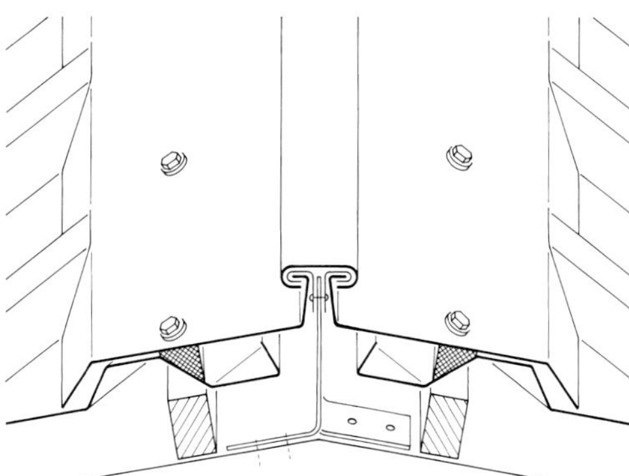

2.4.11.22 Hip detail, with folded sheet metal hip capping

Eaves
Thermal expansion of the profiled sheeting is mainly accommodated at the eaves. Elongated holes or sliding fixings are therefore required here to guarantee the unimpeded expansion of the sheeting.
The sheets should be fixed through every upper rib (corrugation) at the eaves. The bottom of the sheeting can be bent down to form a drip where it overhangs the wall below. Alternatively, a small angle can be attached to act as a rainwater drip.

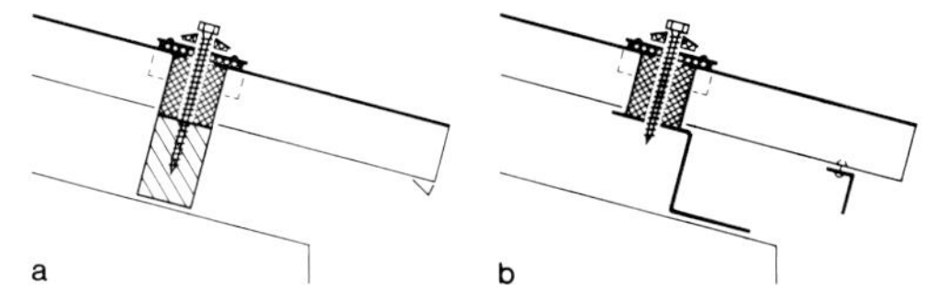


2.4.11.23 Eaves detail: a with bottom ribs folded down to form rainwater drip, b with angle acting as rainwater drip

Valley
Valleys are usually formed as a gutter at a lower level. This improves reliability in the case of a build-up of water, and reduces the risk of water or snow being blown beneath the roof covering. Flashings positioned beneath the sheeting are welted together with the sheet metal gutter. Profile fillers cut on site to suit the respective situation close off the open troughs of the profiled sheeting. This arrangement does not permit any ventilation at the gutter. If vented fillers (carefully cut to suit on site) are incorporated instead of standard profile fillers, the valley can be ventilated (see "Construction details – Metal profiled sheeting").

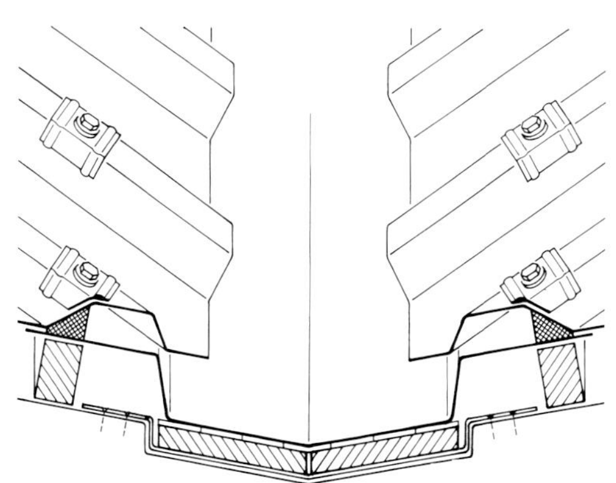

2.4.11.24 Valley detail, with profile fillers

Verge
Folded, flat or profiled verge elements can be used here. They should overlap at least two ribs (corrugations). They are fixed with blind rivets or stainless steel screws with sealing washers. At the top of the gable wall the verge element is folded around a continuous clip.
For details of a verge gutter please refer to "Layers – Drainage").

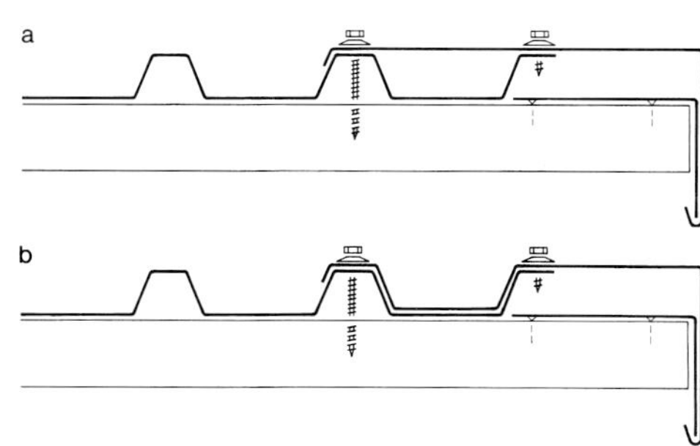


2.4.11.25 Verge detail:
a with plain sheet metal,
b with profiled form to match roofing sheets

Junction with wall at side of slope
This can be made from pieces that follow the profile or from flat sheet metal, in each case overlapping two complete ribs (corrugations) of the sheeting. The junction elements must be fixed to the sheeting with blind rivets or stainless steel screws with sealing washers. The sheet metal is turned up the wall 100–150 mm (depending on pitch), where it is held by a continuous clip or individual fixings (spacing ≤ 500 mm).

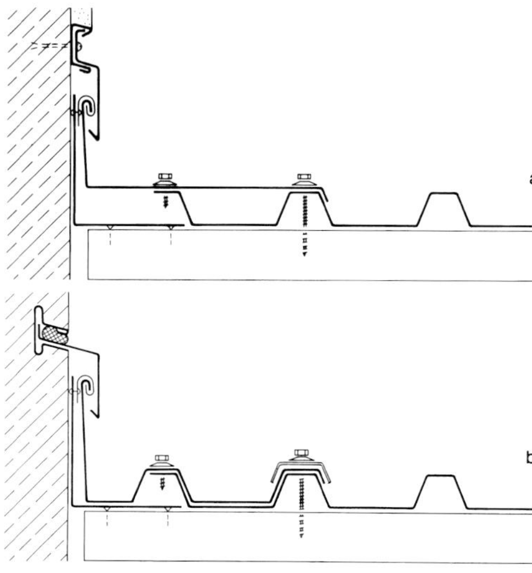


2.4.11.26 Junction with wall at side of slope: a with plain sheet metal, b with profiled form to match roofing sheets [14]

The flashing is completed with a capping strip (overlap ≤ 50, 80, 100 mm). The junction with a wall at the side of a slope can also be carried out using a gutter (see "Layers – Drainage").

Junction with wall at top of slope
This junction is carried out using either flat or profiled sheet metal (overlap 200 mm). The pieces are turned up clear of the wall and covered with a drip flashing (overlap ≥ 50, 80, 100 mm).
Flat sheets are cut and bent to match the roof sheeting. A plastic profile filler is incorporated between the flat sheets and the roof sheeting; in addition, the bottom of the sheeting is bent up near the wall.

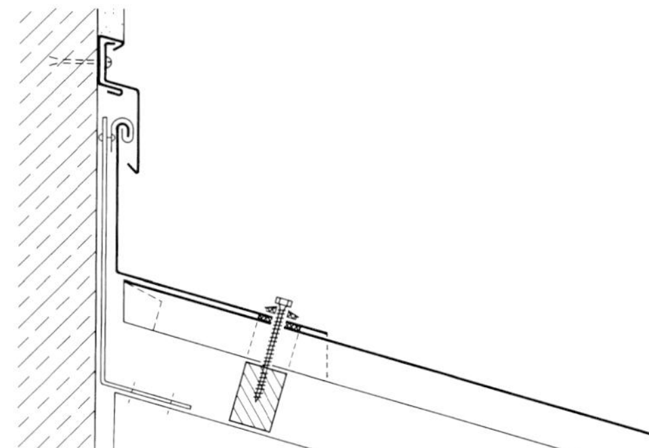

2.4.11.27 Junction with wall at top of slope, with plain sheet metal cut and bent down to close off troughs

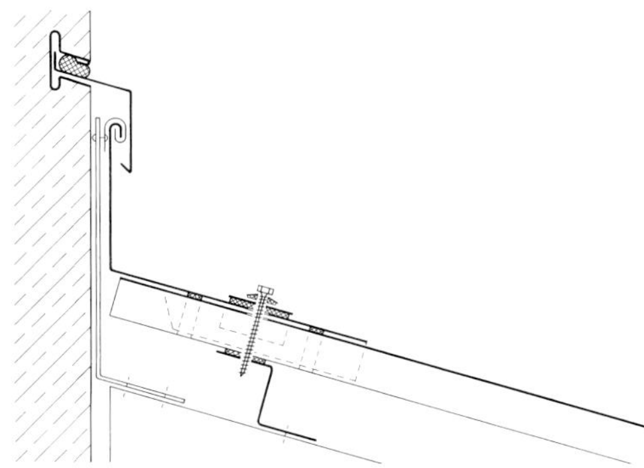

2.4.11.28 Junction with wall at top of slope, with profiled form to match roofing sheets

Trough
The junction at a trough is formed with a flashing. Depending on the roof pitch, this should continue up to 600 mm below the roof covering. The sides of the gutter (≥ 200 mm deep) are welted together with the flashing. The cross-section of the profiled sheets is available for ventilation; mesh screens or perforated sheet metal prevent birds and small animals entering the open ventilation cross-section.

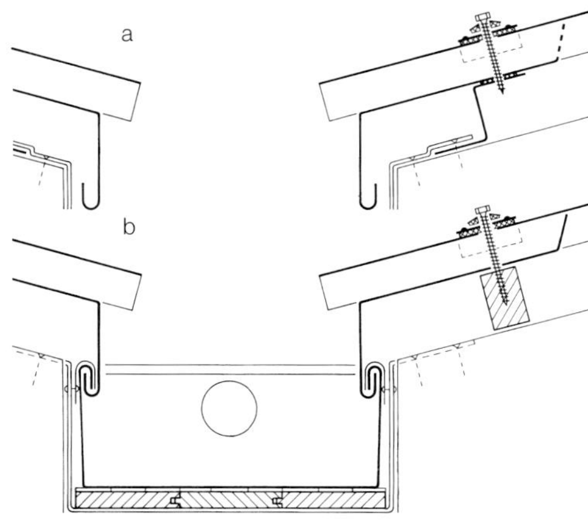


2.4.11.29 Trough detail:
a ventilated, b not ventilated

The gutter at this position may be left unventilated on roofs to ancillary buildings. In this case the flashing is cut and bent up to fit the profiled sheeting. The advantage of this detail is that neither foliage nor driving rain or snow can be driven up below the roof covering.

Penetrations
Roof penetrations measuring up to 150 mm wide can be welded into a profiled sheet. The flashings required must be made by hand to suit.

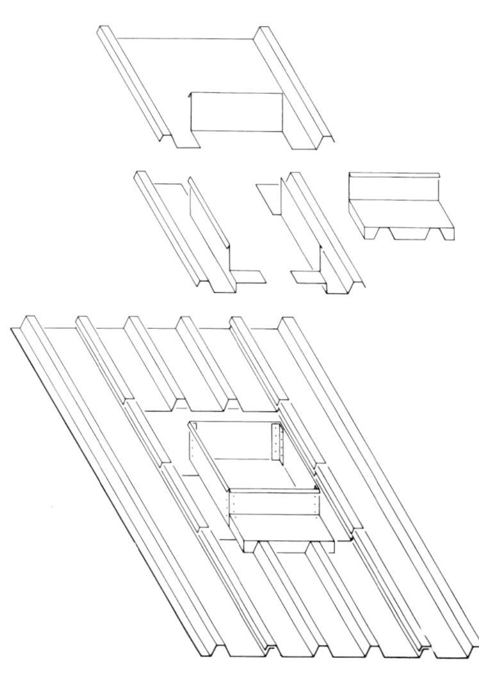

2.4.11.30 Penetration; chimney detail

Even flashings around chimneys are made by hand to suit the particular situation. At the four corners the sheet metal pieces are welted, riveted, soldered/brazed or welded together. They should be turned up at least 150 mm above the roof covering and flashed to prevent ingress of rainwater.

Profiled sheets for rooflights or roof windows are prefabricated and supplied to match the particular profiled sheeting chosen. The position of rooflights or roof windows should be coordinated with the purlins underneath; trimmers may be necessary in certain circumstances.

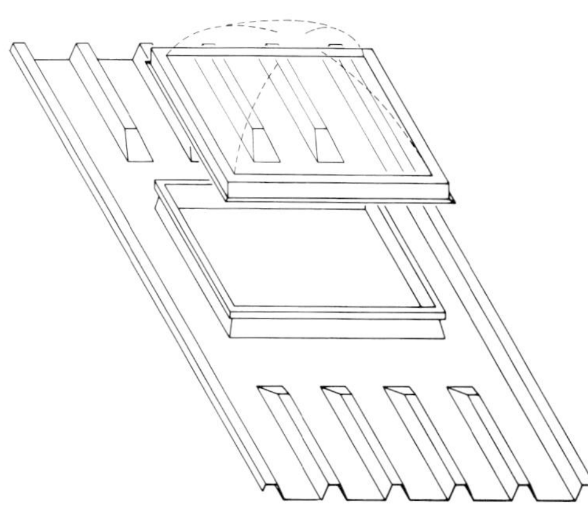

2.4.11.31 Penetration; rooflight detail

**Supporting construction**
Profiled metal sheeting can span between individual or linear supports or can be supported across its entire area on roof decking.

Separating layer
A separating layer, e.g. bituminous felt, bituminous paint, to avoid galvanic corrosion is necessary when the purlins are made from concrete or a different metal from that of the sheeting. A separating layer is not absolutely essential on timber purlins; however, the wood must be free from certain damaging substances (see "Layers – Sheet metal roof coverings"). When supported on flat decking or planks there is a danger that moisture could be retained for longer periods beneath the bottom ribs (troughs of corrugations) of the profiled sheets and the supporting construction. This problem is more likely to occur when the profile cross-section is ventilated and the air carries a lot of moisture from outside below the roof covering.

Purlins
Timber, concrete or steel purlins (≥ 2 mm thick) are met with most frequently in practice, aluminium (≥ 3 mm thick) less often. The width of the bearing for profiled sheets is ≥ 60 mm in the span, ≥ 40 mm at the edges. [05]

| min. support width [mm] | Type of supporting construction | | |
|---|---|---|---|
| | Steel, reinforced concrete | Masonry | Timber |
| End support | 40 | 100 | 60 |
| Intermediate support | 60 | 100 | 60 |

2.4.11.32 Minimum support widths to DIN 18807 [05]

Roof decking
- Tongue and groove boarding of grade 1 softwood, air-dried and unplaned, sawn parallel, without chemical preservative; boards 80–160 mm wide, ≥ 24 mm thick for a rafter spacing ≤ 750 mm, otherwise 30 mm thick.
- Trapezoidal metal sheeting or panels with or without reinforcing ribs; water run-off skin fixed either directly through the thermal insulation to the inner skin or via Z-section or channel spacers.
- Concrete supporting construction with embedded galvanised steel flats (≥ 60 x 80 mm) or continuous timber battens (≥ 60 x 40 mm) to accommodate fixings.

**Maintenance and repair**
Profiled steel sheeting can be walked on without crawling boards to spread the load. However, profiled aluminium sheeting is only accessible with crawling boards; otherwise local deformations will be produced. Point loads ≥ 100 kg should be allowed only on a spreader plate near the supports. If frequent

direct access is required for maintenance purposes, e.g. rooftop structures, a minimum sheet thickness of 0.9 mm should be specified. Rooflights and roof windows cannot support foot traffic.
The service life of profiled metal sheeting is primarily governed by the quality of the coating. Rust films, undermining of the coating at cuts through the material, and damage or cracks and subsequent flaking of the coating can lead to the sheeting being ruined or perforated. If damage is not extensive, it can be repaired by soldering/brazing or welding on a new piece of material, plus renewing the coating. If the supporting construction is damaged or if the underside of the sheeting has corroded due to galvanic corrosion, the local cause should be eliminated because just replacing the sheeting is not enough in such cases. A roof pitch that is too shallow increases the risk of deposits and corrosion due to moisture (puddles) (see also "Layers – Sheet metal roof coverings").

**References**


[01] Alcan Aluminium GmbH: information material; Göttingen
[02] Alusuisse Deutschland GmbH: information material; Constance
[03] Bieber: Bieberal – information material; Bischoffen
[04] Deutscher Verzinkerei Verband e.V.: Wellbleche – moderne Bauelemente mit genormter Tragfähigkeit; Düsseldorf
[05] DIN 18807: Trapezoidal sheeting in building; trapezoidal steel sheeting; Berlin: Beuth-Verlag, 2001
[06] Hoesch Siegerlandwerke AG: information material; Siegen
[07] Industrieverband zur Förderung des Bauens mit Stahlblech e.V.: information material: Düsseldorf
[08] Kabelmetall AG: information material; Osnabrück
[09] Kaiser Aluminium Europe Inc.: information material; Koblenz
[10] Kalzip product information
[11] Rheinzink product information
[12] Thyssen Bausysteme GmbH: information material; Dinslaken
[13] Vereinigte Aluminium Werke Leichtmetall GmbH: information material; Bonn
[14] Weber, H.: Dach und Wand, Planen und Bauen mit Aluminium-Profiltafeln; Düsseldorf: Verlag Aluminium, 1982
[15] Zentralverband des Deutschen Dachdecker Handwerkes: Fachregeln des Dachdeckerhandwerks, Hinweise für Dachdeckungen mit Profilbahnen und -tafeln; Cologne: Müller-Verlag, 1986
[16] Zentralverband Sanitär, Heizung, Klima: information material: Dächer mit profilierten Metalltafeln und -bändern; St Augustin, 1988


## Sheet metal roof coverings

Materials, components, laying

### Aluminium

Raw materials, manufacture, properties

#### Raw materials

Aluminium, at 8% the most common metal in the Earth's crust, is obtained from bauxite (= aluminium ore = $Al_2O_3 \cdot H_2O$ [60%], with $Fe_2O_3$, $SiO_2$ and $TiO_2$). Various decomposition processes are employed to produce aluminium oxide, and aluminium is subsequently obtained through fused-salt electrolysis (4 t bauxite produces 2 t aluminium oxide and 1 t aluminium). Owing to its low strength, aluminium is mainly used in the form of alloys. Elements suitable for use in aluminium alloys are manganese, magnesium, silicon, zinc and copper in various proportions.

| | Alloy metal content [% by wt] | Al content [% by wt] | Applications |
|---|---|---|---|
| Highest purity | – | 99.99 | – |
| Refined aluminium | limited impurities, not alloyed | ≥ 99.50 | sheet and strip |
| Alum. alloys: AlMn1 | Mn 0.9 to 1.5 | ≥ 96.35 | |
| AlMn1Mg0.5 | Mn 1.0 to 1.5<br>Mg 0.2 to 0.6 | ≥ 95.70 | |
| AlMgSi0.5 | Mg 0.35 to 0.6<br>Si 0.30 to 0.6 | ≥ 96.85 | sections |
| AlZn4.5Mg1 | Zn 4.0 to 5.0<br>Mg 1.0 to 1.4 | ≥ 91.40 | |

2.4.12.1 Aluminium and important aluminium alloys for use in roofing [44]

#### Manufacture

Preheated billets are hot-rolled (400–540°C) to a thickness of 6–8 mm. They are then cold-rolled (room temperature) to the required dimension. Thickness tolerances of up to 10% are permissible. [17]

#### Properties

Biological properties

Aluminium and its compounds are non-toxic. The small amounts washed from the roof by rain are no danger to humans and the environment. However, high concentrations of aluminium in the soil can damage the roots of plants. [01]

Chemical properties

Aluminium and its alloys form a thin, natural layer (0.01–0.1 µm thick) of oxide that protects the metal from attack. If this layer is damaged, it re-forms immediately. It takes between two and ten years for this protective layer to form completely.

| | Average rate of corrosion |
|---|---|
| Rural atmosphere | < 0.1 µm/a |
| Urban atmosphere | ~ 0.1 to 1.0 µm/a |
| Industrial atmosphere | ~ 1.0 to 1.5 µm/a |
| Marine atmosphere | ~ 0.5 µm/a |

2.4.12.2 Average rates of corrosion; pure aluminium [09]

This matt grey, natural protection is often insufficient in polluted atmospheres (e.g. industrial atmosphere with high concentration of $SO_2$). Aggressive pollutants in the air – primarily sulphur oxides – together with deposits of dust and dirt and the effects of rainwater, cause local corrosion of the metal's surface. The deposits of dust and dirt lead to the formation of elements on a micro level, which then, helped by the acidic rainwater and enriched with the aggressive acids of exhaust fumes, produce this corrosion (pitting) (see also "Building science").

If a long service life is important, the aluminium must be treated. It is therefore also available anodized, coated or stove-enamelled.

| | Al bright-rolled | Al weathered | Al anodized | Al powder, liquid, coil coating |
|---|---|---|---|---|
| Coating thickness [µm] | – | 0.01 to 0.1 | 10 to 30 | 20 to 25 |
| Colour | silver sparkling | matt grey matt silver | various shades metallic sheen | all bright colours |

2.4.12.3 Thickness of protective treatment; colour [01]

The layer of oxide protecting the aluminium is essentially insoluble over the pH range 4.5–8.5. However, acid and alkaline solutions outside this pH range dissolve the layer of oxide and attack the metal. For the same period of exposure, chemical corrosion worsens with increasing concentration and rising temperature.

Aluminium is resistant to ultraviolet radiation and does not rot.

| | Concentration [%] | Temperature [°C] | Degradation [µm/a] |
|---|---|---|---|
| Hydrochloric acid | 1 | | 113 |
| | 10 | | 250 to 300 |
| Sulphuric acid | 1 | 20 | 100 |
| | 10 | | 200 |
| | 96 | | 3700 |
| Sodium hydroxide solution | 10 | | 2500 |
| | 10 | 40 | 6000 |

2.4.12.4 Examples of chemical resistance [09]

Physical properties

Aluminium is frost-resistant and is classed as an incombustible material of building materials class A 1.

| | Al | AlMn1 | AlMn1Mg0.5 |
|---|---|---|---|
| Density [g/cm³] | | 2.7 | |
| Modulus of elasticity [N/mm²] | | 70 000 | |
| Tensile strength [N/mm²] | 40 to 70 | ≥ 120 | ≥ 150 |
| Elongation at rupture [%] | 6 | 7 | 6 |
| Brinell hardness [N/mm²] | 20 to 30 | 40 | 50 |
| Melting point [°C] | | 655 | |
| Thermal conductivity [W/mK] | 235 | 160 to 200 | 160 to 190 |
| Coefficient of thermal expansion [mm/mK] | | 0.024 | |
| Electr. conductance [m/Ω mm²] | 37 | 22 to 28 | 23 to 25 |

2.4.12.5 Physical properties [44, 46]

## Lead

Raw materials, manufacture, properties

**Raw materials**

Lead occurs in nature in the form of various ores. These lead ores (most common: galena PbS, with 2–10% by wt Pb) are enriched to 60–80% by wt Pb through froth flotation. In the traditional two-stage process, the enriched ore is oxidised by roasting and subsequently reduced to crude lead (95–98% by wt Pb). In the newer one-stage ("QSL") process, production is continuous, which saves energy and results in fewer pollutants. Alloy metals for milled sheet lead in building (refined lead) are primarily copper (0.03–0.06% by wt Cu), antimony (Sb), tin (Sn), zinc (Zn), silver (Ag) and bismuth (Bi) in various proportions. [27] The low proportion of copper (< 0.1%) produces a finer grain structure, which in turn improves the mechanical properties, microstructure strength and corrosion resistance. [34]

| | Alloy metal cont. [% by wt] | Lead cont. [% by wt] | Applications |
|---|---|---|---|
| Commercial-grade lead | – | 99.94 to 99.98 | alloys |
| Lead alloys: Pb-Cu alloys etc. | Cu 0.03 to 0.06<br>Sb ≤ 0.005<br>Ag ≤ 0.005<br>Bi ≤ 0.100<br>Sn ≤ 0.005<br>Zn ≤ 0.001<br>misc. ≤ 0.005 | 99.94<br>or<br>remainder | sheet |
| Pipe lead | Sb 0.2 to 1.25 | 98.75 to 99.80 | waste pipes |

2.4.12.6 Lead and important lead alloys for use in roofing [27, 44]

**Manufacture**

The lead is melted at about 400°C and subsequently rolled to the desired thickness in a continuous casting and rolling process (hot rolling at 100–180°C). Thickness tolerances of up to 5% are permissible. [27] Finally, the rolled strip of lead is trimmed and either wound into coils or cut into sheets.

**Properties**

Biological properties

The small amounts of lead (100–300 µg daily) that we humans absorb, mainly through our food, are considered to be completely harmless. We excrete 90% of it anyway. [05, 07, 37] The practically insoluble lead compounds such as lead hydroxide, lead hydroxycarbonate and basic lead carbonate (white lead) found in neutral water of medium and high hardness decompose under the effects of soft water (dH < 8°) or acidic rainwater (pH < 7) and can then be dangerous. [16, 44, 45] Lead itself vaporises upon welding and in this state is classed as hazardous. [08] When working with the material in these forms, precautions should be taken.

Chemical properties

Lead forms a natural protective surface layer (patina) over time, which provides excellent protection from atmospheric pollutants. Patination begins in the first few days, with the formation of a passive layer of lead oxide that air and water convert over several weeks into the precursor of lead hydroxide. This subsequently reacts with the carbon dioxide and sulphur dioxide in the air over several months to form the highly insoluble lead carbonate and lead sulphate. After 6–12 months this protective layer is complete. During this process the colour of the material changes from bright-rolled silver to silver-grey or dark silver-grey. Eluates of lead ions washed out from the surface of the newly laid sheet lead by the rain can be prevented by treating the lead beforehand with a "weathering" oil. This oil is worn away by the weather after a few months to leave room for the natural protective layer described above.
Up to about 20% of the protective layer itself is worn away. Part is dissolved through chemical reactions, part is loosened by the thermal expansion of the sheet metal and washed away by rainwater. [45]
Lead is not resistant to permanent exposure to moisture and simultaneous exclusion of air (e.g. under puddles, condensation) because it then cannot form a protective layer (shallow pitch, underside of sheet metal).

| | Average rate of corrosion |
|---|---|
| Rural atmosphere | < 0.3 to 1.3* µm/a |
| Urban atmosphere | ~ 0.5 to 3.9* µm/a |
| Industrial atmosphere | ~ 0.5 to 2.0 µm/a |
| Marine atmosphere | ~ 0.5 to 1.0/1.9* µm/a |

2.4.12.7 Average rates of corrosion; *) manufacturer's information [09]

| | Pb bright-rolled | Pb weathered | Pb eroded |
|---|---|---|---|
| Coating thk. | – | up to 6 µm | ~ 6 µm |
| Colour | silver | dark silver-grey | |

2.4.12.8 Thickness of protective treatment; colour [06, 34]

| | Concentration [%] | Temperature [°C] | Degradation [µm/a] |
|---|---|---|---|
| Hydrochloric acid | 1 | 20 | 300 |
| | 10 | | 600 |
| Sulphuric acid | 50 | | ~ 50 |
| | 90 | | ~ 100 to 150 |
| | 96 | | ~ 400 |
| Sodium hydroxide solution | no meaningful information available | | |
| Pb with 5% Sn | 10 | 20 | 500 |

2.4.12.9 Examples of chemical resistance [09, 34]

Resistance to acid and alkaline solutions varies; for the same period of exposure, corrosion increases with the concentration. However, lead is resistant to concentrated sulphuric acid because the ensuing layer of lead sulphate protects the metal, virtually halting further attack at moderate temperatures.

Physical properties

Lead is frost-resistant and is classed as an incombustible material of building materials class A 1.

| | | Lead [Kb-Pb] |
|---|---|---|
| Density | [g/cm³] | 11.34 |
| Modulus of elasticity | [N/mm²] | ~ 17000 |
| Tensile strength | [N/mm²] | ~ 15 |
| Elongation at rupture | [%] | ~ 45 |
| Brinell hardness | [N/mm²] | 4 |
| Melting point | [°C] | 327 |
| Thermal conductivity | [W/mK] | 34 |
| Coefficient of thermal expansion | [mm/mK] | 0.029 |
| Electrical conductance | [m/Ωmm²] | 4.8 |

2.4.12.10 Physical properties [38, 44, 46]

## Copper

Raw materials, manufacture, properties

**Raw materials**

Copper is obtained from copper ores (primarily chalcopyrite $CuFeS_2$ and chalcocite $Cu_2S$, with 0.5–0.8% by wt Cu). An enriched ore is formed with 20–35% by wt Cu in a froth flotation process. The roasting and melting in the fused-salt furnace and subsequent reduction – mostly the introduction of air in the converter – gives crude copper of 97–99% by wt Cu. Further refining, i.e. oxidising of impurities and further reduction, then produces refined copper. The oxygen-free (deoxidised high phosphorus – DHP) copper used exclusively in building has a degree of purity of 99.90% by wt Cu. Alloy metals for copper are primarily aluminium, nickel, zinc and tin.

| | Alloy metal content [% by wt] | Copper content [% by wt] | Applications |
|---|---|---|---|
| Highest purity copper Electrolytic copper | – | 99.90 to 99.99 | raw material for semifinished products and alloys |
| Refined copper | P 0.015 to 0.040; not alloyed | 99.90 to 99.95 | sheet pipes |
| Copper alloys: | Zn 0.5 low alloy var. | 99.5 | gutters |
| Cu-Al alloy | Al 2 to 14 | 76 to 98 | fittings, sheet and sections for facades |
| Cu-Zn alloy | Zn 5 to 45 | 55 to 95 | |

2.4.12.11 Copper and important copper alloys for use in roofing [17, 44]

**Manufacture**

The copper sheets produced by extrusion are heated (800–950°C) and rolled out to form billets 10–20 mm thick. These billets are milled and cold-rolled to form sheets and strips of the required thickness. Thickness tolerances of up to 0.02 mm are permissible. [20]

**Properties**

Biological properties

The amount of copper washed from the roof by rain is no danger to humans and the environment. [10] However, a protective mask must be worn when welding copper to prevent the inhalation of copper vapour. [14] All copper salts are hazardous to microorganisms. [16]

Chemical properties

Copper forms a natural protective surface layer (patina) on both sides, consisting of basic copper salts such as copper carbonate and copper sulphate, and also copper chloride in marine environments. These all provide excellent protection against atmospheric pollution. [14]

This protective layer causes the colour of the copper to change from red-brown to dark brown to green. The rate of formation of the protective layer depends on:

- the composition of the air
- the various moisture phases (rain, snow, melt waters)
- the quantity of solid particles (dust, sand, soot)

| | Rate of formation of protective layer |
|---|---|
| Rural atmosphere | up to 30 years |
| Urban atmosphere | 15 to 20 years |
| Industrial atmosphere | 8 to 12 years |
| Marine atmosphere | 4 to 6 years |

2.4.12.12 Rate of formation of protective layer [10]

| | Average rate of corrosion |
|---|---|
| Rural atmosphere | ~ 0.29/0.36* to 0.75*/1.33 μm/a |
| Urban atmosphere | ~ 0.44 to 1.19 μm/a |
| Industrial atmosphere | ~ 1.0 to 5.0 μm/a |
| Marine atmosphere | ~ 0.5*/0.66 to 0.96/1.43* μm/a |

2.4.12.13 Average rates of corrosion; *) North America [09]

| | Cu bright-rolled | Cu weathered | Cu eroded |
|---|---|---|---|
| Coating thk. | – | up to 50 μm | 50 μm |
| Colour | red | anthracite | green |

2.4.12.14 Thickness of protective treatment; colour [10]

About 25% of the protective layer is worn away. Part is dissolved through chemical reactions, part is loosened by the thermal expansion of the sheet metal and washed away by rainwater. [31]

The corrosion of copper by hydrochloric and sulphuric acid depends very much on the temperature, concentration and aeration of the acid. Copper has a low resistance to sodium hydroxide solution.

| | Concentration [%] | Temperature [°C] | Degradation [μm/a] |
|---|---|---|---|
| Hydrochloric acid | | | |
| w/o ventil. | 20 | | 250 to 300 |
| | 30 | | 880 |
| w. ventil. | 20 | | 5000 |
| Sulphuric acid | | 20 | |
| w/o ventil | 20 | | 72 |
| | 96.5 | | 20 |
| w. ventil. | 20 | | 3380 |
| | 96.5 | | 1040 |
| Sodium hydroxide solution | 50 | 0 | 500 |

2.4.12.15 Examples of chemical resistance [09, 34]

Physical properties

Copper is frost-resistant and is classed as an incombustible material of building materials class A 1.

| | Cu (soft) | Cu-DHP R220 | Cu-DHP R240 |
|---|---|---|---|
| Density [g/cm³] | 8.93 | | |
| Mod. of elasticity [N/mm²] | 100 000–130 000 [1)] | | |
| Tensile strength [N/mm²] | 200 to 240 | 220 to 260 | 240 to 300 |
| Elongation at rupture[2)] [%] | 40 to 60 | ≥ 33 | ≥ 8 |
| Brinell hardness [N/mm²] | 40 to 50 | 40 to 65 | 65 to 95 |
| Melting point [°C] | 1083 | | |
| Thermal conductivity [W/mK] | 385 | 293 to 364 | |
| Coeff. of thermal expansion [mm/mK] | 0.017 | | |
| Electr. conductance [m/Ωmm²] | 60 | 41 to 52 | |

[1)] upper value for cold-formed material, [2)] single value (A 50 mm) depends on sheet thickness

2.4.12.16 Physical properties [11, 13, 14, 44, 46]

## Stainless steel

Raw materials, manufacture, properties

**Raw materials**

Iron occurs in nature in the form of iron ore. Liquid pig iron is obtained from this ore in the blastfurnace through reduction. Carbon and other undesirable trace elements are removed from the pig iron by oxidation in various processes (open-hearth process, Bessemer process etc.). This produces steel. Stainless steels contain at least 10.5% by wt chromium. Higher chromium contents and other alloy constituents such as nickel, molybdenum, titanium or niobium improve resistance to corrosion.

| Steel designation | Material No. | Alloy metal content [% by wt] | Application |
|---|---|---|---|
| X6CrTi 17 Sn coating | 1.4510 (magnetic) | C ≤ 0.06; Cr 17; Ti 0.59 | |
| X5CrNi 18-10 | 1.4301 (~ V2A) | C ≤ 0.07; Cr 17.0 to 19.5; Ni 8.0 to 10.5 | |
| X6CrNiTi 18-10 | 1.4541 (~ V3A) | C ≤ 0.08; Cr 17.0 to 19.0: Ni 9.0 to 12.0; Ti 0.5 | thin sheet and strip |
| X5CrNiMo 17-12-2 | 1.4401 (~ V4A) | C ≤ 0.07; Cr 16.5 to 18.5; Ni 10.0 to 13.0 Mo 2.0 to 2.5; | |
| X6CrNiMoTi 17-12-2 | 1.4571 (~ V5A) | C ≤ 0.08; Cr 16.5 to 18.5; Ni 10.5 to 13.5; Mo 2.0 to 2.5; Ti 0.5 | |

2.4.14.17 Important stainless steels for use in roofing; composition [28, 32, 44]

#### Manufacture

Strips of stainless steel are cold-rolled (at about room temperature) to the required thickness for flat semifinished products. Thickness tolerances of up to 10% are permissible. [25, 26] After trimming the strip, the rolled stainless steel is cut into sheets of the required length.

#### Properties

Biological properties
Stainless steel consists primarily of iron, which is harmless. As the degradation of stainless steel is also negligible, practically no metal enters the groundwater. Nevertheless, measurable concentrations of chromium, nickel and molybdenum can be found in municipal wastewater, possibly from the widespread use of stainless steel in domestic households and industry.

Chemical properties
Due to its content of chemically resistant chromium, untreated stainless steel sheet forms a complete passive layer after just a few hours' contact with the air (oxygen). The colour of the sheet metal remains unchanged – shiny, silvery. However, environmental influences such as soot, dust and dirt lead to a loss of shine over time.

| | st. steel bright-rolled | st. steel weathered | st. steel chemical coating |
|---|---|---|---|
| Coating thickness | – | up to 0.1 µm | up to 0.3 µm |
| Colour | silver shiny | silver shiny | transparent film; blue, gold, red, green sheen |

2.4.12.18 Thickness of protective treatment; colour [01, 28]

| | Suitable steel grades [material No.] |
|---|---|
| Rural atmosphere | 1.4301, 1.4541 |
| Urban atmosphere | 1.4541, 1.4401 |
| Industrial atmosphere | 1.4401, 1.4571 |
| Marine atmosphere | 1.4401, 1.4571 |

2.4.12.19 Use of stainless steel depending on quality of environment

In industrial and marine atmospheres a thin film of rust forms on chrome steels that contain no nickel (magnetic). Sheet metal of this type is therefore available pickled and precoated. [09]
Chrome-nickel steels (non-magnetic) do not exhibit such surface corrosion. Their rates of degradation are very low (0.01 µm/a). [31] However, these chrome-nickel steels – either with a low chromium content or with no molybdenum – exhibit pitting after a short time (in marine atmospheres after just one year). In such cases the passive layer is first penetrated by deposits of airborne particles with which it reacts. Afterwards, corrosion pits or small holes form.

Pitting is caused by chloride ions and acidic solutions that attack the steel. More resistant steels with high chromium and nickel contents plus the addition of molybdenum (2–2.5%) are therefore recommended for polluted industrial and salt-laden marine environments. [09, 29, 33]

| | Concentration [%] | Temperature [°C] | Degradation [µm/a] |
|---|---|---|---|
| Hydrochloric acid | | | |
| CrNi steel | 0.5 | 20 | 420 |
| | | 50 | > 11 000 |
| CrNiMo steel | | 20 | 42 |
| | | 50 | 1100 to 11000 |
| Sulphuric acid | | | |
| CrNi steel | 10 | 38 | 240 |
| | 80 | | 7130 |
| CrNiMo steel | 1 to 10 | 20 | < 110 |
| | 80 | | 110 to 1100 |
| Sodium hydroxide solution | 20 | 20 | 100 |
| | > 40 | 20 | > 1000 |

2.4.12.20 Examples of chemical resistance [09]

"The smoother and more homogeneous the surface of the steel, the better is the resistance to pitting. Mill scale and paint bloom, weld seams and scratches promote pitting. A surface clean in metallurgical terms is therefore the prerequisite for a high resistance to corrosion." [33]

Physical properties
Stainless steel is frost-resistant and is classed as an incombustible material of building materials class A 1.

| | 1.4510 | 1.4301/1.4541 | 1.4401/1.4571 |
|---|---|---|---|
| Density [g/cm³] | 7.70 | 7.90 | 7.98 |
| Modulus of elasticity [N/mm²] | 210 000 | 200 000 | |
| Tensile strength [N/mm²] | 470 | 550 to 750 | 550 to 700 |
| Elongation at rupture [%] | 30 | 45 | |
| Brinell hardness [N/mm²] | | 130 to 180 | |
| Melting point [°C] | 1490 | ~1500 | |
| Thermal conductivity [W/mK] | | 15 | |
| Coeff. of thermal expansion [mm/mK] | 0.0106 | 0.016 | 0.0165 |
| Electrical conductance [m/Ωmm²] | | 1.37 | 1.33 |

2.4.12.21 Physical properties [28, 30, 44, 46]

### Galvanised steel

Raw materials, manufacture, properties

#### Raw materials

The production of steel from iron ore is described under "Stainless steel" above. For a roof covering of galvanised steel the steel grade usually employed is a mechanical bending grade with a zinc coating of 25 µm each side. The galvanising is carried out by immersing the steel in molten zinc; this is a continuous process. Commercial grade zinc with 99.5% by wt Zn or refined zinc with 99.95% by wt Zn is generally used for galvanising. The zinc coating adheres firmly to the steel substrate even during subsequent forming. [23, 50] Besides pure zinc, zinc alloy coatings are also common:

- alloys with additions of aluminium (5% by wt Al, 95% by wt Zn) and rare earths
- aluminium-zinc alloys consisting of 55% by wt Al, 1.6% by wt Si and 43.4% by wt Zn

#### Manufacture

Long blocks or ribbons are heated in the rolling mill (soaking pit furnace or pusher-type heating furnace) to rolling temperature (900°C) and then rolled to form flat sheets. Thickness tolerances of up to 15% are permissible. [22] The zinc coating is added in a modified Sendzimir process. The thin sheet metal coils are unrolled, any impurities adhering to the surfaces are removed by annealing (approx. 700–800°C) and the sheet metal passed through a molten zinc bath (approx. 460°C). The desired zinc coating is regulated by jet processing. A coating of aluminium-zinc is applied in a similar continuous process at a higher temperature (approx. 600°C). [03]

| Galvanised substrate material | Zinc coating (class) [g/m² both sides] | Zinc coating thickness [µm each side] |
|---|---|---|
| Hot-dip galvanised strip and sheet (general mild steels, soft non-alloyed steels) | z 100 | 7 |
| | z 140 | 10 |
| | z 180 | 12,5 |
| | z 200 | 14 |
| | z 225 | 16 |
| | z 275 | 20 |
| | z 350 | 25 |
| | z 450 | 32 |
| | z 600 | 42 |

2.4.12.22 Standardised zinc coating classes [23]

#### Properties

Biological properties
Zinc and iron, the main elements of galvanised steel sheet, are not hazardous in the amounts involved here. The constituents washed out into the soil do not reach dangerous levels. However, a high concentration of aluminium in the soil can damage the roots of plants.

Chemical properties
In contact with the atmosphere, untreated galvanised steel sheet forms a protective layer of zinc carbonate. This also provides protection at any cut edges. The formation of this protective layer brings about a colour change from silvery metallic to matt grey.

| | Average rate of corrosion |
|---|---|
| Rural atmosphere | 1 to 4 μm/a |
| Urban atmosphere | 2 to 6 μm/a |
| Industrial atmosphere | 6 to 13 μm/a |
| Marine atmosphere | 2 to 9 μm/a |

2.4.12.23 Average rates of corrosion [02, 09]

| | galv. steel bright-rolled | galv. steel weathered | galv. steel coated |
|---|---|---|---|
| Coating thickness | – | ~ 10 μm | polyester, 15 to 25 μm; PVF 20 to 25 μm, PVC (0) 30 to 60 μm |
| Colour | silvery metallic | matt grey | all shades |

2.4.12.24 Thickness of protective treatment; colour [01, 28]

However, acid and alkaline solutions do corrode zinc – depending on pH value (see "Zinc" below). As with the environmental influences usual today ("acid rain") galvanising represents protection only for a limited time, further treatment of the galvanised steel sheet is necessary after 2–3 years at the latest, after conclusion of the weathering process. Pre-oxidised sheets can be treated immediately. Plastic coatings are always recommended for this because these prolong the service life of the entire corrosion protection system.

Adding aluminium gives the protective zinc coating better hardness, which reaches its maximum for 55% aluminium-zinc after about six weeks. This brings about a noticeable improvement in the surface corrosion protection. However, the extensibility of this coating is limited and so can present a problem when forming and shaping the material.
Permanently wet deposits of dirt and ponding must be avoided with both these materials. This can be achieved with an adequate roof pitch. [03, 04, 15, 24]

Physical properties
Galvanised steel sheet has good frost resistance and is classed as an incombustible material of building materials class A 1.

| | St 02 Z DX 51 D + Z | St E 250 Z S 250 GD + Z |
|---|---|---|
| Material No. | 1.0226 | 1.0242 |
| Density [g/cm³] | 7.85 | |
| Modulus of elasticity [N/mm²] | 200 000 | |
| Tensile strength [N/mm²] | 270 to 500 | 330 to 470 |
| Elongation at rupture [%] | 22 | 19 |
| Brinell hardness [N/mm²] | – | |
| Melting point [°C] | 1250 to 1460 | |
| Thermal conductivity [W/mK] | 60 | |
| Coeff. of thermal expansion [mm/mK] | 0.012 | |
| Electrical conductance [m/Ωmm²] | 9 to 12 | |

2.4.12.25 Physical properties [15, 30, 44, 46]

## Zinc
Raw materials, manufacture, properties

#### Raw materials
The raw materials for the production of zinc are zinc carbonate $ZnCO_3$ (smithsonite) and sphalerite ZnS. These are roasted to produce zinc oxide ZnO, and vaporised zinc ensues at 1250°C due to the reduction with coke (ZnO + C = Zn + CO). This condenses to form commercial grade zinc and refined zinc. The metals for use in zinc alloys are primarily titanium and copper. Titanium-zinc alloys are characterised, in particular, by improved durability, better edge workability (Cu) transverse or parallel to the direction of rolling, and lower thermal expansion than unalloyed zinc.

| | Alloy metal content [% by wt] | Zinc content [% by wt] | Applications |
|---|---|---|---|
| Refined zinc | – | 99.95 to 99.995 | raw mat. for alloys |
| Commercial zinc | limited impurities, not alloyed | 97.5 to 99.5 | sheet, galvanising |
| Zinc alloys: Ti-Zn | Ti 0.12 to 0.2 Cu 0.12 to 0.2 | 99.6 to 99.9 | sheet |

2.4.12.26 Zinc and important zinc alloys for use in roofing [44]

#### Manufacture
The zinc is melted (510–530°C) and subsequently rolled in a continuous casting and rolling process (100–350°C). Thickness tolerances of up to 0.03 mm are permissible. [19]
Finally, the strip of material is split into the desired width (max. 1000 mm). Sheets are produced by cutting across the split strip. Alloyed zinc is also produced in a "pre-weathered" variety.

#### Properties

Biological properties
Zinc is non-toxic and a small amount (10–20 mg) is required by the human body every day. Degradation products that enter the soil are therefore not undesirable – to provide the daily zinc via the food chain. [39, 42] All soluble zinc salts (e.g. zinc chloride, zinc sulphate) provide protection against rotting. [16]

Chemical properties
Firmly adhering covering layers of zinc oxide and basic zinc carbonate form on the bright-rolled surface upon contact with the atmosphere. This brings about a colour change from silvery metallic to matt grey. The protective layer forms more rapidly with increasing humidity. The formation of this protective layer on a wet surface requires an unimpeded flow of air; otherwise there is an increased risk of corrosion. About 60–70% of the protective layer is worn away. Part is dissolved through chemical reactions, part is loosened by the thermal expansion of the sheet metal and washed away by rainwater. [31]

| | Average rate of corrosion |
|---|---|
| Rural atmosphere | 0.2[1]/0.4[2)3)] to 1.8[2]/4.0[1] μm/a |
| Urban atmosphere | 0.9[2]/1.0[1] to 2.8[2]/6.0[1] μm/a |
| Industrial atmosphere | 1.4[2]/4.0[1)3)] to 5.6[2]/13.0[1] μm/a |
| Marine atmosphere | ~ 0.5[1] to 7.0[1] μm/a |

2.4.12.27 Average rates of corrosion: [1] [09], [2] [31], [3] [42]

Zinc is not resistant to exposure to moisture and simultaneous exclusion of the air (e.g. condensation). The underside of sheet zinc is therefore at great risk of being corroded by condensation or incoming rainwater when there is no flow of fresh air, because the protective layer of zinc carbonate cannot form.

| | Zn bright-rolled | Zn weathered | Zn coated with neoprene paint |
|---|---|---|---|
| Coating thickness | – | 1 to 3 μm | ~ 60 μm |
| Colour | silvery metallic | matt grey-blue | beige, grey shades |

2.4.12.28 Thickness of protective treatment; colour [39, 40]

| | Protective layer starts to form after |
|---|---|
| Dry air | 100 days |
| Air with 33% relative humidity | 14 days |
| Air with 75% relative humidity | 4 days |

2.4.12.29 Formation of protective layer on bright-rolled zinc [35]

Zinc is not resistant to hydrochloric acid, sulphuric acid or sodium hydroxide solution even at very low concentrations, and dissolves. This reaction can take place even at room temperature.
Because of the additives contained in oil, a brown discoloration of the sheet zinc must be expected near oil heating systems.

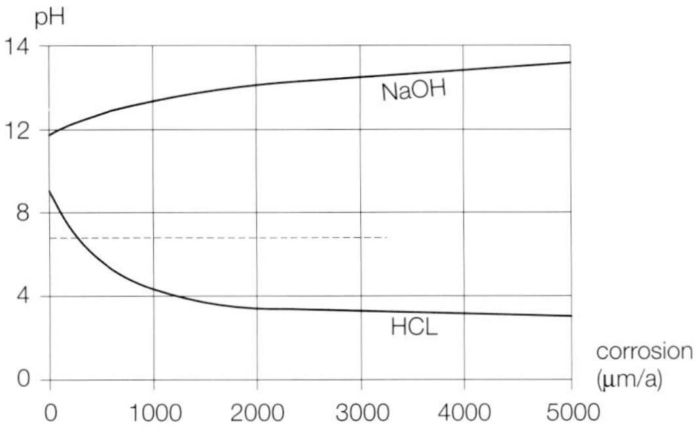


2.4.12.30 Relationship between rate of corrosion and pH for zinc in acid and sodium hydroxide solution at room temperature [09]

Coatings to increase the service life of sheet zinc are required in aggressive industrial atmospheres (e.g. high $SO_2$ content), or where there is a risk of bituminous corrosion. Such coatings can be applied either after a period of natural weathering (2–3 years) or immediately after degreasing the bright-rolled surface. However, they have only a limited effect and must be maintained and renewed at regular intervals.

Physical properties
Zinc is frost-resistant and is classed as an incombustible material of building materials class A 1.

| | | Zinc [D-Zn-bd] |
|---|---|---|
| Density | [kg/m³] | 7150 |
| Modulus of elasticity | [N/mm²] | ≥ 80 000 |
| Tensile strength | [N/mm²] | ≥ 150 |
| Elongation at rupture | [%] | ≥ 40 |
| Brinell hardness | [N/mm²] | 40 |
| Melting point | [°C] | 419 |
| Thermal conductivity | [W/mK] | 109 |
| Coeff. of thermal expansion | [mm/mK] | 0.022 |
| Electrical conductance | [m/Ωmm²] | 17 |

2.4.12.31 Physical properties [30, 42, 44, 46]

## Components

General elements, edge elements, product coding, form of supply

**General elements**
Metal sheet and strip are always available in standard sizes – also with pre-bent edges. Special sizes within the maximum width can be supplied on request.

**Edge elements**
Specially shaped pieces for use at edges and junctions must usually be made by hand. They are cut and bent to suit each particular situation.

| | | Pb [mm] | Cu [mm] | Zn [mm] | Al [mm] | st. steel [mm] | galv. steel [mm] |
|---|---|---|---|---|---|---|---|
| Strip | thick-ness | 0.5 to 6 typical: 2; 2.5 | 0.6 to 2 typical: 0.6; 0.7 | 0.6 to 1.5 typical: 0.7; 0.8 | 0.6; 0.7; 0.8; 1.0 typical: 0.7; 0.8 | 0.3 to 3 typical: 0.5 | 0.4 to 3 typical: 0.6; 0.63 |
| | width | 500, 600, 670, 700 | 500, 600, 670, 700, 800, 1000 | 500, 600, 670, 800, 1000 | 600, 800, 1000 | 800, 100 1250, 1500 | 600, 660, 800, 1000, 1250, 1524, 1650 |
| | length*) | ≥ 2, 4, 40 | ≥ 10, 20, 200 m | | ≥ 25, 50, 500 | ≥ 12.5, 25, 250 | ≥ 10, 20, 200 |
| Sheet | thick-ness | on backing plates for sound insulation and radiation prot. | 0.6 to 2 typical: 0.7 | 0.6 to 15 typical: 0.7; 0.8 | 0.6; 0.7; 0.8; 1.0 typical: 0.7; 0.8 | 0.4 to 4 typical: 0.5 | 0.4 to 3 typical: 0.6; 0.63 |
| | formats | ≤ 1250 · 3000 | 1000 x 2000 1250 x 2500 1000 x 3000 | 1000 x 2000 1000 x 3000 to 6000 | 1000 x 2000 1250 x 2500 1500 x 3000 to 1600 x 6000 | 1000 x 2000 1250 x 2500 1500 x 3000 | 1000 x 2000 1250 x 2500 1500 x 3000 1650 x 6000 |
| Tiles Squares Shingles | | | square: 250 x 250 450 x 450 600 x 600 shingle: 200 x 200 300 x 200 430 x 600 | square: 200 x 200 283 x 283 350 x 350 diamond: 168 x 288 223 x 381 263 x 449 | – | – | overlapping steel panels: 850 wide x max. 2500 long |

2.4.12.32 General elements; standard sizes and formats [01,12, 15, 28, 42, 43, 49]; *) 50, 100 and 1000 kg coils

| | Pb | Cu | Zn | Al | st. steel | galv. steel |
|---|---|---|---|---|---|---|
| Miscellaneous | flashings aprons (roof windows) | sheet f. bending chequered strip b=600, 1000 mm d=0.1; 0.2 mm | sheet f. bending sheet metal flashings | sheet f. bending flashings, frames | sheet f. bending slit strip w ≥ 10 mm d = 0.3–3 mm | sheet f. bending flashings |

2.4.12.33 Edge elements [01, 12, 15, 18, 28, 42, 43, 49];

**Product coding**
Metals are not divided into classes, but are designated using materials numbers to distinguish each alloy. These give information about the constituents of the alloy and hence the mechanical properties of each type of metal.

**Form of supply**
Metal strip is supplied in coils (small: 50 and 100 kg; large: 1000 kg). The coils are delivered in the vertical or horizontal position, with or without a wooden platform. As a rule, the coils are protected by scuffing timbers and covered to keep them clean. Whenever possible, coils should be stored indoors. Otherwise, a waterproof covering with sufficient clearance to the stack or coil of metal should be provided.

## Laying

Conditions for laying, fixing, additional measures, details – standing seams, details – batten roll seams, details – hollow and wood-cored rolls, supporting construction, maintenance and repair

**Conditions for laying**
Metal sheet is laid in rows. Folding up the edges of the sheets produces bays, which are joined together through welting or by covering with metal capping strips. We distinguish between batten roll and standing seam joints for copper, zinc alloy, aluminium and stainless/galvanised steel. Rounded wood-cored and hollow rolls are used only for lead. The side joints (parallel to the slope) always lie above the water run-off level and prevent the ingress of rain and snow. In contrast to this, any transverse joints (across the slope) necessary lie below the water run-off level. Side and transverse joints are not always sufficiently impervious for a build-up of water at certain pitches. Minimum roof pitches are therefore specified to ensure reliable draining of the water, particularly around roof penetrations.

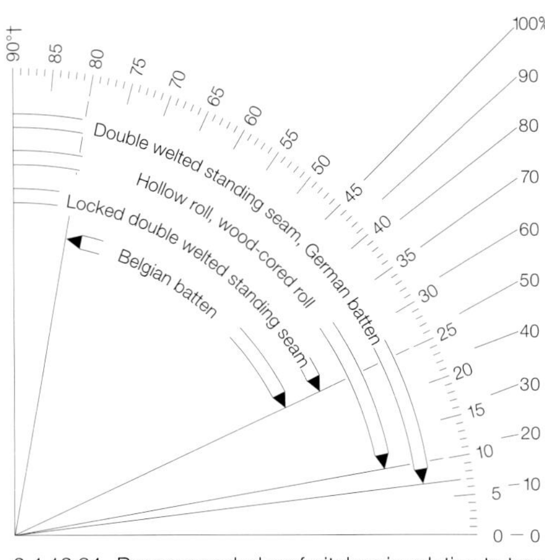


2.4.12.34 Recommended roof pitches in relation to type of roof covering [07, 47, 49]

Roof pitch
The minimum pitch for sheet metal roof coverings is 3°. However, a minimum pitch of 7° is recommended because small inaccuracies or the deflection of the supporting construction may lead to ponding. Such puddles can be blown up the roof by the wind, seep through the joints by capillary action and thus reach the construction underneath. Additional sealing measures are therefore recommended for roof pitches of less than 7°. Aggressive substances in solution are left behind when rainwater evaporates from the surface of the roof; adding a little moisture (drizzle, fog, dew) to these substances can damage the roof covering in high concentrations. [42]

Side joints – standing seams

• Single welt standing seam
The taller (overcloak) of the two bent-up edges is folded tightly over the other (undercloak). A reliable, concealed fixing is not possible; one cut edge remains visible.

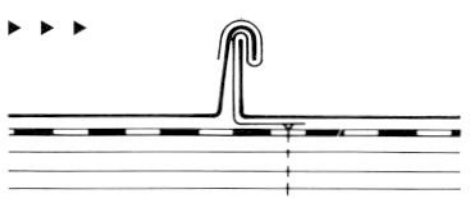

2.4.12.35 Side joint; standing seam with single welt: ▸ prevailing wind direction [49]

The single welt is preferably used for cappings and skirts; it is not suitable for roof surfaces.

• Double welt standing seam
This is an improvement on the single welt standing seam, which is simply folded through 90° to conceal the cut edge. This joint lends the roof surface a distinct texture.

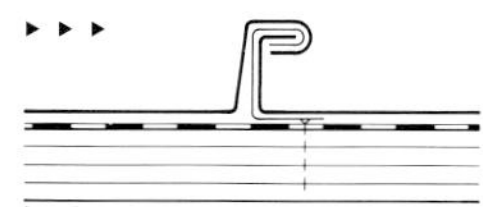

2.4.12.36 Side joint; standing seam with double welt: ▸ prevailing wind direction [49]

The double welt standing seam, up to 35 mm high, may only be used on roof pitches ≥ 25°, and ≥ 35° in regions of heavy snowfall.

• Locked double welt standing seam
The locked double welt standing seam is the most common type of joint. It is formed by simply folding the double welt standing seam through 90° again. This further fold means that the clips along the joints become an integral part of the roofing system and hence all forces are transferred through the joint to the supporting construction.
A locked double welt standing seam is also possible with a lead roof covering. In this case the edges of the two sheets are turned up 75 and 100 mm. The thickness of the lead usually employed (2.25 mm) means there is a large thickness (10x) of material at the joint.

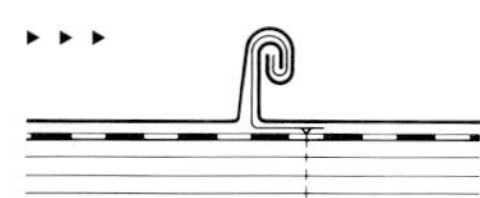

2.4.12.37 Side joint; standing seam with locked double welt: ▸ prevailing wind direction [49]

Side joints – batten roll seams
This type of roof covering uses square or trapezoidal timber battens (40 x 40 mm); the sheet metal is turned up the sides of these battens, straight or at a slight angle. A capping strip covers the top of the batten and overlaps the edges of the sheet metal.

• Belgian batten roll

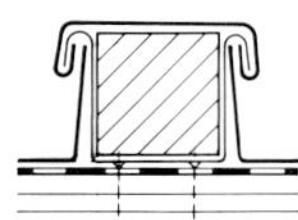

2.4.12.38 Side joint with Belgian batten; only limited rainproofing [49]

The capping strip is not joined to the bent-up edges of the sheet metal but is held in place by clips. This type of joint is not fully watertight and is permitted only on roof pitches ≤ 80°.

• German batten roll

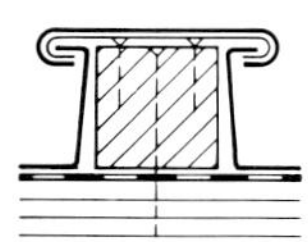

2.4.12.39 Side joint with German batten; rainproof [49]

The bent-up edges of the sheet metal are welted to the capping strip. This is classed as a watertight joint; however, rainwater can enter through capillary action.

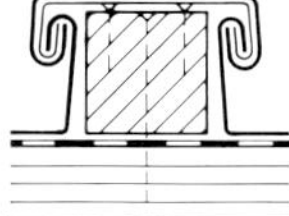

2.4.12.40 Side joint with German batten; improved watertightness

This type of joint can be improved by folding the welted edges downwards through 90°; this produces a particularly watertight joint.

Side joints for lead only

• Hollow roll
The edges of the two sheets of lead are turned up 100 and 125 mm. The taller edge (overcloak) is folded over tightly. This single welt is then turned over with a bossing stick to form a circular hollow roll.

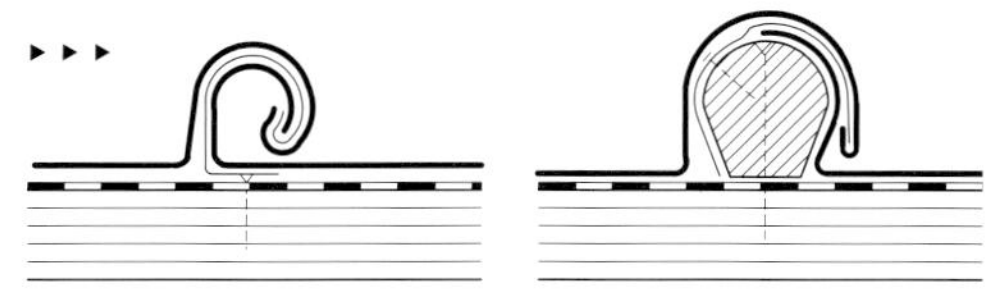

2.4.12.41 Side joint with a) hollow roll, b) wood-cored roll: ▸ prevailing wind direction [07, 47]

This joint is suitable only for steep roofs not subjected to foot traffic.

• Wood-cored roll
First, the shaped timber batten (40 x 40 mm) is fixed to the roof decking with brass screws. The two lead sheets are turned up 55 and 125 mm against the batten; the shorter of the two (undercloak) should cover at least half the batten. The overcloak is folded around a clip fixed to the timber batten or the roof decking. This produces a secure, concealed fixing. This joint is necessary on a shallower roof pitch subjected to foot traffic.

Transverse joints

The type of transverse joint depends on the respective application, the position of the joint and the roof pitch. Transverse joints formed as movement joints, such as laps and single welts, drips and tilting fillets, can compensate for the thermal movement of the sheets. This is necessary for lengths ≥ 10 m.
Sheets are laid offset in order to avoid the transverse joints coinciding at the standing seams.

| Roof pitch [°] | Transverse joint |
|---|---|
| ≥ 25 | single welt |
| ≥ 10 | single welt with additional fold |
| ≥ 7 | double welt |
| < 7 | sealed transverse joint |

2.4.12.42 Types of transverse joints [47, 49]

- Lap

Simple laps usually have a beaded edge for valleys and flashings. Laps in valleys are permitted only for a roof pitch ≥ 15° (see "Valley" below). [47]

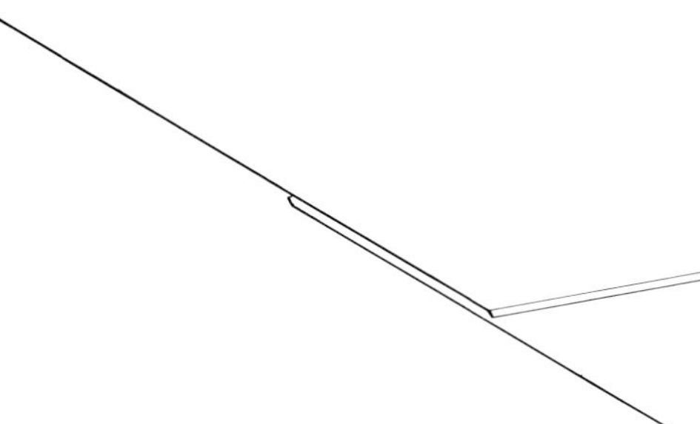

2.4.12.43 Transverse joint; simple lap [49]

When using milled sheet lead, laps between sheets in a bay may be used for roof pitches ≥ 10°, provided the wind load is not excessive. The length of the lap depends on the roof pitch and does not prevent the ingress of water completely. As sheets of lead are limited to a length of 1800–2400 mm, no further joints are necessary for expansion purposes. [07, 47]

| Roof pitch [°] | Lap [mm] |
|---|---|
| ≥ 10 to < 20 | ≥ 290 |
| ≥ 20 to < 30 | ≥ 220 |
| ≥ 30 to < 40 | ≥ 150 |
| ≥ 40 to < 50 | ≥ 115 |
| ≥ 50 | ≥ 100 |

2.4.12.44 Transverse joint; laps between sheets of lead in relation to roof pitch [07, 47, 49]

- Single welt

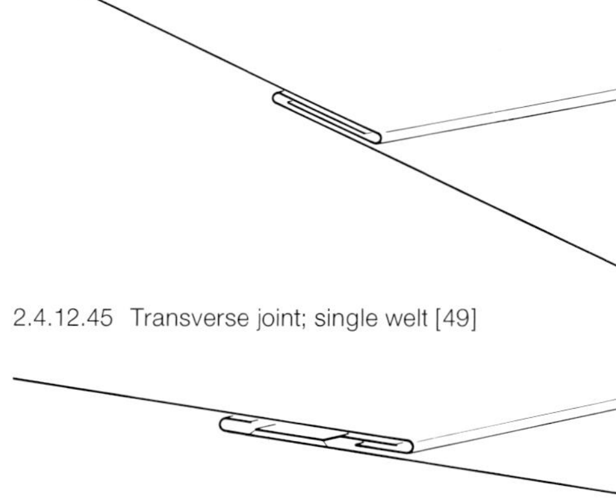

2.4.12.45 Transverse joint; single welt [49]

2.4.12.46 Transverse joint; single welt with additional welt [49]

The minimum overlap for a single welt is 40 mm. The single welt can be provided with an additional welt (adequate expansion possible) for roof pitches ≥ 10°.

- Double welt

The double welt is the standard method of joining sheets without allowing for movement. It is therefore used most frequently at roof penetrations. The welts can be made with or without preformed sealing strips.

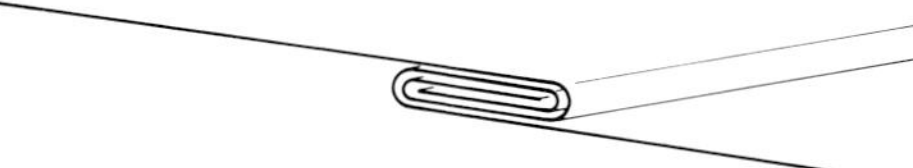

2.4.12.47 Transverse joint; double welt [49]

The minimum overlap is 40 mm, as for a single welt.

- Drip, tilting fillet

The height of the drip should be ≥ 60 mm and must be incorporated into the supporting construction. Tilting fillets can of course be subsequently added to the finished roof decking.

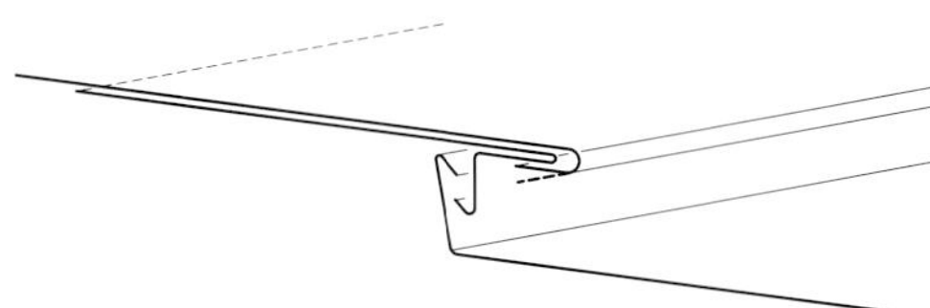

2.4.12.48 Transverse joint; drip [49]

- Sealed transverse joints

These cannot be constructed as movement joints. Depending on the material, these can be welted joints incorporating a preformed sealing strip, riveted joints with a preformed sealing strip, soldered, riveted and soldered, brazed or welded.

| Material | Lap [1] [mm] | Joint |
|---|---|---|
| Pb | 20–40 | • soldered<br>• welded (shielded arc) |
| Cu | 10–40 | • double welt + preformed seal<br>• offset rivets + solder<br>• one row of rivets + solder<br>• brazed<br>• welded (shielded arc) |
| Zn | 10–15 | • soldered |
| Al | 10–40 | • double welt + preformed seal<br>• voffset rivets + preformed seal<br>• welded (shielded arc) |
| st. steel | 10–40 | • offset rivets + preformed seal<br>• one row of rivets + solder<br>• welded (shielded arc) |
| galv. steel | 10–40 | • double welt + preformed seal<br>• offset rivets + preformed seal<br>• one row of rivets + solder<br>• welded [2] |

[1] Corresponding to the type of joint: soldered (≥ 10 mm), one row of rivets + solder (≥ 30 mm), offset rivets + preformed sealing strip (≥ 40 mm)

[2] Condition: pretreatment – removal of zinc coating; subsequent treatment – zinc-based rustproofing

2.4.12.49 Transverse joints; sealed types and minimum laps [47, 49]

Width, length and thickness of sheet metal

The longitudinal movement of the metal with temperature fluctuations governs the maximum length that can be laid. A temperature differential of 100 K is used as a basis here (see also "Material"). The sheet metal must be able to expand and contract if long lengths – according to roof pitch – are to be laid.

| Material | max. strip length [m] |
|---|---|
| Lead | 1.8–2.4 |
| Copper | 10 |
| Zinc | 10 |
| Aluminium | 10 |
| Stainless steel | 14 |
| Hot-dip galvanised steel | 14 |

2.4.12.50 Strip lengths; max. strip length in relation to material [07, 49]

Because of its comparatively high coefficient of thermal expansion, relatively high self-weight and low mechanical strength, sheet lead may be used only in lengths up to 1800–2400 mm. The maximum width is 700 mm and the standard thickness of milled sheet lead is 2.25 mm (see also "Lead" above). [07]

Expansion across the slope of the roof can be allowed for by leaving a gap of 3–5 mm between the bent-up edges of the sheet metal. The bay width is equal to the sheet width minus the bent-up edges on both sides.

| Type of jointing | Strip width [mm] | Finished seam height [mm] | Turned-up edges [mm] | Bay width [mm] |
|---|---|---|---|---|
| Double welt standing seam, locked double welt standing seam | X | 25 | 35/45 | X – 80 |
| | | 30 | 40/50 | X – 90 |
| | | 35 | 45/55 | X – 100 |
| | | 40 | 50/60 | X – 110 |
| | | 45 | 55/65 | X – 120 |
| | | 50 | 60/70 | X – 130 |

2.4.12.51 Strip/bay width; standing seams

| Type of jointing | Strip width [mm] | Finished seam height [mm] | Turned-up edges [mm] | Bay width [mm] |
|---|---|---|---|---|
| Belgian batten | X | 40 | 40/40 | X – 80 |
| | | 60 | 60/60 | X – 120 |
| German batten | | 40 | 60/60 | X – 120 |
| | | 60 | 80/80 | X – 160 |

2.4.12.52 Strip/bay width; seams with battens

| Type of jointing | Strip width [mm] | Finished seam height [mm] | Turned-up edges [mm] | Bay width [mm] |
|---|---|---|---|---|
| Hollow roll | | 50 | 100/125 | X – 225 |
| Wood-cored roll | X | 50 | 55/125 | X – 180 |

2.4.12.53 Strip/bay width; hollow and wood-cored roll seams

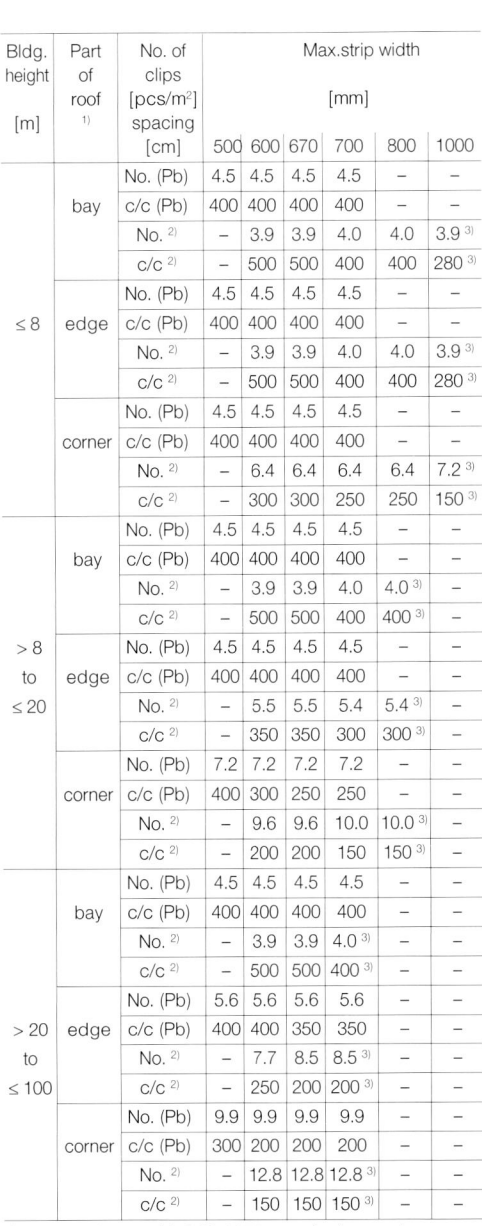

| Bldg. height | max. bay lgth. max. | Ma-terial | Part of roof [1] | Strip width [mm] 500 | 600 | 670 | 700 | 800 | 1000 |
|---|---|---|---|---|---|---|---|---|---|
| [m] | [m] | | | Sheet thickness [mm] | | | | | |
| ≤ 8 | 1.8 | Pb | bay | 2.25 | 2.25 | 2.25 | 2.25 | – | – |
| | to | | edge | 2.25 | 2.25 | 2.5 | 2.5 | – | – |
| | 2.2 | | corner | 2.25 | 2.5 | 3 | 3 | – | – |
| | 10 | Cu | | – | 0.6 | 0.6 | 0.6 | 0.7 | – |
| | 10 | Zn | | – | 0.7 | 0.7 | 0.7 | 0.8 | – |
| | 10 | Al | | – | 0.7 | 0.7 | 0.8 | 0.8 | – |
| | 14 | st. st. | | – | 0.4 | 0.5 | 0.5 | – | – |
| | 14 | g. st. | | – | 0.6 | 0.6 | 0.6 | 0.6 | 0.7 |
| > 8 to ≤ 20 | 1.8 | Pb | bay | 2.25 | 2.25 | 2.25 | 2.25 | – | – |
| | to | | edge | 2.25 | 2.5 | 3 | 3 | – | – |
| | 2.4 | | corner | 2.25 | 3 | 3.5 | 3.75 | – | – |
| | 10 | Cu | | – | 0.6 | 0.6 | 0.6 | – | – |
| | 10 | Zn | | – | 0.7 | 0.7 | 0.7 | – | – |
| | 10 | Al | | – | 0.7 | 0.7 | 0.8 | – | – |
| | 14 | st. st. | | – | 0.4 | 0.5 | 0.5 | – | – |
| | 14 | g. st. | | – | 0.6 | 0.6 | 0.6 | 0.6 | – |
| > 20 to ≤ 100 | 1.8 | Pb | bay | 2.25 | 2.25 | 2.5 | 2.5 | – | – |
| | to | | edge | 2.25 | 2.5 | 3.25 | 3.5 | – | – |
| | 2.4 | | corner | 2.25 | 3.25 | 4 | 4 | – | – |
| | 10 | Cu | | – | 0.6 | 0.6 | – | – | – |
| | 10 | Zn | | – | 0.7 | 0.7 | – | – | – |
| | 10 | Al | | – | 0.7 | 0.7 | – | – | – |
| | 14 | st. st. | | – | 0.4 | 0.5 | – | – | – |
| | 14 | g. st. | | – | 0.6 | 0.6 | 0.6 | – | – |

[1] In accordance with DIN 1055 part 4 edge and corner zones are assumed to be 1/8 x building width (≥ 1 m and ≤ 2 m).

2.4.12.54 Strip width and thickness; permissible strip width and sheet metal thickness in relation to height of building [07, 49]

The permissible width and thickness of the sheet metal are determined by the height of the building.

**Fixing**

Arrangement and number of clips

Clips are required for the indirect fixing of all types of sheet metal roof covering to the supporting construction. To allow for the changes in length due to temperature, expansion clips are needed in addition to fixed clips.

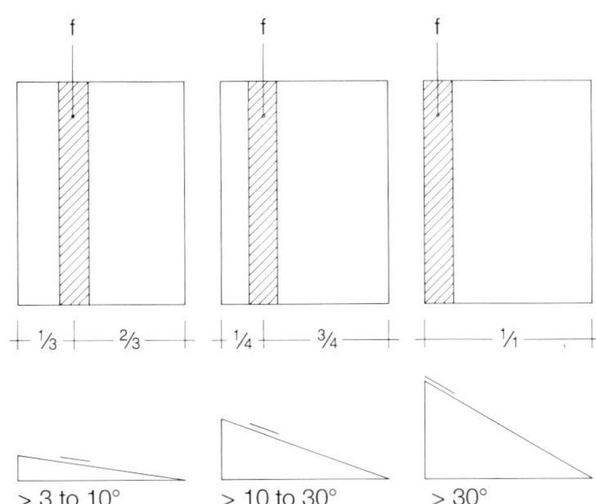


2.4.12.55 Location of fixed clips in relation to roof pitch: f zone for fixed clips [49]

| Bldg. height [m] | Part of roof [1] | No. of clips [pcs/m²] spacing [cm] | Max.strip width [mm] 500 | 600 | 670 | 700 | 800 | 1000 |
|---|---|---|---|---|---|---|---|---|
| ≤ 8 | bay | No. (Pb) | 4.5 | 4.5 | 4.5 | 4.5 | – | – |
| | | c/c (Pb) | 400 | 400 | 400 | 400 | – | – |
| | | No. [2] | – | 3.9 | 3.9 | 4.0 | 4.0 | 3.9 [3] |
| | | c/c [2] | – | 500 | 500 | 400 | 400 | 280 [3] |
| | edge | No. (Pb) | 4.5 | 4.5 | 4.5 | 4.5 | – | – |
| | | c/c (Pb) | 400 | 400 | 400 | 400 | – | – |
| | | No. [2] | – | 3.9 | 3.9 | 4.0 | 4.0 | 3.9 [3] |
| | | c/c [2] | – | 500 | 500 | 400 | 400 | 280 [3] |
| | corner | No. (Pb) | 4.5 | 4.5 | 4.5 | 4.5 | – | – |
| | | c/c (Pb) | 400 | 400 | 400 | 400 | – | – |
| | | No. [2] | – | 6.4 | 6.4 | 6.4 | 6.4 | 7.2 [3] |
| | | c/c [2] | – | 300 | 300 | 250 | 250 | 150 [3] |
| > 8 to ≤ 20 | bay | No. (Pb) | 4.5 | 4.5 | 4.5 | 4.5 | – | – |
| | | c/c (Pb) | 400 | 400 | 400 | 400 | – | – |
| | | No. [2] | – | 3.9 | 3.9 | 4.0 | 4.0 [3] | – |
| | | c/c [2] | – | 500 | 500 | 400 | 400 [3] | – |
| | edge | No. (Pb) | 4.5 | 4.5 | 4.5 | 4.5 | – | – |
| | | c/c (Pb) | 400 | 400 | 400 | 400 | – | – |
| | | No. [2] | – | 5.5 | 5.5 | 5.4 | 5.4 [3] | – |
| | | c/c [2] | – | 350 | 350 | 300 | 300 [3] | – |
| | corner | No. (Pb) | 7.2 | 7.2 | 7.2 | 7.2 | – | – |
| | | c/c (Pb) | 400 | 300 | 250 | 250 | – | – |
| | | No. [2] | – | 9.6 | 9.6 | 10.0 | 10.0 [3] | – |
| | | c/c [2] | – | 200 | 200 | 150 | 150 [3] | – |
| > 20 to ≤ 100 | bay | No. (Pb) | 4.5 | 4.5 | 4.5 | 4.5 | – | – |
| | | c/c (Pb) | 400 | 400 | 400 | 400 | – | – |
| | | No. [2] | – | 3.9 | 3.9 | 4.0 [3] | – | – |
| | | c/c [2] | – | 500 | 500 | 400 [3] | – | – |
| | edge | No. (Pb) | 5.6 | 5.6 | 5.6 | 5.6 | – | – |
| | | c/c (Pb) | 400 | 400 | 350 | 350 | – | – |
| | | No. [2] | – | 7.7 | 8.5 | 8.5 [3] | – | – |
| | | c/c [2] | – | 250 | 200 | 200 [3] | – | – |
| | corner | No. (Pb) | 9.9 | 9.9 | 9.9 | 9.9 | – | – |
| | | c/c (Pb) | 300 | 200 | 200 | 200 | – | – |
| | | No. [2] | – | 12.8 | 12.8 | 12.8 [3] | – | – |
| | | c/c [2] | – | 150 | 150 | 150 [3] | – | – |

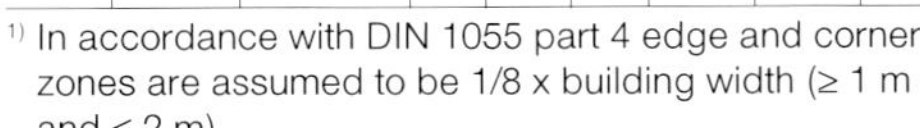

[1] In accordance with DIN 1055 part 4 edge and corner zones are assumed to be 1/8 x building width (≥ 1 m and ≤ 2 m).
[2] Aluminium, copper, zinc, stainless/galvanised steel
[3] (Hot-dip) galvanised steel only

2.4.12.56 Clips; min. number and max. spacing in relation to height of building [07, 49]

For copper, zinc alloy and aluminium such clips are required for bay lengths ≥ 3 m, for stainless and galvanised steel ≥ 6 m. The bays of sheet metal must be secured against slipping by fixed clips so that expansion clips can be used. The fixed clips must be positioned every 1–3 m, according to the roof pitch. The number of clips depends on the forces to be transferred.

Fixing material

Clips are increasingly being used for laying of bays by machine.

However, clips for laying by hand are still common.

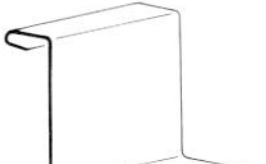
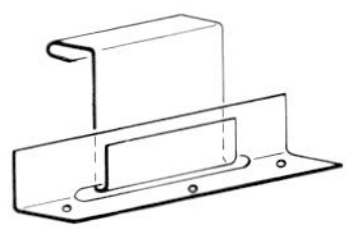

2.4.12.57 Clips; fixed and expansion clips for laying by machine; standing seams [49]

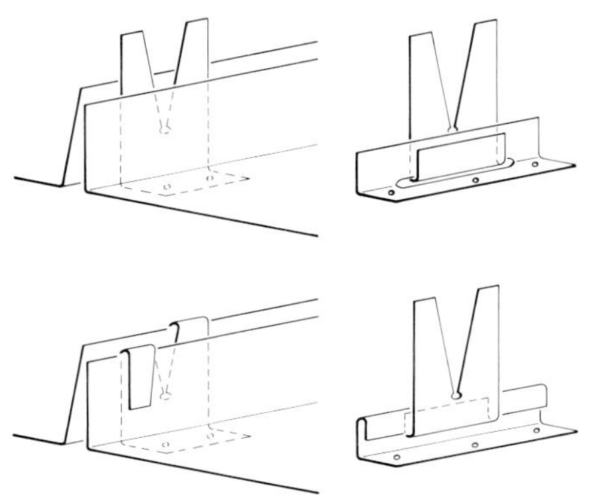

2.4.12.58 Clips; fixed and expansion clips for laying by hand; standing seams [49]

On a standing seam roof the clips are positioned between the bent-up edges of the sheet metal and attached to the supporting construction with at least two nails or screws.

On a batten roll roof the clips are fixed either to the top of the timber battens (German batten roll) or to the supporting construction beneath the timber battens (Belgian batten roll).

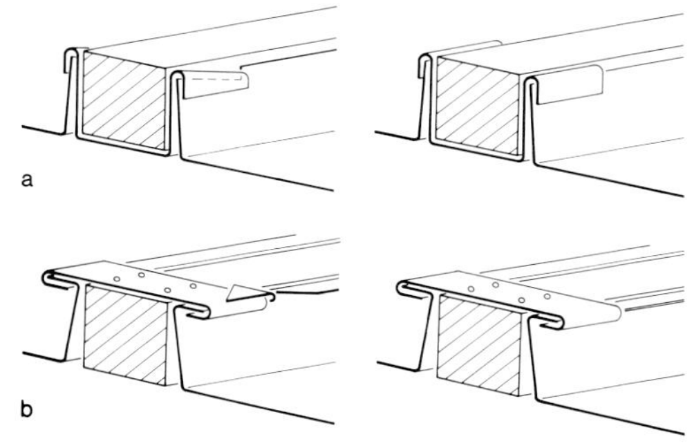


2.4.12.59 Clips; fixed and expansion clips: a Belgian batten, b German batten

Sheets or bays of lead are fixed by two rows of copper or stainless steel nails (9 mm head dia.) near the top in addition to the clips between the bent-up edges of the sheets. The spacing of the nails is approx. 75 mm and the two rows are 25 mm apart; the nails in the two rows are offset.

The nails and screws used for fixing the clips should be compatible with the material of the roof covering and the clips.

| Material of sheet metal to be fixed | Clips | | Fasteners [1] | | | |
|---|---|---|---|---|---|---|
| | | | nails with barbed shank | | countersunk-head screws [5] | |
| | material | min. thckn. [mm] | material | min. [3] dim. [mm] | material | min. dim. [mm] |
| Pb | Cu | 0.7 | Cu | 2.8 x 25 | Cu | 4 x 25 |
| | | | | | brass | |
| | st. st. | 0.4 | st. st. | > 2.5 x 25 | st. st. | |
| Cu | Cu | 0.6 | Cu | 2.8 x25 | Cu | 4 x 25 |
| | | | | | brass | |
| | st. st. | 0.4 | st. st. | > 2.5 x25 | st. st. | |
| Zn | Al [2] | 0.8 | st. st. | > 2.5 x25 [4] | st. st. | 4 x 25 |
| | st. st. | 0.4 | | | | |
| | vSt | 0.6 | g. st. | 2.8 x 25 | g. st. | |
| | Zn | 0.7 | | | | |
| Al | Al [2] | 0.8 | st. st. | > 2.5 x 25 [4] | st. st. | 4 x 25 |
| | st. st. | 0.4 | | | | |
| | g. st. | 0.6 | g. st. | 2.8 x 25 | g. st. | |
| | Zn | 0.7 | | | | |
| st. st. | Cu | 0.6 | Cu | 2.8 x25 | Cu | 4 x 25 |
| | | | | | brass | |
| | st. st. | 0.4 | st. st. | > 2.5 x 25 | st. st. | |
| galv. st. | Al [2] | 0.8 | st. st. | > 2.5 x 25 [4] | st. st. | 4 x 25 |
| | st. st. | 0.4 | | | | |
| | g. st. | 0.6 | g. st. | > 2.8 x 25 | g. st. | |

[1] min. 2 No. off per clip, embedment length ≥ 20 mm
[2] Bottom leg ≥ 1 mm thick for expansion clips
[3] Flat head dia. ≥ 7 mm
[4] Stainless steel annular nail with approx. 9 grooves; max. O.D. 2.8 mm, core dia. 2.5 mm
[5] Preferably stainless steel screws, especially at edges and corners and on taller buildings (> 20 m)

2.4.12.60 Fasteners; materials and sizes [07, 47, 49]

Workability
All the sheet metals described here are relatively easy to work with the right tools and equipment. They can be formed into virtually any shape and joined in a variety of ways. The minimum bending radius depends on the material, its nominal thickness and any coating. "The technological properties of zinc alloys depend on temperature. The material must be at a temperature of 10–12°C in order to bend or fold it. This temperature is reached when the ambient temperature is 2–3 K higher. Because of its higher strength, stainless steel sheet cannot be quite so readily shaped and folded." [49]

| | Pb | Cu | Zn | Al | st. st. | g. st. |
|---|---|---|---|---|---|---|
| Joints | | | | | | |
| welting | • | • | • | • | • | • |
| riveting | – | • | • | • | • | • |
| nailing | • | • | • | • | • | • |
| screwing | • | • | • | • | • | • |
| bonding | • | • | • | • | – | • |
| soldering | • | • | • | • | • | • |
| brazing | • | • | – | • | • | • |
| welding | • | • | – | • | • | • |
| Forming | | | | | | |
| beading | • | • | • | • | • | • |
| bending | • | • | • | • | • | • |
| flanging | • | • | • | • | • | • |
| rounding | • | • | • | • | • | • |
| dressing | • | • | • | • | – | – |
| bossing | • | • | • | – | – | – |

2.4.12.61 Technological properties

**Additional measures**
Additional measures should be allowed for during planning and construction when the reliability of the roof covering has to satisfy enhanced requirements. For example:

- for a roof pitch shallower than recommended,
- with high wind pressures or driving rain,
- when a build-up of water is expected, or
- when several roof surfaces and valleys meet at one point along the eaves.

Additional measures may involve:

- increasing the roof pitch
- increasing the height of the welted seams (see also tables 2.4.12.51 and 2.4.12.52)
- using standing seams with double or locked double instead of single welts
- increasing the overlap of transverse joints
- including an additional welt in a single welt transverse joint
- incorporating preformed sealing strips in the welted joints

**Details – for standing seams**
Ridge, hip, eaves, valley, verge, junctions with walls, trough, penetrations, vents

Ridge with twin double welt standing seam
With a symmetrical arrangement of the bays, the ridge is formed as two double welts (40 mm high). The incoming locked double welt standing seams (≥ 25 mm high) between the bays are bent over at the ridge and integrated into the ridge seam.
This allows the bays to expand unhindered. A batten laid along the ridge can be helpful here (see "Construction details").

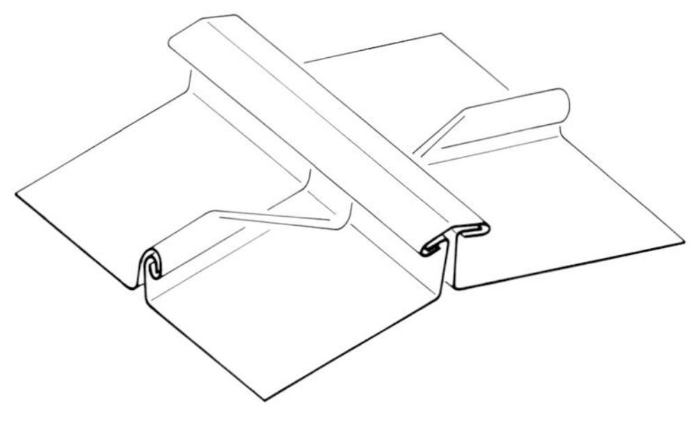

2.4.12.62 Ridge detail with twin double welt

Ridge with locked double welt standing seam
The welted joints between the bays of sheet metal should be arranged not to line up at the ridge seam (40 mm high). This improves the unhindered expansion of the bays and limits the thickness of the welted joint where the joints between the bays intersect with the ridge joint.

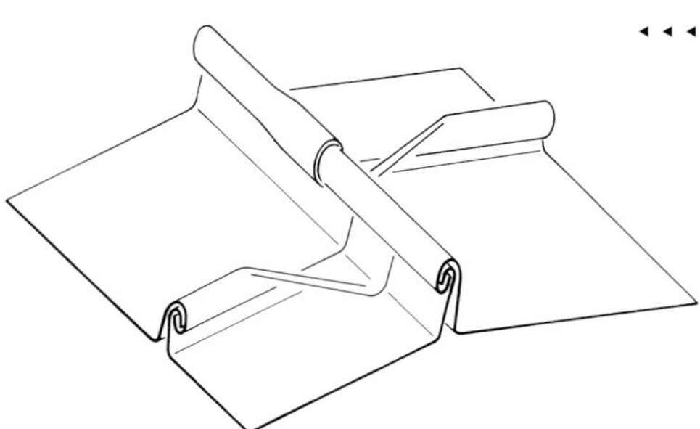

2.4.12.63 Ridge detail with locked double welt standing seam: ▸ prevailing wind direction

The two ridge details described above cannot be ventilated directly. This is not a disadvantage on small roofs or when the eaves-eaves ventilation works well. On larger roofs local ventilation is possible if individual vents are positioned in every bay just below the ridge (see also "Vents" below and "Layers – Ventilation"). However, this form of ventilation is not usually sufficient and is not secure against driving rain and snow.
Continuous ridge ventilation is also possible for sheet metal roofs with welted seams or batten rolls.

Ventilated ridge
The bays of sheet metal are turned up 150 mm at the ridge. The continuous gap along the ridge (≥ 80 mm) is then covered with a separate sheet metal hood.

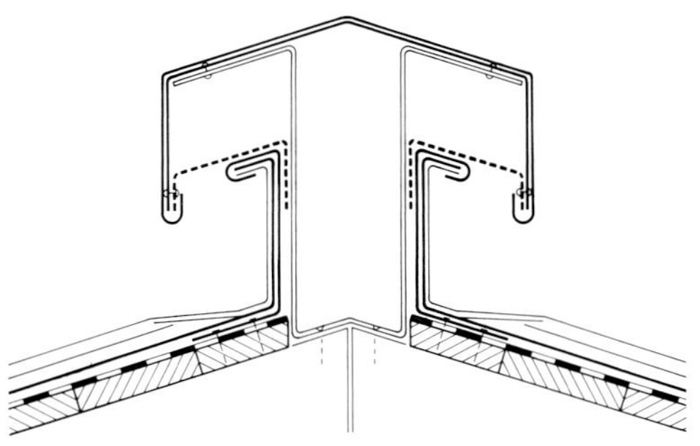

2.4.12.64 Ventilated ridge

The hood is attached to metal mountings fixed to each pair of rafters. A mesh screen or perforated sheet metal prevents birds and small animals entering the ventilation opening.
The separate hood can be laid on boards (any condensation on the inside of the sheet metal can drain via the boards or sheathing; the

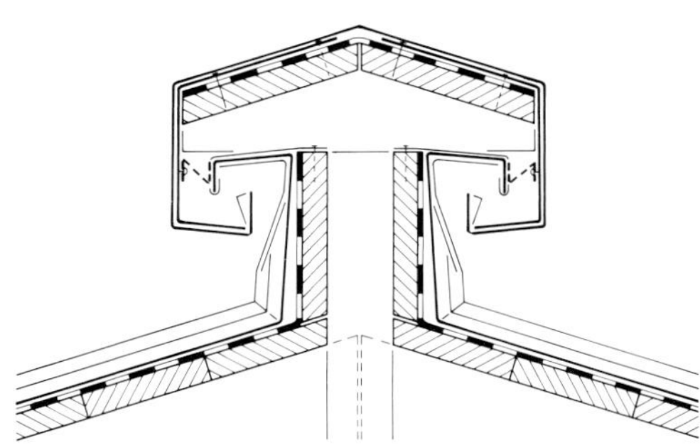

2.4.12.65 Ventilated ridge – protected from ingress of driving rain and snow

boards also help to attenuate noise). Pieces of batten connect the hood to each pair of rafters. Bending over the edges of the hood and the sheet metal upstand redirects the air circulation and helps to secure the ridge against driving rain and snow.

Hip with twin double welt standing seam
(see "Ridge with twin double standing seam")
The locked double welt standing seams of the incoming bays of sheet metal are bent over (closed side upwards) and tucked into the hip seam on both sides. A sheet metal capping finishes the joint. A batten laid along the hip can be helpful here (see "Construction details").

Hip with locked double welt standing seam
The (offset) joints between the bays of sheet metal are bent over (closed side upwards) and tucked into the hip seam. The offset is necessary because the thickness of material may make it impossible to create a decent joint.

Ventilated hip
(see "Ventilated ridge" above)
The hood along the hip does not need to be positioned at an angle.

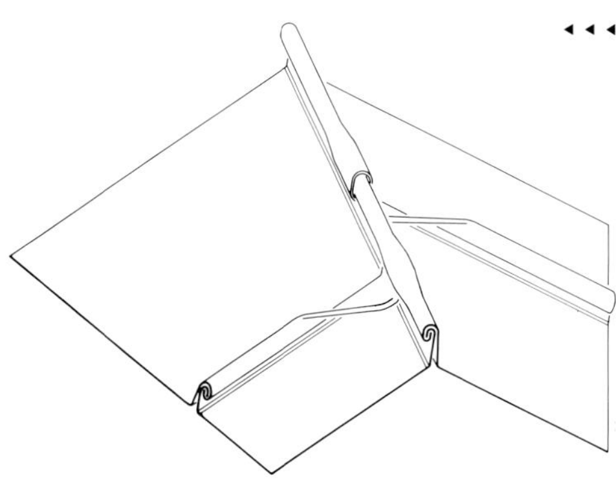


2.4.12.66 Hip detail with locked double welt standing seam: ▸ prevailing wind direction

Eaves
The unhindered movement of the bays of sheet metal – governed by the position of the fixing clips at the ridge – must be guaranteed at the eaves in particular. The ends of the bays are fixed by bending them around the end of the lining plate (35 mm, 0.8 mm) at the eaves. The bent-over end of the bay may not become disengaged from the plate at maximum thermal expansion. There must also be sufficient play to allow for maximum contraction of the bay. The individual pieces of the lining plate at the eaves are not joined together but laid with a small gap, or loosely overlapped and fixed to the fascia board.

Eaves with locked double welt standing seam
The locked double welt standing seam at the eaves can be formed with
- a vertical or
- sloping (especially watertight) end.

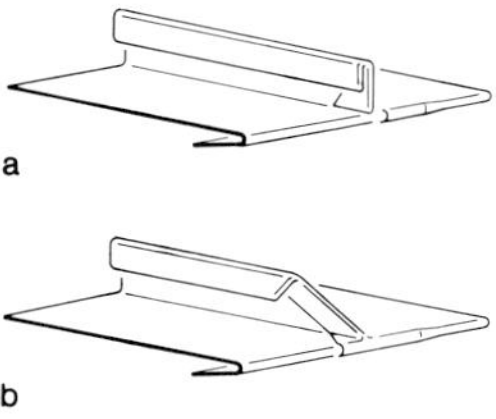


2.4.12.67 Eaves detail: a vertical standing seam, b sloping standing seam [49]

| Valley pitch | Type of valley | Notes |
|---|---|---|
| ≥ 3° | sheet metal channel; sheet metal of roof surface slides in lining plate | good expansion potential, relatively secure against build-up of water |
| ≥ 7° | sheet metal valley with locked double welt standing seam; double welt joint between sheet metal of roof surface and valley | no chance for expansion, small roof areas, short bays (≤ 6 m) |
| ≥ 10° | sheet metal valley with single welt and extra welt, sheet metal of roof surface slides in extra w. | good expansion pot. despite turned-up edge (≥ 40 mm), not secure against build-up of water |
| ≥ 25° | sheet metal valley with single welt, sheet metal of roof surface slides in welt (or sheet metal valley as for 10°) | good expansion pot., not secure against build-up of water |

2.4.12.68 Valley detail; type of valley in relation to pitch of valley [49]

Valley
The valley detail depends on roof pitch and the length of the valley. The junction between the sheet metal of the valley and the incoming bays of sheet metal is achieved with a single welt (≥ 40 mm wide), a single welt with additional welt, or a double welt. Protection against a build-up of water can be improved by including preformed sealing strips in the joints.

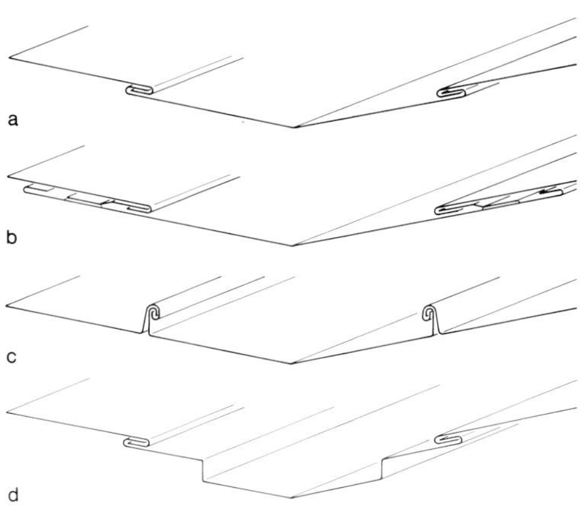


2.4.12.69 Valley detail: a with single welt, b with single welt and additional welt, c with locked double welt, d with deeper central channel [49]

The sheet metal pieces of the valley are simply overlapped (with beaded edges). The length of the lap depends on the pitch of the valley.

| Valley pitch [°] | Lap [mm] |
|---|---|
| ≥ 22 | ≥ 100 |
| ≥ 15 | ≥ 150 |
| < 15 | watertight joint |

2.4.12.70 Laps between sheet metal in valley in relation to pitch of valley [47, 49]

Verge
The edge of the sheet metal is turned up 40–60 mm at the verge (60–100 mm for buildings ≥ 20 m in height). Individual clips, fixed to the roof decking, the barge board or a verge batten, provide a concealed fixing for the edges of the sheet metal and transfer wind suction loads to the roof decking. A gap of 2–3 mm should be maintained between the bent-up edge of the metal and the verge trim or batten to allow for thermal expansion. The metal verge trim is

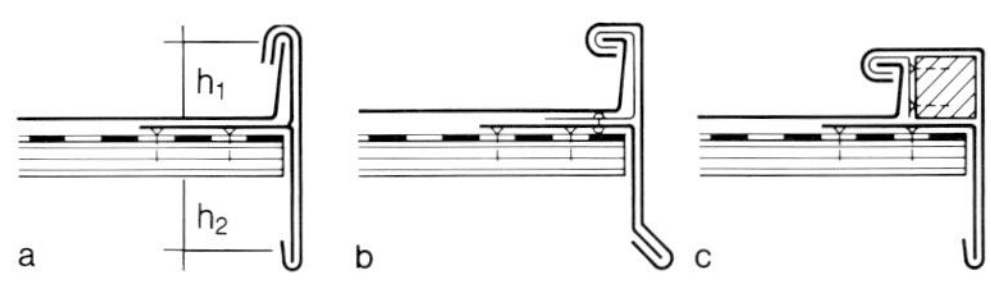


2.4.12.71 Verge detail: a single welt standing seam, b double welt standing seam, c with verge trim [49]

| Building height [m] | Turned-up edge at verge $h_1$ [mm] | Bottom leg of verge trim $h_2$ [mm] | min. clearance between drip edge and building[1] [mm] |
|---|---|---|---|
| ≤ 8 | 40 to 60 | ≥ 50 | 20 to 30 |
| 8 bis 20 | 40 to 60 | ≥ 80 | 30 to 40 |
| ≥ 20 | 60 to 100 | ≥ 100 | 40 to 60 |

2.4.12.72 Verge; spacing and heights in relation to height of building; 1) copper ≥ 40–60 mm [49]

folded around the edge of the sheet metal. An additional fixing is necessary along its bottom edge. This is achieved with a continuous clip (thickness ≥ 0.8 mm for verge trim bent up ≥ 50 mm; thickness ≥ 0.8 mm plus additional fixings for verge trim bent up ≥ 100 mm; without additional fixings the thickness should be ≥ 1.0 mm).

Junction with wall at side of slope
The sheet metal is turned up the wall 100–150 mm according to the pitch. The metal is held there with a continuous clip or individual clips (max. every 300 mm) but allowing for movement, and flashed with a capping strip with sufficient overlap (≥ 50, 80, 100 mm). The sheathing is also turned up the wall to the same height and pressed against the wall by the sheet metal. In this way the wall and the adjoining roof can move independently of each other.

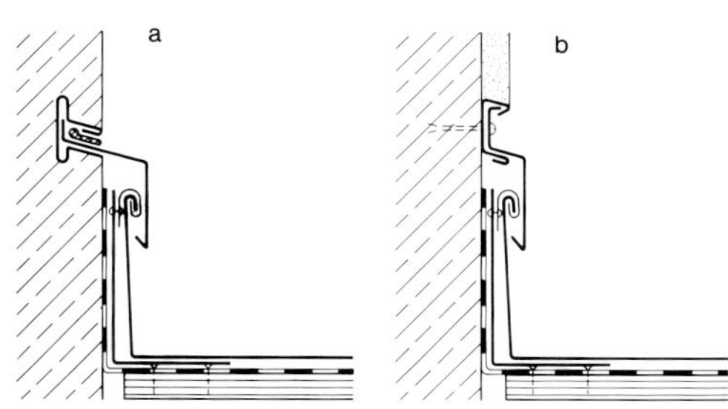


2.4.12.73 Junction with wall at side of slope: a with drip flashing fitted into chase, b with drip flashing combined with rendering bead [49]

Junction with wall at top of slope
If the bay adjoins a drip, a ridge or a wall, the sheet metal must be turned up at least 150 mm (at least 130 mm for a roof pitch ≥ 25°).

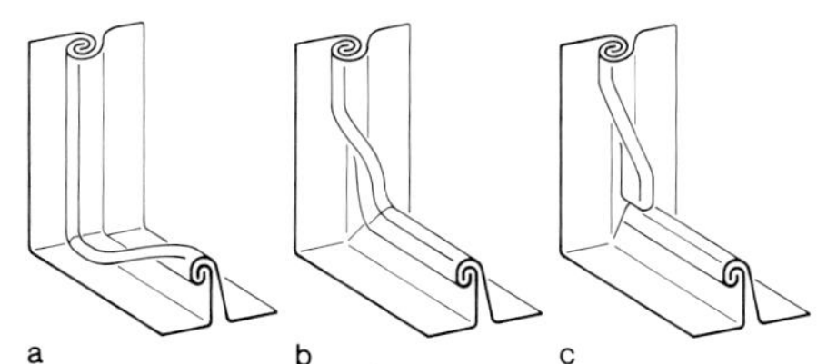


2.4.12.74 Junction with wall at top of slope: a with folded-over double welt, b with uncut (rounded) welted seam, c with cut (angular) welted seam [49]

The end of the sheet metal should have a turned-up edge.

Junction with wall at top of slope – locked double welt standing seams
The form of the locked double welt seam near the turned-up edge:

- as a folded-over locked double welt – watertight, but this joint requires space to produce it; disadvantage: transverse movement of bays is hampered.
- as an uncut (rounded) locked double welt – watertight but requires an adequate height of upstand.
- as a cut (angular) locked double welt – only watertight over height of standing seam, but can be produced for any height of upstand.

Trough

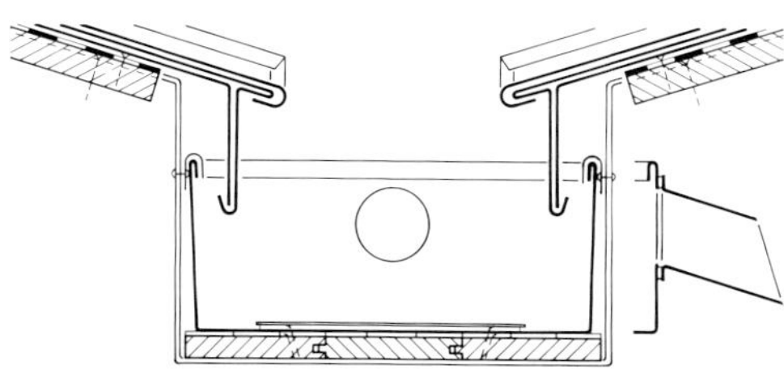

2.4.12.75 Trough detail

The ends of the bays are fixed by bending them around the end of the lining plate (≥ 35 mm). Additional continuous clips secure the lining plate to the sides (200–300 mm high) of the gutter (see also "Layers – Drainage").

Penetrations
Penetrations through the roof surface are sealed by soldered and not by welted joints when the clearance between the penetration and the welted joints on the roof surface permit.

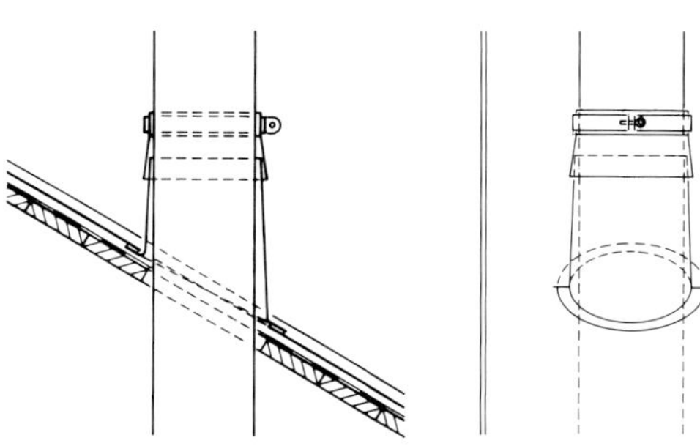

2.4.12.76 Roof penetration; version with soldered flashing [49]

The welted joints on the roof surface may need to be relocated if there are large penetrations. Double welt seams are used to incorporate the penetration. The transverse joint above the penetration is positioned at an angle, bent over to one side and integrated into the side joints. Water can then flow around the penetration. A back gutter is required above the penetration when its width exceeds 1000 mm. To do this, the roof decking should be made into a saddle to suit. Welted seams folded flat below the roof penetration are positioned straight. All penetrations must continue at least 150 mm above the top surface of the roof covering and be flashed watertight. The cover flashing should overlap ≥ 50, 80, 100 mm, depending on height.

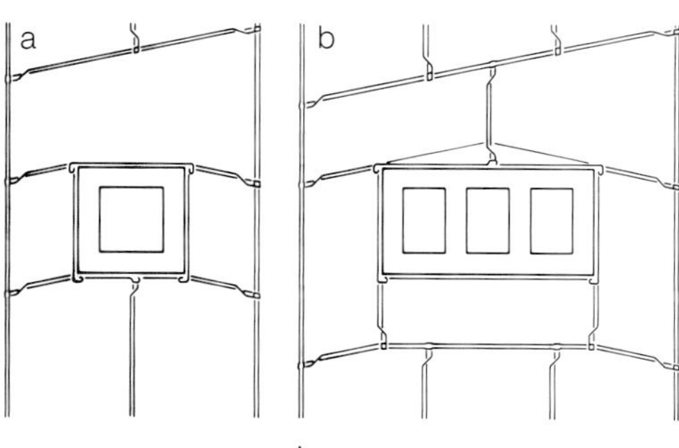


2.4.12.77 Roof penetration (plan views): a layout with transverse joints draining away from penetration, b version with back gutter on higher side of penetration [49]

Vents
Individual vents are used to ventilate the supporting construction. Bending up the edges of the sheet metal at least 15 mm prevents the ingress of driving rain and snow, but does not secure the opening completely. Individual vents are not recommended for roof pitches ≤ 15° (backlog of air). The individual vents are joined to the sheet metal by rivets, soldering or welding. A mesh screen or perforated sheet metal (hole dia. ≥ 5 mm) prevents birds and small animals entering the ventilation opening. The hood/vent opening overlap is 100–150 mm (see also "Layers – Ventilation").

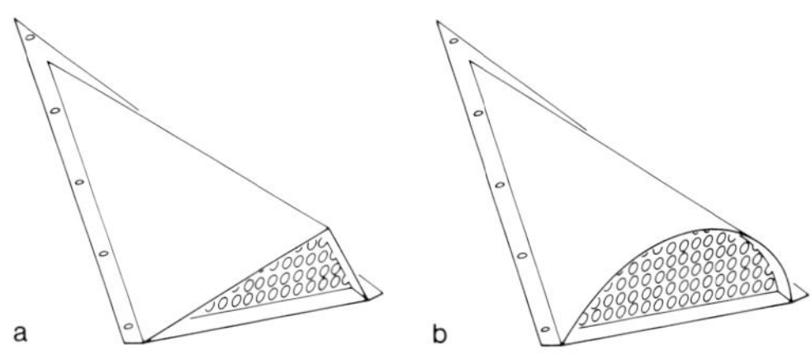


2.4.12.78 Individual vents: a triangular, b rounded [49]

**Details – for batten roll seams**
Ridge, hip, eaves, valley, verge, junctions with walls, trough, penetrations, vents

Ridge

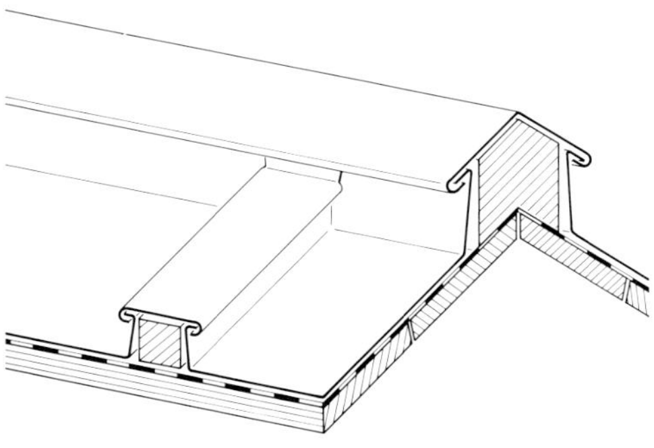

2.4.12.79 Ridge detail, with German batten [49]

The top end of the incoming bay of sheet metal should be turned up at the ridge batten. There should be a clearance of 5–10 mm between this upstand (60–80 mm high) and the ridge batten to allow for thermal expansion. A tilting fillet should be provided at the incoming battens. An angular ridge capping (sloping on both sides to ensure good drainage) is placed over the ridge batten and folded around the turned-up edge of the sheets on the roof surface.

Ventilated ridge
(see "Ventilated ridge" above)

Hip
(see "Ridge" above)
In contrast to the ridge capping, hip capping may be flat.

Ventilated hip
(see "Ventilated hip" above)

Eaves
The capping over the batten slopes down at the eaves and is folded around the lining plate. To do this, the timber batten must be cut at an angle at the eaves. While the turned-up edges of the sheet metal continue to the eaves for a German batten roll, when using a Belgian batten roll, it stops at the point at which the batten starts to taper.

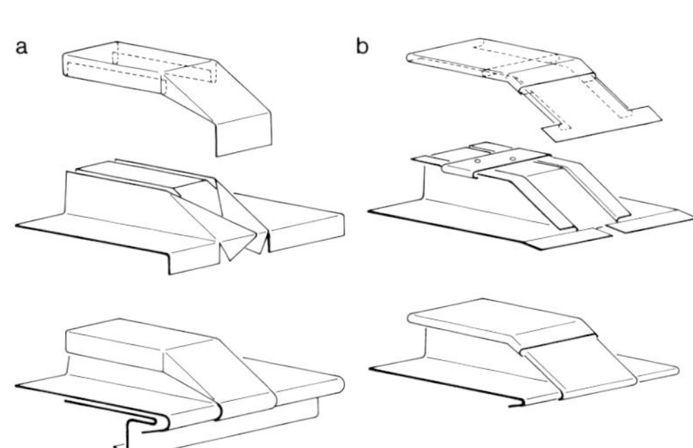

2.4.12.80 Eaves details: a Belgian batten, b German batten [49]

Valley
(see "Valley" above)

Verge
The sheet metal is finished at the eaves by turning up the edge (Belgian batten roll) or by turning up the edge and folding it back (German batten roll). A gap of 2–3 mm should be maintained between the bent-up edge of the metal and the verge batten to allow for expansion. A verge batten should be at least 40 mm high. A metal verge trim is folded around the turned-up edge of the sheet metal and the bottom edge held by a continuous clip (thickness ≥ 0.8 mm for verge trim bent up ≥ 50 mm; thickness ≥ 0.8 mm plus additional

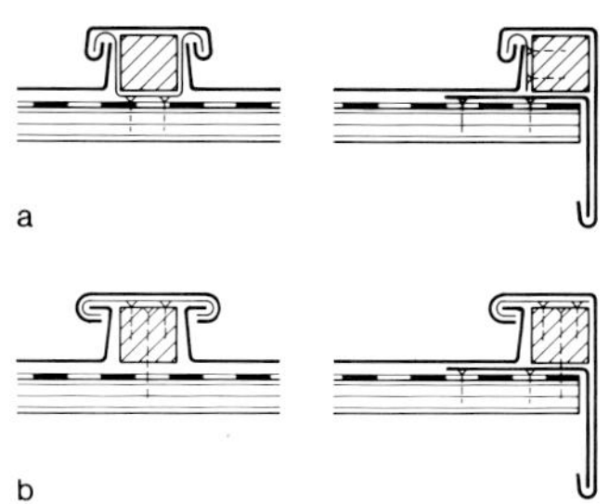

2.4.12.81 Verge details: a Belgian batten, b German batten [49]

fixings for verge trim bent up ≥ 100 mm; without additional fixings the thickness should be ≥ 1.0 mm).
With a Belgian batten roll the verge trim is held in place by individual clips lengthened to form a strip.

Junction with wall at side of slope
(see "Junction with wall at side of slope" above)

Junction with wall at top of slope
(see "Junction with wall at top of slope" above)
Tilting fillets should be provided at the incoming battens.

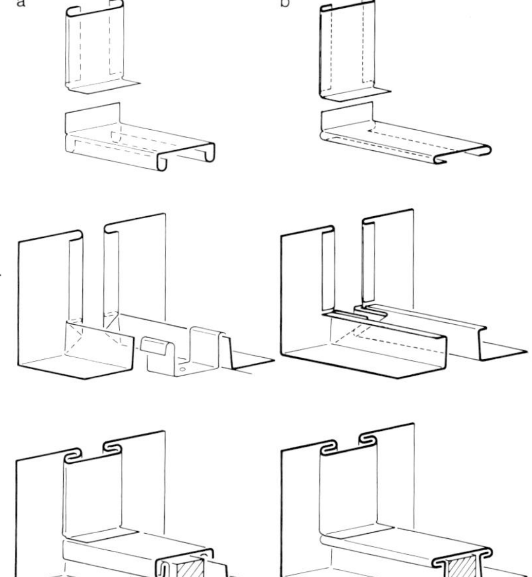

2.4.12.82 Junction with wall at top of slope: a Belgian batten, b German batten [49]

Trough
(see "Trough" above)
With a batten roll roof covering the capping to the batten can be joined to the lining plate. To do this, the timber battens are cut at an angle; however, it is also to possible to cut them off straight just short of the end of the sheet metal bays.

Penetrations
(see "Penetrations" above)

Vents
(see "Vents" above)

**Details – for hollow and wood-cored rolls (lead only)**
Ridge, hip, eaves, valley, verge, junctions with walls, trough, penetrations, vents

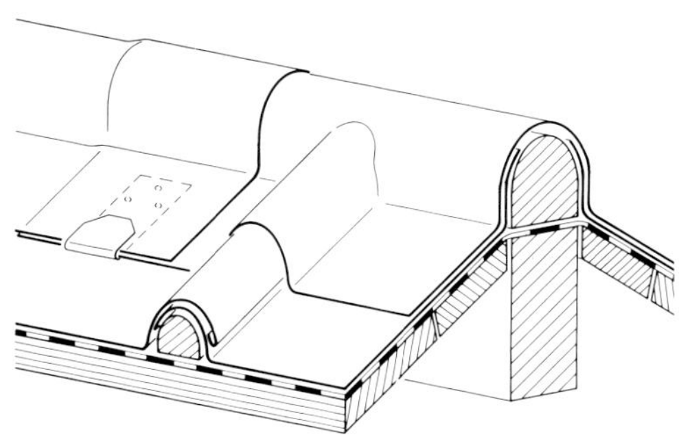
2.4.12.83 Ridge detail, with wood-cored roll [37]

Ridge
The ridge is finished with a ridge roll. This overlaps the sheet metal on the roof surface 120 mm on both sides and is dressed over the roll on the roof surface. The length of the ridge roll is limited to 1500 mm; it is laid with 150 mm laps on a wood core ≥ 60 mm high and secured with clips.

Hip
(see "Ridge" above)
The hip roll overlaps the sheet metal on the roof surface 200 mm on both sides.

Eaves
The eaves flashing of sheet lead (width: 200–250 mm; length: max. 1500 mm; laps: 120 mm) is fixed to the supporting construction along its top edge with two rows of copper nails. The wood core is cut off at a slight angle at the eaves. The incoming sheets of metal are folded down ≥ 75 mm at the eaves and dressed over the core roll.

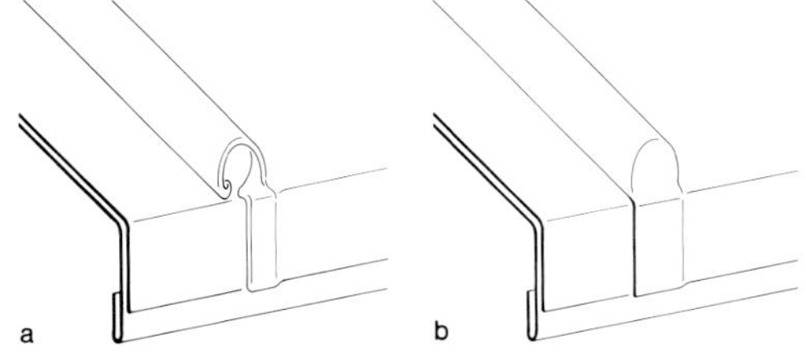

2.4.12.84 Eaves details: a hollow roll, b wood-cored roll [37]

Valley
Valley gutters of milled sheet lead cannot be laid as a strip but must be placed adjacent to each other. They are fixed with nails at the top and joined together with clips.

Verge
The sheets of lead are turned up ≥ 150 mm at the verge and folded around a copper or stainless steel stiffening or lining sheet.

Junction with wall at side of slope
(see "Junction with wall at side of slope" above)

Junction with wall at top of slope
The incoming sheets of lead are turned up the wall 150 mm. The roll, however, ends directly at the wall and is not turned up.
A cover flashing, held by clips and dressed over the roll or "leadburned" around it, covers the junction between the sheet metal roof covering and the wall.

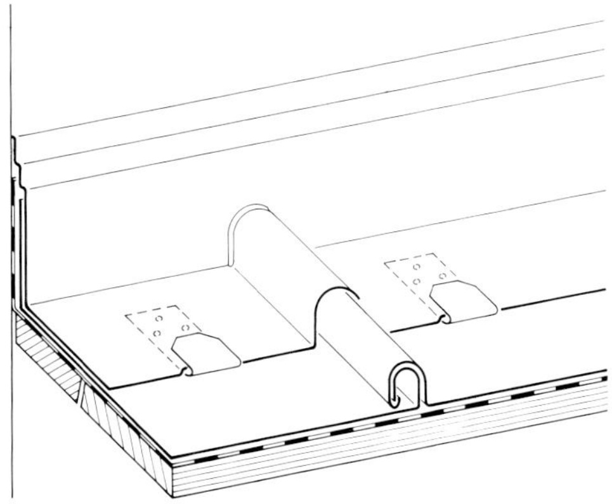

2.4.12.85 Junction with wall at top of slope; hollow roll [37]

Trough
The sheets of lead on the roof surface end at the gutter with a flashing. The sheet metal nailed below the main roof covering overlaps the turned-up edges (≥ 200 mm) of the gutter by at least 75 mm. It is connected to the gutter using clips. The gutter should be at least 225 mm wide.

Penetrations
On a roof covering of sheet lead, the incoming sheets below the penetration are tucked into a apron flashing and those above the penetration into a back gutter. The overlap with the apron flashing and back gutter is at least 250 mm. Apron flashing, back gutter and turned-up edges must be at least 150 mm high and all should be flashed with a cover strip to make them rainproof. At the corners the lead flashings are joined together by "leadburning".

Vents
(see "Vents" above)

**Supporting construction**

Separating layer
A separating layer may be laid between the timber roof decking and the metal roof covering, although this is not compulsory. However, if there is a possibility of a reaction between the sheet metal and acidic substances in the timber, or timber preservatives containing salts, a separating layer must be used. [36, 47, 49]
Materials containing lime and cement underneath sheet aluminium, lead and zinc also require the use of a separating layer because of the possibility of alkaline reactions. [36, 47]
A separating layer is required for drainage purposes below a roof pitch of 15°. It is also generally necessary for roof deckings that are sensitive to moisture or that do not store moisture, e.g. timber derivatives such as building-grade plywood boards. [42, 49]

Suitable separating layers (e.g. braided fibre mat, 8 mm thick) are textured. They protect the metal roof covering against corrosion from the underside by providing a clearance between metal and underlay, as well as unimpeded runoff and ventilation of any incoming rainwater or condensation. They also make it easier for the sheets of metal to slide and thus expand and contract in accordance with the temperature, and they attenuate the impact noise of rain and hail. They also function as sheathing when provided with a film or foil on the underside. Separating layers that absorb and retain water (e.g. felt) are not suitable. [42, 49]
It is possible to omit a separating layer on a non-ventilated timber decking, owing to the good properties of the wood (absorption, distribution, release of moisture), provided the decking does not contain any substances or preservatives that could damage the sheet metal roof covering.

Roof decking
As a rule, timber roof decking is employed as the supporting construction for sheet metal. This enables the roof covering to be fixed easily. The roof decking also intercepts incoming rainwater and condensation and stores it temporarily when it emerges from the underside of the sheet metal.
If the presence of moisture triggers chemical reactions, corrosion-resistant fixings are recommended.
The boards of the roof decking should be laid perpendicular or at an angle (longer span) to the bays of sheet metal so that several boards can be used for fixing the sheet metal.

For standing seams and battens:

- Roof decking laid across the whole of the roof surface, softwood grade 1, sawn smooth S 10, unplaned and air-dried; board thickness ≥ 24 mm for a rafter spacing ≤ 750 mm, otherwise ≥ 30 mm thick; boards 80–160 mm wide with small gaps between them; fixed with at least two corrosion-protected (galvanised steel with 55 µm zinc) or corrosion-resistant (stainless steel) nails per board and rafter. [47, 48, 49]
- Roof decking laid with gaps for roof pitches ≥ 25°, made from battens, softwood grade 1, sawn smooth S 10, unplaned and air-dried; batten thickness ≥ 30 mm, batten width ≥ 80 mm, spacing of battens 100–120 mm; fixings as for sawn boards (see above). [48, 49]
- Tongue and groove boards, softwood grade 1, planed and air-dried; board thickness ≥ 24 mm, board width 95–115 mm; fixings as for sawn boards (see above).
- Waterproof-glued building-grade plywood boards (BFU 100 G), laid in a bond, board thickness ≥ 22 mm, edge length l ≤ 2.5 m; fixed with screws.
- Cement-bound chipboard (incombustible, class A 2) as fire-resistant roof decking (F 90), laid in a bond, board thickness ≥ 25 mm; fixed with screws (galvanised steel with 55 µm zinc, or stainless steel).

For hollow and wood-cored roll seams:

- Roof decking laid across the whole of the roof surface, as described above, except boards ≥ 30 mm thick and 120–160 mm wide, and 2–4 mm gaps between boards; fixed with at least two stainless steel nails.
- Tongue and groove boards as described above, except boards ≥ 30 mm thick. [07]
- Waterproof-glued building-grade plywood boards as described above, except boards ≥ 24 mm thick. [07]

Synthetic resin-bound chipboard (V 100 G) is not suitable as an underlay for sheet metal roofing. It tends to swell when damp, promotes the formation of condensation water owing to its high synthetic resin content, and can trigger chemical reactions with the metals. [07, 49]

Loadbearing planks:

- Concrete planks as a fire-resistant underlay (F 90); roof covering fixed to them with approved plastic anchors and screws (galvanised or stainless steel). [49]
- Aerated concrete planks as a fire-resistant underlay (F 90); roof covering fixed to them with approved special plastic anchors and special screws (galvanised or stainless steel). [49]

**Maintenance and repair**

Copper, lead and stainless steel all have a minimum service life of 80–100 years. A zinc alloy roof covering will also last just as long in a rural or urban environment. We can also assume that aluminium will remain serviceable for up to 50 years. The durability of galvanised steel depends mainly on the thickness of the zinc coating. In industrial atmospheres, additional

coats of paint, which have to be renewed at regular intervals, are absolutely essential to maintain the serviceability of the roof.
Regular cleaning, according to the degree of soiling, reduces the risk of pitting of coated aluminium and stainless steel roof coverings used in industrial atmospheres containing sulphur dioxide, and in salt-laden marine environments. Zinc alloy should be painted, and repainted regularly, in aggressive industrial atmospheres. Installed properly, copper and lead roof coverings do not require any maintenance. Holes in the sheet metal, visible from outside, can be repaired by soldering a piece of appropriate material to an unpainted metal roof, or welding a piece to uncoated metal. Uncontrolled corrosion of the underside of a metal surface – if visible from outside – is probably impossible to repair and the sheet metal will have to be replaced.

However, simply replacing a sheet is only advisable when the local cause of the corrosion (e.g. galvanic corrosion due to contact with another metal) can be eliminated. The positions of the metals in the electrochemical series should be taken into account here.
If the cause of large-scale corrosion of the metal's underside is the presence of moisture and simultaneous exclusion of the air – possibly due to a plastic or even bitumen (ketonic acids) separating layer –, it must be completely removed (above timber boarding), or replaced or supplemented by a permanently rigid textured mat of material that is compatible with the metal.
Large-scale ponding on the surface that causes corrosion from above can be remedied only by increasing the roof pitch to ensure unhindered water run-off.

**References**


[01] Aluminiumzentrale (pub.): Aluminium-Taschenbuch; Düsseldorf: Aluminium-Verlag, 1987
[02] Beratungsstelle für Stahlverwendung (pub.): Merkblatt 400, Korrosionsverhalten von feuerverzinktem Stahl; Düsseldorf, 1983
[03] Bergström, U., Engberg, G.: Zwei Sorten decken alles ab; in: Maschinenmarkt 47/88; Würzburg: Vogel KG, 1988
[04] Biec international (pub.): 55% Aluminium-Zink schmelztauchveredeltes Stahlblech, technical brochure; Bath Pike – Bethlehem: Biec, 1989
[05] Bleiberatung e.V.: information material, European edition – Blei im Bauwesen; Düsseldorf
[06] Bleiberatung e.V.: Blei – Schriftenreihe der Bleiberatung e.V.; Düsseldorf, 1964
[07] Bleiberatung e.V.: Technische Regeln für die Verarbeitung von Saturnblei im Bauwesen, pt 1; Düsseldorf: Gütegemeinschaft Bleihalbzeug e.V., 2001
[08] Federal Ministry for Labour and Social Affairs, Hazardous Goods Committee (pub.): Technische Regeln für Gefahrstoffe 505, Blei und bleihaltige Stoffe; Berlin: BMA, 1996
[09] Dechema: Werkstofftabellen; Weinheim: Verlag-Chemie, 1969, 1976, 1986 & 1995
[10] German Copper Institute: information material and offprints; Düsseldorf
[11] German Copper Institute (pub.): Kupfer-Fachbuch; Berlin/Düsseldorf: DKI, 1982
[12] German Copper Institute: Kupfer im Hochbau; Dachdeckung, Außenwandbekleidung, Klempnertechnik; Düsseldorf, 1999
[13] German Copper Institute (pub.); Kleine-Allekotte, H.; Gressmann, T.: Kupfer im Hochbau; Düsseldorf: DKI, 1999
[14] German Copper Institute (pub.): Kupfer – Vorkommen, Gewinnung, Eigenschaften, Verarbeitung, Verwendung; Düsseldorf: DKI, 1999
[15] Industrieverband zur Förderung des Bauens mit Stahlblech e.V. (pub.): Informationsschriften; Düsseldorf: Stahlinformationszentrum, inter alia 3/1987
[16] Dietrich, A., Müller, P.: Leitfaden der Chemie; Stuttgart: Mundus, 1954
[17] DIN EN 485: Aluminium and aluminium alloys; sheet, strip and plate; pt 1: technical conditions for inspection and delivery; Berlin: Beuth 1994; pt 2: Mechanical properties; Berlin: Beuth, 1995; pt 4: tolerances on shape and dimensions for cold-rolled products; Berlin: Beuth, 1994
[18] DIN EN 612: Eaves gutters and rainwater downpipes of metal sheet – Definitions, classification and requirements; Berlin: Beuth, 1996
[19] DIN EN 988: Zinc and zinc alloys – Specification for rolled flat products for building; Berlin: Beuth, 1996
[20] DIN EN 1172: Copper and copper alloys – Sheet and strip for building purposes; Berlin: Beuth, 1996
[21] DIN EN 10142: Continuously hot-dip zinc coated low carbon steel strip and sheet for cold forming – Technical delivery conditions; Berlin: Beuth, 1995
[22] DIN EN 10143: Continuously hot-dip metal coated steel sheet and strip; tolerances on dimensions and shape; Berlin: Beuth, 1993
[23] DIN EN 10147: Continuously hot-dip zinc coated structural steel strip and sheet – Technical delivery conditions; Berlin: Beuth, 1995
[24] DIN EN 10215: Continuously hot-dip aluminium-zinc (AZ) coated steel strip and sheet – Technical delivery conditions; Berlin: Beuth, 1995
[25] DIN EN 10258: Cold-rolled stainless steel narrow strip and cut lenghts – Tolerances on dimensions and shape; Berlin: Beuth, 1997
[26] DIN EN 10259: Cold-rolled stainless steel wide strip and plate/sheet – Tolerances on dimensions and shape; Berlin: Beuth, 1997
[27] DIN EN 12588: Lead and lead alloys – Rolled lead sheet for building purposes; Berlin: Beuth, 1999
[28] Edelstahl rostfrei: information material, Düsseldorf
[29] Ergang, R.; Rockel, M. B.: Die Korrosionsbeständigkeit der nichtrostenden Stähle an der Atmosphäre. Auswertung von Versuchen bis zu 10-jähriger Auslagerung; in: Werkstoffe und Korrosion, vol. 26, issue 1; Weinheim: Verlag Chemie, 1975
[30] Fachbuchreihe des Stahlhandels: NE Metall Fibel; Düsseldorf
[31] Faller, M.: Metallabtrag und Metallabschwemmung von Metalldächern; in: Baumetall 4/2001
[32] Fischer, U., Kilgus, R., Leopold, B., Röhrer, W., Schilling, K.: Tabellenbuch Metall, 36th ed.; Wuppertal: Nourney, Vollmer, 1987
[33] FMPA Baden-Württemberg, Otto-Graf-Institut, Abteilung Bautenschutz, Bauphysik: Vorlesungsmanuskript "Korrosionsschutz der Metalle im Bauwesen"; Stuttgart: FMPA, 1990
[34] Hofmann, W.: Blei und Bleilegierungen; Berlin, Springer-Verlag, 1962
[35] Holzapfel, W.: Werkstoffkunde für Dach-, Wand- und Abdichtungstechnik, 10th ed.; Cologne: R. Müller, 1999
[36] Hullmann, Willkomm und Partner, Braas Dachsysteme GmbH (pub.): Metalldeckungen – Pro und Contra; Oberursel: Braas, 2000
[37] Lead Development Association: Lead sheet in building, a guide to good practice; London, 1984
[38] Metallgesellschaft (pub.): Blei-Taschenbuch
[39] Metall-Verlag: Zink-Taschenbuch; Düsseldorf: Metall-Verlag
[40] Oeteren, K. A., van: Korrosionsschutz durch Beschichtungsstoffe; Munich: Hanser, 1980
[41] Pohl, W.-H., Behr, R.: Titanzink – Korrosionsverhalten bei atmosphärischer Beanspruchung; in: Metall 5/99;
[42] Rheinzink GmbH (pub.): Rheinzink – Anwendung in der Architektur, 2nd ed.; Datteln: Rheinzink, 2000
[43] Röhr & Stoberg GmbH: Blei im Bauwesen; Krefeld
[44] Scholz, W.: Baustoffkenntnis, 13th ed.; Düsseldorf Werner, 1995
[45] Schulze-Rettmer, R.: Bleidächer und Regenwasser (scientific study), 2nd ed.; Aachen, Düsseldorf: Bleiberatung e.V. (pub.), 2002
[46] Munich Technical University, Institute of Building: material data sheets; Munich, 1986
[47] Zentralverband des Deutschen Dachdeckerhandwerks – Fachverband Dach-, Wand- und Abdichtungstechnik – e.V.: Fachregel für Metallarbeiten im Dachdeckerhandwerk; Cologne: Rudolf Müller, 1999
[48] Zentralverband des Deutschen Dachdeckerhandwerks Fachverband Dach-, Wand- und Abdichtungstechnik e.V.: Hinweise – Holz und Holzwerkstoffe; Cologne: Rudolf Müller, 1997
[49] Zentralverband Sanitär, Heizung, Klima: Richtlinien für die Ausführung von Metalldächern, Außenwandbekleidungen und Bauklempnerarbeiten; St Augustin: ZVSHK, 2002
[50] Zinkberatung e.V. (pub.): Zink als Korrosionsschutz; Düsseldorf: Zinkberatung, 1978
[51] Zinkberatung e.V.: Titanzink im Bauwesen; Düsseldorf, 1987

## Green roof

Materials, components, laying

Rooftop planting is primarily used on flat roofs. However, the advantages can also be exploited on pitched roofs, provided suitable measures are taken to ensure the roof covering, i.e. planting, cannot slide off the roof. As the roof pitch increases, these measures become less and less economic, and the appearance of the planting less and less natural. It is not possible to specify an exact limit, but roofs with a pitch of 15–20° can usually be landscaped without any problems.

We distinguish between two types of rooftop planting, both of which can include diverse types of wild or cultivated vegetation:

- extensive planting
- intensive planting

Extensive rooftop planting

This makes use of less demanding, short, drought-resistant plant varieties. The plant-bearing layer is thin, the water retention and drainage layer not especially effective. Extensive planting requires only minimum effort for its establishment and care; it is therefore particularly suitable for pitched roofs.

Intensive rooftop planting

The choice of plants for intensive planting includes soil cover, short and medium-height grasses, shrubs and bushes that are more demanding in terms of location and care.

Strong and dense-growing, evergreen or perennial plants are preferred. The plant-bearing layer is thicker and has a high level of nutrients. Intensive rooftop planting requires regular care and irrigation during dry periods. Pitched roofs with intensive planting are therefore complicated. Elementary intensive planting is possible, but more elaborate planting is uneconomic.

Layers

Rooftop planting varies according to the number, material and thickness of the individual layers required. The layers provide the plants with room for their roots, contain the necessary nutrients, retain water, drain excess water and seal the roof. Further functions may need to be satisfied, depending on the materials used; the total construction can therefore have the following functional layers:

- plant level
- plant-bearing layer
- filter sheet
- drainage layer
- protection mat
- root barrier
- separating layer
- waterproofing

The different layers are combined in practice according to two different goals: each layer can be allocated a single, particular function, or individual layers can fulfil more than one function.

With a carefully graded mixture of grain sizes, even a single layer can provide a nutrient-rich planting base that retains and drains water. The two-layer make-up includes a separate drainage layer but the plant-bearing layer is designed not to let fine particles be washed out. The three-layer arrangement is augmented by a filter sheet, which permits a different type of soil to be used.

A multi-layer make-up is generally considerably thicker in total. For extensive planting this can be 5–20 cm deep, and for elementary intensive planting must be at least 15 cm. A single layer is always thinner but should be at least 6 cm deep. [15, 23]

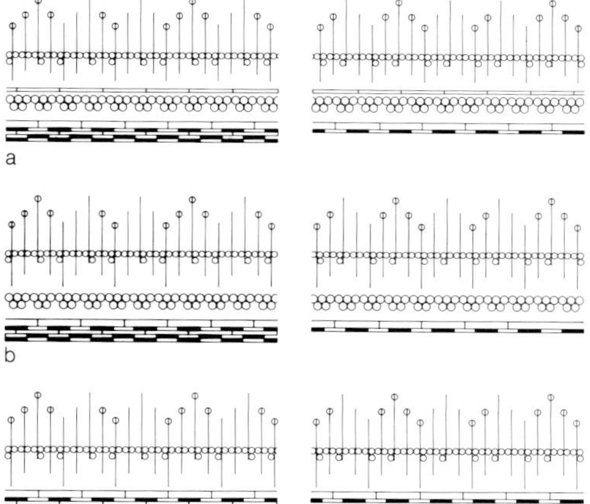


2.4.13.1 Green roof make-up: a three layers, b two layers, c single layer; left: with protection mat, root barrier and bituminous waterproofing; right: with protection mat and root-resistant synthetic waterproofing [23]

### Materials, components

Plants, plant-bearing layer, filter sheet, drainage layer, protection mat, root barrier, separating layer, waterproofing

#### Plants

Rooftop planting calls for plants that can cope with having limited space for their roots, and are not sensitive to extreme temperatures and severe fluctuations in supply of water and nutrients. When choosing the plants, the characteristics of the location (e.g. sunny/shady, facing north/south, high/low winds, protected/unprotected) should be taken into account.

Small plants with small leaves are preferred because less water evaporates from them. Seminiferous plants should be augmented by those that propagate asexually through offshoots, filial generations, bulblets or shoot division.

| | Light | | Water retention | | Nutrients | | layer thickness [mm] |
|---|---|---|---|---|---|---|---|
| | sunny | shady | low | high | low | high | |
| Moss varieties | + | + | + | - | + | - | 10 to 30 |
| Moss-sedum varieties | + | + | + | - | + | - | 20 to 80 |
| Moss-sedum-grass varieties | + | + | + | - | + | - | 30 to 60 |
| Sedum-grass varieties | + | - | + | - | + | - | 40 to 80 |
| Sedum-moss-herb varieties | + | + | + | - | + | + | 50 to 100 |
| Grass varieties | + | - | - | + | + | - | 60 to 100 |
| Sedum-grass-herb varieties | + | - | - | + | + | + | 70 to 150 |
| Grass-herb varieties | + | - | - | + | - | + | 80 to 200<br>120 to 350* |
| Grass-herb-bush varieties | + | + | - | + | + | + | >150* |

2.4.13.2 Requirements of various planting schemes for extensive and elementary intensive (*) rooftop planting in terms of local climate and properties of plant-bearing layer [06, 15, 23]

Mosses are always included in extensive rooftop planting. These drought-resistant plants are not fussy about location and, together with sedum varieties, are ideal for thin (≥ 1 cm) planting layers.

Combinations of plants on extensive rooftop landscapes are not static. They change according to the plants' suitability for the location, the changing seasons and weather conditions, and the composition of the soil. This last factor changes over the long term as a result of decaying vegetation, dust deposits and microorganisms such as fungi, slime fungi and bacteria. An evergreen roof is not possible with extensive planting.

Behaviour in fire

The soil of extensive and elementary intensive planting can dry out from time to time. Plants decaying on the surface, especially tall and dense grass-herb mixtures, bring with them a risk of fire. While intensive rooftop planting, with its thicker plant-bearing layer, is resistant to sparks and radiant heat ("hard roof covering"), extensive planting is sufficiently resistant to sparks and radiant heat only when the following conditions are met [15, 25]:

- plant-bearing layer ≥ 3 cm thick
- plant-bearing layer consists of ≥ 80% mineral constituents and ≤ 20% organic constituents
- low fire load due to short plants (e.g. grasses, sedum or erica varieties)
- clearance of ≥ 50 cm between planting and

roof penetrations (openings) or rooftop structures (with windows ≤ 80 cm from plant-bearing layer) guaranteed by providing paving flags or coarse gravel
- fire compartment walls and party walls extend ≥ 30 cm above plant-bearing layer, or strip ≥ 100 cm wide adjacent to walls kept clear of planting by laying paving flags or coarse gravel
- strip ≥ 100 cm wide adjacent to eaves of gable-end buildings to be kept clear of planting by using incombustible materials

If these conditions are not fulfilled, an analysis of the behaviour in fire must be provided in accordance with DIN 4102 part 7. [09] Tests must be carried out on the complete roof construction at a pitch of 15° with fully grown planting in dry conditions.

**Plant-bearing layer (substrate)**
The plant-bearing layer contains the necessary nutrients, retains water and drains excess water. It must fulfil considerably more demanding requirements than ground-based planting because the nutrient household is restricted by the layer's limited thickness. Furthermore, fluctuations in water content and temperature cannot be fully compensated for.
Within the entire green roof structure, this is the layer that governs the type of planting. It is therefore affected by many factors, such as depth, grain grading and shape, composition, pH value, volume of pores, water retention capacity and permeability, and must be carefully considered in relation to the local circumstances and desired planting.

We distinguish between the following types according to method of manufacture and composition [15, 23]:
- Loose materials

made from improved topsoil and/or subsoil
made from crushed minerals with a high proportion of organic substances
made from crushed minerals with a low proportion of organic substances
made from crushed minerals without organic substances (porous grain structure)
- Sheets

made from mineral wool
made from modified foams enriched with organic substances
- Mats

made from braided fibre and/or non-woven fabrics, also as permanent inlays in vegetation mats

Grain size and shape
The proportion of clay and silt (≤ 0.063 mm) to medium and coarse sand (2–4 mm) should be limited in plant-bearing layers. Owing to the higher flow velocities and washout on steeper roofs, the proportion of the smallest grain sizes should be lower than for shallower roofs.

| | Extensive planting | | Intensive planting |
|---|---|---|---|
| | single layer | multi-layer | not sensitive |
| Grain sizes ≤ 0.063 mm [% by wt] | ≤ 5 | ≤ 15 | ≤ 20 |
| Grain sizes ≥ 2 mm*, ≤ 4 mm** [% by wt] | ≥ 25** | 30 to 60* | ≤ 60* |
| Organic substances [% by wt] | ≤ 4.0 | ≤ 6.0 to ≤ 8.0 | ≤ 6.0 to ≤ 12.0 |
| pH value | 6.5 to 9.5 | 6.5 to 8.0 | 5.5 to 7.0 |
| Salts (for ecological reasons) [g/l] | ≤ 3.5 (≤ 1.0) | | ≤ 2.5 (≤ 1.0) |
| Air content [% by vol.] | ≥ 10 | ≥ 10 | ≥ 10 |
| Water retention [% by vol.] | ≥ 20 | ≥ 35 | ≥ 45 to ≤ 65 |
| Water permeability [mm/s] | ≥ 1.0 | ≥ 0.1 | ≥ 0.05 |

2.4.13.3 Requirements of extensive and intensive rooftop planting in terms of properties of plant-bearing layer (substrate) [15]

The largest grain sizes should be restricted to fine gravel/chippings; ≤ 19 mm for extensive planting and ≤ 16 mm for intensive planting. These grain sizes should be introduced in crushed form so that they create a framework. They must be frost-resistant. [15]

Organic substances
A minimum quantity of organic substances (humus, compost) is required in the plant-bearing layer to initiate the supply of nutrients (nitrogen, phosphorus) through mineralisation processes. However, these substances should be tightly controlled so that moderate decomposition and re-wetting after drying out remains guaranteed.
Care should be taken not to introduce any hazardous substances (seedling test). [23]

pH value
Generally, the pH for extensive planting should be neutral to weak alkaline, for elementary intensive planting weak acidic to neutral. With a higher proportion of organic substances, pH ≤ 6 should keep the biological degradation as low as possible.

Salts
For the sake of the plants, the amount of washed-out salts may not exceed the values given in table 2.4.13.3. Salt-sensitive plants cannot cope with a salt quantity > 1.0 g/l. A value of ≤ 1.0 g/l is also desirable in terms of environmental impact, irrespective of the type of planting. [15]

Lime
The quantity of readily soluble lime should be low to exclude washout and subsequent clogging of drainage channels. [23]

Water retention
With rooftop planting, the volume available for storing water is always very limited. Furthermore, the extreme conditions on the roof – the effects of the wind and (in comparison to ground-based vegetation) more severe heating – lead to increased evaporation. If the supply of water is exclusively in the plant-bearing layer, the plant roots will need more space and hence a relatively high water retention capacity in this layer. Its depth depends on the type of planting (extensive or intensive).
Waterlogging can be expected with a retention volume exceeding 65%. [15]

Water permeability
Plant-bearing layers must be sufficiently and permanently water-permeable so that excess water can drain through to the drainage layer, or – in a single-layer design – drain the water themselves. The required degree of water permeability depends on type of planting and roof pitch. As the roof pitch increases, the value given in table 2.4.13.3 can be reduced. [15, 23]

Loading assumptions
Plant-bearing layers saturated with water exhibit densities ranging from 0.7 to 1.9 g/cm³. In the interests of achieving a low load but maximum depth, low density is desirable. The minimum load in the dried-out condition must be taken into account for uplift due to wind suction.

**Filter sheet**
The filter layer prevents fine particles seeping from the plant-bearing layer (fertile soil) into the drainage layer. A filter layer may consist of loose material, sheets or non-woven fabrics ("filter mats"). With coarsely graded loose material in the plant-bearing layer, a drainage layer of finely graded loose material itself acts as a filter. No-fines materials of comparatively fine-pore drainage sheets function similarily.

| Component Material | Material | Grain size [mm] | Depth [mm] | Width [mm] | Length [mm] | Density[1) ] Bulk density[1)] [g/cm³] | Form of supply |
|---|---|---|---|---|---|---|---|
| Loose soil mixture | soil mixture with mineral/organic enrichment | | | | | 1.6 to 1.9 | loose material |
| Loose mixture with high proportion of organic substances | peat-minerals mixture | 2–11 (expanded shale/clay, crushed) | | | | 1.0 to 1.3 | 50 l sacks on pallets, 1 m³ bags, silo, loose |
| | bark humus-minerals mixture | 4–8 (expanded shale/clay, crushed) | | | | 1.1 to 1.3 | |
| Loose mixture with low proportion of organic substances | lava mixture | ≤ 4.4 to 8 | ≤ 150 | | | 1.5 to 1.8 | 50 l sacks on pallets, 1/1.5 m³ bags, silo, loose |
| | pumice-lava mixture | 2 to 12 | | | | 1.3 to 1.6 | |
| | expanded clay/shale mixture | 2 to 11 | | | | 1.0 to 1.3 | |
| | slag mixture | ≤ 11 | | | | 0.7 to 1.5 | |
| | clay brick-pumice mixture | ≤ 12 | | | | 1.6 to 1.8 | |
| Loose material with porous grain structure | lava mixture | 1 to 12 | | | | 1.1 to 1.4 | 50 l sacks on pallets, 1/1.5 m³ bags, silo, loose |
| | pumice, washed | 1 to 12 | | | | 0.7 to 0.8 | |
| | pumice, unwashed | 1 to 12 | | | | 1.1 to 1.2 | |
| | expanded clay, crushed | 1 to 8 | | | | 0.7 to 0.8 | |
| | expanded shale, crushed | 1 to 11 | | | | 0.7 to 0.8 | |
| | clay brick, crushed | 1 to 12 | | | | 1.0 to 1.3 | |
| Sheets enriched with mineral substances | mineral wool | | 20, 40, 60 | 600 | 900 | 0.8 to 1.0 | sheets on pallets |
| | polyurethane foam, enriched | | 60 | 500 1000 | 1000 | 0.8 to 1.0 | |
| Mats enriched with mineral substances | braided fibres | | 15 to 35 | 1000 | ≤ 30 m | 2.5 to 3.5[2)] | mats in rolls, as constituent of vegetation mats in rolls |
| | natural fibres | | | | | 2.0 to 5.0[2)] | |
| | non-woven fabric | | ≥ 12 | | | 2.0 to 3.0[2)] | |

[1)] at max. water absorption, [2)] g/cm² for total thickness of layer

2.4.13.4 Plant-bearing layer (substrate); dimensions and weights [15, 23]

| | Loose materials mixtures | | | Loose materials | Sheets | Mats |
|---|---|---|---|---|---|---|
| | soils enriched with mineral and organic substances | minerals with high proportion of organic substances | minerals with low proportion of organic substances | minerals with porous grain structure | mineral wool and foams enriched with mineral substances | fibres enriched with mineral substances |
| Properties: | | | | | | |
| Loading assumption[1)] | medium to high | low | low to medium | very low to medium | low | very low |
| Water retention | medium to high | high to very high | medium to high | low to medium | low to very high | low |
| Air content[1)] | low to medium | low to medium | low to high | high | medium to high | high |
| Water permeability | low to medium | medium to high | medium to high | very high | high | very high |
| Stability | medium | low | medium to high | high | high | high |
| Re-wetting capacity[2)] | medium | low to medium | high | very high | very high | very high |
| Nutrients content | medium to high | high | low to medium | low | low to high | very low |
| Special features | Tendency towards hardening, silting up, waterlogging<br>Change of state at higher water content | Sagging<br>Tendency towards waterlogging, acidification Shrinkage and erosion upon drying out | Forms mulch layer upon soaking<br>Low risk of erosion | Self-draining, risk of drying out<br>Wind erosion of light dry minerals | Tendency towards temporary drying out and waterlogging<br>Risk of wind erosion during installation | Extremely thin; fixing at edges/ corners and on steep roofs<br>Suitable as erosion protection in windy locations (precultivated) |
| Main applications: | | | | | | |
| Extensive planting | ± | – | + | + | ± | + |
| Elementary intensive planting | + | + | + | + | + | ± |
| Three-layer make-up | + | + | + | – | – | ± |
| Two-layer make-up | – | – | + | – | + | + |
| Single-layer make-up | – | – | ± | + | ± | + |
| Planting on steep roofs (> 20°) | ± | – | + | ± | ± | + |

[1)] at max. water absorption, [2)] after drying out

2.4.13.5 Comparative review of properties and main applications of plant-bearing layers (substrates): + suitable, ± limited suitability, - unsuitable [23]

Usually, however, the more finely graded plant-bearing layer requires its own filter layer above the more coarsely graded drainage layer. Non-woven fabrics are produced for this – normally 0.7–2.5 mm thick, unless special structural requirements call for a thicker material. [23] These non-woven fabrics are made from the fibres of a number of common materials, e.g. polyamide (PA), polyacrylonitrile (PAN), polyester (PET), polyethylene (PE) and polypropylene (PP), glass fibres or rockwool.

Water permeability
The water permeability of the filter layer must be at least equal to that of the plant-bearing layer. The permeability of non-woven fabric decreases by about 50% over time due to deposits of fine particles. [23, 24] Accordingly, upon installation the water permeability of non-woven fabric must be at least twice the figure required.

Filter size
The effective mesh size of a non-woven fabric should be < 0.2 mm. This ensures that 90% of the particles of the plant-bearing layer (standard test soil) are retained by the filter.
Despite this small mesh size, roots should still be able to pass through the non-woven fabric. The fibres of the fabric must be able to deform so that root growth is not hindered. [15, 23]

Durability
Highly resistant non-woven fabrics (except glass fleece materials and rockwool mats) must be covered by the plant-bearing layer (or some form of temporary protection) within two months to protect them from ultraviolet radiation; less resistant materials within one or two weeks.

Weight
The weight per unit area should be at least 100 g/m²; as a rule it lies between 100 and 200 g/m². A heavier filter sheet may be necessary on steep green roofs (> 20°) to cope with requirements regarding tensile strength and extensibility. [15]

Form of supply
Non-woven filter fabrics are generally supplied in rolls 50–100 m long, 2–3 m wide. [23]

**Drainage layer**
Excess water in the green roof escapes quickly via the drainage layer. Mats, sheets and loose materials with coarse pores but a maximum total pore volume, or profiled mats/sheets with large interconnected voids, are suitable as drainage layers. The weight of the drainage layer should be kept to a minimum, but it must be sufficiently durable and stable in order to maintain its thickness, and hence the total volume of draining voids, under the weight of plants and soil.

Water permeability
The perpendicular water permeability (down the slope) should be ≥ 3 mm/s. The quantity of run-off water that the drainage layer must accommodate, if surface water is to be restricted to a minimum, is calculated as follows [15]:

$$Q = \frac{A \cdot \psi \cdot q}{b}$$

where:
Q = quantity of run-off water [l/sm] in drainage layer
A = surface area to be drained [m²]
y = drainage coefficient (table 2.4.13.6)
q = max. quantity of rainfall (DIN 1986) or local quantity of rainfall [l/sm²] (see "Drainage – Installation")
b = width of run-off surface [m]

| Thickness of layers (d) [cm] | > 50 | > 25 to 50 | > 15 to 25 | > 10 to 15 | > 6 to 10 | > 4 to 6 | > 2 to 4 |
|---|---|---|---|---|---|---|---|
| Drainage coefficient (ψ) | 0.1 | 0.2 | 0.3 | 0.4 | 0.5 | 0.6 | 0.7 |

2.4.13.6 Drainage coefficients (DIN 1986 part 2) for water-saturated layer make-up (d) for rainfall quantity q = 0.03 l/sm² and for roof pitches up to 15°

As the roof pitch increases, so more and more water drains away on the surface, and the flow velocity within the layers increases, meaning that the drainage layer can be thinner or even omitted. The increased surface water is then intercepted by coarse-grained loose materials around the edges of the roof (eaves, trough) and drained from there. [23]

Water retention
It is advantageous for the plants if the drainage layer, besides its draining function, also stores water and provides additional room for the roots of the plants. This is achieved with a large total pore volume but small pore diameters. In addition, the drainage layer must exhibit capillarity so that retained water can rise into the plant-bearing layer.

However, as the drainage function should not be impaired by these other functions, there should be a high pore volume – but graduated in terms of pore size. [23]

pH value, salts, lime
As the roots of the plants can penetrate the drainage layer, the conditions for their growth should be the same here as in the plant-bearing layer. The figures regarding pH value, salts and lime content are therefore the same for both layers.
The drainage layer can be made of various materials and components or combinations thereof: loose materials, sheets and mats.

Loose materials
Good water permeability and a high water retention capacity can be achieved with a corresponding choice of material and appropriate grading. It is sensible to choose a larger grain size for the drainage layer than for the plant-bearing layer. The grading depends on the depth of the layer:

- between 2/8 and 2/12 mm for depths of 40–100 mm
- between 4/8 and 8/16 mm for depths of 100–200 mm
- between 4/8 and 16/32 mm for depths > 200 mm

The proportion of the smallest particles (≤ 0.063 mm) should be ≤ 5% by wt to rule out the possibility of impairing the drainage and clogging roof gullies.

The large volume of voids means that the drainage material contains a lot of plant roots. So that the structure and position of the loose material remains stable from the very start, the grain sizes creating a framework should be of crushed material. For the same reason, they must also be frost-resistant.
Nevertheless, they can only be used on moderate roof pitches (gravel: ≤ 5°; chippings: up to 15–20°).

Sheets
Flat sheets of thermally or bituminously bonded foam beads exhibit a pore content of up to 98%, but only one third of this volume is made up of drainage voids (no-fines pores), so they have limited water retention capacity. Profiled sheets of rigid or foamed plastic have chambers on the upper surface, in which water can collect, plus large-volume continuous voids on the underside to drain the water.
These usually interlock with rebated or tongue and groove edges and provide good mechanical protection for the waterproofing.

The sheets must be sufficiently stable. The maximum permissible creep under load is 20% of the sheet thickness (for thicknesses ≤ 50 mm), or 10 mm (for thicknesses > 50 mm). [15]
As on an upside-down roof, drainage sheets with an acknowledged theoretical thermal resistance value (R) can be employed as additional thermal insulation. [15]

| Component | Material | Grain size [mm] | Depth [mm] | Width [mm] | Length [mm] | Drainage voids [% by vol.] | Density[1] Bulk density[1] [g/cm³] | Remarks | Form of supply |
|---|---|---|---|---|---|---|---|---|---|
| Loose materials | gravel, chippings | 4 to 16 | | | | 25 to 40 | 1.6 to 1.8 | no-fines texture | loose materials, bags, sometimes (small) on pallets, sacks on pallets, |
| | lava | 1 to 12 | | | | 38 to 46 | 1.1 to 1.4 | | |
| | pumice, unwashed | 2 to 12 | | | | 15 to 24 | 1.1 to 1.2 | | |
| | pumice, washed | 2 to 12 | | | | 30 to 38 | 0.7 to 0.8 | | |
| | expanded clay, crushed | 2 to 8 | | | | 34 to 36 | 0.6 to 0.8 | | |
| | expanded shale, crushed | 2 to 11 | | | | 40 to 42 | 0.6 to 0.8 | | |
| | broken clay bricks | 4 to 16 | | | | 35 to 41 | 1.0 to 1.1 | | |
| | expanded clay, uncrushed | 4 to 16 | | | | 45 to 55 | 0.5 to 0.6 | | |
| | expanded shale, uncrushed | 4 to 16 | | | | 40 to 50 | 0.6 to 0.7 | | |
| | foamed glass | 10 to 25 | | | | | 0.25 to 0.3 | | |
| | slag, crushed | up to 32 | | | | | ~ 0.9 | | |
| Sheets | foam beads, thermal or bituminous bonding; polystyrene (EPS) | | 50 to 65 | 1000 | 500 to 750 | 30 to 35 | 0.03 to 0.04 | flat, no-fines texture | sheets on pallets |
| | foamed plastic; polystyrene (XPS) | | 50, 60, 65, 75, 100, 120 | 1000 | 750, 1000 1250 | 6 to 7 | 0.27 to 0.38[2] | foamed plastic; profiled, rebated edges; covered with textile for root retention | |
| | rigid plastic; PE, uPVC, PS | | 25, 40, 60, to 180 | 1000 | 1000, 2000 | 19 to 21[3] | 0.4 to 0.5[2] | profiled, filled with loose material | |
| Mats | textured non-woven fabric | | ~ 10 | ≤ 2000 | 20 m | 53 to 58 | 0.56 to 0.75 | also with ribs on underside | rolls |
| | plastic nodules; polyolefins (PE), rubber | | (12, 20) | 1000 to 2000 | 10 to 20 m | 39 to 41[3] | 0.18 to 0.19 | profiled, top surface laminated with braided fibres | |
| | non-woven fabric polyamide (PA) | | (10, 22) | 1000 | 20 m | 89 to 91 | 0.1 to 0.23 | tangle-woven, laminated on one or both sides | |
| | foam flakes, bonded; polyethylene (PE) | | 35 | 1000 | 20 m | 35 to 40 | 0.16 to 0.17 | top surface laminated with non-woven fabric, underside grooved | |

2.4.13.7 Drainage materials and components; dimensions and weights: [1] at max. water absorption, [2] with build-up, [3] drainage void at top [15, 23, 28, 34]

| | Loose materials | Mats | Flat sheets | Profiled sheets |
|---|---|---|---|---|
| Properties/measures: | | | | |
| Loading assumption (saturated) | low to high | low to medium | low | low to high |
| Water retention | medium to very high | low to high | low | medium to high |
| Structural stability | very high | medium to very high | high | very high |
| Positional stability | low/very high | high | high | very high |
| Thickness of layer [mm] | ≥ 40 | 10–35 | 50–65 | 25–180 |
| Special filter sheet required | yes, except with corresponding grading | no | yes | yes, except with complete covering of foamed elements |
| Protection mat required underneath | yes | no | no | only in special cases |
| Separating layer required | no | only in special cases | frequently | frequently |
| Root penetration capacity | very intensive | moderately intensive | limited | only in some areas |
| Special features | Production- or source-related fluctuations of individual properties | Loading or traffic capacity depends on product | Can be loaded | Rigid grid due to given element dimensions |
| Applications: | | | | |
| Extensive planting | + | + | ± | ± |
| Elementary intensive planting | + | + | + | + |
| Three-layer make-up | + | – | + | + |
| Two-layer make-up | + | + | – | – |
| Planting on steep roofs (> 20°) | + | ± | – | ± |

2.4.13.8 Comparative review of properties and main applications of materials for drainage layers: + suitable, ± limited suitability, – unsuitable [23]

Mats

Mats achieve the necessary drainage performance with a smaller thickness (10-35 mm) and a very low weight. However, they can creep under load, which reduces their volume and hence also their drainage effect. Mats provide good mechanical protection for the layers underneath. Apart from the textured non-woven mats, drainage mats store only little (plastic nodules, foam flakes) or no (braided fibres) water.

**Protection mat**

The waterproofing and hence also the root barrier must be permanently protected from damage. Knocks and impacts during construction are a source of damage, as are adjoining layers made from or containing angular materials.

Depending on the degree of protection necessary, non-woven fabrics, films, mats or sheets can be used. Even with just little chance of damage, a non-woven fabric weighing ≥ 300 g/m² should be selected. [15]

The possibility of smooth films acting as a slip plane must be taken into account.

| Material | T [mm] | W [m] | L [m] | Mass per unit area [g/m²] | Notes |
|---|---|---|---|---|---|
| Separating/protective film: | | | | | |
| synthetic fibres | 2 (4) | 2 | 100 | 300 | with needle-punched back. film, bitumen-compatible; supplied in rolls |
| Protection mats: | | | | | |
| synthetic fibres | 5 | 2 | 25 | 700 | with needle-punched back. film, bitumen-compatible; supplied in rolls |
| polypro-pylene (PP) | 5 | 2 | 50 | 300 to 1 000 | rotproof, water retention capacity 3–8 l/m²; supplied in rolls |
| polyurethane rubber | 6 | 1.25 | 10 | 4 500 | supplied in rolls |
| Protection sheets: | | | | | |
| synthetic fibres | 5 | 2 | 1 | 1 400 | one-side rubberised, rotproof, bitumen-compatible, water retention capacity 2 l/m² |
| polyurethane rubber | 8 | 1.15 | 1.25 | 6 750 | |
| rubber granulate | 10 | 1 | 1 | 9 000 | pressed, bitumen-compatible, nodules on top surface |

2.4.13.9 Protective layers; dimensions and weights

**Root barrier**

The waterproofing of a green roof is at risk of being damaged by the roots of the plants. This is also true for extensive rooftop planting because we can never rule out that the seeds of plants with dangerously rigorous root growth – carried on the wind or by animals – will take root on the roof. If leaks occur, inspection will be almost impossible, and repairs extremely complicated and expensive. It must therefore be ensured that roots can never penetrate the waterproofing layer.
Prevention of root penetration can be achieved either by providing a root-resistant waterproofing layer or by including an additional root barrier.

There is currently no finalised German nor European standard for testing the root resistance of waterproofing and root barrier materials. However, a German agricultural research centre has published a "Method for investigating the root resistance of root barriers". This specifies an outdoor test spanning four years in which the seams should also remain secure. Alternatively, a two-year test can be carried out in a climate-controlled greenhouse. According to this method, various types of PVC, ECB and EPDM sheets, and special bitumen sheets with a metal foil inlay have proved to be effective root barriers. However, the results of these tests are only applicable to sheets produced and joined with the same materials and methods. [14]

Besides the properties of the material, the root resistance also depends on the thickness of the sheet, the method of joining the sheets and the quality of the workmanship.

**Root-resistant bitumen sheets**

| Component | Material | Jointing |
|---|---|---|
| awa root barrier WS-CU S5 | built-up felt roofing/CU copper foil inlay (CU 0.1 mm) 5.0 mm | felt torching |
| Vedaflor WS root-resistant waterproofing | 5.0 mm | |
| Bauder Plant E special board natural slate | PYE elastomer-bitumen with slate chippings 5.0 mm | felt torching |
| awa WS-PYE PV 250 S5 | PYE/PV elastomer-bitumen polyester non-woven fabric inlay 50 mm | felt torching |
| Polyflor-PV | (PV 200 g/m²) with slate chippings 5.2 mm | |
| SKBit 105 PV 200 root barrier | (PV 200 g/m²) 5.0 mm | |
| Vedaflor root barrier WS-X | | |
| dkd Elastik WS root barrier | PYE/PV elastomer-bitumen polyester non-woven fabric composite backing 5.2 mm | felt torching |
| Axtertop Jardin | PYE/PV elastomer-bitumen polyester non-woven fabric 4.2 mm | felt torching |
| Glaser Bituverde WF FLL | 5.2 mm | |
| Sopralene Jardin 200 | | |
| Grünplast 2000 | PYE/PV combination elastomer-bitumen polyester non-woven fabric combination backing 4.0 mm, 5.2 mm | felt torching |
| Kebu Original root barrier PV | 5.2 mm | |
| Bauder plant board | PYE/CU elastomer-bitumen copper foil inlay 5.0 mm | felt torching |
| Hassodritt CU | (CU 0.1 mm) 5.0 mm | |
| Kebu root barrier CU | 5.0 mm | |
| Polyflor CU | 5.2 mm | |
| SKBit 105 CU 0.1 root barrier | (CU 0.1 mm) 5.0 mm | |
| Vedaflor root barrier | PYE/PV + CU elastomer-bitumen polyester non-woven fabric inlay copper vapour deposition both sides | felt torching |
| WS-E | 4.2 mm | |
| WS-I | surfaced with blue-green slate chippings 5.2 mm | |
| Casali Eradix 40200 | PYP/PV plastomer-bitumen polyester non-woven fabric 4.0 mm | felt torching |
| Polygum Roof-garden T Mec | 4.0 mm | |

**Root-resistant bitumen-synthetic sheets**

| Component | Material | Jointing |
|---|---|---|
| O.C.Plan type 2000 | ECB/GV ethylene-copolymer bitumen glass fleece coating 2.0 mm | hot gas welding |
| Binné M | ECB/GV ethylene-copolymer bitumen glass fleece inlay 2.0 mm | hot gas welding |
| Carisma CI | 2.0 mm | |
| O.C.Plan type 3000 | 2.0 mm | |
| O.C.Plan type 4000 | ECB/GV + PV ethylene-copolymer bitumen glass fleece inlay and polyester non-woven fabric coating 3.0 mm | hot gas welding |
| Vedaplan MF | OCB/GV + GG olefin-copolymer bitumen glass fleece and glass mat inlay 2.3 mm | hot gas welding |

**Root-resistant synthetic sheets and coatings**

| Component | Material | Jointing |
|---|---|---|
| Alkorplan | PVC-P plasticised PVC incompatible with bit. | solvent hot gas bonding |
| Typ 35036 | 1.5 mm | |
| Typ 35070 | 1.2 mm | |
| Plastoplan root barrier | 1.0 mm | |
| Optigrün root barrier | 0.8 mm | solvent bonding and seam sealing |
| Optima root barrier | 0.8 mm | |

| Component | Material | Jointing |
|---|---|---|
| Rhenofol C | 1.5 mm | solvent bonding, splayed central sheet edges (T-joints) |
| Trocal<br>type TB<br>type T (opaque)<br><br>type T (translucent) | <br>1.5 mm<br>cloudy translucency,<br>1.5 mm<br>cloudy transparency,<br>1.5 mm | hot gas welding |
| Ursuplast-Folie<br><br><br>type LB<br><br>type W | PVC-P<br>plasticised PVC, (in)-compatible with bit.<br>black,<br>0.8 mm<br>brown,<br>0.8 mm | solvent bonding |
| Trocal<br>type A | PVC-P<br>plasticised PVC<br>compatible with bit.<br>1.5 mm | hot gas welding |
| Wolfin-IB waterproofing sheet | black,<br>1.5 mm | solvent bonding (flat lap areas), hot gas welding (corners and multiple laps), sealed with liquid film (seams) |
| Alkorplan<br>type 35072 | PVC-P/GV<br>plasticised PVC, incompatible with bit.<br>glass fleece inlay<br>1.2 mm | solvent hot gas bonding |
| Rhenofol CG | 1.2 mm | solvent bonding |
| Sarnafil<br>waterproofing sh.<br>G-438-10<br>G-471-24<br>G-476-15 | <br><br>1.0 mm<br>2.4 mm<br>1.5 mm | hot gas welding |
| Trocal<br>type SGmA | <br>1.2 mm | solvent bonding secured with PVC solution (seams), injected with PVC (T-joints) |
| Gekaplan GF 15 | PVC-P/GW<br>plasticised PVC, (in)-compatible with bit.<br>glass cloth inlay<br>1.5 mm | solvent hot gas bonding |
| Alkorplan<br>types 35038 | PVC-P/GV + GG<br>plasticised PVC<br>compatible with bit.<br>glass fleece and glass mat inlay<br>1.2 mm | |
| Bauder Thermoplan SF 15 | PVC-P/PW<br>plasticised PVC<br>incompatible with bit.<br>polyester textile inlay<br>1.2 mm | solvent bonding and seam sealing |
| Cosmofin FG | PVC-P/PW<br>plasticised PVC<br>incompatible with bit.<br>polyester textile inlay<br>1.2 mm | |
| Wepelen<br>waterproofing sh. | PE<br>polyethylene, modified<br>0.5 mm | solvent bonding |
| Alkorplan<br>type 35090 | PE-C/PW<br>polyethylene, chlorinated, polyester textile coating<br>1.5 mm | solvent hot gas bonding |
| Evalon<br>waterproofing sheet | EVA-PVC<br>ethylene vinyl acetate with PVC<br>1.2 mm | solvent hot gas bonding and seam sealing |
| Bauder Thermoplan T TL | FPO<br>polyolefins, flexible<br>1.2 mm | hot gas welding |
| Cutiflex 300 | FPO/GV<br>polyolefins, flexible<br>glass fleece inlay<br>2.0 mm | |
| Sarnafil<br>TG 66-15<br>TG 66-20 | (PE and PP)<br>1.5 mm<br>2.0 mm | |
| Trocal Futura | FPO/GG<br>polyolefins, flexible<br>glass mat inlay<br>1.5 mm | |
| Sarnafil<br>TG 55-20 | FPO/GW<br>polyolefins, flexible<br>(PE and PP)<br>glass cloth inlay<br>2.0 mm | |
| Sarnafil<br>TS 77-12 | FPO/GV + PV<br>polyolefins, flexible<br>(PE and PP), fleece inlay with polyester non-woven fabric inlay<br>1.2 mm | |
| DLW<br>root-resistant waterproofing sh.<br>type EN | EPDM<br>ethylene-propylene-diene copolymer<br>(elastomer-rubber)<br>1.4 mm | vulcanising |
| Prelasti-EPDM | 1.2 mm | |
| Resistit-Perfekt R | 1.2 mm | |
| SG-tan<br>waterproofing sh. | 1.5 mm | vulcanising with hot bond. agent |
| Resitec GD | EPDM/GG<br>ethylene-propylene-diene copolymer<br>glass mat inlay<br>2.0 mm | vulcanising |
| Evalastic | EPDM-PP<br>ethylene-propylene-diene copolymer<br>with polypropylene<br>1.2 mm | hot gas welding |
| DBV<br>synthetic rubber sheet | EPDM-IIR<br>ethylene-propylene-diene copolymer with butyl rubber | vulcanising |
| Büfa<br>Oldoroof<br>(2-part resin) | PUR<br>polyurethane<br>liquid seal<br>2.0–3.0 mm | injection (seamless) |
| Kemperol<br>V 210<br>(3-part resin) | FUP<br>Polyester resin, flexible<br>polyester fleece inlay<br>(PV 165 up to 200 g/m²)<br>1.5–2.0 mm | rolling (seamless) |

2.4.13.10 Root-resistant sheets – bitumen, bitumen-synthetic materials, synthetic materials and coatings; materials, dimensions, jointing [13, 14, 28, 32]; test results according to various testing centres using the FLL method [13, 14, 32]

**Separating layer**

If the materials of neighbouring layers are chemically incompatible, a separating layer is required. In particular circumstances, polyethylene (PE) film and non-woven polypropylene (PP) fabric have proved to be suitable.
The possibility of smooth films acting as a slip plane must be taken into account.

| Material | Thk. [mm] | W [m] | L [m] | Mass per unit area [kg/m²] | Remarks |
|---|---|---|---|---|---|
| Film: | | | | | |
| Polyethylene (PE) | 0.15 to 0.30 | 2 to 4<br>8 (12) | 30 to 50<br>25 | 0.18 | compatible with bitumen, supplied in rolls<br>compatible with bit., supplied in large sheets or folded in rolls |
| Non-woven fabric: | | | | | |
| Polypropylene (PP) | 2 | 2 | 50 (100) | up to 0.25 | compatible with bitumen, strength class III supplied in rolls |

2.4.13.11 Separating layers; dimensions and weights

**Waterproofing**

Waterproofing materials can be divided into two main groups:
- bituminous sheets
- high-polymer synthetic sheets

Bitumen is made from crude oil. The fully synthetic sheets are based on crude oil, coal, natural gas, lime, common salt, water etc.

Bituminous sheets
(see “Layers – Asphalt shingles”)

High-polymer synthetic sheets
The main constituents of these plastics are carbon, hydrogen and oxygen. High-polymer plastics are produced fully synthetically through the bonding of small molecules (monomers) to form macromolecules (polymers).
We distinguish between thermoplastic and elastic materials, according to their mechanical and thermal behaviour.
In terms of method of manufacture we distinguish between calendered, extruded and carded sheets.

- Calendering

The granulate is rolled out to a thickness of about 0.6 mm between hot rolls (nips). If thicker material is required, several layers are produced and then bonded together thermally.

| Backing and DIN No. | Bitumen roofing felt and DIN No. | | glass fleece base 52 143 52 128 | metal foil inlay 18 190 | for water-proofing 52 130 | built-up felt 52 131 | polymer-base felt 52 132 | polymer-base built-up felt 52 133 |
|---|---|---|---|---|---|---|---|---|
| | char. values of sheets | [μ] | 10 000 to 80 000 | 100 000 | 100 000 | 100 000 | 20 000 to 30 000 (PYE) 50 000 to 60 000 (PYP) | |
| | | thermal [°C] | 0 to +70 | 0 to +70 | 0 to +70 | 0 to +70 | -25 to +100 (PYE) -15 to +130 (PYP) | |
| | ten. strength [N/5 cm] | elongation [%] | | | | | | |
| glass fleece 52 141 | II: 400 ⊥: 300 | II: 2 ⊥: 2 | V 13 DIN 52 143 | | | V 60 S 4 | | |
| glass fabric 18 194 (fabric 220 g/m²) | II: 1000 ⊥: 1000 | II: 2 ⊥: 2 | | G 220 D | G 200 DD | G 200 S 4 G 200 S 5 | PYE-G 220 DD PYP-G 200 DD | PYE-G200S4 PYP-G200S4 PYE-G200S5 PYP-G200S5 |
| jute fabric | II: 600 ⊥: 500 | II: 3.5 ⊥: 5 | | J 300 D | J 300 DD | J 300 S 4 J 300 S 5 | PYE-J 300 DD PYP-J 300 DD | PYE-J300S4 PYP-J300S4 PYE-J300S5 PYP-J300S5 |
| polyester fleece 18 192 | II: 800 ⊥: 800 | II: 40 ⊥: 40 | | | PV 200 DD | PV 200 S 5 | PYE-PV200DD PYE-PV200DD | PYE-PV200S5 PYP-PV200S5 |
| felt 52 117 | II: 300 ⊥: 250 | II: 2 ⊥: 2 | R 500 DIN 52 128 | | | | | |
| | II: 200 ⊥: 150 | II: 2 ⊥: 2 | R 333 DIN 52 128 | | | | | |
| aluminium 0.1; 0.2 mm | II: 350 ⊥: 350 | II: 5 ⊥: 5 | AL 0.1 (vapour barr. only) | | | Al 0.1 S4 DIN 52 131 (vapour barrier) | | |
| aluminium 0.2 mm 18 195 pt 2 cl. 3.8 | II: 500 ⊥: 500 | II: 5 ⊥: 5 | | Al 0.2 D | | | | |
| copper 0.1 mm 18 195 pt 2 cl. 3.8 | II: 500 ⊥: 500 | II: 5 ⊥: 5 | | Cu 0.1 D | | | | |
| aluminium 0.1 mm & glass fleece 52 141 | II: 700 ⊥: 500 | II: 2.5 ⊥: 2.5 | | | | Al 0.1 + V 60 S 4 DIN 52 131 (vapour barrier) | | |
| aluminium 0.08 mm & glass fabric 18 191 | II: 1000 ⊥: 1000 | II: 3 ⊥: 3 | | | | Al 0.08 +G 200 S 5 DIN 52 131 (vapour barrier) | | |

2.4.13.12 Waterproofing sheets made of bitumen; make-up, properties: II parallel with sheet direction, ⊥ perpendicular to sheet direction, μ water vapour diffusion resistance factor, PYE/PYP polymer-modified bitumen elastomer/plastomer, modified [01, 16, 17]

| Thermoplastic | Elastomer |
|---|---|
| linear arrangement of thread molecules | wide mesh with three-dimensional interlinking |
| hard to soft elastic to plastic | rubber elastic (insensitive to blunt point loads, high resilience) |
| readily melted insensitive to temperatures up to 70–100°C | cannot be melted insensitive to temperatures up to 200°C |
| welding | bonding, vulcanising |
| softener creates rubber-elastic behaviour | – |
| readily soluble | limited solubility |

2.4.13.13 Thermoplastics and elastomers; properties

• Extruding
In this method appropriate sheet dies can be used to produce films of any thickness. These films can be reinforced with fibres in the form of fabrics or textiles, or laminated with non-woven fabrics or cloths to bind production-related stresses.

• Carding
The viscous plastic paste is spread over a backing material (e.g. glass fleece or polyester lattice fabric) and subsequently bonded in a hot-air tunnel. This method of manufacture enables high-quality films completely free from inherent stresses to be produced. Carded sheets can be made in two, three or even more layers.

Material compatibility
Care must always be taken to ensure that individual materials are compatible with all the other materials in the roof construction. All synthetic waterproofing sheets, apart from plasticised PVC intended for non-bituminous laying, are resistant to hot bitumen. They can all be attacked by substances containing tar or timber preservatives containing oil or solvents. The migration of the less interlinked softeners can be promoted through contact with bitumen and plastic foam (polystyrene) in the case of "softened" thermoplastics (e.g. plasticised PVC, softener content usually 20-40% [28]). If incompatible materials have to be used together, additional measures will be required (see "Separating layer" above).

| | DIN | Tearing resistance | | Elongation at tear | |
|---|---|---|---|---|---|
| | | to DIN 53354, 53455, 53504 | | | |
| | | [N/mm²] | | [%] | |
| | | long. | trans. | long. | trans. |
| Thermoplastics: | | | | | |
| ethylene copolymer bitumen (ECB) | 16 732 | >3 to >3.5 | >3 to >3.5 | 400 to 600 | 400 to 600 |
| ethylene vinylacetate (EVA) | – | >4 to >10 | >4 to >10 | 300 to 500[1] | 300 to 500[1] |
| polyethylene, chlorinated (PE-C) | – | >12 | >12 | >330 | >330 |
| polyisobutylene (PIB) | 16 731 | >4.5 | >4.5 | 350[2] | 350[2] |
| plasticised polyvinyl chloride (PVC-P) | 16 730 | >10 to >18 | >10 to >18 | >250 to >360 | >250 to >360 |
| Elastomers: | | | | | |
| polychloroprene rubber (CR) | 7864 | >8.5 | >6.9 | 280 | 280 |
| chlorosulphonated polyethylene (CSM) | 16 733 | >13 | >15 | >550 | >800 |
| ethylene-propylenediene rubber (EPDM) | 7864 | >5 to >9.8 | >5 to >9.8 | >350 to 540 | >350 to 540 |
| isoprene-isobutene rubber (IIR) | 7864 | 7.5 to 8.0 | 7.5 to 8.0 | >450 | >450 |
| nitrile-butyl rubber (NBR) | 7864 | 8.0 | 8.0 | 280 | 280 |

[1] with fabric: > 15; [2] with fleece: > 50

2.4.13.14 Synthetic waterproofing sheets; materials and properties [02]

## Laying

Waterproofing and root barrier, protection mat, drainage layer, filter sheet, plant-bearing layer, plants, additional measures, details, maintenance and repair

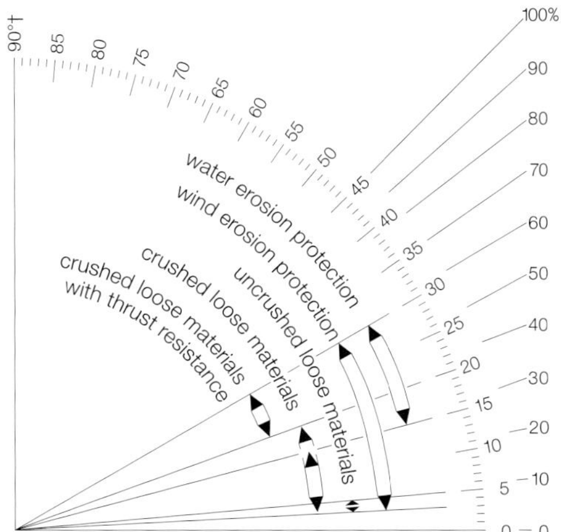


2.4.13.15 Roof pitches

### Waterproofing and root barrier

Sheets acting as waterproofing and root barriers must be laid over the entire roof surface, including the various edge zones. In doing so, all joints must be made resistant to root penetration. It is not sufficient to lay the root barrier below just the planted areas only.
The waterproofing sheets present an upper vapour-proof termination and therefore form a continuous vapour barrier.
It is advisable to employ an additional root barrier only when its dynamic friction on the waterproofing sheets is sufficiently high or when the roof is not too steep (about ≤ 10°).

### Bituminous sheets

A waterproofing layer made from bitumen roofing felt must comprise at least two layers. At least one of these layers must include a backing of jute or glass-fibre fabric, or be made of non-woven polyester fibres.

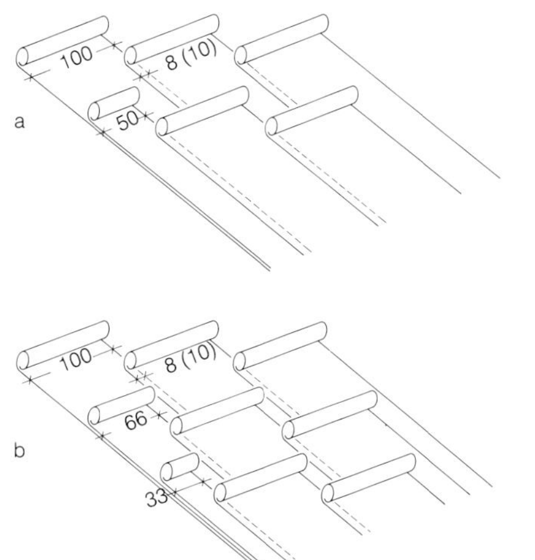


2.4.13.16 Standard laps [cm]: a two layers, b three layers

Two-layer waterproofing is laid offset by half the width of the sheet, three-layer waterproofing offset by one third. The overlap should be at least 80 mm and the third layer should overlap the first by at least 40 mm.

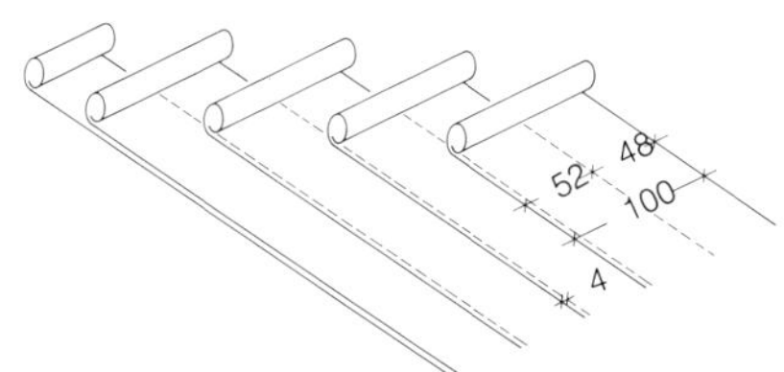


2.4.13.17 Laying in bond with laps [cm]

The first layer of waterproofing material is spot/strip-bonded or nailed to the roof structure. On substrates such as concrete, three or four plate-sized areas of adhesive every square metre or two or three strips of adhesive per metre will hold the material in place. On substrates such as timber galvanised clout nails (or special nails to suit the substrate) are driven in every 10 cm along the laps. Nailed waterproofing layers should have a backing of glass-fibre or jute cloth, or be made of non-woven polyester fibres.
The further layers are attached with bonding compound or by felt torching. The bonding compound used is a blown bitumen with a softening point ≥ 100°C (B 100/25, B 105/15, B 115/15) applied at a temperature of 180–220°C.

Bonding work cannot be carried out during cold weather (≤ 5°C, snow, ice, frost), or wet weather, or in strong winds.

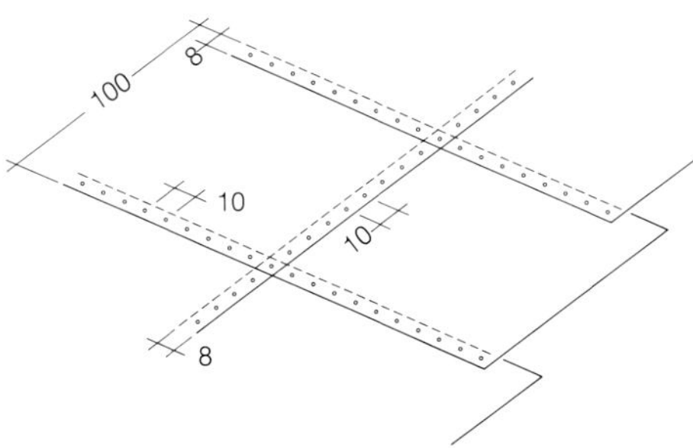


2.4.13.18 Fixing whole sheets with nails [cm] [16]

For roof pitches ≥ 5° the further layers, apart from fully bonded roofing, should also be nailed along the laps – every 5–10 cm depending on pitch and material. All bituminous materials must be stored in a dry place on site. [16]
The waterproofing sheets require additional measures to prevent them slipping:

- the use of sheets with a high tensile strength and low extensibility of the backing
- the use of sheets with a rough surface (granule-surfaced bitumen felt)
- laying the sheets in the direction of the slope 150–200 mm over the ridge, with the uppermost sheet on the side facing the prevailing wind
- securing the sheets with additional nails at 50 mm centres along the top edge
- fixing the sheets with metal strips in the laps
- including additional nailing strips on non-nailable substrates at eaves, ridge and every lap

### High-polymer sheets

These sheets can be laid in one or two layers. They should overlap 40–50 mm when joined by felt torching, ≥ 50 mm when using contact adhesives, and ≥ 100 mm with bitumen bonding compounds.
The joints to be made on site are described in the respective laying instructions. Generally, thermoplastic sheets are welded together and elastomeric sheets vulcanised or bonded.

| | Welding | | | | | | Cold bonding | | | |
|---|---|---|---|---|---|---|---|---|---|---|
| | hot gas welding(hot air) | heated wedge welding | high-frequency torching | solvent bonding (solvents) | vulcanising | hot bonding (bitumen, partial) | bitumen/rubber/ synthetic adhesive | contact adhesive | cover tape, self-adhesive one side | sealing tape, self-adhesive both sides |
| Width of seam [mm] | ≥ 30 | ≥ 30 | – | ≥ 30 | ≥ 30 | ≥ 100 | ≥ 100 | ≥ 50 | ≥ 40 | ≥ 40 |
| Thermoplastics: | | | | | | | | | | |
| ethylene copolymer bitumen (ECB) | • | • | | | | • | | | | • |
| ethylene vinyl-acetate (EVA) | • | • | • | • | | • | • | | | |
| polyethylene, chlorinated (PE-C) | • | • | • | • | | | | | • | |
| polyisobutylene (PIB) | • | | | • | | • | • | | | • |
| plasticised polyvinyl chloride (PVC-P) | • | • | • | • | | (•) | • | | • | |
| Elastomers: | | | | | | | | | | |
| polychloroprene rubber (CR) | | | | | • | • | • | • | | • |
| chlorosulphonated polyethylene (CSM) | • | • | • | • | | • | • | • | | |
| ethylene-propylene-diene rubber (EPDM) | • | | | | • | • | • | • | | • |
| isoprene-isobutene rubber (IIR) | | | | | • | | • | • | • | • |
| nitrile-butyl rubber (NBR) | | | | | • | • | • | • | • | • |

2.4.13.19 Synthetic waterproofing sheets; jointing and laying techniques [02, 33]

The waterproofing sheet must be resistant to bitumen if a bitumen bonding compound is used.
Sheets measuring about 200 m$^2$ can be prefabricated and laid loose. However, it is almost impossible to lay such large sheets without any creases. Five laying techniques are possible with high-polymer sheeting:

- laying loose, with crushed loose material, paving flags or rooftop planting to hold down the sheets (≤ 5°)
- laying loose with mechanical fixings (refer to manufacturer's instructions in material data sheets) (≤ 90°)
- laying in hot bitumen bonding compound (not every bitumen-compatible sheet is suitable for this) (≤ 15°)
- laying and bonding with modified cold bitumen adhesives
- laying and bonding with rubber or synthetic adhesives (≤ 45°)

Thermoplastic sheeting with softeners (plasticised PVC) can shrink considerably after laying. It must therefore be laid loose, held down with heavy materials and fixed with mechanical fasteners at all edges, junctions and penetrations.

Waterproofing sheets are turned up 100–150 mm above the top of the substrate, bonded and fixed with mechanical fasteners. The top edge should be flashed, either with a capping strip or by the wall overhanging the waterproofing.

Cover strips, with their homogeneous connections to thermoplastic high-polymer waterproofing sheets on one side, adhesives and sealing strips combined with connecting strips on the other, are usually materials and components with which or via which a connection to other components, e.g. of metal, timber, timber derivatives, concrete, plastic (glass fibre-reinforced plastic, unplasticised PVC, PMMA) can be made. Cover and make-up pieces must be provided here to suit the detail. [17]

An additional test to ensure the imperviousness of the waterproofing layer (including seams) is required before laying the protection mat.

#### Protection mat

Separating and protective non-woven fabrics should be laid with 100 mm laps. In a waterproofing layer with a rough surface or thick laps, two layers of 200 g/m$^2$ non-woven fabric (laid at 90° to each other) or one 300–500 g/m$^2$ layer can be employed. Films are less suitable as a protection mat on roof pitches > 10° because their smooth surfaces tend to create a slip plane.

#### Drainage layer

Irrespective of whether loose materials, sheets or mats are being used, it is recommended to divide up the roof surface into areas of max. 400 m$^2$ and limit the length of drainage runs to 15 m to ensure a reliable water run-off. [15]

Loose materials
Without additional means of retention, non-crushed materials can be laid on roof pitches ≤ 5°, but only crushed materials on roof pitches up to 15–20°. Humps or grids of battens will be required on steeper roofs (> 20°) [27, 34], depending on the coefficient of friction, the material's angle of repose and the resulting thrust.
Some lighter materials (e.g. expanded clay, expanded shale) can be blown onto the roof through hoses. In order to rule out mechanical damage to the waterproofing layer and root barrier, a protection mat is required beneath crushed loose materials.

Sheets
Drainage sheets are stable and can also be laid on steep roofs (> 20°). The elements are butted tightly together – sometimes as plain butt joints, sometimes with rebates, preferably in a bond – and if laid loose should be weighted down to prevent bulges. Supports at the eaves are adequate to resist the thrust up to a pitch of 20°. At steeper pitches the thrust should be resisted at regular intervals by suitable means [34]:

| Roof pitch [°] | > 20 | > 25 | ~ 30 |
|---|---|---|---|
| Spacing [m] | ~< 10 | ~< 8 | ~< 5 |

2.4.13.20 Drainage sheets; spacing of thrust resistance [34]

Profiled foamed plastic sheets are usually laid with overlapping rebated edges and cut to suit. Profiled rigid plastic sheets are laid with interlocking overlapping edges. When cutting these elements, any sharp edges should be deburred so as not to damage waterproofing layers and root barriers.
The tensile stresses that occur with sheets spot- or strip-bonded to the substrate can damage waterproofing layers and root barriers. This is why laying the sheets loose is preferred.

Mats
Drainage mats should only be laid on roofs with a pitch ≤ 20°. They must accommodate more tension as the pitch increases; and should therefore be "hung" over the ridge. Foamed plastic mats are butted tightly together and joined with adhesive tape. Textured mats (e.g. textured non-woven mats, nodular mats, braided fibre mats) are laid butted tightly together and clipped, or overlapped and screwed or welded together. This prevents the mats coming apart and thus the accidental penetration of the substrate during installation or afterwards.

Where components rise above the roof surface, mats can continue to the top of waterproofing layers and root barriers in order to protect them. If they are not resistant to ultraviolet (UV) radiation, any exposed portions should be protected.
As textured non-woven mats in particular creep under load, the plant-bearing layer should be max. 15 cm deep, depending on the load. [23]

#### Filter sheet

Filter layers – loose materials or non-woven fabrics – are laid in one operation except when the drainage layer doubles as a filter, e.g. with a widely graded loose material, foamed sheets with a no-fines structure or mats laminated with non-woven fabric.

Filters of non-woven fabric must be laid with laps of ≥ 100 mm and turned up at the edges 100–150 mm according to the pitch. Drainpipes should be wrapped in this non-woven fabric. The fabric must be protected directly after laying, either by the plant-bearing layer or by some other means to prevent it being blown away by the wind.

Before roots have penetrated a non-woven fabric filter, it can act as a slip plane on smooth drainage layers (≥ 10°).

#### Plant-bearing layer (substrate)

Loose materials
A plant-bearing layer comprising loose materials should be installed in a moist, lightly crumbling state and kept moist (weight) until the vegetation is added. Only minimal settlement is permitted after installation. Some loose materials can be blown onto the roof through hoses. Care should be taken with mixtures of loose materials to ensure they are adequately compacted so that capillarity ensues within the layers.

The structure and stability of mixtures of loose materials can be guaranteed when the proportion of organic substances is limited to 30% by vol. The properties of the plant-bearing layer should not alter on steep roofs (> 20°). Plastic flow can be prevented by limiting the content of cohesive constituents (≤ 0.063 mm) to ≤ 10% by wt.

As in the drainage layer of a multi-layer roof construction, the plant-bearing layer of a single-layer design for roof pitches exceeding 20° must include means to withstand the thrust on the roof surface and at the eaves (see also "Drainage layer" above).

Sheets
Substrate sheets are best used as a lower plant-bearing layer. They should be protected from becoming saturated prior to installation, laid dry as supplied and wetted prior to applying the upper plant-bearing layer of loose materials. [23]

Mats
Substrate mats are used as an underlay for loose materials or as an intermediate layer within such materials. Together with the loose materials, they create a plant-bearing layer of minimum thickness. [15] In the form of vegetation mats they are laid together with the precultivated plants they contain (see "Plants" below).

If there is a long delay before planting, the plant-bearing layer must be protected from erosion (see "Additional measures" below). On roof pitches > 15° it is not unreasonable to include a protective mesh or fabric (rolled out down the slope) within the plant-bearing layer on any type of green roof to prevent erosion before the plant roots become firmly established within the layer. It is also recommended to prevent erosion through wind and water by covering the whole plant-bearing layer with a vegetation mat. [23, 27, 34]

Additional weight in the form of gravel or paving flags should be provided in zones of high wind suction (edges, corners). [23]

**Plants**
We distinguish between the following methods or combinations thereof for establishing plants on the roof:
- broadcast seeding
- hydroseeding
- planting-out of shoots
- direct planting
- precultivated vegetation mats

Broadcast seeding
Manual sowing can be improved by mixing the seeds with sawdust or fine sand to prevent them being blown away. The use of smaller seed spreaders virtually eliminates the risk of losing seeds to the wind. The seeds should be covered with at least 5 mm of substrate material. Scattering and rolling achieves this cover of fine-grain substrates. The substrate must be kept permanently moist during the initial germination and growth phases.

Hydroseeding
A mixture of seeds, bonding agent, mulch, fertiliser and water is sprayed onto the surface of the substrate in one operation. The seeds are thus bonded in a thin layer of mulch. Hydroseeding methods are particularly suitable for planting larger roof areas; rolling is unnecessary.

Planting-out of shoots
Young shoots of various sedum varieties about 10–40 mm long are used in this method. The young shoots are planted by hand in a second operation following broadcast seeding or in a first operation prior to hydroseeding, or by machine – sprayed mixed in with the liquid mass. Good contact with the plant-bearing layer can be achieved by rolling or covering with a thin layer of substrate or wood-chip mulch.

Direct planting
Generally, about 12–15 plants per $m^2$ are required on shallower roofs and about 25 plants per $m^2$ on steeper ones. In both cases this ensures faster coverage and faster root growth. The plants should have a shallow root ball and the root system should not be too entwined. They must be given enough water until they are firmly established in the substrate.

Precultivated vegetation mats
These vegetation mats are rolled out on a levelled substrate and tightly butt-jointed together in a semi-moist state. Textile inlays or underlays are laid with laps or the edges bonded together (special adhesive). To counteract uplift due to wind suction, gravel or paving flags are laid along the edges (wind suction peaks) or even across the whole roof surface (suction on steeper roofs). Roll turf can be secured against wind suction by means of wire mesh or nets.

Vegetation mats with mosses, succulents, herbs and grasses must be kept moist until the roots have become established within the substrate. Roll turf requires continuous irrigation even after becoming established.

Transport and storage (in a shady place) of mats should not last longer than 2–6 days, depending on the climate.

Early summer is the best time to sow, plant or install mats. This guarantees that late frosts do not damage the germinating seeds and plant roots are well established by the following winter and thus not susceptible to frost.

**Additional measures**
Irrigation
We distinguish between the following types of irrigation:
- via a hose
- via hose and sprinkler
- via an irrigation hose
- via a buried trickle irrigation system
- via an overhead irrigation system
- via water retention in the drainage layer

Combinations of these forms of irrigation are common in practice. Irrigation can be controlled manually or automatically.

Preventing slippage
This can be provided in different layers in different ways.
In strips using:

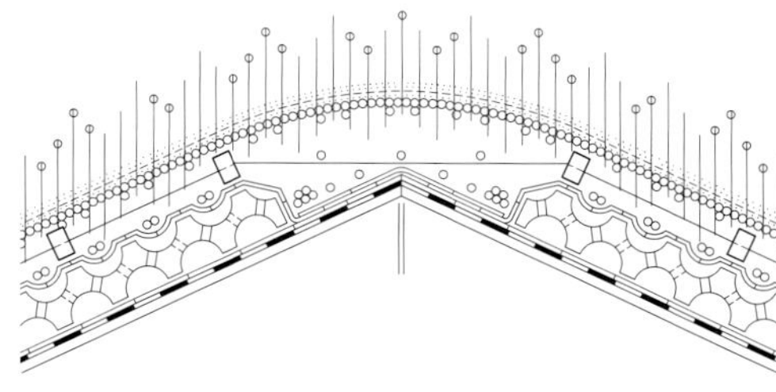

2.4.13.21 Additional measure at ridge; battens connected with plastic cord

- humps
- battens

At individual points using:
- dowels
- individual humps

Over the whole area using:
- graded materials
- stabilised vegetation mats
- textured non-woven mats
- braided fibre mats
- a slope stabilisation textile
- a honeycomb grid
- a grid of battens

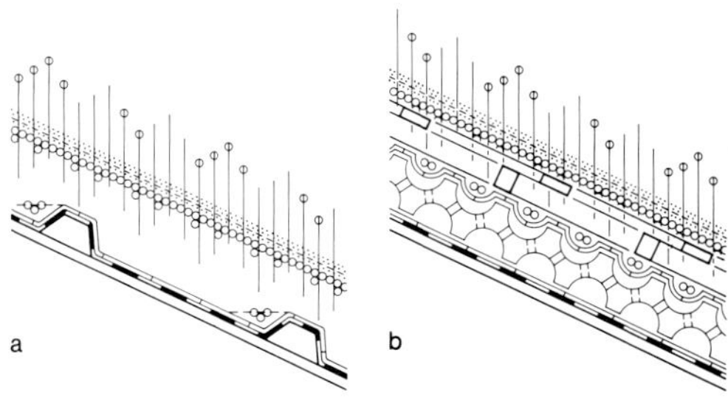


2.4.13.22 Additional measures: a separated into strips by humps, b grid of battens over entire surface

The shape and grading of the grains is crucial in determining the stability of loose materials. Crushed grains exhibit a high loading capacity and reduced risk of erosion owing to their serrated and shear-resistant form. Stability can be improved with a higher proportion of crushed grains and the use of graded mixtures.

Securing against the wind
During construction:
- weighting down temporarily with wooden planks or sandbags
- filling up the drainage and water retention elements with water
- immediately adding the next layer

Prior to root establishment:

- the use of stable loose materials
- keeping the loose materials permanently moist
- the use of textiles to prevent erosion
- including a bonding agent when employing hydroseeding
- the use of precultivated vegetation mats
- by selecting suitable plant varieties
- infill planting

Continuous windy weather can damage plants and erode the substrate even when the rooftop planting is fully established. This is especially the case at the edges and corners (wind suction) of the roof and in other areas subjected to constant wind eddies.

**Details**

Ridge, eaves, junction with wall, trough, verge, penetrations

Ridge

Sheets and mats are "hung" over the ridge. Depending on access or other requirements, protective measures such as splitting up the fertile soil with a layer of chippings or including a walkway may be advisable to prevent the plant-bearing layer being damaged.

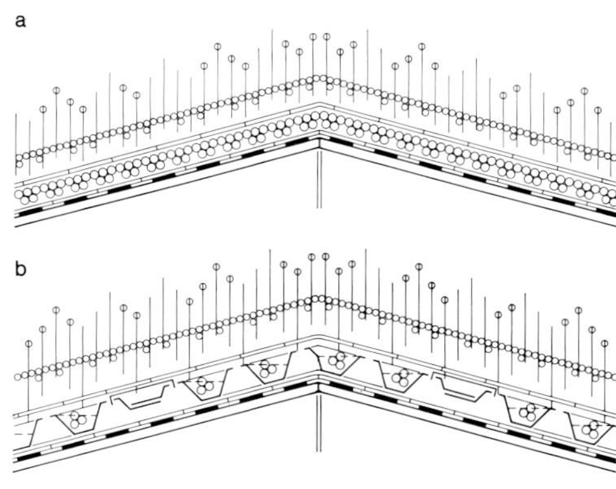


2.4.13.23 Ridge; drainage: a using loose materials, b with profiled drainage sheets

Eaves

A strip of coarse gravel or chippings (32/64 mm) about 25 cm wide should be included along the edges to ensure good drainage of the run-off water. An additional drainpipe within the drainage layer spreads the water across the slope.

When using profiled drainage sheets that have to be held at the eaves, the sheets themselves provide the necessary transverse distribution of the water.

The filter sheet is turned up to the surface to ensure uninterrupted separation between drainage layer and plant-bearing layer.

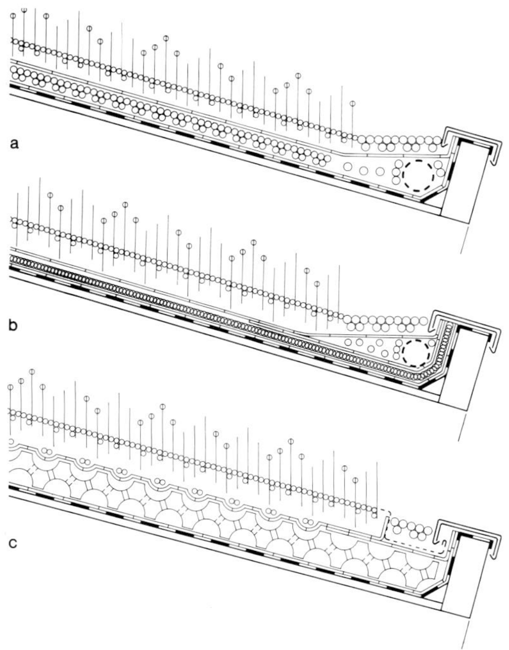


2.4.13.24 Eaves; drainage: a using loose materials, b with profiled drainage sheets, c with drainage elements

Junction with wall

A strip of coarse gravel (≤ 5° roof pitch) or chippings (up to 15–20°) ≥ 50 cm wide should be included adjacent to external walls as a safety measure (fire, water run-off without roots in the soil) and splash protection (fine particles of soil). This strip also provides access for maintenance work (see "Materials, components – Behaviour in fire" above). It is best to increase grain sizes – 16/32 to 32/63 mm – as the roof pitch decreases.

The clearance between planting and wall prevents plant development being adversely affected by water draining or dripping from the wall.

It should always be ensured that the waterproofing and root barrier are turned up the wall for a distance of 100–150 mm above gravel, vegetation, paving flags etc. and suitably flashed. This also applies to other components and roof penetrations, e.g. vents, aerials, rooflights.

If a filter sheet has been included, it should also always be turned up to the surface of the plant-bearing layer. When areas of planting have been arranged with a clearance to the wall, there are three options for drainage [23]:

- providing a continuous drainage layer beneath the area of planting and strips of gravel
- separating the drainage of areas of planting and strips of gravel
- including a drainage channel instead of a strip of gravel

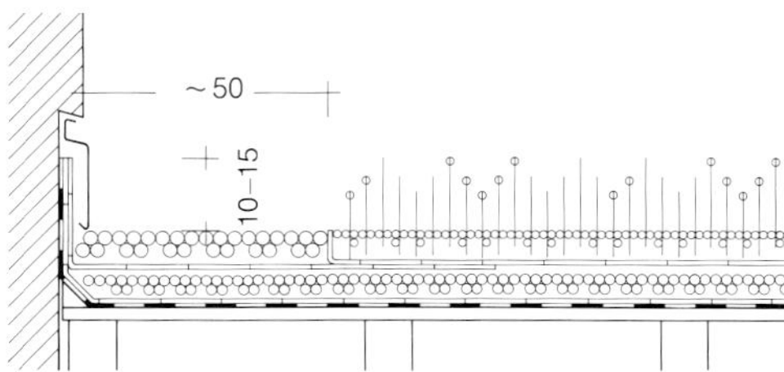


2.4.13.25 Junction with wall at side of slope; continuous drainage layer beneath planting and gravel strip

Trough

A wide strip of gravel or chippings should be provided to avoid a build-up of water. For grain sizes see "Eaves" above. A filter sheet of non-woven material is laid with laps in the direction of flow. Besides adequate means of drainage, a reliable overflow should be included.

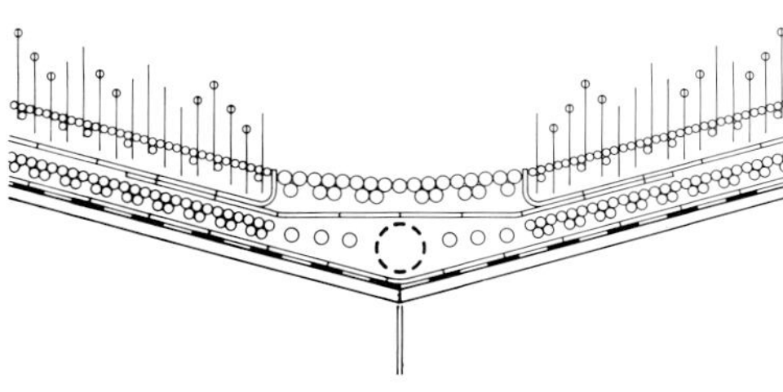

2.4.13.26 Trough; drainage via gravel strip and drainpipe

Verge

The area of planting should be separated from the edge construction by a strip of coarse gravel (≤ 5° roof pitch) or chippings (up to 15–20°). This should be held in place by humps on steeper roofs. For grain sizes see "Junction with wall" above. For details of position of filter sheet and triangular fillet see "Eaves" above.

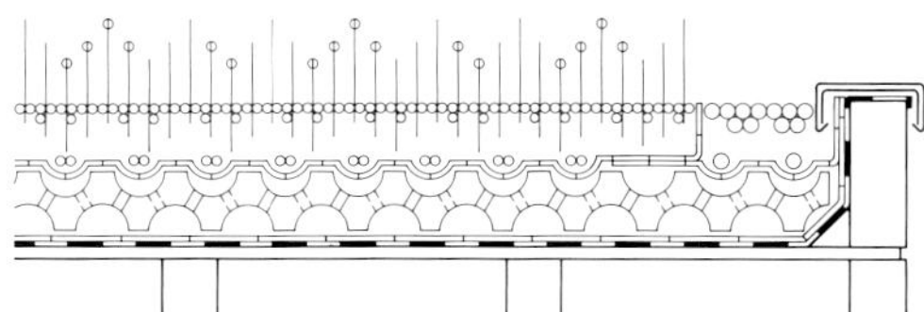

2.4.13.27 Verge; drainage via drainage elements

Penetrations

For details of edge strips see "Junction with wall" and "Verge" above. For details of position of filter sheet see "Eaves" above. The turned-up edges of film should be covered to protect them from ultraviolet radiation.

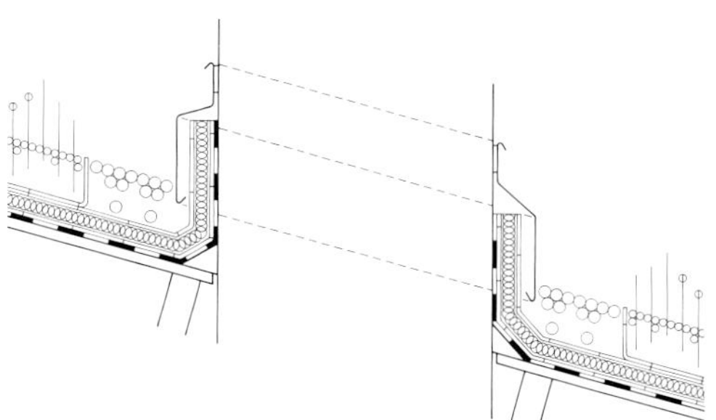

2.4.13.28 Penetration; chimney; drainage via drainagemats

**Maintenance and repair**

After all the layers of a green roof have been installed, initial and follow-up care of the plants is essential.

After handover, the plant development requires attention for a limited period, which can last up to two years. During this phase, in which the plants are becoming established, the surface of the plant-bearing layer should not be allowed to dry out. This applies particularly to methods of planting in which no fully developed plants are used. After this initial phase, care of the plants should continue throughout the service life of the roof. This ensures that the green roof remains functional. According to the plants chosen, this may entail annual sowing. In doing so, young plants that have suffered during dry periods should be removed and replaced.

While this is quite possible with shrubs and bushes, some roots and rhizomes of grasses and herbs remain in the soil, and can develop again into strong plants. Dead parts of plants should therefore be cleared away from extensive or elementary intensive rooftop planting only in exceptional cases.

If the plants chosen prove unsuitable for both the local climatic conditions and the layer make-up, the plant failures to be expected increase the amount of work quite dramatically. It may be necessary to remove and replace the entire vegetation together with some of the mulch and plant-bearing layer.

Plant failures can also damage areas of the plant-bearing layer when it is unable to withstand ultraviolet radiation or heat (e.g. some synthetic materials) as the plants no longer provide the necessary shade and/or there is insufficient cover to the substrate. When this leads to a permanent loss of the necessary cohesion within the layer of loose material, this can slip on a relatively steep roof. In this case the entire roof make-up must be renewed accordingly, together with the planting.

Incorrectly installed vapour barriers lead to condensation problems in sensitive constructions when the moisture cannot escape through ventilation. In these instances a load-bearing timber decking can rot. The decking and entire green roof make-up must then be renewed (expensive). Materials should be reused wherever possible.

| Type of care | Extensive planting | | | Elementary intensive planting |
|---|---|---|---|---|
| | moss-sedum varieties | moss-sedum-herb varieties | sedum-grass-herb varieties | grass-herb varieties |
| Preparatory care: | | | | |
| initial irrigation | + | + | | + |
| irrigation during sowing | | | | + |
| periodic irrigation prior to handover | | | + | + |
| initial fertiliser | | | ± | ± |
| follow-up fertiliser | | | – | – |
| removal of weeds | – | – | ± | – |
| re-sowing | | | ± | ± |
| Care during establishment: | | | | |
| irrigation | – | – | – | + |
| fertiliser | | | ± | – |
| removal of weeds | – | – | – | – |
| re-sowing | | | ± | ± |
| inspections | + | + | + | + |
| Maintenance: | | | | |
| irrigation | | | | + |
| fertiliser | | | – | – |
| removal of weeds | – | – | – | – |
| re-sowing | | | ± | ± |
| inspections | + | + | + | + |

2.4.13.29 Garden care activities for various types of planting: + required regularly or constantly, ± as required, – only in exceptional cases [23]

**References**

[01] Braun, E.: Bitumen; Cologne: Rudolf Müller, 1987

[02] Buss, H.: Bauschäden – beurteilen und beheben durch konkrete Lösungen im Detail: Kissing: Weka Fachverlage GmbH & Co. KG, 1988

[03] DIN 1055: Design loads for buildings; pt 1: Stored materials, building materials and structural members, dead load and angle of friction; Berlin: Beuth, 1978

[04] DIN 1055: Design loads for buildings; pt 4: Imposed loads, wind loads on buildings not susceptible to vibration; Berlin: Beuth, 1986 und 1987

[05] DIN 1055: Design loads for buildings; pt 5: Live loads, snow load and ice load; Berlin: Beuth, 1975 & 1994

[06] DIN 1986: Entwässerungsanlagen für Gebäude und Grundstücke; pt 2: Ermittlung der Nennweiten von Abwasser- und Lüftungseinrichtungen; Berlin: Beuth, 1995

[07] DIN 4102: Fire behaviour of building materials and building components; pt 1: Building materials; concepts, requirements and tests; Berlin: Beuth, 1981

[08] DIN 4102: Fire behaviour of building materials and building components; pt 4: Synopsis and application of classified building materials, components and special components; Berlin: Beuth, 1981

[09] DIN 4102: Fire behaviour of building materials and building components; pt 7: Roofing; definitions, requirements and testing; Berlin: Beuth, 1987

[10] DIN 18195: Waterproofing of buildings and structures; pt 5: waterproofing against water that exerts no hydrostatic pressure; design and workmanship; Berlin: Beuth, 1984

[11] DIN 18195 pt 9: Waterproofing of buildings and stuctures; penetrations, transitions, closures; Berlin: Beuth, 1986

[12] DIN 18195 pt 10: Waterproofing of buildings and structures; protective layers and protective measures; Berlin: Beuth, 1983

[13] FBB Fachvereinigung Bauwerksbegrünung: Wurzelfeste Bahnen und Beschichtungen; Unna: FBB, 2001

[14] Fischer, P., Meinken, E.: Durchwurzelungsfestigkeit von Dachbahnen; in: BBauBl, issue 8, pp. 412–17; 1989

[15] FLL Forschungsgesellschaft Landschaftsentwicklung Landschaftsbau e.V.: Richtlinie für die Planung, Ausführung und Pflege von Dachbegrünungen – Dachbegrünungsrichtlinie; Bonn: FLL, 2002

[16] Industrieverband Bitumen-, Dach- und Dichtungsbahnen e.V., vdd: abc der Bitumenbahnen, Technische Regeln; Frankfurt/M.: vdd, 1991

[17] Institut für das Bauen mit Kunststoffen e.V., IBK: IBK seminar 1977, Gründächer; Darmstadt: IBK, 1986

[18] Kolb, W.: Extensivbegrünung von Dachflächen, Fragen zur Substratwahl; in: Das Gartenamt 31, issue 7, pp. 429–32; 1982

[19] Kolb, W. Schwarz, T.: Dachbegrünung – intensiv und extensiv ("Der Gartenprofi"); Stuttgart: Ulmer GmbH, 1999

[20] Krupka, B.: Handbuch des Landschaftbaues – Dachbegrünungen, Pflanzen- und Vegetationsanwendungen an Bauwerken; Stuttgart: Ulmer GmbH, 1992

[21] Krupka, B.: Moose und Sedum – Überlebenskünstler für extensive Dachbegrünungen in: Gartenpraxis 13, issue 7, pp. 39–41; 1987

[22] Krupka, B.: Standortfaktoren, Pflanzen und Vegetationsformen für extensive Dachbegrünung; in: Das Gartenamt 33, issue 12, pp. 814–22; 1984

[23] Liesecke, H.-J., Krupka, B., Lösken, G., Brüggemann, H.: Grundlagen der Dachbegrünung; Berlin: Patzer, 1989

[24] Liesecke, H. J.: Funktionsgerechter Aufbau von Dachbegrünungen; in: Das Gartenamt 28, issue 5, pp. 277–88; 1979

[25] Ministy of Urban Development, Housing and Transport: Brandverhalten begrünter Dächer; Düsseldorf: Ministerial Gazette for the State of North Rhine-Westphalia, No. 4; Sept 1989

[26] Moritz, K.: Flachdachhandbuch; Wiesbaden, Berlin: Bauverlag GmbH, 4th ed., 1975

[27] Optigrün international AG: planning aid; Krauchenwies, 2001

[28] Scholz, W., et al.: Baustoffkenntnis, 13th ed.; Düsseldorf: Werner GmbH, 1995

[29] Stifter, R.: Dachgarten; Stuttgart: Eugen Ulmer GmbH & Co., 1988

[30] Technischer Arbeitskreis Kunststoff- und Kautschukbahnen e.V., TAKK: Werkstoffblätter Dachbahnen; Darmstadt: TAKK, 1988

[31] Weiser, H.: Durchwurzelungsfeste Bahnen nach dem FLL-Verfahren; in: Deutscher Gartenbau 44, issue 5, pp. 270–75; 1990

[32] Zentralverband des Deutschen Dachdeckerhandwerks: Richtlinien für die Planung und Ausführung von Dächern mit Abdichtungen, Flachdachrichtlinien; Cologne: Rudolf Müller, 1982

[33] Zimmermann, G.: Flachdachabdichtungen mit hochpolymeren Bahnen; in: Deutsches Architekten Blatt; 3/85

[34] ZinCo GmbH: Das grüne Dach, Planungshilfe, 6th ed.; Unterensingen, 1998

## Membranes

Materials, components, laying

### Textiles

Raw materials, manufacture, properties

#### Raw materials

The raw materials for textiles are fibres, which we divide into natural and man-made fibres. Natural fibres are the vegetable, animal and mineral fibres that produce natural growth and fibre-formation processes. They include cotton, silk, hemp and flax, although only cotton is employed for membranes. Man-made fibres are produced in industrial processes and may comprise the following substances:

- Natural polymers

The raw materials for these have a vegetable or animal origin.

- Synthetic polymers

These are also known as synthetic fibres and consist of thermoplastics.

- Inorganic raw materials

These man-made fibres include glass and metal fibres.

#### Manufacture

As the length of natural fibres is limited, they must be spun into threads (staple fibres). Their diameter is usually > 0.1 mm. Man-made fibres can be manufactured practically infinitely long with diameters < 0.1 mm and with any cross-sectional shape. These very fine fibres are twisted into stable yarns.

Further processing to form textiles

Textiles consist of systems of threads crossing at 90°. The threads in the direction of the material or direction of manufacture are called warp threads and perpendicular ones the weft threads. We distinguish between three basic types of weave: plain, twill and satin weave. Numerous other related weaves are derived from them. Visual appearance, texture and mechanical properties depend on the type of weave employed. Plain weave and its derivative, hopsack weave, have become firmly established in the manufacture of membranes. They are characterised by an enhanced surface roughness, which increases the adhesion of the coating and hence the strength of the seams.

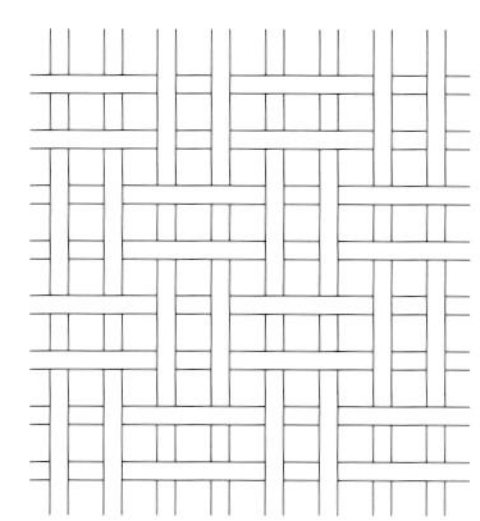

2.4.14.1 Types of weave
Plain weave Hopsack weave

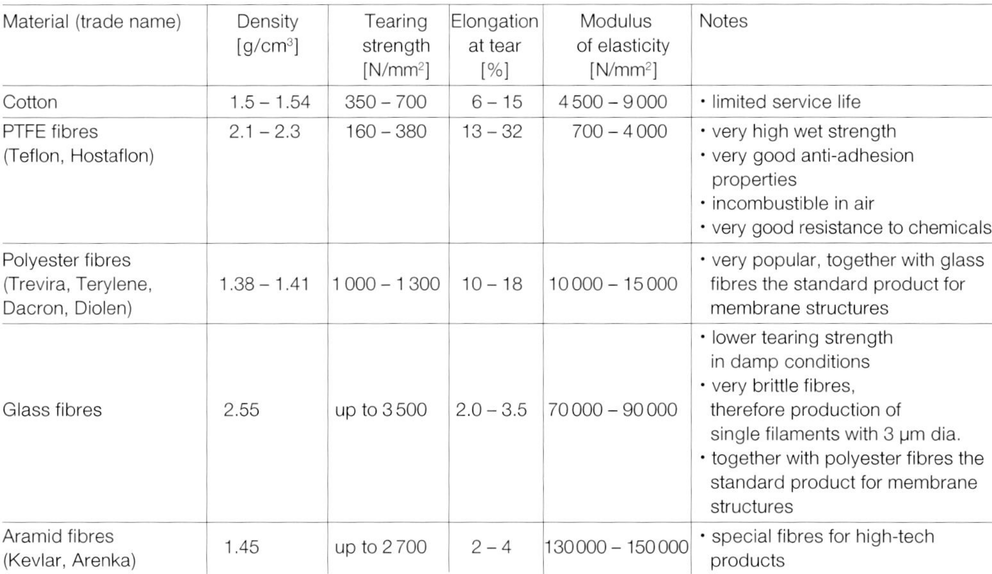

| Material (trade name) | Density [g/cm³] | Tearing strength [N/mm²] | Elongation at tear [%] | Modulus of elasticity [N/mm²] | Notes |
|---|---|---|---|---|---|
| Cotton | 1.5 – 1.54 | 350 – 700 | 6 – 15 | 4500 – 9000 | • limited service life |
| PTFE fibres (Teflon, Hostaflon) | 2.1 – 2.3 | 160 – 380 | 13 – 32 | 700 – 4000 | • very high wet strength<br>• very good anti-adhesion properties<br>• incombustible in air<br>• very good resistance to chemicals |
| Polyester fibres (Trevira, Terylene, Dacron, Diolen) | 1.38 – 1.41 | 1000 – 1300 | 10 – 18 | 10000 – 15000 | • very popular, together with glass fibres the standard product for membrane structures |
| Glass fibres | 2.55 | up to 3500 | 2.0 – 3.5 | 70000 – 90000 | • lower tearing strength in damp conditions<br>• very brittle fibres, therefore production of single filaments with 3 µm dia.<br>• together with polyester fibres the standard product for membrane structures |
| Aramid fibres (Kevlar, Arenka) | 1.45 | up to 2700 | 2 – 4 | 130000 – 150000 | • special fibres for high-tech products |

2.4.14.2 Mechanical properties of selected fibres [23]

Coatings

These textiles do not yet satisfy the requirements placed on a building envelope and must be made weather-resistant in a subsequent step. The textiles first undergo preliminary treatment.

This may be the application of a bonding agent, which improves the chemical adhesion of the textile. Polyester yarns can be treated to achieve an anti-wicking effect, which reduces the capillarity of the material.

After that, the textiles are coated. The following coating materials are employed in the manufacture of membranes:

- Polyvinyl chloride (PVC)

True PVC is hard, very brittle at 0°C and neither heat- nor UV-radiation-resistant. Preliminary processing is therefore necessary. PVC powder, softeners (plastisols, approx. 40% by wt), small amounts of heat and light stabilisers, pigments and additives to decrease combustibility are mixed together to form a paste that is applied to the textile and scraped off with a blade. The paste is thickened at 160– 200°C and subsequently cooled. The procedure is repeated to coat both sides of the material or to achieve a thicker coating. To counteract the migration of the softeners and reduce incident ultraviolet radiation, the surface of the coating is refined. This prevents embrittlement and prolongs service life. It also improves the soiling and cleaning behaviour of the smooth, anti-adhesive surface. [03] The surface refinement processes currently employed are based on acrylic lacquer (thickness of coating 3–8 µm), PVDF lacquer (10 µm) and PVF laminate (25 µm).

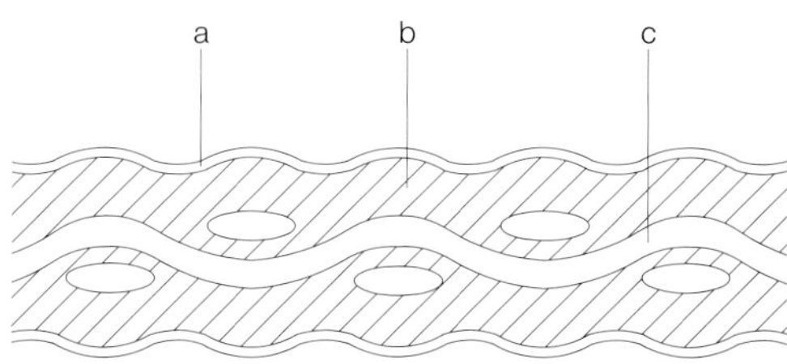


2.4.14.3 Structure of a PVC-coated polyester textile with surface refinement: a surface refinement, b coating, c textile

- Polytetrafluoroethylene (PTFE)

PTFE coatings are possible only on textiles with a higher melting point than the PTFE itself (327°C), i.e. glass-fibre and aramid-fibre textiles.

The PTFE is converted to a dispersion in which its proportion is 50–60%. So that the PTFE particles do not settle in the water, 3–6% wetting agent is mixed into the dispersion. The textile is steeped in this dispersion and the water is evaporated off at > 100°C and the wetting agent decomposed at temperatures exceeding 250°C. Finally, the PTFE is fused onto the textile at temperatures above its melting point. The procedure may need to be repeated to reach the desired coating thickness. [03]

- Silicone

The silicone is liquefied using solvents and subsequently spread over the textile. The coating is heated to evaporate the solvents. The procedure is repeated until the desired thickness is achieved.

**Properties**

Mechanical properties
The textile provides the loadbearing functions and hence governs mechanical properties. Textiles exhibit a non-linear stress-strain progression are non-elastic. They respond anisotropically, owing to the manufacturing process in which the warp threads are tightened (stentered) and the weft threads fed through them from alternate directions.

Physical properties
Textiles are translucent and create diffuse, evenly distributed lighting. The degree of translucency depends on the material and thickness of the textile, and the material and thickness of the coating. Applying a thinner coating does increase the translucency but at the same time reduces ultraviolet radiation resistance and hence tensile strength. The UV radiation resistance of almost all textiles can be regarded as good to very good. Aramid-fibre textiles alone are not resistant to ultraviolet radiation and must be completely covered with an opaque coating.

Behaviour in fire
Virtually all uncoated and coated textiles satisfy the requirements of DIN 4102 building materials class B 1 (not readily flammable, no dripping burning fragments). If there are more demanding fire protection requirements, PTFE or PTFE-coated textiles can be employed, which are classed as incombustible. As they are very thin, membranes have a very low fire load.

Chemical properties
Textiles exhibit good to very good resistance to chemical attack.

Biological properties
Owing to their open structure, uncoated textiles have a very low resistance to fungi and micro-organisms. Cotton textiles can be impregnated to protect them, but only for a limited time. Coated textiles, on the other hand, are highly resistant to biological attack.
A coated textile is a composite material and hence can be recycled only with considerable (uneconomic) effort. Used textiles are either disposed of in landfill sites, incinerated or reprocessed to form granulate.

## Foils

Raw materials, manufacture, properties

**Raw materials**
Various foils are available for use in membranes. Besides thermoplastic foils, metal foils (steel and aluminium) can be employed. Fluoropolymer foils, in particular the ETFE foils, play an outstanding role here. ETFE is a copolymer made from ethylene and tetrafluoroethylene.

**Manufacture**
Generally, fluoropolymer foils can be manufactured using the production methods described earlier (calendering, extruding, carding). ETFE foils are usually produced by means of extrusion, with a maximum width of 1.55 m.

| Material | Designation | Weight per unit area [g/m²] DIN 55 352 | min. tensile strength [N/5cm] warp/weft DIN 53 353 | Elongation at tear [%] warp/weft DIN 53 353 | Tear propagation strength [N] warp/weft DIN 53 363 | Buckling stability | Translucency [%] | UV-radiation resistance | Fire resistance DIN 4102 |
|---|---|---|---|---|---|---|---|---|---|
| Uncoated textiles: | | | | | | | | | |
| Cotton textile | | 350 | 1700/1000 | 35/18 | 60 | ++ | varies | o | B2 |
| | | 520 | 2500/2000 | 38/20 | 80 | ++ | varies | o | B2 |
| PTFE textile | | 300 | 2390/2210 | 11/10 | 500/500 | ++ | up to 37 | ++ | incombustible |
| | | 520 | 3290/3370 | 11/10 | 500/500 | ++ | up to 37 | ++ | incombustible |
| | | 710 | 4470/4510 | 18/9 | 500/500 | ++ | up to 37 | ++ | incombustible |
| Coated textiles: | | | | | | | | | |
| PVC-coated polyester textile | type I | 800 | 3000/3000 | 15/20 | 350/310 | ++ | up to 20 | + | B1 |
| | type II | 900 | 4400/3950 | 15/20 | 580/520 | ++ | up to 17.5 | + | B1 |
| | type II | 1050 | 5750/5100 | 15/25 | 950/800 | ++ | up to 15.0 | + | B1 |
| | type IV | 1300 | 7450/6400 | 15/30 | 1400/1100 | ++ | up to 12.5 | + | B1 |
| | type V | 1450 | 9800/8300 | 20/30 | 1800/1600 | ++ | up to 10.0 | + | B1 |
| | type VI | 2000 | 13000/13000 | | 3000/3000 | ++ | up to 7.5 | + | B1 |
| | type VII | | | | | ++ | up to 5.0 | + | B1 |
| PTFE-coated glass-fibre textile | | 800 | 3500/3500 | 7/10 to 2/17 | 300/300 | o | 15 | ++ | incombustible |
| | | 1150 | 5800/5800 | 7/10 to 2/17 | 500/500 | o | 12 | ++ | incombustible |
| | | 1550 | 7500/6500 | 7/10 to 2/17 | 500/500 | o | 8 | ++ | incombustible |
| Silicone-coated glass-fibre textile | | 800 | 3500/3000 | 7/10 to 2/17 | 300/300 | o | up to 25 | ++ | A2 |
| | | 1270 | 6600/6000 | 7/10 to 2/17 | 570 | o | up to 25 | ++ | A2 |
| PVC-coated aramid-fibre textile | | 900 | 7000/9000 | 5/6 | 700 | + | basically zero | o | B1 |
| | | 2020 | 24500/24500 | 5/6 | 4450 | + | basically zero | o | B1 |
| PTFE-coated aramid-fibre textile | | | limited adjustment options | limited adjustment options | limited adjustment options | + | basically zero | o | incombustible |

2.4.14.4 Mechanical and physical properties of technical textiles [11, 14, 16, 17, 24]: ++ very good, + good, o satisfactory

**Properties**

Mechanical properties
ETFE foils exhibit an approximately bilinear (elastic-plastic) stress-strain progression, and are isotropic and temperature-dependent.

Physical properties
Transparent ETFE foils (up to 95% translucency) can be manufactured. They are also highly resistant to ultraviolet radiation.

Behaviour in fire
ETFE foils are not readily flammable and release no dripping fragments (DIN 4102 class B 1). They represent a low fire load and melt away in the event of a fire, which creates a direct smoke and heat vent.

Chemical properties
ETFE foils are resistant to numerous chemicals.

Biological properties
ETFE foils are highly resistant to fungi and microorganisms.
The special feature of the material is its high permeability for UV-A radiation (100% transmission) and the filtering of hazardous UV-B (50% transmission) or UV-C (0% transmission) radiation. This filtering of hazardous radiation creates a favourable naturally lit climate for living organisms. [13]
As ETFE foils are not composite materials, complete recycling without any waste is possible.

**Components**
General elements

**General elements**
Membranes are supplied as sheets in rolls. Sheet widths vary between manufacturers, but 6 m is the maximum. The sheets are 1000–2000 m long, but even longer sheets can be produced to order. PVC-coated polyester textiles, PTFE-coated glass-fibre textiles and ETFE foils are all standard products and can be supplied "off the shelf". Other membrane materials are manufactured to order.

Colour
Colour can be introduced by dyeing with pigments or by printing. The standard colour of coated textiles is white and foils are normally transparent, but both can be manufactured in numerous other colours upon request.
Coloured PVC-coated textiles gradually fade under the long-term effects of ultraviolet radiation.
PTFE-coated textiles are basically beige in colour, which can be attributed to the decomposition of the wetting agent upon sintering. The membrane turns white under the effects of sunlight, artificial lighting or heat radiation. Prebleached varieties can be supplied on request.

| Material | Type | Weight per unit area [g/m²] DIN 55 352 | Tensile strength [N/mm²] DIN 53 455 | Elongation at tear [%] DIN 53 455 | Tear propagation strength [N/mm] DIN 53 363 | Buckling stability | Translucency [%] | Fire resistance DIN 4102 |
|---|---|---|---|---|---|---|---|---|
| ETFE | 50 µm | 87.5 | 64/56 | 450/500 | 450/450 | o | up to 95 | B1 |
| | 80 µm | 140 | 58/54 | 500/600 | 450/450 | o | up to 95 | B1 |
| | 100 µm | 175 | 58/57 | 550/600 | 430/440 | o | up to 95 | B1 |
| | 150 µm | 262.5 | 58/57 | 600/650 | 450/430 | o | up to 95 | B1 |
| | 200 µm | 350 | 52/52 | 600/600 | 430/430 | o | up to 95 | B1 |
| THV | 500 µm | 980 | 22/21 | 540/560 | 255/250 | + | up to 95 | B1 |

2.4.14.5 Mechanical and physical properties of foils [13, 17]: + good, o satisfactory

Manufacture
Membrane structures have surfaces curving in three dimensions. As membrane materials are produced in flat sheets, it is the task of the manufacturer to design a cutting pattern with which the sheets can be cut to exactly the right size and shape. Prior to the actual cutting, the material has to pass through projection and compensation stages.

• Projection
After the orientation of the sheets has been ascertained, the three-dimensional curved surface is transferred to the flat plane. This complex process is carried out by means of computer-assisted routines. Various criteria must be taken into account during this process:

Surfaces with extreme curvature require relatively narrow strips of material in order to achieve the form with sufficient accuracy. This results in increased wastage and more work for the manufacturer. Allowing for extra material for the seams and selvedge plus cable and edge beading pockets, the maximum width of the strip may not exceed the width of the roll. The warp and weft threads of textiles should follow the direction of the main stresses whenever possible. The strips should be positioned perpendicular to the edges wherever possible to minimise the tangential forces that result from the angle between the direction of main stresses and the edge.

• Compensation
Loadbearing membrane structures are prestressed mechanically or pneumatically. In order to introduce a prestress into the membrane, the planar segments are cut smaller by an amount equal to an elongation factor. Mono-axial and biaxial tests carried out on samples of the material form the basis for the

| | | Availability | Width [cm] | Thickness [mm] | Colour |
|---|---|---|---|---|---|
| Uncoated textiles: | | | | | |
| Cotton | | to order | depends on loom | | large choice of colours |
| PTFE | | to order | depends on loom | | white, other colours on request |
| Coated textiles: | | | | | |
| PVC-coated polyester textile | type I – III | standard | 200 – 300 | up to approx. 1.2 | standard: white; |
| | type IV – VII | to order | | | large choice of colours |
| PTFE-coated glass-fibre textile | | standard | up to 500 | up to approx. 1.0 | standard: white; limited range of colours on request |
| Silicone-coated glass-fibre textile | | to order | depends on loom | | standard: white; limited range of colours on request |
| PVC-coated aramid-fibre textile | | to order | depends on loom | | standard: white; large choice of colours on request |
| PTFE-coated aramid-fibre textile | | to order | up to 500 | | standard: white; limited range of colours on request |
| Foils: | | | | | |
| ETFE | | standard | up to 155 | 0.05 – 0.2 | standard: transparent, white, blue; other colours on request |
| THV | | to order | 50 – 150 | 0.08 to several mm | transparent, other colours on request |

2.4.14.6 Production-related properties of membrane materials [11, 14, 16, 17, 24]

compensation factor. The degree of prestress should be chosen to suit structural and economic requirements. It should not exceed 10% of the short-term strength because this would significantly reduce service life. The degree of prestress is designed for the condition directly after erection. Membranes with a distinct creep behaviour suffer a loss of prestress over time. This can be remedied by overstressing during erection or by including (re)tensioning devices.

| Material | Prestress [% of short-term strength] |
|---|---|
| Cotton textile | 2–8 |
| Polyester textile | 3–8 |
| Glass-fibre textile | 4–9 |
| Aramid-fibre textile | no details available |

2.4.14.7 Typical prestressing values for textiles [10]

• Cutting the sheets
Cutting is carried out according to the compensation values calculated. Small, complicated areas are cut out manually using paper templates, and large areas by means of computer-controlled wheel cutters. The strips should be coordinated with the width of the sheets in order to achieve maximum utilisation of the material.

Special optimisation software is employed to plan the cutting to minimise wastage and hence material consumption.

2.4.14.8 Development and cutting pattern for a stressed skin structure curved in three dimensions [22]

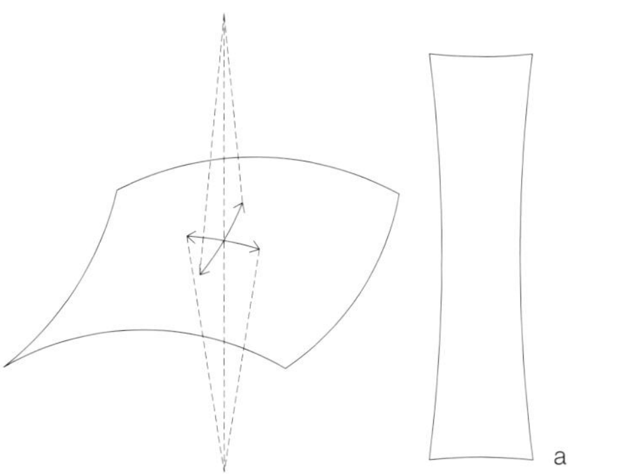


2.4.14.9 Strip forms for a) anticlastic, and b) synclastic surfaces

Thermal performance
Thin membranes react rapidly to climatic changes. Thermal insulation measures are necessary with membrane structures that are exposed to cold weather and heated. In hot weather the heat builds up quickly within a membrane structure. This can be remedied by installing mechanical ventilators or exploiting natural ventilation options.
Thermal insulation can be provided by one of the following means:

• Insulation using multiple skins
Double-skin construction
This consists of two membranes, one (outer or inner) or both of which can provide a loadbearing function. The loadbearing and non-loadbearing membranes must be joined together. The degree of efficiency of the insulation depends on the spacing of the membranes and way in which they are joined together.

Air-filled cushions
The membranes are spanned between a loadbearing structure of linear members and prestressed using high pressure.

Cushions with separate air ducts
Cushions can be square, rectangular or hexagonal on plan and are usually constructed with three plies to reduce the depth of the air layer. Pre-dried air is constantly circulated through the cushions (5–6 air changes per hour) via valves to avoid condensation. In a three-ply cushion the two air chambers are connected together via a hole in the central membrane. The degree of efficiency of the insulation depends on the spacing of the membranes and the size of the cushion.

Variable transmission external skin
Cushions with separate air ducts can have a shading system integrated into the roof. The upper and central membranes of the three-ply design are printed with an offset, reflective pattern. The central membrane is pressed against the external skin by adjusting the air flow, which results in a solid surface that allows very little solar radiation into the interior. If the desire is to admit solar radiation and heat up the interior, the central membrane is shifted to the internal skin.

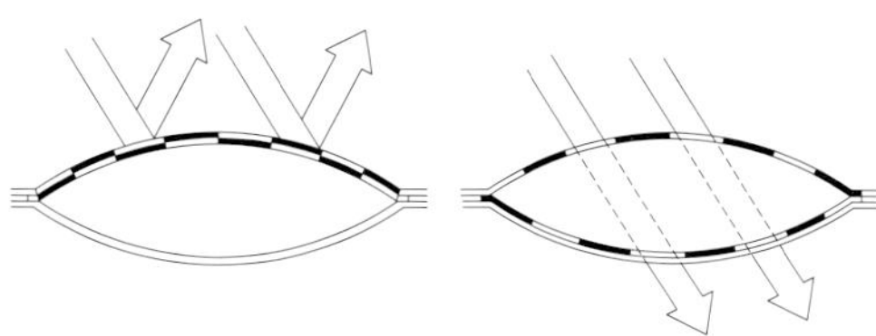

2.4.14.10 Three-ply foil membrane roof with variable transmission [13]

Multi-skin design
Multi-skin membrane designs consist of between three and five membranes. The type of material and sequence of membrane plies can be adapted to suit the particular purpose. The degree of efficiency of the insulation depends on the number and thickness of the air layers. In a multi-skin construction the heat of the outgoing process air can be used for insulation and the incident solar radiation can achieve energy gains.

| Structure | Spacing [mm] | Thermal resistance R [m²K/W] | Thermal transmittance U [W/m²K] |
|---|---|---|---|
| Single layer | 0 | 0.01 | 5.72 |
| Two layers | 10 | 0.15 | 3.2 |
| | 50 | 0.18 | 2.87 |
| | 100 | 0.2 | 2.78 |
| | 200 | 0.21 | 2.71 |
| | 300 | 0.21 | 2.71 |
| Three layers | 200 | 0.43 | 1.67 |

2.4.14.11 Thermal resistance and thermal transmittance values for single- and multi-skin membranes [03]

| Insulation by means of multi-skin structure | Two-skin structure with one air cavity | Cushion with separate air ducts | Multi-skin structure with air cavity |
|---|---|---|---|
| | | | |
| U-value [W/m²K] | approx. 2.7 | approx. 1.0–2.0 | approx. 1.0 and less |
| Insulation by means of insulating batts | Single-skin structure with suspended insulation cut to suit | Two-skin structure with one or two layers of insulation | Transparent thermal insulation |
| | | | |
| U-value [W/m²K] | approx. 0.4–1.5 | approx. 0.4–1.5 | approx. 1.1 |

2.4.14.12 Examples of insulating options [03, 12, 13]

When designing a multi-skin membrane, it should be noted that:

- the insulation effect decreases as the air velocity increases, so this should be limited to 1 m/s
- the inner membrane must show adequate fire resistance

Multi-skin membrane designs without additional thermal insulation are particularly suitable for pneumatically prestressed membrane structures because here the air is already required for stabilising the loadbearing structure.

- Insulation provided by insulating batts

Membrane structures can be provided with opaque or transparent thermal insulation batts. When doing so, it should be ensured that the insulating materials cannot become saturated. If the inner membrane is uncoated, a vapour barrier must be included or adequate ventilation must be guaranteed.

Opaque thermal insulation

Insulating batts can be laid on or hung below the inner membrane. The insulation material must be adaptable to adapt to the shape of the structure, and must be resistant to ultraviolet radiation. Adhesives or mechanical fasteners (spikes, straps) can be used to attach the insulating batts. It should be ensured that the insulating batts are not compressed because that reduces their insulating effect. The degree of efficiency of the insulation depends on the distance between membrane and batts, and on the thickness of the batts.

Transparent thermal insulation

Transparent (or translucent) thermal insulation enables insulated membranes to be constructed that also admit light. They possess both a low thermal conductance and a high light transmittance. Up to now, only insulating materials based on spun glass fibres have been used in conjunction with membranes.

Multi-skin constructions with additional layers of thermal insulation are primarily used for mechanically prestressed membrane structures.

Sound insulation

Owing to their low mass, membranes have poor sound insulation properties. The following measures can be taken to improve the sound reduction value of membranes:

- increase the mass by adding metal chips to the coating
- fill textiles with heavy media, e.g. quartz sand

Thermal insulation batts also have a sound attenuation effect and can thus also be used upon to improve the sound insulation.
All these measures result in a loss of translucency.

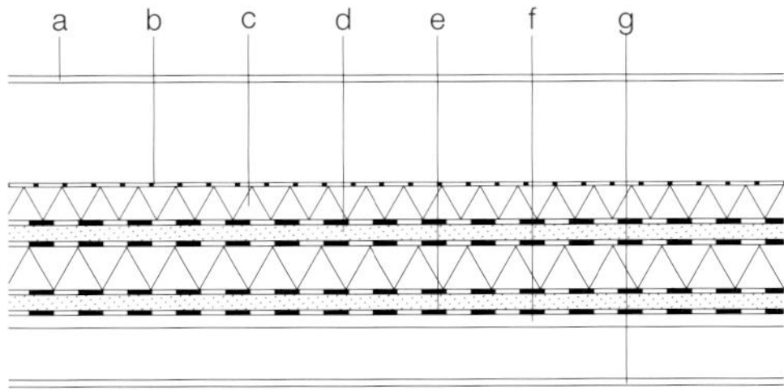


2.4.14.13 Multi-skin membrane roof with thermal insulating batts and textile filled with quartz sand: a outer membrane, b wire mesh fabric, c thermal insulation, d sand-filled fabric, e vapour barrier, f cable lattice, g inner membrane [15]

Moisture control

The water vapour diffusion resistance can be set to virtually any value during the manufacture of the membrane.
The following measures are possible:

- changing the vapour diffusion resistance factor through an appropriate choice of material
- changing the thickness of the foils or textile coatings

## Laying

Joining segments, details, additional measures, maintenance and service life, repair

### Joining segments

The membranes are provided in pieces (cut from sheets) which have to be joined together to form larger membrane areas.
The seams must fulfil certain requirements:

- if possible, strength at least equal to that of the membrane
- membrane and seam to have identical or near identical strain behaviour
- watertight
- airtight in the case of pneumatic structures

We distinguish between detachable and non-detachable joins.

Non-detachable seams

These are usually produced by the manufacturer at the works. Various techniques are employed for joining the material:

- Sewing

In a sewn seam the forces are transferred by way of friction and a direct mechanical interlock. The type of seam, type of thread, number of rows of stitching and number of stitches can vary depending on the loads. The width of the lap depends on the load on the seam, the material of the membrane, the type of thread and the method of production. The number and position of seams are determined by the magnitude of the forces to be transferred and watertightness/airtightness requirements. Normally, sewn seams have 2–4 rows of stitching spaced 8–25 mm apart. Special constructions may have up to 12 rows of stitching. [05]
As the membrane is perforated by the thread and the multi-skin design of the membrane leads to distinct contours, in which rainwater can collect, cover strips or some form of sealing are required.
Temperature, humidity, ultraviolet (UV) and infrared (IR) radiation or chemicals reduce the durability of seams. Black thread is used on structures with longer service lives because it is more resistant to UV radiation than white thread. Hot-cropping tools can be used to cut the edges; these melt the textile and its coating and thus seal the edge.

- Welding

In a welded seam two layers of membrane material are overlapped, heated and pressed together. The force transfer depends on the adhesion of the individual materials. Various welding techniques are available. The width of the seam depends on the loads, the membrane material and the method of welding, and is normally between 30 and 120 mm. Wider seams should be avoided because the outer edges become detached even before the seam can transfer forces. [05] The seam is

prestressed during welding to counteract temperature-related shrinkage (e.g. 1% for PTFE-coated glass-fibre textiles). [18] PTFE coatings are generally very thin and so an additional piece of material (tetrafluoroethylene-hexafluoropropylene or tetrafluoroethylene-perfluoroalkoxy vinyl ether) should be placed between the membrane layers during welding and worked into the join. This technique is known as indirect heated tool welding.
Fluoropolymer seals (e.g. PVDF lacquer) have a higher melting point than the PVC coating. This should be removed first to prevent the seal forming a separating layer during welding. To do so, the coating paste is ground off along the line of the seam.

• Combined seams
These are used for multi-layer and highly stressed seams in particular. They are designated according to the sequence of the joining processes.

Sewn-welded
The plies of membrane material are first sewn together and welded afterwards. This means that the thread lies unstressed within the textile and does not carry any load until the weld fails. This seam is watertight.

Welded-sewn
The plies of membrane material are first welded together and then sewn. The threads are stressed within the textile and carry the forces together with the weld. The perforated seam should be sealed with cover strips or a coating of PVC or fluorocarbon resin.

• Bonding
Welding is not possible with silicone coatings because their decomposition temperature lies below the melting point.
These textiles are joined either by cold welding (with solvents) or with reactive adhesives.

Detachable seams
Larger membrane segments cannot always be handled in one piece on site and often have to be supplied in smaller pieces. The size of the pieces depends on the weight of the material, the facilities available, and transport and erection options. On-site seams are necessary in order to connect these pieces, which have been prefabricated at the works ready for connecting during erection.

| | Cotton textile | PTFE textile | Polyester or aramid fibre textile | | | Glass-fibre textile | | Aramid-fibre text. | ETFE foil | THV foil |
|---|---|---|---|---|---|---|---|---|---|---|
| Coating | | | PVC | PVC | PVC | PTFE | silicone | PTFE | | |
| Surface refinement | impregnation | | Acryl lacquer | PVDF lacquer | PVF laminate | | | | | |
| Sewing[1] | • | • | • | • | • | | | | • | • |
| Hot air welding | | | • | • | • | | | | | |
| Hot element welding | | | • | • | • | •[2] | | •[2] | • | • |
| High-frequency welding | | | • | • | • | | | | | |
| Bonding | | | | | | | • | | | |
| Solvent bonding | | | • | • | • | | | | | |

[1] Employed only when other methods are not feasible
[2] Hot element welding with extra piece of material (FEP or PFA/TFA)

2.4.14.14 Non-detachable jointing techniques [05, 18]

• Clamping plate connection
The membranes are pressed together with metal plates and clamping bolts. Circular sections, known as edge beading, are included alongside the metal plates to prevent the membranes slipping. The clamping plates are made from strip material manufactured from anodized or powder-coated aluminium or stainless steel (V2A, V4A). Their dimensions depend on the loads and the curvature of the surface. Various cross-sectional shapes are available.

| | |
|---|---|
| Length [mm] | 100 – 150 |
| Width [mm] | 30 – 40 |
| Thickness [mm] | 5 – 8 |

2.4.14.15 Recommended dimensions of clamping plates [05]

The clamping bolts (8–12 mm dia.) are made from standard or hot-dip galvanised stainless steel (V2A, V4A). The edge beading (5–10 mm dia.) is made from PVC monofilaments, EPDM, stainless steel or polypropylene. A cover strip over clamping plates and bolts ensures that the seam remains watertight, and can be protected against damage by a foam strip. Seams across the slope should be avoided in order to prevent rainwater collecting there.

• Tied connection
The sheets are tied together via eyes incorporated in the membranes. Edge beading should be included close to the edge of the membranes in order to prevent overloading the eyes.

**Details**
Edges, point supports, linear supports

Edges
Membranes can be connected to the edge construction either by non-rigid members loaded only in tension, or by rigid members. The edge members should have a low weight, require little maintenance, be essentially prefabricated in the works and be easy to erect. The type of connection at the edges depends on the material used, the fixings and the method of erection.

• Non-rigid edge
The non-rigid edge follows a circular or catenary-type segment. Owing to their more favourable loadbearing behaviour, segments with small spans should be preferred to those with larger spans. Tensioning elements are seldom employed because the prestress is introduced by moving the corners.

Linear edge
Various constructions are available for forming the non-rigid edge.

Cable in pocket
The cables made from stainless steel, Galfan-coated stainless steel or synthetic materials have a diameter of 20–40 mm depending on the loading and are laid loose in a membrane pocket. A strip of membrane material or a soft strap can be included between membrane and cable to prevent abrasion.

Cable in pocket with strap
If the cable alone is unable to accommodate the tangential forces parallel to the edge, a strap is included along the pocket. This strap, made from polyester or aramid fibres, measures between 20 x 1 mm and 150 x 8 mm. [05]

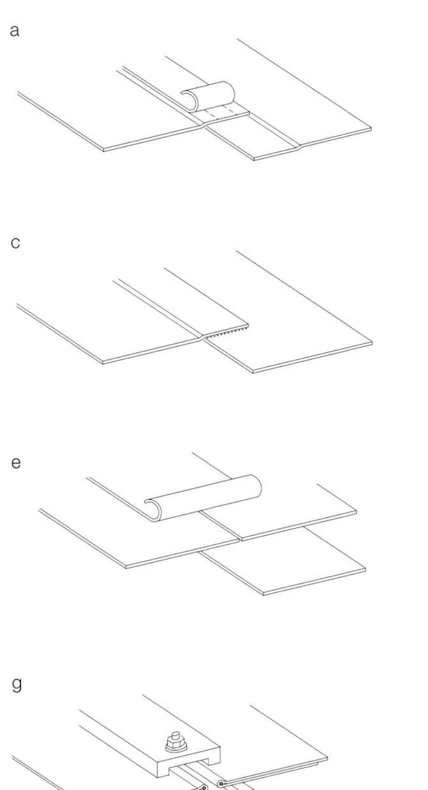


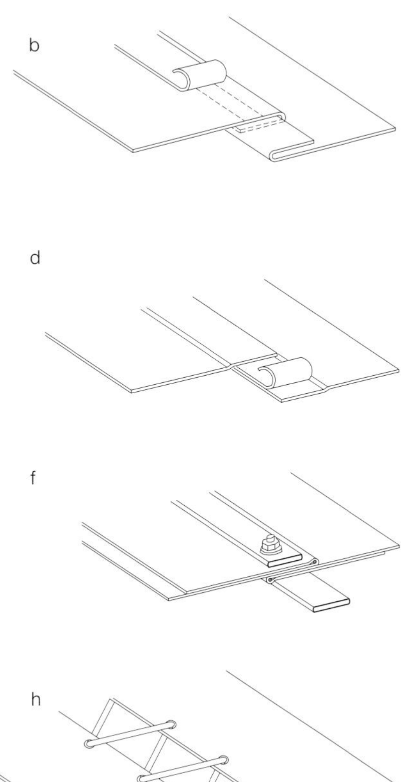


2.4.14.16 Seams and connections between pieces of material

a sewn seam with cover strip
b double lapped seam with cover strip
c welded seam
d welded seam with extra piece of material
e butt joint with cover strips to both sides
f butt joint with clamping plates
g butt joint with clamping plates over edge beading
h tied connection

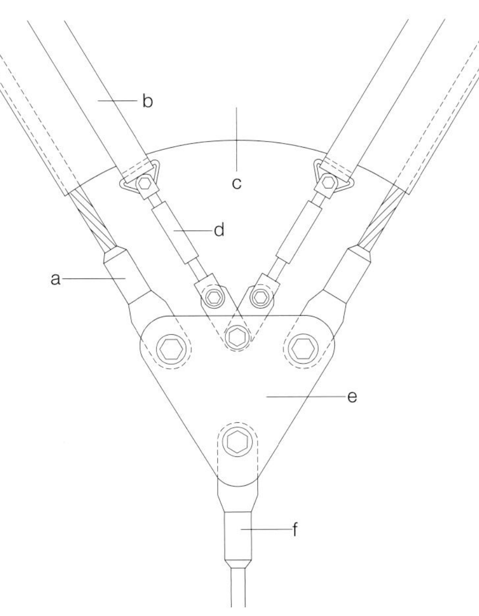


2.4.14.17 Open membrane corner; corner assembly held by eye fittings [06]: a edge cable with eye fitting, b strap, c membrane, d turnbuckle, e metal fitting, f guy cable with eye fitting

In a closed corner the membrane is held from above and below by corner fittings with clamping bolts.

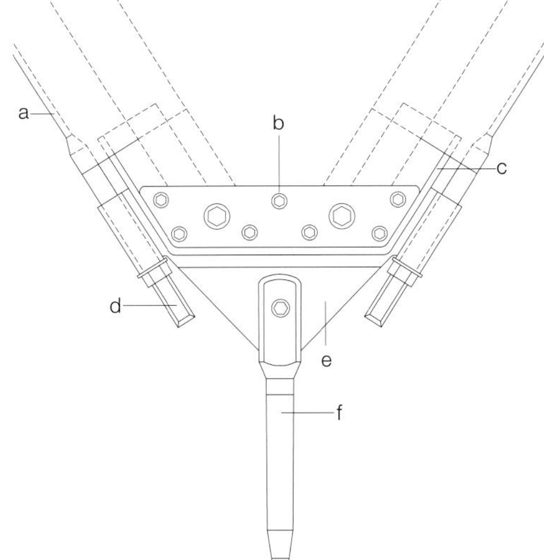


2.4.14.18 Closed membrane corner with corner assembly [15]: a edge cable, b upper section of metal fitting, c edge beading, d clamping bolt, e lower section of metal fitting, f guy cable with fork fitting

Sewn-on strap
With small loads the forces can be transferred by a strap alone to the guying positions. It must be protected against the weather, ultraviolet radiation and moisture by means of membrane pockets or cover strips.

Cable with tied connection
The membrane is tied to the edge cable by UV-stabilised polypropylene cables with a steel core. This type of construction can be tensioned step by step (with a lot of effort). The eyes along the edge are positioned directly adjacent to the edge beading in order to prevent overstressing the membrane. Creases along the edge are prevented by employing short abutting edge beading rods instead of an edge beading cable.

Cable with individual clamped elements
The member is held by edge beading and clamping plates. Cable and membrane are connected via (sheet) metal fittings, which are fixed to the clamping plates by clamping bolts at a regular spacing. The U-shaped fittings are made of galvanised steel or aluminium, but fittings of bendable sheet metal are also available and can be adapted to suit the size of the cable. A profiled strip of rigid plastic (e.g. polyamide) can be inserted between cable and sheet metal to prevent galvanic corrosion. The spacing of the fittings should match that of the clamping bolts.

Corners
Forces from membrane, edge cable and edge strap meet at the corners of the membrane and are diverted into a supporting construction. We distinguish between open and closed membrane corners. In the open membrane corner only the edge cable and edge strap are connected to the edge fitting, while the membrane is cut in an arc around the fitting.
A retainer is required to prevent the membrane slipping. This can be achieved by means of straps parallel with the edge, strips of membrane or flat metal fittings, which are fixed to the edge cable by flat metal clamps. It is also possible to fix them to the corner fitting with metal fasteners and plates or auxiliary cables.

Drainage
Circular sections made of foam material can be included along the edges in membrane pockets to control rainwater run-off. Alternatively, plastic or metal angle sections can be clamped on to discharge the rainwater.
Another possibility is to lay short pieces of pipe in membrane pockets open on the top.

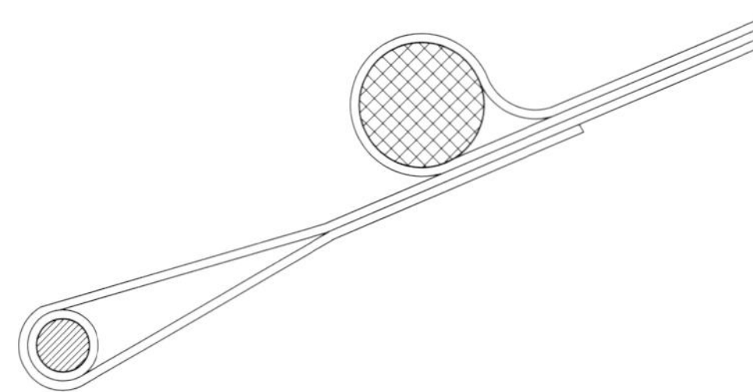

2.4.14.19 Rainwater deflector made of foam profile fitted in membrane pocket

Junction with wall
Transitions between a membrane roof and a wall or facade construction usually employ membrane skirts. These skirts are attached to the roof membrane and the facade by clamping plates, or are formed with a membrane overhanging the edge of the roof. Because the membrane may move, the skirts are fixed without being prestressed. If the movements are small, sponge rubber beads can be used instead.

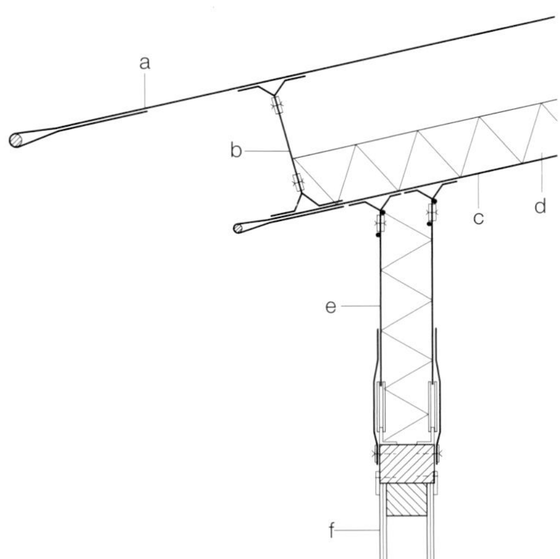


2.4.14.20 Detail of junction with facade, with clamped membrane skirt [07]: a outer membrane, b closure, c inner membrane, d thermal insulation, e insulated membrane skirt, f glass facade

• Rigid edge
Linear edge
Various options are available for the detail at a rigid edge.

Direct clamping plate connection
The membrane is clamped directly to the edge construction (concrete, timber or steel member) by using clamping plates and bolts. The membrane should be protected by a strip of membrane material wherever it passes over an edge turned up or down. To prevent rainwater collecting along the edge, the clamping plates should be spaced further apart or cover strips should be added.

Edge beading rail
The membrane and its edge beading are threaded into a profiled rail of lightweight metal (e.g. aluminium) or plastic. Edge beading rails are available in various designs. They can be fixed directly to a rigid edge member or used as part of an edge fitting.

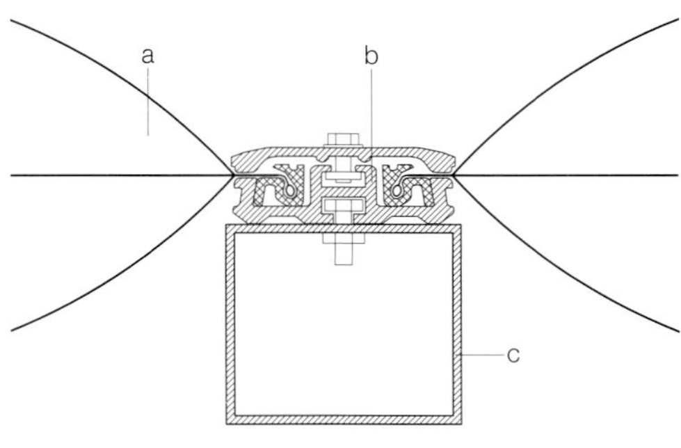


2.4.14.21 Edge beading rail for pneumatic cushions: a three-ply foil cushion, b edge beading rail, c loadbearing member

Tube in pocket
A steel tube subjected to bending, which is assembled from individual segments prior to erection, is permanently connected to the primary loadbearing structure and threaded through a pocket in the membrane.
A semicircle is cut out of the membrane at the anchorage points.
The included angle of the pocket should be kept small so as not to tear open the seam.

Tube with tied connection
As for the cable with tied connection, the membrane is tied tightly to the steel tube edge member.

Connection with metal fittings
The design of the fittings can vary according to application. They can be assembled from U-shaped steel sections, edge beading rails, clamping bolts or other metal fittings. Clamping bolts permit infinite (re)adjustment and compensation for manufacturing tolerances. Pivoted anchor bolts enable the metal fittings to be adapted to match the slope of the membrane.

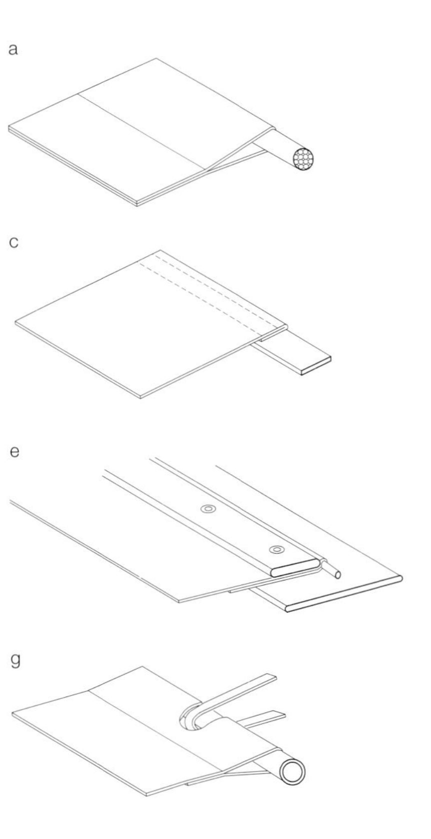


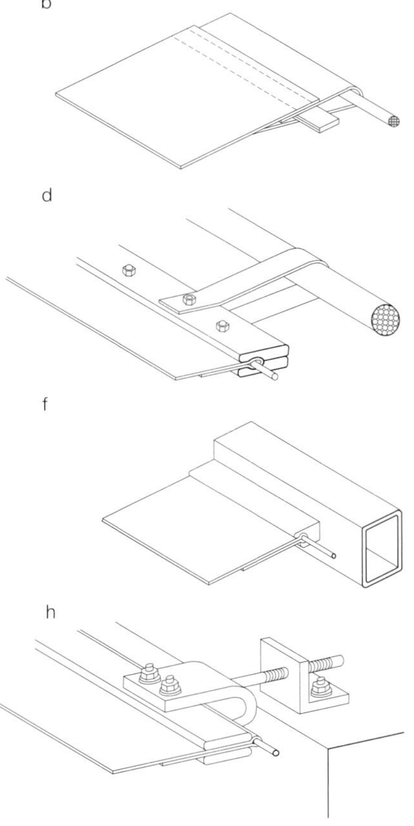


2.4.14.22 Edge construction options

a cable in pocket
b cable in pocket with strap
c sewn-on strap
d cable with sheet metal fittings
e direct clamping plate connection
f connection with edge beading rail
g tube in pocket
h connection with metal fitting

Corners
As a rigid membrane corner involves a change of direction of the membrane edge alone, no special detailing is required. The clamping plates are adapted to suit the angle at the corner.

Drainage
Standard gutters or steel sections, fitted into the membrane, are used for draining the rainwater.

Point supports
High and low points are either linear or spread arrangements in order to avoid stress peaks. A larger bearing surface produces a more even stress distribution. This considerably reduces the risk of local failure.

• High points
Eye loops and rosettes
Linear solutions only subjected to tension are the eye loop and its derivative the rosette. The design principle corresponds to that of a cable in a pocket.

Ring
The membrane is attached to a ring using clamping plates. This ring is either freely suspended, e.g. via cables, or firmly fixed to a loadbearing construction, e.g. mast. Cylindrical rings made from steel flat are used for PVC-coated polyester textiles. Conical rings adapted to suit the incoming angle of the membrane are better for glass-fibre textiles, which are vulnerable to buckling. Various cover arrangements such as steel vessel bases, rooflights of glass fibre-reinforced synthetic resin, Plexiglas or polycarbonate, and non-loadbearing textile membranes may be used to make the construction watertight.

Hump
The planiform humps are primarily subjected to compression and are made from a strong membrane material, leather or metal.
Hump forms are either standardised or adapted to suit the membrane surface. Various forms are employed. Metal vessel bases with welded ribs are suitable for heavy loads. The vessel can be split into individual strips of sheet metal to give the hump a more lightweight appearance.
Another option is to use overlapping lamellae of timber or sheet metal to form a star-shaped, flat support.
The hump surface can also be divided into small, plate-like segments supported by a tree-like structure.

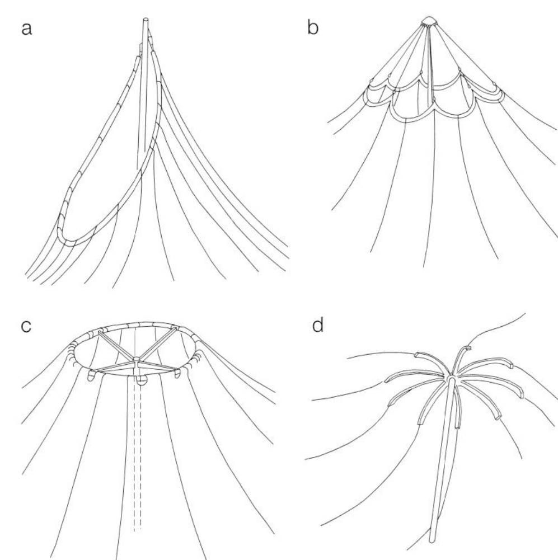

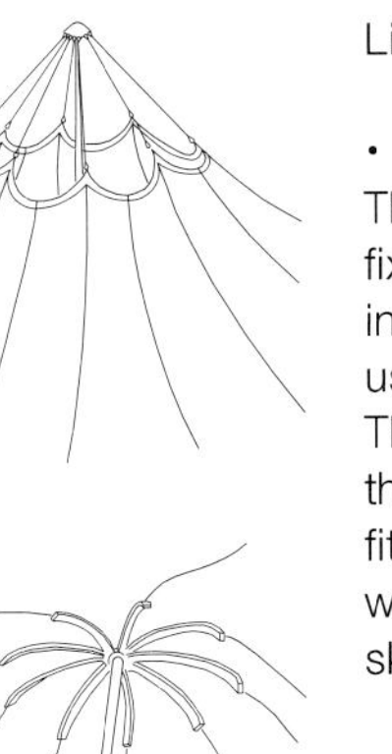


2.4.14.23 High point options

a eye loop
b rosette
c ring
d hump

• Low points
Low points use the same design principles as high points, but also have to provide for drainage.
Besides the direct connection between the low point and the foundation, an inverted eye loop or rosette is also possible. In these open constructions the cable guys should be provided at an adequate spacing so that snow traps are not created.
Inverted umbrella membrane canopies are usually drained via downpipes integrated into the columns, or via the columns themselves. To prevent the water freezing, the pipe can be insulated and heated. The rainwater flows into the downpipe via membrane skirts clamped on and via gullies. Inverted humps are drained via hoses.

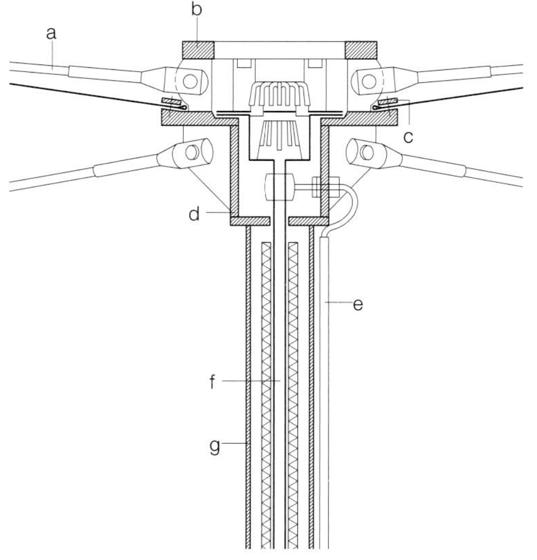


2.4.14.24 Drainage via column: a steel cable, b steel flat ring, c clamping ring, d head of column, e cable for electric heating, f rainwater downpipe, g pin-jointed column

Linear supports

• Arch
The membrane can be draped over the arch, fixed with edge beading rails and edge beading, or be clamped directly to the arch member using clamping plates.
The membrane can also be fixed at points on the arch in catenary fashion using special fittings. This type of connection must be made watertight with non-loadbearing membrane skirts.

2.4.14.25 Arch construction; membrane attached with clamping plates: a outer membrane, b cover strip, c glulam arch, d thermal insulation, e vapour barrier, f inner membrane

• Hip and valley cables
Hip and valley cables differ only slightly in terms of detailing.
They lie above or below the membrane, which is strengthened at this point, and are fixed by way of loops or membrane pockets. Straps made from steel flat, membrane retainers from sheet metal or sections of steel tube are other options for fixing the membrane to the cable.

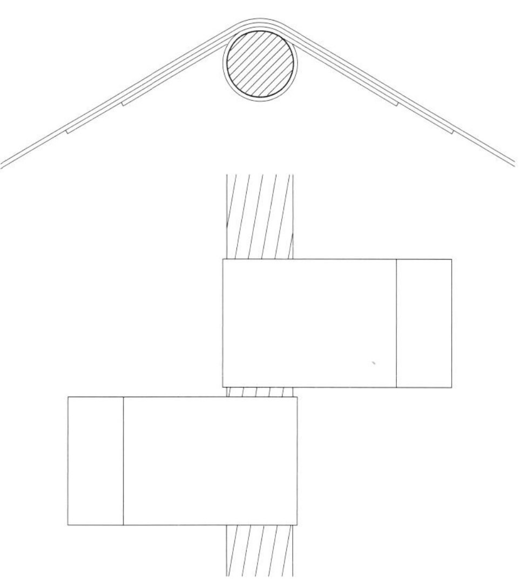

2.4.14.26 Hip cable with loops [05]

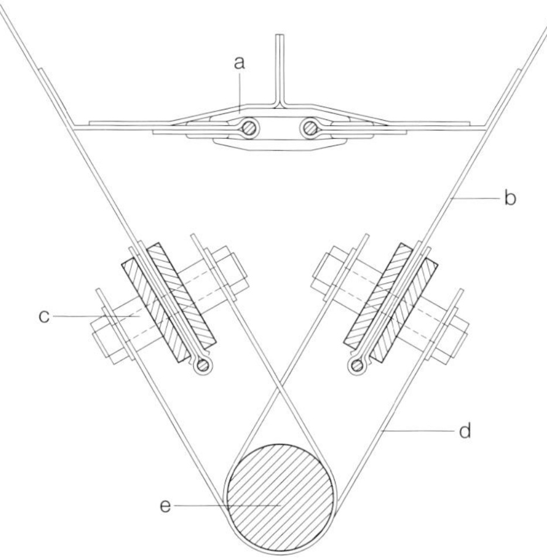


2.4.14.27 Valley cable with membrane retainers made of sheet steel [05]: a tied gutter with cover strip, b membrane, c clamping arrangement, d sheet metal shackle, e valley cable

| | Cotton textile | PTFE textile | Polyester or aramid-fibre textile | | | Glass-fibre textile | | Aramid-fibre text. | ETFE foil | THV foil |
|---|---|---|---|---|---|---|---|---|---|---|
| Coating | | | PVC | PVC | PVC | PTFE | silicone | PTFE | | |
| Surface refinement | impreg-nation | | acrylic lacquer | PVDF lacquer | PVF laminate | | | | | |
| Soiling behaviour | 0 | ++ | 0 | + | ++ | ++ | + | ++ | ++ | ++ |
| Life expectancy [years] | < 5 | > 25 | > 20 | > 20 | > 20 | > 25 | > 20 | > 25 | > 25 | > 20 |

2.4.14.28 Maintenance requirements and life expectancy [11, 14, 16, 17, 24]
++ very good, + good, o satisfactory

**Additional measures**

Snow

It may be necessary to clear the snow from shallow roof surfaces, valleys etc. This can be done by hand in accessible areas. On multi-skin (above all pneumatic) constructions heated air (e.g. process air) can be pumped into the outer cavity to melt the snow. However, the melt water must be able to drain away properly.

Adaptable or mobile membrane structures, e.g. folding inverted umbrella canopies, should be folded down or removed and stored during the winter so that they are not exposed to snowfall.

Sunshading

Membrane structures heat up rapidly and considerably when exposed to solar radiation. Besides air conditioning or similar measures and the provision of sunshades, adequate natural/mechanical ventilation must be possible.

• Choice of material

Opaque, reflective membranes (mostly white) reduce the heat absorption in hot climates, i.e. they minimise the amount of ambient heat entering the interior.

• Sunshading measures

In hot and tropical regions, nets suspended above the membrane can provide shade. Another advantage of this is the attenuation of impact noise during heavy rainfall.

Adequate clearance between membrane and nets is required to avoid a build-up of heat and guarantee adequate ventilation.

The mesh of the nets should not be too small because otherwise rainwater creates additional loads (wind loads) due to its surface tension.

• Ventilation

Thermal currents can be exploited to ventilate the interior by placing exhaust-air outlets at the highest and fresh-air inlets at the lowest points. If the outlets are larger than the inlets, this creates a negative pressure in the interior, which improves the ventilation.

**Maintenance and service life**

Maintenance

The amount of maintenance required by a membrane roof depends on the surface characteristics of the material or the coating. The customary membrane materials exhibit a good to very good soiling behaviour; the low adhesion of the materials results in a "self-cleaning effect", where dust and dirt are washed away by the rain. Membrane materials exposed to more severe soiling are either replaced (cotton) or cleaned regularly in accordance with the manufacturer's instructions.

Service life

Membrane materials, apart from cotton, will last at least 20 years.

**Repair**

As membranes embody both covering and loadbearing functions, any repair measures must also be considered in terms of their effect on the membrane's structural behaviour. While minor damage may be rectified by on-site welding, more serious damage will probably mean that segments or indeed the entire membrane will have to be replaced. Metal components (e.g. clamping plates, steel cables) should be checked for corrosion during repair work and replaced as required (see also "Metal profiled sheeting and metal panels").

**References**

[01] Battle, G.: Membranen für eine wohltemperierte Umwelt; Arch-plus 107/1991
[02] Brinkmann, G.: Leicht und weit – Zur Konstruktion weitgespannter Flächentragwerke; Weinheim; VCH Verlags-GmbH; 1990
[03] Bubner, E.: Membrankonstruktionen – Leichtbaukonstruktionen pt 1; Cologne-Braunsfeld; Verlagsgesellschaft Rudolf Müller; 1979
[04] Bubner, E.: Membrankonstruktionen 2; Cologne-Braunsfeld; Verlagsgesellschaft Rudolf Müller; 1981
[05] Bubner, E.: Membrankonstruktionen – Verbindungstechniken; Essen; Druckerei Wehlmann GmbH; 1999
[06] CENO TEC GmbH: product information
[07] Dangl V., Kagerer F., Kettenberger J.: Studienarbeit – Doppellagige und wärmegedämmte Membrankonstruktionen; Faculty of Architecture – Chair of Structural Engineering; Munich Technical University; 2000
[08] Der Weg zum textilen Bauwerk: pub. Arbeitskreis Textile Architektur
[09] DIN 4134: Air-supported structures; structural design, construction and operation; Berlin; Beuth Verlag; 1983
[10] Drüsedau, H.: IL 15 – Lufthallenhandbuch, Mitteilungen des Instituts für Leichte Flächentragwerke; Stuttgart University; 1983
[11] Ferrari S. A.: product information
[12] Flontex Walter Weissinger GmbH: product information
[13] Foiltec GmbH: product information
[14] Heytex Julius Heywinkel: product information
[15] Klein,R.: Unverwechselbares Membrandach – Kulturzentrum in Puchheim; Deutsche Bauzeitschrift 12/1999
[16] Mehler Haku GmbH: product information
[17] Moritz, K.: Membranwerkstoffe im Hochbau; Detail 06/2000
[18] Moritz, K.: Materialeinsatz und Konfektion von Membranwerkstoffen; Stahlbau 69/2000
[19] Rein, A.; Wilhelm V.: Das Konstruieren mit Membranen; Detail 06/2000
[20] Schock, H.-J.: Segel, Folien und Membranen – Innovative Konstruktionen in der textilen Architektur; Basel/Berlin/Boston; Birkhäuser Verlag; 1997
[21] Skyspan GmbH: product information
[22] Sobek, W.: Technologische Grundlagen des textilen Bauens, Detail 06/1994
[23] Sobek, W.; Speth M.: Textile Werkstoffe; Bauingenieur 70/1995
[24] Verseidag Indutex GmbH: product information

## Energy production

Photovoltaic and thermal energy systems

The energy provided by incident solar radiation in Europe is adequate for realistic active uses. However, its intensity is diminished by seasonal and weather-related fluctuations.

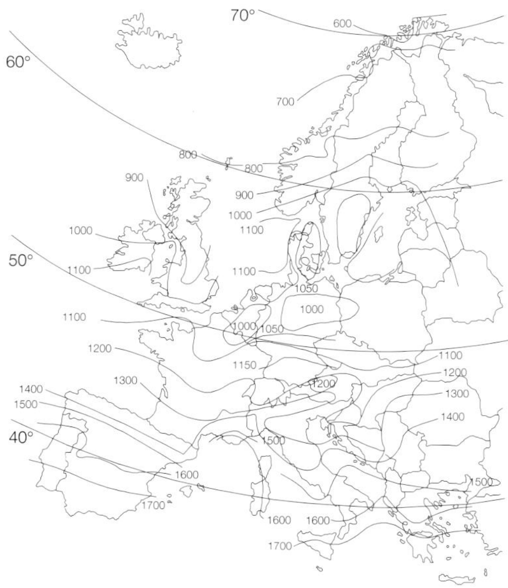


2.4.15.1 Average annual incident radiation figures for Europe [kWh/m²a] [11]

For the roof there are two forms of energy production to consider: photovoltaic systems, in which solar cells convert light energy directly into an electric current, and thermal energy systems, in which collectors generate usable heat.

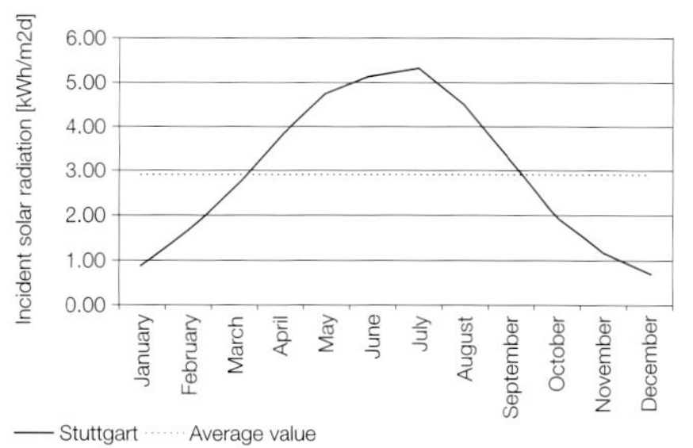


2.4.15.2 Average daily incident solar radiation level for Stuttgart [39]

## Photovoltaic systems

Raw materials and manufacture, properties, components

### Raw materials and manufacture

We distinguish between crystalline cells and thin-film cells. Crystalline solar cells are produced from thin slices (approx. 0.3 mm) of monocrystalline or polycrystalline silicon. The slices are given a dark antireflective coating, which can be in a variety of colours. The lighter the colour, the lower the degree of efficiency. These cells have a metallic sheen. In thin-film cells, glass or plastic in a rigid or flexible form is coated directly with thin solar cells (approx. 0.002 mm). [12, 20, 31] Thin-film cells have a dark, non-shiny colouring.

### Properties

Biological and chemical properties

The silicon used for crystalline and amorphous cells is non-toxic. Some of the materials used in the production of thin-film cells are toxic but are not hazardous, because only small quantities are used and the finished cells are hermetically sealed. [31]

Physical properties

The output of photovoltaic cells is specified in $W_{Peak}$. This output allows us to estimate the annual electricity yield. The service life of solar cells is at least 25 years, and the energy used in their production is recovered within 2–4 years. [31]

Solar cells deliver a d.c. voltage, which increases the risk of arcing. This arcing is not self-extinguishing during exposure to radiation and can lead to fires. As normal fuses do not work with photovoltaic systems, special attention must be paid to short-circuit safety. [12]

In Germany the net energy yield of photovoltaic systems is about 600 kWh/kWpa in the north and about 900 kWh/kWpa in the south. [31]

### Components

Crystalline solar cells are made in sizes of max. 15 x 15 cm. To create larger systems, cells are grouped in laminated components with a visible grid arrangement. These are usually assembled on a multi-ply plastic film and always covered with panes of toughened safety glass. Thin-film components have a distinct grid and a uniform dark colouring. There is a connection box, 20–35 mm high, at the rear of each component. Components are often provided with a peripheral aluminium frame 35–50 mm high to provide better fixing options and add some stability.

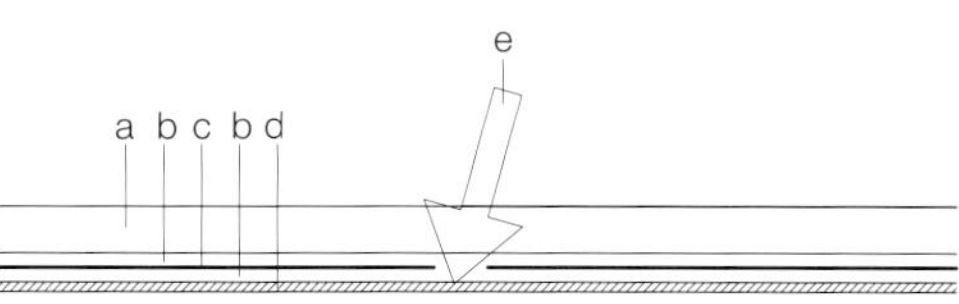


Glass-plastic component

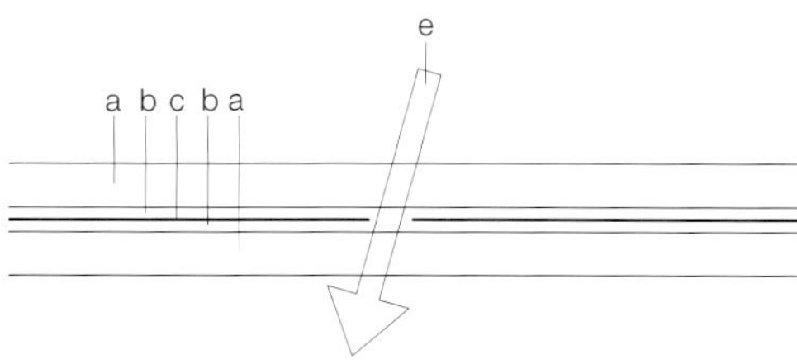


Double glazing component

2.4.15.4 Structure of glass-plastic and double glazing components with crystalline cells: a toughened safety glass, b plastic embedment layer (ethylene vinyl acetate), c crystalline silicon cell, d opaque plastic composite film (polyester and polyvinyl fluoride), e incident solar radiation

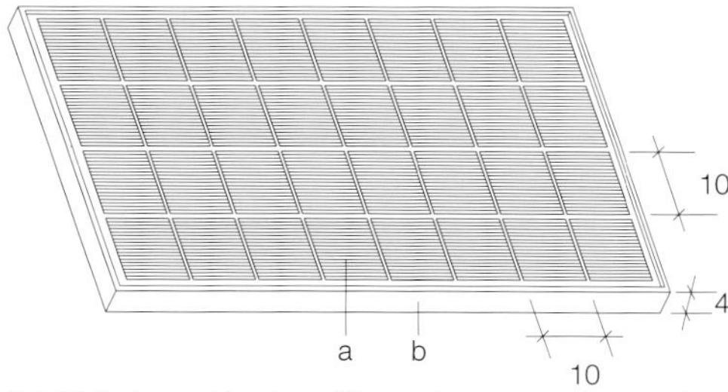


2.4.15.5 Isometric view of framed component comprising crystalline cells: a solar cell, b aluminium frame

| | Weight [kg/m²] | Thickness [mm] |
|---|---|---|
| Glass-plastic component | 11–14 kg/m² | 4–5 |
| Double glazing component | 17–22 kg/m² | 8–9 |

2.4.15.6 Weights and thicknesses of photovoltaic components

| Type | Std. area/ max. area | Cell type | Materials | Degree of efficiency | Cell colour |
|---|---|---|---|---|---|
| crystalline cells | 0.5–1.0 m²/ 6 m² | monocrystalline | silicon (Si) | 11.4–14.0% | dark blue to black |
| | | polycrystalline | silicon (Si) | 9.4–12.9% | dark blue, silver-grey |
| thin-film cells | 0.6–1.2 m²/ 1.2 m² | amorphous silicon | silicon (Si) | 6.8–8% | red-brown |
| | | copper-indium-diselenite (CIS) | copper (Cu) indium (In) selenium (Se) | 10–13% | black |
| | | cadmium-telluride | cadmium (Cd) tellurium (Te) | 9–10% | black with green |

2.4.15.3 Types and properties of solar cells

| | Width [mm] | Length [mm] | Manufacturer |
|---|---|---|---|
| Components with crystalline cells | 483 | 1200 | [01] |
| | 502 | 1105/1456 | [14] |
| | 652 | 526/751/976 | [21] |
| | 654 | 1470 | [27] |
| | 731 | 1456/1909 | [14] |
| | 805 | 1350 | [05] |
| | 981 | 1097 | [28] |
| | 1283 | 1892 | [04] |
| Thin-film components | 329 | 748/1239 | [25] |
| | 600 | 1000/1200 | [04], [02] |

2.4.15.7 Dimensions of framed photovoltaic components

Double glazing units are not laminated glazing units in accordance with the standards, but can be made into laminated safety glass units. Building authority approval is then required on a case-by-case basis when using such glass for overhead glazing.

Sizes of components
Dimensions vary widely according to the manufacturer. Custom-made components are possible using the forms and sizes of glass typical in building work. The maximum dimensions of thin-film cells are governed by the production plant.

Light transmittance
Solar energy components are not translucent, but can be produced in semi-transparent forms if a lower degree of efficiency is acceptable. To do this, crystalline cells in double glazing units can be spaced further apart. Cells can also be perforated to introduce a degree of transparency (degree of transmission approx. 20%). This does not alter the colour spectrum of the incoming light. Thin-film components made of amorphous silicon can be produced in a direct semi-transparent form or spaced out on a grid.

## Thermal energy systems

Physical properties, components

The energy of the absorbed radiation heats a liquid or gaseous medium. Besides systems for providing hot water, there are also systems for backing up space heating, with long-term storage, and systems for generating hot air.

### Physical properties

Degree of efficiency
The degree of efficiency of solar collectors decreases as the temperature differential increases with respect to the ambient temperature. If there is no circulation of the heat transfer medium, temperatures of up to 250°C can occur at the connections.

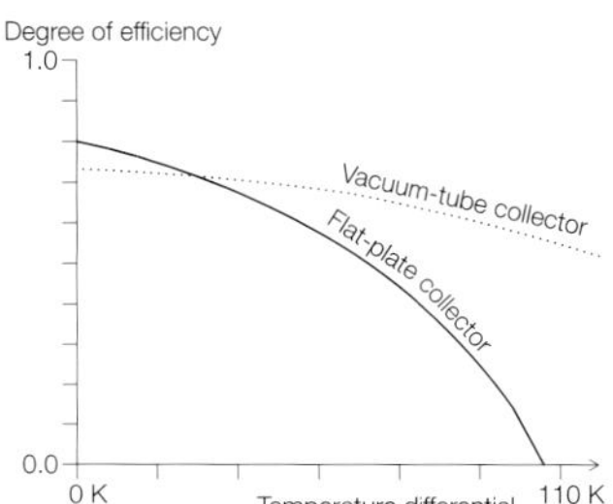


2.4.15.8 Degrees of efficiency of flat-plate collectors and vacuum-tube collectors in relation to temperature differential between heat transfer medium and ambient temperature

Energy yield
The annual energy yield from flat-plate collectors, for an annual incident radiation figure of 1040 kWh/m²a, is at least 525 kWh/m²a, minus system losses of approx. 30%. Short-term storage can store the energy for 2–3 days; longer storage is not normally advisable for hot water systems. Owing to seasonal fluctuations, without long-term storage approx. 60% of the annual energy required for hot water can be generated using solar energy. In Germany a flat-plate collector measuring about 1.5–2.0 m² can provide the hot water requirements of one person; a vacuum-tube collector need only be 1.0–1.5 m². [22]

### Components

We distinguish between flat-plate and vacuum-tube collectors.

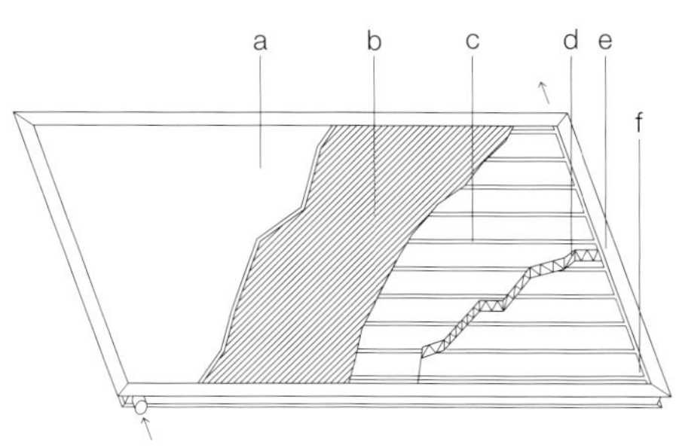


2.4.15.10 Isometric view of a flat-plate collector: a glass cover, b absorber, c pipes conveying heat transfer medium, d insulation, e aluminium frame, f rear panel

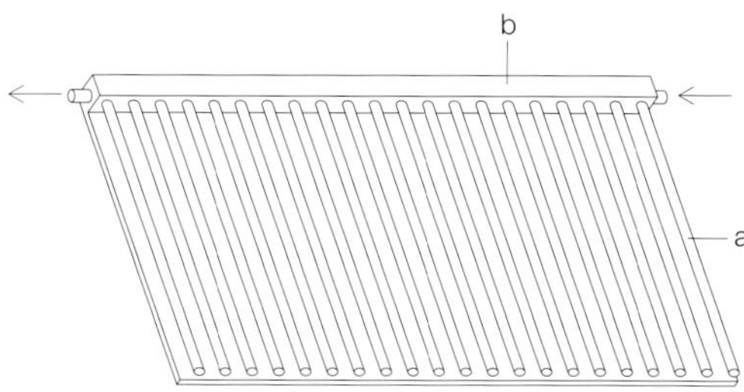


2.4.15.11 Isometric view of a vacuum-tube collector: a vacuum tubes, b manifold housing

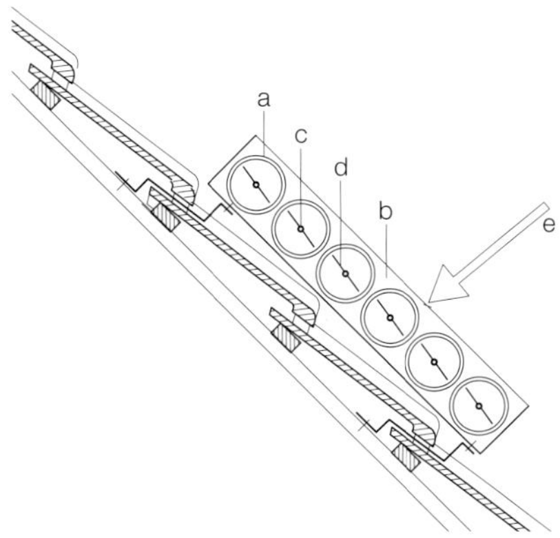


2.4.15.12 Section through a vacuum-tube collector with tubes arranged horizontally: a evacuated glass tube, b manifold housing, c pipes conveying heat transfer medium, d absorber, e incident solar radiation

| Type of collector | Area [m²] | Width [mm] | Length [mm] | Thickness [mm] | Manufacturer | Weight [kg/m²] |
|---|---|---|---|---|---|---|
| Flat-plate collectors | 0.6–6 | 753 | 2385 | 102 | [28] | 20–25 |
| | | 1083 | 2090 | 105 | [29] | |
| | | 1180 | 1880 | 105 | [30] | |
| | | 1215 | 2151 | 110 | [31] | |
| | | 1238 | 2077 | 100 | [32] | |
| | | 1978 | 1008 | 78 | [33] | |
| | | 2115 | 1135 | 112 | [34] | |
| Vacuum-tube collectors | 1.5–4.5 | 741 | 2028 | 138 | [28] | 15–22 |
| | | 730 | 2920 | 120 | [36] | |
| | | 1540 | 1650 | 137 | [30] | |
| | | 1830 | 1638 | 120 | [32] | |
| | | 2124 | 1960 | 130 | [39] | |

2.4.15.9 Selected sizes of solar collectors

Form and dimensions
Flat-plate collectors consist of a thermally insulated housing, usually with a dark grey absorber, pipes and a transparent cover.
Besides square and rectangular panels, other shapes are also possible.
Vacuum-tube collectors consist of almost completely evacuated glass tubes about 2 m long, which contain the absorber and the pipes filled with the heat transfer medium. The tubes can be positioned horizontally or vertically. They achieve higher yields than flat-plate collectors, especially with a low level of incident radiation, and are also suitable for unfavourable roof pitches because the tubes can be aligned to suit the incident radiation.

## Photovoltaic and thermal energy systems

Laying, maintenance and repair

### Laying

Orientation
Solar cells or collectors should be aligned perpendicular to the incident solar radiation. The optimum angle depends on the geographical position, the particular application and the deviation from due south. The panels should be positioned at a steeper angle when facing

north and where increased winter usage is expected. A minimum angle of 25° is required to guarantee an adequate self-cleaning effect for the panels. Very good yields are generally achieved with panels mounted at an angle of about 35° and facing southeast to southwest. [11]

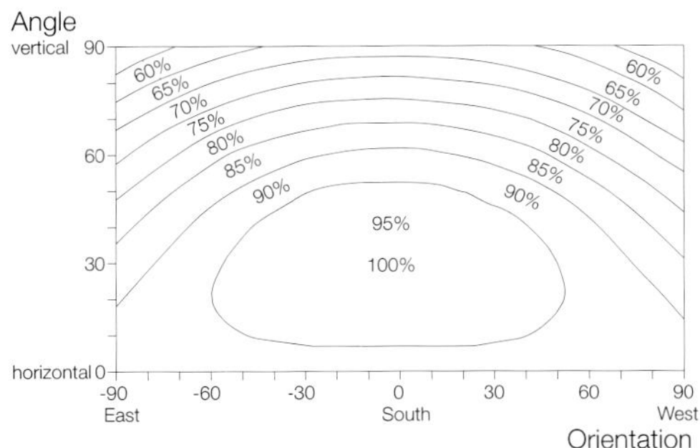


2.4.15.13 Relative incident solar radiation on surfaces in relation to angle and orientation (Central Europe) [07]

| System | Applications | Operating period | Orientation | Angle |
|---|---|---|---|---|
| Photovoltaic | electricity supplies | whole year | south ± 35° | 22°–45° |
| Thermal energy | general hot water | April–October | south ± 45° | 15°–45° |
| | | whole year | south ± 30° | 30°–50° |
| | swimming pool heating | April–October | south ± 90° | 0°–30° |
| | solar heating | October–April | south ± 15° | 45°–70° |
| | solar local heating | whole year | south ± 30° | 15°–35° |
| | cooling | May–September | south ± 15° | 30°–40° |

2.4.15.14 Favourable orientation and angle of energy production surfaces [22]

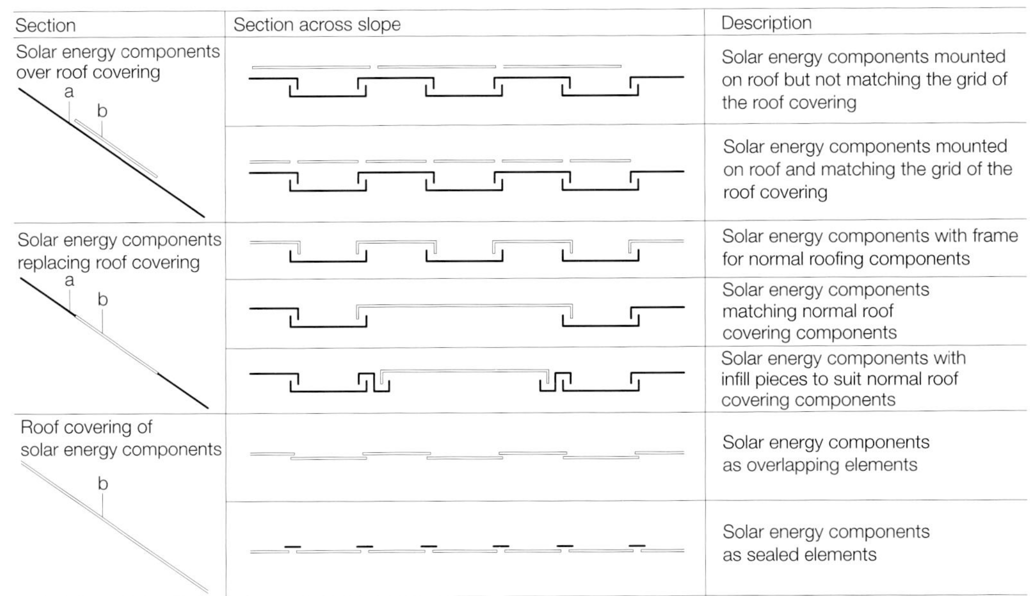

Section
Section across slope
Description
Solar energy components over roof covering
a
b
Solar energy components mounted on roof but not matching the grid of the roof covering
Solar energy components mounted on roof and matching the grid of the roof covering
Solar energy components replacing roof covering
a
b
Solar energy components with frame for normal roofing components
Solar energy components matching normal roof covering components
Solar energy components with infill pieces to suit normal roof covering components
Roof covering of solar energy components
b
Solar energy components as overlapping elements
Solar energy components as sealed elements


2.4.15.15 Arrangement of energy production components on a pitched roof: a normal roof covering component, b energy production component

Shading
Shadow falling on components or cells of photovoltaic systems can greatly reduce the output of the system and even lead to heat damage of the modules in the shade. The loss in yield of solar collectors is proportional to the area in the shade. [31]

Ventilation
As solar cells can heat up by 50°C when exposed to solar radiation and the degree of efficiency drops by up to 25% in these conditions, the underside of such panels should be well ventilated. The output of solar collector systems actually benefits from some heat dissipation.

Lightning protection
As a rule, photovoltaic systems do not increase the risk of lightning striking the building. If the building has an external lightning protection system, the photovoltaic system should be connected to it. Care should be taken to ensure that lightning conductors do not cast a shadow over the solar cells. A safety clearance of at least 200 mm should be maintained between lightning conductors and solar panels. [07, 09]

Safety
Rooftop photovoltaic components for protected low-voltage systems (≤ 120 Vdc) can also be installed by experienced DIY enthusiasts familiar with electrical systems. However, a high degree of safety must then be incorporated into the system to allow for installation errors. [35]

Arrangement
There are three principal approaches to positioning roof-mounted energy production components on a pitched roof. Covering components that are not part of the energy production system are designated here as normal components.

• Supplementary to normal roof covering
The energy production components are positioned above a complete roof covering, and may be coordinated with the grid of the normal roof covering.

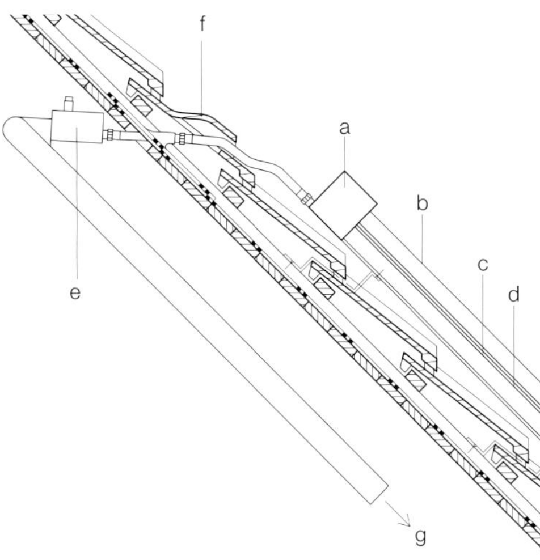


2.4.15.16 Rooftop mounting and connection of a vacuum-tube collector: a evacuated glass tube, b manifold housing, c pipes, d absorber, e bleed valve, f ventilating tile, g return line

• As substitute for normal roof components
Parts of the normal roof covering are removed and replaced by energy production components.

Solar energy components matching normal roof covering components
The solar energy components are based on normal components but have been converted and supplemented to contribute to energy production. This approach is mainly suitable for photovoltaic applications.
The edge and special components of the normal roof covering can still be employed.

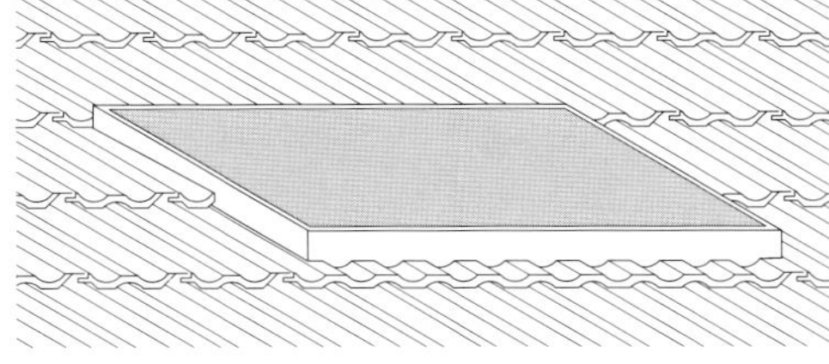

2.4.15.17 Energy production component fitted into normal roof covering

Solar energy components with peripheral frame to suit normal roof covering
On roof coverings of small-format components, several of these are replaced by a solar energy

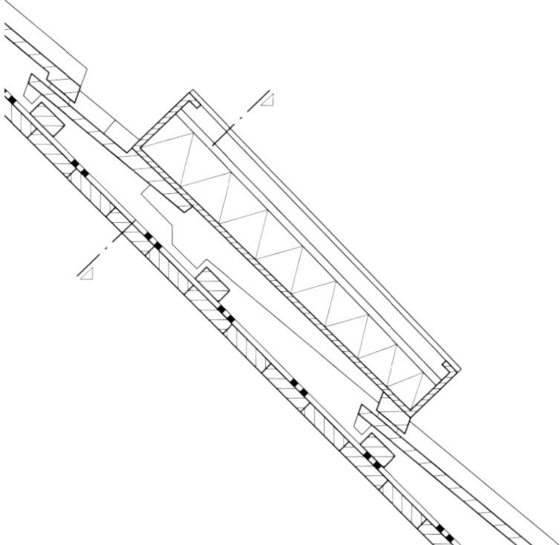

2.4.15.18 Longitudinal section through a collector with frame to suit normal roof covering [03]

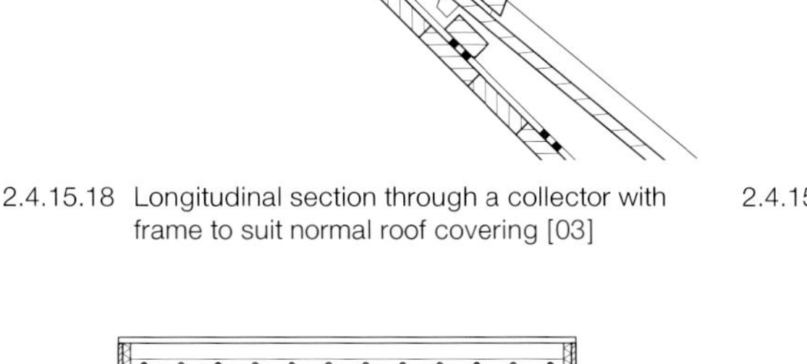

2.4.15.19 Transverse section through a collector with frame to suit normal roof covering [03]

component with a peripheral frame that fits exactly into the surrounding normal components. This approach is suitable when only some areas are required for energy systems.

Solar energy components with infill pieces
A large area of the normal roof covering is replaced by large-format solar energy components, which are then joined to the normal roof covering using infill pieces. Rainwater can drain over or under the energy production components. This approach is very popular for thermal energy systems. Prefabricated subassemblies are available to suit the solar energy components and the normal roof covering employed. In some cases complete collectors and peripheral frames are supplied ready for installation.

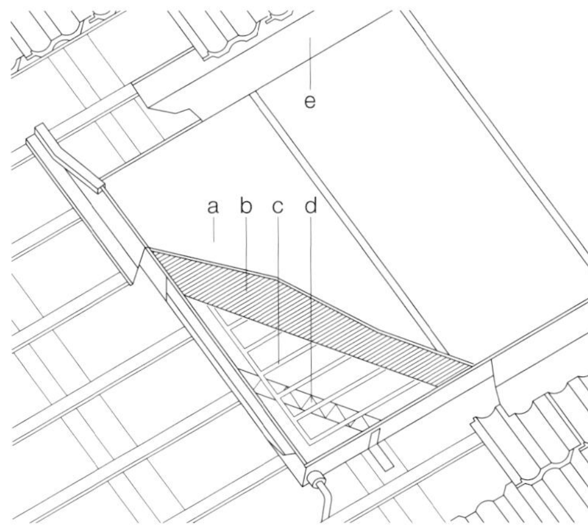


2.4.15.20 Solar energy component with infill pieces: a glass cover, b absorber, c pipes conveying heat transfer medium, d insulation, e sheet metal infill piece (flashing)

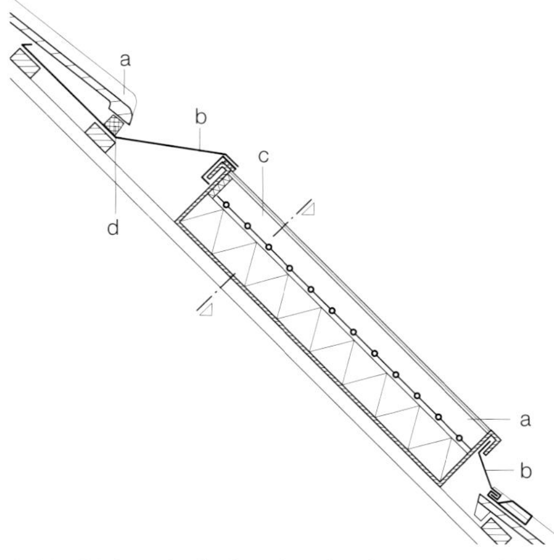


2.4.15.21 Longitudinal section showing upper and lower edge details, with water run-off over the collector: a, b, c, d – see figure 2.4.15.22 below

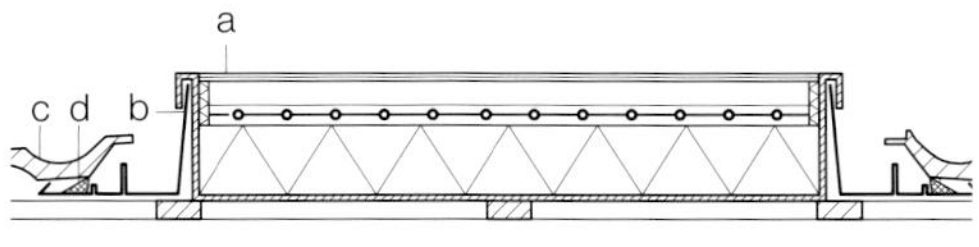
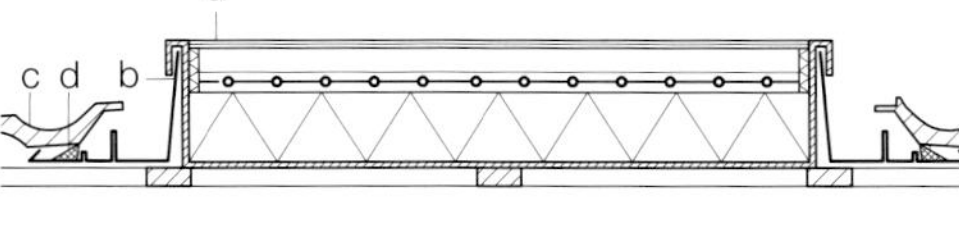


2.4.15.22 Transverse section showing edge details, with water run-off over the collector: a collector, b sheet metal perimeter flashing, c roof covering, d closure piece [17]

**Roof covering of solar energy components**
Here, the energy production components also act as the roof covering layer. This creates a uniform appearance.

Overlapping photovoltaic panels
The flat panels are laid with overlaps. The transverse joints are complicated and usually require the use of additional profiles.

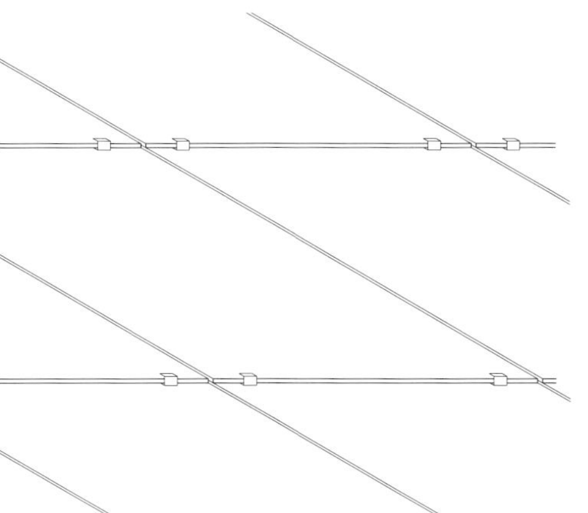

2.4.15.23 Photovoltaic roof panels laid as an overlapping roof covering

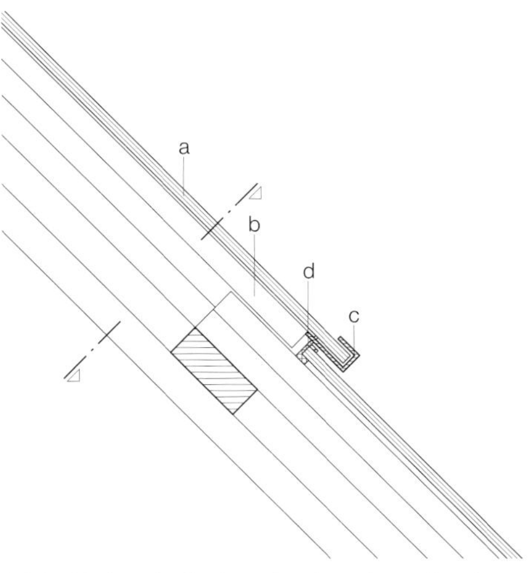


2.4.15.24 Longitudinal section through overlapping components [23]: a, b, c, d – see figure 2.4.15.25 below

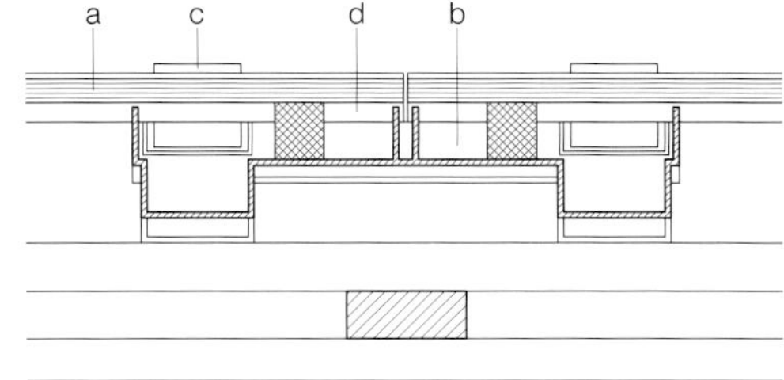


2.4.15.25 Transverse section through the roof covering: a solar panel, b aluminium section, c mounting, d preformed seal [23]

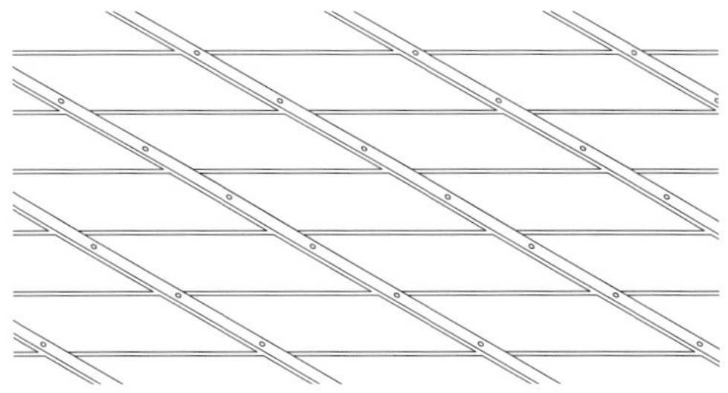

2.4.15.26 Thin-film components laid as a sealed roof covering with patent glazing caps [22]

Sealed covering of photovoltaic panels

The elements are laid in a similar fashion to patent glazing, generally with a further waterproofing layer and thermal insulation below the roof covering.

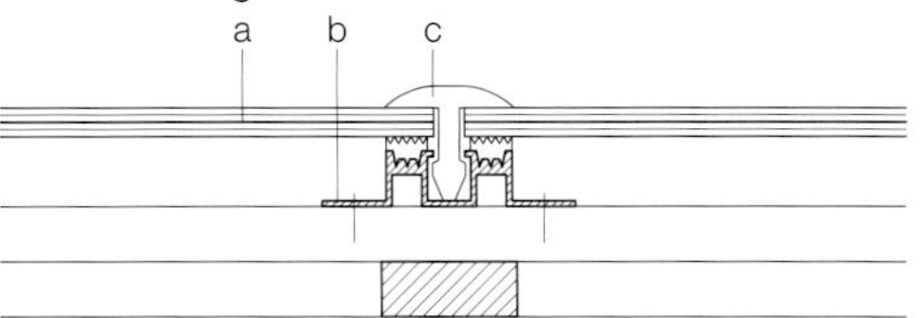


2.4.15.27 Transverse section through the roof covering: a photovoltaic panel, b aluminium section, c self-clamping preformed seal

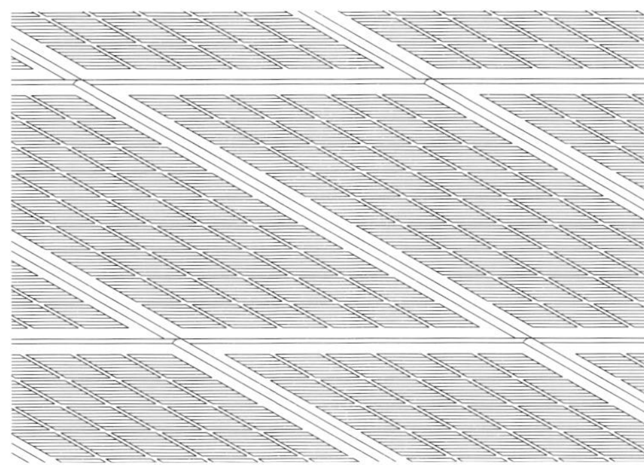

2.4.15.28 Photovoltaic roof panels laid as sealed roof covering

Collector components as roof construction
If more heat is required, the roof covering can be designed to act as a large-scale collector. The covering of the collector then forms the covering layer of the roof, and the collector insulation contributes to the roof's thermal insulation.
In addition to those assembled manually on site, fully or partly prefabricated solutions are also available.
The structure of the roof covering is generally identical to that of a flat-plate collector. [19, 26]

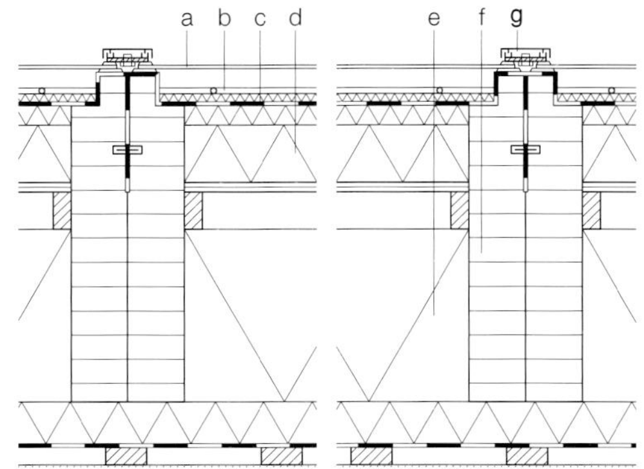


2.4.15.29 Transverse section through prefabricated flat-plate collector system forming the roof construction: a glass cover, b absorber, c waterproofing sheet, d collector insulation, e building insulation, f loadbearing rafter, g patent glazing cap [19]

**Maintenance and repair**

Photovoltaic and thermal energy systems require hardly any maintenance. Regular inspections should be carried out about once a year. The system functions can be monitored regularly to assess output.
Malfunctions in photovoltaic systems are mostly caused by the ingress of water and corrosion of the electrical connections.
In a thermal energy system the level of antifreeze agent and the operating pressure are among the items that must be checked regularly. A bleed valve – accessible from the roof or from inside – should be included at the highest point.

The energy production components should be cleaned regularly in regions of low rainfall or when the angle of installation is < 20°. [11, 31]

Standard dimensions have not yet been established for photovoltaic panels or collectors. It is therefore often difficult to obtain replacement elements that fit exactly. However, it should not be at all difficult to connect new energy production components to existing systems.

**References**

[01] AEG product information
[02] Antec product information
[03] Alligator product information
[04] ASE product information
[05] BP Solar product information
[06] Buderus product information
[07] Delzer, T.: Die Solardachfibel; Basel: Die Solarpraxis, 1995
[08] DIN 4757: Solar heating plants, parts 1-5: Beuth Verlag, 11/1982
[09] DIN VDE 0100 part 712 (draft): Erection of low-voltage installations — requirements for special installations or locations; photovoltaic power supply systems, vol. 6/1998
[10] Elco Klöckner product information
[11] Fox, U.: Sonnenkollektoren, Thermische Solaranlagen; Stuttgart: Kohlhammer-Verlag, 1998
[12] Hofmann, V.: Photovoltaik: Strom aus Licht; Stuttgart: Teubner-Verlag, 1996
[13] Humm, O.: Photovoltaik und Architektur; Birkhäuser-Verlag, 1993
[14] IBC Solar product information
[15] IEC 61215
[16] IEC 61646
[17] Energy Information Centre, Baden-Württemberg Trading Standards Dept: Energie Photovoltaik, Architektonische Gebäudeintegration, Stuttgart 2000
[18] Energy Information Centre, Baden-Württemberg Trading Standards Dept: Energie Sonne, Wasser erwärmen und heizen mit der Sonne, Stuttgart 2000
[19] ITW, Stuttgart University: Zentrale Nahwärmeversorgung mit Solaranlage und Langzeitspeicher in Neckarsulm; in: Detail 3/1999: Solares Bauen
[20] Kaltschmitt, M.: Erneuerbare Energien: Systemtechnik, Wirtschaftlichkeit, Umweltaspekte; Berlin: Springer-Verlag 2000
[21] Kyocera product information
[22] Pistohl, W.: Handbuch der Gebäudetechnik, vol. 2; Düsseldorf: Werner Verlag, 2000
[23] ReGen product information
[24] Schweizer product information
[25] Siemens Solar product information
[26] Solar-Energie-Technik product information
[27] Solarfabrik product information
[28] Solarworld product information
[29] Sonnenkraft product information
[30] Stiebel Eltron product information
[31] Staiß, F.: Photovoltaik, Ein Leitfaden für Anwender; Cologne: TÜV-Verlag, 2000
[32] Thyssen Bausysteme product information
[33] UFE Solar product information
[34] Vaillant product information
[35] VDI Energy Technology Association: Technische Regeln zur Photovoltaik: Bestand und Bedarf; Düsseldorf: VDI-Verlag, 2000
[36] Viessmann product information
[37] Viva solar product information
[38] Wolf product information
[39] German Solar Energy Association: Report 1995

## Ventilation

Air circulation, air passages and ventilation openings

Roof designs involving complex multi-layer constructions made from numerous individual parts are almost exclusively assembled on site by workers from different trades. This results in dimensional deviations, errors at interfaces and make-up pieces that allow air and water vapour to penetrate the construction. Roof covering and thermal insulation should therefore be ventilated using air layers or spaces linked to the external air via openings at the edges of the roof. This principle allows heat, water vapour, condensation and residual water/gases from the construction to escape (see "Building science" and "Design principles"). Detailed information on ventilated and non-ventilated designs can be found in the section "Design principles". The reader is recommended to read the information given here in conjunction with that section.

**Air circulation**

The movement of air within the roof is caused either by wind pressure due to differential air pressures, or by thermal convection currents due to air temperature differentials. If wind pressure and thermal convection currents act simultaneously, they have either an additive effect (stronger air circulation) or a subtractive effect (diminished air circulation).

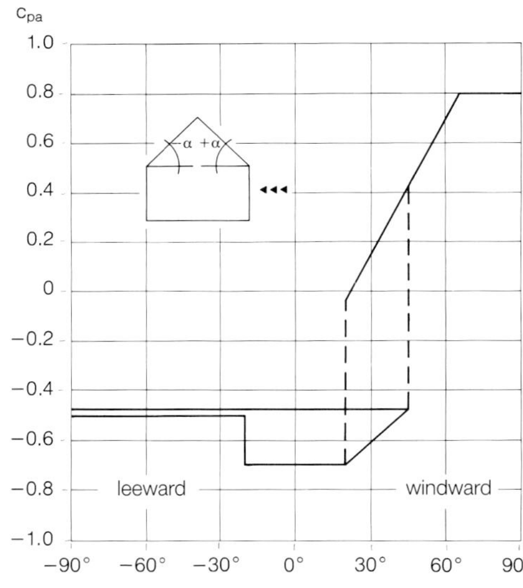


2.4.16.1 Pressure and suction coefficients in relation to roof pitch: ◂ prevailing wind direction [07]

Air movements due to pressure differentials
The pressure and suction conditions around the building depend on the direction of the wind, the wind force, the form of the building and the roof pitch. While the form of the building and its position relative to the direction of the wind determine the size of the suction zone on the leeward side [10], the roof pitch influences both the distribution of pres-

sure and suction zones and the magnitude of these forces on the roof.
The wind forces acting at the edges and corners of roof surfaces are considerably higher than those acting on the roof surface itself (see "Loadbearing structure").

| Roof pitch $\alpha$ | Suction peak coefficient $c_p$ corner | edge |
|---|---|---|
| ≤ 25° | – 3.2 | – 1.8 |
| 25° < $\alpha$ ≤ 35° | –1.8 | – 1.1 |
| ≥ 35° | no suction peaks | |

2.4.16.2 Suction peaks in relation to roof pitch [03]

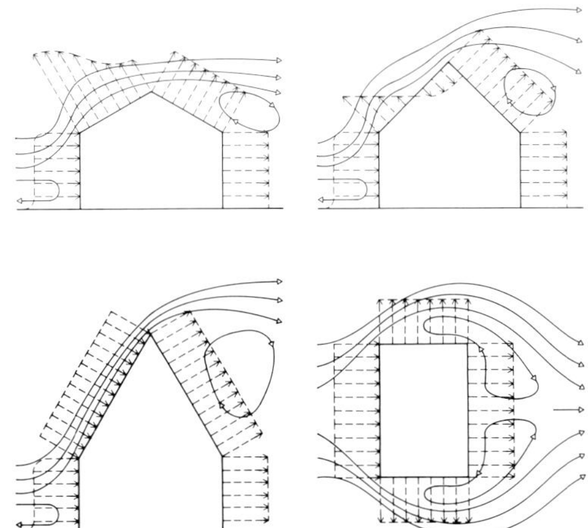

2.4.16.3 Distribution of pressure and suction zones on a duopitch roof in relation to roof pitch; sections and plans

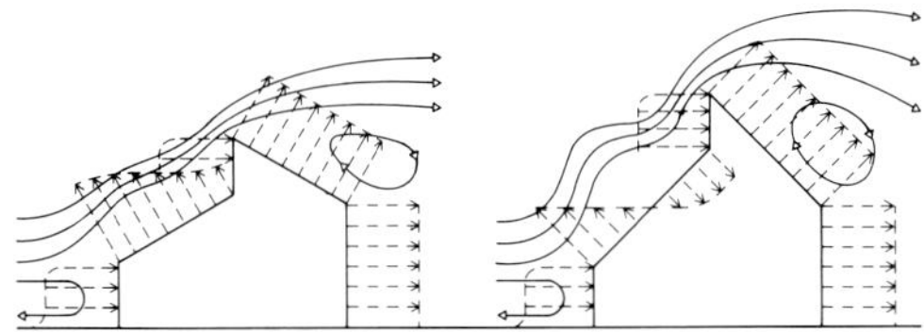

2.4.16.4 Distribution of pressure and suction zones on a clerestory roof in relation to roof pitch; sections

When the wind strikes the building at an angle, pressure in a trough is also possible.
Calm air (no wind movement) prevails on about 30 days in the year. On these days there is no air flow due to pressure differentials.
It is advisable to position the building with one of its pitched roof surfaces facing the prevailing wind. However, changing wind directions can reverse the distribution of pressure and suction zones temporarily. The local environment (e.g. dense, tall developments) also affects air circulation within the roof (see "Building science").

**Air movements due to temperature differentials**

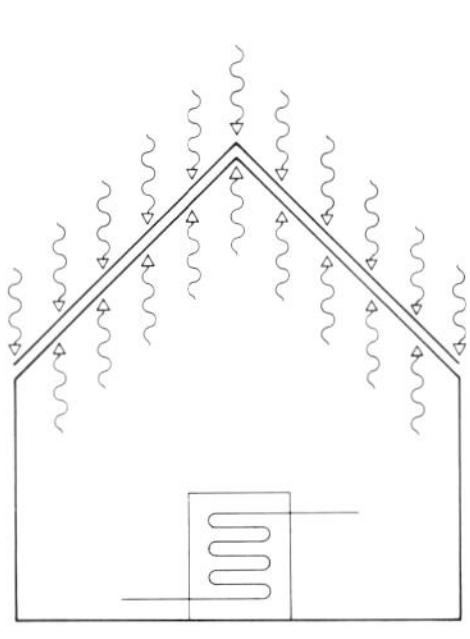

2.4.16.5 Movement of air due to air temperature differentials (incident solar radiation in summer, space heating in winter)

A density differential is set up between the warm air in the roof and the colder air outside. The resulting difference in mass leads to thermal convection and hence to a flow of air (see "Building science"). The steeper the roof, the greater this effect. On a shallow pitch, with correspondingly lower thermal convection currents, it is therefore advisable to increase the depth of the air circulation layers to reduce the friction of the air on the enclosing surfaces. Inlets and outlets should also be enlarged.

Laminar and turbulent air flows
The flow of air in ventilation layers is either laminar (streamline) or turbulent.
Laminar flow means that the individual particles of the moving air move in an orderly manner and retain the same relative positions in successive cross-sections. No eddies are produced in the ventilation space. Eddies occur at the boundaries of the ventilation space due to the air making contact with the "rough" surfaces of the components enclosing the space.
In turbulent flow at least some of the individual particles of the moving air move in a disorderly manner and occupy different relative positions in successive cross-sections. This produces eddies throughout the ventilation space.
The state of the air flow in the ventilation space depends on:
- the throughflow velocity
- the temperature of the air (density, pressure, movement of air particles)
- the cross-sectional area of the ventilation space
- the form and surfaces of components enclosing the ventilation space

**Air passages and ventilation openings**

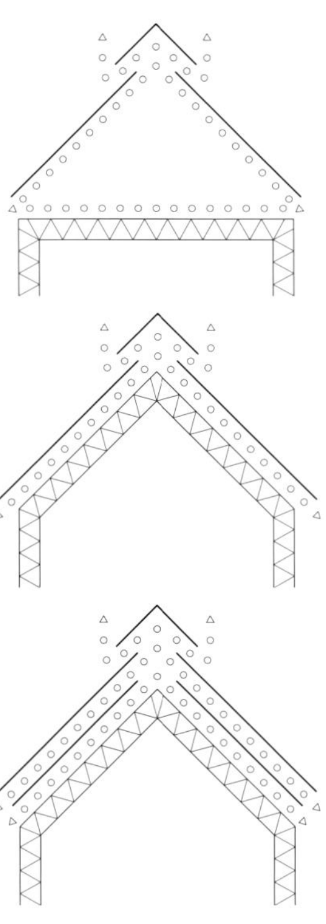

2.4.16.6 Air flows: a unoccupied roof space, b occupied roof space with non-ventilated roof design, c occupied roof space with ventilated roof design

a Unoccupied roof space:
The volume of air is large, producing good roof ventilation even at high temperatures; large enough openings should be provided.
b Occupied roof space with non-ventilated roof design:
DIN 4108 part 3 distinguishes between roof covering and roof sealing:
- Roof covering

Various roof covering designs are listed to which pairs of values are allocated for the water vapour-equivalent air layer thickness outside ($s_{de}$) and inside ($s_{di}$) the thermal insulation. Designs with non-ventilated roof coverings and a diffusion-retardant layer below the thermal insulation should always have an $s_{di} \geq 100$ m. The thermal resistance below the diffusion-retardant layer for all the roof covering designs listed should never exceed 20% of the value for the total roof construction. The DIN standard also mentions an aerated concrete construction without stipulations for the vapour permeability of the thermal insulation, and an upside-down roof with such stipulations.
- Roof sealing

In terms of $s_{di}$ and thermal resistance, the same applies as for a roof covering with a diffusion-retardant layer below the thermal insulation.

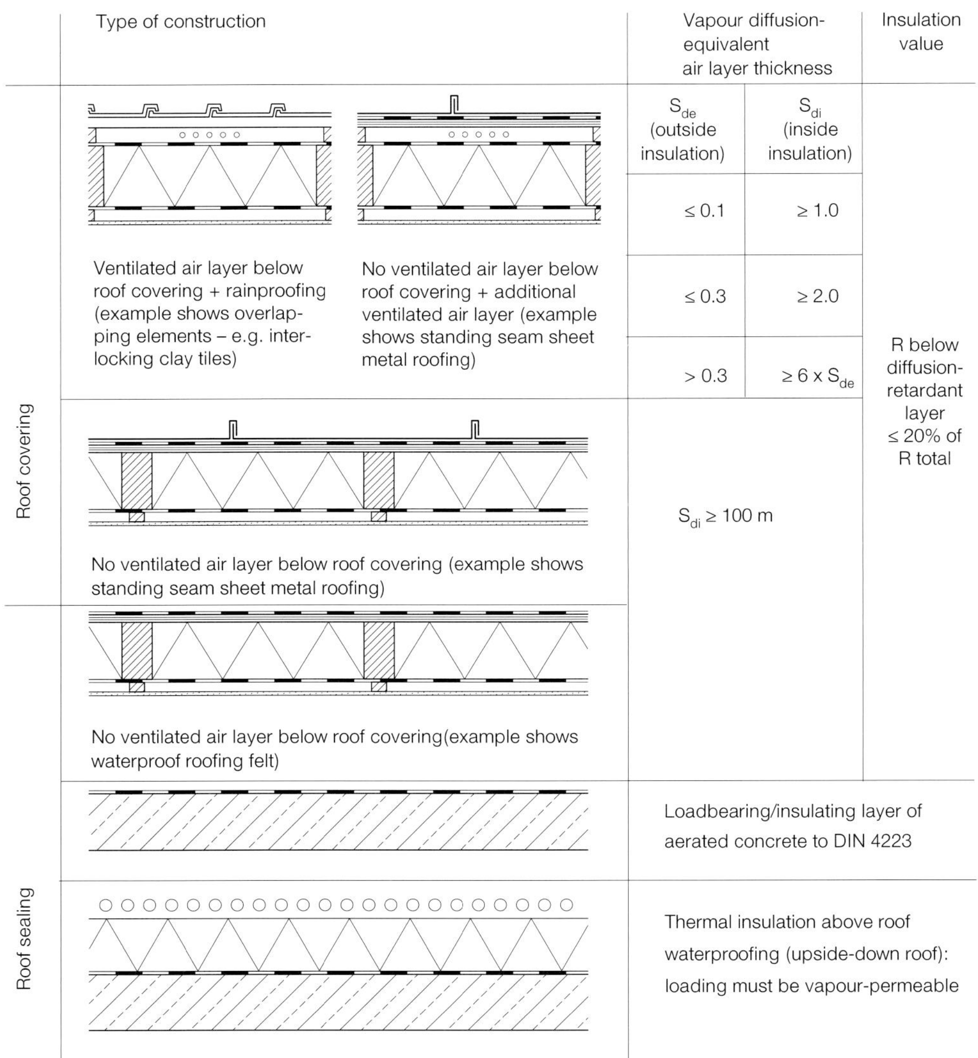

| | Type of construction | Vapour diffusion-equivalent air layer thickness | | Insulation value |
|---|---|---|---|---|
| | | $S_{de}$ (outside insulation) | $S_{di}$ (inside insulation) | |
| Roof covering | Ventilated air layer below roof covering + rainproofing (example shows overlapping elements – e.g. interlocking clay tiles); No ventilated air layer below roof covering + additional ventilated air layer (example shows standing seam sheet metal roofing) | ≤ 0.1 | ≥ 1.0 | R below diffusion-retardant layer ≤ 20% of R total |
| | | ≤ 0.3 | ≥ 2.0 | |
| | | > 0.3 | ≥ 6 x $S_{de}$ | |
| | No ventilated air layer below roof covering (example shows standing seam sheet metal roofing) | $S_{di}$ ≥ 100 m | | |
| | No ventilated air layer below roof covering(example shows waterproof roofing felt) | | | |
| Roof sealing | | Loadbearing/insulating layer of aerated concrete to DIN 4223 | | |
| | | Thermal insulation above roof waterproofing (upside-down roof): loading must be vapour-permeable | | |

2.4.16.7 Minimum requirements for non-ventilated roof designs without a theoretical analysis to DIN 4108 part 3

c Occupied roof space with ventilated roof design:
DIN 4108 part 3 distinguishes between roofs with a pitch greater or less than 5° and stipulates minimum requirements for the water vapour-equivalent air layer thickness $s_d$, the cross-sectional area for ventilation and the thermal resistance R of the various parts of the roof when a theoretical analysis is not provided.

The required minimum cross-sectional area for ventilation must be guaranteed in the finished condition. However, it is advisable to provide larger cross-sections because
- thermal insulation materials can swell, distort or bunch up after installation;
- installation errors and tolerances can reduce the cross-sectional area of the ventilation layers;

| Roof pitch | Area | Equivalent air layer thickness | Area of ventilation opening | Thermal resistance |
|---|---|---|---|---|
| < 5° | within area of roof | below therm. insul. $s_{di}$ ≥ 100 m | | R below diffusion-retardant layer ≤ 20 % of total R |
| ≥ 5° | within area of roof | below air layer $s_d$ ≥ 2.0 m | ≥ 2 cm | |
| | eaves • duopitch roof • monopitch roof ridge • monopitch roof | | ≥ 2 ‰ of associated roof surface, min. 200 cm²/m | |
| | ridge + eaves • duopitch roof | | ≥ 0.5 ‰ of associated roof surface, min. 5 cm²/m | |

2.4.16.8 Minimum requirements for ventilated roof designs without a theoretical analysis to DIN 4108 part 3

- meshes, screens and perforated sheet metal can reduce the unobstructed cross-sectional area for ventilation quite considerably in some cases; placing these at an angle can limit this restriction. The opening size of fine-mesh screens and sheet metal with small perforations can be reduced simply by painting them. Therefore, mesh or holes should not be less than 5 mm in size.

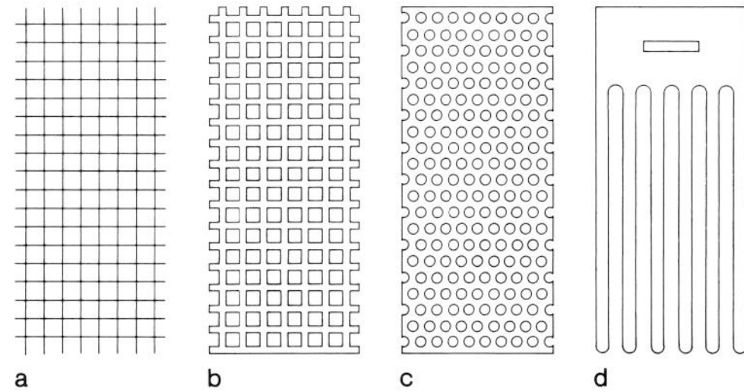


2.4.16.9 Standard protective screens; forms: a mesh, b and c perforated sheet metal, d comb filler [01]

**Roof surface**

Individual vents may be used near all roof edges. Ventilation openings must be protected against the ingress of driving snow and rain by redirecting the air flow once or (better) several times within the vent. As pressure and suction effects often change with the wind conditions, some form of safeguard is always sensible.

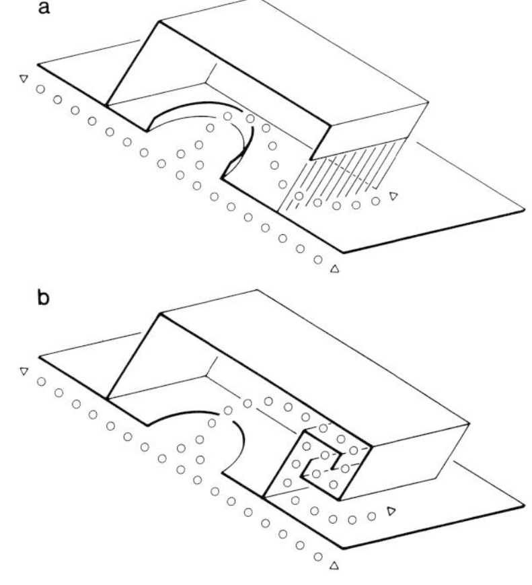


2.4.16.10 Individual vents in a pressure zone: a rainproof, b protected against driving rain and snow

Simple vents allow more air through than those protected against driving snow and rain because they create less friction and hence fewer eddies. They are, however, not as secure.
A wind deflector attached in front of the ventilation opening deflects the wind and creates a small suction zone on its rear face. Unguarded ventilation openings can therefore be included even in pressure zones.

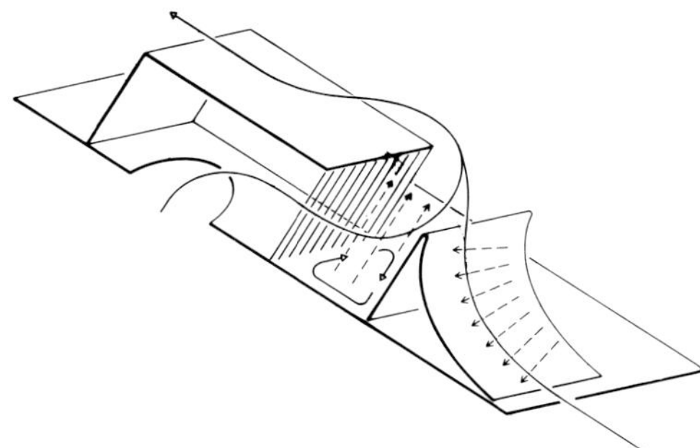

2.4.16.11 Individual vent with wind deflector

| Material | Roof covering component | Ventilation opening [cm² each] |
|---|---|---|
| Clay and loam | bullnose tiles | 7.5–15 |
| | pantiles | 8–25 |
| | interlocking tiles | |
| Concrete | interlocking tiles | 15–32 |
| Metal | sheet metal | made by hand; size of opening varies |
| | wooden shingles | |
| | slates | |
| Man-made | fibre-cement sheets | 75, 180 |
| | fibre-cement corrugated sheets | |
| | asphalt shingles | 135, 175 |
| | corrugated bitumen sheets | |
| | slates | |

2.4.16.12 Individual vents; area of ventilation opening [01, 02, 06]

**Ridge**

The area of the unobstructed ventilation opening at the ridge for a ventilated roof design without a theoretical analysis according to DIN 4108 part 3 is given in table 2.4.16.8. As the highest point of the roof, the ridge must expel the air that entered at the eaves. This is achieved by way of specially designed ridge cappings. However, the air often bypasses the ridge and does not escape until it reaches the eaves on the other side (eaves-eaves ventilation). But as described in the "Design principles" section, in certain situations (e.g. roof surfaces facing north and south) this can lead to moist warm air being conveyed from the southern to the northern side, where it condenses on cold components. It is therefore advisable to separate the air layers at the ridge when the roof surfaces are subjected to different climatic conditions. Although this gives a lower level of through-ventilation (which can be compensated for by enlarging the cross-sectional area of ventilation layers), it does prevent the thermal insulation from becoming saturated.

The roofing components that permit air exchange with the surroundings can be individual units positioned at certain intervals along the ridge, or be laid to form a continuous ventilation opening. Multiple redirection of the air flow within the component prevents the ingress of driving rain and snow. Without this, the vent is less secure.

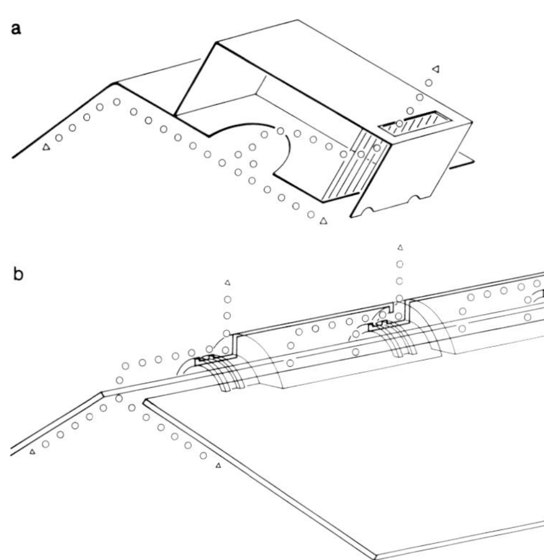


2.4.16.13 Individual ridge vents in a pressure zone: a and b secure

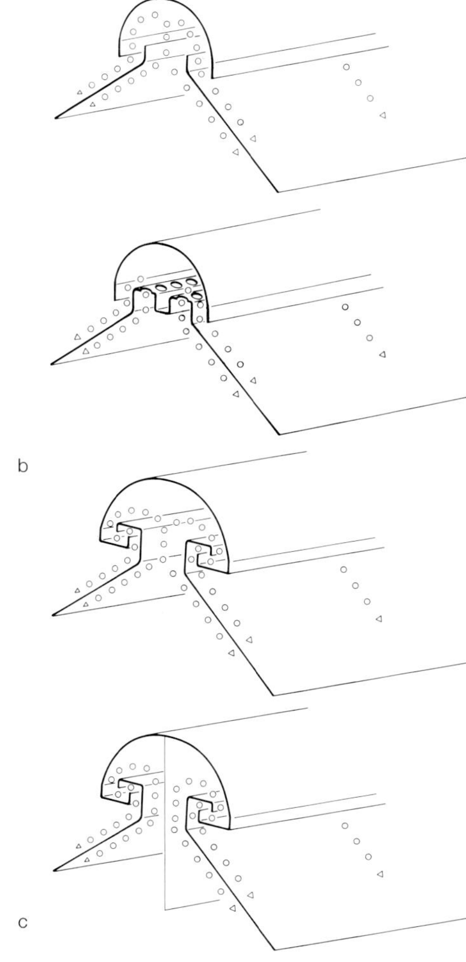


2.4.16.14 Continuous ridge vent in a pressure zone: a rainproof, b protected against driving rain and snow, c with air layers separated at ridge of duopitch roof

| Type of ridge ventilation | Material | Ventilation opening [cm²/m each side] |
|---|---|---|
| Individual | clay tiles: ridge-ridge ventilation | 90–150 |
| | corr. fibre-cement: ridge hoods | with screen: 162 cm² each<br>with box: 122 cm² each |
| Continuous | clay tiles: ridge-top course ventilation | 75–150 |
| | plastic vent | 80–200 |
| | concrete: plastic vent | 280, 380 |
| | corr. fibre-cement: ventilated ridge | 500 |
| | sheet metal and metal sheeting: ventilated ridge | depends on details |

2.4.16.15 Ridge vent elements; area of ventilation opening [01, 02, 06]

Ridge, upper/lower air layers

So that there is a connection between the upper and lower air layers, boarding stops at least 30 mm short of the ridge, roofing felt at least 50 mm.

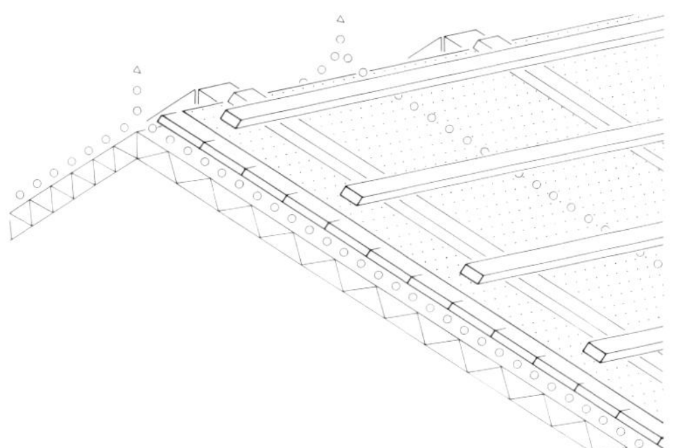

2.4.16.16 Ventilation of upper and lower air layers at ridge; battens and counter battens

**Ridge to monopitch roof**

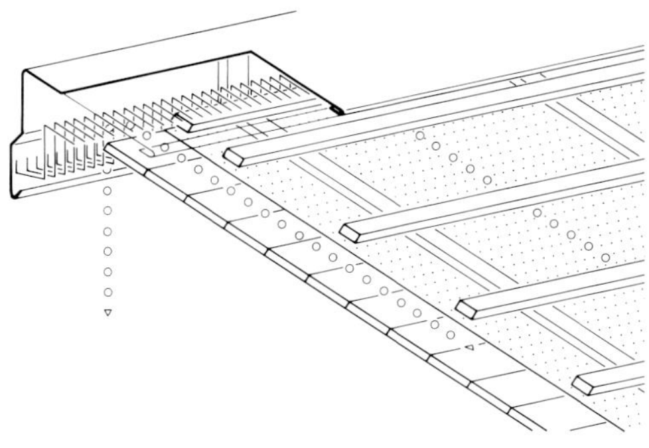

2.4.16.17 Ventilation of upper air layer at ridge to monopitch roof; battens and counter battens. The perforated sheet metal is fixed to a separate roof covering batten directly at the ridge and protected by the flashing.

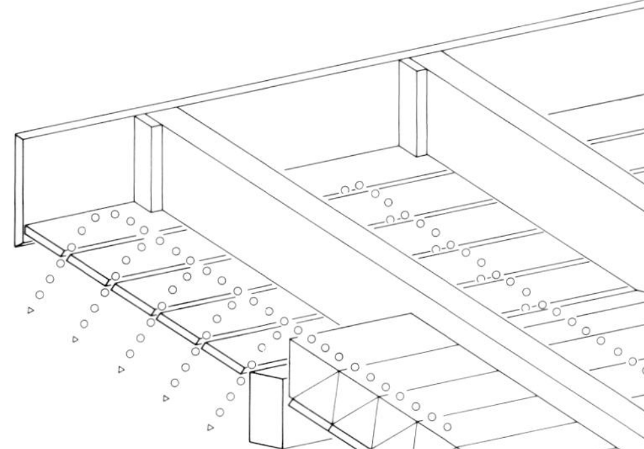

2.4.16.18 Ventilation of lower air layer at ridge to monopitch roof; spaces between soffit boards

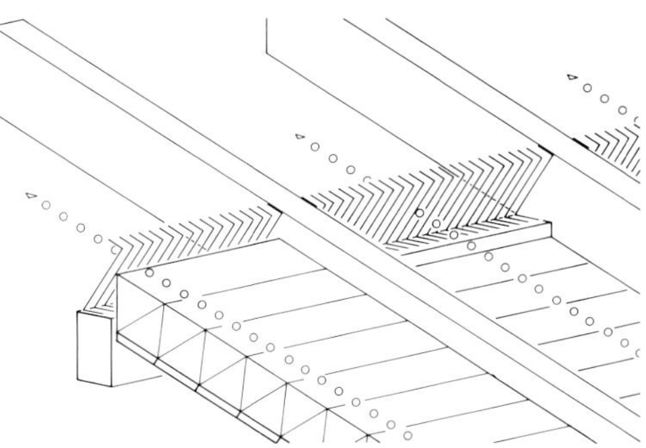

2.4.16.19 Ventilation of lower air layer at ridge to monopitch roof; perforated sheet metal

The ventilation openings along the ridge of a monopitch roof should be the same size as those at the eaves. As there is only one roof surface to be ventilated, the cross-sectional area required for ventilation is greater than at the ridge of a duopitch roof.

Ridge to monopitch roof, upper air layer
Perforated sheet metal protects the ventilation opening between rafters/decking and flashing from birds and small animals. The resulting reduction in the size of the opening must be taken into account when sizing the ventilation gap.

Ridge to monopitch roof, lower air layer
Soffit boards laid with gaps between guarantee ventilation of the lower air layer. If the gap between the boards is too wide, they are closed off with perforated sheet metal. Pieces of perforated sheet metal fixed at an angle between the rafters protect the ventilation opening against birds and small animals.

**Hip**
The ventilation requirements at a hip are identical to those at the ridge. The exchange of air with the surroundings can take place either directly via special ventilating components (see "Ridge" above) or through design measures. The latter involves directing the air along the hip to the outlets at the ridge.

Hip, upper air layer

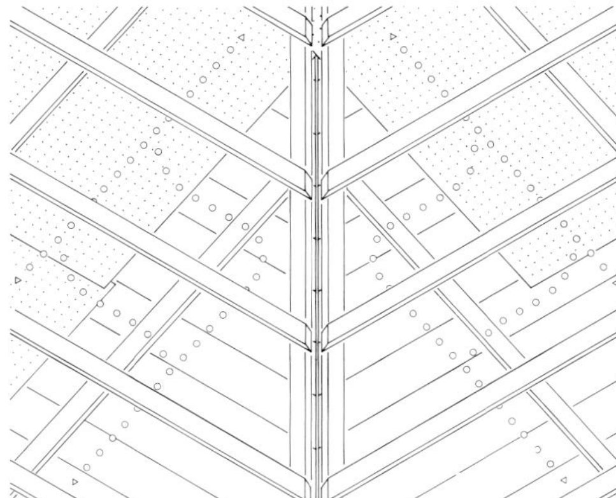

2.4.16.20 Ventilation of upper air layer at hip; battens and counter battens

If the roof design includes battens and counter battens, the air flow in the upper air layer can be channelled in a zigzag fashion, directed over the counter battens and under the battens carrying the roof covering.

If decking has been provided instead of battens (e.g. with metal sheeting), the counter battens can be interrupted near the hip. The air flow is therefore directed along the hip.

As this widens the space between the supports for the roof covering, additional pieces of batten may need to be fixed between counter battens and hip batten. Another option is to interrupt the counter batten acting as a hip batten. Air then flows over the hip into the neighbouring roof surface (e.g. on a pavilion roof).

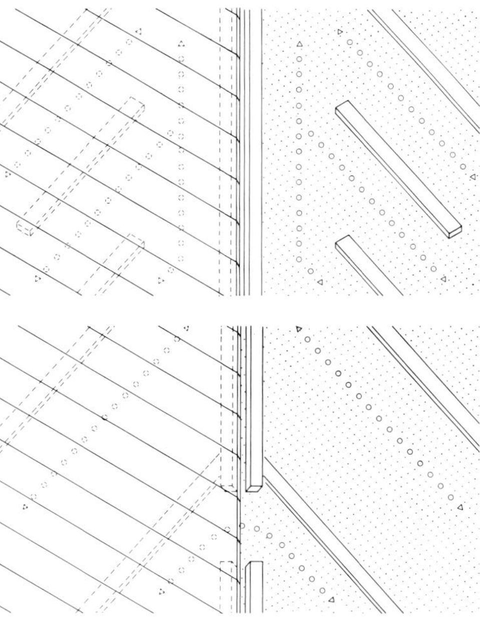

2.4.16.21 Ventilation of upper air layer at hip; roof decking and counter battens

Hip, lower air layer
The depth of the jack rafters is reduced by the thickness of a batten over about 200 mm at the hip. (This does not cause any structural weakness because the rafters are the same size as their standard full-length counterparts and thus oversized.) This guarantees an unobstructed air flow towards the ridge. Another possibility is to include additional battens on top of the standard, jack and hip rafters to ensure ventilation of the lower air layer. These battens are interrupted at the hip to guarantee the passage of air.

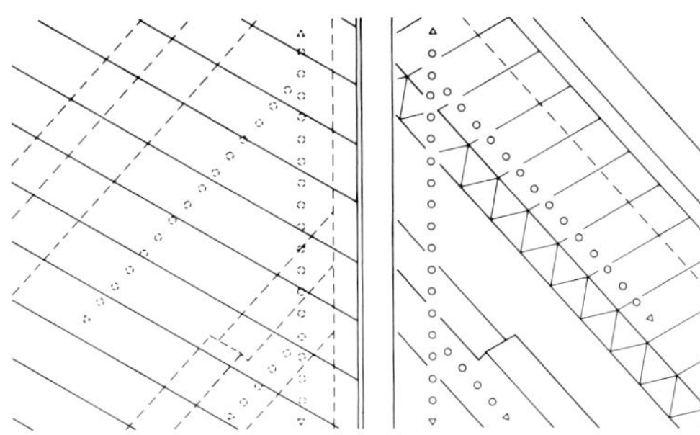

2.4.16.22 Ventilation of lower air layer at hip; jack rafters cut out to suit

Hip, upper/lower air layers
There are various ways of directing the air from one air layer into another:

- By using roofing felt vents at the laps in the roofing felt; water drains around these elements.
- By adding counter battens parallel to and about 20 mm from the hip batten. The roofing felt is folded around them and fixed in place, giving a continuous air gap from the eaves to the ridge.

These two solutions are suitable only for simple designs with very low demands.

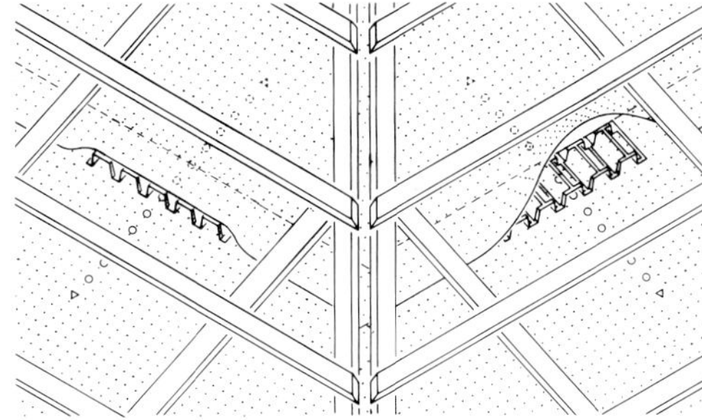

2.4.16.23 Ventilation of upper and lower air layers at hip; roofing felt and special vents in lap of roofing felt

- By redirecting the air flow through vents integrated in the decking. Flanges ($h \leq 20$ mm) on the vents ensure that water is drained around the openings.

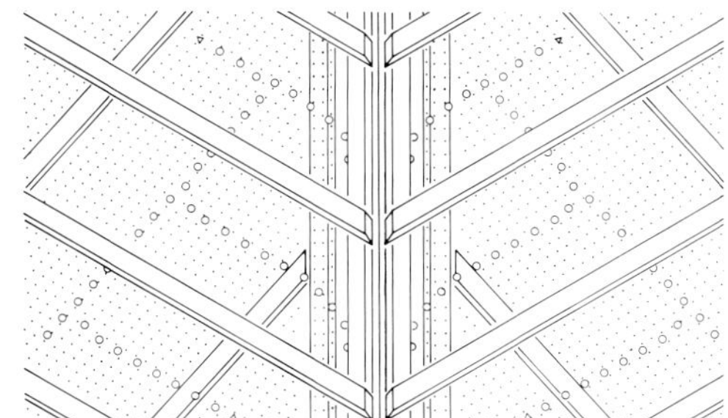

2.4.16.24 Ventilation of upper and lower air layers at hip; roofing felt and additional counter battens [05]

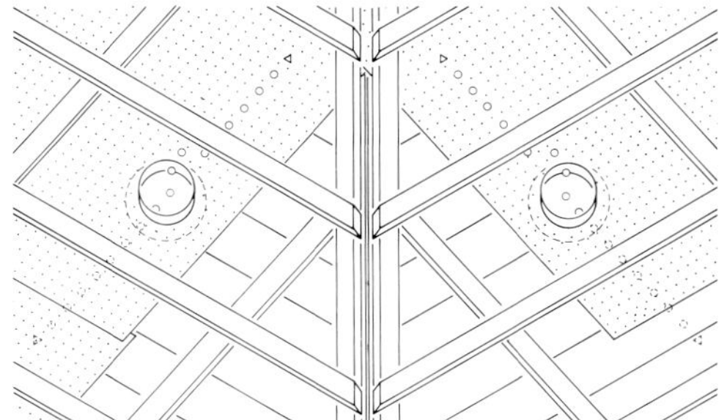

2.4.16.25 Ventilation of upper and lower air layers at hip; vents

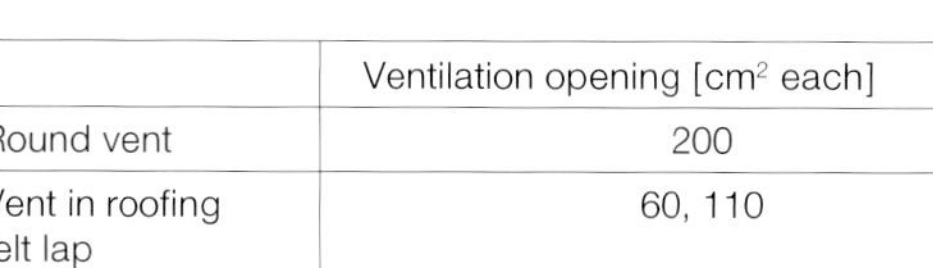

| | Ventilation opening [cm² each] |
|---|---|
| Round vent | 200 |
| Vent in roofing felt lap | 60, 110 |

2.4.16.26 Area of ventilation opening [01]

**Eaves**

The unobstructed cross-sectional area for ventilation at the eaves (required) for ventilated designs according to DIN 4108 part 3 should be 20‰ of the associated roof surface but not less than 200 cm²/m of eaves. As the lowest point of the roof, the eaves usually supply fresh external air to the roof construction.

Eaves, upper air layer

An eaves comb filler or strip of perforated sheet metal protects the upper air layer from birds and small animals.

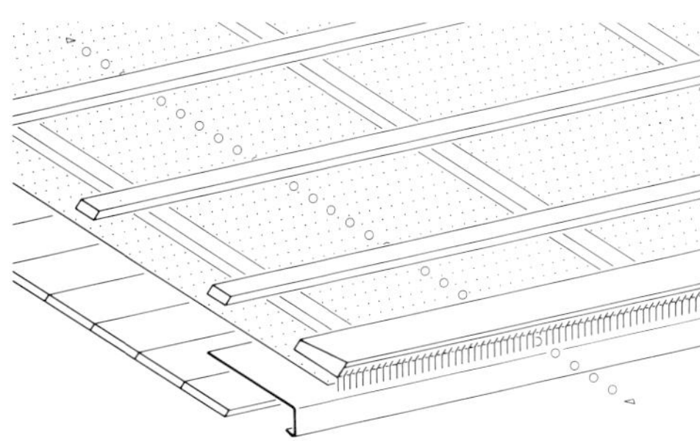

2.4.16.27 Ventilation of upper air layer at eaves; eaves filler comb

A perforated strip attached directly to the decking and eaves flashing acts as a sprocket, as well as permitting an inflow of air.

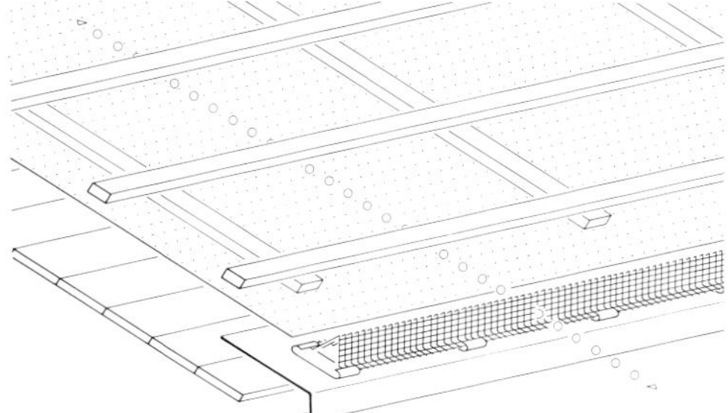

2.4.16.28 Ventilation of upper air layer at eaves; perforated strip

2.4.16.29 Ventilation of upper air layer at eaves; perforated sheet metal

Eaves, lower air layer

The opening to the lower air layer at the eaves is protected by perforated sheet metal, fitted at an angle between the rafters.

The size of the ventilation opening for perforated sheet metal, strips and eaves filler combs depends on the height and the size of the holes in the respective product; values lie between 200 and 300 cm²/m.

For further ventilation options see "Ridge to monopitch roof".

**Valley**

A valley should be treated in the same way as a hip with respect to ventilation openings.

Valley, upper air layer

The counter battens stop at the valley short of the valley batten, so as to drain water on the lower waterproofing level reliably. The air flows in the direction of the ridge or eaves – over the counter batten acting as a valley batten and below the battens carrying the roof covering.

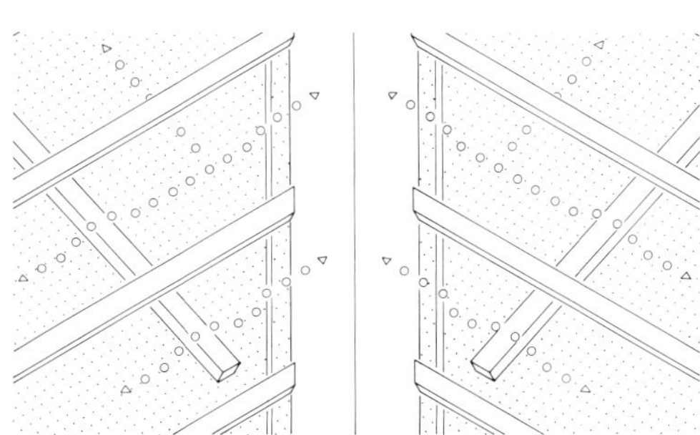

2.4.16.30 Ventilation of upper air layer at valley; roof covering battens, counter battens and valley battens

Another design option is to run the counter battens right up to the sheet metal of the valley gutter. A continuous perforated sheet metal or continuous filler comb is fixed to the packing batten running parallel to the valley to keep out birds and small animals.

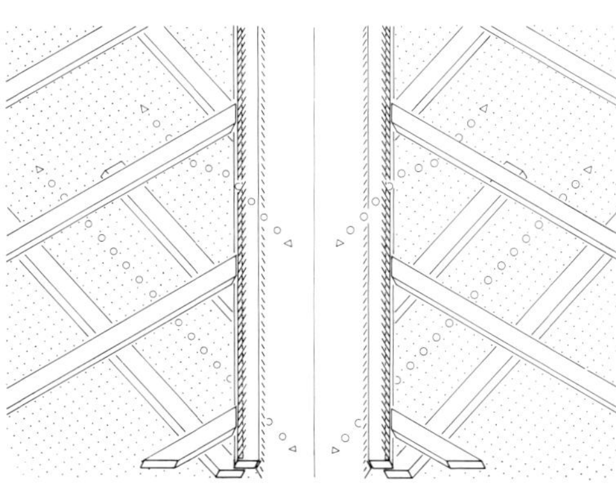

2.4.16.31 Ventilation of upper air layer at valley; roof covering battens, counter battens and valley battens

Valley, lower air layer
(see "Hip" above)

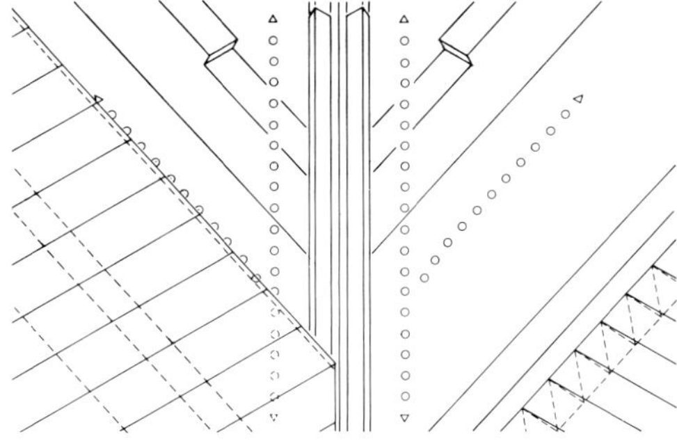

2.4.16.32 Ventilation of upper air layer at valley; jack rafters cut out to suit

Valley, upper/lower air layers
(see "Hip" above)

Pieces of batten are required to support the battens carrying the roof covering if the spacing becomes too wide. The pieces of batten should be attached to two or more battens, depending on the load.

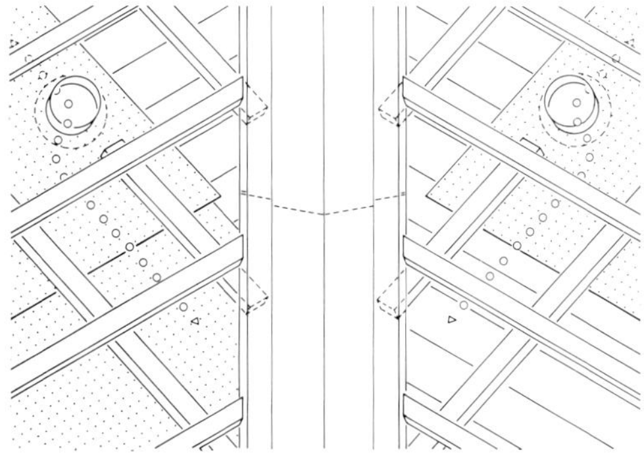

2.4.16.33 Ventilation of upper and lower air layers valley; vents

As these measures are sometimes very involved and can lead to diminished through-ventilation with unfavourable pressure ratios, DIN 4108 part 3 states that ventilation of the valley is not possible and proposes a non-ventilated design.

**Trough**

The trough is the part of the roof most at risk because both waterproofing and ventilation problems must be solved (see also "Drainage"). As the ventilation openings can become constricted due to foliage etc., troughs should always be accessible for cleaning, and should be able to carry the weight of persons and plant. Where a trough is combined with a shallow roof pitch, a non-ventilated design without a ventilated air layer above the insulation is often more prudent than a ventilated design with a ventilated air layer above the insulation. The design of the ventilation openings at a trough is so complicated that it can be illustrated only in conjunction with the respective design principles and materials (see "Construction details").

**Wall at top/bottom of slope**

(see "Eaves" above and "Construction details")

**Penetrations**

Ventilation should always continue around penetrations. If the penetration is very wide, however, it might prove more prudent to opt for a non-ventilated construction (no ventilated air layer above insulation).

Penetration, upper air layer

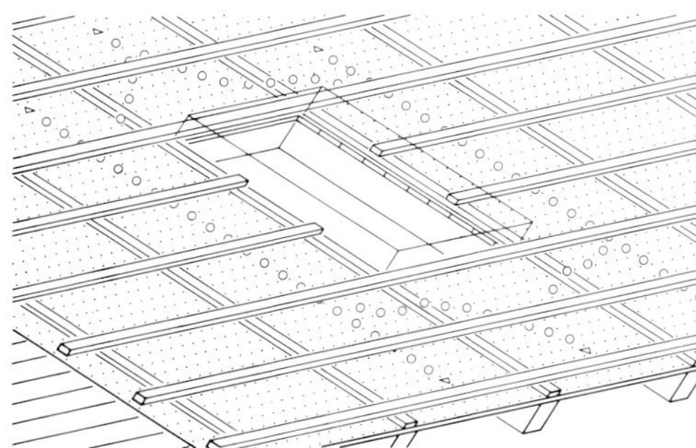

2.4.16.34 Ventilation of upper air layer at penetration; battens and counter battens [07]

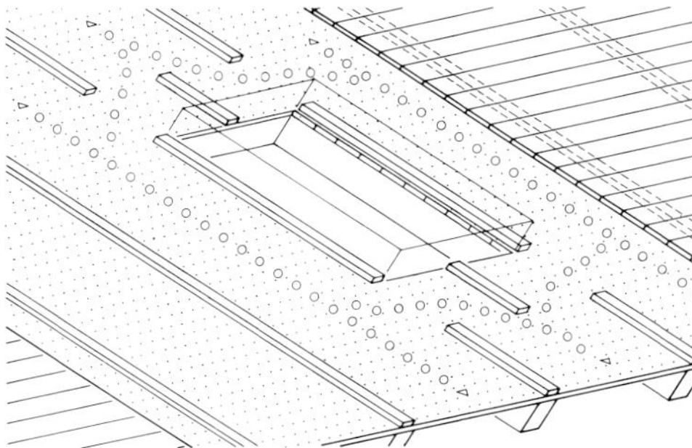

2.4.16.35 Ventilation of upper air layer at penetration; roof decking and counter battens

The air flow is redirected into the adjoining areas before reaching the penetration and fed around the sides of the obstruction. After passing the penetration, the air is fed back into its original path.
The counter battens are interrupted above and below the penetration. They redirect the air into the neighbouring areas. Additional pieces of batten can be incorporated to support the decking.

Penetration, lower air layer

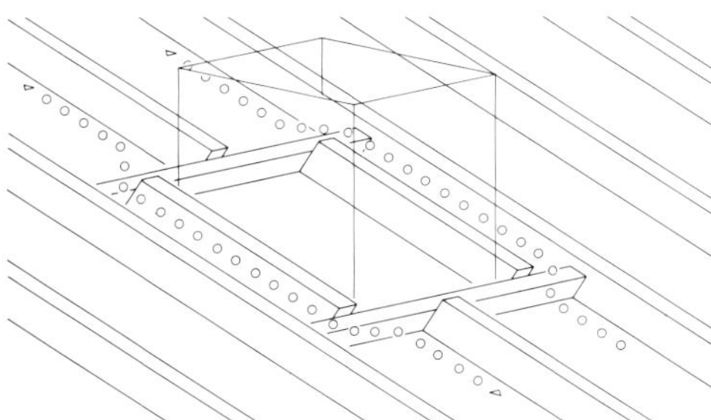

2.4.16.36 Ventilation of lower air layer at penetration; depth of trimmers

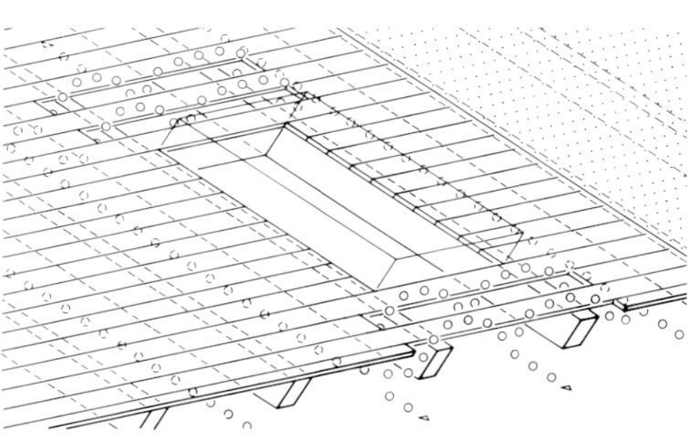

2.4.16.37 Ventilation of lower air layer at penetration; boards omitted from roof decking

If trimmers are necessary, their depth should be less than that of the rafters. The lower level can thus also be ventilated. The air flows around the sides of the obstruction. The unobstructed cross-sectional area required for ventilation should be maintained.
If a penetration blocks an entire bay between rafters, some boards can be omitted from the decking above and below the obstruction ($\geq$ 20 cm wide in the bay). The air can thus escape over the rafters into the neighbouring bay. As the cross-sectional area for ventilation is quite small, at least two or (better) more boards of the decking should be left out. The disadvantage is that a soft decking material could be inadvertently pushed inwards by persons working on the roof.

**Dormer window**

The information regarding troughs and wide penetrations also applies to dormer windows: here too, it may be more prudent to choose a non-ventilated design without a ventilated air layer over the insulation.

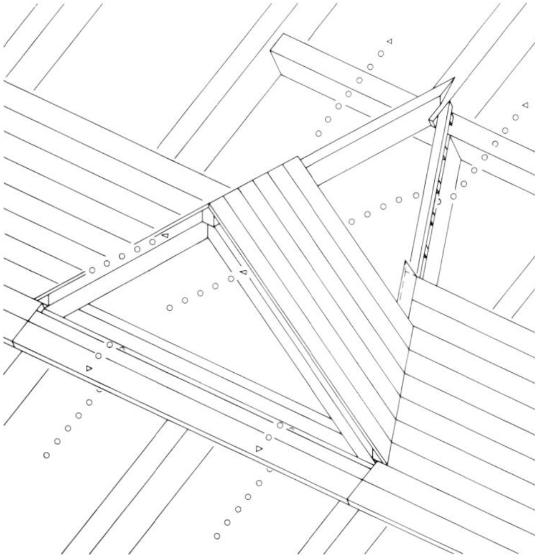

2.4.16.38 Ventilation of lower air layer at dormer window; battens and pieces of batten

Dormer window, lower air layer
Both the cheek members and the upper dormer window trimmer can have a smaller cross-section than the rafters. Packing up the cheek members with battens and pieces of batten allows the air entering at the verge of the dormer window to be channelled into the normal roof surface.

**References**


[01] Braas & Co. GmbH: Handbuch 89/90 – Geneigte Dächer; Oberursel 1998
[02] Dachziegelwerke Mayr GmbH: information material for architects and users; Straubing
[03] DIN 1055, pt 4: Design loads for buildings – Imposed loads, wind loads on buildings not susceptible to vibration; Berlin: Beuth-Verlag, 1986
[04] DIN 4108: Thermal insulation and energy economy in buildings; pt 3: protection against moisture subject to climate conditions; requirements and directions for design and construction; Berlin: Beuth-Verlag, 2001
[05] Dörken, E. AG: information material; Herdecke 1985
[06] Eternit AG: Planung und Anwendung, Well-Eternit Dächer; Berlin 1995
[07] Liersch, K. W.: Belüftete Dach- und Wandkonstruktionen, B3 Dächer; Wiesbaden: Bauverlag; 1986
[08] Velux: Informationsmaterial; Hamburg 1988
[09] Wolfseher, U.; Gertis, K.: Bodennahe Aerodynamik, offprint from "Gesundheits-Ingenieur", 1978
[10] Informationsdienst für neuzeitliches Bauen, d-extrakt Arbeitsblätter 1985/86 & 1994

**Secondary waterproofing/covering layer**
Actions, boarding and roofing felts, laying

The secondary waterproofing/covering layer is made of boarding and/or roofing felt.

**Actions**
Roofs with a covering of overlapping elements are rainproof but not waterproof, owing to the high proportion of joints. Driving rain, a build-up of water and condensation may make additional measures necessary. These measures are also taken in certain circumstances, e.g. on large roofs, where pitches are below the recommended minimum, or when several roof surfaces meet at one point.

Dust and dirt
Dust and dirt can enter the roof space through the joints in the roof covering. If the roof space is to be used for anything other than storage of unimportant items, protection from dust, dirt and soot is required.

Driven water
Driving rain and snow can be blown through the joints in the roof covering. On shallow pitches the wind can drive surface water up the roof, through the joints and into the roof construction. The ingress of snow and rain at ventilation openings cannot be entirely avoided.

Ponding
On a poorly designed roof snow can melt due to the flow of heat from the interior of the building. This melt water freezes again at the colder eaves and the ensuing ice blocks further drainage. More melt water collects behind the ice and seeps through the joints in the roof covering into the roof construction. Especially frequent freeze-thaw cycles produce "ice dams".

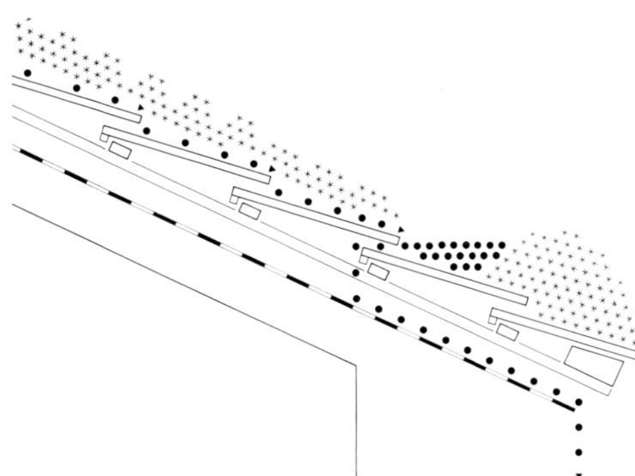

2.4.17.1 Roof covering with build-up of water behind "ice dam"

This problem can be avoided by employing the following measures:
- reducing the flow of heat from the interior of the building by providing adequate thermal insulation
- dissipating the heat through adequate ventilation underneath the roof covering

On large, shallow roof surfaces water also builds up at eaves and valleys.

Condensation
Condensation forms on the top surface of the roof covering and on the underside when heat radiates skywards during cloudless nights and the temperature at the surface drops below the dew point. This can happen with a temperature difference as small as 3°C. A thunderstorm can also cause the roof covering to cool down below the temperature of the external air. Here again, if the humidity of the air is relatively high at the same time, the surface temperature can drop below the dew point. If additional thermal currents or wind are not available to generate through-ventilation, the moisture cannot be carried away.

At temperatures below 0°C the condensation turns to frost. As the sun rises, the layer of frost gradually melts and the ensuing quantity of condensation considerably exceeds the amount expected in the form of water vapour diffusion from the interior of the building. This water drips or drains onto the thermal insulation and the roof timbers, thus increasing moisture levels substantially. [07] Materials that cool rapidly, radiate considerable quantities of heat and absorb little water as a result of their low heat capacity are particularly vulnerable, above all when good thermal insulation prevents the roof covering from warming.

**Boarding and roofing felts**
One possible measure to counteract these actions is to provide a second water run-off level beneath the roof covering. The unavoidable incoming water can thus drain safely over this layer. It can either flow into the gutter or drip from a flashing at a safe distance from the face of the external wall (figure 2.4.17.2).

This second water run-off level should be fitted around penetrations for chimneys, roof/dormer windows etc. in such a way that no water can enter the roof construction.

As already mentioned under "Design principles", boarding and roofing felts are often known by various names. We shall use the following definitions in this book:

- Secondary waterproofing layer in this case is an independent waterproofing layer that could also constitute a functioning roof without the roof covering layer above it.

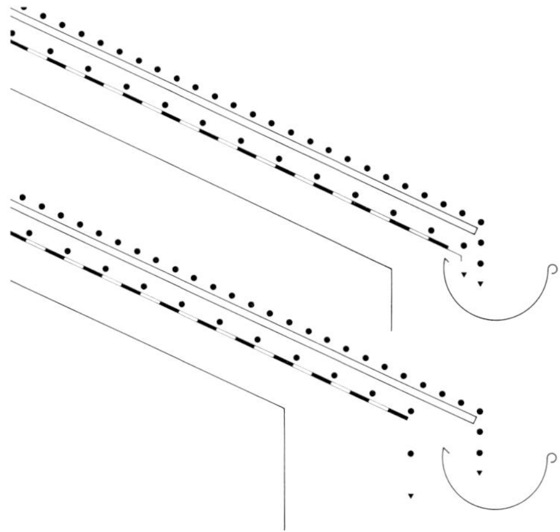

2.4.17.2 Water discharge from secondary waterproofing or covering layer

Many of the permanent functions of a secondary waterproofing layer are normally provided by roof coverings with or without an underlying covering layer or by a waterproofing layer.

Roof coverings always require an underlying waterproofing layer when for some reason the roof covering is not sufficiently watertight, e.g. on a shallower pitch than recommended.
In such cases the roof covering drains most of the rainwater, protects the underlying components against ultraviolet radiation and mechanical damage, provides colour and satisfies aesthetic needs.
- Secondary covering layer is an independent roof covering layer. It is not a watertight arrangement but is formed by overlapping or butt-jointed sheeting or boards.
- Sheathing is a type of underlay that can function as a temporary roof covering and serve as an "emergency roof" prior to and during roofing, as it is able to withstand the rigours of the weather for this period. Afterwards, it serves as a secondary water run-off layer, prevents the ingress of dust and dirt, or serves as a separating layer (timber constituents).

Secondary waterproofing/covering layers and sheathing can initially be laid over all the openings that will be required later. As construction work progresses, the necessary openings, e.g. at the ridge, for chimneys, roof windows etc., are made in the material.

Ventilated secondary waterproofing/covering layer
Ventilating the secondary waterproofing/covering layer is an effective way of avoiding damage due to moisture transport from the interior of the building. However, as with the roof covering itself, water in the external air can condense on the underside of the boarding or roofing felt. This happens when moist warm

external air passes over a secondary waterproofing/covering layer that has been overcooled as a result of night-time skyward radiation.

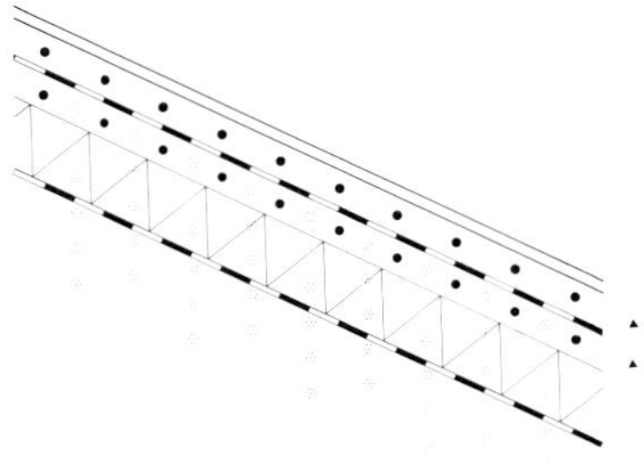

2.4.17.3 Ventilation underneath secondary waterproofing or covering layer

Overcooling occurs less often with impervious layers laid on timber boards, owing to the heat capacity of the wood. In addition, the boards function as a moisture buffer; condensation is temporarily absorbed by the timber boards and does not drip off. [06] If ventilation to the underside of the boards is supplemented by ventilation above the insulation, the information given in the sections "Design principles" and "Ventilation" applies.

Non-ventilated secondary waterproofing/covering layer
Besides the disadvantages mentioned under "Design principles", this approach also has advantages:

- Thermal insulation placed between the rafters can exploit the full depth of the rafters.
- The details at eaves, ridge and roof penetrations can be made simpler.
- No moisture from the external air can condense on the underside.

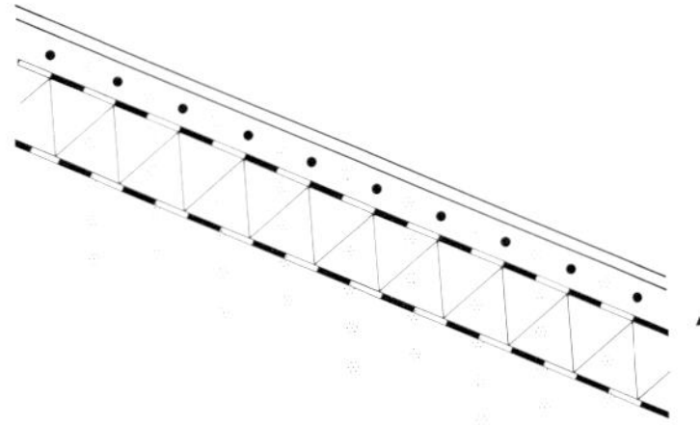

2.4.17.4 Secondary waterproofing or covering layer without extra ventilation

However, the following recommendations should be observed in order to avoid damage due to condensation:

- There may be no moisture transport in air flows from the inside to the outside. The inner lining or the vapour barrier must be installed absolutely airtight (see "Vapour barrier and airtight membrane"). [09]
- The diffusion resistance ($s_d$-value) of the vapour barrier must be compatible with the external covering to the layer of the thermal insulation (see "Building science" and "Ventilation"). DIN 4108 part 3 (July 2001 edition) specifies pairs of values for diffusion barriers inside and outside the thermal insulation for designs without a theoretical analysis. It also prescribes a vapour diffusion-equivalent air layer thickness $s_d \geq 100$ m for roof covering or roof sealing without ventilation underneath (see "Ventilation"). When using a vapour barrier with a lower $s_d$-value, it must be proved that no condensation forms or any that does form is rendered harmless by subsequent evaporation. DIN 4108 part 3 specifies the method of analysis for this. [01] The use of sheets open to diffusion (fibre-cement sheets, bituminous fibre board) or flexible sheeting on top of the thermal insulation is compulsory under DIN 4108. [04, 05]

## Laying

Secondary covering layer, secondary waterproofing layer

#### Secondary covering layer

Rigid sheets

Butted joints
Relatively thick sheets are laid in one plane and held in place by continuous counter battens. The joints are rebated or in tongue and groove form, through which any incoming water can drain.

Thermal insulation batts
When laid over the rafters, rigid foam insulating batts of polystyrene or polyurethane can also act as boarding.
The joints are rebated or in tongue and groove form. The minimum pitch of the sheets depends on the type of joint.

The disadvantages of such insulating batts are their low capacity to accommodate structural movement, their sensitivity to compression and the fact that the pitch depends on the type of joint. The insulating batts should be factory-laminated with a waterproofing layer of bituminous sheeting, plastic film, aluminium foil or timber derivative material.

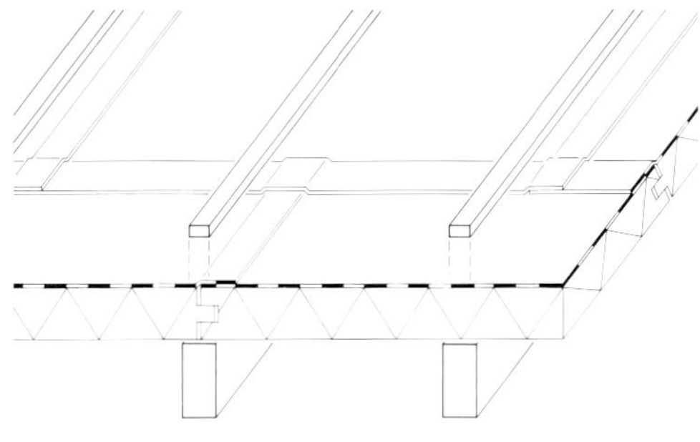

2.4.17.5 Rigid insulation with laminated vapour barrier

Bituminous fibreboard
The sheets for use as a secondary covering layer have a bitumen content of 10–15% by wt. When laid over the rafters, the sheets are held in place with clout nails and the counter battens. A watertight joint is achieved by means of the V-shaped edge profile. However, this joint can accommodate only minimal structural movement.
To prevent excessive deflection between the rafters, the roof pitch should be ≥ 20° and the spacing of the rafters ≤ 700 mm. Bituminous fibreboard are open to diffusion and have a low thermal conductance (see "Layers – Thermal insulation"). [12]

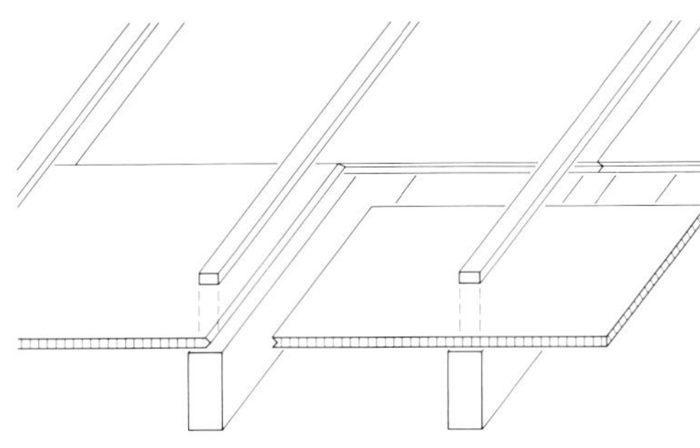

2.4.17.6 Bituminous fibreboard with rebated edge joints

Overlapping joints
Relatively thin sheets can be laid as overlapping elements. The corners must be cropped where otherwise four sheets would overlap. The sequence of laying and cutting of corners can be carried out in one of two ways:

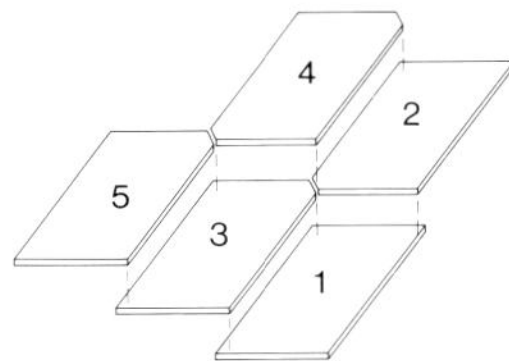


2.4.17.7 Cutting of corners and sequence of laying (1)

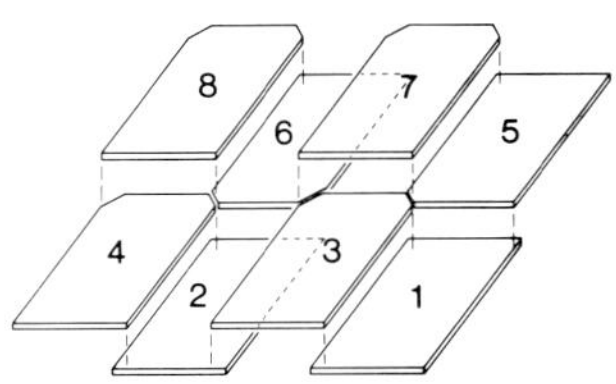


2.4.17.8 Cutting of corners and sequence of laying (2)

Hardboard
These sheets are lapped ≥ 100 mm and the fixing nails covered by the lap. The side laps are made at the rafters and are also ≥ 100 mm. Its hygroscopic properties mean hardboard has to be properly ventilated. [03]

Fibre-cement sheets
These sheets are laid parallel to the eaves and in the opposite direction to the prevailing wind. They are fixed to the rafters with galvanised clout nails (no predrilled holes). Counter battens are nailed on immediately after laying the sheets to prevent uplift due to wind suction. The side laps coincide with the rafters and should be ≥ 50 mm. The sides of the sheets are trimmed to match the spacing of the rafters, or the side laps are increased accordingly. End laps are ≥ 50 mm. [11]

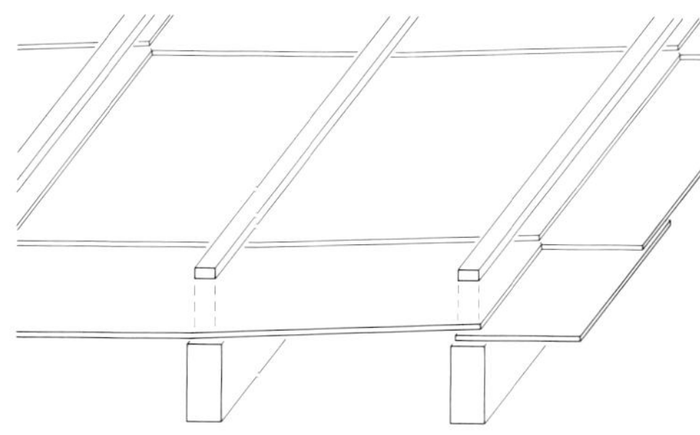

2.4.17.9 Fibre-cement sheets with cropped corners, laid overlapping in two directions

For enhanced watertightness requirements, e.g. if the roof pitch is shallower than recommended, the sheets are fixed to the rafters with gaps of 3–5 mm. The joints are then sealed with double-sided adhesive tape between the sheets pressed down by the counter battens.

End laps are ≥ 100 mm. Double-sided adhesive tape can also be laid in these laps if required.

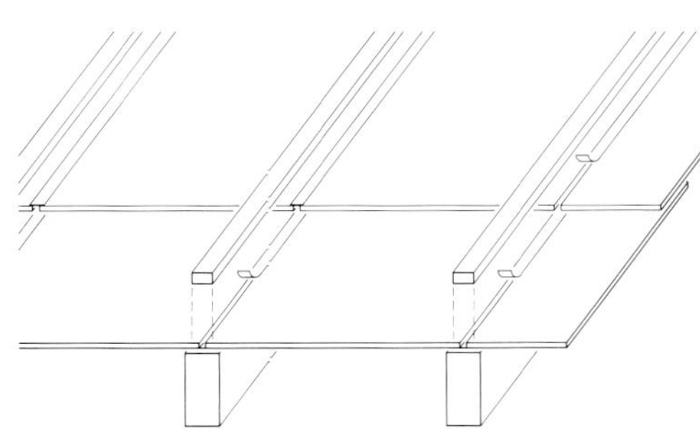

2.4.17.10 Fibre-cement sheets with double-sided self-adhesive tape, laid overlapping in one direction

The largest possible sheet formats should be employed to reduce the proportion of joints. [10, 11] Water deflectors are necessary above roof penetrations. Deflectors of sheet metal or battens embedded in putty and nailed to the trimming members are required around larger openings. A bead of putty is adequate around smaller openings. [10, 11]

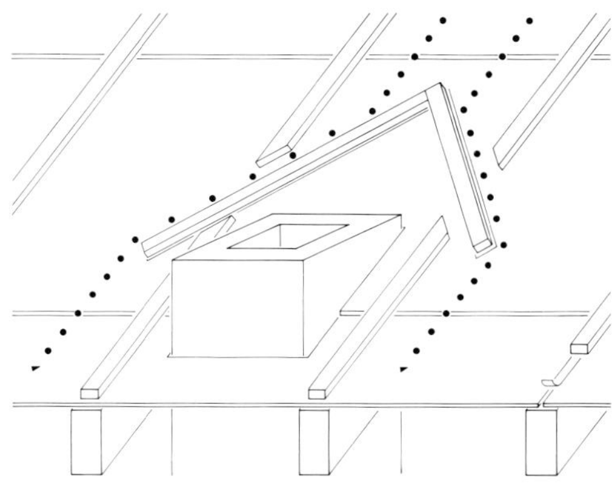

2.4.17.11 Run-off water being channelled around a roof penetration

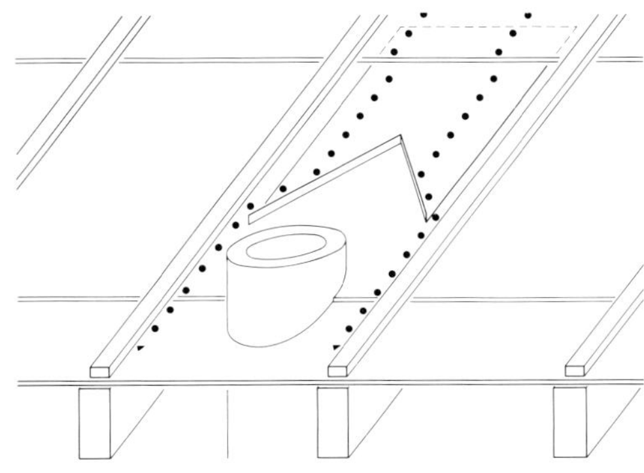

2.4.17.12 Sheet metal flashing above roof penetration

Flexible sheeting

Roofing felt
This is the simplest form of secondary covering layer. The sheets are laid parallel to the eaves over the rafters and fixed every 100–200 mm. Allowing the sheets to sag very slightly means that any moisture can drain between the rafters without saturating the counter battens.

The minimum roof pitch is 16°. The lap between adjacent sheets is 100 mm; but this should be increased to 150–200 mm for roof pitches ≤ 22°. [09]

With ventilation underneath, the last sheet ends ≥ 50 mm below the ridge (see "Layers – Ventilation"). Any driving rain or snow entering at this point can be intercepted by an additional sheet along the ridge.

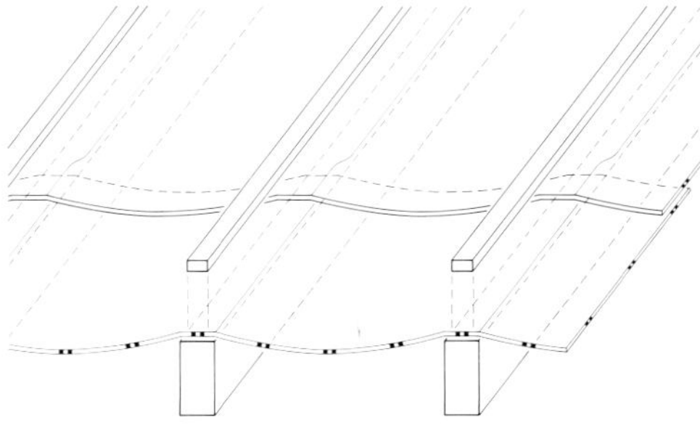

2.4.17.13 Roofing felt laid with laps

At hips the sheets are always laid over the hip itself, fixed to the hip rafter and held in place by hip battens (see "Construction details – Profiled clay and concrete tiles – Roof covering with roofing felt underneath"; for ventilated hip see "Layers – Ventilation").

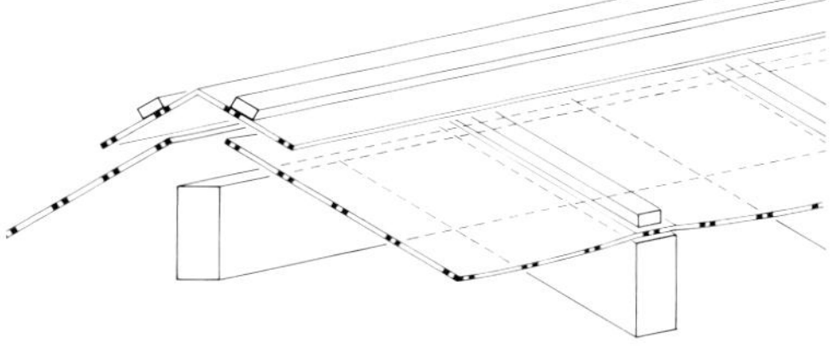

2.4.17.14 Ridge sheet laid on counter battens

The sheets at the eaves are laid on an eaves board (≥ 24 mm) or over the fascia board and simply hung over the gutter or drip flashing. They are pulled taut to prevent ponding.

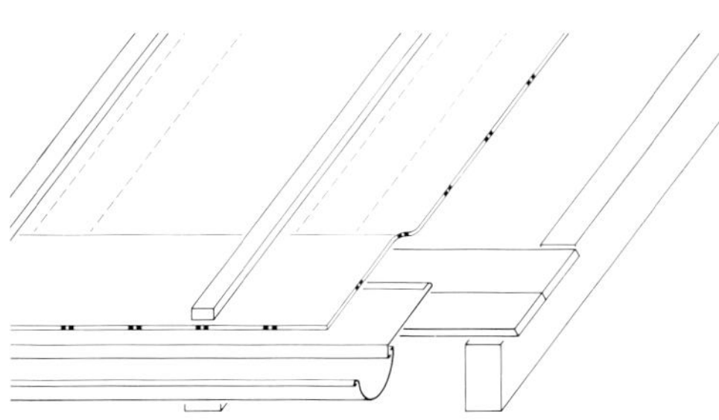

2.4.17.15 Eaves sheet laid loose

At a valley the sheets are laid on the valley board and overlap the sheet metal of the valley gutter. They are fixed to the boards and held in place by counter battens.

At verges the sheets are laid over the last rafter, continue up to the masonry of the gable and are wrapped around the battens.

The sheets should be carefully turned up and joined to chimneys, vent pipes, roof windows etc. Foil channels intercept water above the roof penetrations and discharge it safely to the sides.

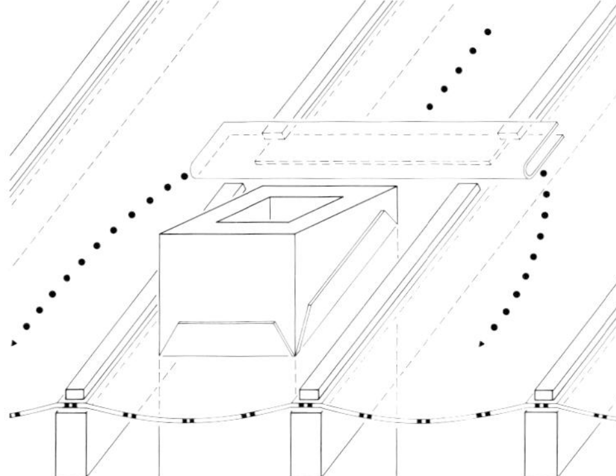

2.4.17.16 Foil channel fitted into roofing felt

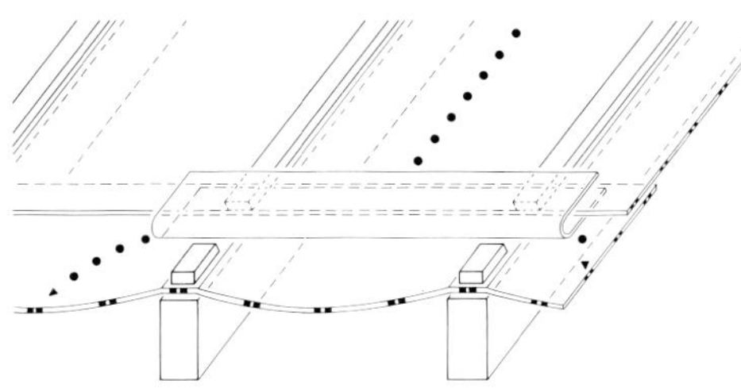

2.4.17.17 Foil channel at roofing felt lap

Moisture from the external air can condense on roofing felt with ventilation underneath. Roofing felts open to diffusion, laid directly on the insulation, are an alternative (see also "Design principles").

Special papers made of a mixture of wool fibres, cellulose fibres and impregnation substance are also open to diffusion. Their disadvantage is that they are not resistant to rain and wind during installation.

Flexible sheeting on roof decking
Bitumen or synthetic roofing felts laid on timber decking parallel to the eaves and with loose laps of ≥ 80 mm can suffice as a secondary covering layer. They are nailed (every approx. 100 mm) along their top edges and the nails are covered by the laps.

Both roof decking and roofing felt stop ≥ 30 mm below the ridge. [02]

At hips and valleys care should be taken to ensure that the sheets, including those on the hip or in the valley, overlap in the direction of the fall.

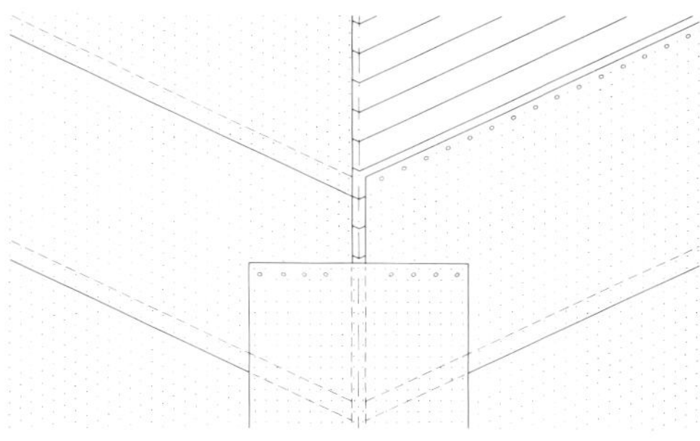

2.4.17.18 Roofing felt cut to suit at hip

If water can collect at valley battens, it will be necessary to bond or weld the sheets together at that point, even if they are otherwise laid with loose laps.

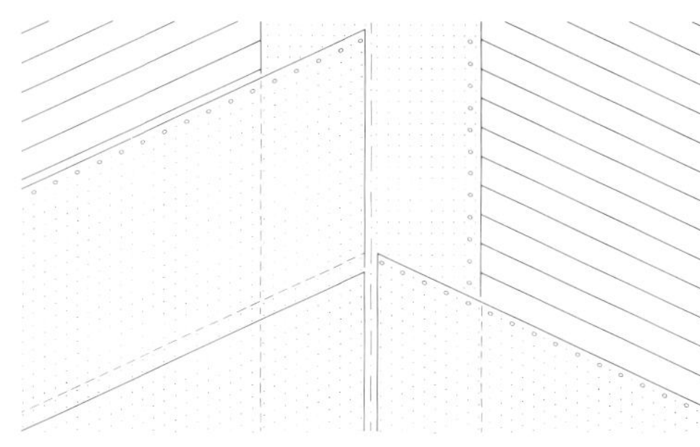

2.4.17.19 Roofing felt cut to suit at valley

**Secondary waterproofing layer**
A secondary waterproofing layer should consist of two layers of bitumen roofing felt, one layer of built-up roofing felt, or one layer of polymer base roofing felt, and a flat supporting construction. [02] A two-layer waterproofing arrangement on a substrate that accepts nails requires the first layer to be nailed in position and the second to be fully bonded but with the joints offset with respect to the first layer.

When using just one layer of material the nails should be covered by the laps. Seams and joints must be carefully welded or bonded together. The seams of bitumen roofing felt should overlap ≥ 80 mm, polymer base roofing felt 20–50 mm depending on the particular material. On roof decking treated with a timber preservative containing oil, PVC roofing felt (DIN 16 735) requires a suitable separating layer (synthetic non-woven fabric). It is welded to plastic-coated metal foil attached along the top edges. [08]

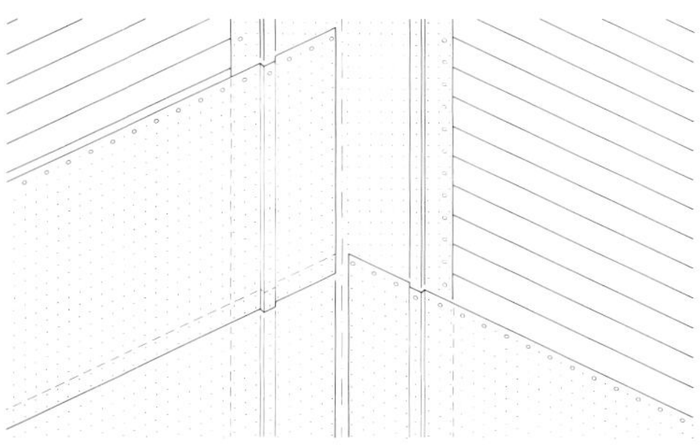

2.4.17.20 Arrangement of roofing felt and counter battens at valley

A timber boarding underlay consists of 24 mm thick, finish-sawn boards that fit tightly together. To prevent springiness of individual boards, tongue and groove joints are preferred. The counter battens are laid on the waterproofing and fixed.
On a shallow pitched roof with a rapid water run-off over the waterproofing, air must be able to circulate around the counter battens.
On a very shallow pitched roof with a slow water run-off it is advisable to protect the battens against long-term moisture.
If moisture seeps beneath the waterproofing, it ruins the counter battens because it cannot escape again.
With ventilation underneath, roof decking and waterproofing stop ≥ 30 mm below the ridge. For safety, the sheets of the secondary water run-off level should always be bonded or welded around shallow valleys and troughs ("safety channel") (see also "Layers – Green roof – Laying – Waterproofing and root barrier").

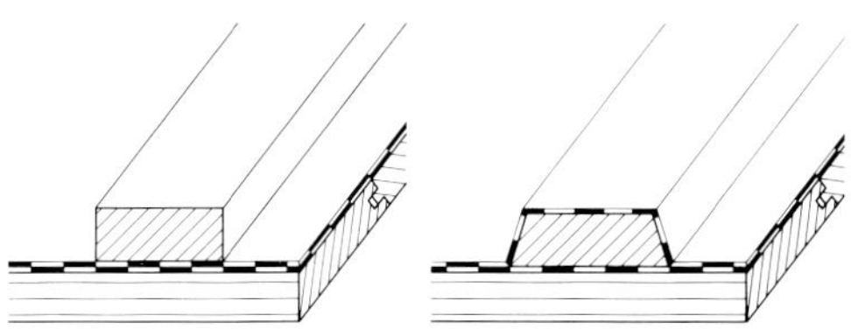

2.4.17.21 Counter batten above and below waterproofing layer

**References**
[01] DIN 4108: Thermal insulation and energy economy in buildings; pt 3: protection against moisture subject to climate conditions; requirements and directions for design and construction; Berlin: Beuth-Verlag; 2001
[02] pub. Zentralverband des Deutschen Dachdeckerhandwerks (Fachverband Dach-, Wand- und Abdichtungstechnik) e.V.: Fachregeln des Dachdeckerhandwerks; Cologne: Müller, 1992
[03] Hungerbühler, Ruedi: Konstruktion im Hochbau, vol. 2 Rohbauelemente, Montagebau, Ausbau. Zürich: Baufachverlag 1983
[04] Kasper, F.-J.: Erhöhung des Feuchterisikos bei Volldämmung zwischen den Sparren; in: DAB 3, 1990
[05] König, N.: Wärme- und Feuchtetransport bei unterschiedlichen Schrägdachdämmungen; in: Altbau-Modernisierung: bauphysikalische Aspekte beim Ausbau von Dachgeschossen; pub. Fraunhofer Institute for Building Science, Stuttgart
[06] Künzel, H.: Wärmegedämmte Satteldächer ohne Belüftung. Mitteilung 173, Fraunhofer Institute for Building Science, Stuttgart
[07] Liersch, Klaus W.: Belüftete Dach- und Wandkonstruktionen. Wiesbaden, Berlin: Bauverlag 1986, vol. 3, Dächer: bauphysikalische Grundlagen des Wärme- und Feuchteschutzes
[08] Braas product information
[09] Dörken product information
[10] Eternit product information
[11] Fulgurit product information
[12] Gutex product information

## Vapour barrier and airtight membrane

Actions, requirements, components, laying

**Actions**

During winter a water vapour partial pressure gradient from inside to outside usually prevails, meaning that water vapour diffusion occurs. Condensation forms where the air in the temperature gradient that exists in the roof construction reaches its water vapour saturation level.

If the inner layers of the roof construction are not airtight, thermal convection currents and/or wind suction force warm interior air through the joints. Compared to water vapour diffusion, the outward air flow can convey far more water vapour (1000x) to the outside. This depends on:

- the relative humidity in the interior
- the pressure differential between inside and outside
- the size of the joints

Such air flows also cause ventilation heat losses, which can also be considerably higher (2x to 30x) than the heat losses due to conduction. [15]

**Requirements**

In a multi-layer roof construction no condensation forms through water vapour diffusion when the layers are arranged according to the following basic principles:

- The thermal resistance $1/\Lambda$ of the individual layers must increase from outside to inside.
- The water vapour diffusion-equivalent air layer thickness ($s_d$) of the individual layers must decrease from inside to outside. [11]
- The effect of vapour-resistant roof coverings or secondary covering layers is cancelled out by a moving layer of air underneath.
- The flow in this air layer and the $s_d$-value of the layers on the inside of this must be related to each other; the smaller the air movements, the greater the $s_d$-value must be. [08]

The yardstick for measuring the vapour resistance effect of a component is its "diffusion-equivalent air layer thickness" ($s_d$). If several layers are present, their $s_d$-values are added together. The following equation applies:

$$s_d = \mu \cdot s$$

where:
$s_d$ = diffusion-equivalent air layer thickness [m]
$\mu$ = diffusion resistance index [dimensionless]
s = thickness of material [m]

DIN 4108 part 3 specifies the requirements for the individual layers. It gives the necessary $s_d$-values of "ventilated roofs" (ventilated air layer over thermal insulation) and "non-ventilated roofs" (no ventilated air layer over thermal insulation) in relation to sequence of layers, roof pitch and size of roof (eaves-ridge length).

If the conditions outlined below are satisfied the absence of condensation does not need to be checked in a theoretical analysis:

- Ventilated roofs with roof pitch ≥ 5°:
Unobstructed cross-sectional area for ventilation ≥ 2 cm high, or ≥ 2‰ of associated roof surface but not less than 200 cm²; inner layers with higher $s_d$-values will be required for a smaller ventilation cross-section or larger roofs (see "Layers – Ventilation"). [12]
- Ventilated roofs with roof pitch < 5°:
$s_d$ of internal vapour barrier ≥ 100 m.
- Non-ventilated roofs with ventilated roof covering:
Ratio of external vapour barrier $s_{de}$ to internal vapour barrier $s_{di}$ ≤ 1:6 (table 2.4.18.1).

| Diffusion-equivalent air layer thickness $s_d$ [m] outside $s_{de}$ | inside $s_{di}$ |
|---|---|
| ≤ 0.1 | ≥ 1.0 |
| ≤ 0.3 *) | ≥ 2.0 |
| > 0.3 | ≥ 6 $s_{de}$ |

*) It is not necessary to use a chemical timber preservative on non-ventilated roofs with $s_{de}$ ≤ 0.2 m when protection of the timber is achieved through preventive detailing measures (to DIN 68 800 part 2).

2.4.18.1 Vapour diffusion resistance of non-ventilated roofs with ventilated roof covering; water vapour diffusion-equivalent air layer thickness [03

- Non-ventilated roofs without ventilated roof covering:
$s_{di}$ of internal vapour barrier ≥ 100 m.
- Non-ventilated roofs with sealed roof covering:
$s_{di}$ of internal vapour barrier ≥ 100 m.
- Non-ventilated roofs with sealed waterproofing layer below thermal insulation (upside-down roof):
vapour-permeable layer on top of insulation.

If vapour control layers are positioned both above and below the thermal insulation, the diffusion resistance of the inner lining should be compatible with the outer covering of the insulation layer.

An approximation for avoiding condensation water is:

$$s_{di} = 10s_{de} \text{ to } 14s_{de} \text{ [13]}$$

Various materials used for the inner lining have a high thermal resistance $1/\Lambda$. In this case the vapour barrier lies between two thermal insulation layers. The temperature gradient means condensation water can form on the inside of the barrier. To prevent this, the thermal resistance of the layers on the inside of the vapour barrier may not exceed 20% of the total resistance of the roof (see "Layers – Thermal insulation"). [08]

**Components**

Properties

Roof coverings of normal-weight, lightweight or aerated concrete and layers of plaster are regarded as airtight membranes. Timber derivative boards, plasterboard, gypsum wallboard and fibre-cement sheets are also airtight. However, these components – like trapezoidal or corrugated metal sheeting – are not laid sufficiently airtight owing to the number of joints (when these joints are not additionally sealed). Perforated synthetic roofing felts or films are not airtight.

| Material | DIN No. | Density [g/cm³] | water vapour diffusion resistance index μ min. | max. |
|---|---|---|---|---|
| Timber boards, spruce/fir | | 0.47/0.45 | 40 | |
| Timber derivative boards: | | | | |
| plywood | 68 705/EN 315 | 0.8 | 50 | 400 |
| laminated particle boards | EN 312-2, -3, -5 | 0.7 | 50 | 100 |
| extruded particle boards | 68 764 | 0.7 | 20 | |
| hardboard | 68 754/EN 622-2 | 1.0 | 70 | |
| porous ("soft") wood-fibre boards<br>bituminous fibreboard | EN 622-1, -4<br>68 752 | ≤ 0.20<br>≤ 0.30 | 5<br>5 | |
| Cement-bound boards: | | | | |
| wood-wool lightweight boards<br>d ≥ 25 mm<br>d = 15 mm | 1101/1102 | <br>0.36 to 0.48<br>0.57 | <br>2<br>2 | <br>5<br>5 |
| fibre-cement sheeting | | 2.0 | 20 | 50 |
| Multi-ply boards: | | | | |
| plasterboard | 18 180 | 0.9 | 8 | |
| lightweight boards with rigid plastic foam core | 1101/1102 | 0.46 to 0.65 | 20 | 50 |

2.4.18.2 Inner linings; materials, characteristic values [02]

| Material | DIN No. | Density [g/cm³] | water vapour diffusion resistance index μ min. | max. |
|---|---|---|---|---|
| Bitumen flexible sheeting: | | | | |
| bitumen roofing felt | 52 128 | 1.2 | 10 000 | 80 000 |
| non-coated bitumen roofing felt | 52 129 | 1.2 | 2000 | 20 000 |
| glass fleece bitumen roofing felt | 52 143 | | 20 000 | 60 000 |
| built-up roofing felt | | | 60 000 | 10 0000 |
| Synthetic flexible sheeting: | | | | |
| polyisobutylene | 16 731 | | 400 000 | 1 750 000 |
| plasticised PVC | 16 730 | | 40 000 | 30 000 |
| ethylene copolymer bitumen 2.0 K | 16 729 | | 50 000 | 75 000 |
| ethylene copolymer bitumen 2.0 | 16 729 | | 70 000 | 90 000 |
| chlorinated polyethylene | | | 40 000 | |
| neoprene rubber | 7 864 | | 38 000 | |
| chlorosulphonated polyethylene | 16 733 | | 50 000 | 58 000 |
| EPDM | 7 864 | | 65 000 | 75 000 |
| isoprene-isobutene rubber | 7 864 | | 165 000 | 400 000 |
| acrylonitrile butadiene rubber | 7 864 | | 10 000 | |
| Plastic foil: | | | | |
| PVC, ≥ 0.1 mm thk. | | | 20 000 | 50 000 |
| Polyethylene, ≥ 0.1 mm thk. | | | 100 000 | |
| Metal foil: | | | | |
| aluminium, ≥ 0.05 mm thk. | | | vapour-proof | |
| other metal foils, ≥ 0.1 mm thk. | | | vapour-proof | |

2.4.18.3 Flexible sheeting, film and foil; characteristic values [01, 02]

**Rigid sheets**

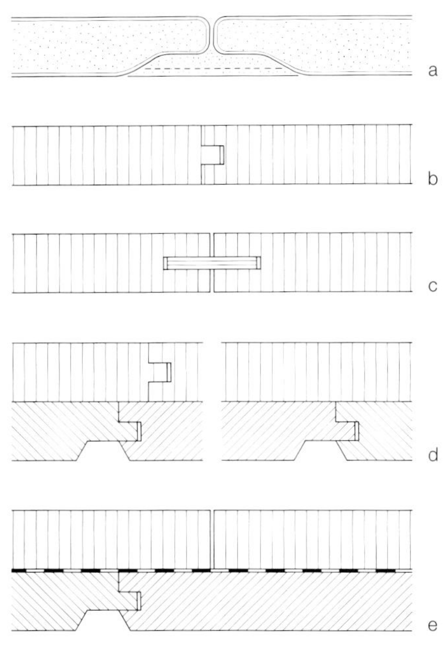


2.4.18.5 Inner linings; airtight joints [13, 14]: a plasterboard with filled joints, b pressed particle board with tongue and groove edge joint, c timber derivative boards with groove and loose tongue, d profiled boards beneath pressed particle board with tongue and groove edge joint, e profiled boards with laminated foil

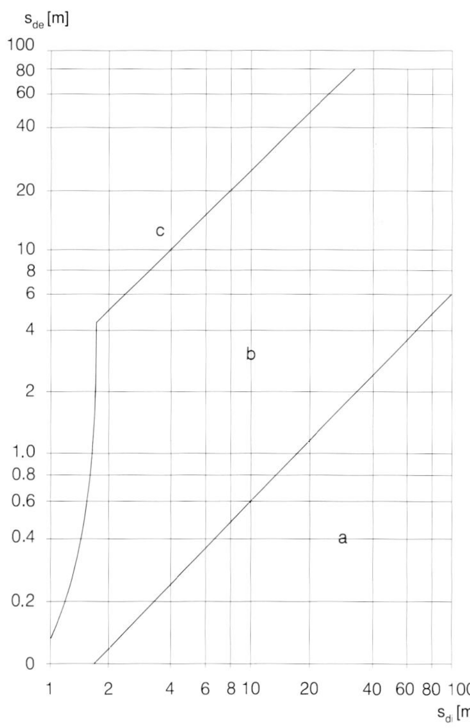


2.4.18.4 Formation of condensation water in non-ventilated roofs with different $s_d$-values inside and outside (climatic conditions and method of analysis to DIN 4108)[09]: a no condensation, b condensation dries out in following summer, c complete drying of condensation not guaranteed

As the materials traditionally used for the inner linings of roofs (table 2.4.18.2) do not have a high vapour diffusion resistance, an internal vapour barrier has to be included as well. This also acts as an airtight membrane.

Films and foils with a sufficiently high $s_d$-value are also suitable vapour control components (provided the number of joints is not excessive) (table 2.4.18.3). It may also be possible to use insulating components – laminated with foil on the underside – which also have a high $s_d$-value (see "Layers – Thermal insulation").

Vapour control layers with $s_d \geq 1500$ m are designated as "water vapour-proof" to DIN EN ISO 12572. However, vapour barriers with lower $s_d$-values allow the passage of only small amounts of water vapour. This means that if the basic principles are adhered to, condensation does not form and water vapour is carried away with the air flow.

## Laying

Rigid sheets, flexible sheeting

Airtight joints can be achieved with sheets in one or more layers and with film or foil.

A layer of plasterboard with filled joints is airtight. Strips of textile or glass fibre should be laid over the joints to accommodate movement. [13]
Sheets made of timber derivatives with a tongue and groove or similar edge joint are regarded as being virtually airtight when there is a firm connection at all joints. However, this is barely possible in practice. [13, 14]

Sheets with simple butt joints and timber boards are not suitable. They may exhibit a high air permeability because the proportion of joints is high and the joints widen as the material dries out. An inner lining of timber boards must therefore be attached underneath timber derivative sheets with airtight joints or some other form of completely airtight barrier. [13]
The joints between rigid foam sheets are also insufficiently airtight, even when the edges are joined with adhesive or the sheets are laid in two layers with the joints offset. [09, 10]

**Flexible sheeting**

Foil is laid from ridge to eaves without joints so that the side laps (≥ 100 mm) can be pressed against the rafters with counter battens. In addition, double-sided adhesive tape should be laid in the laps.
Joints across the slope should be avoided. If they are unavoidable, they should be lapped and pressed together in the same way.

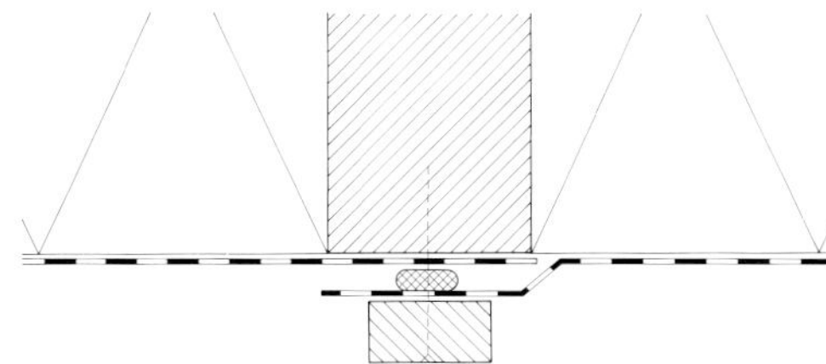

2.4.18.6 Side lap of foil under rafter, with sealing strip in lap [05]

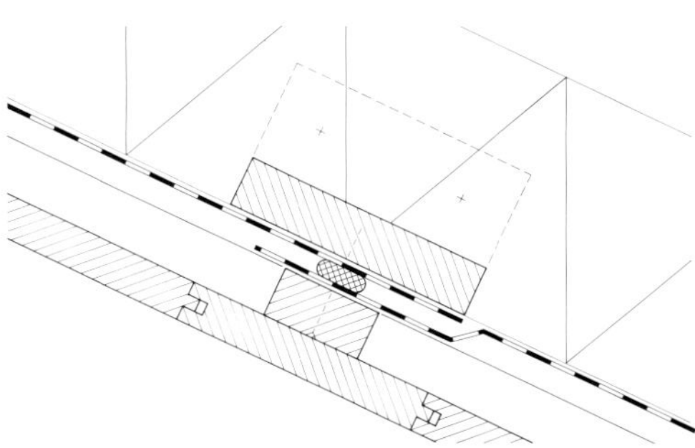

2.4.18.7 Transverse joint with sealing strip and board to apply pressure under soft thermal insulation [05, 11]

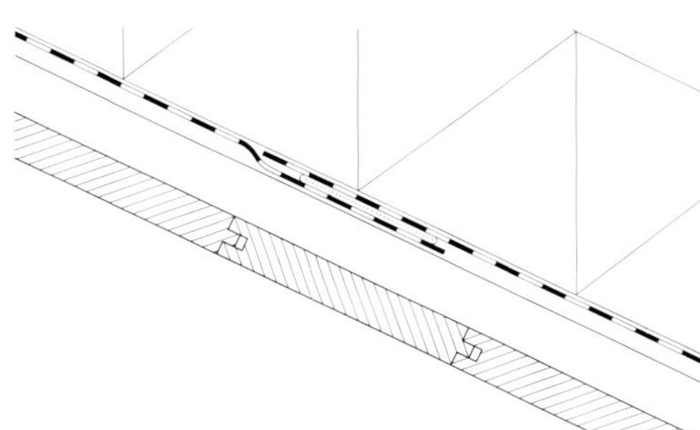

2.4.18.8 Transverse joint with self-adhesive tape beneath rigid thermal insulation [05, 12]

Airtight joints between the rafters are difficult because this doubles the number of joints. A permanently elastic sealing strip must be pressed between foil/film and rafters and held in place by the jointing strip of the inner lining.

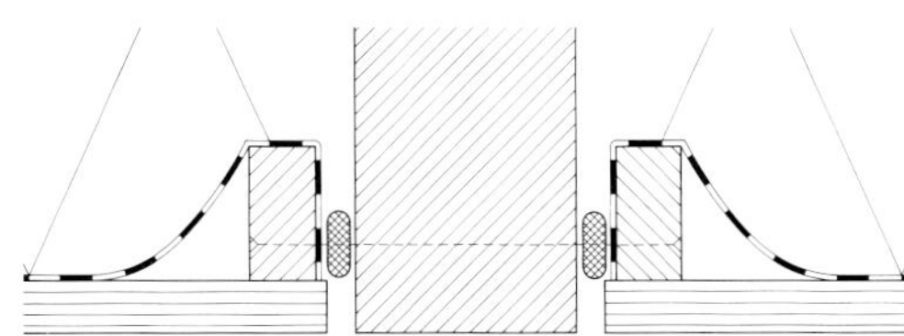

2.4.18.9 Junction with rafter, with batten applying pressure and sealing strip [12]

At adjoining elements, e.g. floor slabs, walls, foil should be held in position with battens over the full length. The joints between foil and an uneven component will also require a permanently elastic sealing strip. The joint between gable wall and rafters should be packed tight with mineral wool. [12]

The exposed edges (at laps) of fibre insulation laminated with aluminium foil acting as a vapour barrier require additional measures to render them airtight. Attaching these edges to the rafters is not adequate, even when this is done at very close centres. Side and end laps can be sealed with timber strips nailed or screwed on, or with wide adhesive tape. [09, 10]

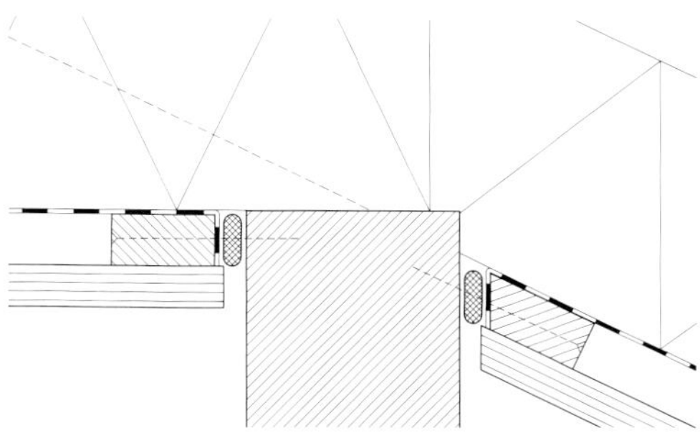

2.4.18.10 Junction with purlin, with batten applying pressure and sealing strip [12]

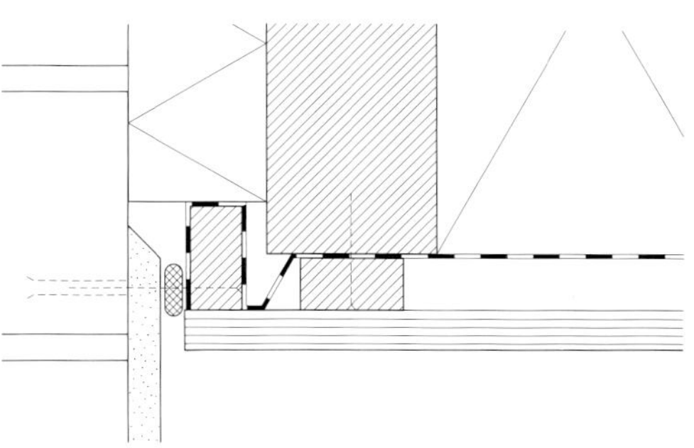

2.4.18.11 Junction with wall, with batten applying pressure and sealing strip [05]

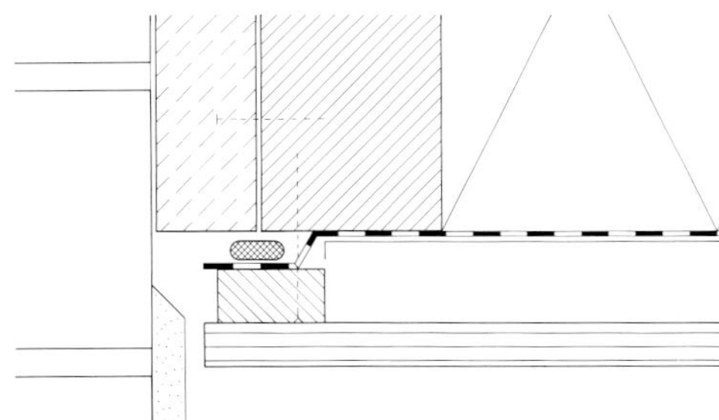

2.4.18.12 Junction with chimney stack, with batten applying pressure and sealing strip [05, 12]

Pipes and similar items penetrating the vapour barrier should be flashed with a collar, which is bonded or welded to the vapour barrier and tightened around the pipe etc. together with a sealing strip. Mechanical fasteners that penetrate the inner lining or vapour barrier do not normally present any problems. The air permeability and the water vapour diffusion remain practically unchanged. The same is true for minor damage to the vapour barrier, provided the inner lining underneath is airtight across its whole surface. [02, 13]

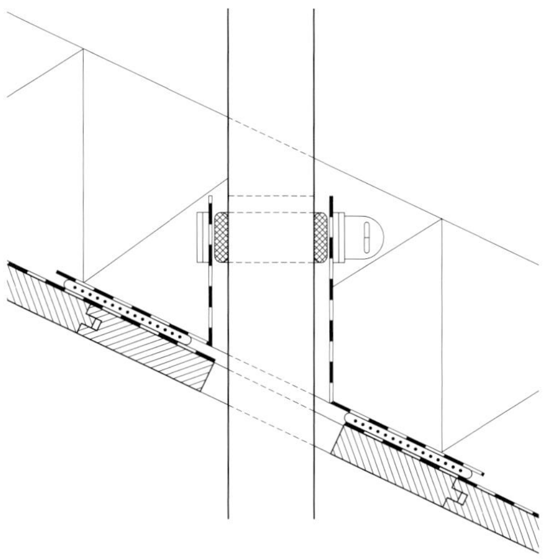

2.4.18.13 Pipe penetration with self-adhesive flange, collar and sealing strip

**References**


[01] Buss, Harald: Feuchteschäden – Flachdachkonstruktionen. Kissing, Zürich, Paris, Mailand, Amsterdam, Vienna, London, New York: WEKA Fachverlag, 1988

[02] DIN 4108: Thermal protection and energy economy in buildings; pt 2: minimum requirements for thermal insulation; Berlin: Beuth, 1996

[03] DIN 4108: Thermal insulation and energy economy in buildings; pt 3: protection against moisture subject to climate conditions; requirements and directions for design and construction; Berlin: Beuth, 2001

[04] DIN 4108: Thermal insulation and energy economy in buildings; pt 4: characteristic values relating to thermal insulation and protection against moisture; Berlin: Beuth, 2002

[05] DIN V 4108 (prelim.): Thermal insulation and energy economy of buildings; pt 7: Airtightness of building, requirements, recommendations and examples for planning and performance; Berlin: Beuth, 1996

[06] DIN 68800: Protection of timber; pt 2: preventive constructional measures in buildings; Berlin: Beuth, 1996

[07] DIN EN ISO 12572: Building materials – determination of water vapour transmission properties; Berlin: Beuth, 2001

[08] Grassnick, Arno, ed.: Der Schadenfreie Hochbau: Grundlagen zur Vermeidung von Bauschäden, vol. 3: Pohlenz, Rainer: Wärmeschutz, Tauwasserschutz und Schallschutz. Cologne: R. Müller, 1987

[09] Jablonka, Dieter: Tauwasser beim luftdurchlässigen geneigten Dach; in: DDH 3, 1987

[10] Knublauch, E.; Schäfer, H.; Sidon, S.: Über die Luftdurchlässigkeit geneigter Dächer; in: Gesundheitsingenieur 108/issue 1, 1987

[11] Pohl, W.-H.: Belüftete Dächer mit Metalldeckung, Feuchteschutz, bauphysikalische Grundlagen; Datteln: Rheinzink, 1991

[12] Grünzweig & Hartmann product information

[13] Schulze, Horst: Hausdächer in Holzbauart: Konstruktion, Statik, Bauphysik. Düsseldorf: Werner, 1987

[14] Schulze, Horst: Holzwerkstoffe, Konstruktionen, Bauphysik; pub. by Entwicklungsgemeinschaft Holzbau (EGH), Deutschen Gesellschaft für Holzforschung, Munich

[15] Zimmermann, Klaus: Zum Ausbau geneigter Dächer für Wohnzwecke; in: Bauwelt 9, 1989

## Thermal insulation

Materials, manufacture and properties, laying

### Materials, manufacture and properties

Granulates and flakes

- Expanded perlite is made from the volcanic rock perlite; it is non-toxic and environmentally compatible. Used expanded perlite products can be crushed and fed back into the production of new products. [06]
- Expanded clay is produced by milling and granulating natural clay. It is light in weight, has a good compressive strength, good thermal insulation properties and is resistant to virtually all types of acids and alkalis, moisture and frost; it is also non-toxic and environmentally compatible. Used material can be crushed and reutilised as raw material for new components or as a loose filling material.
- Vermiculite belongs to the group of hydrated sheet silicates and is found mainly in South Africa. In its exfoliated state vermiculite is very light, has a good compressive strength, excellent thermal insulation properties and is fire-resistant (class A 1); it is also non-toxic and environmentally compatible. After use, vermiculite can be reused as a loose filling material or crushed and fed back into production, or employed as a recycled material for ground improvement works. [19]

| Insulating material | | Density [kg/m³] | Type of application | Water vapour diffusion resistance index μ min. | max. | Water absorption [% by vol., 28 days] | Thermal conductance $\lambda_R$ [W/mK] | Coefficient of thermal expansion[1/Kx10⁻⁶] | Short-term thermal stability [°C] | Long-term thermal stability [°C] | Low-temperature stability [°C] | Behaviour in fire [building mat. class] | Compressive stress at 10% compression [N/mm²] |
|---|---|---|---|---|---|---|---|---|---|---|---|---|---|
| Expanded perlite | | ≤ 100 | S/W | 1 | | | 0.060 | | | | | A1 | |
| Expanded clay | | 400–1800 | S/W | 2 | 8 | | 0.13–0.25 | | | | | A1 | |
| Exfoliated vermiculite | | 60–140 | | | | | 0.063–0.069 | | 1200 | 1000 | | A1 | |
| Cellulose fibres | | 35–60 | S/W/WL | 1–1.5 | | | 0.040/0.045 | | | | | B2/B1 | |
| Cork DIN 18161 part 1 | expanded cork agglomerate | ≥ 80 | WD | 5 | 10 | | 0.045/ 0.050/0.055 | 40 | 180 | 100 | | B2 | 0.05–0.11 |
| | | ≥ 120 | | | | | | | | | | | |
| | impregnated cork | ≥ 120 | WD | | | | | | 170 | 120 | | | |
| | | ≥ 200 | WDS | | | | | | | | | | |
| Foamed glass DIN 18174 | | 100–150 | WDS/ WDH | practically vapour-proof | | | 0.045/0.050/ 0.055/0.060 | 8.5 | 430 | 400 | -260 | A1 | |
| Foamed plastics DIN 18164 part 1 Rigid foams | polystyrene particle foam | ≥ 15 | W | 20 | 50 | 2 – 3 | 0.025 | 67–98 | 100 | 75 | | B1 | 0.07–0.12 |
| | | ≥ 20 | WD | 30 | 70 | | 0.030 | | | | | | 0.12–0.16 |
| | | ≥ 30 | WS | 40 | 100 | | 0.035 | | | | | | 0.18–0.26 |
| | extruded polystyrene foam | ≥ 25 | W/WD | 80 | 300 | 2 | 0.040 | 67–76 | 100 | 85 | | B1 | |
| | | ≥ 30 | WS | | | | | | | | | | |
| | polyurethane | ≥ 30 | W/WD/ WS | 30 | 100 | 2 – 5 | 0.020/0.025 0.030/0.035 | 50–80 | 250 | 100 | -180 | B1/ B2 | 0.10–0.15 |
| | phenolic resin | ≥ 30 | W | 30 | 50 | 7 – 12 | 0.030/0.035/ 0.040/0.045 | 23 | 200 | 130 | -200 | B1/ B2 | 0.10–0.35 |
| | | ≥ 35 | WD/WS | | | | | | | | | | |
| Rigid melamine resin foam | | 8–11 | | 1–2 | | | < 0.035 | | ~ 200 | ~ 150 | | B1 | 0.04–0.2 |
| Polyester fibres | | 15–40 | W/WL | | | 1 | 0.035/0.040/ 0.045 | | 250 | 100 | | B1 | |
| Coconut fibres | | 75–85 | W/WL | 1 | | | 0.045 | | | | | B1/B2 | |
| Porous wood-fibre boards DIN 68 750 | | | ≤ 200 | W/WL | 5 | | 0.045 | | | | | B1/B2 | |
| | | ≤ 300 | | | | | 0.056 | | | | | | |
| Wood-wool lightweight build. boards DIN 1101 | d ≥ 25 mm thk | 360–480 | W/WD/WS/ WV/WB | 2 | 5 | | 0.093 | | | 150 | | B1 | 0.15–0.2 |
| | d = 25 mm thk | 570 | | | | | 0.15 | | | | | | |
| Multi-ply lightweight building boards DIN 1104 part 1 | polystyrene particle f. | ≥15 | W/WD/WS/ WV/WB | 20 | 50 | | 0.04 | | | | | B1/B2 | |
| | wood-wool d = 10–25 [mm] | 460–650 | | 2 | 5 | | 0.15 | | | | | | |
| | d ≥ 25 | 360–460 | | | | | 0.095 | | | | | | |
| | Mineral-fibre layer | 50–250 | | 1 | | | 0.040/0.045 | | | | | | |
| Sheep's wool | | 20–80 | W/WL | 1–2 | | | 0.037 | | 500–600 | | | B2 | |
| Straw | | 220 | W | 2 | | | ~ 0.050 | | 170 | 100 | | B2 | |
| Reed | | 120–200 | W | 2 | 5 | | 0.042–0.073 | | | | | B2 | |
| Flax | | 20–80 | W/WL | 1 | | | 0.035–0.045 | | | | | B2 | |
| Cotton wool | | 20–30 | W-w | 1–2 | | | 0.040 | | | | | B2 | |
| Hemp | | 100–140 | W/WL | 1–2 | | | 0.039–0.060 | | | | | B2 | |
| Mineral fibres DIN 18165 part 1 | rock wool | 8–500 | W/WD/ WS/WV | 1 | | | 0.035/0.040/ 0.045/0.050 | 0–7 | 900 | 600 | | A1/A2 | |
| | glass wool | | | | | | | | 500 | 500 | | | |

2.4.19.1 Materials; characteristic values [06, 08, 14, 19, 25]
S: loose material; W, WL: cannot support compressive loads; WD: can support compressive loads; WS, WDS: with increased loading capacity for special applications; WDH: with increased compressive loading capacity; WV: can withstand pull-off and shear loads; WB: can withstand bending loads

- Cellulose fibres are obtained from sorted, mechanically crushed newspaper. These fibres contain no inhalable fine dust and do not release any hazardous substances. However, the very high proportion of flame-retardant agent (boric salt content up to 20%) should not be ignored. Cellulose insulating materials are available as batts or loose material. Classed as not readily flammable (class B 1), cellulose insulation waste is therefore unsuitable for incineration, so that only reuse or disposal in a landfill site can be considered. Cellulose insulating batts may help to channel the flood of scrap paper into better controlled uses. [14]

Granulate batts
Cork is obtained from the bark of the cork oak tree (debarking is carried out every 8–12 years).

- Expanded cork is made by expanding scrap cork in steam.
- Expanded cork agglomerate is made by milling cork bark to a granulate and treating it in autoclaves. The suberin resin contained in the virgin cork bark binds the expanded granulate into blocks, which can then be cut into sheets.
- Impregnated cork is made by mixing expanded granulate with hot bitumen to form blocks. [08]

From an ecological viewpoint cork is not completely unproblematic. The unnecessary transport from its countries of origin around the Mediterranean Sea and the associated environmental impact are no longer justifiable. The availability of cork is extremely limited. Some cork products are made in processes that are not entirely without their environmental problems. The manufacture of expanded cork gives off toxic vapours whose accumulation in the cork products cannot always be ruled out. Scrap cork can be crushed and reused in the manufacturing process. [06]

Foam batts
- Foamed glass is made by foaming pulverised, silica glass while adding a propellant (carbon). It has a good compressive strength and long service life, is moisture-resistant, vapour-proof, incombustible and biologically stable. But the installation of foamed glass is not without its health hazards. Pieces of foamed glass are bonded with hot bitumen or bitumen cold-bonding agents. If bitumen adhesives contain used oil, vapours with carcinogenic constituents may be released during hot bitumen bonding. As foamed glass contains no additives, its disposal in landfill sites presents no problems. Foamed glass can also be crushed for reuse as a filling material in paving works.

- Rigid polystyrene (PS) foam consists principally of closed-cell, rigid expanded styrene or copolymers. We distinguish between particle foam made from bonded, expanded polystyrene granulate, and extruded foam, according to the method of manufacture:

- Polystyrene particle (EPS) foam is made by treating polystyrene granulate with steam. Blocks, sheets or mouldings are given their shape in a second, continuous or discontinuous steam process. [08] The lightweight, inexpensive sheets have good to very good thermal insulation properties. Clean production residue, waste from on-site cutting and used packaging can be collected and fed into recycling schemes. [25] In milled form it can be used as a lightweight aggregate in concrete, mortar and plaster. Polystyrene particle foam insulating materials can be converted back into the polystyrene from which they were originally made by a simple melting process, which renders the production of injection-moulded polystyrene components possible. Chemical processes (pyrolysis, hydrogenation) can break down polystyrene particle foam into its constituent materials again. Disposal in landfill sites and incineration in modern waste incineration plants continues.

- Extruded rigid polystyrene (XPS) foam is produced as a continuous ribbon of foamed material. Polystyrene is first melted in the extruder and the melt is then pressed to form a ribbon after adding partially halogenated chlorofluorocarbon (CFC) or carbon dioxide ($CO_2$) as a propellant. Owing to its closed-cell structure, extruded rigid polystyrene absorbs hardly any water, is rotproof and has a very good compressive strength, but is not resistant to ultraviolet light; it has good to very good thermal insulation properties. When no longer required, extruded rigid polystyrene can be reused, even when very old. It can be disposed of in landfill sites for domestic waste without any environmental problems. Extruded rigid polystyrene can also be disposed of in modern waste incineration plants or in waste-burning power stations. [07]

- Rigid polyurethane (PUR) foam is a principally closed-cell, rigid foam material made from liquid raw materials (isocyanate, polyhydric alcohol) to which a propellant has been added. The principal propellants in Germany are hydrocarbons (pentane), small amounts of carbon dioxide ($CO_2$) and partially halogenated CFC. Rigid polyurethane foam has excellent thermal insulation properties, is rotproof, can be walked on without damage and is moisture-resistant, but has problems with ultraviolet radiation. Owing to the high cost of disposal, attempts should always be made to utilise residue on the same building site. The chemical disposal methods include glycolysis, which enables the raw materials to be extracted. However, this method can be used only on clean waste whose chemical composition is known. [11] The pressure-bonding method for recycling clean rigid polyurethane foam continues to be suitable. This method produces good-quality pressed sheets, which can be used on their own or in multi-ply format. Disposal in modern waste incineration plants is, in ecological terms, the best method of dealing with soiled (with bitumen or roofing felt residue) or old insulating materials containing CFC.

- Rigid melamine resin foam is a flexible, open-cell foam material made of melamine resin, a duroplastic synthetic material which belongs to the group of aminoplastics. [16] During use, rigid melamine resin foam can be classed as non-toxic and environmentally compatible. It can be recycled by crushing to form flakes, and then further treated to form a foam. Melamine resin is also used as the binding agent here. [16]

- Perlite insulating batts are produced by mixing inorganic and/or organic fibres and binding agents into expanded perlite. The manufacture of the insulating batts, from the preparation of the fibres up to the finished, shaped product, is carried out using the wet process. After drying, the batts are cut to size. [08] Perlite insulating batts have moderate thermal insulation properties and a reasonable compressive strength. They are employed in areas with possible moisture problems. [10] Used material can be crushed and fed back into the production of new products. Crushed scrap material can also be used as a filler or for ground improvement works in landscaping.

- Polyester (PET), a raw material obtained from crude oil, in granulated form is melted down in the extruder and subsequently spun out in the melt extrusion/spinning process. The fibres are compressed under the action of heat and mechanical pressure to form blocks which are wedged between the rafters. Polyester is a very new building material and its use is not yet very widespread. It is a non-composite material, rotproof, stable in ultraviolet light and resistant to moisture, bio-organisms and pests. Polyester sheets are mainly employed as insulation between the rafters of pitched roofs. [24] Polyester fibres present no disposal problems because, worldwide, all the material can be fed back into closed material life cycles. Incineration also presents no problems because only carbon and water are given off.

Fibre materials

- Coconut fibres (coir) are obtained from the outer shell of the coconut. After storage in water for several weeks, only the rotproof residue remains, and can be impregnated with ammonium sulphate to make it fire-retardant. Coconut fibres are used only rarely in Europe owing to their poor availability. The fibres cannot be composted and incineration is not desirable because of the high ammonium sulphate content. Coconut fibre materials are either reused or disposed of in landfill sites. [06]

- Wood-fibre batts are produced from waste materials, i.e. from fibres made of sawmill residue, mixed with wood's own resin (lignin) or synthetic resin (casein glue) as a binding agent. They are also available with a bitumen additive to provide moisture protection. Aluminium sulphate is the only additive in the batts, which means they can be certified as biologically compatible. With bitumen added they can also be used as airtight moisture protection above the rafters. Wood-fibre batts can be reused or hacked into small pieces for use as an environmentally compatible compost. [14]

- Wood-wool lightweight building boards are made from wood-wool shavings approx. 500 mm long, 5 mm wide and 0.5 mm thick, together with mineral binding agents.

- Multi-ply lightweight building boards are made from a layer of rigid foam or mineral fibres faced on one (2-ply board) or both (3-ply board) sides with mineral-bound wood-wool. The high content of cement or magnesia cement [06] for bonding the individual plies together or bonding the material to other components makes recycling uneconomic at present. Depending on how they were fixed, the boards can be removed and reused, but if they were bonded to and are contaminated with other materials, they must be disposed of in a landfill site. [17]

- Sheep's wool is an insulating material made from natural fibres that exhibits good technical properties such as low weight, a low thermal conductance and very good vapour permeability. Sheep's wool can be protected against moth attack and its behaviour in fire improved (class B 2) by treating it with borax, a natural salt. Besides the insulation of steep roofs and suspended ceilings, sheep's wool is suitable for filling voids in floor slabs (sound absorption). It can be completely recycled [03] and its non-composite nature means that it is readily composted, provided no polyester fibres have been added. [06]

- Reed, without the addition of other substances, is moisture-resistant, open to diffusion and has sound attenuation properties. Reed insulating batts are made from an untreated natural raw material, require very little energy during production and are fully recyclable. Reed is thus a healthy, ecologically viable insulating material. [03]

- Straw can be used both as a loose material and in the form of sheets. The sheets are made by crushing the straw, drying it, milling it to form a dust and then adding appropriate binding agents and additives (cellulose, lignin, silicic acid compounds and glue). The heated straw mass is then cut to size. [03] Straw is ideal for thermal and sound insulation, is open to diffusion and is water vapour-permeable. Insulating products made of straw can be employed throughout the interior of a building and as wall systems, and in conjunction with plaster for insulating facades. Straw products can be composted.

- Flax insulating materials comprise short fibres (bast fibres from the flax plant) and oiled flax fibres that cannot be used in the manufacture of textiles. After impregnation with an aqueous borax solution, flax is not readily flammable (class B 2) and is protected against pests. Flax insulating materials can store moisture and release it later. As the non-woven fabrics or felts contain only small amounts of boric salt and no other additives, flax is ideal for composting or forming mulches. Flax fibres are taken back by manufacturers for reuse.

- Cotton wool for use as non-woven fabric and loose material is grown in Asia and Egypt. The raw material is compressed under mechanical pressure to form insulating batts. Owing to the long delivery chain, the monocultures of the growing regions and the use of pesticides, cotton wool for use as an insulating material is not justifiable in ecological terms. Composting is hampered by the amount of boric salt that has to be added, which means that incineration is the principal means of disposal. [15]

- Non-woven hemp fabrics have only recently been introduced as a thermal insulation material. Used hemp insulating materials can be composted or incinerated without any ecological problems. [03] It is also possible to recycle old, used hemp materials.

Mineral-fibre insulating materials

- Mineral-fibre insulating materials are divided into three groups according to their raw materials: rockwool, glass wool and slag wool. The method of manufacture is the same for all three groups. After melting down, the raw mass is drawn out into fibres 6–50 mm long and cured in a furnace with binding agent and slip additive. The binding agent and slip additive are thereby converted into duroplastics. The ribbon of insulating material is cut into standard formats.

- Mineral wool is moisture-repellent, rotproof and exhibits good sound and thermal insulation properties. Mineral wool fibres present no health problems and are recyclable. Production residue and clean waste from building and demolition sites can be fed back into the production process. Soiled insulating batts contaminated with other materials are disposed of in landfill sites.

- Glass wool consists of up to 70% scrap glass, sand, soda and lime. A small quantity of synthetic resins (0.5–7%) is added as a binding agent to form the wool-like structure, and mineral oil (approx. 0.5%) is added to suppress dust during production and handling. After removing the residual moisture in drying ovens, the synthetic resins (phenol, formaldehyde with the addition of urea, ammonia and ammonium sulphate) are irreversibly cured so that there are no hazardous emissions during installation and use. [18]

- Slag wool is only produced in small quantities. In terms of recycling, there are no independent concepts at present. Used slag wool is disposed of in landfill sites.

- Rock wool is primarily produced from the volcanic rocks diabase and basalt. A defibration machine produces fibres 3–6 mm along from the melt. These are then sprayed with an aqueous binding agent solution (mixture of phenol-urea-formaldehyde resins with ammonia additive) and immediately vitrify. In a hardening furnace the duroplastic resins are virtually irreversibly cured and almost all volatile components driven off. The remaining odorous gases are removed in a cooling zone.

## Laying

Loose materials, sheets and batts, refurbishment

#### Loose materials

The use of loose materials enables roofs with complicated shapes and inaccessible roof surfaces to be easily insulated.

- Mineral and cellulose fibres are blown through hoses into enclosed voids between the rafters. Turbulent air compacts the fibres and fits them around uneven components. The enclosing surfaces must be airtight.

Cellulose fibres can also be blown into stable paper and jute sacks. This enables an air layer to be included above the insulation. [20]

- Perlite granulate is blown through metal foil hoses into the space between the rafters. [21]

#### Sheets and batts

Laying over the rafters

Single layer with spacer rafters
Spacer rafters are positioned over the loadbearing rafters on a decking with a vapour barrier. The insulation is fitted tightly between the spacer rafters.

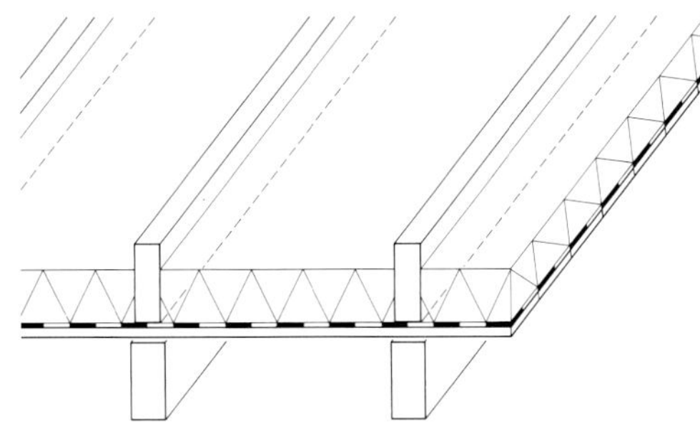

2.4.19.2 Insulation laid between spacer rafters

Single layer with short battens
The battens are cut to match the width of the batts and are attached above the roof decking and vapour barrier at twice the rafter spacing. The insulation is fitted tightly between these battens. The next row of insulating batts is laid offset by one rafter bay. [23]

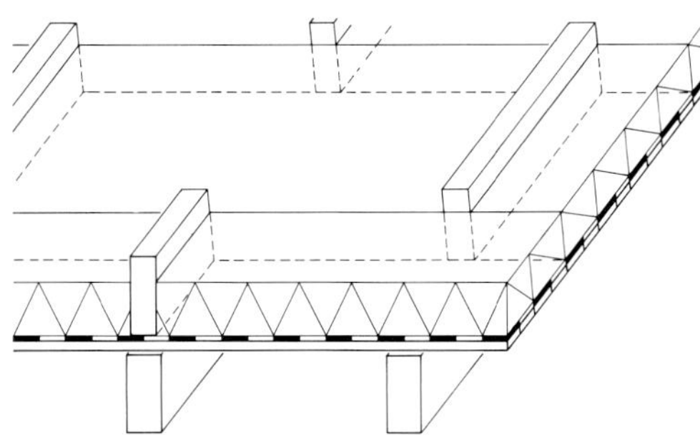

2.4.19.3 Insulation laid between short battens

Single layer with transverse battens
Battens (≥ 60 mm wide) parallel to the eaves are laid on the roof decking and vapour barrier at a spacing equal to the width of a batt. The insulation is fitted tightly between these battens. The spacing of the battens can be increased to twice the width of a batt on roofs with a low pitch and/or no snow load.

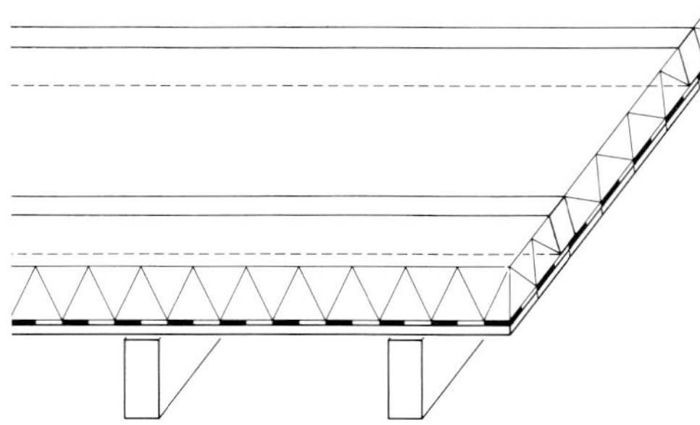

2.4.19.4 Insulation laid between transverse battens

Two layers with battens in both directions
The lower battens are attached parallel to the eaves at a spacing equal to the width of a batt. After installing the insulation tightly between them, the second layer of battens is fixed perpendicular to the eaves. These upper battens must be aligned with the rafters on steep roofs and/or roofs with a high snow load. Deeper upper battens can be provided to create a ventilation space. [23]

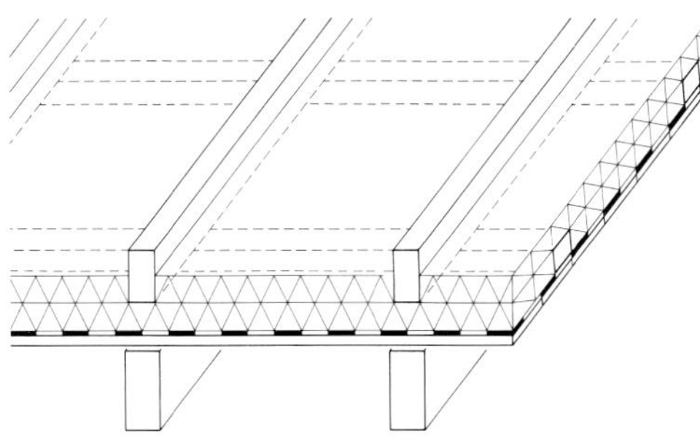

2.4.19.5 Two layers of insulation laid between battens in both directions

Continuous insulation systems
A continuous layer of insulation in couple and collar roofs means that the battens carrying the roof covering and the counter battens are separated from the rafters. The compressive forces perpendicular to the roof surface are transmitted through the layer of insulation to the rafters. The insulating material takes on a loadbearing function, which requires insulating materials with a suitable compressive strength. The forces parallel to the roof surface (shear forces) are resisted by the counter battens, which are thus subjected to axial compression; sections measuring 40 x 80 mm or 30 x 100 mm are therefore necessary. In order to avoid bending stresses in the nails fixing the counter battens to the rafters, an interlocking connection between the counter battens and the rafters is essential at the eaves to transfer the axial forces to the rafters. Roofs with little or no overhang will require a suitable member along the eaves. The use of thrust blocks is preferable on roofs with a long overhang. [04, 11, 12, 27]

Laying between the rafters

Laying thermal insulation between the rafters is primarily employed when the roof covering is already in place. However, in existing buildings the depth of the rafters is often insufficient to ensure an adequate ventilation void, making it necessary to attach battens to the underside of the rafters. The insulation is always fitted flush with the underside of the rafters or the extra battens.
Various components have been developed to match the different rafter spacings and to simplify installation.

- Mineral felts supplied in rolls. Pieces at least 10 mm wider than the spacing of the rafters are cut from the roll and fitted tightly between the rafters. [02]

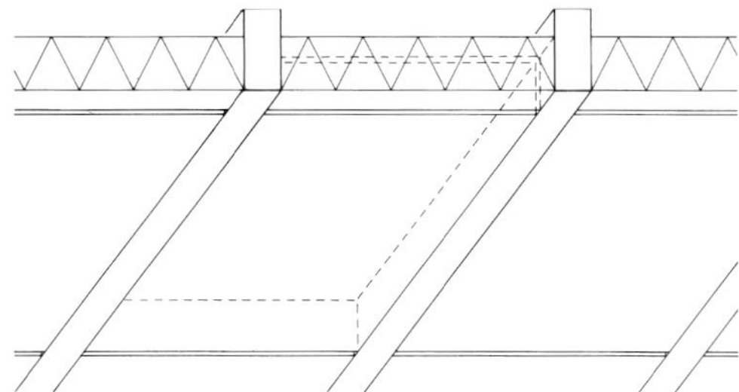

2.4.19.6 Mineral felt wedged between rafters

- Mineral-fibre felts with a laminated paper or mesh-reinforced aluminium foil backing. Pieces are cut at least 10 mm wider than the spacing of the rafters and are fixed using the folding strips on both sides. The aluminium foil functions as a vapour barrier. [02]

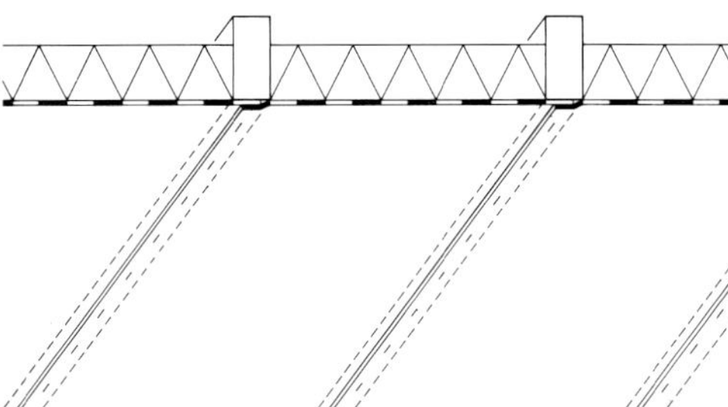

2.4.19.7 Mineral-fibre felt with laminated paper or mesh-reinforced aluminium foil backing, wedged between rafters

- Longitudinal slits in rigid foam sheets enable them to be bent one way. They are cut at least 5 mm wider than the rafter spacing and fitted tightly between the rafters. Sheets with rebates on two edges are used when providing a single layer of insulation. If providing two layers, sheets without rebated joints are installed with the joints offset. [02, 04]

- Insulating wedges are uncoated mineral-fibre batts cut diagonally (at least 10 mm wider than the spacing of the rafters) to form two opposing wedges. These are jammed between the rafters from above with a small board. [02, 22]

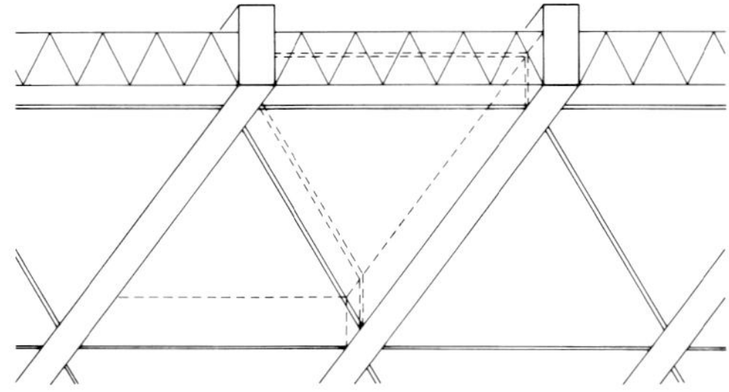

2.4.19.8 Installing wedge-shaped insulating batts

Laying beneath the rafters
This arrangement is primarily chosen when fitting out a roof space at a later date, where the rafters are not deep enough but there is sufficient space within the roof void. The insulation can comprise insulating material with sufficient stiffness (rigid foam sheets) or composite elements with an inner lining of timber derivative boards or plasterboard.

A single layer of insulation is fitted with counter battens, and composite elements attached to the rafters with clout nails or clips.
A double layer of insulation is feasible on a framework of battens in both directions. The layers of insulation are fitted into this framework; the first layer is fixed to the rafters, the second to the framework.

Laying between and beneath the rafters
This arrangement is employed when fitting out a roof space at a later date.

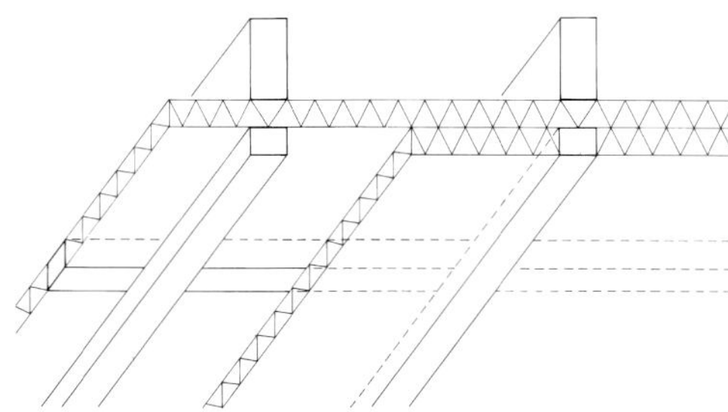

2.4.19.9 Two layers of insulation installed between framework of battens

#### Refurbishment

Insulation that proves to be inadequate can be upgraded by adding additional layers of insulation above or below the loadbearing structure. If the insulation has been ruined by small animals or moisture, its replacement by a material with a higher insulating value is advisable in order to satisfy more stringent requirements. The relationships are explained in more detail in section "Refurbishment".

#### References


[01] Bartl, J.: ISOFLACHS, ein neuer Stern am Dämmstoffhimmel, aus Wohnung und Gesundheit, vol. 16, No. 71, 1994
[02] Busch, K.: Dämmstoffe im Steildach; in: DBZ 9, 1988
[03] CMA-Centrale Marketing-Gesellschaft der deutschen Agrarwirtschaft mbH (pub.): Dämmstoffe aus der heimischen Natur, information brochure in conjunction with Fachagentur nachwachsende Rohstoffe e.V. and C.A.R.M.E.N Centrales Agrar-Rohstoff-Marketing und Entwicklungsnetzwerk e.V.
[04] Dämmpraxis 3.211 Geneigtes Dach: Styropor als Wärmedämmung zwischen und unter den Sparren; pub. Industrieverband Hartschaum
[05] Dämmpraxis 3.212 Geneigtes Dach: Styropor als Wärmedämmung über den Sparren; pub. Industrieverband Hartschaum
[06] Epinatjeff, P.: Ökologische Verwendung von Baustoffen; from: DBZ-Deutscher Bauzeitschrift, vol. 44, No. 10, 1996
[07] FPX Fachvereinigung Polystyrol-Extruderschaumstoff: Verwertung oder Entsorgung gebrauchter extrudierter Polystyrol-Hartschaumstoffe; information 1/97, position as of 2000, FPX Technical Committee
[08] GDI-Gesamtverband Dämmstoffindustrie: Dämmstoffe für den baulichen Wärmeschutz – Übersicht über genormte Produkte, position as of 1999, 2nd, rev. ed.
[09] Gefäller, H.; Warnken, A.: Wärmedämmstoffe und ihre Anwendung; pub. Arbeitsgemeinschaft Wohnberatung e.V.
[10] Grote, M.: Dämmstoffe im Vergleich; from: Wohnen, No. 4 1999
[11] IVPU-Industrieverband Polyurethan-Hartschaum e.V.: Verwertung (Recycling) und Entsorgung von PUR-Hartschaum-Abfällen; from: IVPU Nachrichten, No. 54, Oct 1996
[12] Kallweit, G.: Auf-Sparren-Dämmsysteme mit nicht brennbaren Mineralwolle-Dämmstoffen; in: DBZ 10, 1989
[13] Klose, G.-R.: Sind Faserdämmstoffe aus künstlichen Mineralfasern gesundheitsgefährdend? in: Baustofftechnik 4-6, 1985
[14] Morgenweck, G.: Wo bleiben ausgebrauchte Dämmstoffe? from: Baugewerbe, No. 1/2, 1992
[15] Nachwachsende Rohstoffe e.V.
[16] BASF product information
[17] Fibrolith Dämmstoffe, Wilms GmbH: product information
[18] Product information: Isover-Grünzweig+Hartmann: Ökologische Aspekte, information brochure, position as of 2000
[19] Mandoval product information
[20] Ökologische Bautechnik Hirschhagen: product information
[21] Perlite product information
[22] Rockwool product information
[23] Sarna product information
[24] ri/ws: Allergikerfreundlicher Dämmstoff; from: Bauzeitung, vol. 50, No. 5, 1996, p. 29
[25] Schönell, H.: Recycling von Dämmsystemen aus Styropor; from: Baustoffrecycling + Deponietechnik, 12/95
[26] Scholz, W.: Baustoffkenntnis: ed. Knoblauch, issue 13., new, rev. & updated ed., Düsseldorf: Werner, 1995
[27] Schulze, H.: Hausdächer in Holzbauart: Konstruktionen, Statistik, Bauphysik, Düsseldorf: Werner, 1987
[28] Wendehorst, R.: Baustoffkunde; intro. by R. Wendehorst; new, fully rev. ed. by H. Spruck, 22nd, rev. ed., Hannover: Vincentz, 1986
[29] Zimmermann, G.: Harte Schaumkunststoffe im Bauwesen; in: DAB 2, 1987
[30] Studentenarbeitsgruppe Wärmedämmstoffe, Basel School of Engineering, Muttenz; Wärmedämmstoffe, 2nd ed., Feldbach: Graf, 1989


## Drainage

Materials, components, installation

The precipitation falling on the roof is drained via suitably sized and suitably installed gutters and downpipes into the public sewage system (combined system) or into the local groundwater (separate systems).

### Materials

Gutters and pipes and their associated fittings are primarily made of thin sheet metal (aluminium, copper, zinc, galvanised and stainless steel), or from cast iron and plastic (unplasticised PVC). Gutters and pipes made of fibre-cement, gutters made of timber boards nailed together and lined with a waterproofing membrane, and gutters of hollowed-out pieces of round timber, play only a minor role. Cast iron is employed for pressurised drainage systems for large roofs.

| Gutters/pipes | Gutter brackets, pipe clips |
|---|---|
| aluminium (Al) | galvanised steel<br>aluminium |
| copper (Cu) | galv. steel with copper coating<br>copper |
| zinc (Zn) | galvanised steel<br>galv. steel with zinc coating |
| stainless steel (st. st.) | stainless steel<br>galvanised steel with stainless steel coating |
| galv. steel (galv. st.) | galvanised steel |
| cast iron | cast iron |
| unplasticised PVC (PVC-U, formerly uPVC) | galvanised steel<br>plastic-coated galvanised steel |

2.4.20.1 Materials [05, 11]

#### Components

Gutters and pipes

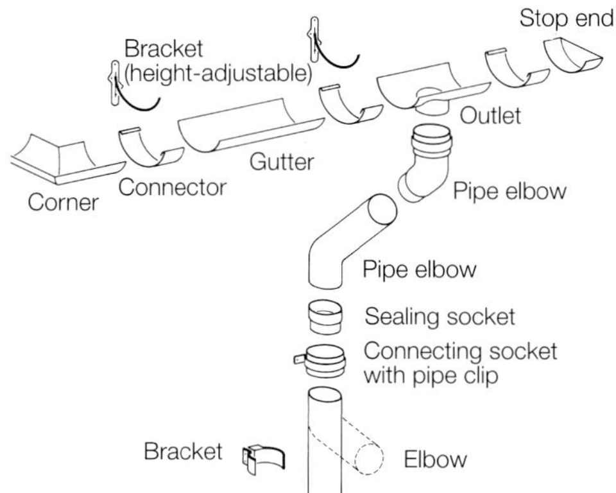


2.4.20.2 Modular drainage system; components; cast iron [07]

Together with their accessories, gutters and pipes form a modular system for draining the rainwater. Gutters are defined according to position and cross-section, pipes according to their cross-section.

**Gutters**

Eaves gutters

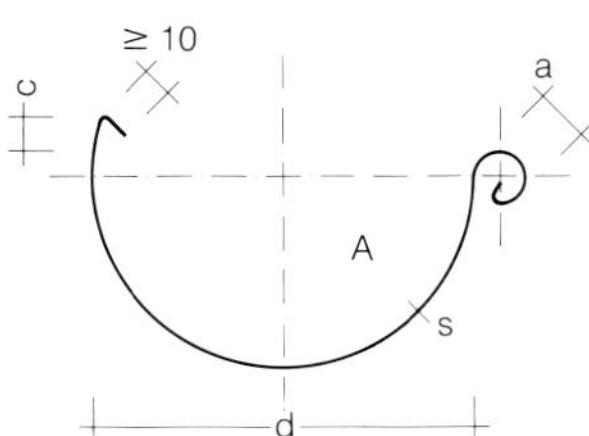


| Nom. size Ng | d +2 0 [mm] | a ±1 [mm] | c min. [mm] | Material thickness s min. [mm] Al | Cu | Zn | st.st. | galv. steel | PVC | A [cm²] |
|---|---|---|---|---|---|---|---|---|---|---|
| 200 | 80 | 16 | 8 | 0.7 | 0.6 | 0.65 | 0.4 | 0.6 | – | 25 |
| 250 | 105 | 18 | 10 | 0.7 | 0.6 | 0.65 | 0.4 | 0.6 | – | 43 |
| | 104 | – | – | – | – | – | – | 1.4 | – | |
| 280 | 127 | 18 | 11 | 0.7 | 0.6 | 0.7 | 0.4 | 0.6 | – | 63 |
| | 129 | – | – | – | – | – | – | 1.5 | – | |
| 333 | 153 | 20 | 11 | 0.7 | 0.6 | 0.7 | 0.4 | 0.6 | – | 92 |
| | 154 | – | – | – | – | – | – | 1.6 | – | |
| 400 | 192 | 22 | 11 | 0.8 | 0.7 | 0.8 | 0.5 | 0.7 | – | 145 |
| | 184 | – | – | – | – | – | – | 1.7 | – | |
| 500 | 250 | 22 | 21 | 0.8 | 0.7 | 0.8 | 0.5 | 0.7 | – | 245 |

2.4.20.3 Half-round gutter of thin sheet metal or plastic; form, dimensions, materials [01, 06, 11]

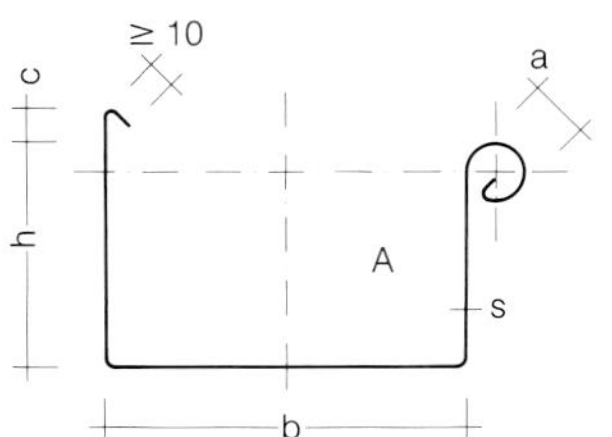


| Nom. size Ng | b 0 −1 [mm] | h ±1 [mm] | a ±1 [mm] | c min. [mm] | Material thickness s min. [mm] Al | Cu | Zn | st.st. | galv. steel | A [cm²] |
|---|---|---|---|---|---|---|---|---|---|---|
| 200 | 70 | 42 | 16 | 8 | 0.7 | 0.6 | 0.65 | 0.4 | 0.6 | 29 |
| 250 | 85 | 55 | 18 | 10 | 0.7 | 0.6 | 0.65 | 0.4 | 0.6 | 47 |
| 333 | 120 | 75 | 20 | 10 | 0.7 | 0.6 | 0.7 | 0.4 | 0.6 | 90 |
| 400 | 150 | 90 | 22 | 10 | 0.8 | 0.7 | 0.8 | 0.5 | 0.7 | 135 |
| 500 | 200 | 110 | 22 | 20 | 0.8 | 0.7 | 0.8 | 0.5 | 0.7 | 220 |

2.4.20.4 Rectangular gutter of thin sheet metal; form, dimensions, materials [06, 11]

| | Length of gutter |
|---|---|
| Thin sheet metal | 3.0 m |
| Cast iron | 0.6; 0.9; 1.2; 1.8 m |
| Plastic | 2.0; 4.0 m |

2.4.20.5 Eaves gutters; materials, dimensions

All cross-sections different from the two standard forms shown above must be made by hand.

Trough gutters

Trough gutters are available with half-round or rectangular profiles. These thin sheet metal (≥ 0.8 mm) gutters are supplied in 3 m lengths

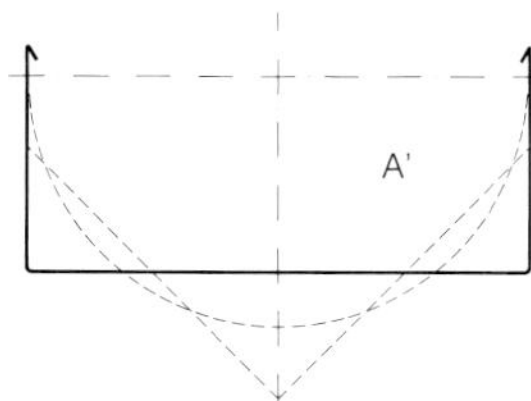


2.4.20.6 Trough gutter of thin sheet metal; forms

in a limited range (see "Layers – Sheet metal roof coverings – Components"). Trough gutters should be constructed so that they are accessible and can carry the loads of cleaning operatives. The rectangular form is best for this.

Valley gutters

Besides sheet metal valley gutters there are also ready-made valley gutters for when larger quantities of water are anticipated. They are produced in standard shapes to suit the application:

a simple sheet metal valley gutter for short valleys

b sheet metal valley gutter with baffle for short, steep valleys

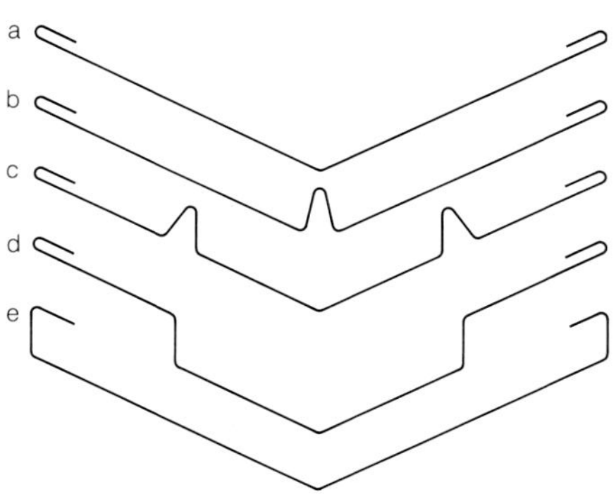


2.4.20.7 Valley gutters of thin sheet metal; forms

c valley gutter with baffles and overflows for long, steep valleys

d valley gutter with deep central channel for shallow valleys

e deep valley gutter for long, shallow valleys

Verge/junction gutters

Factory-prefabricated gutters are available for verges and wall junctions in addition to those produced by hand.

Simple form for small quantities of water:

- for profiled roof covering (little driving rain)
- for a low wall (little driving rain)

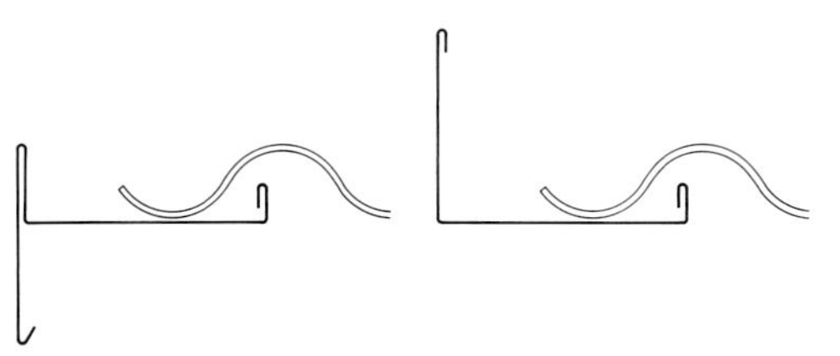

2.4.20.8 Verge/junction gutter of thin sheet metal; simple form

Deeper form for large quantities of water:

- for flat roof covering (severe driving rain)
- for a high wall (severe driving rain)

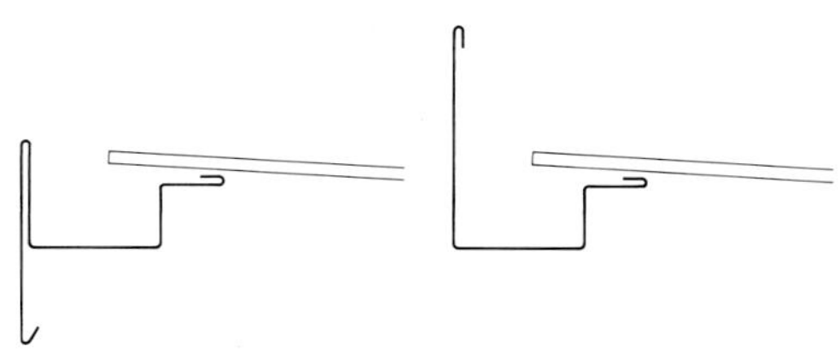

2.4.20.9 Verge/junction gutter of thin sheet metal; deeper form

**Standard gutter elements**

Corners

Internal and external corner pieces are factory-produced (deep drawn) from one piece in each case. Corners made by hand have a mitred seam (soldered, riveted or welded). Plastic corners are produced by injection moulding.

| Nom. size Ng | d [mm] metal | d [mm] plastic | Leg length int. angle [mm] metal | int. angle plastic | ext. angle [mm] metal | ext. angle plastic | Material thickness [mm] metal | plastic |
|---|---|---|---|---|---|---|---|---|
| 250 | 105 | 104 | 210 | 239 | 225 | 236 | 0.7 | 1.4 |
| 280 | 127 | 129 | 235 | 265 | 250 | 261 | 0.7 | 1.5 |
| 333 | 153 | 154 | 280 | 301.5 | 300 | 298 | 0.7 | 1.6 |
| 400 | 192 | 184 | 310 | 333 | 325 | 330 | 0.8 | 1.7 |

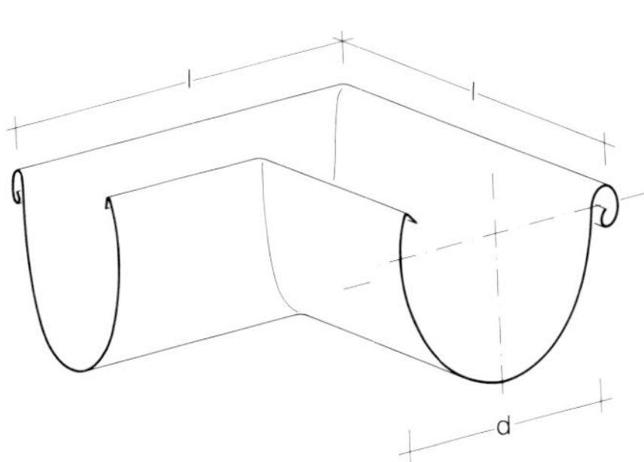


2.4.20.10 Gutter corner for half-round gutters of thin sheet metal and plastic; form (external angle), dimensions [01, 08, 11]

Stop ends

These are connected to the end of the gutter by soldering or welting (with preformed sealing strip in joint).

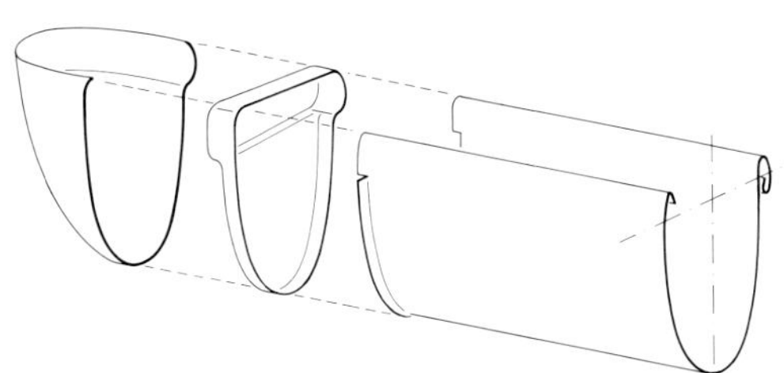

2.4.20.11 Gutter stop ends of thin sheet metal; forms [07]

## Headers

| Nom. size gutter | pipe g | pipe s | d [mm] g | d [mm] s | $d_1$ ±1 [mm] g | $d_1$ ±1 [mm] s | h min. [mm] g | h min. [mm] s | width min. [mm] metal g | width min. [mm] metal s | width min. [mm] plastic g | t [mm] |
|---|---|---|---|---|---|---|---|---|---|---|---|---|
| 200 | 60 | – | 80 | – | 58 | – | 60 | – | 115 | – | – | 35 |
| 250 | 80 | – | 105 | – | 78 | – | 65 | – | 140 | – | – | 40 |
| | 70 | – | – | – | 75 | – | – | – | – | – | 264 | – |
| 280 | 80 | | 127 | | 78 | | 80 | | 165 | 120 | – | 40 |
| | 70 | – | – | | 75 | – | – | | – | | 290 | – |
| | 100 | – | – | | 110 | – | – | | – | | 290 | – |
| 333 | 100 | | 153 | | 98 | | 95 | 93 | 185 | 140 | – | 45 |
| | 100 | – | – | | 110 | – | – | | – | | 300 | – |
| 400 | 120 | | 192 | | 118 | | 105 | 113 | 210 | 170 | – | 50 |
| | 125 | – | – | | 125 | – | – | | – | | 320 | – |

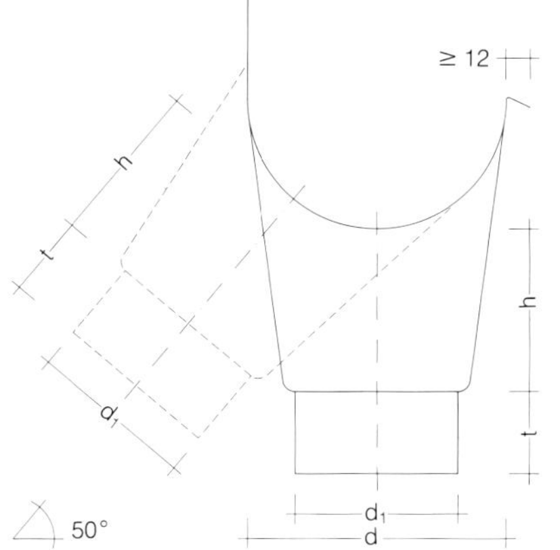


2.4.20.12 Gutter header of thin sheet metal; straight (g), tapered (s) and – of plastic – straight (g); form, dimensions [01, 06, 11]

Headers are produced in cylindrical, tapering and tank-shaped forms.

**Gutter brackets**

Gutter brackets are supplied with nib and clip or with two clips. They are made of aluminium, copper, galvanised and stainless steel, or of galvanised steel with a copper or zinc alloy coating. The gutter brackets for plastic gutters are made of galvanised steel with a plastic coating. The thickness of the zinc or aluminium-zinc coating on the steel should be ≥ 20 µm.

Gutter brackets for half-round gutters may include a strengthening rib.

Other shapes must be produced by hand.

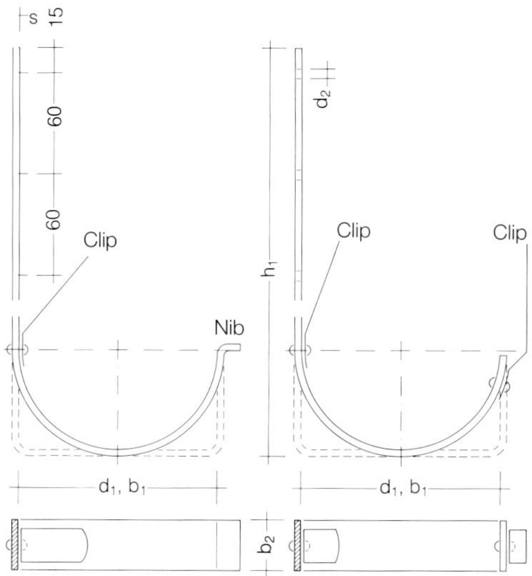


| Nom. size Ng | $d_1$ 0 +2 [mm] | $b_1$ 0 +2 [mm] | $h_1$ ±3 mm half-round | | rec-tangular | | $b_2 \cdot s$[1)] [mm] 1 | 2 | 3 | 4 | $d_2$ ±1 [mm] |
|---|---|---|---|---|---|---|---|---|---|---|---|
| 200 | 80 | 70 | 230 | 270 | 230 | 270 | 25·4 | 25·4 | 25·4 | – | |
| 250 | 105 | 85 | 280 | 330 | 280 | 330 | 25·4 | 30·4 | 25·6 | – | |
| | | | 410 | 500 | – | – | 25·4 | – | – | – | 6 |
| 280 | 127 | – | 290 | 350 | – | – | 30·4 | 30·5 | 25·6 | 25·8 | for |
| | | | 390 | 480 | – | – | 30·4 | – | – | – | s≤5 |
| 333 | 153 | 120 | 300 | 370 | 300 | 370 | 30·5 | 25·6 | 40·5 | 30·8 | 7 |
| | | | 450 | – | – | – | 30·5 | – | – | – | for |
| 400 | 192 | 150 | 340 | 430 | 330 | 420 | 30·5 | 40·5 | 25·8 | 30·8 | s>5 |
| | | | 410 | – | – | – | 30·5 | – | – | – | |
| 500 | 250 | 200 | 375 | 515 | 350 | 490 | 40·5 | 40·5 | 30·8 | 30·8 | |

1) see table 2.4.20.28

4.20.13 Gutter brackets for half-round (d) and rectangular (b) gutters of thin sheet metal; form: nib-clip; dimensions [06]

**Pipes**

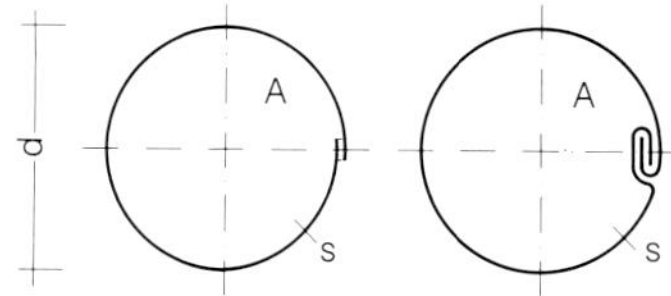


| Nom. size Ng | d ±1 [mm] | Al | Material thickness s min. [mm] Cu | Zn | st. st. | gal. st. | PVC | A [cm²] |
|---|---|---|---|---|---|---|---|---|
| 60 | 60 | 0.7 | 0.6 | 0.65 | 0.4 | 0.6 | – | 28 |
| 70 | 75 | – | – | – | – | – | 1.7 | – |
| 80 | 80 | 0.7 | 0.6 | 0.65 | 0.4 | 0.6 | – | 50 |
| 100 | 100 | 0.7 | 0.6 | 0.65 | 0.4 | 0.6 | – | 79 |
| | 110 | – | – | – | – | – | 1.9 | – |
| 120 | 120 | 0.7 | 0.7 | 0.7 | 0.5 | 0.7 | – | 113 |
| 125 | 125 | – | – | – | – | – | 2.1 | – |
| 150 | 150 | 0.7 | 0.7 | 0.7 | 0.5 | 0.7 | – | 177 |

2.4.20.14 Round rainwater downpipes of thin sheet metal and plastic; form, dimensions, materials [01, 06, 11]

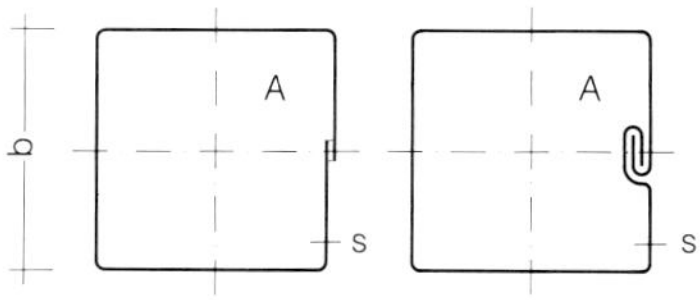


| Nom. size Ng | b ±1 [mm] | Material thickness s min. [mm] Al | Cu | Zn | st. st. | galv. st. | A [cm²] |
|---|---|---|---|---|---|---|---|
| 60 | 60 | 0.7 | 0.6 | 0.65 | 0.4 | 0.6 | 36 |
| 80 | 80 | 0.7 | 0.6 | 0.65 | 0.4 | 0.6 | 64 |
| 100 | 100 | 0.7 | 0.7 | 0.7 | 0.4 | 0.7 | 100 |
| 120 | 120 | 0.7 | 0.7 | 0.8 | 0.5 | 0.7 | 144 |

2.4.20.15 Square rainwater downpipes of thin sheet metal; form, dimensions, materials [06]

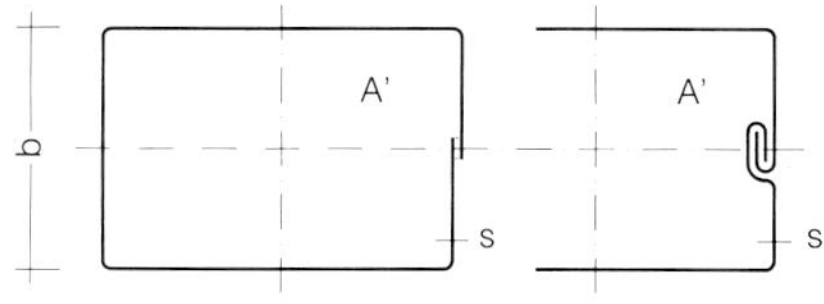


2.4.20.16 Rectangular rainwater downpipes of thin sheet metal [06]

Rainwater downpipes made of sheet metal are supplied already welded or soldered, occasionally soldered and riveted, in round or square/rectangular profiles. Welded pipes are also available.

| | Al | Cu | Zn | st.st. | galv. st. | min. welt/seam width [mm] |
|---|---|---|---|---|---|---|
| Soldered | – | • | • | – | – | 5 |
| Brazed | – | • | – | – | – | 3 |
| Welted | • | • | • | • | •[1)] | 6 |
| Welded | • | • | • | • | •[1)] | depends on method of welding |

[1)] subsequently hot-dip galvanised

2.4.20.17 Type of seam for rainwater downpipes of thin sheet metal [10, 11]

Rainwater downpipes have one narrow and one wide end (difference: 2 x material thickness) in order to form a spigot-and-socket connection.

The diameter d and the width b are inside dimensions; they correspond to the wide end of the pipe. Straightness tolerance: 5 mm over a 2 m length of pipe, measured in the middle.

| | Length of pipe |
|---|---|
| Thin sheet metal | 2.0; 3.0 m |
| Cast iron | 0.6; 0.9; 1.2; 1.8; 2.0 m |
| Plastic | 0.5; 1.0; 2.0; 2.5; 4.0 m |

2.4.20.18 Rainwater downpipes; materials, dimensions

The length of the short side of a rectangular rainwater downpipe corresponds to the size of the square form. The length of the long side is determined by the size of the original sheet.

**Standard pipe elements**

Elbows
Pipe elbows are available for all the standard downpipe sizes; 40°, 60° and 72° elbows are industrially prefabricated. Elbows can also be made by hand (swan-neck).

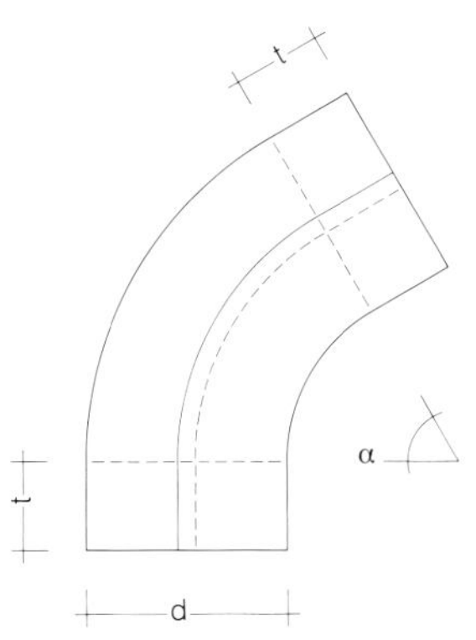


| Nom. size Ng | d ±1 [mm] | α [°] | t min. [mm] | Material thickness s min. [mm] Al | Cu | Zn | st.st. | galv. st. | PVC |
|---|---|---|---|---|---|---|---|---|---|
| 60 | 60 | 40; 60; 72 | 30 | 0.7 | 0.6 | 0.7 | 0.5 | 0.6 | – |
| 70 | 75 | 15; 30; 45; 67 | – | – | – | – | – | – | 1.7 |
| 80 | 80 | 40; 60; 72 | 35 | 0.7 | 0.6 | 0.7 | 0.5 | 0.6 | – |
| 100 | 100 | 40; 60; 72 | 35 | 0.7 | 0.6 | 0.7 | 0.5 | 0.6 | – |
| | 110 | 15; 30; 45; 67 | – | – | – | – | – | – | 1.9 |
| 120 | 120 | 40; 60; 72 | 40 | 0.7 | 0.7 | 0.8 | 0.6 | 0.6 | – |
| 125 | 125 | 30; 45 | – | – | – | – | – | – | 2.1 |
| 150 | 150 | 40; 60; 72 | 40 | 0.7 | 0.7 | 0.8 | 0.6 | 0.7 | – |

2.4.20.19 Pipe elbows of thin metal and plastic; form, dimensions, materials [01, 06]

Spouts
Rainwater downpipes with an integral spout are available for 60, 80, 100 and 120 mm pipes. They must be made specially for larger downpipe sizes.

Pipe clips

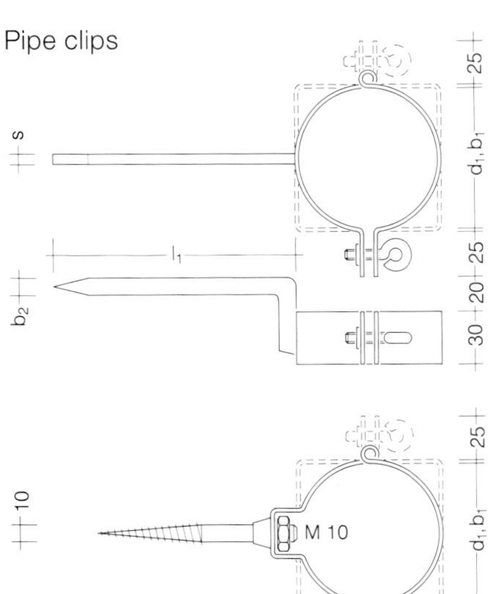


| Nom. size Ng | $d_1$ +1 0 [mm] | $b_1$ +1 0 [mm] | Driven in $l_1 \pm 5$ [mm] | Driven in $b_2 \cdot s$ [mm] | Screwed in $l_2 \pm 5$ [mm] | Screwed in Ø [mm] |
|---|---|---|---|---|---|---|
| 60 | 60 | 62 | 140 | 10·6 | 100 | 10, M 10 |
| 80 | 80 | 82 | | | 100 | 10, M 10 |
| 100 | 100 | 102 | 140 | 10·6 | 200 | 10, M 10 |
| 120 | 120 | 122 | 200 | 8·8 | 250 | 10, M 10 |
| 150 | 150 | – | | | | 10, M 10 |

2.4.20.20 Pipe clips for round (d) and square (b) pipes of thin sheet metal; forms, dimensions [06]

There are versions available with a spike that is driven into the wall, or those with an interchangeable screw.
Pipe clips made from material < 2 mm thick are produced with a strengthening rib for both round and square/rectangular pipes.

## Installation

Design, installation of gutters, installation of pipes

**Design**

The design of rainwater drainage systems begins at the rainwater downpipe. Rainwater gutters are open channels; they are assigned to a designed downpipe cross-sectional area and not calculated separately. The design of downpipes is carried out according to the assumed rainfall load [l/s·ha]. Generally, at least 300 l/s·ha is assumed, but this can be higher depending on local circumstances. Weather centres can provide information on levels of rainfall.
Important: The design assumes tapering headers. The use of cylindrical headers means that the permissible roof area must be reduced by 30%, which translates into using the next larger downpipe diameter. And when the gutter outlets are protected by gratings, the permissible roof area must be reduced by 50%. The short side of a rectangular downpipe must be at least equal to the diameter of the corresponding downpipe with a round cross-section.

Other information required for the design:

- The run-off value [dimensionless]; this includes a factor for the water retention capacity (pitch, surface characteristics).

| Type of roof surface | | | Coefficient |
|---|---|---|---|
| Covering | steep | ≥ 15° | 1 |
| Covering | shallow | < 15° | 0.8 |
| Loose mat. | coarse (gravel) | < 10° | 0.5 |
| Loose mat. | fine (roof garden) | > 3° | 0.3 |

2.4.20.22 Run-off coefficients [04, 11]

- Calculation of rainwater run-off [l/s], which is the quantity of water flowing into the rainwater drainage system per second.
- Size of the roof surface to be drained by the system [m²].

| Rain-water run-off [l/s] | max. roof area[1)] [m²] | Downpipe Ng | Downpipe A [cm²] | Associated gutter half-round Ng | half-round A [cm²] | rectangular Ng | rectangular A [cm²] |
|---|---|---|---|---|---|---|---|
| 1.1 | 37 | 60 | 28 | 200 | 25 | 200 | 28 |
| 1.7 | 57 | 70 | 38 | – | – | – | – |
| 2.5 | 83 | 80 | 50 | 250, 280 | 43, 63 | 250 | 42 |
| 4.5 | 150 | 100 | 79 | 333 | 92 | 333 | 90 |
| 7.3 | 243 | 120 | 113 | 400 | 145 | 400 | 135 |
| 8.1 | 270 | 125 | 122 | – | – | – | – |
| 13.3 | 443 | 150 | 177 | 500 | 245 | 500 | 220 |

[1)] Applies only to a local rainfall level of 300 l/sha

2.4.20.23 Rainwater downpipes with round cross-section; design; allocation of half-round and rectangular metal gutters (tapering headers) [04, 10]

Additional safety measures must be taken with trough gutters (see below).

| Local peak rainfall [l/sha] | | 25 | 50 | 100 | 150 | 200 | 300 | 400 | 500 |
|---|---|---|---|---|---|---|---|---|---|
| | | Rainwater run-off [l/s] | | | | | | | |
| Augsburg | 333 | 0.83 | 1.66 | 3.33 | 4.99 | 6.66 | 9.99 | 13.32 | 16.65 |
| Bonn | 532 | 1.33 | 2.66 | 5.32 | 7.98 | 10.64 | 15.96 | 21.28 | 26.60 |
| Frankfurt | 370 | 0.92 | 1.84 | 3.68 | 5.52 | 7.36 | 11.04 | 14.72 | 18.50 |
| Hannover | 490 | 1.22 | 2.45 | 4.90 | 7.35 | 9.80 | 14.70 | 19.60 | 24.50 |
| Karlsruhe | 532 | 1.33 | 2.66 | 5.32 | 7.98 | 10.64 | 15.96 | 21.28 | 26.60 |
| Kassel | 203 | 0.51 | 1.02 | 2.03 | 3.05 | 4.06 | 6.09 | 8.12 | 10.15 |
| Mönchengladbach | 300 | 0.75 | 1.50 | 3.00 | 4.50 | 6.00 | 9.00 | 12.00 | 15.00 |
| Munich | 416 | 1.04 | 2.08 | 4.16 | 6.24 | 8.32 | 12.48 | 16.64 | 20.80 |

(Column headings 25–500: Area of roof surface to be drained [m²])

2.4.20.21 Rainfall levels; local peak values; rainwater run-off in relation to size of roof surface to be drained

**Installation of gutters**

Eaves gutters
Positioning gutters
Water flowing off the roof covering should discharge into the gutter at the third point so that fast-flowing water does not overshoot the front edge of the gutter.
The gutter should be positioned such that snowboards pass over the top of it.

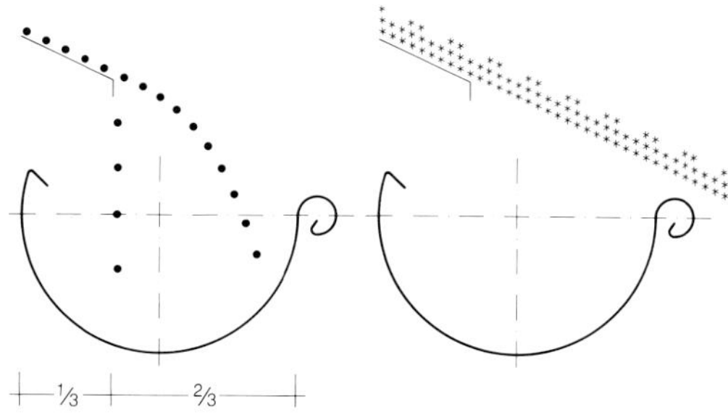


2.4.20.24 Position of gutter

Fall of gutter
Eaves gutters should be fitted so that an adequate transverse fall is guaranteed. The top edge of the side fitted to the building should be 6–21 mm – depending on size of gutter – higher than the front edge of the gutter (for gutters suspended along the eaves).
Gutters should be laid with a minimum longitudinal fall of 0.1–0.5%, i.e. 1–5 mm/m.

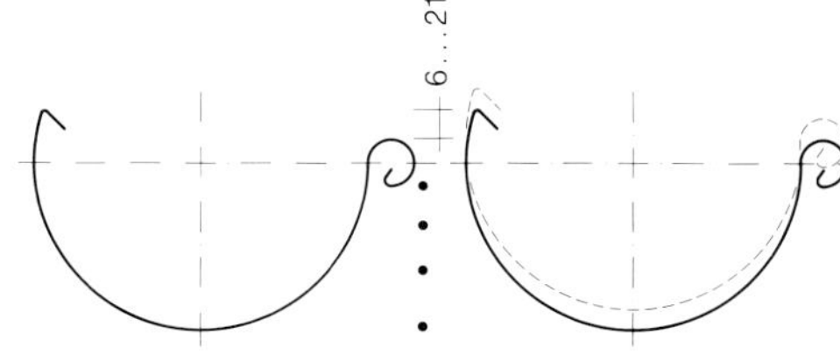


2.4.20.25 Transverse and longitudinal falls [06, 11]

Expansion joints in gutters
Segments of guttering should not exceed a length of 15 m owing to thermal movement effects. This length should be measured around corners.
Measures to allow for thermal movement include:

- sliding joints with two overlapping gutter bases at the highest point
- connecting clips for plastic gutters that can accommodate thermal movement as well as connect the individual lengths of guttering; these can be positioned at any point
- expansion pieces made of synthetic rubber fitted at any point and able to provide a sealing function at the same time
- a movable inlet to the gutter outlet at the lowest point

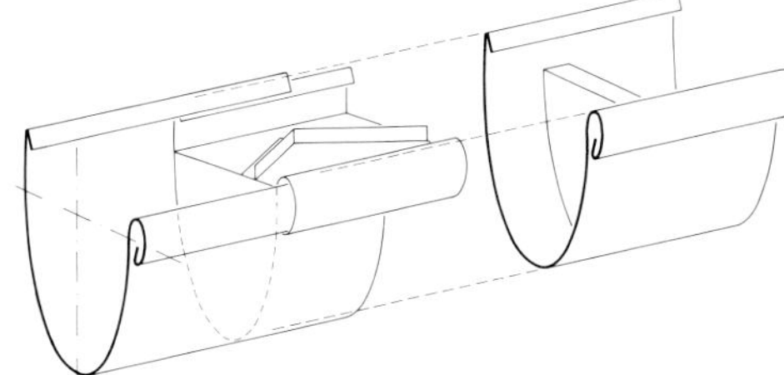

2.4.20.26 Expansion joint [11]

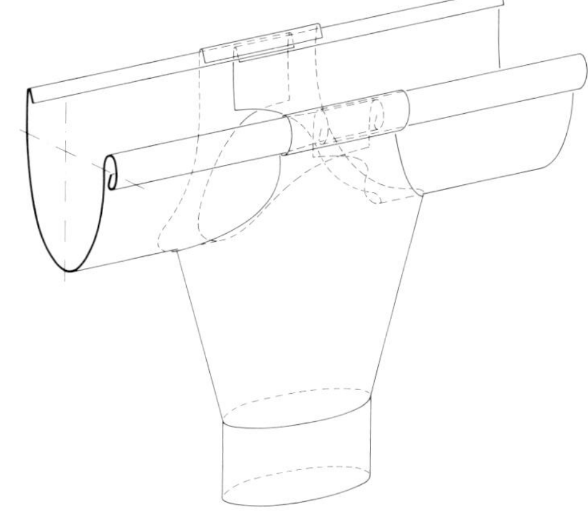

2.4.20.27 Outlet with expansion joint [11]

Fixed gutter connections
Segments of guttering can be joined together by soldering or riveting. The lap should be ≥ 10 mm for soldered and ≥ 30 mm for riveted joints. Riveted joints are sealed with a preformed sealing strip (two rows of offset rivets) or with solder (one row of rivets).

Gutter brackets
Gutter brackets are fixed with two or three nails or screws. They should be let into a notch in the board to fit flush where covered by roofing materials. Bracket cross-section, bracket spacing and weight of gutter must be coordinated with each other. [11]

| Spacing of brackets ± 50 [mm] | Loading group | |
|---|---|---|
| | standard | high |
| ≤ 700 | 1 | 3 |
| ≤ 800 | 2 | 4 |
| ≤ 900 | 3 | – |

2.4.20.28 Gutter brackets; loading groups and spacings (see table 2.4.20.13) [11]

Gutter outlets
These ensure the reliable discharge of water into the header. To do this, an oval hole (diameter 10–15 mm smaller than diameter of outlet) is cut out of the bottom of the gutter and the edge turned downwards to form a flange.

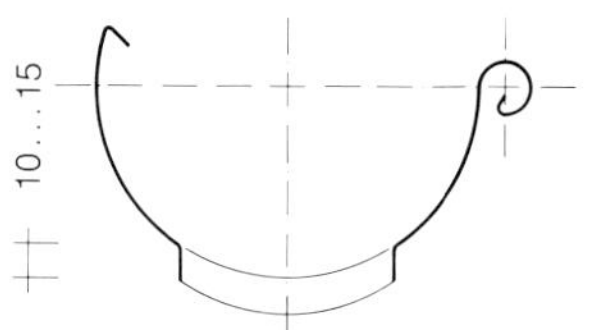


2.4.20.29 Outlet in thin sheet metal gutter

Trough gutters
Trough gutters should be laid with a minimum longitudinal fall of 0.5%, preferably 1–1.5%, i.e. 10–15 mm/m. For safety, gutter materials should be laid continuous. However, the widths of sheet metal available (see "Layers – Sheet metal roof coverings – Components") mean that only limited gutter widths are feasible without the sheet metal having to be joined. As soldering is not permissible on sheet metal trough gutters, wider metal gutters can only the produced in weldable sheet metal. Safety gutters made from flexible sheeting can be bonded or welded together. Twice the number of downpipes calculated must be provided for internal gutters, and at least two outlets, or outlet plus additional safety overflow. Every outlet must be able to discharge the full amount of rainfall alone. Internal gutters must always have tapering headers. If a safety gutter has been included, ventilation between it and the main gutter must be guaranteed.

Valley gutters
If a semi-swept valley is not possible, valley gutters must be provided. These require support and should therefore be laid on timber boarding ≥ 24 mm thick. Valley gutters should be fixed indirectly to the supporting construction with clips. They do not normally have their own outlet but discharge into another gutter.

Verge/junction gutters
These are fixed to battens or roof decking with individual clips and/or continuous clips. Gutters adjacent to a wall are traditionally fixed to the rising wall and covered with a capping strip or rendering bead. They do not have their own outlet but discharge into another gutter.

**Additional measures**

- A metal rod can be inserted into the beaded edge of the gutter to strengthen it against impact loads (sliding masses of snow, ladders). It is also possible to fit a metal strap to the beaded edge of the gutter.

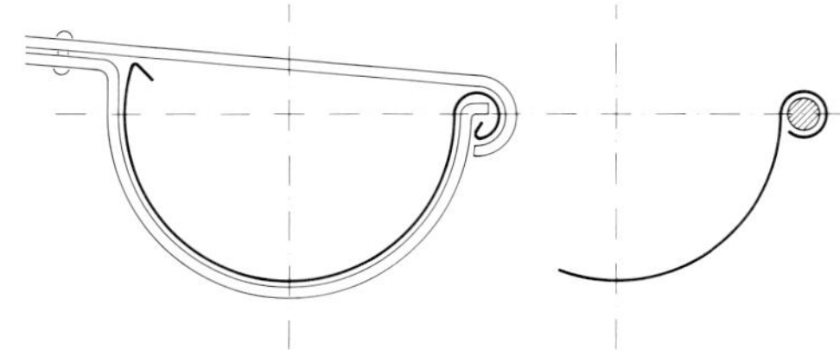

2.4.20.30 Gutter strengthening; strap, rod

- The inclusion of gutter heating can prevent the formation of ice. The heating may not be adequately designed for extremely cold weather. There is a danger of damaging the heating when cleaning out the gutter.

- To prevent blockages, gratings with a wide mesh should be fitted over the outlets. These gratings must, however, allow the passage of suspended matter and small particles.

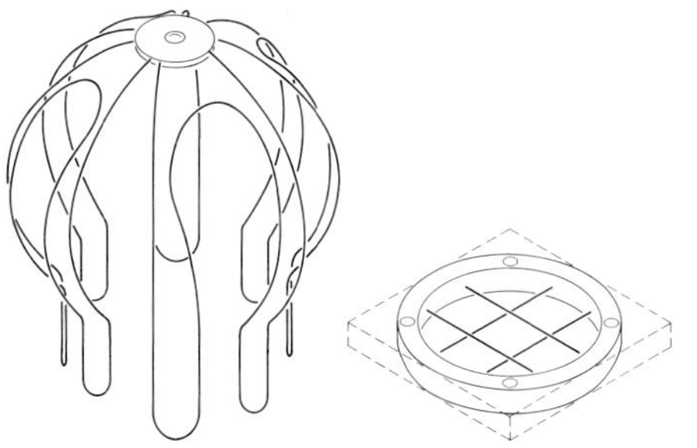

2.4.20.31 Outlet grating

**Installation of pipes**

Positioning pipes

Rainwater downpipes should be attached with a clearance of ≥ 20 mm between pipe and building component.

To enable easier inspection and prevent the wall from becoming saturated if the pipe is damaged the longitudinal seam should be positioned where it can be seen – either at the side or facing away from the building. Plastic pipes are seamless.

Internal rainwater downpipes should be insulated for about 2–3 m below the inlet to avoid condensation forming on the outside of the pipe.

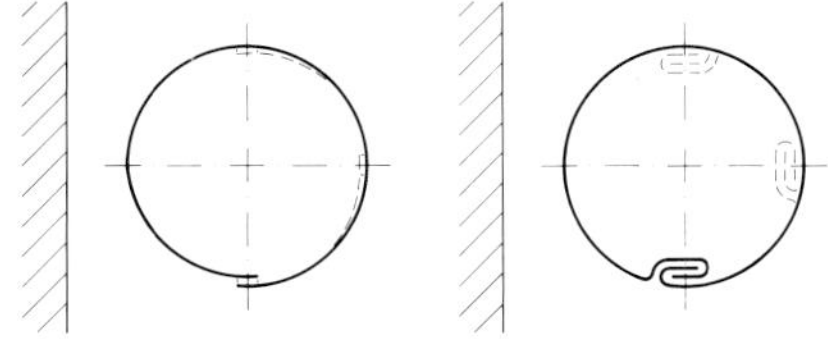

2.4.20.32 Position of pipe and pipe seam

Pipe connections

The overlap at the spigot-and-socket joint should be ≥ 50 mm for metal, ≥ 44 mm for plastic.

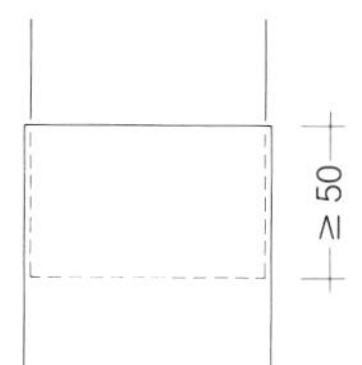


2.4.20.33 Pipe connection

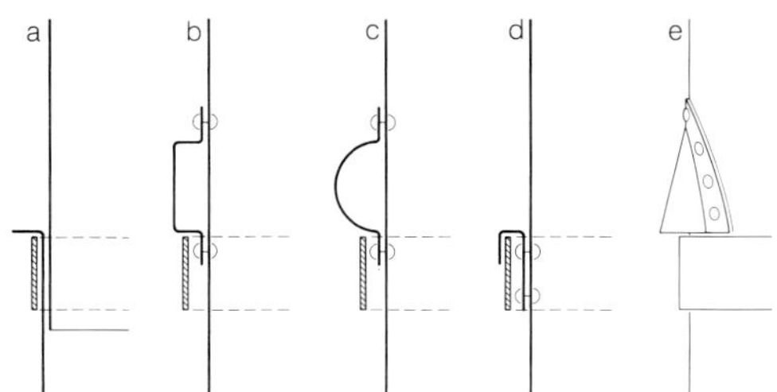


2.4.20.34 Pipe fixings; clip: a with pipe flange, b square bead, c rounded bead, d clip, e nib [02]

Pipe clips

Pipe clips should be fixed every max. 3 m for metal pipes ≤ 100 mm dia., max. 2 m for metal and plastic pipes > 100 mm dia. Beads, clips or nibs to support pipe liners at pipe clips and cornice penetrations are required above the pipe clips to metal rainwater downpipes.

**Additional measures**

- Foliage interception devices in the downpipe; in conjunction with a spout for better accessibility.
- Spout for drawing off water
- Rainwater downpipes in areas where they could suffer mechanical damage (300-1500 mm above ground/floor level) should be made from a suitable material, e.g. cast iron, steel, polyethylene.
- Inclusion of pipe heating

**References**

[01] Braas & Co GmbH: Braas Handbuch 98/2000 – geneigte Dächer; Oberursel, 2000
[02] German Copper Institute: Kupfer im Hochbau; Berlin, 1984
[03] Dierks, K.; Hermann, H.-J.; Tietge, H.-W.; Wormuth, B.; Wiethüchter, H.: Baukonstruktion; Düsseldorf: Verlag Werner, 1990
[04] DIN 18460: External rainwater pipes and eaves gutters; concepts and design principles
[05] DIN EN 607: Eaves gutters and fittings made from PVC-U – Definitions, requirements and testing; Berlin: Beuth-Verlag, 1996
[06] DIN EN 612: Eaves gutters and rainwater downpipes of metal sheet – Definitions, classification and requirements; Berlin: Beuth-Verlag, 1996
[07] Glynwed Foundries: Rainwater Systems; Ketley-Telford (GB), 1989
[08] Rheinzink GmbH: Rheinzink-Anwendung im Hochbau; Datteln, 2000
[09] Täumer, H.: Spengler- und Dachdeckerarbeiten; Munich, 1978
[10] Zentralverband des deutschen Dachdeckerhandwerks – Fachverband Dach-, Wand- und Abdichtungstechnik – e.V.: Fachregel für Metallarbeiten im Dachdeckerhandwerk, Technische Hinweise Hängedachrinnen, Regenfallrohre und Zubehör; Cologne: Rudolf Müller Verlag 1999
[11] Zentralverband Sanitär, Heizung, Klima: Richtlinien für die Ausführung von Metalldächern. Außenwandbekleidungen und Bauklempnerarbeiten; St Augustin: ZVSHK, 2002

The following section illustrates construction details and examples in which a legend of 100 designations is used. These are subdivided into six groups depending on their function:

00 to 09 Retaining
10 to 34 Supporting
35 to 69 Covering
70 to 79 Sealing
80 to 89 Insulating
90 to 99 Drainage, ventilation

# Part 3 Construction details

**Eberhard Schunck and Hans Jochen Oster**

The sequence of construction details presented here follows the system of form/shape used throughout this book. Within the individual forms, the materials are arranged according to their occurrence in building work and hence roughly according to their potential. Concessions have been made where this system would have disrupted continuity. The principal idea behind the selection of the construction details was to round off, as far as possible, the treatment of the various roof covering materials and forms. The long history of building therefore makes it necessary to include some traditional materials and methods of laying that some may consider outdated. Of course, the design principles given on pp. 97–100 could not be illustrated in all possible configurations. It is presumed that the reader can translate them from one type of roof covering to another.
The details have been drawn for the main parts of the roof (surface, eaves, ridge and verge) and their variations for all the roof covering materials and forms dealt with in this book. But space constraints will certainly have meant the exclusion of some desirable additional variations of some details. The fact that more complicated parts of the roof at greater risk (e.g. trough gutters) have been included does not mean they are also recommended. However, in situations where such difficult details are unavoidable, the details shown here may help the engineer or architect find a workable solution.
A "Refurbishment" section has been included for the first time. This topic has been given its own section because dividing it according to layers and types of construction would have obstructed the necessary clarity.
One important requirement was to show the relationship between the respective design principle, the chosen type of roof covering and the external wall. This was done not only to reflect usage requirements but also to show the degree of technical progress and round off the functional aspects.
As there is no system that could manage without overlaps, it was also impossible here to avoid "Layers" and "Construction details" overlapping. Where problems were encountered that could not be sensibly separated, they have been covered in both chapters. This intensification of the treatment of these problems proved to be a welcome byproduct.

## Thatch

Stitched and tied thatch

### Ridge

**1** Ridge with upright ridge layer, stitched thatch

The ridge requires no additional measures to make it rainproof. The ridge layers of short, thin material are laid – with the tips facing down the slope – on both sides on the topmost courses (lanes), and stitched with galvanised or stainless steel wire (left exposed) to the ridge battens. They are held at close centres (60–80 mm) by the stitches (suction peaks). The filling gives the ridge its shape and is jammed under the topmost courses, which are essentially identical to the normal courses on the roof but are cut shorter to fit under the ridge. A layer of thinner and hence more tightly packed thatch (undercoat) is laid below the topmost and the normal courses, and serves everywhere as a slip plane for the overlying layers. Ridge ventilation is not absolutely essential with a thatched roof because the thatch itself is air-permeable and has a cooling effect in summer.

### Eaves

**2** Eaves with tilting board, stitched thatch

The eaves, ≥ 400 mm wide, consists of two layers of long material. Here, the first layer is laid on the tilting board and battens and fixed with binding wire (pulled tight) every 150–200 mm. The second and third layers determine the pitch and line of the roof.
At the verge the thatch does not follow the line of the fall but is laid ≤ 60° to the line of the eaves (horizontal) and gradually returns to its normal position towards the middle of the roof. Double stitching is required on the outside.
If the roof space contains accommodation, the ventilation layer between thermal insulation and battens should be ≥ 60 mm deep, and even larger when swelling of the thermal insulation is to be expected. Ventilation openings should be covered with a mesh screen to prevent birds and small animals gaining access.
The covering layer here is thicker than at the ridge – reed 350 mm, straw 300 mm – owing to the increased water run-off.
If the roof space is used only for storage and has through-ventilation even during the winter, which is particularly beneficial for a roof covering of natural materials, the floor below should be designed to stop the passage of heat and water vapour. The junction of the vapour barrier with the wall should be made airtight with a timber batten.

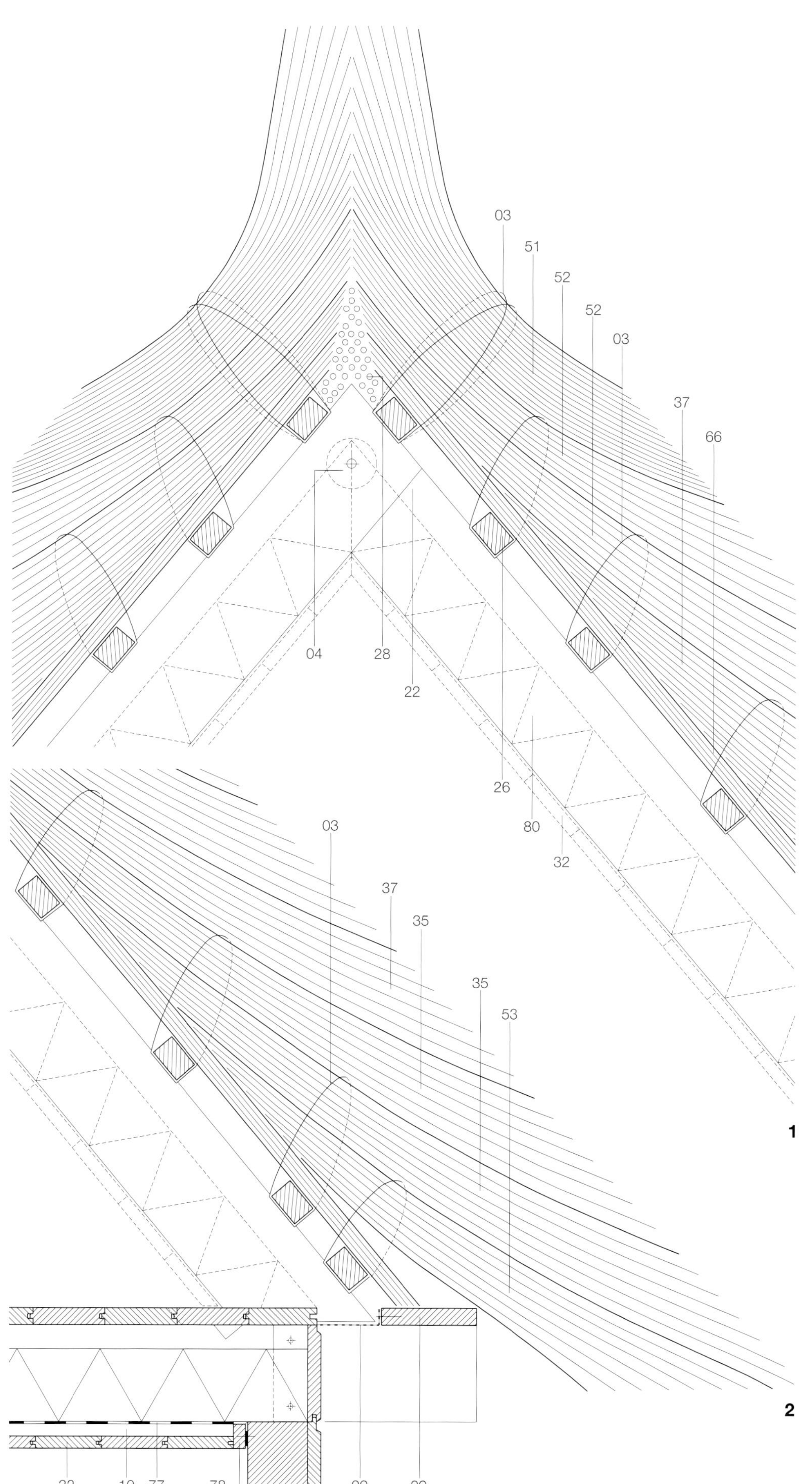

**Verge**

**3** Verge with bargeboard, stitched/tied thatch

At the verge all the layers of thatch are laid at an angle (≤ 60°) to the horizontal to achieve a rainproof roof covering. The angle becomes shallower towards the ridge, where the layers are horizontal. Here too, the thatch is pressed against a tilting board (bargeboard) and held under tension with close or double stitching (suction peaks). Stitching produces indents at the stitching points in the middle of the roof covering – more frequently at the edge of the roof (60–80 mm), less often on the roof surface (150–200 mm) – which must be well covered. Conversely, tying sways and liggers or metal rods forces the thatch down evenly. Binding wire and metal rods are made from rustproofed – preferably non-corrosive – steel. Fixings such as ladder hooks and supports for snowguards should not be incorporated into a thatched roof because they create weak points through which rainwater can enter the construction.

**Penetrations**

**4** Chimney with shouldered stack and overlapping timber boards, tied thatch

The chimney stack is always positioned to pass through the ridge and project ≥ 800 mm above the ridge. The shouldered arrangement cantilevers over the roof covering and thus protects the junction from the ingress of rainwater. Timber boards ≤ 200 mm wide, overlapping ≥ 50 mm and screwed down, are tucked beneath the shoulder on the eaves side of the chimney stack. The final normal course of thatch approx. 100 mm thick overlaps these timber boards at the sides. The advantage of timber boards over other materials (e.g. sheet metal) is that they do not release condensation onto the roof covering. A clearance of 300 mm for reed and 250 mm for straw should be maintained between battens and chimney stack. For safety, the chimney stack walls should be widened for up to 500 mm below the roof construction and finished with ≥ 10 mm plaster. There should be a clearance of ≥ 50 mm between loadbearing members and the chimney stack.

Details scale 1:10
00 Loop of binding wire
03 Stitch
04 Dowel
08 Sway/metal rod
09 Eaves board
10 Spacer batten
13 Cantilevering brick course
14 Chimney stack, widened
22 Rafter
26 Batten
28 Ridge filling
29 Bargeboard
32 Timber boarding
35 Thatch course laid at an angle
37 Normal course of thatch
40 Overlapping timber boards
51 Ridge course
52 Topmost course
53 Upper eaves course
66 Undercoat (viewed partly from below)
72 Plaster
77 Vapour barrier
78 Preformed seal clamped behind batten
80 Thermal insulation
99 Mesh screen to ventilation opening

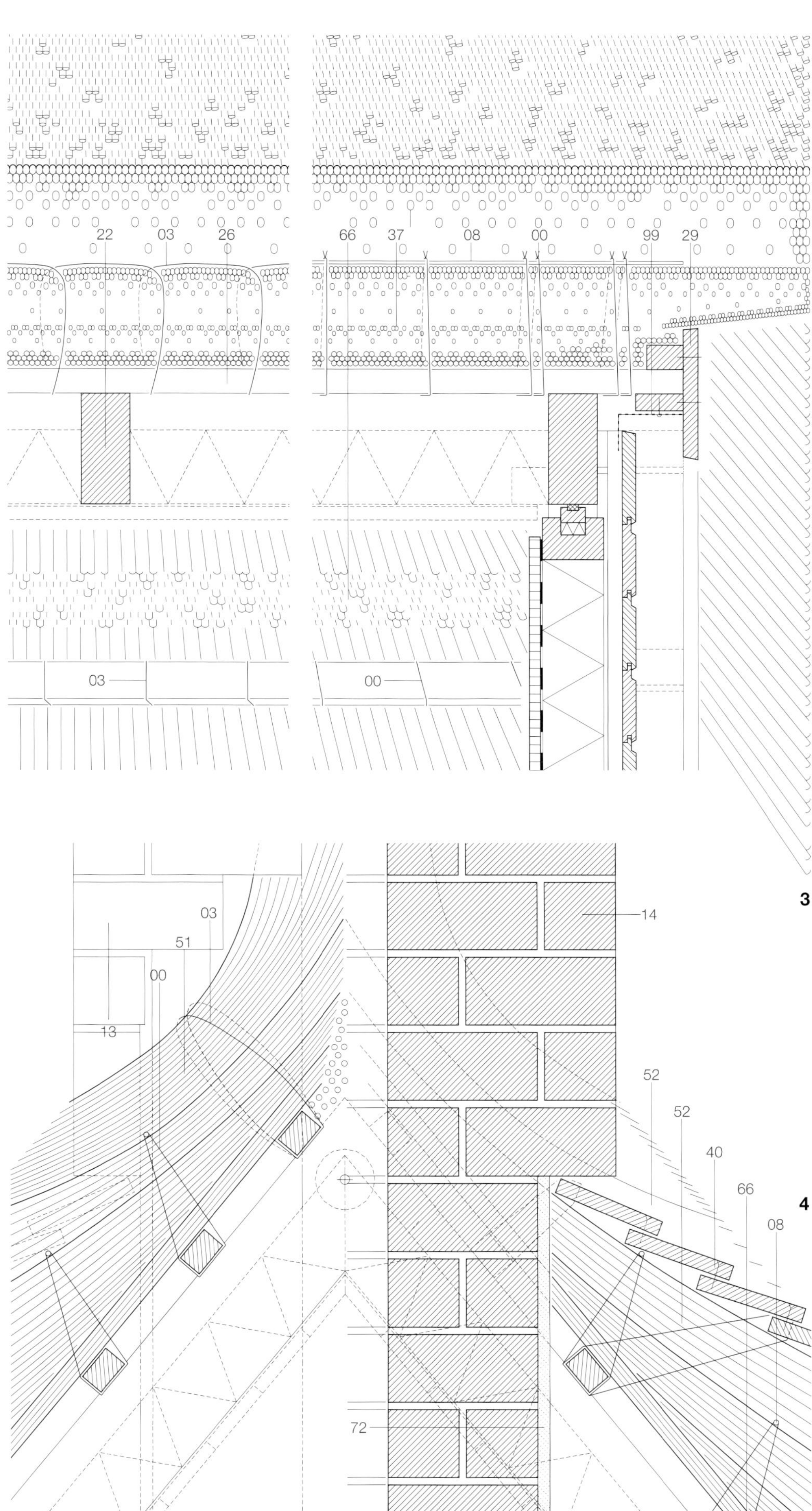

## Wooden shakes and shingles

Ventilated roof covering, roofing felt on timber boarding, ventilated thermal insulation

#### Ridge

**1** Ventilated ridge with overlapping shakes/shingles
**2** Overhanging ridge to monopitch roof with fascia board and overlapping shakes/shingles

**1** The ridge is covered in three layers in the opposite direction to the prevailing wind. The shakes/shingles on the ridge overlap alternately and each is secured with two nails (positioned offset).
Ridge vent openings should be on the leeward side of the roof. As they cannot prevent the ingress of driving rain and snow, any moisture must be able drain away safely on the roofing felt below. The ventilation openings in the roof covering and the timber boarding should be offset by a considerable distance. Battens clamp the vapour barrier tightly to the purlin.

**2** The ridge to a monopitch roof is also covered with three layers in the opposite direction to the prevailing wind. The ridge shakes/shingles and the last course on the roof surface cantilever 50–90 mm beyond the upper fascia board.
To pack up the ridge, an additional course of shakes/shingles is laid underneath with its butt end uppermost.
A fascia board closes off the airspace below the shakes/shingles and overlaps the underlying roofing felt and timber boarding ≥ 50 mm. Additional strips of sheet metal are inserted – as weather protection and to spread the load – where ladder hooks are required.

#### Hip

**3** Mitred hip

In contrast to the ridge of a duopitch roof, the hip involves a mitred arrangement. The shakes/shingles at the hip are displaced by one course towards the eaves and thus function like overlapping elements. Vents in the roofing felt and boarding below the roof covering ensure ventilation to the bays between the jack rafters.

Details scale 1:10
00 Ladder hook
03 Vapour barrier clamped behind batten
06 Gutter bracket
10 Valley board
21 Purlin
22 Rafter, jack rafter
23 Hip/valley rafter
25 Spacer batten
26 Batten
27 Feather-edge board
28 Rafter extension
29 Upper fascia board
31 Strengthening rod
32 Timber boarding
35 Packing shake/shingle
40 Fascia board
49 Vent
51 Ridge/hip element
53 Eaves element
62 Drip flashing
63 Gutter flashing
67 Sheathing, roofing felt
77 Vapour barrier
80 Thermal insulation
93 Vent
95 Gutter
98 Snowguard (fence/pole)
99 Mesh screen to ventilation opening

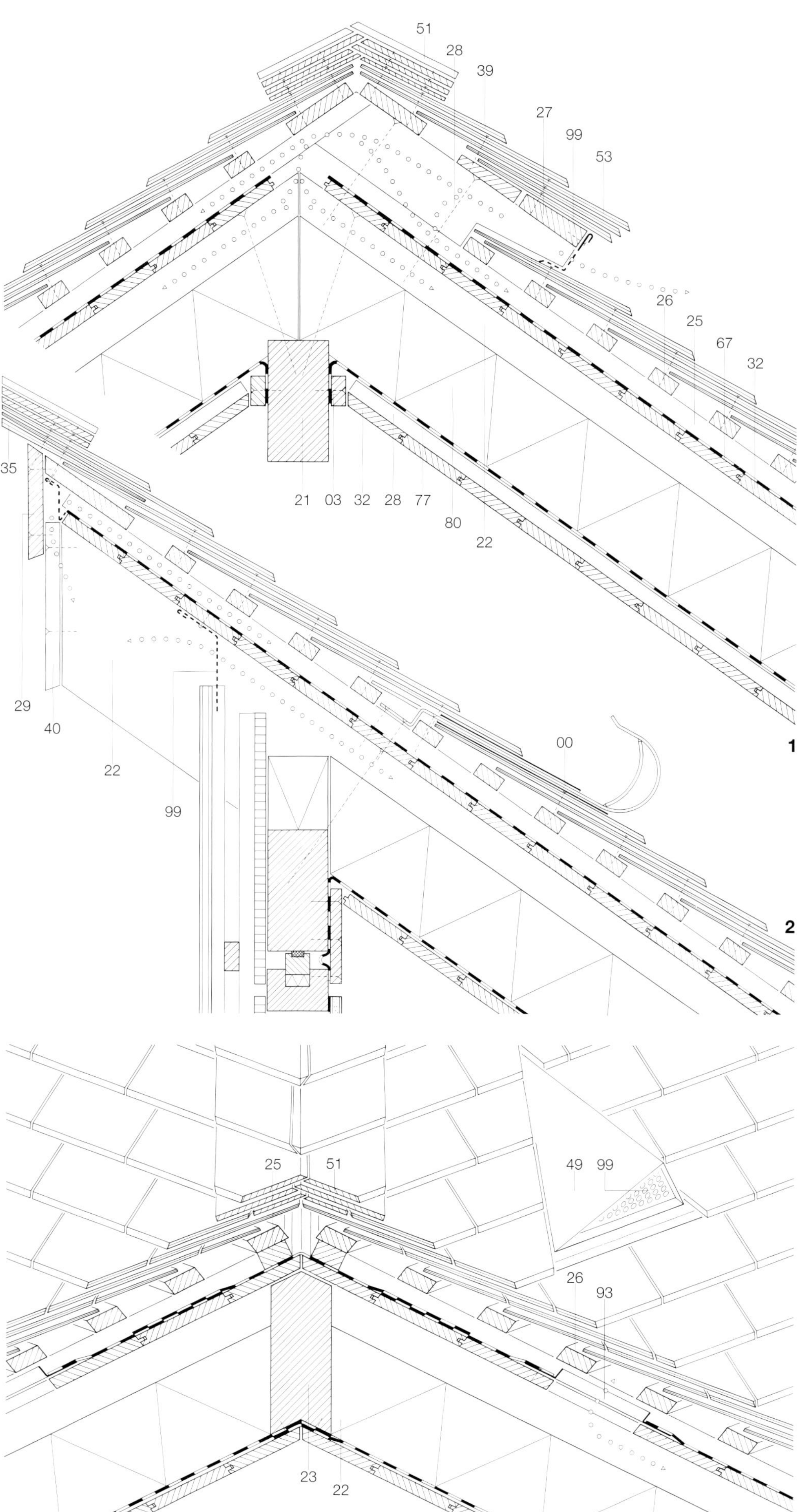

**Valley**

**4** Semi-swept valley

The valley is formed with four layers of shakes or shingles equal in length to those used on the roof surface. A wide valley board and adjoining feather-edge boards pack up the supporting construction (see sketch). The boards lie on the end of the battens, which are supported on

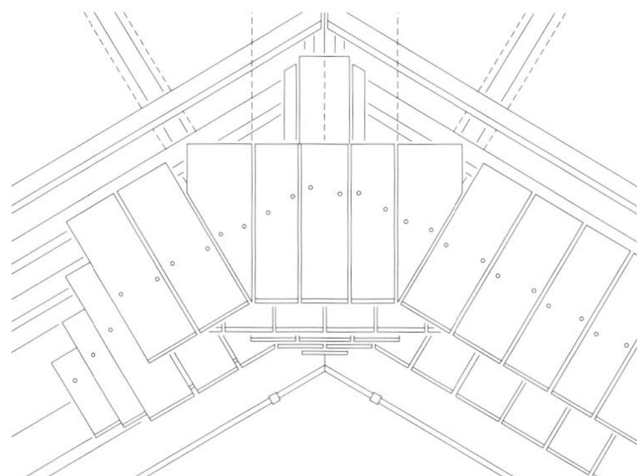

counter battens (if necessary, additional pieces thereof); these create a void for draining possible moisture. Vents permit through-ventilation of the isolated spaces between the jack rafters. Below the roof covering, the air flows alternately underneath between the counter battens and on top between the roof covering battens. The vapour barrier is pulled below the valley rafter and pressed down by battens.

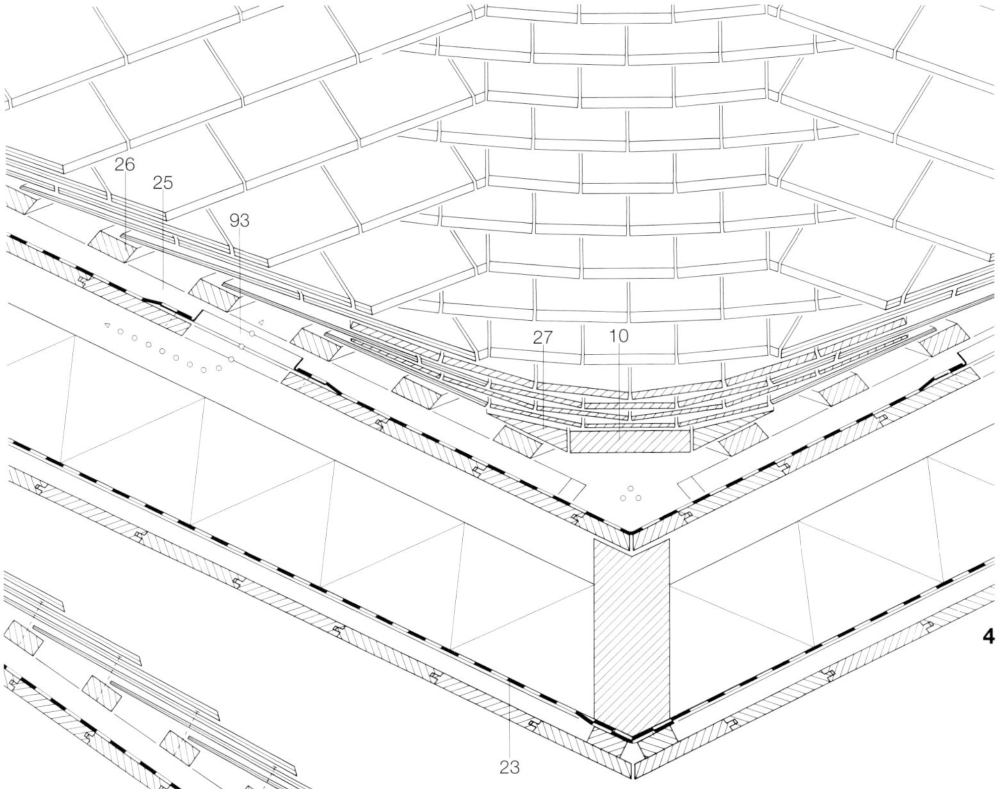

**Eaves**

**5** Eaves with low-level gutter, fence-type snowguard

**6** Eaves with high-level gutter, timber pole as snowguard

The eaves course consists of shakes/shingles of various lengths laid in a stepped arrangement. Rainwater drips from the butt ends of the shakes/shingles and so cannot be drawn up between them by capillary action. The shakes/shingles project 10–20 mm beyond the eaves flashing. Two feather-edge boards provide a means of fixing for the flashing (150– 200 mm wide depending on pitch) and the shakes/shingles themselves. There is a gap of 10–20 mm between these boards, which allows air to circulate below the roof covering. In regions with heavy snowfall, where gutters are often blocked with snow and ice, it is advisable to fix the gutter at a higher level. This allows melt water and excess water that seeps through the roof covering to drain away unhindered on the roofing felt. A metal rod can be incorporated into the bead of the gutter to strengthen it. Snowguards in the form of fences or timber poles require sheet metal flashings and an underlay to spread the load. Ventilation openings should be protected against birds and small animals by mesh screens.

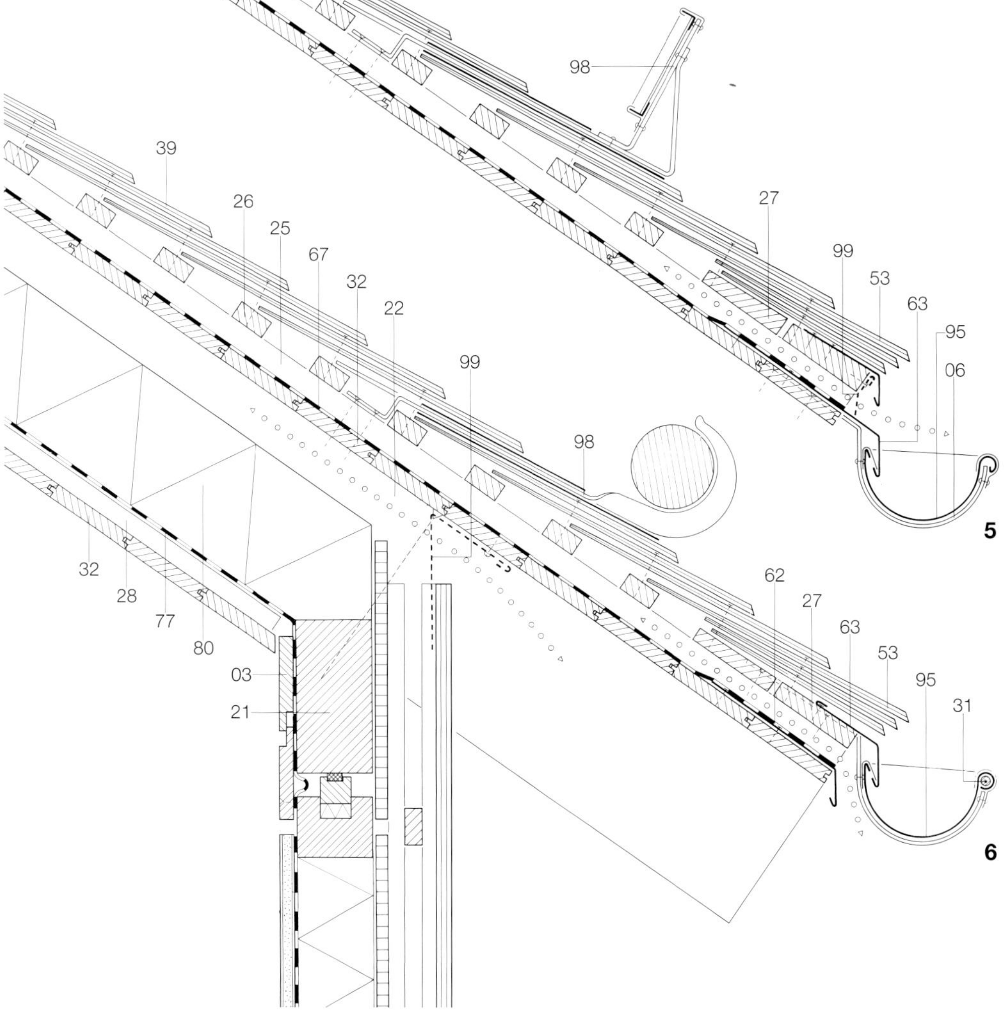

**Verge**

**7** Overhanging verge

At the verge the shakes/shingles project about 30 mm beyond the bargeboard. The outer corner of each butt end is cropped so that water draining down the edge of the roof flows back onto the roof surface. An extra counter batten retains and tensions the bargeboard. Wide and narrow shakes/shingles are laid with long enough side laps (≥ 30 mm) (see "Layers – Flat overlapping shakes/shingles – Wooden shakes and shingles – Laying").

**Junction with wall**

**8** Junction with wall at side of slope, deep gutter
**9** Junction with wall at side of slope, swept gutter
**10** Junction with wall at top of slope, sheet metal flashing

**8** A deep gutter is employed primarily where much water is expected. On one side it has a turned-up edge tucked under the roof covering. This gives the overlying shakes/shingles a transverse fall, which directs rainwater back onto the roof surface. On the other side the sheet metal is turned up the wall ≥ 150 mm above the roof covering and overlapped by the wall construction ≥ 50 mm.

**9** The swept gutter is rainproof. Four layers of shakes/shingles are laid on a rounded construction. Both gutter board and secondary waterproofing layer underneath can be adjusted for height and thus accommodate adjoining components without needing to be cut. The vapour barrier is pressed tightly onto the rafter with a batten and the joint between it and the wall tightly sealed with a preformed sponge rubber strip.

**10** The last course is shorter. The sheet metal flashing overlaps the shakes/shingles by their length. It is pressed into position by its fixing and overlapped by the wall construction ≥ 50 mm. The sheet metal chosen must be compatible with the wood used for the shakes or shingles (see "Layers – Flat overlapping shakes/shingles – Wooden shakes and shingles – Materials").

Details scale 1:10

00 Spacer
03 Vapour barrier
05 Clip
06 Fixing for flashing
07 Auxiliary timber for fixing batten
10 Feather-edge board
20 Tapering frame
22 Rafter
24 Trimmer
25 Spacer batten
26 Batten, glulam batten
27 Feather-edge board, glulam feather-edge board
28 Rafter extension
29 Bargeboard, fascia board
31 Strut
32 Timber boarding
35 Narrow valley shake/shingle
39 Wooden shake/shingle
51 Ridge element
53 Eaves element, shortened
61 Flashing
67 Sheathing, roofing felt
77 Vapour barrier
78 Permanently elastic seal
80 Thermal insulation
93 Vent
95 Gutter
99 Mesh screen

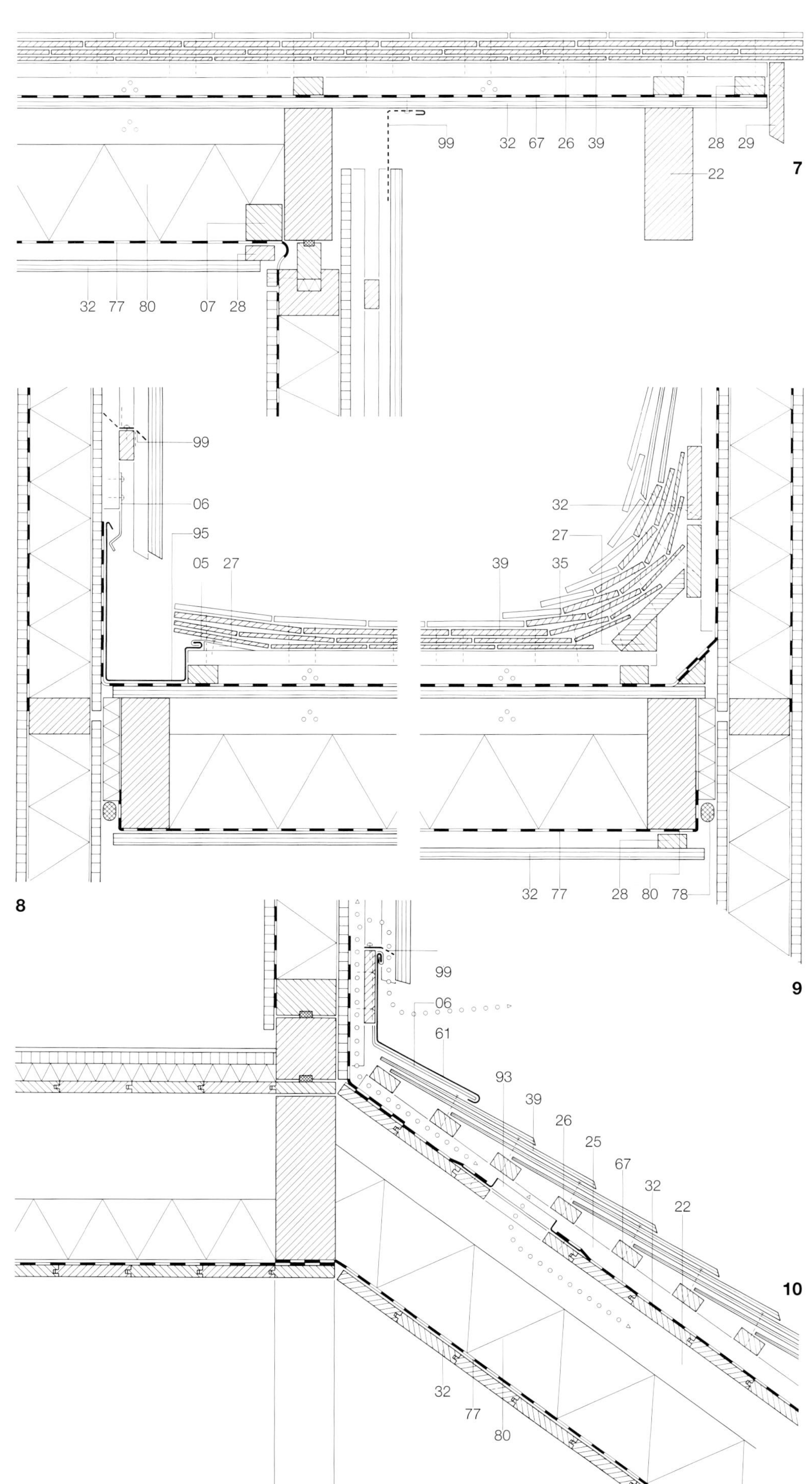

**Dormer window**

**11, 12, 13** Eyebrow dormer window with ventilation openings

The height-to-width ratio of an eyebrow dormer window should not exceed 1:5 (see "Layers – Flat overlapping shakes/shingles – Wooden shakes and shingles – Details"). A more pronounced curve leads to excessively bulky side joints in which the overlap of ≥ 30 mm is not achieved.
The wooden shakes or shingles are laid on glulam battens around the dormer window; their flexibility allows them to be adapted to the form of the window (see sketch). The feather-edge eaves boards are also given this treatment. The gaps between them – as at the eaves – allow air to circulate below the roof covering. A steeper angle at the start of the eyebrow

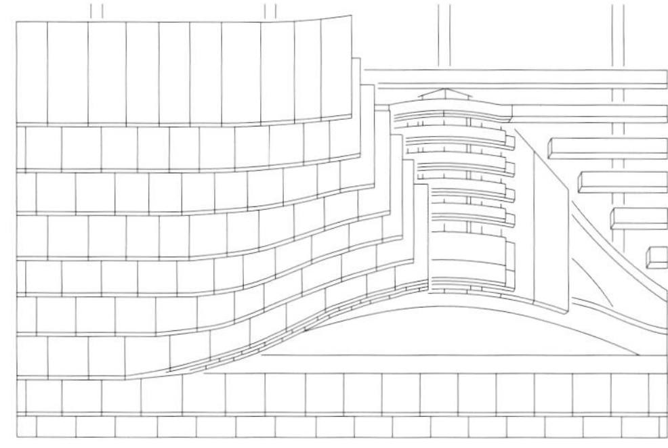

dormer window requires the use of wedges below the counter battens to prevent gaps appearing between the butt ends of the shakes or shingles.
The roof structure is interrupted at the dormer window; trimmers, struts and roof decking frame the opening. Tapering and chamfered boards form the bearing for the window construction and – together with the curving frame – produce its internal and external form.
At a height:width ratio of 1:5 a low window calls for a wide opening between the rafters and only by cutting through two rafters is it possible to achieve a window height of about 600 mm.
As with the other details, the eyebrow dormer window has two ventilation levels. Below the roof covering, counter battens create a space for air circulation, and above the thermal insulation the air flows between the individual parts of the roof structure. However, both the continuous support board standing on the struts and the timber spacer blocks obstruct the air flow.
The openings to both ventilation levels are covered with feather-edge boards and given a mesh screen to prevent birds and small animals from entering.
The ventilation to the roof surface below the dormer window is comparable to that at the ridge. The ventilation openings in the roof covering and secondary waterproofing layer should be offset from each other.

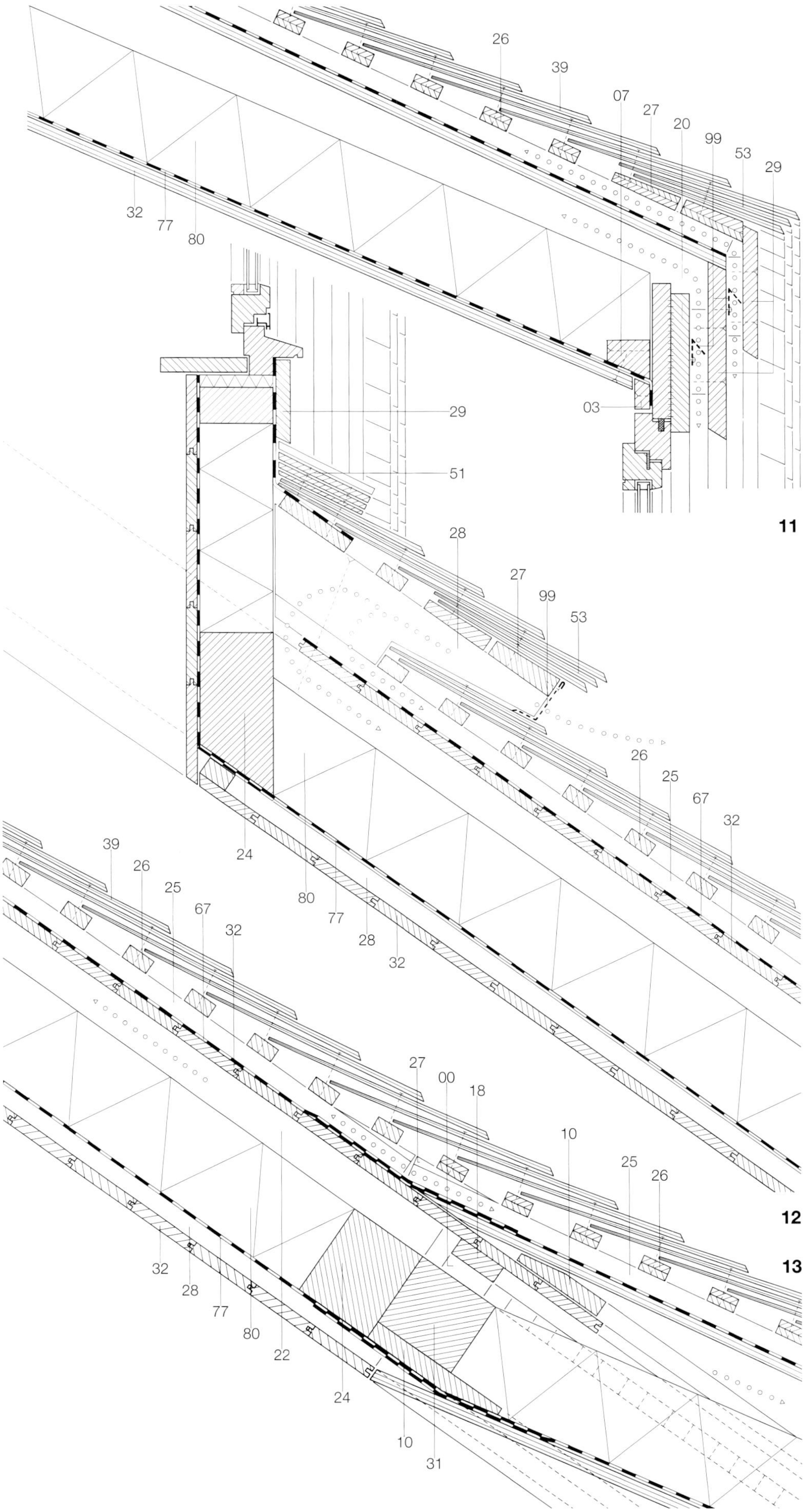

11

12

13

**Natural and fibre-cement slates**

Ventilated/non-ventilated roof covering on roofing felt/sheathing on timber boarding, ventilated thermal insulation and vapour barrier

**Ridge**

**1** Ventilated ridge and overlapping ridge slates, rectangular double-lap slating
**2** Ridge with ventilation hood and overlapping ridge slates, single-lap non-horizontal slating

**1** Overlapping slates on the ridge are laid in the opposite direction to the prevailing wind. The courses on both sides are laid with regard to the prevailing wind direction. The courses on the windward side must project beyond those on the leeward side by 50–70 mm. Nails under the laps hold them in place. The key slate alone is fixed with stainless steel nails that remain visible.
Simple ridge vents should be positioned on the leeward side. As they cannot prevent the ingress of driving rain and snow, any moisture must be able drain away safely on the roofing felt below. The ventilation openings in the roof covering and the timber boarding should therefore be offset by a considerable distance. Additional protection is provided by a featheredge board fixed to the roof boarding.

**2** Ventilation to both sides must include measures to exclude driving rain and snow. Standard and top course slates are used in the courses below the ridge to finish off the non-horizontal courses in a straight line.

**Ridge to monopitch roof**

**3** Ridge to monopitch roof with overlapping ridge slates, double-lap non-horizontal slating

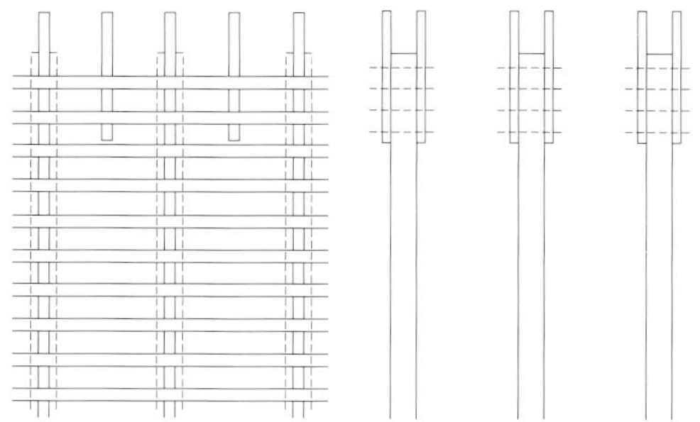

The ridge to a monopitch roof is covered in the same way as a duopitch roof. As with double-lap slating on the main surface of the roof, large slates are used here. Milled sheet lead is used as an underlay to spread the load from ladder hooks. It is advisable to strengthen the supporting construction by doubling up the members or providing additional members in the centre of each bay (see sketch).

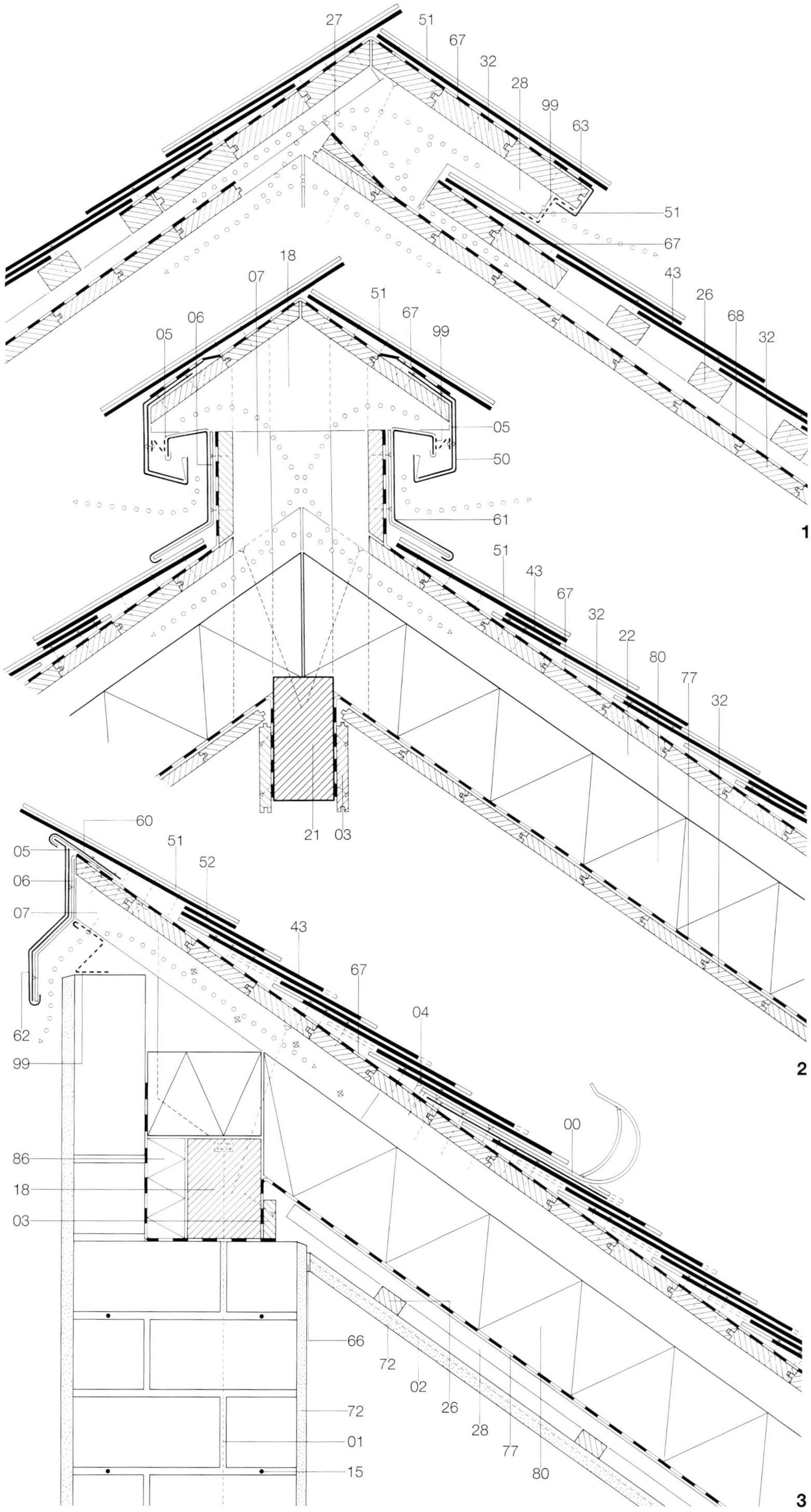

**Hip**

**4** Mitred hip, rectangular double-lap slating
Each course at a mitred hip ends with a cut hip slate that projects over the leeward side by 50–70 mm. Roof decking is required in the plane of the battens for fixing the edge slates with three or more (annular) nails.
Ventilation to the bays between the jack rafters is through vents in the secondary waterproofing layer and a "maze" of battens and counter battens; additional vents are required on long hips.

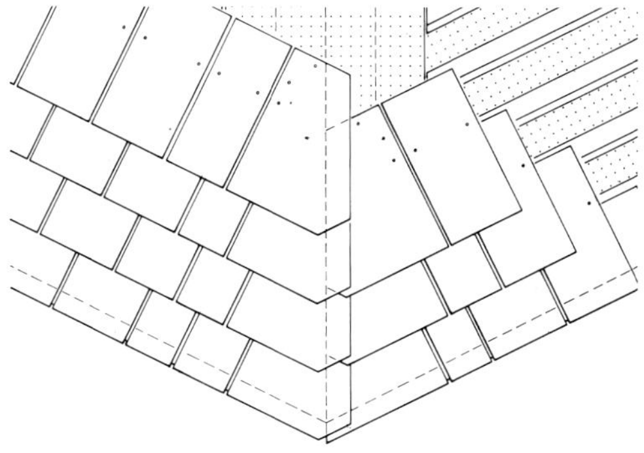

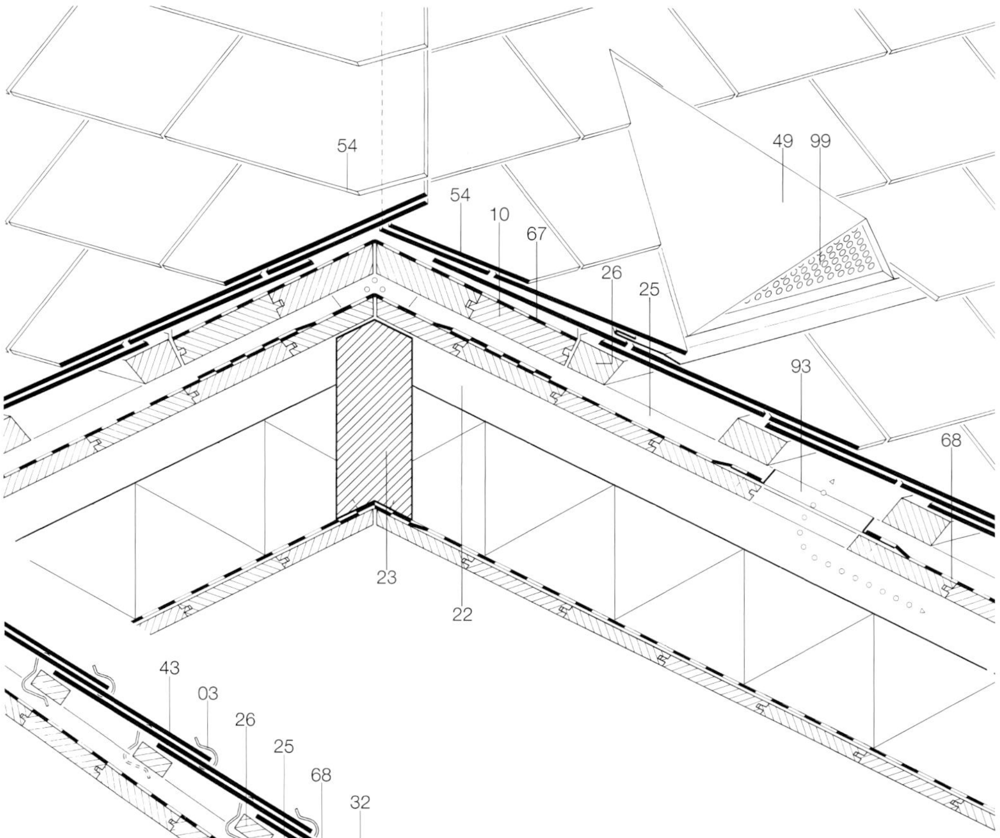

**Eaves**

**5** Eaves with low-level gutter, clipped rectangular double-lap slating
**6** Eaves with strengthened high-level gutter, single-lap non-horizontal slating with mitred eaves
**5** Clips (copper or stainless steel) fix rectangular double-lap slating when laying narrow slates (length > width). The eaves course consists of shortened undereaves slates covered completely by standard slates. A feather-edge board maintains the pitch at the eaves.
**6** Each course of non-horizontal slating starts at the eaves with a special coursing slate and two or three eaves slates of different length (see "Layers – Natural and fibre-cement slates – Laying").

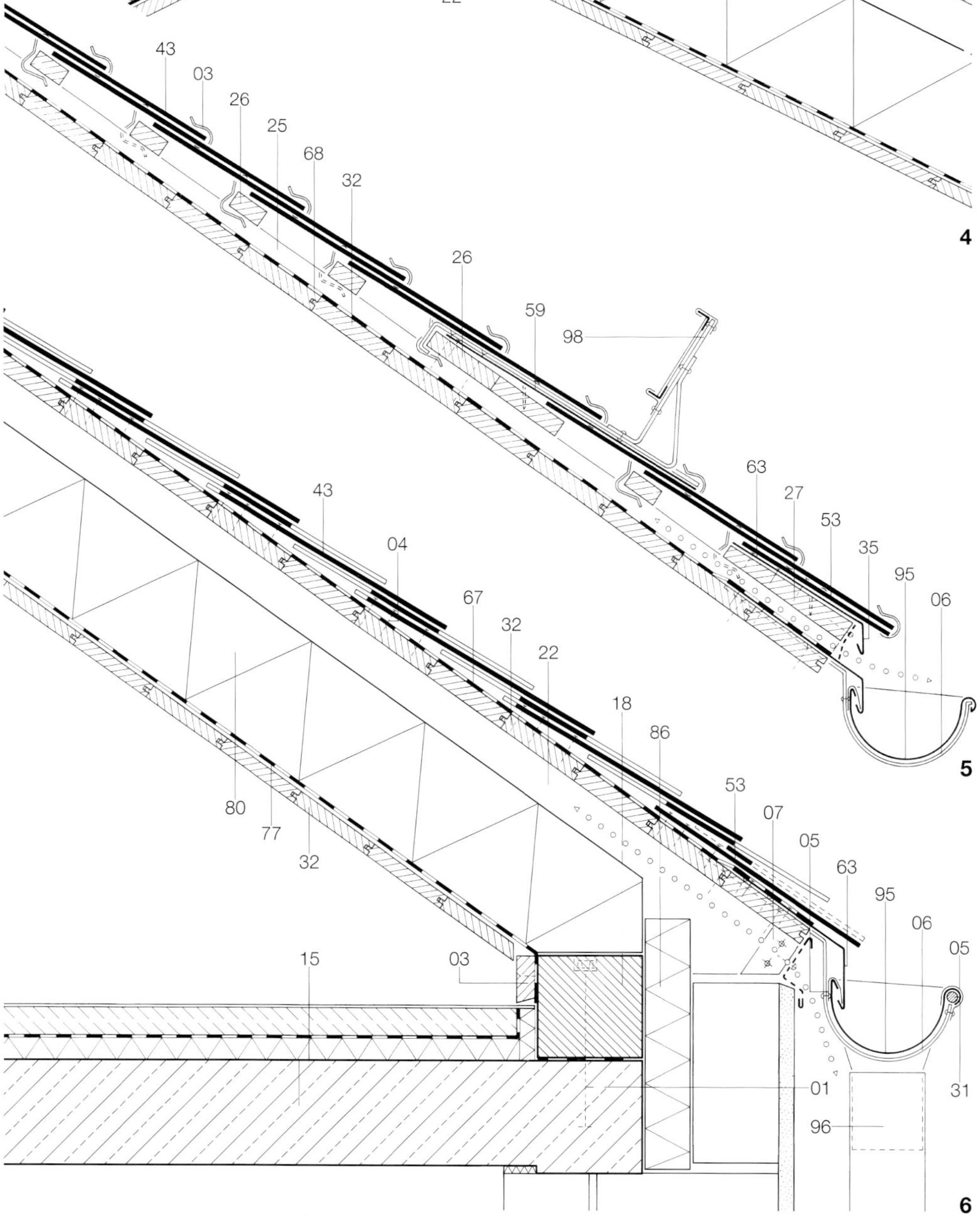

Details scale 1:10
00 Ladder hook
01 Masonry anchor
02 Plaster background
03 Vapour barrier clamped behind batten/board
04 Nail, annular nail
05 Clip, continuous clip
06 Fixing for flashing, gutter bracket
07 Timber member
10 Hip boards
15 Peripheral reinforcement (in bed joint or floor slab)
18 Wall plate, hood support
21 Purlin
22 Rafter, jack rafter
23 Hip rafter
25 Spacer batten
26 Batten
27 Feather-edge board
28 Rafter extension
31 Strengthening rod
32 Tongue and groove boarding
35 Drip flashing
43 Standard slate
49 Vent
50 Ventilation hood
51 Ridge slate
52 Top course slate
53 Eaves slate
54 Verge slate
59 Sheet metal underlay
60 Cover flashing
61 Apron flashing
62 Drip flashing
63 Flashing
66 Separating layer
67 Sheathing (laid with laps)
68 Sheathing/roofing felt (laid with laps)
72 Plaster
77 Vapour barrier
80 Thermal insulation
86 Thermal insulation
93 Vent
95 Gutter
96 Rainwater downpipe
98 Snowguard and mounting
99 Mesh screen

4

5

6

**Valley**

**7** Valley with soakers, diagonal slating
**8** Swept valley, rectangular double-lap slating
**9** Swept valley, single-lap non-horizontal slating

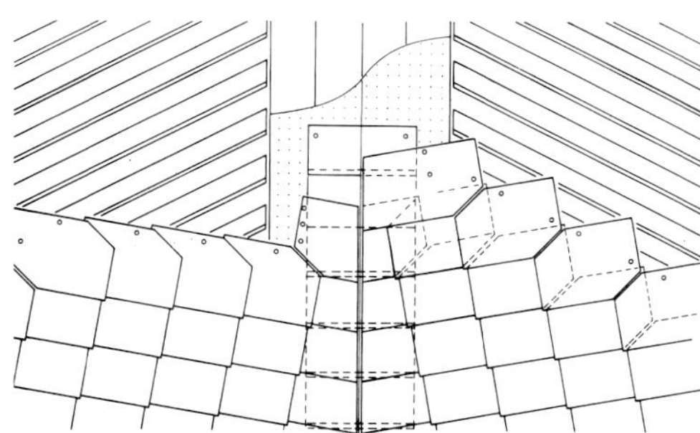

**7** The valley with soakers can be laid rainproof at a pitch of ≥ 25°. The pieces of sheet metal (soakers) ≥ 330 mm wide are incorporated with single-laps and are overlapped ≥ 150 mm by the adjacent roofing slates. Special formats in different sizes are cut from standard slates. They must be fixed to timber boarding along the valley. A roof covering over roofing felt and timber boarding is specially ventilated underneath via the battens and counter battens, and is ideal for laying on battens (see sketch).

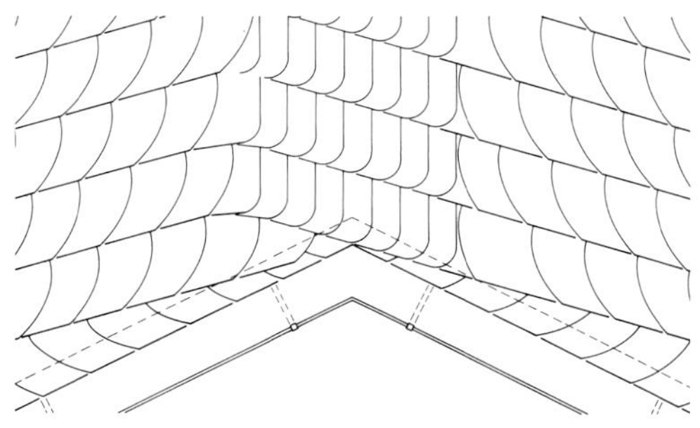

**8** The swept valley with covering and underlying layers of slate can be laid rainproof at a pitch of ≥ 30°. Standard slates are used, but with a lap one third greater than normal. All valley slates are laid on timber boarding, which is given a rounded shape with a valley board and tapering battens, and is covered with sheathing. The two air layers are interconnected by vents.

**9** This left-hand swept valley is suitable for accommodating large amounts or faster flowing water coming from the left. The rounding is shifted to the left. Battens – omitted at the valley – are attached to the rafters to make them deeper and thus enable the bays between the jack rafters to be ventilated.

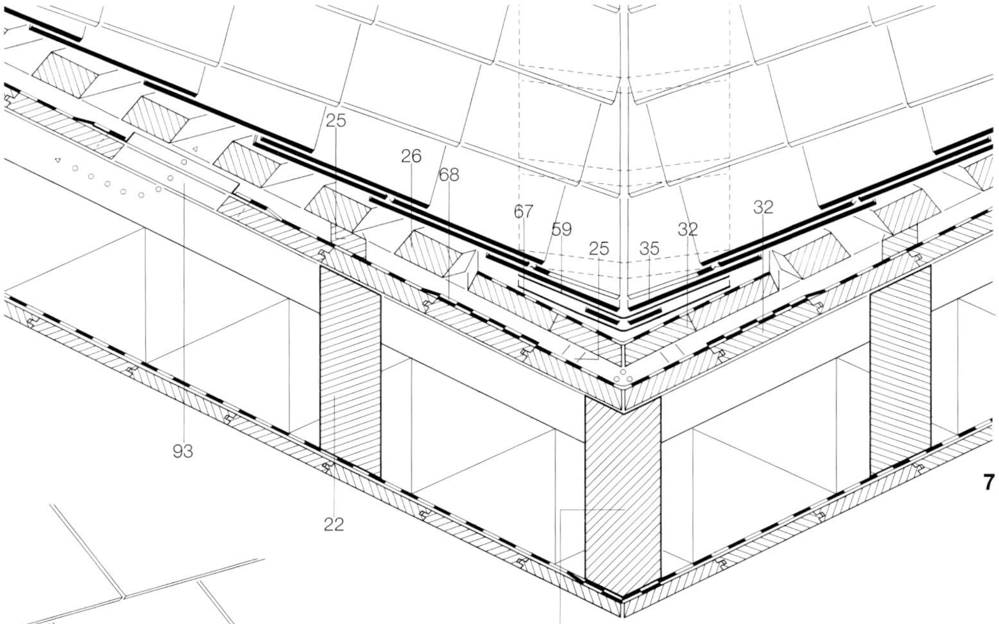

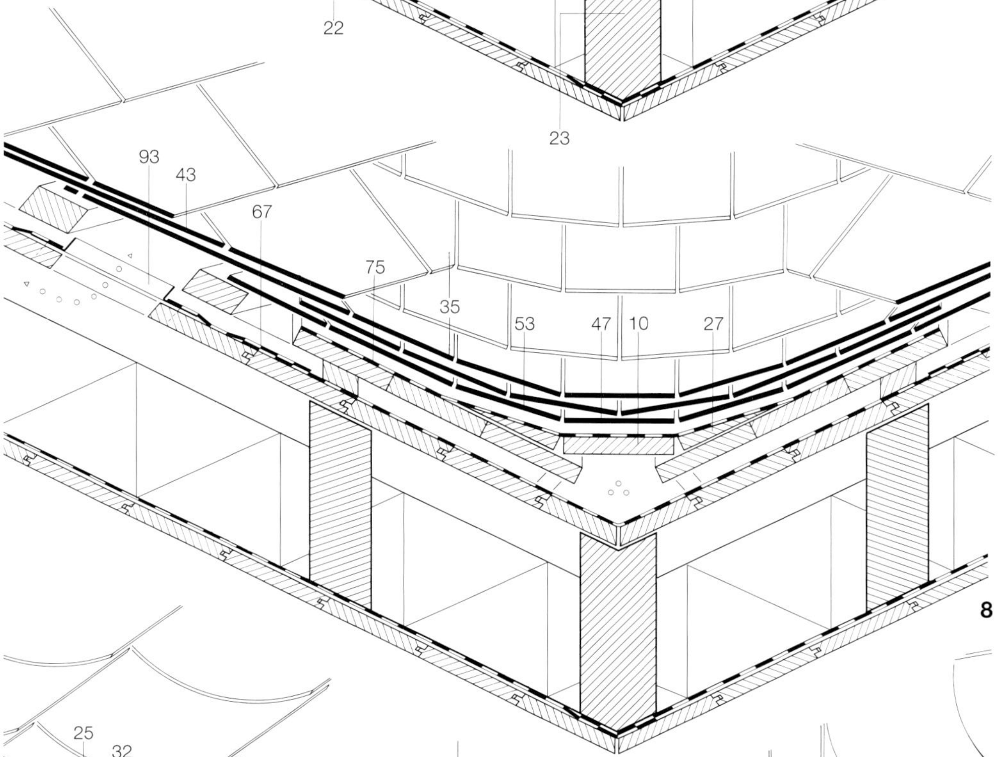

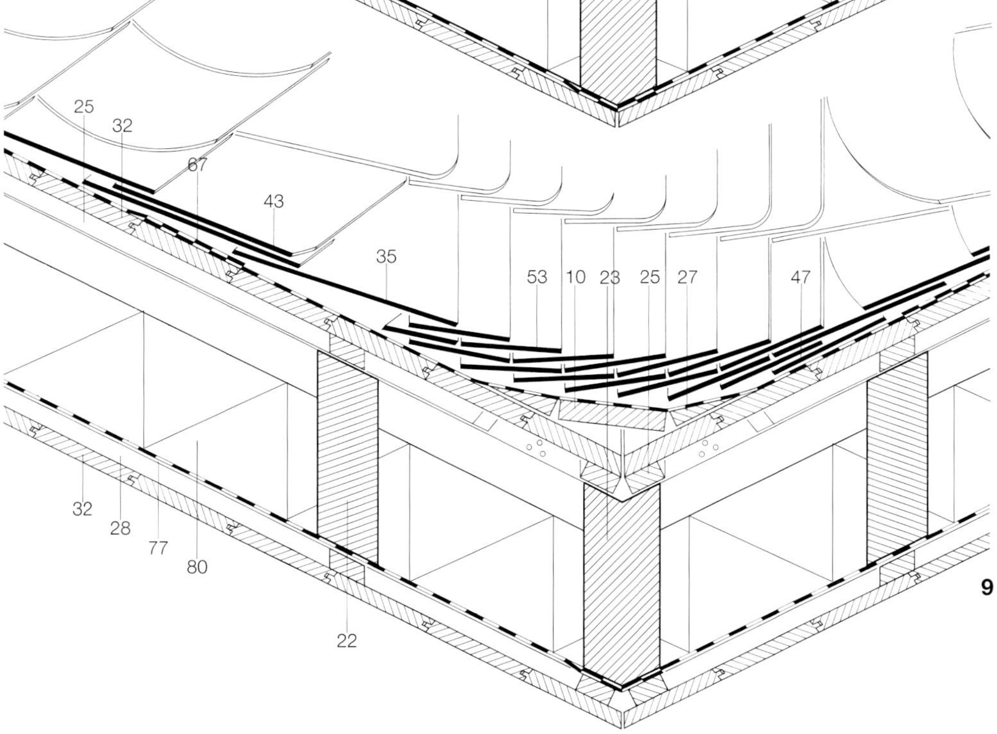

**Verge**

**10** Verge with gutter, clipped rectangular double-lap slating
**11** Verge with flashing, single-lap non-horizontal slating

**10** The roof covering should overhang the verge by ≤ 50 mm. The slates are laid on the turned-up edge of the verge gutter, which produces a slight reverse fall back onto the roof surface. Slates along the edge are fixed to a board with hooks (whole slates) or nails (half slates), but other slates are clipped to the battens. Gutter and flashing are kept separate. The sheet metal flashing is held and stiffened by clips and continuous clips.

**11** Three verge slates of different sizes are required to begin the non-horizontal courses. They are laid on the turned-up edge of the verge flashing and are each fixed with at least three nails to the continuous timber boarding. Battens hold the vapour barrier in place in both verge details. These battens compensate for the different deflections of the rafters.

**Junction with wall**

**12** Junction with wall at side of slope, swept arrangement, single-lap non-horizontal slating
**13** Junction with wall at side of slope, with soakers, rectangular double-lap slating

**12** The swept (left-hand) valley forms a gentle transition between the roof and the wall. It is seven valley slates wide and is laid from the roof (channel slate) to the wall (draining slate). The supporting construction consists of a valley board and two feather-edge boards, and is covered with a layer of sheathing to drain the water temporarily (e.g. during construction).

**13** The roof adjoins the wall with narrow and wide rectangular slates. The metal soakers are laid with single laps and are tucked beneath the roof covering for half a slate's width. The drip flashing above overlaps the soakers by ≥ 50 mm.

Details scale 1:10

00 Plaster background
03 Tile clip
05 Clip, continuous clip
06 Fixing for flashing
10 Valley board
15 Peripheral reinforcement (in bed joint or capping beam)
18 Wall plate
22 Rafter, jack rafter
23 Valley rafter
25 Spacer batten
26 Batten
27 Feather-edge board
28 Rafter extension
29 Stop bead
32 Tongue and groove boarding
35 Special make-up slate, valley transition slate
43 Standard slate
47 Channel slate
53 Valley slate
54 Verge slate
59 Soaker
60 Cover flashing
62 Drip flashing
66 Separating layer
67 Sheathing (laid with laps)
68 Sheathing/roofing felt (laid with laps)
72 Plaster/rendering
75 Water check, bonded
77 Vapour barrier
78 Permanently elastic seal
80 Thermal insulation
86 Thermal insulation
93 Vent
95 Gutter

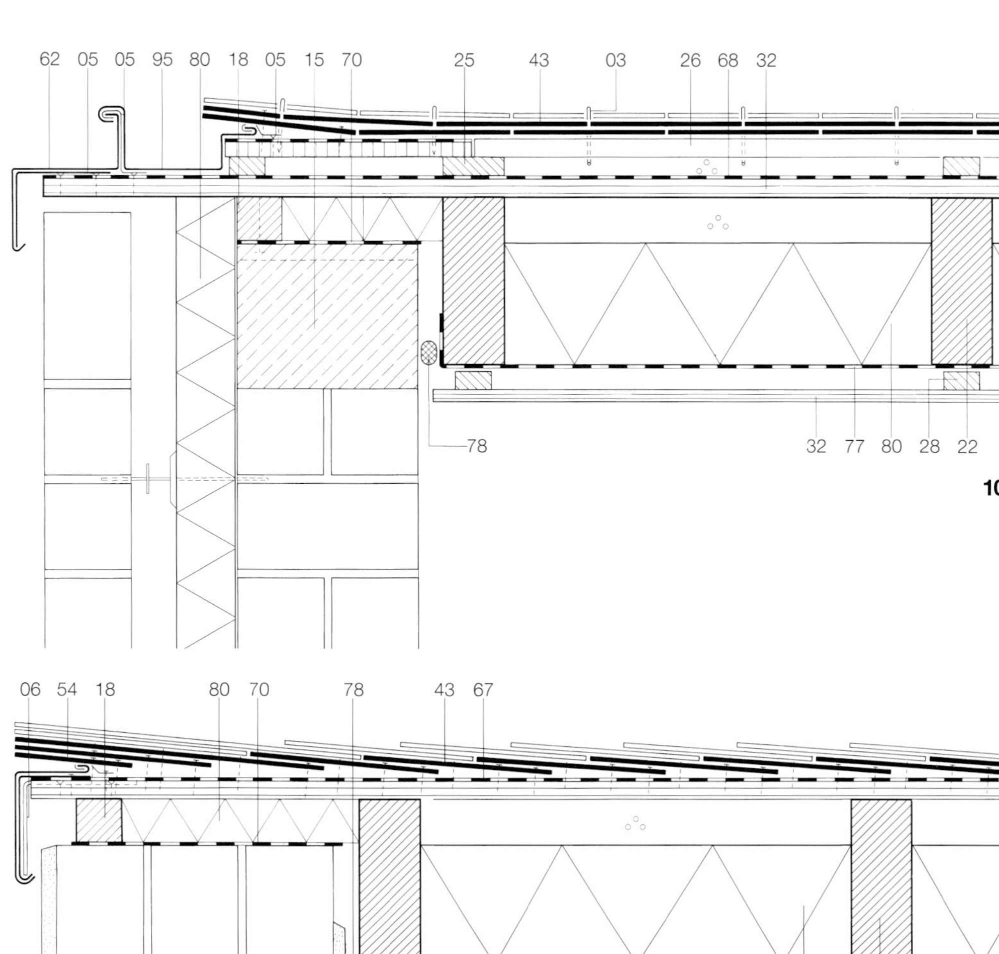


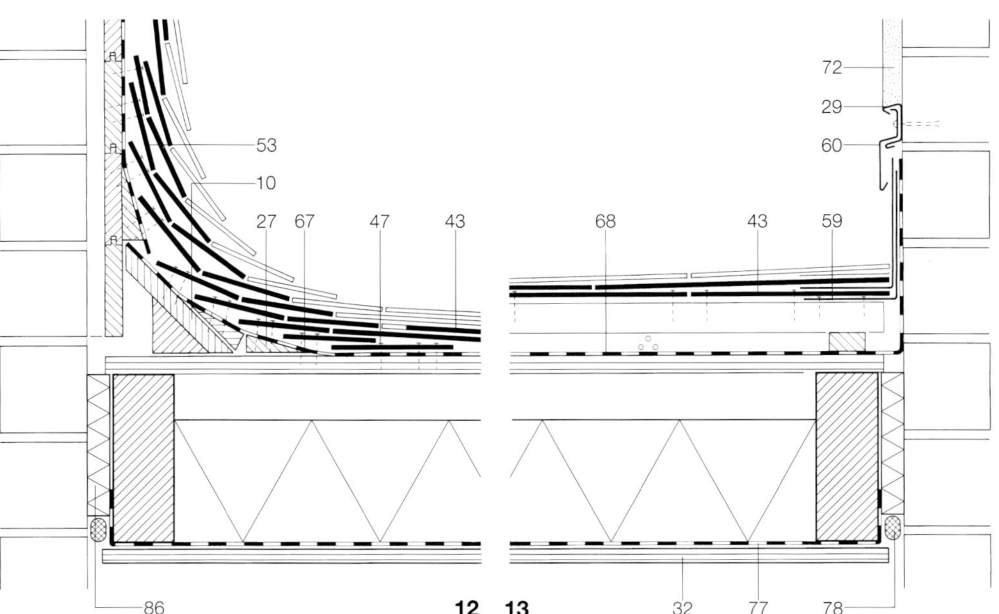

**Penetrations**

**14** Slated chimney stack, single-lap non-horizontal slating

A "saddle" with swept slating is provided on the ridge side of the chimney stack. Its apex is horizontal and its sides are inclined at ≤ 45°. On the eaves side the junction with the roof surface is rounded with a valley board and feather-edge board; slating to the chimney thus overlaps the – independent – slating on the roof surface.
The chimney slating is supported by timber boarding on battens (see sketch).

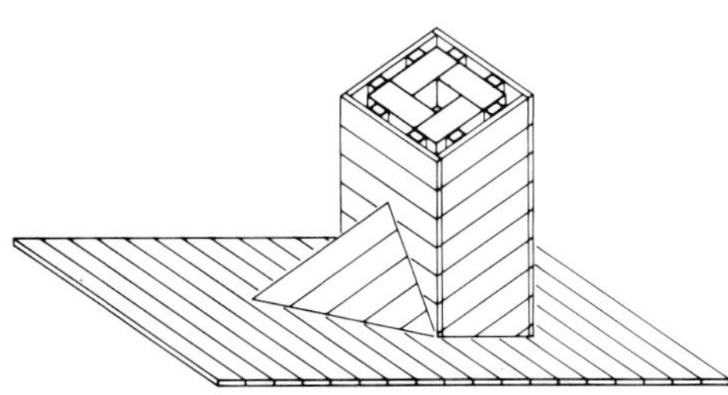

**Junction with wall**

**15** Junction with wall at top of slope, simple vent, rectangular double-lap slating
**16** Junction with wall at top of slope, secure vent, single-lap non-horizontal slating

**15** The roof covering finishes at the wall with overlapping top course slates. The laps of these slates depend on the weather and are fixed to a board with at least three nails. These are in turn flashed with sheet metal.
The ventilation opening redirects the air only once and is constricted only very little by the mesh screen (fitted at an angle). However, it cannot prevent the ingress of driving rain or snow. Water that does enter the vent drains away safely on the roofing felt, which is turned up the wall. Sheet metal is laid beneath the ladder hooks to distribute the load.

**16** The roof covering finishes at the wall as at the ridge, with overlapping top course slates. Top course slates of different sizes finish off the non-horizontal courses in a straight line. The sheet metal flashing (100–150 mm) forms part of a vent in which the air is redirected more than once. This is in turn protected by a drip flashing above.
Roof covering and vent are laid on sheathing turned up the wall. A board presses the vapour barrier tightly against the purlin.
A preformed foam rubber strip seals the joint between masonry and purlin; its flexibility compensates for the unevenness of the masonry.

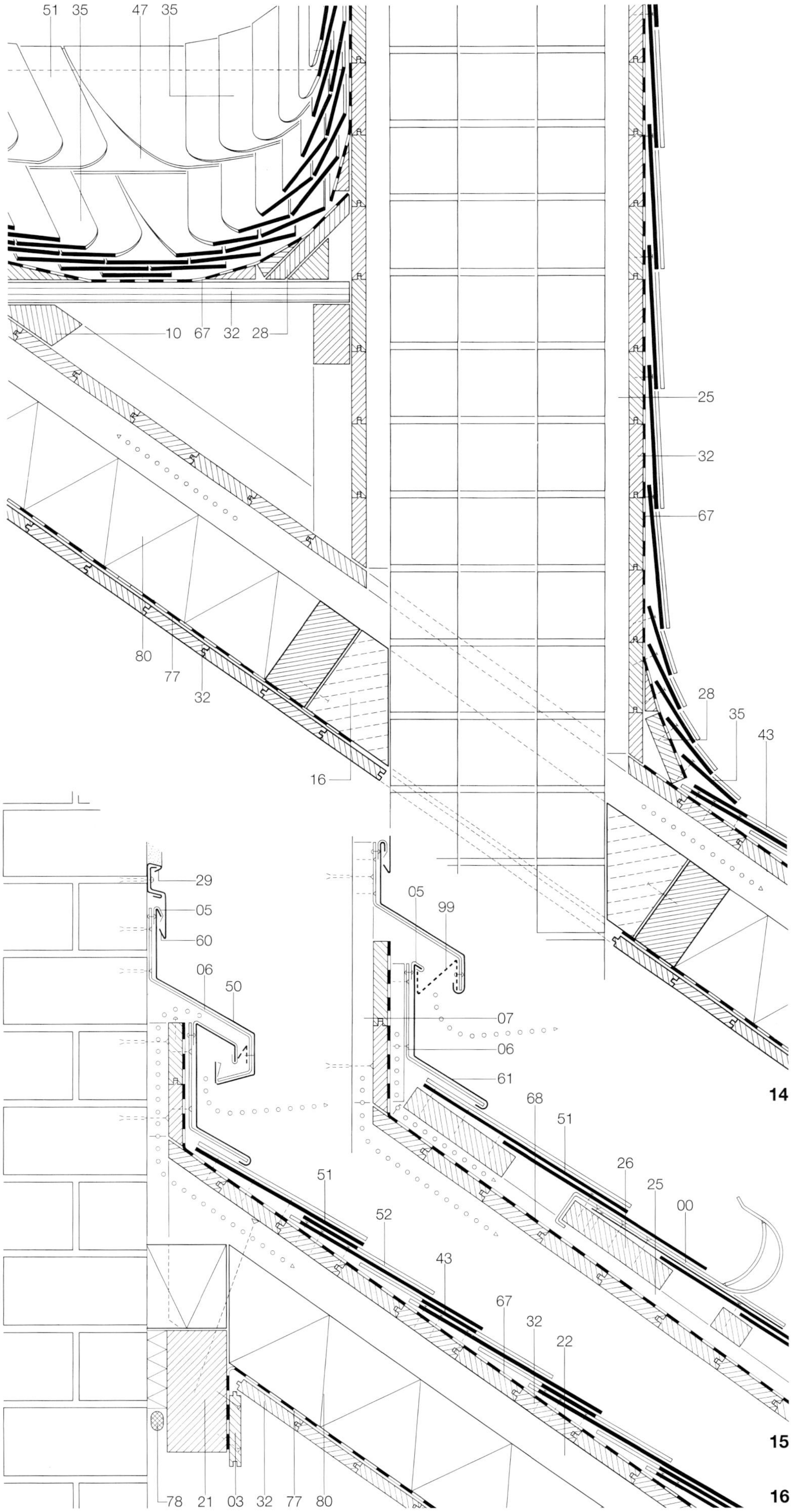

**Dormer window**

**17, 18** Gablet, junction with window and ventilation openings, single-lap non-horizontal slating

The pitch of the gablet roof surfaces should match that of the main roof surface. The two valleys are covered as left- and right-hand valleys using 7–9 slates each. Along the ridge

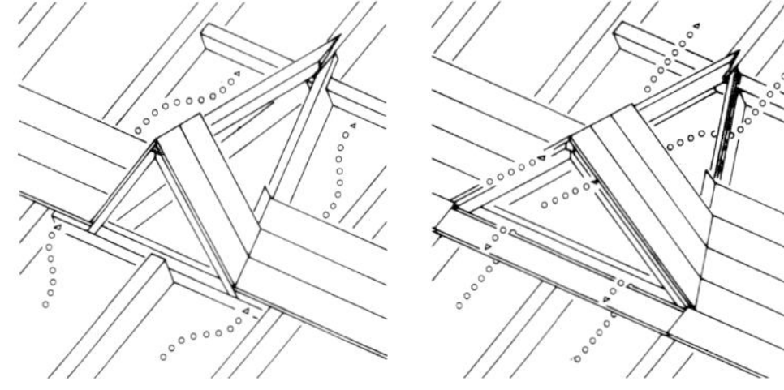

of the gablet the slates on the windward side project beyond those on the leeward side by 50–70 mm.

The supporting construction comprises sheathing on timber boarding. Trimmers, cross-members and struts frame the opening. Chamfered boards and a ridge purlin form the bearing for the dormer window boarding.
Air flows towards the roof surface in one level (see "Construction details – Wooden shakes and shingles – Dormer window").

**Change of slope**

**19** Mansard roof, rectangular double-lap slating

At the change of slope the lower roof surface ends with an overlapping top course – as at a ridge. The slates overlap according to the prevailing wind and are fixed with at least three nails. The upper roof surface starts on a feather-edge board – as at the eaves – with a course of shorter undereaves slates and the bottommost course of (whole) standard slates. The air layer of the lower roof surface is connected to the large void in the attic but separated from it by a mesh screen.

Details scale 1:10

00 Ladder hook
01 Anchor bolt
03 Vapour barrier
05 Clip, continuous clip
06 Fixing for flashing
07 Batten
10 Timber member
16 Concrete
17 Column
18 Wall plate
20 Frame
21 Purlin
22 Rafter
24 Trimmer
25 Spacer batten
26 Batten
27 Feather-edge board
28 Valley board
29 Stop bead
31 Strut
32 Tongue and groove boarding
35 Valley slate
43 Standard slate
47 Channel slate
49 Vent
50 Vent
51 Ridge slate
52 Top course slate
53 Eaves slate
54 Verge slate
60 Cover flashing
61 Apron flashing
63 Eaves flashing
67 Sheathing (laid with laps)
68 Sheathing/roofing felt (laid with laps)
77 Vapour barrier
78 Permanently elastic seal
80 Thermal insulation
93 Vent
99 Mesh screen

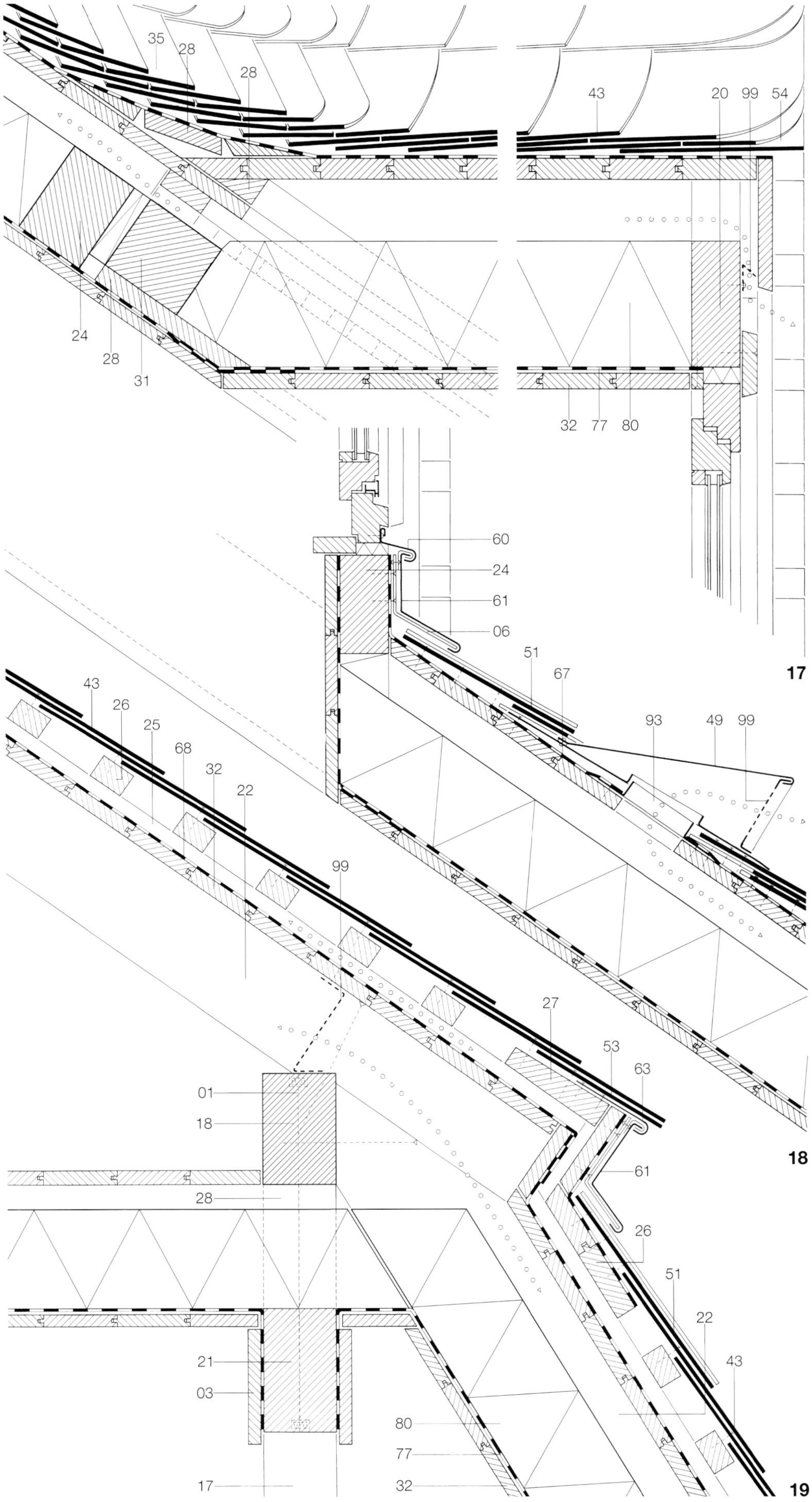

**Asphalt shingles**

Roof covering on sheathing and timber boarding, ventilated thermal insulation and vapour barrier

**Ridge**

**1** Ridge with ventilation hood and capping of asphalt shingles

**2** Ridge with vent and capping of asphalt shingles

The ridge capping is laid in the opposite direction to the prevailing wind. Pieces the width of one "tab" are used here and laid in a double-lap arrangement with laps ≥ 10 mm. The topmost course is a double-lap standard course but with the top edge of the shingles cut back to fit under the ridge.

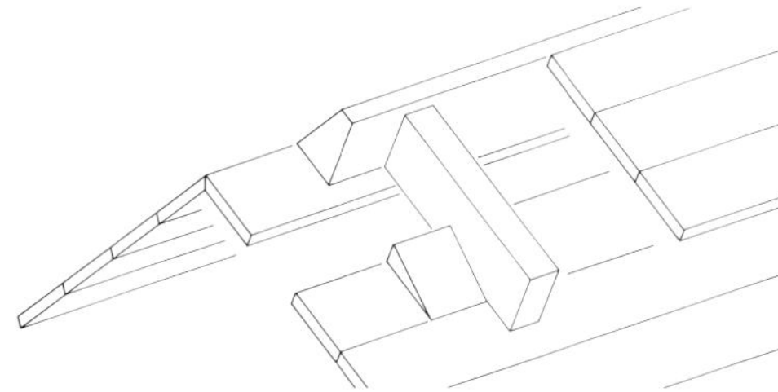

Ridge ventilation is possible on one or both sides. Vents on one side only should be positioned on the leeward side. They are simple to construct (see sketch) but cannot prevent the ingress of driving rain and snow. Any water that enters here should drain away safely on roofing felt that is open to diffusion.
A ventilation hood with openings on both sides must be designed to prevent driving rain and snow from entering. The air flow must be redirected more than once. The opening is protected from birds and small animals by a mesh screen.

**Hip**

**3** Hip with capping of asphalt shingles

Pieces the width of one tab are used on this type of hip, laid in a double-lap arrangement with laps ≥ 10 mm. Underneath, the asphalt shingles on the main roof surface are cut to suit at the hip parallel to it. The ventilation at the hip also runs parallel to it, past the spacer battens, which stop short of it, and is not affected by driving rain and snow. The air passage is determined by the possible spans of the boards forming the roof decking. It remains the same size as it passes through the bay between the rafters and is therefore large enough to ventilate only a limited number of bays.

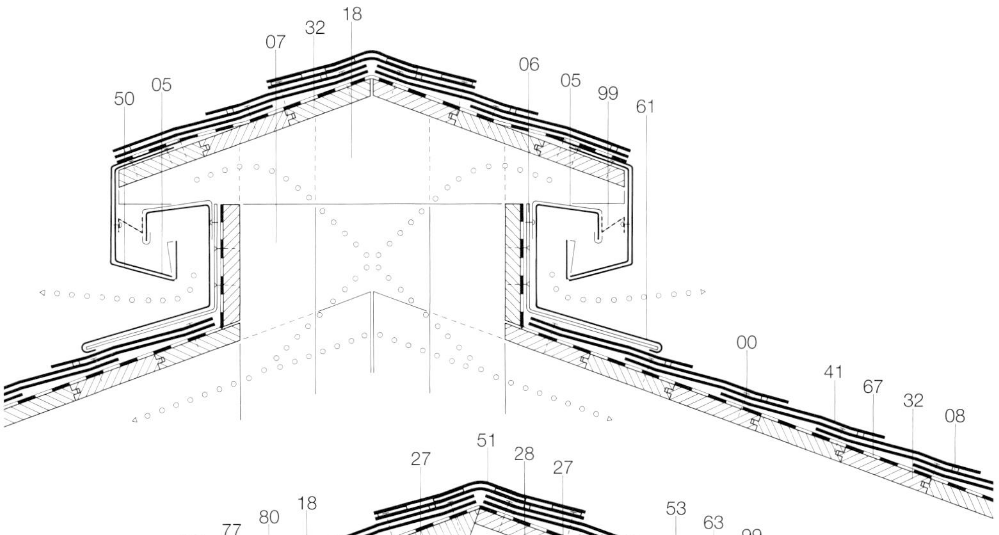

1

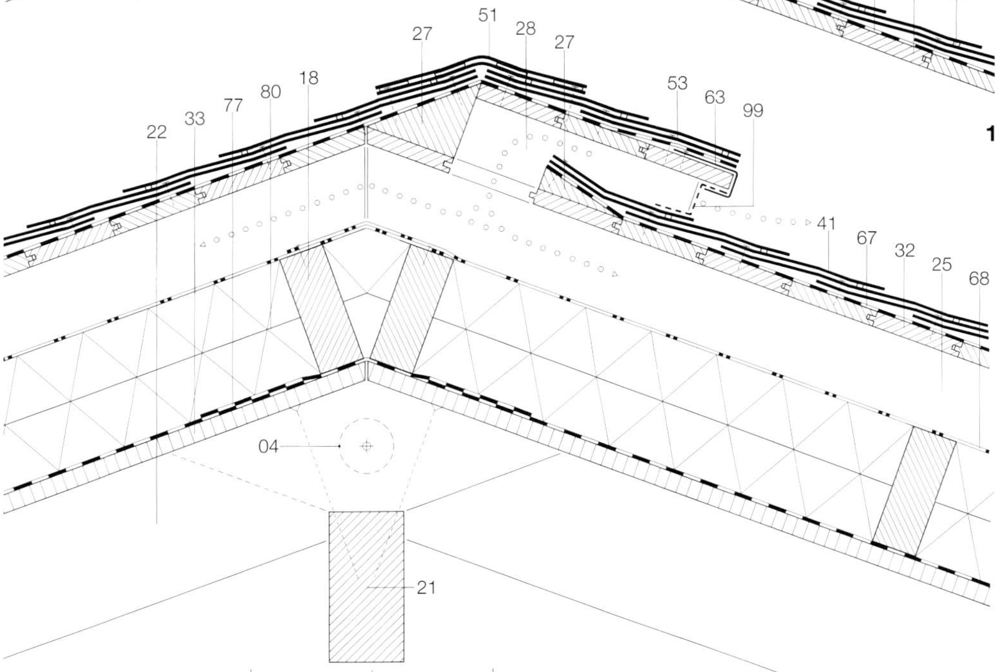

2

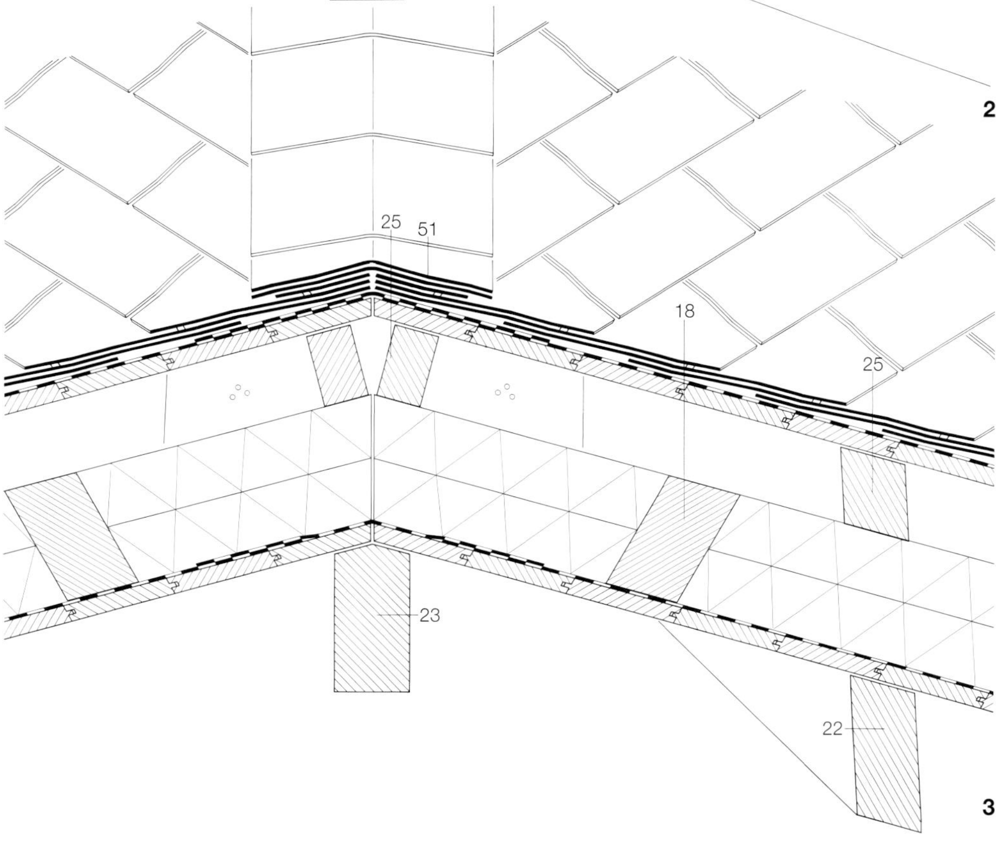

3

**Valley**

**4** Valley with underlay of asphalt shingles
**5** Laced valley with alternately overlapping asphalt shingles

Valleys adjacent to small roof surfaces with short valley rafters can be designed as "lined" valleys. They are made with pieces two tabs wide laid with triple laps to form a valley one tab wide. There should be no nails in the valley over a width of 300 mm. The courses on the roof surface overlap the valley courses at the sides by ≥ 120 mm. The pitch of the valley is ≥ 30°. Valleys on larger roofs with longer valley rafters need to be constructed as "semi-swept" and "laced" valleys employing standard asphalt shingles (see "Layers – Asphalt shingles"). This valley should also be without nails over a width of 300 mm. Here, the method of laying makes the laps greater. The pitch of the valley should match the recommended pitch. A valley board is required for a pitch ≥ 25°. Valleys are ventilated in a similar fashion to hips (see above).

**Eaves**

**6** Stepped eaves

Shingles at the eaves should stop ≥ 10 mm back from the edge. An eaves flashing is therefore necessary to form a drip edge. A shorter undereaves shingle is used, with the tabs of the first course of shingles bonded to it. This relatively stiff edge should not be bonded to the eaves flashing because the different thermal expansion of the two materials will deform the asphalt shingles. A feather-edge board adjusts the height.
The step in the roof levels – due to the omission of thermal insulation – is rainproofed with an apron flashing (100–150 mm according to pitch) and a long drip flashing. It can be secured against driving rain and snow only when the flow of air is redirected more than once. All sheet metal parts must be protected from bituminous corrosion. A mesh screen keeps out birds and small animals. The ends of the rafters (end grain) are protected from rain by timber capping pieces.

Details scale 1:10
00 Clout nail
04 Split-ring connector with bolt
05 Clip, continuous clip
06 Fixing for flashing
07 Timber post
08 Adhesive tape
18 Wall plate, hood support
21 Purlin
22 Rafter, jack rafter
23 Hip/valley rafter
25 Spacer batten
27 Triangular fillet
28 Vent side panel (timber)
29 Feather-edge board
32 Timber boarding
33 Laminated board
41 Asphalt shingle
50 Ventilation hood
51 Ridge/hip shingle
52 Top course shingle
53 Undereaves shingle
61 Apron flashing
63 Eaves/gutter flashing
67 Sheathing (laid with laps)
68 Roofing felt (laid with laps)
77 Vapour barrier, bonded or welded
80 Thermal insulation
95 Gutter
99 Mesh screen to ventilation opening

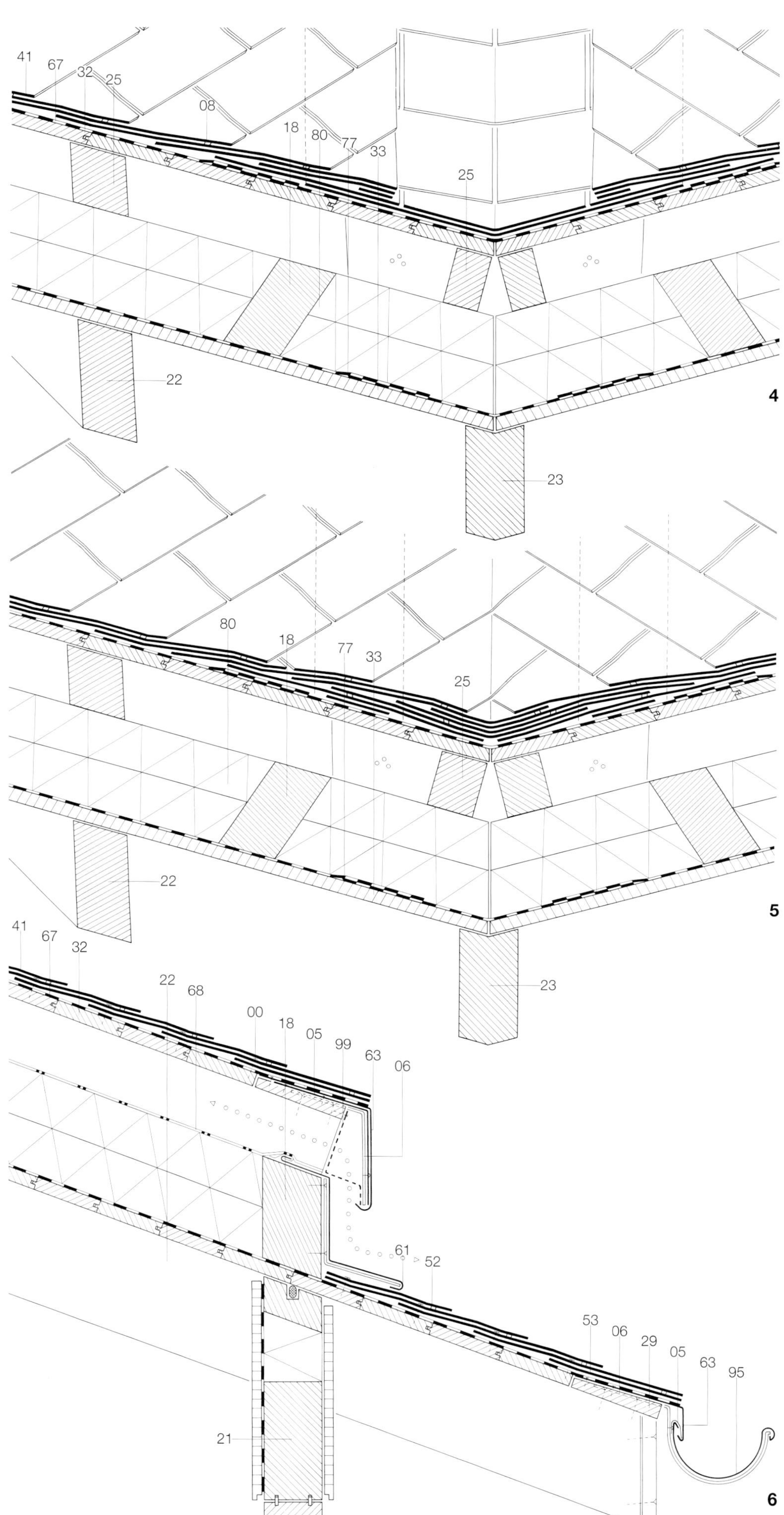

**Verge**
**7** Stepped verge with capping of asphalt shingles
**8** Verge with sheet metal flashing
**9** Verge with drip flashing and gutter

All verges are designed for water draining down the edge of the roof to be directed back onto the roof surface. The edge of the roof should therefore be raised by ≥ 30 mm.
A verge capping is made with pieces the width of one tab. These are laid with double laps ≥ 50 mm (depending on pitch). The verge capping is fixed to the top and side of the feather-edge board forming the edge of the roof and forms a drip edge with an overhang of ≥ 50 mm. The overlap with the shingles on the lower roof surface is also ≥ 50 mm. Both sheet metal and asphalt shingle cappings extend back down the feather-edge board as far as the roof surface.
Sheet metal with a turned-up edge tucked under the asphalt shingles (≥ 100 mm) raises the edge of the shingles and forms a shallow gutter. The shingles overlap the side of the sheet metal by ≥ 80 mm.
A small parapet relieves the shingles near the verge from increased wind suction loads. The edge of the sheet metal is held in place by continuous clips (height ≥ 50 mm) and additional clips (height ≥ 100 mm). Instead of continuous sheet metal, separate pieces (soakers) may be employed (see "Layers – Asphalt shingles – Laying"). To prevent the wind blowing into the roof construction (roof space), both the airtight membrane and the joints between the timber boards must be tightly sealed.

**Junction with wall at side of slope**
**10** Wall junction with shingles
**11** Wall junction with sheet metal gutter

A junction detail employing asphalt shingles requires the shingles to be turned up the wall 100–150 mm (depending on pitch) on a 45° triangular fillet. If roof and wall move differently because of deflection or settlement, the top end of the shingles should be attached to a separate board fixed to the roof construction.
A sheet metal gutter tucked under the shingles on the roof surface (≥ 100 mm) must have a turned-up edge, be overlapped by the shingles ≥ 80 mm and turned up the wall 100–150 mm (depending on pitch). Instead of continuous sheet metal, separate pieces (soakers) may be employed. These are tucked under the asphalt shingles ≥ 150 mm and are the most reliable type of junction (see "Layers – Asphalt shingles – Laying"). The joints between vapour barrier or airtight membrane and wall are sealed with a preformed plastic profile and can thus accommodate movement.

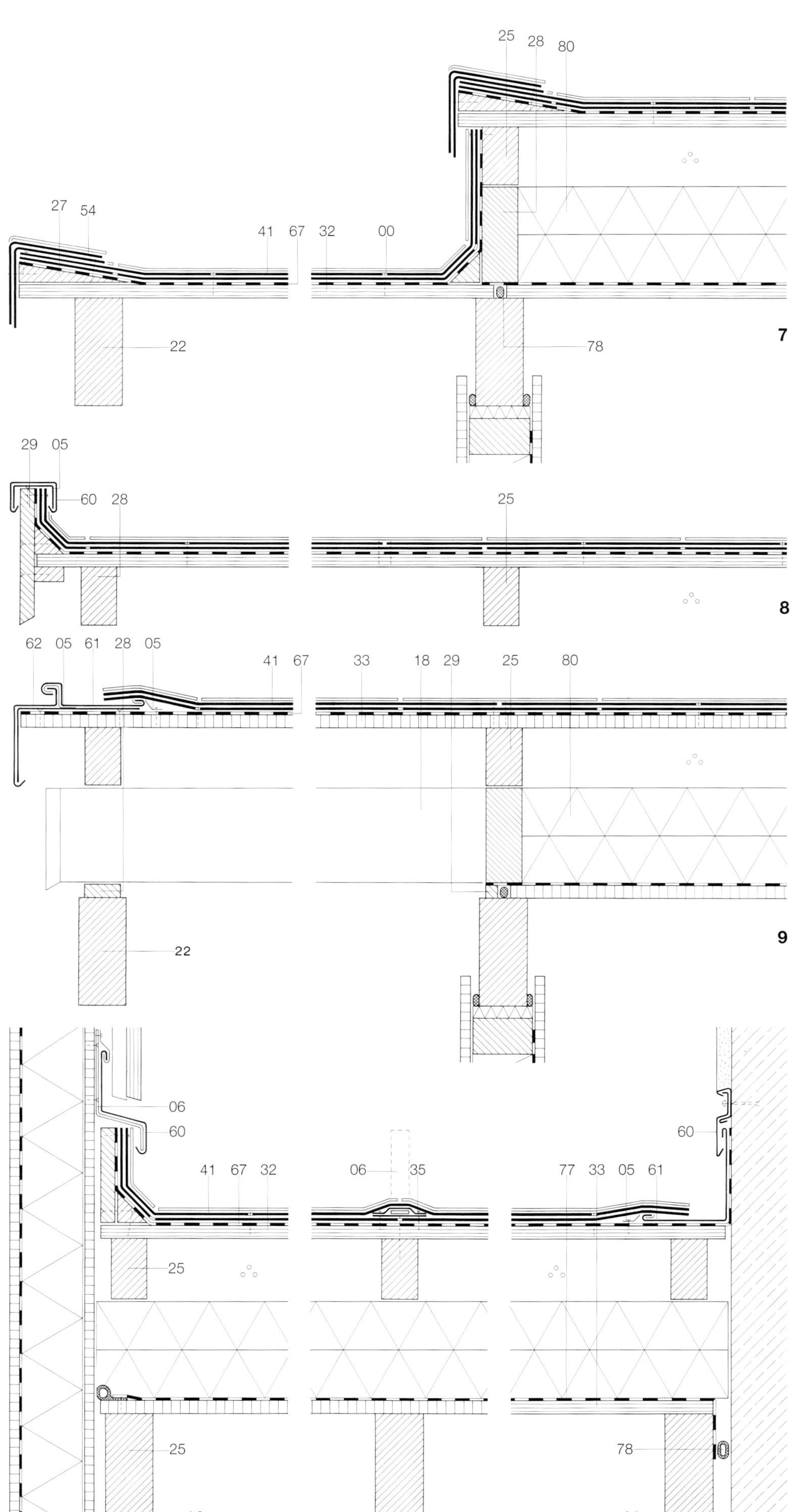

**Junction with wall at top of slope**

**12, 13** Wall junction with vent

A junction with a wall at the top of a roof slope must allow for ventilation and accommodate movement. A simple vent cannot prevent the ingress of driving rain and snow without an additional secondary waterproofing layer underneath the roof covering. This is unnecessary if the air flow is redirected more than once within the vent. A mesh screen keeps out birds and small animals. The sheathing and shingles are turned up the wall ≥ 150 mm on a board placed at an angle and fixed in place. The shortened top course of shingles may be replaced by a sheet metal apron flashing. Ladder hooks are incorporated into the double-lap roof covering as the shingles are laid, fixed securely and flashed with milled sheet lead.

**Penetrations**

**14** Chimney with support sleeve and collar

Small-diameter flues pass through the roof between two rafters and are held in place by cross-members. The flue support sleeve, partly above, partly below, is riveted/soldered or welded, and joined to a flange plate, which is incorporated into the asphalt shingle roof covering. The flange has a turned-up edge on three sides and the shingles overlap ≥ 100 mm at the sides, ≥ 50 mm at the top.
The flue support sleeve itself projects, together with the sheathing, ≥ 150 mm above the roof

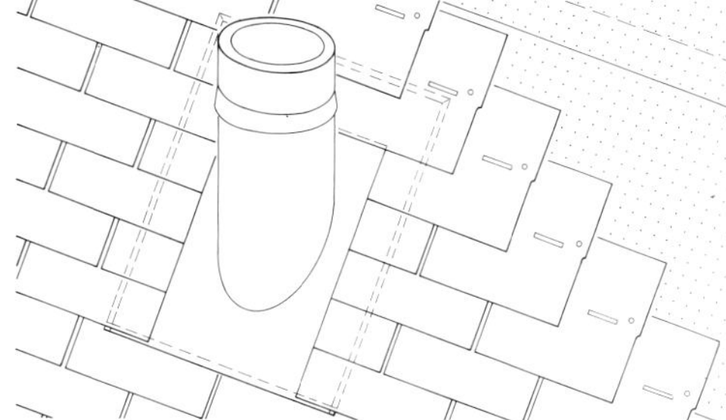

surface. This is flashed with a skirt that overlaps ≥ 50 mm, with a permanently elastic seal between skirt and flue (or welded). Flange plate and shingles should not be bonded together.

Details scale 1:10

00 Clout nail
03 Collar
04 Rivet and soft solder
05 Clip, continuous clip
06 Fixing for flashing, ladder hook
07 Steel angle
08 Adhesive tape
18 Timber member
22 Rafter
24 Cross-member
25 Spacer batten
27 Feather-edge board
28 Timber member, make-up piece
29 Bargeboard
32 Timber boarding
33 Laminated board
35 Milled sheet lead
41 Asphalt shingle
50 Ventilation hood
52 Top course shingle
53 Undereaves shingle
54 Verge shingle (capping)
59 Soaker
60 Sheet metal capping, skirt
61 Apron flashing
62 Verge flashing
67 Sheathing (laid with laps)
68 Roofing felt (laid with laps)
77 Vapour barrier
78 Permanently elastic seal
80 Thermal insulation
93 Flue
96 Flue support sleeve
99 Mesh screen

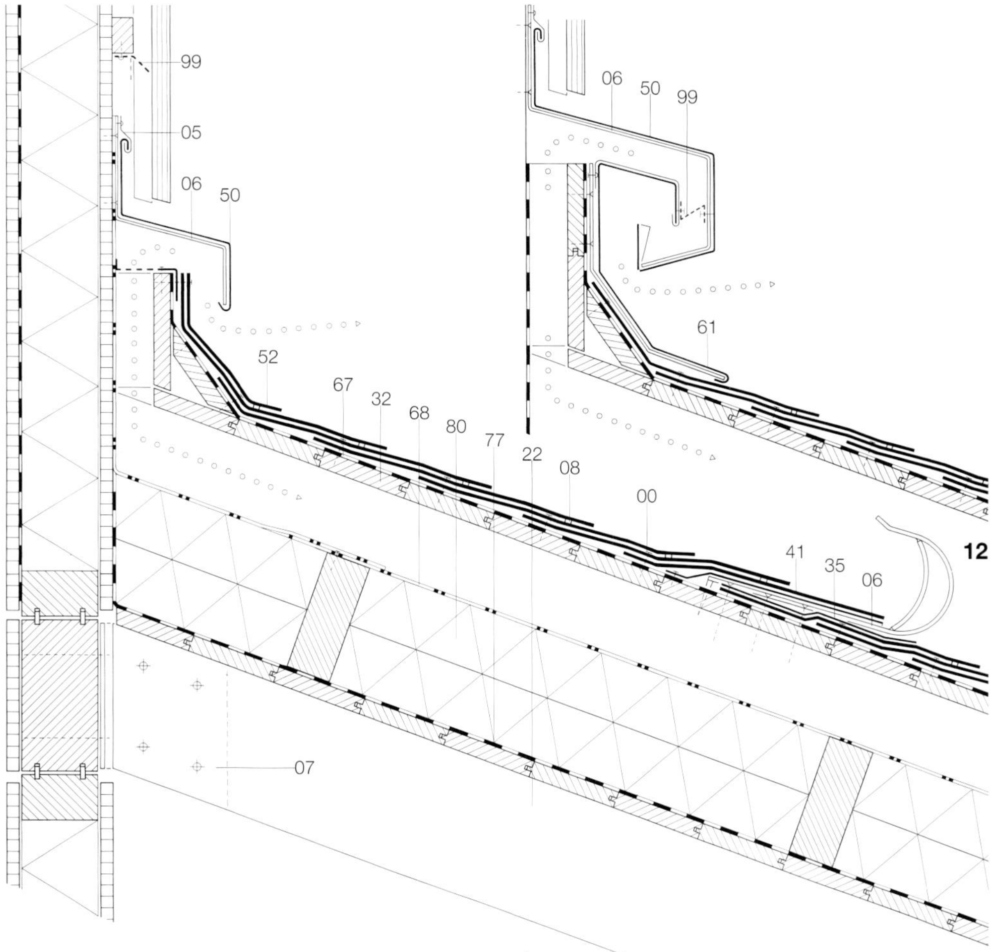

12

13

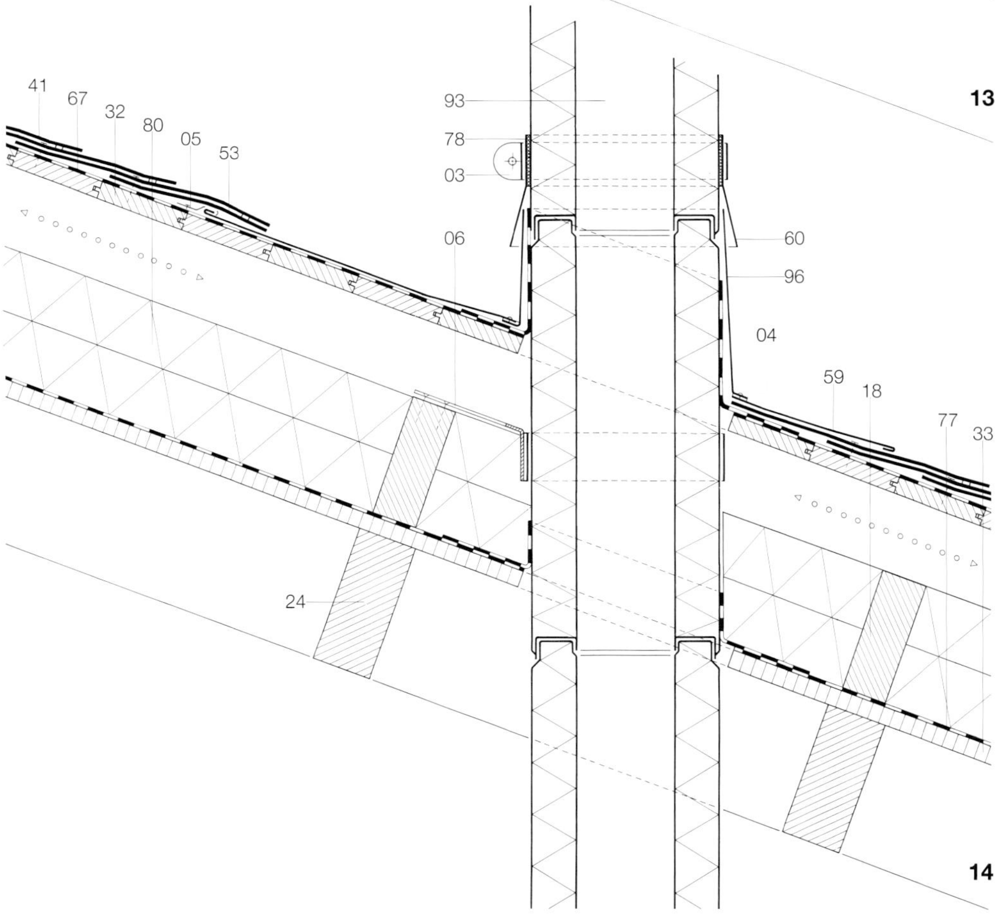

14

**Flat clay and concrete tiles**
Roof covering on secondary waterproofing/covering layer
Ventilated thermal insulation with vapour barrier
Double-lap tiling and crown tiling

**Ridge**
**1** Double-lap tiling with ventilating bullnose tile, duopitch roof with ridge capping bedded in mortar and secured with wire
**2** Double-lap tiling and ventilating component, duopitch roof with ridge capping bedded in mortar and secured with clips
**3** Crown tiling, duopitch roof with clipped ventilating ridge capping

This design principle can be employed for demanding situations. The secondary covering layer comprises loose overlapping bitumen or synthetic roofing felt. If a better-quality solution is chosen (e.g. built-up roofing felt), this layer can be improved to form a secondary waterproofing layer.

**1** The uppermost course of double-lap tiling must be laid as crown tiling because otherwise one part of the side joint remains uncovered. The ridge capping is bedded in mortar, which is pushed back to create a drip edge along the bottom of the ridge capping. This minimises the risks of freezing and long-term saturation. The ridge capping should be laid in the opposite direction to the prevailing wind. A ventilating bullnose tile provides the ventilation outlet (min. ventilation opening 0.5‰ of area of sloping surface); and as it is thicker than standard tiles, the top two tiling battens are deeper than the others. To ventilate the lower air layer, boarding, felt and battens must stop about 50 mm back from the apex.

**2** The topmost course is again laid as crown tiling but the bullnose tiles here are of different lengths. This ensures that the appearance of the double-lap tiling is not disturbed. If the purlins are to remain exposed internally, the vapour barrier must be connected to the purlins along their full length.

**3** This detail shows crown tiling combined with a clipped ventilating ridge capping. As all side joints are covered in crown tiling, the roof covering remains the same right up to the topmost course. The ventilating ridge capping is fixed to the counter battens via a ridge batten. This continuous vent along the ridge is the most effective form of ventilation because air can escape from the highest point of the roof – through the specially designed joints between the individual capping elements. As an alternative to an exposed roof structure, the ridge purlin is shown here behind a fire-retardant lining. The advantage of this is that the vapour barrier can easily be installed as a continuous layer.

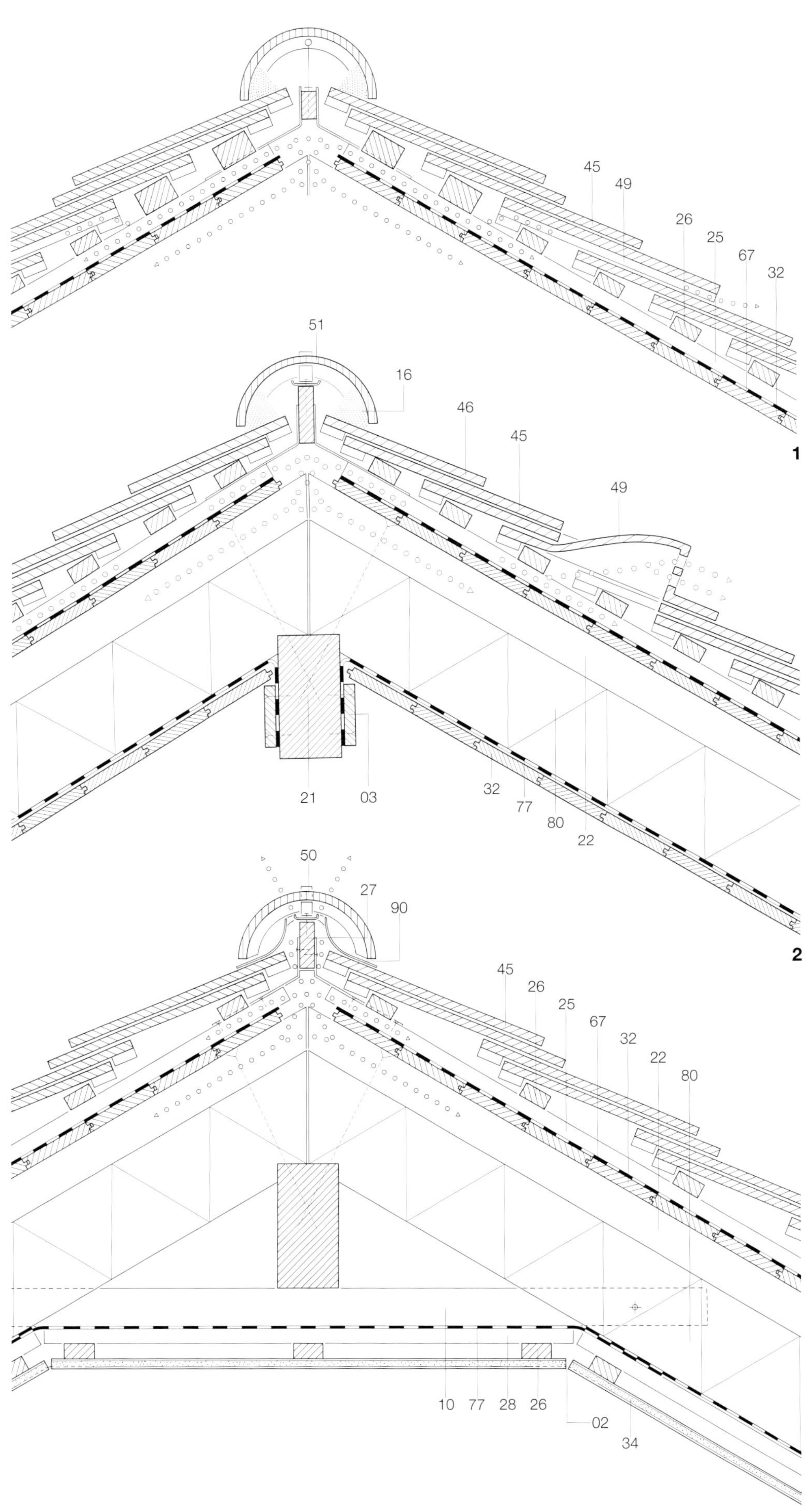

**Ridge to monopitch roof**

**4** Double-lap tiling, ridge to monopitch roof with small overhang and mono ridge tiles
**5** Crown tiling, ridge to monopitch roof with large overhang and sheet metal capping

**4** The mono ridge tiles are positioned as close as possible to the external wall but with sufficient clearance to allow proper ventilation of both air layers (min. ventilation opening 2‰ – preferably more – of area of sloping surface; see "Ventilation").
The mono ridge tiles secured against uplift are of two different lengths, thus maintaining the appearance of the double-lap tiling along the ridge as well. To protect the edge of the roof against wind uplift and protect the construction against driving rain and snow there is a sheet metal soffit to the overhang (instead of timber boarding). Another advantage is that it spreads the load for the cantilevering counter battens. To guarantee ventilation to the underside of the roof covering in this area as well, perforated metal strips are used instead of timber battens. The ladder hooks must be screwed through the counter battens or timber boarding into the rafters.

**5** The topmost course of a roof with crown tiling is also rainproof. The overlap of the sheet metal capping must be the same as the normal end lap between roof tiles. Sheet metal capping and apron flashing are held in place with fixings of flat metal attached to the fascia board and an additional, wider "ridge batten". However, it may be necessary to include a continuous ridge board with larger rafter spacings. The fixings for the step mounting must extend into the rafters. The ventilation outlet can be larger here than with a small overhang because it is well protected against rain. However, like all openings, it must be protected against birds and small animals with a mesh screen.

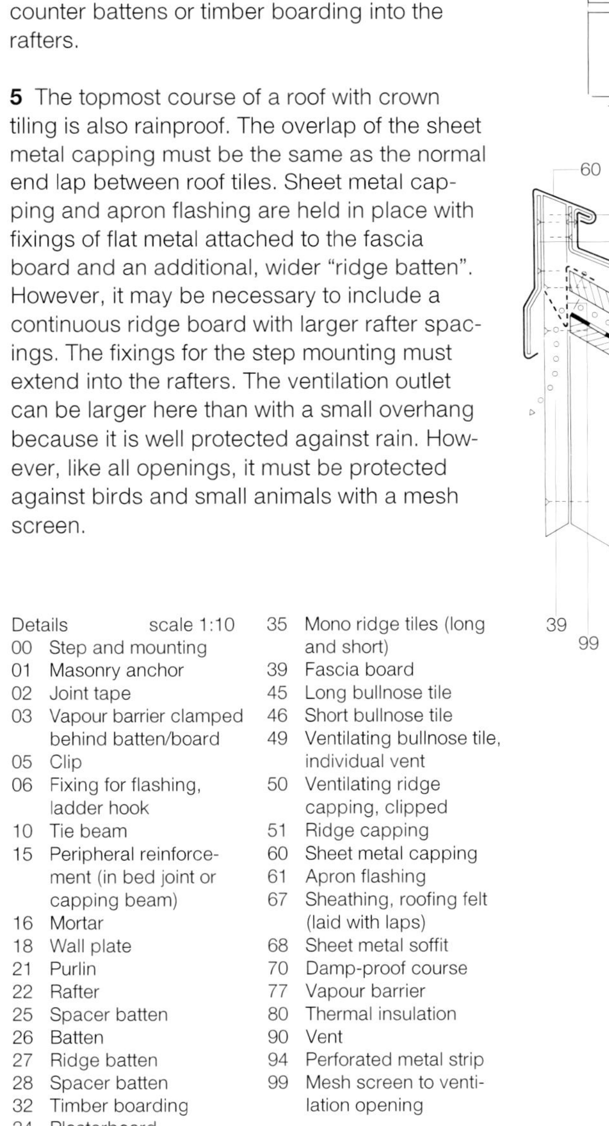

Details scale 1:10
00 Step and mounting
01 Masonry anchor
02 Joint tape
03 Vapour barrier clamped behind batten/board
05 Clip
06 Fixing for flashing, ladder hook
10 Tie beam
15 Peripheral reinforcement (in bed joint or capping beam)
16 Mortar
18 Wall plate
21 Purlin
22 Rafter
25 Spacer batten
26 Batten
27 Ridge batten
28 Spacer batten
32 Timber boarding
34 Plasterboard
35 Mono ridge tiles (long and short)
39 Fascia board
45 Long bullnose tile
46 Short bullnose tile
49 Ventilating bullnose tile, individual vent
50 Ventilating ridge capping, clipped
51 Ridge capping
60 Sheet metal capping
61 Apron flashing
67 Sheathing, roofing felt (laid with laps)
68 Sheet metal soffit
70 Damp-proof course
77 Vapour barrier
80 Thermal insulation
90 Vent
94 Perforated metal strip
99 Mesh screen to ventilation opening

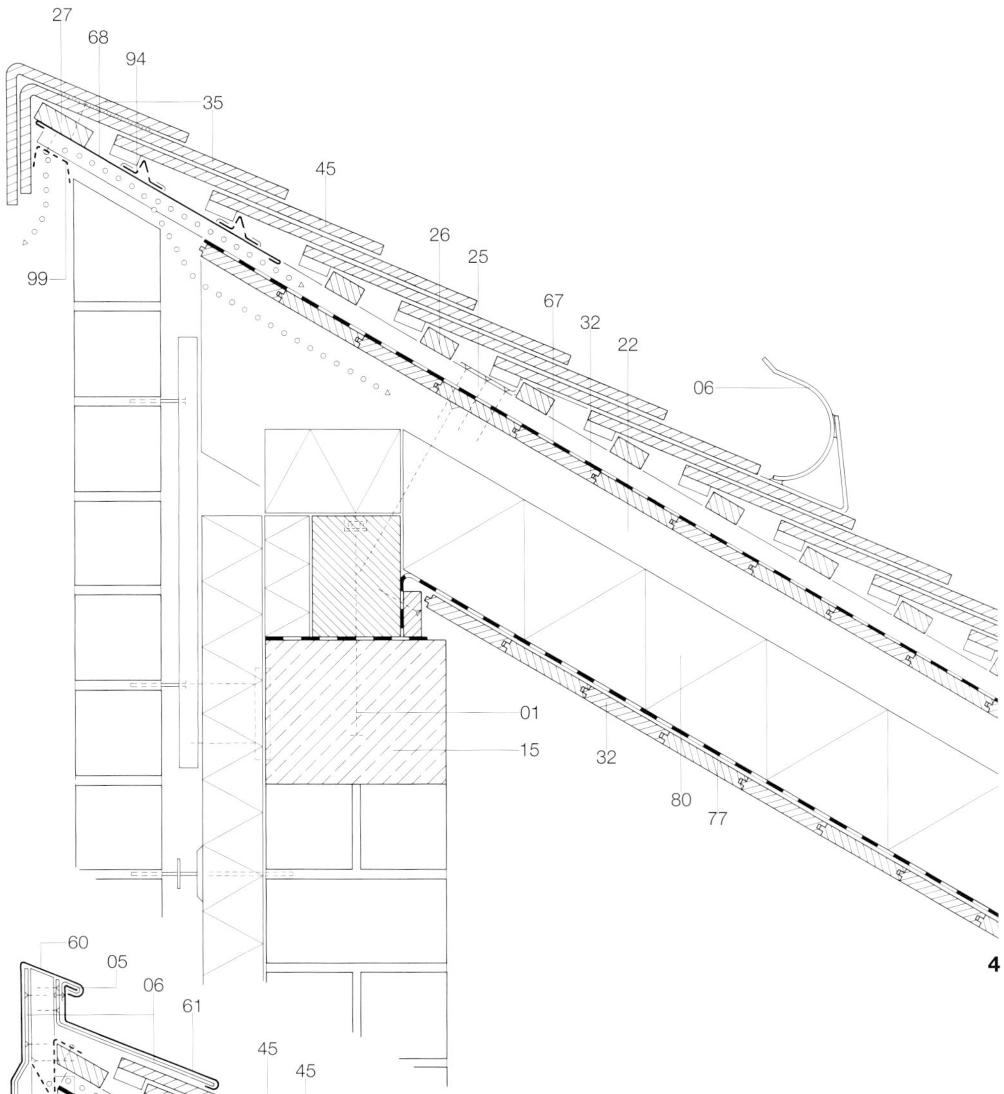

4

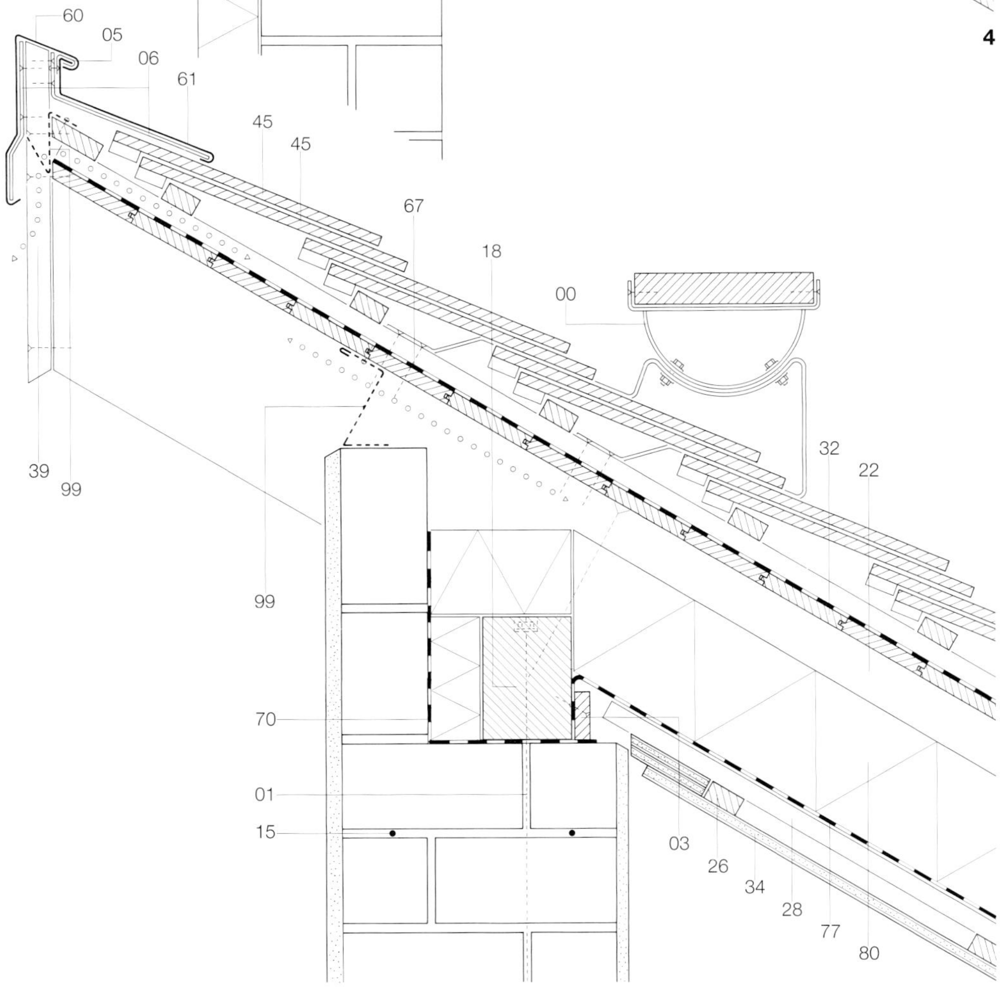

5

**Hip**

**6** Double-lap tiling, hip secured with clips
**7** Crown tiling, hip bedded in mortar

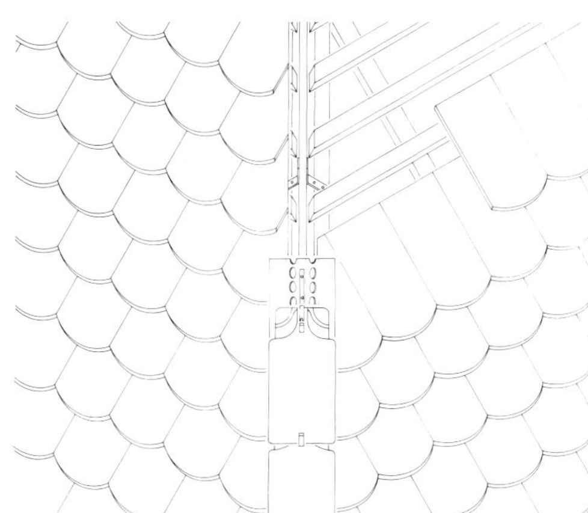

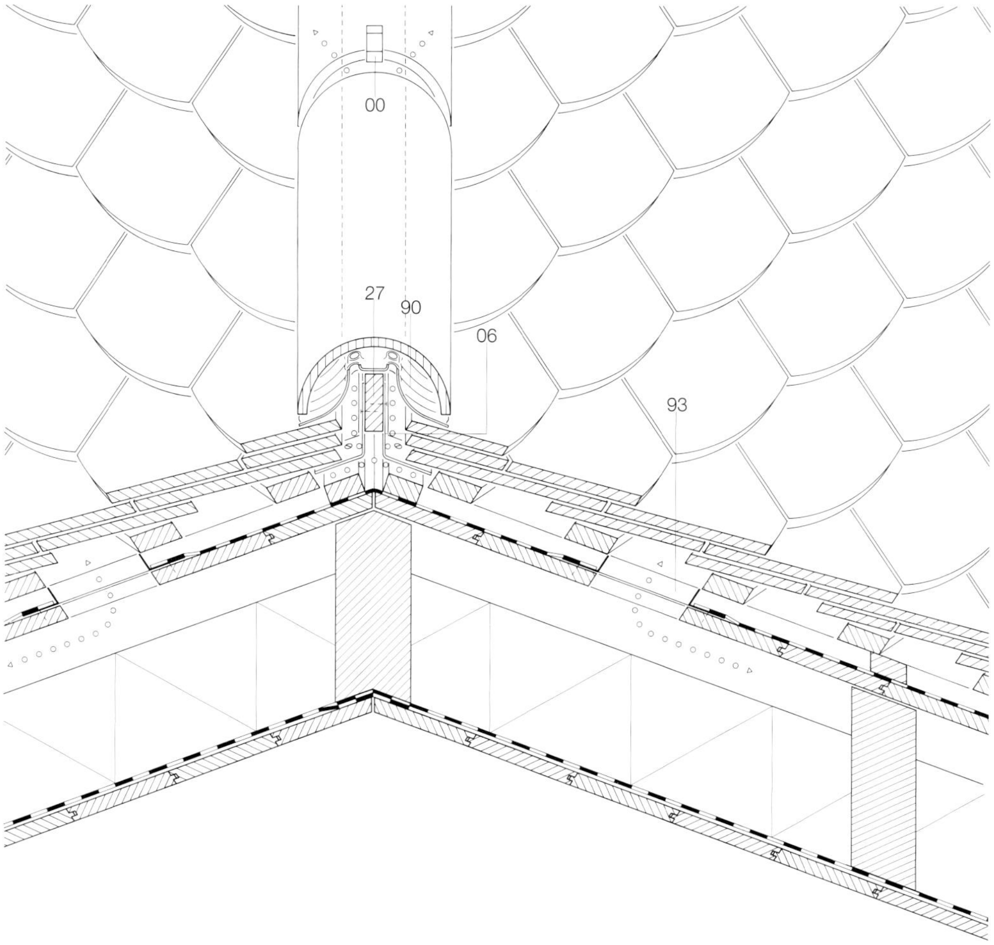

**6** The clay or concrete roof tiles adjacent to the hip must be cut to fit and additionally secured. The hip capping is laid over the ventilating/junction component and fixed to the hip batten with clips. Metal straps secure the hip batten to a pair of battens on the hip rafter. The secondary waterproofing/covering layer continues past the hip, so that the lower ventilation layer has to be connected to the upper layer via vents (for other options see "Ventilation").

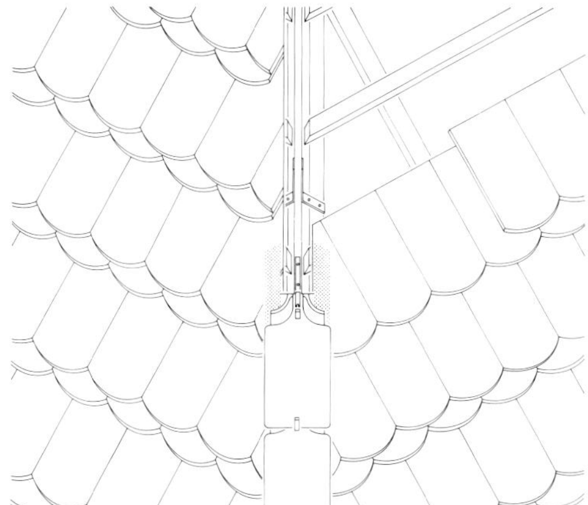

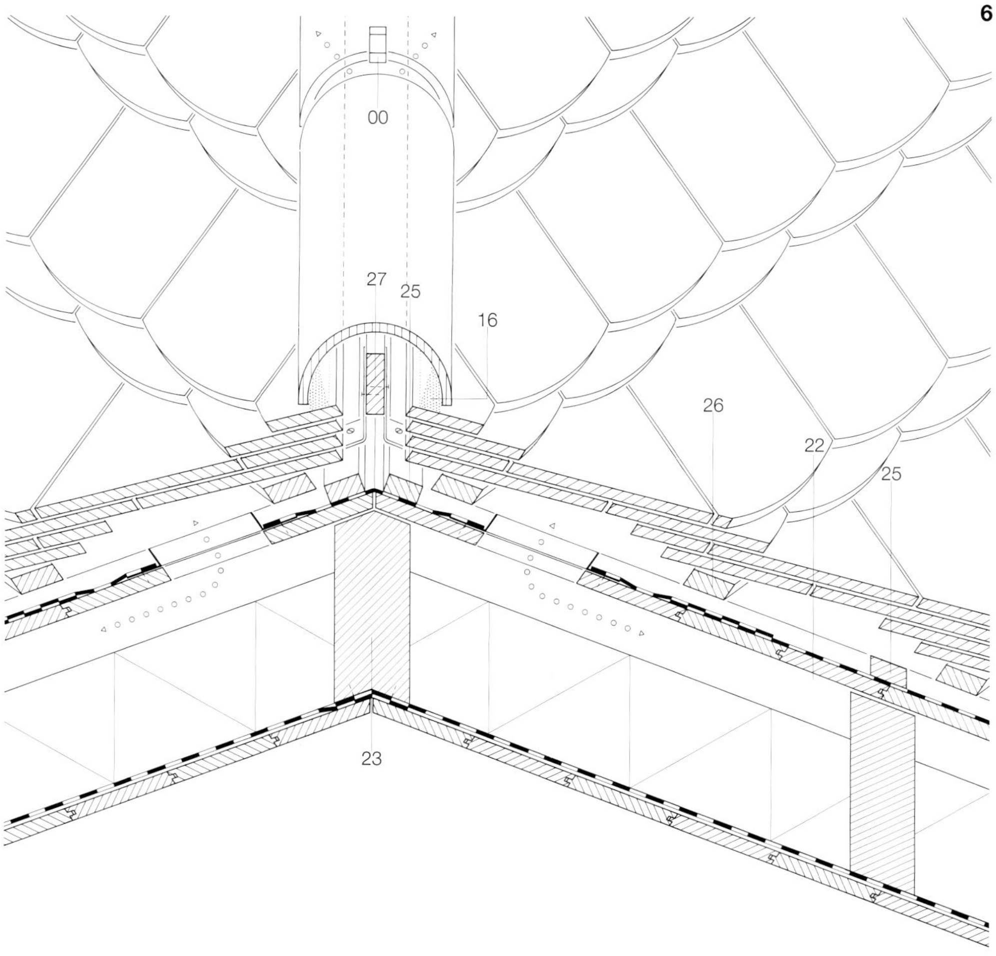

**7** When the hip capping is bedded in mortar – shown here on a roof with crown tiling – the capping is still fixed to the hip battens with clips as well. As at the ridge, the mortar must be pushed back behind the drip edge of the hip capping (saturation). The triangular gap at the side between roof covering and hip capping is somewhat larger with crown tiling than with double-lap tiling. A hip capping bedded in mortar is therefore preferable with crown tiling.

**Eaves**

**8** Double-lap tiling, eaves without overhang
**9** Crown tiling, eaves with overhang

**8** As at the ridge, double-lap tiling results in an uncovered side joint at the eaves; crown tiling is therefore used here. Additional fastenings (clips, wire, screws) to prevent wind uplift are necessary at the eaves. A tilting board higher than the battens is required to compensate for the thickness of three clay or concrete roof tiles and thus retain the standard roof pitch. The screw fixings for the snowguard extend below the roof covering and the counter battens to the rafters. The eaves detail must permit the entry of fresh air to both ventilation layers. Such openings are always protected by a mesh screen. Connecting the cavity of the external wall with the ventilation layer in the roof construction produces no problems.
The timber boarding is notched out to accommodate the gutter brackets, which are screwed to the rafters. Any water that collects on the secondary waterproofing layer drains into the gutter via a drip flashing. However, this means that the gutter has to be fitted at such a low level that water discharging from the roof covering during heavy rainfall can overshoot it. One solution is to use a wider gutter. At the eaves too, the vapour barrier must be securely joined to the enclosing elements of the interior – in this case a wall plate.

**9** Crown tiling can continue right down to the eaves course because the side joints of the tiles underneath are always covered. Here again, a tilting board higher than the battens ensures that the bottommost course has the same slope as the rest of the roof surface. The boarding continues the full extent of the overhang so that the roof covering cannot be lifted off by the wind.
The gutter brackets are screwed to the tilting board in this detail. Any water that collects on the secondary waterproofing layer drips off the flashing behind the gutter, but with such a large overhang it does not cause damage.

Details scale 1:10
00 Clip
01 Masonry anchor
03 Vapour barrier clamped behind batten
05 Clip
05 Clip, continuous clip
06 Hip batten fixing strap, gutter bracket
13 Facing brickwork
14 Brickwork
15 Peripheral reinforcement (in capping beam)
16 Mortar
18 Wall plate
22 Rafter, jack rafter
23 Hip rafter
25 Counter batten
26 Batten
27 Hip batten, tilting board
28 Spacer batten
29 Make-up piece
31 Strengthening rod
32 Timber boarding
34 Plasterboard
35 Drip flashing
45 Bullnose tile
63 Eaves/gutter flashing
67 Sheathing, roofing felt (laid with laps)
70 Damp-proof course
77 Vapour barrier
80 Thermal insulation
90 Ventilating element
93 Vent
95 Gutter
96 Rainwater downpipe
98 Snowguard and mounting
99 Mesh screen to ventilation opening

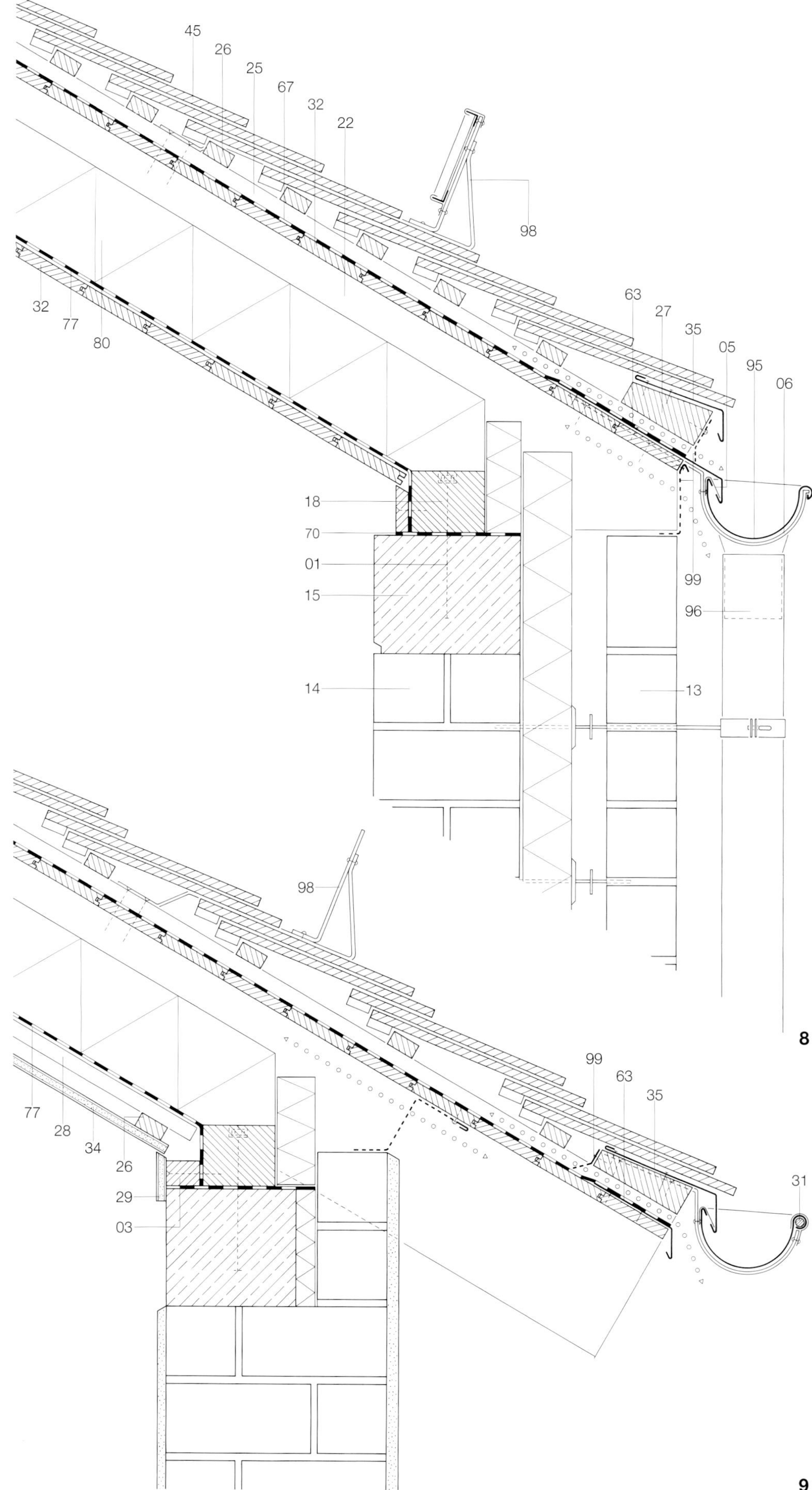

**Valley**
**10** Double-lap tiling, semi-swept valley
**11** Crown tiling, closed valley with soakers

**10** When the roof pitch is steep enough, a semi-swept valley is preferable because it can be covered with the same material as the roof surface. The clay or concrete roof tiles cut at the intersection of the roof surfaces require additional fixings. A valley board, on which the roof covering is laid, is incorporated to round off the valley. As there is no ventilation to the underside of the roof covering at this point, it is best to lay roofing felt – with a granule surface finish if possible – under the valley. The risks in this area are high and so the felt must be especially carefully laid, if possible with fully sealed (bonded) joints. The geometry of the valley allows the lower air layer to be ventilated only when it is connected to the upper layer via vents. The air flow in the upper ventilation layer is channelled along the valley board towards the ridge or the eaves (see sketch).

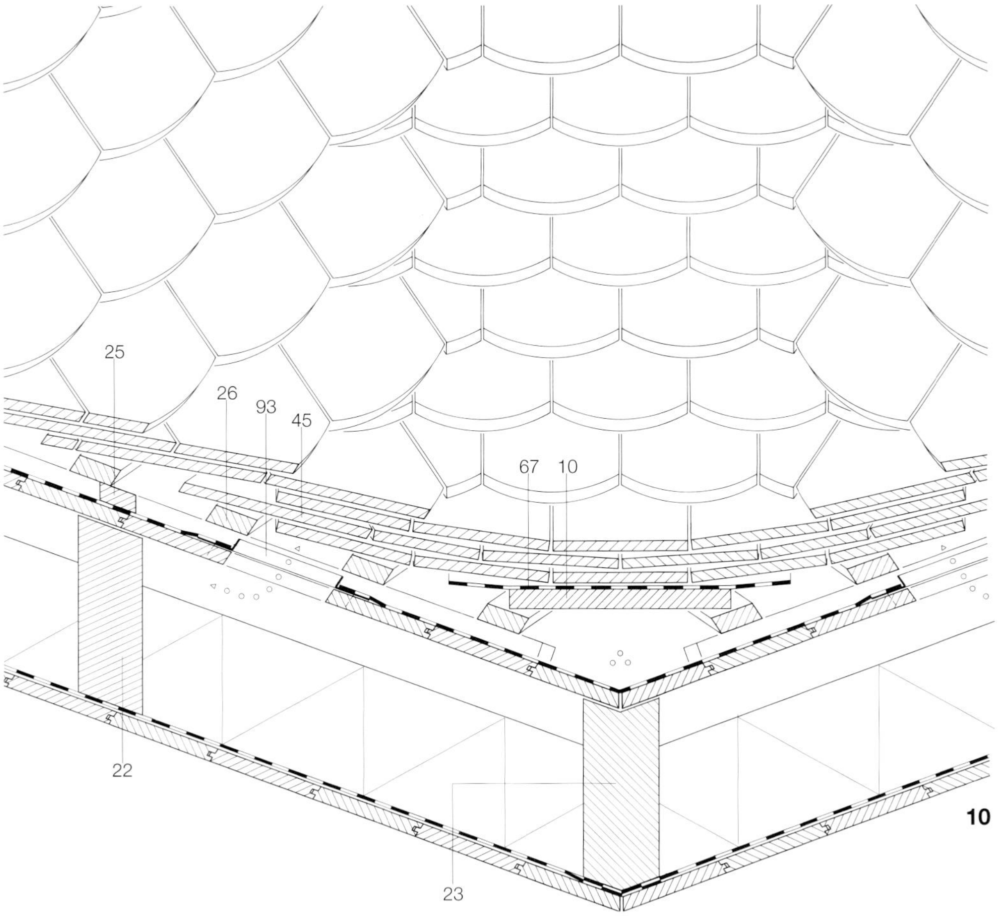

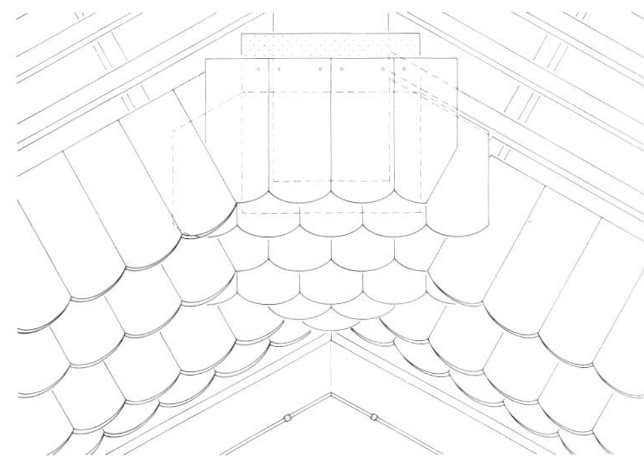

**11** In a closed valley with soakers the pieces of sheet metal overlap the courses of roof tiles. The tiles are cut at the intersection of the roof surfaces. This type of valley is very efficient; it can be used with flat overlapping elements for valleys with a pitch as shallow as 25°. Both types of valley are suitable for double-lap or crown tiling. The ventilation problems are the same in both cases (see also "Layers – Flat overlapping elements" and "Ventilation").

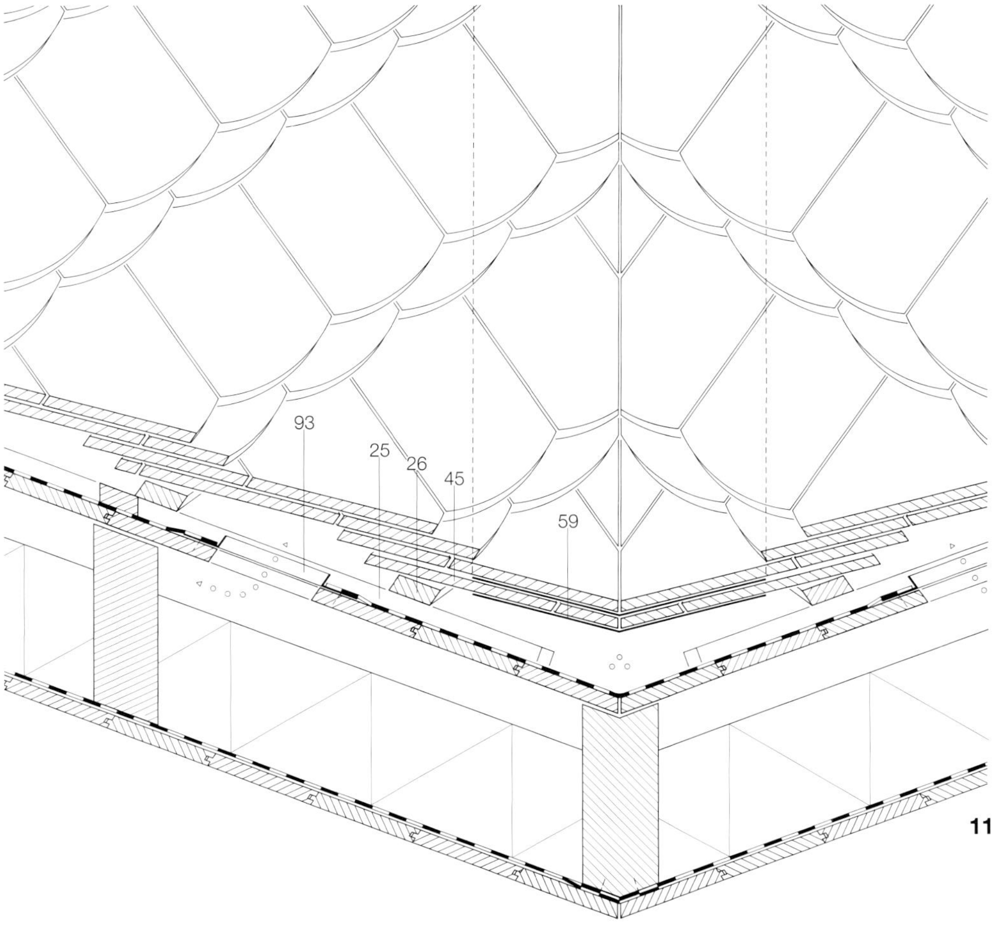

Details scale 1:10
01 Cast-in channel
05 Clip, continuous clip
06 Fixing for flashing
10 Valley board
15 Peripheral reinforcement (in bed joint)
18 Make-up batten
22 Rafter, jack rafter
23 Valley rafter
25 Spacer batten
26 Batten
28 Spacer batten
29 Bargeboard
32 Timber boarding
34 Plasterboard
45 Bullnose tiles, some cut
46 Bullnose half tile
54 Cloaked verge tile
59 Soaker
62 Verge flashing
67 Sheathing, roofing felt (laid with laps)
70 Damp-proof course
77 Vapour barrier
78 Permanently elastic seal
80 Thermal insulation
93 Vent
95 Gutter

10

11

**Verge**

**12** Verge without overhang, with cloaked verge tiles
**13** Verge without overhang, with gutter
**14** Verge with overhang

**12** The advantage of the verge detail with cloaked verge tiles is the homogeneous appearance of the roof covering. The small overhang does not afford much protection to the external wall, however, but allows water on the surface of the roof to be blown over the verge. Additional fastenings are necessary to secure the cloaked verge tiles against uplift. The battens cantilever beyond their support on the capping beam on top of the loadbearing wall and over the external leaf, where they can accommodate some movement.

Ventilation via the verge is possible but not absolutely necessary. Connecting the cavity of the external wall to the roof ventilation layer(s) produces no problems. As with all edges of the roof, the vapour barrier must be carefully connected to the inside wall.

**13** The verge detail with a gutter, together with the small cross-fall in the roof covering, ensures that no surface water is blown over the verge. The deeper gutter provides extra security. The flashing along the edge is a two-part construction screwed to the gutter board and stiffened with a continuous clip.

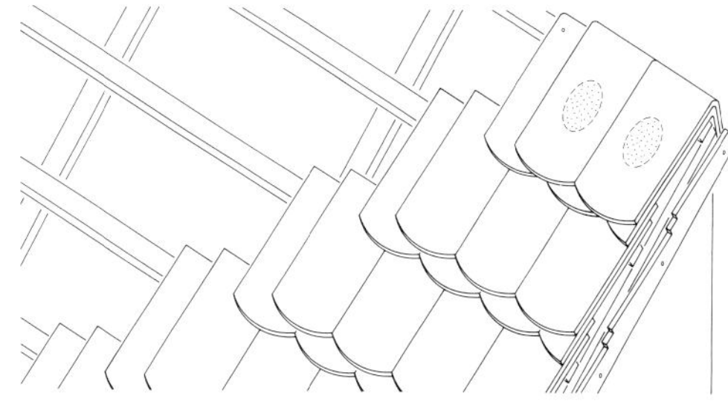

**14** The cantilevering roof surface protects the external wall better. The raised edge ensures that surface water is directed back onto the roof. The verge tiles, some of which are half tiles, require additional fastenings (screws; clips and wire with analysis). Soffit boards – or battens at least – are required underneath to prevent the roof covering lifting off.

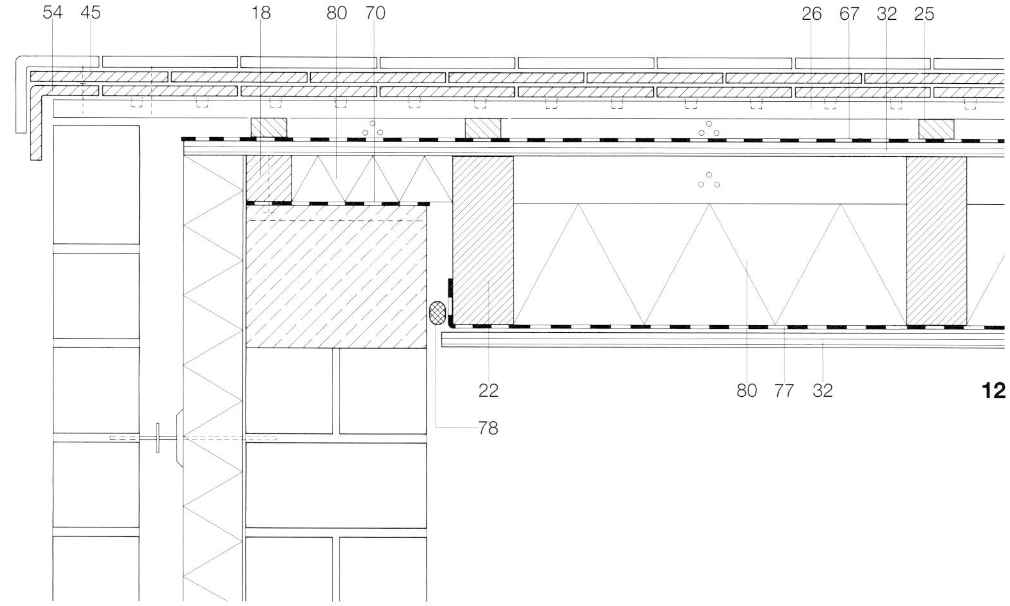

12

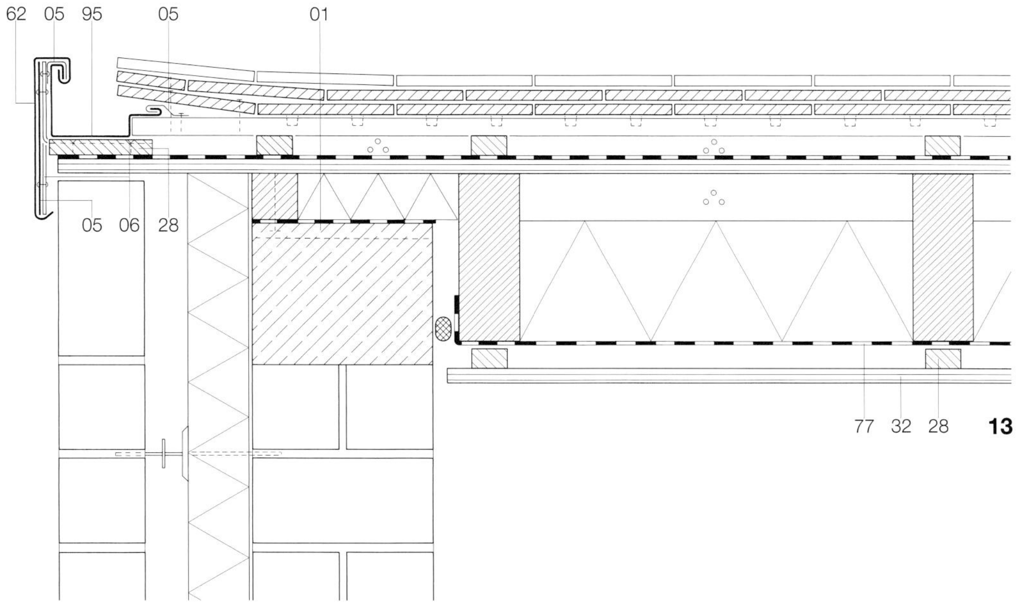

13

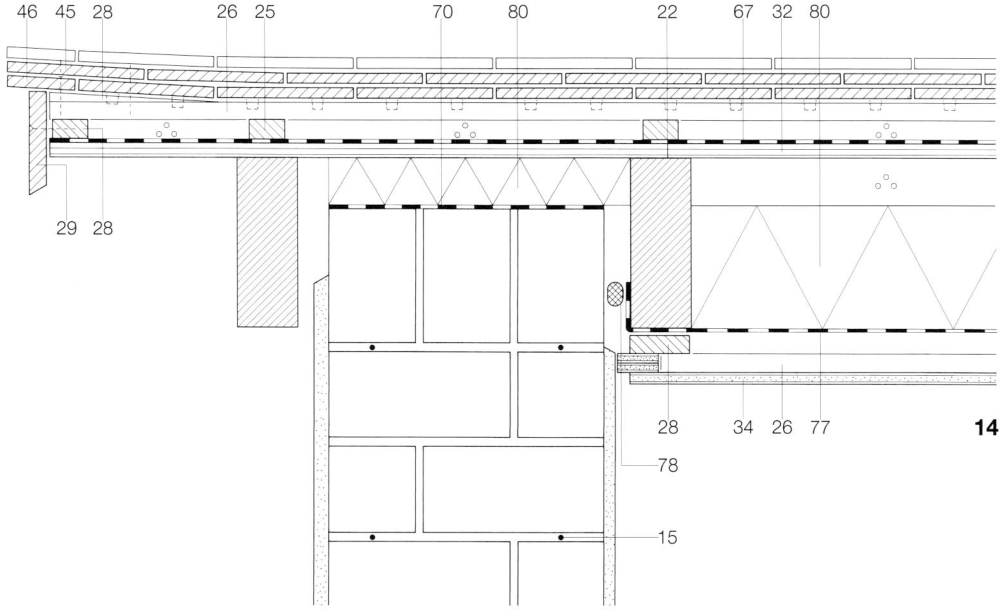

14

**Junction with wall**

**15** Junction with wall at side of slope, with deeper gutter
**16** Junction with wall at side of slope, with soakers
**17** Junction with wall at side of slope, with flat gutter

**15** A deeper gutter is better for situations where movement between the roof structure and the adjoining wall must be accommodated. The tiles (standard and half tiles) at the edge of the gutter are laid on the turned-up edge of the sheet metal and so create a slight cross-fall in the roof covering, which helps to keep rain-water away from the wall. The joint between gutter and wall – facing brickwork in this example – is covered by a stepped flashing let into the bed joints. The roofing felt is turned up the wall to the full height of the gutter (approx. 150 mm above roof surface).

As with all edges of the roof, the vapour barrier must be carefully joined to the wall.

**16** One tried-and-tested method is to use soakers for this detail. The bent pieces of sheet metal are integrated into the roof covering like overlapping elements. The joint between the soakers and the wall is the same as described above.

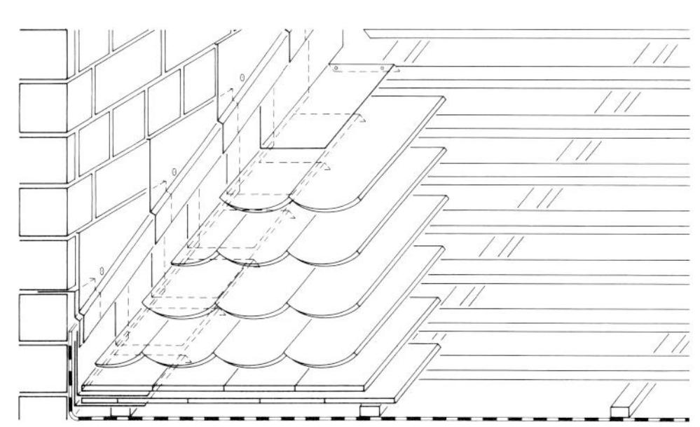

**17** In this detail the gutter is laid on the tiling battens. As with the deeper gutter, the tiles alongside the gutter are laid on the turned-up edge of the sheet metal and so create a slight cross-fall in the roof covering. Here, the gutter is connected to the wall via a wall gutter fixing which, as part of the roof construction, guarantees independent movement of roof and wall. The joint at the wall is protected by a drip flashing in conjunction with a stop bead. This detail can also incorporate ventilation below the gutter.

Details scale 1:10
03 Vapour barrier clamped behind board
05 Clip
06 Fixing for flashing
07 Batten
13 Facing brickwork
14 Brickwork
21 Purlin
22 Rafter
25 Spacer batten
26 Batten
27 Tilting board
28 Triangular fillet
29 Stop bead
32 Timber boarding
35 Stepped flashing
45 Bullnose tile

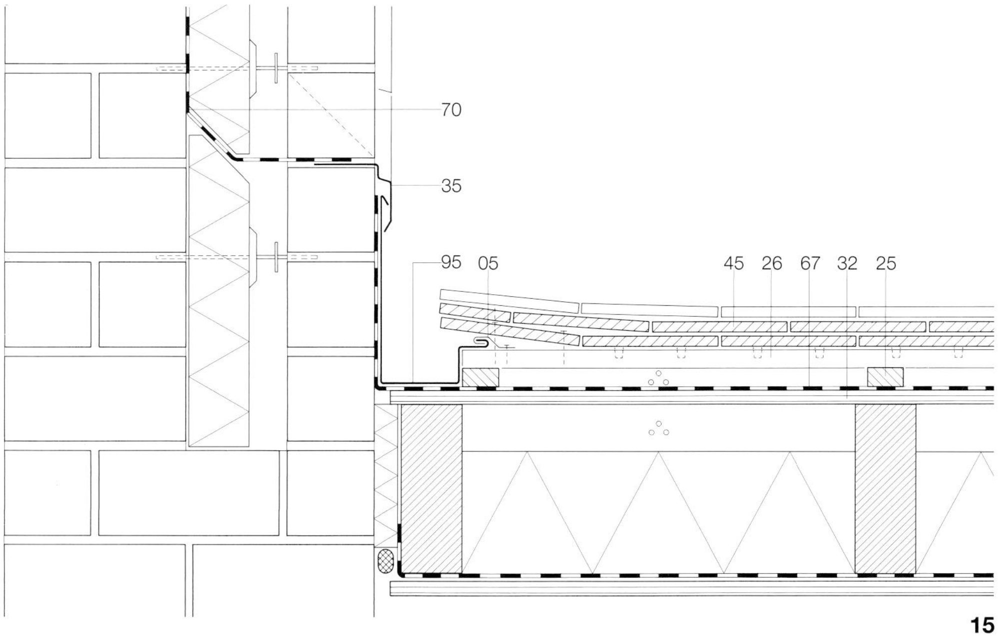

70 35 95 05 45 26 67 32 25

15

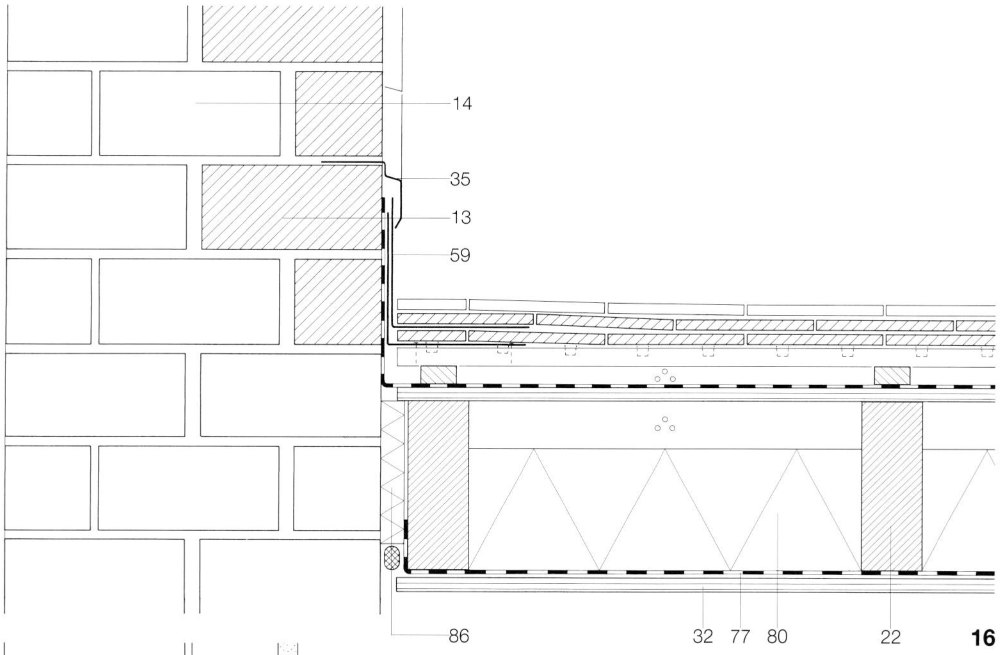

14 35 13 59 86 32 77 80 22

16

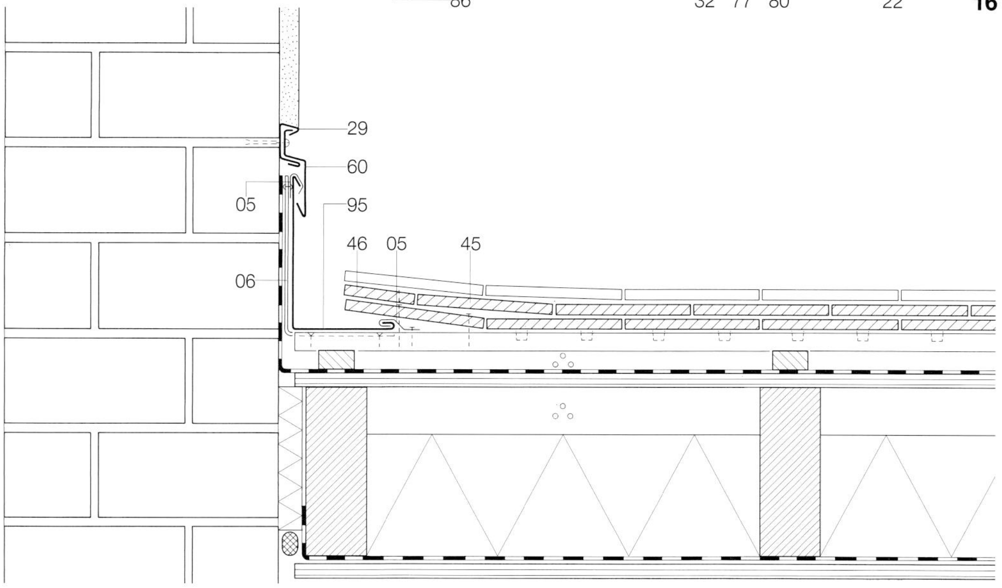

29 60 05 95 46 05 45 06

17

**Junction with wall**

**18** Junction with wall at bottom of slope, ventilated back gutter
**19** Junction with wall at top of slope, with secure vent
**20** Junction with wall at top of slope, with simple vent

**18** The junction with a wall at the bottom of a slope is the part of the roof most at risk. If it is unavoidable, the following measures are recommended:

- a wide enough back gutter (min. 200 mm)
- extending gutter components up the wall and up the roof, and including permanently elastic seals between gutter and flashings
- providing an emergency overflow when the back gutter is near the edge of the roof
- gutter heating to avoid ice forming if the ventilation fails
- secondary waterproofing layer instead of a secondary covering layer (two layers of bitumen roofing felt or one layer of built-up roofing felt) extending up the wall and up the roof higher than the gutter.

Both ventilation layers pass below the gutter and up the wall. The ventilation opening is secured against driving rain and snow by redirecting the air flow in accordance with the standard. The capping strip over the joint at the wall is let into the bed joints of the masonry. Sometimes a non-ventilated design is preferred above the connection with the wall. The vapour barrier must be especially carefully connected.

**19** The apron flashing must be turned up the wall at least 100 mm and ventilated. Here, the upper air layer is ventilated via a ventilating bullnose tile and the lower layer via a secure vent at the wall. The sheet metal flashing on the roofing provides additional protection from snow or rain driven through the ventilating tile or beneath the apron flashing. Moisture drains onto the secondary waterproofing layer.

**20** A simple vent can be provided instead, but is not completely secure against driving rain and snow. The secondary waterproofing layer is turned up the wall and pressed against the timber boarding by the mesh screen protecting the ventilation opening.

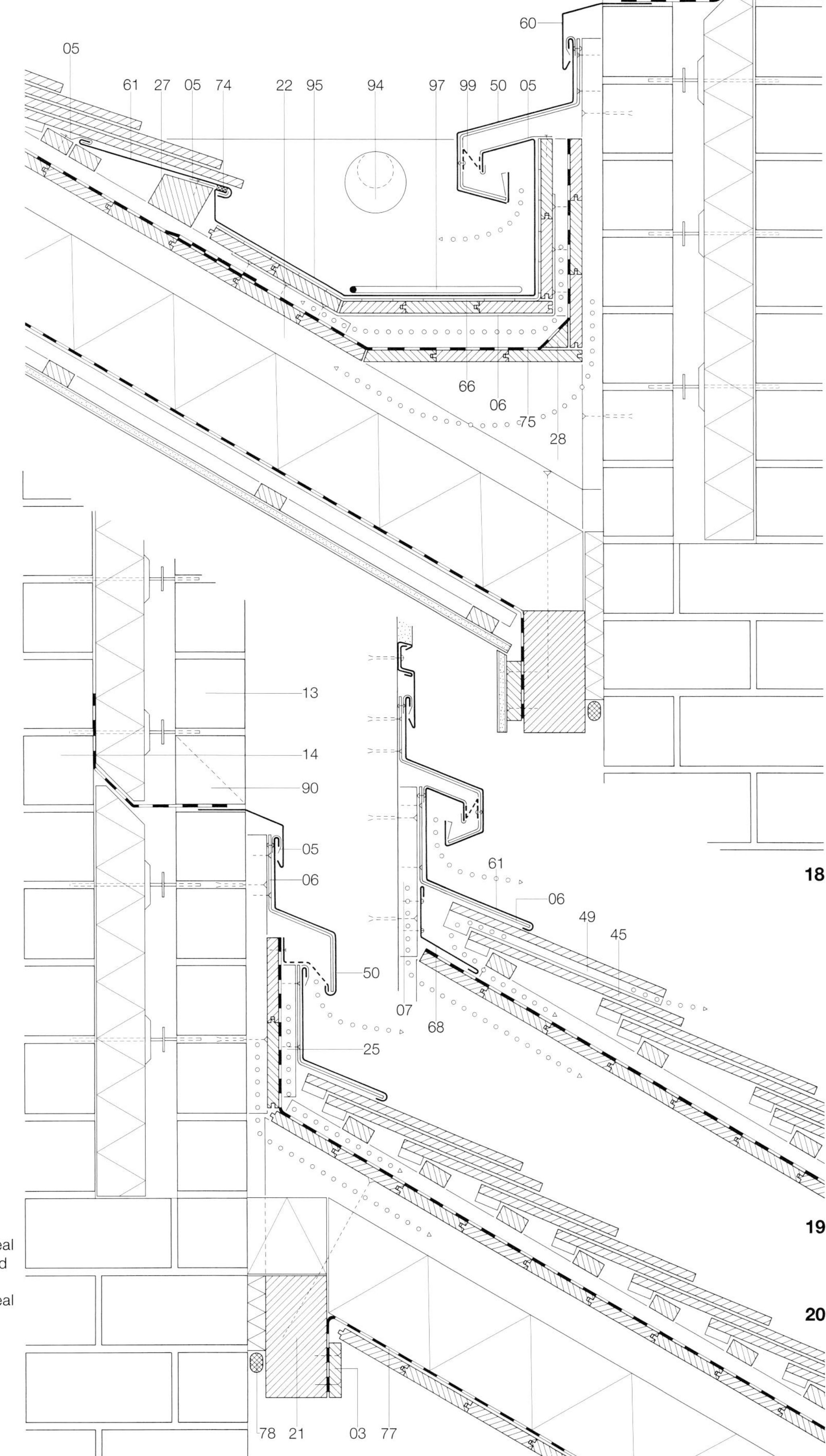


Details scale 1:10
46 Bullnose half tile
49 Bullnose ventilating tile
50 Ventilation hood
59 Soaker
60 Cover flashing
61 Apron flashing
66 Separating layer
67 Sheathing, roofing felt
68 Apron flashing
70 Damp-proof course and cavity tray
74 Permanently elastic seal
75 Waterproofing, bonded
77 Vapour barrier
78 Permanently elastic seal
80 Thermal insulation
90 Weephole
94 Overflow
95 Gutter
97 Gutter heating
99 Mesh screen

**Penetrations, openings**
**21** Double-lap tiling, chimney with soakers
**22** Double-lap tiling, roof window

**21** Penetrations unite all the problems of the junction with wall at top, bottom and side of a slope. However, the junctions are of limited width and do not have to satisfy any ventilation requirements. The course above the chimney is laid as at the eaves (on a double batten in this example). On the ridge side the roof is finished with a flashing acting as a back gutter, which is turned up the chimney stack (min. 200 mm above roof surface). This flashing should also extend up beneath the roof covering to the same height. To achieve better water run-off, it has a raised "saddle" in the middle. At the sides the joint is formed by a stepped flashing (soakers) let into the bed joints of the masonry. On the eaves side of the chimney the apron flashing is welted to the projecting side flashings (soakers) and pressed down onto the roof covering with a minimum overlap. The flashings turned up the chimney stack are protected with capping strips let into the bed joints of the masonry. The roofing felt is turned up the chimney stack to the same height as the sheet metal flashings, fastened in place and pressed against the chimney by the flashings. On the ridge side of the chimney a channel is formed with welded roofing felt or metal foil so that any moisture beneath the roof covering drains to either side of the chimney.

Instead of the soakers at the side, it is also possible to incorporate a gutter (see sketch).

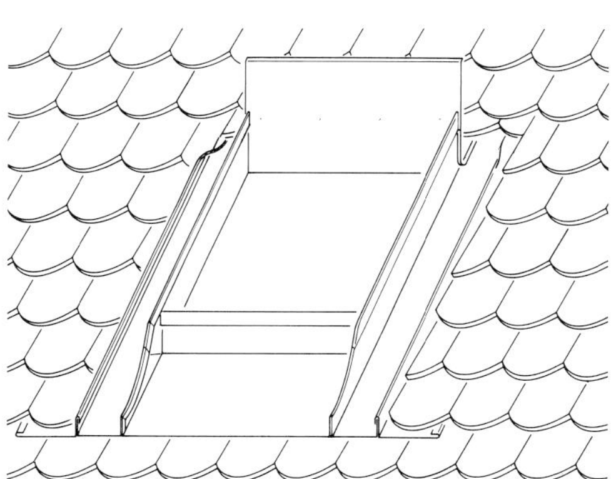

**22** The last course on the ridge side of a roof window is laid on folded sheet metal so that the roof pitch is not altered. The flashings are turned up the window frame on all sides and covered by the frame flashing typical of this type of window. The secondary waterproofing/covering layer is treated in the same way as with the chimney stack. The flashings to the sides include a gutter beneath the roof covering (see also "Junction with wall at side of slope" above).

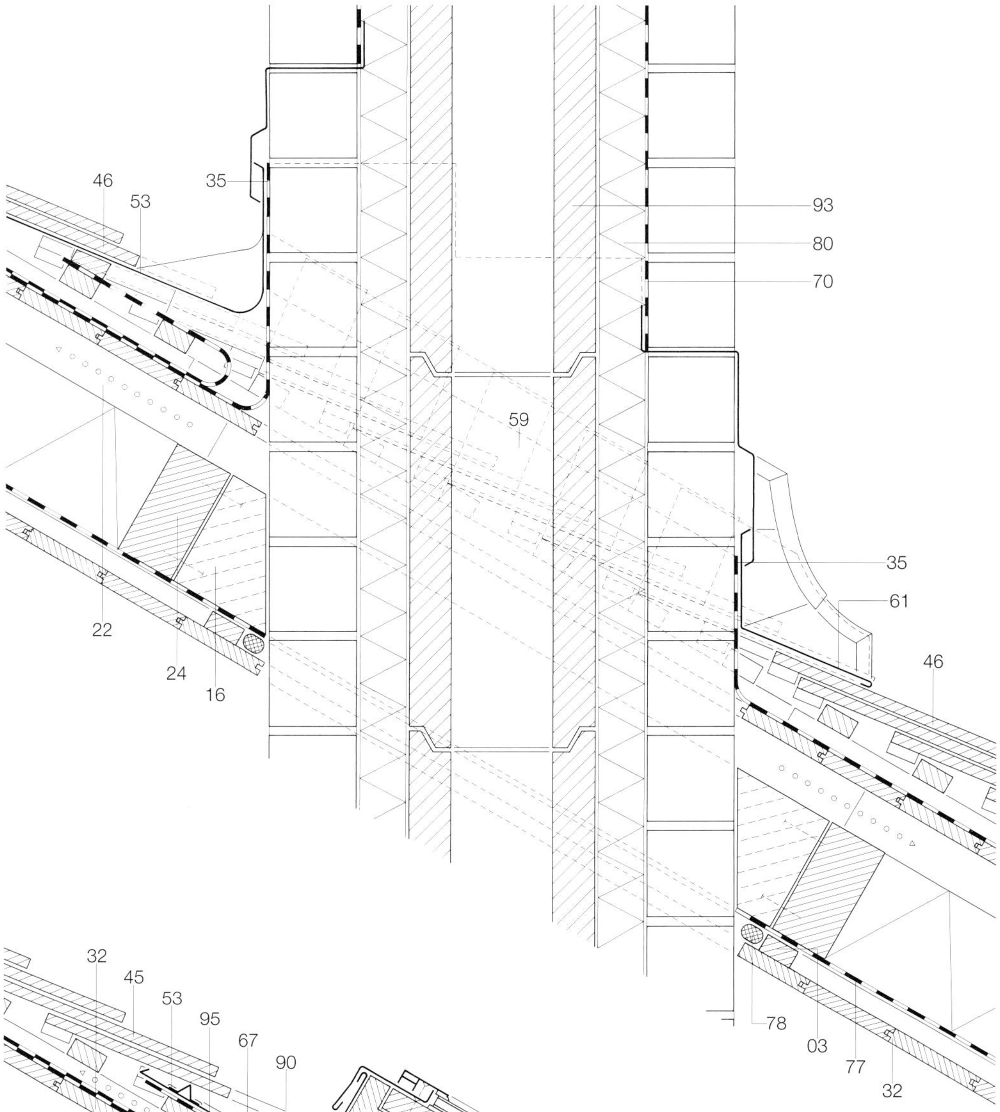

21

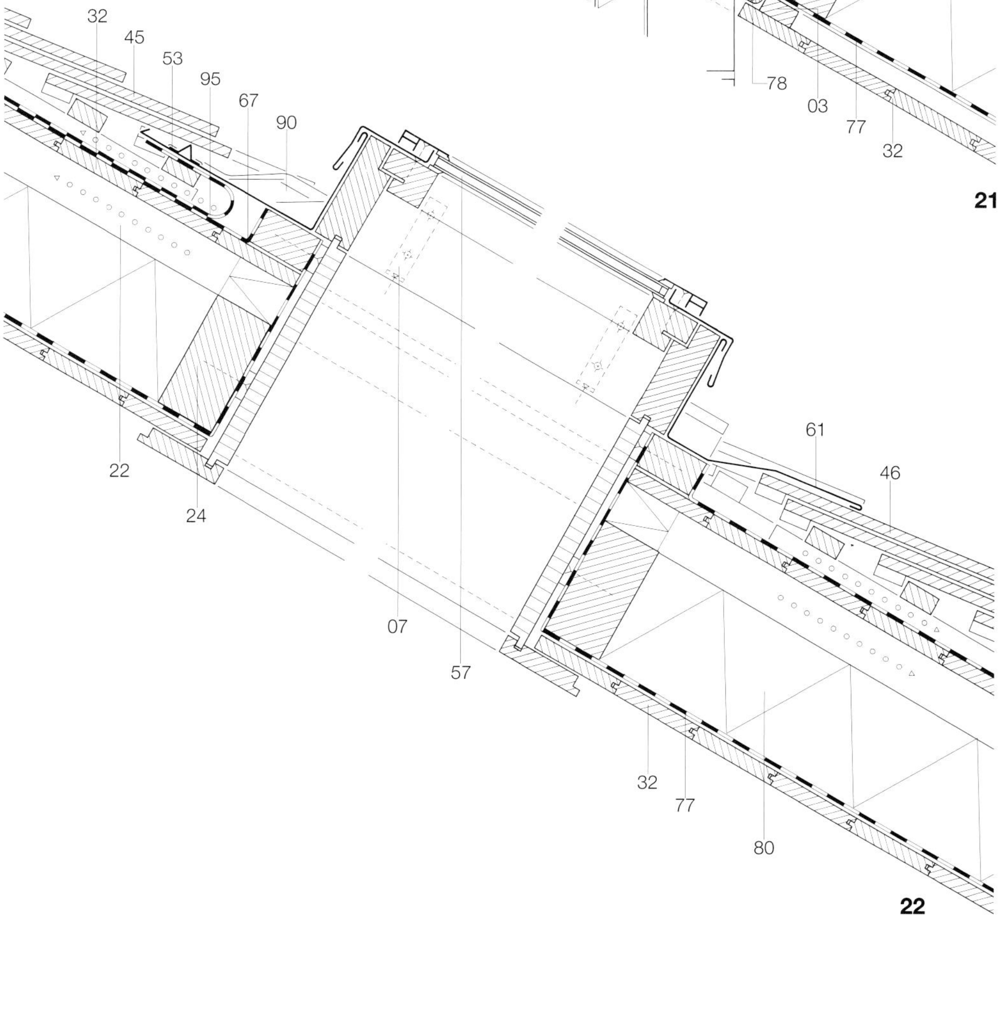

22

**Dormer window**

**23** Double-lap tiling, eyebrow dormer window, section through window head

**24** Crown tiling, eyebrow dormer window, section through window sill

**23** The eyebrow dormer window is the most elegant way of protecting a vertical roof opening with coverings of flat overlapping elements. This is because the junction with the roof above and to the sides of the window is made using the same materials as the roof surface. The "kink" between dormer window and roof surface is positioned between two tiling battens. The eaves course (as crown tiling) is laid on a deeper tilting fillet (glulam feather-edge board); it requires additional fixings. The over-

hang of the dormer window eaves tiles is variable so that the position of the dormer window can match the courses on the roof surface. Both ventilation layers are required at the eaves over the window.

**24** The junction at the window sill can be constructed like the junction with a wall at the top of a slope (see drawings 19 and 20). In this case air escapes via ventilating bullnose tiles. Incoming moisture can be drained away on the roofing felt because it extends up beneath the window sill. The sill is welted to an apron flashing on the roof covering.

Details scale 1:10

00 Spacer
03 Vapour barrier clamped behind batten
05 Clip
06 Fixing for flashing
07 Fixing bracket
10 Curving valley board
16 Concrete
18 Support board
20 Curving frame
22 Rafter
24 Trimmer
25 Spacer batten
26 Batten, glulam batten
27 Feather-edge board
28 Curving ridge board
29 Curving fascia board
31 Strut
32 Timber boarding
35 Cover flashing
45 Bullnose tile
46 Bullnose tile, crown tiling course
49 Ventilating bullnose tile
53 Back gutter with saddle
57 Double glazing
59 Soakers (at sides) with cover flashing
61 Apron flashing
63 Sheet metal window sill
67 Sheathing, roofing felt
70 Vapour check, air-permeable
77 Vapour barrier
78 Permanently elastic seal
80 Thermal insulation
90 Back gutter
93 Flue lining
95 Foil gutter
99 Mesh screen

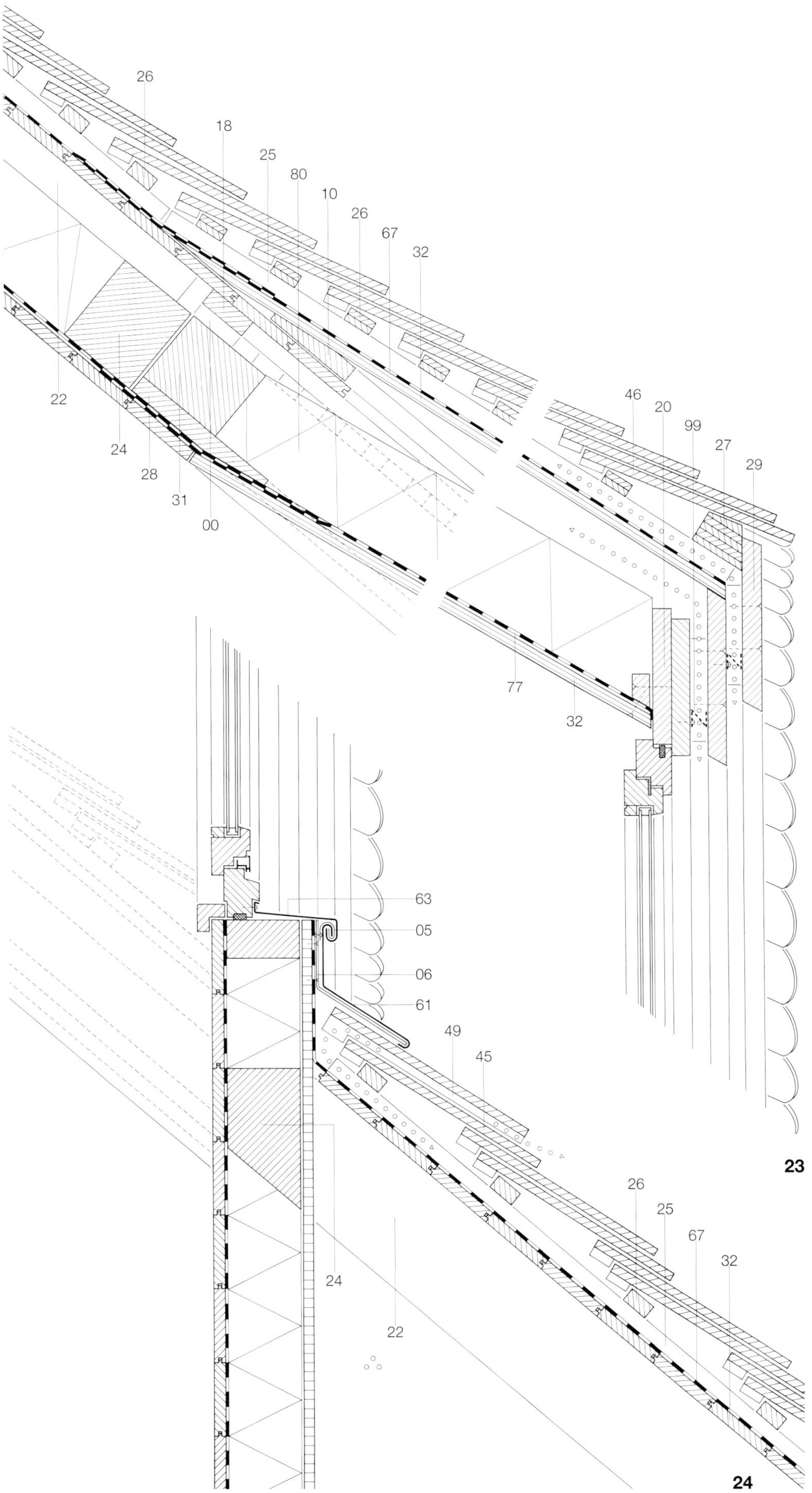

23

24

**Profiled clay and concrete tiles**
Roof covering over open roof space (identical details for clay or concrete)

In order to illustrate the laying of profiled tiles of both clay and concrete, the details reflect a hybrid approach common to both materials.

**Ridge**
**1** Ridge to duopitch roof, with ridge capping bedded in mortar
**2** Ridge to monopitch proof, with mono ridge tiles

A roof covering over an open roof space is not protected against dust and dirt or driving snow. This aspect and the fluctuating temperatures that prevail in a non-insulated roof space permit its use for simple purposes only.

**1** When bedding the ridge capping in mortar, care must be taken to ensure that the mortar does not protrude beyond the edges of the capping and thus spoil the drip edge effect. Special ventilating tiles should be used at the ridge, when the ridge capping is bedded in mortar. All the ridge capping elements must be fixed with screws.

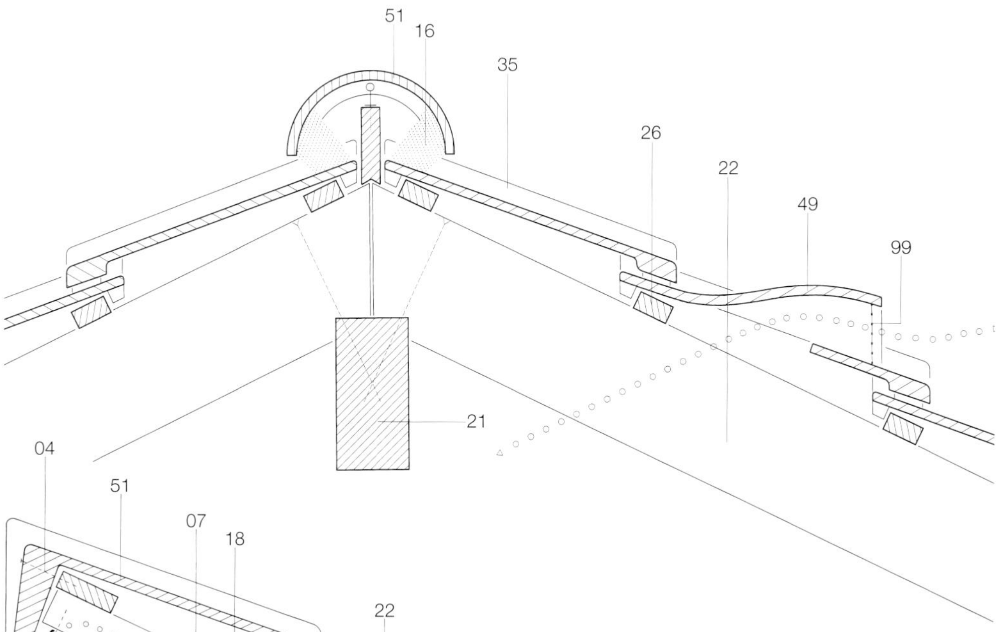

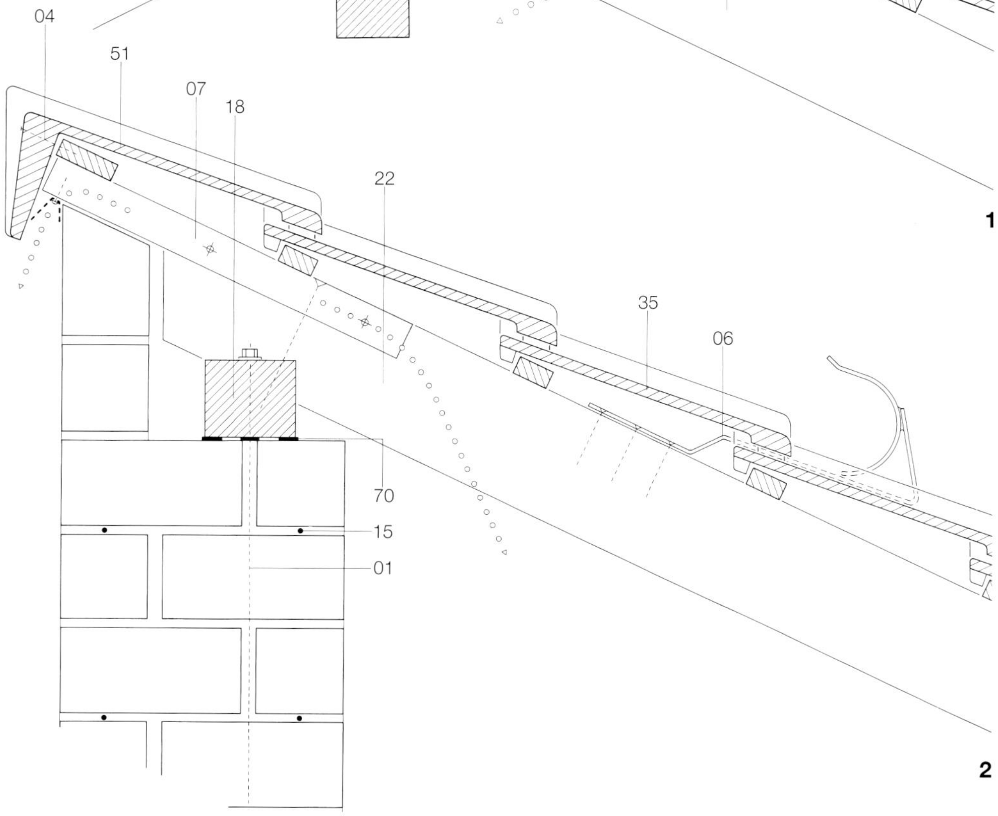

**2** The use of mono ridge tiles is well suited to single-lap tiling. All the ridge tiles must be secured. Additional battens or other small timber members support the tiles cantilevering over the external wall. A large enough overhang ensures ventilation.

**Hip**
**3** Hip, with capping bedded in mortar

The hip capping is fitted over a hip board, which is fixed to the hip rafter with metal straps. Each capping is secured with a clip before the mortar is laid. The roof tiles adjacent to the ridge must be cut to suit and additionally secured. Ventilation can be via the hip capping.

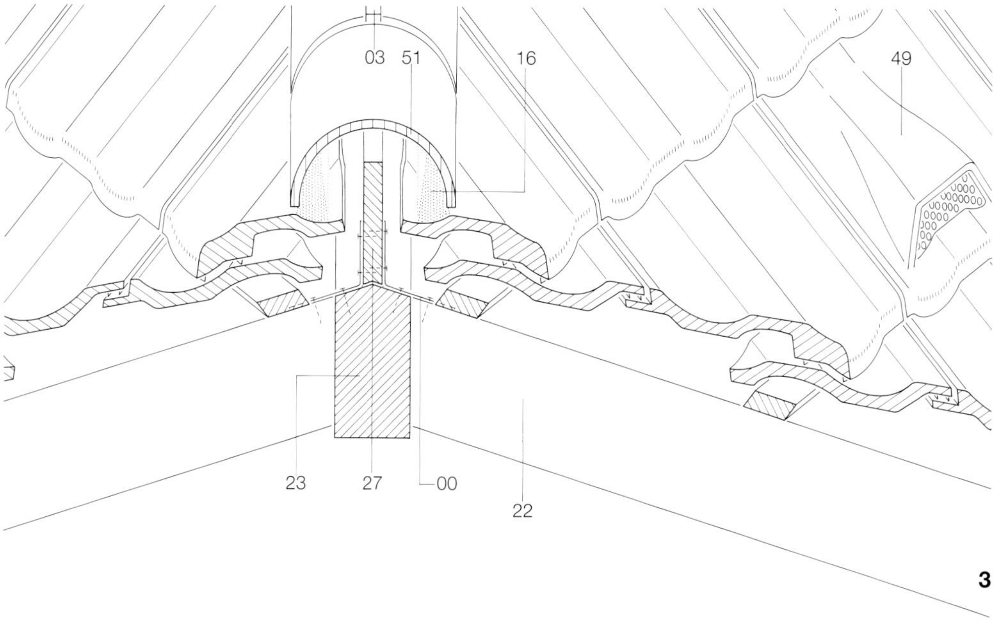

**Verge**

**4** Verge without overhang, with cloaked verge tiles

A verge that matches the roof surface is possible using cloaked verge tiles. However, this means that the length of the building must be an exact multiple of the width of the proposed roof tiles, especially with an almost flush design. The cloaked verge tiles must be secured against uplift (screws). The overhang of the cloaked verge tiles should allow for movement tolerances and possibly for moisture rising via the rendering (min. overhang 10 mm).

**Eaves**

**5** Eaves without overhang

The use of profiled and interlocking roof tiles means that the eaves course is also rainproof. A tilting board must be used and secured against uplift. An eaves flashing (gutter flashing) protects the tilting board against the weather and discharges any water passing through the side joints directly into the gutter.

**Valley**

**6** Lined valley

The roof tiles meeting at the valley are cut to suit and additionally secured. The jack rafters at the valley are notched to accommodate the boards supporting the sheet metal gutter, which is fixed with clips to the pair of rafters parallel to the line of the valley. The sheet metal gutter has turned-up edges to prevent water building up on long shallow gutters. These edges may also have a zigzag form to match the roof covering. The ventilating tiles fitted above the valley gutter ensure ventilation.

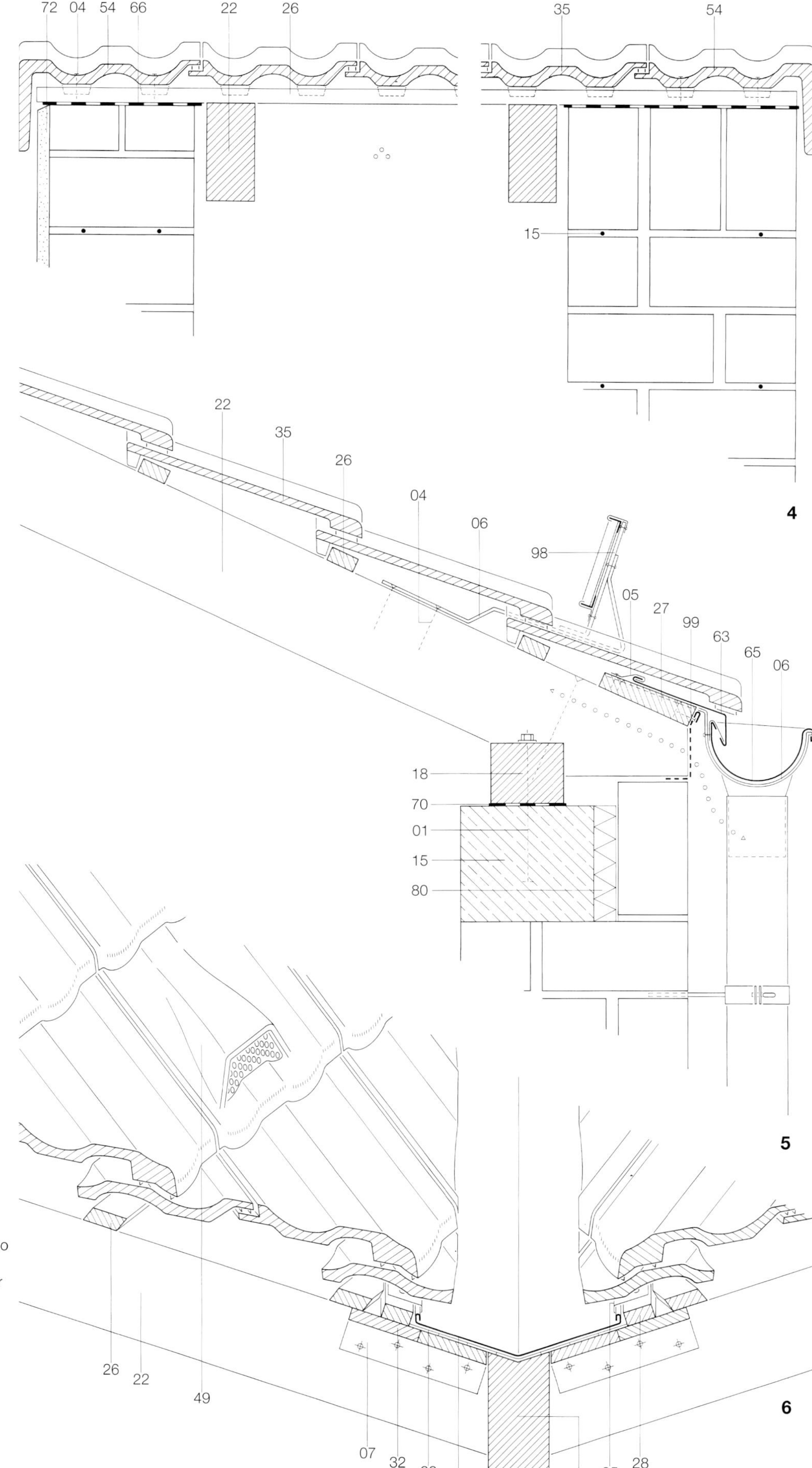


Details scale 1:10

00 Metal strap
01 Masonry anchor
03 Tile clip
04 Wood screw
05 Clip
06 Gutter bracket, ladder hook, snowguard mounting
07 Additional batten
15 Peripheral reinforcement (in bed joint or capping beam)
16 Mortar
18 Wall plate
21 Purlin
22 Rafter, jack rafter
23 Hip/valley rafter
26 Batten
27 Hip batten, tilting board
28 Valley batten
32 Timber boarding
35 Interlocking profiled tile
49 Ventilating tile
51 Ridge/hip capping, mono ridge tile
53 Sheet metal valley gutter
54 Cloaked verge tile
63 Eaves/gutter flashing
66 Separating layer
70 Damp-proof course
72 Rendering
80 Thermal insulation
95 Gutter
98 Snowguard
99 Mesh screen to ventilation opening

## Profiled clay and concrete tiles

Roof covering with roofing felt underneath (identical details for clay or concrete)

**Ridge**
**1** Ridge to duopitch proof, ventilating ridge capping secured with clips
**2** Ridge to monopitch proof, with mono ridge tiles
**3** Ridge to monopitch proof, with overhang

Roof coverings with a roofing felt underneath are suitable over roof spaces with only simple uses. They provide protection from wind, driving snow, dust and dirt. Only in exceptional cases and after consultation with the tile manufacturer may a roofing felt be used in laying the roof covering at a pitch shallower than recommended.

**1** In this example the ridge capping is clipped to the ventilating elements, which are fixed to the ridge batten – although cappings from some manufacturers can be clipped directly to the ridge batten. Here, metal straps fix the ridge batten to the rafters. This is more secure and requires less maintenance than a ridge capping bedded in mortar. The roofing felt stops about 50 mm back from the apex so that the roof space can be ventilated via the ridge as well.

**2** Ventilation to DIN 4108 must be guaranteed, so the mono ridge tiles project further beyond the external wall than in an open roof space. Cantilevering battens can be used to support the mono ridge tiles, which require additional fixings (screws). The ventilation opening is protected from birds and large insects by a mesh screen.

**3** A larger roof overhang is preferred because it provides better protection for the external wall, and it can accommodate movement between wall and roof more easily. The roof covering is protected against the wind from below by a soffit of timber boards supported on the cantilevering rafters (notched to accommodate boards). The roofing felt continues over the boarding as far as the fascia board. The ridge detail is finished with a sheet metal capping, which is fixed to the upper fascia board with a continuous clip. A strip of milled sheet lead dressed over the roof tiles is connected to the apron flashing below the sheet metal capping. The upper fascia board is screwed to the main fascia board, which is in turn screwed to the ridge batten and the ends of the rafters. The space between soffit, rafters and top of masonry wall is closed off with sheet metal (partly perforated), which provides protection against rain and snow, as well as birds and small animals.

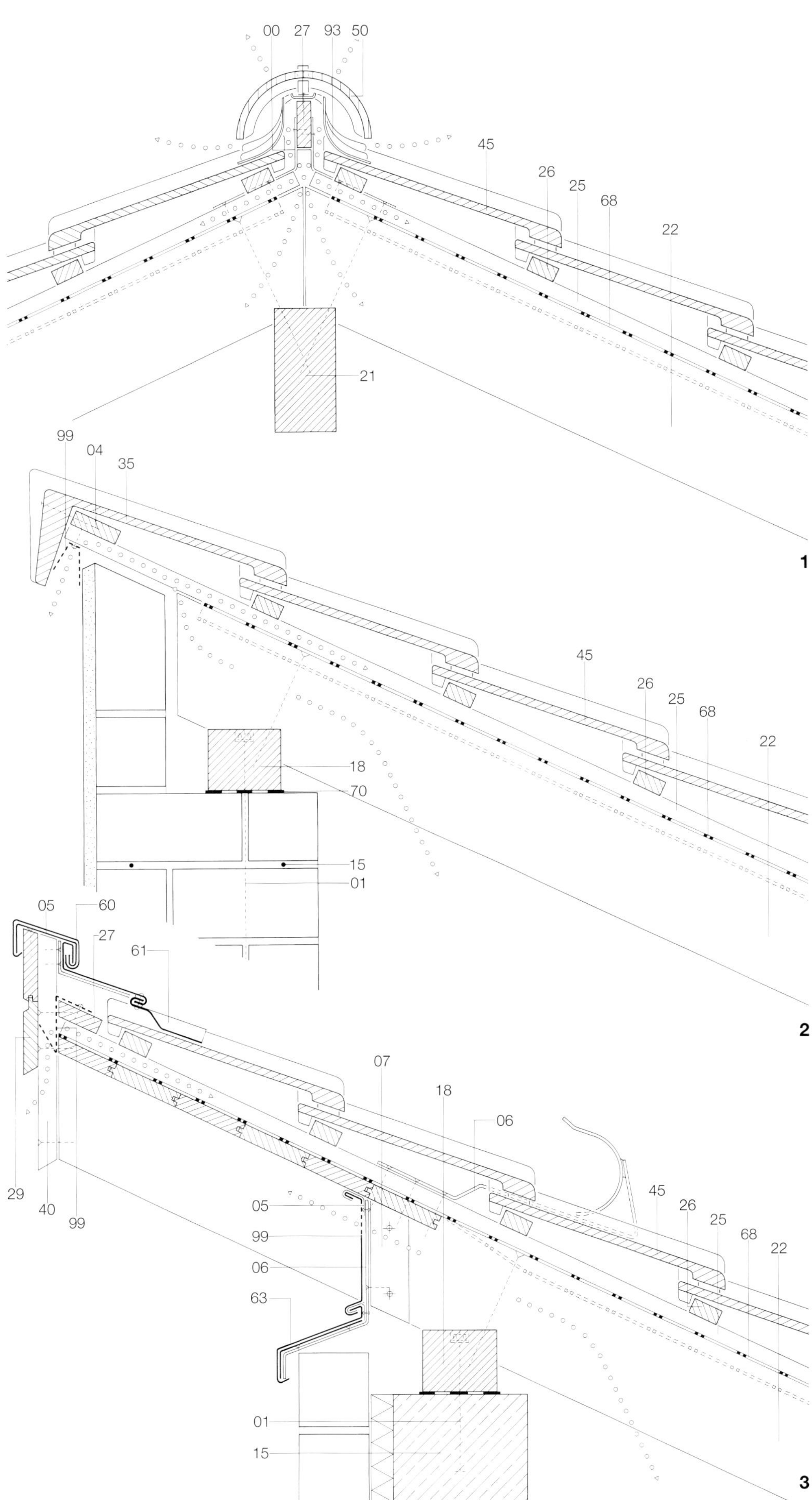

**Hip**

**4** Hip, with capping bedded in mortar

It is easier to seal the joint between hip capping and roof tiles with mortar. Each hip capping must be clipped to the hip batten to prevent it slipping down the hip. Metal straps are used to fix the hip batten to a pair of counter battens parallel to the line of the hip. The roofing felt continues over the hip.

**Eaves**

**5** Eaves without overhang

**6** Eaves with overhang

**5** The eaves course is laid on a feather-edge board (tilting board) protected by a sheet metal flashing. The gutter brackets are screwed into the rafters through the boards along the edge of the roof (rafters notched to accommodate boards). The gutter is positioned so that it catches any water draining down the roofing felt, but is well below the surface of the roof so water draining down the roof covering can overshoot during heavy rainfall. This problem can be solved by fitting a larger gutter or fixing the gutter further out. The snowguard in this example is fitted only to a tiling batten, which therefore has to be screwed to the rafters. The ends of the rafters are only partly protected from the weather by the gutter, so particularly good impregnation with preservative is necessary.

**6** An overhang at the eaves is better. Here, the gutter brackets are attached to the tilting board. The roof covering is protected against wind uplift by soffit boards (rafters notched to accommodate them). The roofing felt is laid on these soffit boards and any moisture on the felt drains via a drip flashing. The snowguard here is screwed directly to the rafters – a preferable solution to the one described above. The space between soffit, rafters and top of masonry wall is closed off as described under "Ridge to mono-pitch roof" above.

Details scale 1:10

00 Metal strap
01 Masonry anchor
03 Tile clip
04 Wood screw
05 Clip, continuous clip
06 Fixing for flashing, gutter bracket
07 Plate
15 Peripheral reinforcement (in bed joint, capping beam, floor slab)
16 Mortar
18 Wall plate
21 Purlin
22 Rafter, jack rafter
23 Hip rafter
25 Counter batten
26 Batten
27 Ridge/hip batten, tilting board
29 Upper fascia board
31 Strengthening rod
32 Timber boarding
35 Mono ridge tile
40 Fascia board
45 Interlocking profiled tile
46 Interlocking profiled tile, cut to suit
51 Ventilating ridge capping
60 Sheet metal capping
61 Milled sheet lead flashing
63 Flashing
68 Roofing felt
70 Damp-proof course
72 Rendering
93 Vent
95 Gutter
98 Snowguard
99 Mesh screen

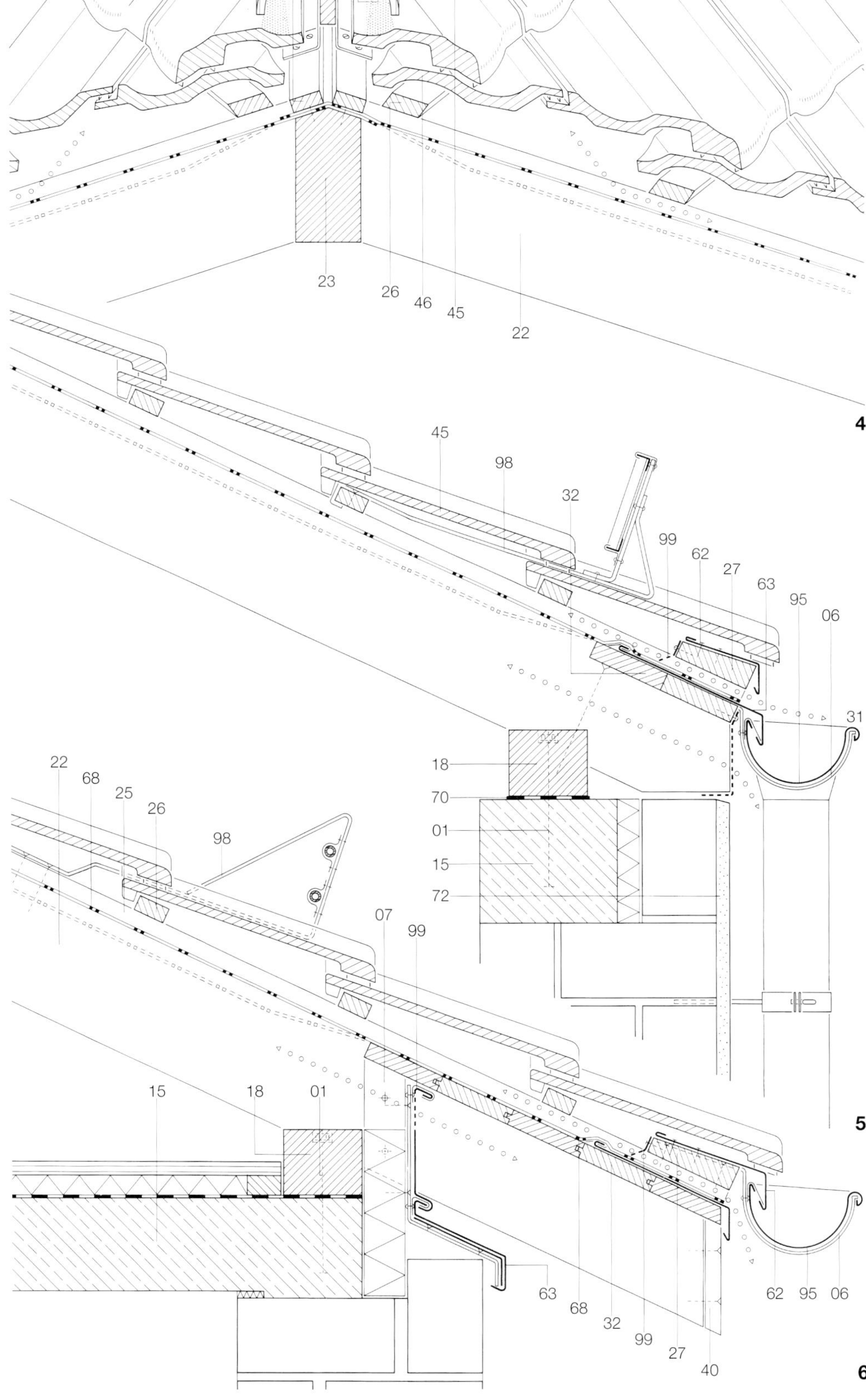

**Valley**
**7** Lined valley

A valley to a roof with roof tiles and roofing felt underneath must satisfy both waterproofing and ventilation requirements. The clay or concrete roof tiles at the intersection of the roof surfaces must be cut to suit and each piece fixed separately; they are supported on a pair of battens running parallel to the valley. The flat sheet metal gutter, with turned-up edges, is fixed to a bonded/welded waterproofing layer of film/foil laid on boards. The roofing felt overlaps the sheet metal and is held in place by the counter battens.

**Verge**
**8** Verge without overhang, with cloaked verge tiles
**9** Verge with overhang and double-roll verge tiles

**8** A flush verge with cloaked verge tiles calls for the length of the building to be an exact multiple of the width of the proposed roof tiles. The verge need not provide ventilation transverse to the roof slope. This means that the distance of the cloaked verge tiles from the external wall is determined solely by tolerance and saturation considerations (min. 10 mm). The roofing felt continues over the top of the external wall.

**9** If an overhang is desired at the verge, the length of the building no longer needs to be an exact multiple of the width of the roof tiles. This arrangement also affords better protection to the external wall. The double-roll verge tile requires additional fixings (screws); this also applies to the tiles in the previous detail. The soffit boards below the roof overhang protect the roof covering against wind uplift. A bargeboard – with its top edge shaped to fit the verge tiles – finishes off the detail. The roofing felt continues over the top of the external wall and the soffit boards right up to the bargeboard. It therefore protects them from moisture sleeping through the roof covering.

Details scale 1:10
04 Wood screw
05 Clip
06 Fixing for flashing
07 Batten
15 Peripheral reinforcement (in bed joint)
16 Water-repellent mortar in 20 mm wall joint
21 Purlin
22 Rafter, jack rafter
23 Valley rafter
26 Batten
28 Make-up piece
29 Bargeboard
32 Timber boarding
35 Cover flashing
45 Interlocking profiled tile
46 Interlocking profiled tile, cut to suit
53 Sheet metal valley gutter
54 Cloaked verge tile, double-roll verge tile
60 Sheet metal capping
61 Milled sheet lead flashing
66 Separating layer
68 Roofing felt
72 Rendering
74 Solder, rivet
76 Waterproofing
80 Thermal insulation
94 Overflow
95 Gutter
97 Gutter heating
99 Mesh screen to ventilation opening

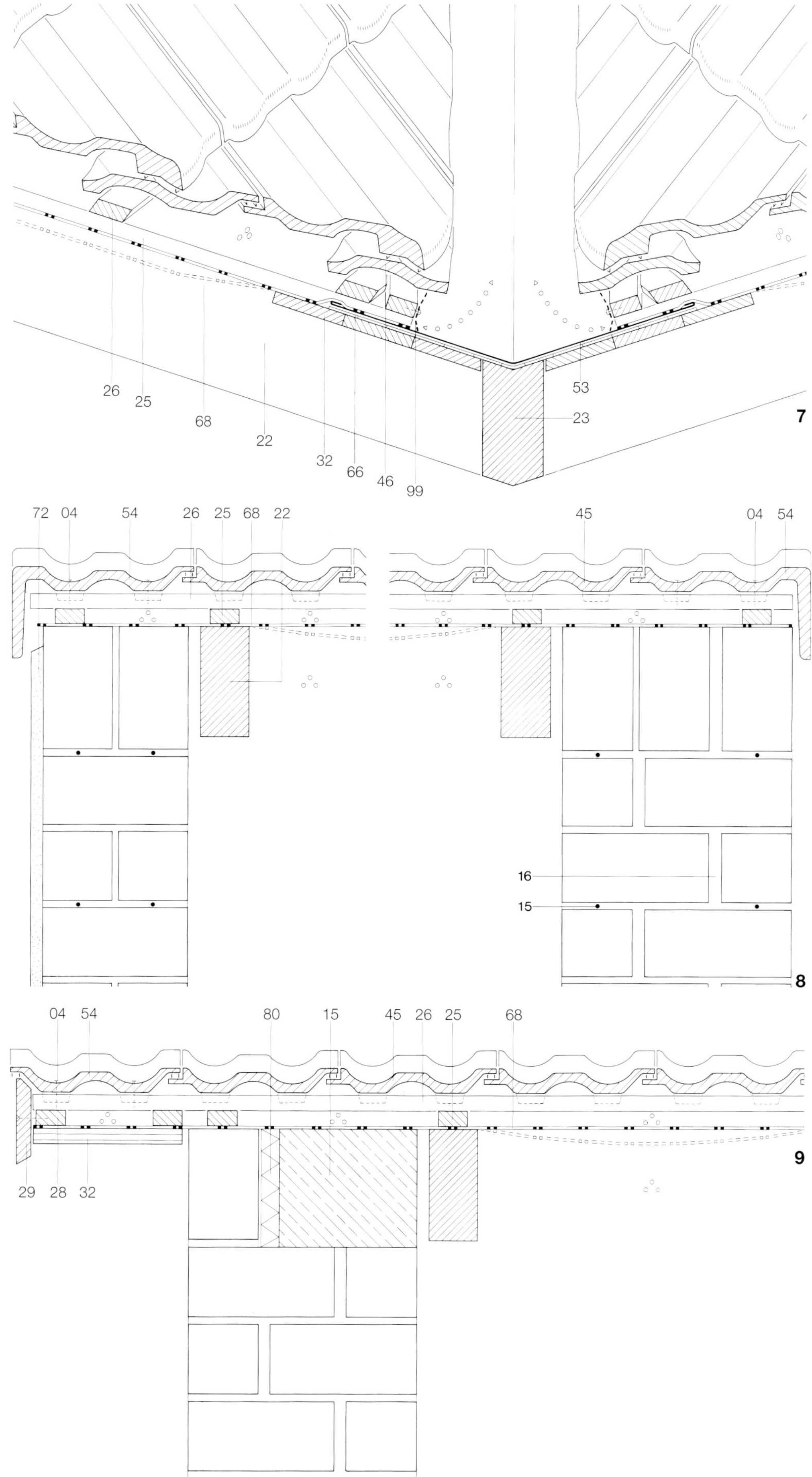

**Junction with wall**

**10** Junction with wall at bottom of slope, ventilated back gutter
**11** Junction with wall at side of slope, with deeper gutter
**12** Junction with wall at side of slope, with milled sheet lead flashing

**10** As mentioned above under "Flat clay and concrete tiles" (drawing 18), this detail – if unavoidable – must be designed and built with extreme care. In straightforward situations the contradiction between waterproofing and ventilation requirements may be solved by omitting the ventilation at this junction and ensuring good transverse air flows elsewhere.
The final course of tiles above the back gutter is shown in this example raised up on a mesh strip that permits ventilation. Timber boards supported on make-up pieces on the rafters form the base for the sheet metal gutter, which continues up the wall (min. 200 mm) on a batten to permit ventilation. Here again, a waterproofing layer is recommended. The roofing felt overlaps the sheet metal gutter and is held in place by the counter battens. The simple vent, shown here formed by the folded edge to the vertical part of the gutter and the insect screen, does not protect fully against driving rain and snow, but is conceivable for a relatively simple construction with roofing felt. The sheet metal capping is fixed to the batten on the wall with a flat metal strap and is protected by a cover flashing in conjunction with a stop bead.

**11** A deeper gutter can carry more water and is therefore useful on shallower pitches. The double-roll verge tile alongside must overlap the gutter sufficiently. This detail is similar to the verge gutter detail in some respects. The self-supporting gutter is fixed to the counter battens with clips. The top edge of the gutter on the wall side is bent over and protected by a stepped flashing let into the bed joints of the masonry. The roofing felt, which need not satisfy any ventilation requirements at this junction, is turned up the wall, fastened in place and pressed against the wall by the vertical leg of the gutter. Movement between roof and wall is accommodated by leaving a loop in the roofing felt. A loop of material should always be provided in such situations (even if the working drawings do not indicate it!).

**12** The horizontal leg of the milled sheet lead flashing must be dressed over at least one roll of the roof tiles. The top edge of this flashing is protected (left) by a cover flashing in conjunction with a stop bead and (right) by a cover flashing (serving as stop bead) tucked into a chase cut in the brickwork. The roofing felt is laid and fixed as described above.

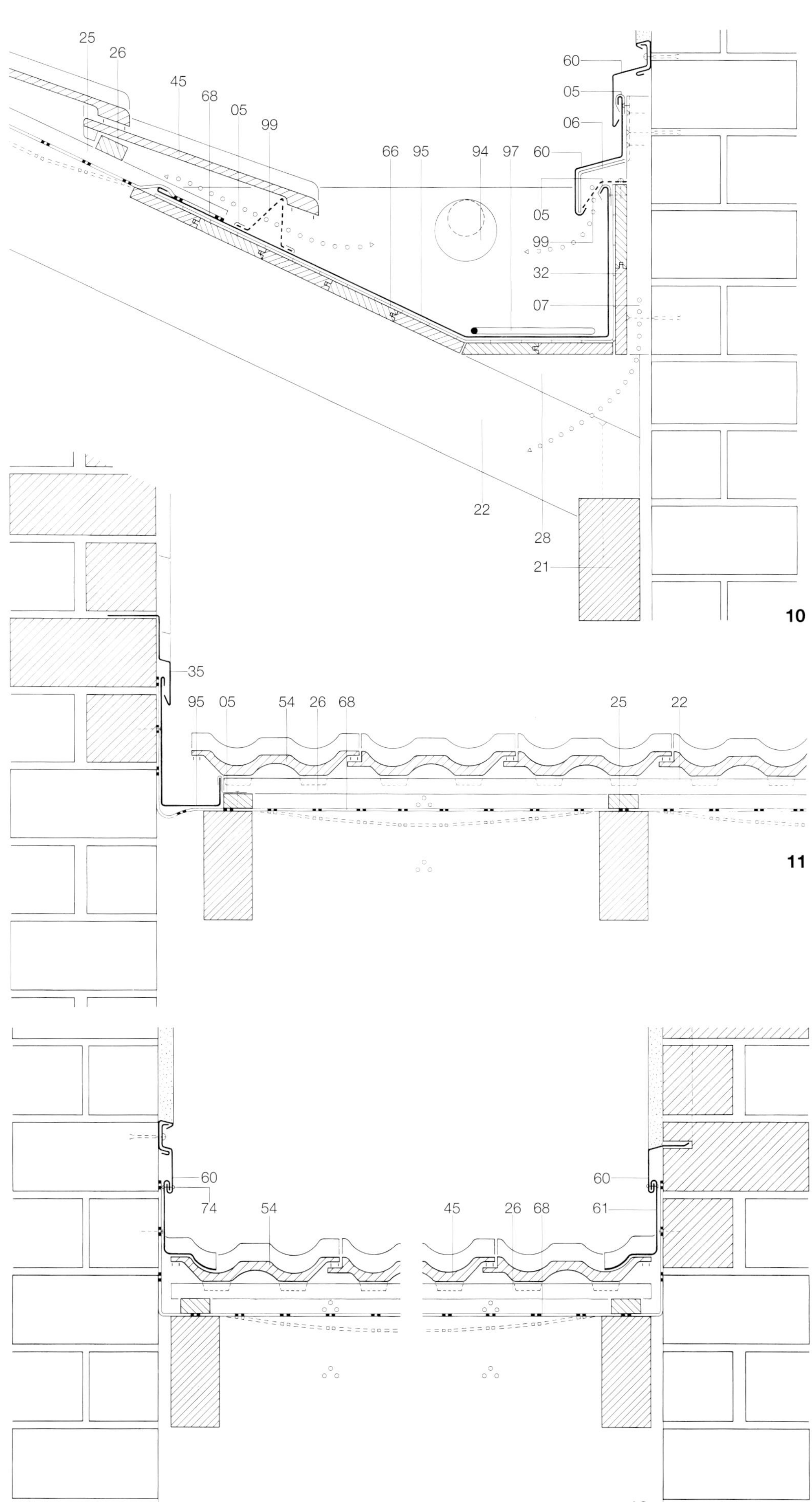

**Junction with wall**

**13** Junction with wall at top of slope, ventilated

This junction, like the ridge to a monopitch roof, must be ventilated in accordance with DIN 4108. A secure vent is provided here to prevent the ingress of driving rain and snow. Both parts of the vent are fixed to battens attached to the wall to create an air gap. The bottom part of the secure vent is welted (and secured with rivets and solder) to a strip of milled sheet lead dressed over the roof tiles. A cover flashing let into a masonry bed joint protects the top part of the vent.
The roofing felt stops 50 mm short of the wall so that the roof space can be ventilated.

**Penetrations**

**14** Chimney with deep gutter on both sides

As already mentioned under "Flat clay and concrete tiles" (drawing 21), the chimney detail unites all the wall junction details. However, its width is limited and so ventilation requirements can be ignored. The tails of the tiles immediately behind the chimney are supported on a double batten. The flashing on the ridge side (with raised "saddle" in the middle) acts as a back gutter. The apron flashing at the front, combined with milled sheet lead dressed over the roof tiles, is welted to the flashings at the side, which thus hold it in place. The cover flashing is welted to the gutter on the ridge side and simply overhangs the apron flashing on the eaves side. It is fixed into the chimney through the stop bead. The roofing felt is turned up the masonry on all sides. On the ridge side of the chimney a channel is formed with welded roofing felt or metal foil so that any moisture beneath the roof covering drains to either side of the chimney.

**Roof window**

**15** Simple roof window, roof access hatch

This is a roof penetration of limited height. The sheet metal flashing is turned up the frame on all sides. It has a turned-up edge on the ridge side, is shaped to fit under the roof tiles at the sides and is attached on the eaves side to a strip of milled sheet lead dressed over the roof tiles.
The last course of roof tiles above the window is supported on a strip of mesh to allow ventilation.
The roofing felt on the ridge side is formed into a channel wider than the penetration itself. At the sides and front the roofing felt is turned up the frame. This detail is simpler but less secure than the chimney detail shown above.

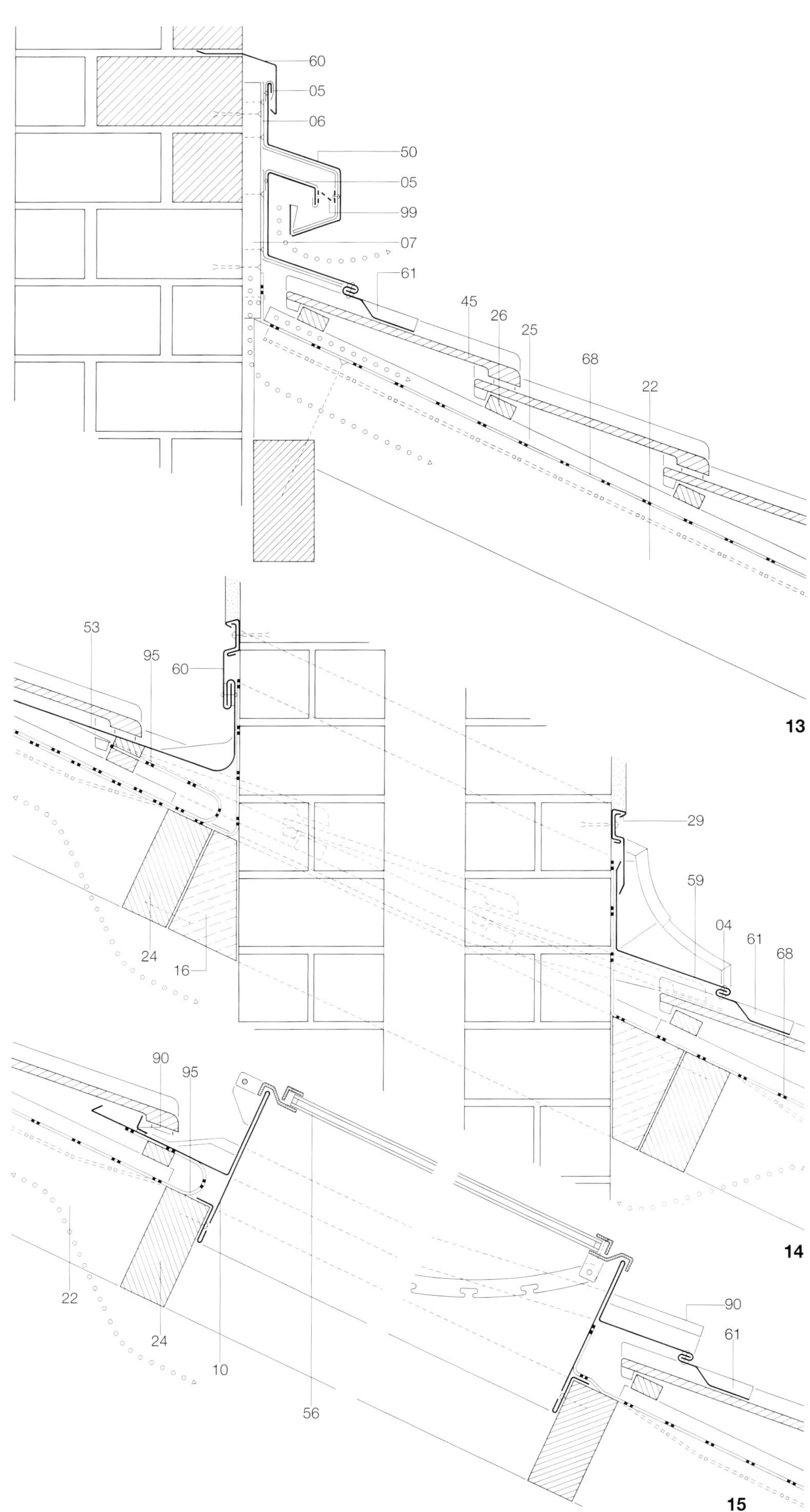

**Dormer window**

**16** Shed dormer window, section through window head
**17** Shed dormer window, section through window sill
**18** Junction between main roof surface and roof to dormer window

A shed dormer window is the best way of incorporating a vertical window into a roof covering of profiled clay or concrete tiles. A low window is preferred because this softens the angle between main roof surface and roof over dormer window, and is thus easier to integrate into the roof surface. The lateral position of the shed dormer window is governed by the pattern of the overlapping roof tiles. However, its vertical position is not so constrained because the overhang of the tiles along the eaves of the dormer window can be varied.

**16** The eaves detail to the dormer window should fulfil the same tasks as the main eaves.

**17** The junction between the roof surface and the sill of the dormer window is treated in the same way as the detail at the top of a slope except that, to minimise the height of the sill detail, ventilation is achieved here through ventilating tiles. The roof space can be ventilated via the other ventilation openings at ridge and eaves. The roofing felt continues up as far as the sheet metal window sill.

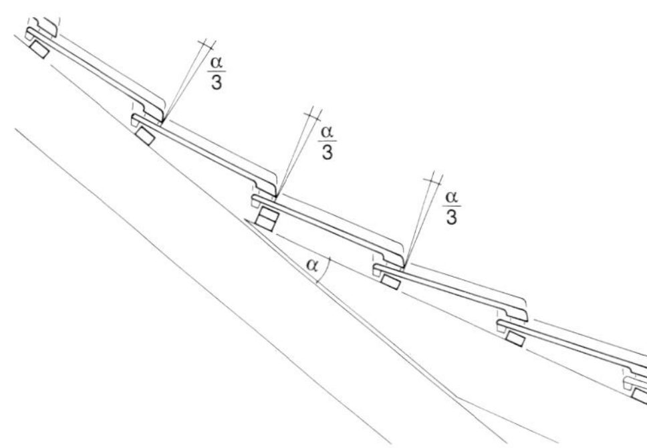


**18** In contrast to the detail shown for flat clay and concrete tiles, a tiling batten coincides with the "kink" in the roof surface. Including a double batten at this point enables the angle to be softened even further and spread over three transverse joints (see sketch).

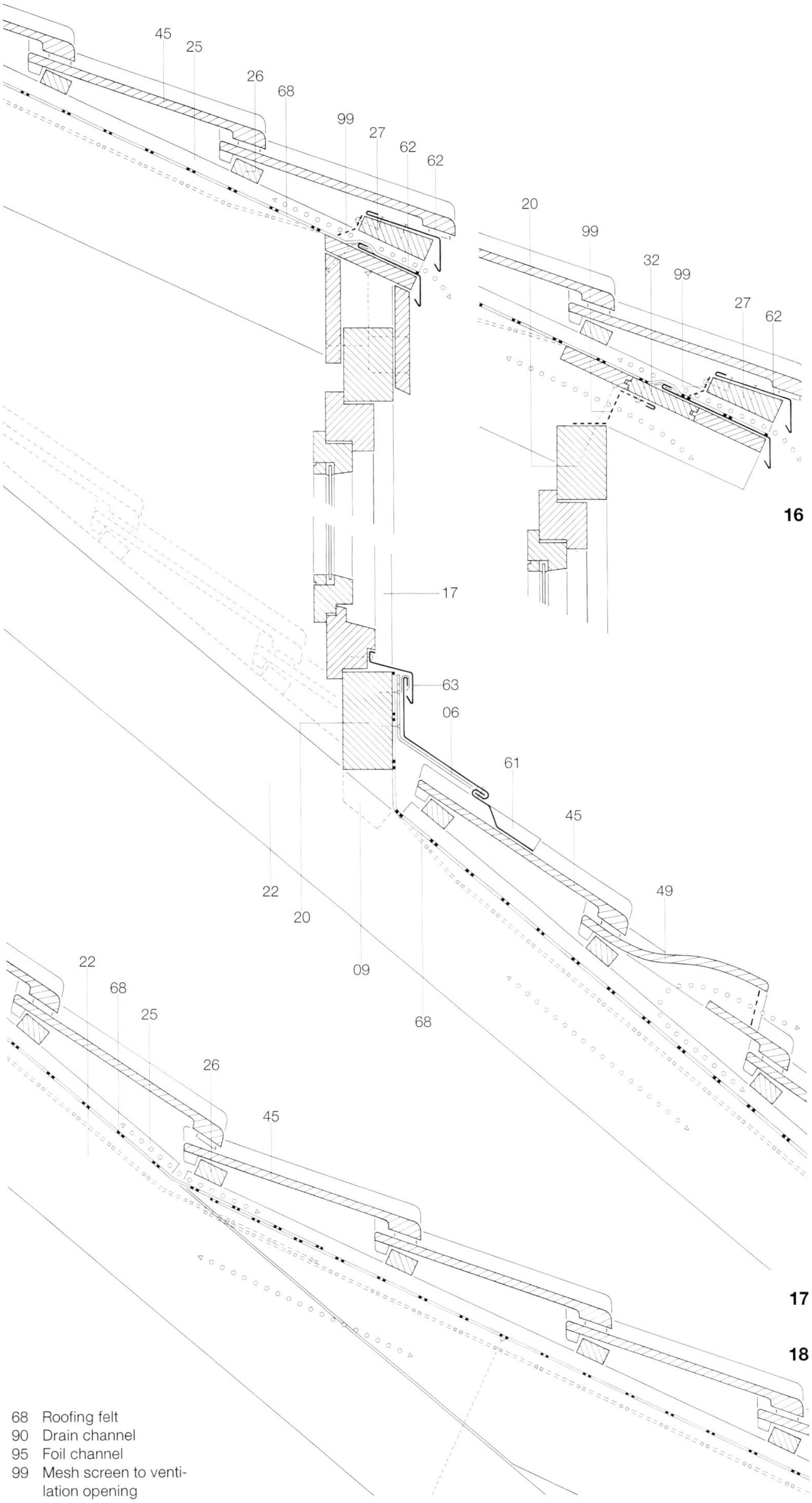

Details scale 1:10
04 Rivet and solder
05 Clip
06 Fixing for flashing
07 Batten
09 Tenon
10 Window frame
16 Concrete
17 Mullion
20 Framing member
22 Rafter
24 Trimmer
25 Counter batten
26 Batten
27 Feather-edge board
29 Stop bead
32 Timber boarding
45 Interlocking profiled tile
49 Ventilating tile
50 Ventilation hood
53 Back gutter
56 Single glazing
59 Apron flashing
60 Cover flashing
61 Milled sheet lead flashing
62 Drip flashing
63 Sheet metal window sill
68 Roofing felt
90 Drain channel
95 Foil channel
99 Mesh screen to ventilation opening

16

17

18

**Profiled clay and concrete tiles**
Roof covering with secondary waterproofing layer underneath
Ventilated thermal insulation with vapour barrier above loadbearing structure
(identical details for clay or concrete)

In order to illustrate the laying of profiled tiles of both clay and concrete, the details reflect a hybrid approach common to both materials.

**Ridge**
**1** Ridge to duopitch roof, with ventilating capping secured with clips
**2** Ridge to monopitch proof, with overhang and mono ridge tiles

A roof construction with a secondary waterproofing layer, ventilated thermal insulation and vapour barrier is suitable over roof spaces destined for more demanding uses, e.g. living accommodation. The provision of a secondary waterproofing layer allows pitches a little shallower than those recommended to be employed. The position of the insulation above the loadbearing structure creates good conditions for laying the insulation and for the vapour barrier, but leads to a deep overall construction.

**1** The fixing of the ridge capping and ventilating elements has already been described (see, for example, "Flat clay and concrete tiles"). In order to connect both ventilation layers to the ridge ventilation, roof decking and roofing felt should stop 30 mm below the apex on both sides. This "weak point" in the secondary waterproofing layer calls for the seal between ridge capping and topmost course of tiles to be carefully executed. This example shows – in simplified form – a type of ventilating element whose plastic skirts follow the profile of the tiles. The depth of the spacer rafters required for thick insulation plus a ventilation layer can be minimised by including spacer purlins half as deep as the insulation. This type of construction allows the vapour barrier to be laid uninterrupted over the entire roof before the rest of the overlying construction.

**2** The long cantilever of this roof overhang to a monopitch roof in this detail is supported on spacer rafters. This means the edge of the roof can be slimmer than if the main loadbearing rafters were used. The fixings for the mono ridge tiles and the ladder hook are described above. The roof decking of timber boards continues out beyond the external wall to form a soffit, which protects the roof covering against wind uplift. Here again, the vapour barrier should continue as far as the capping beam, where it is clamped firmly in position.

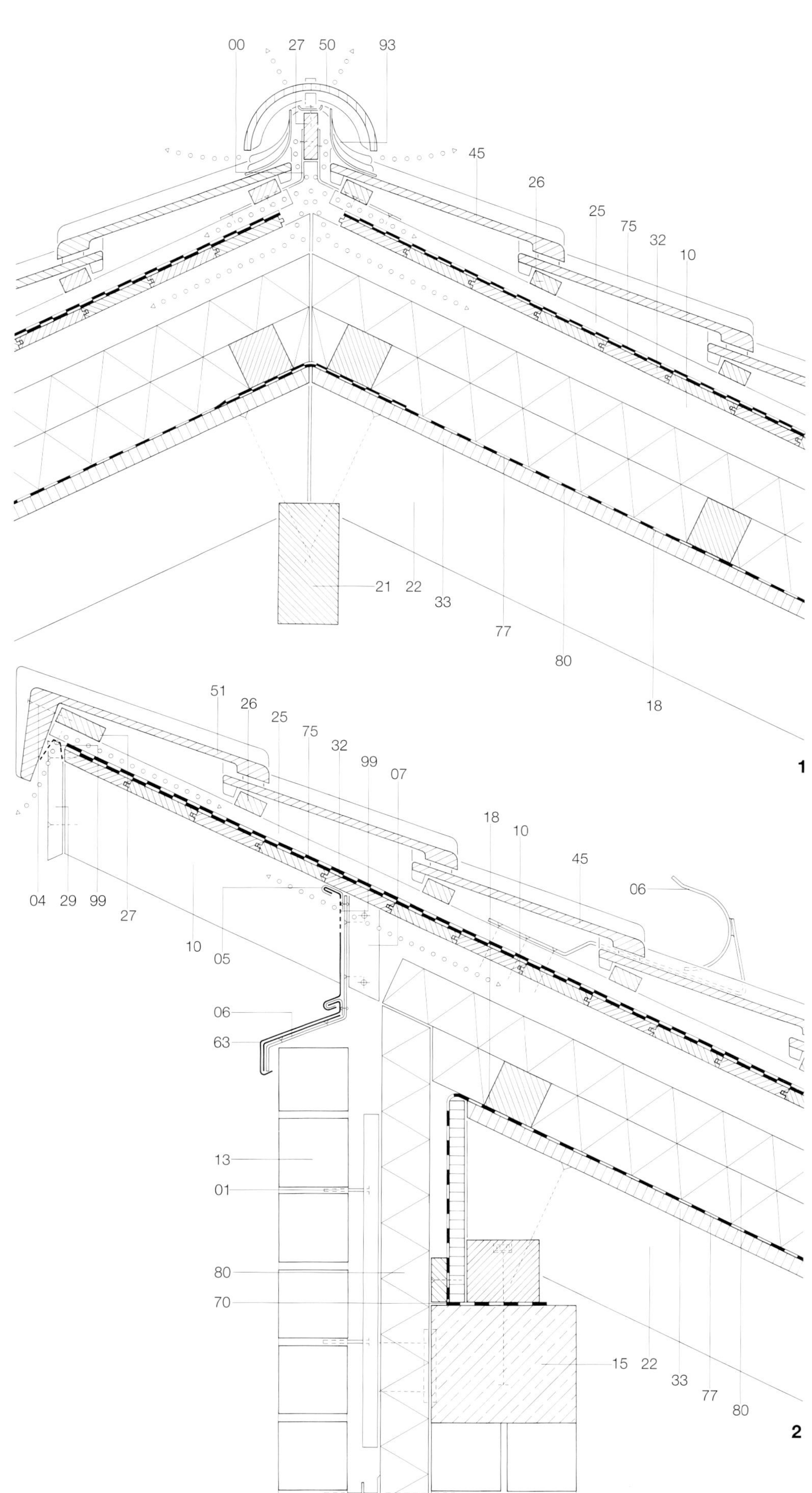

**Hip**

**3** Hip, with ventilating capping secured with clips

The clay or concrete hip capping is fixed to the hip batten via a ventilating element, whose metal mounting straps are screwed to a pair of battens parallel to the ridge. Each roof tile cut at an angle to fit the hip is fixed separately. The ventilating element follows the profile of the roof tiles as at the ridge. In order to ventilate the lower air layer, it must be connected to the upper layer via vents. The air in the upper layer then flows towards the ridge or the eaves as described in the "Ventilation" section.
In this example the two-layer supporting construction for the insulation and ventilation layers is clearly discernible.

**Eaves**

**4** Eaves with overhang

Here too, the long cantilever of the roof overhang is carried by spacer rafters. In other respects the detail is very similar to the one for flat clay and concrete tiles. One variation shown here is the snowguard tile (instead of a fence or pole). The roofing felt and boarding beneath the roof covering continues the full length of the overhang so that the roof tiles are protected against wind uplift and water draining down this layer is discharged as far as possible from the external wall. The roof insulation, as at the ridge to a monopitch roof, is joined to the insulation in the external wall to form a continuous insulating envelope. The information given above for the vapour barrier applies here as well. If masonry external leaves continue up to the underside of the rafters, they must be restrained suitably – in this and similar cases via a dovetail slot fixed back to the capping beam. Connecting the cavity in the external wall to the lower ventilation layer in the roof has neither advantages nor disadvantages.

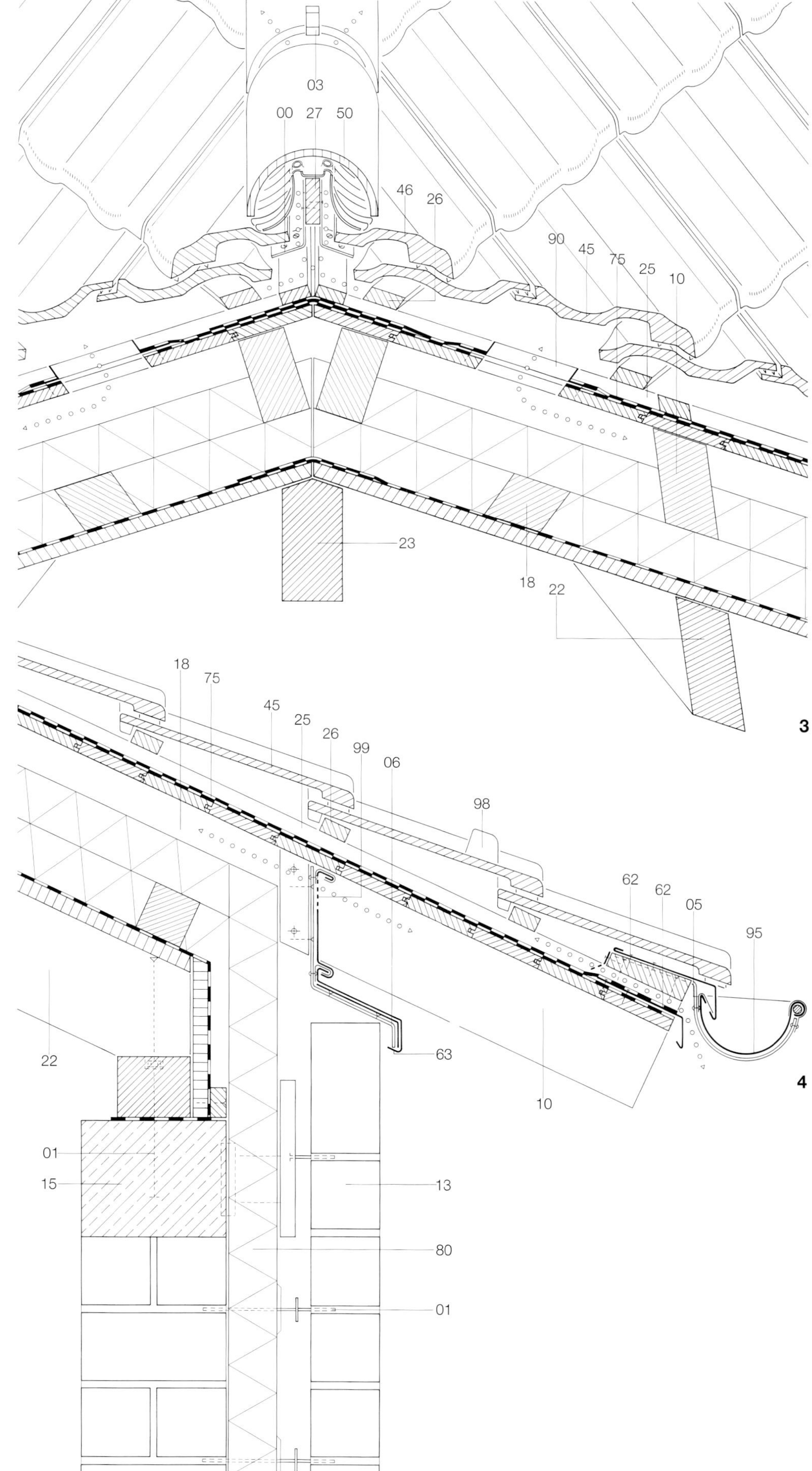


Details scale 1:10
00 Metal strap
01 Masonry anchor, wall tie in dovetail slot
03 Tile clip
04 Wood screw
05 Clip, continuous clip
06 Fixing for flashing, ladder hook
07 Timber block
10 Spacer rafter
13 Facing brickwork
15 Capping beam
18 Spacer purlin
21 Purlin
22 Rafter, jack rafter
23 Hip rafter
25 Counter batten
26 Batten
27 Ridge/hip batten
29 Fascia board
32 Timber boarding
33 Timber derivative board
45 Interlocking profiled tile
46 Interlocking profiled tile, cut to suit
50 Ventilating ridge capping
51 Mono ridge tile
62 Drip flashing
63 Flashing
70 Damp-proof course
75 Bitumen roofing felt, two layers
77 Vapour barrier
80 Thermal insulation, two layers
90 Vent
93 Ventilating element
95 Gutter and bracket
98 Snowguard tile
99 Mesh screen to ventilation opening

**Valley**

**5** Lined valley

Only lined valleys are feasible with profiled clay or concrete tiles. The tiles at the intersection of the two roof surfaces must be cut to suit and each fixed separately. Adjacent to the valley they are supported on the folded edge of the sheet metal valley gutter, which is fixed with clips. This edge treatment provides a certain degree of protection if there is a backlog of water.
However, the real safety factor is the layer of waterproofing material underneath.
Some air can flow through the gap between the underside of the profiled tiles and the edge of the sheet metal gutter. Laying the valley boards on the counter battens creates an uninterrupted ventilation space underneath. This lower ventilation layer is connected to the upper one via vents (for further information see "Layers – Ventilation").
As at the hip, the vapour barrier continues right across the valley.

**Verge**

**6** Overhanging verge with bargeboard

In contrast to the eaves and the ridge, where the cantilever is carried on spacer rafters, the purlins are extended at the verge. These gain extra support from exposed rafters beyond the external wall and are secured against uplift by the counter battens and tiling battens. This example employs double-roll verge tiles instead of cloaked verge tiles.
A bargeboard protects the edge of the construction.
The roof decking extends to form a soffit and thus protect the roof covering against wind uplift. The thermal insulation in the roof is joined to that in the external wall.
The vapour barrier is carefully joined to the top of the external wall.

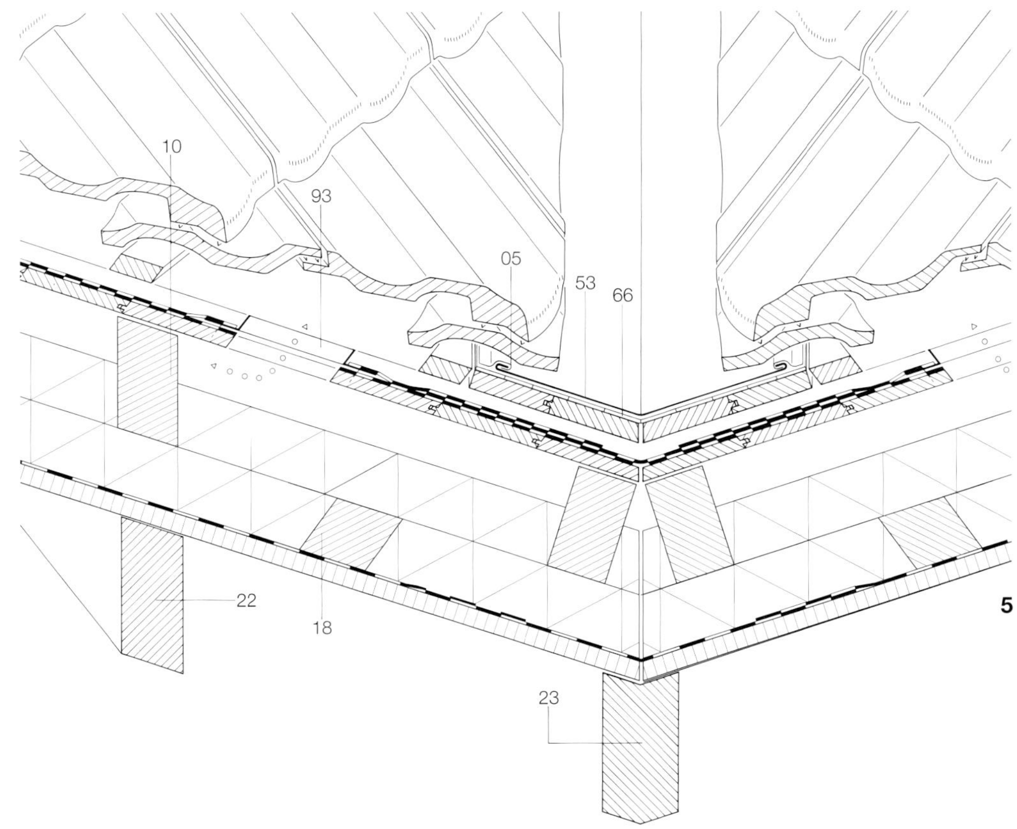


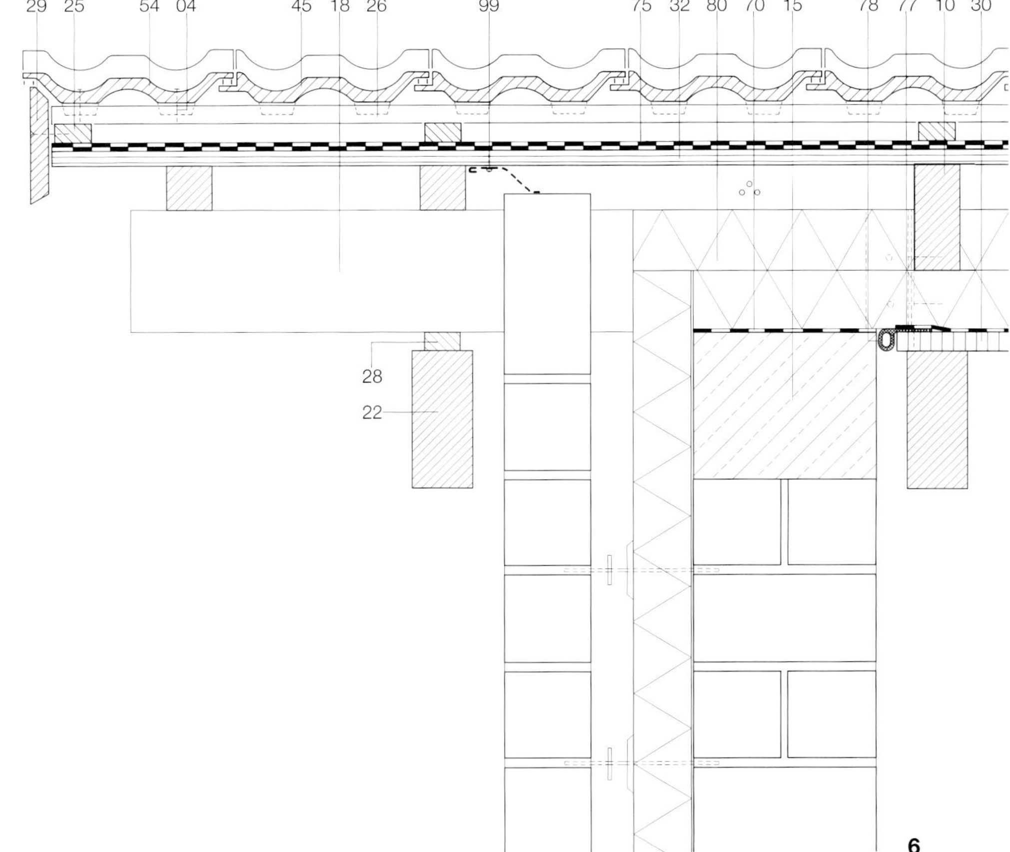


Details scale 1:10

00 Bracket
01 Anchor
04 Wood screw
05 Clip
06 Fixing for flashing
07 Batten
10 Spacer rafter, spacer
15 Capping beam
18 Spacer purlin
21 Purlin
22 Rafter, jack rafter
23 Valley rafter
25 Counter batten
26 Batten
28 Make-up piece
29 Bargeboard
32 Timber boarding
33 Timber derivative board
45 Interlocking profiled tile
50 Ventilation hood
53 Sheet metal valley gutter
54 Double-roll verge tile
61 Milled sheet lead flashing, riveted and soldered to capping strip
66 Separating layer
70 Damp-proof course
75 Bitumen roofing felt, bonded
77 Vapour barrier
80 Thermal insulation
90 Perforated metal strip
93 Vent
94 Overflow
95 Gutter
97 Gutter heating
99 Mesh screen to ventilation opening

**Junction with wall**

**7** Junction with wall at bottom of slope, ventilated back gutter
**8** Junction with wall at side of slope, with deeper gutter
**9** Junction with wall at side of slope, with milled sheet lead flashing

**7** Attention has been drawn in previous examples to the disadvantages of the back gutter, with its ventilation and waterproofing requirements. It is always true to say that the higher the gutter and waterproofing continue up the wall and back up the slope, the safer the detail is.
This design principle with a waterproof underlay, which in fact seals the whole roof right up to the ridge, offers the greatest protection. At the back gutter the design is similar to the one already discussed for roof tiles with roofing felt underneath.
However, as there are two air layers needing ventilation, the gutter is placed on timber boards over the counter battens. The multiple redirection of the air flow at the ventilation hood, which protects against driving rain and snow, governs the size of the vent and hence the depth and capacity of the back gutter.
The counter battens clamp the secondary waterproofing layer to the vertical part of the timber boarding. As the upper air layer is ventilated above the level of the gutter via a perforated metal strip supporting the tail of the bottom course of tiles, the vertical air layer behind the gutter need not be very wide.
As already mentioned, gutter heating and an overflow provide extra security for this risky detail. (The dotted circle in the drawing represents the overflow diameter specified in the standard, and the solid line that recommended by the authors.) It is advisable to fit a rainwater drip collar to the bracket supporting the external leaf of the wall above the gutter so that any water that does penetrate the masonry can drain safely onto the ventilation hood. In this example insulation without an overlying ventilation layer is recommended.

**8, 9** The junction with a wall at the side of the slope, which does not have to satisfy any ventilation requirements, can be realised in the same way as a design with roof tiles plus roofing felt (see "Profiled clay and concrete tiles – Roof covering with roofing felt underneath", drawings 11 and 12). So it is sufficient here to point out that the layer of waterproofing (foil/film, built-up roofing felt or synthetic roofing felt) turned up the wall must be securely clamped to the rising wall construction. This is achieved by a cover flashing, which in drawing 8 protects the top edge of the gutter and in drawing 9 is fixed to the milled sheet lead flashing.

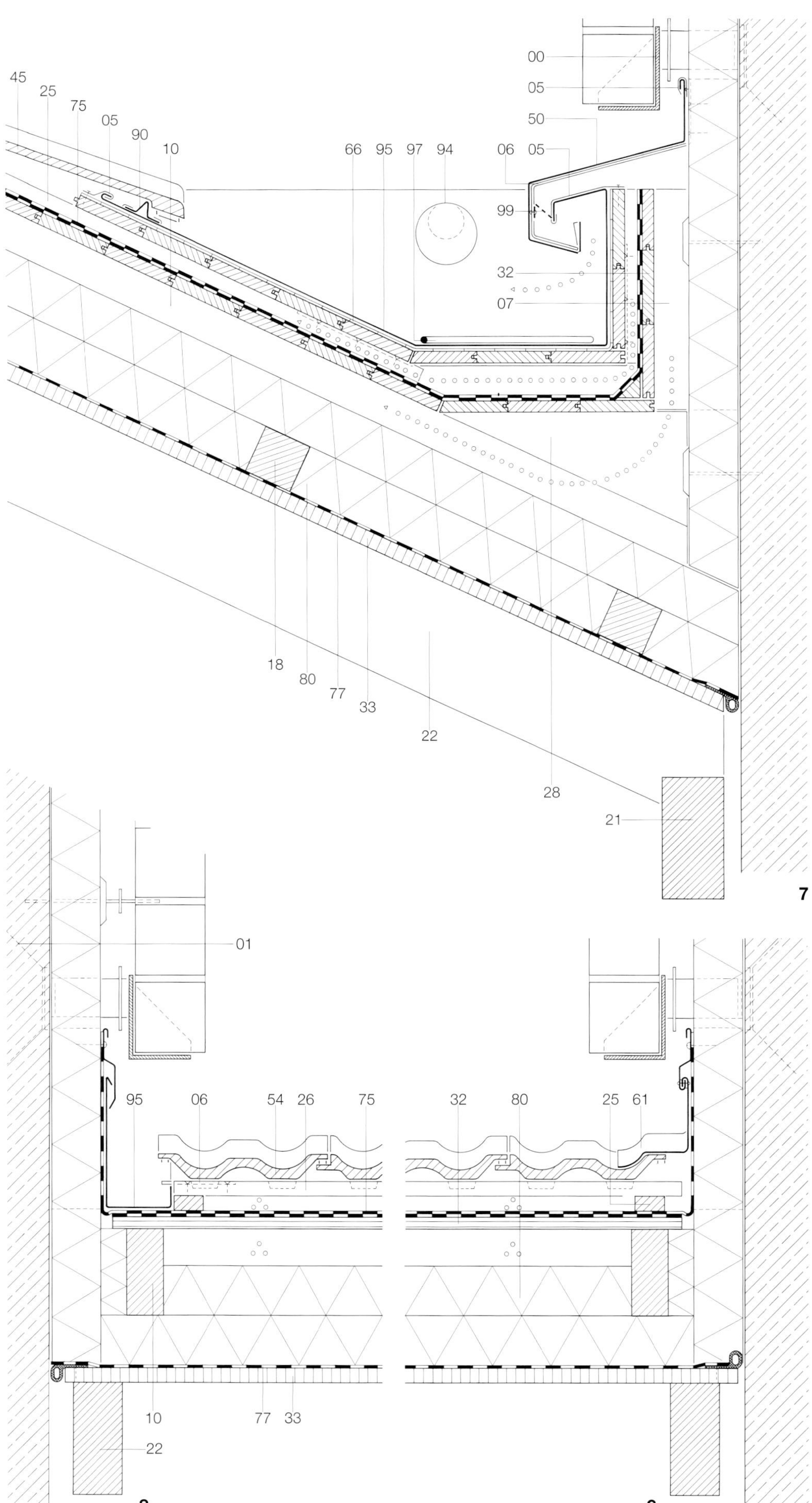

**Penetrations**

**10** Chimney stack

This detail differs only slightly from the solutions shown earlier (see "Profiled clay and concrete tiles – Roof covering with roofing felt underneath", drawings 14 and 15). As with the back gutter detail, the secondary waterproofing layer provides extra protection.
The chimney stack penetration with a chimney clad in sheet metal is seldom a problem. The flashing on the ridge side is formed like a back gutter and is supported on a double batten, together with the last course of tiles above the chimney. The apron flashing at the front of the chimney is welted to the sheet metal cladding around it, like the flashings at the back and the sides. The connection to the milled sheet lead flashing dressed over the profiled roof tiles roof is secured, as in other, similar details, with rivets and solder. The layer of waterproofing is fixed to the sides of the chimney by the continuous clips that hold the flashings in place.
Ventilation needs not be considered in this detail because the air flow is deflected around the chimney.
The vapour barrier must be carefully connected.

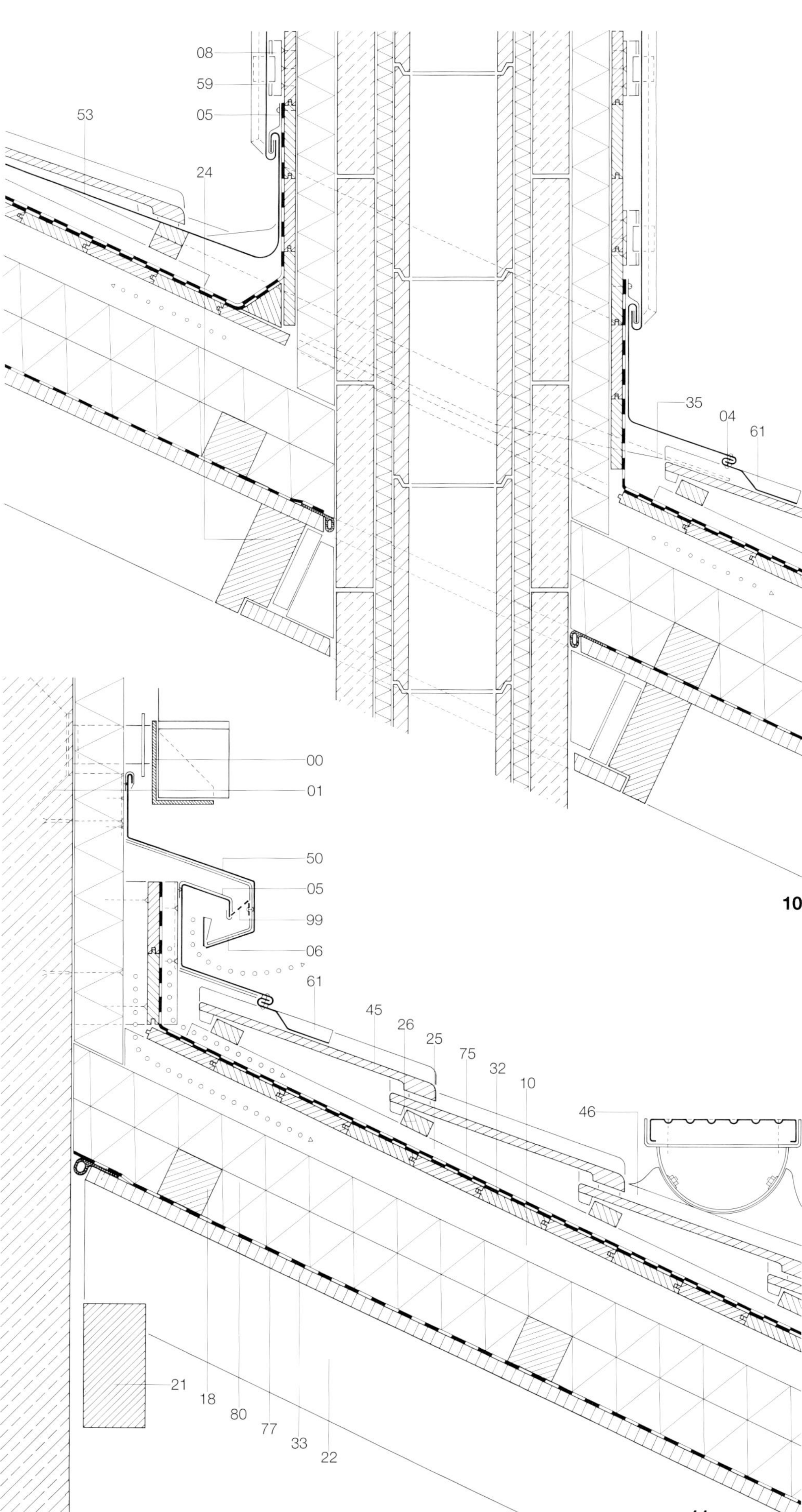


**Junction with wall**

**11** Junction with wall at top of slope, with secure vent

This detail has to ventilate two air layers. This example employs the back gutter solution. The ventilation hood must be very large, or the upper and lower ventilation layers must be joined by vents. Battens, boarding and waterproofing layer – fixed to vertical spacer battens within the thermal insulation – are turned up the wall as far as the top of the lower part of the ventilation hood, which is also screwed to these spacer battens.
If more pronounced roof movements need to be taken into account, it is advisable to include a loop in the waterproofing material at the transition from the slope to the vertical.
The thermal insulation in the roof is joined to that of the external wall to form a continuous envelope.
The vapour barrier is connected to the rising external wall.

**Dormer window**

**12** Shed dormer window, section through window head with overhanging eaves
**13** Shed dormer window, section through window sill
**14** Junction between main roof surface and roof to dormer window

**12** It has already been stated that the shed dormer window is the best form for use with profiled clay or concrete tiles. The provision of an overhanging eaves protects the window below and also eases the vertical positioning of the dormer window within the pattern of the roof covering. The dormer window eaves should fulfil the same requirements as the eaves to the main surface of the roof. If the height of the window is kept to a minimum, which is desirable for the softer transition to the roof surface at the back of the window and better integration within the roof surface, an eaves gutter is unnecessary.

**13** The junction at the sill of the window can be executed similarly to the junction with a wall at the top of a slope. However, to minimise the height of the sill above the roof covering, ventilating tiles are installed instead of a ventilation hood. As the lower air layer has to be ventilated as well, the waterproofing layer stops short of the vertical thermal insulation. The last course of tiles below the window sill stops even further back so that any water that manages to seep through the flashing (secured with rivets and solder) can drip down onto the waterproofing. An alternative detail would be to take the waterproofing layer up to the window sill and join the lower ventilation layer to the upper one by way of vents. The vapour barrier must continue right up to the window frame.

**14** As described under "Profiled clay and concrete tiles – Roof covering with roofing felt underneath", this transition coincides with a transverse joint in the roof covering. It can be made even softer by including a double batten, which spreads the transition over three transverse joints.

Details scale 1:10
00 Bracket
01 Anchor
04 Rivet and solder
05 Clip
06 Fixing for flashing
09 Tenon
10 Spacer rafter
18 Spacer purlin
20 Framing member
21 Purlin
22 Rafter
24 Trimmer
25 Counter batten
26 Batten
27 Feather-edge board
29 Fascia board
32 Timber boarding
33 Timber derivative board
35 Side flashing, with deeper gutter
45 Interlocking profiled tile
46 Step support tile with step
49 Ventilating tile
50 Ventilation hood
53 Back gutter
59 Metal cladding
61 Milled sheet lead flashing
62 Drip flashing
63 Sheet metal window sill
75 Bit. roofing felt, two layers
77 Vapour barrier
80 Thermal insulation, two layers
99 Mesh screen to ventilation opening

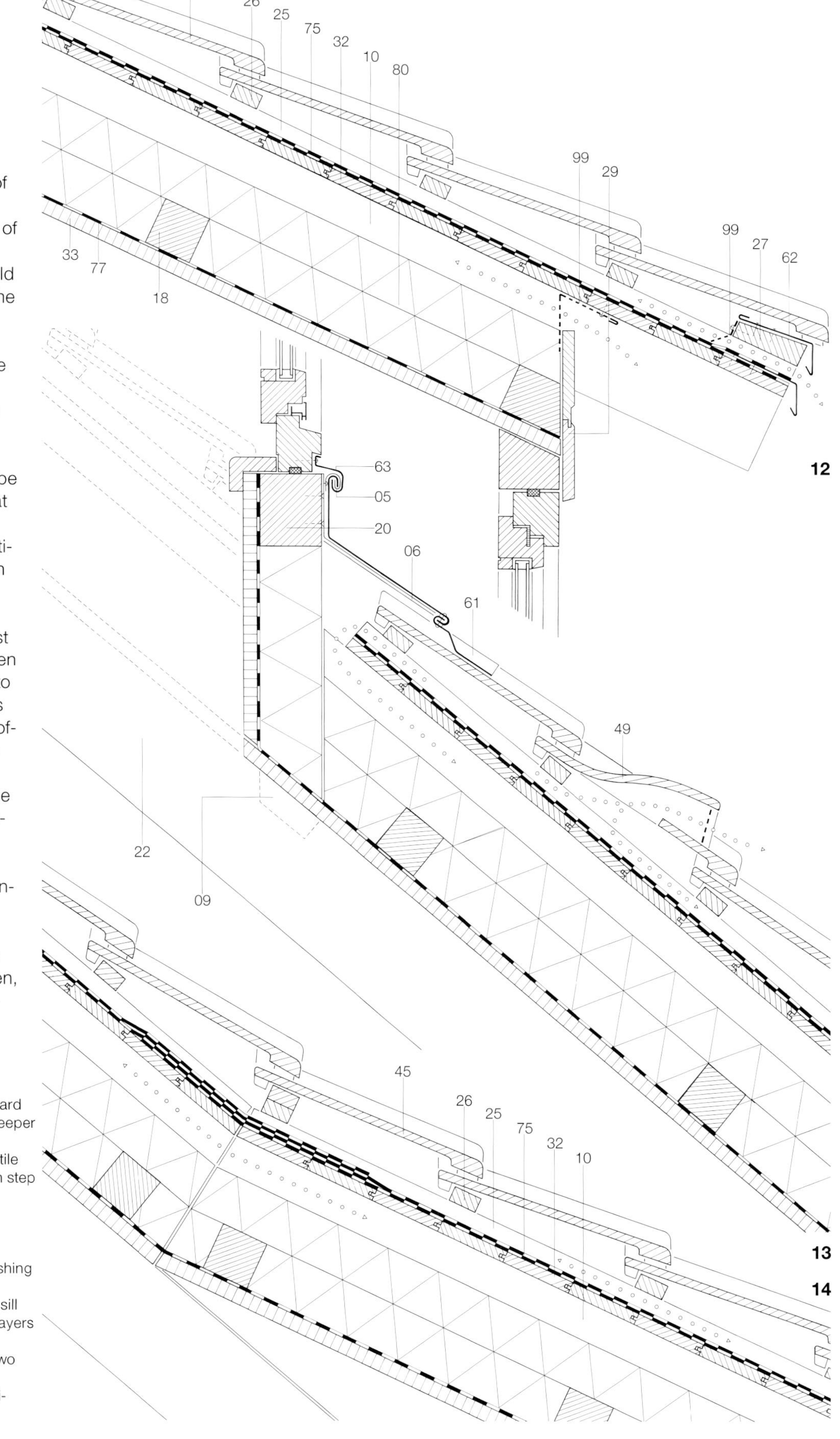

### Insulating glass

Overlapping and sealed designs with preformed seals and glazing bars

**Ridge**

**1** Overlapping panes, ridge to duopitch roof with ventilation louvres
**2** Sealed panes, ridge to duopitch roof
**3** Sealed panes, ridge to monopitch roof

The difference between an overlapping and a sealed design can be found in the transverse joints. In the two cases illustrated here the roof loads are carried by the loadbearing glazing bars parallel to the slope of the roof. The panes of glass are held tightly on the glazing bars by the glazing caps/wings with their integral preformed seals. The sections below the transverse joints have no loadbearing functions.

**1** The overlapping stepped insulating glass units are fitted on wedge-shaped loadbearing glazing bars. The transverse section is also in the form of a step. The panes overlap by at least 30 mm. As the transverse joint is not covered, the hermetic edge seal here must be protected against ultraviolet radiation (e.g. with a metallic coating). Preformed seals are included to prevent capillary action and keep water out in the case of ponding. The louvres guarantee effective ventilation around the ridge. Adapted from louvres commonly found on facades, they have not yet been used extensively.

**2** The sections employed along the transverse joints of sealed panes are very slim and have a bevel on the ridge side so that run-off water can drain over them easily. The section at the ridge to the duopitch roof is a variation on the standard transverse section. Preformed seals are either simply butted together or joined with a form of scarf joint; however, moulded parts (L-, T-, X-piece) are preferable, or better still, vulcanised preformed gasket meshes. The sunshading often necessary with glass roofs – here in the form of louvres – can be supported on the loadbearing longitudinal glazing bars.

**3** The ridge to a monopitch roof shown here is formed by a sandwich panel as thick as the insulating glass units; it can therefore be clamped onto the sealed glazing bars of the roof and the facade. Its size and shape depends on the requirements of the building and the loadbearing structure. At this ridge it is advisable to integrate the ventilation into the facade (louvre window).

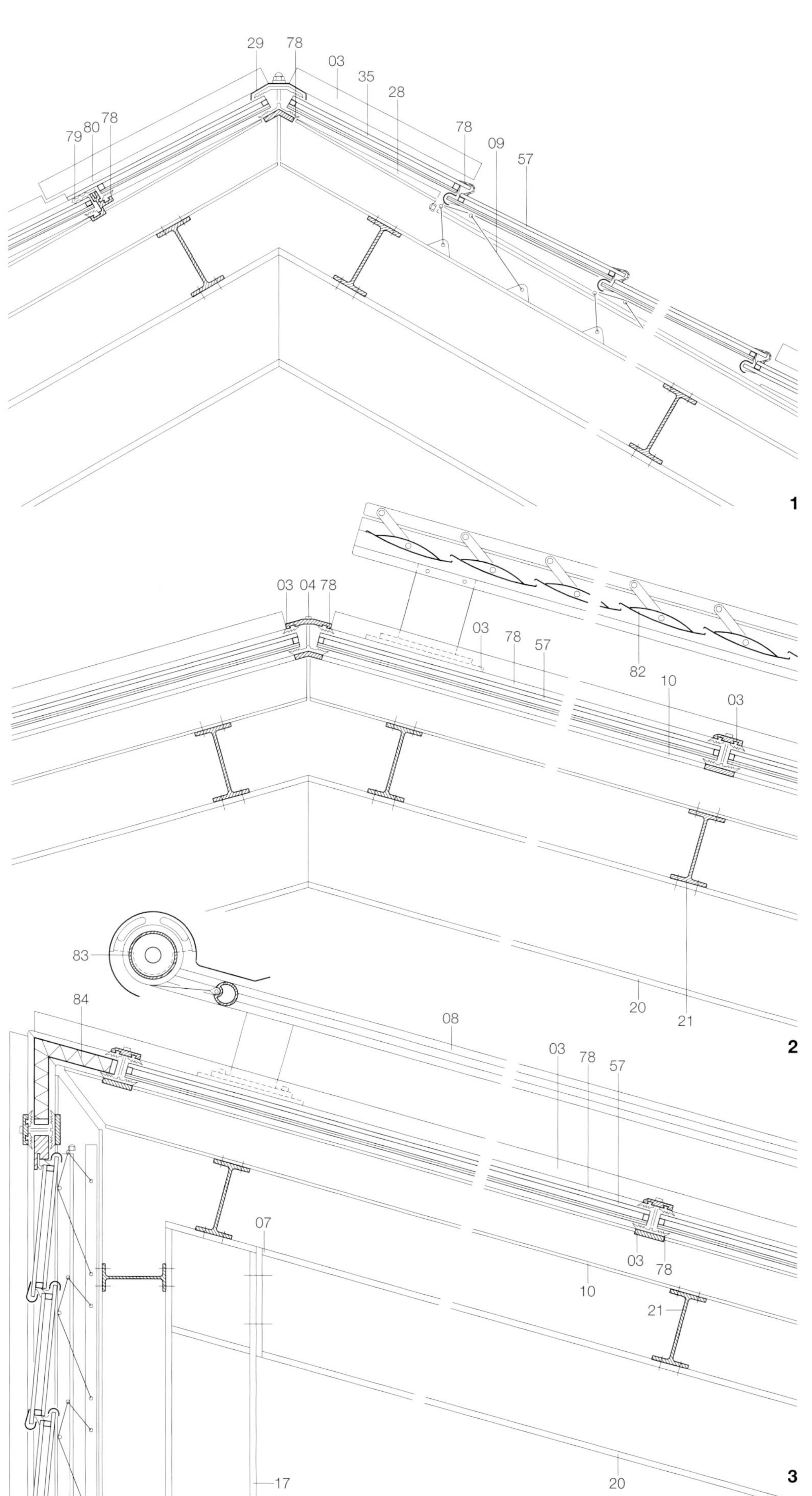

**Hip**

**4** Overlapping panes

As with other types of roof covering, the hip detail is very similar to the ridge detail on a duopitch roof. The details correspond to the principle of overlapping panes with stepped insulating glass units, stepped transverse sections and preformed seals. The hermetic edge seal must be protected against ultraviolet radiation because it is not covered by fixing or sealing components; otherwise it must be made from a UV radiation-resistant material (see "Layers – Glass roof coverings").

**Eaves**

**5** Overlapping panes

**6** Sealed panes

The detail at the eaves can employ either overlapping or sealed panes.

**5** In this example the support along the eaves for the stepped insulating glass units is in the form of an angle section bent to the shape of the corner. The setting blocks prevent the glass sliding down the slope. In order to relieve the shear load on the hermetic edge seal, the upper pane is additionally held at the bottom edge. The cantilever should be at least 200 mm and the overhanging pane made from toughened safety glass. The glazing bar at the eaves also holds the topmost section of the facade (in this case a sandwich panel). The screw attaching the glazing wing/cap to this eaves glazing bar also fixes a flashing pressed up tight against the underside of the upper pane. The gutter is supported on a bracket carrying a gutter bearer; the bracket is screwed to a vertical post in the facade. If these posts are not too far apart, the gutter bearer can be screwed directly to the posts.

**6** The eaves with sealed glazing units may have a corner that is transparent (bent glass) or opaque (as shown here). The water discharges over the edge during heavy rain; but during more moderate rainfall the dirty run-off water is directed via a condensation water channel to the (U-shaped) facade glazing wings/caps.

Details scale 1:10

00 Setting block
03 Glazing wing/cap
04 Machine screw
05 Clip
06 Glass holder
07 End plate, web stiffener
08 Guide rail
09 Spring clip
10 Loadbearing glazing bar
17 Column
18 Bracket with gutter bearer
20 Roof beam
21 Purlin
22 "Jack" glazing bar
23 Hip beam
26 Transverse glazing bar
28 Make-up piece
29 Glazing cap/wing
35 Ventilation element
57 Insulating glass
63 Gutter flashing
78 Permanently elastic preformed seal
79 Permanently elastic sealing strip
80 UV radiation protection
82 Movable louvre
83 Sunblind
84 Sandwich panel
94 Condensation channel
95 Gutter

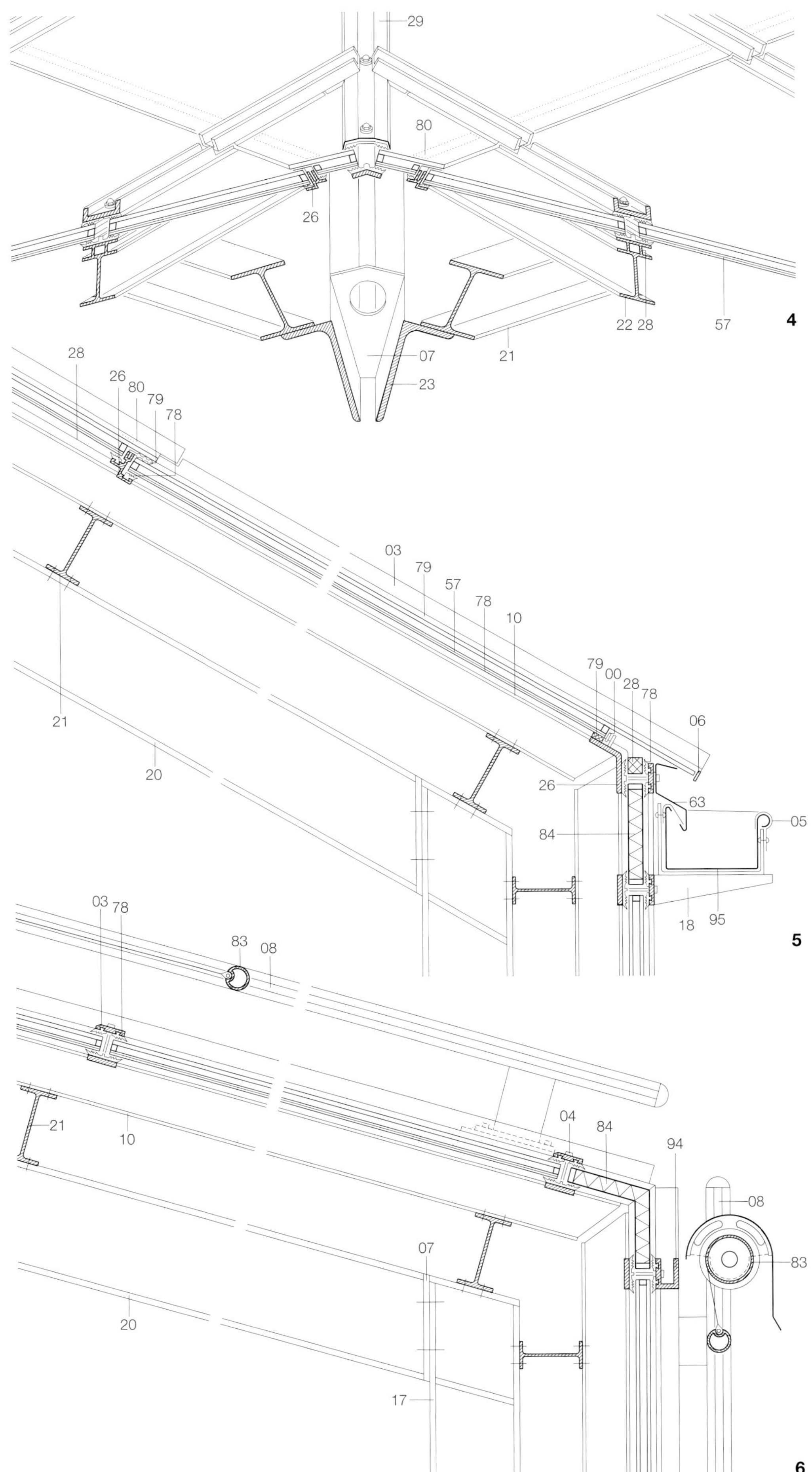

**Valley**
**7** Sealed panes

In order to illustrate the full extent of the problem at the valley, the transverse glazing bars are shown with their intersection with the valley glazing bar clearly visible. This results in a very small pane of glass that should be avoided when planning the grid of the glazing bars.
The valley is more secure with sealed panes than with overlapping ones. As at the ridge, the valley section is merely a variation on the transverse section. The preformed seals at the intersections in the valley area must be very carefully fitted. The use of a vulcanised preformed gasket mesh is conceivable.

**Verge**
**8** Sealed panes

The verge is similar to the ridge of a monopitch roof. The arrangement with sealed panes can accommodate custom-made pieces of any size and shape (according to building and loadbearing structure) or even a transparent solution. The information given above regarding preformed seals applies here too. The louvre sunshade is supported on brackets fixed to the loadbearing glazing wings/caps, or, if necessary, directly to the loadbearing glazing bars.

**Junction with wall**
**9** Junction with wall at side of slope, sealed panes
**10** Junction with wall at side of slope, sealed panes, with gutter and roof vent

**9, 10** The junction with a wall at the side of a slope may or may not include a gutter. In the left-hand drawing (9) a sandwich panel (thickness equal to that of glazing units) is clamped onto the glazing bar and supported at the wall on a sealing strip fitted to an angle. Also clamped to the glazing bar is a flashing, which is turned up the wall and clipped in place. This detail allows roof and wall to move independently of each other.
The depth of the loadbearing glazing bars is exploited in the deeper gutter shown on the right (10). The space between the sheet metal gutter and the internal soffit plate is filled with insulating material. Thicker insulation is also feasible here.
Windows in the roof surface are designed so that the frame projects high enough above the water run-off level (optimum dim. 150 mm). Frame and opening light are then clamped, like all such components, onto the glazing bars.

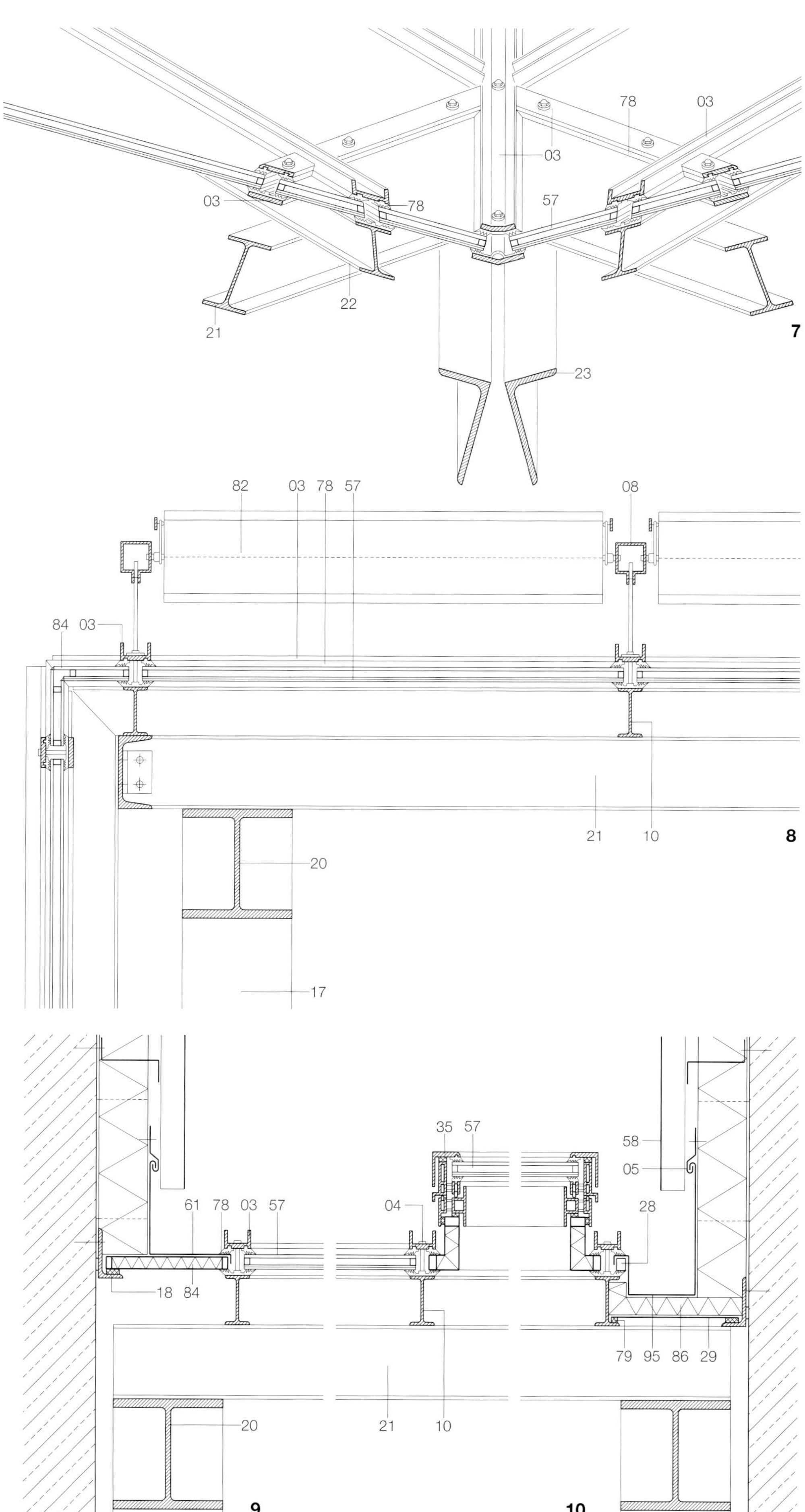

**Junction with wall**

**11** Junction with wall at top of slope, sealed panes

This detail is similar to the junction with a wall at the side of a slope.

**Penetrations**

**12** Chimney, sealed panes

A bay for the chimney penetration is created with two transverse glazing bars. A sandwich panel with a cut-out matching the shape of the flue is then clamped into this bay and the joint between flue and panel sealed on the inside with a preformed ring. A two-piece flashing is clamped onto this sandwich panel such that the ridge side lies over, and the eaves side under, the flange of the flue support sleeve. The flashing is soldered to the flange. The two halves of the flashing overlap on both sides. The flue support sleeve is flashed with a skirt, with a permanently elastic performed seal between skirt and flue.

**Step**

**13** Overlapping panes, ventilated step

The change in roof level can be regarded as a combination of the eaves detail and internal angle – "kink" – detail. This eaves, too, has a holder for the upper pane. It could be omitted on shallow roof pitches, but the hermetic edge seal between the panes would then have a shorter service life because of the shear load effect. The hermetic edge seal should be protected against ultraviolet radiation or be made of a material resistant to UV radiation (see "Layers – Glass roof coverings"). The seal between the vertical glazing and the underside of the upper glass pane is shown here in the form of a flexible sealing lip, which is clamped into the corner glazing bar with a packing piece. The vertical part of the step includes opening lights for ventilation. Condensation collects in a channel from where it can evaporate. The detail at the bottom of the vertical section includes a sandwich element as at the ridge to a monopitch roof.

Details scale 1:10

00 Setting block
03 Glazing wing/cap
04 Machine screw
05 Clip
06 Glass holder
07 End plate, web stiffener
08 Guide rail
09 Spring clip
10 Loadbearing glazing bar
17 Column
18 Bracket with gutter bearer
20 Roof beam
21 Purlin
22 "Jack" glazing bar
23 Hip beam
26 Transverse glazing bar
28 Make-up piece
29 Glazing cap/wing
35 Ventilation element
57 Insulating glass
63 Gutter flashing
78 Permanently elastic preformed seal
79 Permanently elastic sealing strip
80 UV radiation protection
82 Movable louvre
83 Sunblind
84 Sandwich panel
94 Condensation channel
95 Gutter
96 Flue support sleeve

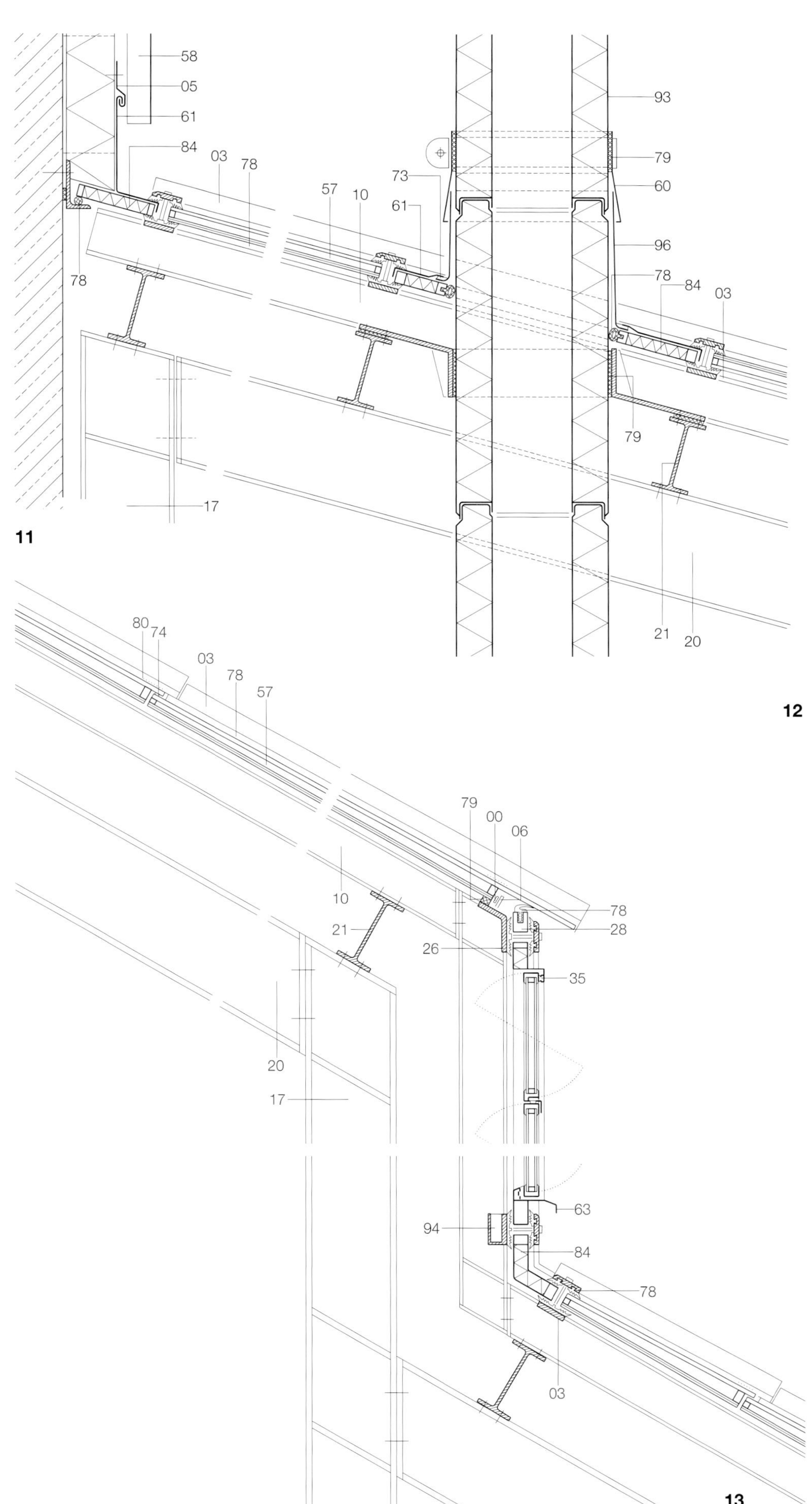

**Fibre-cement corrugated sheeting**

Sheeting on battens, roofing felt on timber boarding, ventilated thermal insulation and vapour barrier

**Ridge**

**1** Ridge with one-piece corrugated capping
**2** Ridge with two-piece corrugated capping
**3** Ridge with two-piece corrugated ventilating capping
**4** Ventilated ridge with hood

End laps between fibre-cement corrugated sheets are ≥ 150 mm or ≥ 200 mm, according to pitch. At pitches ≤ 10° an additional 8 mm dia. preformed sealing strip is required in the end laps. The ridge is generally laid in the opposite direction to the prevailing wind.

**1** A ridge with a one-piece corrugated capping, in contrast to two- and three-piece ridges, requires the sheeting on both sides of the ridge to be laid with all corrugations exactly aligned.

**2, 3** When using a two-piece corrugated capping or ventilating capping, the upper piece of each pair should be laid on the side facing the prevailing wind. A preformed sealing strip laid in the lap between the pieces prevents the ingress of driving rain and snow.

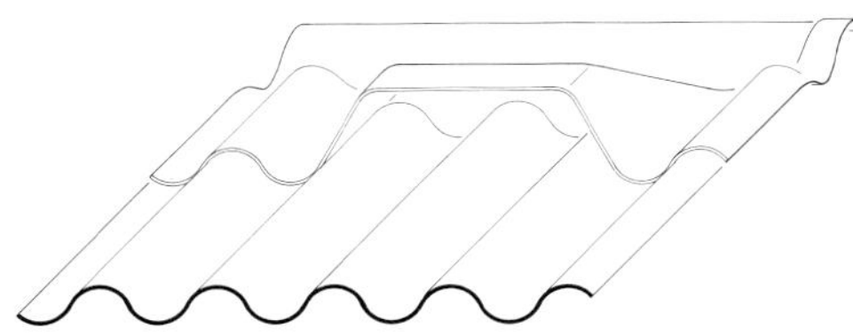

**4** The ventilated ridge with a hood is joined to the corrugated sheeting on both sides by way of fibre-cement apron flashing pieces. The corrugated sheets are laid on purlins or battens depending on the load and the span. A layer of roofing felt laid across the slope prevents the ingress of driving rain and snow and catches any condensation water dripping from the underside of the roof covering. Below the roof covering, timber boarding (≥ 19 mm) capable of supporting foot traffic eases erection and repair work.
The depth of the ventilation layer above the single layer of thermal insulation laid between the rafters should be ≥ 60 mm, depending on the pitch. The vapour barrier ($s_d$ ≥ 10 m) also functions as an airtight membrane.
Ventilation at the ridge can be by way of individual vents inserted into the sheeting, special ridge vents protected by a mesh screen or mesh box, or a ventilation hood arrangement. All ventilation measures call for roofing felt to be laid below the roof covering, and the ventilation hood also requires a sheet metal flashing underneath the ridge.

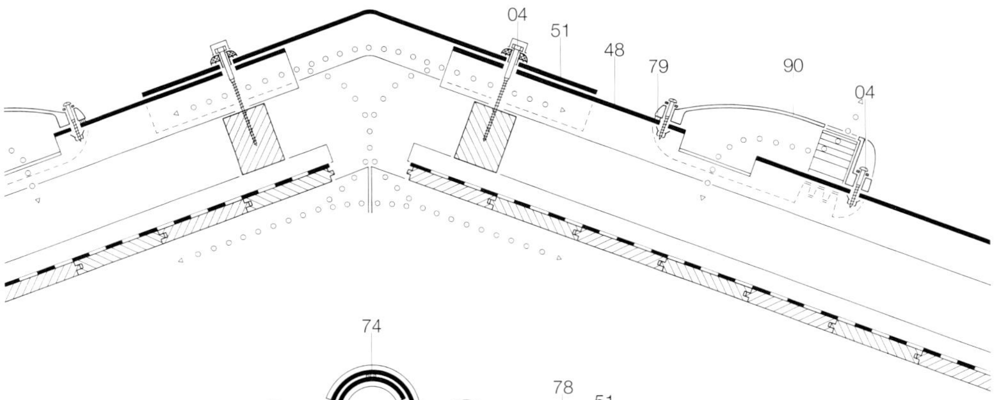

1

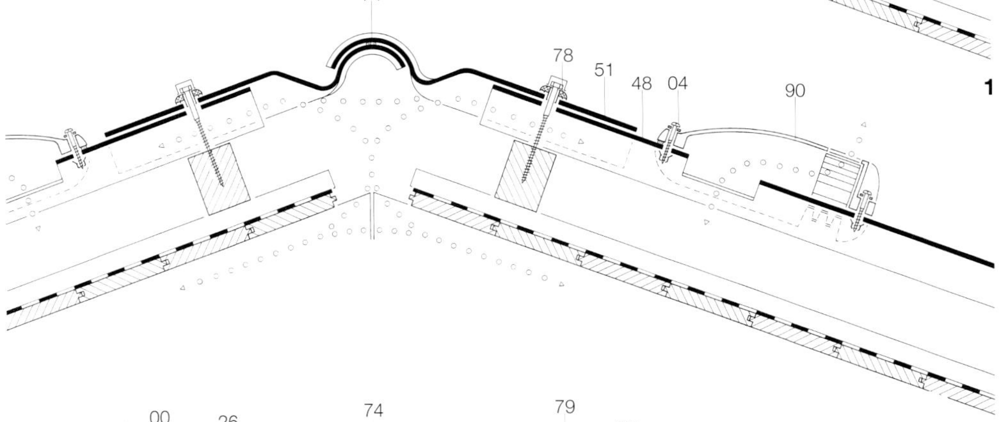

2

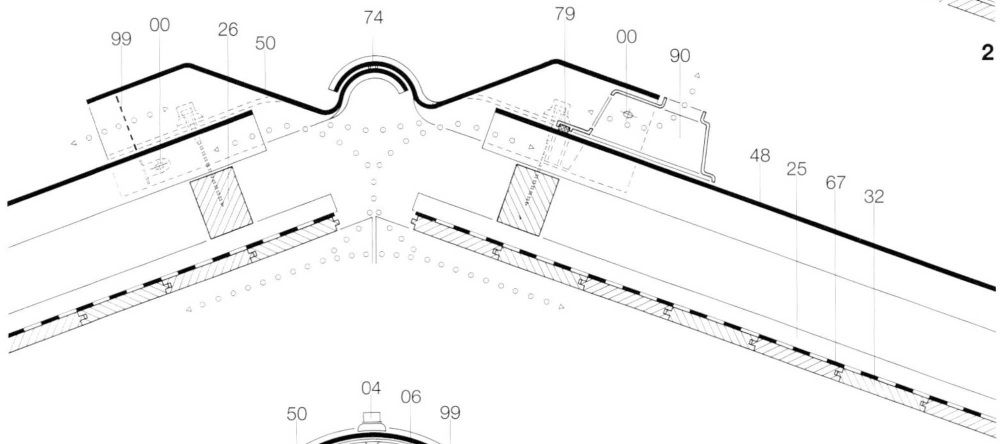

3

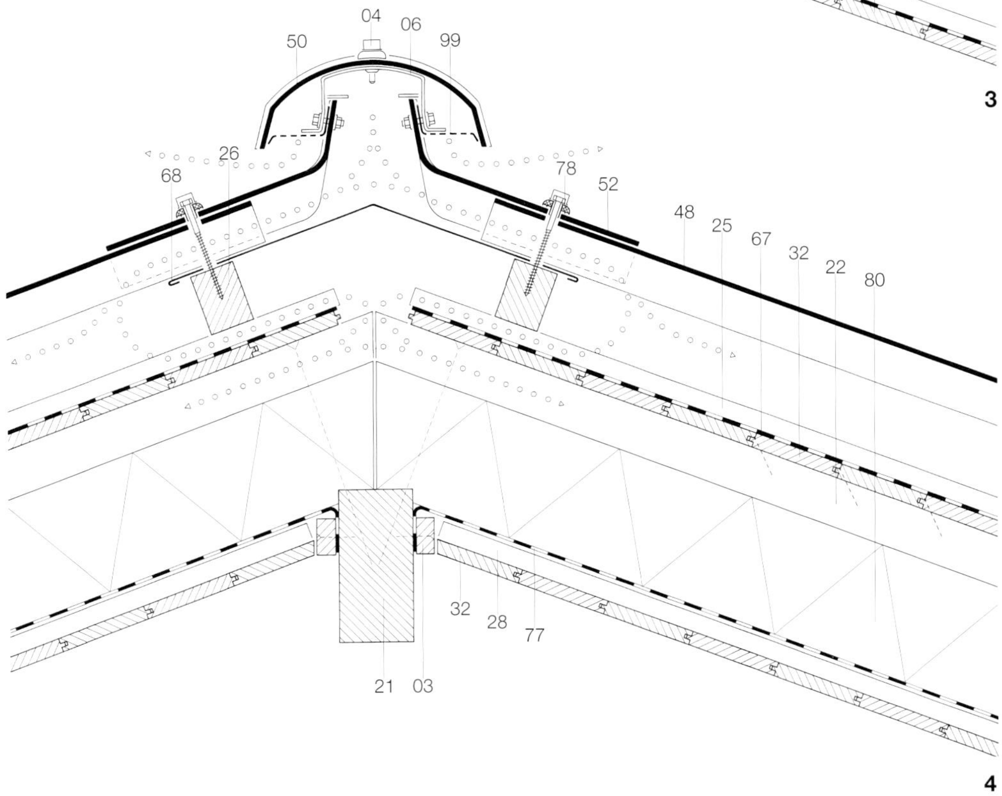

4

**Further ridge details**

**5** Ridge to duopitch roof, mono ridge capping
**6** Ridge to monopitch roof, with mono ridge capping
**7** Ridge to monopitch roof, with profile filler fascia board

The mono ridge capping overlaps the outer leaf of the external wall by 50–100 mm and the profile filler fascia board overlaps the soffit of the roof overhang to a similar degree. While water drips safely off the mono ridge capping, in the case of the overhanging corrugated sheets water can penetrate to the inside on the underside of the sheets. At a low pitch (≤ 10°) rainwater can be driven over the edge of the ridge by the wind; at steeper pitches (25–30°) driving rain can reach the underside directly. Shallower and steeper pitches than these call for the joint between corrugated sheeting and profile filler fascia board to be sealed with a permanently plastic material or for the inclusion of an eaves closure piece, likewise sealed. The end of the rafter (end grain) should be protected by a timber capping.
The joint between mono ridge capping and corrugated sheeting must be sealed with a permanently plastic material because there is no roofing felt or timber boarding underneath this point. Projecting spacer battens prevent the roof loads being transferred to the outer leaf. Their load-carrying capacity determines the length of the cantilever, and can be increased by using larger or additional battens. The cantilever of the corrugated sheeting must be ≤ 1/4 of the maximum permissible batten/purlin span.
Ladder hooks (max. every 1500 mm) are screwed to the batten/purlin (hole cut through crest in end lap). A special bearing distributes the load evenly over the corrugation.

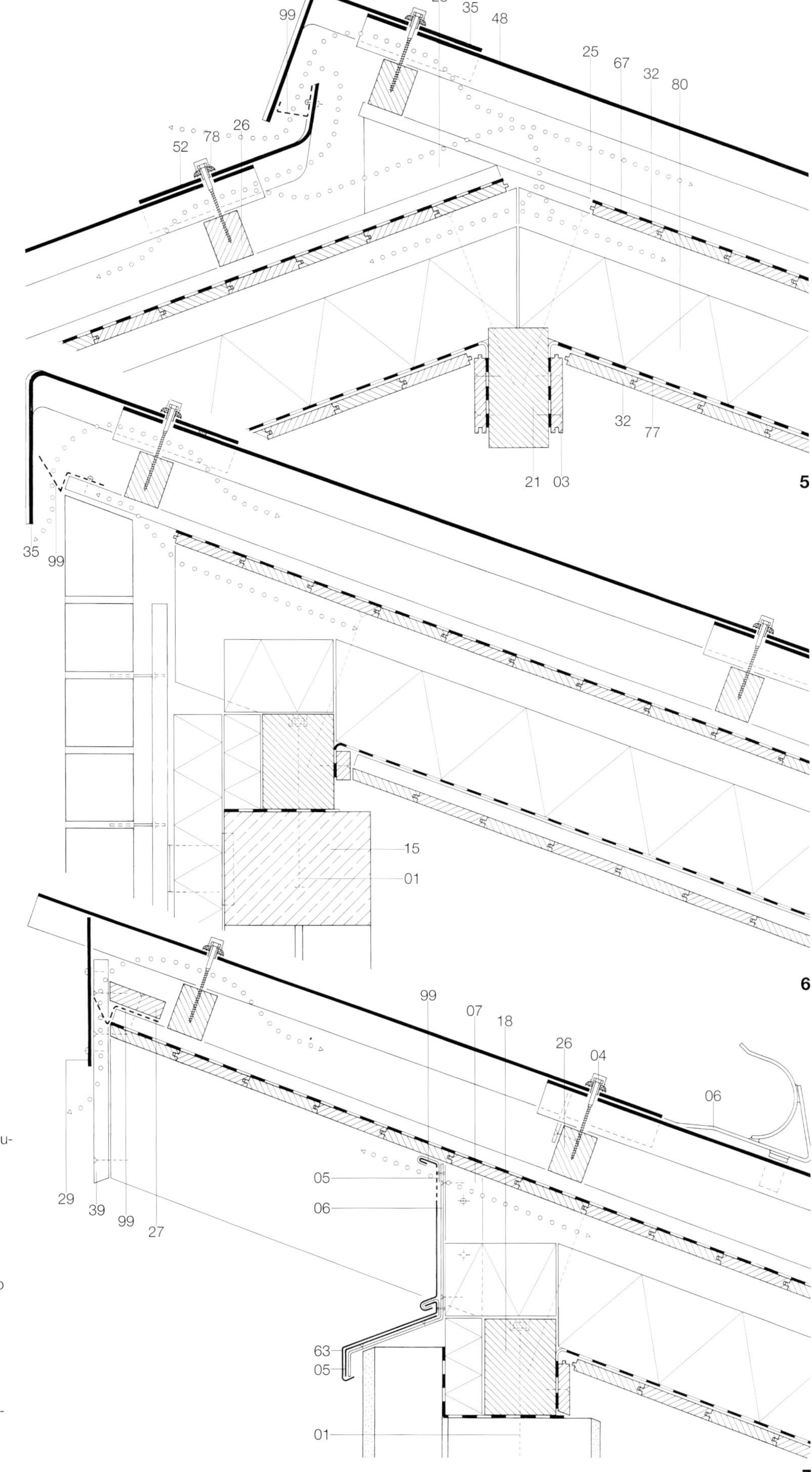


Details scale 1:10

00 Plastic rivet
01 Masonry anchor
03 Vapour barrier clamped behind batten/board
04 Screw
05 Clip, continuous clip
06 Fixing for flashing
07 Timber block
15 Peripheral reinforcement (in capping beam)
18 Wall plate
21 Purlin
22 Rafter
25 Spacer batten
26 Batten
27 Ridge board
28 Make-up piece
29 Fibre-cement upper fascia board
32 Timber boarding
35 Mono ridge capping
39 Fascia board
48 Fibre-cement corrugated sheet
50 Ventilation hood, two-piece ventilating capping
51 One- or two-piece corrugated capping
52 Fibre-cement apron flashing piece
63 Flashing
67 Roofing felt (laid with laps)
68 Flashing
74 Preformed sealing strip
77 Vapour barrier
78 Plastic washer with metal inlay
79 Sealing strip
80 Thermal insulation
90 Vent
99 Mesh screen to ventilation opening

**Hip**

**8** Hip with milled sheet lead flashing and individual vents
**9** Hip with ventilating capping
**10** Hip with capping bedded in mortar

In contrast to the ridge, the hip is covered with a special hip capping. Each capping piece is shaped like a socket at its eaves end. The capping is laid on a hip board and attached with screws, nails or clips.
To create a rainproof roof covering, the hip capping is laid on milled sheet lead dressed over the profiled sheeting, or bedded in lime or lime-cement mortar. This bed should be formed so that the bottom edges of the hip capping create a 20 mm rainwater drip. An alternative is to employ hip ventilating elements with flexible skirts that adapt to the shape of the corrugations.

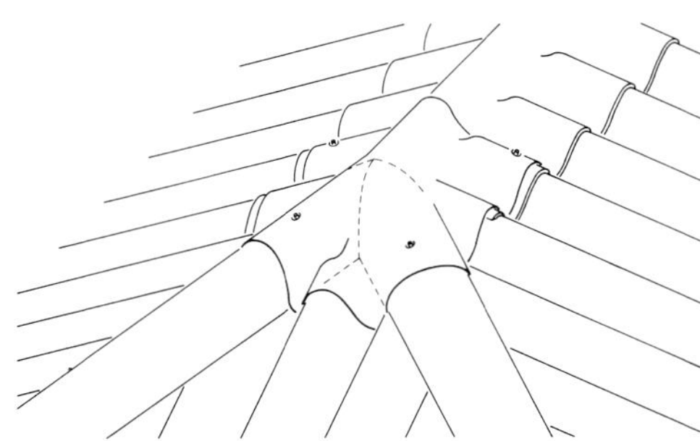

The hip-ridge intersection is protected by a milled sheet lead flashing (1.0–2.0 mm thick), which is fastened together with the fibre-cement sheeting (see sketch).
The hip ventilation on a pavilion roof (no ridge) is feasible only with individual vents (75–150 cm² per vent) and ventilating hip cappings (100 cm²/m). On other types of roof (with ridge) the advantage of continuous spacer battens and sheeting battens with ventilation below the roof covering can be exploited.
The ventilation layer above the thermal insulation is connected to the ventilation layer below the roof covering at the hip by a sufficient number of vents (see "Layers – Ventilation").

Details scale 1:10
05 Clip, continuous clip
06 Fixing for flashing
07 Timber block, metal angle bracket
10 Fixing board
15 Peripheral reinforcement
16 Mortar
18 Wall plate
22 Rafter, jack rafter
23 Hip/valley rafter
25 Spacer batten
26 Batten
27 Tilting board
31 Strengthening rod
32 Timber boarding
48 Fibre-cement corrugated sheet
49 Vent
51 Hip capping, with "socket"
53 Fibre-cement eaves closure piece
61 Milled sheet lead
63 Eaves/gutter flashing
66 Separating layer
67 Roofing felt
77 Vapour barrier
80 Thermal insulation
90 Ventilating element
93 Vent
95 Gutter
96 Rainwater downpipe
98 Snowguard (fence/tube)
99 Mesh screen to ventilation opening

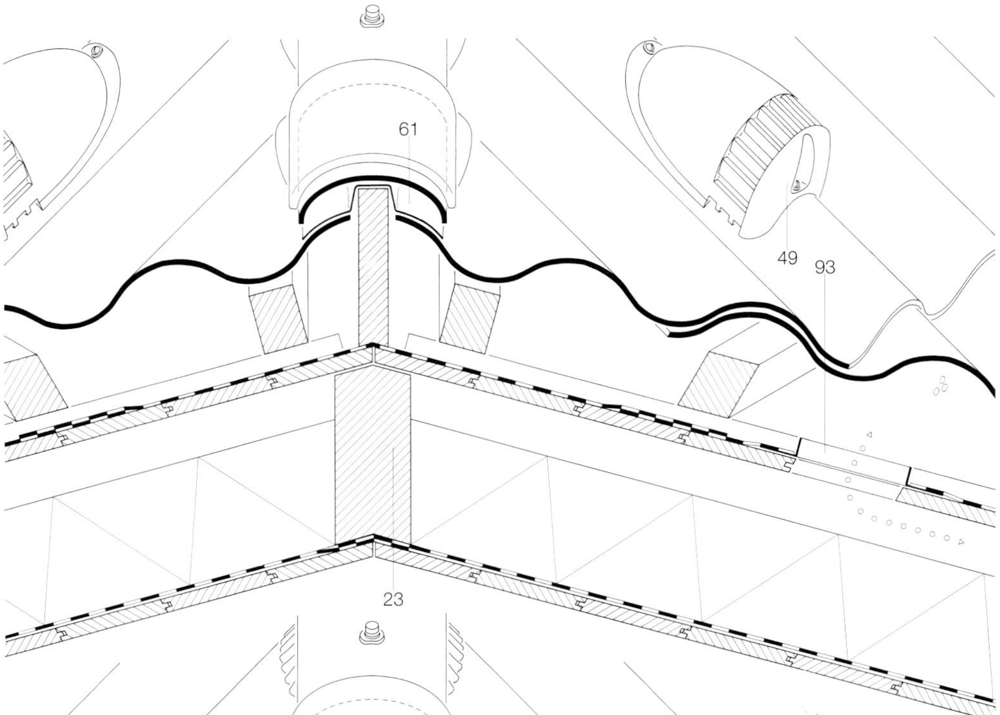

8

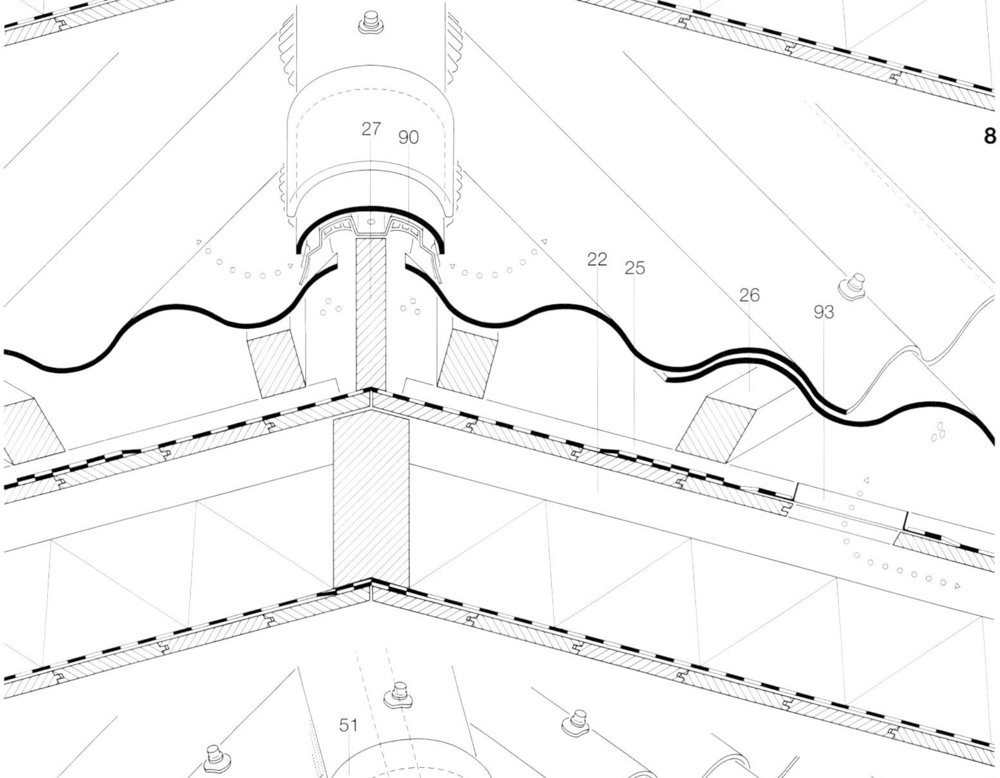

9

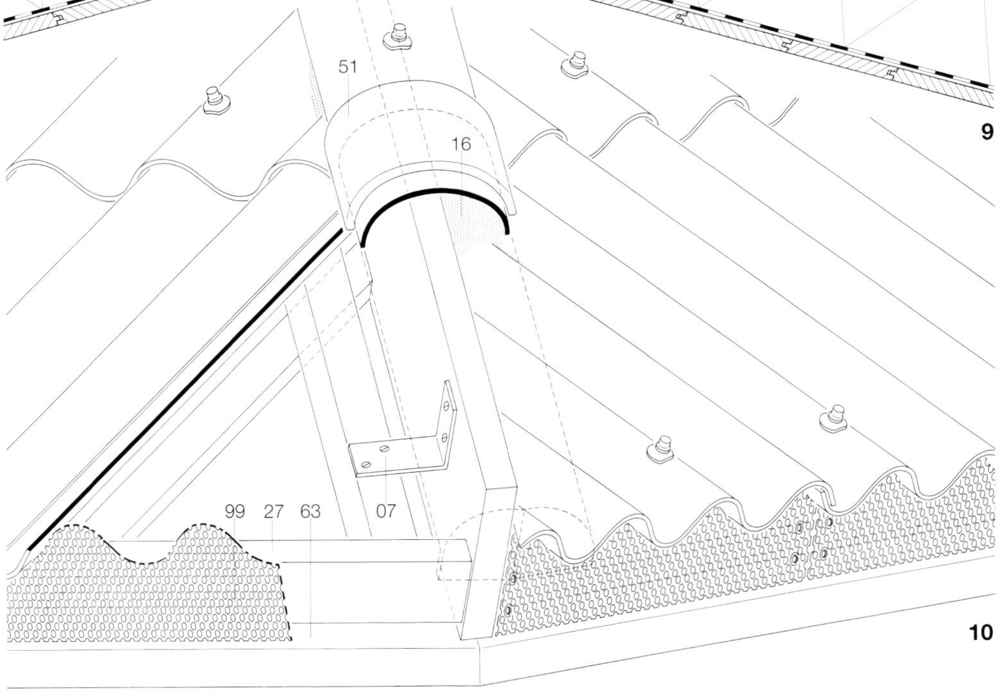

10

#### Eaves

**11** Eaves with closure piece and tubular snowguard
**12** Eaves with gutter flashing and fence-type snowguard

Here, as at the ridge, the corrugated sheeting may cantilever ≤ 1/4 of the maximum permissible batten/purlin span. A board supports the bottom end of the sheets and packs them up to maintain the roof pitch. The gutter flashing is fixed to this board, which is notched to accommodate the gutter brackets. Protection against splashing water is achieved at the eaves gutter by means of the eaves closure piece or the gutter flashing with turned-up top edge.
For details of the longitudinal and transverse falls of the gutter see "Layers – Drainage". Snowboards should slide over the gutter. Snowguards should be fixed through each crest (see sketch) with one screw (≥ 10 mm dia.) to an existing batten/purlin or one inserted for the purpose. If the formation of ice and ponding of melt water is anticipated, a piece of corrugated sheeting 2500 mm long can be employed, with a permanently plastic seal in the side laps.
On shallow roofs without an overhang at the eaves it is recommended to position the gutter at a lower level to drain water from the underlying roofing felt into the gutter as well.
Even a snow-filled gutter may not hinder the ventilation below the roof covering. This is guaranteed by providing sufficiently deep spacer battens to ensure a large air gap below the gutter.

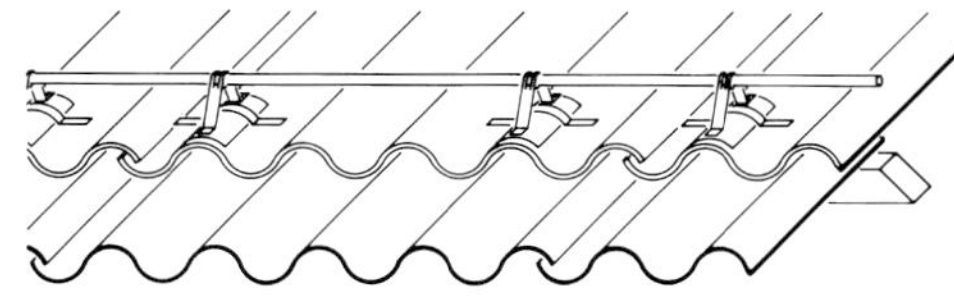

A mesh screen protects the ventilation opening against birds and small animals. The end of the rafter exposed to the rain (end grain) should be protected by a timber capping.

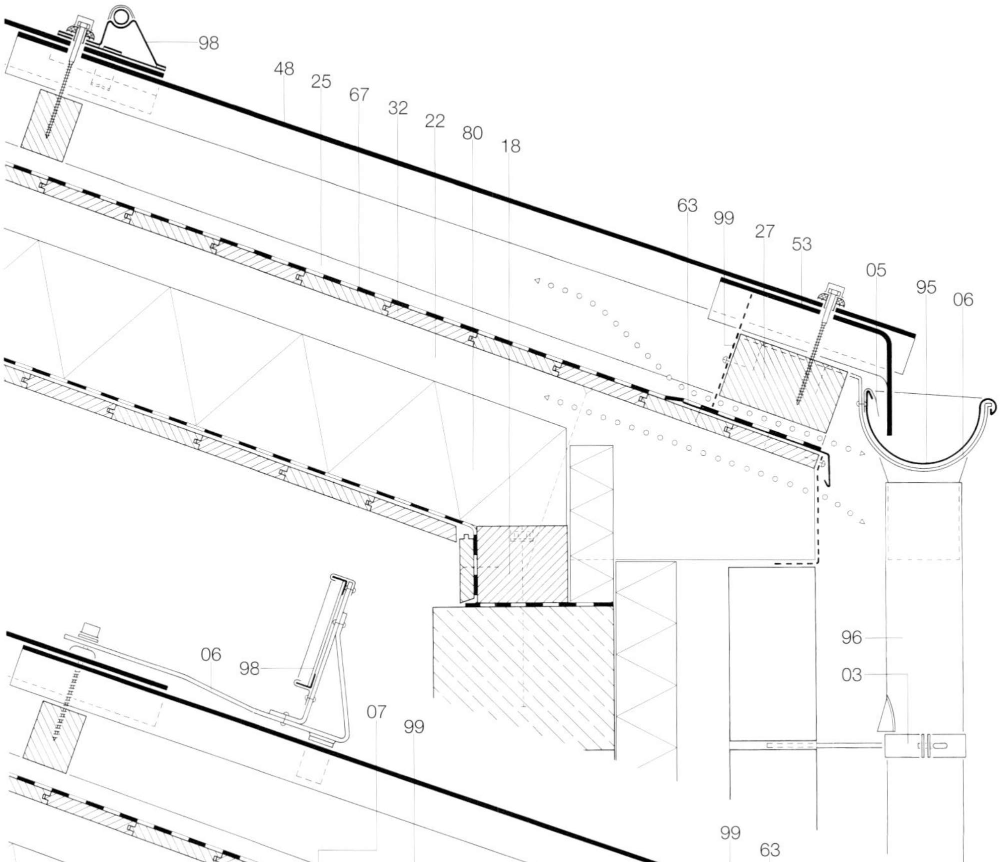

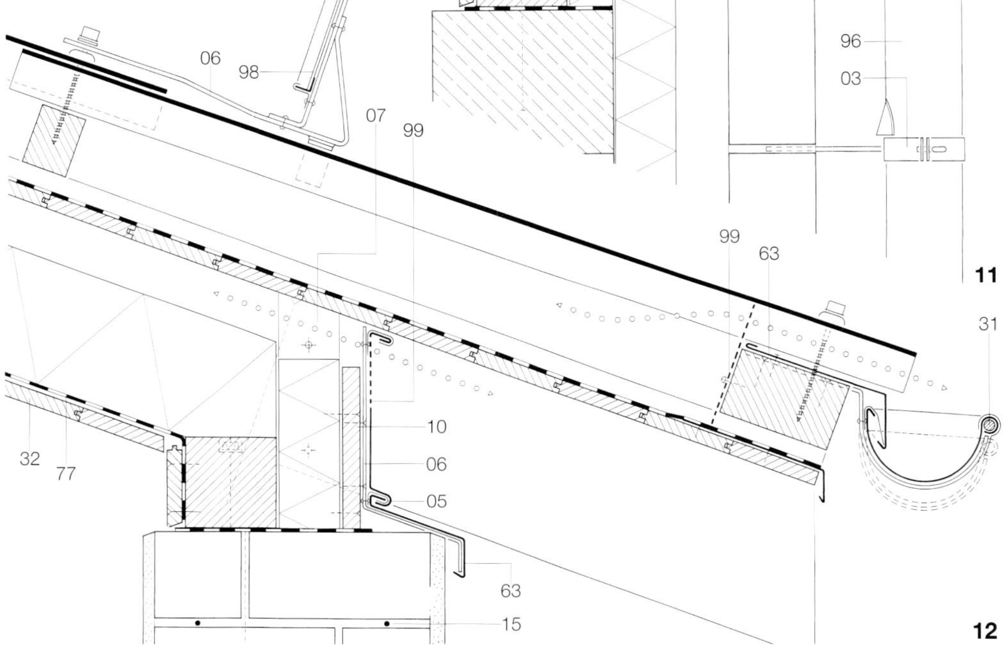

#### Valley

**13** Valley with deeper gutter

Deeper valleys are always specified. This involves a sheet metal gutter with a deeper central section (≤ 40 mm) and turned-up edges on both sides. If necessary, an additional baffle can be included in the centre of the gutter to help channel the flow of large amounts of fast-flowing water. The corrugated sheeting overlaps the sheet metal ≥ 100 mm and the deeper centre channel itself ≥ 50 mm. This section should remain open ≥ 150 mm to enable self-cleaning or ≥ 200 mm if manual cleaning is necessary. The top end of the valley should be flashed and secured with milled sheet lead (1.0–2.0 mm) as at the hip-ridge intersection.

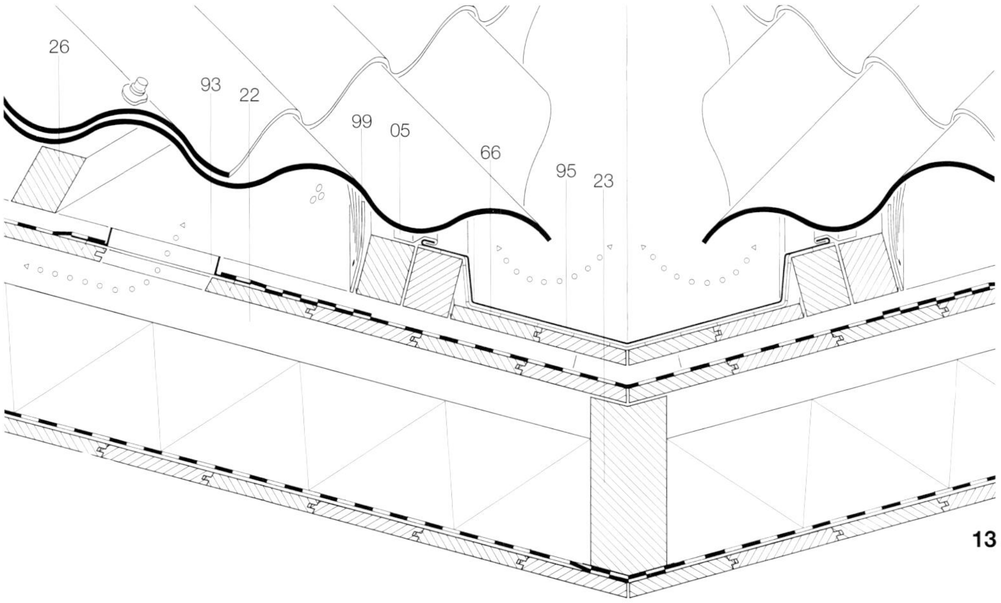

**Verge**

**14** Verge with special verge element
**15** Verge with fibre-cement bargeboard
**16** Overhanging verge with timber bargeboard

**14** The special verge element is corrugated to match the sheeting and overlaps the final sheet by one whole corrugation. It is supported by a batten on edge to prevent it deflecting under load. The cloak of the verge element is positioned ≥ 10 mm clear of the external wall so that rainwater can drip off unhindered. However, it may be necessary to increase this clearance for tolerance reasons.

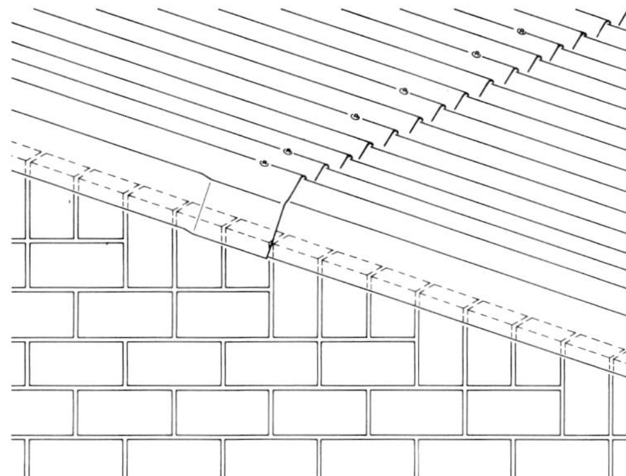

**15, 16** The final trough of the sheet at a verge must be fully supported and end with a downward corrugation. The fibre-cement or timber bargeboard is held in tension with a packing batten or board.
Side laps should be 50–100 mm, depending on type of sheeting.
The thermal insulation on top of the external wall is not ventilated. It should therefore be water-repellent.
Elsewhere, the air flows in both ventilation layers in the direction of the slope, which means that no extra ventilation arrangements are required at the verge. A sponge rubber seal closes off the joint between vapour barrier and masonry wall. The suspended sealing has a smoke-tight joint at this position and provides the necessary fire protection.

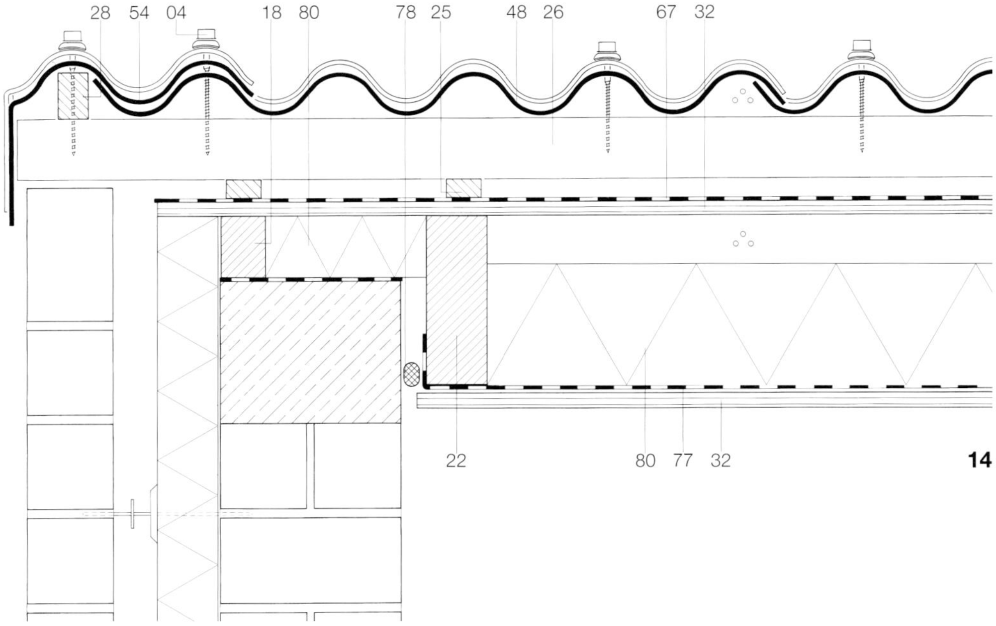

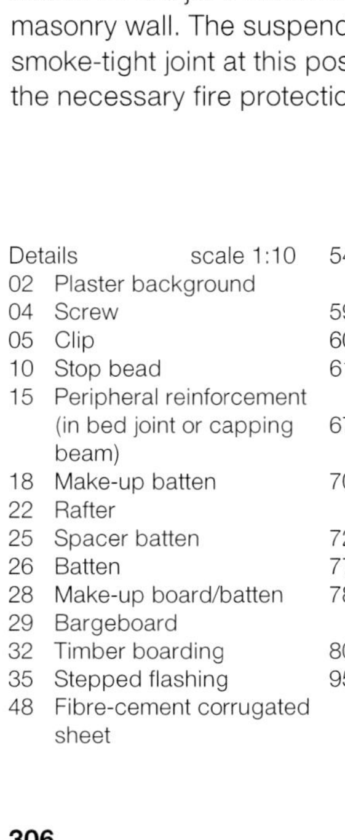

Details scale 1:10

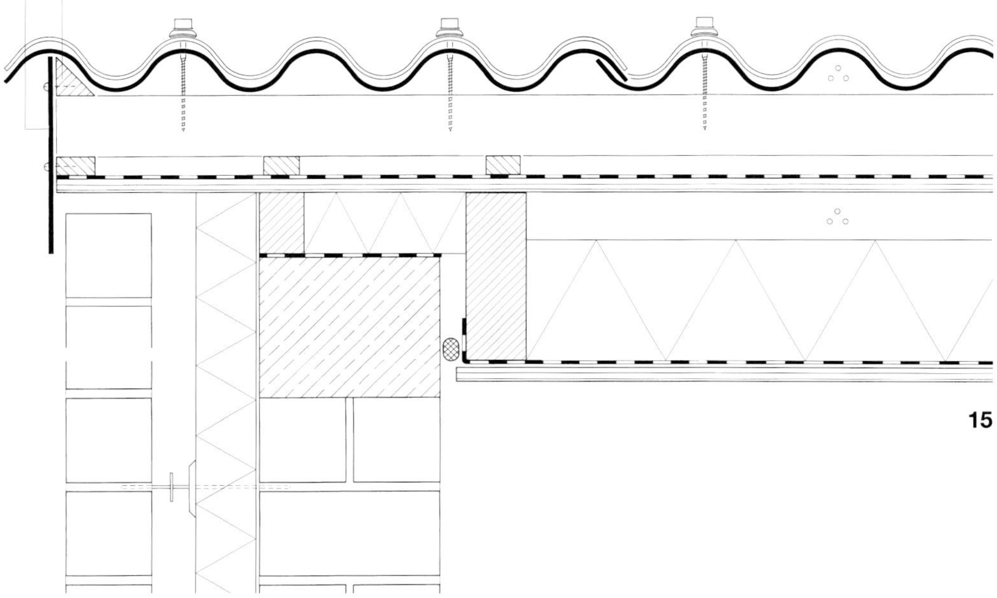

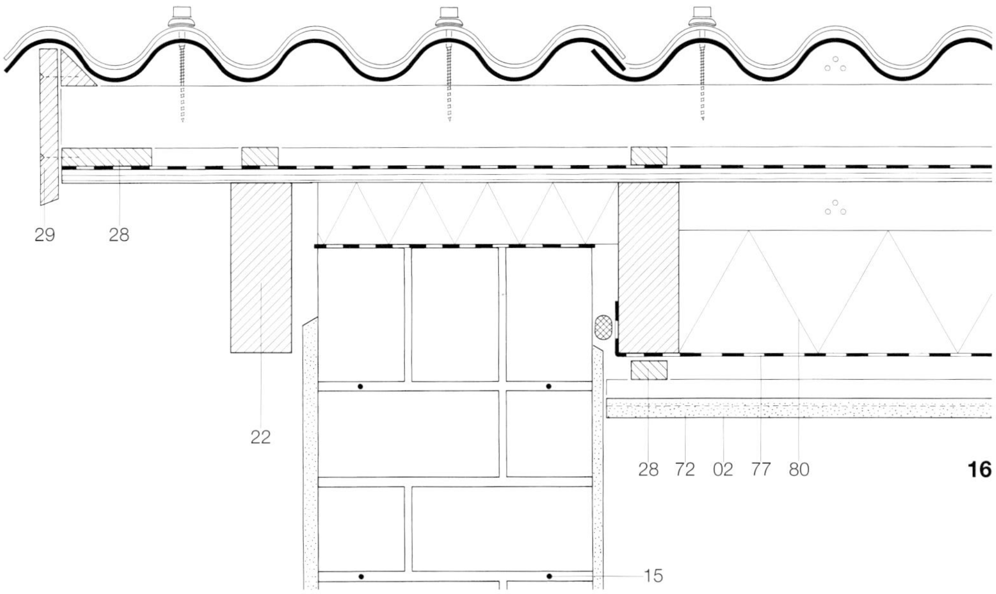

02 Plaster background
04 Screw
05 Clip
10 Stop bead
15 Peripheral reinforcement (in bed joint or capping beam)
18 Make-up batten
22 Rafter
25 Spacer batten
26 Batten
28 Make-up board/batten
29 Bargeboard
32 Timber boarding
35 Stepped flashing
48 Fibre-cement corrugated sheet
54 Fibre-cement verge element
59 Sheet metal gutter
60 Sheet metal capping
61 Flashing plus milled sheet lead, riveted
67 Roofing felt (laid with laps)
70 Damp-proof course and cavity tray
72 Rendering
77 Vapour barrier
78 Permanently elastic seal
80 Thermal insulation
95 Gutter

14

15

16

**Party wall**

**17** Party wall detail with gutter

For reasons of sound insulation, terraced houses are built with separate party walls. Accordingly, no loadbearing members extend across the joint. The party walls are protected by a sheet metal gutter that extends on both sides below the first trough of the fibre-cement sheeting. The roofing felt extends across the joint with a generous overlap. The loadbearing members cantilever up to the joint, across the tops of the party walls, and can move independently. The sheet metal gutter and the roofing felt deform to accommodate any horizontal movements of the loadbearing members. The thermal insulation continues across the two walls without joints in order to prevent cold air reaching the non-insulated walls.

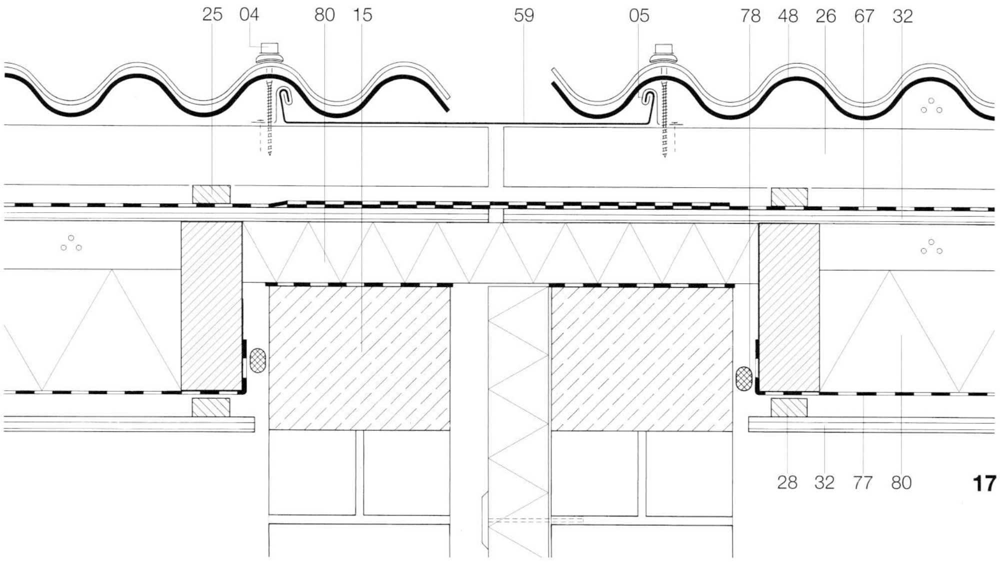

25 04 80 15 59 05 78 48 26 67 32

28 32 77 80

17

**Junction with wall**

**18** Junction with wall at side of slope, with gutter

**19** Junction with wall at side of slope, with milled sheet lead flashing

**18** The shallow gutter shown here is adequate for small amounts of driving rain draining down the wall. A deeper gutter is required when larger amounts of water are anticipated.

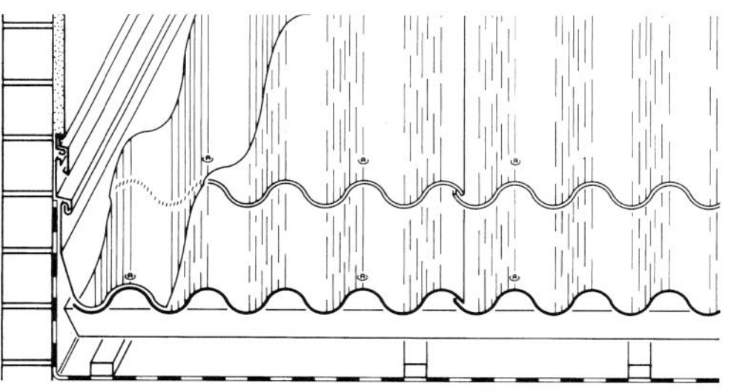

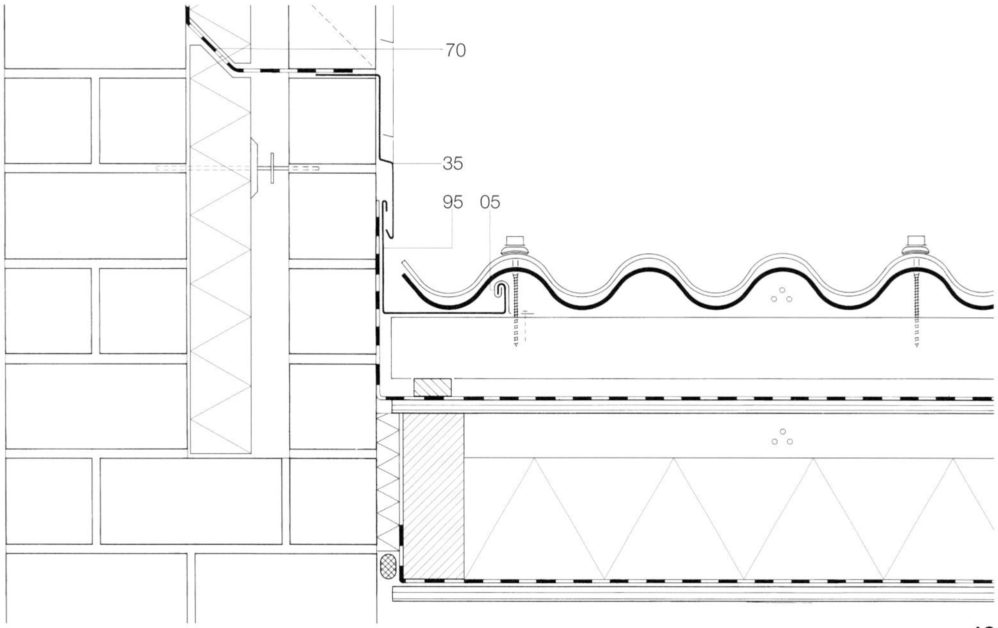

The bent-up edge of the gutter is fitted behind the first trough. It is pressed down by the corrugated sheeting and fastened with clips. The side of the gutter is turned up the wall 100–150 mm together with the roofing felt, and covered by a stepped flashing let into the bed joints of the masonry. Vertical movement is possible.

**19** If the wall is not parallel to the corrugations, a milled sheet lead flashing should be dressed over the corrugations (see sketch). This strip of lead is easily moulded to follow the shape of the corrugations, and extends over the first crest into the neighbouring trough. It must be welted to a stiffer sheet metal flashing over its whole length and additionally secured with rivets (loadbearing function) and solder (sealing function).

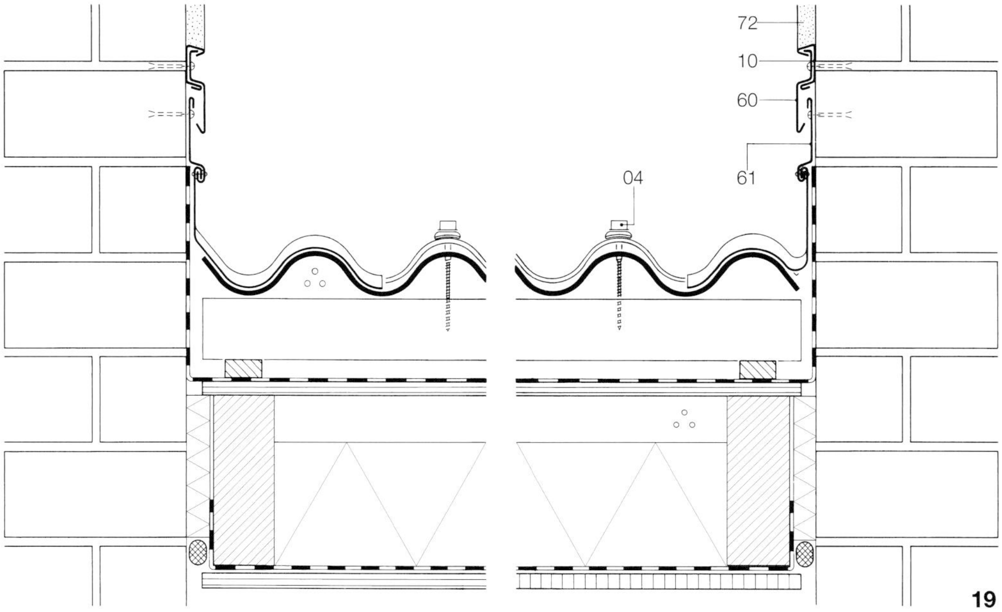

70 35 95 05

18

72 10 60 04 61

19

**Junction with wall, back gutter**

**20** Back gutter, secure vent, junction with window sill

**21** Back gutter capable of carrying foot traffic, plus safety gutter

**20** Back gutter constructions are particularly at risk because water can collect in them.
A reasonable number of outlets, adequately sized overflows (60–100 mm dia.), generous dimensions, and extending the gutter and underlying waterproofing layer up the wall and up the roof (250–300 mm) are measures that increase the reliability of back gutters.
The back gutter illustrated here is a simple version. Various materials can be used and the width of the gutter is limited only by the material chosen (≤ 1000 mm or ≤ 1500 mm).
The sheet metal should be continued as a bonded (sealed) bitumen gutter wherever water can back up.
A triangular fillet packs up the boarding and rounds off the shape of the gutter.
Gutter heating is indispensable for ensuring that the gutter continues to function during the winter.
Multiple redirection of the air flow in the ventilation hood ensures that the lower air layer is reliably ventilated. The upper ventilation layer receives a supply of fresh air at counter batten level. A fibre-cement eaves closure piece closes off the openings on the underside of the corrugated sheeting.

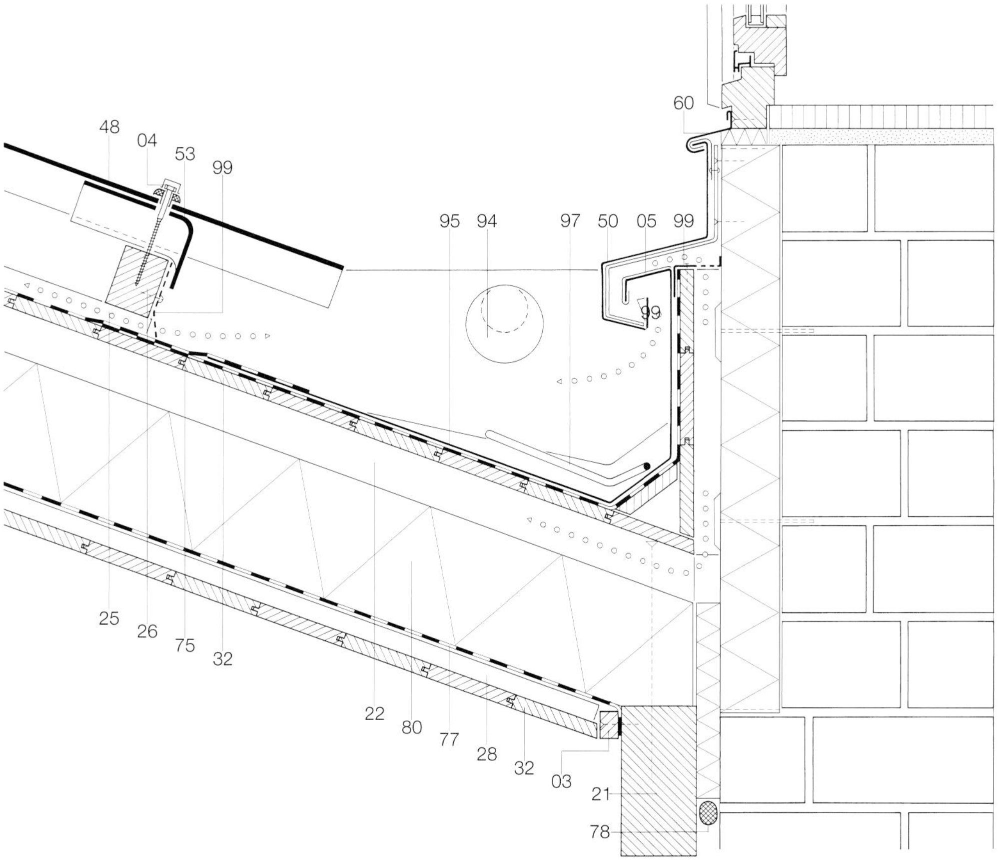

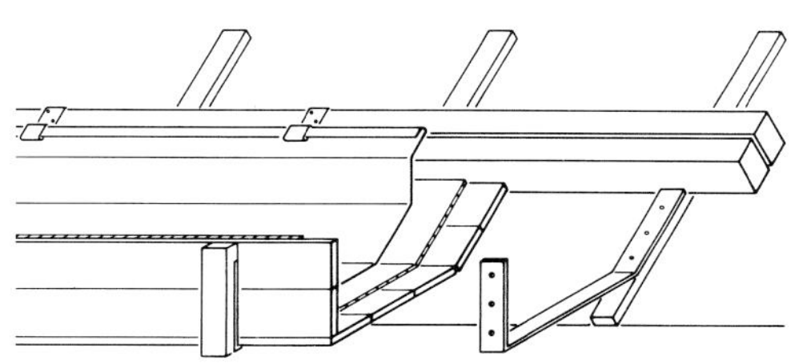

**21** A safety gutter can be included below the back gutter to minimise the risk of water build-up. It consists of two layers of bonded bitumen roofing felt or one layer of built-up roofing felt. The roofing felt is laid on its own timber boarding and continues beyond the area at risk of ponding. A triangular fillet rounds off sharp corners < 45°. The back gutter is laid on a separating layer plus timber boarding and is supported on steel straps (see sketch). The safety gutter thus remains uncluttered by other components. Both gutters are protected by a common ventilation hood. This redirects the air flow only once and is not secure against driving rain and snow, but any incoming moisture is reliably intercepted by the safety gutter.
Back gutters should be maintained at regular intervals and should therefore be accessible (≥ 200 mm, preferably 300 mm) and able to withstand the weight of operatives.

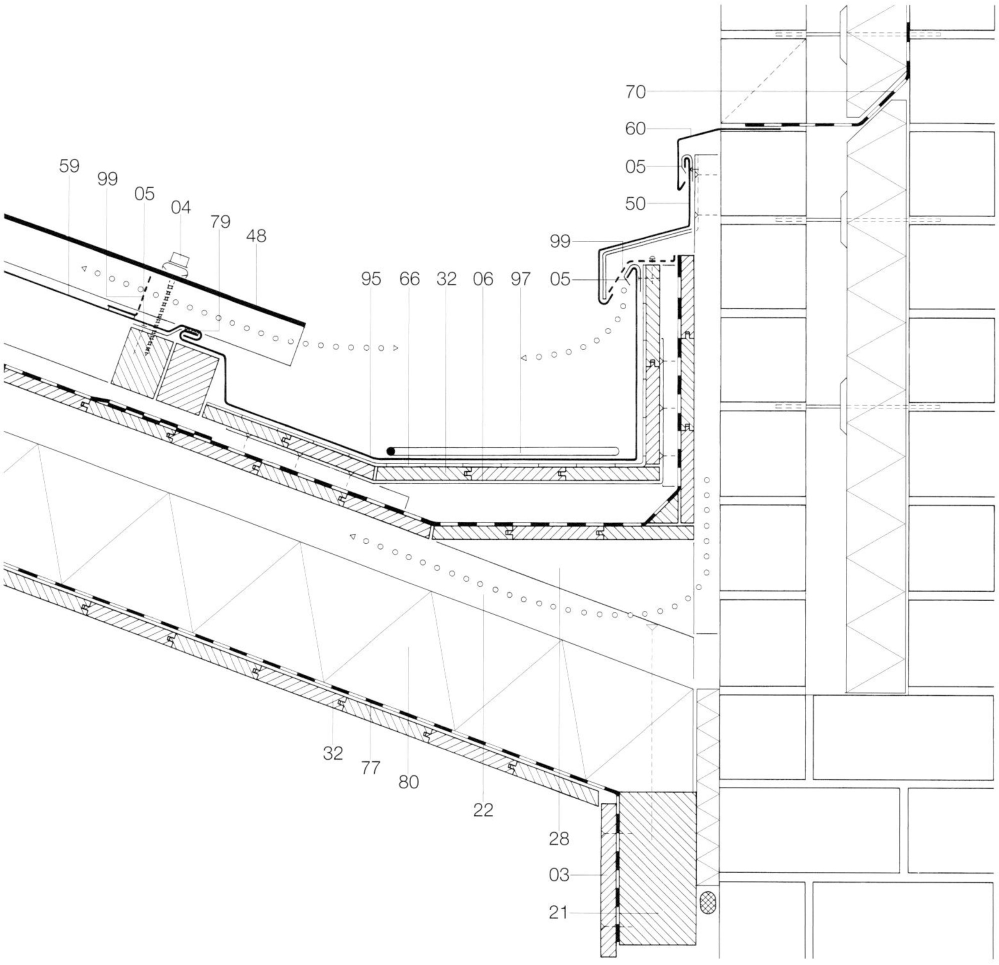

20

21

**Junction with wall**

**22** Junction with wall at top of slope, with ventilation hood

**23** Junction with wall at top of slope, with metal capping, apron flashing piece, wind deflector

**24** Junction with wall at top of slope, with metal capping and apron flashing piece

**22** The junction with a wall at the top of a slope uses a strip of milled sheet lead, which is dressed over the corrugations. It overlaps the fibre-cement sheeting 150–200 mm, depending on pitch, and is secured to the sheet metal apron flashing with rivets and solder. The apron flashing is in turn stiffened and held in place by continuous and individual clips (see sketch). It continues up the wall 100–150 mm and forms the lower part of the ventilation hood. This redirects the air flow more than once and is thus secure against driving rain and snow. Any moisture drains away on the roofing felt, which is supported on timber boarding and is turned up the wall as far as the ventilation hood.

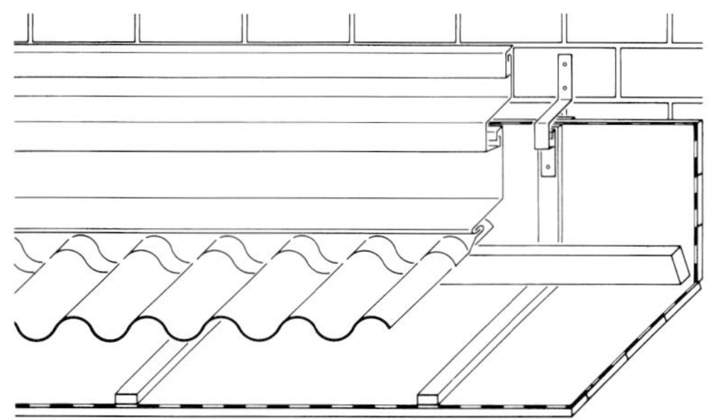

**23** This detail is also secure against driving rain and snow. It comprises a standard fibre-cement apron flashing piece, a simple sheet metal capping and a fibre-cement profile filler positioned as a wind deflector in front of the ventilation opening (see "Layers – Ventilation").

**24** A simple wall junction detail is feasible in areas subject to wind suction. Incoming rain is again intercepted by a sheet metal apron flashing overlapping the roofing felt underlay.

Details scale 1:10

03 Vapour barrier clamped behind batten/board
04 Screw, sealing washer
05 Clip
06 Fixing for flashing, gutter bracket
07 Batten
10 Stop bead
21 Purlin
22 Rafter
25 Counter batten
26 Batten
28 Make-up piece, spacer batten
32 Timber boarding
48 Fibre-cement corrugated sheet
50 Ventilation hood
52 Fibre-cement apron flashing piece
53 Fibre-cement eaves closure piece
59 Gutter extension, with welted joint
60 Cover flashing
61 Apron flashing and milled sheet lead
66 Separating layer
67 Roofing felt
68 Flashing
70 Damp-proof course and cavity tray
72 Rendering
75 Bitumen roofing felt, welded
77 Vapour barrier
78 Permanently elastic seal
80 Thermal insulation
94 Overflow
95 Gutter
97 Gutter heating
98 Wind deflector
99 Mesh screen

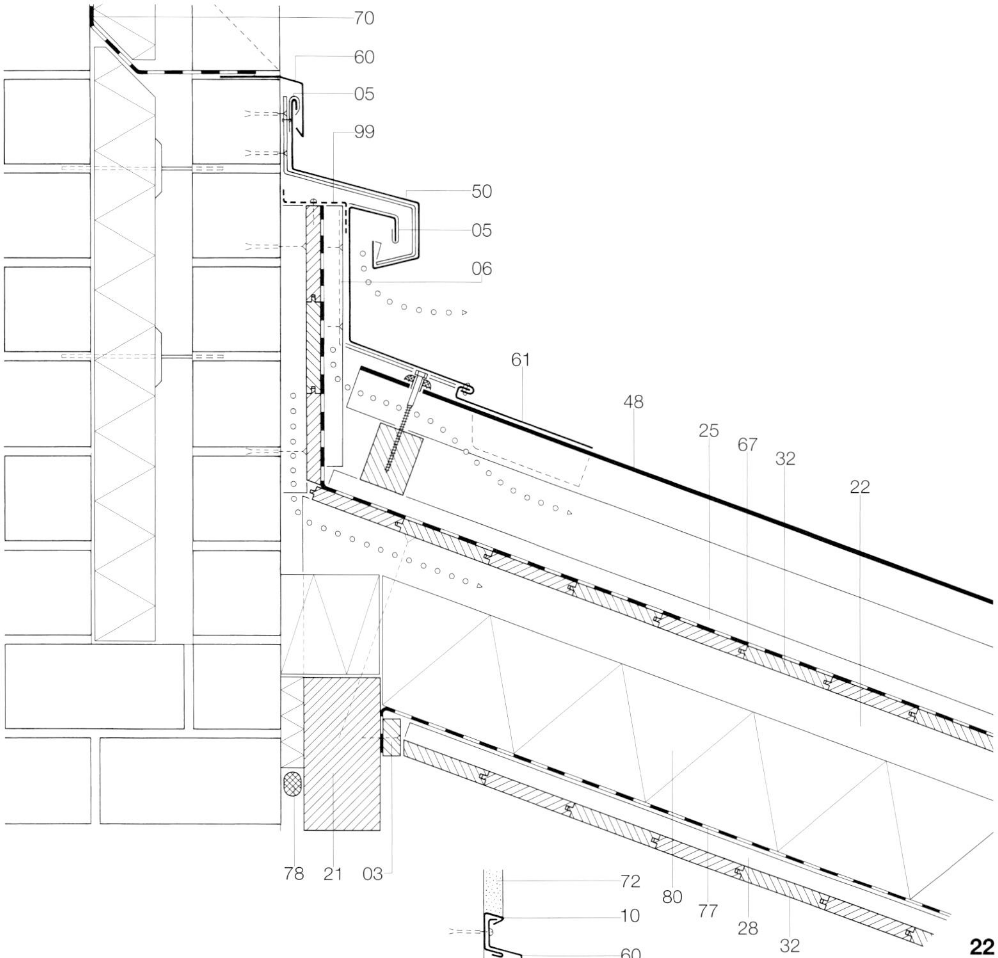

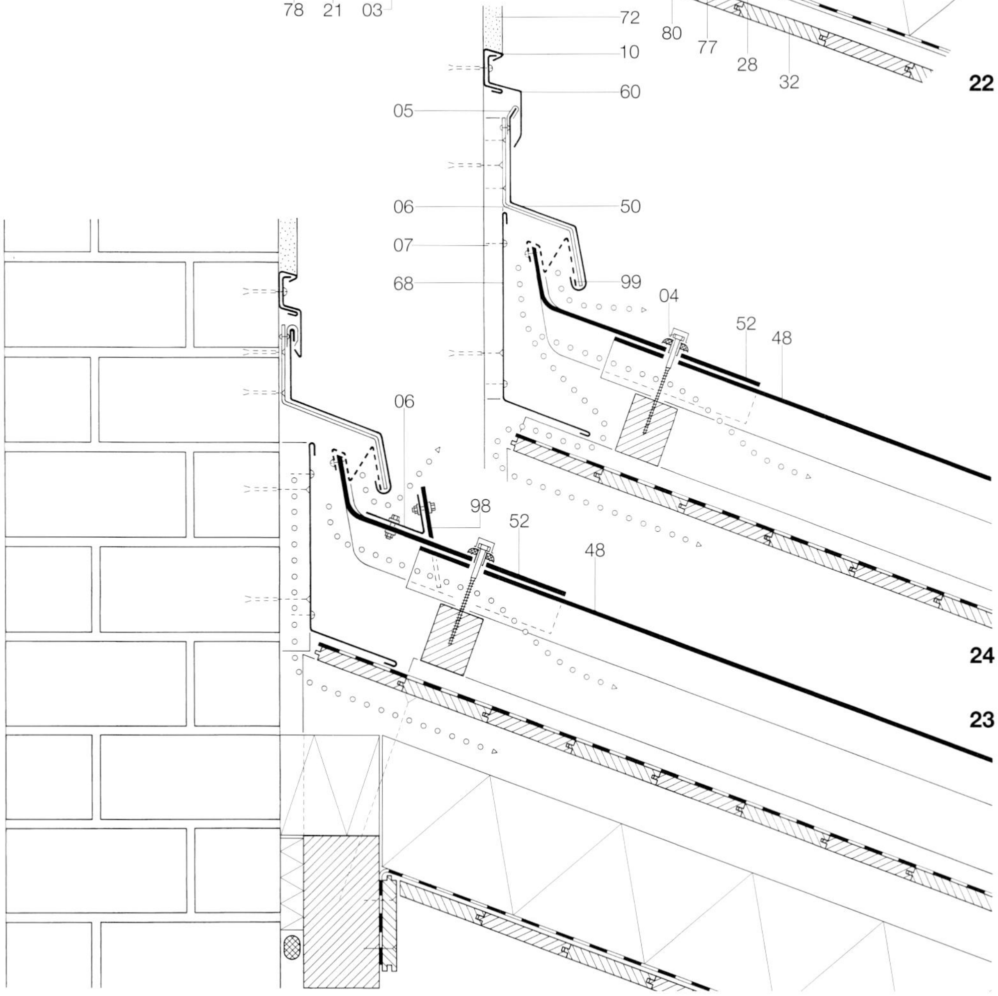

**Penetrations**

**25, 26** Chimney stack with various junction details

**25, 26** A chimney stack with half-brick-thick walls allows water to penetrate the joints as far as the vertical plane in front of the thermal insulation, where it drains downwards and outwards. The flashing at the rear extends ≥ 200 mm below the fibre-cement sheeting, where it is held in place by clips. A profile filler soldered to the gutter closes off the space below the covering. Run-off water is directed around the sides of the chimney by a "saddle" soldered into the flashing behind the chimney. In front of the chimney, a strip of milled sheet lead can be dressed over the corrugations (lap ≥ 200 mm) and fixed to the apron flashing with a welted, riveted and soldered joint.
The joint at the side can be formed with milled sheet lead or a sheet metal shallow gutter. A stepped flashing let into the bed joints of the masonry protects the top edge of the sheet metal gutter. However, an easier solution is to provide a capping strip fixed to the masonry in conjunction with a stop bead.
The roofing felt is turned up on all sides of the chimney and clamped in position behind the respective flashings. An additional film/foil channel on the ridge side intercepts any residual water and directs it away from the chimney.
The roof structure can provide lateral restraint for a chimney (≥ 5 m tall), if necessary with a concrete infill between the timber roof members and the chimney brickwork. The joint between vapour barrier and chimney is sealed with a preformed strip on all sides. The air in the ventilation layers flows around the chimney (see sketch).

Details scale 1:10

00 Split-ring connector
03 Vapour barrier clamped behind batten/board
04 Screw, sealing washer
05 Clip
06 Ladder hook
10 Stop bead
16 Concrete
18 Timber member
21 Purlin
22 Rafter
23 Trimming rafter
24 Trimmer
25 Counter batten
26 Batten
28 Spacer batten
29 Inner lining
32 Timber boarding
34 Plasterboard
35 Stepped flashing
48 Fibre-cement corrugated sheet
51 Fibre-cement transition piece
53 Back gutter with saddle
57 Insulating glass
59 Back gutter with saddle and profile filler
60 Cover flashing
61 Apron flashing and milled sheet lead, riveted and soldered
67 Roofing felt (laid with laps)
70 Damp-proof course
72 Rendering
74 Preformed sealing strip
77 Vapour barrier
80 Thermal insulation
81 Sunblind
93 Flue liner
94 Foil/film channel
95 Gutter

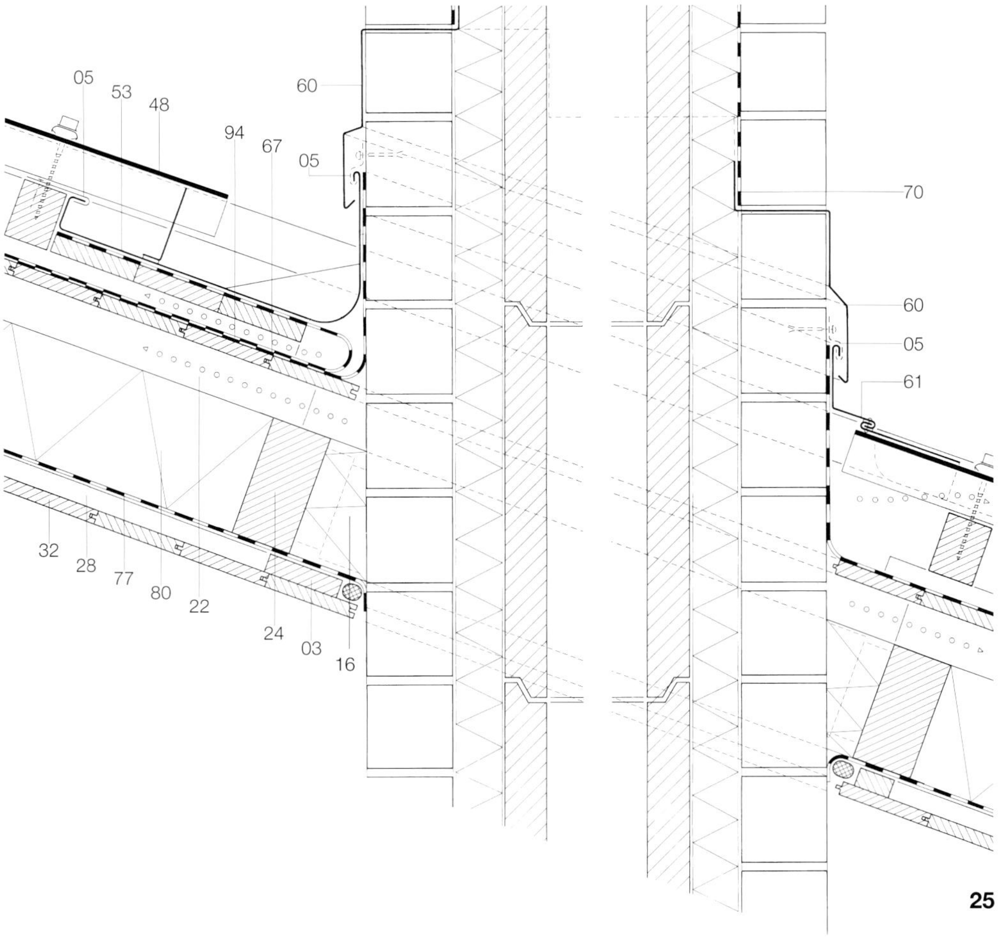

25

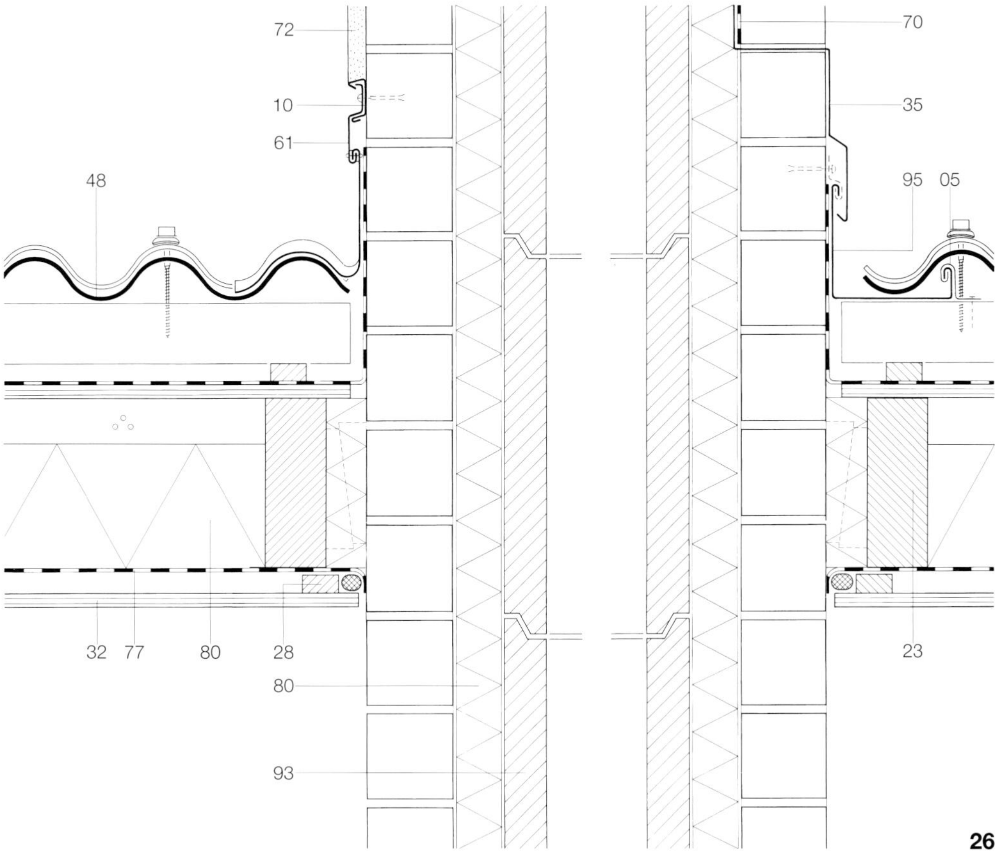

26

**Roof window**

**27** Roof window with sheet metal flashing

The flashing on the ridge side of the window extends 150–200 mm (depending on pitch) beneath the roof covering, where it terminates with a turned-up edge. A profile filler soldered to this flashing closes off the space below the roof covering.
Run-off water is directed around the sides of the window by a "saddle". At the sides the flashing extends beneath the first trough and, as at the chimney, is bent up below the first crest to form a gutter. Water collecting on the flashing on the eaves side of the window drains onto the fibre-cement corrugated sheeting below the window.
Above the window a foil/film channel intercepts any water draining down the roofing felt and directs it to either side of the window (see sketch).
The window frame is fixed directly to timber trimmers or via angles screwed to the side. Infill pieces and inner lining cover the supporting construction at this cut-out in the roof surface. The vapour barrier continues up as far as the window frame. The air in both ventilation layers flows around the chimney (see "Layers – Ventilation").

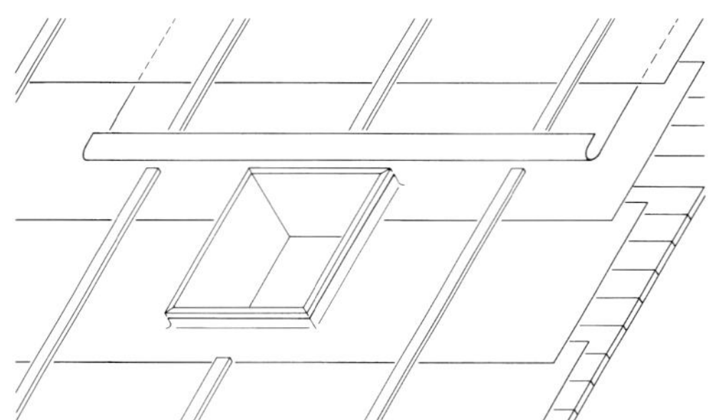

**Change of slope**

**28** External angle with transition piece > 180°
**29** Internal angle with transition piece < 180°

Special transition pieces are required when the change in roof pitch is ≥ 15°. These fibre-cement corrugated pieces can be produced with any angle (preferably in 5° steps). The leg length is always 300 mm.
Ladder hooks are positioned over a crest and fixed through the end lap. A special bearing distributes the load evenly over the corrugation. All the layers of the roof construction, apart from vapour barrier and soffit boards, continue past the purlin at the change of slope. Boards or battens clamp the vapour barrier tightly to the purlin and the soffit boards stop either side of the purlin. Differential deflection in the rafters is compensated for by packing pieces and battens.

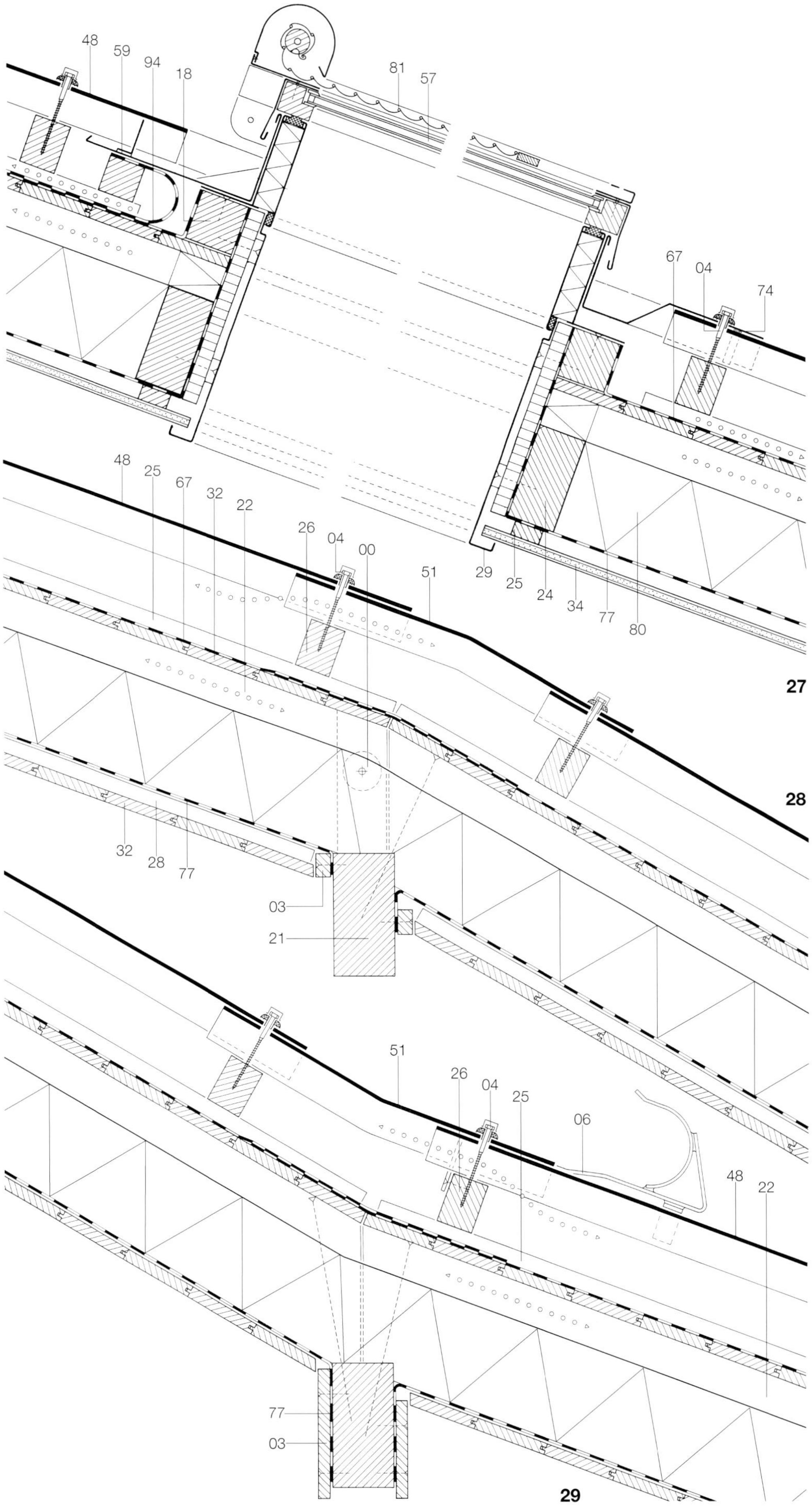

27

28

29

## Metal profiled sheeting

Ventilated roof covering, roofing felt on thermal insulation, loadbearing skin acting as vapour barrier

#### Ridge

**1** Ridge with plain sheet metal capping
**2** Ridge with ventilation hood

**1** The ridge termination in this detail employs two pieces of plain sheet metal cut and bent down to close off the troughs of the trapezoidal sheeting. A foam profile filler seals the junction against driving rain and snow (see sketch). Minor thermal movement of the metal roof covering can be accommodated by deformation of the Z-section loadbearing rails.

**2** The apron flashing pieces forming the lower part of the ventilation hood are profiled to match the trapezoidal sheeting. Under normal conditions this joint is rainproof without additional measures (see “Layers – Metal profiled sheeting – Laying”). Separating the ventilation layers on the two sides of the roof prevents the formation of condensation on the underside of the roof covering in the colder half of the roof. Condensation dripping from the underside of the metal roof covering drains away on the roofing felt. This is laid directly over the thermal insulation and should not have significant resistance to vapour diffusion ($s_d \leq 10$ m). Joints in the layer of the loadbearing trapezoidal sheeting are made airtight and watertight by including metal closure pieces and preformed seals.

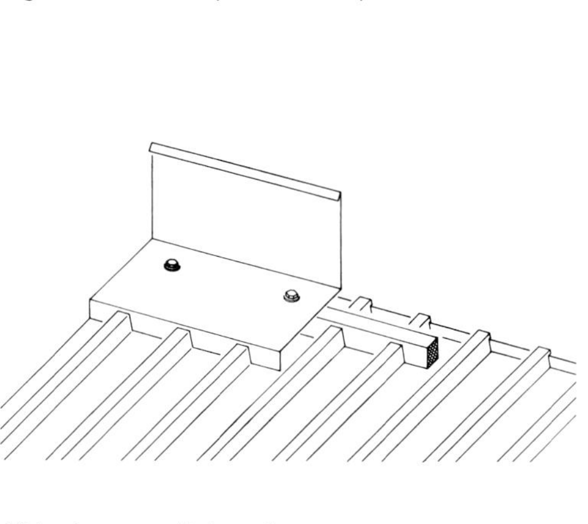

#### Ridge to mono pitch roof

**3** Overhanging ridge

On a ridge with a shallow pitch the water driven over the ridge drips off the underside of the roof covering. Any water that enters the roof construction drains away on the roofing felt, which is joined securely to the external wall. Thermal movement of the metal roof covering is accommodated at the top of the roof by elongated holes. The roof covering and the supporting construction are made from different metals and thus have different electric potentials, so they must be separated by an intermediate layer.

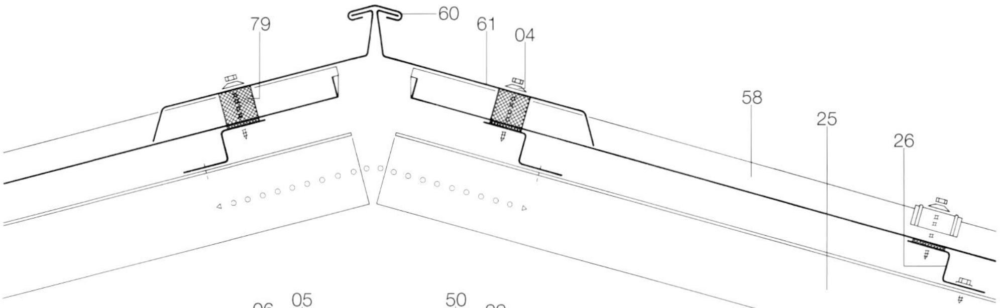

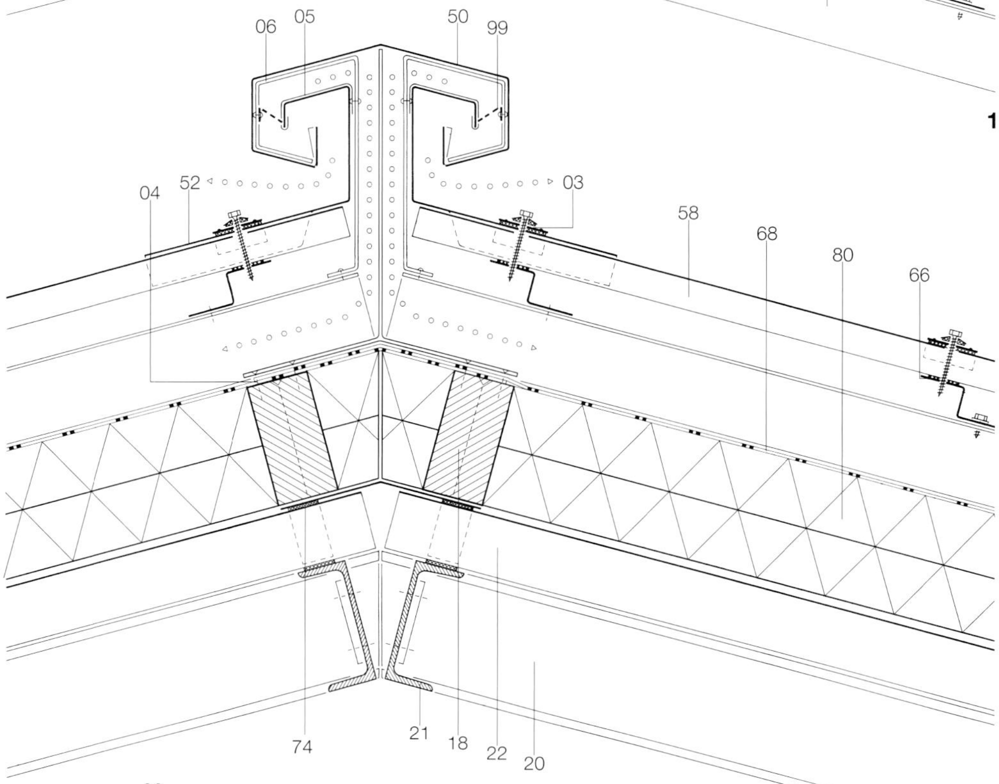

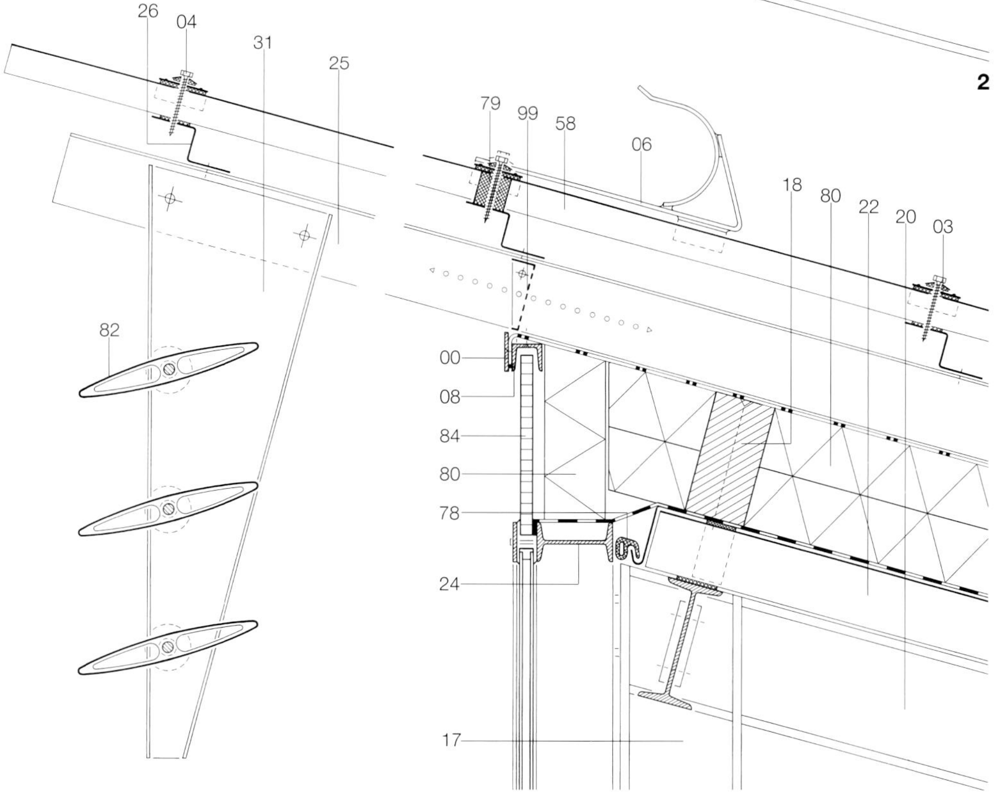

**Eaves**

**4** Eaves with tubular snowguard, ice stop and rainwater drip
**5** Overhanging eaves with gutter

**4** The roof covering is fixed in the bays through every second rib, and at the edges through every rib, using special pressure and capping pieces. The mountings for the snowguard are also attached to these fixings.
A small angle prevents rainwater from being blown back up the underside of the sheeting on shallow roof pitches.

**5** As at the ridge, thermal movement of the metal roof covering at the eaves is accommodated by elongated holes. A ventilation layer ≥ 100 mm deep below the trapezoidal sheeting ensures that heat gains are dissipated. The two layers of thermal insulation below the roofing felt, which is joined securely to the external wall construction, are laid with offset joints and are supported by timber members that stop heat flow into the loadbearing construction. The loadbearing trapezoidal metal sheeting functions as a vapour barrier and has a closure plate, sealed tightly with a foam strip that follows the profile; the peripheral preformed seal is attached to this.

**Valley**

**6** Open valley

The metal roof covering is fixed here through every rib – with a pressure and capping piece – to the loadbearing sections, which are positioned parallel to the line of the valley. The valley and the ventilation openings are protected against birds and small animals with a comb filler. The sheet metal valley gutter is laid on tongue and groove boarding. The gutter is ≥ 200 mm wide to provide access for cleaning. The sheeting overlaps the gutter ≥ 100 mm, depending on depth of profile. At low valley pitches the gutter is deepened.

Details scale 1:10

00 Clamping strip
03 Pressure and capping piece
04 Self-tapping screw
05 Clip
06 Fixing for flashing, ladder hook
08 Guide rail
17 Column
18 Timber member
20 Roof beam
21 Purlin
22 Trapezoidal profile sheeting, loadbearing
23 Valley beam
24 Facade beam
25 Spacer section
26 Sheeting rail
27 Rainwater drip
31 Fin
32 Timber boarding
50 Ventilation hood
52 Profiled apron flashing
53 Valley gutter
58 Trapezoidal profile sheeting, roof covering
60 Ridge capping
61 Apron flashing, cut and bent down to close off troughs
62 Closure plate
66 Separating layer
68 Roofing felt, vapour-permeable
74 Preformed sealing strip
77 Vapour barrier (sheet metal)
78 Permanently elastic preformed seal
79 Sealing strip
80 Thermal insulation
82 Louvre
84 Sandwich panel
95 Gutter
98 Tubular snowguard with ice stop
99 Mesh screen

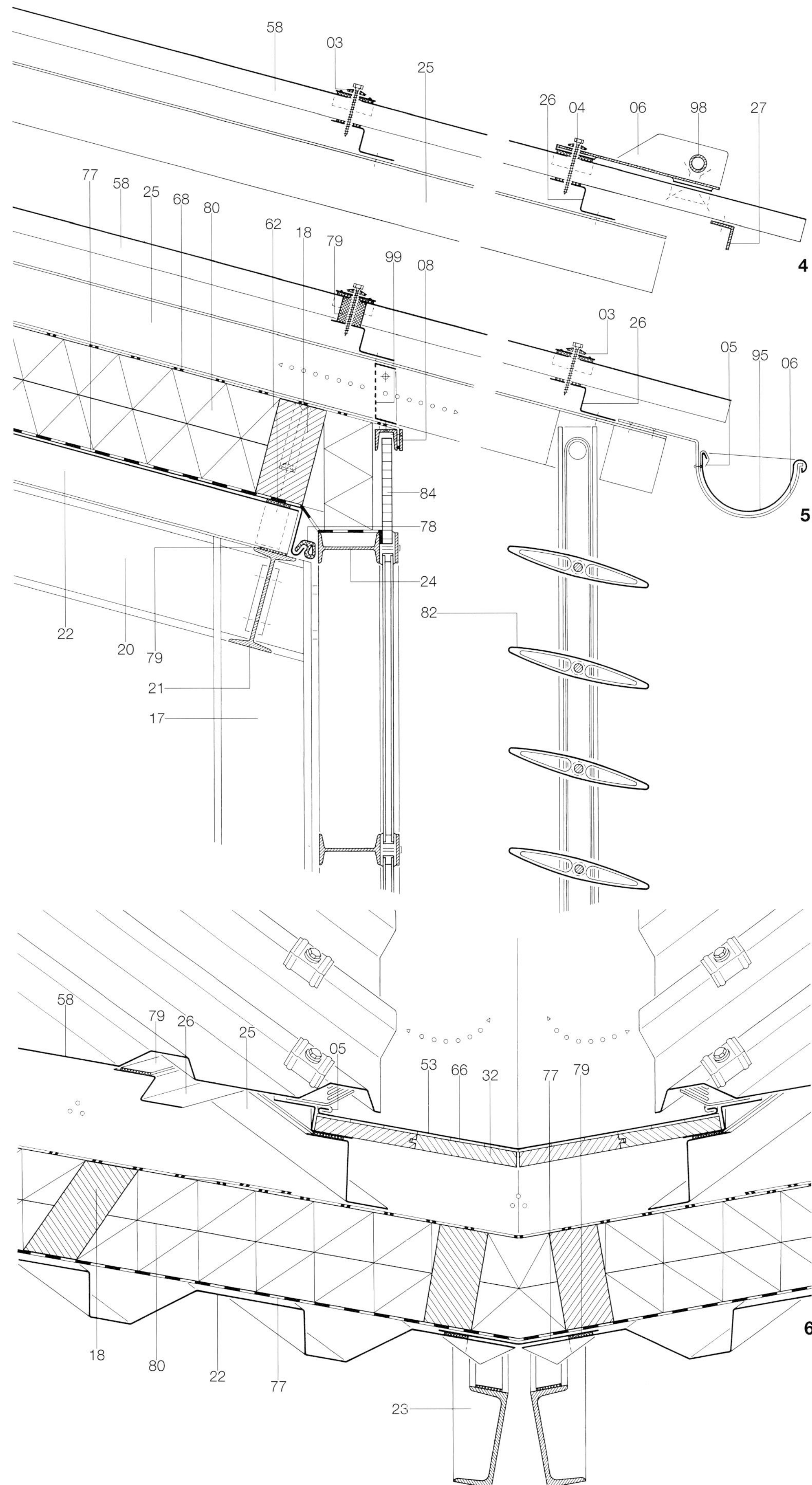

**Verge**

**7** Overhanging verge

With small sheeting rails the verge cannot overhang as far as the ridge (monopitch roof) or the eaves. The roof covering is firmly fixed through the two outer ribs using appropriate pressure and capping pieces.
The roofing felt underneath (open to vapour diffusion) continues over the external wall and is clamped in place there with a metal strip. The side joints between the roof covering sheets are fixed at least every 500 mm with self-drilling screws. The loadbearing trapezoidal sheeting is fixed to the purlins through every trough.

**Wall junction**

**8** Junction with wall at side of slope, with profiled apron flashing

Both the apron flashing and the roofing felt underneath continue 100–150 mm above the water run-off level of the roof covering and are overlapped ≥ 50 mm by the external leaf of the wall. The thermal insulation to the wall continues down to the underside of the loadbearing sheeting, where it is supported on a Z-section rail. A preformed seal forms the joint between this rail and the trapezoidal profile sheeting.

**Trough**

**9** Trough gutter with safety gutter

The gutter at this position is supported – on a separating layer to isolate it from the timber derivative board underlay – on steel gutter brackets, and is held in place by vented sheet metal eaves filler pieces. The outlet and the V-shaped overflow are necessary for the serviceability of the gutter. The heat flow through the loadbearing construction is limited by including a timber member. More heat passes through the single layer of insulation below the gutter and so helps to warm up the gutter. Nevertheless, heating elements are required in the gutter to prevent the formation of ice in winter.

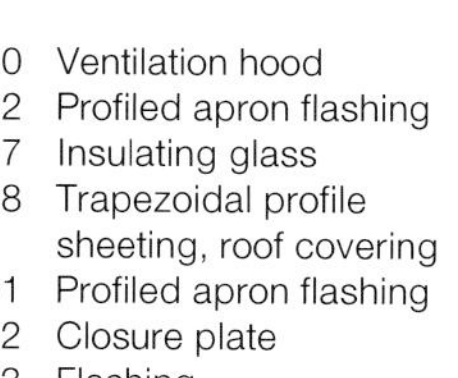

Details scale 1:10

00 Clamping strip
03 Pressure and capping piece
04 Self-tapping screw
05 Clip, continuous clip
06 Fixing for flashing, gutter bracket
08 Guide rail
17 Column
18 Timber member
20 Roof beam
21 Purlin
22 Trapezoidal profile sheeting, loadbearing
24 Facade beam
25 Spacer section
26 Sheeting rail
29 Z-section rail
33 Timber derivative board
35 Opening light in frame
50 Ventilation hood
52 Profiled apron flashing
57 Insulating glass
58 Trapezoidal profile sheeting, roof covering
61 Profiled apron flashing
62 Closure plate
63 Flashing
66 Separating layer
68 Roofing felt
77 Vapour barrier
78 Permanently elastic preformed seal
79 Sealing strip
80 Thermal insulation
82 Sunblind
84 Sandwich panel
94 Safety gutter
95 Gutter with outlet
98 Grating
99 Mesh screen

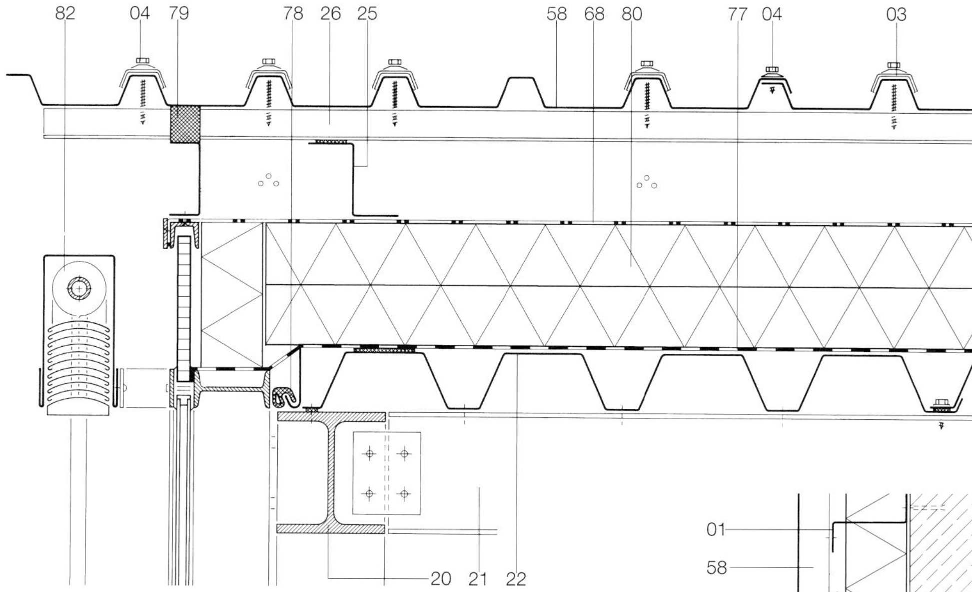

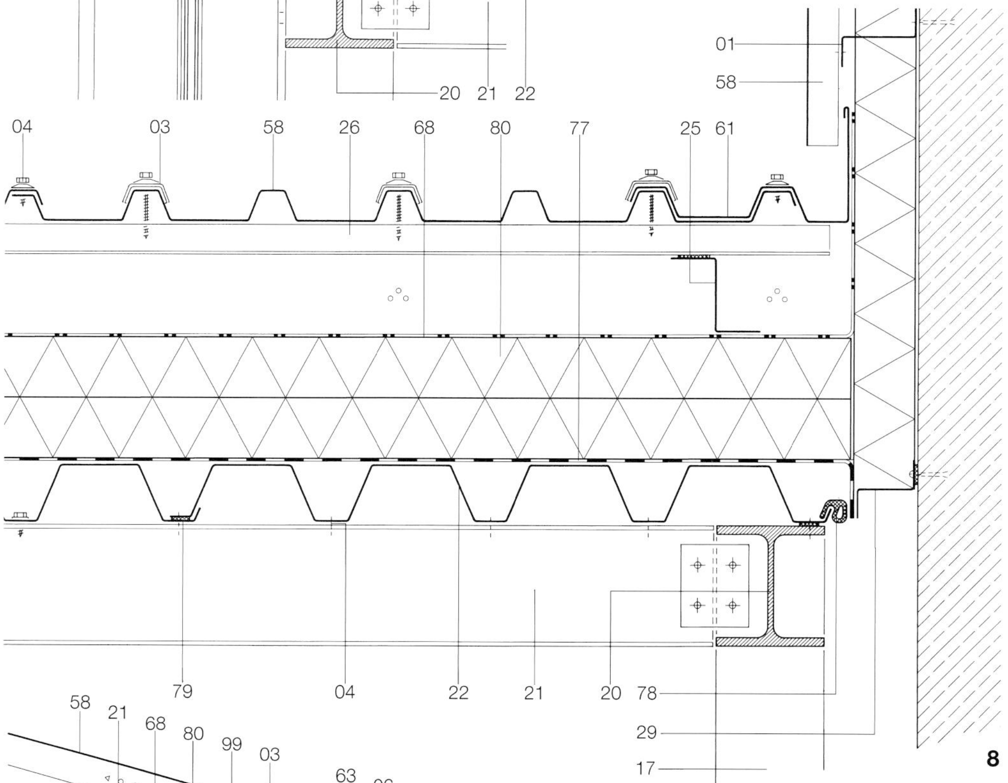

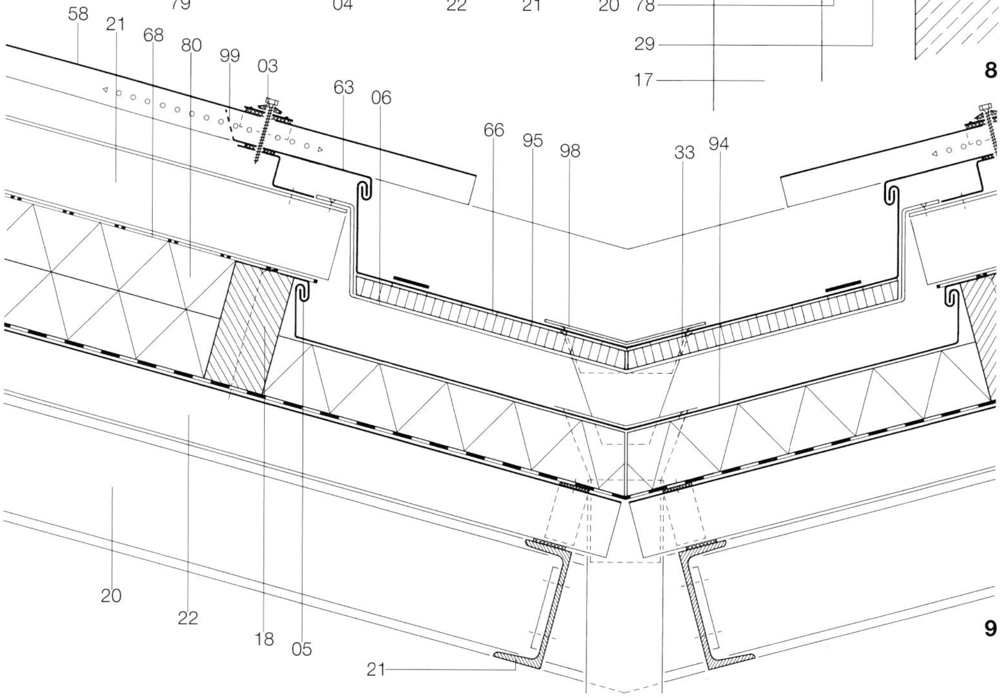

**Step, wall junction**

**10, 11** Change in roof level, with clerestory window and secure ventilation hood

The roof covering, together with spacer and ventilation sections, cantilevers over the window and thus protects it against driving rain. There is sufficient clearance in front of the window for the water to discharge over the edge; on larger roofs an eaves gutter may be more advisable at this position.
The junction between the lower roof surface and the panel below the window includes a ventilation hood with multiple redirection of the air flow to protect against driving rain and snow.
Mesh screens keep small animals, birds and large insects out of the ventilation openings.
The thermal insulation continues without interruption, apart from strips for the timber members. The heat flow through the steel loadbearing construction is essentially prevented by the timber spacer members.

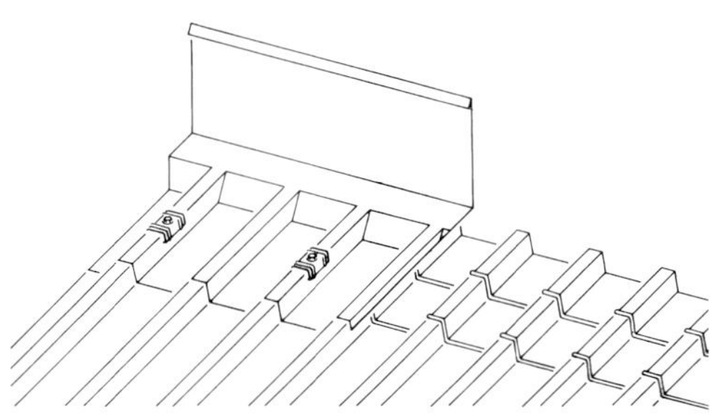

**Wall junction**

**12** Junction with wall at top of slope, with profiled apron flashing

An apron flashing with a profile matching that of the incoming sheeting can be used. It overlaps the trapezoidal sheeting 150–200 mm, depending on pitch. At roof pitches ≤ 8° an additional preformed seal between apron flashing and sheeting is necessary to rainproof the joint (see sketch).
Both apron flashing and roofing felt underneath are turned up the wall 100–150 mm and overlapped by the external leaf of the wall 50–100 mm, depending on the risk of a water build-up.
Driving rain and snow can penetrate this joint depending on wind pressure/suction, but any moisture that enters drains away on the roofing felt.
Thermal movement of the metal roof covering is accommodated by elongated holes.
The loadbearing trapezoidal metal sheeting functions as a vapour barrier and has a closure plate tightly sealed with a foam strip following the profile; the peripheral preformed seal is attached to this.

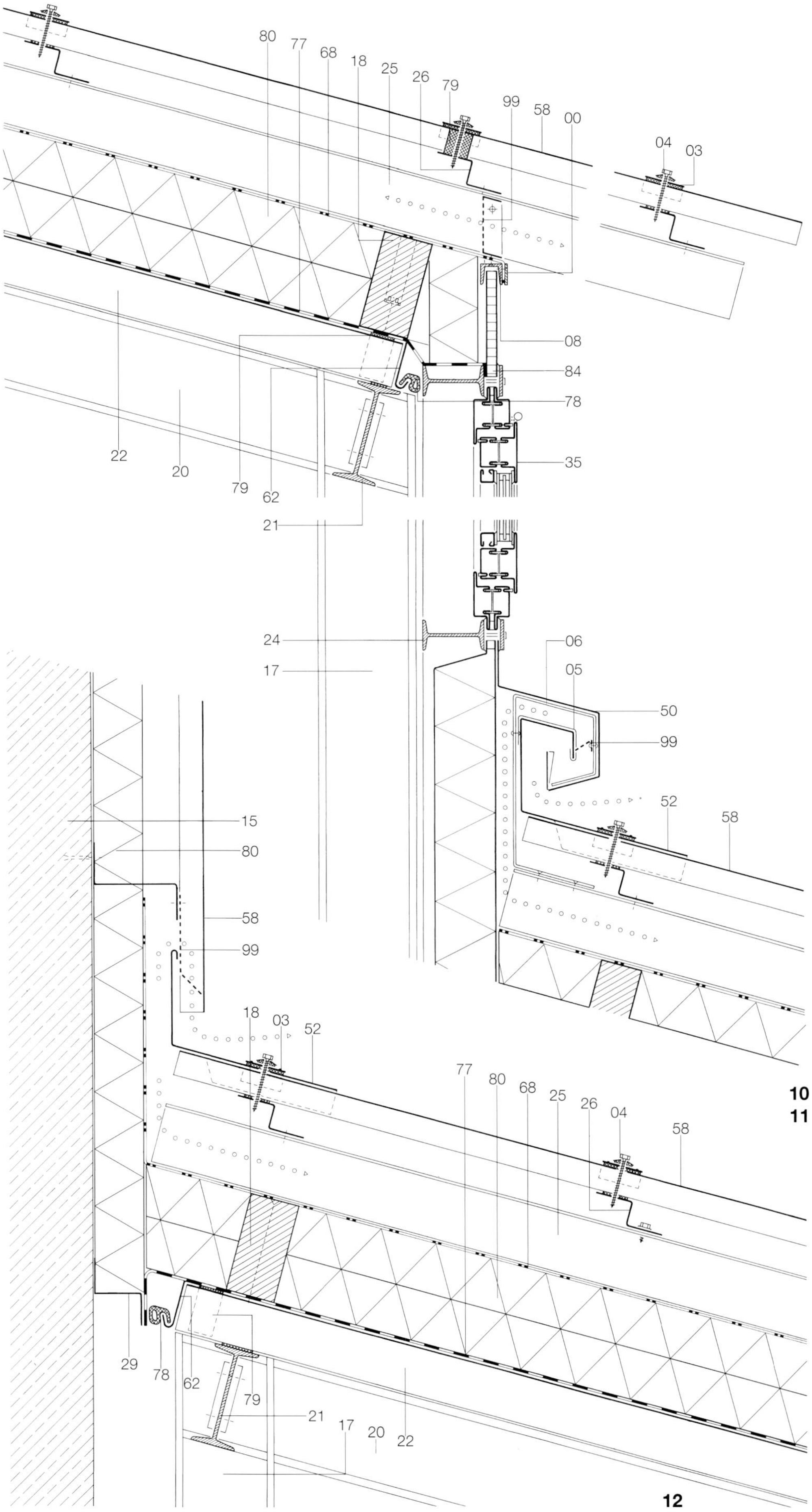

**10**
**11**

**12**

**Sheet metal roof coverings**
Roof covering on sheathing and roof decking, ventilated thermal insulation and vapour barrier

**Ridge**
**1** Ridge with twin double welt standing seam
**2** Ridge with batten, roof covering with batten rolls
**3** Ridge with secure ventilation hood, locked double welt standing seam roof covering, with uncut (rounded) seam

Symmetrical arrangements at the ridge require a twin double welt standing seam (≥ 40 mm) or a ridge batten (60 mm). The locked double welt standing seams (25 mm) between the bays of sheet metal are folded "inwards" at the ridge and integrated into the ridge capping. The bays of sheet metal thus have no transverse movement options; uncut (rounded) or cut (angular) welted seam transitions (≥ 60 mm) would be better here.
The capping strip is bent over the batten and welted to the bent-up edges of the sheet metal. Individual vents restrict the air flow and require additional measures. These are unnecessary with a ventilation hood, provided the air flow is redirected more than once.

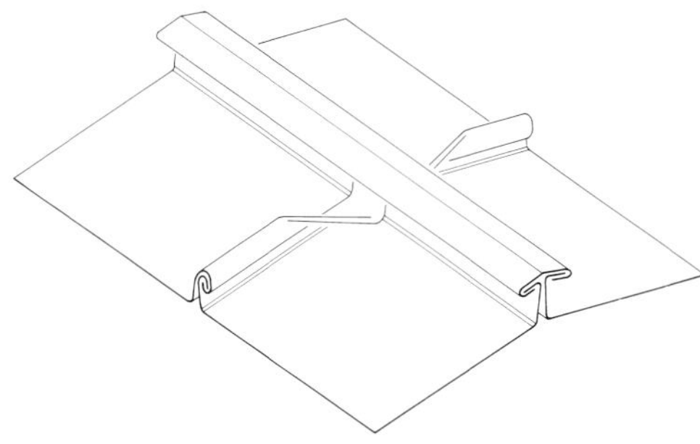

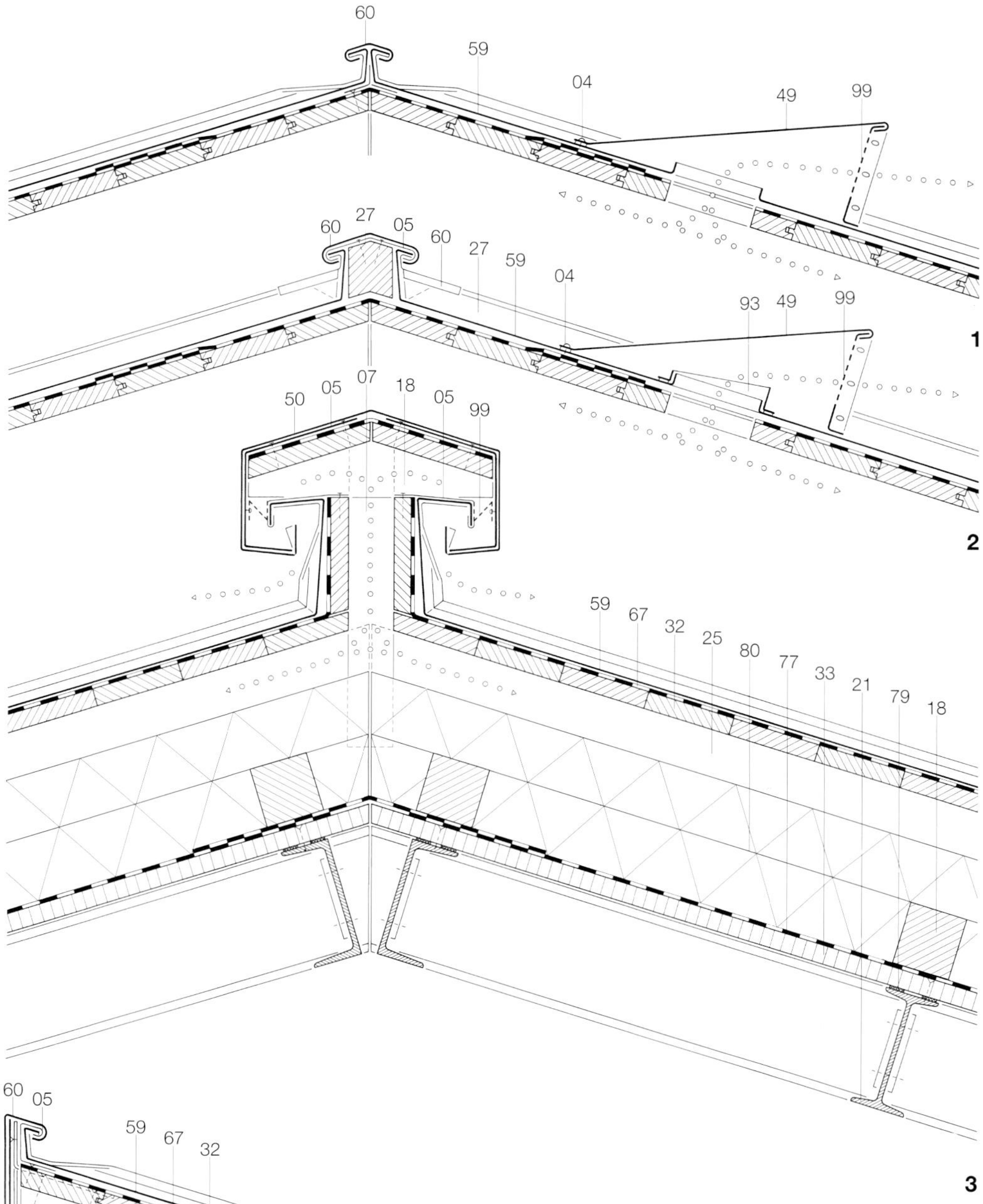

**Ridge to monopitch roof**
**4** Ridge with double welt standing seam
**5** Ridge with batten, roof covering with batten rolls

Monopitch roofs should be positioned facing the prevailing wind to minimise the ingress of driving rain.
On steep or short roof surfaces fixed clips should be specified for the upper part of the roof so that the bays of sheet metal can expand down the slope. The fixed clips for longer, shallow bays of sheet metal are positioned in the top quarter or third, depending on pitch, so that the metal can expand both up and down the slope; expansion options are provided at ridge and eaves (clearance, lining plate).
Ladder hooks (every max. 1500 mm) are fitted adjacent to the fixed clips through the sheet metal or batten capping strip to the load-bearing construction and flashed with riveted/soldered or welded sheet metal.

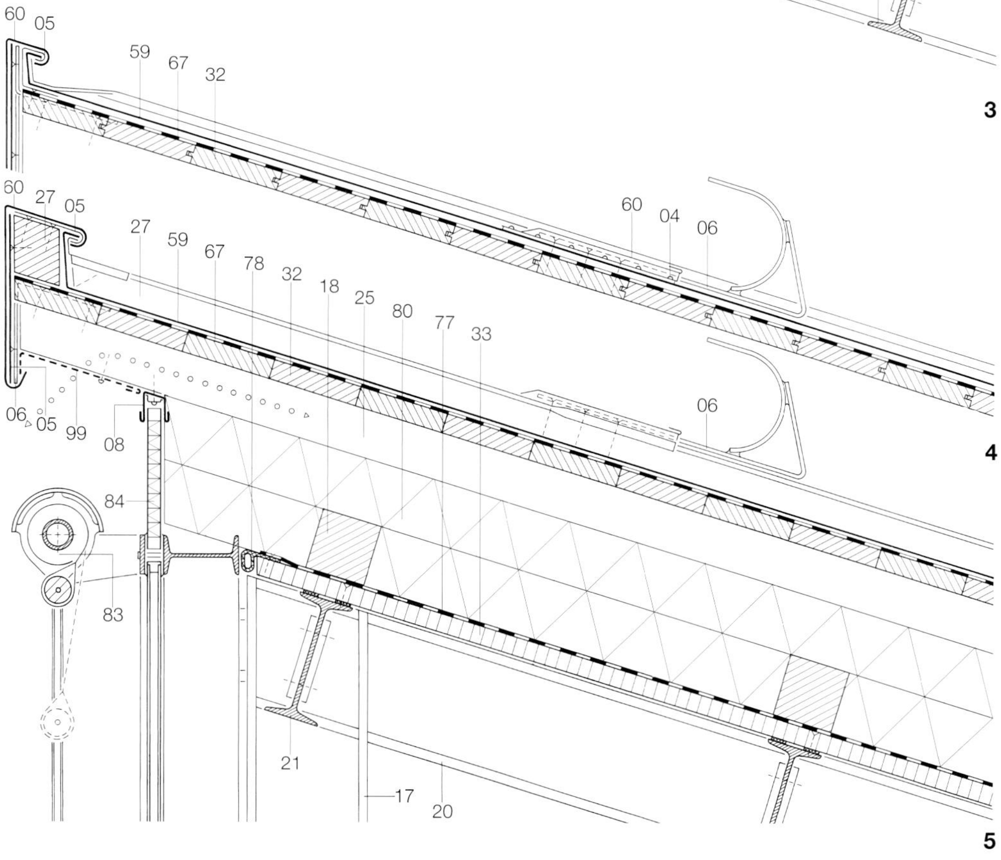

**Hip**

**6** Hip with batten, roof covering with batten rolls

The detail at the hip can employ a locked double welt standing seam, a twin double welt standing seam or a batten. The incoming locked double welt standing seams between the bays of sheet metal are folded over here and integrated into the hip seam in an asymmetric (offset) or symmetric arrangement (see "Layers – Sheet metal roof coverings"). The closed side of the bent-over seams must always point up the slope so that run-off water cannot seep into the joint.
It is better to channel the air flow parallel to the hip. The opening for the air flow is the same size all the way from eaves to ridge and serves only a limited number of bays (see "Layers – Ventilation").

**Eaves**

**7** Eaves with lining plate, locked double welt standing seam roof covering, vertical end to seam

**8** Eaves with lining plate, roof covering with batten rolls

Thermal expansion (≤ 15 mm) of the bays of sheet metal (≤ 10-14 m long) has to be accommodated at the eaves (fixed clips near the ridge). There must therefore be a corresponding clearance between the bottom end of the sheet metal and the eaves flashing. A lining plate with end folded over ≥ 30 mm serves as the eaves flashing. The locked double welt standing seams are not folded over, so that transverse movement of the bays of sheet metal is unhindered. The tubular snowguard and roof access steps are permanently clamped to the locked double welt standing seams by means of special mountings. On a roof covering with batten rolls the special mountings are screwed through the batten capping strip and flashed with a cap to allow movement. The fixed end of the batten capping strip provides space for the bays of sheet metal to move.

Details scale 1:10

03 Clamp mounting, pipe clip
04 Rivet and soft solder
05 Clip, continuous clip
06 Fixing for flashing, ladder hook, gutter bracket
07 Timber post
08 Guide rail
10 Step
17 Column
18 Spacer purlin, hood support
20 Roof beam
21 Purlin
23 Hip beam
25 Spacer rafter
27 Batten roll
31 Strengthening rod
32 Timber boarding
33 Laminated board
49 Vent
50 Ventilation hood
59 Sheet metal roof covering
60 Capping strip, verge capping
63 Lining plate
67 Sheathing (laid with laps), textured top surface
77 Vapour barrier
78 Permanently elastic seal
79 Permanently elastic bearing pad
80 Thermal insulation
83 Sunblind
84 Sandwich panel
93 Vent
95 Gutter
96 Rainwater downpipe
98 Tubular snowguard with ice stop
99 Mesh screen

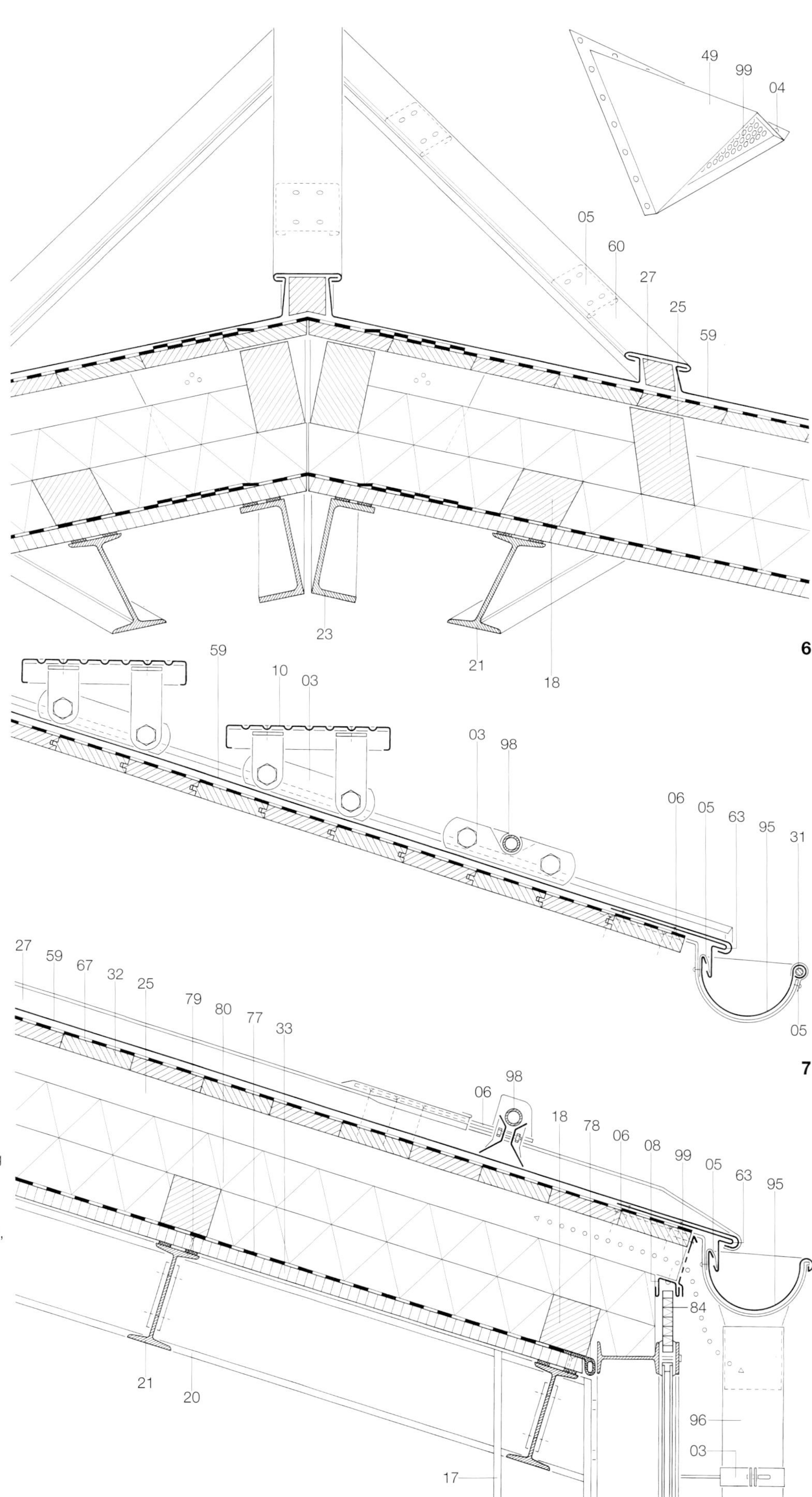

**Valley**

**9** Valley gutter with sliding seam and additional turned-up edge
**10** Deeper valley gutter with lining plate, roof covering with batten rolls

Valleys should have a fall of ≥ 10°, unless a deeper valley has been incorporated.
Small roof areas with short bays of sheet metal can be joined to the sheet metal in the valley with locked double welt standing seams (see sketch). In this arrangement the expansion of the bays of sheet metal down the slope can be accommodated only at the seam.
It is better to join large roof areas with long bays of sheet metal by means of a sliding seam and turned-up edge, so that the sheet metal in the valley and in the bays can expand and contract unhindered.

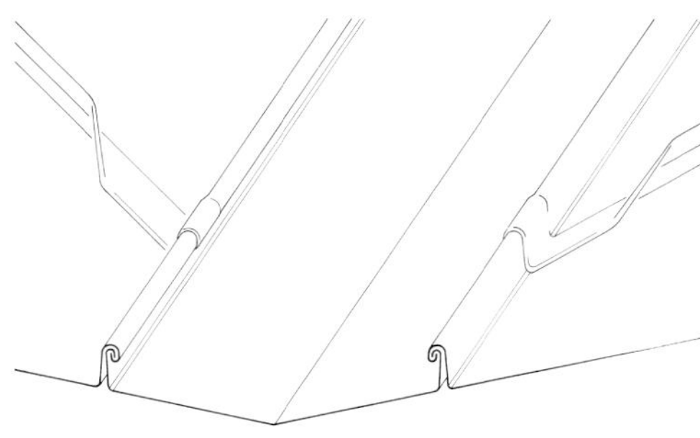

However, despite its turned-up edge (≥ 40 mm), this solution is not secure against a build-up of water on shallow roof pitches (≤ 10°).
Long, shallow valleys usually employ a deeper valley gutter, where the bays of sheet metal and the batten capping strips connect directly to the projection of the lining plate.
To increase reliability with respect to a backlog of water, preformed sealing strips can be laid in the seams, or bitumen roofing felt can be bonded or welded to the sheathing to form a sealed "overflow gutter". The valley is ventilated as for the hip (see above).
The timber boarding and the separating layer with its textured top surface prevent the formation of condensation and the transmission of impact sound.

Details scale 1:10

01 Cast-in channel, expansion anchor
03 Clamp mounting
04 Rivet and soft solder
05 Clip, continuous clip
06 Fixing for flashing, ladder hook
18 Spacer purlin
20 Roof beam
21 Purlin
23 Valley beam
25 Spacer rafter
27 Batten roll
29 Stop bead
32 Timber boarding
33 Laminated board
49 Vent
53 Valley gutter with turned-up edge and sliding seam
59 Sheet metal roof covering
60 Capping strip
62 Verge flashing
63 Lining plate
67 Sheathing (laid with laps), textured top surface
72 Rendering, two coats
77 Vapour barrier
78 Permanently elastic seal
79 Permanently elastic bearing pad
95 Deeper central channel
98 Tubular snowguard

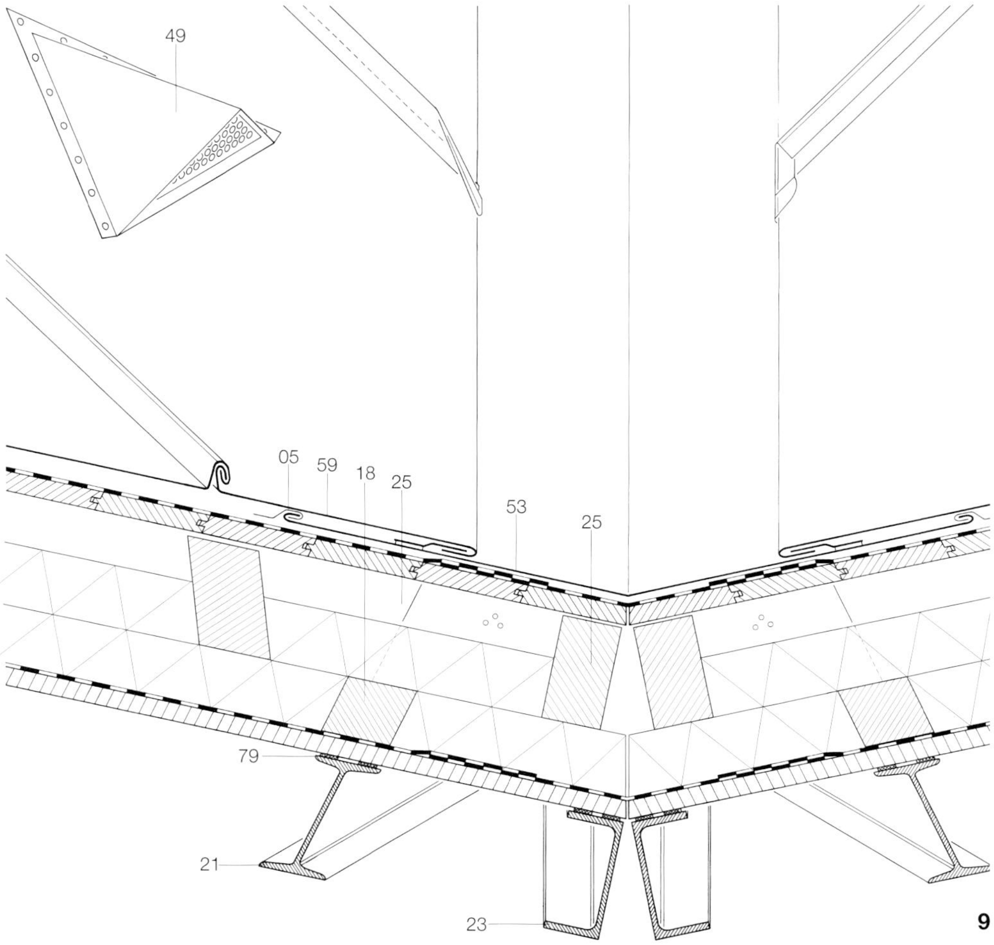

9

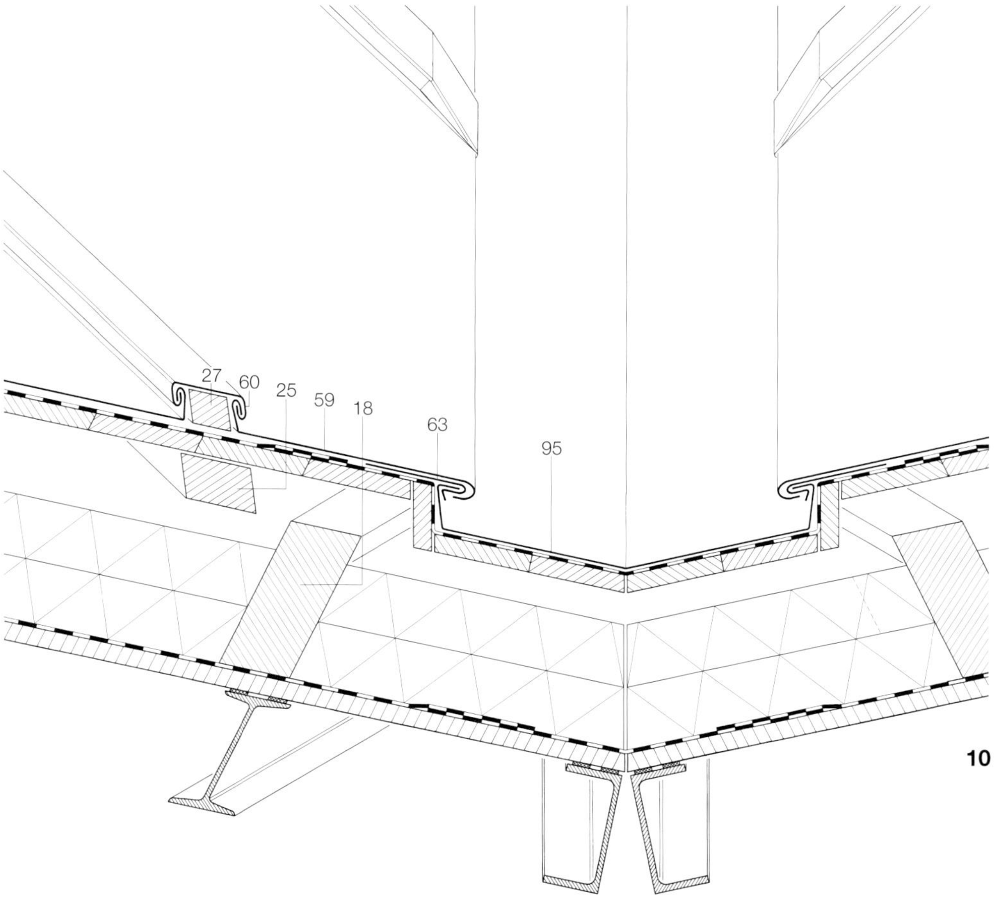

10

**Verge**

**11** with double welt standing seam, locked double welt standing seam roof covering

**12** with batten, roof covering with batten rolls

The normal bay width is 600 mm, irrespective of roof covering; widths from 420 to 920 mm are possible (see "Layers – Sheet metal roof coverings"). Transverse movement is allowed by folding up the edges at seams, or fitting battens at a slight angle (leaving a 2–3 mm gap) and not vertically.

Individual clips positioned every max. 500 mm hold the edges of the sheet metal bays and transfer wind suction forces to the roof decking. The verge is finished with a double welt standing seam (40 mm) or a verge capping strip (40 mm batten). This holds the sheet metal "bargeboard" in position and stabilises it without introducing restraint stresses. The verge must overhang the external wall 50–100 mm, depending on height above the ground. The bottom edge must be stiffened with a continuous clip for a leg length ≥ 50 mm, with additional clips for a length ≥ 100 mm. The overall depth of this verge trim can be reduced by moving the seam or batten back from the edge of the roof (see sketch).

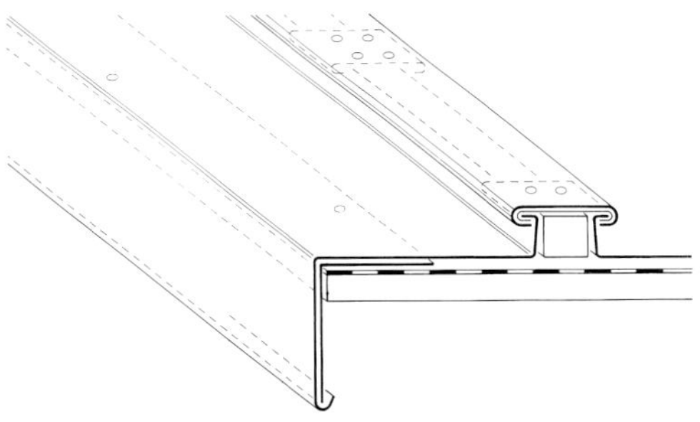

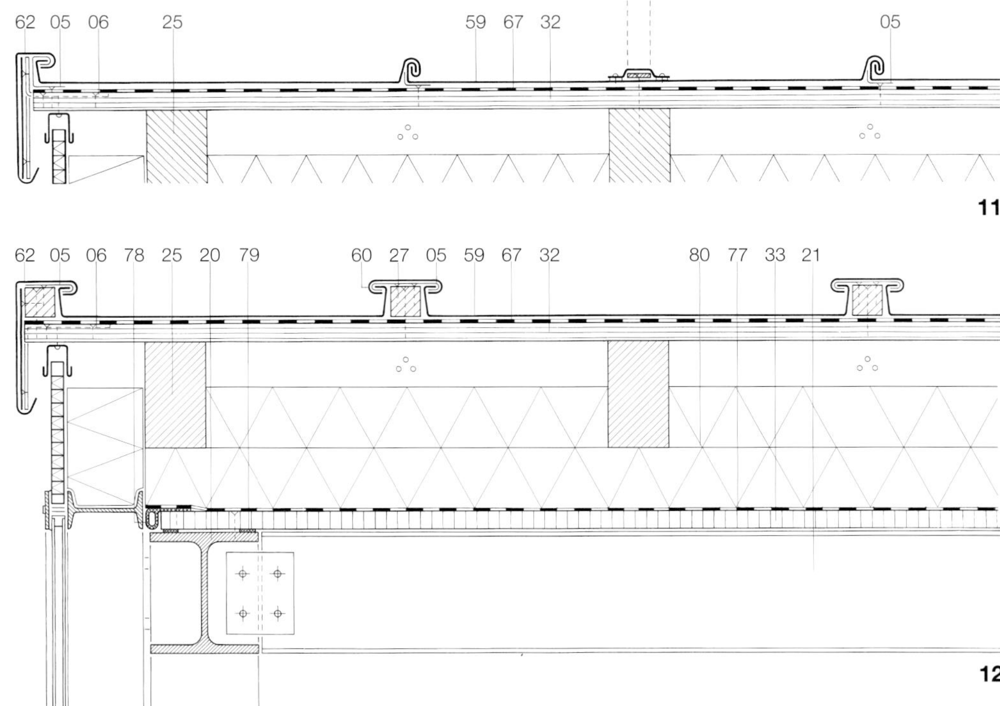


11

12

**Junction with wall**

**13** Junction with wall at side of slope, with cover flashing tucked into channel cast into wall, locked double welt standing seam roof covering

**14** Junction with wall at side of slope, with stop bead and cover flashing, roof covering with batten rolls

The bay of sheet metal adjacent to the wall is turned up the wall 100–150 mm, depending on pitch. The top edge is held by clips, but can still move, and is protected by a flashing that overlaps 50–100 mm. The sheathing is also taken up the wall for the same distance and pressed against it by the sheet metal. Wall and adjoining roof can therefore move independently. Tubular snowguard mountings and ladder hooks are either permanently clamped to the standing seam or screwed to the batten. The screw fixing must be flashed with a riveted/soldered or welded cap, or – preferably – positioned at a transverse joint in the capping strip and overlapped (150–200 mm) by that part of the capping strip on the ridge side.

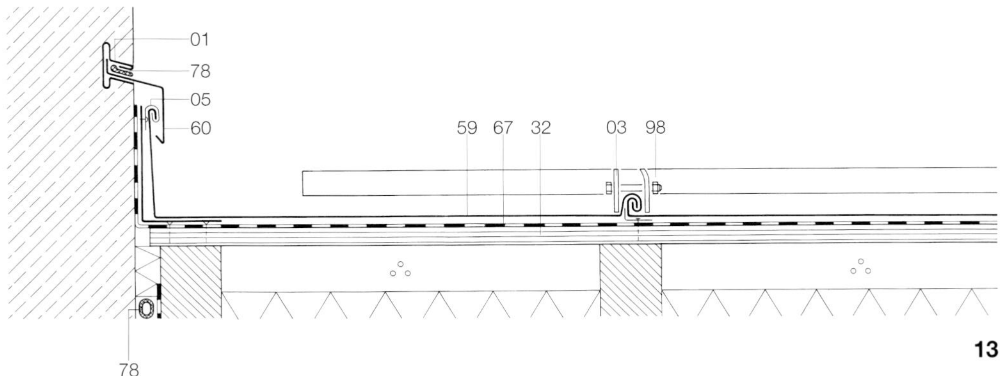


13

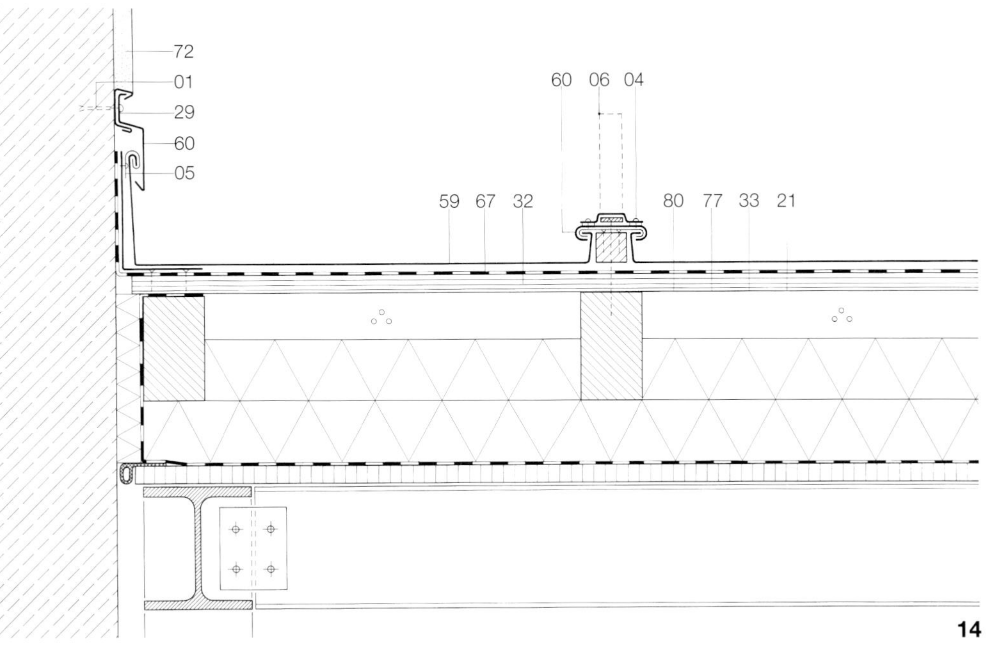


14

**Trough, junction with wall**

**15** Trough with gutter and overflow gutter, locked double welt standing seam roof covering, vertical end to seam

**16** Junction with wall at bottom of slope, back gutter with sliding seam, turned-up edge, locked double welt standing seam roof covering

Trough and back gutters should only be included when the risk of a backlog of water remains calculable. Internal gutters of this type are given a longitudinal fall of 1–1.5%. Heating coils prevent layers of ice and snow forming. For safety, twice the number of downpipes calculated should be provided. Outlets are covered with a flat (coarse) mesh grating. The depth of the gutter and the overflow ("safety") gutter (sheet metal or roofing felt) should be 200–300 mm. Overflows should have an unobstructed opening greater than the size of the downpipe. It should be noted that the width of sheet copper and titanium-zinc available is ≤ 1000 mm and soldered seams in the gutter itself are not permitted. Aluminium, stainless steel and galvanised steel (sometimes) are available in wider pieces and may be welded together along the length of the gutter. However, welding damages the galvanising.

**Junction with wall**

**17** Junction with wall at top of slope, with ventilation hood, locked double welt standing seam roof covering, with uncut (rounded) seam

The bays of sheet metal are turned up the wall 100–150 mm (depending on pitch); the small clearance allows for movement. An uncut (rounded) fold is used to turn the locked double welt standing seam up the wall; this permits transverse movement of the sheet metal. The ventilation hood is held with clips every 500–600 mm, and is overlapped 50–100 mm by the cover flashing. Multiple redirection of the air flow within the hood minimises the ingress of driving rain and snow.

Details scale 1:10

00 Roof window
01 Expansion anchor
03 Collar
04 Soft solder
05 Clip, continuous clip
06 Fixing for flashing
08 Guide rail
10 Inner lining
17 Column
18 Spacer purlin, hood support
20 Roof beam
21 Purlin
22 Cantilevering rafter
24 Trimmer
25 Spacer batten
28 Timber member
29 Stop bead
32 Timber boarding
33 Laminated board
35 Transverse seam, standing/folded over
50 Ventilation hood
57 Insulating glass
59 Sheet metal roof covering
60 Capping strip, skirt
63 Lining plate
67 Sheathing (laid with laps), textured top surface
70 Waterproofing, bonded/welded
72 Rendering, two coats
77 Vapour barrier, bonded or welded
78 Permanently elastic preformed seal
79 Permanently elastic bearing pad
80 Thermal insulation
93 Flue
94 Overflow
95 Foil channel
95 Gutter with outlets
96 Rainwater downpipe
97 Gutter heating
98 Grating
99 Mesh screen

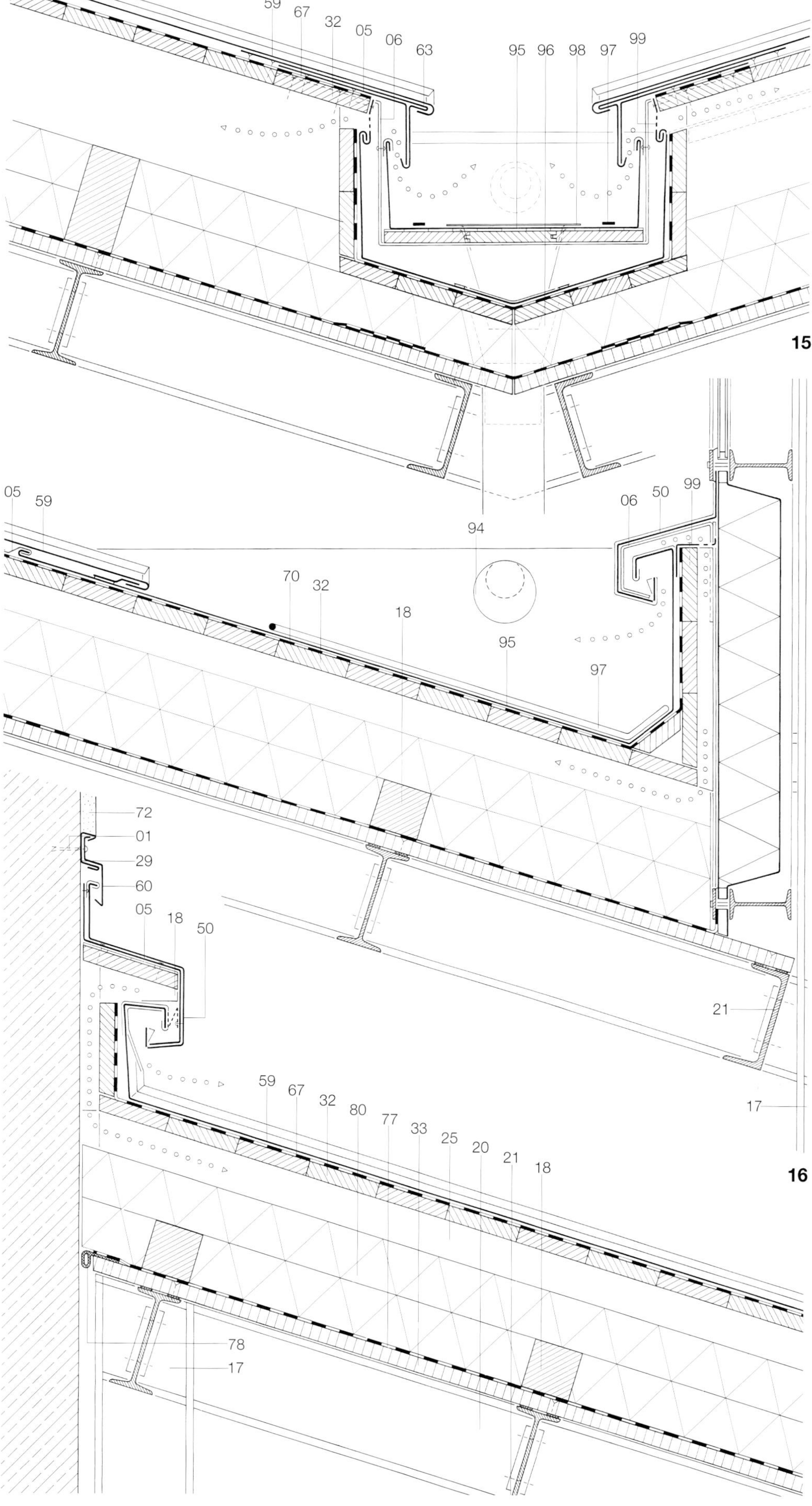

**Penetrations**

**18** Flue with support sleeve and skirt, locked double welt standing seam roof covering with trimmer seams

Flues and pipes are incorporated into the bay of sheet metal without trimmer seams when the distance to the seams on both sides is ≥ 200 mm. For larger pipes or rectangular ducts, trimmers are required in both the roof structure and the seams on the roof surface. Standing seams folded over at the ends direct water away from the penetration (see sketches). Rectangular ducts ≥ 1 m also have a "saddle". The flue support sleeve (≥ 150 mm) is fitted half above, half below, and riveted/soldered or welded in position. The top of the sleeve is flashed with a skirt (overlap 50–100 mm depending on height). The air flows around the penetration between the rafters/trimmers. The vapour barrier is clamped tightly around the flue.

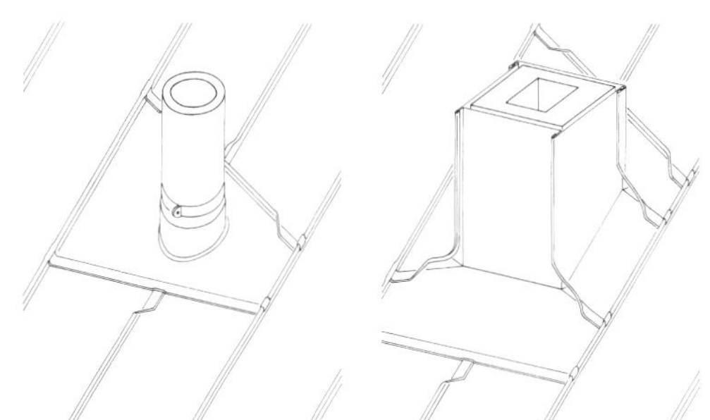

**Roof window**

**19** Window with curb and "saddle", locked double welt standing seam roof covering with trimmer seams

Curb and sheet metal cladding project ≥ 150 mm above the roof surface to prevent a build-up of water. Trimmer seams and sheet metal saddle should be provided as for a roof penetration. The spacer battens fitted above the rafters (creating an air space) stop above and below the window.

**Step**

**20** Change in roof level, with separate canopy

The roof level steps down and continues on the roof decking. This offset is made rainproof by turning up the bays of sheet metal 100–150 mm and providing a deep eaves flashing. Thermal movement of the sheet metal on the higher roof level is accommodated by a sliding seam (≥ 30 mm) on the lining plate, and on the lower roof level by leaving a gap between the timber member at the back edge of the canopy and the sheet metal. The uncut (rounded) transition as the standing seam turns up permits transverse movement.

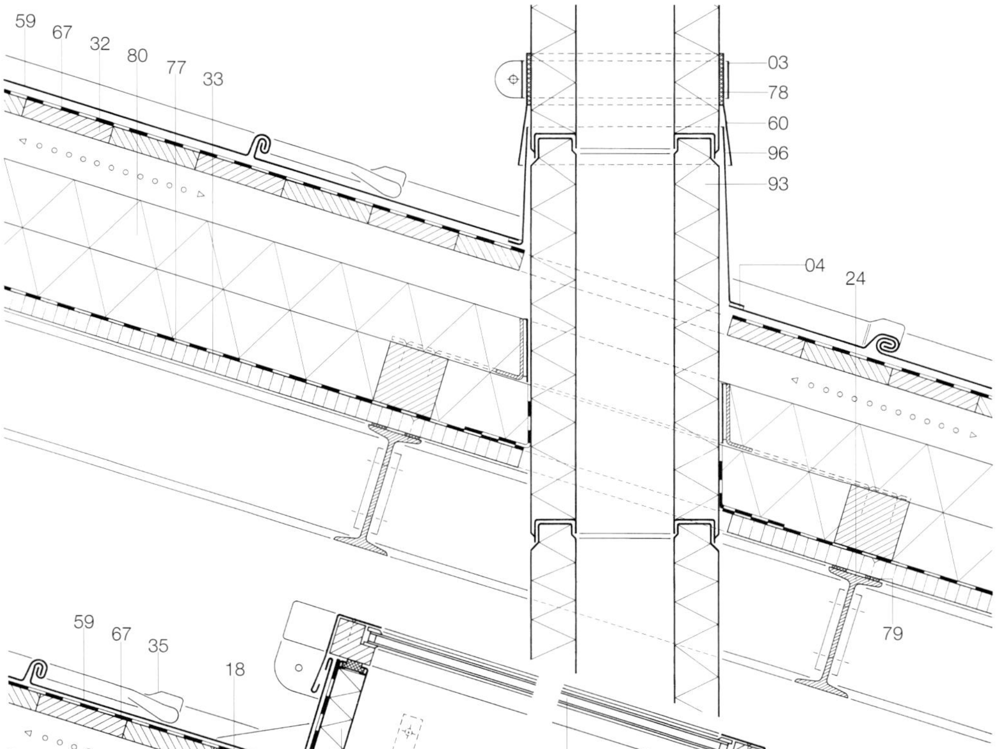

18

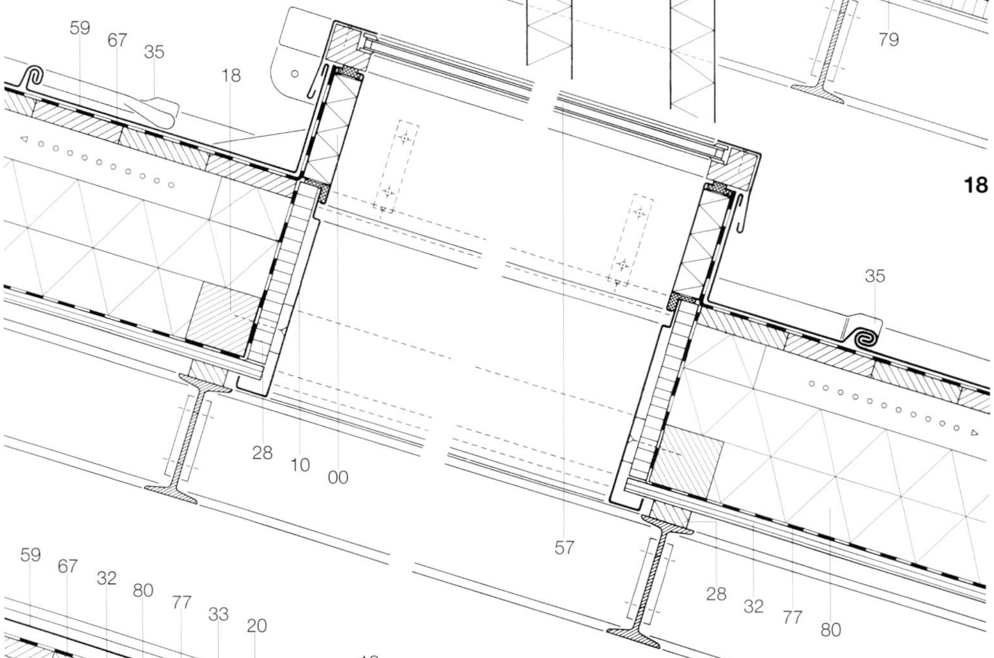

19

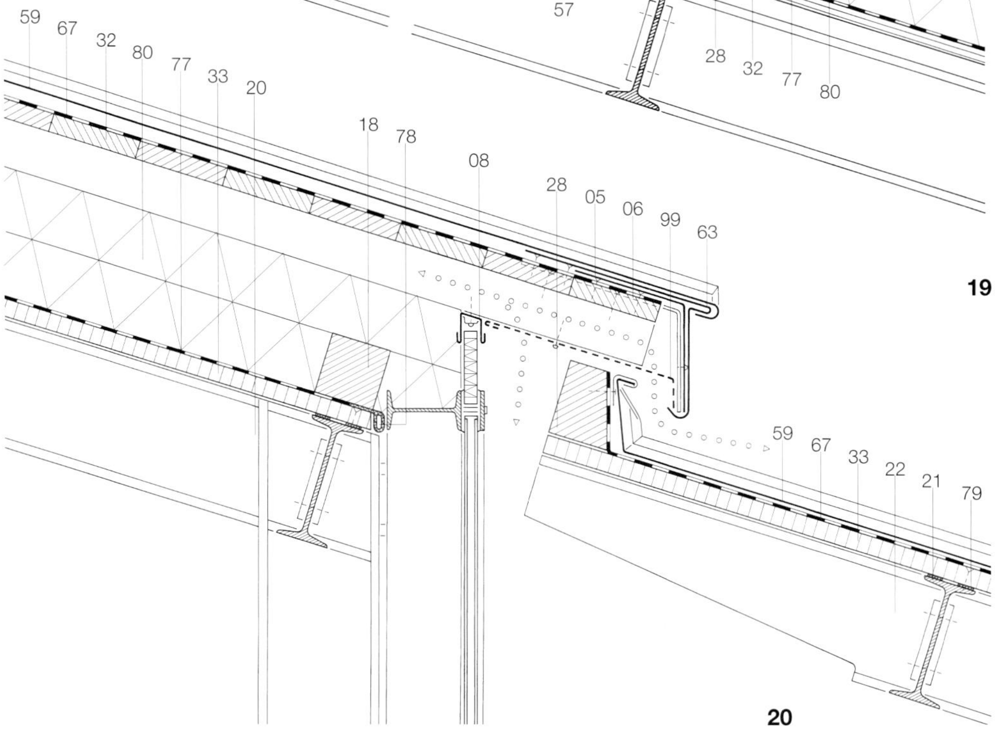

20

**Green roof**
Roof covering on plant-bearing layer, drainage layer, waterproofing, ventilated thermal insulation and vapour barrier

**Ridge**
**1** Roof covering continuing over ridge

All sheet materials are wrapped over the ridge to secure them against slippage. The waterproofing material overlaps the layers on the other side of the ridge by 150–200 mm; the upper edges are fixed with mechanical fasteners. However, it is better to lay the sheets in one piece from eaves to eaves with sealed side laps (waterproofing, root barrier) or loose side laps (protection mat, filter sheet, erosion protection textile).
Ventilation at the ridge is unnecessary because both plants (evaporation) and loose materials (storage mass) cover thermal performance requirements in summer. The pressure differential between windward and leeward sides enables the ventilation layer to remove any internal moisture via the eaves over the whole year – apart from a few days of totally calm air in summer.

**Eaves**
**2** Eaves with opening and gutter
**3** Eaves with outlet and chain "downpipe"

**2** The run-off water is discharged into the gutter along the full length of the eaves. A perforated metal strip or timber plank raised clear of the roof decking keeps the loose drainage material in position. Both are securely fixed (shear-resistant) to the roof decking, and the fixings are well sealed. At the eaves, surface water seeps into a narrow drainage channel filled with coarse material. A filter sheet (non-woven fabric) separates the drainage channel from the soil and thus prevent fine particles being washed out. Draining and overflow water are discharged into the gutter via a generously sized eaves flashing. All sheet metal components must be rustproof or treated to prevent corrosion.

**3** A timber parapet at the eaves requires a wide drainage channel behind it. Loose materials laid flat (≤ 5°) may include coarse gravel. The loose materials of the plant-bearing layer are separated from those of the drainage layer by a filter sheet (non-woven fabric) so that fine particles are not washed out. The waterproofing is pulled gently upwards and over the timber parapet so that excess surface water can drip to the outside. An additional drainpipe can help to remove water quickly.
Shifting loose materials and (temporary) hydrostatic pressures demand a substantial parapet member, fixed to the rafters with rigid, shear-resistant connections.

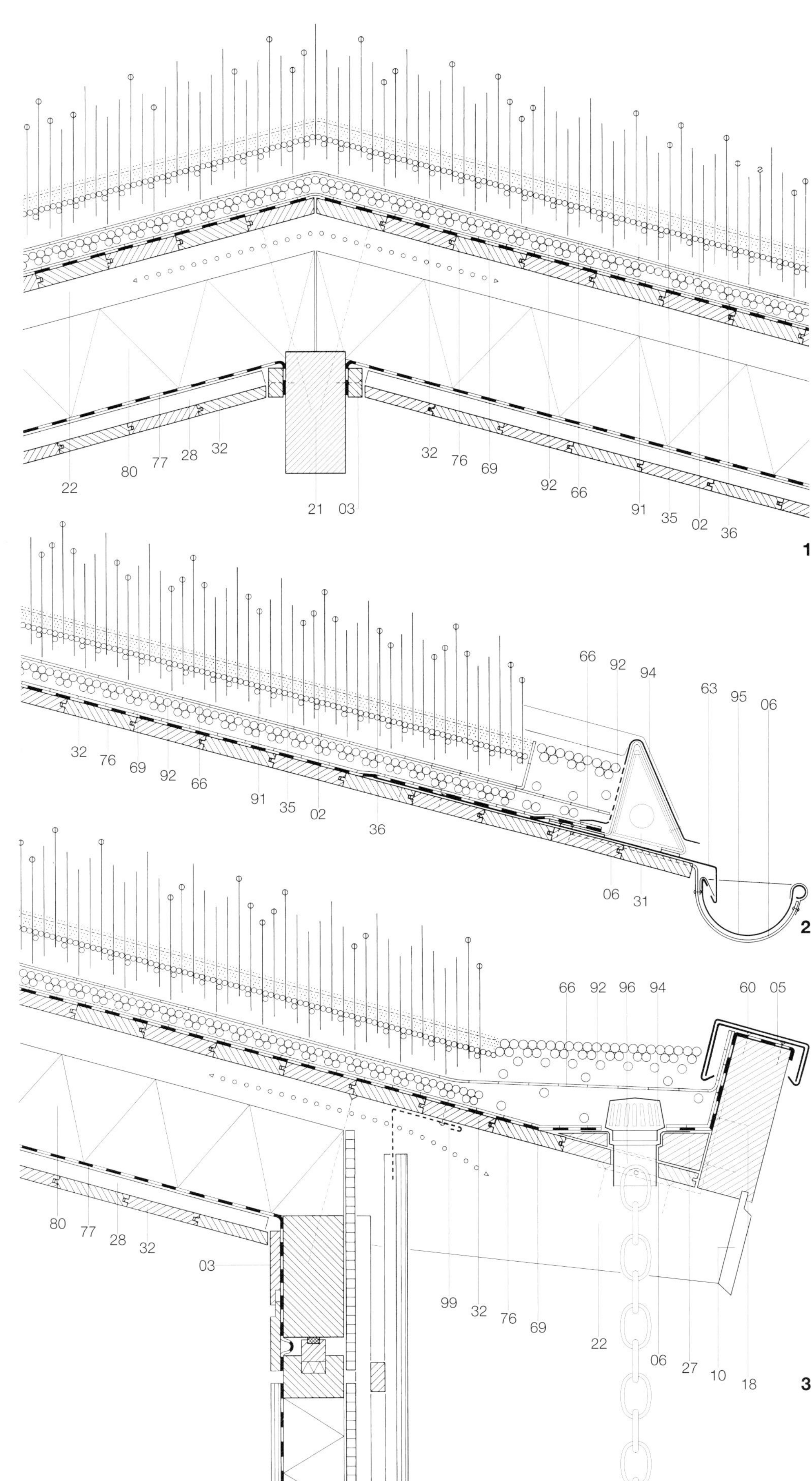

**Verge**

**4** Verge with sheet metal parapet
**5** Verge with timber parapet

At the verge the plant-bearing layer is separated from the parapet by a narrow strip of coarse, stable material. This drains excess surface water, but itself stores only little moisture and so helps to keep the roots away from the vulnerable edge of the roof.

**4** To keep the edge strips free from fine mulch particles, the upper layer of the filter sheet (non-woven fabric) is turned up to separate the drainage strip from the planting area. The lower layer of this filter sheet – overlapped in the direction of flow – protects the actual drainage layer. Non-woven fabric, protection mat and waterproofing are all turned up the inside of the stable sheet metal parapet; the waterproofing material is wrapped over the top of it. A sheet metal capping finishes of the parapet construction. This capping is forced over the parapet and laid on the perforated metal strip.

**5** Relatively shallow roofs with less surface water do not require special protection for the upper layer of loose material along the edge. The interior is carefully sealed, the vapour barrier clamped on securely and airtight.

**Penetrations**

**6** Chimney, with sheet metal flashings

The sheet metal flashings (sandwich plate) are welded to the waterproofing material and turned up the chimney ≥ 150 mm. The top edges are protected by a separate flashing. A strip of loose material laid around the chimney prevents a build-up of water at the rear flashing. The filter sheet (non-woven fabric) is also turned up the chimney to prevent fine particles being washed out of the soil into the drainage layer. A batten on each side presses the vapour barrier tightly against the chimney.

Details scale 1:10

02 Erosion protection textile
03 Vapour barrier clamped behind batten/board
05 Continuous clip
06 Fixing for flashing
07 Additional batten
09 Wedge of insulating material
10 Fascia board
18 Timber parapet
20 Timber parapet
21 Purlin
22 Rafter
24 Trimmer
27 Feather-edge board, triangular fillet
28 Spacer batten
29 Stop bead
31 Fin
32 Timber boarding
35 Mulch layer
36 Plants
59 Apron flashing
60 Capping strip
62 Drip flashing
63 Eaves flashing
66 Filter sheet (non-woven fabric)
69 Protection mat
72 Rendering
76 Waterproofing, root-resistant
77 Vapour barrier
78 Permanently elastic preformed seal
80 Thermal insulation
91 Plant-bearing layer
92 Drainage layer (chippings/gravel)
94 Outlet grating, perforated sheet metal
95 Gutter
96 Outlet with chain "downpipe"
99 Mesh screen

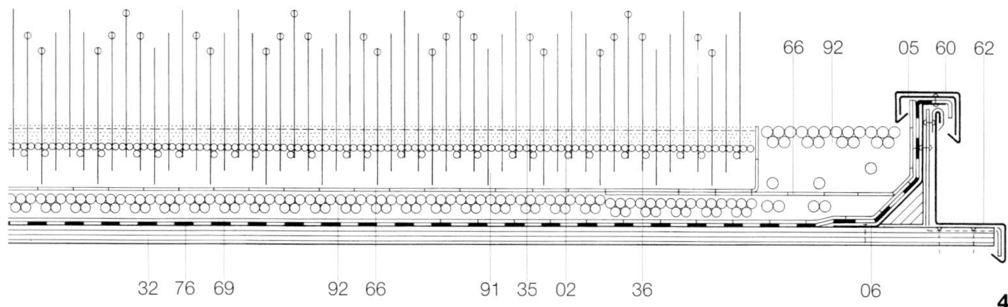

4

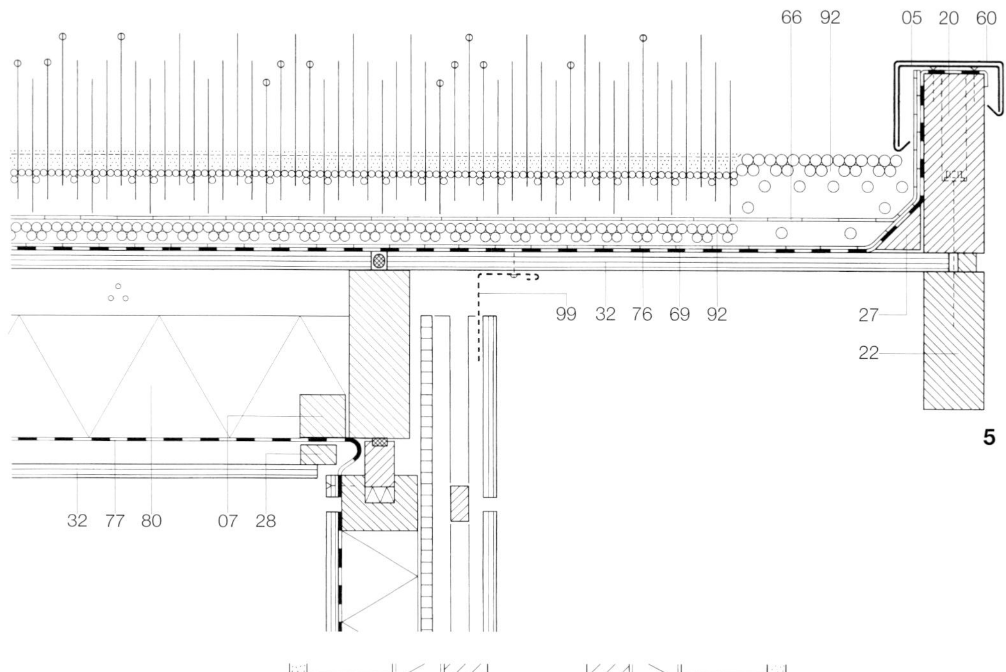

5

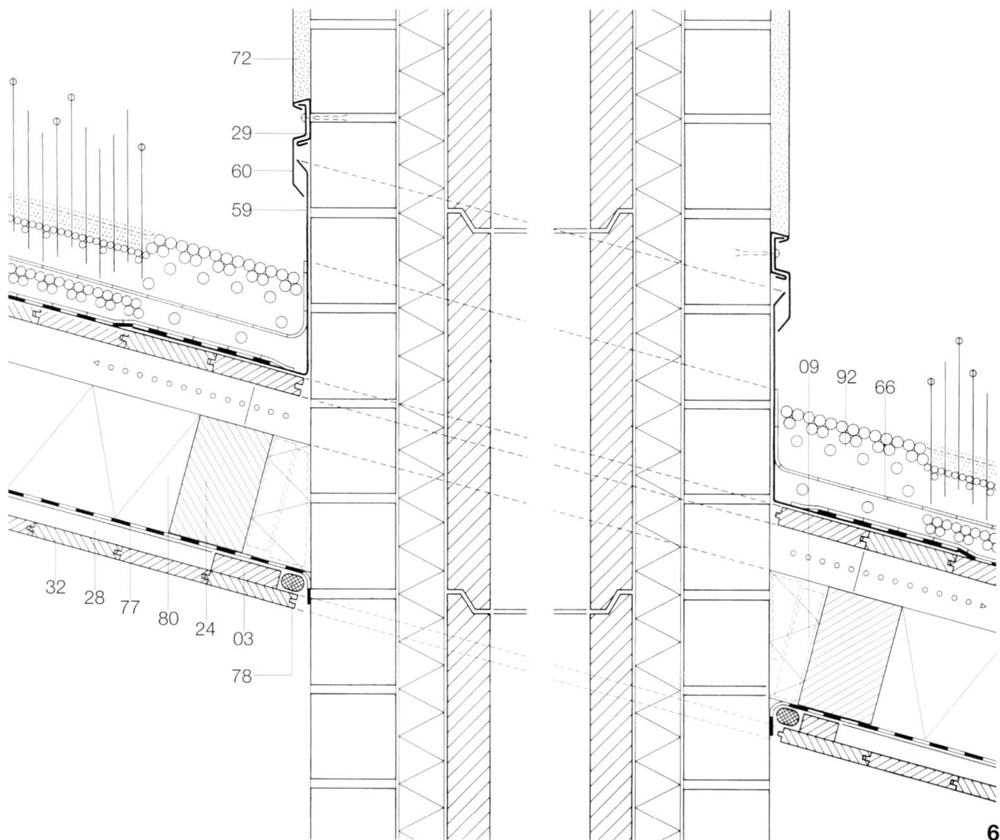

6

## Green roof

Roof covering on plant-bearing layer, drainage layer, non-ventilated thermal insulation and waterproofing

On an upside-down roof the thermal insulation is on top of the waterproofing – in the "wet" part of the roof – and is therefore included in the thermal performance calculation with a U-value of 0.05 W/m²K. Its water absorption should not exceed 2% by vol. The insulating components should have rebated edges to interrupt the water circulation at the joints, and should be laid in a single layer to minimise water run-off layers. Water vapour that penetrates into the thermal insulation can escape upwards via the drainage layer. The thermal insulation is a protection mat for the waterproofing, which also acts as a vapour barrier.
All metal components must be rustproof or treated to prevent corrosion.

#### Ridge to monopitch roof

**1** Ridge to monopitch roof, with parapet and sheet metal capping

The thermal insulation in the roof directly joins the cavity insulation of the external wall. At the ridge the waterproofing is turned up the parapet ≥ 100 mm above the plant-bearing layer on the rigid foam insulation. It is protected against damage by the filter sheet (non-woven fabric) and covered by the sheet metal parapet capping. A narrow strip of gravel keeps this edge dry and also helps to keep the roots of the plants clear of the edge of the roof.
The masonry outer leaf, like the parapet board, is supported by a dovetail slot anchored back into the concrete roof slab. The parapet board provides a stable base for the steel straps holding the sheet metal capping.
A peripheral sealing strip closes of the joint between the window frame and the reinforced concrete roof.

#### Eaves

**2** Eaves with twin outlets and gutter

Drainage mat and waterproofing both drain into the box gutter formed by the waterproofing material. This is turned up and over the edge plate so that overflowing water can drain.
A drainage strip provides space for fast-flowing run-off water and transfers the thrust to the roof structure. Perforated sheet metal keeps the loose material (gravel) of the drainage strip in place.
The upper layer of the filter sheet (non-woven fabric) separates the drainage strip from the soil and thus prevents fine particles being washed out. The lower layer of the filter sheet separates it from the drainage mat so that even if surface water overflows, only very few fine particles reach the actual drainage layer.

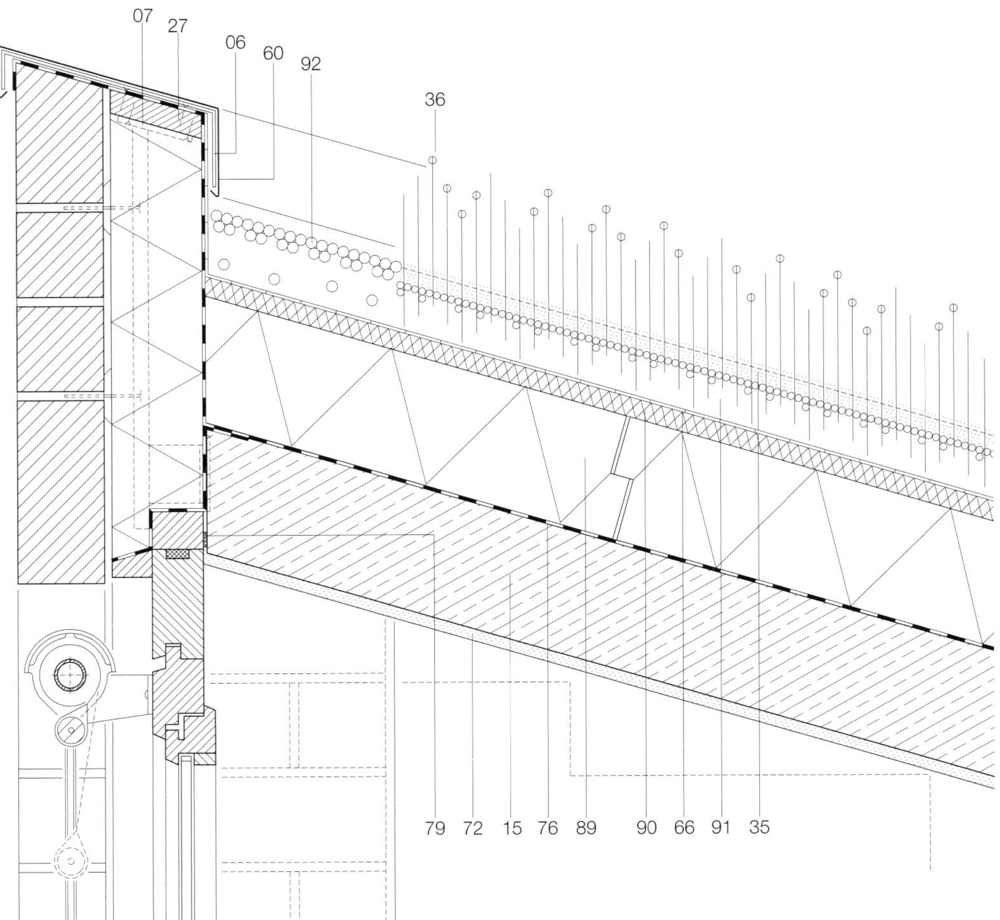


1

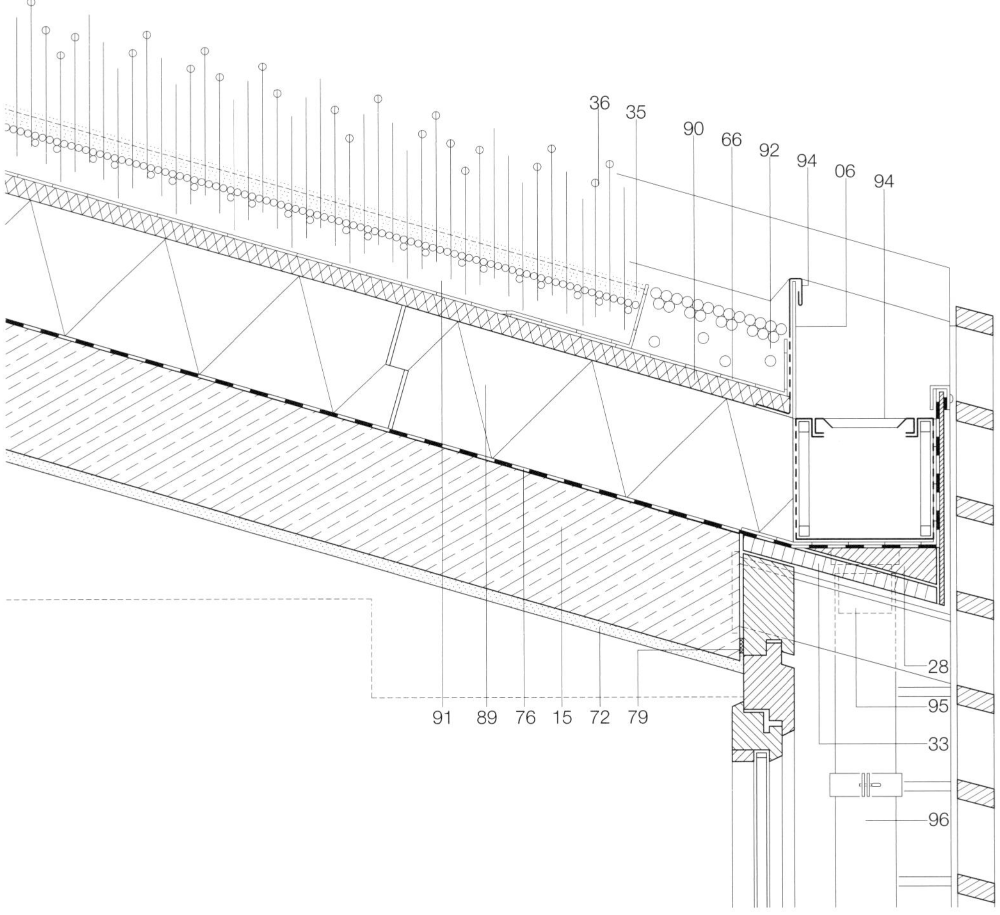


2

**3** Eaves with twin outlets and canopy

The water run-off layers – drainage mat and waterproofing – discharge directly to the outside along the full length of the eaves. The surface water seeps into a strip of gravel along the edge, which – like the drainage mat – is protected by the filter sheet (non-woven fabric) from becoming clogged by fine particles from the plant-bearing layer. Perforated sheet metal keeps the loose material of the drainage strip in place. A raised member made of moisture-resistant material withstands the thrust from the roof construction. This is firmly anchored (shear-resistant) in the reinforced concrete roof slab. There must be a generous overlap of material over these anchors, which must be very carefully sealed. The canopy of large timber derivative sheets supported on steel cantilever brackets protects the external wall. The length of this canopy depends on the height and number of storeys and terminates with a sheet metal drip flashing.

**Verge**

**4** Verge with parapet and sheet metal capping

A narrow, stable gravel drainage strip conveys excess surface water quickly into the drainage layer. The gravel itself stores no moisture and hence helps to prevent roots reaching the vulnerable edge of the roof. The drainage mat and the gravel are both separated from the fine particles in the plant-bearing layer (fertile soil) by a filter sheet (non-woven fabric).
Stiff bitumen roofing felt is turned up the parapet over a triangular fillet, ≥ 100 mm above the plant-bearing layer, and over the top of the parapet. At the top of the parapet the lower layer of roofing felt is nailed to a board, and the upper layer is fully bonded. Both layers continue over the full width of the parapet. The filter sheet and the sheet metal capping protect the waterproofing against damage.
The reinforced concrete roof slab (edge stepped to match brickwork courses) is supported on the inner leaf and also acts as a ring beam.

Details scale 1:10

00 Dovetail slot
01 Wall tie
02 Erosion protection textile
06 Fixing for flashing, steel strap
07 Steel plate
09 Wedge of insulating material
12 Inner leaf of masonry
13 Facing brickwork
15 Reinforced concrete
22 Cantilever bracket
27 Parapet board
33 Timber derivative board
35 Mulch layer
36 Plants
60 Sheet metal capping
63 Eaves flashing
66 Filter sheet (non-woven fabric)
72 Plaster
75 Damp-proof course
76 Waterproofing, root-resistant; root barrier
79 Permanently elastic sealing strip
80 Cavity insulation
89 Thermal insulation
90 Drainage mat
91 Plant-bearing layer
92 Drainage layer (chippings)
94 Drainage strip
95 Foil channel, outlet
96 Rainwater downpipe

3

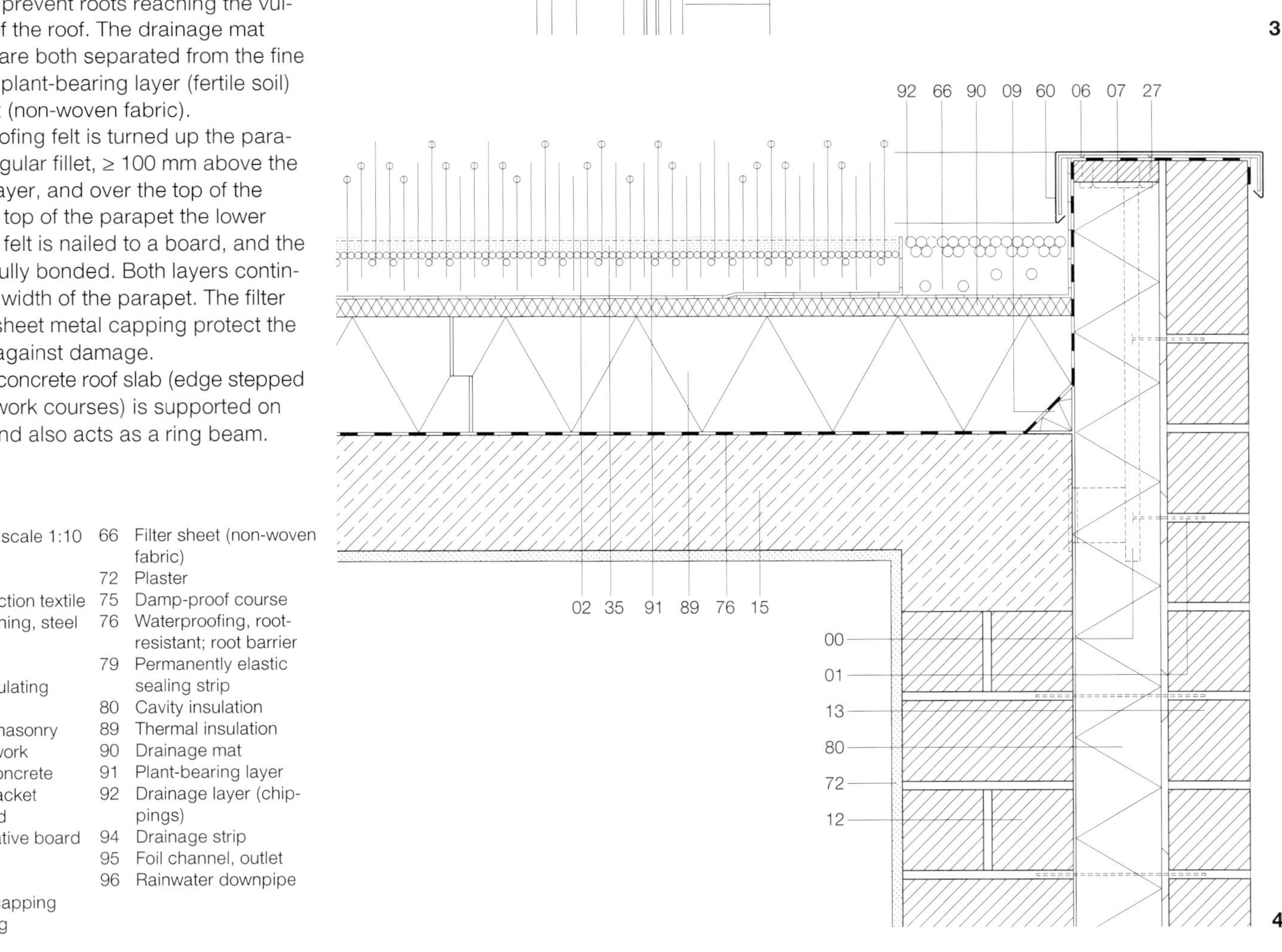


4

**Junction with wall**

**5** Junction with wall at side of slope, with sheet metal flashing

Rainwater striking and draining down the external leaf of the wall above roof level is intercepted by a wide strip of coarse, loose material and transferred from there to the drainage layer. The waterproofing is turned up the wall ≥ 150 mm above the plant-bearing layer, where it is protected by the filter sheet (non-woven fabric) and the sheet metal flashing. The sheet metal continues up behind the bracket supporting the external leaf and thus prevents water penetrating the cavity insulation. The flashing is fixed to vertical battens let into the insulation.
The reinforced concrete roof slab (edge stepped to match brickwork courses) is supported on the inner leaf and also acts as a ring beam. The joint between the concrete and the masonry does not have to accommodate movement because good thermal insulation and the rest of the roof construction, providing extra thermal insulation in winter and good heat capacity plus cooling evaporation in summer, ensures that the roof slab is not subjected to significant thermal movements.

**Penetrations**

**6** Flue, with support sleeve and skirt

The gas flue consists of long sections of pipe that must withstand the thrust of the plant-bearing layer and the drainage strip where they pass through the reinforced concrete roof slab. The flue passes through an opening in the roof slab fitted with a sheet metal sleeve. The deep roof construction of the upside-down green roof requires a long flue support sleeve. It projects ≥ 150 mm above the plant-bearing layer (surface water) and the drainage strip. Half of the flange to the support sleeve is above, half below the sheet metal flashing, to which it is riveted/soldered or welded. The skirt around the flue overlaps the support sleeve 50–100 mm and thus accommodates the thermal expansion of the sections of pipe. The root barrier is firmly welded to the plastic-coated sheet metal flashing. The joint around the flue is closed off with a permanently elastic, vapour-tight preformed rubber sealing strip.

Details scale 1:10
03 Collar
12 Inner leaf of masonry
13 Facing brickwork
15 Reinforced concrete
18 Steel bracket
28 Batten, sleeve
35 Mulch layer
36 Plants
59 Flashing
60 Sheet steel skirt
61 Flashing
66 Filter sheet (non-woven fabric)
72 Plaster
75 Damp-proof course and cavity tray
76 Waterproofing, root-resistant; root barrier
78 Permanently elastic preformed seal
80 Cavity insulation
89 Thermal insulation
90 Drainage mat
91 Plant-bearing layer
92 Drainage strip (gravel)
93 Flue
95 Steel flue support sleeve

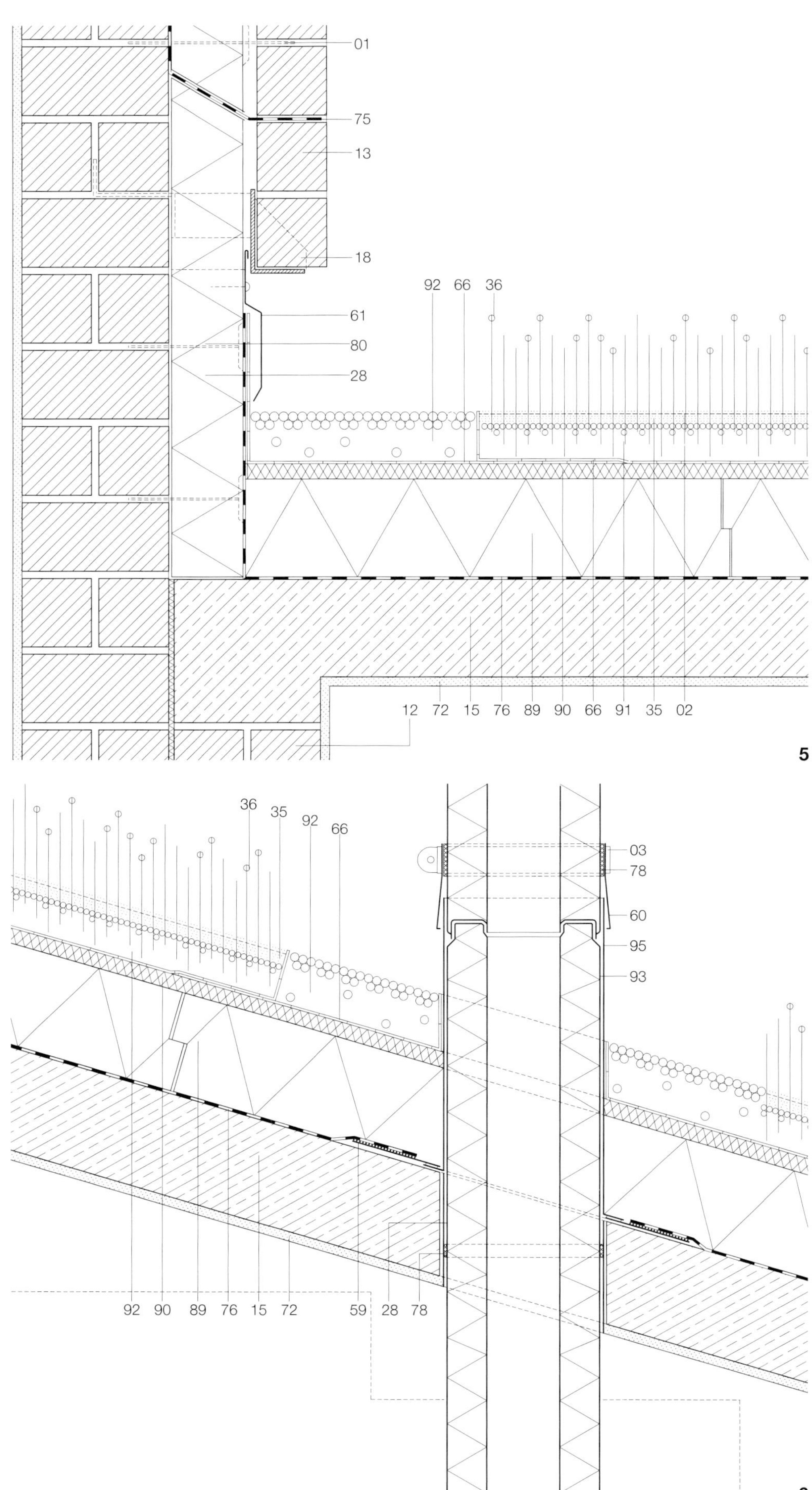

## Refurbishment

**Significance**
The maintenance and repair of roof surfaces has already become a major source of work in the building industry, and is set to take on even greater significance in the future. The reasons for this are:
- Building fabric

Besides the buildings that survived the war, more than 50% of Germany's current building stock was built between the years 1949 and 1975. In line with a refurbishment cycle of 30 years, the great majority of these structures are due for refurbishment, regardless of any new building regulations.
- Energy economy

As outlined in the chapter "Changes in the 20th century", efficient resource management and energy saving are becoming increasingly important. The introduction of the Energy Economy Act in Germany once again raised the standards. Upgrading roofs in terms of their energy efficiency has become an important requirement in our society.
- New living accommodation

Using the roof space is not without its problems (see "Use and form"). However, in Germany there is a large stock of existing, convertible roof spaces, which can be made habitable economically.

**Definitions**
The term "refurbishment" is linked with a permanent improvement of the building fabric. Whether the refurbishment is carried out for aesthetic, functional or structural reasons is irrelevant. Refurbishment includes the continued use of any part of the existing fabric suitable for the purpose.
"Repair" is different from refurbishment in that it attempts only to preserve the state of the existing fabric and is hence a short-term measure. Of course, the transition between repair and refurbishment is fluid. However, in this chapter we shall primarily be talking about the long-term improvement of the building fabric.

**Approach**
Below, we look at the layers of the roof construction – singly or in combination – in accordance with the above definitions. Maintenance and repair of the roof covering materials themselves have been described in the individual sections on those materials. It was felt that the special aspects of the materials and forms could be treated better in that way. Roofs requiring refurbishment differ greatly in terms of their form, condition and intended usage. To simplify our treatment of refurbishment principles, we assume a roof with a covering of profiled roof tiles and a pitch of 30°. We also assume a ventilation layer below the roof covering and above the thermal insulation, plus roofing felt, in line with current DIN standards. Vapour barrier and inner lining are assumed to be fitted below the loadbearing structure.
As is more common in practice, a verge without overhang but eaves and monopitch roof ridge with overhang have been assumed. Normal internal temperatures apply. As energy economy refurbishment measures are generally more sensible when the entire building envelope is involved, the refurbishment details for the roof take into account the increase in thickness of the external walls due to additional thermal insulation. Refurbishment work can and may be visible after completion.

**Case studies**
Overview

**Overview**
The columns give the various defects or reasons for refurbishment and their possible combinations. The rows show the minimum work involved and the refurbishment options when the roof surface is raised or left in position. The titles of the rows designate the layers that are missing, inadequate or defective; these parts are shown in red. The parts already included in the roof construction and which are to be retained are shown in black. New additions are shown in blue.
A few general notes about the solutions illustrated in the overview on pp. 328–29:
The refurbishment options include both ventilated and non-ventilated insulation. Empty boxes mean that no reasonable solution has been found for this particular refurbishment principle or that the solution involves even more work (and costs) and is not feasible without causing damage.
Refurbishment is not always the perfect answer. This applies in particular to the associated external walls.

**Minimum work**
To illustrate the range of options, column A shows solutions involving the minimum amount of work (and costs). This has been considered for the roof surface only because a "true" refurbishment, with the associated energy economy and functional improvements, is always preferable.

Secondary waterproofing/covering layer A1
The minimum work required for this type of problem involves removing the roof covering and its supporting members (battens) from above. After laying a new roofing felt (open to diffusion), there is the opportunity to replace critical parts of the roof covering and improve the fixings along the edges of the roof in accordance with newer, more stringent requirements. All in all, this is a relatively complicated and expensive measure, which is only justified when the roof covering allows rainwater to reach the thermal insulation because the roof pitch is too shallow.
If it is possible to raise the roof surface, a true secondary waterproofing/covering layer consisting of roof decking and waterproof roofing felt can be incorporated instead of just replacing the roofing felt. Another alternative is described under "Secondary waterproofing/ covering layer plus thermal insulation A4" below.

Thermal insulation A2
The minimum work required here can at best consist of thickening the insulation from below. To do this, the inner lining must be removed together with supporting construction, vapour barrier and any existing insulation. It is recommended to remove the old insulation completely and not just add to it because new insulation materials in a better heat conduction class can then be selected. This very involved and costly process also brings to light the problem that current energy economy requirements cannot be fulfilled with the depth of rafter generally available.
Simply blowing cellulose fibres into the roof construction without incorporating any other measures should be regarded with scepticism because the existing roofing felt probably has a high diffusion resistance. This, together with the existing – probably defective – vapour barrier, can lead to saturation of any materials between the rafters.

Vapour barrier A3
It is adequate here to remove the inner lining and its supporting construction to install a new vapour barrier. This enables the new vapour barrier to be carefully joined to the existing components in order to protect the insulation against saturation from inside and to achieve the airtightness required by the new Energy Economy Act.

Secondary waterproofing/covering layer plus thermal insulation A4
As described above under "Secondary waterproofing/covering layer", this refurbishment work is carried out from above. Non-ventilated thermal insulation is shown here as an alternative. This is possible because a new roofing felt open to diffusion can be selected.
This alternative presents the opportunity of gaining more depth for the layer of thermal insulation. However, this presupposes a reliably functioning vapour barrier, an assumption that should never be made.

Thermal insulation plus vapour barrier A5
This solution is covered by the measures described under "Thermal insulation A2" and "Vapour barrier A3".

Secondary waterproofing/covering layer plus thermal insulation plus vapour barrier A6
This complex damage situation makes it necessary to deal with the problem both from above and from below. It is almost the same as rebuilding the whole roof. Part of the thermal insulation – if still serviceable – can be retained. However, it is recommended to remove this as well because new insulation materials in a better heat conduction class can then be selected. The considerable improvement in energy economy performance justifies the amount of work and the expense.

**Refurbishment without changing the position of the roof surface**
Where it is not possible to raise the roof surface, the refurbishment measures must be carried out underneath and between the loadbearing members. The solutions show that the measures are often identical to minimal solutions. Only in the case of ventilated roof designs with defective thermal insulation is it necessary to add framing to the underside of the loadbearing structure in order to achieve the necessary depth for the insulation. The ridge and eaves details are shown and discussed on the following pages. Here, too, it is possible to derive solutions for situations not actually shown.

**Refurbishment with a change in the position of the roof surface**
When it is possible to raise the roof surface, this type of refurbishment should be preferred over all others because it embodies all the right conditions for a sensible design. If only the vapour barrier is defective it is more sensible to work from below. As outlined in the section "Design principles", the advantages are:

- The loadbearing structure is protected against temperature stresses and fluctuations.
- The thermal insulation can be laid in one plane.
- The vapour barrier can be laid from above in good working conditions and in one plane without interruptions.

However, the solutions involve more work and higher costs, and a deeper overall roof construction. Some potential solutions for ventilated/non-ventilated designs are shown and discussed on the following pages. Those situations not shown can be assumed to be similar.

| Defective component | | Minimum work |
|---|---|---|
| Secondary waterproofing/ covering layer | | 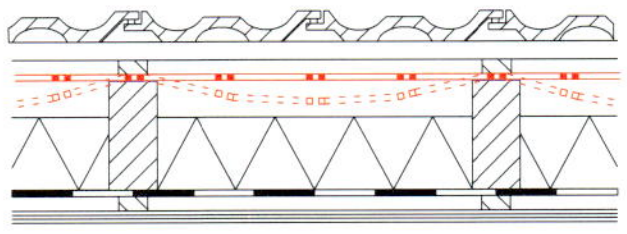 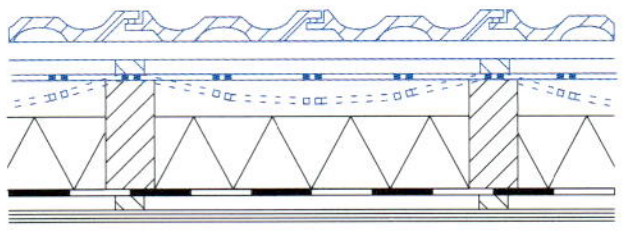 A1 |
| Thermal insulation | | 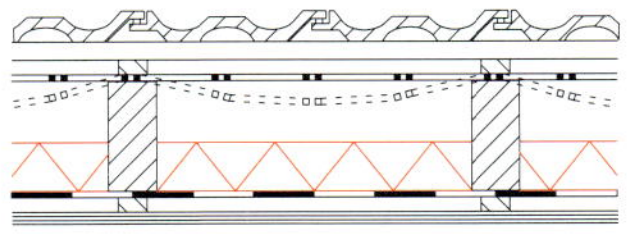 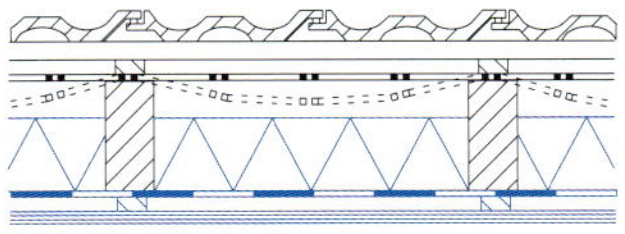 A2 |
| Vapour barrier | | 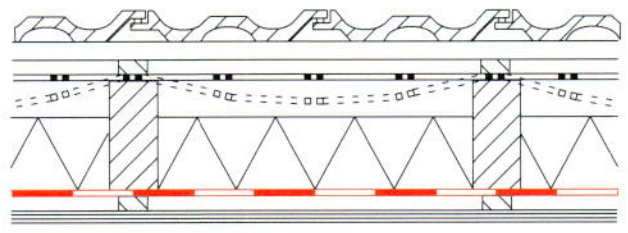 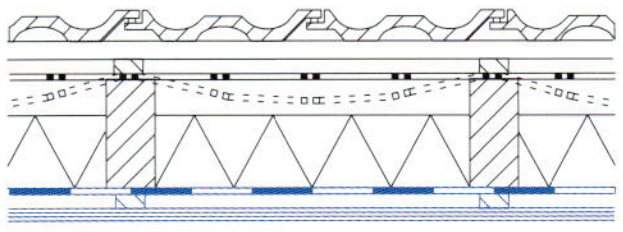 A3 |
| Secondary waterproofing/ covering layer<br>Thermal insulation | | 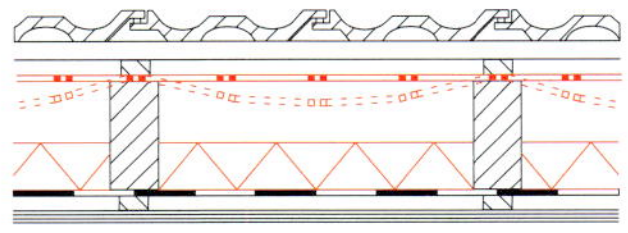 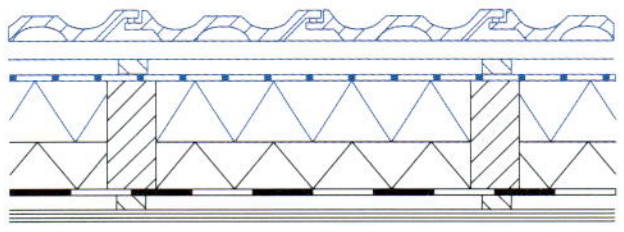 A4 |
| Thermal insulation<br>Vapour barrier | | 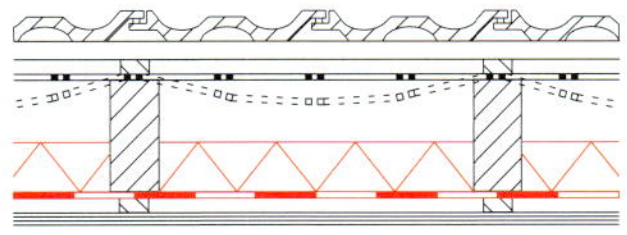 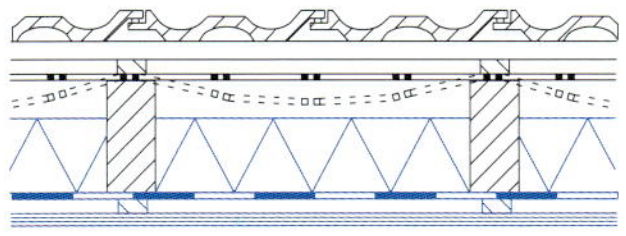 A5 |
| Secondary waterproofing/ covering layer<br>Thermal insulation<br>Vapour barrier | | 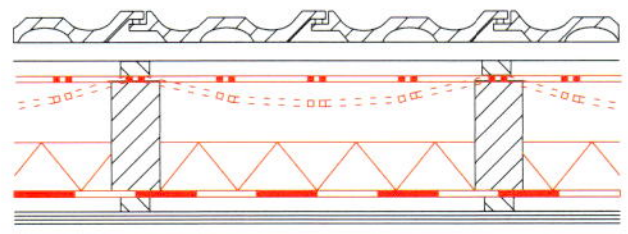 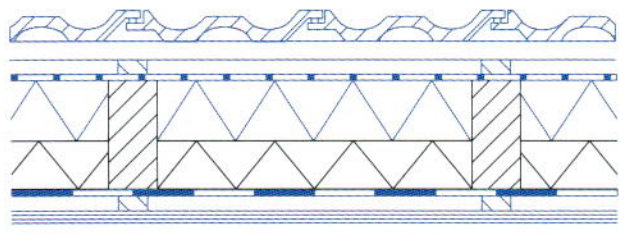 A6 |

| Position of roof surface unchanged | | Roof surface raised | |
|---|---|---|---|
| ventilated | non-ventilated | ventilated | non-ventilated |
| B1 | C1 | | |
| Details, see pp. 334-35 B2 | C2 | Details, see p. 333 D2 | E2 |
| B3 | | | |
| B4 | C4 | Details, see pp. 330-31 D4 | Details, see pp. 332-33 E4 |
| B5 | | Details, see pp. 330-31 D5 | Details, see pp. 332-33 E5 |
| B6 | C6 | Details, see pp. 330-31 D6 | Details, see pp. 332-33 E6 |

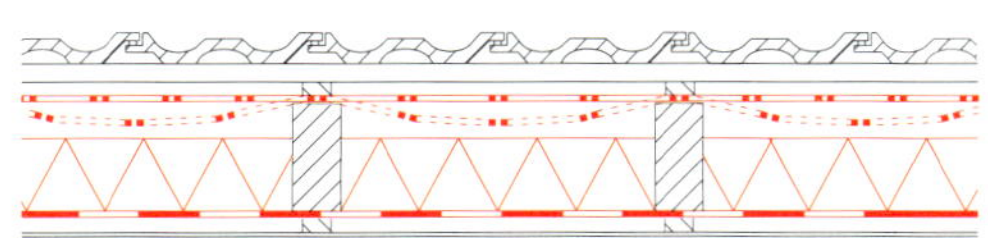

**D4 Defective secondary waterproofing/covering layer and thermal insulation**
**D5 Defective thermal insulation and vapour barrier**
**D6 Defective secondary waterproofing/covering layer, thermal insulation and vapour barrier**
Roof surface raised
Ventilation layer over thermal insulation above loadbearing structure

In these situations, the roof surface must be raised. However, this does create space underneath the roof construction because the existing inner lining, vapour barrier and insulation are removed. Rafters can be clad if their appearance makes them unsuitable for being left exposed in the roof space.

**Ridge**
**1** Ridge to duopitch roof, with separated ventilation layers
**2** Ridge to monopitch roof, with overhang

**1** It is very easy to lay the vapour barrier, even at the ridge, when the thermal insulation is positioned above the loadbearing structure. As at the verge and eaves, the ridge is finished with a sheet metal capping. The ventilation hood, with its multiple redirection of the air flow, is secure against driving rain and snow. If the roof surfaces are subject to different climatic conditions, it is recommended to separate the ventilation layers above the insulation at the ridge so that moist, warm air cannot flow from the warm side to the cold side, where it could condense under a roof surface covered with frost or snow.

**2** If the existing rafters cantilever beyond the external wall, they should be trimmed back. After refurbishment, the cantilever is formed by the new spacer rafters and the roof covering alone. This full thickness of the roof construction is thus understated at the edge. The sheet metal capping to the ridge matches the height of the verge capping. The metal panels covering the edge of the roof construction below the ridge can also help to conceal the energy economy improvements to the external wall. The rest of the roof construction is as shown on p. 292.

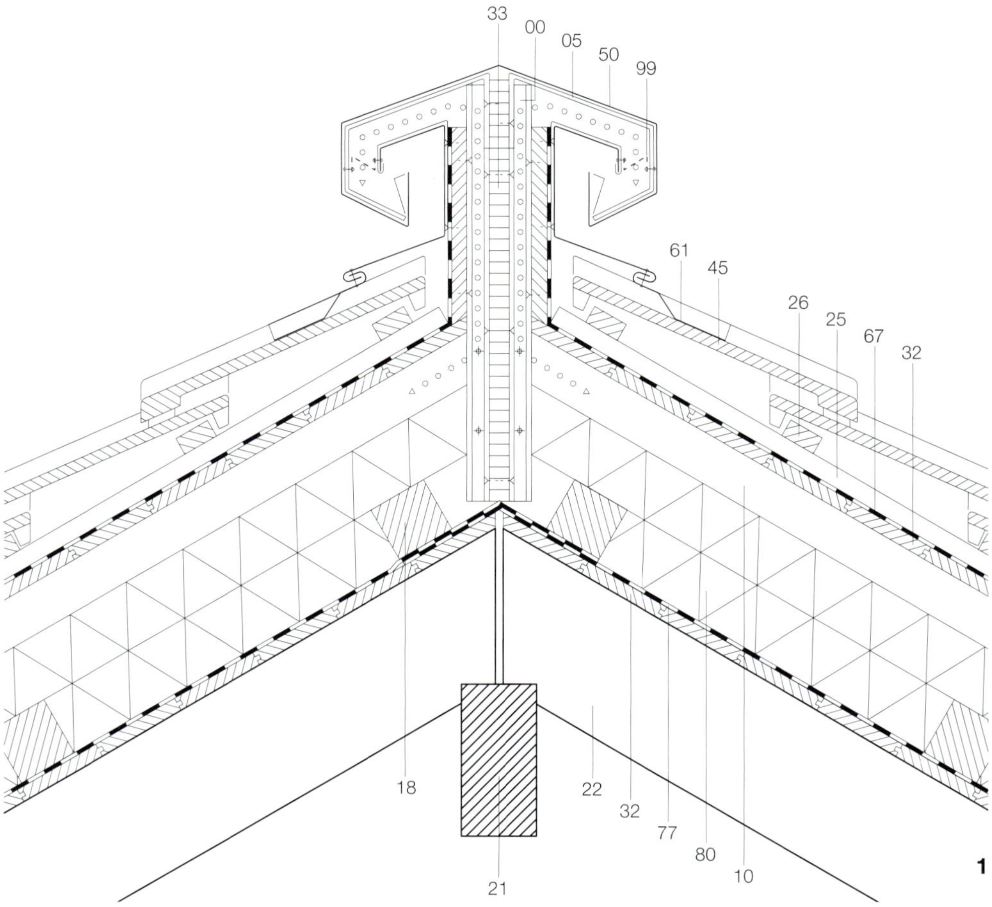

1

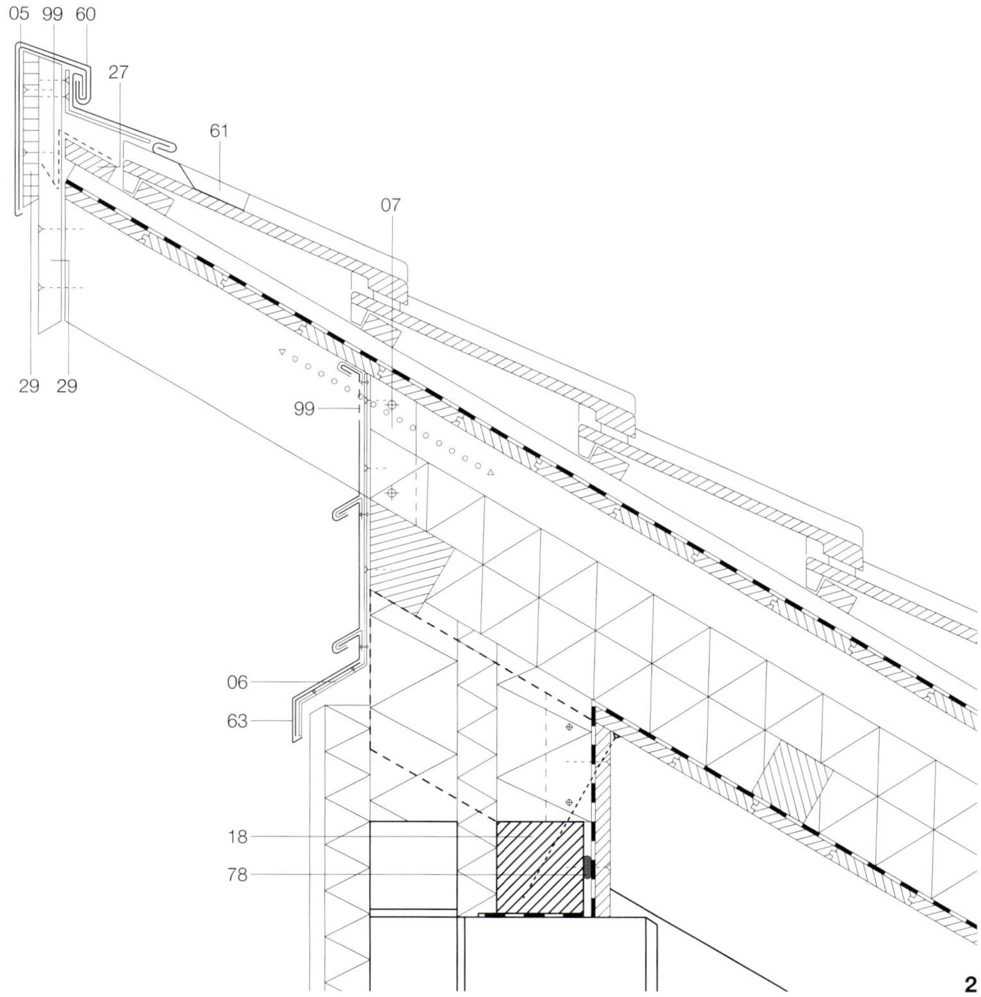

2

## Eaves

**3** Eaves with overhang

The existing rafters together with the roof decking and the locked double welt standing seam sheet metal covering create a slender edge to this roof, because the new construction continues only as far as the external wall. As with the other edges in this refurbishment situation, the roof covering at the eaves employs sheet metal. It is laid to match the detail at the verge. As with the ridge to the monopitch roof, the vapour barrier is clamped to the wall plate. Here again, sheet metal panels can be used to conceal the thicker external wall.
As for the ridge detail shown in drawing 2, the primary loadbearing rafters could be cut back instead and the overhang carried on the spacer rafters.

## Verge

**4** Verge without overhang

The existing roof covering must be removed completely. A roof decking, extending beyond the gable wall, is laid on the existing loadbearing structure. The vapour barrier can now be laid on top, over the entire area of the roof. A strip of film/foil should be clamped between the existing rafters and the new roof decking, and the joint between it and the inside of the external wall sealed. This avoids the need for a stepped gable wall. Spacer purlins on the roof decking plus spacer rafters on top of these raise the roof construction above the thick layers of thermal insulation. A layer of timber boarding and roofing felt closes off the ventilation layer above the thermal insulation. If the old roof covering is to be replaced as before and the external wall is now thicker to cope with enhanced energy economy requirements, it is advisable to incorporate a verge gutter to close off the gap between the old roof covering and the new verge. The edge of the deep roof construction is protected along the verge with a timber bargeboard and sheet metal capping.
A verge without an overhang is the most typical case in practice.

Details scale 1:10

00 Spacer
05 Clip, continuous clip
06 Fixing for flashing, gutter bracket
07 Additional batten
10 Spacer rafter
18 Spacer purlin, wall plate
21 Purlin
22 Rafter
25 Counter batten
26 Batten
27 Feather-edge board, ridge board
28 Verge board
29 Bargeboard, capping piece
32 Timber boarding
33 Laminated board
35 Drip flashing
45 Interlocking profiled tile
50 Ventilation hood
59 Sheet metal roof covering
60 Sheet metal capping
61 Milled sheet lead
62 Verge flashing
63 Cover flashing
67 Roofing felt
70 Damp-proof course
77 Vapour barrier
78 Preformed seal
80 Thermal insulation
90 Tangle fleece
95 Gutter
99 Mesh screen

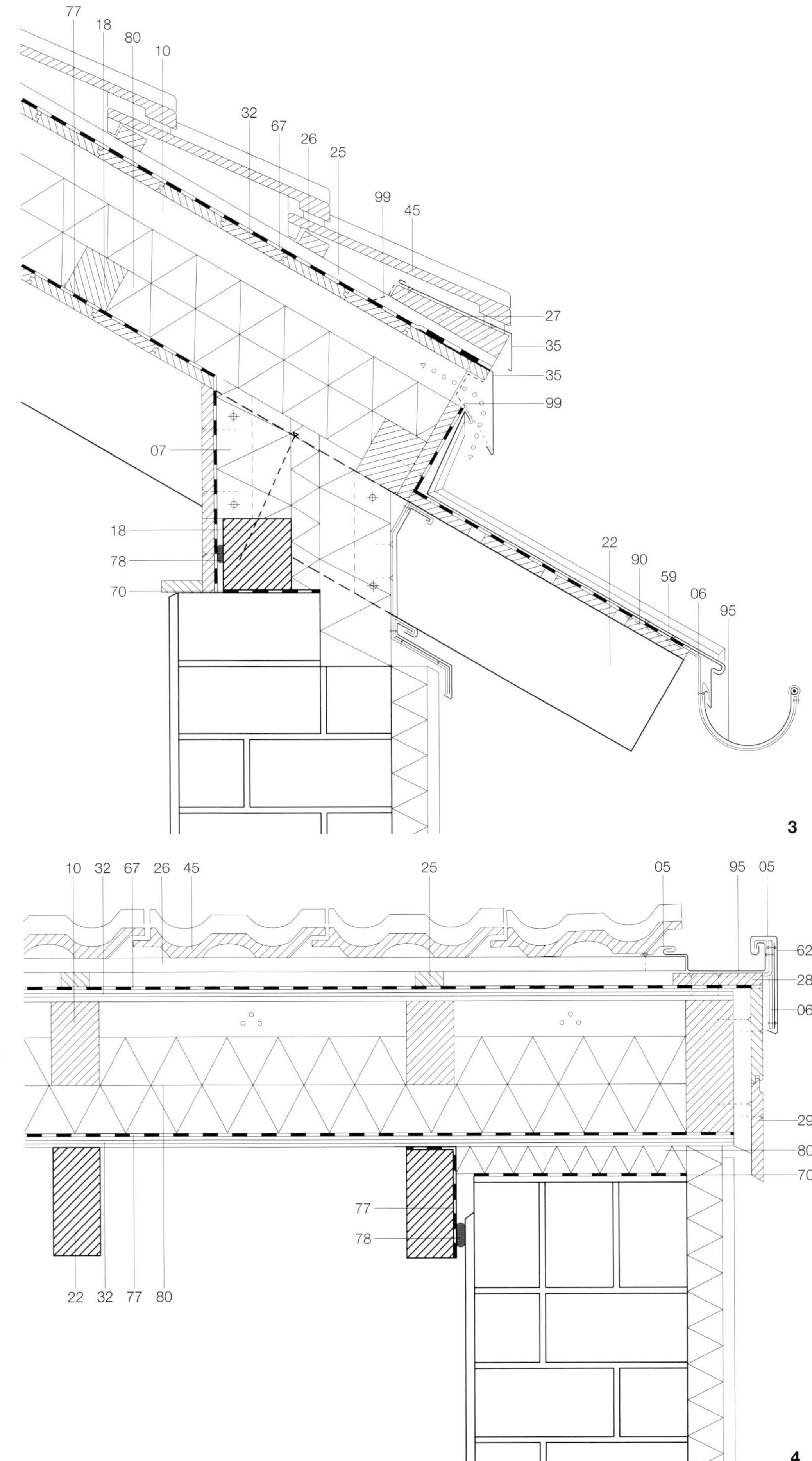

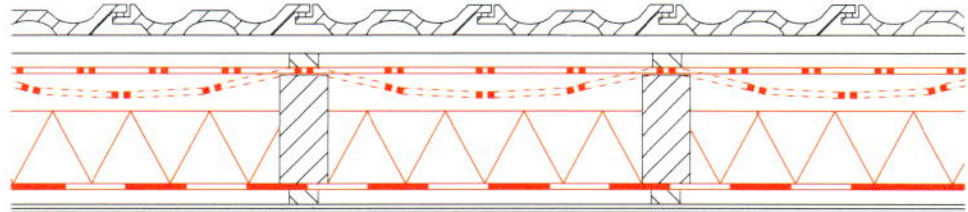

**E4 Defective secondary waterproofing/ covering layer and thermal insulation**
**E5 Defective thermal insulation and vapour barrier**
**E6 Defective secondary waterproofing/covering layer, thermal insulation and vapour barrier**
Roof surface raised
No ventilation layer over thermal insulation above loadbearing structure

The refurbishment options for a roof without a ventilation layer above the thermal insulation are very similar to the previous details when the problems are the same and the roof surface can be raised. Roof covering, thermal insulation, vapour barrier and inner lining must be removed before work commences.
The details – not illustrated here – for the eaves and a ridge to a monopitch roof can be refurbished similarly by simply omitting the ventilation layer.

**Ridge**
**1** Ridge to duopitch roof, with ventilation

The construction illustrated here shows that it is easy to lay the vapour barrier even at the ridge. There is no ventilation layer directly above the thermal insulation itself, but moisture can escape through the waterproofing layer (open to diffusion) into the overlying ventilation layer. A ridge detail with an appropriate ventilation opening supports this.
The problems of non-ventilated thermal insulation have been discussed in detail in the section "Design principles".

**Verge**
**4** Verge without overhang

The roof decking and the vapour barrier are installed and connected to the external wall as described for D4, D5 and D6 above. According to DIN 4108 the diffusion-equivalent air thickness layer of the material covering the insulation may not exceed 1/6 of that of the vapour barrier below the insulation. The total thermal resistance of the layers below the insulation must be ≤ 20% of the thermal resistance of the entire roof construction. The ventilation layer above the insulation carries away any residual moisture from between the rafters and condensation forming on the underside of the roof covering. Apart from the thinner overall roof construction, the verge detail is as in B1.

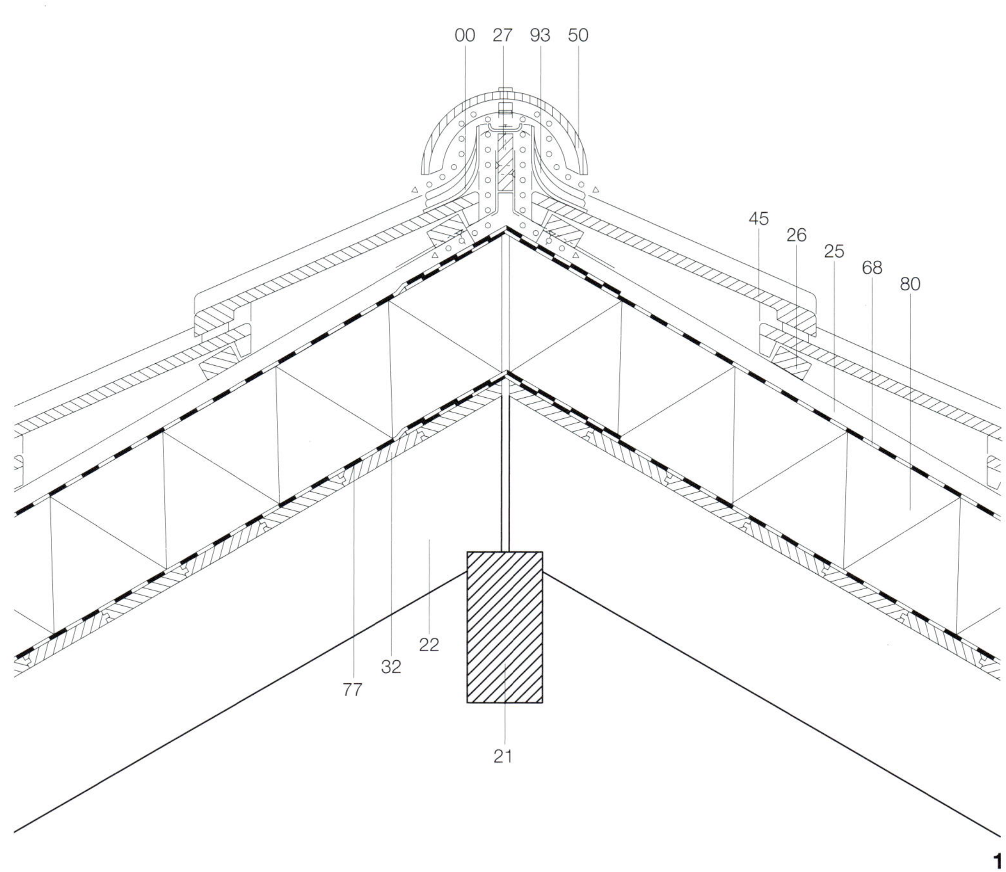


1

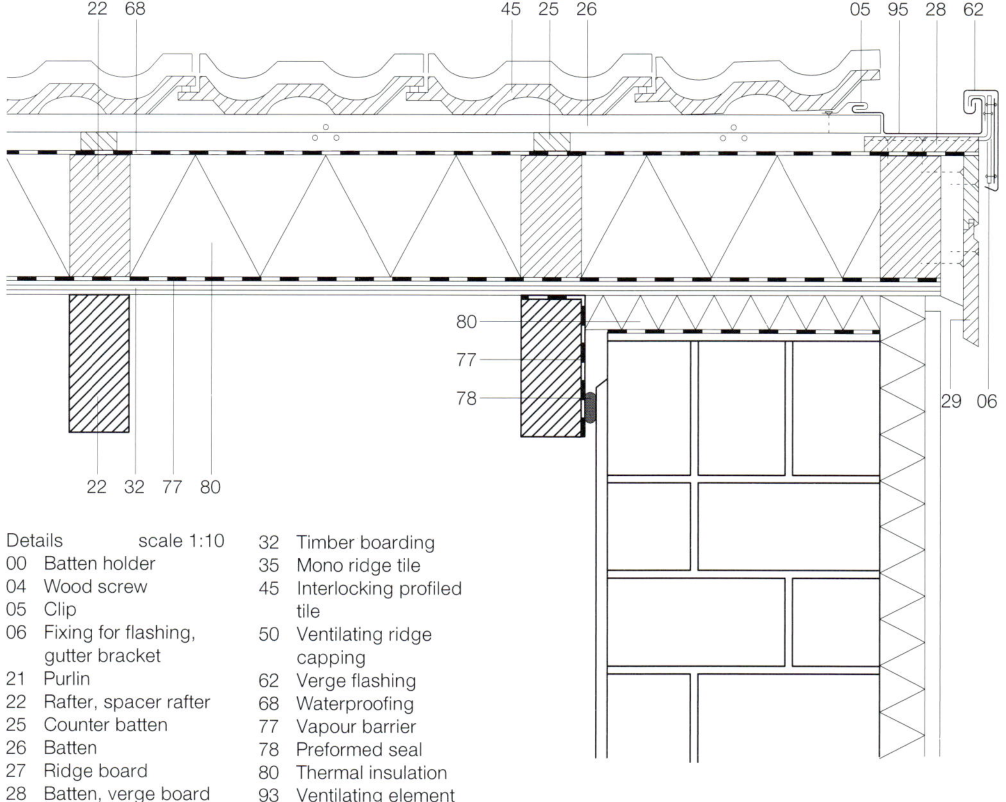


Details scale 1:10
00 Batten holder
04 Wood screw
05 Clip
06 Fixing for flashing, gutter bracket
21 Purlin
22 Rafter, spacer rafter
25 Counter batten
26 Batten
27 Ridge board
28 Batten, verge board
29 Bargeboard, capping piece
32 Timber boarding
35 Mono ridge tile
45 Interlocking profiled tile
50 Ventilating ridge capping
62 Verge flashing
68 Waterproofing
77 Vapour barrier
78 Preformed seal
80 Thermal insulation
93 Ventilating element
95 Gutter
99 Mesh screen

2

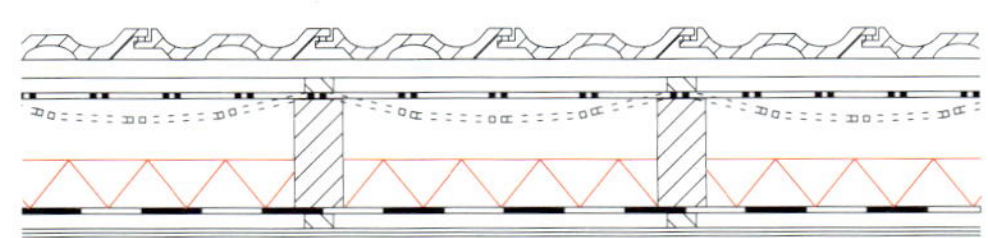

**D2 Defective thermal insulation**
Roof surface raised
Ventilation layer over thermal insulation between loadbearing members

This assumes a roof in which the thermal insulation is defective or is no longer adequate, but the other parts of the construction are still fully serviceable. There is an overhang at the ridge and at the eaves. Refurbishment can be carried out from above by removing roof covering, battens, counter battens and roofing felt; the roof surface can be raised. Extra members are attached to the existing rafters to increase their depth for the thermal insulation plus ventilation layer.

**Ridge**
**1** Ridge to monopitch roof, with overhang and mono ridge tiles

As mentioned above, the existing roof covering must be removed completely and temporarily stored ready for reuse. The depth of the rafters is increased over their full length so that sufficient depth is available for the thicker thermal insulation and the recommended ventilation layer above it. The insulation is laid from above between the loadbearing members and thickened on the ridge side in front of the existing wall plate. Timber boarding plus roofing felt is attached to the top of the deeper rafters. The former roof covering can then be reused because the length of the roof slope is maintained. The sheet metal panels covering the edge of the roof construction are fixed to timber battens fitted to both sides of each rafter. Perforations in the top part of these panels create a ventilation opening. They also help to conceal the thicker external wall construction. The sheet metal at the verge is tucked under the side of the ridge tile.
The ridge to a duopitch roof is very similar to this detail and is therefore not illustrated here.

**Eaves**
**2** Eaves with overhang

After increasing the depth of the rafters, installing the insulation and fixing the boarding and roofing felt (as described above), the roof covering is extended down to the bottom (eaves) end of the rafters. The sheet metal panels between the rafters can also cover the thicker external wall (for energy economy reasons). Perforations in the top part of these panels create a ventilation opening.

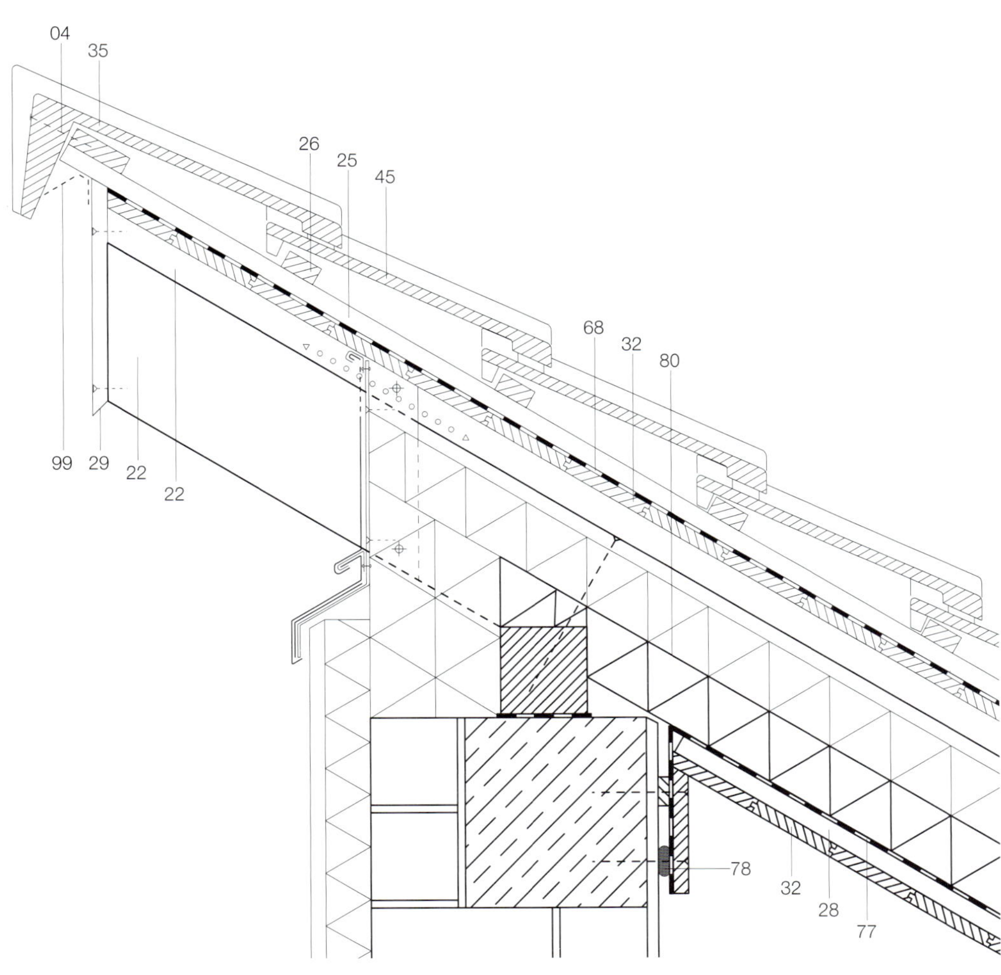


1

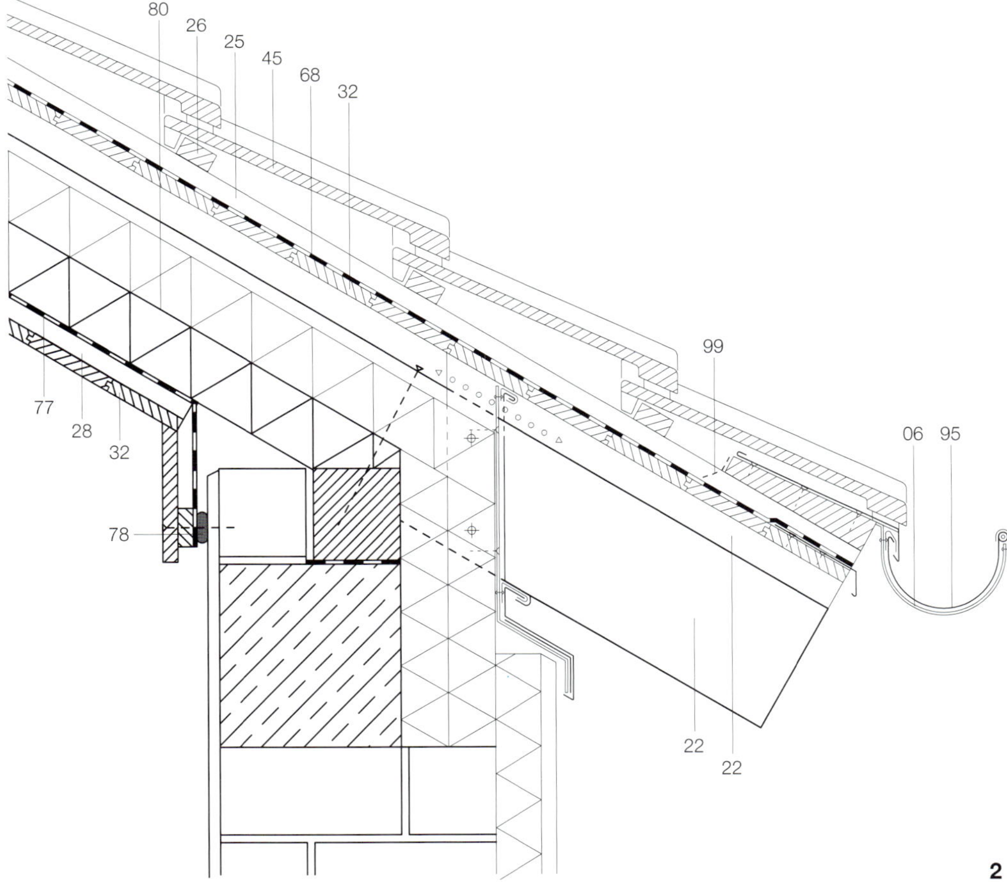


2

**Verge**
**3** Verge without overhang

The new roof decking of the secondary waterproofing/covering layer is laid over the top of the gable wall. It should be supported on a spacer batten on the outside edge of the wall. A verge gutter should be included if the former roof covering material is to be reused without modifications because the roof is now wider due to the additional thermal insulation to the external walls. T-shaped fixings hold the gutter in place. The gutter profile is visible at the ridge and tucks under the ridge tile.

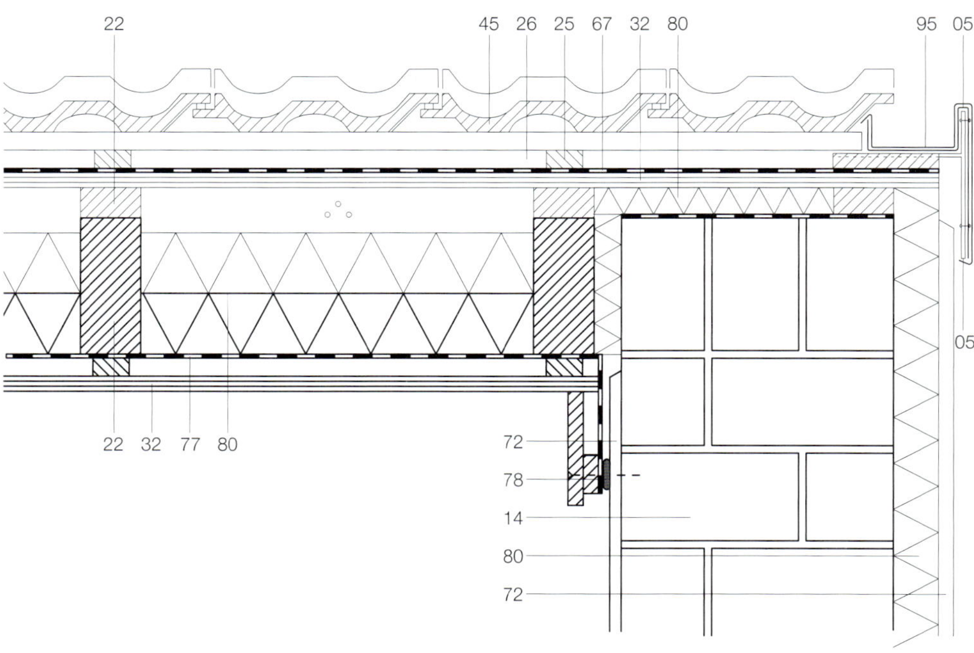


3

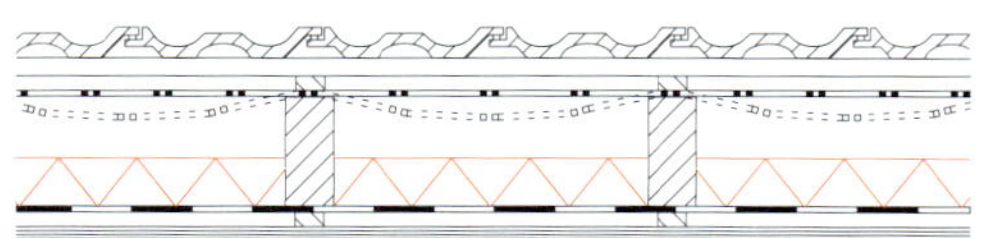

**B2 Defective thermal insulation**
No change to position of roof surface
Ventilation layer above thermal insulation laid between loadbearing members

As in the previous damage case (D2), the thermal insulation is defective or is no longer adequate, but the other parts of the construction are still fully serviceable. These details show the ridge to a duopitch roof and an overhanging eaves. However, as in this case the roof surface cannot be raised, all refurbishment work must be carried out from below. The depth necessary for the thermal insulation and the overlying ventilation layer is achieved here with framing below the loadbearing members.

**Ridge**
**1** Ridge to duopitch roof, with ventilation

In order to gain access to the roof construction from inside, the inner lining and vapour barrier must be removed. Extra members are added to the underside of the rafters to increase their depth over the full length. After installing the new thermal insulation, the vapour barrier can be laid below the ridge purlin in one plane; this avoids having to connect it to the purlin – a detail vulnerable to problems. Ventilation of the insulation via the ridge capping must be guaranteed.
The roof surface also remains in place when dealing with the ridge to a monopitch roof. The detail is therefore similar to this one.

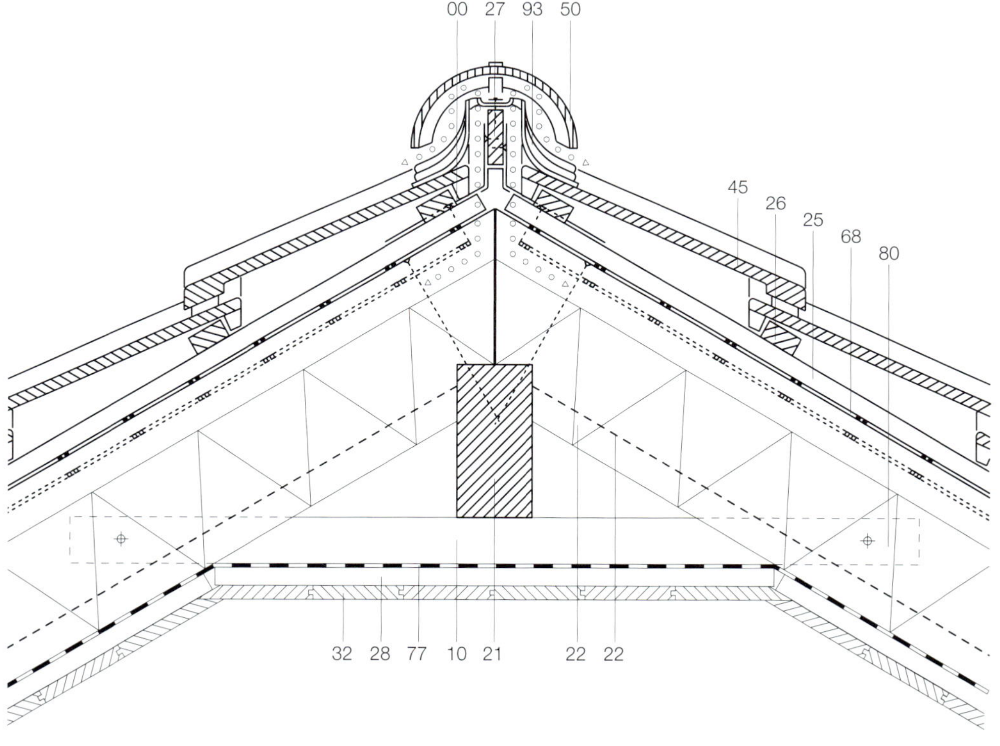


1

**Eaves**

**2** Eaves with overhang

As described above, the thermal insulation is installed from below and continues around the wall plate at the eaves. The vapour barrier is connected to and pressed against the inside face of the external wall with a new inner lining plus preformed seal. The space between the rafters and the insulation is protected by sheet metal panels. These are fixed to timber battens fitted to both sides of each rafter. Perforations in the top part of these panels create a ventilation opening. The panels also help to conceal the thicker external wall construction. This detail is otherwise similar to that shown on p. 293.

**Verge**

**3** Verge without overhang

After the inner lining and vapour barrier have been removed, extra members are added to the underside of the rafters to increase their depth over the full length. Thermal insulation is also inserted into the space between the trimming rafter and the inside face of the external wall. A good airtight joint between roof and external wall is achieved here by ensuring that the inner lining presses the vapour barrier and the preformed sealing strip against the wall. A verge gutter is required to finish off the roof surface, which is now wider owing to the thicker external walls (for energy economy reasons).

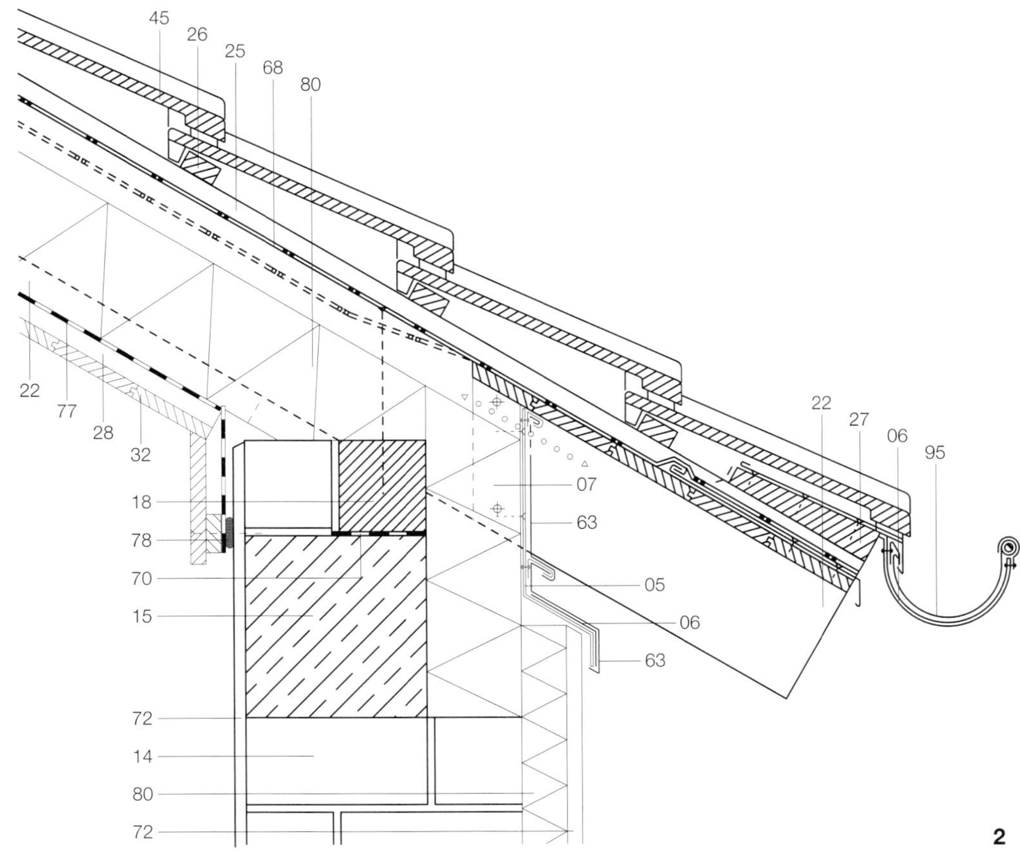

2

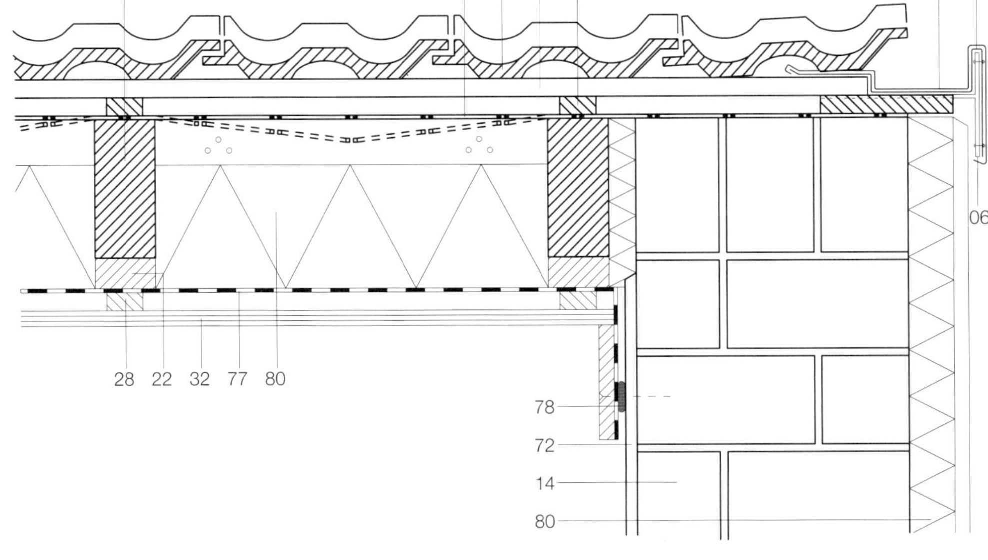

3

Details scale 1:10

00 Batten holder
05 Clip, continuous clip
06 Fixing for flashing, gutter bracket
07 Additional batten
10 Tie beam
14 Brickwork
15 Capping beam
18 Wall plate
21 Purlin
22 Rafter, rafter make-up piece
25 Counter batten
26 Batten
27 Feather-edge board, ridge board
28 Spacer batten
32 Timber boarding
45 Interlocking profiled tile
50 Ventilating ridge capping
63 Cover flashing
67 Waterproofing
68 Roofing felt
70 Damp-proof course
72 Plaster/rendering
77 Vapour barrier
78 Preformed seal
80 Cavity insulation
93 Ventilating element
95 Gutter
99 Mesh screen

# Part 4 Built examples

**Eberhard Schunck and Hans Jochen Oster**

In this section, too, the examples are arranged according to type of roof, for easier orientation.

As in part 3, the aim here is to present as wide a selection of roof materials and forms as possible. Accordingly, some of the coverings illustrated will no longer be in common use. It follows, too, that other roofs in the selection will feature materials for which techniques in their application have not existed for long. The selection of the latter was admittedly driven by a curiosity about certain architectural prototypes, and a wish to use them as an opportunity for a closer study of roof function and form.

In addition to constructional issues and details, the selection underlines how roof, building volume and surroundings are inseparable. For this reason, plans and sections of the buildings are included, along with informative site plans. This strong relationship to the urban context led to many simple building volumes and roof forms featuring in the selection.

Inevitably, some of the examples are of constructions that no longer conform to present-day standards, but excluding them would not necessarily have been desirable. If only faultless constructions had been chosen, a certain amount of interest would have been lost. In these instances careful corrections have been made – without falsifying the original. Where such amendment was inadvisable, information is given about the conflict with today's techniques.

The scale used for the detail drawings is, wherever possible, the same as in part 3. This facilitates comparisons. Likewise, the captions are collated in an overall index, organised in groups. Great efforts have been made to define the materials used precisely. However, in one or two cases this endeavour failed due to lack of corresponding source information.

**Holiday home in Korshage, Sjaelland**
1960

Architect: E. Korshagen, Copenhagen
Structural engineer: J. Nielsen
Client: E. Korshagen, Copenhagen

East side

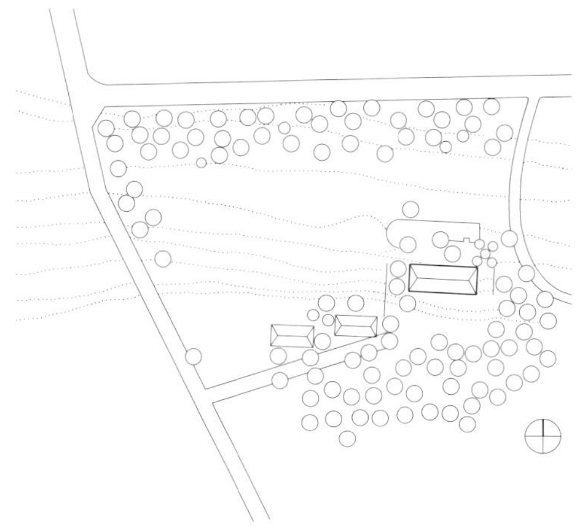

Site plan scale 1:2500

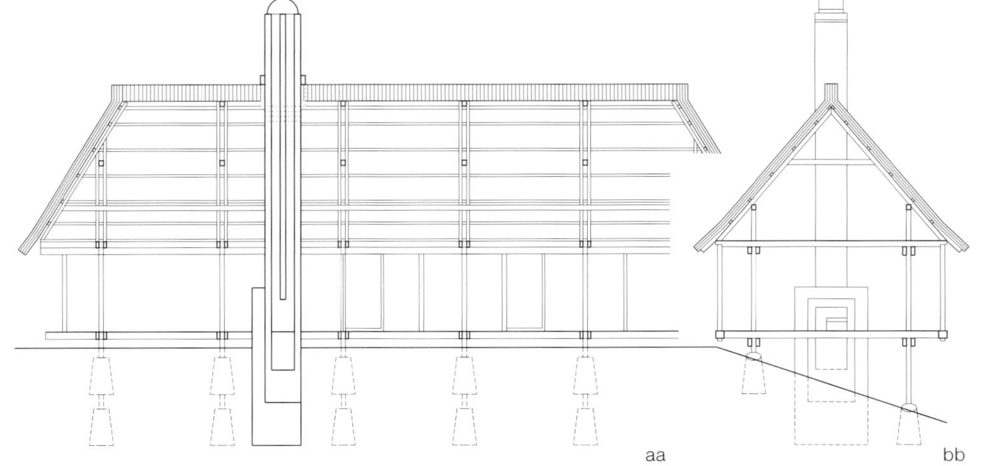


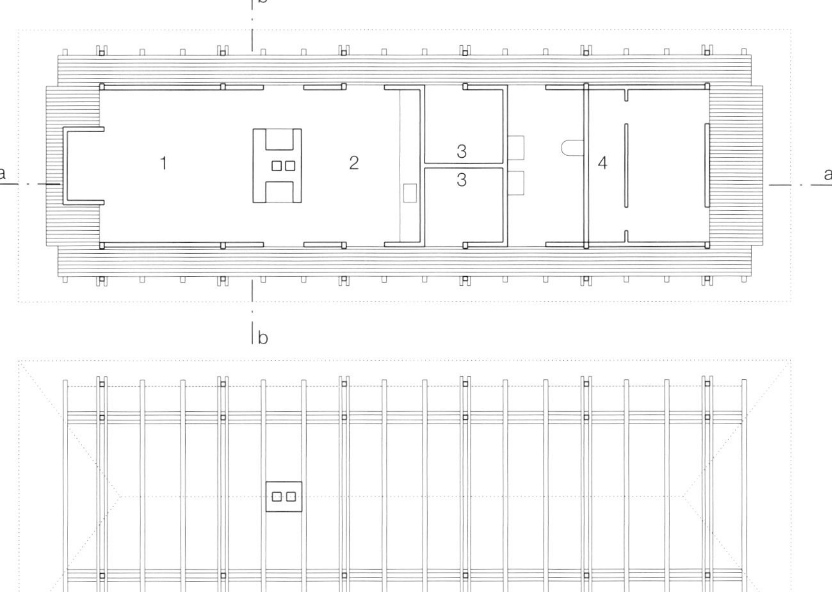


Plan• Position of beams • Sections scale 1:200

1 Living area
2 Kitchen/dining room
3 Bedroom
4 Bedroom and dressing room

This holiday home is located on a peninsula on the Danish island of Sjaelland, where the Ise Fjord meets the Kattegat. It stands on a sloping site, at the edge of a wood, in an area of grass, bushes and trees; a few other houses are dotted nearby. The open sea is only about one hundred metres away. The use of natural materials on the linear building, which rests on stilts, is in keeping with the setting, allowing the house to blend well with its surroundings.

Designed as a holiday home, the rooms are positioned one after the other. All rooms are accessed only from the veranda; there are no connecting doors between the rooms. The enormous roof space is used for storage. Access to it is also from the veranda, via hatches in the ceiling.

With a pitch of 50° the roof covering is watertight and windproof, even in stormy conditions, as at this steep angle wind does not lift under

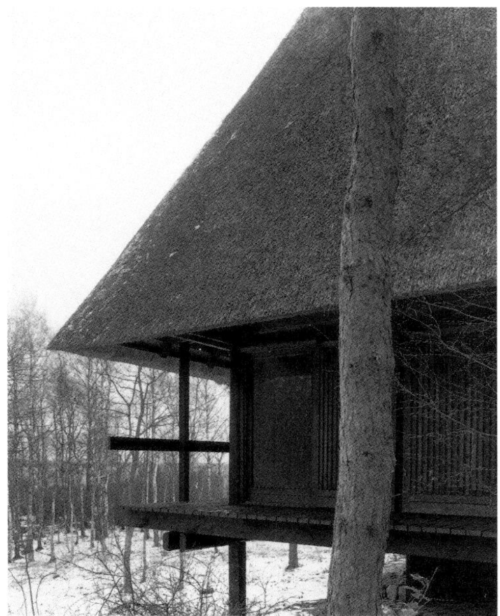

North side

Details scale 1:10
00 Stitching
03 Metal hook
08 Sway
10 Reed ridge filling
17 63.5 x 127 mm suspended timber column, every 3 m
20 51 x 127 mm tie, every 3 m
22 63.5 x 127 mm rafter, every 1 m
26 40 x 60 mm batten
27 Eaves batten, tilting fillet
28 Jack rafter
32 Spruce board
35 Eaves course
37 Facing course
51 Ridge course
52 Wrap-over course
53 Undereaves course
66 Backfilling

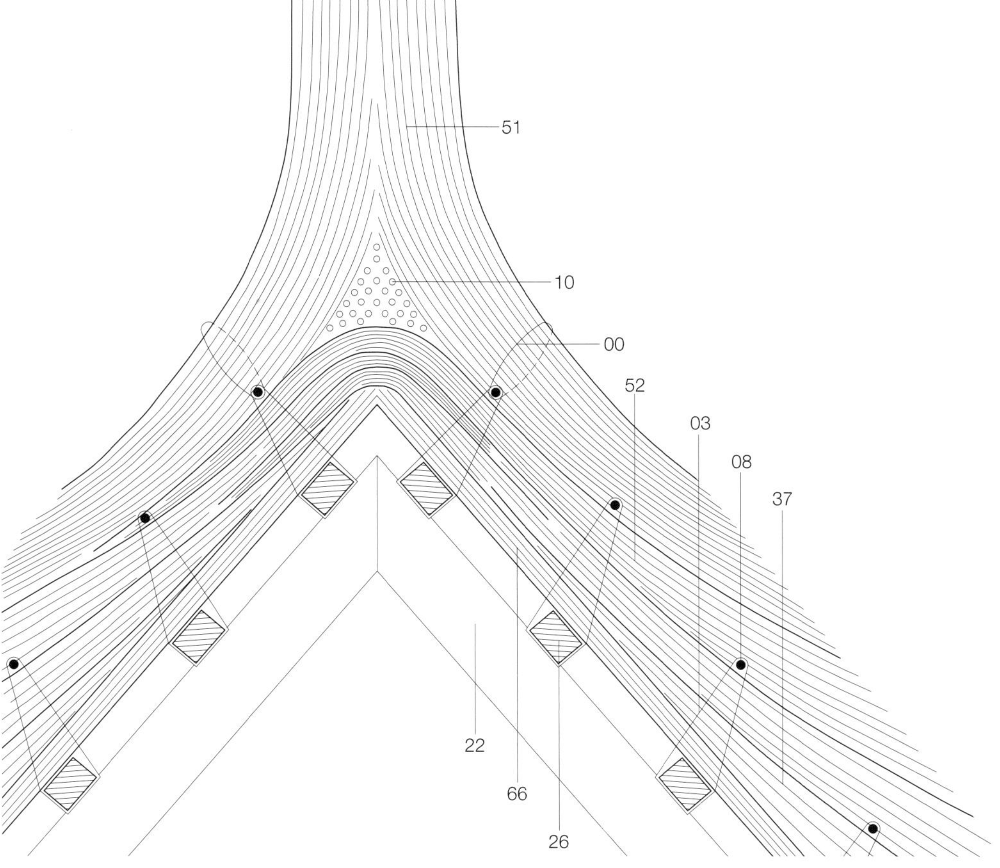


Ridge

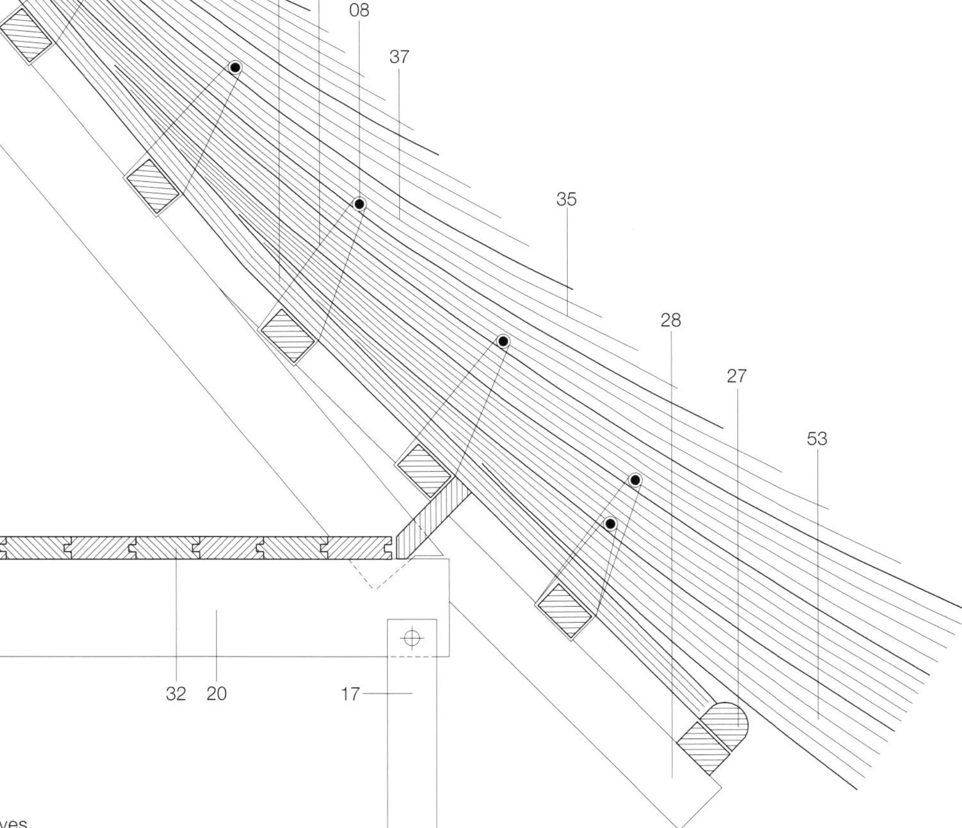


Eaves

the thatch but presses down on top of it. The covering therefore has a thermal insulation effect, making an additional layer of insulation at ceiling level unnecessary. In summer the reed thatch works superbly as a climate buffer.

The building's frame, a timber post-and-beam construction with six bays, consists of columns, tie-like longitudinal and transverse girders with simple crossbracing in between. The roof is a collar roof with cantilevered frame, the rafters of which are additionally supported by purlins. Concrete cores, timber walls that structurally have a plate effect, and twelve columns that extend right up under the purlins, provide bracing for the building volume.

The roof is covered with reed, the individual courses secured with sways. The ridge courses are stitched. As is customary in Denmark, the covering is laid to an average thickness of 250 mm.

**The Sea Ranch, Condominium 1, California**
1965

Architects:
Charles W. Moore, Donlyn Lyndon, William Turnbult Jr., Richard Whitaker
Structural engineer: Davis & Morreau
Building science: Matthew Sylvia
Landscape architect: Laurence Halpren
Client: Oceanic Properties, Inc.

View from the ocean

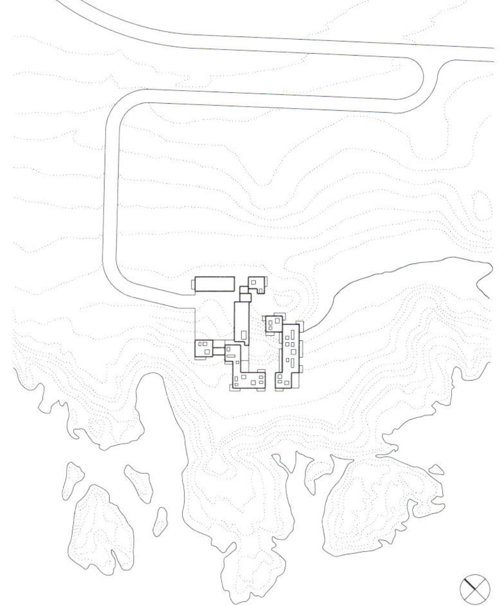

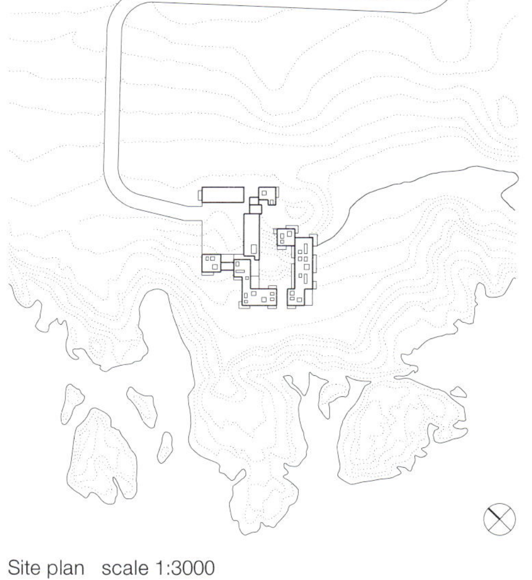

Site plan scale 1:3000

Plans of upper floor, ground floor• Section scale 1:400

The Sea Ranch is located on the Pacific coast of California, north of San Francisco, in a beautiful landscape of grassland, woods and cliffs. This condominium of ten apartments stands in an exposed position right by the ocean. Simple and barn-like in design, the building is the kind of structure that best suits this setting. The large monopitch roof brings together the ensemble, its angle of pitch tracing the line of the slope. Because of the high winds experienced here on the coast, roof overhangs are of little use. This explains the clipped, edgy profile of the buildings, which gives the Sea Ranch its distinctive look.

1 Living area
2 Dining area
3 Oriel
4 Gallery

Southeast side

The roof and the building's load-bearing frame are ribbed constructions with timber boards for the crosswalls, a typical style of building in the USA. The roof frame is of Douglas fir purlins. Outer walls and the roof skin are built on the same principle. The inner load-bearing decking is designed with sawn tongue and groove boards measuring 50 x 200 mm. Bituminous felt is used as an intermediate layer. While the outer skin of the wall is weatherboarding (25 x 200 mm), the roof skin is made up of wooden shingles. No additional thermal insulation was needed, because of the mild maritime climate.

The homogeneous outer envelope of untreated Red Cedar takes on a shimmering silver-grey tone over time, bringing the house into an even closer relationship with the natural setting.

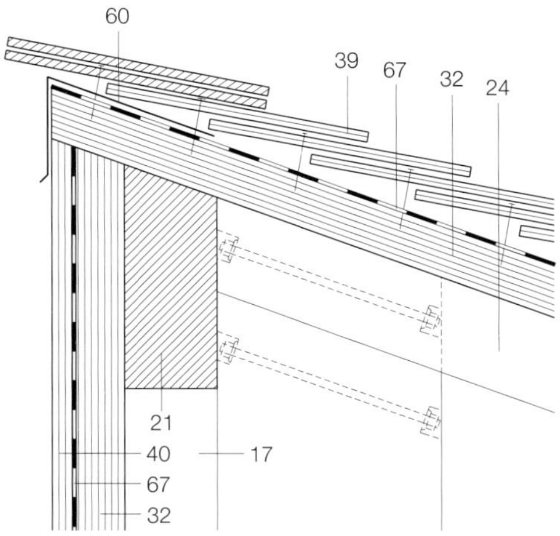

Ridge of monopitch roof

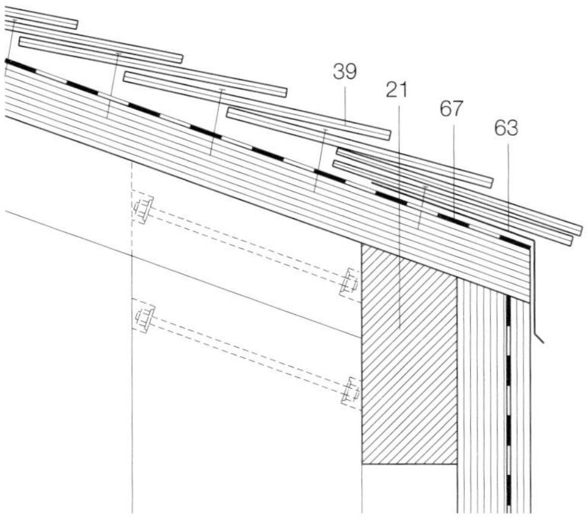

Eaves

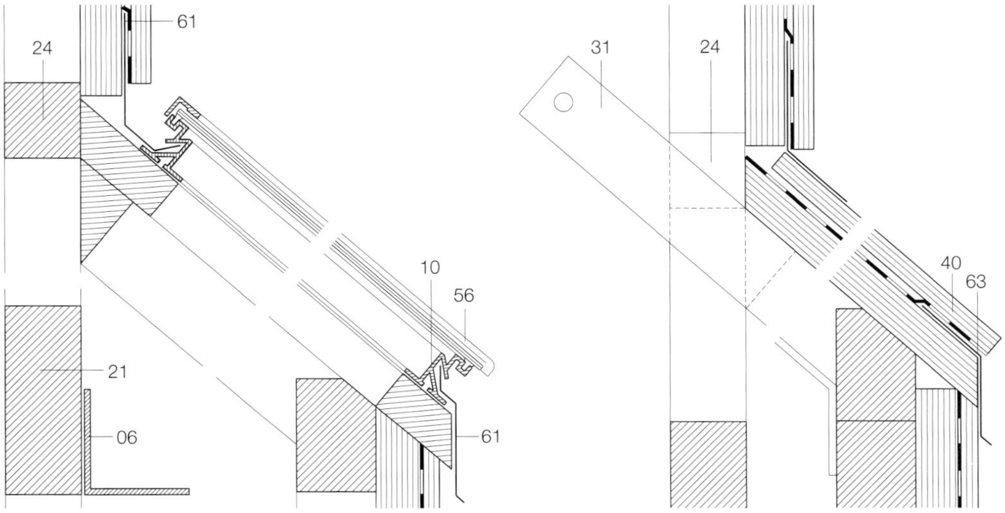

Wall junctions

Rooflights, roof penetrations

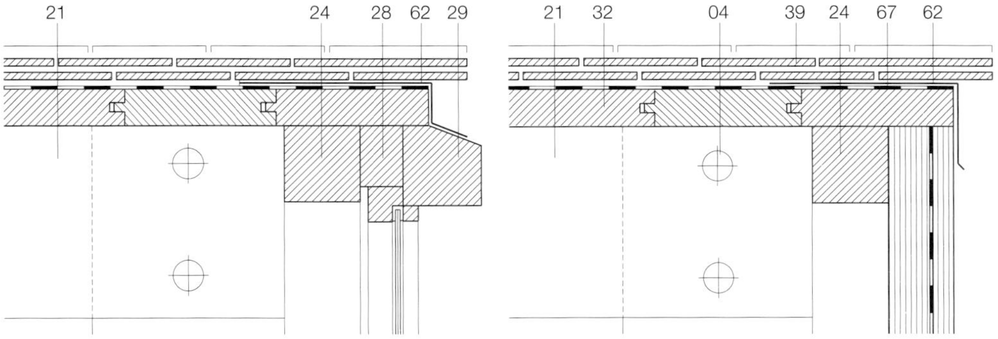

Verges

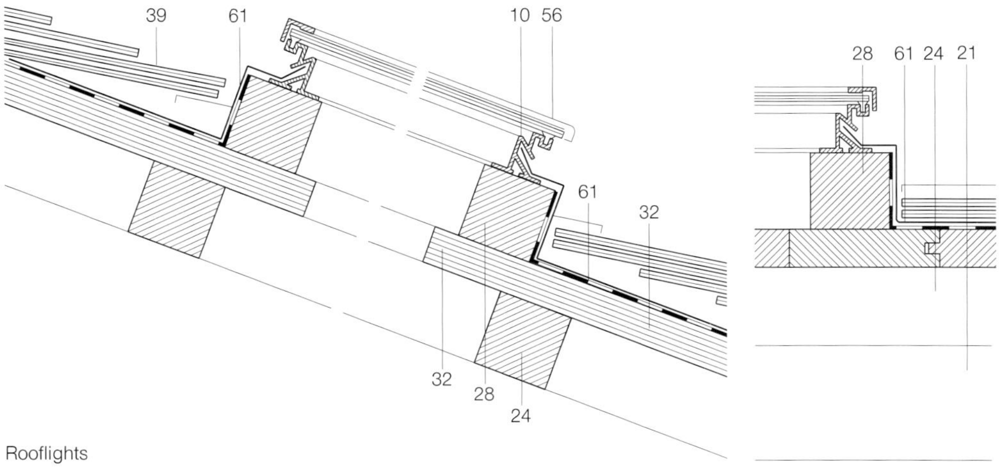

Details scale 1:10
04 Bolt and dowel
06 Steel angle
10 Aluminium casement
17 100 x 100 mm (4″ x 4″) vertical member
21 Douglas fir purlin, 100 x 250.5 mm (4″ x 10″)
24 Horizontal member in outer wall, 100 x 100 mm (4″ x 4″)
28 100 x 100 mm (4″ x 4″) firring / filler frame
29 Timber facing
31 100 x 100 mm (4″ x 4″) strut
32 50 x 200 mm (2″ x 8″) tongue and groove decking
39 Red Cedar shingles ~ 400 mm
40 20.5 x 200 mm (1″ x 8″) Red Cedar weatherboarding
56 Aluminium sash frame with single glazing
60 Copper ridge plate
61 Copper connecting plate
62 Copper verge flashing
63 Copper eaves flashing
67 Overlapping bituminous felt

Rooflights

**House and studio in Gleissenberg**
2001

Architect: Florian Nagler Architekten
Assistants: Stefan Lambertz, Felix Lukasch, Mathias Pätzold
Structural engineer: Büro Merz, Kaufmann and Partner
Clients: Gabriele and Peter Lang

Southwest side

Site plan scale 1:2000

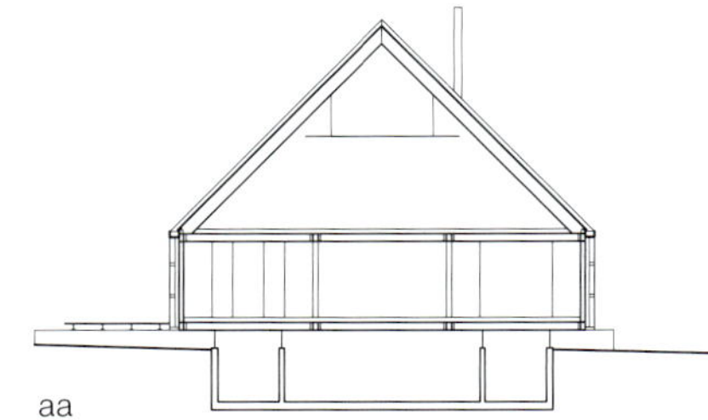

aa

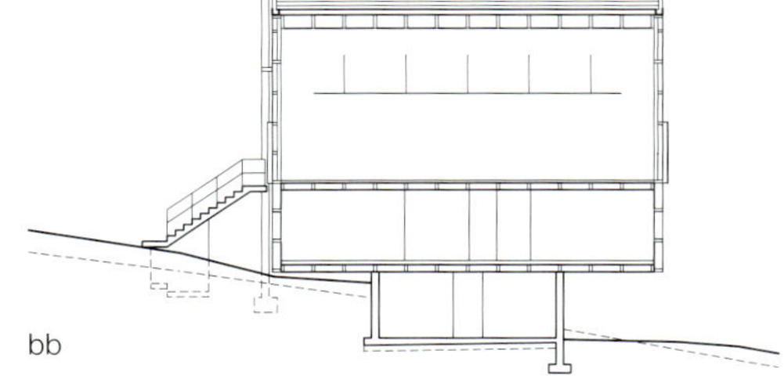

bb

This house is located in the Bavarian town of Gleissenberg. The building is divided into two zones, each with a different function: a living area on the ground floor, and a studio, which occupies the whole of the roof storey.

In designing the building, ecological aspects were important, other key factors being the tight budget and ease of construction.

The house is distinctive for the unusual choice of materials. The building's core is constructed of prefabricated timber wall panels, made up of 160 mm mineral wool insulation sandwiched between oriented strand board. Triple-walled polycarbonate panels form the outer skin of the double-layer facade, the air space between playing a role in heat insulation.

Vents in the upper part of the facade prevent overheating in summer. Shingles of red cedar were used as the covering on the gable roof with 45° pitch.

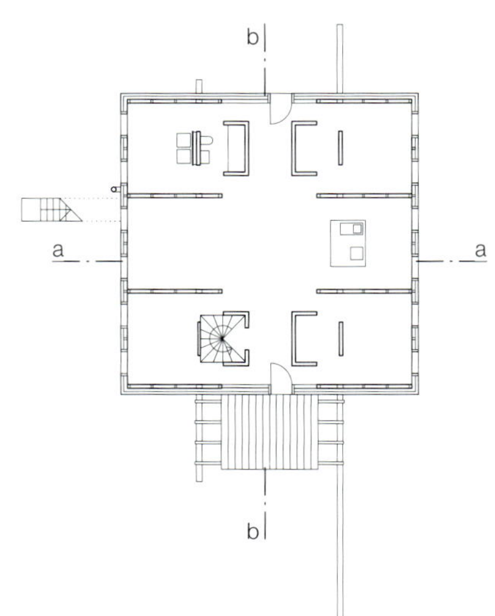



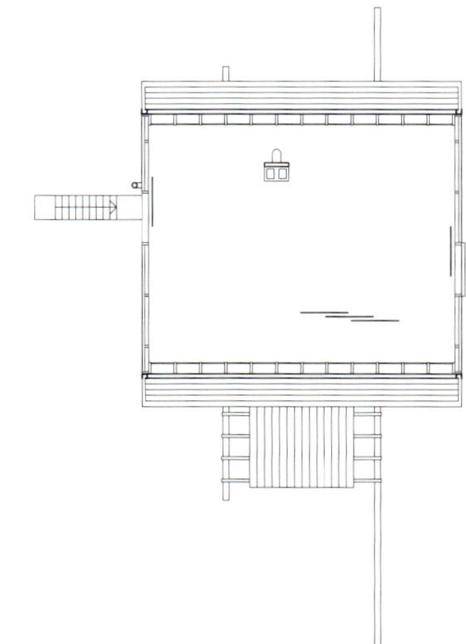

Plans of ground floor, roof floor Sections scale 1:400

Details scale 1:10
00 Steel angle
18 80 x 100 mm timber
20 120 x 240 mm glued laminated timber truss
22 10 x 320 mm rafter
25 40 x 60 mm counter battens
26 60 x 60 mm battens
27 Ridge timber, 60 x 240 mm verge timber
32 160 x 24 mm sawn timber decking
33 22 mm oriented strand board
39 12 mm red cedar shingles, 120-150 mm wide x 600 mm
51 Galvanised steel section
60 Flashing
62 Verge flashing
64 Triple-walled poly-carbonate panel
68 Vapour-diffusing roofing felt
77 Vapour barrier, vapour-tight bonded edges
86 160 mm mineral wool
90 Perforated, mill-finished 2 mm aluminium sheet, 50 x 30 x 50 mm, bent to fit
95 184 x 184 mm titanium-zinc sheet rainwater gutter
99 Galvanised steel sheet insect screen, bent to fit

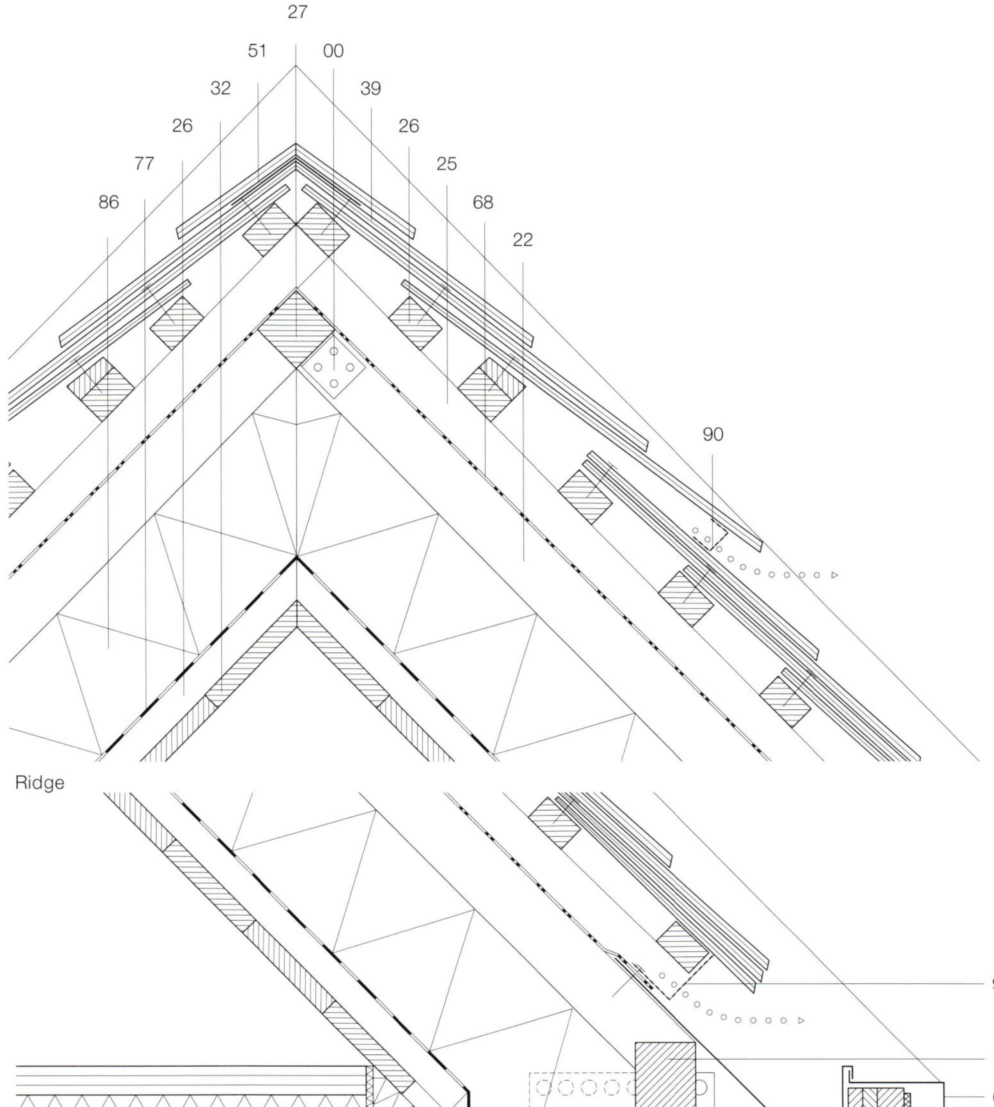


Ridge

Eaves

The ventilated roof frame has 160 mm mineral wool insulation between the rafters and is fitted with rough board decking.

Towards the ridge, perforated metal sheet, bent to shape, ventilates the space below the roof covering. A square-section box gutter with an overflow pipe directs rainwater away. Collector panels mounted on the roof provide hot water, and can also be used to heat the living area and studio.

South side

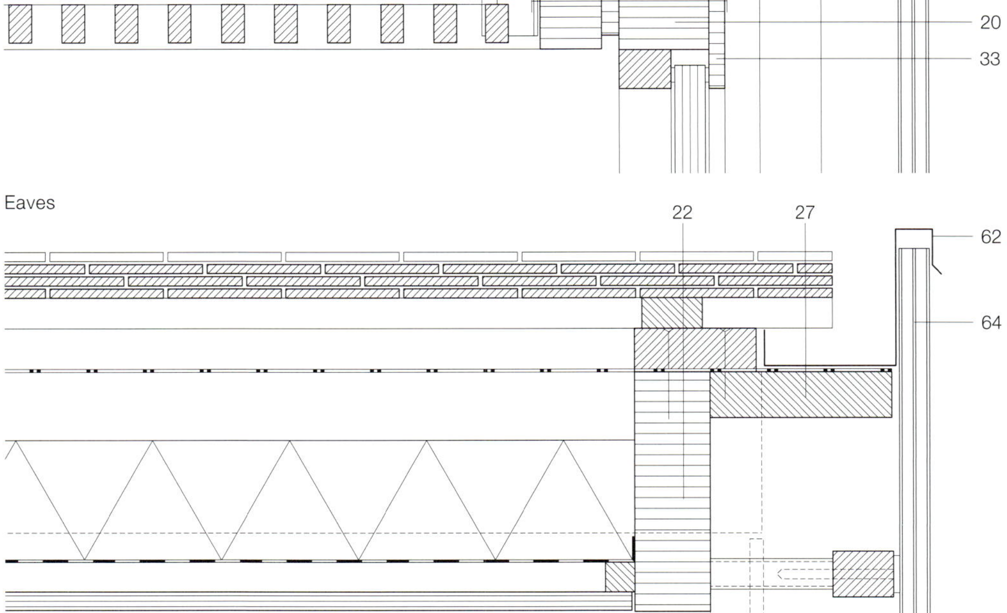


Verge

**Holiday home in Normandy**
1994

Architect: Gerhard Kalhöfer; Kalhöfer – Korschildgen, Cologne
Assistant: Christèle Jany
Clients: Ulrich Kalhöfer, Jörg Schröder

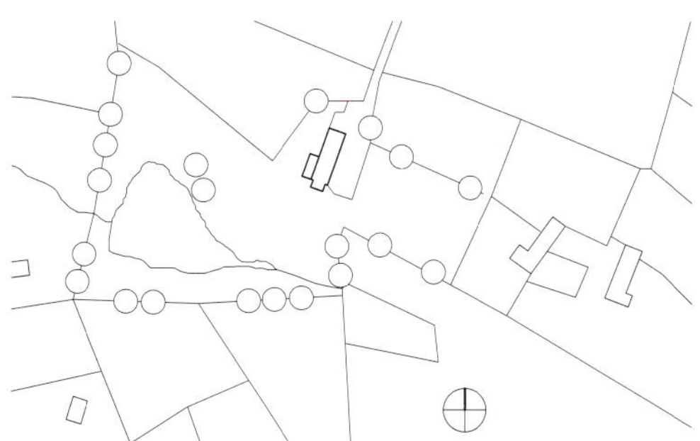

Site plan scale 1:4000

East side

This old Norman farmhouse is located close to Villedieu, a village 30 kilometres from the Atlantic coast of France. Before extensive renovation and conversion into a holiday home, the building was only a skeleton of rubble walls.

Viewed from the outside, two entirely different sections are evident. In the renovated old part the historic character has been maintained through the use of traditional materials and details, while a steel-framed construction and almost exclusively prefabricated components were chosen for the new annex, which houses all the domestic installations such as WC, shower and kitchen.

The old part has a purlin roof with a 50° pitch, with one ridge purlin and three intermediate purlins on each side, plus two eaves purlins. The gable end walls and the intermediate walls – all of rubblestone masonry – and the collar beam frames inserted into the middle of each roof space support the purlins. Regularly spaced on the purlins are the rafters, which bear the load of the roof covering. Dark-coloured slate was chosen for the roofing, to blend with the rubble walls and give the building a harmonious appearance. The rectangular double-lap slating is supported on roof battens. The roof structure is ventilated and has individual vents located towards the top. For thermal insulation, 90 mm mats of fibrous mineral wool were laid between the rafters.

aa

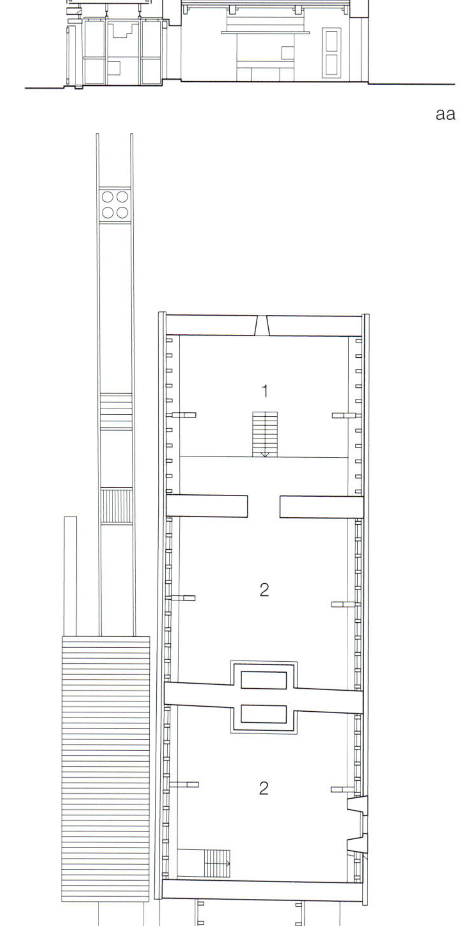


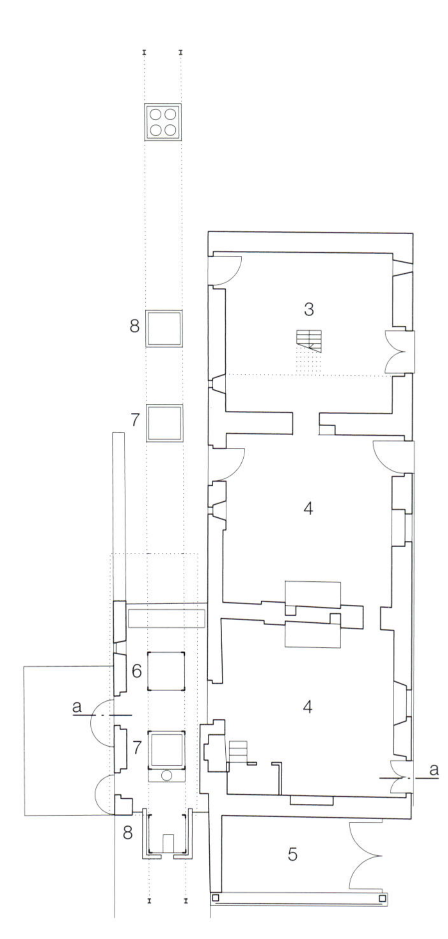

Plans of upper floor, ground floor • Section scale 1:250

South side

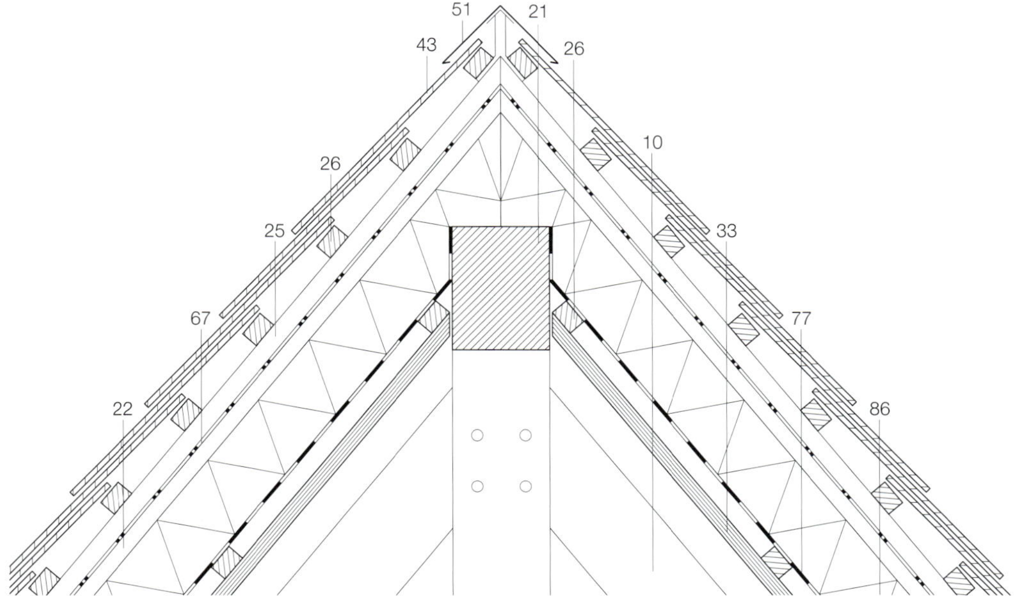


Ridge

1 Void
2 Bedroom
3 Barn
4 Living area
5 Studio
6 Kitchen
7 Shower
8 WC

Details scale 1:10

06 Bracket
10 120 x 160 mm collar roof
11 600 mm rubble walls, pointed
15 600 x 100 mm peripheral tie beam
18 120 x 300 mm eaves purlin
21 120 x 160 mm ridge purlin
22 60 x 110 mm rafter
25 24 x 36 mm counter battens
26 24 x 36 mm battens
27 Feather-edge board
33 20 mm sawn Douglas fir decking
43 Slates
51 Zinc ridge capping, with bracket
62 Verge flashing
63 Zinc flashing
67 Roofing felt
74 Sealant
77 Vapour barrier
86 Mineral fibre material
95 Sheet zinc rainwater gutter

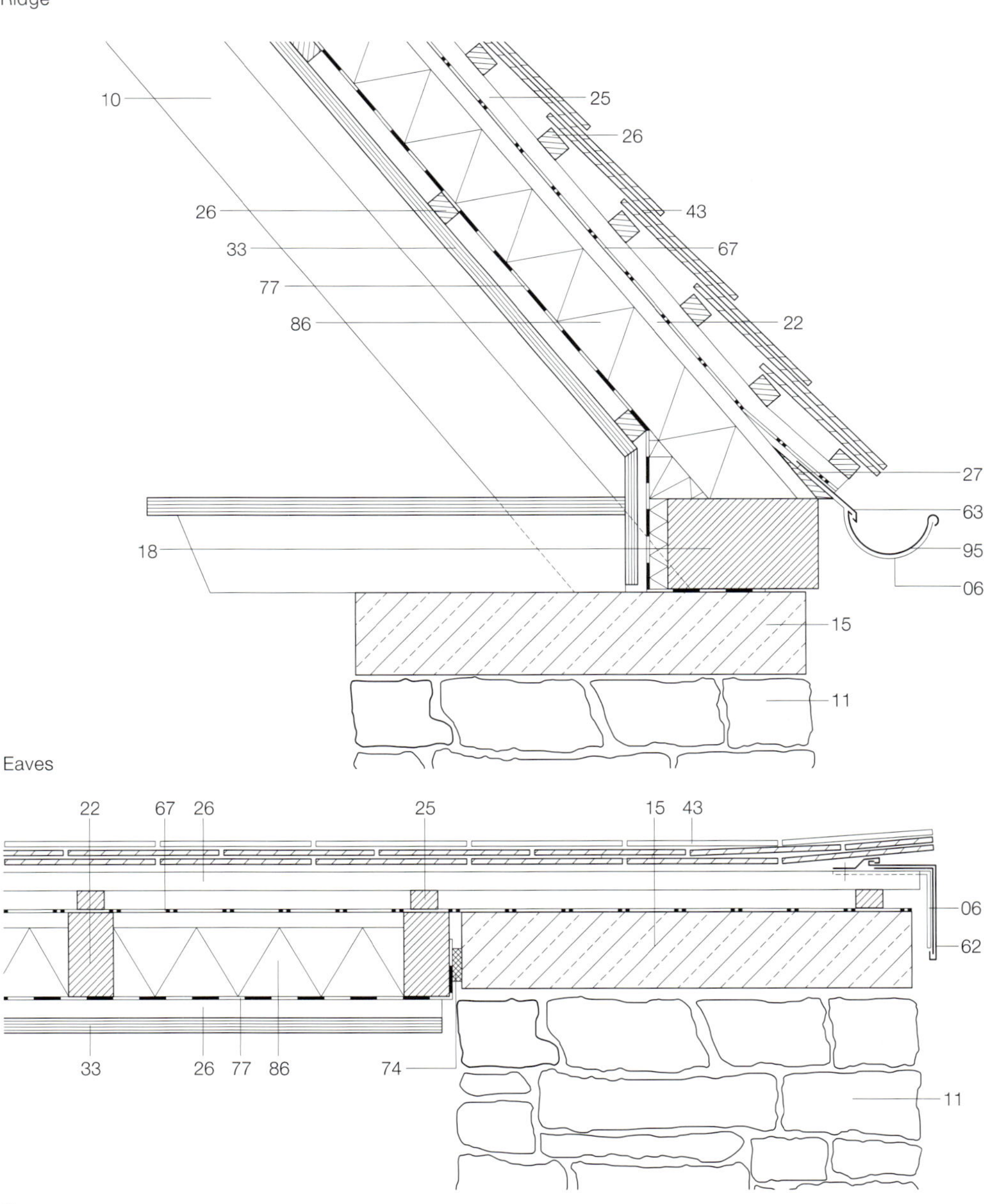


Eaves

Verge

**Søholm houses in Klampenborg, Sjaelland**
1950

Architect: Arne Jacobsen, Copenhagen
Structural engineer: K. Norup and Birch & Krogboe
Clients: O. W. Madsen and J. Thaarup, Copenhagen

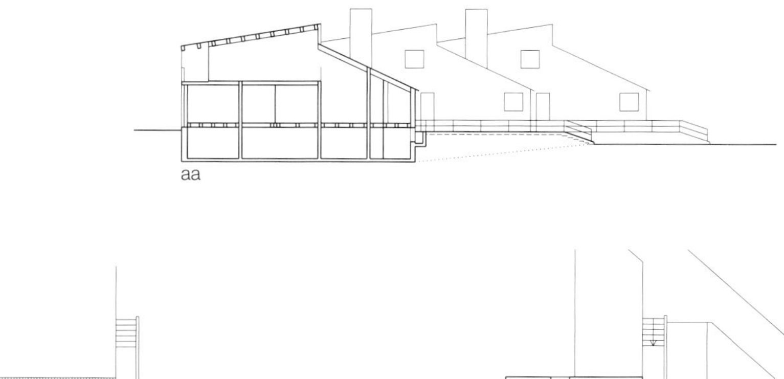


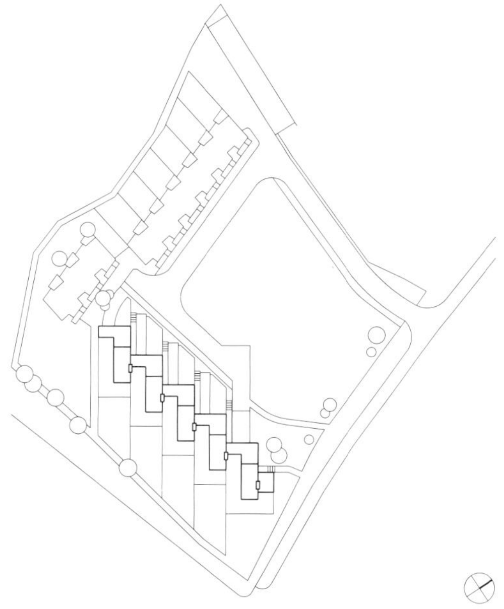

Site plan scale 1:2000

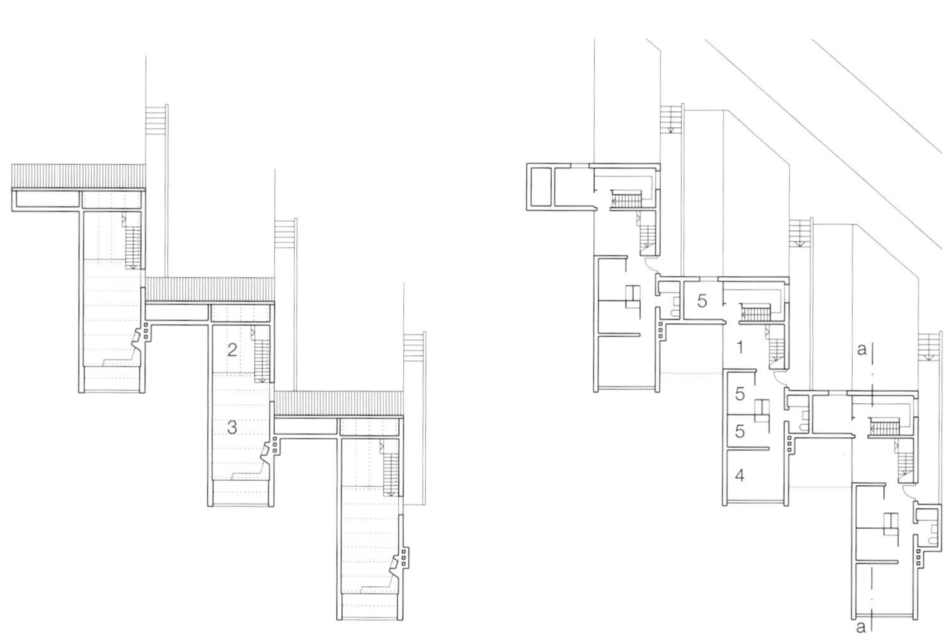


Plans of upper floor, ground floor • Section scale 1:500

The site on which these five interlinked houses stands is to the north of Copenhagen on the Øresund, which separates Denmark from Sweden.
A busy main road runs between the houses and the sea.
The houses are staggered in relation to each other, set at an angle to the edge of the plot, facing the open water. Making the most of this aspect, they have a double-height living space facing southeast, with a single-height entrance storey on the side away from the sea.
The roof follows this thinking, as it has clerestory glazing between the offset slopes of the roof, bringing more light into the high living room from the northwest. It is this response to the requirements of the interior that gives the row of houses its characteristic form, one that was often imitated in the 1950s.
Resting on the walls of yellowish fair-faced masonry is a roof with pitches of 9° and 22° covered with double-lap fibre-cement slating.

1 Dining area
2 Void
3 Living room
4 Bedroom
5 Child's bedroom

Street side with garden path and garage entrance

Details scale 1:10
01 Fixing strip
02 Lathing
03 Galvanised steel pipe bracket
05 Galvanised steel sheet retainer strip
06 Galvanised steel gutter bracket
10 19 mm open decking
13 Frost-resistant brick
17 60 x 120 mm shaped timber raking support
20 140 mm channel-section, 120 mm T-section
21 150 x 150 mm purlin
22 75 x 150 mm, 90 x 180 mm rafters
25 Triangular fillet
26 38 x 57 mm batten
27 Feather-edge board
32 25 mm sawn decking
47 Asbestos-cement slates
56 Rolled glass or wired rolled glass
60 Zinc flashing
61 Zinc connection sheet
63 Zinc eaves flashing
67 Bitumen sheeting with dry felt
72 Plaster
75 Built-up dry felt roofing
86 20 mm rock wool
95 Zinc sheet rainwater gutter, 280 mm
96 Rainwater downpipe

Balcony, projecting roof

The eaves on the one-storey entrance facade and the verge are kept very narrow. A slight overhang at the ridge provides modest protection against the weather for the clerestory glazing below, while a projecting glass roof gives cover to the balcony on the two-storey south side.

For proper protection against rain, the 9° pitch of the roof is too shallow for the rectangular tiles used. Built-up roofing felt was therefore laid under the tiles.

Both parts of the roof lie immediately above living areas. By today's standards of building science, the roof construction is inadequate. It lacks a vapour barrier below the insulation, and ventilation above it. The thermal insulation would nowadays also be insufficient, even for Danish conditions. It can be assumed that the moderating influence of the maritime climate and the ever-present wind pressure prevents the formation of condensation.

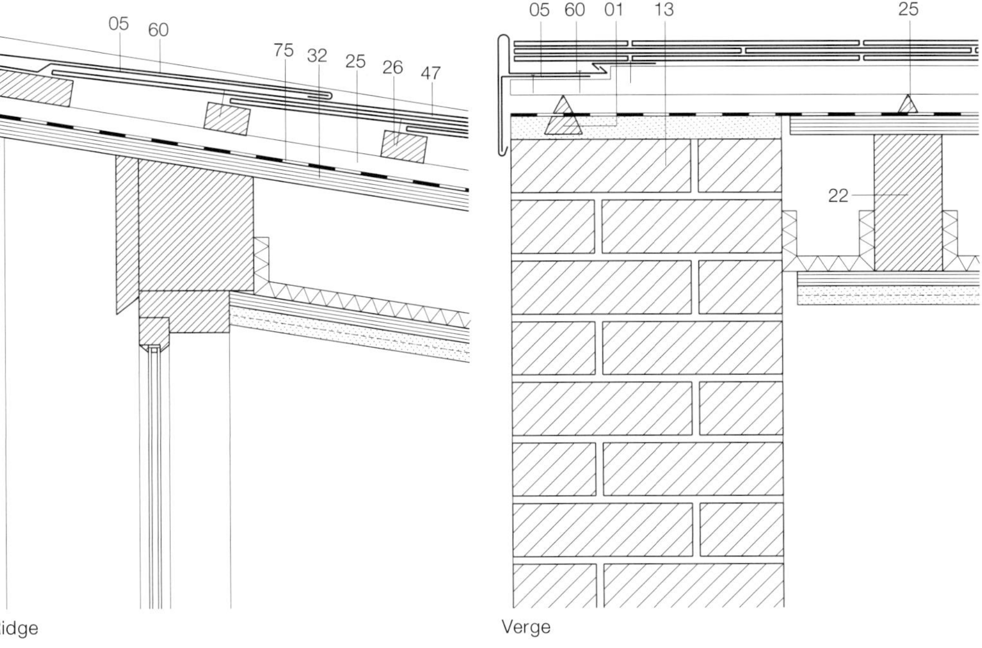


Ridge

Verge

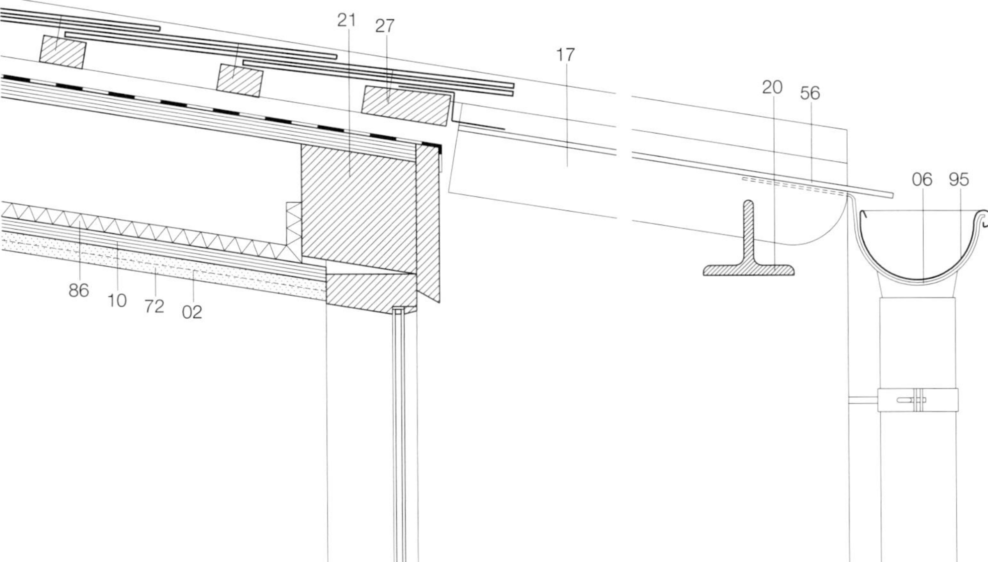


Eaves, garden side

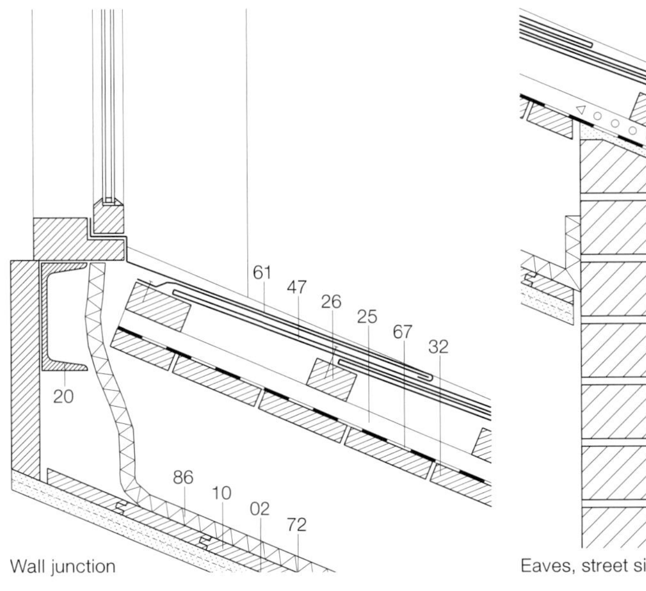


Wall junction

Eaves, street side

**Detached house in Büren-Steinhausen**
1996

Architect: Reinhold Tobey, Detmold
Clients: Andreas and Gabriele Tobey

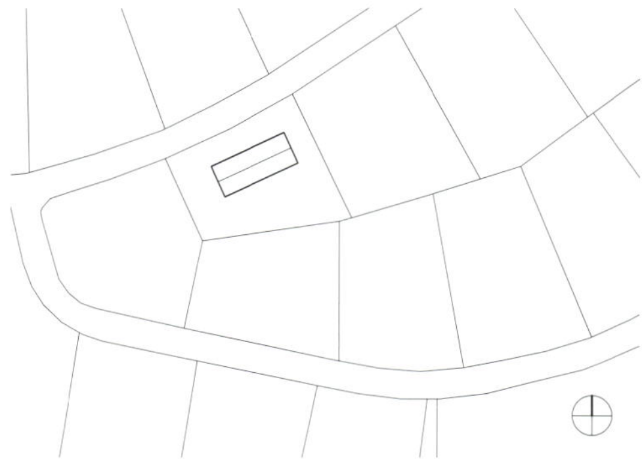

Site plan scale 1:2000

North side

This house, built in 1996, stands on an estate of detached houses. It provides space for a family with two children. The ground plan is very simple: crosswalls, regularly spaced at 3.15 metres, divide both ground floor and first floor into five equal-sized rooms. A central corridor runs down the middle of each floor, linking the rooms. At ground floor level are the living and working spaces, including kitchen and dining room. The bedrooms are on the upper floor.

The building frame consists of prefabricated wall and roof panels, and a timber joist floor above the ground floor. The panel elements consist of load-bearing ribs faced with synthetic resin-bound chipboard, and mineral fibre insulation in between.

The south-facing facade is fully glazed, giving an unhindered view of the terrace and garden. All other facades have minimal openings, and are clad with weatherboarding. Glazed strips along the jamb wall bring natural light into the roof storey.

The gable roof with 45° pitch is covered with black asphalt shingles affixed to timber decking covered with sheathing. Spacer rafters and a ridge ventilator cap ensure adequate ventilation of the roof. Like the walls, the roof frame itself is also made of prefabricated timber panels. A conventional semicircular rainwater gutter takes care of roof drainage.

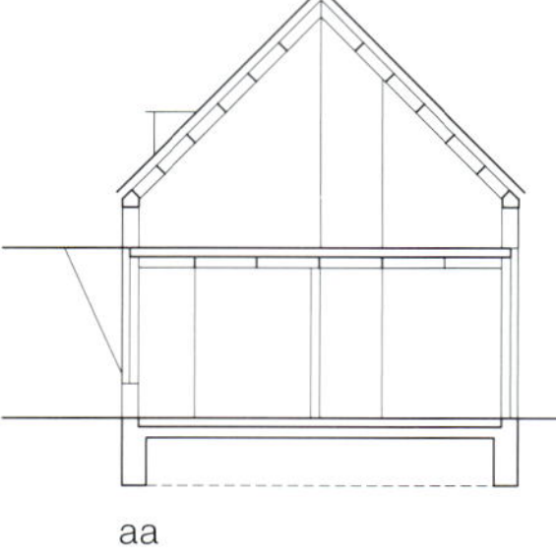

aa

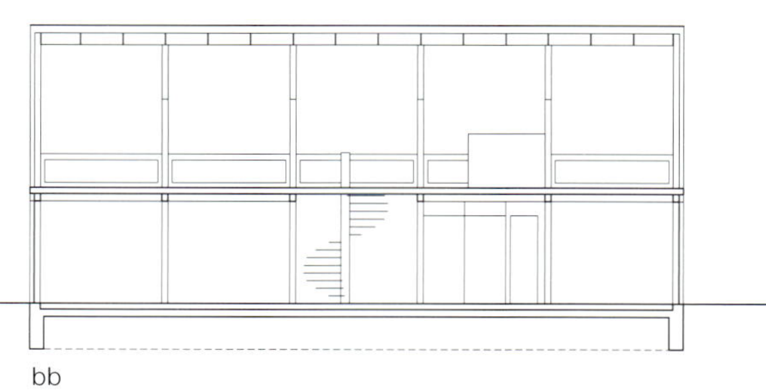

bb

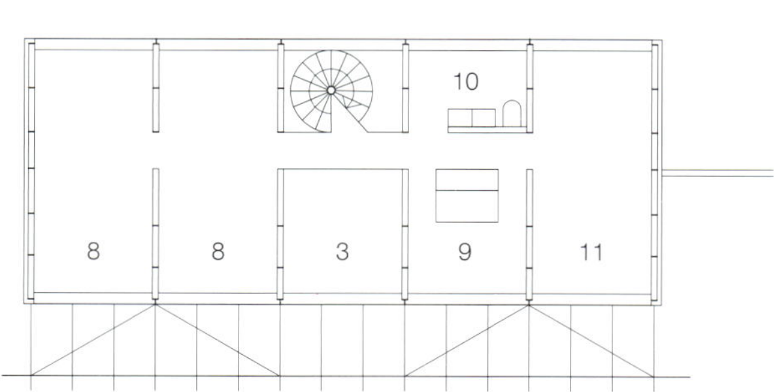


Sections
Ground plans
Upper floor
Ground floor
scale 1:250

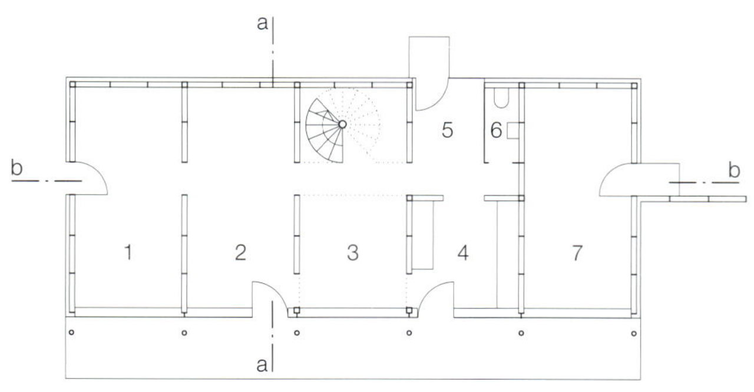


1 Study
2 Living room
3 Dining room/staircase
4 Kitchen
5 Lobby
6 WC
7 Laundry/bicycles
8 Child's bedroom
9 Walkway
10 Bathroom
11 Bedroom

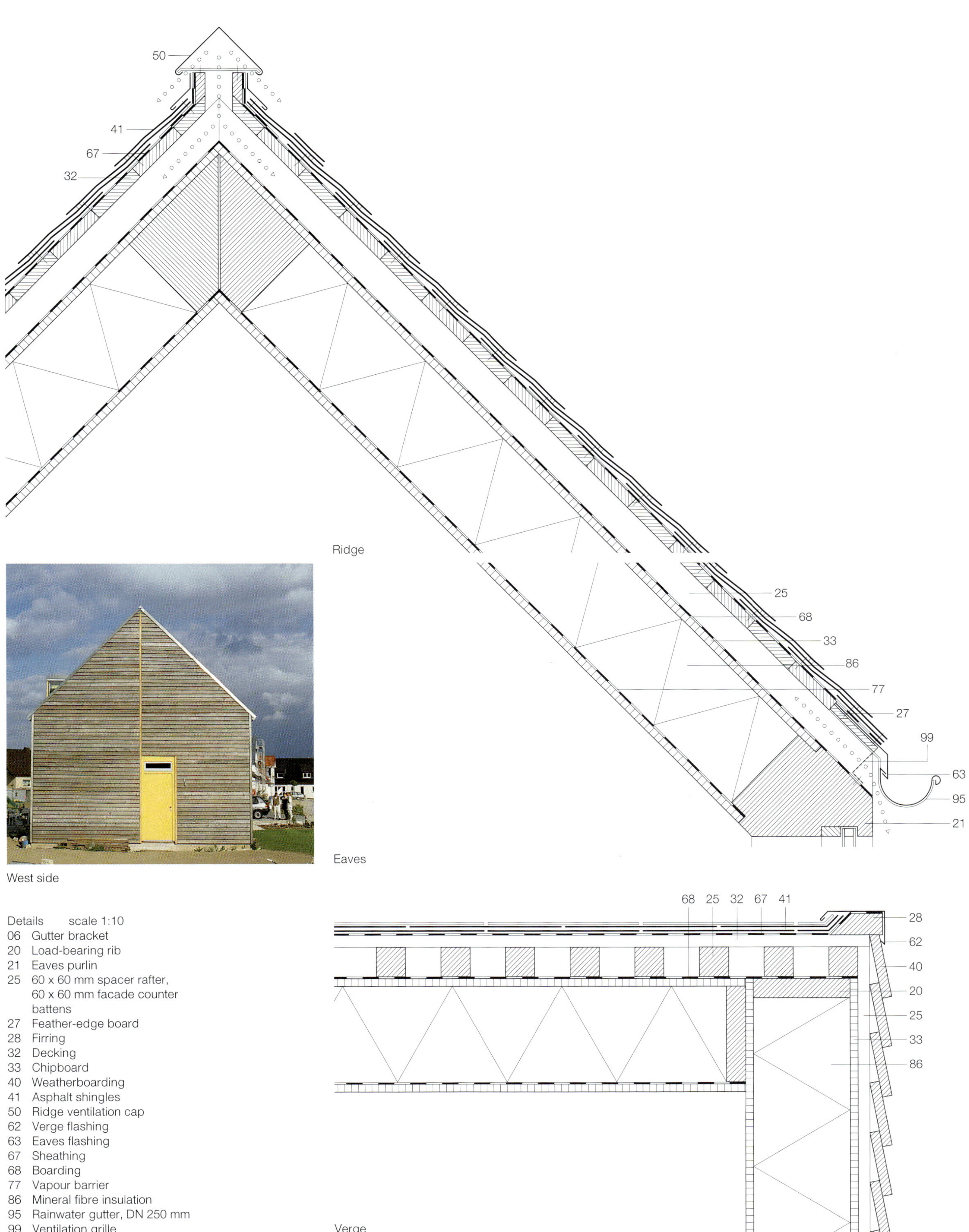


Ridge

Eaves

West side

Verge

Details scale 1:10
06 Gutter bracket
20 Load-bearing rib
21 Eaves purlin
25 60 x 60 mm spacer rafter, 60 x 60 mm facade counter battens
27 Feather-edge board
28 Firring
32 Decking
33 Chipboard
40 Weatherboarding
41 Asphalt shingles
50 Ridge ventilation cap
62 Verge flashing
63 Eaves flashing
67 Sheathing
68 Boarding
77 Vapour barrier
86 Mineral fibre insulation
95 Rainwater gutter, DN 250 mm
99 Ventilation grille

**Student housing in Ingolstadt**
1999

Architect: Andreas Meck, Munich
Structural engineer: Ingenieurbüro Schittig, Ingolstadt
Client: Gemeinnützige Wohnungsbaugesellschaft Ingolstadt

North side

This hall of residence was completed as the last of three phases in the redevelopment of an inner-city area of Ingolstadt. The tapering shape of the plot determined the outline of the building. Within this outline is a rectangular block with 24 student rooms, leaving space on the north side for corridors and communication zones. The ground floor and first floor are combined in maisonette apartments, with the upper level designed as a quieter area for working and sleeping. On the second and third floors are one-room apartments, all identical in plan. A tight budget prompted the choice of in-situ concrete for the whole building. Further cost savings came from deciding to fit a composite thermal insulation system only to the rectangular section containing the student rooms. The communication zones have a non-ventilated flat roof, while living areas are finished with a monopitch roof.

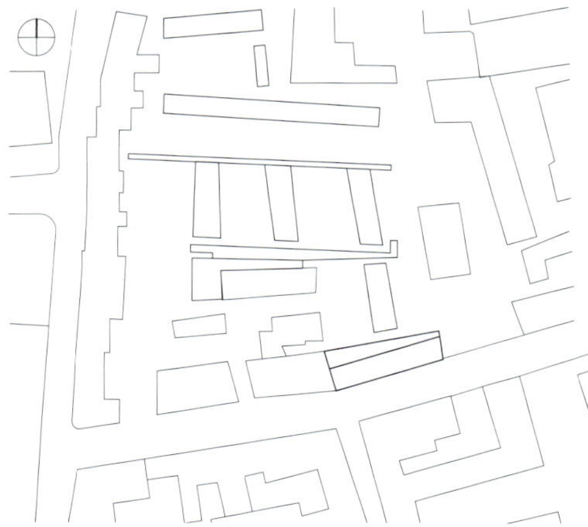
Site plan scale 1:2500

Plans • Elevation scale 1:400

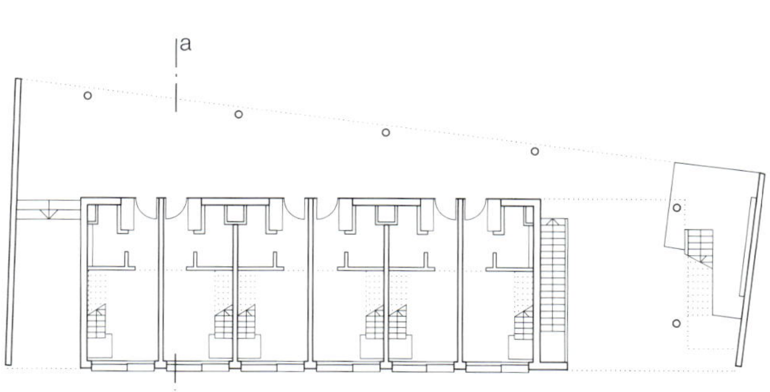

Ground floor

South elevation

1st floor

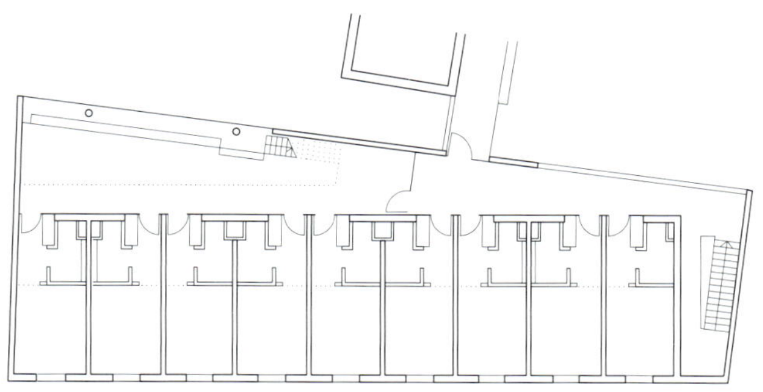
2nd floor

South side

The monopitch roof has a pitch of 30° and is covered with flat, overlapping bullnose tiles. The roof covering and the battens to which it is affixed rest on rafters, which are themselves supported by purlins. The purlins span between reinforced concrete crosswalls, which form the partition walls between the individual apartments. A layer of mineral wool 140 mm thick between the purlins provides adequate thermal insulation. The roof overhang protects the north-facing windows which let light into the upper apartments.

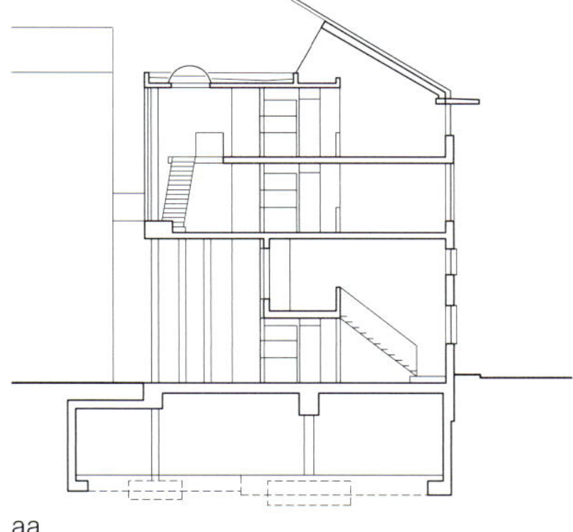

aa

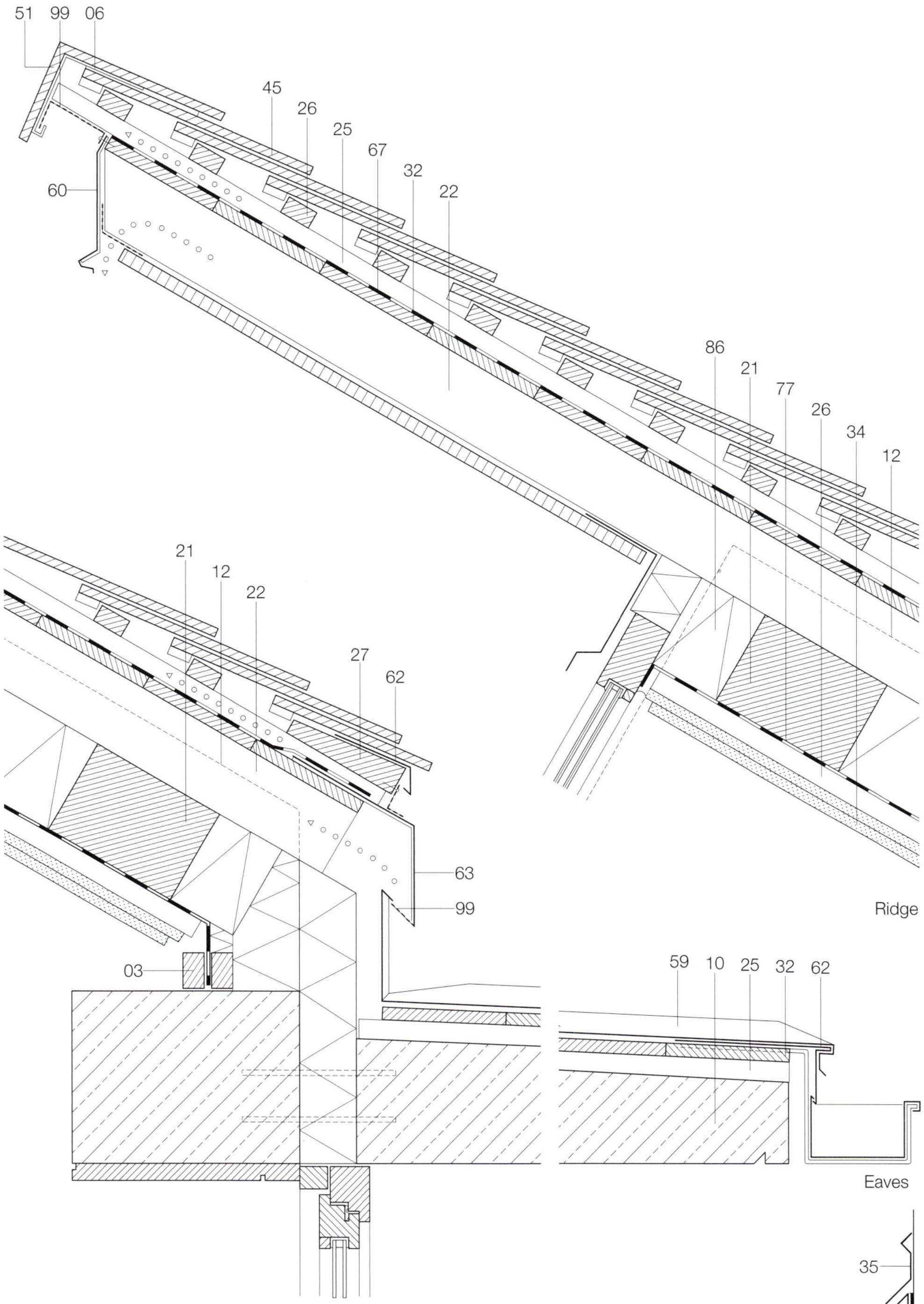

Details scale 1:10

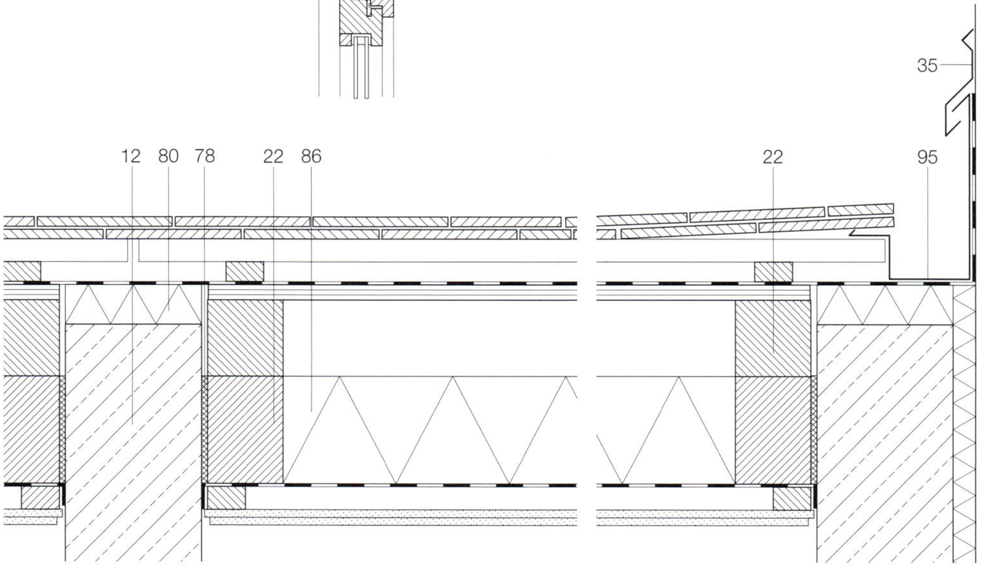

- 03 Clamping strip
- 06 Bracket
- 10 Precast reinforced concrete component
- 12 Reinforced concrete wall
- 21 140 x 200 mm purlin
- 22 100 x 140 mm, 100 x 100 mm rafters
- 25 25 x 45 mm counter batten
- 26 25 x 45 mm support batten
- 27 Tilting board
- 32 18 mm roof decking
- 34 15 mm gypsum fibre-board
- 35 Sheet-metal cap
- 45 Bullnose clay tile
- 51 Angle ridge tile
- 59 Eaves flashing
- 60 Cover sheet
- 62 Drip sheet
- 63 Eaves flashing, lining plate
- 67 Roofing felt
- 77 Vapour barrier
- 78 Permanently elastic seal
- 80 50 mm thermal insulation
- 86 140 mm mineral wool
- 95 Rainwater gutter
- 99 Ventilation grille

Ridge

Eaves

Wall connection

**Detached house in Eckenthal**
1998

Architect: a.ml Architekturwerkstatt
Matthias Loebermann, Nuremberg
Assistant: Eric Alles
Structural engineer: Wolfrum Ingenieurbüro, Nuremberg
Client: Majer family

West side

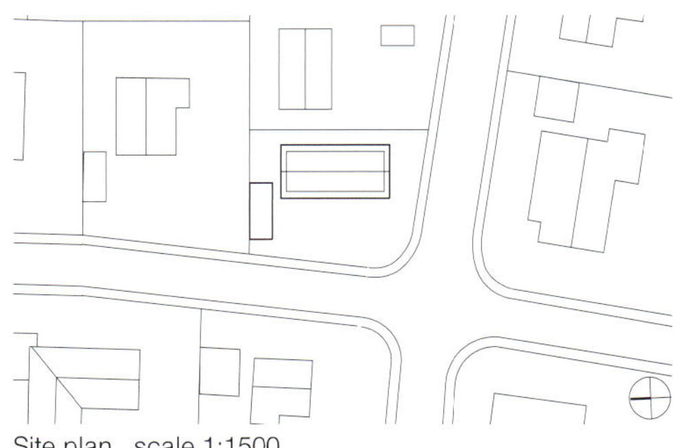

Site plan scale 1:1500

The long, narrow envelope of this detached house is oriented east-west. Living and sleeping areas are positioned across the width of the building, at both ends, minimising the space taken up by communication zones. An open plan distinguishes clearly between areas for communal use or private retreat.

The facade of the house stretches around the building like a multi-layered skin. Horizontal louvres can be opened or closed as required, to regulate incoming light or ventilate the interior space. The entire building envelope is a ventilated, vapour-diffusing construction. Low-energy standards were observed throughout. In addition to its highly insulated skin, the house also has a system for using rainwater, and solar panels fitted to the roof of the garage.

The house has a timber post-and-beam frame, which was entirely prefabricated. The 65 cm structural grid continues on all four external walls and also on the gable roof.

The roof structure consists of a purlin roof with an ultra-slim roof overhang. Because of the material used in its construction, this overhang forms a visual transition between the walls and the roof. It also protects the facade from rain and snow. Over the main body of the house, the roof is covered with grey concrete roof tiles. In the non-insulated area a perimeter strip of boards of untreated (sensitive) laminated veneer lumber protects the timber.

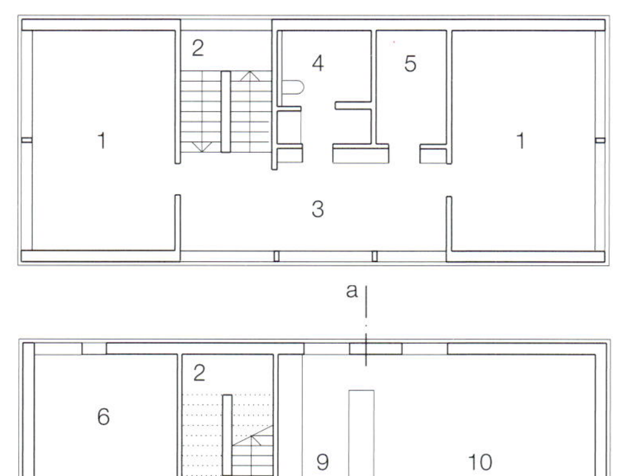


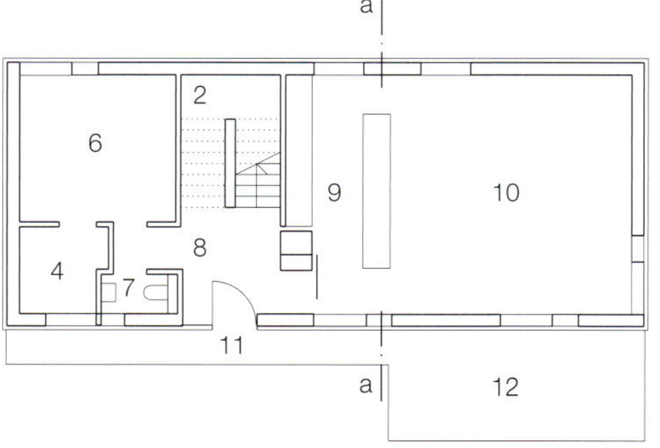


1 Child's bedroom
2 Stairwell
3 Playing area
4 Bathroom
5 Dressing room
6 Parents' bedroom
7 WC
8 Hallway
9 Kitchen
10 Lounge/dining room
11 Wooden walkway
12 Terrace

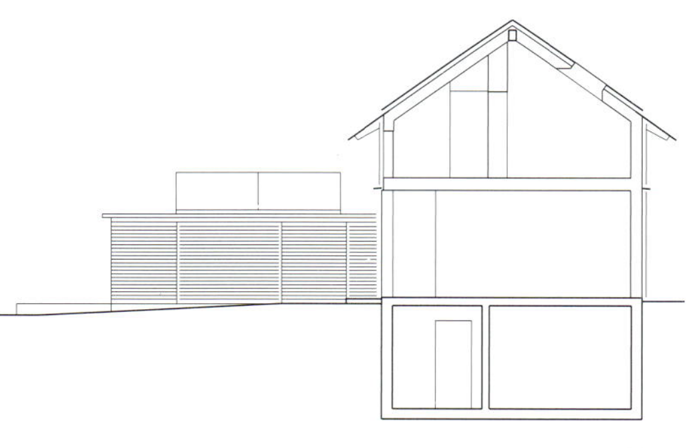

Plans of upper floor, ground floor • Section scale 1:250

aa

East side

South side

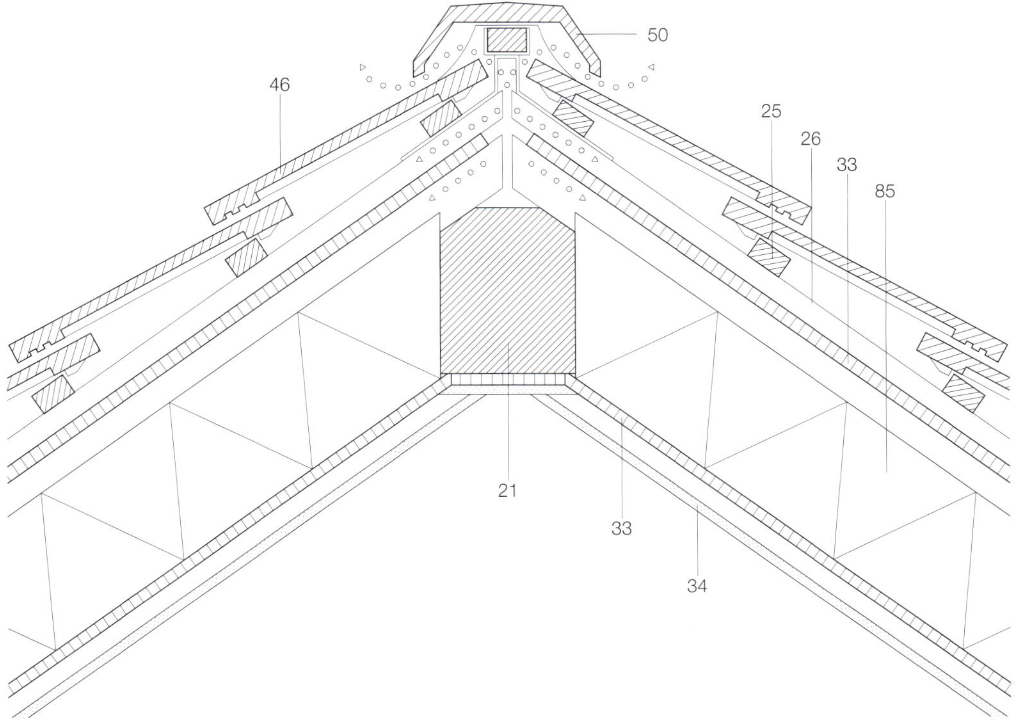

Ridge with ventilated layer above thermal insulation

Details scale 1:10

18 40 x 80 mm timber
20 120 x 160 headrail of post-and-beam wall
21 180 x 220 mm ridge purlin, 80 x 160 mm eaves purlin
22 80 x 220 mm rafter, 80 x 200 mm on outside, (timber grade: GK II)
24 60 x 160 mm horizontal member
25 30 x 50 mm counter batten
26 30 x 50 mm batten
27 Tilting board
29 Vertical board
32 26 mm larch decking
33 18 mm multiplex plywood, 15 mm OSB, 37 mm laminated veneer lumber
34 12.5 mm plasterboard
46 Concrete roof tile
50 Ridge ventilation tile
75 Facade waterproofing, windproof acrylic-coated polyester
85 Thermal insulation, flax: roof 180 mm, wall 160 mm + 60 mm
95 Titanium-zinc rainwater gutter
99 Insect screen

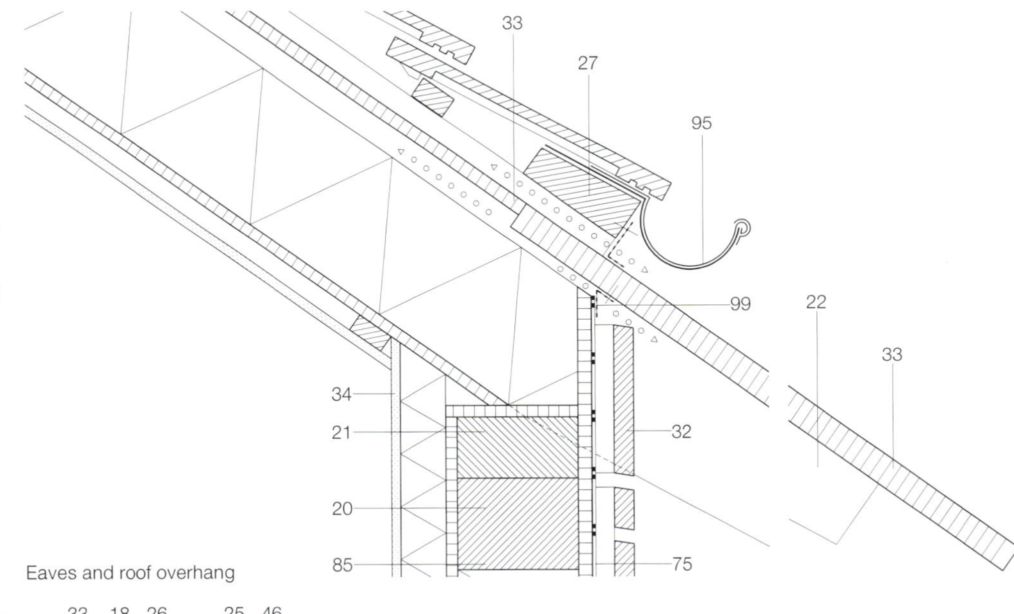

Eaves and roof overhang

Terrace on west side

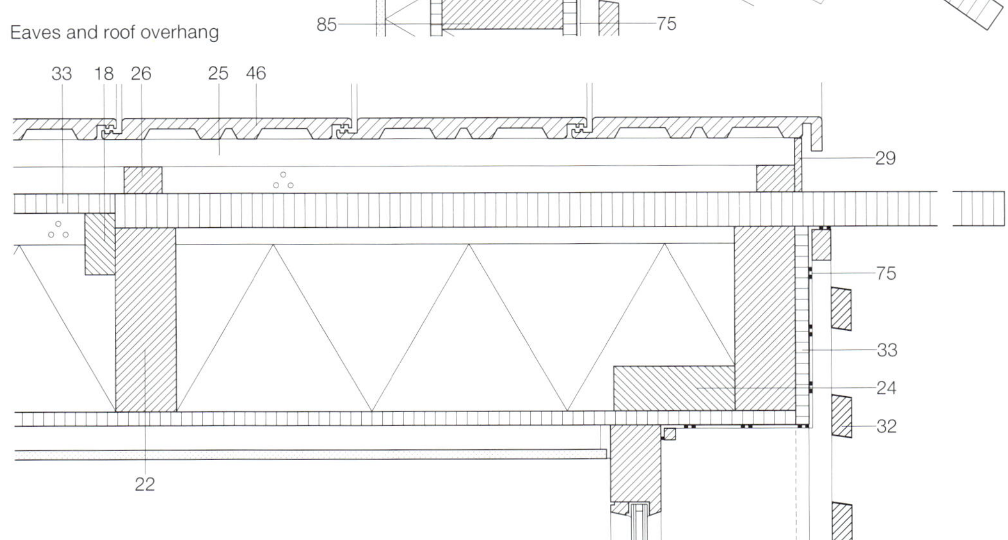

Verge and window junction

**Office building, University of Eichstätt**
1980

Architects: K. J. Schattner and J. Homeier, Eichstätt
Structural engineer: Sailer, Stepan, Munich
Client: Stiftung Katholische Universität Eichstätt

Street side

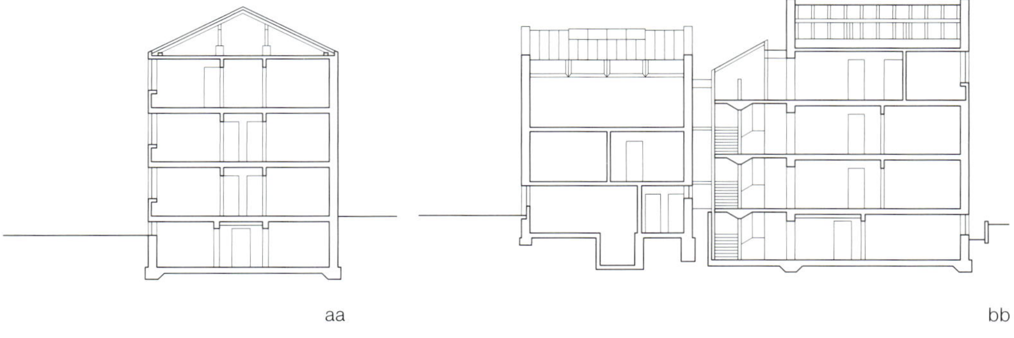


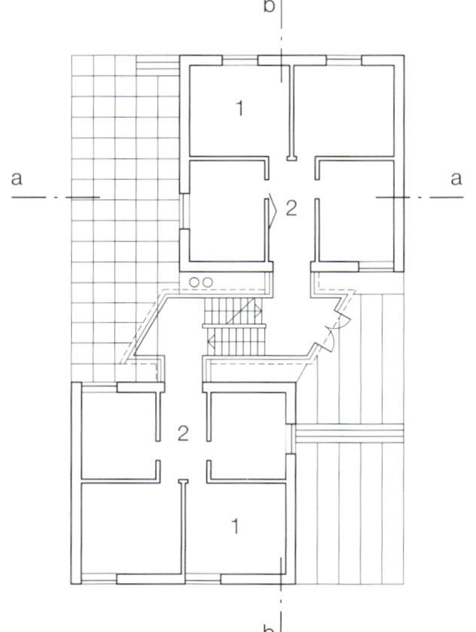


1 Office
2 Hallway
3 Conference room
4 Director's office

Sections • Plans of ground floor, roof floor scale 1:400

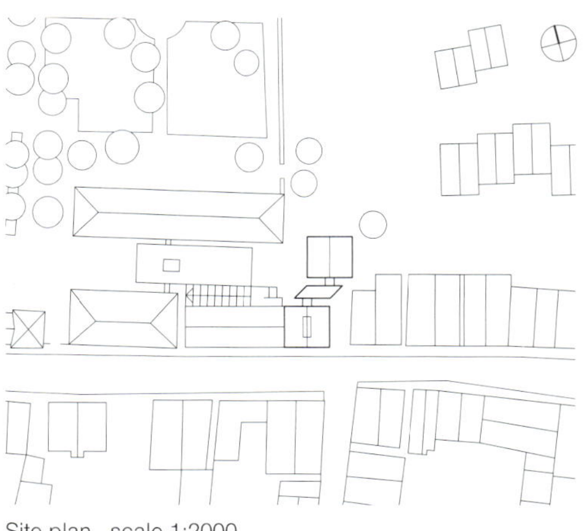
Site plan scale 1:2000

This building, which houses offices for the university, is situated on a main road leading into the centre of Eichstätt. Its outer form blends well with the neighbouring two- and three-storey buildings, which have pointed gables. A glass staircase separates the building in two, the part facing the street harmonising in its dimensions with the surrounding development. Distinctive features on the outside are the clean, clear lines marking out the edges of the building, and a skin of lightweight concrete with joints articulating the facade. The roof shape, too, takes its cue from the neighbourhood, harmonising well with the overall roof landscape.

The southern block is an open-plan design with a timber purlin roof. A steel frame was used in the northern block, where the conference room extends up into the roof. Throughout, the underside of the roof is ventilated between the rafters, but extract ventilation below the ridge rooflight is very close to the roof surface. Untreated, flat concrete roof tiles were used for the roof covering, an echo of the local tradition in Eichstätt of using Jurassic slate. It was not until the introduction of mass-produced clay tiles that this practice was discontinued. An overall homogeneity in the appearance of this building is maintained through the choice of the same material on both roof and outer walls.

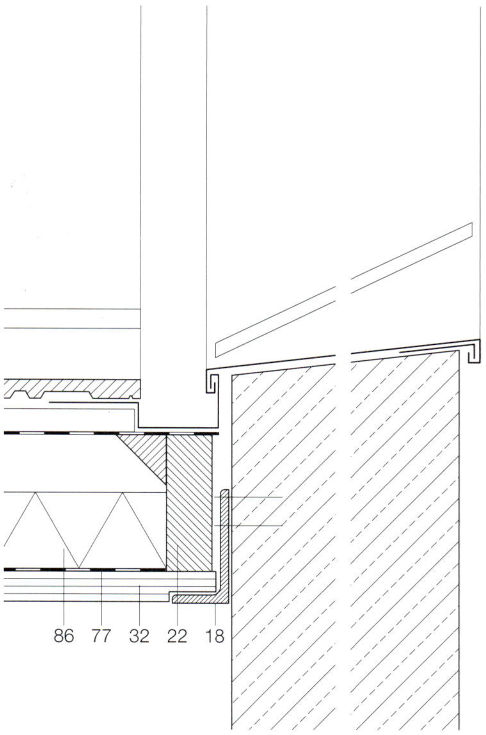

Verge, northern block

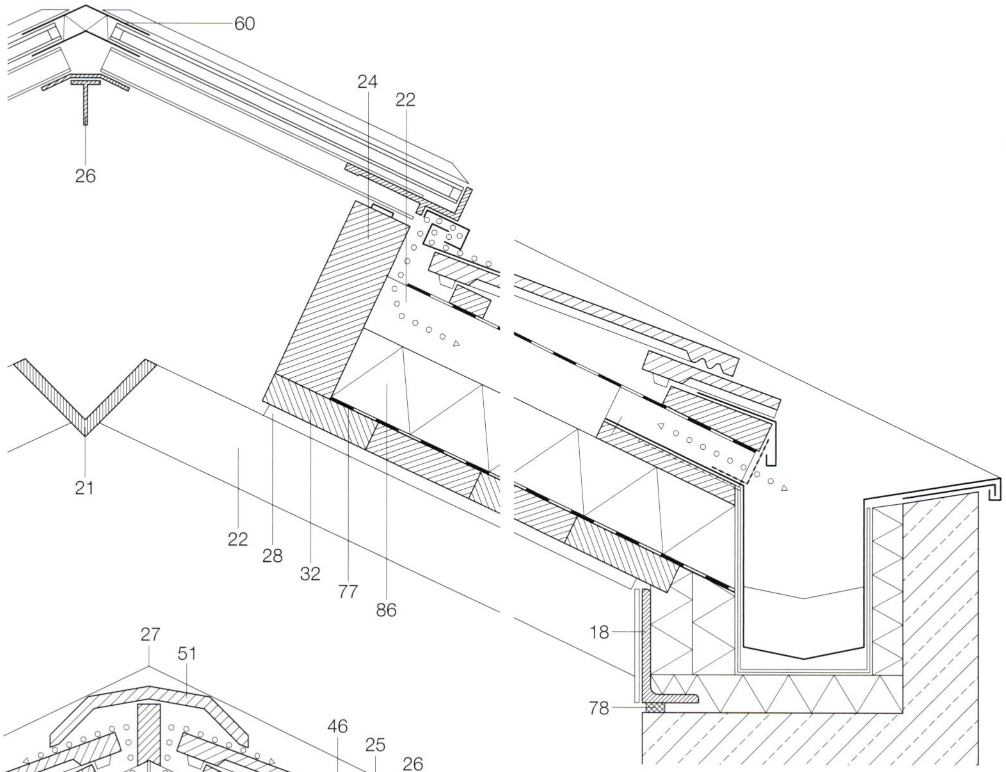

Ridge and eaves, northern block

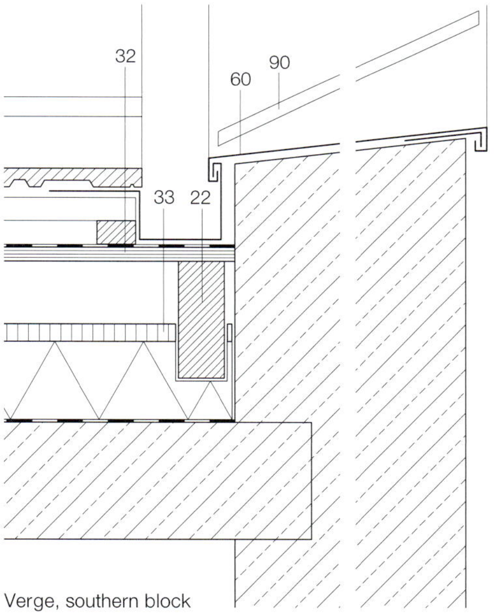

Verge, southern block

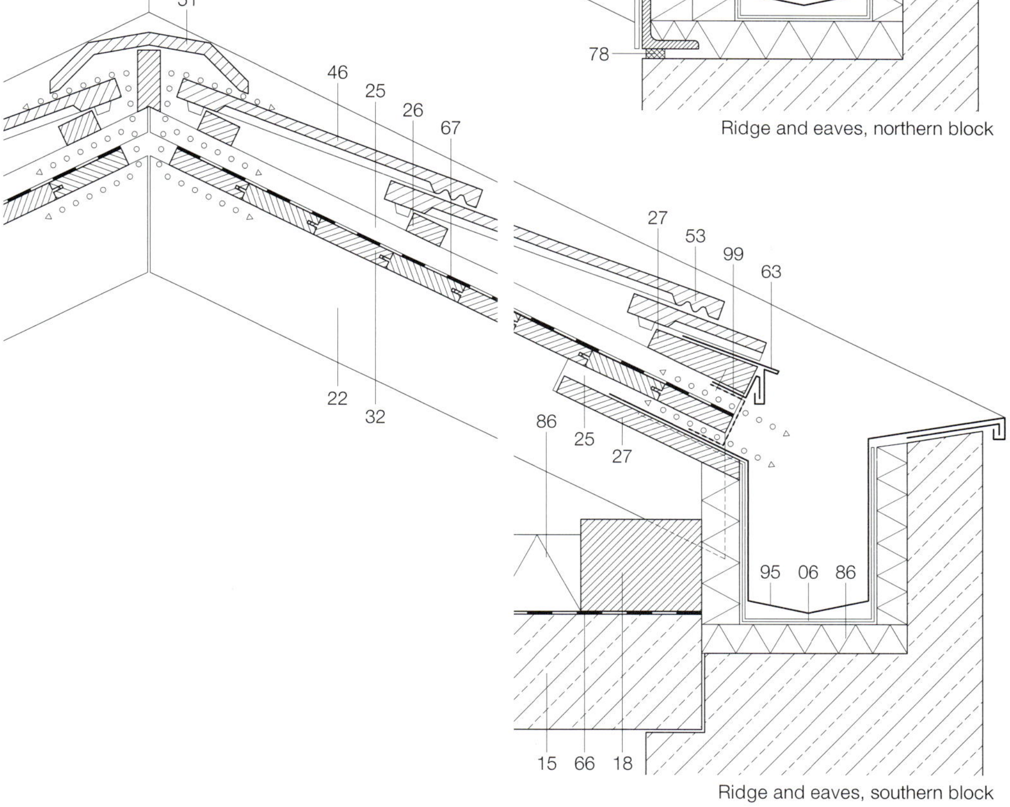

Ridge and eaves, southern block

Details scale 1:10

06 40 x 5 mm galvanised steel gutter bracket
15 150 mm concrete floor
18 150 x 75 x 11 mm steel angle, 160 x 120 mm wall plate
21 Steel angle ridge purlin
22 80 x 140 mm rafter, steel angle rafter
24 80 x 345 mm glued laminated timber frame
25 30 x 50 mm spacer rafter
26 Batten, IPE 80 halved
27 30 x 40 x 150 mm feather-edge board, 30 x 70 mm ridge board, fascia board
28 Filler strip
32 Spruce decking
33 22 mm chipboard (type V 100)
46 Flat concrete roof tiles, low interlock
51 Ridge tile
53 Shortened eaves tile
60 0.7 mm titanium-zinc cover sheet
63 0.7 mm titanium-zinc eaves flashing
66 Felt underlay
67 Sand-surfaced bituminous felt
77 Aluminium-coated vapour barrier
78 Permanently elastic seal
86 100 mm mineral fibre mat, aluminium-coated
90 1.0 mm titanium-zinc angled water guide
95 500 mm titianium-zinc gutter
99 Anodised aluminium ventilation grille

Verge

## Semi-detached house in Allensbach

1998

Architects: Schaudt Architekten, Konstanz
Assistant: Helmut Hagmüller
Structural engineer: Ingenieurbüro Leisering, Konstanz
Client: Andrea Hagmüller-Hahn

West side

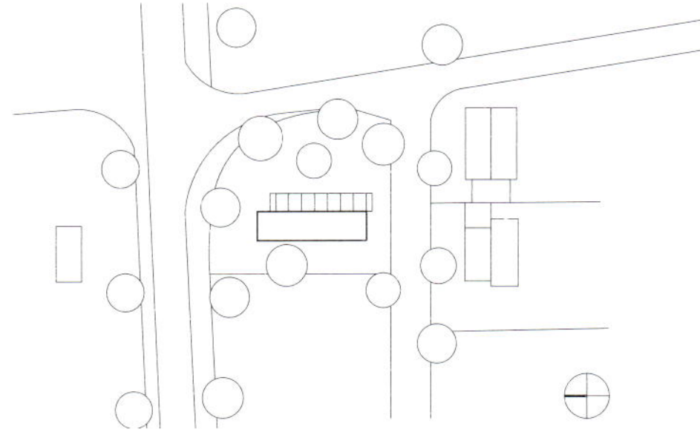

Site plan
Scale 1:2000
Sections

Plans
Upper floor
Ground floor
Parking level
Scale 1:400

1 Lounge/dining room
2 Kitchen
3 Terrace
4 Bedroom with flexible cupboard units
5 Cisterns for rainwater utilisation
6 Storage
7 Parking

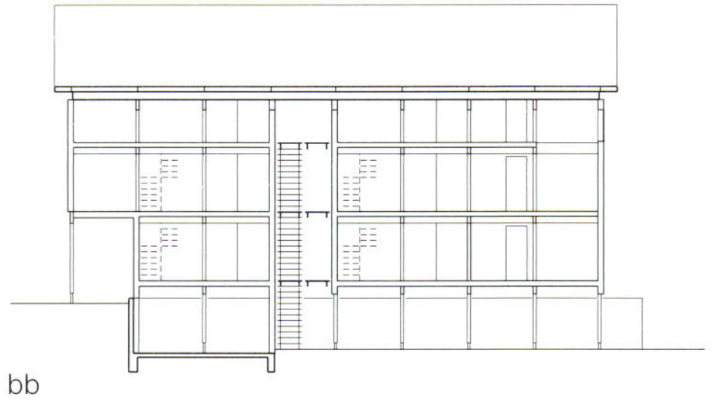


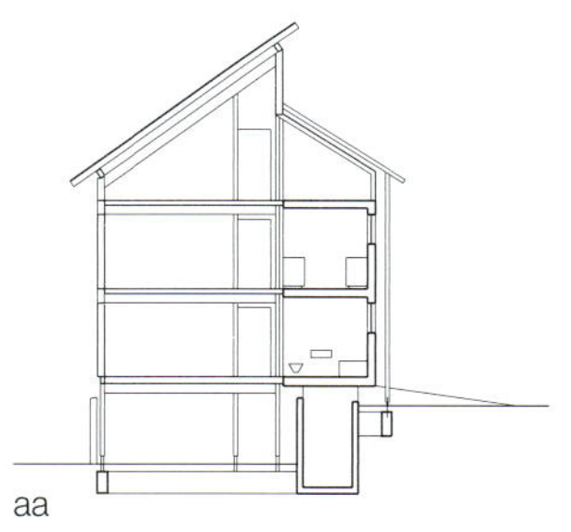


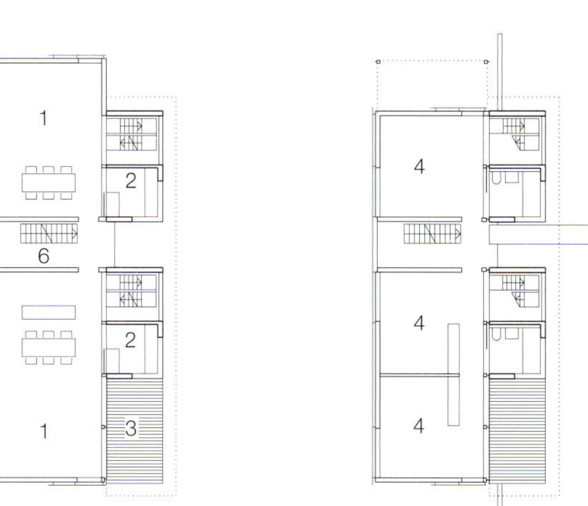


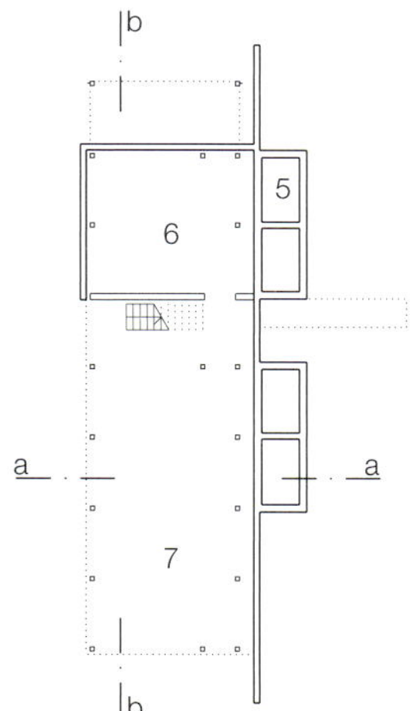


This building stands on the edge of an area of new residential developments, overlooking Lake Constance. An external staircase, running across the building volume, divides it into two separate houses. The three floors in each section are further connected by means of an internal staircase; this is intended to simplify combining or diving living space later, without major structural interventions. A further division is evident in the construction: the west side, containing living areas and bedrooms, is timber-framed, while the east side consists of two solid-walled concrete cubes housing ancillary facilities. The cubes are integrated into a fine steel structure, which supports terraces facing the lake. The roof construction, too, has a distinct east-west divide. The two monopitch roofs, rising towards each other, are different in both material and size. On the west side the timber frame continues into a close-couple roof with no ventilation layer above the insulation, and the roof covering is concrete tiles. The steel frame on the east side carries a lamella roof of larchwood, which was designed to facilitate later mounting of solar panels.

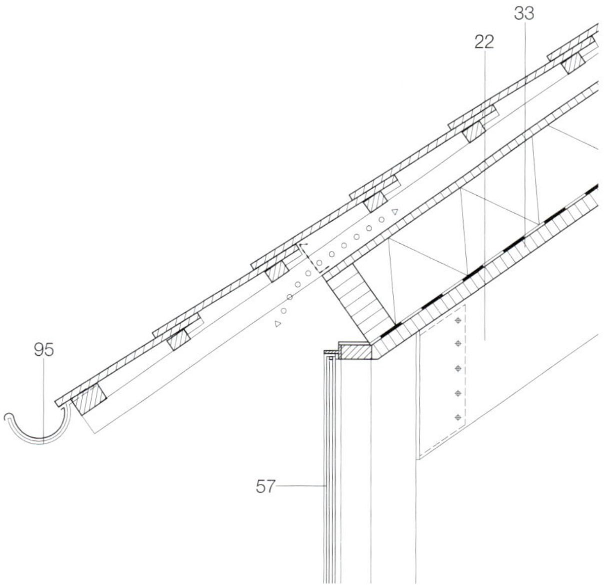

Eaves and roof overhang

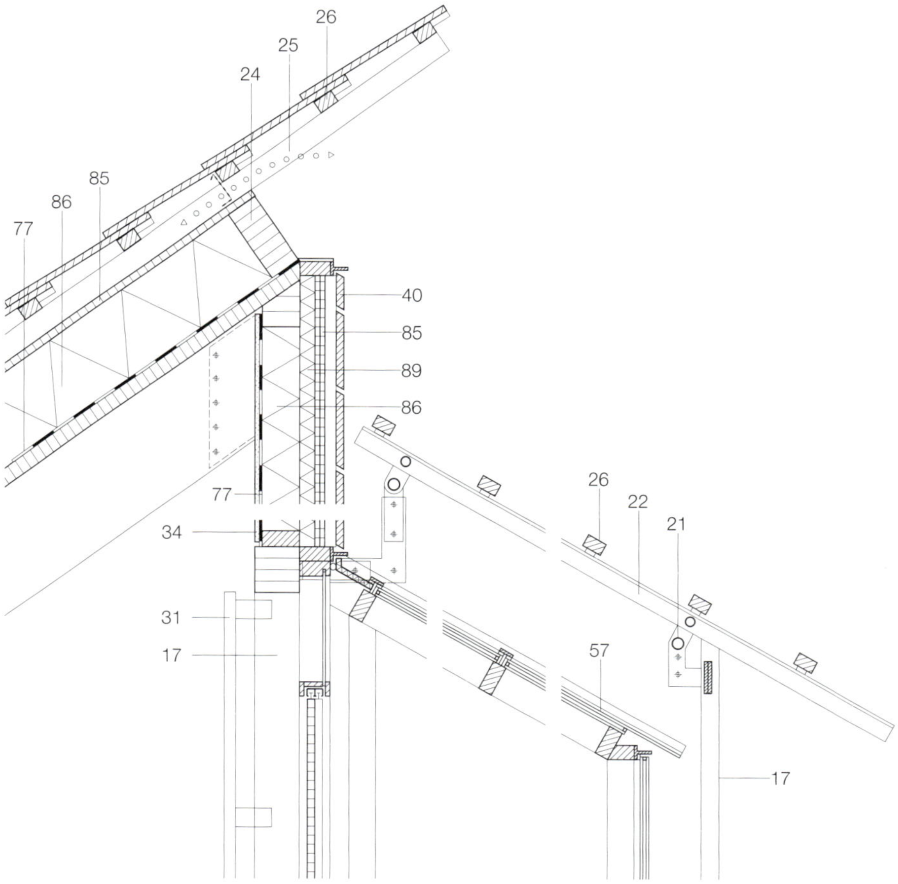

Ridge with no ventilation layer above thermal insulation

Southside

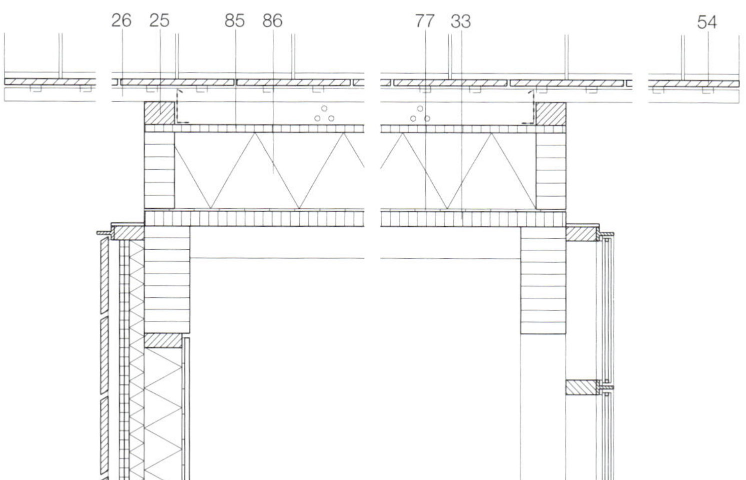


Verge-facade junction

Details scale 1:20

17 Column, inside: 120 x 120 mm glued laminated timber; outside: double column, 2 x 48.3 mm dia. x 4.5 mm galvanised steel tube

21 30 mm dia. x 3.2 mm galvanised steel tube at ridge/eaves

24 80 x 200 mm glued laminated horizontal timber

25 60 x 80 mm counter battens

26 30 x 50 mm larchwood battens

31 Structural reinforcement of column in roof storey: 31.8 mm dia. x 2.6 mm galvanised steel tube

33 40 mm plywood construction board

34 12.5 mm gypsum fibreboard

40 20 mm red cedar decking on 40 x 60 mm laths

54 Verge tile

57 Insulating glass, on roof: laminated safety glass

85 Fibreboard, roof: 25 mm; wall: 2 x 13 mm

86 Mineral wool, roof: 200 mm; wall: 100 mm

89 40 mm rigid foam

77 0.4 mm polyethylene sheet vapour barrier

95 Rainwater gutter

**Detached house near Bad Tölz**
1997

Architects: Fink + Jocher, Munich,
Dietrich Fink, Thomas Jocher
Assistants: Nicole Hemminger, Thomas Pfeiffer
Structural engineer: Toni Staudacher, Tegernsee
Clients: Ursula and Alexander Schroth

East side

Site plan scale 1:4000

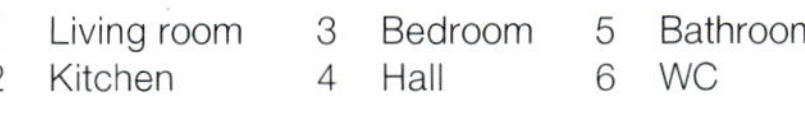


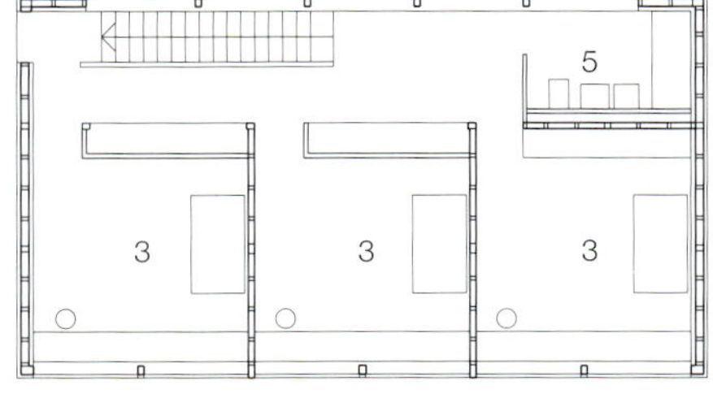


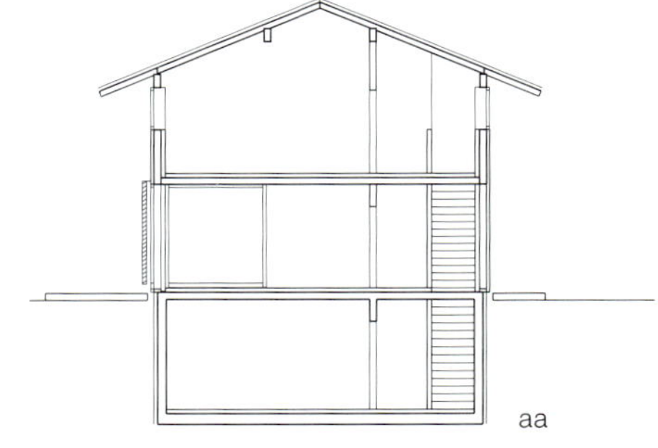


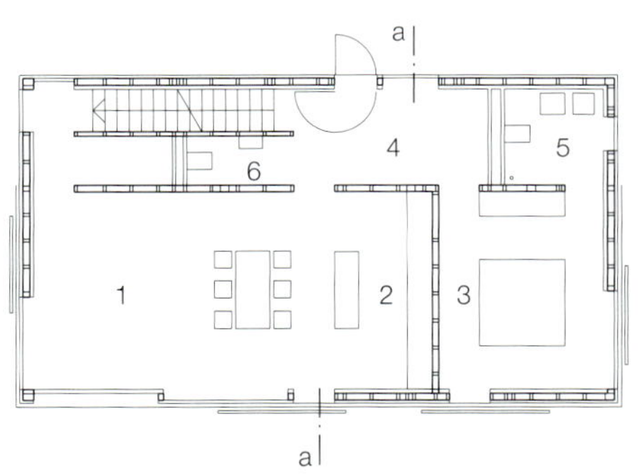


Plans of upper floor, ground floor Section scale 1:250

This low-energy house stands on the edge of a small village in Upper Bavaria. The two-storey building, which also has a full-size cellar, is distinctive for its simple wooden facade, wide overhanging roof and shallow roof pitch. All of these elements draw their inspiration from the simple forms of the surrounding farmhouses.

The plan is divided clearly into northern and southern sections. On the northern side, behind an energy-efficient closed facade, are the functional zones and entrance area. The house opens up towards the south, east and west. At ground floor level it is glazed from floor to ceiling. Sliding panels of larchwood, suspended in front of the generous expanse of windows in the living room, provide screening and prevent interior temperatures rising too high in summer. The ground floor leaves scope for easy rearrangement to create an integrated one-room apartment, by combining the bedroom and bathroom, and fitting a kitchen.

South side

Gable overhang, south

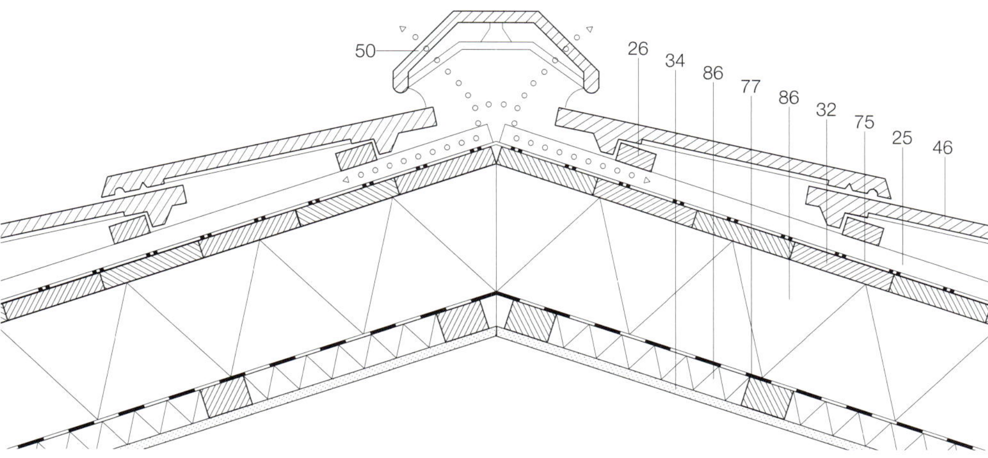

Ridge, no ventilated air layer above insulation

The building's frame and walls are built in the panel construction method. Mainly prefabricated, storey-high elements with continuous timber uprights, in combination with the inner plywood panel, form the basic framework of the double-layered outer wall. By choosing larchwood, it was possible to avoid using timber preservatives on walls and roof.

The roof has a purlin roof frame with an overhanging roof edge that affords weather protection for the wooden facade. Concrete roof tiles were used for the roof covering, placed above the insulation with no ventilated air layer. 20% of the thermal insulation is located here underneath the vapour barrier.

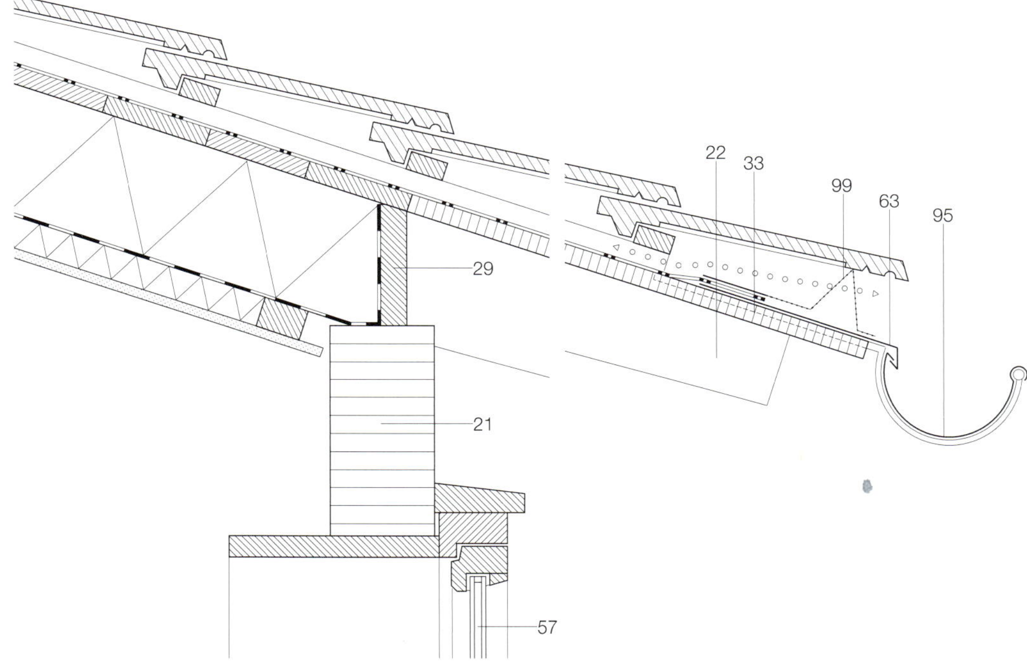

Eaves, roof overhang and window detail

Details scale 1:10

21 140 x 280 mm purlin
22 60 x 160 mm rafter
24 60 x 60 mm horizontal member
25 24 x 48 mm counter batten
26 30 x 50 mm batten
29 Fascia board
32 24 mm rough tongue and groove decking
33 12 mm plywood panel (AW 100), visible underside of eaves 24 mm maritime pine board, scumbled white
34 12.5 mm plasterboard
40 24 mm tongue and groove pine decking, outside 30 x 50 mm larch
46 Concrete roof tile
50 Ridge ventilation tile
57 Insulating glass
62 Verge flashing
63 Eaves flashing
75 Vapour-diffusing roof seal, wall: vapour-diffusing windproof building paper
77 Vapour barrier, aluminium on roof, polyethylene sheet on walls
86 Cellulose fibre thermal insulation, roof 160 + 40 mm, wall 160 + 60 mm
95 Titanium-zinc rainwater gutter
99 Insect screen

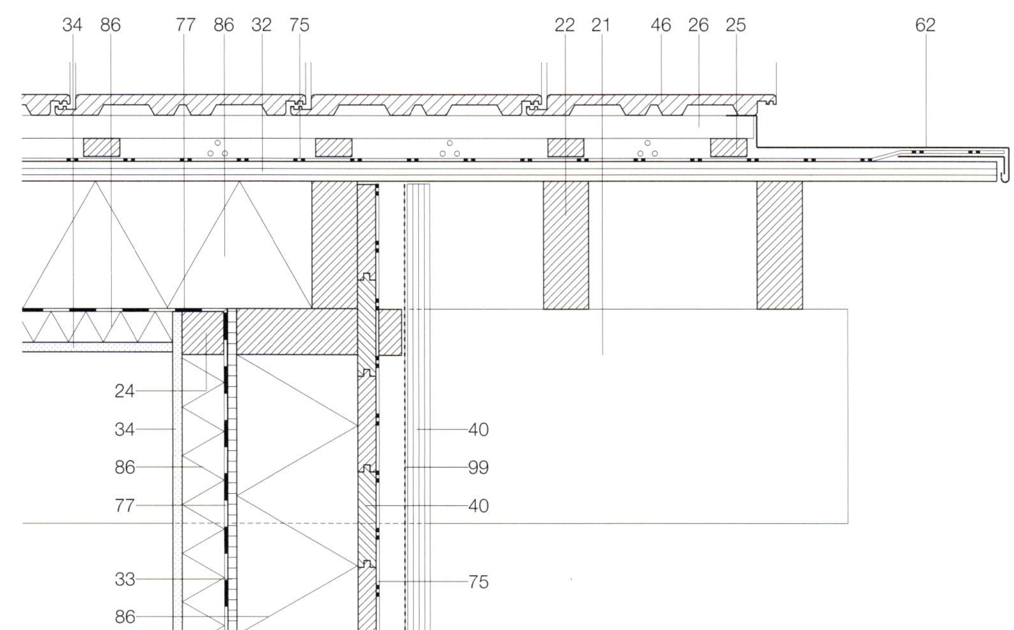

Verge-facade junction

**Casa Rurale in Italy**
2000

Architects: Döring, Dahmen, Joeressen, Düsseldorf
Wolfgang Döring, Michael Dahmen, Elmar Joeressen
Assistant: Mark Altgassen
Structural engineer: Giorgio Marziali, Acquapendente Prov. Viterbo

East side

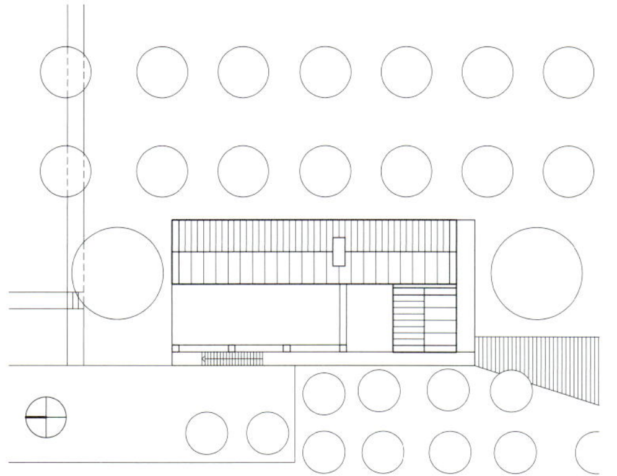
Site plan scale 1:1000

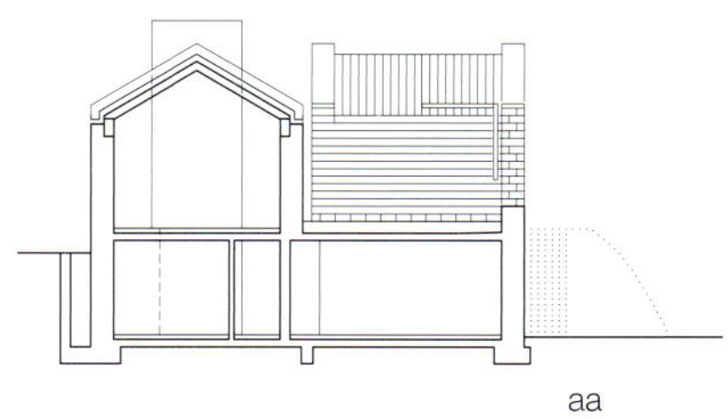
aa

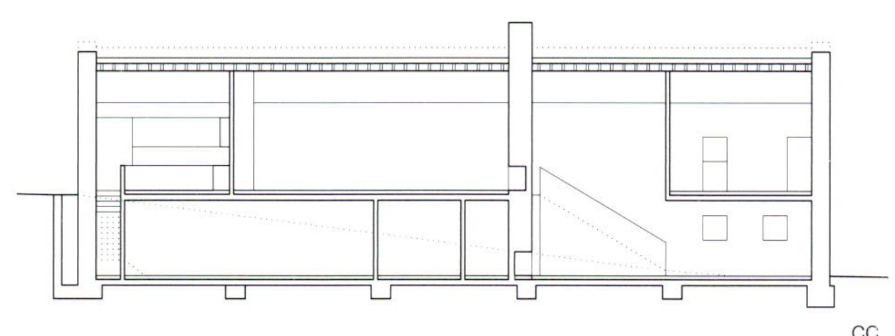
cc

The main house in this agricultural business in Latium is a geometrically shaped volume built on a slope. The two-storey building follows the local tradition with its tuff masonry, shallow pitched roof and extended gable wall. The cavity wall, which is 65 cm thick and has few window openings, acts as a thermal storage mass, preventing overheating of the interior in summer and rapid cooling in winter.

The geometry of the building is based on a basic module of 5.40 x 5.40 m, the length, width and height deriving from the sloping site.

The entrance is on the valley side, at the lower level. Leading off the courtyard, which functions as an open-air reception space, are the office and work areas.

On the upper floor, which is also the ground floor on the slope side, are the living areas, fronted by a terrace.

The building's load-bearing structure is a reinforced concrete frame and panel construction that continues up into the roof. In the roof area the frame is infilled with prefabricated brick panels. Applied on top of this is a vapour barrier, insulation and screed. The custom-made under-and-over roof tiles were laid directly onto the wet screed.

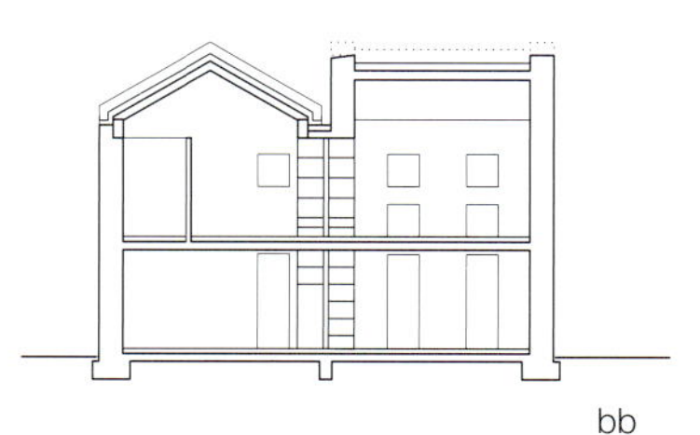
bb

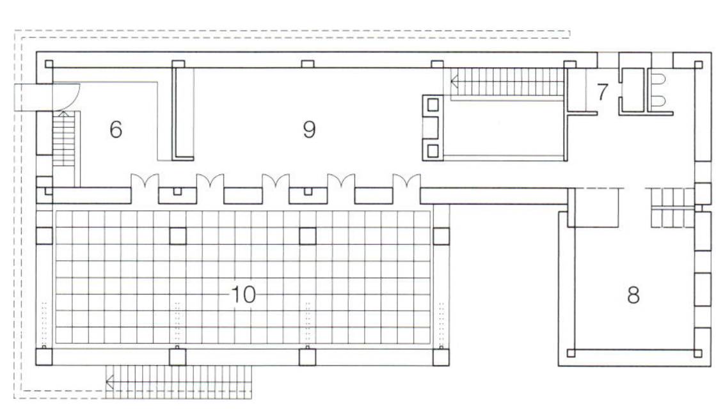


Sections
Plans
scale 1:400

1 Entrance
2 Guest room
3 Office
4 Wine cellar
5 Store room
6 Kitchen
7 Bathroom
8 Room
9 Living room
10 Terrace

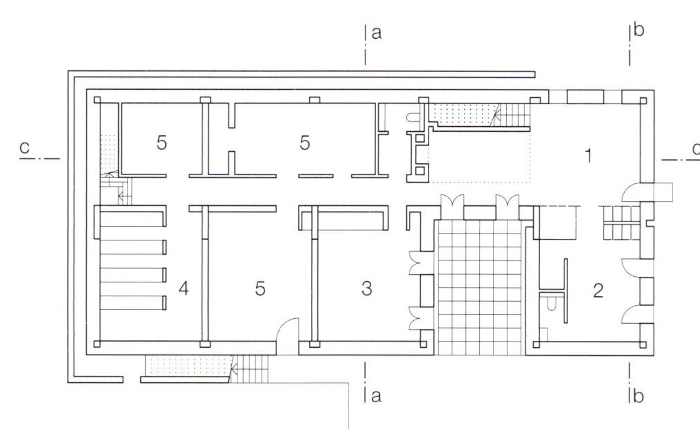

Northwest side

Details scale 1:20
04 Welded pins
11 250 mm tuff masonry, 50 mm Basaltino stone wall coping
13 300 mm brick panels, 220 mm brick components
15 Reinforced concrete frame
16 60 mm screed
34 Plaster
45 Flat over-and-under tiles
51 Ridge tile, set in mortar
60 Zinc sheet flashing, bent to fit
77 Vapour barrier
86 80 mm compression-resistant thermal insulation
95 Rainwater gutter
96 Rainwater downpipe

## Housing estate in Fredensborg, Sjaelland

1963

Architect: Jørn Utzon, Copenhagen
Client: A Danish local community

Courtyard side

This estate is located on a south-facing slope near to Lake Esrum in the picturesque landscape of northern Sjaelland. The 48 atrium houses and 30 terrace houses were built for Danish citizens returning home to live in their native country. Nearby Fredensborg Castle lent its name to the estate.

The single-storey atrium houses sit on square plots. They are strung together in a meandering line, a simple arrangement that facilitates their close integration into the surrounding landscape. The fair-faced brickwork of the outer walls tones with the almost identical yellow of the roof covering of interlocking clay pantiles. At the ridge and eaves, the roof covering overhangs, but the gable walls are continued up above the roof surface. They follow the slope of the roof in a distinctive stepped formation.

The roof frames are constructed as simple timber purlin roofs. The roof structure is ventilated. Both the ventilation cross-section and the insulation are more than adequate for the mild maritime climate of Denmark.

The charm of this residential estate, which is closely related to the Kingohus estate north of Copenhagen, lies in the lively configuration of basically standard units. Their arrangement in this Arcadian landscape gives the estate a unique impression.

Site plan scale 1:6000

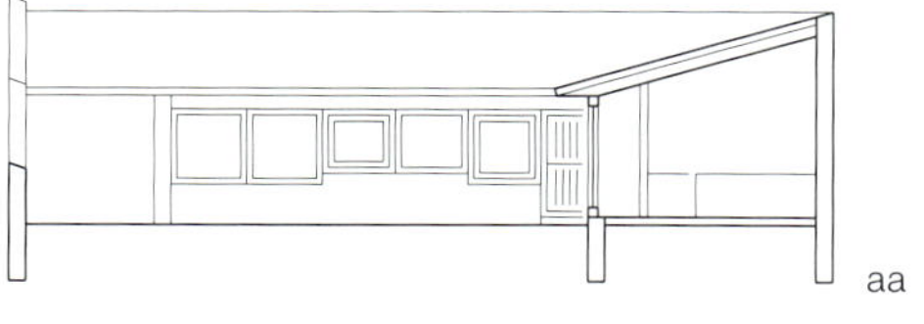


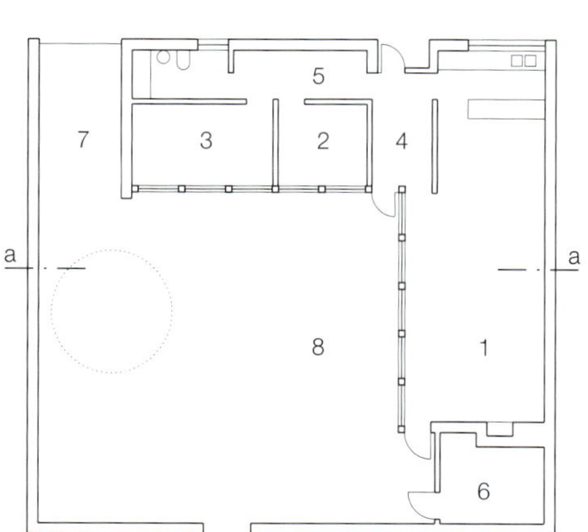


Plan of ground floor • Section scale 1:300

1 Lounge/dining area
2 Lounge/sleeping area
3 Bedroom
4 Hall
5 Cloakroom
6 Storage
7 Garage
8 Courtyard

View of roofs

View of roofs

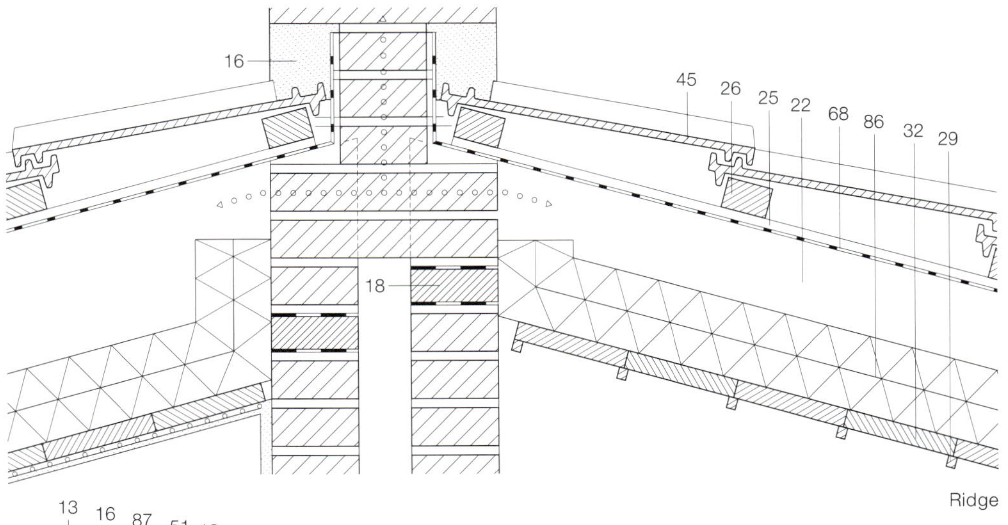


Ridge

Details scale 1:10

13 Wall brickwork
16 Mortar
17 120 x 120 mm timber post
18 Wall plate
21 Purlin, 2x 120 x 120 mm, 120 x 120 mm
22 Rafters, 100 x 200 mm, 100-200 x 280 mm, 50 x 200 mm
25 12 x 50 mm spacer batten
26 40 x 60 mm batten
27 2x 24 x 100 mm eaves boards
29 12 x 15 mm cover strip
32 24 x 150 mm boards, 24 mm decking
45 Ochre-brown interlocking clay tile
51 Ridge tile
61 Copper connector sheet
68 Roofing felt
72 Plaster on reed mat
75 Waterproofing, triple-layer bitumen sheeting, bonded
86 Thermal insulation, 2 x 50 mm glass wool
87 70 mm polystyrene panels
95 Copper rainwater gutter

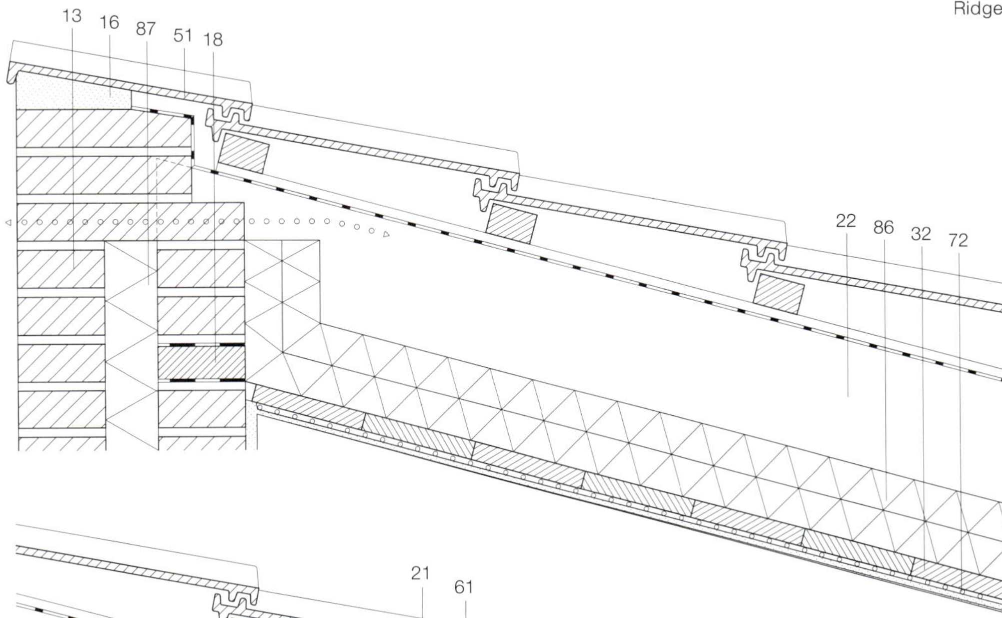


Eaves

Passageway

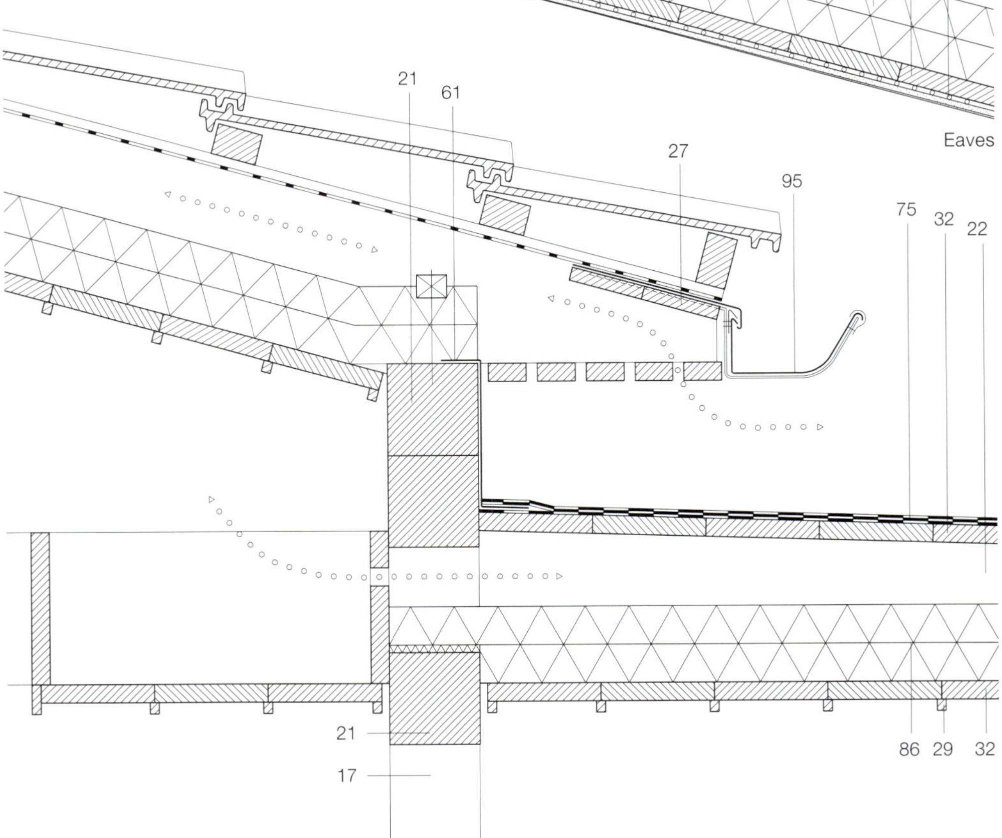


Wall junction

## Detached house in Brühl

1997

Architect: Heinz Bienefeld, Swisstal Ollheim
Assistant: J. Siller
Structural engineer: R. Mertens, Cologne
Client: Babanek family

Northeast side

Site plan scale 1:2000

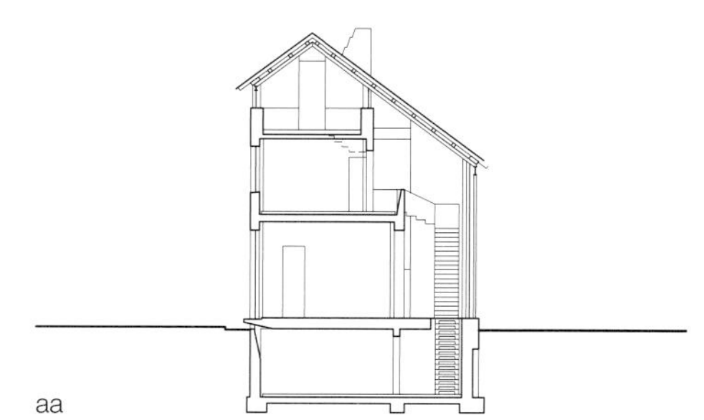

aa

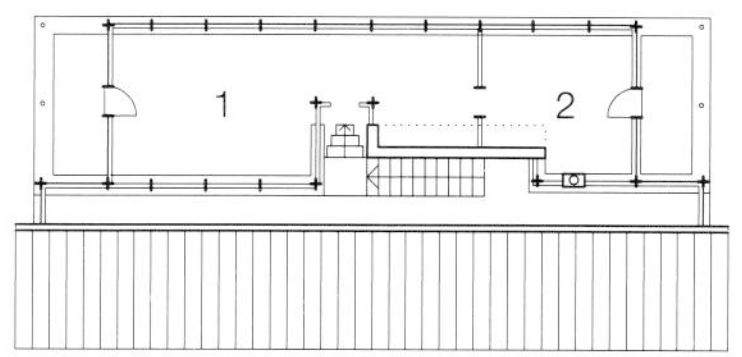


The building is divided into two parts: living areas and communication zones, an arrangement clearly legible on the outside as different materials were used for each. The southwest-facing lobby, with entrance hall and staircase, is a steel and glass construction, while the main part of the building is built of 500 mm solid brickwork. The northeast facade is clearly articulated with regularly spaced openings. On the layered gable walls, the different levels of ground floor, first floor and roof storey are easily identifiable. A continuous strip of glazing separates the gable roof with 33° pitch from the brick-built part of the house, bringing daylight into the upper rooms.

The purlin roof construction, which extends over both parts of the building, is covered with profiled overlapping tiles. Hollow clay blocks were used on the visible underface of the roof, where they also play a role in thermal insulation. Shallow box gutters, also acting as open downpipes, are used for roof drainage.

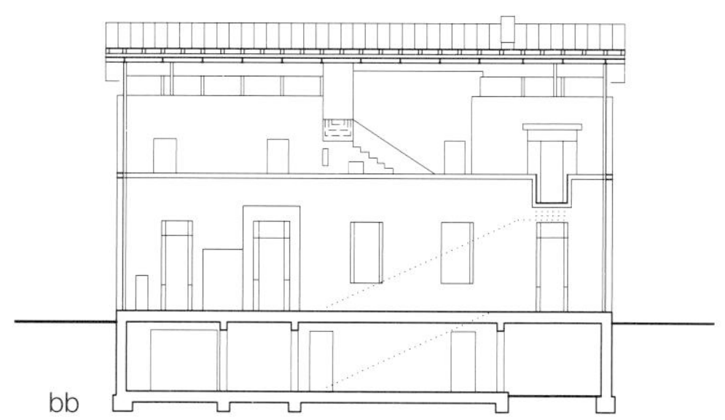

bb

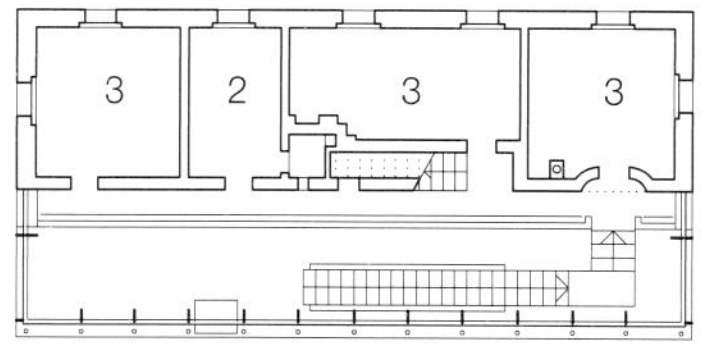


Sections • Plans scale 1:400

1 Parents' bedroom
2 Bathroom/WC
3 Child's bedroom
4 Kitchen
5 Living room
6 Study
7 Entrance hall
8 Guest WC

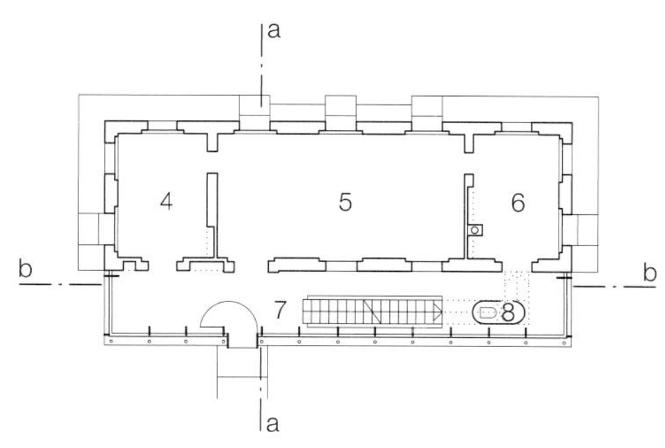

Details scale 1:10

06 6 mm stainless steel binder
07 Ridge gusset plate, welded steel sheet
18 80 x 100 mm timber bearer
21 2x 80 x 80 x 10 mm steel angle purlin
22 80 x 100 mm spacer rafter, IPE 140 steel section, steel section rafter extension
25 24 x 48 mm counter battens
26 24 x 48 mm battens
30 Tie
45 Interlocking tile
68 Roofing felt
77 Vapour barrier
80 Hollow clay block
86 Thermal insulation
95 140 mm box gutter
99 Ventilation grille

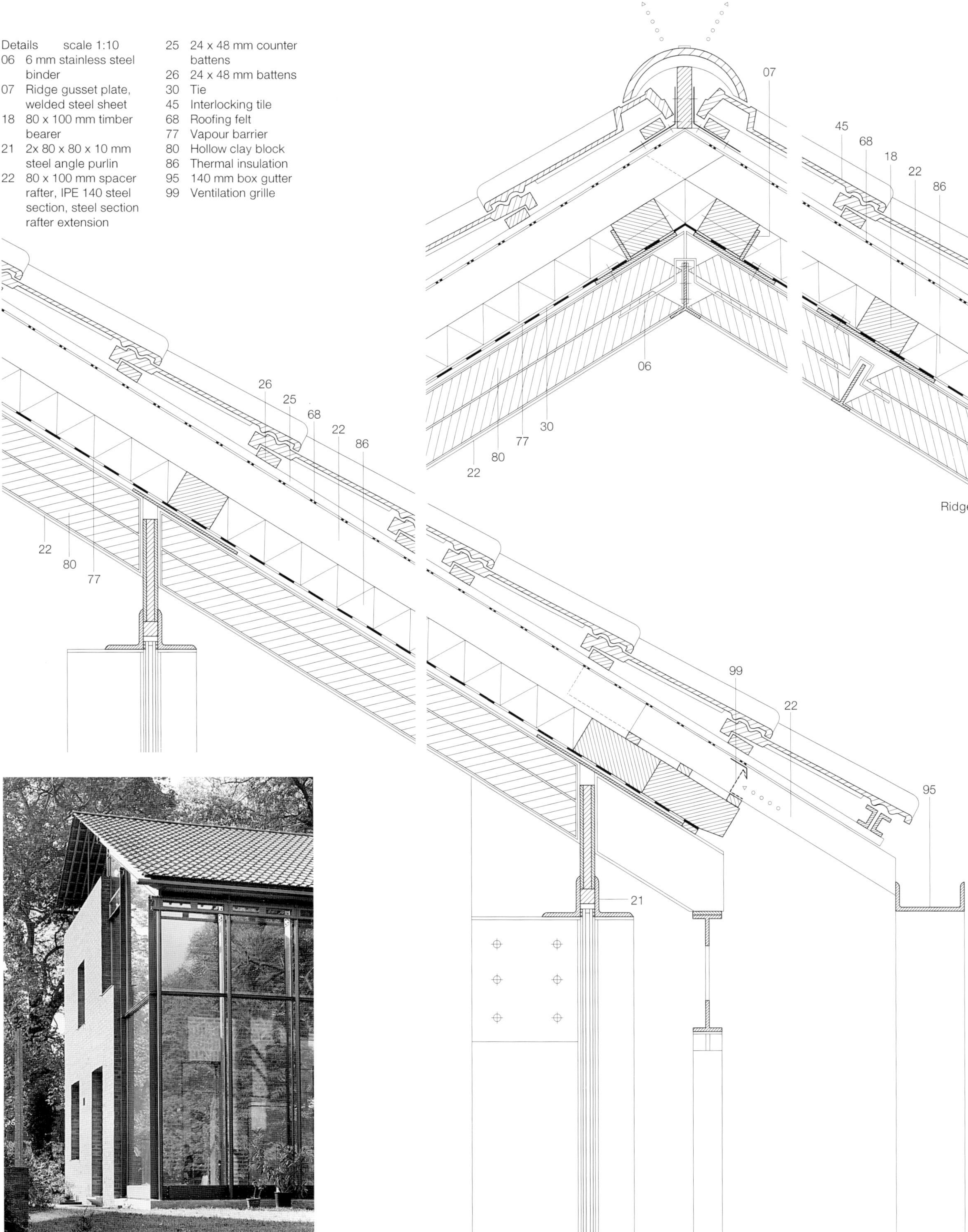

Ridge

Southwest side

Eaves

**Hotel in Mainz-Weisenau**
1999-2001

Architect: Max Dudler, Berlin/Zurich
Assistant: Thomas Kröger
Structural engineer: Büro Idstein-Hof, Mainz
Clients: Rosemarie and Rainer Schreeb, Mainz

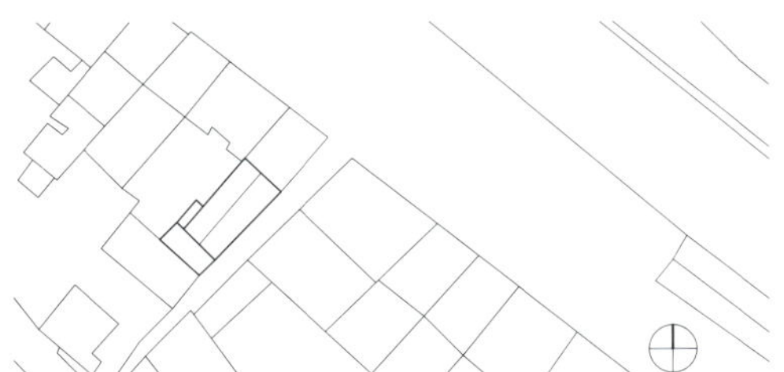

Site plan scale 1:1500

This new building lies close by the Rhine, within a conservation area of the town of Mainz. Visitors enter the hotel via a forecourt surrounded by low walls.

At ground floor level are the foyer, reception area, bar and breakfast room, plus an office and the cleaner's room. On each of the three upper floors are two guest rooms, all furnished simply. Reinforced concrete was used for the walls, columns and floors of the building.

The narrow structure is clad entirely in Portuguese granite, which gives a monolithic impression. Only on the end walls is the envelope pierced by narrow, high-format windows, set flush with the facade.

The covering for the close couple roof is also of granite, the slabs fixed in a staggered arrangement on a frame of steel sections. The joints between the slabs are left open. The non-ventilated roof structure has 180 mm of mineral wool insulation, laid between the rafters.

The rainwater deflected by the roof seal is carried away along a box gutter, which is invisible from the outside of the building.

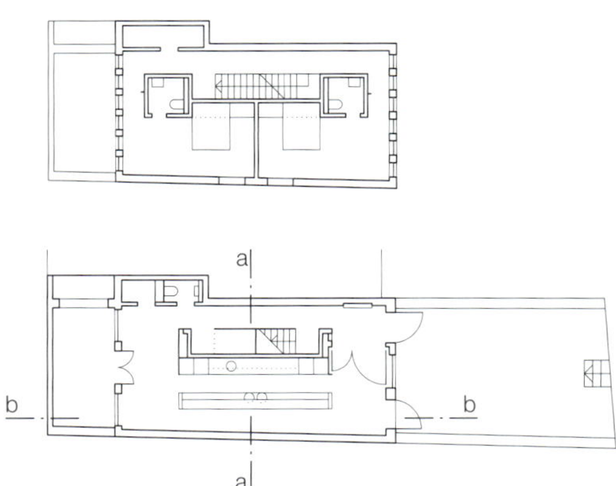


Sections • Upper floor, ground floor scale 1:250

Side facing the River Rhine

Details scale 1:10

00 80 x 8 x 140 mm flat steel
01 Dowel
06 Bracket
07 2x 90 x 140 x 3 mm steel struts
15 160 mm reinforced concrete wall
18 120 x 120 x 15 mm continuous steel angle
22 180 x 8 mm rafter
26 Metal frame, 36 x 48 mm support battens
28 24 x 48 mm filler batten
32 28 mm timber decking
34 10 mm plasterboard panels, laid double and crosswise
44 30 mm Portuguese granite tile
60 Cover sheet
63 Drip sheet
75 Polymer base roofing felt
77 Vapour barrier
79 Silicon seal
80 Thermal insulation
86 180 mm mineral wool
95 Rainwater gutter

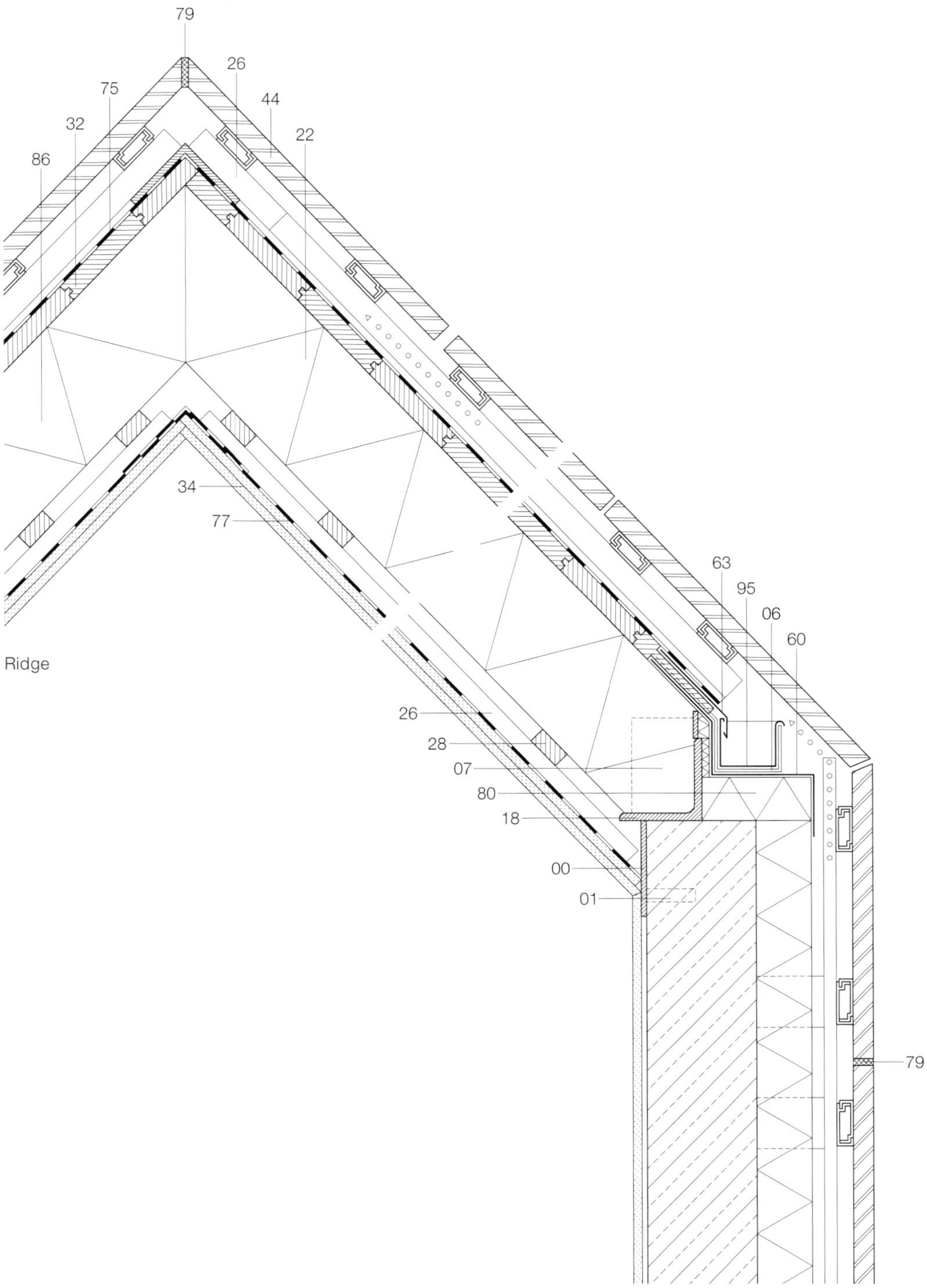

Ridge

Eaves

View towards the Rhine

Passageway

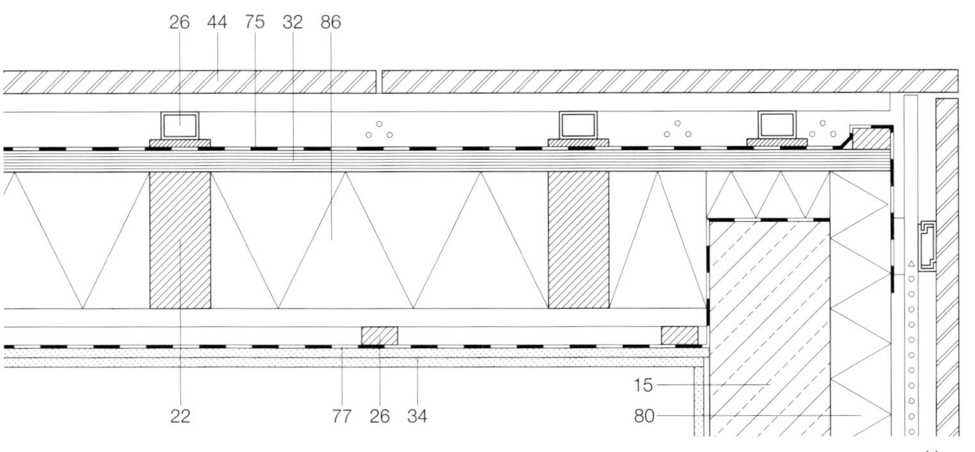

Verge

**Holiday home by Lake Ossiach, Carinthia**
1977

Architect: Manfred Kovatsch, Munich
Structural engineer: H. Lintl, Munich
Client: C. Kolig

Southeast side

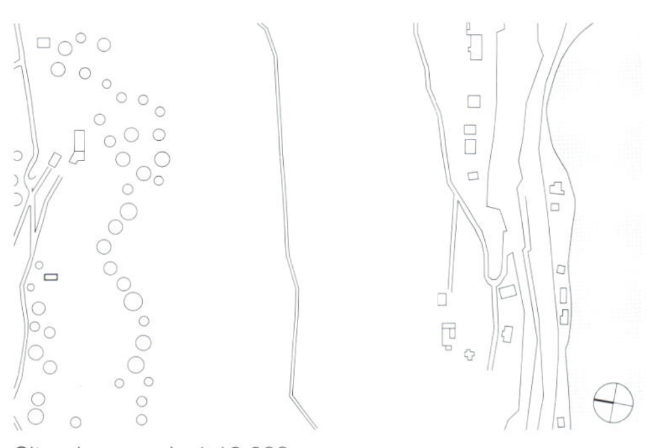
Site plan scale 1:10 000

This holiday home stands on a steep slope about 300 metres above Lake Ossiach, a position that affords wonderful views of the Karawanken mountain range and the Julian Alps. The ridge line of the farmhouses and hay barns in the surrounding district is at right angles to the gradient, the narrow sides of the buildings backed onto the precipitous slope. Taking up this idea, the house is designed to disturb the terrain as little as possible. Its entrance is at the top, the height of the building determined by the angle of the slope and the depth of the house. The exterior walls are clad with larchwood, in keeping with the materials commonly used in the area. In form, the roof also follows the vernacular, with a wide overhang to the south, protecting the terraces and the fully glazed south side.

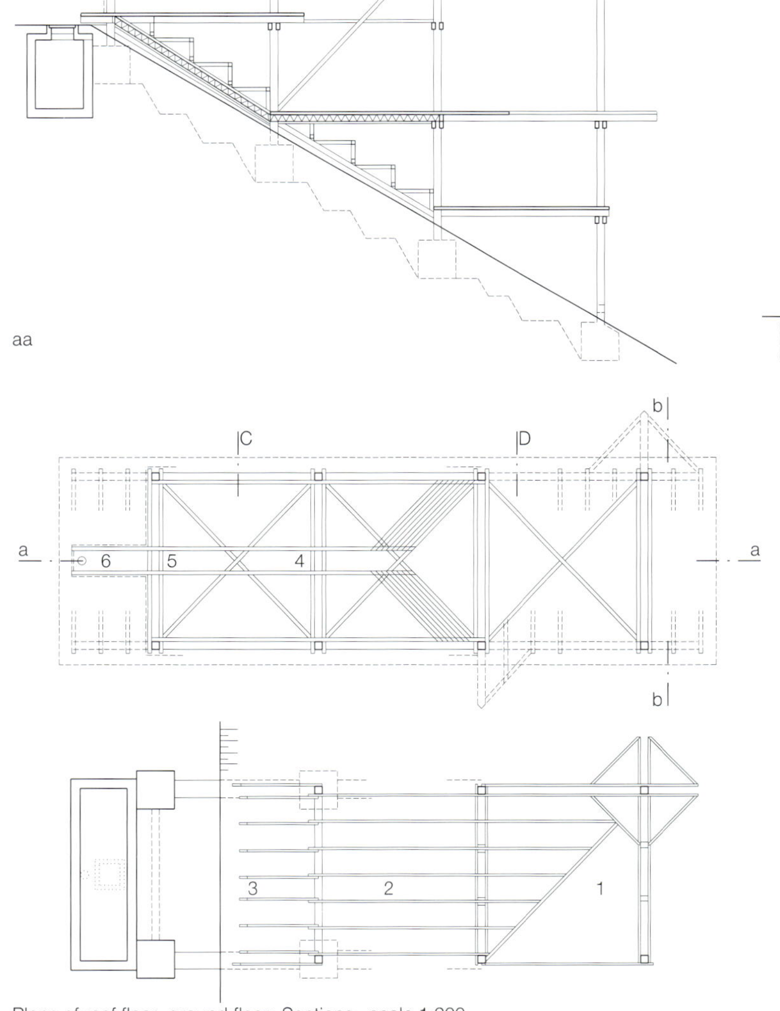


1 Terrace
2 Living area
3 Kitchen/dining area
4 Sleeping area
5 Bathroom
6 WC

Plans of roof floor, ground floor • Sections scale 1:200

The roof is a purlin roof made of spruce, a good choice for the cantilever in the direction of the ridge. To keep the roof structure visible on the inside as well as on the outside, the rafter structure is two-layer. Roof and building skeleton form a single entity.

In order to achieve this uniformity on the building envelope, too, the covering chosen for the roof was the same as the cladding used on roofs of old barns in the surrounding area. It consists of a triple-layer ventilated larchwood construction. Below this, another layer of decking and roofing felt provides additional sealing, while two 60 mm mats of rock wool take care of thermal insulation.

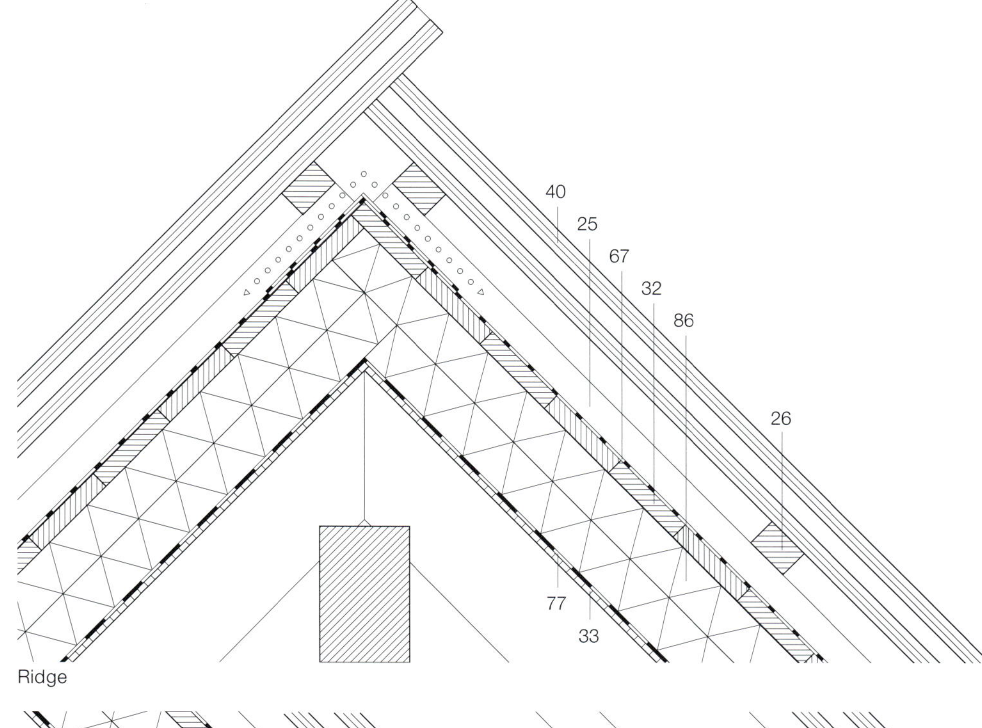


Ridge

South side

99
33
86
40
24

Eaves section C-C

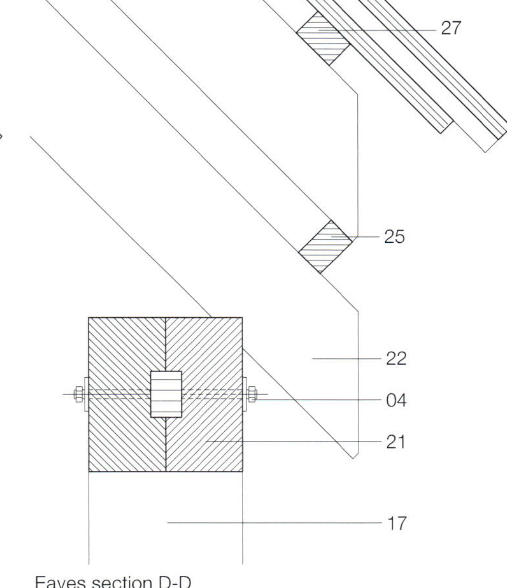


Eaves section D-D

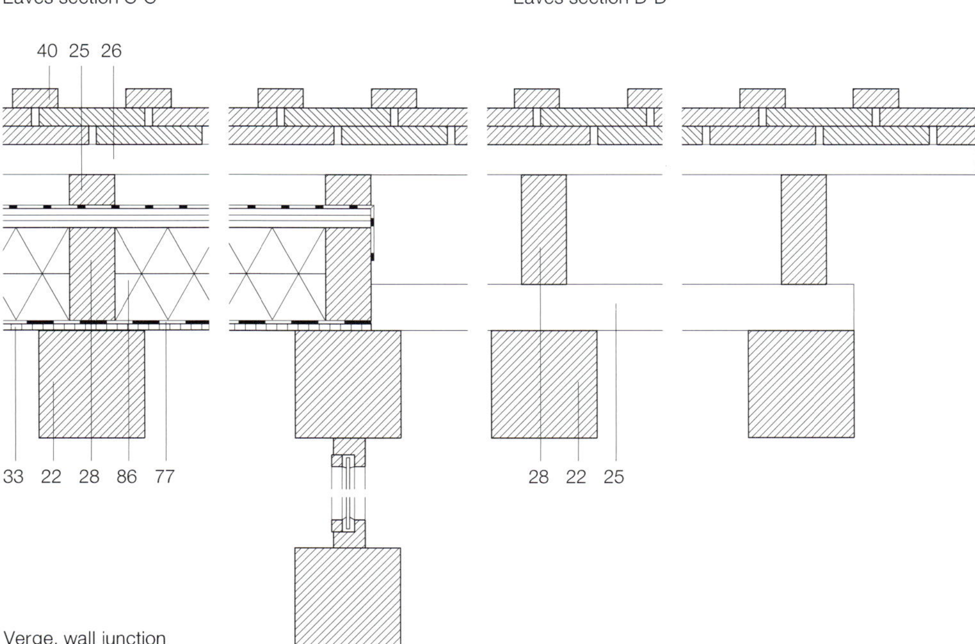


Verge, wall junction

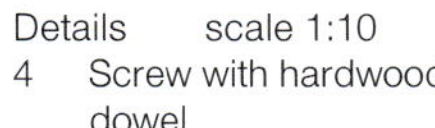

Details scale 1:10

- 4 Screw with hardwood dowel
- 17 200 x 200 mm glued laminated spruce column
- 21 2 x 100 x 200 spruce eaves purlins
- 22 140 x 140 mm spruce rafter
- 24 50 x 100 mm horizontal member
- 25 40 x 60 mm spacer batten
- 26 40 x 60 mm batten
- 27 Eaves batten
- 28 60 x 120 mm filler
- 32 24 mm decking
- 33 8 mm spruce plywood panel
- 40 Roof covering, 24 x 140 mm larch, triple-layer (roof), 22 x 140 mm tongue and groove larch boarding (wall), impregnating scumble
- 67 Bitumen sheeting
- 77 Synthetic sheeting
- 86 Rock wool, 2x 60 mm in roof
- 99 Ventilation grille

### Holiday home in Elvenes, Steindalen

Architect: Tord Kvien, Oslo
Structural engineer: Ivar Johansen
Storsteinnes Trelasthandel as, Storsteinnes
Client: Marit and Asbjørn Kvien

Site plan scale 1:4000

This holiday home is located in the far north of Norway, on the edge of a tiny settlement of farmhouses on Lyngenfjord near Troms. It is built on a slope leading straight down to the sea.

The southeast side, with its glazed living room, looks onto the fjord and to the sea and mountains beyond. The bedrooms in the northwest corner are buried almost entirely into the slope. They are lit and ventilated by means of recesses in the middle of the house, a feature that also protects the entrance and forms a terrace. Above the bedrooms is a boat shed accessible from the outside.
The roof is a close couple roof. In the remaining part of the house the rafters rest on timber columns, to provide extra storage space. As the roof storey is used as a boat shed rather than a living space, the deck above the ground floor is insulated, and not the roof. The roof decking consists of pressure impregnated spruce boards fitted with expansion joints; the boards are laid in two offset overlapping layers, and nailed to the counter battens. This prevents water penetration and also provides for the weather-related deformation of the wood.

North side

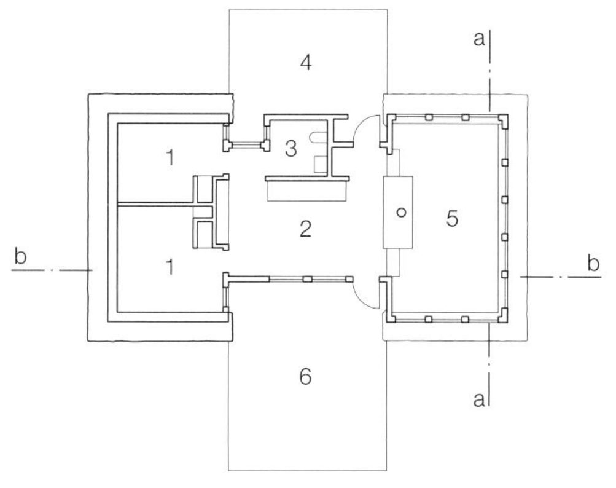


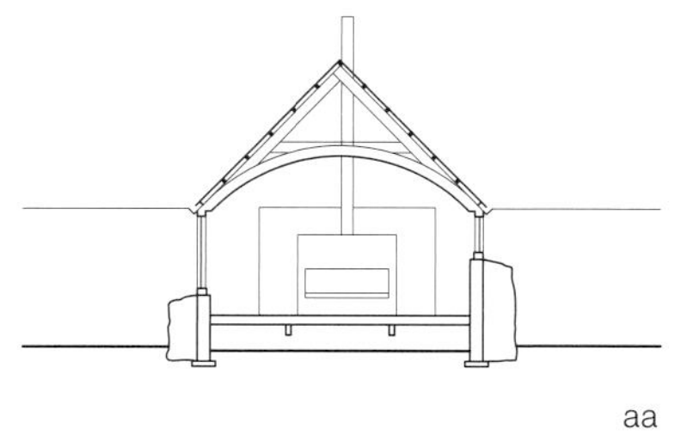


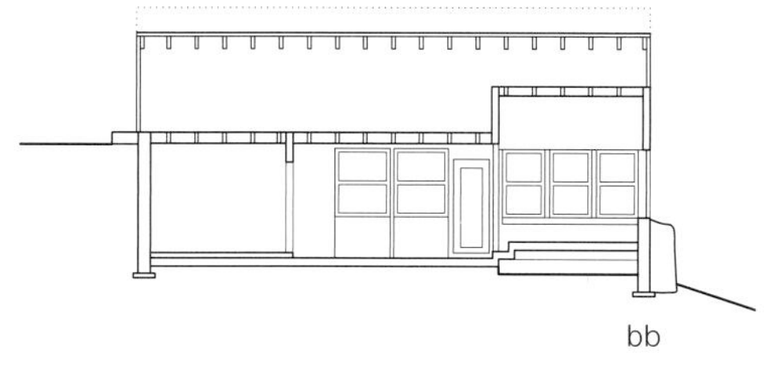


Plan • Sections scale 1:250

1 Bedroom
2 Kitchen
3 Bathroom
4 Terrace
5 Living room
6 Entrance

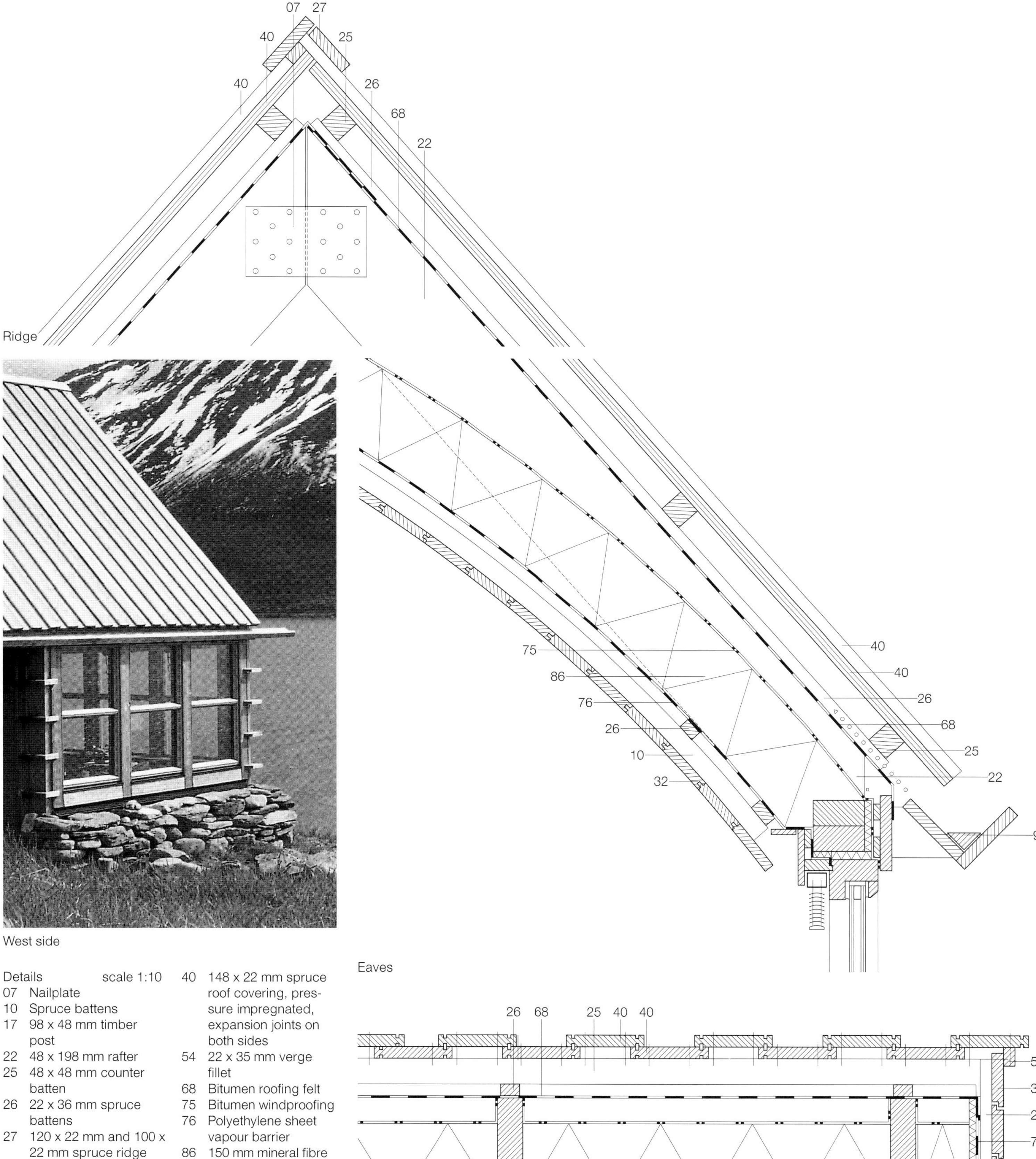


Ridge

West side

Eaves

Verge

Details scale 1:10

07 Nailplate
10 Spruce battens
17 98 x 48 mm timber post
22 48 x 198 mm rafter
25 48 x 48 mm counter batten
26 22 x 36 mm spruce battens
27 120 x 22 mm and 100 x 22 mm spruce ridge board, pressure impregnated
32 18 mm tongue and groove spruce decking
33 13 mm bituminised soft fibreboard
35 22 x 100 mm timber panel
40 148 x 22 mm spruce roof covering, pressure impregnated, expansion joints on both sides
54 22 x 35 mm verge fillet
68 Bitumen roofing felt
75 Bitumen windproofing
76 Polyethylene sheet vapour barrier
86 150 mm mineral fibre mat
95 184 x 22 mm spruce rainwater gutter, pressure impregnated, triangular fillet to create slope, silicone sealed joints, oil-based paint on inside

**Detached house in Regensburg**
1979

Architect: Thomas Herzog, Munich
Assistant: V. Herzog-Loibl
Structural engineer: Natterer & Dittrich, Planungsgesellschaft, Munich
Client: W. and M. Burghardt

Garden side

Site plan scale 1:3000

The wedge-shaped house stands in a 1950s residential area featuring some high-rise buildings. A stream runs through the plot, and a number of mature trees stand within the boundaries. Both the shape of the building and the covering materials used form a sharp contrast to the natural surroundings. Built on a 900 x 900 x 450 mm structural grid, the geometry is clear to see on both the inside and the outside.

The house is divided linearly into four zones, each with a different function: the access path between the house wall and the plant trellis; ancillary rooms with domestic installations; the main rooms; and the temperature buffer zone with its two conservatories.

The building and roof frames, both of glued laminated timbers, form a constructional and structural unit.

The load-bearing frame consists of triangular trusses, with additional support for the rafters

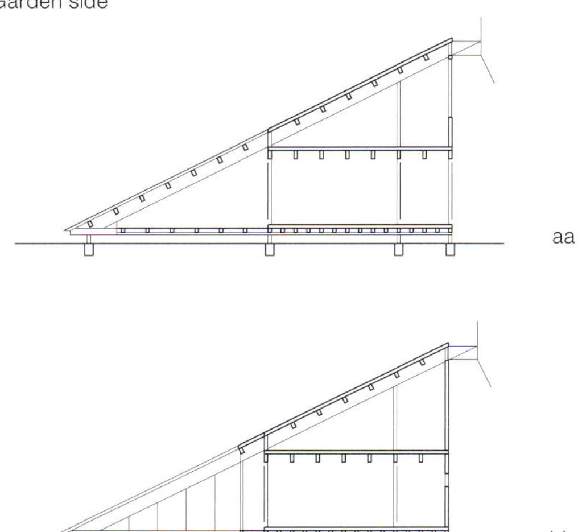


Plans of ground floor, upper floor, sections
scale 1:300
1 Entrance hall, lobby
2 Living room with fireplace
3 Dining room
4 Bedroom
5 Dressing room
6 Sauna
7 Heating
8 Conservatory
9 Veranda
10 Gallery
11 Guest area
12 Integrated one-room apartment
13 Void
14 Glass roof

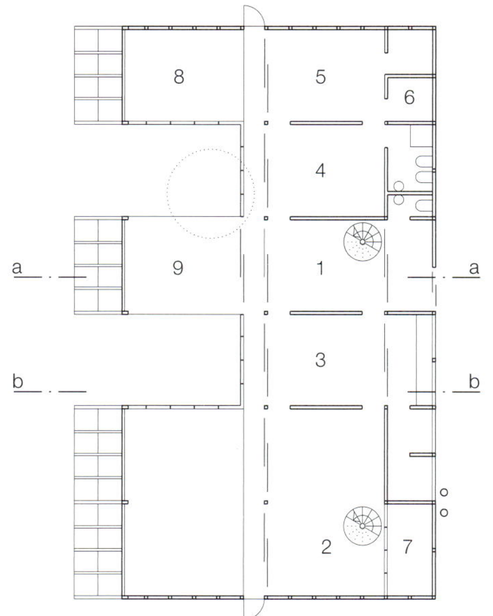


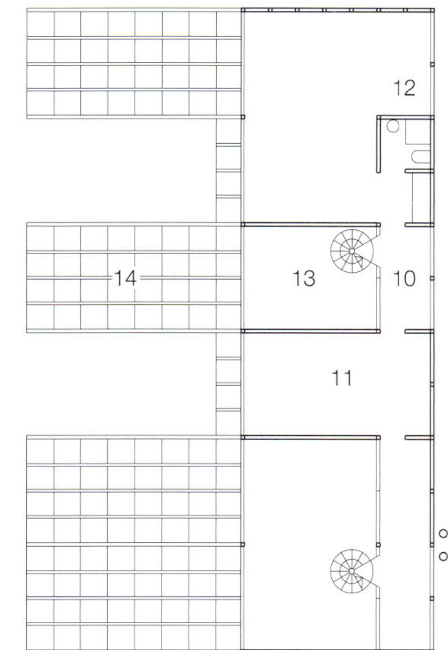


Plans of ground floor, upper floor• Sections scale 1:300

Entrance side

Details scale 1:10

00 Railing frame, 60 x 30 x 3 mm galvanised steel angle
06 Galvanised steel gutter bracket
20 Spruce cantilevered beam, glued laminated spruce section, 2x 70 x 400 mm, all 3.60 m
21 80 x 160 mm glued laminated purlin, all 1.0 m
22 Softwood rafter (grade: GK II), 60 x 140 mm, all 0.9 mm
24 Glued laminated horizontal member, 40 x 140 mm and 120 x 290 mm
28 Filler board
29 Galvanised steel cover strip (St 37)
33 18 mm chipboard (20 mm larch veneer on inside)
35 4 mm galvanised steel channelled plate
40 22 mm Oregon pine weatherboarding
56 Safety glass
59 Locked double welt titanium-zinc sheeting
60 1 mm titanium-zinc cover sheet
77 Aluminium-coated vapour barrier
78 Polychloroprene section
86 100 mm glass wool thermal insulation
95 Titanium-zinc sheet rainwater gutter
99 Perforated aluminium sheet

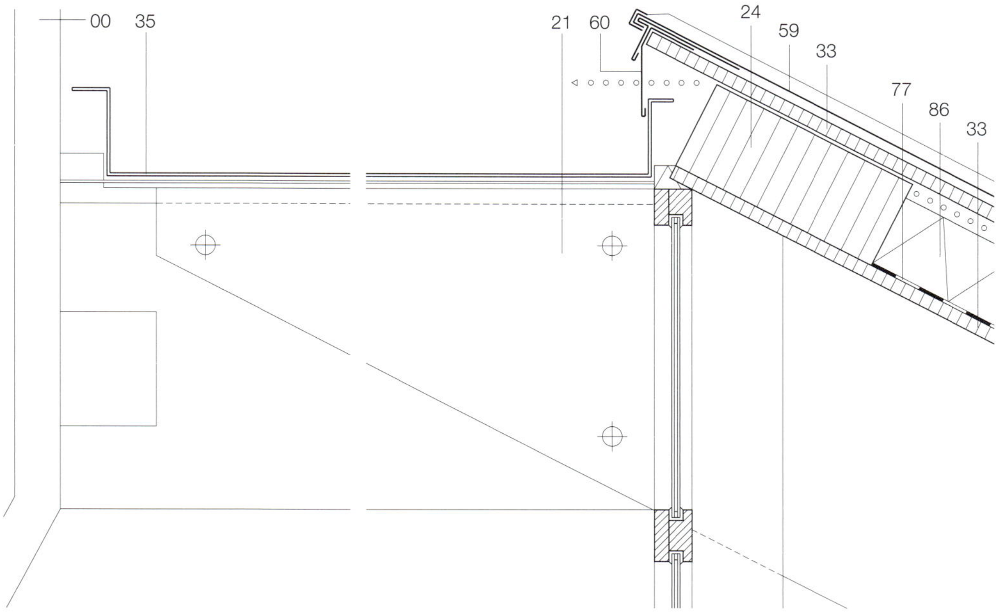

at the centre. Between the ceiling joists or rafters are purlins or secondary beams. The load-bearing structure is braced transversely by its triangular shape, longitudinally by a steel cross, and in the roof plane by veneered panels. The upper area of the monopitch roof is covered with locked double welt zinc sheeting on veneered panels, and the lower part is covered with toughened safety glass. Pressed steel battens coated in zinc sheet run the length of the fall line, holding the eaves flashing in place in the middle of the surface and the glass panes at the edge.

There is a narrow ventilation layer above the insulation. Cross ventilation in the rooms below the roof helps cool the house in summer. Energy gain in winter is limited through the relatively shallow angle of inclination of the toughened glass.

Ridge with walkway

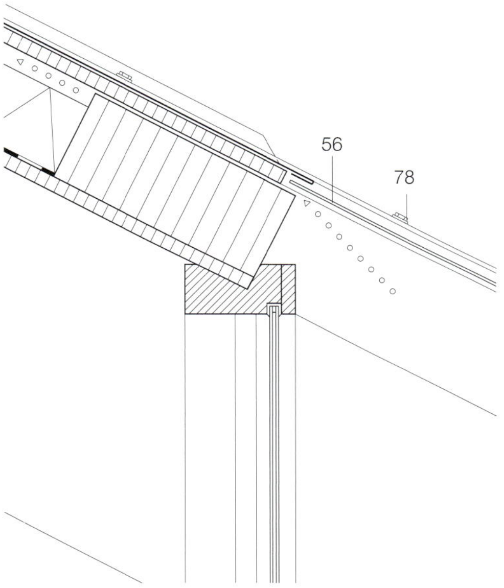

Window-wall junction

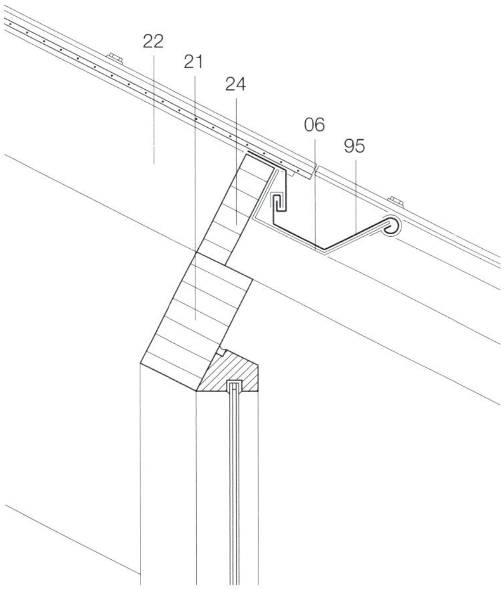

Eaves

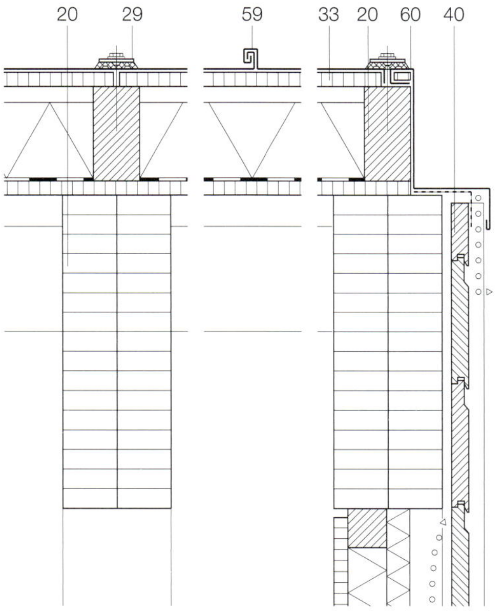

Eaves

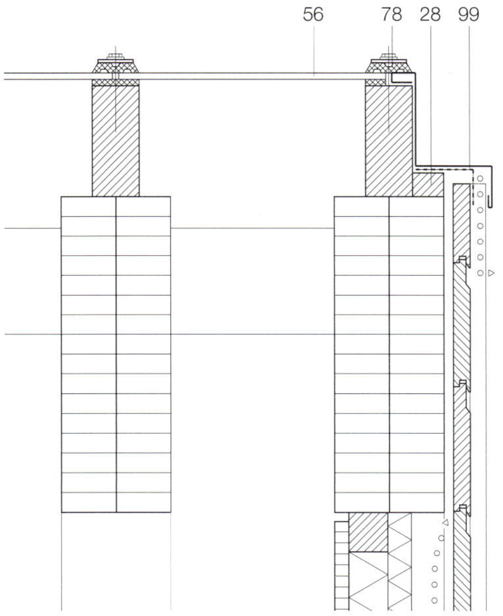

Verge, conservatory

**The Reichstag in Berlin**
1999

Architects: Foster and Partners, London
Norman Foster, David Nelson, Mark Braun
Assistants: Christian Hallmann, Ulrich Hamann, Dieter Müller, Ingo Pott
Structural engineers: Leonhard und Andrä, Stuttgart
Ove Arup Partnership, London
Schlaich, Bergermann + Partner, Stuttgart
Client: Federal Republic of Germany, represented by the Bundesbaugesellschaft Berlin

East side

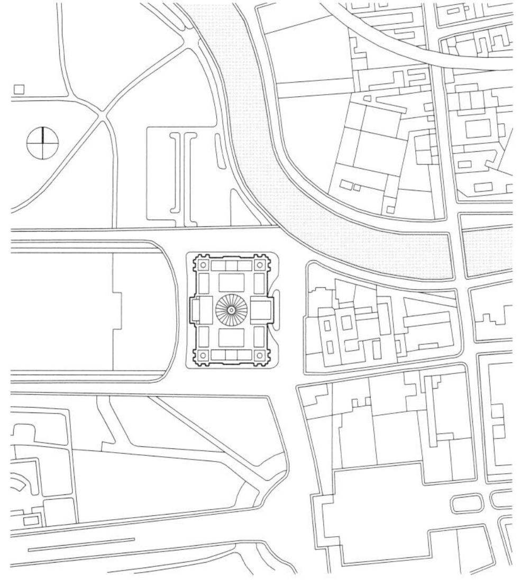
Site plan scale 1:10 000

The design for the plenary hall of the Bundestag, the lower house of the German parliament, emerged from an architectural competition in 1992. One criterion was that the building should be accessible for the public. For this purpose, a glazed dome with viewing platform and access ramps was proposed for the roof of the old Reichstag building; visitors have a view from the ramps down through a glass ceiling into the plenary hall. The dome performs key functions in the building's systems as well: a cone-shaped structure inside the dome directs daylight down into the hall below, and is important for ventilation and heating. The electrically operated solar shading element prevents overheating in summer and protects against glare.

The dome is open at the top and unheated. The actual weather-protected part of building begins at the level of the rooflight of the plenary hall.

The steel frame, measuring 38 metres in diameter at its base, and 23.5 metres in height, rests on a space frame with rotational symmetry. The 24 triangular, welded hollow-section ribs are arranged radially with 15° spacing. They are linked by 17 polygonal rings of hollow sections with trapezoidal cross section, spaced horizontally at 1.7 metres. The ribs and rings are welded to each other with cast steel components. At the upper end, the ribs are connected, via rigid connections, to a ring girder with triangular cross-section. At the base point, rigid connections link the ribs to a box-section ring; the ribs are also welded firmly to a continuous floor plate.
24 reinforced elastomer supports are arranged as an extension of the ribs, taking up horizontal loading in a tangential direction but allowing translational movement in a radial direction, to avoid problems with temperature differences.

The ramps lead upwards in a double helix, offset at 180° to each other, encircling the dome two and a half times en route. They are divided into 10.8 metre long sections rising at a gradient of 8%, and alternating with 1.2 metre long platforms. The ramps are supported by radial tension and compression members affixed to every second rib.

The viewing platform, located 16 metres above the roof terrace of the old Reichstag building, has a diameter of 17.4 metres and a central opening 6.6 metres across. It is made up of an outer and an inner ring girder welded into a box section, and a slab with cover plate. Welded between the two girders are radial and tangential ribs, made up of I-sections and plates.

The platform is suspended from a box ring girder by twelve steel reinforcing bars. On the ends are screwed fork connections of cast steel, with bolts connected to eye plates with hinged bearings.

The light cone is a funnel-shaped steel construction with a maximum diameter of 16 metres, and a height of 23.3 metres. Mounted around the cone are mirror louvres for light deflection (30 rows of mirrors, 12 mirrors in each row). The cone, which pierces the rooflight over the plenary hall, also houses
systems for ventilation, heating and smoke-venting. To assist venting of waste air, a wind-deflecting profile is mounted at the opening of the cone. This directs the stream of air over the apex of the dome.

The solar shading element consists of a spatially curved frame structure with horizontal aluminium tubes. It is electrically operated and tracks the sun fully automatically. All steel components have a base coat and three finishing coats, to protect against corrosion. All site welds are also protected against corrosion.

Laminated safety glass, made of two 12 mm panes of toughened glass, form the shingle-like covering of the dome. The maximum size of pane is 1.70 x 5.10 metres. The 17 rows of panes and the supplementary horizontal glass panes are held in place by means of aluminium glazing profiles, cast steel brackets and steel plates. Horizontally the panes of glass are connected to each other with an EPDM lip seal.

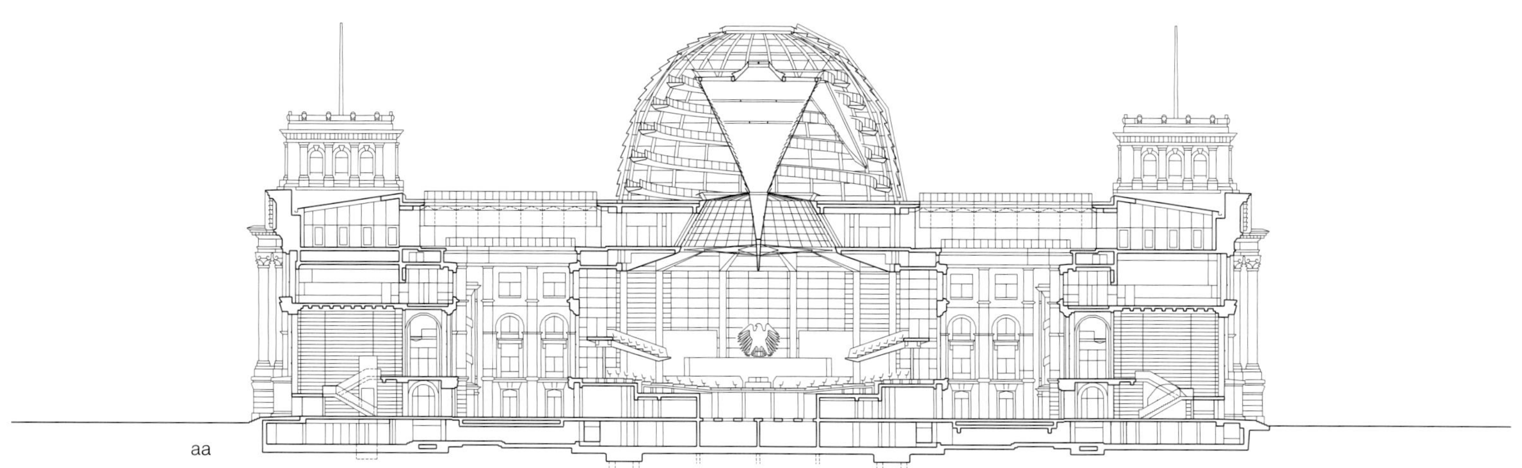


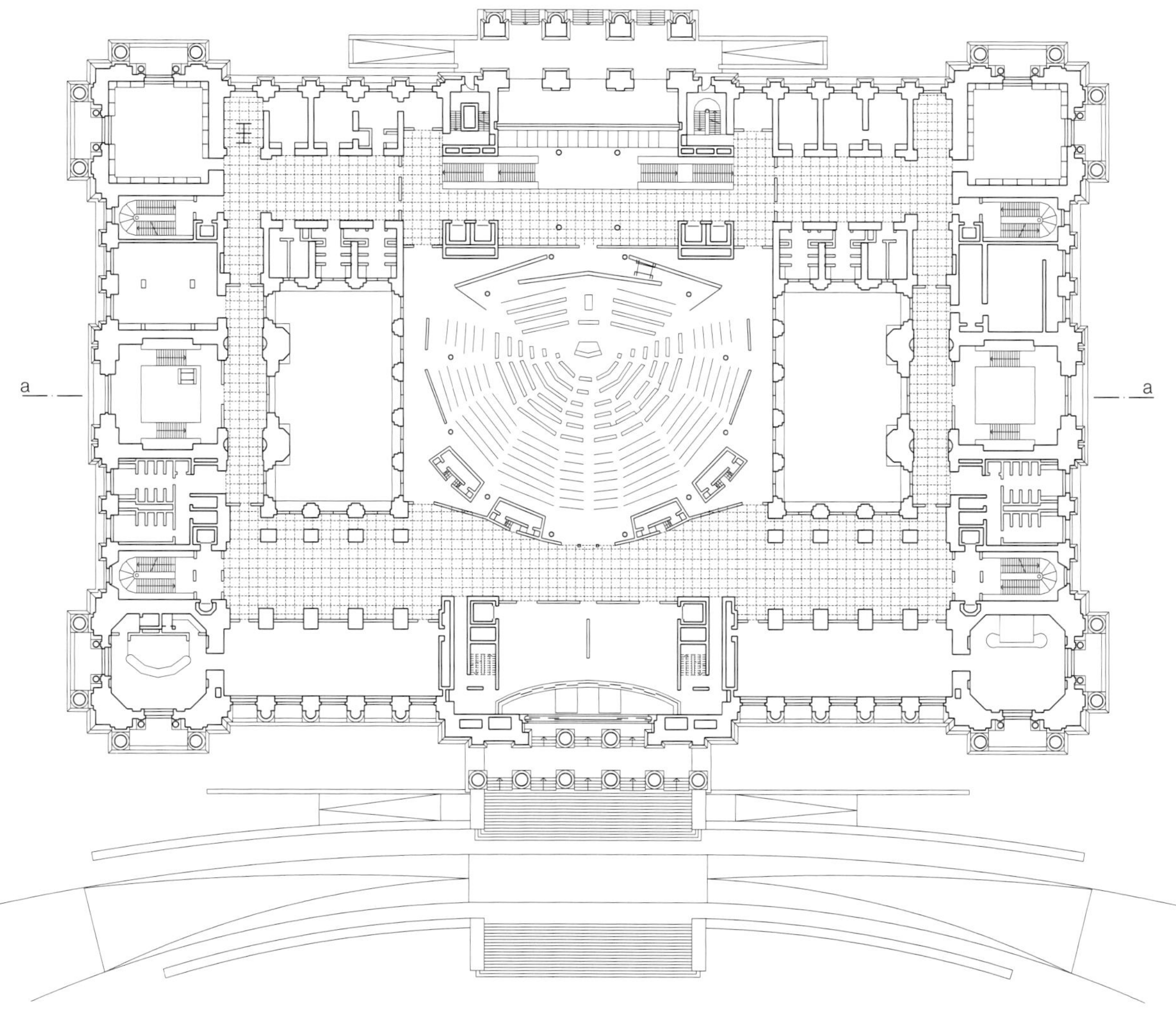


Section • Plan of plenary hall level (1st floor) scale 1:1000

Dome, partial elevation

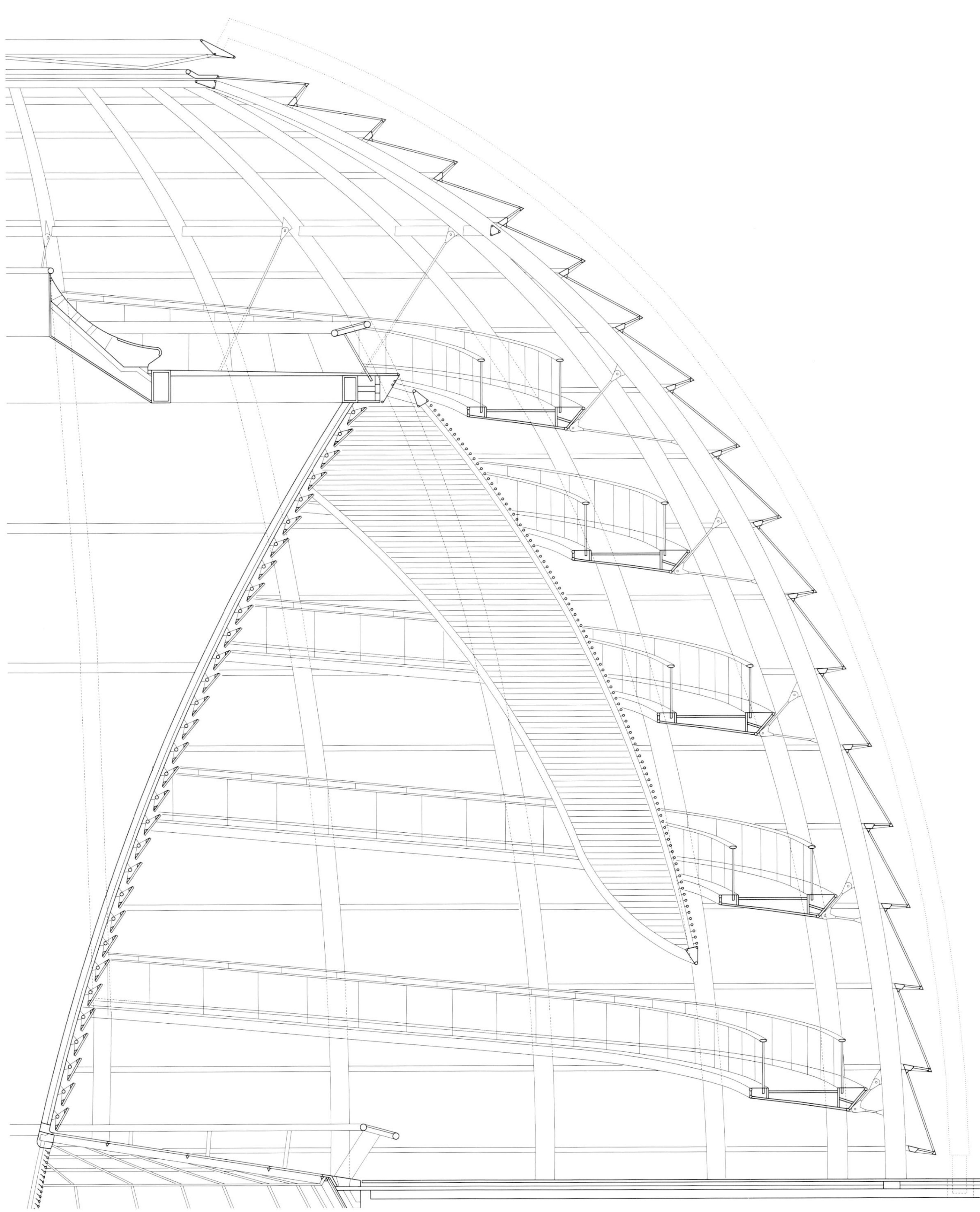

Dome, partial section scale 1:100

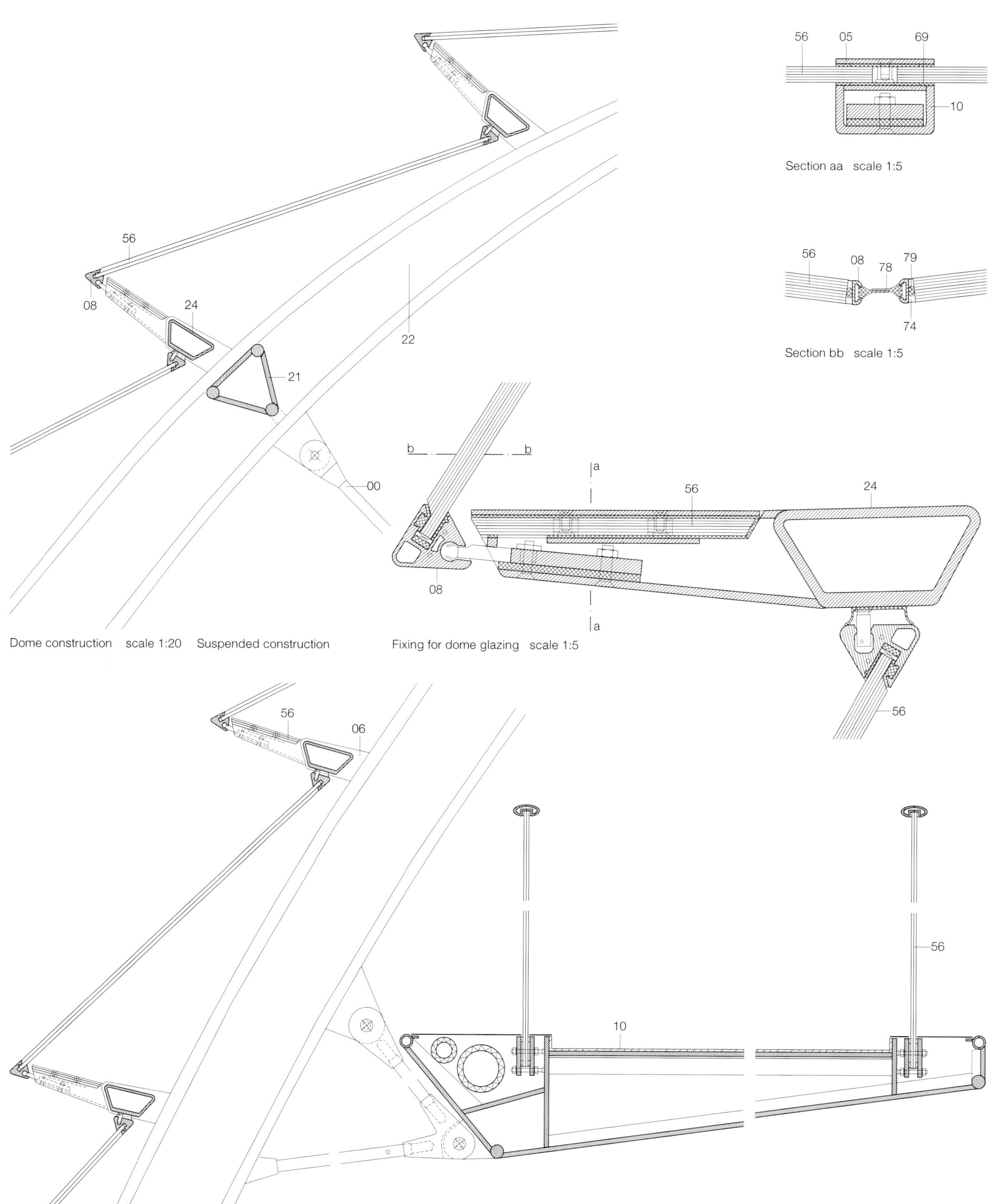


Section aa scale 1:5

Section bb scale 1:5

Dome construction scale 1:20 Suspended construction

Fixing for dome glazing scale 1:5

Dome construction scale 1:20 Ramp fixing

Apex of dome with ring girder and wind-deflecting profile

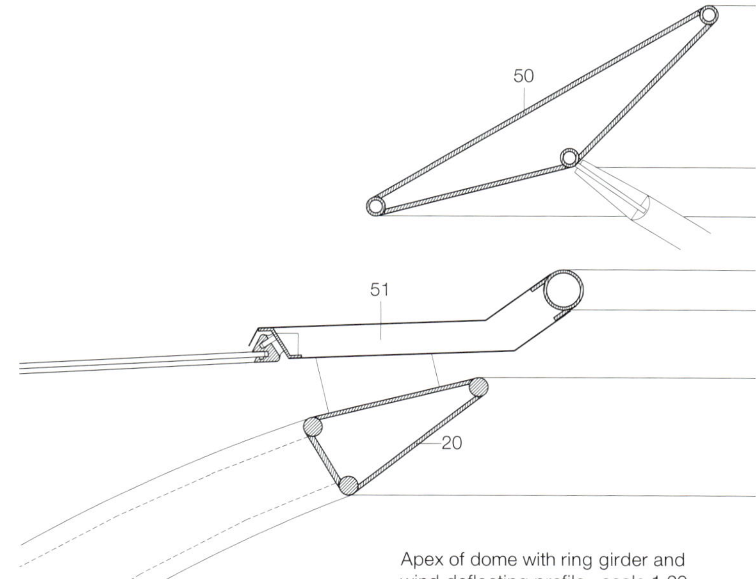

Apex of dome with ring girder and wind-deflecting profile scale 1:20

Details scale 1:5 and 1:20
00 Suspension of viewing platform, 60 mm dia. steel reinforcing bars
05 Steel batten: 3 mm steel sheet, 20 mm floor plate
06 Cast steel junction element
08 Aluminium glazing profile
10 10 mm plastic mortar on 15 mm steel plate with 4 mm damping sheet bonded on underside, cast steel bracket
18 Steel base ring, elastomer support consisting of 2 steel rings and 3 layers of elastomer
20 Ring girder: 50 mm dia. steel bar, 10 mm steel plate
21 Ring girder: 50 mm dia. steel bar, 20 mm steel plate
22 Rib of dome: 50 mm dia. steel bar, 23 mm flat steel
24 Steel section, 210 x 100 mm trapezoidal section steel
50 Wind-deflecting profile, 6 mm steel sheet
51 3 mm steel sheet, 114.3 mm dia. x 4 mm steel tube
56 Laminated safety glass: 2 panes of 12 mm toughened glass with PVG interlayer, laminated safety glass: 2 panes of 8 mm toughened glass with PVG interlayer
69 EPDM support, cellular rubber support, filler plate, built-in component
74 Elastoplastic joint seal
78 EPDM lip seal
79 Backing strip

Glass covering

Base point of rib

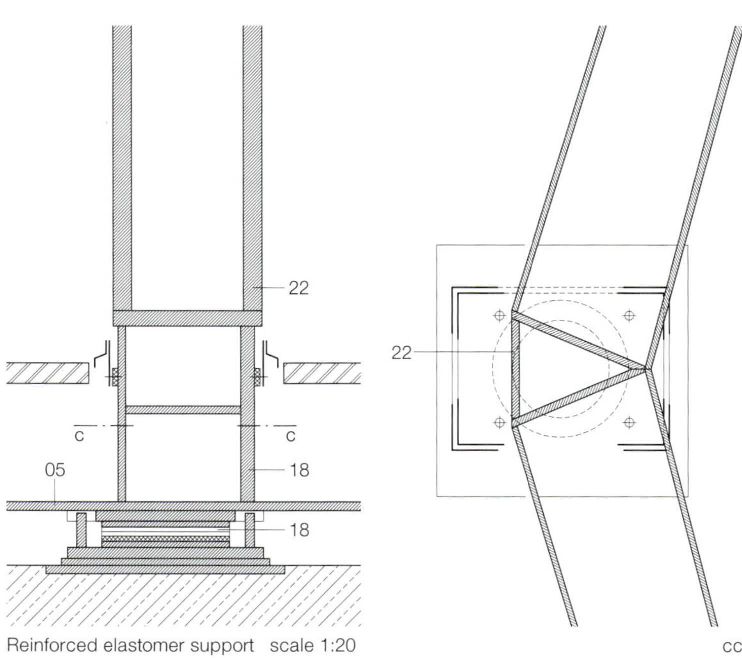

Reinforced elastomer support scale 1:20

## Roof over museum courtyard, Hamburg

1989

Architects: von Gerkan, Marg + Partner, Hamburg
Assistant: Klaus Lübbert
Structural engineer: Schlaich, Bergermann + Partner, Stuttgart
Assistant: Karl Friedrich
Design: Volkwin Marg, Jörg Schlaich
Client: Verein der Freunde des Museums für Hamburgische Geschichte e.V.

View of roof

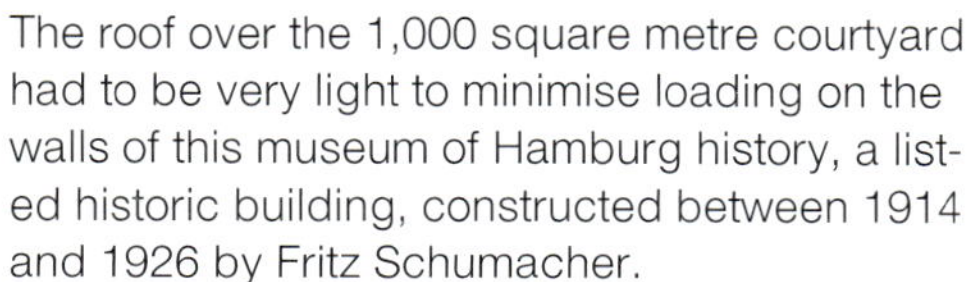

The roof over the 1,000 square metre courtyard had to be very light to minimise loading on the walls of this museum of Hamburg history, a listed historic building, constructed between 1914 and 1926 by Fritz Schumacher.

The design was a lattice shell with two barrel-vaulted sections (spans of 14 and 18 metres), connected at their intersection with a dome. With this arrangement, the loads are distributed largely through membrane compression forces, and bending stresses are avoided.

The lattice shell is made up of galvanised, white-painted flat steel sections connected to each other by pivoting joints to form a load-bearing network with a mesh size of 1.17 x 1.17 m. At 60 x 40 mm in cross-section the profiles have the minimum dimensions required to support the 10 mm thick panes of laminated safety glass, secured at the nodes with point fixings. Condensation is prevented by means of heating wires placed between the edge bearing of the glazing and the supporting bars. To ventilate the space, air exchange takes place via the edge of the roof and air vents at the apex of the barrel vault.

To prevent any skewing of the mesh structure, it was necessary to introduce diagonals, but they had to be as slim in profile as possible. It was decided to use cables, prestressed in both directions and thus able to take compression forces. The structurally "softer" barrel-vaulted areas were additionally braced with a radial arrangement of cables to cope with any high uneven loads resulting from pockets or drifts of snow building up on the roof. The lattice is supported by a steel I-section purlin 160 mm deep (HEB) which runs 70 to 90 mm above the roof of the building itself, through which it is affixed at intervals to the reinforced concrete floor and walls within. A gutter heating system ensures trouble-free drainage as the water is directed away via the museum's roof.

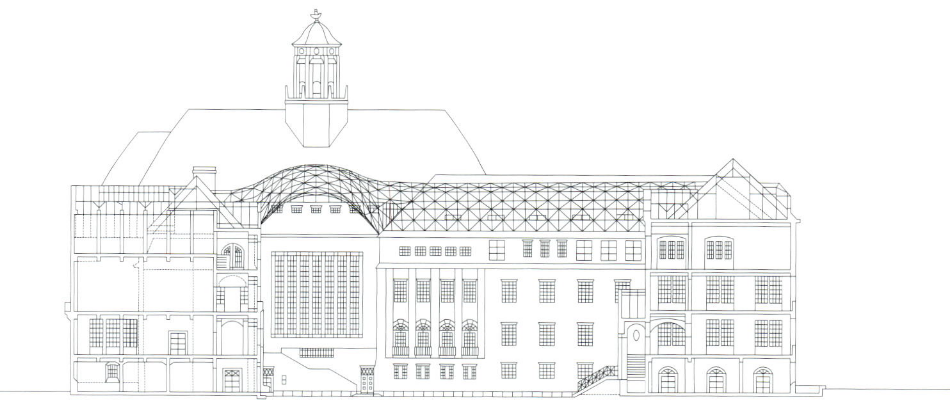


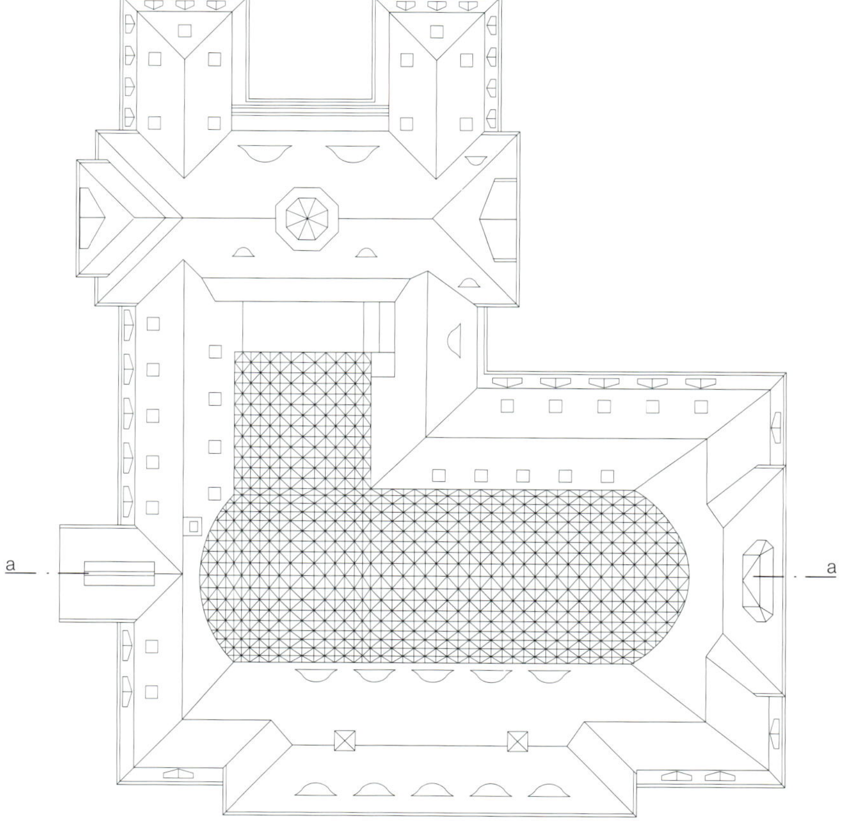


Section • Top view scale 1:750

Inner courtyard

Node

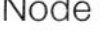

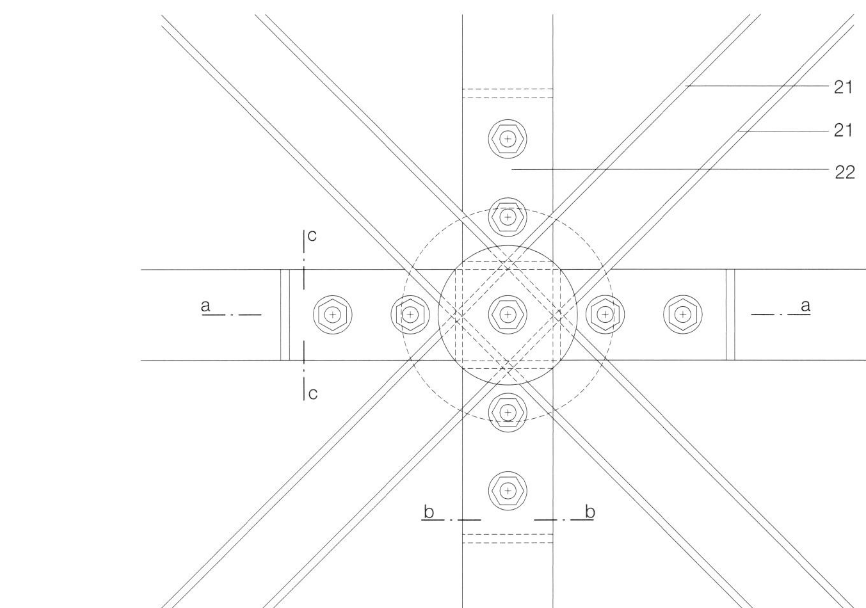

Bottom view of node scale 1:5

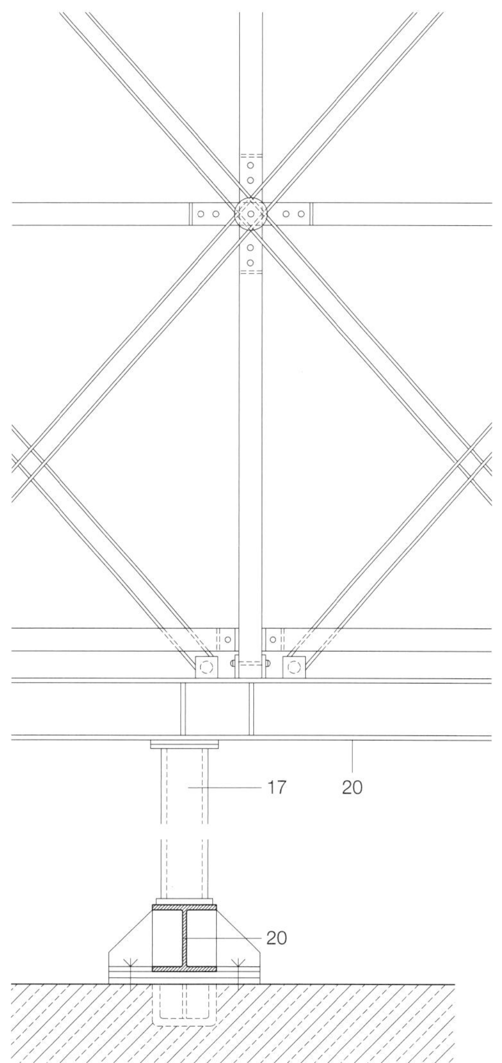

Purlin elevation scale 1:20

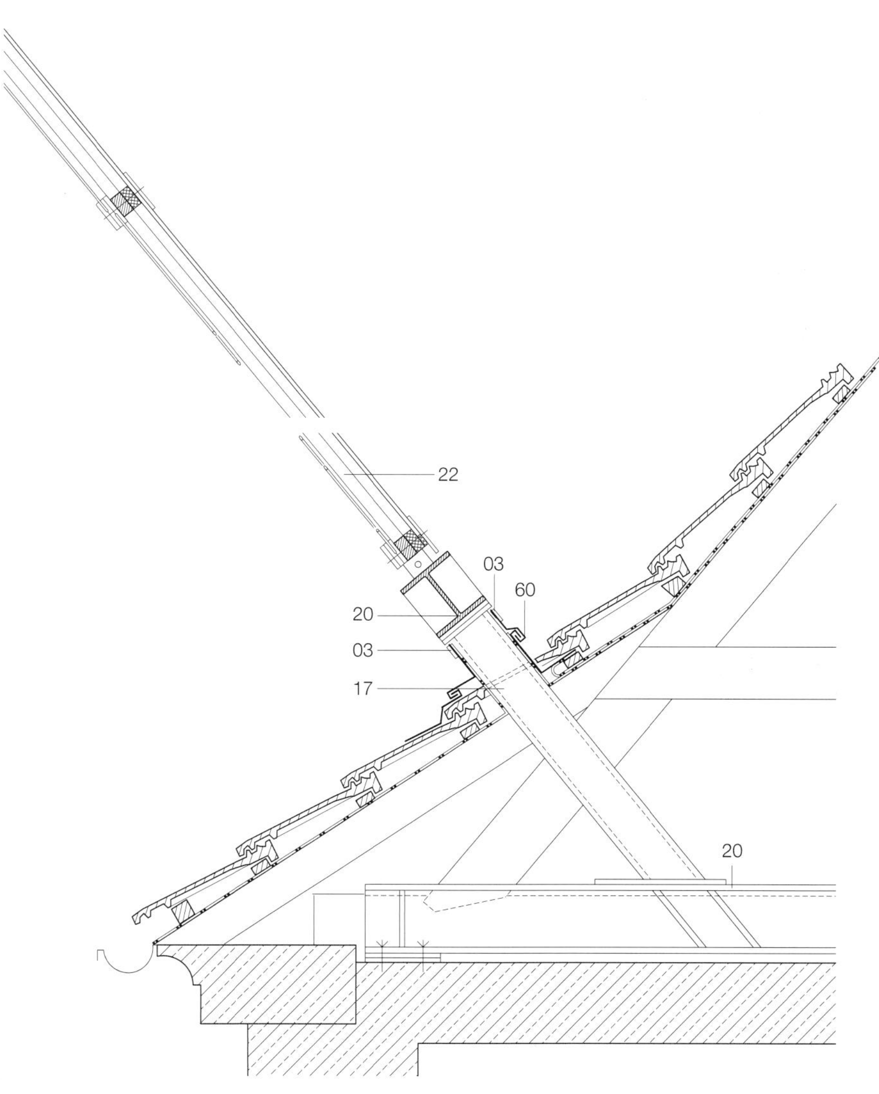

Purlin section scale 1:20

Hub

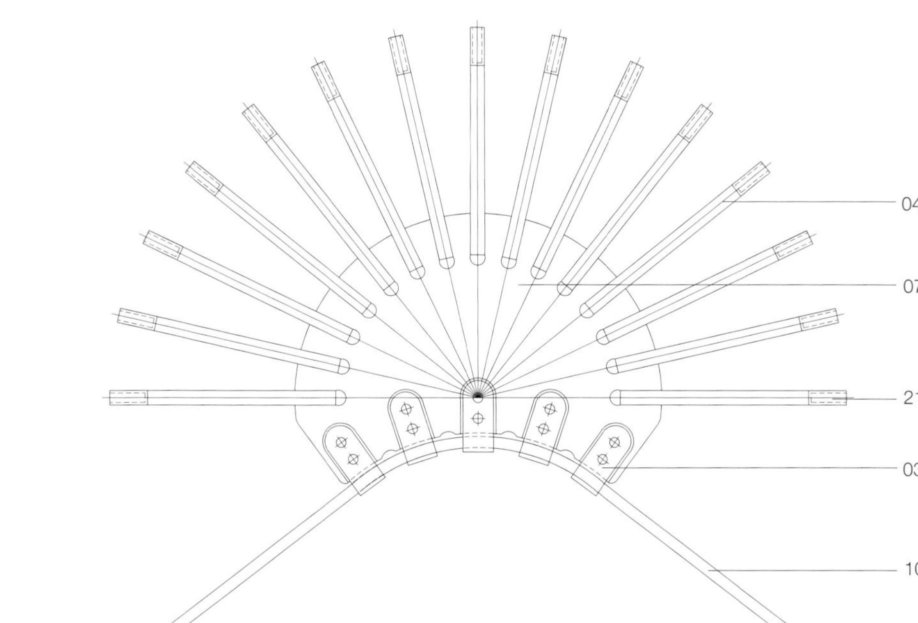


Hub scale 1:10

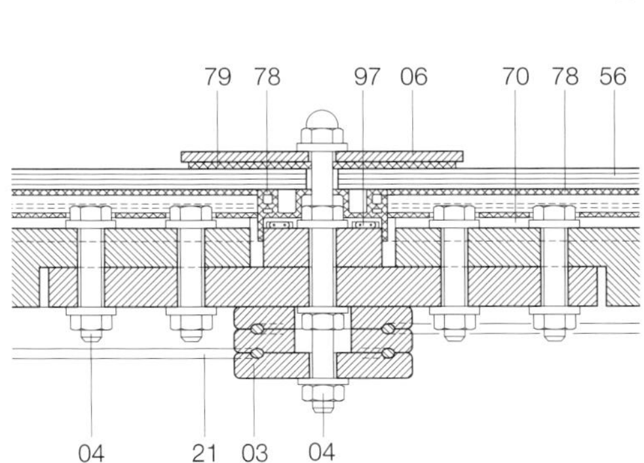


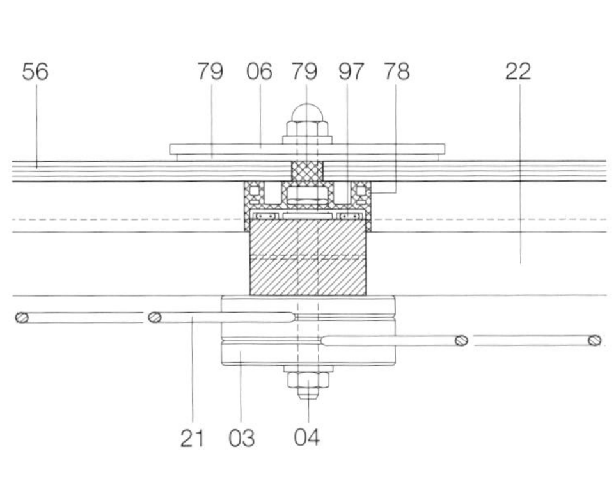


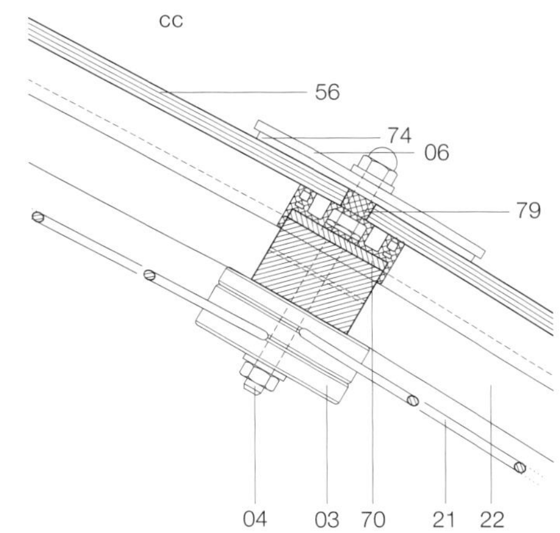


Node scale 1:5

Purlin scale 1:20
Hub scale 1:10
Node scale 1:5

03 90 mm dia. clamping discs for diagonal cables 40 x 4 mm clamping piece, pipe clamp
04 Stainless steel screws (M12), threaded bolts (M12), left-handed thread (M16) 50 mm long
06 140 mm dia. x 5 mm external plate
07 20 mm node plate
10 16 mm dia. stainless steel tension cable
17 127 mm dia. x 10 mm steel tube
20 Steel I-section support 180 mm deep (HEA), steel I-section purlin 160 mm deep (HEB)
21 2x 6 mm stainless steel diagonal tension cables, 16 mm stainless steel spokes, 16 mm stainless steel tension cable
22 Galvanised, white-painted 60 x 40 mm flat steel section
56 2 panes 5 mm laminated safety glass
60 Sleeve
70 4.5 mm spacer
74 Silicone seal
78 Neoprene section glass bearing
79 EPDM seal
97 Heating wire

Underside of roof

## Juval Castle, South Tyrol, Italy
1996

Architect: Robert Danz, Schönaich
Site manager: Konrad Bergmeister, Brixen
Structural engineer: Delta-X, Stuttgart
Albrecht Burmeister, Ekkehard Ramm, Stuttgart
Client: Reinhold Messner

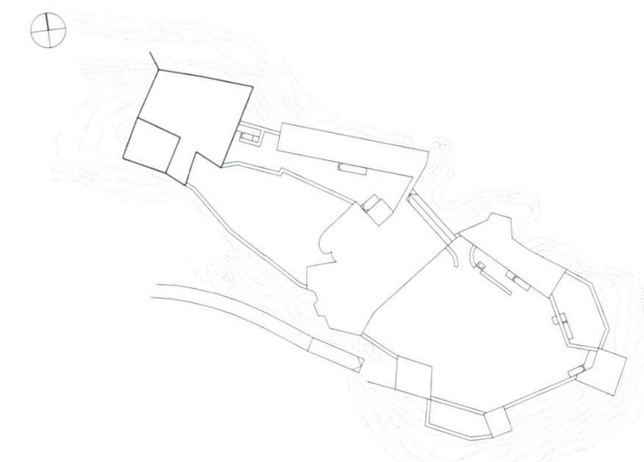

Site plan scale 1:1500

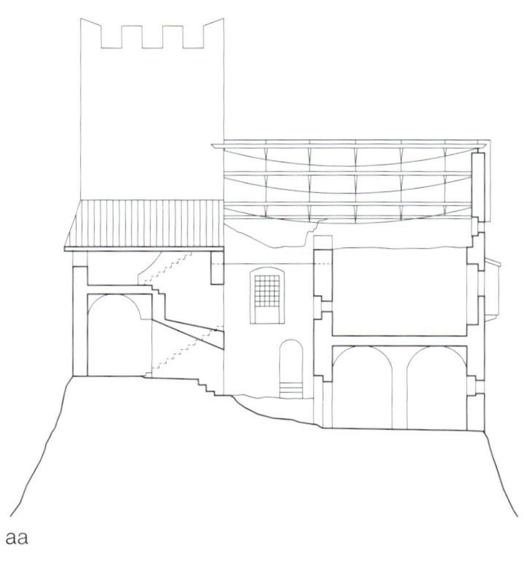

aa

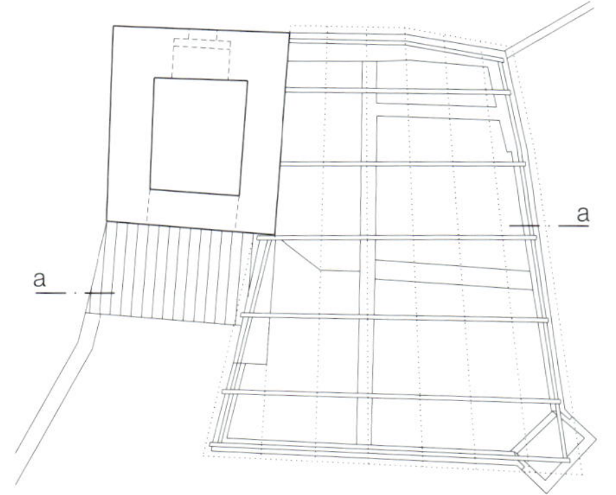


Northeast elevation • Section • Plan scale 1:400

North side

Underside of roof

Thought to have been built in the 13th century by Hugo von Montalban, the fortress has changed owners many times over the years. In 1983 it was acquired by the mountaineer Reinhold Messner, who began to renovate it.
A lightweight glass roof now prevents further deterioration of the walls, and protects Messner's exhibition.
The duopitch roof takes its cue from the shape of the original roof of the castle. Steel I-beams (HEB) were laid on the rubblestone walls to act as wall plates; they are welded at intervals to steel tubes drilled into the walls, and fixed to the upper chords of the girder trusses that span the whole space.
The overlapping glass panels, supported on four hinged point fixings and horizontal balancing arms, are also trussed on the underside in the direction of the roof pitch. Covering the entire roof, the panels are laid in a radiating pattern; different dimensions were required for each pane of glass. The roof overhangs 250-400 mm on all sides. Around the keep the upper chords of the trussed beams were set into the wall; the spacing between the glass and the wall is approximately 30 mm.

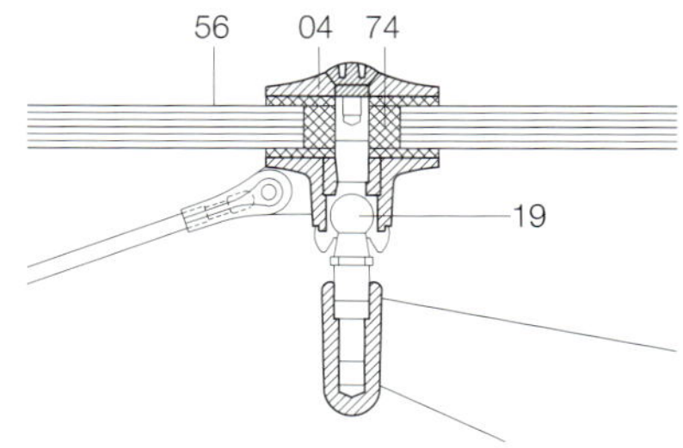


Point fixing

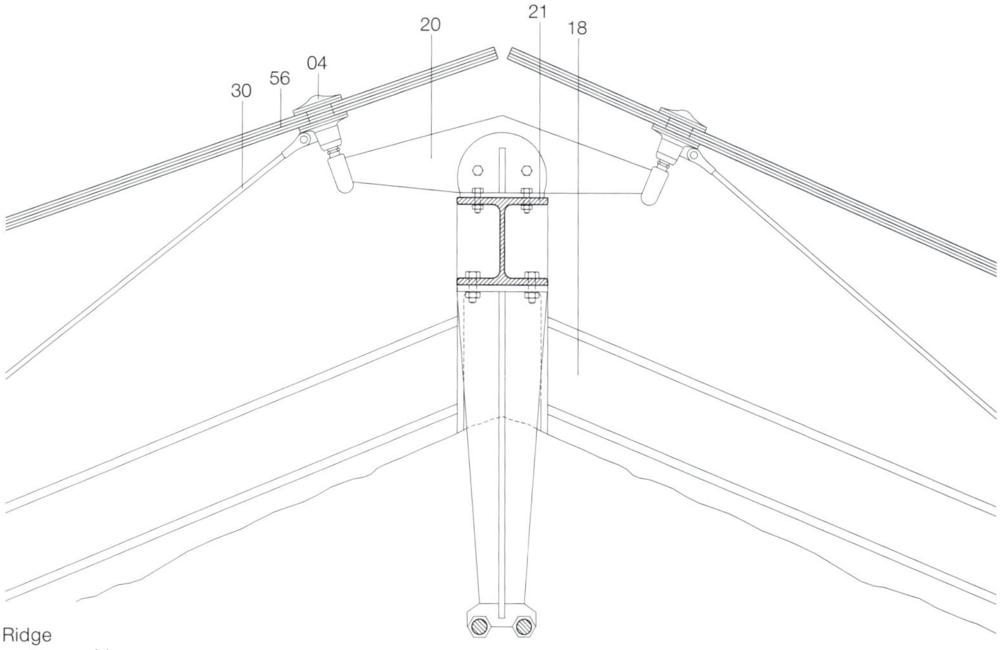

Details scale 1:10
01 50 mm dia. steel tube
04 Stainless steel point fixing
11 Rubblestone masonry
16 Levelling mortar
17 16 mm dia. x 2 mm posts
18 Steel I-section wall plate 120 mm deep (HEB)
19 Ball and socket joint
20 8 mm steel plate balancing arm
21 Steel I-beam 120 mm deep (HEA) trussed on underside
30 6 mm dia. steel tension rod
56 2 panes 8 mm laminated safety glass with PVB interlayer
74 Epoxy resin

Ridge

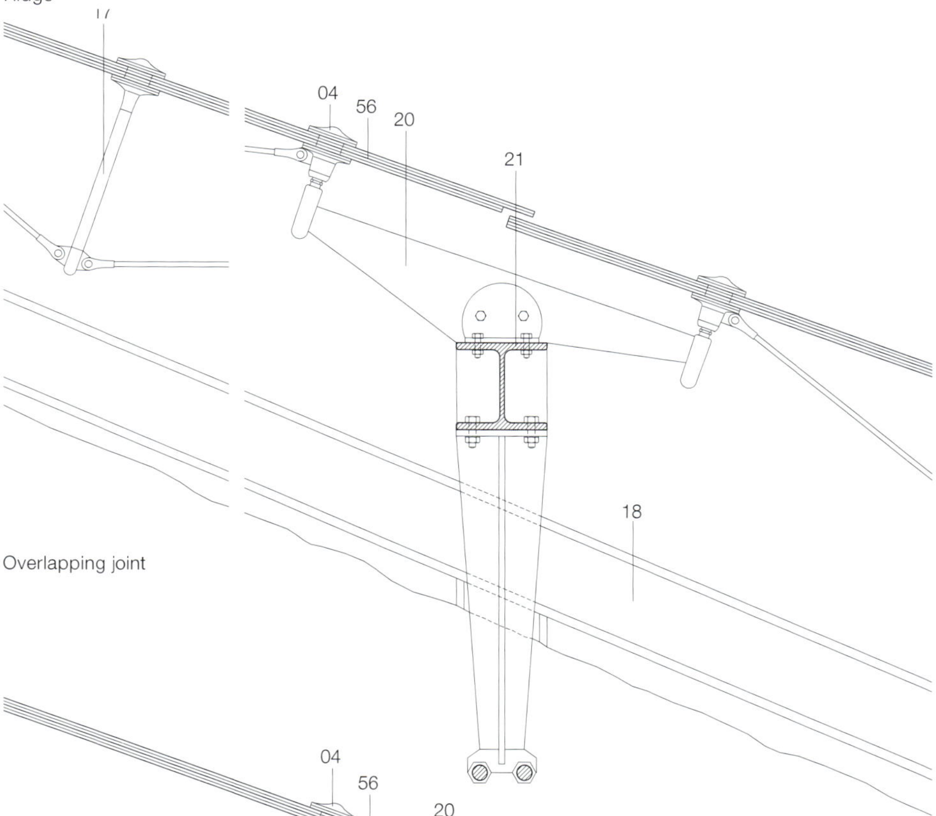

Overlapping joint

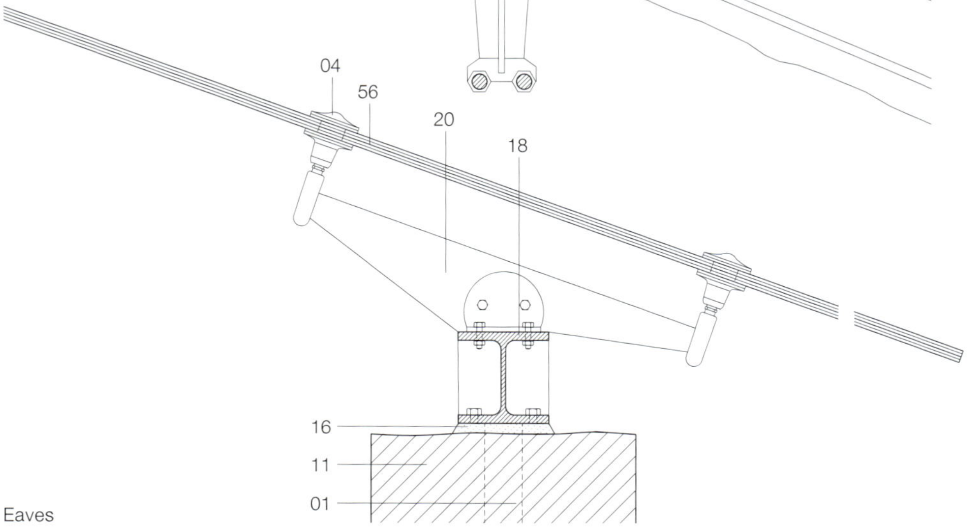

Eaves

**Olympic Swimming Pool in Munich**
1972

Architects: Behnisch und Partner, Stuttgart
Behnisch • Auer • Büxel • Tränkner • Weber
Project manager: J. Bauer
Assistants: G. Haberer, P. Rogge, W. Wolf
Landscaping: with G. Grzimek, Pfeffenhausen
Roof: Behnisch und Partner, F. Otto, Leonhardt und Andrä (Chief engineer: J. Schlaich)
Masonry: O. Höllerer
Client: Olympia-Baugesellschaft, Munich

Entrance area, view from east

The swimming pool at the southeast end of the tented landscape of Munich's Olympic sports ground has a freely designed stressed-skin geometry. Fixed in numerous places at the edges, the membrane surface is suspended from a single mast and anchored at two troughs. The roof rises towards the lake side. A pre-tensioned steel cable net with a mesh size of 750 x 750 mm forms the support structure. Aluminium clamps at the junctions of the mesh create sliding connections between the cables. Principal cables fix the cable net to the mast, which in turn is anchored to the ground with tension cables. The roof covering consists of 300 x 300 mm extruded polymethacrylic panels (Plexiglas) mounted on the junctions in the cable net via metal vibration buffers, which permit adequate movement. The panels are connected to each other with strips of chloroprene, clamped in place with aluminium battens. The chloroprene strips form channels 50 mm deep and 140 mm wide, which prevent the transverse movement of snow and rainwater. A layer of honeycomb-structure material developed from PVC sheeting is used as translucent insulation. This layer is suspended from the roof skin, on the same structural grid, with a gap of 50 cm. Air is drawn in at the edges through this air space and blown out at the highest point. This stream of air transports any moisture diffusing through the roof covering. Apron walls form the connection between the roof and the facade and absorb any differential movement. The roof of this swimming pool shows that the basic structural requirements of a pitched roof, such as shedding and ventilation, can be applied using completely new materials and under extreme load-bearing conditions.

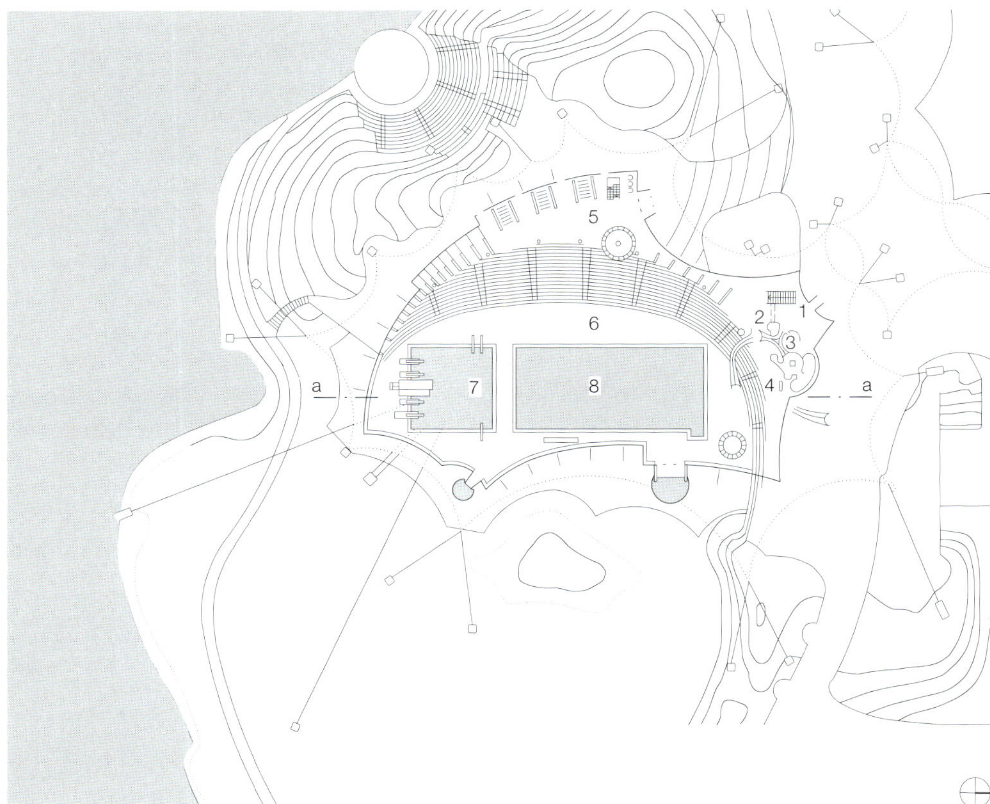

Plan • Section scale 1:2000

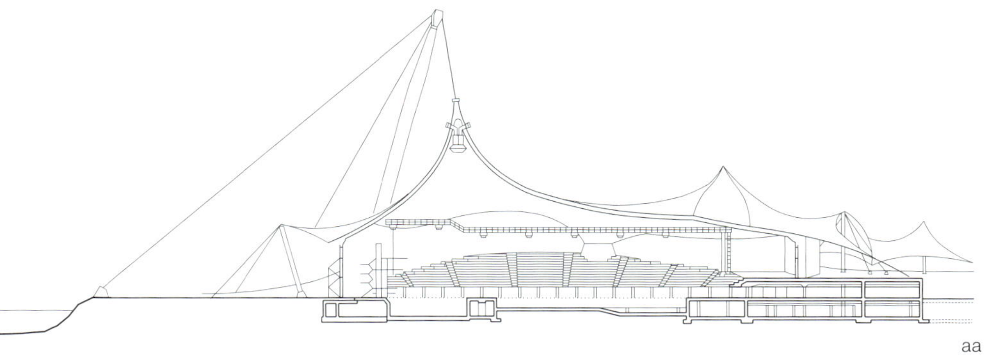
aa

1 Entrance, foyer
2 Information, kiosk
3 Post office, administration
4 Restaurant
5 Cloakroom
6 Spectator seating
7 Diving pool, diving tower
8 Competition pool

Swimming pool, view from south

Details scale 1:10

00 Articulated suspension point
03 Aluminium clamping batten
04 Screw with 78 mm dia. aluminium washer
06 Steel membrane fixing
07 Suspension plate
08 Hinge, guide rail
09 Galvanised steel tension spring (securing against wind suction), covered in plastic, steel clamp clip (St 52)
10 Deflection bracket, cable head
18 Polychloroprene-metal buffers, 16 per acrylic plastic panel, 11.7 and 16.5 mm dia. cable net junctions
20 Steel I-section columns, 240 mm deep (IPB), 240 mm deep (IPE)
21 2.3 to 3.4 mm dia. galvanised 19-strand cables
24 280 mm steel channel section with 200 x 100 x 10 mm angle section
27 45 x 45 x 3 mm hollow-section steel cantilever arm
30 Steel wire suspension point
57 Insulating glass
64 Extruded acrylic plastic panels, 300 x 300 x 4 mm (roof), double glazed (wall)
68 PVC sheeting with mesh inlay
69 Reinforced supporting membrane
70 Chloroprene vacuum profile
78 Chloroprene sealing disc
79 Chloroprene profiles
84 Multiple-layer PVC insulation
95 Chloroprene gutter
97 Heating cable

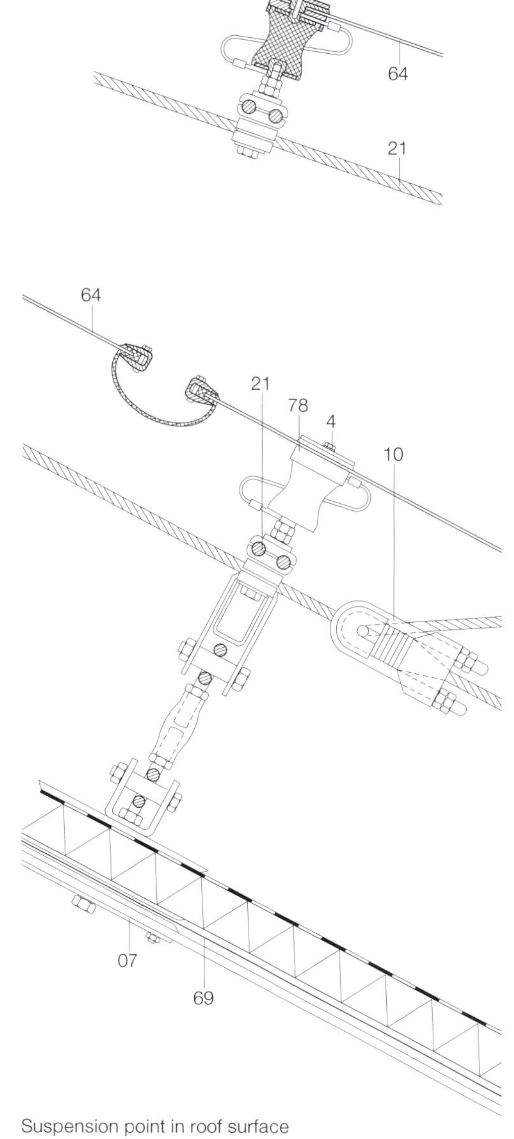


Suspension point in roof surface

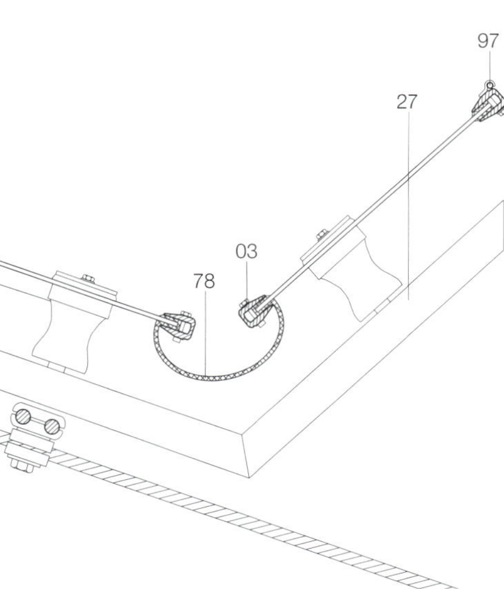

Eaves; eaves and gutter

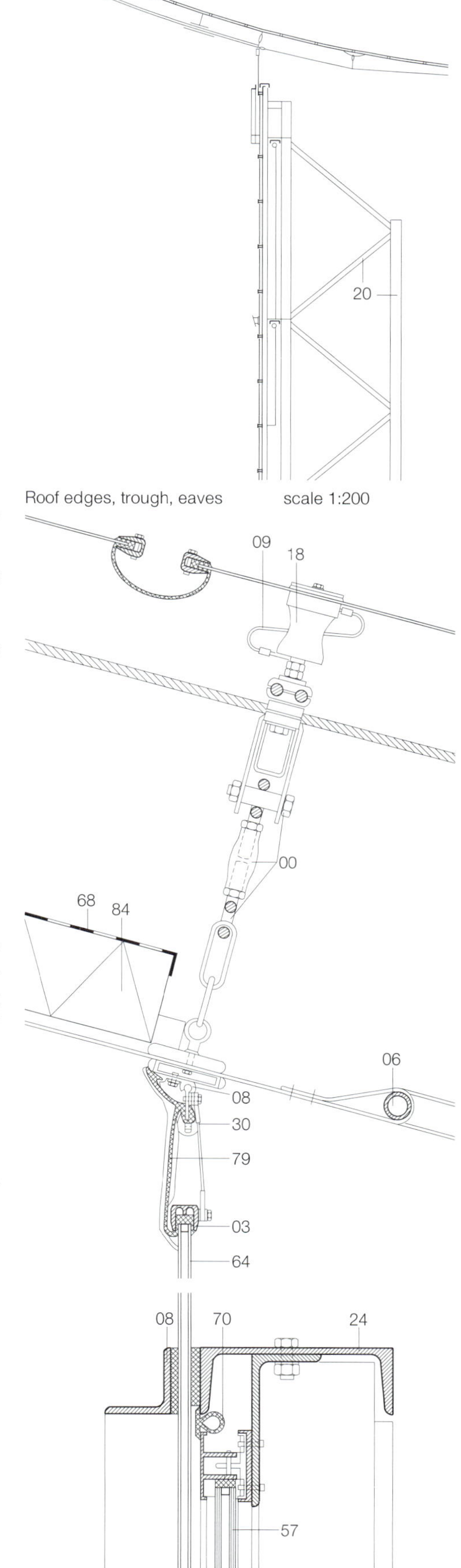


Roof edges, trough, eaves scale 1:200

Facade connection

Eaves anchor point

**House and studio house in Baden-Baden**
1962

Architect: Egon Eiermann, Baden-Baden
Structural engineer: Karl Winkelmann
Client: E. Eiermann, Baden-Baden

Site plan scale 1:4000

Studio house

aa

The house stands above the town of Baden-Baden on a southwest-facing slope leading down to the Oos valley. It is situated in an area of irregularly spaced villas, amidst mature trees. The original idea of the architect was to create a "house" for each family member. The crosswall construction, with walls spaced at 4 metres, achieves this only partly. Because of the steeply sloping site, two- or three-storey heights were necessary. Distinctive features of the building volumes are the extensive glazing between the crosswalls, and the second facade layer, consisting of roof edge, slender white piers, sun blinds, cross beams, wires and flower boxes.

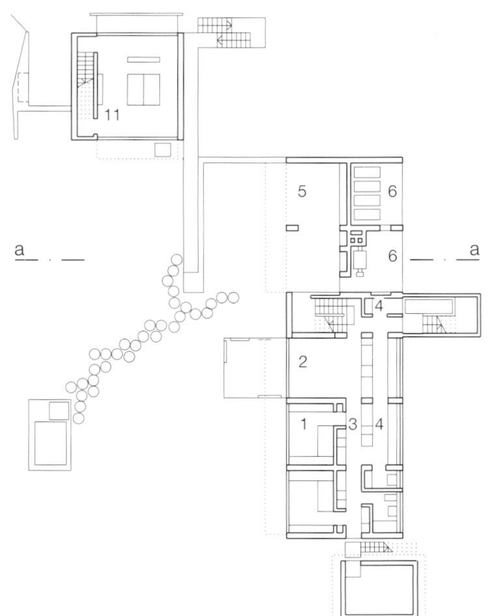

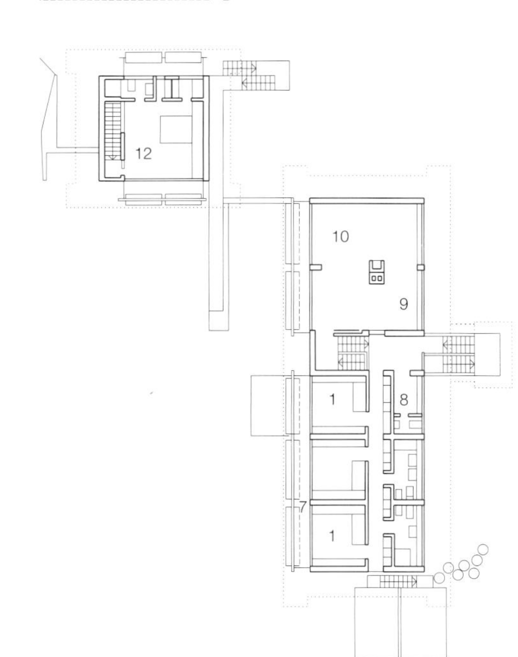

1 Living rooms, bedrooms
2 Dining area
3 Hall
4 Storage room, pantry
5 Covered terrace
6 Fuel storage, boiler room
7 Balcony
8 Cloakroom
9 Kitchen/dining area
10 Living area
11 Office
12 Guest apartment

Plans of ground floor, upper floor • Section scale 1:500

As in many other projects, the architect has created an original form that derives from a thorough analysis of function. The construction of the ridge, for example, is developed from the requirements of ridge ventilation, which explains its asymmetric arrangement. At the verges and eaves the edge of the roof appears particularly light, thanks to the projecting roof parts.
The shallow pitched roof rests on wooden rafters fixed directly to concrete purlins. The slim piers are attached to the two-part rafters, which cantilever out almost two metres.
The roof is covered with white-painted, corrugated asbestos-cement sheets. The ventilation layer is limited to the depth of the corrugations. This is possible because the thermal insulation of mineral wool is protected against moisture penetration by a vapour barrier.
To keep a narrow profile for the edge of the roof at the eaves, the architect separated the overhang from the insulating, weatherproofing part of the roof. He could then make provision for the differing stresses deriving from temperature and wind acting on those parts. The wide projecting roof also enabled him to dispense with a roof gutter and envelop his house with a "curtain of pearls" when it rained.

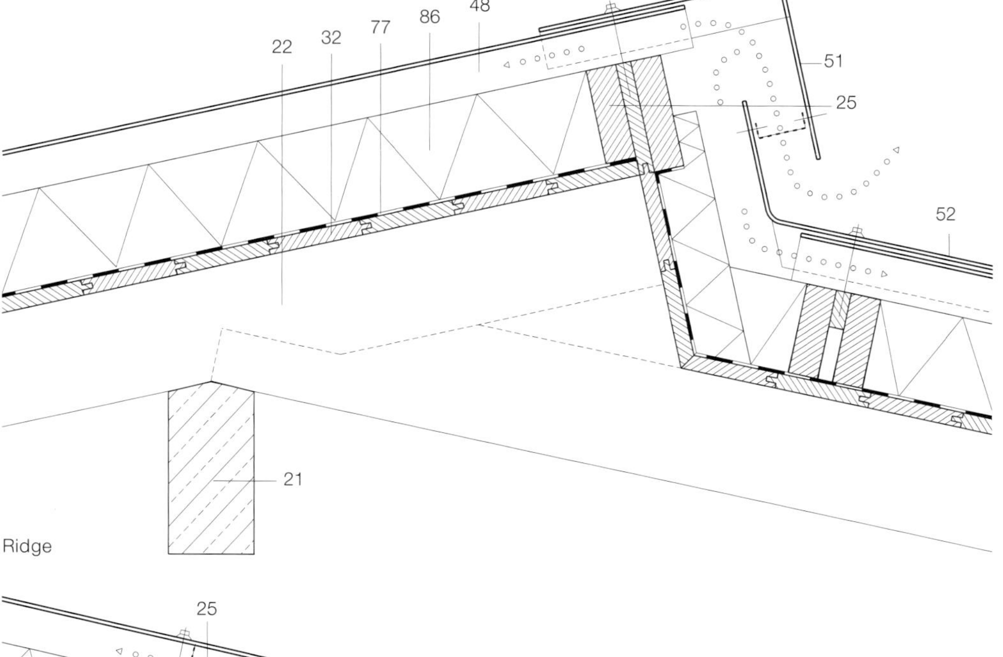


Ridge

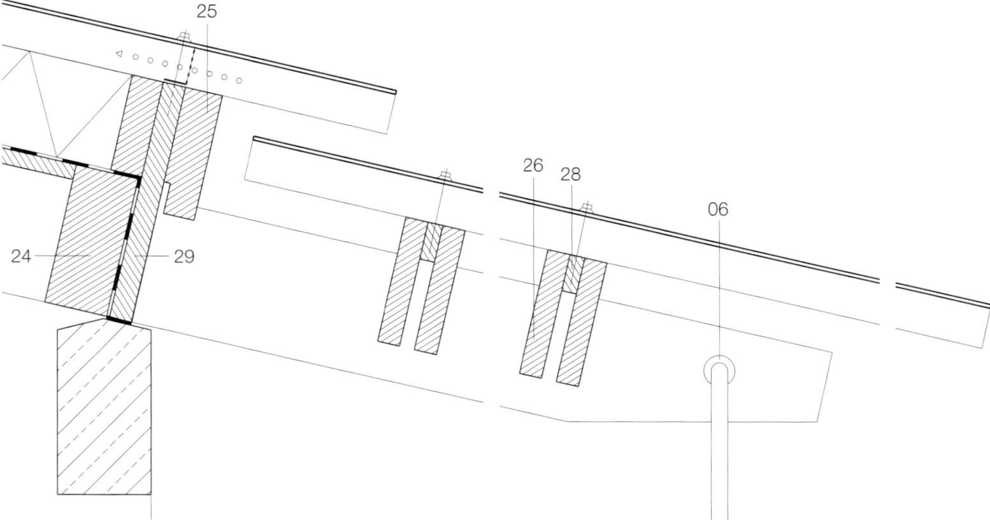


Eaves and roof overhang

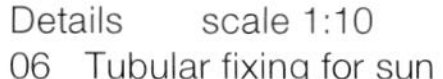

Details scale 1:10
06 Tubular fixing for sun blind
13 Clay brickwork, painted anthracite grey
21 Concrete purlin
22 Clear-varnished Oregon pine rafter
24 Clear-varnished Oregon pine horizontal timber
25 Spacer batten
26 Load-bearing board
28 Filler board
29 Fascia board
32 Clear-varnished Oregon pine decking
48 Corrugated asbestos-cement panel (profile 5)
51 Shaped monoridge capping
52 Apron flashing piece
77 Vapour barrier
86 Mineral wool

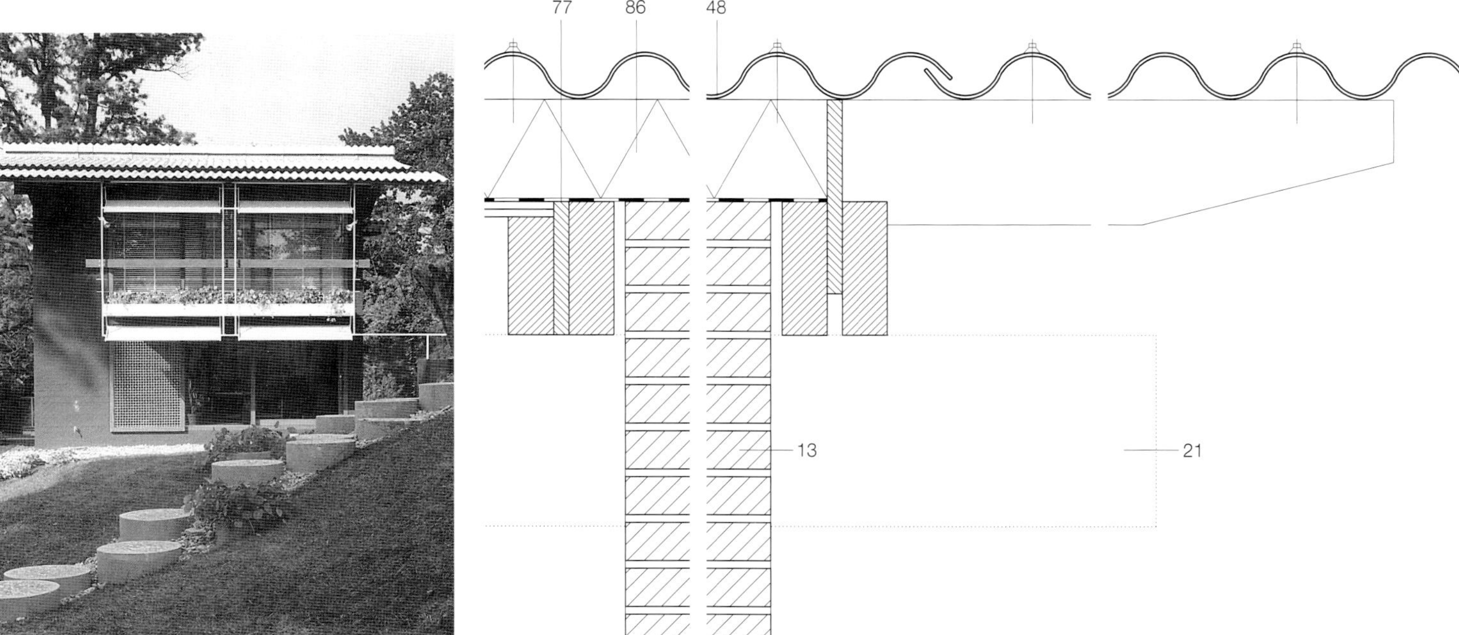


Projecting roofs of both houses

Verge and cantilevered roof

**Moruya detached house in New South Wales**
1985

Architects: Glenn Murcutt and Partner, Mosman
Structural engineer: Tailor and Partner, Mosman
Client: D. and T. Magney

The house stands isolated on the top of a treeless slope dotted with clumps of grass and rocks. It affords an unhindered view of the undeveloped coast and a lake to the north.

Inside the house the curved roof marks out a clear division of space. All rooms are arranged in a line and oriented towards the north, facing the sun. A long corridor runs the length of the building, connecting the two entrances on the narrow end walls. This corridor divides the main rooms from the sanitary facilities and built-in cupboards along the south wall. The house is divided into two independent areas, used by the owners and their adult children. A terrace, covered along its length, connects both these parts.

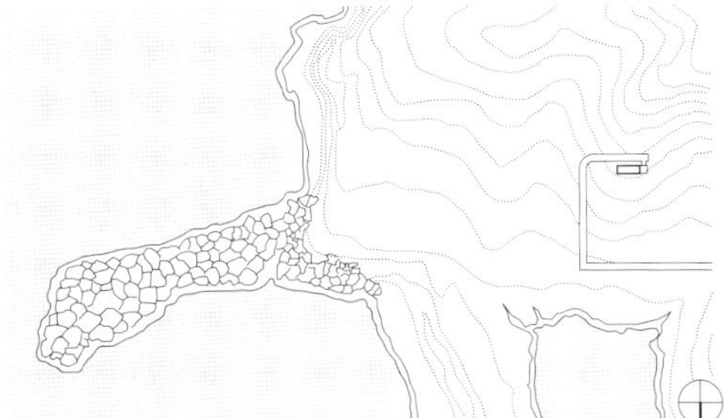

Site plan scale 1:25 000

Main approach, west side

Curved tubular steel beams, with flexurally rigid connections to steel columns, form the loadbearing frame in a transverse direction. Channel sections span between them at the same height from bay to bay. Gusset plates connect them to the tubular sections to form a frame. At the end the channel sections are welded onto the steel tubes and cantilever out. The corrugated sheet covering also projects, in the direction of the corrugations, and is supported by a thin tubular purlin and struts arranged in a V-shape. The only bracing comes through the frames. In the moderate-to-warm (monthly average 12 to 22°C), damp (monsoon) climate, summer cooling is more important than winter heating, particularly as the daily temperatures are very high, but freezing point is never reached (daily extremes 2 to 45°C).

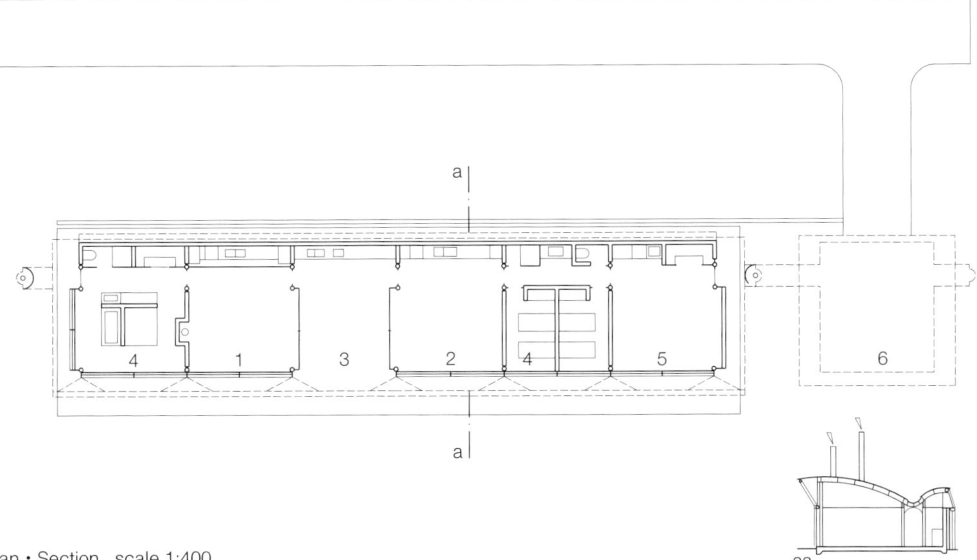


Plan • Section scale 1:400

North side, terrace

1 Parents' living room
2 Children's living room
3 Covered terrace
4 Bedroom
5 Laundry, multi-purpose room
6 Garage (planned, fabric)

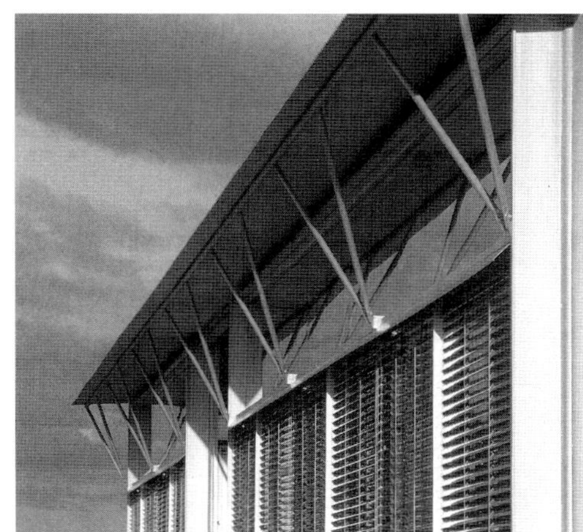
Roof edge and bracing, ridge

Roof overhang, verge

The roof construction, with a thick outer layer of thermal insulation directly below the covering, therefore fulfils its purpose.
For the few hours during the rainy season when the house needs to be heated, the narrower, inner layer of thermal insulation is adequate. At this time of year the vapour diffusion flow reverses and makes an inner vapour barrier unnecessary.
Also, masonry partition walls and a masonry rear wall (cold south wind) play their part in storing heat and balancing the temperature inside.

Details scale 1:10

00 1 screw per corrugation
02 Galvanised wire mesh
04 Screws (M12), M16 (beams), M16 (columns)
07 10 mm welded gusset plate
08 Channel profile rail (below), 2x anodised aluminium angles (above)
10 Cantilevered purlin, 152 x 89 x 10 mm hot-dip galvanised steel angle
17 114 mm dia. x 4.5 mm tubular steel column
19 10 mm welded steel end plate
20 114 mm dia. x 4.5 mm tubular steel frame
21 Hot-dip galvanised steel purlins, 2 x 100 x 50 x 20 mm channel, 150 x 70 x 16 mm channel
24 76 x 152 mm horizontal timber
28 Filler board
31 Strut
34 Plasterboard
56 Toughened glass, silicone
58 Galvanised corrugated steel, r = 1.80 m (south), l = 9.33 m (north)
74 Silicone rubber
82 Anodised aluminium louvre screen
86 Mineral wool, 75 mm (upper), 50 mm (lower)
95 1.6 mm zinc sheet gutter, r = 550 mm

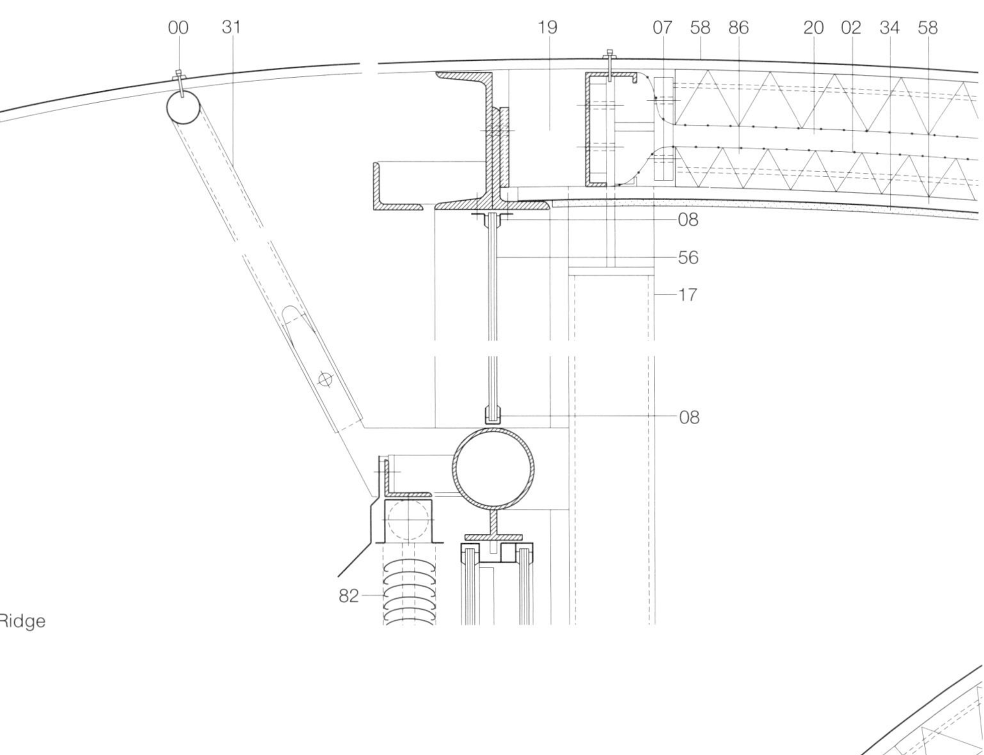

Ridge

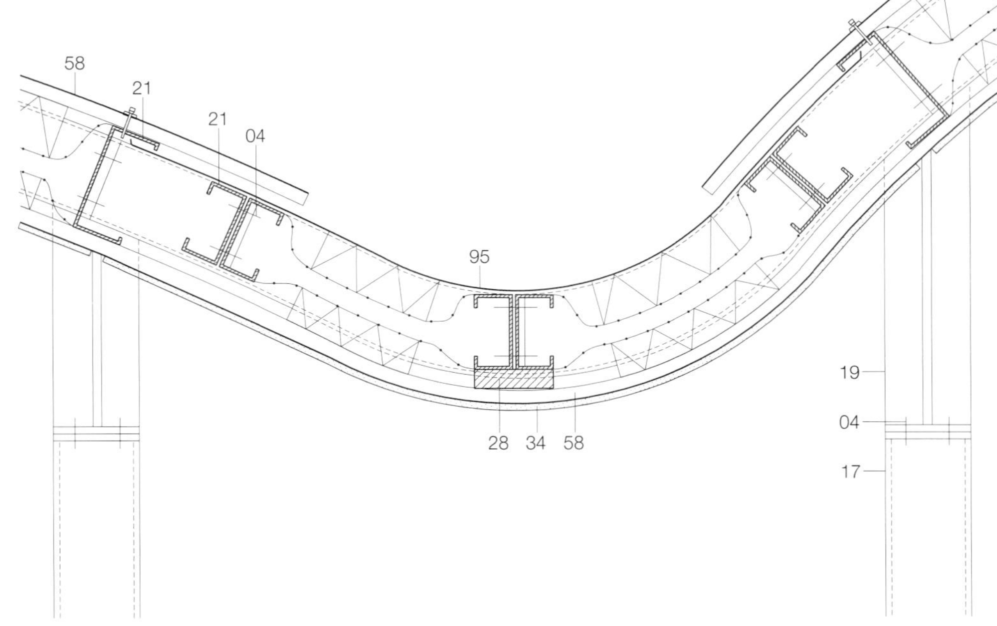

Trough

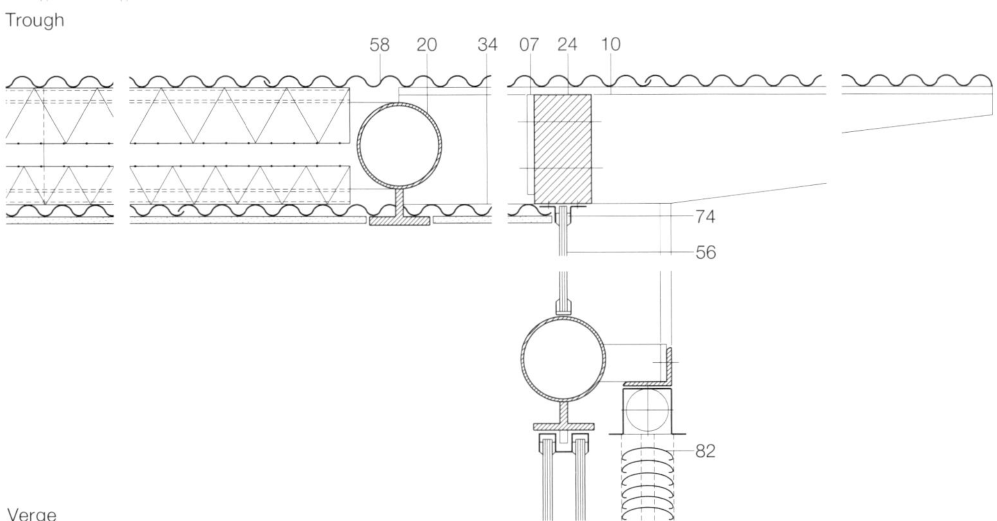

Verge

**Information Centre in Fetsund**
1996

Architect: Askim/Lantto, Oslo
Jens Petter Askim, Niels Marius Askim, Lars Lantto
Client: Fetsund Lenser (Rafting Museum)

West side

The building is located on the banks of the river Glomma in a nature conservation area close to the Norwegian town of Fetsund. It is part of a 2.5 km long museum complex containing exhibits mostly connected with timber rafting and its associated crafts, once common in the region. The information centre puts on temporary exhibitions on history, natural science and art. In designing the centre it was intended to bring out the contrast between the ever-changing natural environment and the historic building structures on the site. While the timber post-and-beam construction of the main loadbearing frame consists of fixed sections, the facade is built of modules that can be interchanged or removed. The fittings inside the building are also independent of the primary construction, enabling flexible utilisation.
The roof construction, pitched towards the building's main axis, is covered with corrugated metal sheet towards the edge. In the air-conditioned section, prefabricated roof panels of trapezoid sheet with integrated thermal insulation were used. The central drainage gutter, fitted with additional mineral wool insulation, directs rainwater into hoppers feeding into drainage pipes. The roof is sealed with synthetic roofing felt.

Site plan
scale 1:4000

1 Information centre
2 Workshops
3 Storage
4 Wooden barrier

Plan • Sections
scale 1:400

1 Foyer
2 Cafeteria
3 Exhibition
4 Kitchen
5 Cloakroom
6 WC
7 Storage

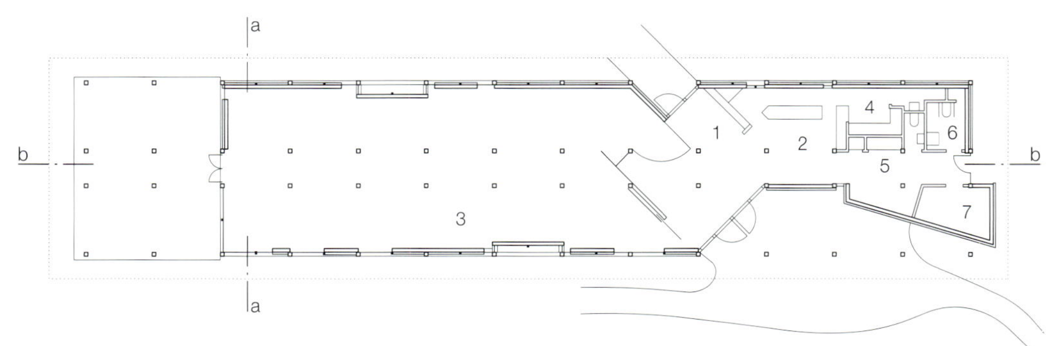


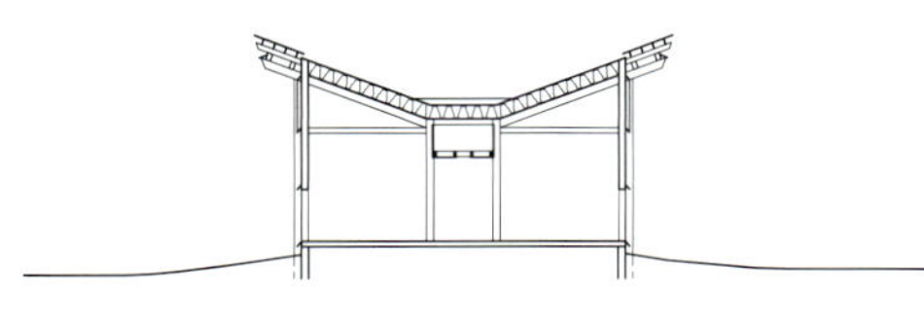

aa

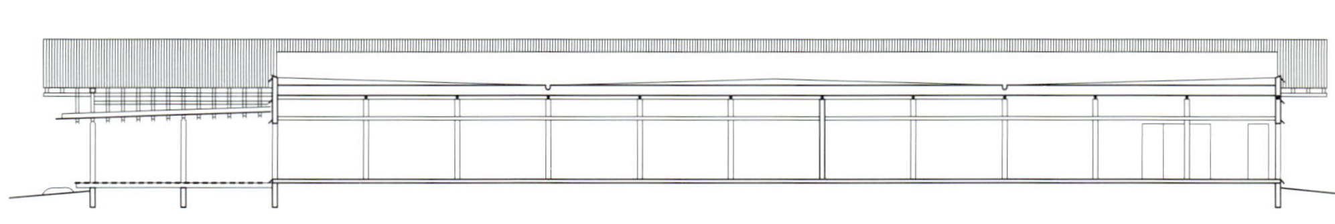

bb

Details scale 1:20
17 98 x 98 mm post
20 98 x 198 mm beam (frame), 98 x 120 mm timber (ridge)
21 98 x 198 mm purlin
22 98 x 198 mm rafter
26 Battens, 48 x 48 mm, 12 x 12 mm
28 Filler wedge
29 73 x 23 mm cladding on profiled batten
32 23 x 98 mm decking
33 15 mm oriented strand board (ridge), 16 mm birch plywood panel (verge)
34 9 mm plasterboard
40 Cover board
56 Insulating glass
58 Corrugated sheet-metal panel
60 Aluminium sheet vapour barrier
76 Synthetic roofing felt
77 Vapour barrier
80 Prefabricated panel: trapezoidal profile sheet with a core of mineral wool
86 Mineral wool

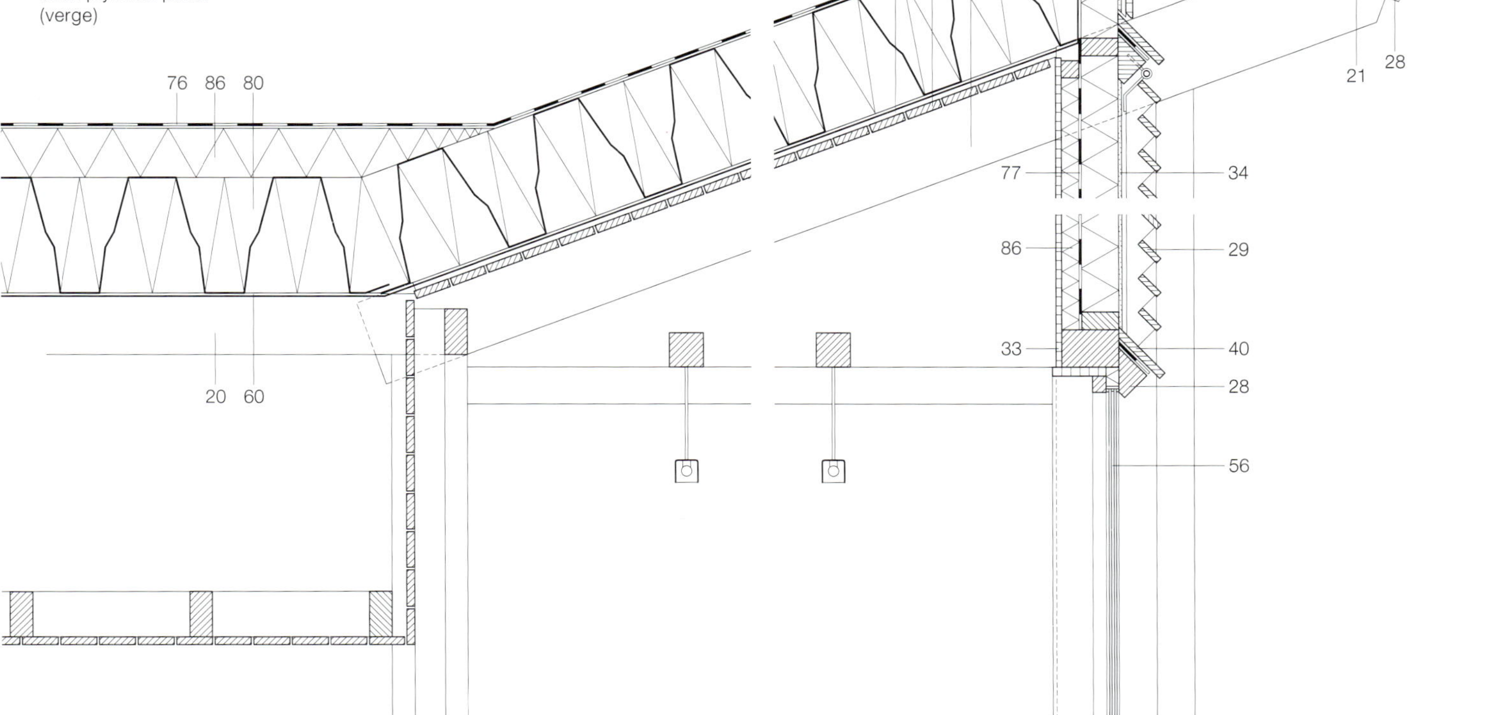


Ridge and gutter

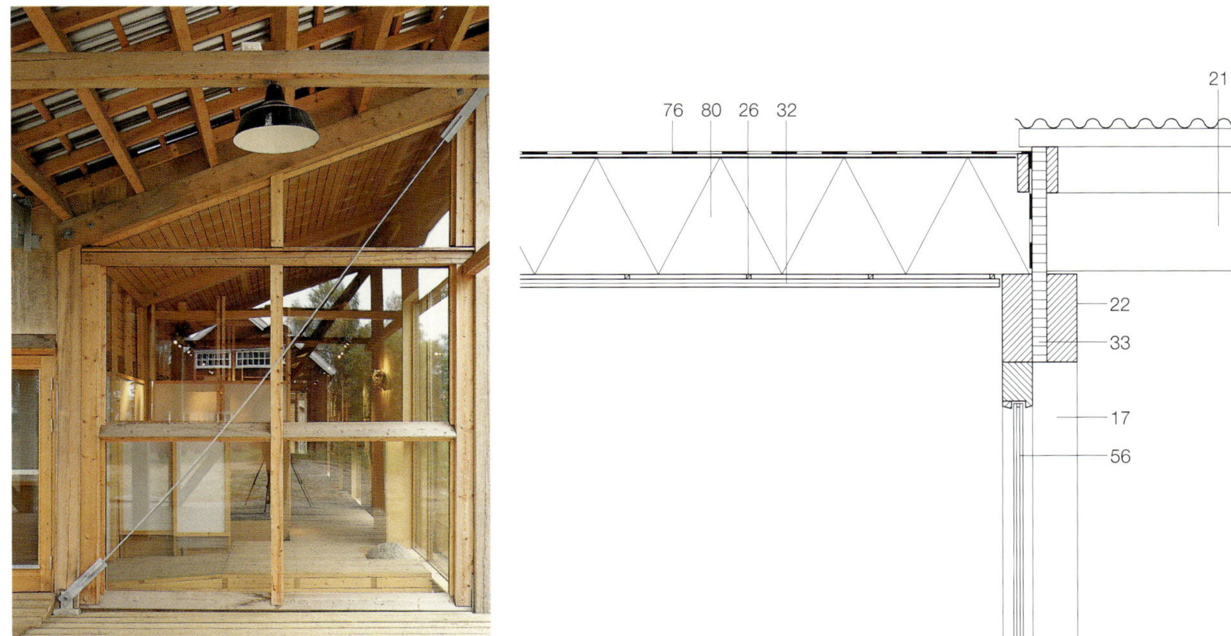


View from the terrace into the exhibition rooms

Verge

**Semi-detached houses in Munich**
1997

Architect: Werner Bäuerle, Konstanz
Assistants: Gunther Braun, Katja Pochert, Biggy Gittl
Structural engineer: Helmut Fischer, Bad Endorf
Client: Paul Dahl, Landstuhl

North side

Site plan scale 1:2000

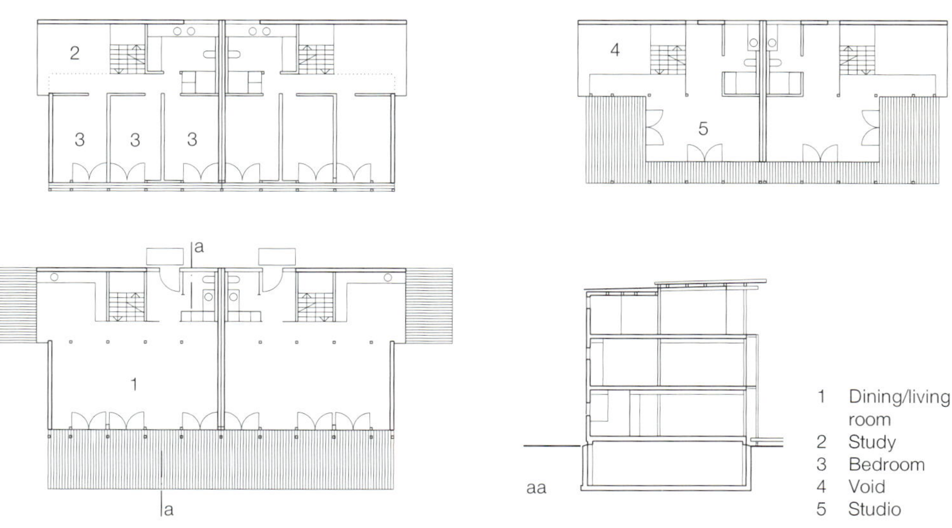


Plans of ground floor, 1st floor, 2nd floor • Section scale 1:400

Tall, mature beech trees dominate this site in the Munich suburb of Solln, a feature that made development difficult, particularly as strict tree protection regulations dictated a very limited building space. It was not even permitted to drive or walk on the root areas of the trees during building work. These restrictions all led to the choice of a skeleton frame and the material wood.
On the northern side of the symmetrical building volume are the kitchens, bathrooms and staircases. The rooms are behind a closed, wooden-clad front with narrow window openings facing the street. The living areas and bedrooms overlooking the garden on the south side have full-height glazing.
The projecting parts of the gable-end walls are fully glazed, affording extensive views over the park-like garden. Ventilation is controlled through a combination of fixed glazing, opening sashes and louvred windows. The roof storey, which is set back on the south facade, is fully glazed on three sides.
The houses are built on a 2 m grid. The timber frame with continuous girders stands on imper-

South side

West-facing gable facade

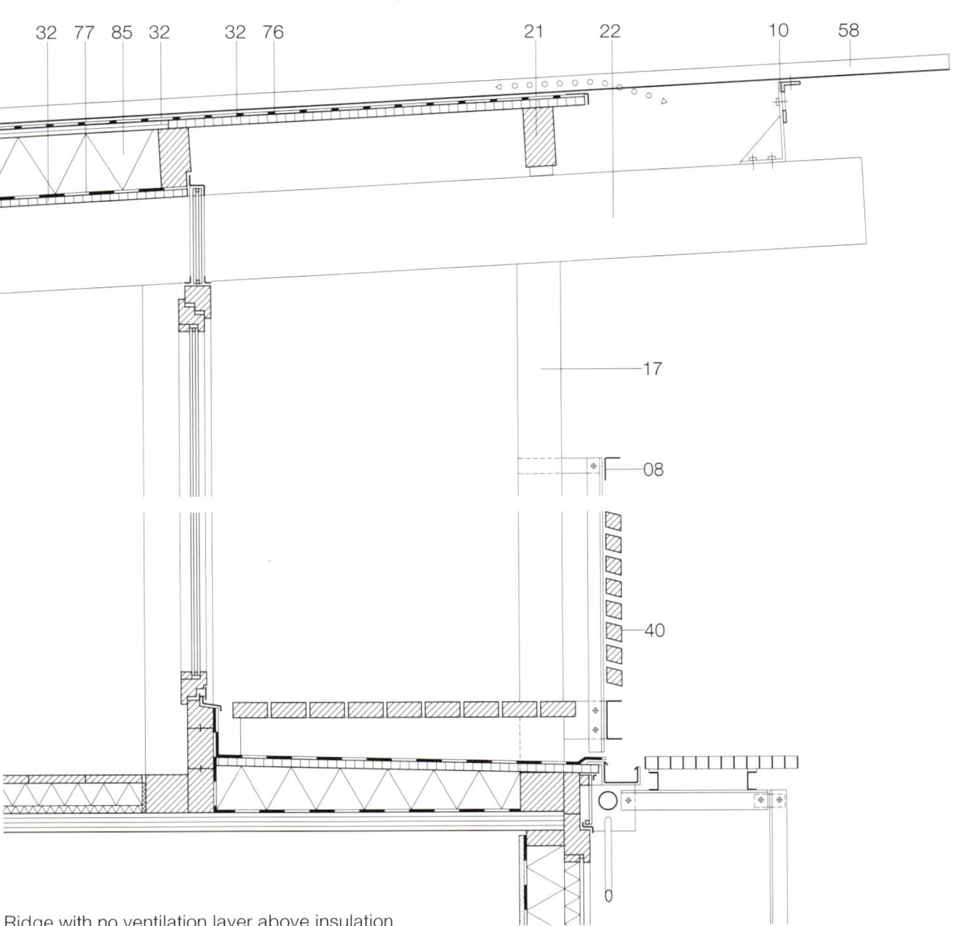

Ridge with no ventilation layer above insulation

meable reinforced concrete. It is braced by multiplex building board in the transverse axis and by the slim cross-pieces in front of the south facade. The monopitch roof is insulated with flax, with no ventilation layer above, and a covering of corrugated aluminium panels.

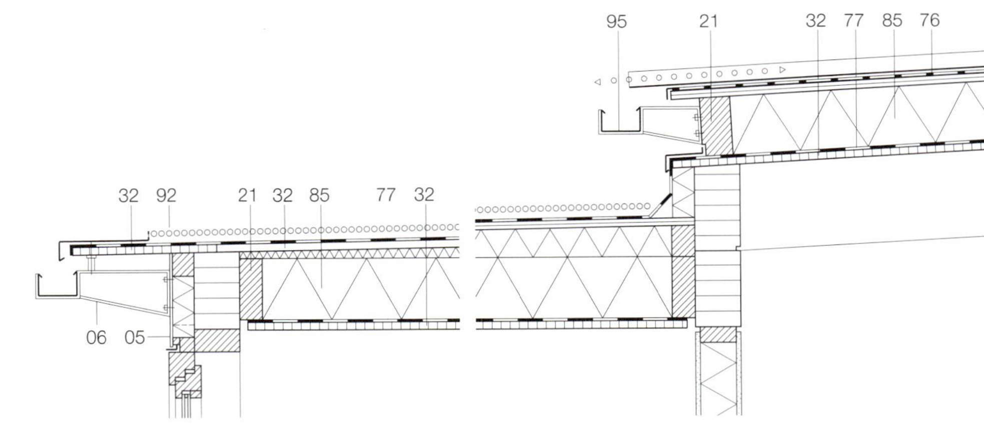

Eaves and step in roof

Details scale 1:20

05 4 mm aluminium retainer sheet
06 5 x 30 mm steel flat gutter bracket
08 40 x 60 mm steel angle-section handrail, two 20 x 40 mm angle posts
10 50 x 100 x 8 mm perforated steel angle section
17 120 x 120 mm glued laminated timber post
21 80 x 160 mm, 60 x 160 mm timber rib
22 120 x 220 mm glued laminated timber rafter
40 40 x 40 mm larchwood cladding
32 19 mm rough tongue and groove decking, 19 mm three-ply panel (in visible area)
58 55 x 177 x 0.8 mm corrugated aluminium panel
76 Roofing felt, fireproof at fire wall
77 Vapour barrier, polyethylene sheeting under corrugated sheet, composite aluminium sheeting under gravel
85 Thermal insulation, 160 mm flax
86 Mineral wool
92 30 mm gravel layer
95 Rainwater gutter

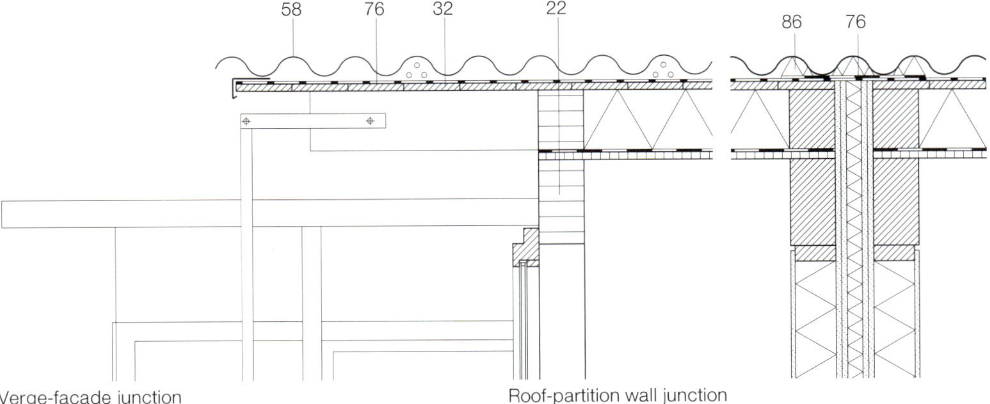

Verge-facade junction

Roof-partition wall junction

**Schäferwiese primary school in Munich**
1999

Architects: Schunck-Ullrich-Krausen, Munich
Project partner: Norbert Krausen
Project manager: Martin Kerling
Assistants: Robert Kellner, Martina Wulf
Structural engineer: Stepan und Partner, Munich
Client: Landeshauptstadt Munich

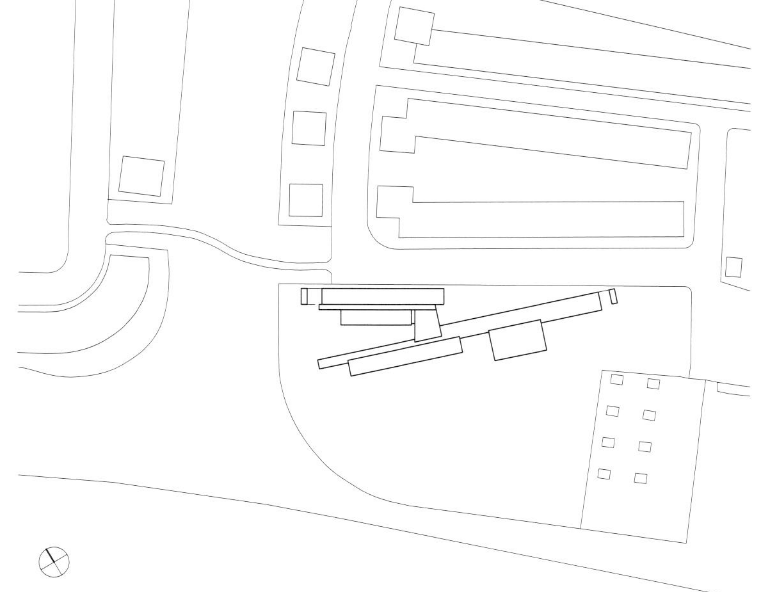

Site plan scale 1:4000

This primary school with day nursery and sports facilities is situated on a former meadow in west Munich. On the southern edge of the site is a wall that keeps out the noise of the Munich-Augsburg railway line, and on the north is a high-rise residential development. The school building is backed up against the northern border. The areas used by the pupils at breaktimes open up to the green spaces to the southwest. The two building volumes are angled towards each other, defining the entrance area and main courtyard. Between the two buildings is the transparent, two-storey hall used by the pupils at break times. The open spaces around the school and the adjacent small park can be glimpsed through it. The hall forms the focal point of the school; it extends over two floors, connecting the more public-oriented entrance courtyard, and the break areas inside. Here, too, is the point at which all communication routes in the school converge. A free-standing staircase connects the two levels. For school functions, this hall can be used in combination with the multi-purpose hall to provide more space. Walls are either opaque or open, depending on facade orientation. The roof surfaces are separated from the walls and they cantilever out on all sides, a design that gives them a protective character and makes them appear lighter. The classrooms and day nursery rooms face south towards the sun; north-facing rooflights ventilate the classrooms on the side away from the noise. Lighting from two sides ensures even illumination and helps save electricity. The halls are lit by means of generous rooflights and storey-high internal glass facades. The fair-faced brickwork of the building is designed to be legible in its texture and material.

Entrance side

It was intended that the children should be able to understand the work processes that went into making the building - the "building blocks" should be clear to see. The roofs are covered in profiled aluminium panels in sine-wave corrugations. As this covering cantilevers out on all sides, it was necessary to use multi-layered support frames. Above the classroom wings, glued laminated timber purlins rest on steel beams. Insulating purlins and spacer rafters provide ventilation above the insulation layer. Above this is boarding that was used during the construction phase for winter protection, but which now gives additional protection against driving rain and noise. I-section purlins resting on trussed rafters are used for the roof of the break hall and sports hall. The visible soffit of the roof is a profiled aluminium panel with perforated sine-wave corrugations. Multiple-layer aluminium profiles are used for load transfer, ventilation and the cantilevered verge. For noise insulation and added protection in the winter, mineral-bound chipboard was used here as boarding, plus a layer of bitumen sheeting. Above this, double-layer fixing profiles support the ventilated covering.

School yard

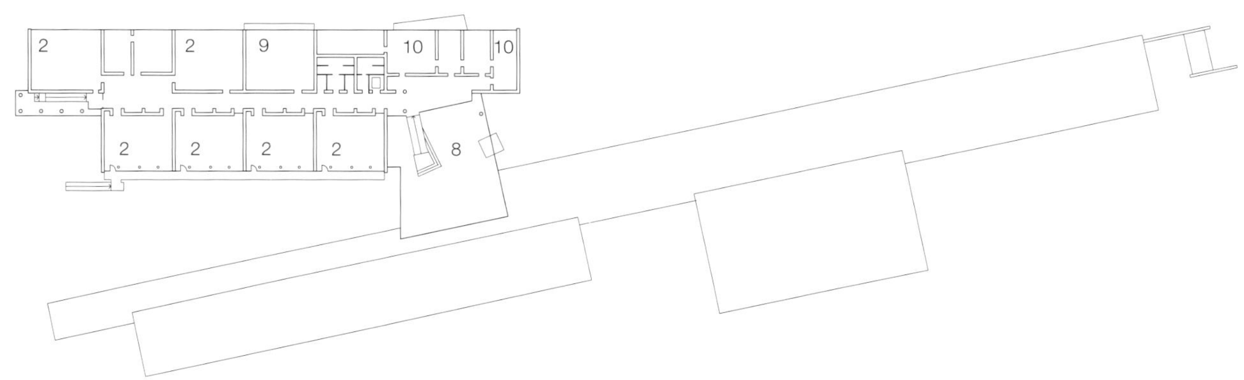

Upper floor

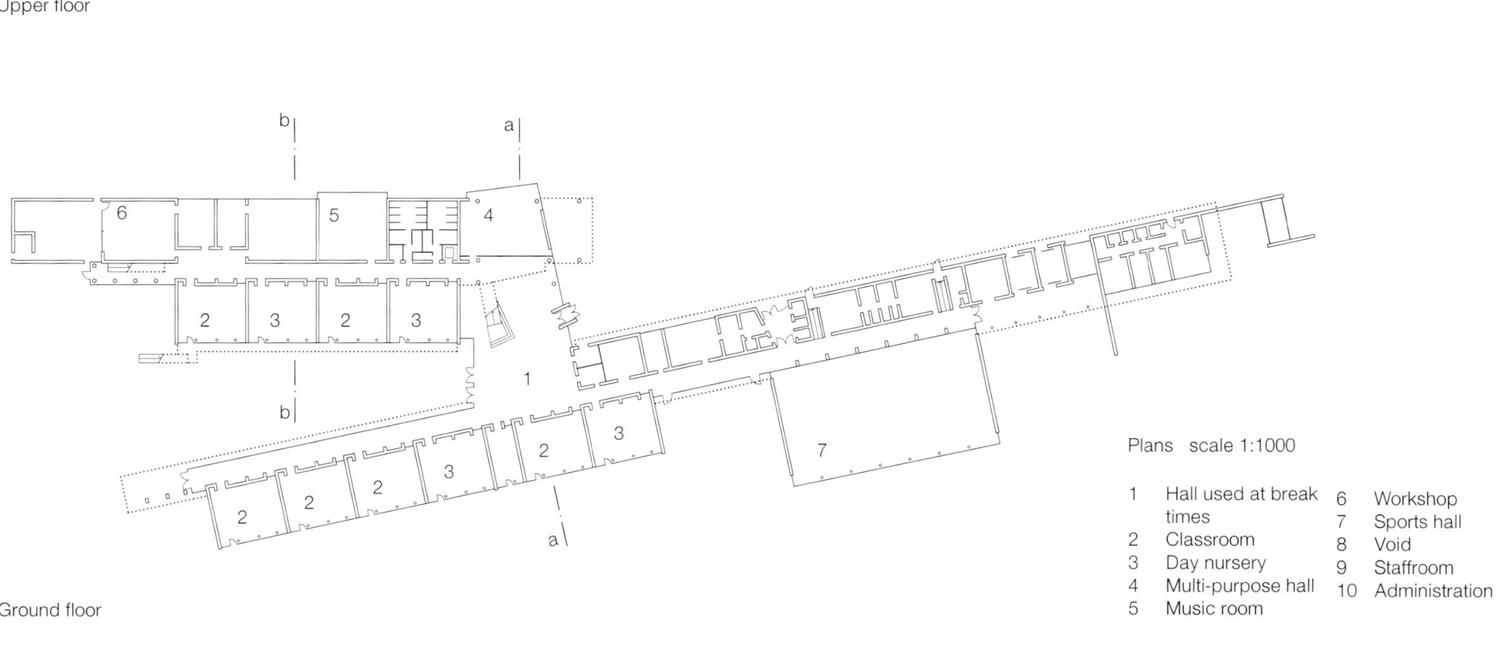

Ground floor

Plans scale 1:1000

1 Hall used at break times
2 Classroom
3 Day nursery
4 Multi-purpose hall
5 Music room
6 Workshop
7 Sports hall
8 Void
9 Staffroom
10 Administration

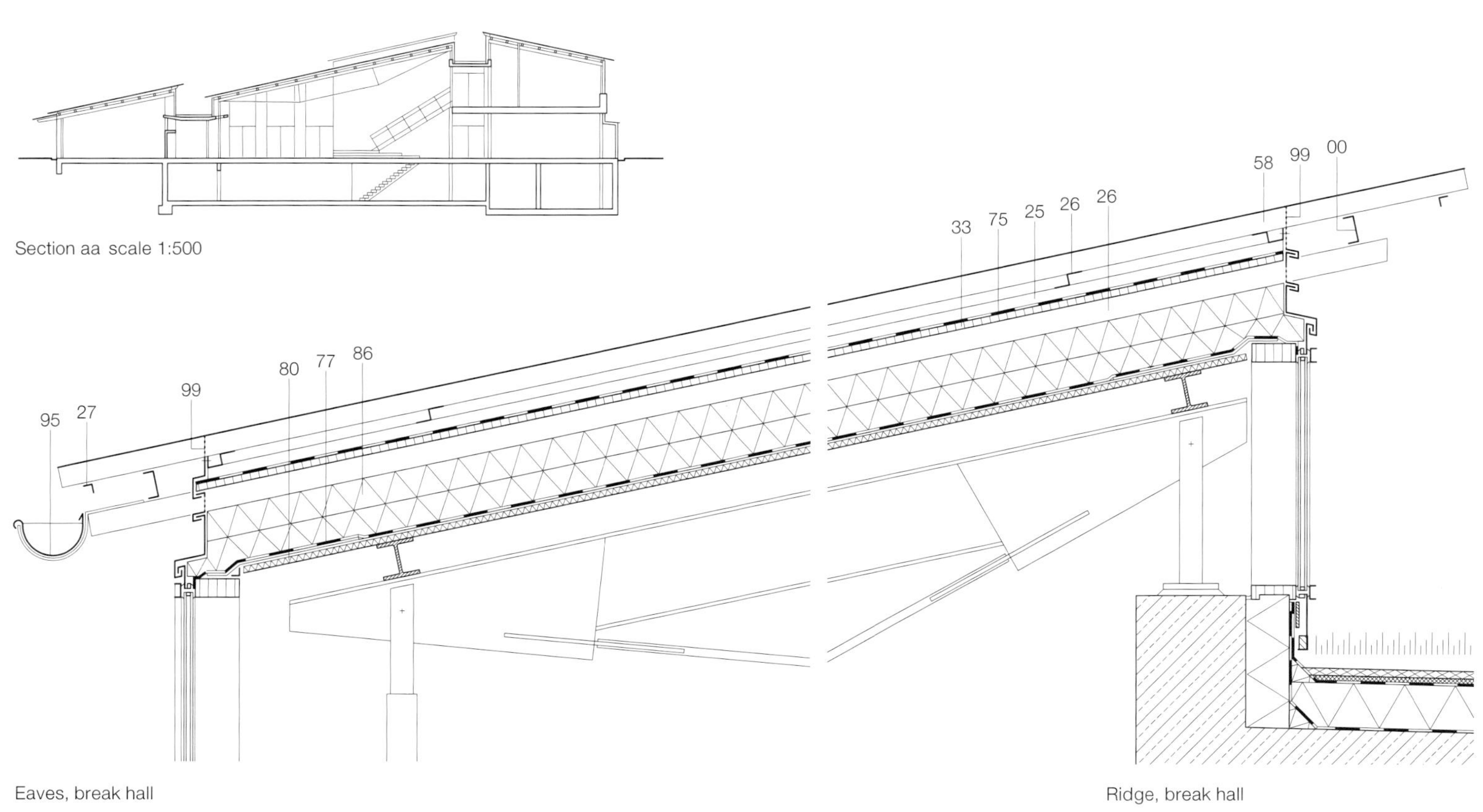


Section aa scale 1:500

Eaves, break hall

Ridge, break hall

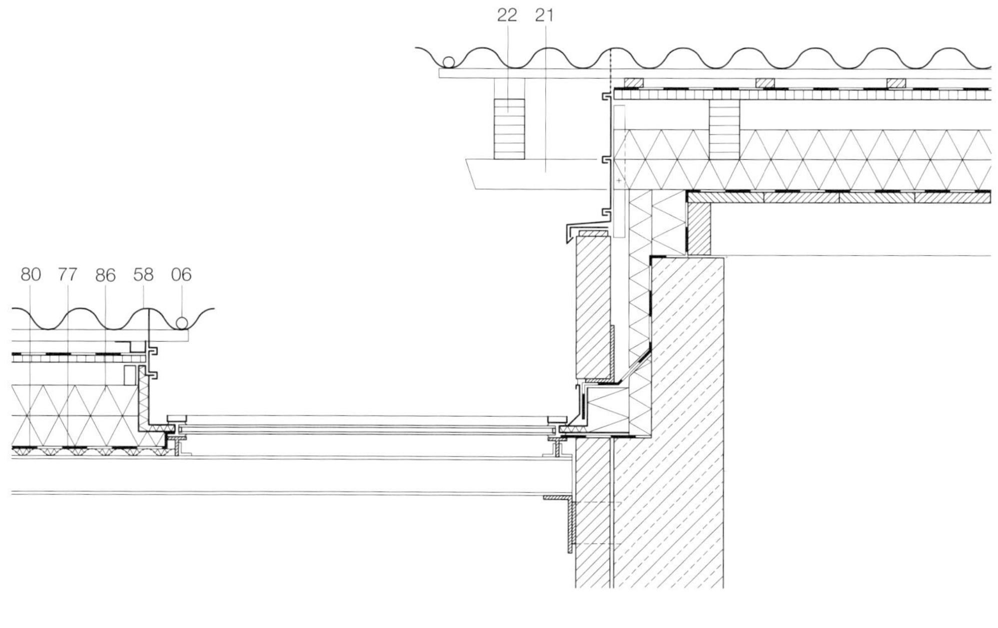


Verge, break hall

Break hall

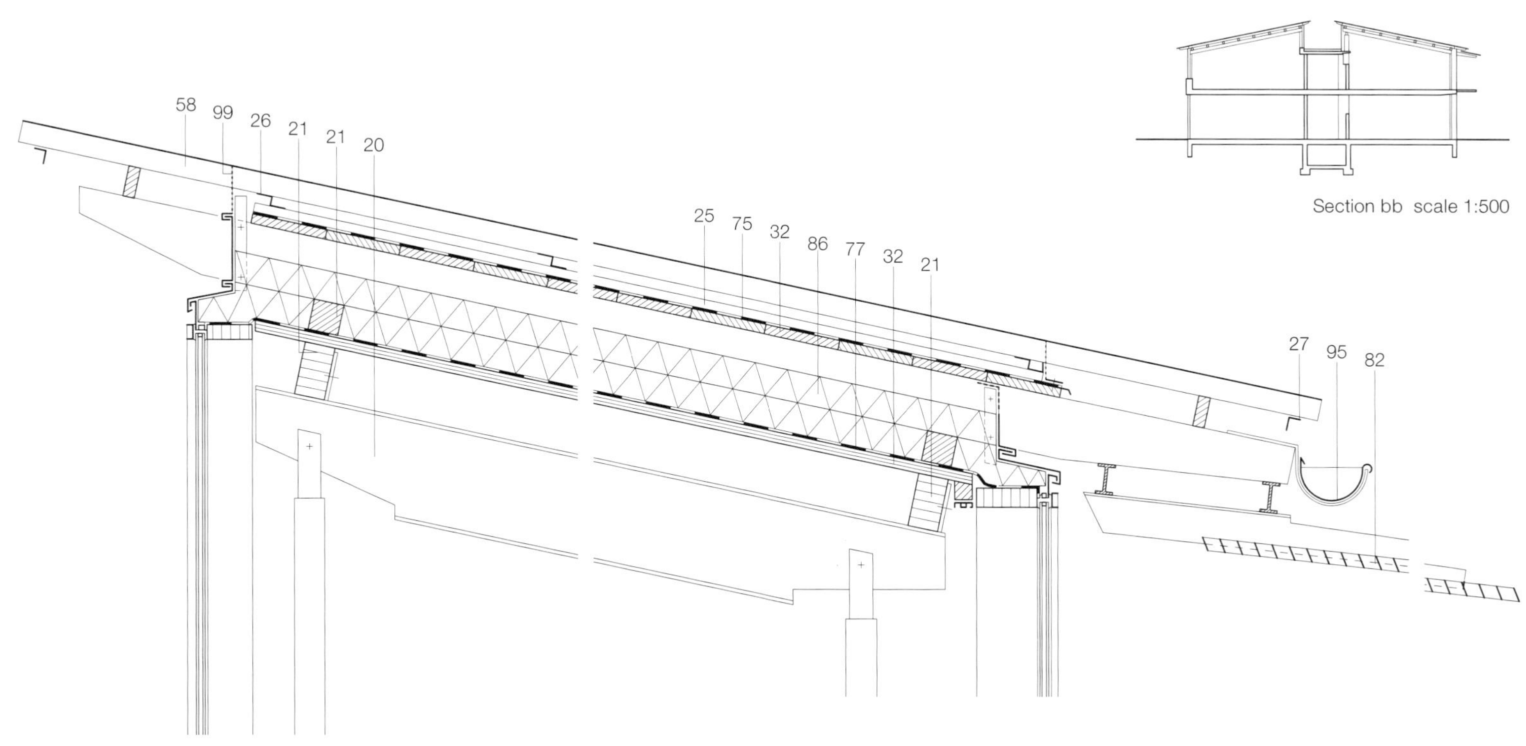


Section bb scale 1:500

Ridge, classroom

Eaves

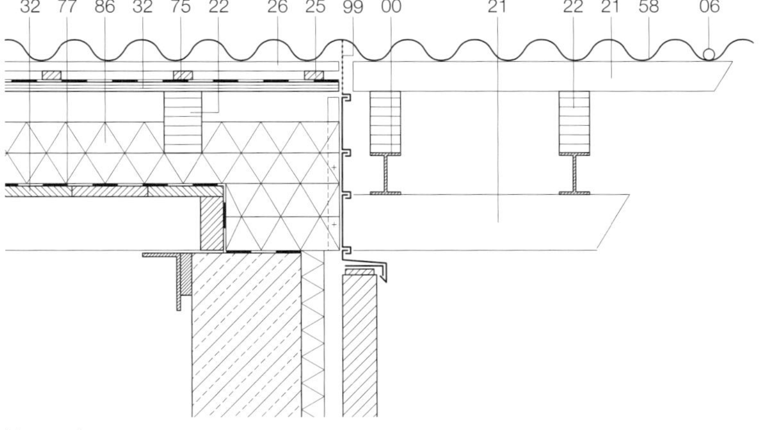


Verge, classroom

Details scale 1:20

00 5 mm welded steel sheet spacer, 80 mm steel channel section
06 Retainer profile, 28 mm dia. steel tube
20 Steel I-section 270 mm deep (IPE)
21 80 x 140 mm purlin, 80 x 80 mm spacer purlin, 30 x 80 mm purlin (verge), 100 x 140 glued laminated timber eaves purlin
22 100 x 160 mm spacer rafter, 80 x 160 mm glued laminated timber rafter (verge)
25 22 x 48 mm counter battens, 30 mm ventilating profile
26 30 mm Z-section aluminium battens, aluminium hollow section/ 60 mm air space
27 Drip profile
32 Sawn decking, matchboarding
33 19 mm mineral-bound chipboard
58 55 x 177 mm corrugated aluminium sheet
60 Cover sheet
75 Roofing seal, bitumen sheeting
77 Polyethylene sheet vapour barrier
80 18 x 76 mm corrugated, perforated aluminium sheet with core of acoustic foam
82 Solar shading screen
86 2 x 80 mm mineral-fibre insulation
95 Aluminium sheet rainwater gutter
99 Ventilation grille

Corner detail

**Old people's home in Neuenburg**
1998–99

Architects: Mahler, Günster, Fuchs, Stuttgart
Assistants: Michael Peters, Karin Schmid-Arnold, Heike Woller-Fuchs
Structural engineer: Wolfgang Beck, Dennach
Client: Stadt Neuenburg

Site plan scale 1:3000

This old people's home with 28 residential units is located on the banks of the river Enz in the town of Neuenburg in southwest Germany. The units are divided into four almost identical residential blocks, resulting in an arrangement that blends well with the surrounding development. The individual apartments are accessed via external corridors and a staircase on the north side. As this obviates the need for an internal corridor, these essentially quite large buildings have a slim profile.
Solar collectors are mounted on the southwest face of the roof, for heating water and as auxiliary support for the central heating system. The high transmission values of the corrugated acrylic plastic roofing ensure the system achieves a high degree of operating efficiency. The collectors are integrated into the roof design, and the transparency of the acrylic plastic panels reveals the geometry of the timber construction below the covering.
The space beneath the simple purlin roof is unheated; it contains services and storage areas.

Northwest side

1 Hall
2 Living room
3 Bedroom
4 Storage
5 Bathroom
6 Kitchen
7 Balcony
8 Stairwell

Section • Plans scale 1:100

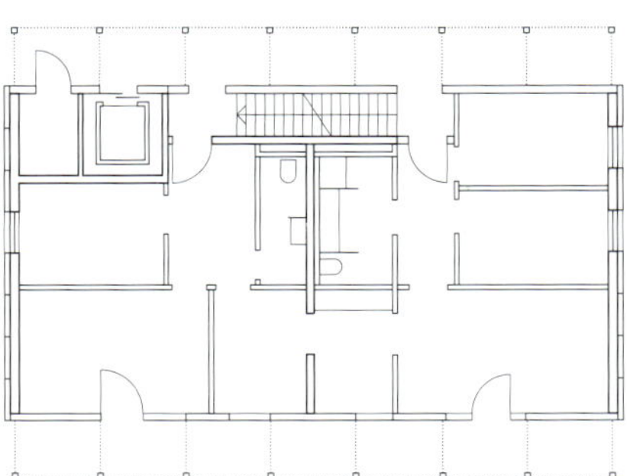
Ground floor

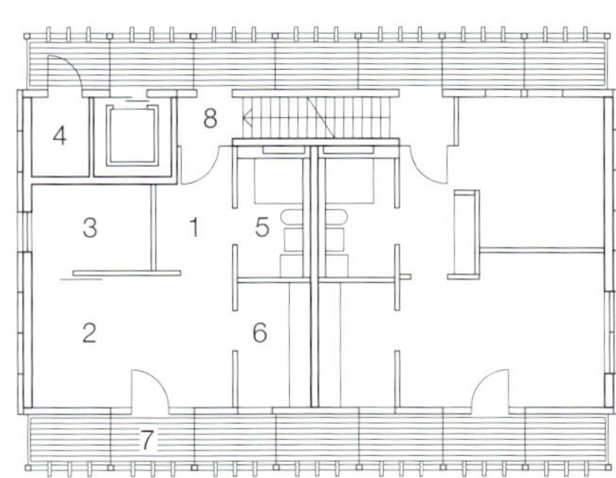

Residential floor

North side

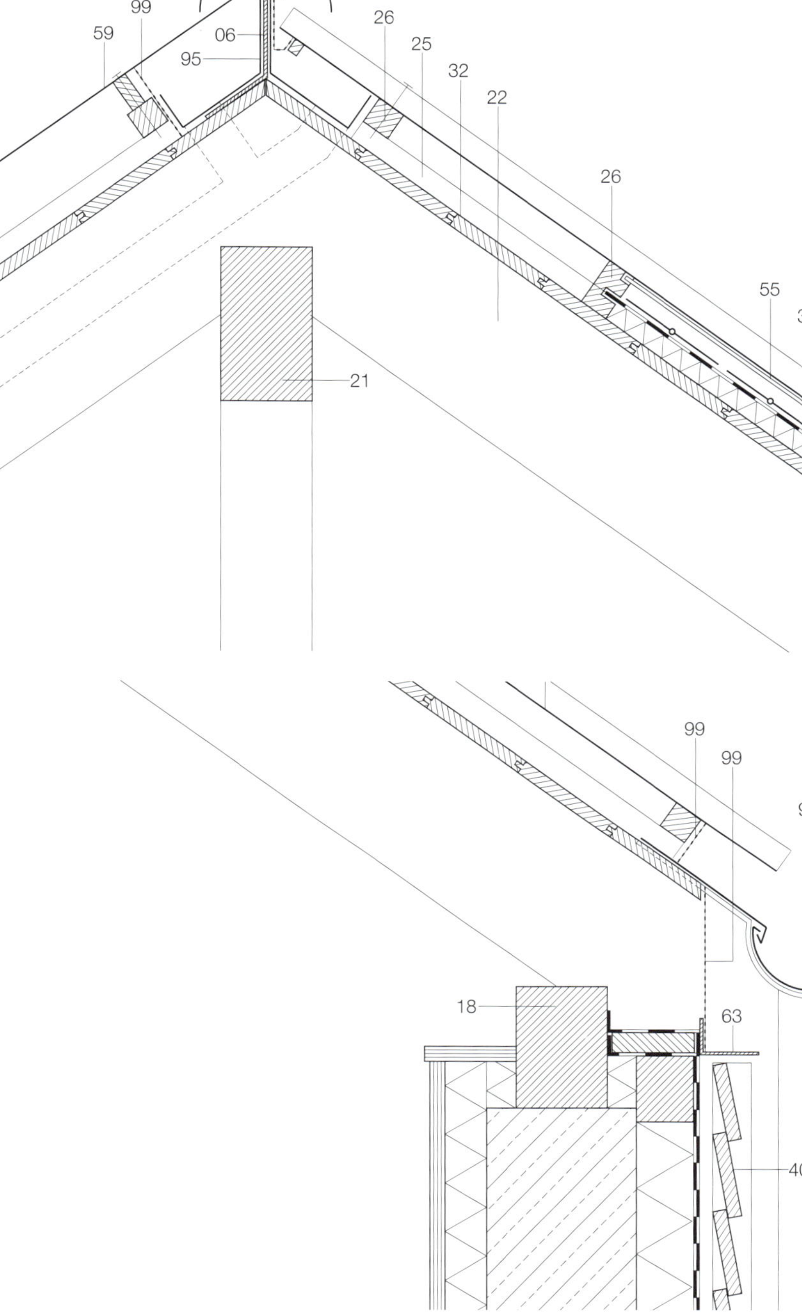


Details scale 1:10

06 Galvanised steel sheet, bent to fit
18 120 x 160 mm softwood wall plate
21 160 x 220 mm purlin
22 100 x 200 mm rafter
24 40 x 40 mm header
25 30 x 40 mm counter batten
26 40 x 40 mm batten, batten with 15 x 15 mm countersinking for fixed glazing of toughened glass
27 50 x 50 mm ridge board
29 Cover strip, windproofing batten
32 155 x 19.5 mm decking
35 Collector, copper profile flange-mounted on copper pipe
40 Softwood weatherboarding
55 Fixed glazing of toughened securitiy glass with perimieter strip and silicone seal
51 180 mm dia. acrylic plastic semicircular ridge capping
59 Metal flashing, titanium-zinc chimney stack flashing with rain guard
63 80 x 50 x 5 mm angle water bar
65 130 x 30 mm corrugated acrylic plastic panel
77 Teflon sheeting
86 30 mm heat-resistant thermal insulation
95 Rainwater gutter, storm gutter (ridge area)
99 Insect screen

Southeast side

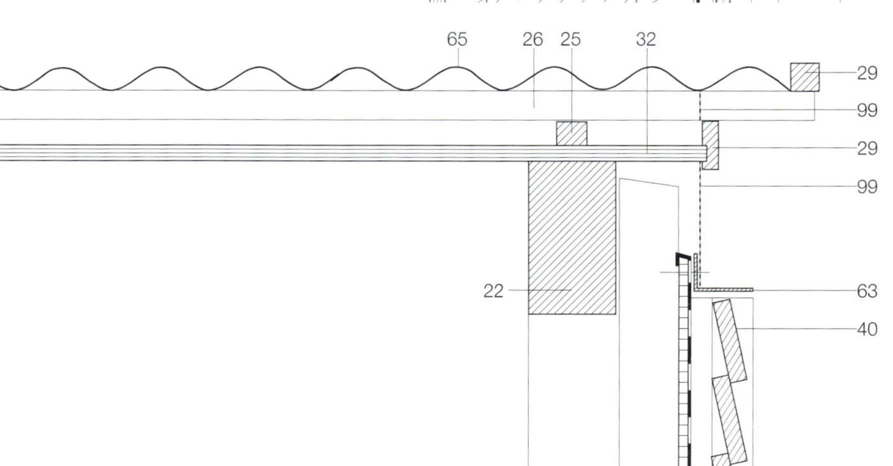

**Sydney Opera House**
1973

Architects: Jørn Utzon, P. Hall, E.-H. Farmer, D.S. Littlemoore, L. Todd, Copenhagen/Sydney
Structural engineer: Ove Arup & Partners, London
Client: Sydney Opera House Trust

Harbour promenade, north side

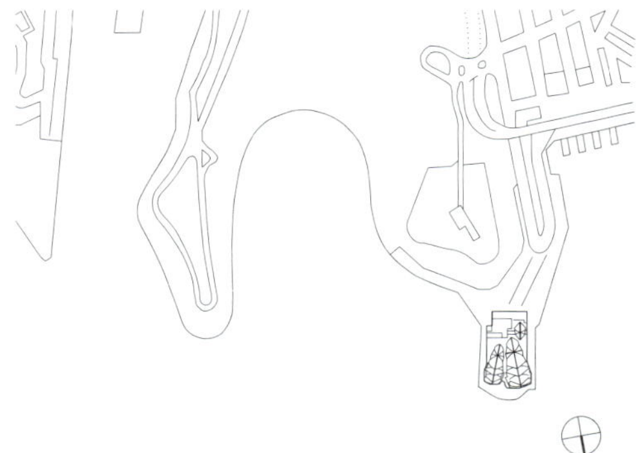

Site plan scale 1:20 000

Three main components of the shells can be distinguished: the "main shells", the tallest of which is 54.6 metres high, the "side shells" in between, and the "louvre shells" supporting the main shells. Each cut triangle vertical to the ridge is part of a sphere surface with a diameter of 75 metres. Each "shell" consists of a series of pairs of rigid concrete arch ribs, which develop from a T-shape at the bottom, where they are supported, to a Y-shape at the ridge.

The uppermost layer of the roof consists of white ceramic tiles measuring 120 x 120 mm. To allow for prefabrication, the tiles were inset into concrete panels that follow the line of the arch ribs. The size of these "ceramic lids" thus varies, according to position, from 2270 x 450 mm to 3500 x 3800 mm. The joint vertical to the direction of the meridian is angled. The ceramic lids are multi-layered precast concrete com-

West side

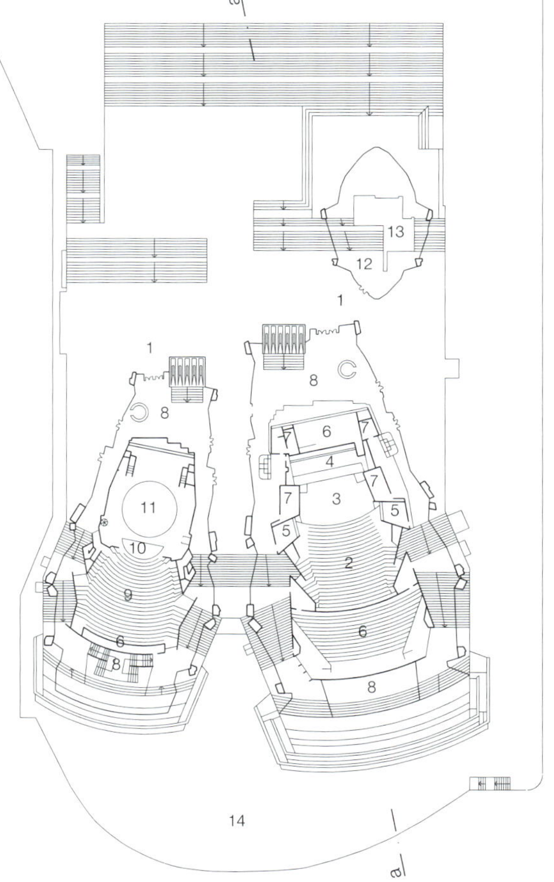


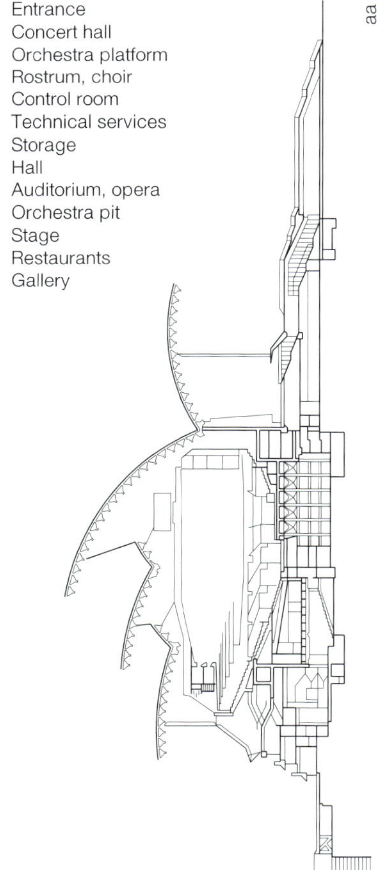


1 Entrance
2 Concert hall
3 Orchestra platform
4 Rostrum, choir
5 Control room
6 Technical services
7 Storage
8 Hall
9 Auditorium, opera
10 Orchestra pit
11 Stage
12 Restaurants
13 Gallery

Plan Level 6 • Section scale 1:1500

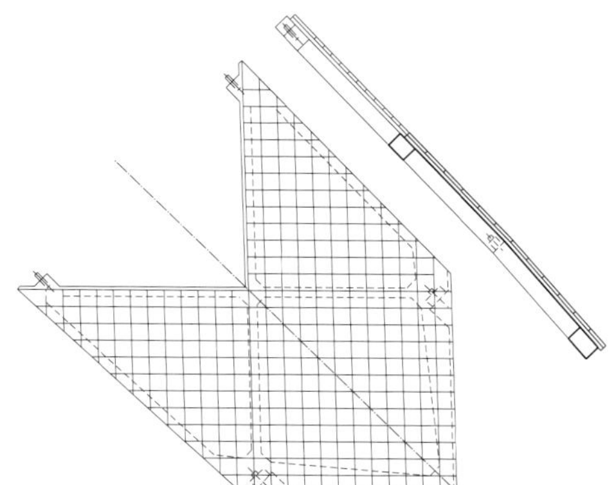

Ceramic panels

Erection of roof covering

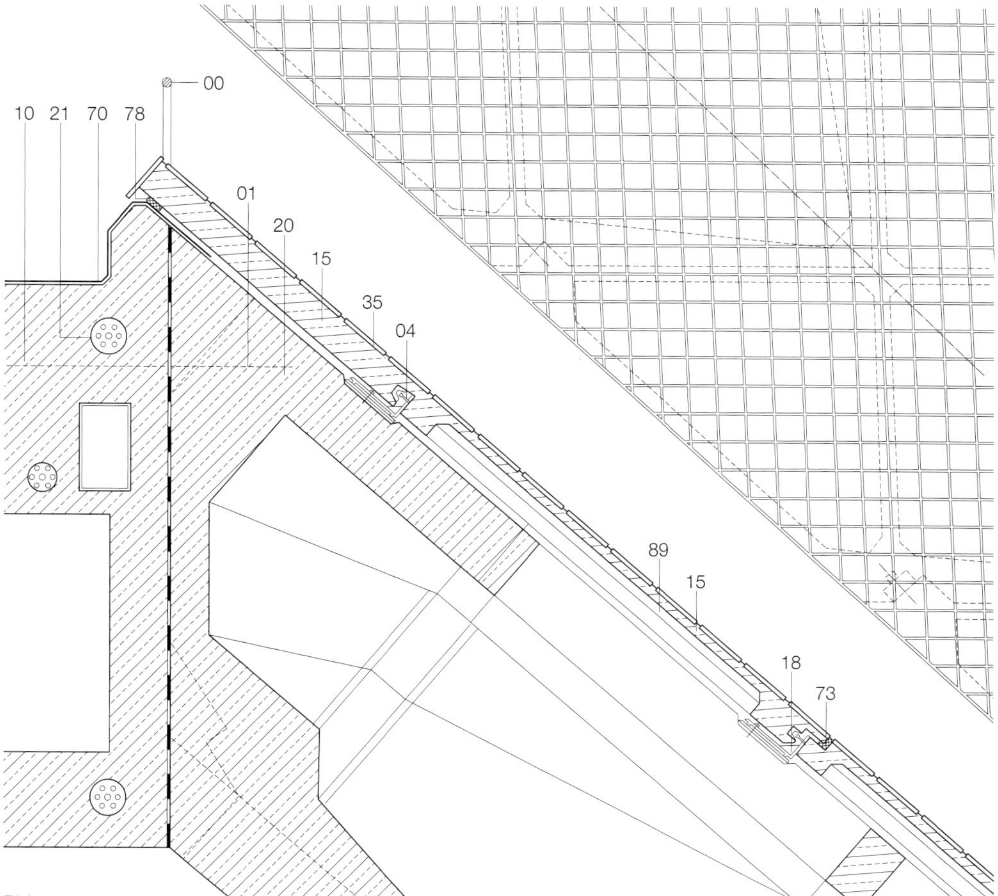

ponents, steam-cured and reinforced with three layers of galvanised reinforcing mat; they are 44 mm thick. The relationship between these "ceramic lids" and the underlying rib support structure is highlighted by the contrast between the matt finish around the edges of the lids and the gloss finish on the main part.

To permit thermal movement of the panels, each is fixed independently of its neighbour to a support bracket with an adjustable bolt. The insulation underneath the ceramic lids consists of self-extinguishing polyurethane panels 20 mm thick. The joints between the tiles are sealed. The joints between the ceramic lids are finished with PVC strips and grouted with a two-component acrylic mixture. The roof posed an enormous technical challenge to both architects and engineers. Only when the constructional details were resolved could this symbol of Sydney come into being.

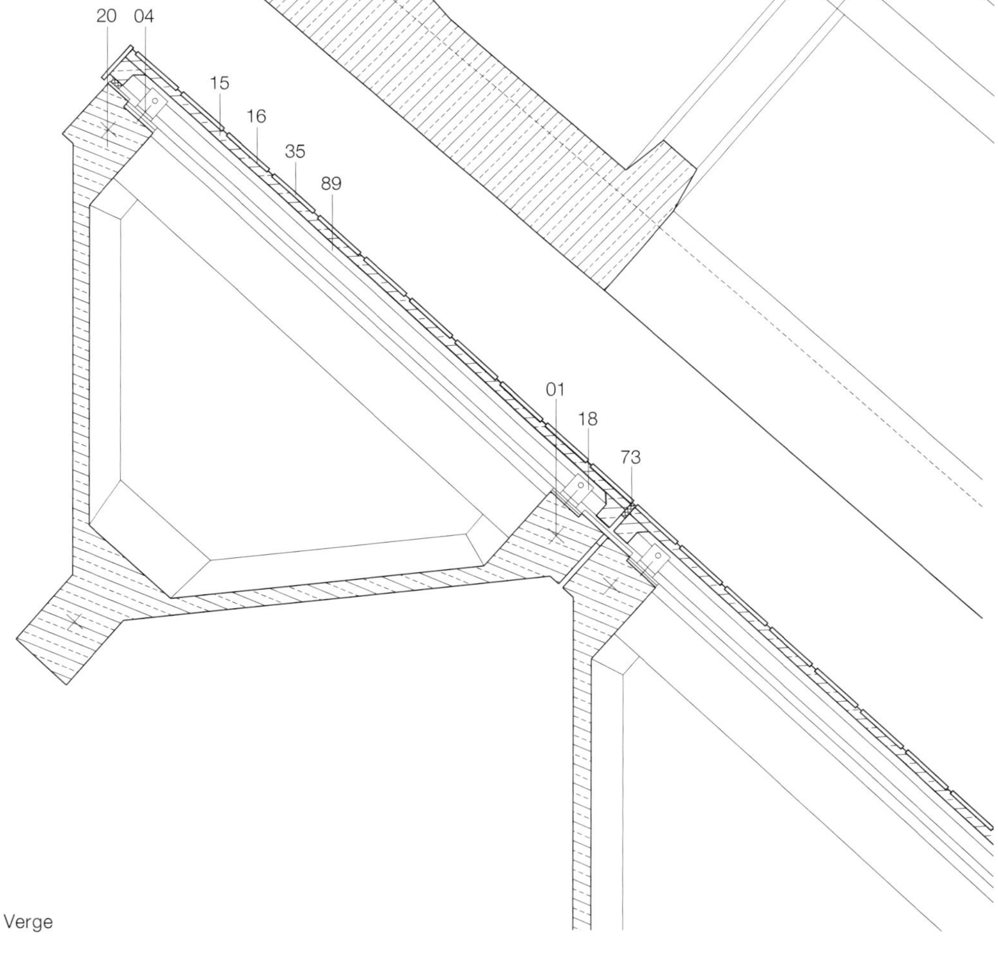

Details scale 1:33.3

00 Railing
01 Anchor
04 Bolt
10 Precast reinforced concrete ridge
15 Reinforced concrete frame panel
16 Sand-cement mortar with supporting interlayer
18 Angle bracket
20 Precast reinforced concrete rib support
21 Pretensioned cable
35 120 x 120 x 10 mm glazed ceramic tile
70 Sealing layer
73 Acrylic resin joint seal
78 Chloroprene sealing strip
89 Polyurethane foam thermal insulation

Ridge

Verge

View onto roof

**School building, Eichstätt**
1993

Architects: Schunck und Partner, Munich
Eberhard Schunck, Dieter Ullrich, Norbert Krausen
Assistant: Sandra Weimar
Structural engineer: Martinka and Grad, Gaimersheim

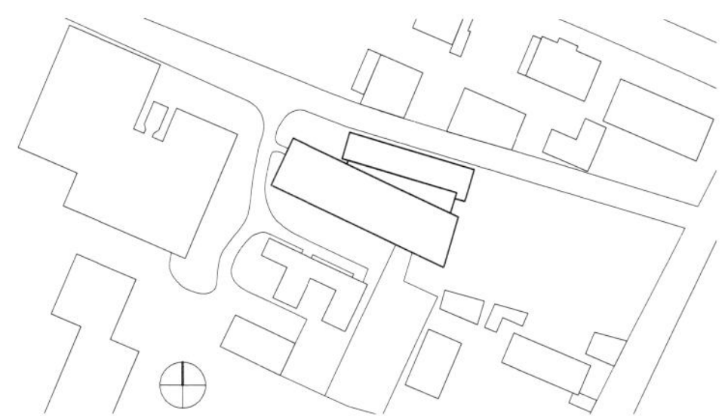
Site plan scale 1:3000

Entrance side

This building stands on a narrow plot on a schools campus in the Schottenau suburb of Eichstätt. It consists of two structures - a southern two-storey block with classrooms and small-group rooms, and a northern single-storey block with administration areas, staff-rooms and classrooms. The outward-facing long facades trace the line of the neighbouring development, the differing angles producing a wedge-shaped space in between, widening to the east. This area is used by the pupils at breaktime. While the north side is protected mostly by masonry wall slabs, the south side opens up in a finely articulated, multi-layer metal facade overlooking the playground and break areas. On the west side is the later addition of a (sadly not very transparent) corridor connection to the main building.

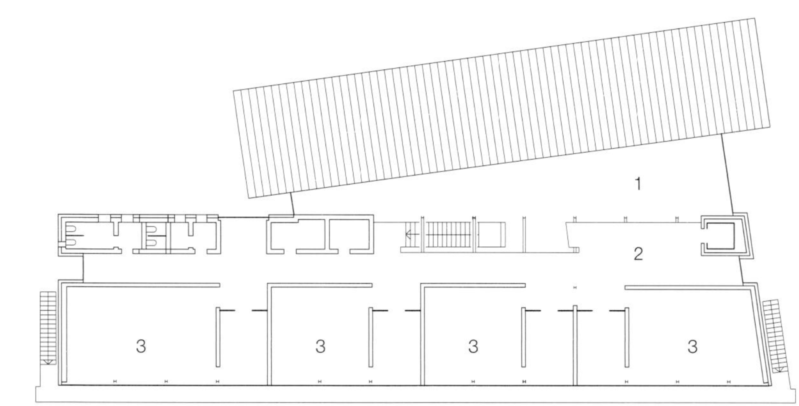
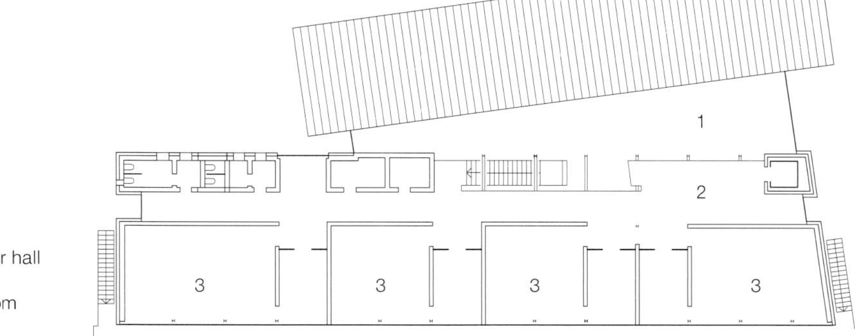

Upper storey
scale 1:500
1 Void over hall
2 Hall
3 Classroom

The steel frame of simple rolled sections as the primary loadbearing structure made it possible to divide the space freely, according to use. Only the reinforced concrete floor above the ground floor is made of a composite of semi-precast slabs and steel beams. The underside has a corrugated structure. The steel frame is infilled with pale-grey modular concrete blocks. These large-format blocks between the linear steel components create a very emphatic wall-like impression.

The external walls are a cavity construction with two layers of ventilated modular masonry blocks, and the facades are a framed construction of steel profiles. On the south facade a canopy of printed glass protects the classrooms on the upper floor from the sun, while not noticeably reducing light levels. The first-floor escape and maintenance balcony, a lightweight structure suspended on steel members, leads to steps at the gable ends. Its white mesh structures appear as a transparent veil in front of the masonry.

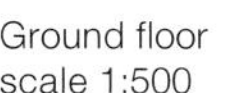

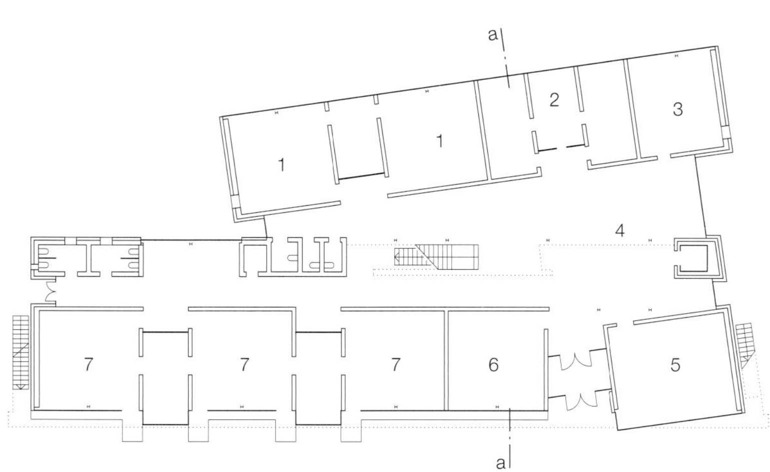

Ground floor
scale 1:500
1 Classroom
2 Administration
3 Staffroom
4 Hall
5 Gymnasium
6 Multi-purpose hall
7 Kindergarten

Corner detail

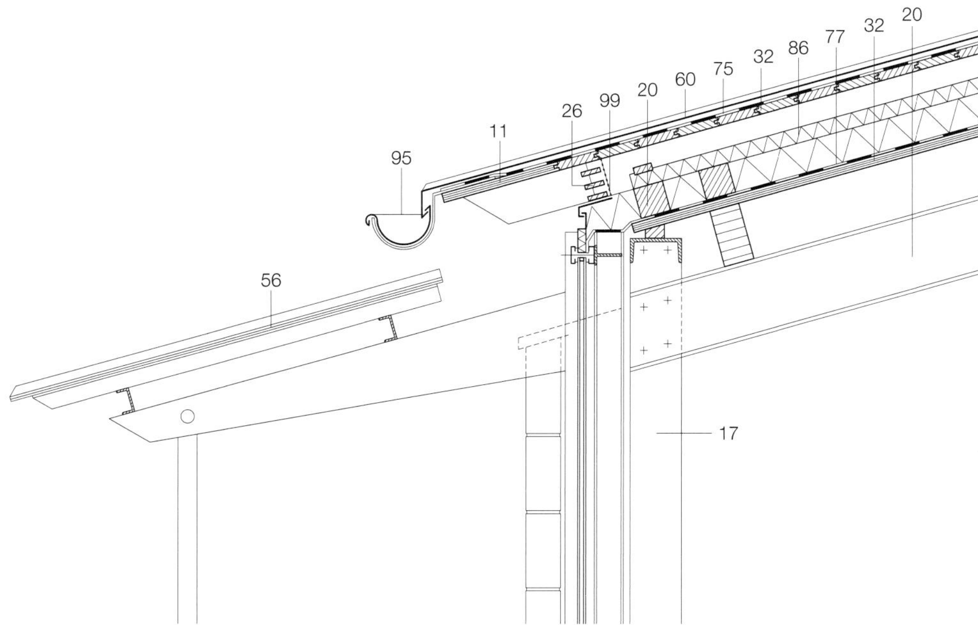


Eaves, balcony

Eaves, main roof

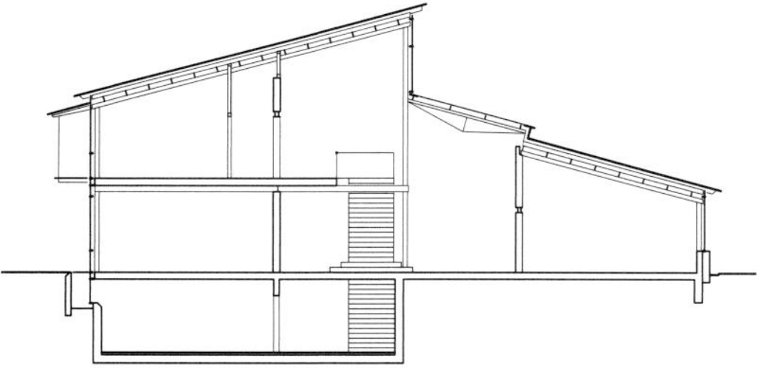

Section aa scale 1:400

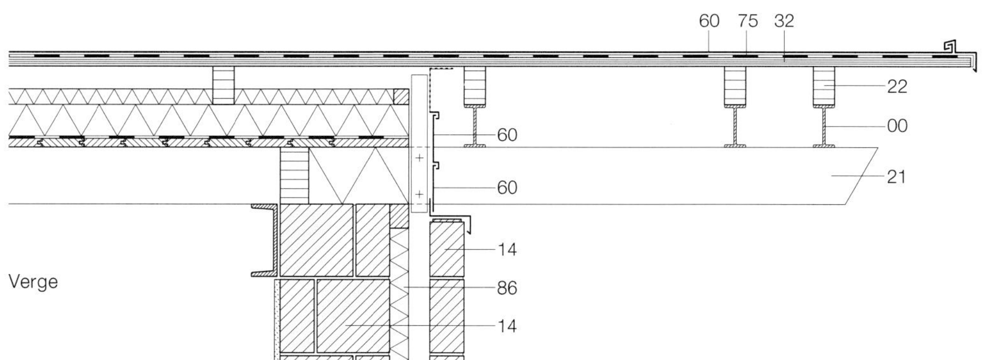


Verge

The roof frame is made of steel beams and timber purlins. The roof construction, with a ventilation layer above the insulation, lies above the loadbearing frame. To make the ventilation space as large as possible, the spacer rafters were mounted on timber wall plates positioned in the plane of the insulation. The position of the main purlin permits a roof overhang at the verge. In keeping with the pale grey modular facade, the roof covering is titanium-zinc sheeting with double-lock welts. The glass roof over the hall used for break periods rests on a pressed steel frame. To protect against diffuse light on the north side, the glass is printed in parts with a grid of white dots.

Details scale 1:20

00 Spacer of 5 mm welded steel sheet, 108 x 60 mm, l = 80 mm
11 Eaves trimmer
14 90 mm concrete block, 290 mm concrete block
17 I-section steel column 140 mm deep (IPE)
20 80 x 80 timber; main roof: two 180 mm steel channel sections; break hall: upper chord: two 80 x 40 x 8 mm steel angle, tensioned underneath with 10 mm dia. steel bar
21 80 x 150 mm glued laminated timber purlin, I-section steel purlin 100 mm deep (IPE)
22 60 x 100 mm rafter, 60 x 120 mm rafter
26 45 mm steel T-profile glazing bars, 15 x 50 mm spruce louvres
32 24 mm decking, 28 mm decking
56 Insulating glass: printed solar glass + laminated safety glass
60 Standing-seam titanium-zinc sheet, 105 x 15 x 1.5 mm and 150 x 15 x 1.5 mm aluminium cover sheet bent to fit
75 Bituminous felt
77 Vapour barrier
86 Mineral-fibre thermal insulation, 40 mm, 50 mm, 80 mm
85 Sheet-aluminium rainwater gutter
99 Ventilation grille

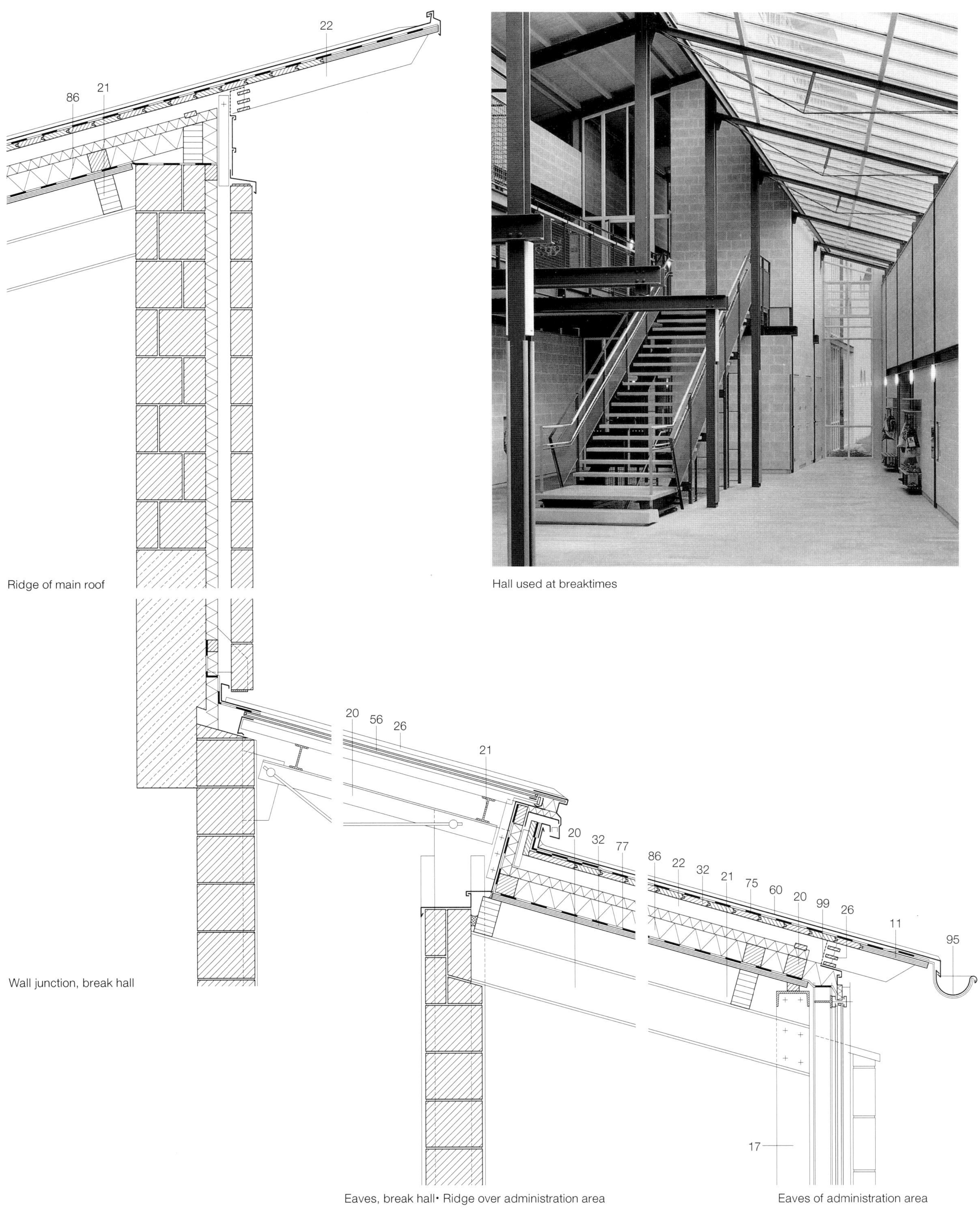


Ridge of main roof

Hall used at breaktimes

Wall junction, break hall

Eaves, break hall • Ridge over administration area

Eaves of administration area

**Museum in Henley-on-Thames, Oxfordshire**
1999

Architects: David Chipperfield Architects, London
Assistants: Renato Benedetti, Peter Crompton, Rebecca Elliot, Spencer Fung, Alec Gillies, Harvey Langston-Jones, Genevieve Lilley, Andrew Llowarch, Rik Nys, John Onken, Viktoria Pike, Maurice Shapiro, Mechthild Stuhlmacher, Simon Timms
Structural engineer: Whitby, Bird & Partner, London
Client: River and Rowing Museum Foundation

Northeast side

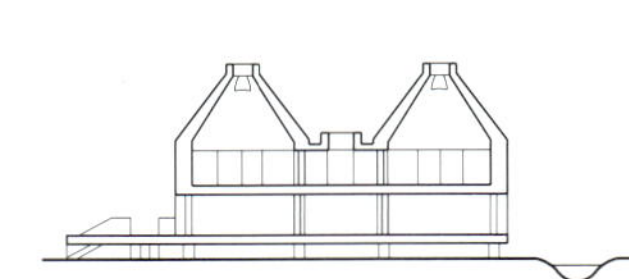
aa

1 Entrance
2 Exhibition space
3 Library
4 Office
5 Meeting room
6 Restaurant
7 Terrace

Site plan scale 1:6000

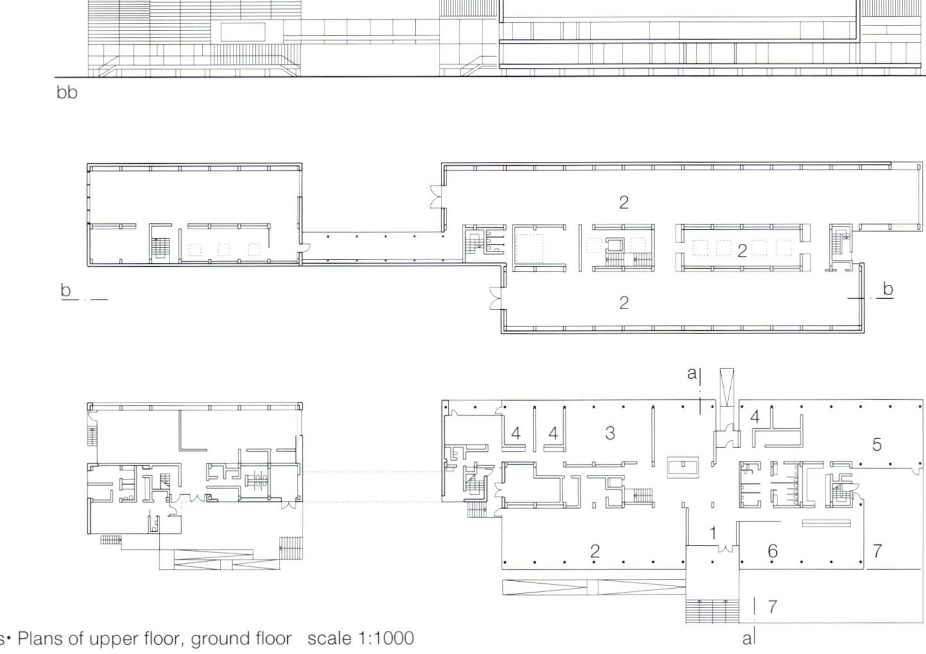

Sections• Plans of upper floor, ground floor scale 1:1000

The museum, situated on the banks of the River Thames, documents the history of rowing, the river and the town of Henley. The design was influenced by the traditional wooden barns and boathouses found in the county of Oxfordshire, and the tents which provide cover for spectators at the annual Henley Regatta. In this new interpretation of local building forms, the transparent entrance level is lifted above the ground and the wooden-clad boat halls are raised on stilts. The seemingly enclosed upper floor has a steel frame with trusses at 3.90 m centres. Shear walls and round reinforced concrete columns support the trusses and the floor slabs. In the interior the steel roof frame disappears behind thermally insulated panels; on the outside, the roof is covered with stainless steel.

South side

Steel truss roof frame

Details scale 1:20

05 6 mm steel plate welded in steel frame
20 Steel truss, 51 x 102 mm channel section upper and lower chords, 70 x 70 x 6 mm steel angle struts
24 I-section, channel-section, horizontal members
57 Insulating glass: toughened security glass + laminated safety glass
58 0.4 mm terne-coated stainless steel sheet standing seam roofing
85 18 mm plywood
86 Aluminium-lined structural tray with 100 mm thermal insulation and 40 mm ventilation space
95 Stainless steel rainwater gutter
98 Perforated sheet-metal leaf screen
99 Insect screen

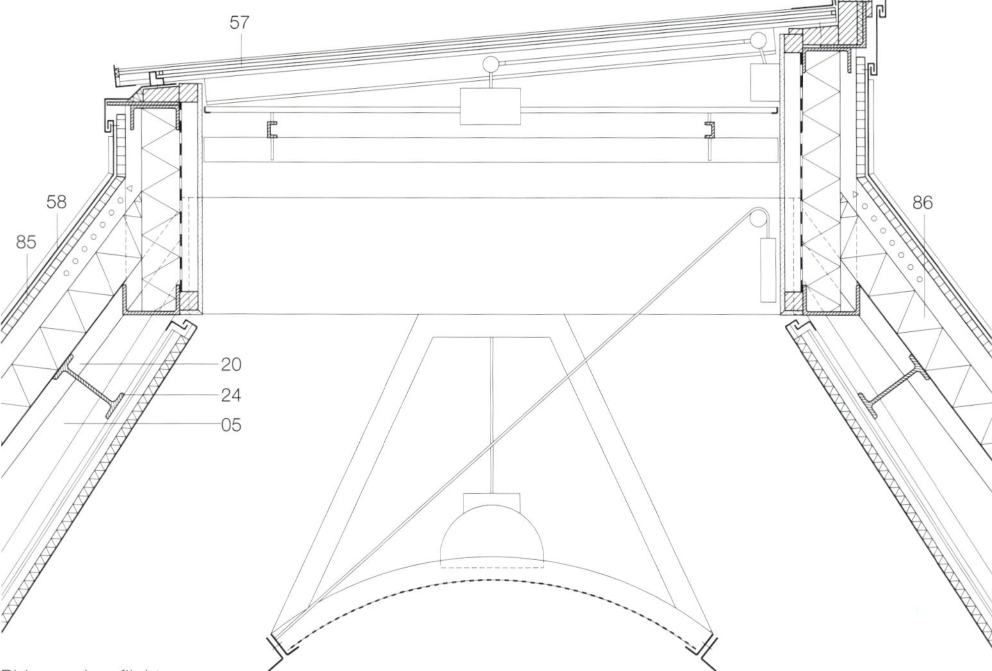


Ridge and rooflight

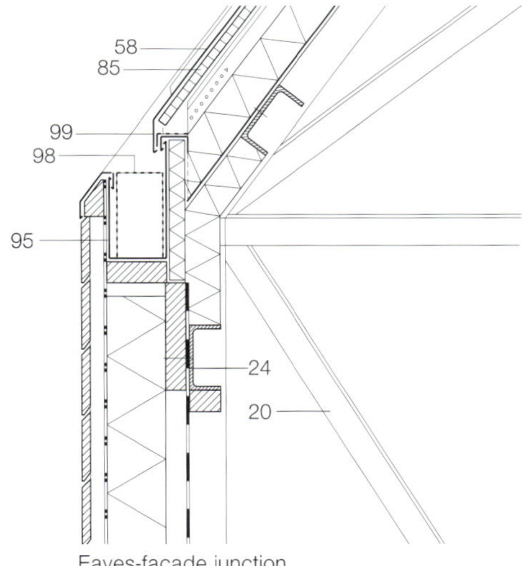


Eaves-facade junction

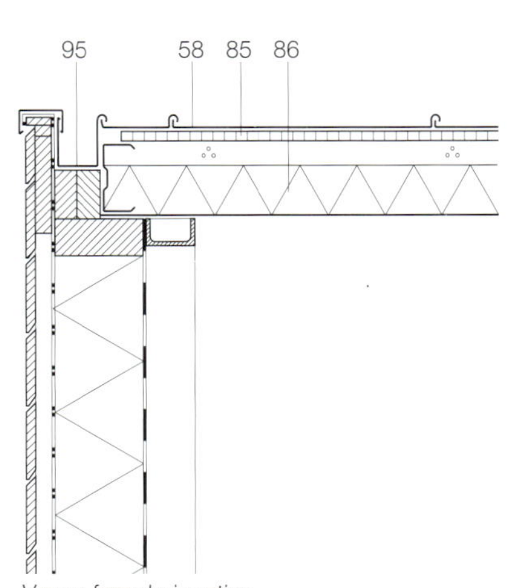


Verge-facade junction

Southeast side

## House in Flawil

1998–99

Architects: Markus Wespi and Jérôme de Meuron, Gaviano and Zurich
Structural engineer: Fritz Allenbach, Frutigen

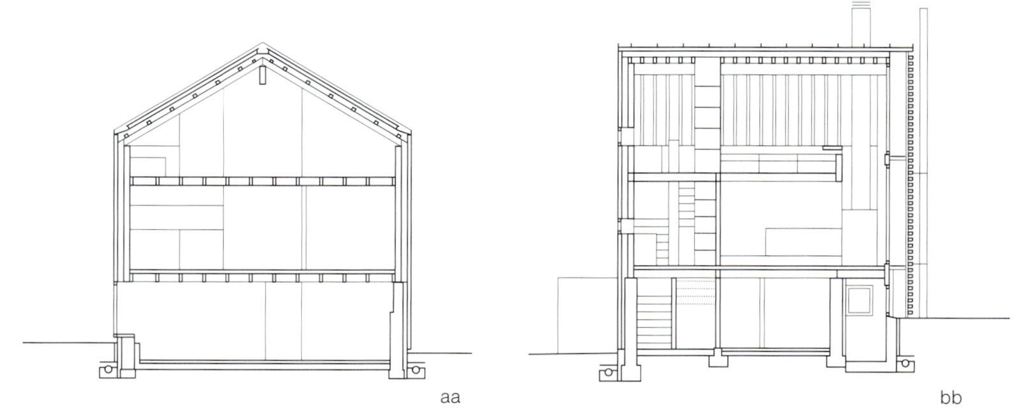


Sections • Plans scale 1:200

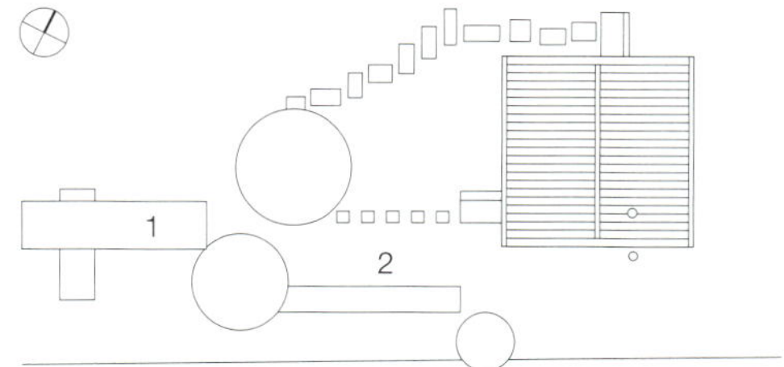


Site plan scale 1:500

Southeast side

1 Covered bicycle stand
2 Garden courtyard
3 Entrance
4 Bathroom/WC
5 Guest room
6 Storage
7 Boiler room/laundry
8 Kitchen/dining
9 Living room
10 Fireplace
11 Study
12 Sleeping deck
13 Void

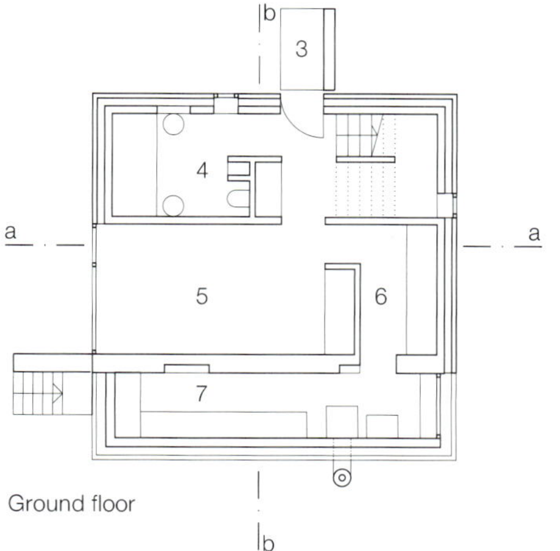


Ground floor

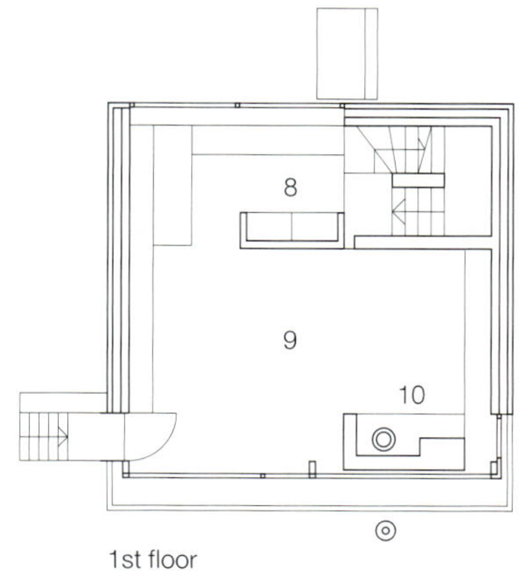


1st floor

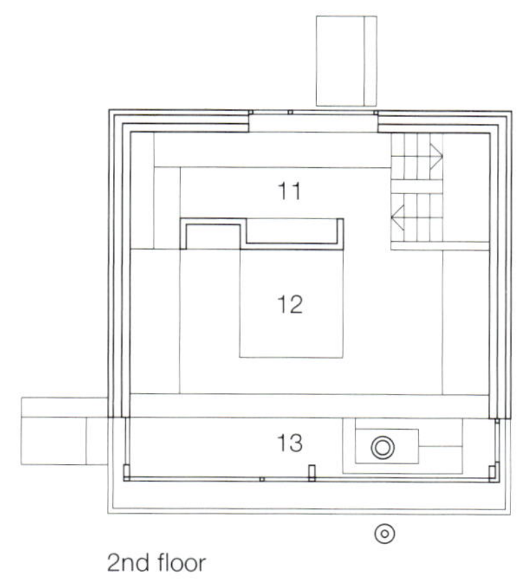


2nd floor

Southwest side

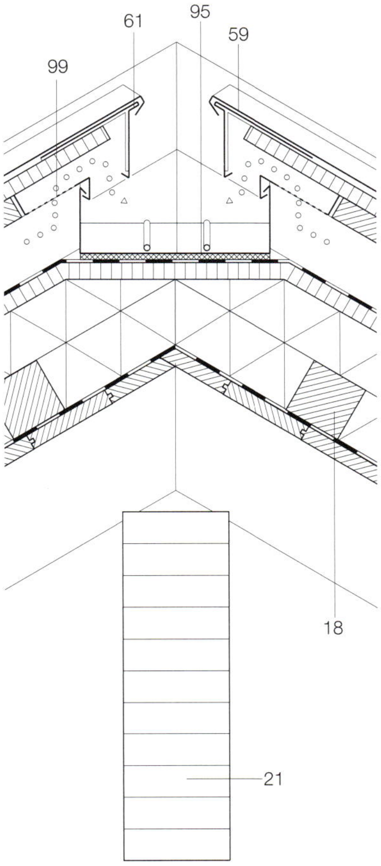

This detached house in Flawil was one of the first prefabricated Swiss houses and, in line with tastes at the time, its facades were rendered, as it was supposed to look like a masonry construction. Today, after renovation, the materials chosen and the simple form echo the design of barns found in the surrounding countryside.

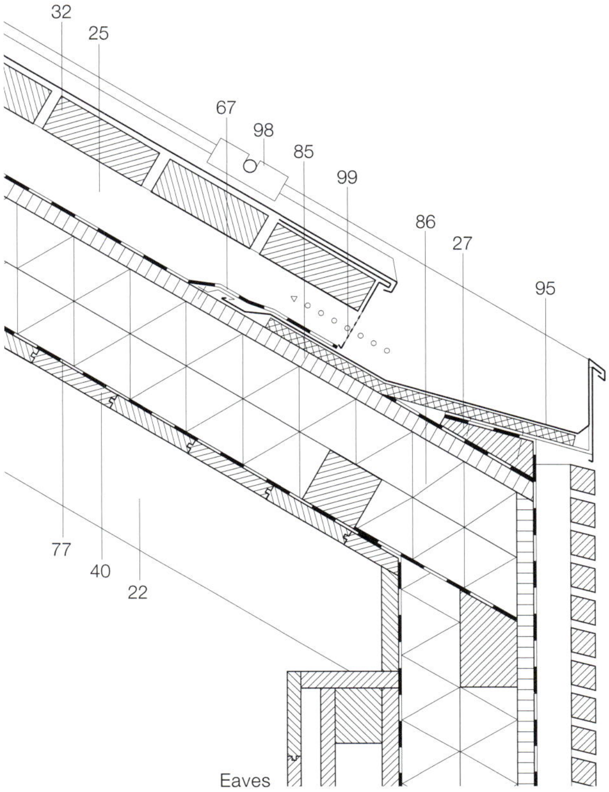

For the renovation, the external rendering was removed and the facade fitted with thermally insulated, ventilated larchwood cladding. The closed facade breaks up on the south side into a screen of Douglas fir battens fixed horizontally. This screen affords protection against direct solar radiation on this south-facing side, and thereby enables the entire facade to be glazed, with insulating glass. The purlin roof is covered with titanium-zinc sheet ventilated underneath. Its design, with integrated box gutters, reinforces the impression of restraint created by the simple lines of the house itself. The special construction of the ridge as a gutter that also performs a ventilation function was possible because a second layer of roofing felt was provided.

Details scale 1:10

- 03 55 x 22 mm clamping batten
- 05 Clip
- 17 42 mm dia. steel tube
- 18 80 x 80 mm wall plate
- 21 140 x 460 mm pine ridge purlin
- 22 80 x 140 mm glued laminated pine rafter
- 25 Counter battens/80 mm ventilation space
- 27 Feather-edged board
- 32 50 mm pine decking
- 40 Spruce decking, 20 mm on roof, 16 mm on wall
- 59 Titanium-zinc roofing sheet
- 61 Connecting plate
- 62 Verge flashing
- 67 Roofing felt
- 77 Vapour barrier
- 85 22 mm soft fibreboard
- 86 2 x 80 mm thermal insulation
- 95 Rainwater gutter with heating wire, ridge and eaves
- 98 Snowguard
- 99 Ventilation grille

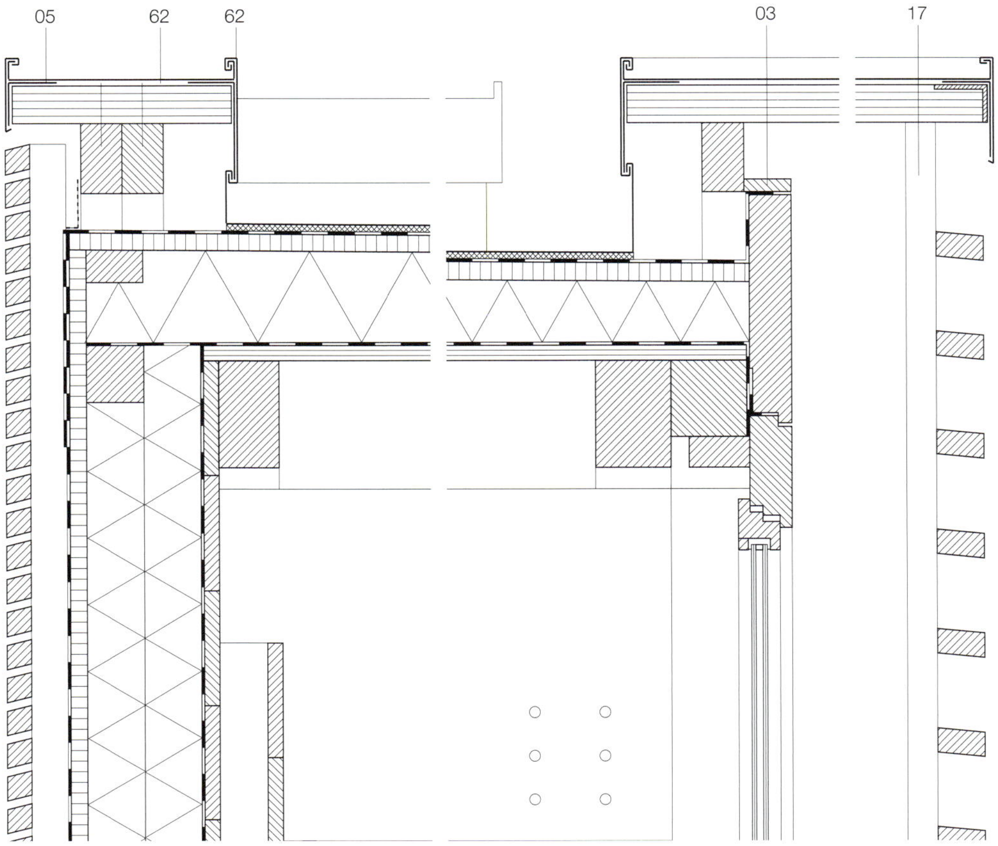

Ridge

Eaves

Verge and louvre facade

**Sauna in Finland**
1994–95

Design: Jaakko Keppo / Holzstudio, Technical University of Helsinki
Consultants: Jan Söderlund, Seppo Häkli, Hannu Hirsi
Client: Marja Kanervo

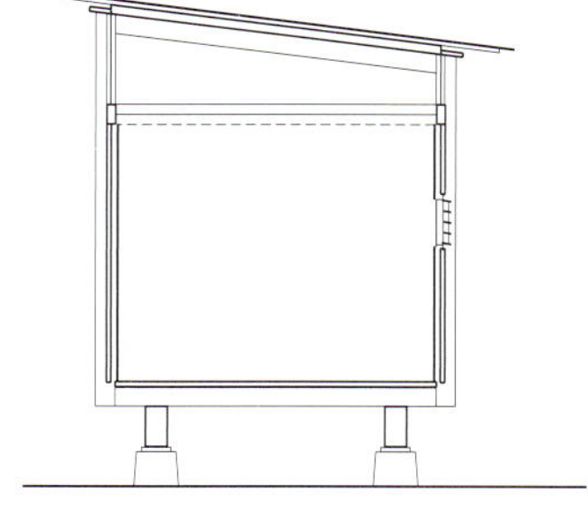


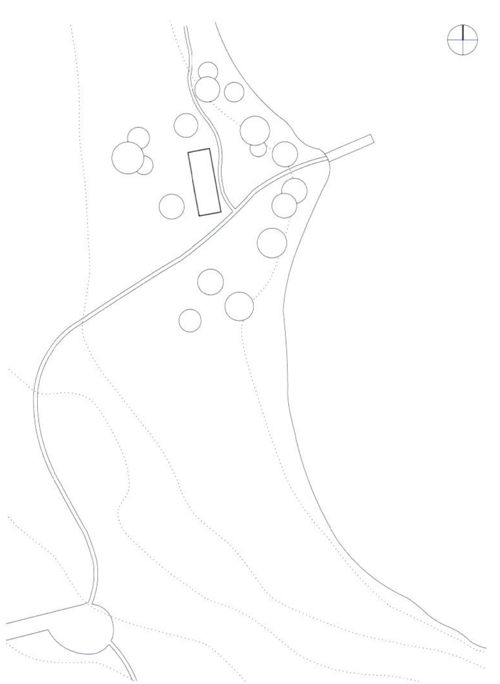

Site plan scale 1:1000

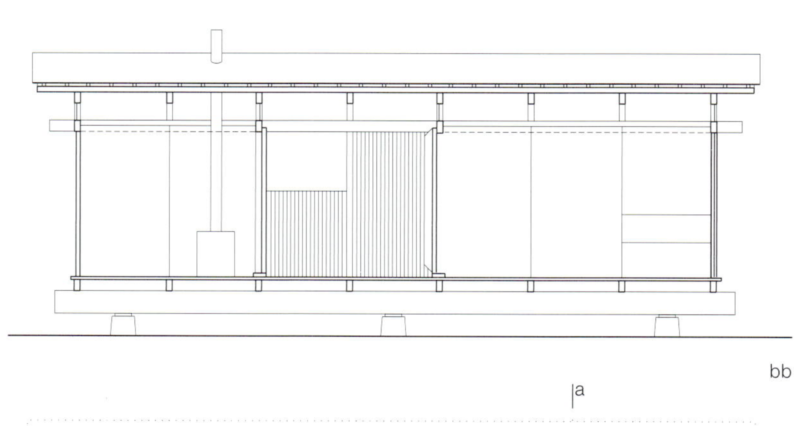


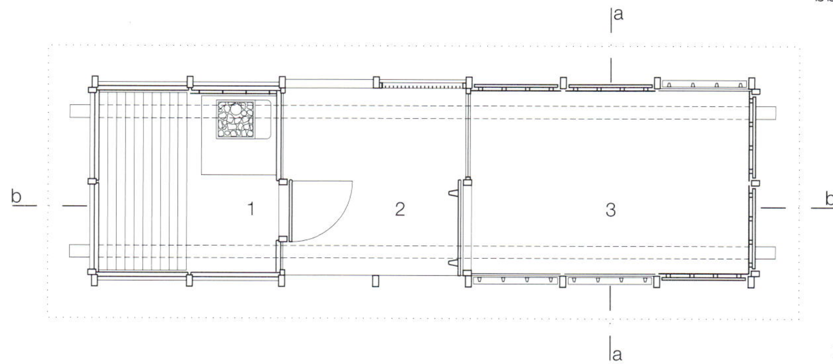


Plan • Sections scale 1:100

1 Sauna
2 Terrace
3 Rest room

West side

Details scale 1:10

08 Fitting for sliding door, sliding door: 45 x 45 mm glued laminated pine and 15 x 42 mm glued laminated alder
20 76 x 150 mm glued laminated pine frame
25 45 x 45 mm pine batten
28 50 x 50 mm filler board
29 Cover board
32 18 mm birch plywood panel
33 Birch plywood roofing panel, upper layer 9 mm, lower layer 15 mm
34 15 mm birch plywood wall cladding, colour-waxed
40 28 x 80 mm aspen cladding
67 Waterproofing, bitumen sheeting
86 50 mm mineral-fibre thermal insulation

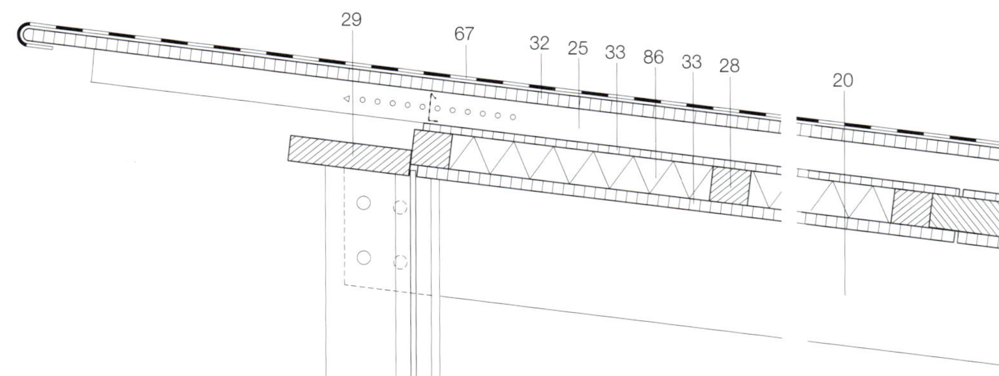

Ridge with no ventilation layer above the insulation

The design for this sauna, built by the shore of a lake in the middle of a wood, won a student competition at the Technical University of Helsinki. It had to demonstrate sustainability, ecological compatibility and prefabrication. The resulting small, simple, framed construction was built on a 20 square metre plot. It has prefabricated floors and wall units. Only native woods were used on the roof and the walls: Lapland pine, birch, alder and aspen. The basic unit is a rigid frame of glued laminated pine, with infill panels of various types of wood. It is fitted with a strip of single-glazed windows under the eaves.

The roof is made of prefabricated panels of birch plywood, which are butted over the frame or joined together with connection pieces. The roof covering, consisting of simple bitumen roofing sheet, has a ventilation layer underneath. Because of the building's restricted use and the high ventilation layer, it was not necessary to incorporate a vapour barrier.

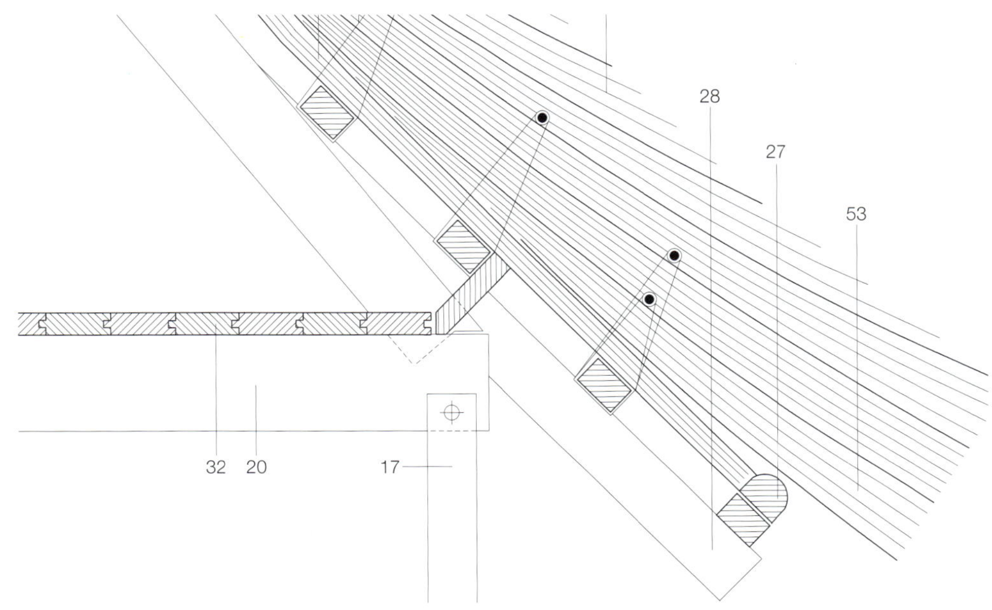

Eaves with roof overhang

Southeast side

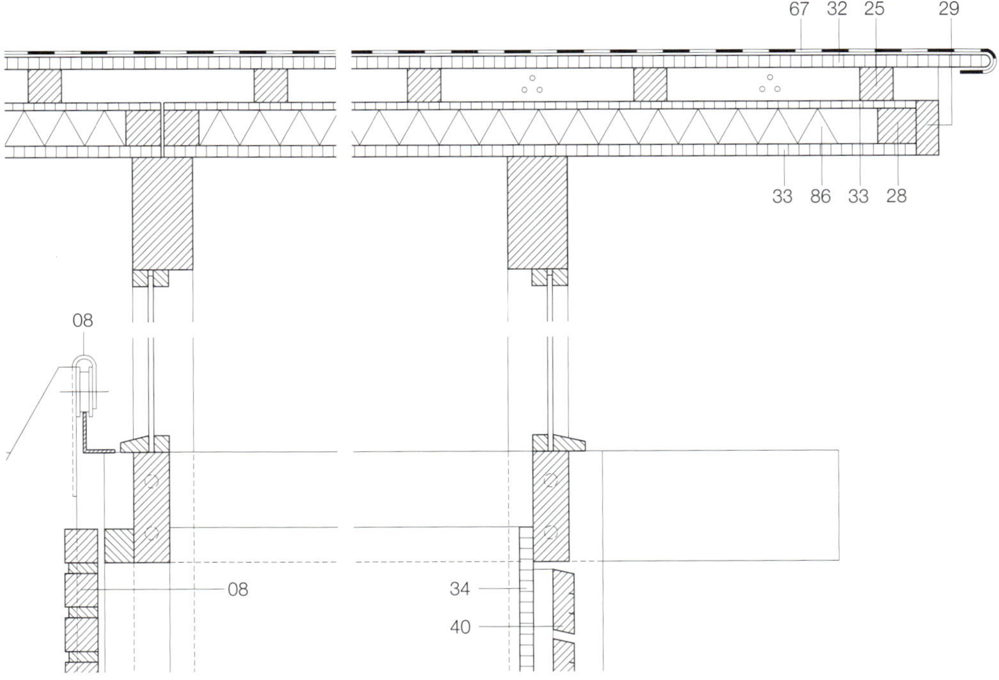

Verge with connection to facade

**Exhibition Hall 26 in Hannover**
1996

Architects: Herzog + Partner, Munich
Thomas Herzog, Hanns Jörg Schrade, Michael Volz
Structural engineer: Schlaich, Bergermann und Partner, Stuttgart
Jörg Schlaich, Andreas Keil, Frank Simon
Client: Deutsche Messe AG, Hannover

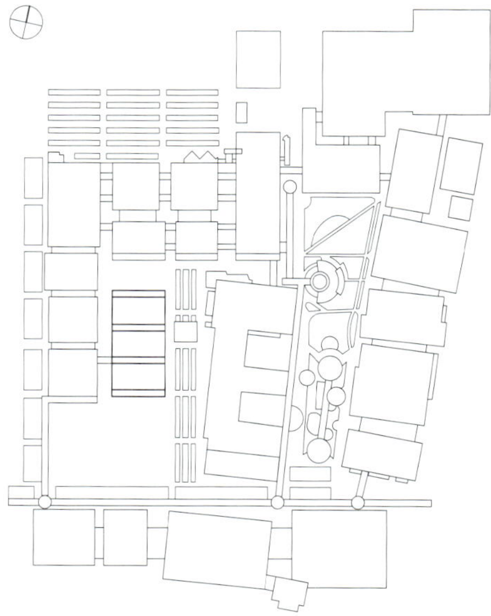
Site plan scale 1:15 000

It took just nine months to build this 25,400 m² hall at Hannover's exhibition centre. Its roof form and the ventilation and lighting concept deriving from it are particularly striking. Measuring 220 metres long by 115 metres wide, the hall is divided into three sections. Each section is spanned by a suspended steel-framed roof fitted with prefabricated wooden panels. A-frames were used as abutments for the tensile system. Vehicle access is located below these struts, while inside the halls, the exhibition areas under the suspended roof are column-free. Along the sides of the hall are six smaller volumes housing catering operations, toilet facilities, supply installations, waste disposal collection and air-conditioning plant.

The A-frames consist of two adjacent trussed frames connected to each other horizontally via tubular sections and stabilised with wind bracing. The pairs are connected in turn by tubular steel sections. The main loadbearing part of the suspension system consists of strips of steel flats with a cross section of 300 x 40 mm. Fixed at 5.5 metres spacing to trussed girders running across the width of the hall (height 26.5 m and 14.0 m), these strips span over 55 metres and have a sag of 7.0 metres.
Laid on top of these steel tie rods are 2.0 x 5.5 m timber panels, which function as secondary beams, bracing, thermal insulation and decking for the roof seal.

The hollow box units have a vapour barrier, a filling of chippings and a layer of mineral-wool insulation. The units were nailed together and attached to the steel tie rods by a combination of nail and screw connections. Mechanically applied synthetic roofing felt forms the final covering layer.
The high self-weight of the roof, unusual for such a tensile construction, is intended to prevent vibration under wind load and limit deformation under uneven vertical loads (snow on one side). For additional stabilisation of the roof surface, cable guys with integrated springs were slung across to the A-frames. The fire-resistance period of the roof is about 60 minutes. A convex counter-curvature of the roof

Northwest elevation

North side

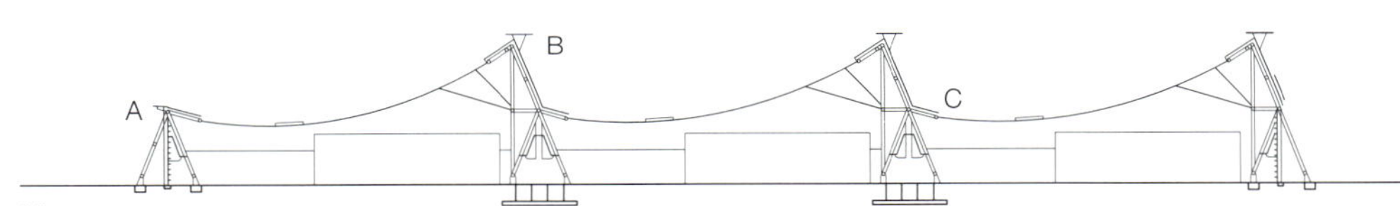


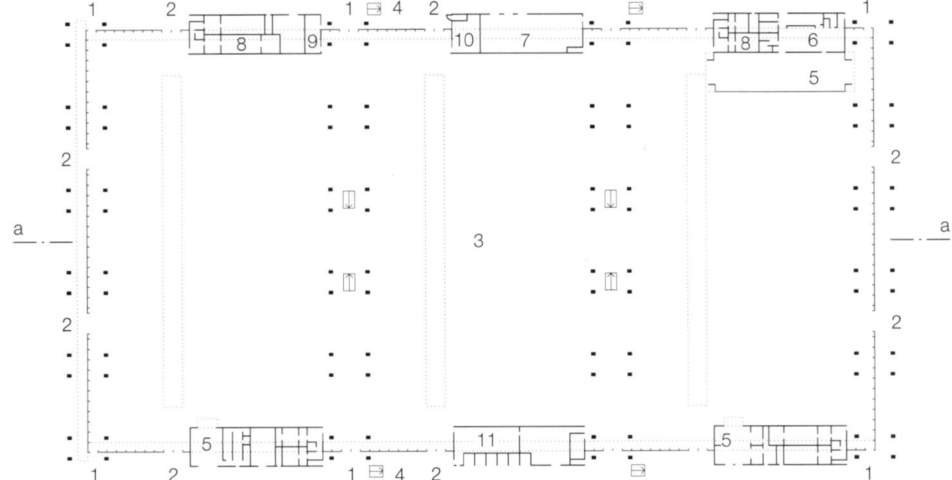


Plan • Section scale 1:2000

1 Entrances
2 Vehicle access and emergency exits
3 Exhibition areas
4 Escape tunnel access
5 Restaurant
6 Kitchen
7 Air-conditioning plant
8 WCs
9 Hall caretaker
10 Telecommunications systems
11 Electrical systems

surface ensures that rainwater runs off to the sides. The rise in height towards the centre is achieved using shortened steel tie rods in this area.

The post-and-beam facade along the roof edges is supported by a frame of two I-sections put together and fixed to the outer tie rods via spreader bars. The sections are pretensioned, which ensures that the outer tie rods are under tension as well. In this way the roof edge remains virtually unmoveable.

Fresh air is drawn in through openings 4.7 m high and distributed evenly to the lower levels. Used air rises through convection, and is vented through openings near the ridge that are fitted with individually controlled flaps. Horizontal covers above the openings enhance the suction effect. To heat the hall, prewarmed air is blown in horizontally through wide-angle nozzles. Extensive north-facing glazing on the ends with the struts brings natural daylight into the space, while avoiding direct solar radiation. Additionally, rooflights with integrated light grids are fitted at the troughs of the suspended roof structure. Light-deflecting elements on the inside of the suspended roof scatter both natural light entering via the glass facade and artificial light. The curved shape of the roof surface underpins this effect.

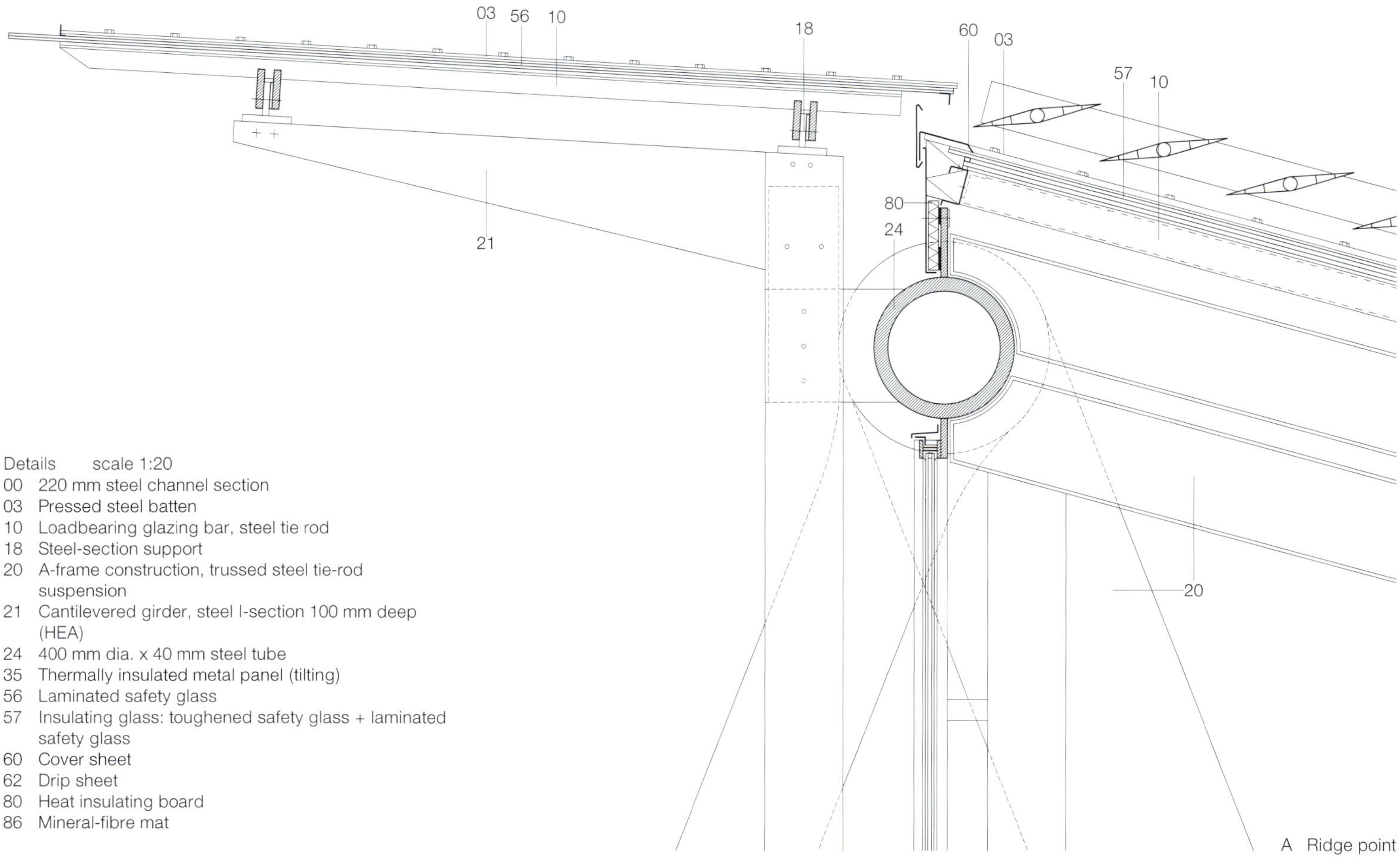

Details scale 1:20

00 220 mm steel channel section
03 Pressed steel batten
10 Loadbearing glazing bar, steel tie rod
18 Steel-section support
20 A-frame construction, trussed steel tie-rod suspension
21 Cantilevered girder, steel I-section 100 mm deep (HEA)
24 400 mm dia. x 40 mm steel tube
35 Thermally insulated metal panel (tilting)
56 Laminated safety glass
57 Insulating glass: toughened safety glass + laminated safety glass
60 Cover sheet
62 Drip sheet
80 Heat insulating board
86 Mineral-fibre mat



A Ridge point

Interior/underside of roof

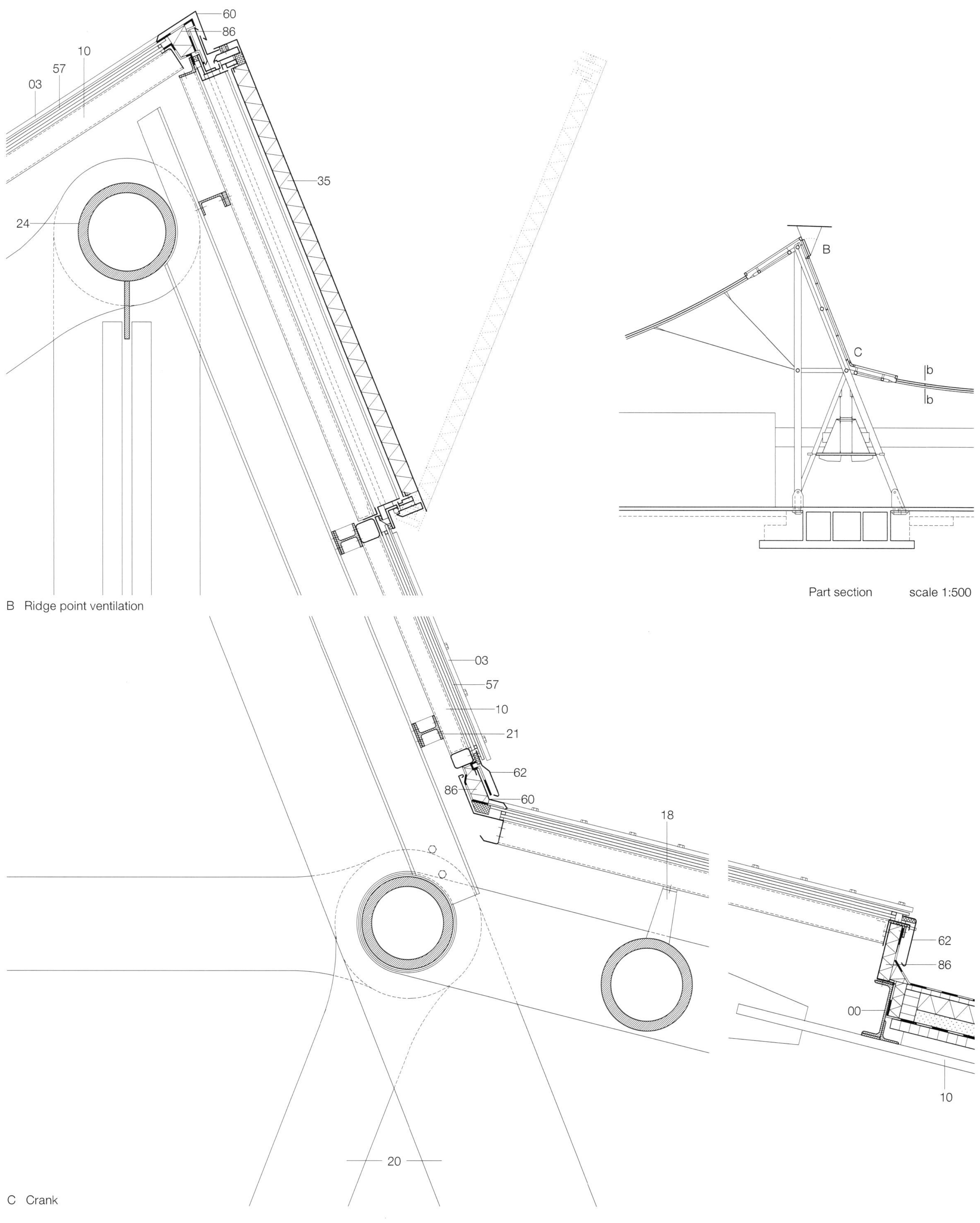


B Ridge point ventilation

Part section scale 1:500

C Crank

Details scale 1:20
00 Welded head bolt with interior thread
04 Nail, bolt
06 Metal angle
09 Insulating wedge
10 Timber, steel tie rod
20 40 x 115 mm glued laminated timber ribs (BS11)
21 Spreader bar
32 Timber profile cladding
33 Timber derivative board
60 Cover sheet
66 65 mm chippings infill
73 Jointing mortar
76 Synthetic roofing felt
77 Vapour barrier
79 Waterstop, sealing strip
86 50 mm mineral wool insulation

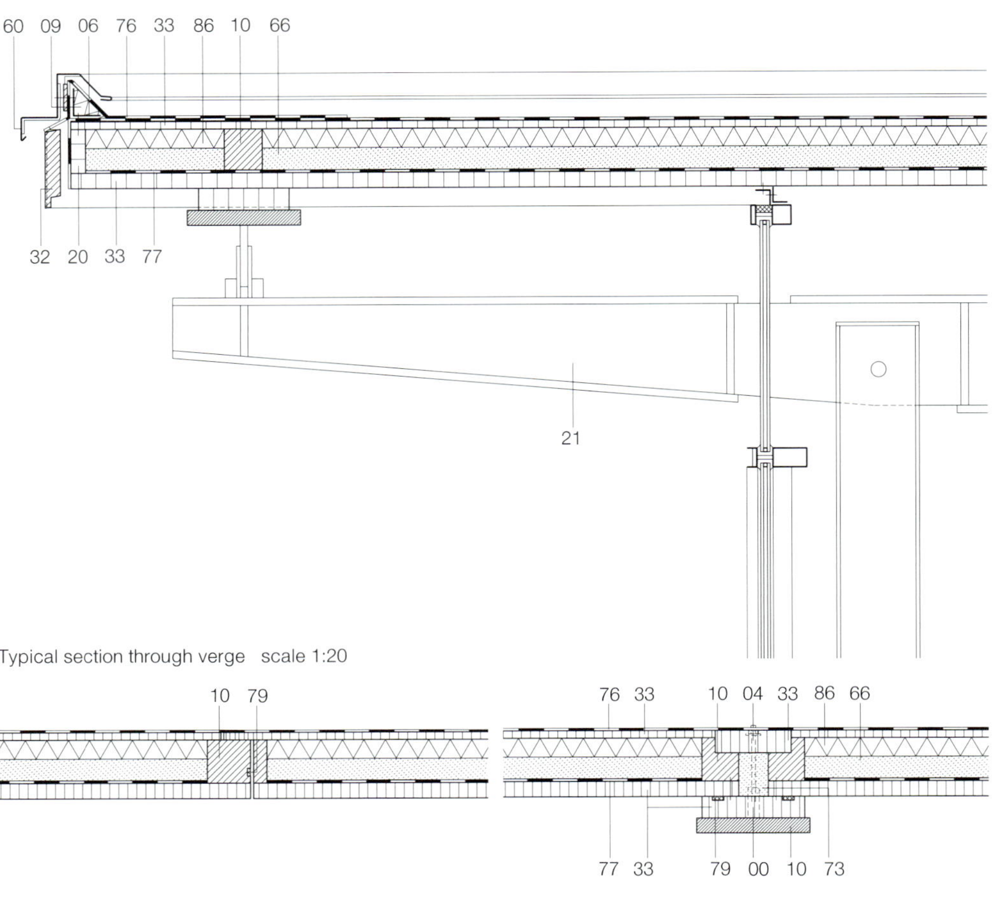


Typical section through verge scale 1:20

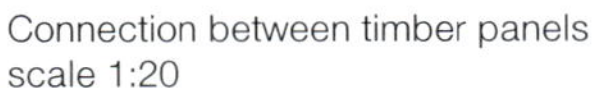

Connection between timber panels
scale 1:20

Connection to steel tie rods
scale 1:20

Southwest side

**University Library in Delft**
1997

Architects: Mecanoo architecten, Delft
Project managers: Francine Houben, Chris de Weijer
Structural engineer: ABT, Delft
Client: ING Vastgoed Ontwikkeling, Den Haag

The library stands close to a 1960s reinforced concrete lecture building. To counteract its solid impression, the library was designed as an extension of the site's green spaces.
A sloping grass roof forms the outer skin and provides space for recreation. The north, east and south sides are finished with a glass facade. The double-skin facade is tilted outwards and angled along its line. In elevation it is a parallelogram. A funnel-shaped approach to the main floor is faced with concrete. In the large hall are open shelves of books and a four-tier unit for magazines. An additional million works of reference are stored in the moisture- and temperature-controlled basement archives. Grouped around the hall are a book store, a café, computer workplaces and offices. The turfed roof is pierced by a 40 m high, grey rendered cone of reinforced concrete. Its tip is a steel frame. This structurally independent construction is supported on A-frames. A ring-like glazing strip between the edge of the roof and the outer wall of the cone brings daylight into the spaces below. Towards the east facade, starting at the highest point of the roof, the concrete roof structure becomes a frame of steel beams and trapezoidal metal sheeting.
The entire roof is supported on reinforced concrete columns. Raking steel supports outside the facade transfer the load of the cantilevered roof down into the ground. 90 mm thick foam glass, sandwiched between an EPDM seal and a vapour barrier of polyethylene sheet, satisfies Dutch thermal insulation requirements. The upper roof consists of a layer of gravel, a filter mat and extensive turfing on top of a substrate. Excess water runs off into a drainage pipe along the edge of the roof. The high storage mass of the roof creates a pleasant indoor climate, and in summer evaporation in the layer of vegetation helps keep temperatures down.

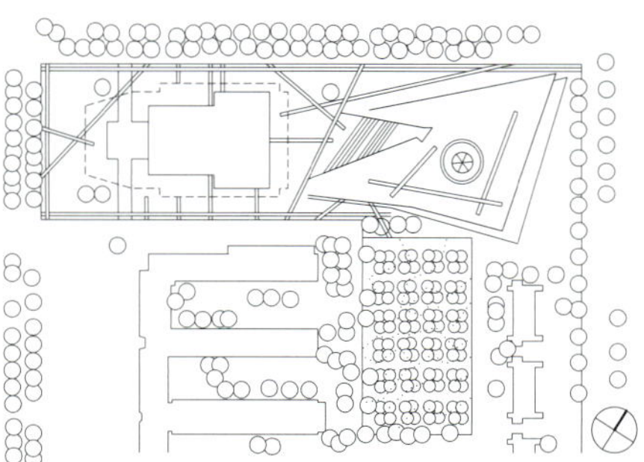

Site plan scale 1:7500

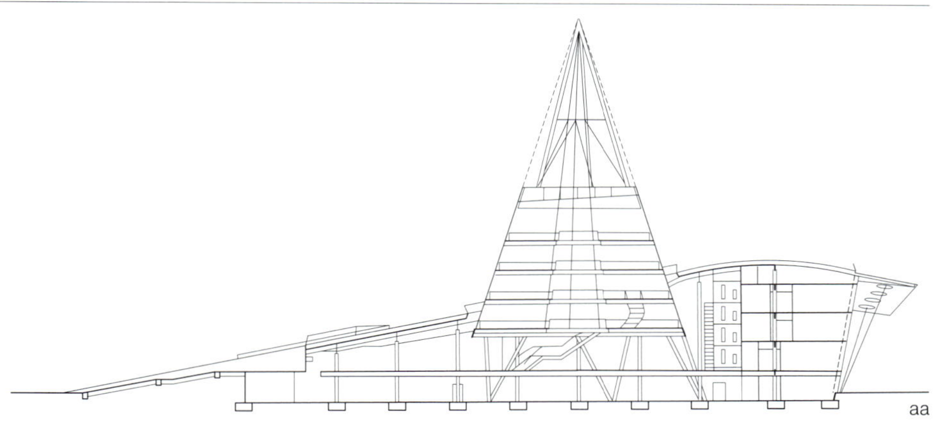

North side

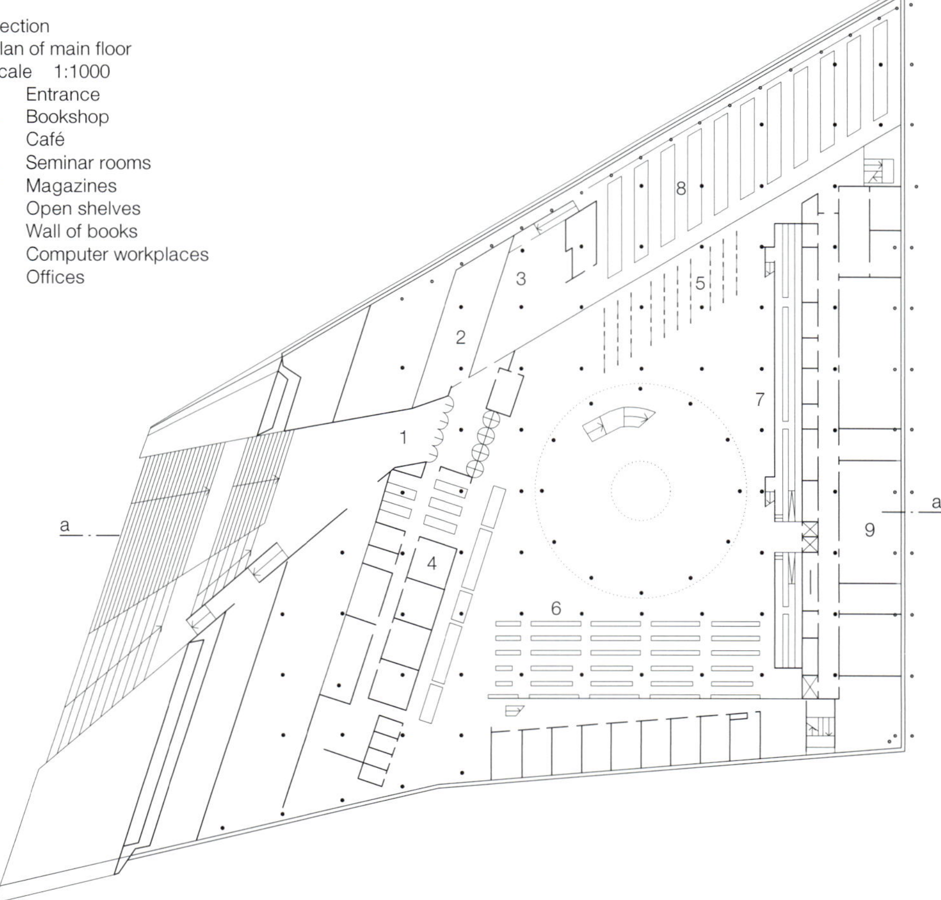


Section
Plan of main floor
scale 1:1000
1 Entrance
2 Bookshop
3 Café
4 Seminar rooms
5 Magazines
6 Open shelves
7 Wall of books
8 Computer workplaces
9 Offices

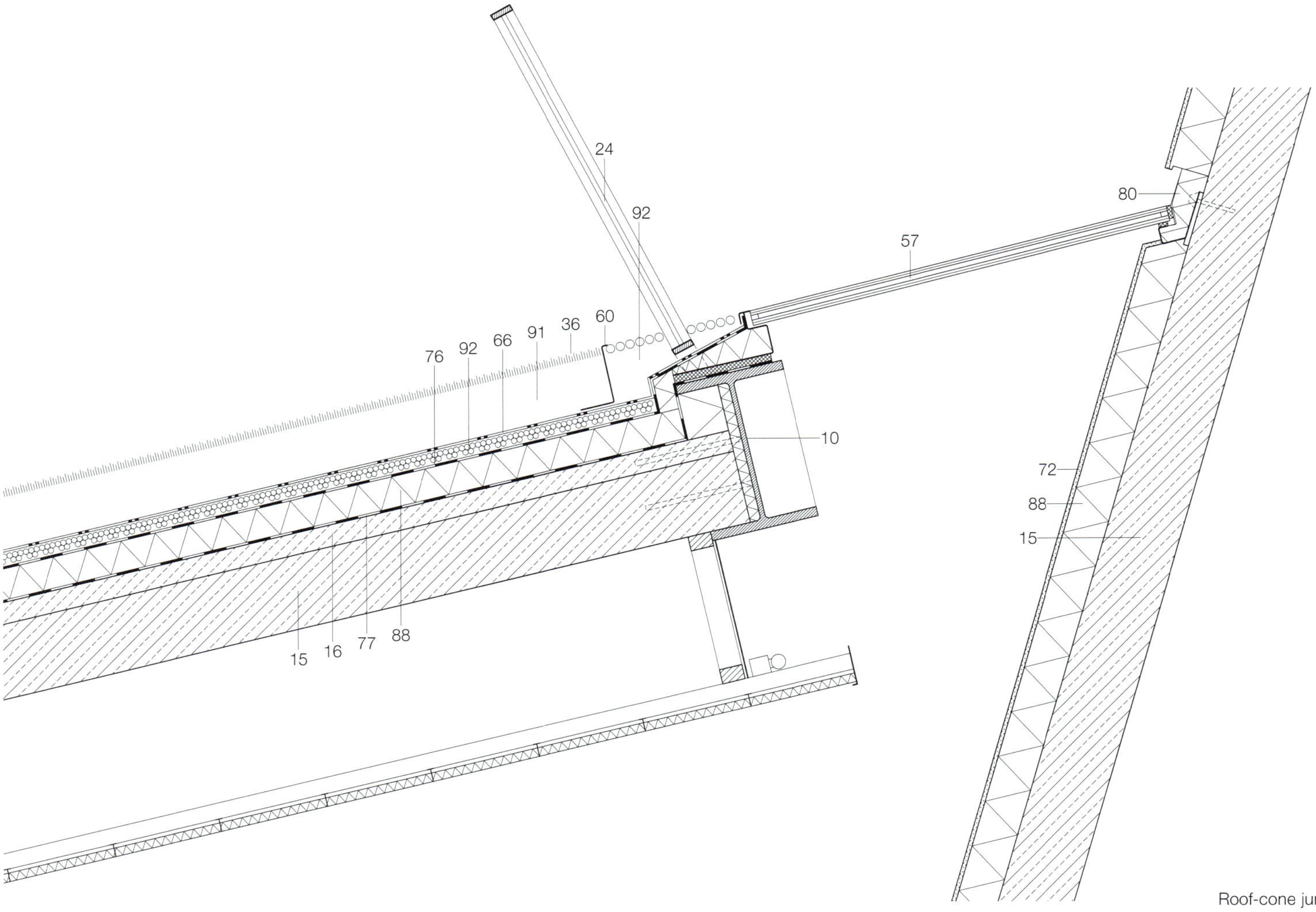

Roof-cone junction

Reinforced concrete cone and reading rooms

Details scale 1:20

10 Steel I-section 460 mm deep (IPE)
15 220 mm reinforced concrete
16 60 mm concrete topping
17 Reinforced concrete column
20 Steel I-section 260 mm deep (HEB)
24 Railing
36 Extensive turfing
57 Insulating glass: 12 mm toughened glass + 2 panes of 8 mm laminated glass
58 70 mm trapezoidal sheet
59 3 mm aluminium sheet
60 90 x 180 x 20 mm Cor-Ten steel angle, cover sheet
66 Filter mat
72 Rendering
76 6 mm root-resistant sheeting, 1.2 mm EPDM seal
77 0.2 mm polyethylene sheet vapour barrier
80 Thermally insulated rooflight support
88 90 mm foam glass thermal insulation
91 Substrate
92 40 mm gravel layer, drainage chippings
94 Drainage pipe

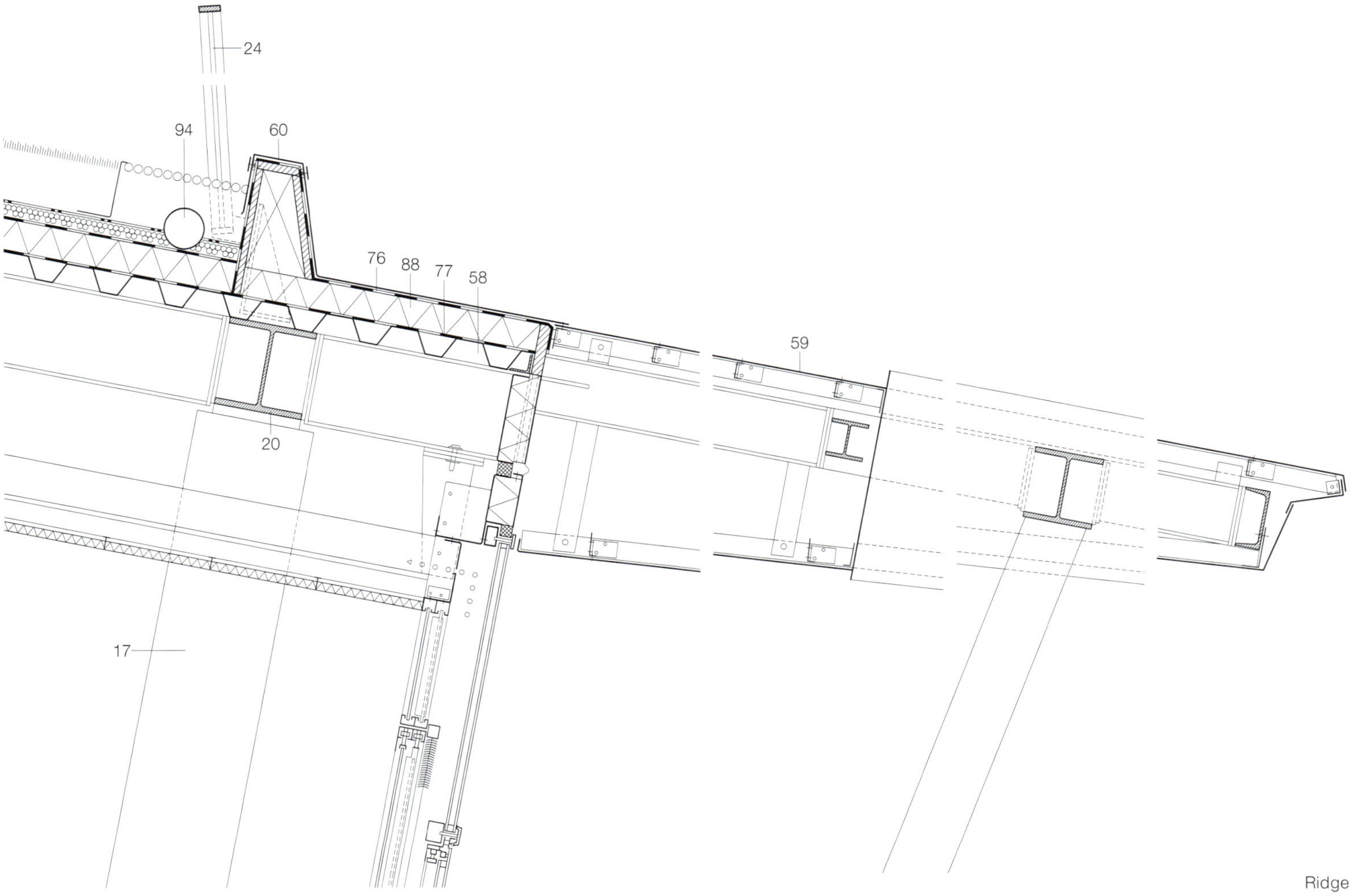

24

94 60

76 88 77 58

59

20

17

Ridge

East elevation

**Skating Rink, Olympiapark in Munich**
1983

Architect: Kurt Ackermann und Partner, Munich
J. Feit, P. Jaeger, R. Martin
Structural engineer: Schlaich, Bergermann und Partner, Stuttgart; J. Seidel
Landscape architect: G. Grzimek, Pfeffenhausen
Client: München Olympiapark GmbH

Membrane and row of "eyes" for light and air

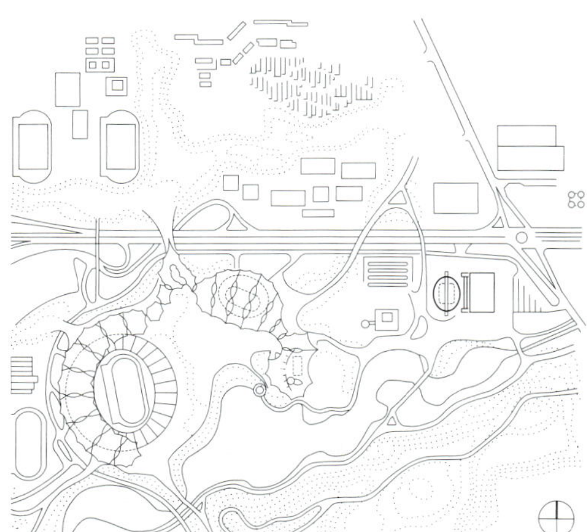

Site plan scale 1:20 000

Underside of roof showing cable net and timber grid

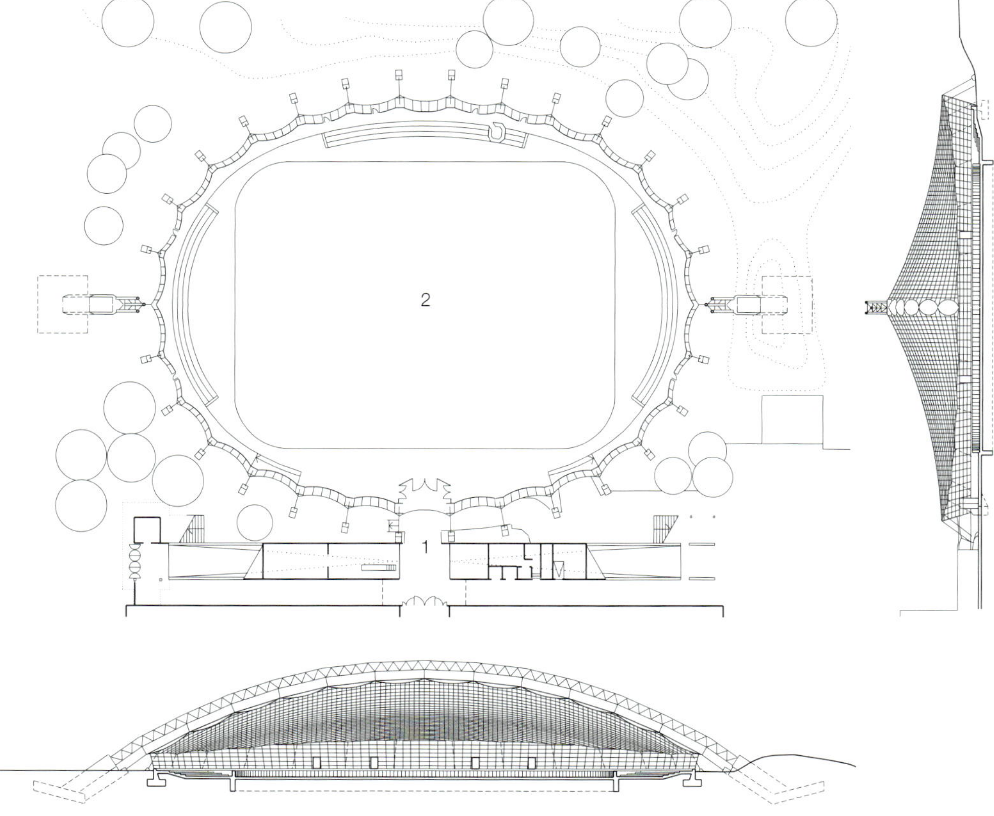


Plan • Elevations scale 1:1200

The task here was to build a simple roof over an existing ice rink. The strictly geometric shape of the adjacent ice sports hall and the tented landscape of the surrounding Olympic facilities influenced the design.

The roof shape responds with a contemporary loadbearing construction. The architects and engineers developed an almost 100-m long triangular steel arch truss spanning the length of the skating rink, leaving a column-free space below.

A net of reverse-curved (and therefore stabilising) cables was extended outwards from this arch. The cables carry a wooden grid, its mesh becoming denser in the flatter part where the higher roof loads occur. On this wooden grid rests the covering layer, a membrane of polyester coated with PVC.

For ventilation and illumination, a chain of lens-shaped rooflights covered with transparent polycarbonate panels is cut out at the "ridge" of the net and the membrane. No thermal insulation is needed on the roof as the structure is intended to protect only against rain and snow.

The roof structure is the dominant feature of the skating rink. Inside, the timber grid opening up towards the chain of rooflights creates an impression of amazing lightness. Seen from the outside the large, pale roof surface nestles modestly among the landscaped slopes and other roofs on the Olympic site. At night, the lights inside set the skating rink aglow.

1 Entrance
2 Ice rink

Steel arch truss, erecting the cable net

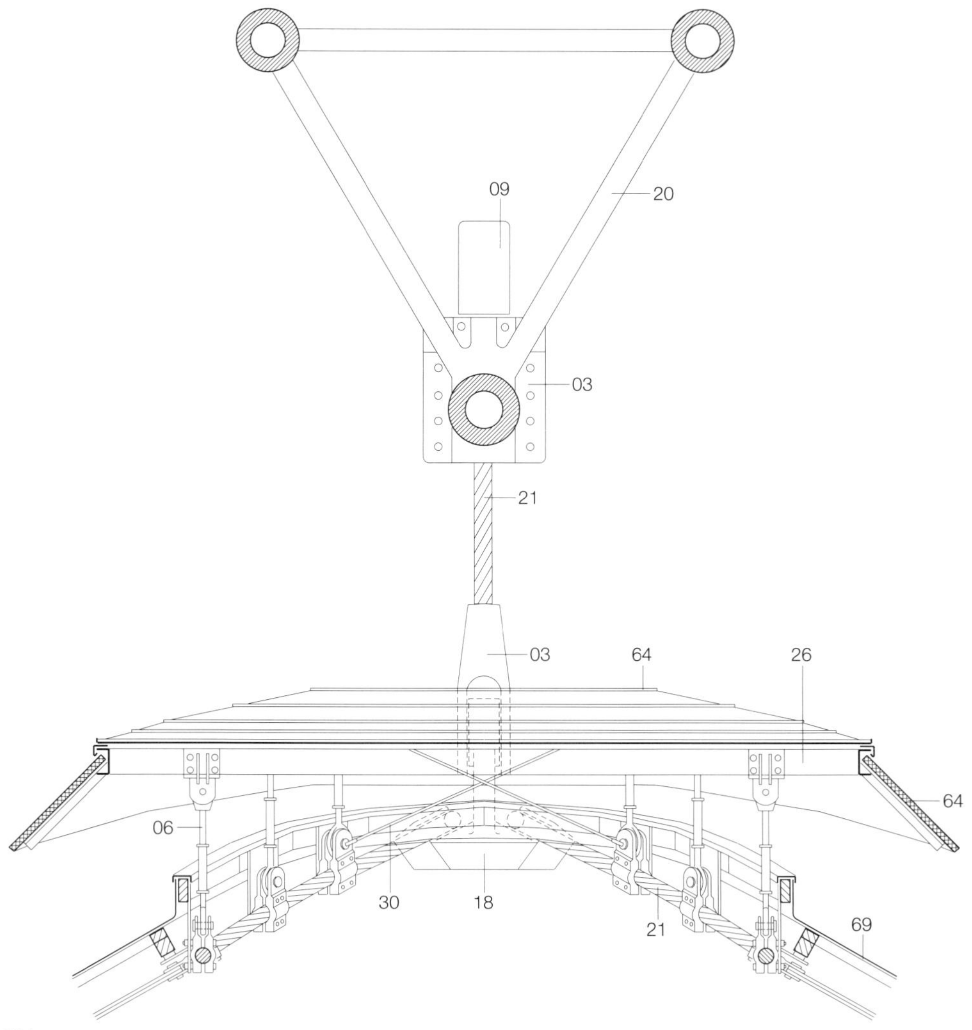


Ridge

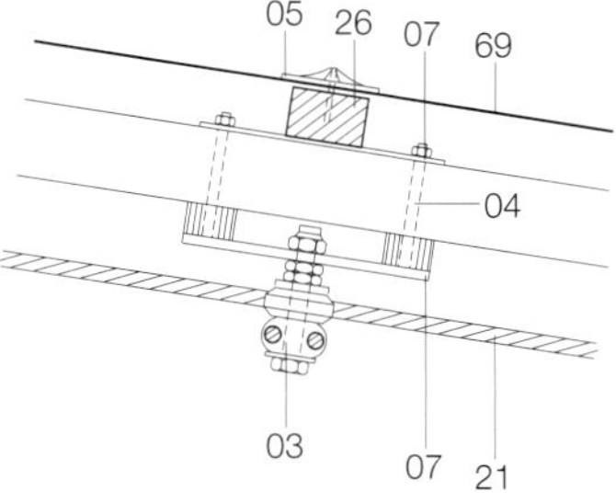


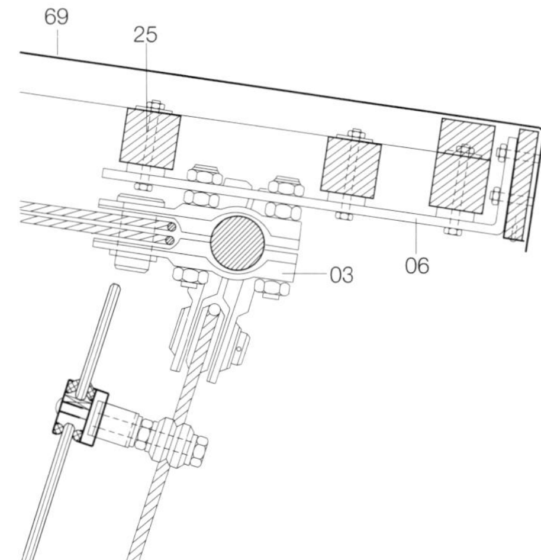


Eaves

Details scale 1:30, scale 1:10

03 Suspension clamp, fork head, cable clamp, edge-cable clamp
04 Threaded bolt (M8)
05 Plastic cramp washer
06 Threaded rod and bush, eaves angle
07 200 x 50 x 2.5 mm and 200 x 60 x 8 mm connecting straps
09 Tensioning device
18 Hip cable bracket
20 Triangular steel arch truss (St 52), 244.5 mm dia. x 60 mm, 267 x 60 mm, 88.5 x 25 mm, 82.5 mm x 25mm
21 60 mm dia. suspension, "eye" and edge cable, 11.5 mm dia. mesh cable
25 60 x 60 mm edge battens
26 100 x 60 x 5.6 mm rectangular hollow section, 40 x 60 mm batten
30 Transverse reinforcement
64 Polycarbonate panels
69 PVC-coated polyester membrane

**Waste disposal services depot in Munich**
1999

Architects: Ackermann und Partner, Munich
Assistants: Eoin Bowler, Frank Höreth, Peter Jaeger, Brigitte Kiermaier, Dieter Kiermaier, Horst Raab, Monika Stegmann, Jens Viehweg
Structural engineer (roof): Schlaich, Bergermann und Partner, Stuttgart
Knut Göppert, Kirsten Martin
Client: Landeshauptstadt Munich

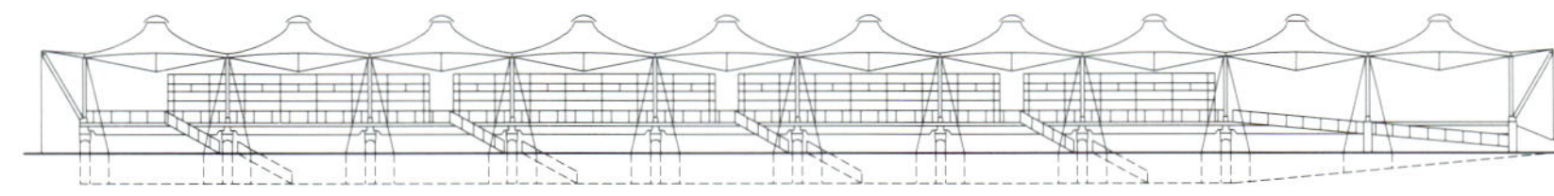

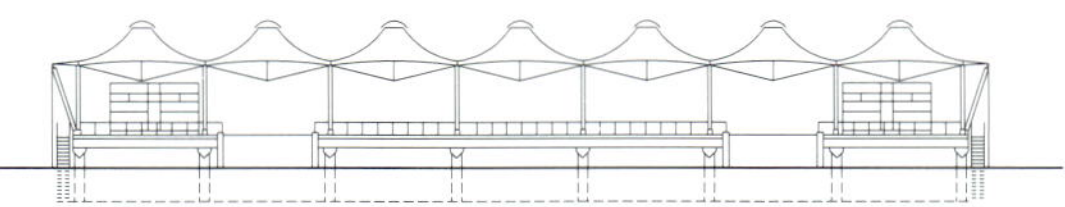

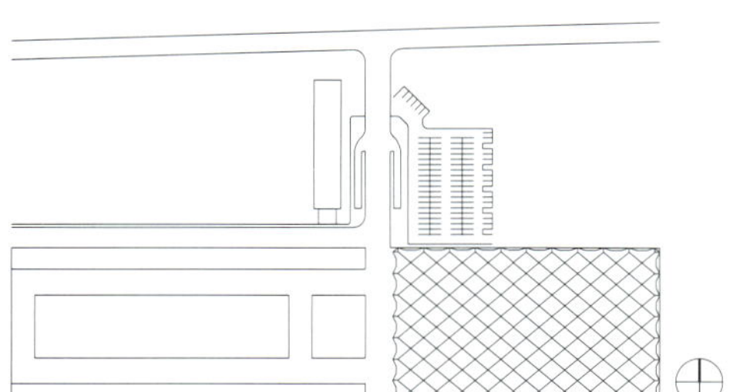

Site plan scale 1:1000

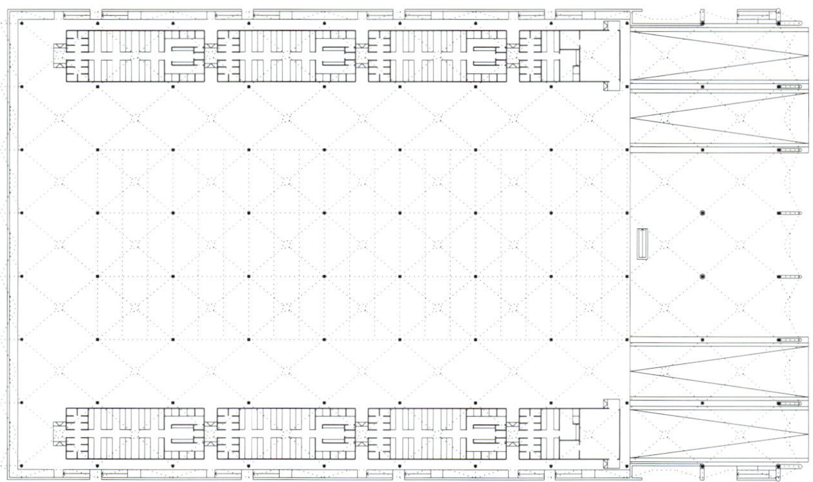

North elevation, West elevation Ground plan scale 1:1200

Underside of roof

Details scale 1:20
00 108 mm dia. x 7.1 mm tubular steel tensioning element
17 Suspended support, 127.7 mm dia. x 7.1 mm steel tube
19 Cast steel node
20 101.6 mm dia. x 5 mm tubular steel compression ring
21 Steel cable, aluminium-zinc coated in membrane pockets: 21 mm dia. stainless steel cable
59 40 x 90 mm flat steel section
69 Glassfibre textile membrane, 1 mm PTFE-coated, tear strength 130 kN/m

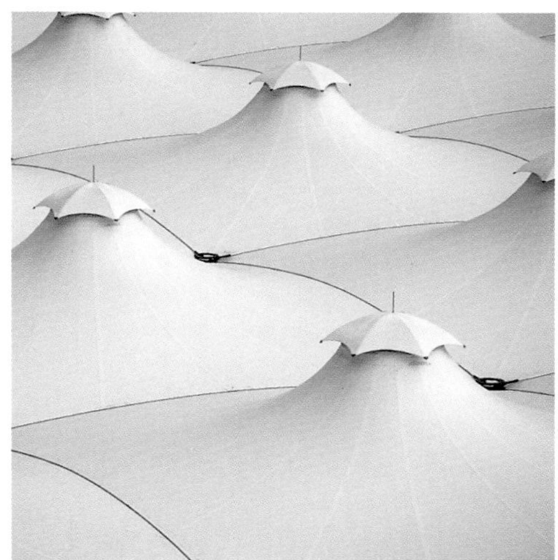
Top view of roof

This covered vehicles park is located at the waste disposal services depot of the City of Munich. On two levels it provides parking space for 150 refuse collection trucks. Its roof is an open membrane structure covered with PTFE-coated glassfibre textile. Also located beneath this roof are changing rooms and showers for the 500 refuse workers.

The construction consists of a waterproofed basement in which a concrete floor slab is inserted, leaving a gap around its edges. Standing on the floor slab are 88 steel columns arranged in a 10 x 12 m grid. These columns support the 8,400 square metres of membrane roof surface. The textile roof covering was welded together on site from 12 metre wide, prefabricated membrane strips. Each membrane bay is tensioned by a "floating" steel support trussed on the underside, directing the vertical forces into the columns. Articulated joints connect the columns to their bases, made of concrete to protect against impact. The horizontal forces in the roof structure are directed into the basement level via the raking columns at the edges. The entire construction was erected without any supporting elements subject to bending stresses; this lends lightness to the overall impression. A vacuum system inside the columns provides for drainage of the roof surface.

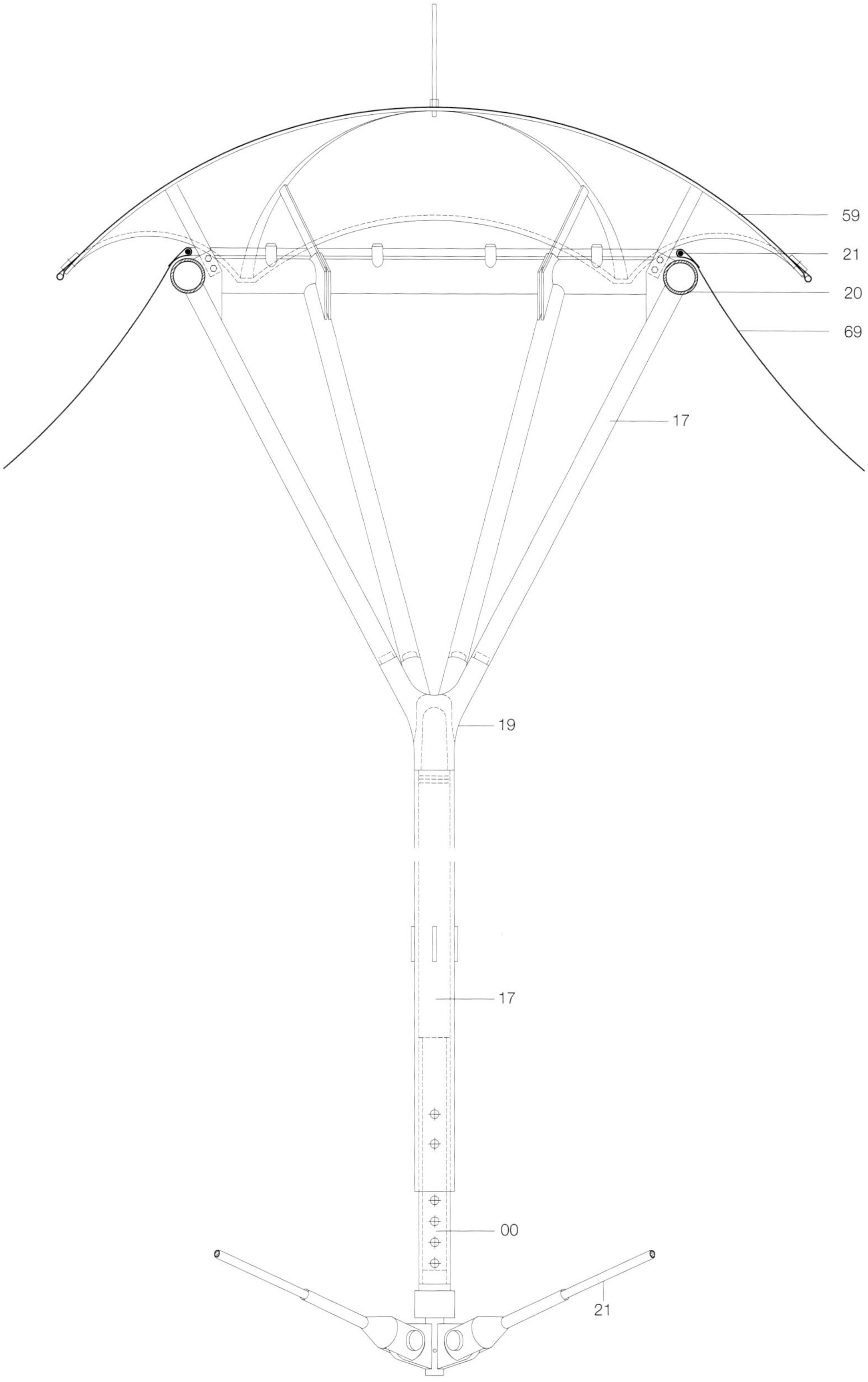

59
21
20
69
17
19
17
00
21

High point

Edge column and underside of roof

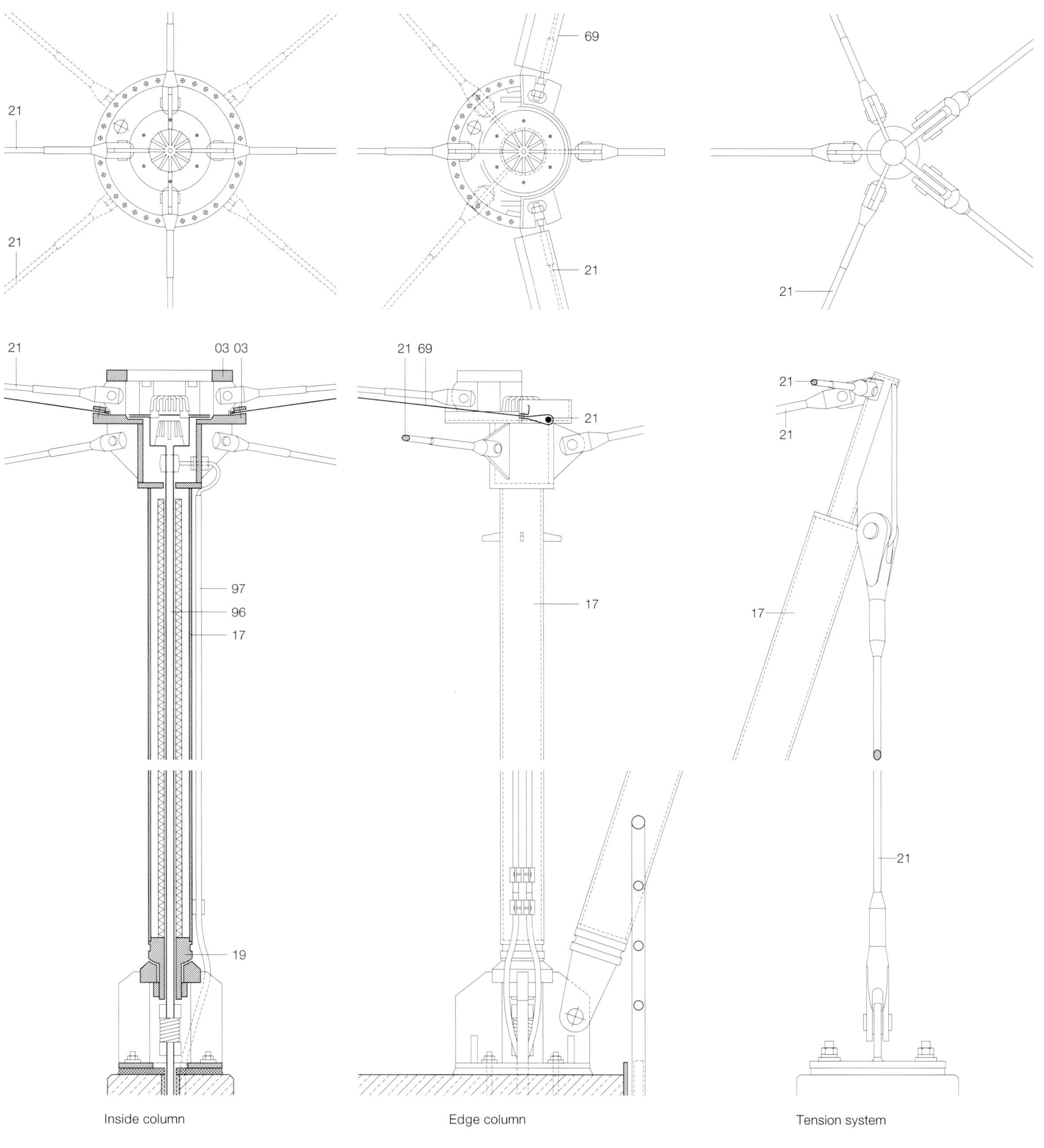


Inside column

Edge column

Tension system

Details scale 1:20

03 40 x 6 mm flat steel clamping ring, 80 x 40 mm flat steel ring
17 60.3 mm dia. x 7.1 mm tubular steel suspended support, 177.8 mm dia. x 5 mm tubular steel hinged column, 193.7 mm dia. x 20 mm tubular steel edge column
19 Steel pivot
21 Aluminium-zinc (Al 5 %) coated steel cable, horizontal tensioning: 22 mm dia. open spiral strands; vertical tensioning: 40 mm dia. fully locked strands; in membrane pockets: 21 mm dia. stainless steel cable
69 Glassfibre textile membrane, 1 mm PTFE-coated, tear strength 130 kN/m
96 Insulated and heated 50 mm downpipe
97 Electrical cabling for heating

**CargoLifter hangar, Berlin**
2000

Architects: SIAT Architektur + Technik, Munich
Assistants: Martin Hautum, Verena Thiels, Jürgen Grothe
Structural engineer: Arup GmbH, Düsseldorf
Client: CargoLifter AG

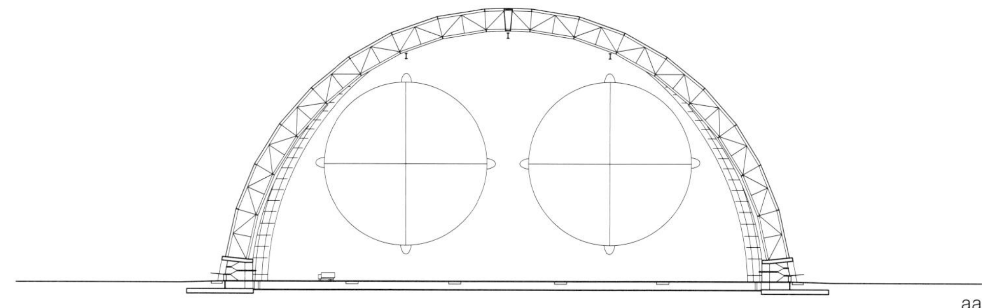


CargoLifter AG, which builds, maintains and operates a new generation of airships, built its base 60 km south of Berlin on the former military airfield Briesen-Brand. On the 580-hectare site are two anchoring areas, a power plant, a visitors' centre and the "Lighter than Air" Academy, alongside the biggest hangar in Europe: a "supershed", 107 x 360 x 210 metres, with space to house two airships.

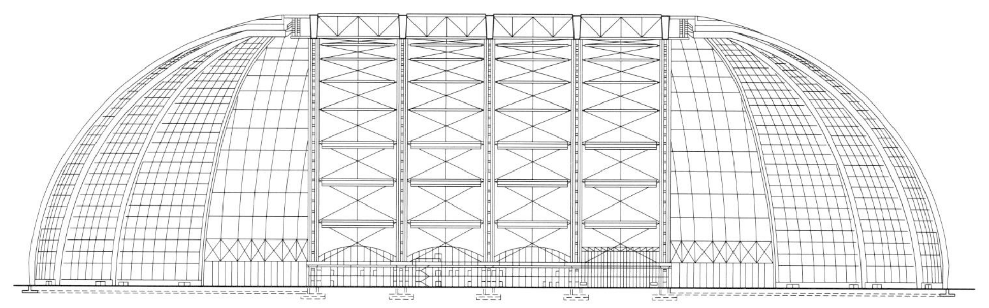


The hangar consists of five 4-chord arch trusses with a multi-shell membrane construction spanning between them to form a recumbent half-cylinder. The arches are spaced at 35 metre centres, and are formed from a polygonal tie consisting of 18-metre long elements. Each arch is 8 metres between upper and lower chord. Along the length of the hall the arches are linked by a continuous ridge girder, and at the eaves point they are anchored into a reinforced concrete base. Office and rest areas, with glazed inner and outer facades, are located in the 8.6 to 9.2 metre high base level. The 31-metre span between the arch trusses is covered with a self-supporting, multi-shell membrane construction, consisting of an inner and an outer membrane, both fixed to the upper chord. The PVC-coated polyester outer skin distributes wind and snow loads via the arch trusses. The inner skin is concentrically applied to the outer membrane, and, when the outer skin is renewed, it serves as a weather-protection layer. A further, lighter membrane is suspended from each of the two load-bearing membranes. The air pocket provides thermal insulation. The membrane construction achieves a U-value of 0.9. The garland-shaped membrane edge is point-fixed to the upper chords of the adjacent arches and the ridge girder via metal fittings, piping and turnbuckles. Non-loadbearing membrane aprons form the topmost surface and seal the roof.

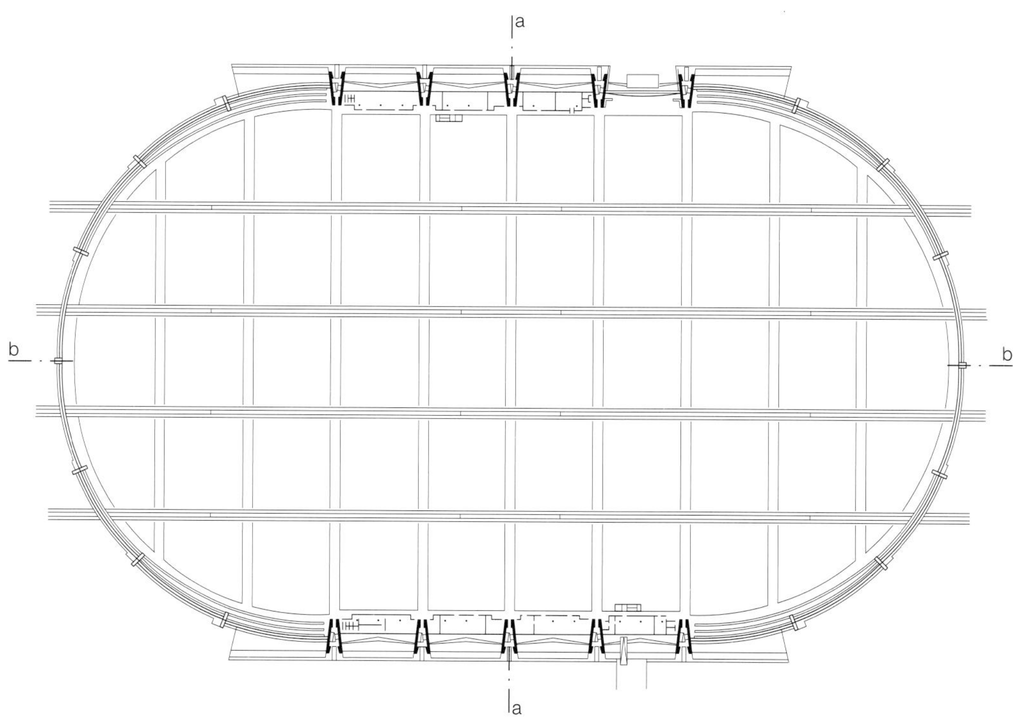


Plan • Sections 1:3000

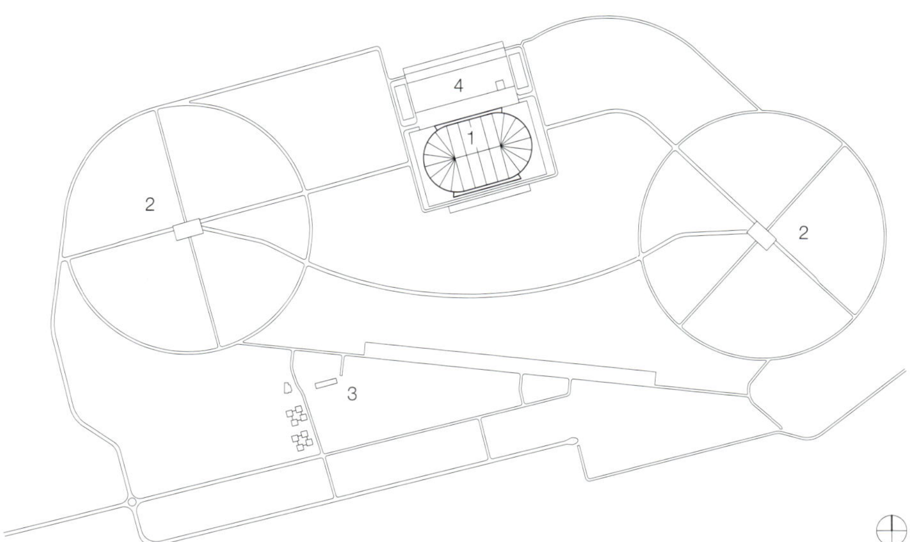


Site plan scale 1:25 000

1 Hangar
2 Anchoring area
3 Visitors' centre and "Lighter than Air" Academy
4 Power plant

South side

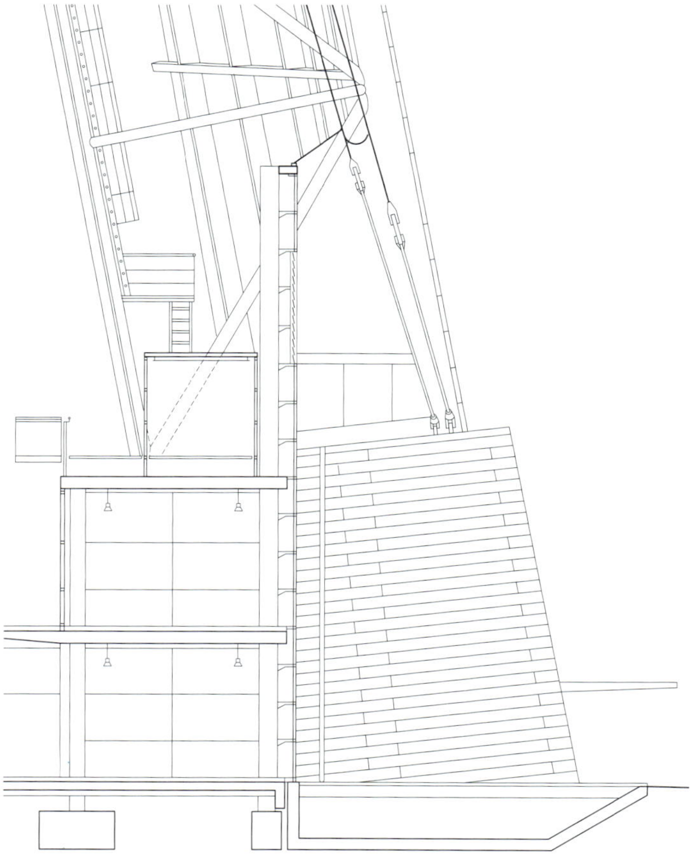

Facade section scale 1:200

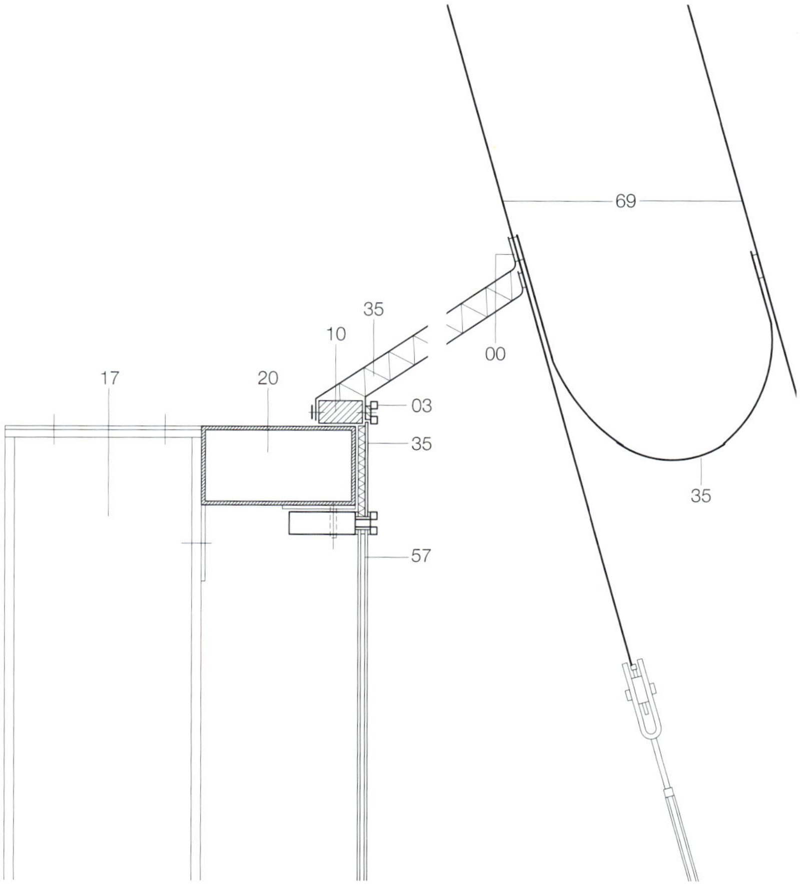

Membrane-facade junction scale 1:20

Glazed offices and rest areas in front of the opening gate

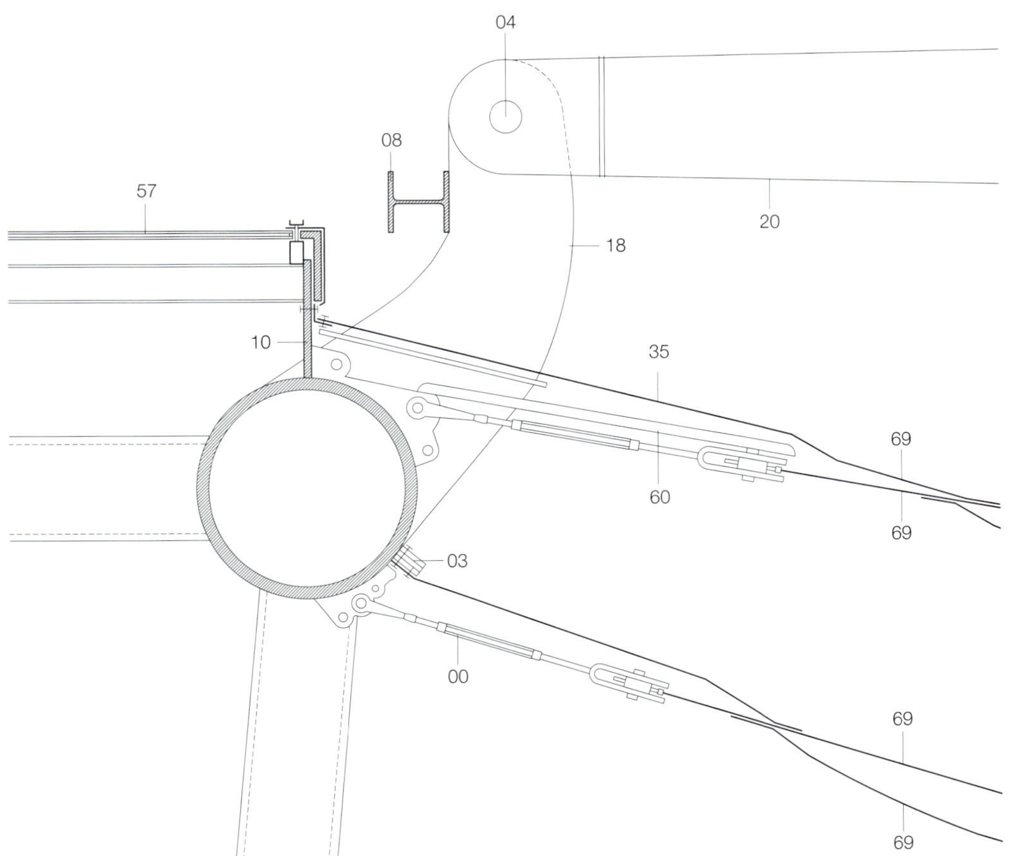


Membrane-arch junction scale 1:20

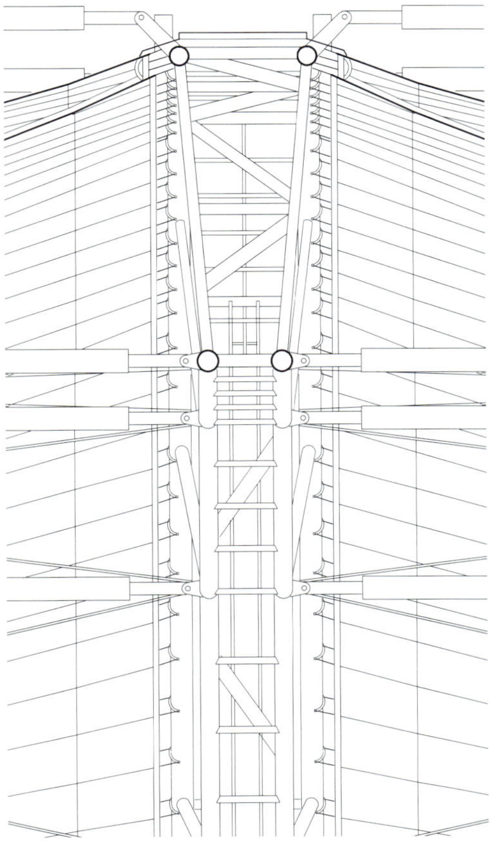

Section through 4-chord arch truss scale 1:200

Maintenance gantry

Details scale 1:20

00 Velcro fastening, stainless steel turnbuckle
03 Clamping strip and bolt, clamping plate and bolt
04 Bolt connection
08 Guide rail of maintenance trolley, steel I-section 160 mm deep (HEA)
10 60 x 120 mm timber, stop between membrane and skylight, welded flat steel section
17 Steel I-section stanchion 500 mm deep (HEA)
18 Support, welded flat steel torsional reinforcement
20 400 x 200 x 12.5 mm hot-dip galvanised steel section, welded steel section torsional reinforcement, galvanised
35 Thermally insulated aluminium panel, thermally insulated polyester textile membrane apron, polyester textile membrane apron
57 Solar glazing, rooflight glazing
60 Protective cover
69 Outer membrane: PVC-coated polyester (grade V), painted light grey; inner membrane: PVC-coated polyester (grade III), liner (grade II)

The lower edge of the membrane is fixed to a steel cable by metal fittings. To prevent the membrane coming through, a suction cable is attached in the middle; this also enables a controlled run-off of rainwater. To take up the immense quantities of rainwater running off the 66,000 square metres of sealed roof space, water basins, which can be filled up to a depth of 1.5 metres, are sunk between the foundations for the base level. This water reservoir can also be used for extinguishing any fire. Evaporation in summer from the water surface helps cool the adjacent office areas, and reflections from it raise light levels inside all year round.

The segmented gates consist of two vertical and one horizontal edge girders (3.0 x 1.0 m box girder) and the shell itself. This shell consists of horizontal, vertical and diagonal steel beams with flexurally rigid connections. Trapezoidal steel sections, thermal insulation and clip-fixed aluminium panels form the covering above the movable segments.

The fixed gate segments are covered with flexible sheeting (trapezoidal steel sections, thermal insulation, Evalon seal). For opening, the movable segments are moved underneath the fixed segments. At the ridge point, the movable segments pivot on a pin 1.0 metre in diameter and 6.0 metres high.

At 12 metres high, in the base level and at the gates, there is a ring of opening ventilation units, which ensure a smoke-free zone above the floor in case of fire. Smoke extraction is also aided by glass ventilation louvres above the ridge girders. The strips of glazing above the arched frames help prevent fire spreading from one membrane surface to the other; the glazing strips themselves are a low fire risk. The translucence of the membrane, the glazing over the arches and the ridge girder, and the glazed facades at base level, reduce the need for artificial lighting, bringing cost savings in terms of energy consumption. When daylight conditions are poor, a deflector system of mirrors ensures adequate brightness. In addition, spots are directed onto light-scattering mirrors (3 x 3 m) attached to the arch trusses to enhance levels of diffuse light in the hangar.

View of opening gate

**Eden Project in St Austell**
2000
Architect: Nicholas Grimshaw & Partners, London
Project manager: Andrew Whalley
Assistants: Jolyon Brewis, Michael Pawlyn, Perry Hooper, William Horgon, Oliver Konrath
Structural engineer: Anthony Hunt, Cirencester
Client: The Eden Project Ltd, Cornwall

Site plan scale 1:10 000

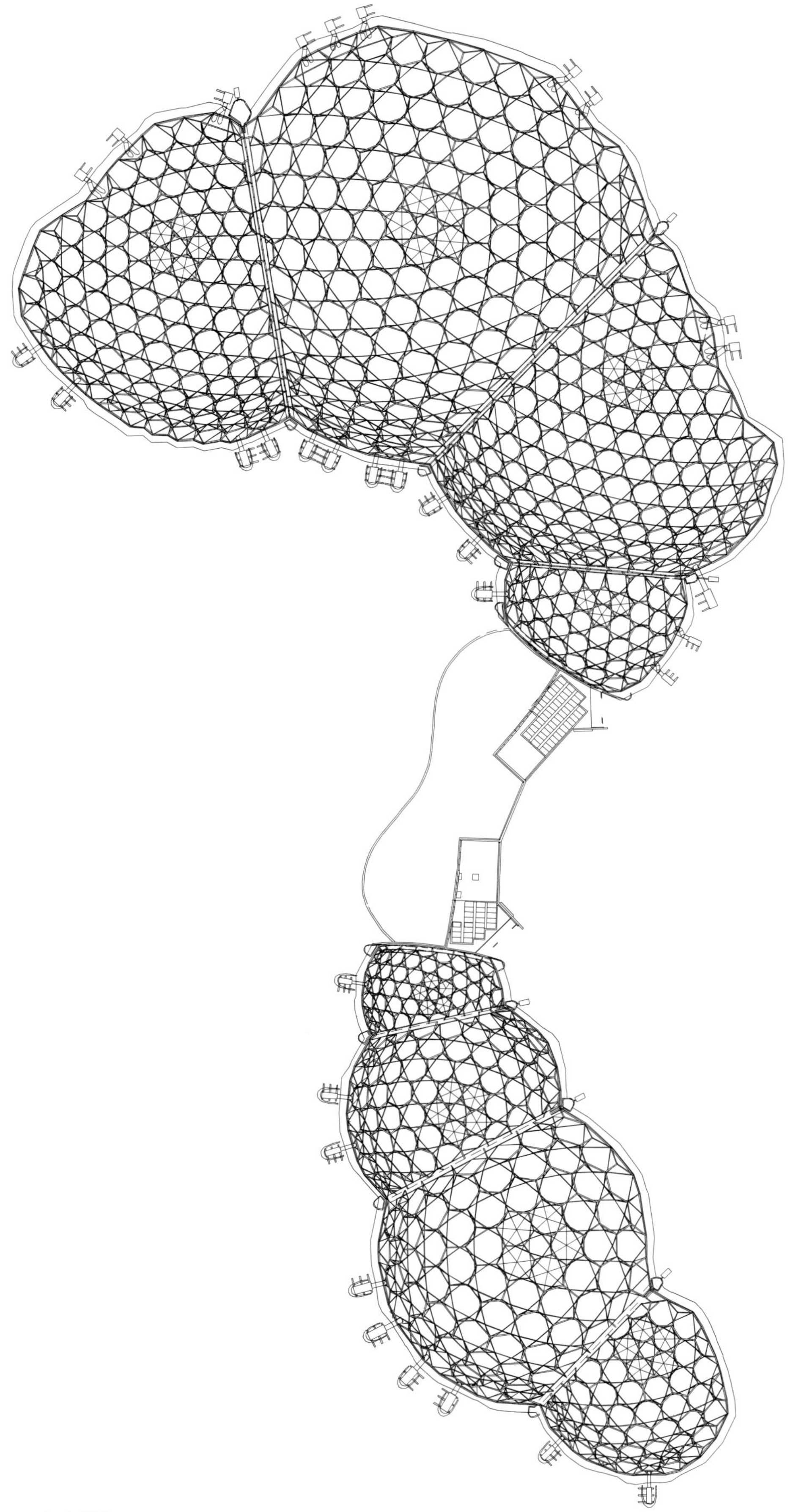

The Eden Project is a huge botanical garden, constructed in an old china clay pit in Cornwall, in southwest England. It was one of a number of projects built to mark the millennium. Its greenhouses are strung in two chains, each made up of four intersecting domes ("biomes"). The four western-most domes provide an equatorial rainforest-type climate and the four eastern-most ones a warm Mediterranean-type climate.

Linking the two greenhouses is a flat building with a green roof. This is the main entrance.

Plan scale 1:1500

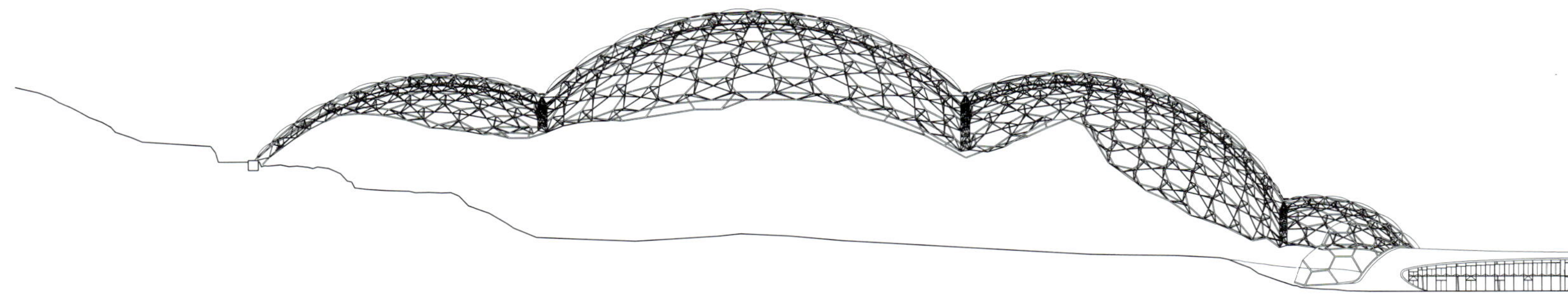

Section scale 1:1500

The dome shape permitted a very light, rigid construction, which could be prefabricated and delivered in sections. It also created a column-free interior, which gives maximum flexibility for plant placement and grouping.

Dome diameters vary from 37 to 124 m, the apex of the highest dome reaching 40 m. Trees have ample space to grow freely in the interior. The honeycomb structure affords good lighting for the plants below.

The loadbearing structure of the individual domes is a double-layer steel curved space frame. The inner skin is made up of a series of triangles and hexagons, and the outer one is composed of hexagons that are visible from the outside. Diagonal ties connect these two layers to the space frame.

Steel arch trusses support the intersection of the domes. These span over 100 metres and are anchored to the foundation strips via articulation joints. It was possible to add or subtract whole hexagons or parts thereof, so as to adapt the chain of buildings to the irregular geometry of the site. Each of the 187 bearing points has a different design. In total the space frame contains around 4,000 junctions and 11,000 steel tubes.

The triangular steel arch trusses follow a continuous radius, but the intersection points between the individual surfaces are different, because of their geometry. To compensate for this the trusses are not located directly at the intersection of the two domes.

The large size of the hexagonal panels resulted in a very lightweight structure. Cable net reinforcement on the inside of the cushions is required to support the high loads generated by drifting snow.

South side

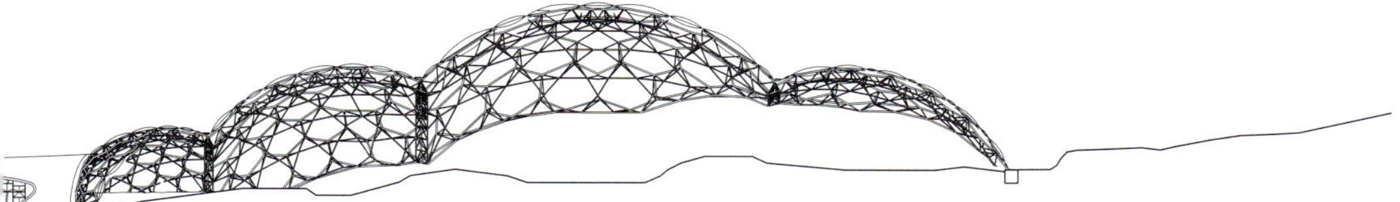

The panels are covered with triple-layer ETFE (ethyltetrafluoroethylene) foil filled with air; panel edge dimensions reach 5.20 metres. The upper and lower layers of foil have a loadbearing function; the middle one, separating the two, plays a role in thermal insulation. The inflated ETFE cushions are highly effective insulators. Also, as ETFE foils are more permeable to UV light than glass, the germicidal effect of the UV light promotes an ideal environment for the plants. The high tear resistance of the foil reduces the risk of storm damage. ETFE foil has a high surface tension and is very slippery, which helps keep it clean. The cushions are clipped to extruded aluminium frames, which are then bolted to the hexagons of the loadbearing frame. Each cushion element is inflated to a nominal pressure of about 300 Pa. The domes are ventilated by means of triangular louvres located at the apex. Each dome has 30 remote-controlled opening louvres, also coated with ETFE foil. For additional loads the hexagons below the vents were fitted with extra reinforcement in the form of a secondary steel frame of rectangular hollow sections. Air is introduced at the base of the domes through glass louvres in the sides.

The bearing points consist of a pipe cross and a base plate with shear cleat. Depending on the position, one or two upper chord bars on the arched trusses are connected to this cross. Water falling on the roof runs down into the dome intersections, where aluminium-sheet gutters, on a layer of insulation and foil, direct it away in a controlled fashion. This run-off is collected and used to water the plants.

Ventilation louvres

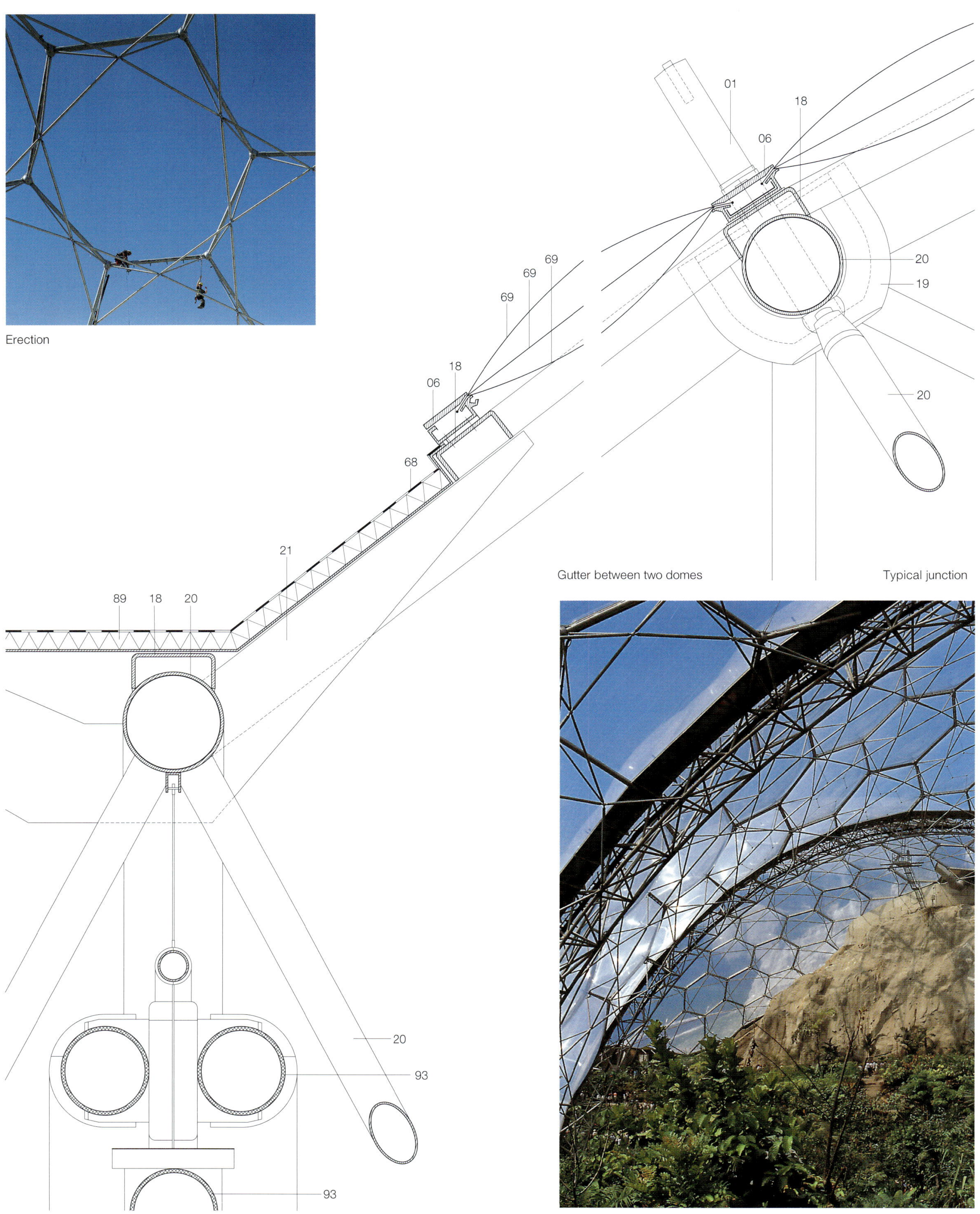


Erection

Gutter between two domes

Typical junction

ETFE cushions

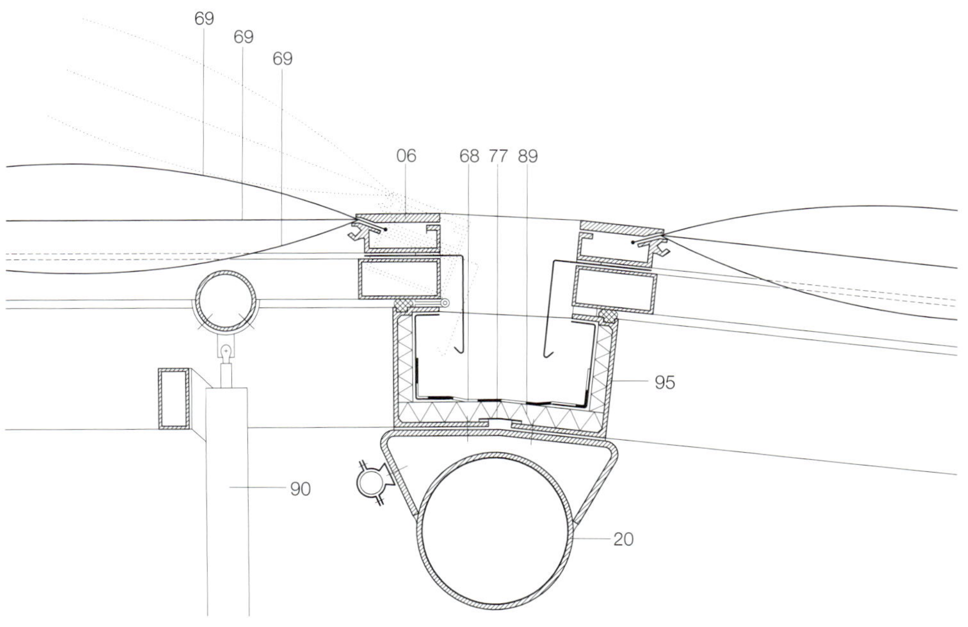


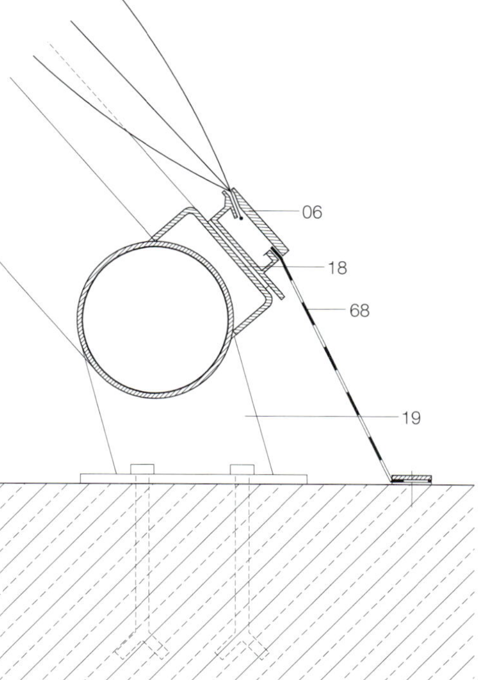

Ventilation louvre

Details scale 1:10

01 Fall guard, 70 mm dia. steel bar
05 4 mm aluminium retaining strip for gutter
06 Frame for opening louvre, aluminium, extruded profiles, clamping profile
16 140 x 70 mm steel rectangular hollow section
18 6 mm steel sheet bent to fit
19 Cast iron connecting junction
20 Tubular steel arch truss: 219.1 mm dia.; 159.6 mm; 101.6 mm
21 10 mm steel section cantilevered arm
68 PVC roofing sheet
69 Triple-layer ETFE foil: inner layer 0.1 mm, outer layer 0.2 mm
77 Aluminium sheet vapour barrier
89 High-strength thermal insulation
90 Pneumatically operated opening cylinder, flexible pressure tubing for louvre drive
93 PVC ventilation pipe fixed with polyethylene clips
95 Steel section rainwater gutter

Gutter between two domes

## Legend

**00 Retaining**
00 Bracket
00 Clamping strip
00 Clip
00 Clout nail
00 Dovetail slot
00 Ladder hook
00 Loop of binding wire
00 Metal strap
00 Plaster background
00 Plastic rivet
00 Setting block
00 Spacer
00 Split-ring connector
00 Step and mounting
00 Velux-type roof window with frame and opening light
01 Anchor
01 Anchor bolt
01 Cast-in channel
01 Cast-in channel, expansion anchor
01 Expansion anchor
01 Masonry anchor
01 Masonry anchor, wall tie in dovetail slot
01 Wall tie
02 Erosion protection textile
02 Joint tape
02 Plaster background
03 Clamp mounting
03 Clamp mounting, pipe clip
03 Collar
03 Glazing wing/cap
03 Pressure and capping piece
03 Stitch
03 Tile clip
03 Vapour barrier clamped behind batten
03 Vapour barrier clamped behind board
04 Dowel
04 Machine screw
04 Nail, annular nail
04 Rivet and soft solder
04 Rivet and solder
04 Screw
04 Screw, sealing washer
04 Self-tapping screw
04 Soft solder
04 Split-ring connector with bolt
04 Wood screw
05 Clip
05 Clip, continuous clip
05 Continuous clip
06 Fixing for flashing
06 Fixing for flashing, gutter bracket
06 Fixing for flashing, ladder hook
06 Fixing for flashing, steel strap
06 Glass holder
06 Gutter bracket
06 Gutter bracket, ladder hook, snow-guard mounting
06 Hip batten fixing strap, gutter bracket
06 Ladder hook
07 Auxiliary timber for fixing batten
07 Batten
07 End plate, web stiffener
07 Plate
07 Steel angle
07 Steel plate
07 Timber block
07 Timber block, metal angle bracket
07 Timber member
07 Timber post
08 Adhesive tape
08 Guide rail
08 Sway/metal rod
09 Eaves board
09 Spring clip
09 Tenon
09 Wedge of insulating material

**10 Supporting**
10 Fascia board
10 Feather-edge board
10 Fixing board
10 Hip board
10 Inner lining
10 Loadbearing glazing bar
10 Spacer batten
10 Spacer rafter
10 Step
10 Stop bead
10 Tie beam
10 Timber member
10 Valley board
10 Window frame
12 Inner leaf of masonry
13 Cantilevering brick course
14 Brickwork
14 Chimney stack, widened
15 Capping beam
15 Peripheral reinforcement (in bed joint or capping beam)
15 Peripheral reinforcement (in bed joint or floor slab)
15 Peripheral reinforcement (in bed joint)
15 Peripheral reinforcement (in bed joint, capping beam, floor slab)
15 Reinforced concrete
16 Concrete
16 Mortar
16 Water-repellent mortar in 20 mm wall joint
17 Column
17 Mullion
18 Bracket
18 Bracket with gutter bearer
18 Make-up batten
18 Spacer purlin
18 Spacer purlin, hood support
18 Steel bracket
18 Timber member
18 Timber parapet
18 Wall plate
18 Wall plate, hood support
20 Frame
20 Framing member
20 Roof beam
20 Tapering frame
20 Timber parapet
21 Purlin
22 "Jack" glazing bar
22 Cantilever bracket
22 Cantilevering rafter
22 Rafter
22 Rafter, jack rafter
22 Trapezoidal profile sheeting, load-bearing
23 Hip beam
23 Hip rafter
23 Hip/valley rafter
23 Trimming rafter
23 Valley beam
23 Valley rafter
24 Cross-member
24 Facade beam
24 Trimmer
25 Counter batten
25 Spacer batten
25 Spacer rafter
25 Spacer section
26 Batten
26 Batten, glulam batten
26 Sheeting rail
26 Transverse glazing bar
27 Batten roll
27 Feather-edge board
27 Feather-edge board, glulam feather-edge board
27 Feather-edge board, triangular fillet
27 Hip batten, tilting board
27 Parapet board
27 Rainwater drip
27 Ridge batten
27 Ridge board
27 Ridge/hip batten
27 Ridge/hip batten, tilting board
27 Tilting board
27 Triangular fillet
28 Batten, sleeve
28 Make-up board/batten
28 Rafter extension
28 Ridge filling
28 Spacer batten
28 Timber member
28 Timber member, make-up piece
28 Triangular fillet
28 Valley batten
28 Valley board
28 Vent side panel (timber)
29 Bargeboard
29 Fascia board
29 Feather-edge board
29 Fibre-cement upper fascia board
29 Glazing cap/wing
29 Inner lining
29 Stop bead
29 Upper fascia board
29 Z-section rail
31 Fin
31 Strengthening rod
31 Strut
32 Timber boarding
32 Tongue and groove boarding
33 Laminated board
33 Timber derivative board
34 Plasterboard

**35 Covering**
35 Cover flashing, stepped flashing
35 Drip flashing
35 Special make-up slate, valley transition slate
35 Interlocking profiled tile
35 Milled sheet lead
35 Mono ridge capping
35 Mono ridge tile
35 Mono ridge tiles (long and short)
35 Mulch layer
35 Narrow valley shake/shingle
35 Opening light in frame
35 Packing shake/shingle
35 Roof vent in frame
35 Side flashing, with deeper gutter
35 Stepped flashing
35 Thatch course laid at an angle
35 Transverse seam, standing/folded over
35 Valley slate
35 Ventilation element
36 Plants
37 Normal course of thatch
39 Fascia board
39 Wooden shake/shingle
40 Fascia board
40 Overlapping timber boards
41 Asphalt shingle
43 Standard slate
45 Bullnose tile
45 Interlocking profiled tile
45 Long bullnose tile
46 Bullnose half tile
46 Interlocking profiled tile, cut to suit
46 Short bullnose tile
46 Step support tile with step
47 Channel slate
48 Fibre-cement corrugated sheet
49 Bullnose ventilating tile
49 Vent
49 Ventilating bullnose tile, individual vent
49 Ventilating tile
50 Ventilating ridge capping
50 Ventilating ridge capping, clipped
50 Ventilation hood
50 Ventilation hood, two-piece ventilating capping
51 Fibre-cement transition piece
51 Hip capping, with "socket"
51 Mono ridge tile
51 One- or two-piece corrugated capping
51 Ridge capping
51 Ridge course
51 Ridge element
51 Ridge slate
51 Ridge/hip capping, mono ridge tile
51 Ridge/hip element
51 Ridge/hip shingle
51 Ventilating ridge capping
52 Fibre-cement apron flashing piece
52 Profiled apron flashing
52 Top course shingle
52 Top course slate
52 Topmost course
53 Back gutter
53 Back gutter with saddle
53 Eaves element
53 Eaves slate
53 Fibre-cement eaves closure piece
53 Sheet metal valley gutter
53 Undereaves shingle
53 Upper eaves course
53 Valley gutter
53 Valley gutter with turned-up edge and sliding seam
53 Valley slate
54 Cloaked verge tile
54 Cloaked verge tile, double-roll verge tile
54 Double-roll verge tile
54 Fibre-cement verge element
54 Verge shingle (capping)
54 Verge slate
56 Single glazing
57 Insulating glass
57 Insulating glass, some panes wedge-shaped
58 Trapezoidal profile sheeting
59 Apron flashing
59 Back gutter with saddle and profile filler
59 Flashing
59 Gutter extension, with welted joint
59 Metal cladding
59 Sheet metal gutter
59 Sheet metal roof covering
59 Sheet metal underlay
59 Soaker
60 Capping strip
60 Capping strip, skirt
60 Capping strip, verge capping
60 Cover flashing
60 Ridge capping
60 Sheet metal capping
60 Sheet steel skirt
60 Skirt
61 Apron flashing
61 Apron flashing and milled sheet lead
61 Apron flashing and milled sheet lead, riveted and soldered
61 Apron flashing, cut and bent down to close off troughs
61 Flashing
61 Flashing plus milled sheet lead, riveted
61 Milled sheet lead
61 Milled sheet lead flashing, riveted and soldered to capping strip

61 Profiled apron flashing
62 Closure plate
62 Drip flashing
62 Flashing
62 Verge flashing
63 Eaves flashing
63 Eaves/gutter flashing
63 Gutter flashing
63 Lining plate
63 Sheet metal window sill
63 Sill
66 Filter sheet (non-woven fabric)
66 Separating layer
66 Undercoat (partly viewed from below)
67 Roofing felt
67 Sheathing (laid with laps)
67 Sheathing (laid with laps), textured top surface
67 Sheathing, roofing felt
67 Sheathing, roofing felt (laid with laps)
68 Apron flashing
68 Flashing
68 Roofing felt
68 Roofing felt (laid with laps)
68 Roofing felt, vapour-permeable
68 Sheathing/roofing felt (laid with laps)
68 Sheet metal soffit
69 Protection mat

**70 Sealing**
70 Damp-proof course
70 Damp-proof course and cavity tray
70 Waterproofing, bonded/welded
72 Plaster
72 Rendering
72 Rendering, two coats
73 Soldered joint
74 Permanently elastic seal
74 Preformed sealing strip
74 Putty seal
74 Solder, rivet
75 Bitumen roofing felt, bonded
75 Bitumen roofing felt, two layers
75 Bitumen roofing felt, welded
75 Damp-proof course
75 Damp-proof course and cavity tray
75 Water check, bonded
75 Waterproofing, bonded
76 Waterproofing
76 Waterproofing, root-resistant
76 Waterproofing, root-resistant; root barrier
77 Vapour barrier
77 Vapour barrier (sheet metal)
77 Vapour barrier, bonded or welded
78 Permanently elastic preformed seal
78 Permanently elastic seal
78 Plastic washer with metal inlay
78 Preformed seal clamped behind batten
79 Permanently elastic bearing pad
79 Permanently elastic sealing strip
79 Sealing strip

**80 Insulating**
80 Cavity insulation
80 Thermal insulation
80 Thermal insulation, two layers
80 UV radiation protection
81 Sunblind
82 Louvre
82 Movable louvre
83 Sunblind
84 Sandwich panel
86 Thermal insulation
89 Thermal insulation

**90 Drainage, ventilation**
90 Drain channel
90 Drainage mat
90 Perforated metal strip
90 Vent
90 Ventilating element
90 Weephole
91 Plant-bearing layer
92 Drainage layer (chippings)
92 Drainage strip (gravel)
93 Flue
93 Flue liner
93 Vent
93 Ventilating element
94 Condensation channel
94 Drainage strip
94 Foil/film channel
94 Outlet grating, perforated sheet metal
94 Overflow
94 Perforated metal strip
94 Safety gutter
95 Deeper central channel
95 Foil channel
95 Foil channel, outlet
95 Gutter
95 Gutter and bracket
95 Gutter with outlet
95 Steel flue support sleeve
96 Flue support sleeve
96 Outlet with chain "downpipe"
96 Rainwater downpipe
97 Gutter heating
98 Grating
98 Snowguard
98 Snowguard (fence/pole)
98 Snowguard (fence/tube)
98 Snowguard tile
98 Tubular snowguard
98 Tubular snowguard with ice stop
98 Wind deflector
99 Mesh screen to ventilation opening

**References**

To improve clarity, the lists of references in this book have been included at the end of each individual section. These references also serve as a bibliography for further reading.

The following publications contain further information about the building techniques in use around the turn of the 20th century:


- Handbuch der Architektur, ed. Josef Durm: die Hochbau-Constructionen, Dachdeckungen von Hugo Koch; Stuttgart, 1899
- Schrader, Fritz; Reim, Hugo: Der Deutsche Dachdeckermeister, vol. 1, Leipzig: Engelmann, 1911, 612 pp., numerous illustrations
- Schrader, Fritz; Reim, Hugo: Der Deutsche Dachdeckermeister, vol. 2, Leipzig: Engelmann, 1911, 104 plates


**Index of architects and engineers**

**Index and Glossary**

## Picture credits

Photographs that are not specifically acknowledged were supplied by the architect or owner, or from the archives of the journal DETAIL.

**Part 1**
**Pitched roofs – past and present**
Aidelsburger, Erika; Munich: 1.22
Bednorz, Achim; Cologne: 1.1, 1.35
Bower, Dave; London: 1.33
Courtesy of the Estate R. Buckminster Fuller: 1.18
Darsow, Marliese; Krefeld: 1.28
Degonda, Lucia; Zürich: 1.13
Flabeg Solar; Cologne: 1.39
Gauls Die Fotografen; Koblenz: 1.46
Helfenstein, Heinrich; Zürich: 1.27
Kaltenbach, Frank; Munich: 1.21
Kandzia, Christian; Stuttgart: 1.52
Kavin, Anders; Aarhus: 1.17
Kitajima, Toshiharu; Tokyo: 1.26
Luftbild Nikolaus Fricke; Salzburg: 1.6
Neuendorf, Horstheinz; Baden-Baden: 1.24
Richters, Christian; Münster: 1.31
Riedel, Christian; Dresden: 1.20
Ruault, Philippe; Nantes: 1.50
Schittich, Christian; Munich: 1.19, 1.40, 1.44, 1.48
Schunck, Eberhard; Munich: 1.8, 1.23, 1.25, 1.30, 1.53
Weiss Werbefotografie; Gersthofen: 1.29
Wessely, Heide; Munich: 1.34
Zuuk, Rene; Almere: 1.51

**Part 4**
**Built examples in detail**
Aumer, G.; Hamburg: p. 380
Blunck, Reiner; Tübingen: pp. 356, 357, 368, 369
Brunsendorf, Rolf; Cologne: p. 344
Burg, Barbara & Schuh, Oliver (Palladium Photodesign); Cologne: pp. 429–432
Cook, Peter (View); London: p. 436 top
Dupain, A; Artarmon, Australia: p. 390
Esch, Hans Georg; Hennef/Sieg: pp. 381–383, 402, 404
Frederiksen, Jens; Copenhagen: pp. 362, 363
Freeman, Michael; London: p. 340
Gabriel, Andreas; Munich: pp. 354, 355, 379 centre, 425
Havran, Jiri; Oslo: pp. 392, 393
Heinrich, Michael; Munich: pp. 350, 351
Henz, Hannes; Zürich: pp. 410, 411
Kandzia, Christian; Stuttgart: pp. 41, 386
Kinold, Klaus; Munich: pp. 364, 365, 396–399, 406, 407, 424
Krausen, Norbert; Munich: pp. 405
Leistner, Dieter (artur), Mainz: pp. 414–418
Meisen, Manos; Düsseldorf: pp. 360, 361
Müller-Naumann, Stefan; Munich: pp. 394, 395
Nemec, Ivan; Frankfurt/Main: pp. 366, 367
Neubert, Sigrid; Munich: p. 422 bottom
Neudecker, Hans; Rotis: p. 426
Neuendorf, Horstheinz; Baden-Baden: pp. 388, 389
Richters, Christian; Münster: pp. 400, 401, 419–421
Schenkirz, Richard; Regensburg: pp. 372, 373
Schittich, Christian; Munich: pp. 374, 384, 385
Schuster, Oliver; Stuttgart: pp. 352, 353
Seidel, Michael; Vienna: p. 379 bottom
Sessner, Paul; Munich: p. 423
Strüwing, Aage; Seeland: pp. 346, 347
Suzuki, Hisao; Barcelona: pp. 408, 409 bottom
Thurmann, Stefan (Picture Press); Hamburg: p. 345
Tiainen, Jussi; Helsinki: pp. 412, 413
Werner, Heike; Munich: pp. 422 top, 387
Wessely, Heide; Munich: pp. 434–437
Young, Nigel; London: pp. 376, 379 top

**Full page plates**
Page 9
Roof landscape in Siena, Italy
Photo: Christian Schittich, Munich
Page 43
Clay tile roof in San Stefano, Italy
Photo: Christian Schittich, Munich
Page 257
dvg headquarters in Hannover
Architects: Hascher + Jehle, with Heinle, Wischer & Partner
Photo: Frank Kaltenbach, Munich
Page 337
Waste Management Department in Munich
Architects: Ackermann & Partner
Photo: Klaus Kinold, Munich